Proceedi

Third IEEE International Conference on Data Mining

ICDM 2003

Proceedings

Third IEEE International Conference on Data Mining

ICDM 2003

19-22 November 2003 • Melbourne, Florida

Editors
Xindong Wu and Alex Tuzhilin, *Program Chairs*
Jude Shavlik, *Conference Chair*

Sponsored by
IEEE Computer Society Technical Committee on Computational Intelligence (TCCI)
IEEE Computer Society Technical Committee on Pattern Analysis and Machine Intelligence (TCPAMI)

Los Alamitos, California

Washington   •   Brussels   •   Tokyo

IEEE Computer Society Order Number PR01978
ISBN 0-7695-1978-4
Library of Congress Number: 2003105566

Additional copies may be ordered from:

IEEE Computer Society	IEEE Service Center	IEEE Computer Society
Customer Service Center	445 Hoes Lane	Asia/Pacific Office
10662 Los Vaqueros Circle	P.O. Box 1331	Watanabe Bldg., 1-4-2
P.O. Box 3014	Piscataway, NJ 08855-1331	Minami-Aoyama
Los Alamitos, CA 90720-1314	Tel: + 1-732-981-0060	Minato-ku, Tokyo 107-0062
Tel: + 1-714-821-8380	Fax: + 1-732-981-9667	JAPAN
Fax: + 1-714-821-4641	http://shop.ieee.org/store/	Tel: + 81-3-3408-3118
E-mail: cs.books@computer.org	customer-service@ieee.org	Fax: + 81-3-3408-3553
		tokyo.ofc@computer.org

Editorial production by Stephanie Kawada
Cover art production by Joe Daigle/Studio Productions
Printed in the United States of America by The Printing House

ICDM 2003
Proceedings

Third IEEE International Conference on Data Mining

Table of Contents

Research-Track Regular Papers

Research-Track Short Papers

Industry-Track Papers

Author Index

Welcome to ICDM 2003

Welcome to IEEE Data Mining 2003, the Third IEEE International Conference on Data Mining (ICDM '03). We would like to thank you for coming to ICDM '03. We hope that your time in Melbourne, Florida, is very enjoyable and that you have fond memories of the technical and social programs of the conference, including the memorable tour of the NASA Kennedy Space Center.

The third meeting of the IEEE ICDM conference series follows the success of ICDM '01 in San Jose, California, USA in 2001, and ICDM '02 in Maebashi City, Japan in 2002. ICDM '03 brought together researchers and practitioners to share their original research results and practical development experiences in Data Mining technology. Attendees came from many related data-mining areas such as machine learning, automated scientific discovery, statistics, pattern recognition, knowledge acquisition, soft computing, databases, data warehousing, data visualization, and knowledge-based systems.

Data mining is an emerging and highly interdisciplinary field. The ICDM '03 conference and workshop proceedings cover a broad and diverse range of topics related to data-mining theory, systems, and applications. These include, but are not limited to, the following areas:

- Foundations of data mining
- Data-mining and machine-learning algorithms and methods in traditional areas (such as classification, regression, clustering, probabilistic modeling, and association analysis), and in new areas
- Mining text and semi-structured data, and mining temporal, spatial and multimedia data
- Data and knowledge representation for data mining
- Complexity, efficiency, and scalability issues in data mining
- Data pre-processing, data reduction, feature selection and feature transformation
- Post-processing of data-mining results
- Statistics and probability in large-scale data mining
- Soft computing (including neural networks, fuzzy logic, evolutionary computation, and rough sets) and uncertainty management for data mining
- Integration of data warehousing, OLAP and data mining
- Human-machine interaction and visualization in data mining, and visual data mining
- High performance and distributed data mining
- Pattern recognition and scientific discovery
- Quality assessment and interestingness metrics of data mining results
- Process-centric data mining and models of the data-mining process
- Security, privacy, and social impact of data mining
- Data-mining applications in electronic commerce, bioinformatics, computer security, Web intelligence, intelligent learning database systems, finance, marketing, healthcare, telecommunications, and other fields

With the support, contributions, and participation of both world-renowned experts and new researchers from the international data-mining community, ICDM has received an overwhelming response every year since its establishment in 2001, and has become a premier conference in Data Mining. This year, we received a record number of 501 paper submissions from 46 different countries, including Australia, Austria, Bangladesh, Belgium, Brazil, Canada, China, Czech Republic, Egypt, Finland, France, Germany, Greece, Hong Kong, India, Iran, Ireland, Israel, Italy, Japan, Korea, New Zealand, Pakistan, Poland, Portugal, Romania, Russia, Singapore, Slovak Republic, Slovenia, Spain, Switzerland, Taiwan, Thailand, Turkey, UK, USA, Vietnam, and Tunisia.

One of the 501 submissions was withdrawn after the submission deadline, and each of the remaining 500 submissions went through a rigorous review process. Each paper was sent to at least three Program Committee members for review, and every effort was made to obtain as many reviews from the Program Committee members as we could. These reviews were supplemented by subsequent e-mail discussions to resolve any disagreements among the reviewers, and were further discussed by the Program Committee Chairs, Conference Chair, and several Vice Chairs at a Program Committee meeting on 5 August 2003. The final acceptance decisions were made at the Program Committee meeting based on the reviews, feedback from the Vice Chairs, and additional discussion at the meeting. Of the 501 submissions, 58 regular papers, 61 short papers, and 9 industry-track papers were selected for presentation at the conference and for publication in these proceedings. In addition, our technical program also features five invited talks, six workshops, four tutorials, and one panel discussion.

A large conference like ICDM always requires tremendous efforts from various individuals. We would like to thank the Vice Chairs, Industry Track Chair, Workshops Chair, Tutorials Chair, Panels Chair, Publicity Chair, members of the Program Committee, and additional reviewers, for their countless hours devoted to various conference activities (their names all appear elsewhere in these proceedings). The Program Committee members have put in extra effort to review the record number of submissions this year. Some of them as well as additional reviewers were asked to provide last-minute reviews on a very short notice. Ning Zhong and his Web development staff deserve a particular mention for the invaluable support that the Cyberchair system provided for paper and registration management. We would also like to express our special thanks to Philip Chan for his great work in local arrangements. During the course of the year, the Steering Committee provided valuable feedback and discussions on important aspects of the conference.

We would like to express our special appreciation to our world-class invited speakers: Thomas Dietterich (Oregon State University), Usama M. Fayyad (digiMine, Inc.), Heikki Mannila (University of Helsinki), Gene Myers (University of California, Berkeley), and Philip Yu (IBM T. J. Watson Research Center).

We are grateful to the ICDM '03 corporate sponsors for their support: Computer Science Innovations, Inc., IBM Research, the *Knowledge and Information Systems* journal, and Web Intelligence Consortium.

Last, but not least, we thank all of the authors and conference attendees for their contributions and participation. ICDM '03 maintains the important ICDM traditions of (a) being truly international, (b) having exciting social programs as well as impressive technical programs, and (c) being designed and organized by a broad collection of people. We look forward to seeing you again at ICDM '04 in Brighton, UK, and at ICDM '05 back in North America.

Xindong Wu and Alex Tuzhilin
Program Chairs

Jude Shavlik
Conference Chair

Conference Organization

Conference Chair

Jude Shavlik, *University of Wisconsin-Madison (shavlik@cs.wisc.edu)*

Program Committee Chairs

Xindong Wu, *University of Vermont (xwu@cs.uvm.edu)*
Alex Tuzhilin, *New York University (atuzhili@stern.nyu.edu)*

Vice Chairs

Christopher W. Clifton, *Purdue University, USA*
Douglas H. Fisher, *Vanderbilt University, USA*
Paolo Frasconi, *Università di Firenze, Italy*
Dunja Mladenic, *J. Stefan Institute, Slovenia*
Raghu Ramakrishnan, *University of Wisconsin-Madison, USA*
Rajeev Rastogi, *Lucent, USA*
Michele Sebag, *Université Paris-Sud, France*
Dale Schuurmans, *University of Waterloo, Canada*
Jaideep Srivastava, *University of Minnesota, USA*
Mohammed Zaki, *Rensselaer Polytechnic Institute, USA*

Industry Track Chair

Roberto Bayardo, *IBM Almaden Research Center, USA (bayardo@almaden.ibm.com)*

Panels Chair

Nick Cercone, *Dalhousie University (nick@cs.dal.ca)*

Workshops Chair

David Page, *University of Wisconsin-Madison (page@biostat.wisc.edu)*

Tutorials Chair

Martin Ester, *Simon Fraser University (ester@cs.sfu.ca)*

Publicity Chair

Balaji Padmanabhan, *University of Pennsylvania (balaji@wharton.upenn.edu)*

Local Arrangements Chair

Philip Chan, *Florida Institute of Technology (pkc@cs.fit.edu)*

Web Master

Ning Zhong, *Maebashi Institute of Technology (zhong@maebashi-it.ac.jp)*

Steering Committee

Xindong Wu (Chair), *University of Vermont, USA*
Max Bramer, *University of Portsmouth, UK*
Nick Cercone, *Dalhousie University, Canada*
Ramamohanarao Kotagiri, *University of Melbourne, Australia*
Vipin Kumar, *University of Minnesota, USA*
Katharina Morik, *University of Dortmund, Germany*
Gregory Piatetsky-Shapiro, *KDnuggets, USA*
Philip S. Yu, *IBM T. J. Watson Research Center, USA*
Benjamin W. Wah, *University of Illinois, Urbana-Champaign, USA*
Ning Zhong, *Maebashi Institute of Technology, Japan*

Program Committee

Program Chairs
Xindong Wu, *University of Vermont*
Alex Tuzhilin, *New York University*

Program Committee
Gedas Adomavicius, *University of Minnesota, USA*
Kamal Ali, *Yahoo, USA*
Aijun An, *York University, Canada*
Peter Andreae, *Victoria University of Wellington, New Zealand*
Hiroki Arimura, *Kyushu University, Japan*
Rohan Baxter, *CSIRO, Australia*
Stephen Bay, *Institute for the Study of Learning and Expertise, USA*
Roberto Bayardo, *IBM Almaden Research Center, USA*
Kristin P. Bennett, *Rensselaer Polytechnic Institute, USA*
Paul Bradley, *Microsoft Research, USA*
Max Bramer, *University of Portsmouth, UK*
Carla Brodley, *Purdue University, USA*
Mary Elaine Califf, *Illinois State University, USA*
Claire Cardie, *Cornell University, USA*
Rich Caruana, *Cornell University, USA*
Nick Cercone, *Dalhousie University, Canada*
Philip K. Chan, *Florida Institute of Technology, USA*
Hsinchun Chen, *University of Arizona, USA*
Ming-Syan Chen, *National Taiwan University, Taiwan*
Ken Church, *AT&T Labs-Research, USA*
Chris Clifton, *Purdue University, USA*
Diane Cook, *University of Texas at Arlington, USA*
Mark Craven, *University of Wisconsin, USA*
Honghua Dai, *Deakin University, Australia*
Gautam Das, *Microsoft Research, USA*
Ayhan Demiriz, *Verizon Communications, USA*
Inderjit Dhillon, *University of Texas at Austin, USA*
Chris Ding, *Lawrence Berkeley National Laboratory, USA*
Guozhu Dong, *Wright State University, USA*
Saso Dzeroski, *Jozef Stefan Institute, Slovenia*
Tina Eliassi-Rad, *Lawrence Livermore National Laboratory, USA*
Charles Elkan, *University of California, San Diego, USA*
Vladimir Estivill-Castro, *Griffith University, Australia*
Theodoros Evgeniou, *INSEAD, France*
Wei Fan, *IBM T. J. Watson Research, USA*
Usama M. Fayyad, *DMX Group, USA*
Ronen Feldman, *Bar-Ilan University and ClearForest Corporation, Israel*
Douglas H. Fisher, *Vanderbilt University, USA*
Peter A. Flach, *University of Bristol, United Kingdom*
Paolo Frasconi, *Universita di Firenze, Italy*

Dmitry Pavlov, *Yahoo! Inc, USA*
Jian Pei, *State University of New York at Buffalo, USA*
Gregory Piatetsky-Shapiro, *KDnuggets, USA*
Will Potts, *Data Miners, USA*
Vijay V. Raghavan, *University of Louisiana at Lafayette, USA*
Sridhar Rajagopalan, *IBM Almaden Research Center, USA*
Naren Ramakrishnan, *Virginia Tech, USA*
Raghu Ramakrishnan, *University of Wisconsin-Madison, USA*
Zbigniew W. Ras, *University of North Carolina, USA*
Rajeev Rastogi, *Bell Labs, Lucent, USA*
Greg Ridgeway, *RAND, USA*
John Roddick, *Flinders University, Australia*
Maytal Saar-Tsechansky, *University of Texas-Austin, USA*
Lorenza Saitta, *University of Torino, Italy*
Dale Schuurmans, *University of Waterloo, Canada*
Michele Sebag, *LRI, Universite Paris-Sud Orsay, France*
Jude Shavlik, *University of Wisconsin-Madison, USA*
Shashi Shekhar, *University of Minnesota, USA*
Olivia Sheng, *The University of Utah, USA*
Kyuseok Shim, *Seoul National University, Korea*
Arno Siebes, *Utrecht University, Netherlands*
David Skillicorn, *Queen's University, Canada*
Andrzej Skowron, *University of Warsaw, Poland*
Kate A. Smith, *Monash University, Australia*
Myra Spiliopoulou, *Otto-von-Guericke University Magdeburg, Germany*
Nicolas Spyratos, *University of Paris-Sud, France*
Jaideep Srivastava, *University of Minnesota and Yodlee, Inc, USA*
Salvatore Stolfo, *Columbia University, USA*
Nick Street, *University of Iowa, USA*
Einoshin Suzuki, *Yokohama National University, Japan*
Pang-Ning Tan, *University of Minnesota, USA*
Takao Terano, *Tsukuba Univeristy, Japan*
Cindy Thompson, *University of Utah, USA*
Hannu T. T. Toivonen, *University of Helsinki, Finland*
Shusaku Tsumoto, *Shimane Medical University, Japan*
Peter D. Turney, *National Research Council, Canada*
Jeffrey D. Ullman, *Stanford University, USA*
Benjamin W. Wah, *University of Illinois, Urbana-Champaign, USA*
Haixun Wang, *IBM T. J. Watson Research, USA*
Jason Wang, *New Jersey Institute of Technology, USA*
Ke Wang, *Simon Fraser University, Canada*
Lipo Wang, *Nanyang Technological University, Singapore*
Takashi Washio, *I.S.I.R., Osaka University, Japan*
Geoff Webb, *Monash University, Australia*
Graham J. Williams, *CSIRO Australia, Australia*
Stefan Wrobel, *University of Bonn, Germany*
Takahira Yamaguchi, *Shizuoka University, Japan*
Qiang Yang, *Hong Kong University of Science and Technology, China*
Xin Yao, *University of Birmingham, UK*
Yiyu Yao, *University of Regina, Canada*
Philip S. Yu, *IBM T. J. Watson Research Center, USA*
Osmar Zaiane, *University of Alberta, Canada*

External Reviewers

A. Giacometti
Aleksander Lazarevic
Alexandre Evfimievski
Alin Dobra
Amit Mandvikar
Amol Ghoting
Anca Doloc-Mihu
Andre Elisseeff
Andrew Foss
Angelina Tzacheva
Antonin Rozsypal
Ari Rantanen
Arkadiusz Wojna
Asad Satti
Aysel Ozgur
Bernard Zenko
Bi-Ru Dai
Bianca Zadrozny
Biren Shah
Bob Price
Carl Mooney
Carmel Dumshlak
Carson K. Leung
Chi-Ming Chao
Chienting Lin
Ching-Huang Yun
Christophe Rigotti
Claudia Perlich
Cliff Brunk
D. Laurent
Damjan Demsar
Daniel Lizotte
Daniel McDonald
David Bodoff
Daxin Jiang
Ding Yuan
Dong Xin
Edda Leopold
Elias Gyftodimos
Eric Eilertson
Eugene Fink
Faliang Huang
Ganesh Ramesh
Gang Li
Gang Wang

Gerhard Paass
Greg Hamerly
Haimonti Dutta
Hathai Tanta-ngai
Hong Yao
Hongxing He
Hui Wang
Hui Xiong
Hui Yang
Huiyuan Shan
Ingo Schwab
Ioannis Ioannidis
J. F. Boulicaut
Jack Newton
Janez Brank
Jaroslaw Stepaniuk
Jeffrey Xu Yu
Jennifer Xu
Jialun Qin
Jianghui Liu
Jie Chen
Jinbo Bi
Jingli Lu
JingTao Yao
Jiye Li
Joerg Kindermann
Jukka Kohonen
Jun He
Kaan Ataman
Kamran Karimi
Kari Laasonen
Kevin Yip
Krishna Kummamuru
Kun Liu
Kun-Ta Chuang
Kunal Punera
Kyoung-Mi Lee
Lalita Narupiyakul
Lavinia Egidi
Lei Yu
Lellahi
Levent Ertoz
Li Niu
Lifang Gu
Lin Lin

Liqiang Geng
Ljupco Todorovski
Luis Perez-Breva
Luiza Antonie
Lukas C. Faulstich
Maja Pusara
Mark-A. Krogel
Marko Salmenkivi
Martin Scholz
Massimiliano Pontil
Matthew Otey
Mehmet Koyuturk
Meiling Liu
Michael Chau
Michael Steinbach
Michael Wurst
Michinari Momma
Miho Ohsaki
Mika Raento
Ming-Jyh Hsieh
Mirek Riedewald
Mohammad El-Hajj
Moshe Fresko
N. Novelli
N. Shiri
Naoki Fukuta
Nguyen H. Son
Nguyen S. Hoa
Parag Kanade
Pavel Berkhin
Qian Wan
Ravi Kothari
Robert Banfield
Rohit M. Lotlikar
Ronaldo A. Ferreira
Ruchita Bhargava
Rui Miguel Forte
Russell Greiner
Ryan G. Benton
Ryan Rifkin
Sachindra Joshi
Sameep Mehta
Sandeep Narravula
Sarah Coppock
Sedar Cabuk

Sen Zhang
Shoji Hirano
Sidi Goutam
Sofus A. Macskassy
Soumya Ray
Souptik Datta
Srihari Venkatesan
Srujana Merugu
Stanley Oliveira
Stefan Haustein
Stefan Rueping
Stefania Montani
Steven Eschrich
Steven X. Wang
Susanne Hoche
Suvrit Sra
Tamas Horvath
Taneli Mielikäinen
Tao Li
Thian-Huat Ong
Thomas Gaertner
Thorsten Schnier
Timm Euler

Todd Olsen
Tom Johnsten
Tony Abou-Assaleh
Tuan Trung Nguyen
V. Phan-Luong
Vitor Santos Costa
Wai Lam
Wai-Shing Ho
Walker White
Wei-Guang Teng
Weiqiang Lin
Willi Kloesgen
Wingyan Chung
Xia Yi
Xiang Hu
Xiangji Huang
Xiangyang Xue
Xiaodong Zhou
Xiaoshu Hang
Xiaowei Yan
Xifeng Xan
Xifeng Yan
Xin Wang

Y. Loyer
Y. Tzitzikas
Yaling Pei
Yi Zhang
Yifan Li
Yilu Zhou
Ying Yang
Yinghui Yang
Yinliang Zhao
Yiwen Zhang
YongSeog Kim
Yu-Chen Mao
Yuan Shen
Yuanyuan Wang
Yuming Ou
Yun Chi
Yunfei Yin
Yuqiang Guan
Zan Huang
Zhiqiang Zheng
Zhixiang Chen
Zonghuan Wu

Corporate Sponsors

Computer Science Innovations, Inc.

IBM Research

Knowledge and Information Systems

Web Intelligence Consortium

Research-Track Regular Papers

Efficient Multidimensional Quantitative Hypotheses Generation

Amihood Amir*
Department of Computer Science
Bar-Ilan University,52900 Ramat-Gan, Israel
(972-3)531-8770, amir@cs.biu.ac.il
and College of Computing, Georgia Tech, Atlanta, GA 30332-0280

Reuven Kashi†
RUTCOR-Rutgers Center for Operations Research
Rutgers, The State University of New Jersey
640 Bartholomew Rd, Piscataway, NJ 08854-8003
kashi@cs.biu.ac.il

Nathan S. Netanyahu
Department of Computer Science
Bar-Ilan University
52900 Ramat-Gan, Israel
(972-3)531-8865, nathan@cs.biu.ac.il
and Center for Automation Research, Univ. of Maryland, College Park, MD 20742

Abstract

Finding local interrelations (hypotheses) among attributes within very large databases of high dimensionality is an acute problem for many databases and data mining applications. These include, dependency modeling, clustering large databases, correlation and link analysis. Traditional statistical methods are concerned with the corroboration of (a set of) hypotheses on a given body of data. Testing all of the hypotheses that can be generated from a database with millions of records and dozens of fields is clearly infeasible. Generating, on the other hand, a set of the most "promising" hypotheses (to be corroborated) requires much intuition and ingenuity.

In this paper we present an efficient method for ranking the multidimensional hypotheses using image processing of data visualization. In the heart of the method lies the use of visualization techniques and image processing ideas to rank subsets of attributes according to the relation between them in the databases. Some of the scalability issues are solved by concise generalized histograms and by using an efficient on-line computation of clustering around a median with only five additional memory words. In addition to presenting our algorithmic methodology, we demonstrate its efficiency and performance by applying it to real census data sets, as well as synthetic data sets.

1. Introduction

Given very large databases, the main goals of *knowledge discovery in databases* (KDD) and *data mining*, consist of automatic hypothesis-generation and recognition of data subsets where the hypothesis holds, and where it is considered useful for the user, in an appropriate context. More specifically, data mining deals with the search for interesting patterns and structures in large data sets and with the discovery of useful information not explicitly present in the data.

There has been extensive work towards answering the major problem of identifying what should be considered as "interesting" patterns and information within vast amounts of data. Many metrics for measuring interestingness in specific

---

* Partially supported by NSF grant CCR-01-04494 and ISF grant 282/01.

† part of this work was done while the author was a Ph.D. student at Bar-Ilan University and supported by ISF grant 282/01.

contexts where suggested. Notable examples involve evaluating the most interesting rules [3], and assessing, via visual feedback, the relevance of answers to given queries [4]. A major issue is whether such patterns can be defined independently of the data set domain. It is also essential to test the validity of the patterns being discovered by the proposed methods, since in any large volume of data there can be patterns that are reported by the extracting process to be interesting although they are spurious and of no real interest. Thus, the usefulness of the discovered patterns and subsequently, the whole mining process, is negligible if meaningful information or interesting knowledge cannot be extracted from it.

Approaches for solving this problem vary. Traditional statistical methods are concerned with the corroboration of (a set of) hypotheses on a given body of data. Brute force testing of all hypotheses is clearly imposible for very large data sets. The challenge is to generate a set of "promising" hypotheses.

Attempts to bridge this gap have led to active research in data mining techniques, data visualization, and geometric clustering techniques.

It is important to note that while visualization techniques have the advantage of suggesting hitherto unknown hypotheses, they are slow, imprecise, and confusing in the case of high dimensional data. For example, if a record consists of 30 fields, then just viewing all of the relationships regarding triples involves 24,360 visualizations. This is clearly not feasible for a human user.

Some heuristics for extracting local interrelations use geometric clustering techniques, but they may not be capable of finding the appropriate semantics of an interrelation between the attributes since such a semantic connection may not manifest as a "cluster".

1.1. Image Processing of Visualized Data

A promising methodology for automated hypothesis-ranking in large databases was presented in [1]. The approach pursued was based on the usage of visualization, as well as image processing techniques, for ranking subsets of fields according to the significance of their relation in a given database. The method first labels certain hypotheses as "invalid", and then ranks the valid ones by order of "interest". The ranking is expected to yield a subset of (the more interesting) hypotheses, which can then be further investigated by statistical, visualization, or any other available tools.

The method was tested on some census databases and seemed to predict hypotheses well. The algorithm as described in that paper, performed well but did not seem to scale well. Even for three-dimensional correlations, the algorithm could not handle very large databases with a large number of fields.

In this paper we introduce an efficient algorithm for ranking hypotheses (henceforth the AKN method). This efficiency allows analyzing huge numerical databases having records with a high number of fields.

The main theoretical contributions of this paper are:

1. The introduction of a multidimensional histogram that visually captures data interrelations in a manner that lends itself to analysis by image processing tools. This allows using the AKN method successfully while scanning the database serially only two times. It should be noted that sampling algorithms do not always fare well on clusters, especially if indeed they do cluster together. A total database scan will, naturally, be able to handle clusters of data equally well as data that are randomly distributed. The cost of a total database scan, though, is generally high. We mitigate this cost by minimizing the number of disk swaps. Our algorithm reads the database serially, and does that only twice.

2. Using an algorithm to determine the neighborhood of a median on-line using a very small constant amount of extra space (a handful of bytes).

We compare the quality and efficiency of our algorithm with that of [1]. The qualitative comparison is done on the same census datasets used by [1]. The efficiency is tested both on the census databases with more fields and on much larger synthetic databases.

The rest of the paper is organized as follows. Section 2 provides background, regarding the approach and methodology that were pursued. Section 3 discusses the problems of scalability and provides proposed solutions. Section 4 gives an efficient, on-line algorithm for our median-based, robust clustering procedure that is incorporated into the hypothesis ranking scheme of [1]. Section 5 contains empirical results obtained by testing our method on real Census Bureau databases and testing its scalability on synthetic datasets. Section 6 contains concluding remarks.

2. Background: The AKN Methodology

The AKN method considers all triplets X, Y, Z, and attaches a measure of interestingness according to the relatedness of the (dependent) attribute Z to the attributes X and Y. More specifically, the method works by converting each

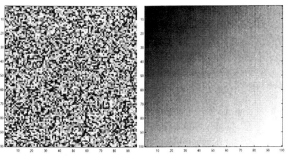

(a) *A "noisy" image*   (b) *A continuous image*

Figure 1. Assessing local relation between variables via data visualization

triplet to an image, such that the Z-value at each (X, Y) location can be viewed as the gray level assigned to that pixel. Once a triplet of attributes is mapped onto a gray level image, various image processing techniques can be employed for automatically assessing the "continuity" of the image, or the degree of interestingness of the corresponding subset of attributes. If the image is "noise-like', as in Figure 1a, it is unlikely that there is a relation between X, Y, and Z. However, if the image is (piecewise) smooth, as in Figure 1b, it is likely that the value of Z is related to the values of X and Y. The idea is to use image processing techniques to automatically assess the piecewise smoothness of a given image. In particular, the *contrast* measure associated with the texture [2] of a given image was used to rank its continuity. It should be noted that this measure is computed in *local* regions over the entire image and thus enables to find local and non-linear correlation in subsets of the data.

The above general procedure is an over simplification of the actual AKN method. In particular, there were a number of database-specific issues that needed to be reckoned with, before assessing the continuity of an image could take place. Such sticking issues included, e.g., large value ranges of X, Y, and Z (which could result in infeasible image size and gray level range), and the possible mapping of many Z-values onto the same (X, Y) image pixel. Handling the first issue was done as follows. The image size was limited to 500×500 and the X- and Y-ranges were each mapped in a linear manner to the desired range $1..500$. Treating the Z variable was done by *generalized histogram trimming*, i.e., by trimming the least frequent values and mapping the rest of the values onto a gray level range of $(10..230)$ in a distance-preserving manner. (See [1] for a detailed discussion.)

The possibility of many Z-values mapping onto the same image pixel raises the crucial issue of a *pixel's validity*. A pixel is defined valid if (at least) 50% of its Z-values are congregated within a relatively small interval surrounding the median of the set of Z-values of that pixel. (Otherwise, it is labeled invalid.) This definition was motivated by the fact that the median – unlike the mean – is a *robust estimator*, i.e., an estimator that is immune to noisy/outlying data.

Once all of the pixels are labeled, the AKN method tests whether the entire image (and the triplet it represents) should be accepted or rejected. For example, an image is rejected if it contains a relatively large number of invalid pixels or if its entropy is relatively small (see [1] for further details). If, however, the image is accepted, the method invokes texture analysis for ranking it. This is done by first computing a *co-occurrence matrix* of the image [2].[1] A contrast measure (or the variance of gray level spatial dependencies) is then computed from the co-occurrence matrix. The latter measure serves for ranking the image; the smaller the variance, the more continuous the image, i.e., the more likely the hypothesized relation between Z and the attributes X and Y.

3. The Scalability Problems and Solutions

We are opting for a total database scan in order to rank our hypotheses. This decision is based on the fear that data are not randomly distributed and thus sampling may miss clustered data that imply some local relation. The compromise we make is that, while we scan the entire database, we want to minimize swaps and thus improve the running time. Scanning the database with a minimum number of swaps can be naturally done by reading it sequentially.

It is therefore necessary to be able to distill data during one run for *all possible relations*. These data need to be concise since they needs to fit in memory. Otherwise, our goal of minimizing disk swaps will not be attained. Through the rest of this paper we concentrate on three-dimensional inter-relations, i.e., correlations between triples of variables (fields). The theory presented in the paper applies to higher dimensional relations, although practically, higher dimensions will cause an explosion since the dimension of the relation is an exponent in our running time.

Nevertheless, it is very difficult for humans to conceptualize relations in very high dimensions. Thus even three- or four-dimensional correlations are important, and the field is still seeking good solutions for finding unknown local relations even in two and three dimensions. We stress again that when we talk of three dimensions, those are the dimensions

---

1   A co-occurrence matrix captures certain properties of the gray level distribution, e.g., the probability of two pixels having certain gray levels occurring at a particular spatial relationship.

of the *relation*, as opposed to the dimension of the database (the number of fields in a record) which can be quite large but still be handled by our algorithm.

As mentioned in the previous section, the main idea of the AKN algorithm was to construct an image for each triple of variables, and then analyze those images using image processing techniques. We will show a method for constructing very small images (50×50) that still allows us to rank hypotheses well. We call these images *multidimensional generalized trimmed histograms*. Although these histograms distort the image, as will be seen in Section 5.1, the ranking they produce compares very favorably to the ranking of [1].

As previously mentioned, the idea of the generalized trimmed histogram was introduced in [1]. However, there it was applied only to the grey levels, and only in a high resolution. We propose using the general trimming as a mapping on variable values. This mapping distorts the values, especially when used with a low resolution. However, it turns out to be distance-preserving in a manner that allows surprisingly good hypothesis-ranking. It should be noted that specialized histograms (e.g. [7, 6]) do not answer all our needs.

3.1. The General Trimmed Mapping

We seek a mapping $T : V \rightarrow K$, where V is the domain V of variable values, and $K = \{1, ..., k\}$, where k will be a small number, say 50. This mapping is to preserve distances in the domain V in the sense that a close clustering of many values will map to distinct numbers, whereas large empty areas will be clumped together.

An uncommon situation that needs to be addressed as well is the case where the original range of V-values is smaller than k. Let the range be defined by $z_{\min}$ and $z_{\max}$. A value z ($z_{\min} \leq z \leq z_{\max}$) is mapped to

$$T(z) = \left(\frac{z - z_{\min}}{z_{\max} - z_{\min}} \right) \cdot k.$$

In general, however, the range might be very large. We then apply generalized histogram trimming.

Let t denote the number of V-values that constitute, say, 90% of the generalized trimmed histogram, let b denote the remaining number of V values, and let nc denote the number of values in K that are allocated for the above t values. (Typically, if we trim the least frequent 10% of the data, then nc is set to 45, i.e., roughly 90% of the range.) We distinguish between the following two cases:

1. $t \geq$ nc. In this case, we simply assign $t/$nc V-values to each element in K, where smaller values assigned to smaller K values. The distance between K elements assigned to the t values is computed relative to the b values, i.e., we assign $b/(k - \text{nc})$ V elements to one K value.

2. $t <$ nc. In this case every one of the t values is assigned a distinct K element. The distance between K elements assigned to the t values is computed relative to the b values, similarly to the case before. Specifically, we assign $b/(k - t)$ elements per one value.

4. The Median Problem

The multidimensional histogram theoretically enables the construction of all images of triples in memory during a single scan. The idea is to use a small enough histogram per triple and compute all images in a single data base scan. As an example, consider a database with records having 30 fields. Using 50×50 histograms with 4 bytes per pixel requires less than 250MB for creating the images of all triples, regardless of the size of the database. These 250MB can reside in memory and be all filled simultaneously during a single serial database scan.

This strategy would seem to solve the problem except for the following snag. In the algorithm presented in [1], a two-step pixel validity procedure was proposed. In the first step, the median of a sequence of elements was found, and in the second step it was verified whether a certain interval around the median contained at least 50% of the sequence elements. The problem we are faced with, then, seems rather formidable. How does one compute a median on-line having only a small constant (in our calculation we used 4) number of bytes?

The selection problem of finding medians and other quantiles has been studied over several decades. It had and still has a tremendous importance both theoretically, in determining upper and lower bounds, and practically, in many database and data mining applications that require computation of quantiles, e.g., query optimization, histogram construction, and computation of association rules. However, the major drawback with current algorithms is that they still require much memory in scenarios where concurrent computing of several medians of several data streams is needed. This is exactly the scenario in our automatic generation of multidimensional hypothesis in the database.

The suggested algorithms and approaches towards the selection problem can be divided into the theoretical oriented work and into databases oriented techniques, that offer feasible solutions for applications involving very large data sets.

4.1. New Proposition: Finding Median Neighborhood

All currently known methods for finding the median require space that is dependent on the database size and is far too large for our purposes. Our idea of computing all valid pixels online with small extra memory will not be able to be implemented if the medians can not be computed.

An immediate suggestion may be to compute neighborhoods around the average, rather than the median. This can surely be done efficiently online but as was pointed out in [1], the average is not a robust estimator (see [8]). Consider the following easy example. Let nine values be 1 and one outlier with a value of 40. The average is 4.9 and its neighborhood has no values, thus would be declared invalid. However, choosing the median would guarantee that the neighborhood of the median indeed is crowded. Thus, the choice of median is far better as it captures an adequate estimate of the majority of the data.

Fortunately, we do not really need to compute the median. Rather we are interested in finding out whether the majority of values are clustered around the median. It is possible to change the Misra and Gries majority algorithm [5] in a manner that allows us to use it for finding clusters around the median. This is an important new non-trivial application of the algorithm. The *majority problem* is defined as follows:

INPUT: An array of n integers.
OUTPUT: If integer i appears at least $n/2$ times, then output i, else output: no majority.

Misra and Gries give an algorithm that solves the majority problem. Their algorithm scans the list serially twice using 2 working variables.

We adapt the Misra and Gries algorithm for our purpose. For ease of exposition we first describe an inaccurate naive idea of the adaptation necessary, and then "fix" it.

Let r be the range of possible values the variable may get. Assume that the distance around the median in which we require a clustering of 50% of the values is (r/α). Map database value i to $\lceil \frac{\alpha i}{r} \rceil$. On this mapping, run the majority algorithm.

The obvious pitfall of the above adaptation is that it implicitly assumes that the median is in the center of one of the α

Figure 2. Partitioning the variable range.

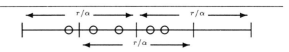

Figure 3. The overlapping partitions are too small.

partitions. This is certainly not generally the case!

A simple fix, that is still not the final one, is to consider two overlapping partitions of the variable range, as in Figure 2.

Note that there may still be valid cases that we will consider invalid, as in the example of Figure 3. The five dots are variable values. Assume that these five values are 50% of all values. They are clustered within r/α of each other, and hence of the median, but they do not all occur within any single interval of length r/α, thus the majority algorithm will declare this block invalid.

To solve this problem we will err on the side of leniency. We choose to declare some invalid pixels as valid rather than vice-versa. Thus we partition the value range into overlapping intervals of length $2r/\alpha$ each. This guarantees that any cluster of 50% of the values around r/α of the median will be identified. The payment is that some clusters of 50% of the values in larger distances around the median (up to $2r/\alpha$) may also be declared valid. We can afford to pay this price since, in any event, the α is a parameter that can be changed depending on the implementation.

4.2. Analysis of Time Complexity

The two main keys to the our algorithm are the multidimensional general trimmed histograms that allow construction of relatively small images per variable triple, and the online median neighborhood computation. In the next section we show that smaller generalized trimmed histograms do not greatly degrade the ranking. We also show excellent running times on real census data as well as very large synthetic data sets.

Theoretically, our algorithm has two independent contributors to its complexity; the number of variables per record, and the number of records in the database.

Number of Variables per Record: Our algorithm tries to construct all images simultaneously in memory. If the records have d variables, there will be $(d(d-1)(d-2))/2$ images for variable triples. If the histogram is a 50×50 array, and we need 5 words per pixel. In our implementation we used 10 bytes per pixel. Therefore the necessary number of bytes per image is 25,000. Working back from, say 1GB RAM, we can construct in core histograms for a database whose records have over 40 fields.

Number of records in database: A great advantage of the algorithm is that once the record size is shown to fit in memory, the database needs to be scanned serially twice, which minimizes swapping and greatly contributes to efficiency from a practical point of view.

5. Experimental Results

We have made a conceptual change to the AKN method by allowing small multidimensional histograms. It is necessary to check that these changes do not cause degradation in the ranking quality. To prove this we use the ranking of [1] as a benchmark. These comparisons are described in Section 5.1. These rankings were done on two datasets of the Census Bureau. The datasets are also described in Section 5.1.

Our tests compare both time and quality of results with the AKN algorithm. The quality of the AKN algorithm's results was compared and validated to statistical methods (for small data sets – where it was feasible to run these tests) in [1] and performed very well. Therefore, it is sufficient to compare our results to AKN. As far as speed, we are not aware of a system capable of producing comparable results to ours on databases of this size. Thus, we present running times of our algorithm on very large data sets. As will be shown, even the AKN algorithm was incapable of running on such large data.

The theoretical efficiency analysis separated our complexity contributors to two classes: the number of fields per record, and the number of records in the database. In Section 5.2 we use again the AKN results as a benchmark. We compare the running times of our algorithm against the AKN algorithm, gradually increasing the number of fields (dimension). Again we ran our tests on the two census datasets.

Finally, in Section 5.3 we test the performance of our algorithm on increasingly large databases having the same number of fields per record. As expected, the increase is linear in the size of the database. We compare the performance to that of the AKN algorithm.

The platform we ran our experiments on is a Pentium

Code	Description	Range
AGE	Person's age	0..90
AGI	Adjusted gross income	$-9999..99,999$
CAPGAIN	Amount of capital gain	0..99,999
DIVVAL	Stock dividends	0..99,999
UCVAL	Unemployment benefits	0..99,999
WSALVAL	Total wage and salary	0..199,998

Table 1. The selected parameters of dataset 'cpsm93p'

III 700MHZ computer with 1GB of memory and running Linux. The algorithms were written in C and all the databases resided on an external hard disk drive.

5.1. Quality Tests

Two datasets were used in [1]. The first dataset was cpsm93p, Current Population Survey of 1993 of personal records, which has 3 types of file groups of the March Questionnaire Supplement. The Person Data Files group was used in [1]. The dataset is available from the DES - Data Extraction System on http://www.census.gov/pub/DES/www/welcome.html. It has 413 attributes, both numeric and nominal. Six numeric attributes were selected. These attributes are described in Table 1.

Only non-empty personal records which had values for the selected attributes were chosen. The total number of records was 155198.

For these 6 attributes there are 60 possible triples. The validity check of AKN rejected 51 of the 60 images and accepted 9. The top 10 selections are described in Table ??. Using histograms of size 100×100 and 50×50 our algorithm accepted 24 triples, including all of the 9 that were accepted by the AKN algorithm. These 9 triples ranked among the top 12. We conclude that while our histogramming method is more lenient as far as accepting hypotheses, it still ranks the top triples very closely to the AKN ranking.

Our experiments also showed that histograms of size 100 and of size 50 accepted the same triples. Their relative rankings were almost identical. This is strong evidence for not needing huge histograms.

The second dataset used by [1] was the census dataset nhis93ac, National Health Interview Survey 1993 (NHIS). The data set is available from http://ferret.bls.census.gov/

Code	Description	Range
AGE	Person's age	0..99
BDDAY12	Bed Days in Past Year	0..365
DV12	Doctor Visits in Past Year	0..997
EDUC	Years of Education	0..18
INCFAMR	Family Income Level	0..8
NCOND	Number of Conditions	0..14
WEIGHT	Weight Without Shoes	$-1, 50..500$

Table 2. The selected parameters of dataset 'nhis93ac'

by using the FERRET data system. It has several hundred numeric and nominal attributes and consists of 45951 records. The numerical attributes described in Table 2 were selected.

For these 7 attributes there are 105 possible triples. The validity check of AKN rejected 86 of the 105 images and accepted 19.

Here also our algorithm accepted more triples. Using histograms of size 100×100 the algorithm accepted 51 triples and using size 50×50 our algorithm accepted 43 triples, including all 19 accepted by the AKN algorithm. The top 10 AKN triples rank in the top 10 triples of our algorithm with both histogram sizes, with only one exception in each case. Again we can conclude that our generalized trimming does not significantly perturb the high ranking.

The relative rankings using the different histogram sizes can be seen in table 3. Again the relative rankings are quite close.

5.2. Scalability Tests on the Dimension

We present running times of the AKN algorithm on the cpsm93p compared with the running times of our algorithm. The object of this test is twofold. The first is to exhibit the time complexity of our algorithm when the size of the database is fixed while the record dimension varies. The second test compares the running times of our algorithm versus the running time of the AKN algorithm.

The numerical results appear in Table 4 and are plotted in Figure 4. We did not test the AKN algorithm for higher dimensions than 15 because even 15 dimensions took two hours and a quarter to run. Our algorithm ran on 28 variables for less than 42 minutes.

Triple			Hist. (100)	Hist. (50)
AGE	INCFAMR	EDUC	1	1
INCFAMR	WEIGHT	EDUC	2	4
DV12	WEIGHT	EDUC	3	6
AGE	NCOND	EDUC	4	3
INCFAMR	NCOND	EDUC	5	5
BDDAY12	WEIGHT	EDUC	6	19
NCOND	WEIGHT	EDUC	7	8
AGE	BDDAY12	EDUC	8	12
AGE	DV12	EDUC	9	2
DV12	INCFAMR	EDUC	10	7
BDDAY12	WEIGHT	NCOND	11	13
BDDAY12	WEIGHT	DV12	12	9
BDDAY12	WEIGHT	AGE	13	33
BDDAY12	INCFAMR	NCOND	14	16
EDUC	WEIGHT	INCFAMR	15	15
DV12	WEIGHT	AGE	16	17
BDDAY12	DV12	NCOND	17	10
BDDAY12	EDUC	AGE	18	18
NCOND	WEIGHT	AGE	19	11
BDDAY12	EDUC	INCFAMR	20	53

Table 3. The relative rankings of the accepted triples using different histogram sizes

dims.	AKN Alg.	New Alg.
4	48.5	5.1
6	251	13
8	771	29.2
10	1745	58.3
15	7740	221
20		582
25		1472
28		2497

Table 4. Running time on cpsm93p. Fixed dataset, variable dimension.

Figure 4 clearly shows what our analysis predicted, i.e., that the running time is $O(d^3)$, where d is the number of dimensions.

5.3. Scalability Tests on Synthetic Data

As previously mentioned, our analysis shows that for a fixed record dimension the complexity of our algorithm grows linearly with the size of the database. We have run

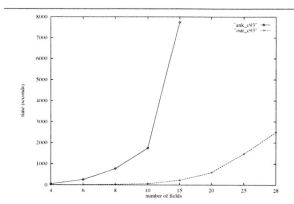

Figure 4. Plot of the AKN running time vs. our running time as a function of the dimension.

Num of rec.	Time (sec.)
100,000	56.4
500,000	269
1,000,000	537
10,000,000	4936

Table 5. Running time as a function of the database size

our algorithm on databases with number of records ranging from $100,000$ to $10,000,000$ (the database sizes range from 5MB to 0.5GB). The records contained 10 fields and we sought all three-dimensional relations. We have used a synthetic data generator similar to the one described in [?] to generate the data. We generated three dimensional clusters in a 10-dimensional space. Every triple of variables that creates a cluster will be accepted by our algorithm in all combinations, thus the algorithm ran on large data sets that have local three dimensional correlations.

Table 5 gives the running times on the various database sizes. It shows that the growth is, indeed, linear.

6. Conclusions

The AKN method proposed in [1] has some advantages over seeking clusters. However, its time complexity was rather high both with respect to the database size and to the number of attributes in a record.

We have shown an efficient implementation of the AKN method. This implementation minimizes the number of disk swaps and allows finding correlations between triples of variables in high dimensional databases.

We presented a scalable, incremental and interruptible algorithm. We tested our algorithm both for quality of results and for efficiency in database size and in database dimension.

We have also shown that a rather small histogram size still achieves good results. This offers possibilities for hybrid solutions in even larger dimensions. One may start with a very small histogram, establish the accepted triples, and then run the algorithm again only on the accepted triples with a larger histogram. Thus, our system will automatically point out to the investigator "interesting" subsets of variables with local (non liner) correlations in a given large multivariate database, so that these subsets can be further explored.

7. Acknowledgments

The authors gratefully thank Daniel Keim and Markus Wawryniuk for providing use of the synthetic data generator and for helpful discussions.

References

[1] A. Amir, R. Kashi, and N. S. Netanyahu. Analyzing quantitative databases: Image is everything. In *VLDB 2001, Proceedings of the 27th International Conference on Very Large Data Bases*, pages 89–98, Rome, Italy, September 11–14 2001.

[2] R. M. Haralick. Statistical and structural approaches to texture. *Proceedings of the IEEE*, 67(5):786–804, May 1979.

[3] R. J. Bayardo Jr. and R. Agrawal. Mining the most interesting rules. In *Proc. of the fifth ACM SIGKDD Int'l Conf. on Knowledge Discovery and Data Mining*, pages 145–154, 1999.

[4] D. A. Keim, H-. P. Kriegel, and T. Seidl. Supporting data mining of large databases by visual feedback queries. In *Proc. 10th Data Engineering*, pages 302–303, Housten, TX, 1994.

[5] J. Misra and D. Gries. Finding repeated elements. *Science of Computer Programming*, 2(2):143–152, November 1982.

[6] V. Poosala. *Histogram-based Estimation Techniques in Databases*. PhD thesis, Univ. of Wisconsin, Madison, 1997.

[7] V. Poosala, Y. Ioannidis, P. Haas, and E. Shekita. Improved histograms for selectivity estimation of range predicates. In *Proc. of ACM SIGMOD Conf.*, pages 294–305, June 1996.

[8] P. J. Rousseeuw and A. M. Leroy. *Robust Regression and Outlier Detection*. Wiley Series in Probability and Mathematical Statistics. John Wiley and Sons, 1987.

ExAMiner:
Optimized Level-wise Frequent Pattern Mining with Monotone Constraints

Francesco Bonchi, Fosca Giannotti
Pisa KDD Laboratory
ISTI - C.N.R. Area della Ricerca di Pisa
Via Giuseppe Moruzzi 1, 56124 Pisa, Italy
bonchi@di.unipi.it, f.giannotti@cnuce.cnr.it

Alessio Mazzanti, Dino Pedreschi
Pisa KDD Laboratory
Dipartimento di Informatica, Università di Pisa
Via F. Buonarroti 2, 56127 Pisa, Italy
mazzanta@cli.di.unipi.it, pedre@di.unipi.it

Abstract

The key point of this paper is that, in frequent pattern mining, the most appropriate way of exploiting monotone constraints in conjunction with frequency is to use them in order to reduce the problem input together with the search space. Following this intuition, we introduce ExAMiner, a level-wise algorithm which exploits the real synergy of anti-monotone and monotone constraints: the total benefit is greater than the sum of the two individual benefits. Ex-AMiner generalizes the basic idea of the preprocessing algorithm ExAnte [4], embedding such ideas at all levels of an Apriori-like computation. The resulting algorithm is the generalization of the Apriori algorithm when a conjunction of monotone constraints is conjoined to the frequency anti-monotone constraint. Experimental results confirm that this is, so far, the most efficient way of attacking the computational problem in analysis.

1. Introduction

Constrained itemset mining i.e., finding all itemsets included in a transaction database that satisfy a given set of constraints, is an active research theme in data mining [6, 8, 11, 12]. The class of anti-monotone constraints is the most effective and easy to use in order to prune the search space. Since any conjunction of anti-monotone constraints is in turn anti-monotone, we can use the *Apriori pruning method*: the more anti-monotone constraints are available, the more selective the *Apriori pruning method* will be. The dual class, monotone constraints, has been considered more complicated to exploit and less effective in pruning the search space. The problem of mining itemsets which satisfy a conjunction of anti-monotone and monotone constraints has been studied for a long time [8, 11], but all these studies have failed in finding the real synergy be-

tween the two opposite pruning opportunities. All the authors have stated that this is the inherent difficulty of the computational problem: when dealing with a conjunction of monotone and anti-monotone constraints we face a tradeoff between anti-monotone and monotone pruning. Our observation is that this prejudice holds only if we focus exclusively on the search space of the itemsets, which is the approach followed by the work done so far. In [4] we have shown that a real synergy of the two opposite pruning exists, and can be exploited by reasoning on both the itemsets search space and the transactions input database *together*. In this way, pushing monotone constraints does not reduce anti-monotone pruning opportunities, on the contrary, such opportunities are boosted. Dually, pushing anti-monotone constraints boosts monotone pruning opportunities: the two components strengthen each other. On the basis of these considerations we have introduced ExAnte [4], a pre-processing data reduction algorithm which reduces dramatically both the search space and the input dataset in constrained frequent pattern mining.

In this paper we show how the basic ideas of ExAnte can be generalized in a level-wise, Apriori-like computation. The resulting algorithm can be seen as the real generalization of Apriori, able to exploit both kind of constraints to reduce the search space. We named our algorithm **Ex-AMiner** (**ExA**nte **Miner** in contrast with ExAnte preprocessor, but also **Miner** which **Ex**ploits **A**nti-monotone and **M**onotone constraints together). Since the most appropriate way of exploiting monotone constraints in conjunction with frequency is to reduce the problem input, which in turn induces a reduction of the search space, the mining philosophy of ExAMiner is to reduce as much as possible the problem dimensions at all levels of the computation. Therefore, instead of trying to explore the exponentially large search space in some smart way, we massively reduce such search space as soon as possible, obtaining a progressively easier mining problem. Experimental results confirm that this is, at this moment, the most efficient way of attacking the computational problem in analysis. Moreover, ExAMiner makes it feasible the computation of *extreme patterns*, i.e. extremely long or extremely costly patterns, which can be found only at very low support levels where all the other known mining approaches can not always complete the computation. Even if the support threshold is very low, ExAMiner, exploiting the extremely strong selectivity of the monotone constraint, reduces drastically the problem dimensions and makes the computation affordable.

2. Problem Definition

Let $Items = \{x_1, ..., x_n\}$ be a set of distinct literals, usually called **items**. An **itemset** X is a non-empty subset of $Items$. If $|X| = k$ then X is called a **k-itemset**. A **transaction** is a couple $\langle tID, X \rangle$ where tID is the transaction identifier and X is the content of the transaction (an itemset). A **transaction database** TDB is a set of transactions. An itemset X is **contained** in a transaction $\langle tID, Y \rangle$ if $X \subseteq Y$. Given a transaction database TDB the subset of transaction which contain an itemset X is named $TDB[X]$. The **support** of an itemset X, written $supp_{TDB}(X)$ is the cardinality of $TDB[X]$. Given a user-defined **minimum support** δ, an itemset X is called **frequent** in TDB if $supp_{TDB}(X) \geq \delta$. This defines the frequency constraint $\mathcal{C}_{freq}[TDB]$: if X is frequent we write $\mathcal{C}_{freq}[TDB](X)$ or simply $\mathcal{C}_{freq}(X)$. Let $Th(\mathcal{C}) = \{X | \mathcal{C}(X)\}$ denotes the set all itemsets X that satisfy constraint $\mathcal{C}$. The *frequent itemset mining problem* requires to compute the set of all frequent itemsets $Th(\mathcal{C}_{freq})$. In general given a conjunction of constraints $\mathcal{C}$ the *constrained itemset mining problem* requires to compute $Th(\mathcal{C})$; the *constrained frequent itemsets mining problem* requires to compute $Th(\mathcal{C}_{freq}) \cap Th(\mathcal{C})$.

We now formally define the notion of anti-monotone and monotone constraints.

Definition 1. *Given an itemset X, a constraint $\mathcal{C}_{AM}$ is anti-monotone if:* $\forall Y \subseteq X : \mathcal{C}_{AM}(X) \Rightarrow \mathcal{C}_{AM}(Y)$.

The frequency constraint is clearly anti-monotone. This property is used by the Apriori algorithm with the following heuristic: if an itemset X does not satisfy $\mathcal{C}_{freq}$, then no superset of X can satisfy $\mathcal{C}_{freq}$, and hence they can be pruned. The Apriori algorithm operates in a level-wise fashion moving bottom-up on the itemset lattice, and each time it finds an infrequent itemset it prunes away all its supersets.

Definition 2. *Given an itemset X, a constraint $\mathcal{C}_M$ is strongly monotone if:* $\forall Y \supseteq X : \mathcal{C}_M(X) \Rightarrow \mathcal{C}_M(Y)$ *independently from the given input transaction database.*

Note that in the last definition we have required a strongly monotone constraint to be satisfied independently from the given input transaction database. This

is necessary since we want to distinguish between simple monotone constraints and global constraints such as the *"infrequency constraint"* ($supp_{TDB}(X) \leq \delta$). This constraint is still monotone but has different properties since it is dataset dependent and it requires dataset scans in order to be computed. Since our algorithm reduces the transaction dataset, we want to exclude the infrequency constraint from our study. In the rest of this paper, we write, for the sake of brevity, monotone instead of strongly monotone.

The general problem that we consider in this paper is the mining of itemsets which satisfy a conjunction of monotone and anti-monotone constraints: $Th(\mathcal{C}_{AM}) \cap Th(\mathcal{C}_M)$. Since any conjunction of anti-monotone constraints is an anti-monotone constraint, and any conjunction of monotone constraints is a monotone constraint, we just consider two constraints: one per class. In particular, we choose frequency ($\mathcal{C}_{AM} \equiv supp_{TDB}(X) \geq \delta$) as anti-monotone constraint, in conjunction with various simple monotone constraints: $Th(\mathcal{C}_{freq}) \cap Th(\mathcal{C}_M)$.

3. Related Work

In [11] a FP-tree based algorithm for mining frequent itemset with monotone constraints, is introduced. Strictly speaking, this algorithm, named $\mathcal{FIC}^\mathcal{M}$, can not be considered a constraint-pushing technique, since it generates the complete set of frequent itemsets, no matter whether they satisfy or not the monotone constraint. The only advantage against a pure *generate & test* algorithm is that it only tests some of frequent itemsets against the monotone constraint. Once a frequent itemset satisfies the monotone constraint, all frequent itemsets having it as a prefix also are guaranteed to satisfy the constraint.

In [7] it is shown that pushing monotone constraints can lead to a reduction of anti-monotone pruning. Therefore, when dealing with a conjunction of monotone and anti-monotone constraints we face a tradeoff between anti-monotone and monotone pruning. This work has a pure theoretical value, as no practical algorithm is proposed.

The first work trying to find an amalgam between anti-monotone and monotone pruning is **DualMiner** [5]. However, DualMiner does not compute all solution itemsets with their support and thus can not be used for constrained frequent pattern mining in contexts where the support of each solution is required, for instance when we want to compute association rules. Moreover, the dual top-down bottom-up exploration of the search space, performed by DualMiner, faces many practical limitations. First it uses multiple scan of the database, even to compute supports of itemsets of the same size. This is due to inherent *divide-et-impera* strategy characterizing the DualMiner computation. For the same reason, it can not exploit data reduction techniques as those ones introduced in this paper. Finally, in real-world problems, even on dense datasets, or at very low support levels, frequency remains always a very selective constraint: the DualMiner top-down computation, exploiting $\mathcal{C}_M$ pruning, will usually perform a huge number of useless tests on very large itemsets, inducing a degradation of the performance.

In [3] we have introduced a general adaptive constraint pushing (*ACP*) strategy. Both monotone and anti-monotone pruning are exploited in a level-wise computation. Level by level, while acquiring new knowledge about the dataset characteristics and selectivity of constraints, *ACP* adapts its behavior giving more power to one pruning over the other in order to maximize efficiency. The proposed algorithm exhibits interesting performances when attacking very dense datasets, on which data reduction strategies are less effective. Thus, *ACP* more than a concurrent of ExAMiner can be seen as an alternative when the input dataset is very dense.

4. Search Space and Input Data Reduction

In order to obtain a real amalgam of the two opposite pruning strategies we have to consider the constrained frequent patterns problem in its whole: not focussing only on the itemsets lattice but considering it together with the input database of transactions. In fact, as proved by the following key theorem [4], monotone constraints can prune away transactions from the input dataset *without losing solutions*.

Proposition 1 (μ-reduction). *Given a transaction database TDB and a monotone constraint $\mathcal{C}_M$, we can prune from TDB the transactions that do not satisfy $\mathcal{C}_M$, without changing the supports to solutions itemsets.*

This monotone pruning of transactions has got another positive effect: while reducing the number of transactions in input it reduces the support of items too, hence the total number of frequent 1-itemsets. In other words, the monotone pruning of transactions strengthens the anti-monotone pruning. Moreover, infrequent items can be deleted by the computation and hence pruned away from the transactions in the input dataset (we named this pruning α-reduction). This anti-monotone pruning has got another positive effect: reducing the size of a transaction which satisfies a monotone constraint can make the transaction violates the monotone constraint. Therefore a growing number of transactions which do not satisfy the monotone constraint can be found. We are clearly inside a loop where two different kinds of pruning cooperates to reduce the search space and the input dataset, strengthening each other step by step until no more pruning is possible (a fix-point has been reached). This is the key idea of ExAnte preprocessing [4] which is generalized to a level-wise computation in this paper.

In a level-wise computation, we collect new information level by level. If we can exploit such information to prune items from the transactions, we obtain new opportunities to μ-reduce again the transaction database.

After the introduction of Apriori [1], a lot of other algorithms, sharing the same level-wise structure, have been proposed. Even if usually proposed as new algorithm with their own names, they can essentially be considered optimizations to the basic Apriori schema. Some of these proposed optimizations are data-reduction techniques, which, if exploited alone, bring little benefit to the computation. But if we couple such anti-monotonicity based optimizations with ExAnte's μ-reduction we can obtain dramatically effective optimizations. In the rest of this section we review all possible data reduction strategies which are based on the anti-monotonicity of frequency. Coupling them with a monotone constraint, and thus with the μ-reduction, we obtaini the ExAMiner algorithm.

In the following propositions [9], we indicate with k the actual iteration, where frequent k-itemsets are computed.

Proposition 2 (Anti-monotone global pruning of an item). *At the iteration k, a singleton item which is not subset of at least k frequent k-itemsets, will not be subset of any frequent $(k + 1)$-itemset, and thus it can be pruned away from all transactions in the input database.*

In the pseudo-code of the algorithm, we use an array of integers V_k (of the size of $Items$), which records for each item the number of frequent k-itemsets in which it appears. While the last proposition induce a pruning which is global to the whole database, the next two propositions [10] induce pruning which are local to a transaction.

Proposition 3 (Anti-monotone local pruning of a transaction). *Given a transaction $\langle tID, X \rangle$, if X is not superset of at least $k + 1$ candidate k-itemsets, then the transaction can be pruned away since it will never be superset of any frequent $(k + 1)$-itemset.*

This property can be checked locally for each transaction t, during the support counting phase, by keeping track of the number of candidate k-itemsets covered by t ($t.count$ in the pseudo-code).

Actually, we can perform more local pruning in a transaction $\langle tID, X \rangle$. Suppose, we know for each item $i \in X$, the number of candidate k-itemsets which are superset of $\{i\}$ and subset of X. We call this number multiplicity of i w.r.t. X at the iteration k and indicate it as $M(i, X)_k$.

Proposition 4 (Anti-monotone local pruning of an item). *Given a transaction $\langle tID, X \rangle$, for each $i \in X$, if $M(i, X)_k < k$ then i can be pruned from X.*

In the pseudo-code of the algorithm, for each transaction t at the iteration k, and for each item in t, we use a counter *i.count* for computing the multiplicity of i w.r.t. t at the iteration k.

Clearly, every time we reduce the size of a transaction we create a new opportunity of pruning the transaction (μ-reduction of the dataset).

5. Further Pruning Opportunities

In this section we introduce novel powerful pruning strategies, which couple more tightly the anti-monotone and monotone pruning.

When the monotone constraint is a cardinality constraint $\mathcal{C}_M \equiv card(S) \geq n$, the following proposition can be used to obtain a stronger pruning at a very low computational price. The following is a generalization of Proposition 2.

Proposition 5 (Enhanced global pruning of an item). *At the iteration k, a singleton item which is not subset of at least $\binom{n-1}{k-1}$ frequent k-itemsets (where $1 < k < n$), will not be subset of any frequent n-itemset.*

The same condition can be further exploited. Consider a generic iteration k of a generic level-wise computation. At the end of the count phase, we have generated the set of frequent k-itemsets L_k, which normally would be used to generate the set of candidate itemsets for the next iteration. For each item i, which does not satisfy the condition in the above proposition, we can prune from the set of generators L_k, each k-itemset containing it, before the generation phase starts. The following corollary of Proposition 5, represents the first proposal of a strategy for pruning the generators, since usually pruning strategies are defined for pruning the candidate itemsets (the generated ones).

Corollary 1 (Generators Pruning). *Consider the computational problem $Th(\mathcal{C}_{freq}) \cap Th(\mathcal{C}_M)$ where $\mathcal{C}_M \equiv card(S) \geq n$. At the iteration k ($1 < k < n$) of the level-wise computation, consider the set S_k of itemsets in L_k which contain at least a singleton item which does not appear in at least $\binom{n-1}{k-1}$ itemsets of L_k.*

$$S_k = \{X \in L_k | \exists i \in X, V_k[i] < m\} \text{ where } m = \binom{n-1}{k-1}$$

In order to generate the set of candidates for the next iteration C_{k+1}, we can use as generators the itemsets in $L_k \setminus S_k$ without losing solutions to the given problem.

Analogously, the same kind of enhancement can be applied to the local pruning of an item from a transaction. The next corollary of Proposition 5, enhances Proposition 4, when we have to deal with a cardinality constraint.

Corollary 2 (Enhanced local pruning of an item). *Consider the computational problem $Th(\mathcal{C}_{freq}) \cap Th(\mathcal{C}_M)$ where $\mathcal{C}_M \equiv card(S) \geq n$. At the iteration k ($1 < k < n$) of the level-wise computation, consider a transaction $\langle tID, X \rangle$, for each $i \in X$, if $M(i,X)_k < \binom{n-1}{k-1}$ then i can be pruned from X.*

Similar pruning enhancements can be obtained also for all monotone constraints, inducing weaker conditions from the above propositions on cardinality.

Consider, for instance, $\mathcal{C}_M \equiv sum(S.price) \geq m$, and suppose that we are at the end of iteration k of the level-wise computation. As usual, we have recorded in $V_k[i]$ the number of frequent k-itemsets in which i appears. It is always possible to compute the maximum value of n for which continues to hold: $V_k[i] \geq \binom{n-1}{k-1}$. This value of n represents an upper-bound for the maximum size of a frequent itemset containing i. In the pseudo-code we use a function **determine_max_n**$(V_k[i], k)$ to determine such upper-bound. Therefore, if we sum the *price* of i with the prices of the $n-1$ most expansive items which are still alive, we can obtain an upper-bound for the total sum of prices of a frequent itemset containing i. In the pseudo-code we use a function **optimistic_monotone_value**$(i, Items, n, \mathcal{C}_M)$ to compute such upper-bound. If this sum is less then the monotone constraint threshold m, the item i can be globally pruned away, with all its supersets which are in L_k, since they can not be solutions.

This generators pruning techniques is twofold benefic. In fact, the proposed technique, not only reduces the generators, and hence the number of candidates at the next iteration, but it also reduces the number of checking of $\mathcal{C}_M$: in fact we prune itemsets from L_k which can not be solution, before the checking of $\mathcal{C}_M$.

A similar reasoning can be done to enhance the local pruning of items from a transaction for all kinds of monotone constraint.

6. ExAMiner Algorithm

Essentially ExAMiner is an Apriori-like algorithm, which exploits anti-monotone and monotone constraints to reduce the problem dimensions level-wise. Each transaction, before participating to the support count, is reduced as much as possible, and only if it survives to this phase, it is used to count the support of candidate itemsets. Each transaction which arrives to the counting phase at iteration k, is then reduced again as much as possible, and only if it survives to this second set of reductions, it is written to the transaction database for the next iteration. Therefore, in order to describe the proposed algorithm, is sufficient to provide the pseudo-code for the procedure which substitutes the counting phase of the Apriori algorithm. This new procedure is named *count&reduce*. In the following with TDB_k we indicate the transaction database at the iteration k.

As already stated, each transaction t in the database passes through two series of reductions and tests. The first reduction (lines 3 and 4 of the pseudo-code) is the global pruning of items (Proposition 2 and 5) which exploits the in-

14

Procedure: **enhanced_local_pruning**$(Items, \mathcal{C}_M, t)$	Procedure: **enhanced_global_pruning**$(Items, \mathcal{C}_M, V_k)$
1. **forall** $i \in t$ **do** $drop_L[i] = false$;	1. **forall** $i \in Items$ **do** $drop_G[i] = false$;
2. **if** $\mathcal{C}_M \equiv card(X) \geq n$ **then**	2. **if** $\mathcal{C}_M \equiv card(X) \geq n$ **then**
3. **forall** $i \in t$ **do**	3. **forall** $i \in Items$ **do**
4. **if** $i.count < \binom{n-1}{k-1}$ **then** $drop_L[i] = true$;	4. **if** $V_k[i] < \binom{n-1}{k-1}$ **then** $drop_G[i] = true$;
5. **else forall** $i \in t$ **do**	5. **else forall** $i \in Items$ **do**
6. $n = determine\_max\_n(i.count, k)$;	6. $n = determine\_max\_n(V_k[i], k)$;
7. **if** $optimistic\_monotone\_value(i, t, n, \mathcal{C}_M) \not\vDash \mathcal{C}_M$	7. **if** $optimistic\_monotone\_value(i, Items, n, \mathcal{C}_M) \not\vDash \mathcal{C}_M$
8. **then** $drop_L[i] = true$	8. **then** $drop_G[i] = true$
9. **return** $drop_L[\,]$	9. **return** $drop_G[\,]$

Procedure: **count&reduce**$(min\_supp, C_k, TDB_k, \mathcal{C}_M, V_{k-1})$

1. **forall** $i \in Items$ **do** $V_k[i] = 0$;
2. **forall** tuples t in TDB_k **do**
3.   **forall** $i \in t$ **do if** $((V_{k-1}[i] < k-1)$ **or** $drop_G[i])$
4.   **then** remove i from t; remove i from $Items$;
5.   **else** $i.count = 0$;
6.   **if** $|t| \geq k$ **then**
7.   **if** $\mathcal{C}_M(t)$ **then**
8.   **forall** $X \in C_k, X \subseteq t$ **do**
9. $X.count++$; $t.count++$;
10.   **forall** $i \in X$ **do** $i.count++$;
11.   **if** $X.count == min\_supp$ **then**
12. $L_k = L_k \cup \{X\}$;
13.   **forall** $i \in X$ **do** $V_k[i]++$;
14.   **if** $|t| \geq k+1$ **then**
15.   **if** $t.count \geq k+1$ **then**
16. $drop_L[\,]$=**enhanced_local_pruning**$(Items, \mathcal{C}_M, t)$;
17.   **forall** $i \in t$ **if** $((i.count < k)$ **or** $drop_L[i])$
18.   **then** remove i from t;
19.   **if** $|t| > k$ **then**
20.   **if** $\mathcal{C}_M(t)$ **then** $write(t, TDB_{k+1})$;
21. $drop_G[\,]$=**enhanced_global_pruning**$(Items, \mathcal{C}_M, V_k)$;
22. **forall** $X \in L_k$ **do**
23.   **if** $\exists i \in X : drop_G[i]$ **then** remove X from L_k;

formation in the array V_{k-1}. After this reduction the transaction is first tested for its cardinality (line 6), and then it's tested against the monotone constraint (line 7, μ-reduction). Only if both tests are passed the transaction t is matched against candidate itemsets to increase their support counts (lines from 8 to 12). During this phase we collect other information regarding t and each item i in t: the number of candidates itemset contained in t (line 9), the multiplicity of i w.r.t. t at the current iteration (line 10), and the number of frequent itemsets containing i (line 13).

If the transaction t has arrived alive to this point, it has still to pass some tests in order to enter into the database for the next iteration. First of all we check if its cardinality is at least $k + 1$ (line 14). Then we check if during the counting phase it has participated to the count of at least $k + 1$ can-

didate k-itemsets (line 15, Proposition 3). After this, if the transaction is still alive, it is further reduced by enhanced local pruning of items (lines 16, 17 and 18). After this reduction we check again the size of the transaction t and if it satisfies the monotone constraint. If also these last two tests are positive the transaction t enters in the database for the next iteration. Finally, we collect information for the enhanced global pruning (line 21), and we perform the pruning of generators (line 23).

6.1. Moving Through the Levels

The proposed data reduction strategy, when instantiated at the first iteration, corresponds to the ExAnte algorithm, with the unique difference that, in ExAnte, the computation starts again and again from the same level until there are pruning opportunities. This approach can be exploited also at the other levels of the ExAMiner level-wise computation. In fact, since during a *count&reduce* round, we reduce the input dataset, as well as the search space, we could start again with another *count&reduce* round at the same level with the reduced transaction dataset. Therefore, we face a choice between different strategies. On one hand, we can have a strictly level-wise computation, in the style of Apriori. On the other hand, we can stand for more than one *count&reduce* round on each level. Between these two extremes we can have a whole range of computational strategies. Essentially we have two dimensions: (i) how many *count&reduce* rounds we admit, (ii) and for which levels of the level-wise computation. We have implemented and tested (see Section 7) three different versions of ExAMiner:

- **ExAMiner$_0$**: it strictly moves on level-wise, allowing only one *count&reduce* round for each level. This is the real generalization of the Apriori algorithm which uses the monotone constraint to reduce the input data and the search space.

- **ExAMiner$_1$**: it allows an undefined number of rounds, until a fix point is reached, only at the first level. This corresponds to an ExAnte preprocessing followed by a strictly level-wise ExAMiner computation.

15

- **ExAMiner$_2$**: it allows an undefined number of *count&reduce* rounds, until a fix point is reached, only at the first two levels. Then, from the third iteration, the computation becomes strictly level-wise.

The rationale behind these implementation choices is that the first two iterations of the usual level-wise algorithm, are the most efficient, since the count can be performed directly, without using complex data structures. From the third iteration, the count become very expensive. Therefore, we have decided to reduce as much as possible the problem during the first two iterations, and then go on directly to compute the solution of the problem.

6.2. Run-through Example

We now show an example of execution of $ExAMiner_2$. Suppose that the transaction and price dataset in Figure 1 (a) and (b) are given. Suppose that we want to compute frequent itemsets ($min\_supp = 3$) with a sum of prices ≥ 30. During the first iteration the total price of each transaction is checked to avoid using transactions which do not satisfy the monotone constraint. All transaction with a sum of prices ≥ 30 are used to count the support for the singleton items. Only the first transaction is discarded.

At the end of the count we find items b, d and h to be infrequent. Note that, if the first transaction had not been discarded, item h would have been counted as frequent. At this point we perform an α-reduction of the dataset: this means removing b, d and h from all transactions in the dataset.

After the α-reduction we have more opportunities to μ-reduce the dataset. In fact, transaction 3, which at the beginning has a total price of 34, now has its total price reduced to 29 due to the pruning of h. This transaction can now be pruned away. The same reasoning holds for the transactions number 3 and 5. At this point we count once again the support of alive items with the reduced dataset. The item f which initially has got a support of 3 now has become infrequent due to the pruning of transaction 5. We can α-reduce again the dataset, removing f from all transactions. Then we can μ-reduce again. In fact, after the removal of f, transactions 9 and 10 have a total price which is less than 30, and thus they are pruned too. We count once again the support of all itemsets and no one has become infrequent. We have reached a fix-point for level one. At this point the input transaction database is as in Figure 1(c). Moreover we have $L_1 = \{a, c, e, g, i, j, k, l\}$, and C_2 which contains all possible couples of items from L_1.

We start with the second level of the level-wise computation. The first set of reductions and tests (lines from 3 to 5 of the pseudo-code) produce no pruning at the beginning of the second level. The support counting phase starts. At the end of this phase we have $L_2 = \{ak, ce, cg, cj, eg, ei, gi, ij, jk, jl\}$.

Item	Price
a	10
b	20
c	8
d	22
e	15
f	10
g	6
h	5
i	10
j	5
k	18
l	14

(a)

tID	Itemset	Total
1	g,h,i	21
2	a,d,i,k	60
3	a,c,g,h,j	34
4	i,l,j,k	47
5	f,h,k	33
6	c,e,j,k	46
7	a,c,g,l,j,k	61
8	c,e,g,i,j	44
9	f,g,i,j	31
10	c,f,g,i,j	39
11	b,c,e,g,i	59
12	a,d,g,k	56
13	e,g,i	31
14	a,b,i,l,j	59

(b)

tID	Itemset	Total
2	a,i,k	38
4	i,l,j,k	47
6	c,e,j,k	46
7	a,c,g,l,j,k	61
8	c,e,g,i,j	44
11	c,e,g,i	39
12	a,g,k	34
13	e,g,i	31
14	a,i,l,j	39

(c)

tID	Itemset	Total
8	e,g,i	31
11	e,g,i	31
13	e,g,i	31

(d)

Figure 1. Run-through Example

The second part of reductions and test produces no pruning since we are at the second level. We start another *count&reduce* round at the second level. Items a and l are globally pruned from all transactions because they appear in only one frequent 2-itemset: $V_2[a] = 1, V_2[l] = 1$. This pruning gives us more opportunities of μ-reducing the dataset. Transactions number 2, 12 and 14 can be pruned away since they no longer satisfy the monotone constraint. Thanks to this data reduction, at the end of another counting phase, we have a smaller set of frequent 2-itemsets: $L_2 = \{ce, cg, cj, eg, ei, gi, jk\}$. At this point item k appears in only one frequent 2-itemset, and hence is globally pruned from the transactions. Due to this pruning, transactions number 4, 6 and 7 satisfy no longer the monotone constraint and they are pruned too. The input transaction database has reduced from 14 to 3 transactions. We count using only these 3 transactions and find that $L_2 = \{eg, ei, gi\}$. Items c and j do not appear in any frequent 2-itemsets and they can be pruned away. The resulting transaction database is as in Figure 1(d). Essentially, only the solution to the problem (egi) is alive in the database.

6.3. Dataset Rewriting

ExAMiner at each iteration rewrites a dataset of smaller size. The next iterations has thus to cope with a smaller input dataset than the previous one. The benefits are not only in term of I/O costs, but also of reduced work in subset counting due to the reduced number and size of transactions.

It is worth to observe that, as shown in [2], when a dataset is sequentially scanned by reading fixed blocks of data, one can take advantage of the OS *prefetching*. Overlapping between computation and I/O activity can occur, provided that the computation granularity is large enough. Moreover, OS buffer caching and pipelining techniques virtualize I/O disk accesses, and, more importantly, small datasets (that we can obtain after few iterations from the initial dataset) can be completely contained in buffer cache or in main memory. In

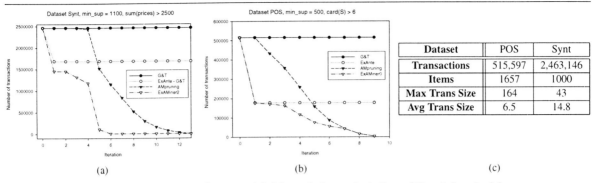

Figure 2. Data reduction rate (a) (b), and characteristics of the datasets (c).

Dataset	POS	Synt
Transactions	515,597	2,463,146
Items	1657	1000
Max Trans Size	164	43
Avg Trans Size	6.5	14.8

summary, if granularity of computation is large enough and datasets are sequentially scanned, prefetching and buffer cache are able to hide I/O time.

In our first implementation we have chosen to rewrite the dataset at each iteration, no matter whether the benefit of the data reduction is worth the I/O cost. This choice was done to concentrate our study on data reduction. However, we can improve our algorithm by forcing it to rewrite the dataset only when the reduction is substantial. For instance, the data reduction rate shown in Figure 3(a) for the $ExAMiner_2$ algorithm suggests to quit rewriting the dataset after the big drop at the fifth iteration.

7. Experimental Results

The test bed architecture used in our experiments was a Windows2000 PC with a Pentium III processor running at 1000MHz and 320MB RAM.

In our experiment we used two different datasets with different characteristics. The first dataset, named "POS", was used in the KDD-Cup 2000 competition and it is described in [13]. The dataset is available from the KDD-Cup 2000 home page[1]. "POS" is a real world dataset containing several years worth of point-of-sale data from a large electronic retailer, aggregated at the product category level. The second dataset, named "Synt" is a synthetic dataset obtained with the most commonly adopted dataset generator, available from IBM Almaden[2]. We associated a price to each item using a uniform distribution.

Figures 2 (a) and (b) report the number of transactions considered, iteration by iteration, by different algorithms. $G\&T$ (generate and test) is a usual Apriori computation, followed by the filtering based on the monotone constraint; $G\&T$ does not exploit any data reduction technique, as it uses the whole initial dataset during the level-wise com-

putation. $ExAnte$-$G\&T$ is a computation composed by an ExAnte preprocessing followed by a $G\&T$ computation: it reduces the dataset as much as possible at the first iteration. With $AMpruning$ we denote a level-wise computation which uses the anti-monotone pruning only: it corresponds to $ExAMiner$ with a trivial monotone constraint, e.g. $sum(prices) \geq 0$. The different behavior of this computation and $ExAMiner_2$ indicates how the pruning is boosted when a monotone constraint is coupled with the frequency constraint.

A run-time comparison between different algorithms on dataset POS, with a monotone cardinality constraint, is reported in Figure 3(a). We have experimented also $\mathcal{FIC}^{\mathcal{M}}$ and $ExAnte$-$\mathcal{FIC}^{\mathcal{M}}$ (i.e. ExAnte preprocessing followed by $\mathcal{FIC}^{\mathcal{M}}$). We have avoided experimenting DualMiner on this dataset, since its dual pruning strategy performs very poorly with the cardinality constraint. It is interesting that, even with a scarcely selective monotone constraint, such as the cardinality constraint, $ExAMiner$ outperforms significantly all other competitors.

The performance improvements become clearer as the monotone constraints become more selective and/or the transaction database larger. In Figure 3(b) and (c) run-time comparisons on the $Synt$ dataset with a $sum(prices) \geq m$ constraint are reported. On this dataset, in our test-bed, $\mathcal{FIC}^{\mathcal{M}}$ was not able to complete the computation due to the excessive memory request to allocate the FP-tree. The $ExAMiner$ computation cut times by the half, and performance improves as the monotone constraint gets more selective (Figure 3(b)) or the minimum support threshold gets more selective (Figure 3(c)).

8. Conclusion and Future Work

This paper introduced ExAMiner, a fast algorithm for frequent pattern mining that exploits anti-monotone and monotone constraints to optimize a level-wise, Apriori-like computation. The strength of the algorithm lies in the

---

1   http://www.ecn.purdue.edu/KDDCUP/
2   http://www.almaden.ibm.com/cs/quest/syndata.html#assocSynData

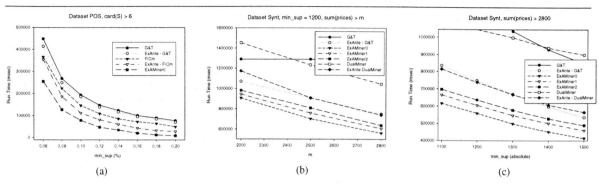

Figure 3. Runtime comparison between different algorithms.

fact that the two kinds of constraints are used synergistically to reduce both the itemset search space and the input database as the computation proceeds. As observed in the suite of experiments, ExAMiner exhibits a sensible improvement with respect to existing algorithms, from the different points of view of performance, reduction of the search space, and the ability to cope with extremely large transaction databases and extremely low support thresholds. Also, in its distinctive feature of dynamically reducing the transaction database, the new algorithm exhibits such dramatic reduction to make it convenient to pay for the extra I/O overhead. We found this results striking, especially in view of the fact that the current implementation of ExAMiner is rather naive, and can be engineered, in principle, to further improve its performance. One possible improvement would be to avoid to dynamically change the transaction database if its reduction rate falls below some given threshold. Another improvement could be obtained by dynamically shifting to the vertical representation of the transaction database (TID lists) as soon as it fits into main memory, as done in [9]. Also, the new algorithm is in principle well-suited to parallel or distributed implementations, which are worth considering in the future. The achieved results and the possibility for further improvements bring us to the conclusion that ExAMiner may enable to deal with frequent pattern queries that are, to date, considered untractable.

Acknowledgements. We are indebted with Laks V.S. Lakshmanan, who first suggested the problem to the first author. This work was supported by "Fondazione Cassa di Risparmio di Pisa" under the "WebDigger Project".

References

[1] R. Agrawal and R. Srikant. Fast Algorithms for Mining Association Rules in Large Databases. In *Proceedings of the Twentieth International Conference on Very Large Databases*, pages 487–499, Santiago, Chile, 1994.

[2] R. Baraglia, D. Laforenza, S. Orlando, P. Palmerini, and R. Perego. Implementation issues in the design of I/O intensive data mining applications on clusters of workstations. In *Proc. of the 3rd Workshop on High Performance Data Mining, LNCS 1800*, pages 350–357, 2000.

[3] F. Bonchi, F. Giannotti, A. Mazzanti, and D. Pedreschi. Adaptive Constraint Pushing in frequent pattern mining. In *Proc. of the 7th Europ. Conf. on Principles and Practice of Knowledge Discovery in Databases (PKDD03)*, 2003.

[4] F. Bonchi, F. Giannotti, A. Mazzanti, and D. Pedreschi. ExAnte: Anticipated data reduction in constrained pattern mining. In *Proc. of the 7th Europ. Conf. on Principles and Practice of Knowledge Discovery in Databases (PKDD03)*, 2003.

[5] C. Bucila, J. Gehrke, D. Kifer, and W. White. DualMiner: A dual-pruning algorithm for itemsets with constraints. In *Proceedings of the 8th ACM SIGKDD International Conference on Knowledge Discovery and Data Mining*, 2002.

[6] J. Han, L. V. S. Lakshmanan, and R. T. Ng. Constraint-based, multidimensional data mining. *Computer*, 32(8):46–50, 1999.

[7] B. Jeudy and J.-F. Boulicaut. Optimization of association rule mining queries. *Intelligent Data Analysis Journal*, 6(4):341–357, 2002.

[8] R. T. Ng, L. V. S. Lakshmanan, J. Han, and A. Pang. Exploratory mining and pruning optimizations of constrained associations rules. In *(SIGMOD-98)*, pages 13–24.

[9] S. Orlando, P. Palmerini, R. Perego, and F. Silvestri. Adaptive and Resource-Aware Mining of Frequent Sets. In *(ICDM'02)*, pages 338–345, Maebashi City, Japan, 2002.

[10] J. S. Park, M.-S. Chen, and P. S. Yu. An effective hash based algorithm for mining association rules. In *SIGMOD95*, pages 175–186, 1995.

[11] J. Pei, J. Han, and L. V. S. Lakshmanan. Mining frequent item sets with convertible constraints. In *(ICDE'01)*, pages 433–442, 2001.

[12] R. Srikant, Q. Vu, and R. Agrawal. Mining association rules with item constraints. In *Proc. 3rd Int. Conf. Knowledge Discovery and Data Mining, KDD*, pages 67–73, 1997.

[13] Z. Zheng, R. Kohavi, and L. Mason. Real world performance of association rule algorithms. In *Proceedings of the Seventh ACM SIGKDD International Conference on Knowledge Discovery and Data Mining*, 2001.

Mining High Utility Itemsets

Raymond Chan
Department of Computer Science
Hong Kong University of
Science & Technology
Hong Kong
raymond.chan@ieee.org

Qiang Yang
Department of Computer Science
Hong Kong University of
Science & Technology
Hong Kong
qyang@cs.ust.hk

Yi-Dong Shen
Laboratory of Computer Science
Institute of Software
Chinese Academy of Sciences
Beijing 100080, China
ydshen@ios.ac.cn

Abstract

Traditional association rule mining algorithms only generate a large number of highly frequent rules, but these rules do not provide useful answers for what the high utility rules are. In this work, we develop a novel idea of top-K objective-directed data mining, which focuses on mining the top-K high utility closed patterns that directly support a given business objective. To association mining, we add the concept of utility to capture highly desirable statistical patterns and present a level-wise itemset mining algorithm. With both positive and negative utilities, the anti-monotone pruning strategy in Apriori algorithm no longer holds. In response, we develop a new pruning strategy based on utilities that allow pruning of low utility itemsets to be done by means of a weaker but anti-monotonic condition. Our experimental results show that our algorithm does not require a user specified minimum utility and hence is effective in practice.

1. Introduction

Association mining is an important problem in data mining. Given a historical dataset of an application, we derive frequent patterns and association rules from the dataset by using some thresholds, such as minimum support and minimum confidence. Since Agrawal's pioneer work [1], a lot of research has been conducted on association mining [2, 3, 5, 6, 7, 8, 9, 11, 14, 15, 16, 17, 18]. Existing approaches to association mining are itemset-correlation-oriented in the sense that they aim to find out how a set of items are statistically correlated by mining association rules of the form

$$I_1, \ldots, I_m \rightarrow I_{m+1}(s\%, c\%) \qquad (1)$$

where $s\%$, the *support* of the rule, is the probability of all items $I_1, \ldots, I_{m+1}$ occurring together, and $c\%$, the *confidence* of the rule, is the conditional probability of I_{m+1} given the itemset $\{I_1, \ldots, I_m\}$.

Although finding itemsets correlations is important in some applications, in many situations people are more in-terested in finding out how a set of items that is useful by some measure. This concept was first introduced in [13]. "Useful" is defined as an itemset that supports a specific objective *Obj* that people want to achieve, and we define association rules in the form of

$$I_1, \ldots, I_m \rightarrow Obj(s\%, c\%, u) \qquad (2)$$

where $s\%$ (support of the rule) is the probability that all items $I_1, \ldots, I_m$ together with *Obj* hold, $c\%$ (confidence of the rule) is the conditional probability of *Obj* given the itemset $\{I_1, \ldots, I_m\}$, and u is the *utility* of the rule showing to what degree the pattern $\{I_1, \ldots, I_m\}$ semantically supports *Obj*. Due to its focus on an objective and the use of utility as key semantic information to measure the usefulness of association patterns, we refer to this new type of association mining as *Objective-Oriented utility-based Association* (OOA) mining, as opposed to traditional *Itemset-Correlation-Oriented Association* (ICOA) mining.

Table 1. A medical dataset *DB*.

R#	tmt	med	eff	sid	R#	tmt	med	eff	sid
1	1	1	2	4	9	4	2	5	2
2	2	1	4	2	10	4	2	4	2
3	2	1	4	2	11	4	2	4	2
4	2	1	2	3	12	4	2	3	1
5	2	1	1	3	13	5	2	4	1
6	3	1	4	2	14	5	2	4	1
7	3	2	4	2	15	5	1	4	1
8	3	2	1	4	16	5	1	3	1

Table 2. Degrees of effectiveness and side-effects.

Effectiveness		Side-effect	
5	Getting much better	4	Very serious
4	Getting better	3	Serious yet tolerable
3	No obvious effect	2	A little
2	Getting worse	1	Normal
1	Getting much worse		

Example 1 Let us consider a simplified dataset *DB* on medical treatments for a certain disease as shown in Table 1, where *Treatment* (tmt), *Medicine* (med), *Effectiveness* (eff), and *Side-effect* (sid) are attributes with domains $\{1, 2, 3, 4, 5\}$, $\{1, 2\}$, $\{1, 2, 3, 4, 5\}$, and $\{1, 2, 3, 4\}$ respectively. R# is not an attribute of *DB*. It is a unique

number to identify each record. Table 2 shows the degrees of effectiveness and side-effects which are assigned by domain experts. The doctor may want to discover from *DB* the best treatment with high effectiveness and low side-effect. The objective *Obj* can be formulated as: (Effectiveness > 3) ∧ (Side-effect < 3). Table 3 shows the supports, confidences and utilities for all rules of the form "Treatment = i → *Obj*" where i is the treatment number.

Table 3. Supports, confidences and utilities.

Obj: (Effectiveness > 3) ∧ (Side-effect < 3)			
OOA Rules	*s%*	*c%*	*u*
Treatment = 1 → *Obj*	0%	0%	−1.6
Treatment = 2 → *Obj*	12.5%	50%	−0.25
Treatment = 3 → *Obj*	12.5%	66.67%	−0.067
Treatment = 4 → *Obj*	18.75%	75%	0.8
Treatment = 5 → *Obj*	18.75%	75%	1.2

OOA mining derives patterns that both statistically and semantically support a given objective *Obj*. Informally, $I = \{I_1, ..., I_m\}$ is said to *statistically support Obj* if the support $s\%$ and confidence $c\%$ of the rule in Eq. (2) are not below a user specified minimum support $ms\%$ and a user specified minimum confidence $mc\%$ respectively, and I is said to *semantically support Obj* if the utility u of the rule in Eq. (2) is not below a user specified minimum utility mu. The resulting patterns from OOA mining must be interesting to an enterprise since when employed, they would increase the (expected) utility above the user specified minimum level. Therefore, OOA mining has wide applications in many areas where people are looking for objective-centered statistical solutions to achieve their goals. Unfortunately, OOA mining is associated with the following two problems.

First, in order to mine all the patterns I statistically supporting *Obj* (I is called a frequent pattern), we may need to generate a lot of patterns, and mining a long frequent pattern requires the generation of many sub-patterns due to the downward closure property of the mining process [9]. Second, setting a minimum utility mu is by no means an easy task and one may need to perform a series of trial and error runs in order to obtain a suitable value. Setting mu to a too small threshold may lead to the generation of many useless rules, whereas a too big threshold may lead to too few rules or even worse no rules at all.

The first problem has been looked at by a couple of researchers previously [9, 11, 18]. Instead of mining frequent patterns, frequent closed patterns should be mined because a closed pattern is a pattern that includes all of its sub-patterns with the same support. For the second problem, it would be advantageous for us if we do not need to specify a minimum utility. In fact it is preferable to mine the top-K utility frequent closed patterns, where K is the desired number of frequent closed patterns (or rules) to be mined, and top-K refers to the K most useful mined rules. K is easy to specify or set default. For example, it would be more natural for a user to specify "give me the 10 most

useful rules" than "give me all rules that have utilities higher than 1.5". The main contribution of this paper is a novel algorithm for discovering the top-K high utility and closed OOA rules without minimum utility.

The organization of the paper is as follows. Section 2 contains a summary of related work. Section 3 defines the concepts of objective, support, confidence, utility, utility lower bound and utility upper bound in OOA mining. In Section 4, we develop algorithms for mining OOA frequent closed patterns and rules. Experimental results are presented in Section 5. Section 6 concludes this paper.

2. Related work

In OOA mining the utility constraint is neither monotone nor anti-monotone. Our algorithm makes use of a weaker but anti-monotonic condition based on utility so that we can prune the search space in order to efficiently derive all OOA rules. Our work also does not need the user to provide the minimum utility and all frequent patterns produced are closed patterns.

Our work is different from existing research on "interestingness" [7, 14], which focuses on finding "interesting patterns" by matching them against a given set of user beliefs. A derived association rule is considered "interesting" if it conforms to or conflicts with the user's beliefs. In contrast, OOA mining measures the interestingness of OOA rules in terms of their probabilities as well as their utilities in supporting the user defined objective.

Sese and Morishita [12] studied mining N most correlated association rules, which is different from our work in two aspects. First, they measure the usefulness of association rules by the significance of the correlation between the assumption and the conclusion whereas we use utility to measure the usefulness of association rules. Second, they do not generate closed itemsets.

Han, et al. [6] proposed a new mining task to mine top-k frequent closed patterns of length no less than *min_l*, where k is the desired number of frequent closed patterns to be mined, and *min_l* is the minimal length of each pattern. Their algorithm is based on the FP-tree mining strategy [5] and does not require the user to specify a minimum support. Their work is different from ours in two different manners. First, their algorithm is based on the construction of an FP-tree whereas ours is Apriori-based. Second, they do not provide a measure to justify the usefulness of all the mined association rules whereas we use the utility concept as the measure.

3. Definitions and concepts

3.1. Objective, support, and confidence

Let *DB* be a dataset with a finite set of attributes DB_{att}. Each attribute $A_i \in DB_{att}$ has a finite domain V_i (continuous attributes can be discretized [4]). For each domain value $v \in V_i$, $A_i = v$ is called an item I_i. An itemset is a set of items, and we denote a k-itemset I as an itemset with k items. DB consists of a finite set of records built from DB_{att}, with each record being a set $\{A_1 = v_1, ..., A_m = v_m\}$ of items where $A_i \neq A_j$ for any $i \neq j$. We use $|DB|$ to denote the total number of records in DB. For any itemset I the function $count(I, DB)$ returns the number of records in DB that are supersets of I. An objective Obj is defined as a logic formula over one or more *objective relation*(s) $A \theta v$ where A is an attribute, θ is a relation symbol such as $\geq, \leq,$ $=$, etc., and v is a domain value. Formally, we have

Definition 1 (Objective) An objective Obj over a dataset DB is a disjunctive normal form $C_1 \vee ... \vee C_m$ ($m \geq 1$) where each C_i is a conjunction $D_1 \wedge ... \wedge D_n$ ($n \geq 1$) with each D_j being an objective relation or the negation of an objective relation.

Example 2 Consider the objective Obj used in Example 1, two objective relations are required, D_1 is Effectiveness > 3, D_2 is Side-effect < 3, and $C_1 = D_1 \wedge D_2 =$ (Effectiveness > 3) $\wedge$ (Side-effect < 3).

The set of attributes DB_{att} can be partitioned into two disjoint non-empty subsets, $DB_{att} = DB_{att}^{Obj} \cup DB_{att}^{nObj}$, where attribute $A \in DB_{att}^{Obj}$ contributes to Obj is called the objective attribute, and attribute $A \in DB_{att}^{nObj}$ does not contribute to Obj is called the non-objective attribute.

In OOA mining, we say an objective Obj holds in a record r in DB (or r supports Obj) if Obj is true given r. Furthermore, for any itemset $I = \{I_1, ..., I_m\}$ we say $I \cup \{Obj\} = \{I_1, ..., I_m, Obj\}$ holds in r if both Obj and all I_is are true in r. The function $count(I \cup \{Obj\}, DB)$ returns the number of records in DB in which $I \cup \{Obj\}$ holds.

Definition 2 (Support and confidence) Let $I = \{I_1, ..., I_m\}$ be an itemset and $I_1, ..., I_m \rightarrow Obj(s\%, c\%, u)$ be an association rule in OOA mining. The support and confidence of the rule are defined as

$$s\% = supp(I, Obj) = \frac{count(\{I_1, ..., I_m, Obj\}, DB)}{|DB|} \times 100\% \quad (3)$$

$$c\% = conf(I, Obj) = \frac{count(\{I_1, ..., I_m, Obj\}, DB)}{count(\{I_1, ..., I_m\}, DB)} \times 100\% \quad (4)$$

3.2. Utility

Let A be an objective attribute and V be its domain. For each $v \in V$, $A = v$ is called an objective item. Based on an objective Obj, the utility of an objective item is given by a utility function $U: f(A = v) \rightarrow \Re$, where $\Re$ is the set of real numbers. The utility function maps to the set of positive real numbers $\Re^+$ (including zero) for each objective item that shows positive support for Obj, and the utility function maps to the set of negative real numbers $\Re^-$ for each objective item that shows negative support for Obj.

Definition 3 (OOA itemset) An *OOA itemset* (or *OOA pattern*) is a set $\{A_1 = v_1, ..., A_m = v_m\}$ of items with $A_i \in DB_{att}^{nObj}$ and $A_i \neq A_j$ for any $i \neq j$.

Example 3 Consider the dataset DB in Example 1. The objective Obj divides the set of attributes DB_{att} into $DB_{att}^{Obj} = \{$eff, sid$\}$ and $DB_{att}^{nObj} = \{$tmt, med$\}$. $\{$tmt = $i\}$, $\{$med = $j\}$, and $\{$tmt = i, med = $j\}$ are all OOA itemsets/patterns, where $i = 1, ..., 5$ and $j = 1, 2$.

Let I be an OOA itemset and r be a record in DB with $I \subset r$. The utility of record r in DB is given by

$$u(r) = \sum_{A \in DB_{att}^{Obj} \wedge A = v \subset r} f(A = v) \quad (5)$$

The total utility of I over DB is then

$$u_{DB}(I) = \sum_{r \in DB \wedge I \subset r} u(r) \quad (6)$$

Definition 4 (Utility) Let $I = \{I_1, ..., I_m\}$ be an OOA itemset and $I_1, ..., I_m \rightarrow Obj(s\%, c\%, u)$ be an association rule in OOA mining. The (expected) utility of the rule (or itemset I) is defined as

$$u = util(I, Obj) = \frac{u_{DB}(I)}{count(I, DB)} \quad (7)$$

Table 4. Utility of objective items.

Effectiveness (eff)	f(eff=v)	Side-effect (sid)	f(sid=v)
5	1	4	−0.8
4	0.8	3	−0.4
3	0	2	0
2	−0.8	1	0.6
1	−1		

Table 5. Utility of record for Treatment = 2.

R#	eff	f(eff=v)	sid	f(sid=v)	u(R#)
2	4	0.8	2	0	0.8
3	4	0.8	2	0	0.8
4	2	−0.8	3	−0.4	−1.2
5	1	−1	3	−0.4	−1.4

Example 4 Table 4 defines the utility function and it shows the utility value associated with each objective item. The objective items that show positive and negative support for Obj are $\{$eff = 5, eff = 4, eff = 3, sid = 1, sid = 2$\}$ and $\{$eff = 1, eff = 2, sid = 4, sid = 3$\}$ respectively. Suppose we look at treatment 2 in Table 1 (records 2 to 5), the utility of each record line is calculated and shown in Table 5. The utility of $I = \{$tmt = 2$\}$ over DB is

$$u = \frac{0.8 + 0.8 + (-1.2) + (-1.4)}{4} = -0.25$$

Definition 5 (OOA frequent itemset) Let $ms\%$ be a user specified minimum support. I is an *OOA frequent itemset/pattern* in DB if $s\% \geq ms\%$.

Definition 6 (OOA frequent closed itemset) Let I be an OOA frequent itemset, i.e. I satisfies the support constraint. I is known as an *OOA frequent closed itemset* if there does not exist an itemset J such that (1) $I \subset J$, and (2) $\forall r \in DB, I \subset r \Rightarrow J \subset r$. In other words, the support of I is the same as the support of I' for any $I' \subset I$.

Example 5 For the dataset DB shown in Table 1, the OOA itemset $I = \{$tmt = 2$\}$ is not a closed itemset because

$J = \{\text{tmt} = 2, \text{med} = 1\}$ exists. In fact J is an OOA closed itemset. $\{\text{tmt} = 3\}$, $\{\text{tmt} = 3, \text{med} = 1\}$ and $\{\text{tmt} = 3, \text{med} = 2\}$ are also OOA closed itemsets.

Definition 7 (OOA rule) Let $mc\%$ and mu be a user specified minimum confidence and minimum utility respectively. Let $I = \{I_1, \ldots, I_m\}$ be an OOA frequent itemset. $I_1, \ldots, I_m \rightarrow Obj(s\%, c\%, u)$ is an *OOA rule* if $c\% \geq mc\%$ and $u \geq mu$.

Theorem 1 below establishes the fact that the support constraint of OOA frequent itemsets is anti-monotone [10], and Theorem 2 states that the utility constraint for OOA rules is neither monotone [10] nor anti-monotone.

Theorem 1 If I is an OOA frequent itemset and $J \subset I$ with $J \neq \varnothing$, J is also an OOA frequent itemset.
Proof: From Eq. (3), $supp(J, Obj) \geq supp(I, Obj) \geq ms\%$ since $J \subset I$ and $J \neq \varnothing$.

Theorem 2 The utility constraint ($u \geq mu$) for OOA rules is neither monotone nor anti-monotone.
Proof: Let us consider treatment 5 in Table 1 (records 13 to 16). Let $I = \{\text{tmt} = 5\}$, $J_1 = \{\text{tmt} = 5, \text{med} = 1\}$, and $J_2 = \{\text{tmt} = 5, \text{med} = 2\}$. The utilities of I, J_1 and J_2 are
$$util(I, Obj) = 1.2$$
$$util(J_1, Obj) = \frac{0.8 + 0.6 + 0 + 0.6}{2} = 1$$
$$util(J_2, Obj) = \frac{0.8 + 0.6 + 0.8 + 0.6}{2} = 1.4$$
It can be seen that the utility of any superset of I can increase or decrease, and hence the utility constraint is neither monotone nor anti-monotone.

3.3. Top-*n* utility and bottom-*n* utility

Although the utility-based OOA itemsets do not satisfy the anti-monotone restriction, we can look for upper or lower bounds of the utilities that do satisfy this condition. If we could do this, we can potentially prune a large set of items that are of low utility early in the search process.

Let S be the set of records $\{r_1, \ldots, r_N\}$ in DB consisting of an OOA k-itemset I, that is
$$S = \{r_1, \ldots, r_N\} = \{r_i \mid I \subset r_i\} \quad (8)$$
where $i = 1, \ldots, N$, and $N = |S|$ is the number of records in S. Suppose we sort the records in S in decreasing order of utility, that is, $u(r_1) \geq u(r_2) \geq \ldots \geq u(r_N)$.

Definition 8 (Top-*n* utility) The top-*n* utility of I is defined as
$$u^{(n)}(I) = \frac{1}{n} \sum_{i=1}^{n} u(r_i) \quad \text{where } n = 1, \ldots, N \quad (9)$$

Definition 9 (Bottom-*n* utility) The bottom-*n* utility of I is defined as
$$u_{(n)}(I) = \frac{1}{n} \sum_{i=N-n+1}^{N} u(r_i) \quad \text{where } n = 1, \ldots, N \quad (10)$$

If we choose $n = ms\% \times |DB|$, the top-*n* utility and bottom-*n* utility become the tightest upper bound and lower bound of any OOA frequent itemset J that is a superset of I respectively. Formally, we have

Theorem 3 Let I be an OOA frequent itemset. For any OOA frequent itemset $J \supset I$, the utility of the itemset J, $util(J, Obj)$, satisfies the following inequality.
$$u_{(n)}(I) \leq util(J, Obj) \leq u^{(n)}(I) \text{ where } n = ms\% \times |DB| \quad (11)$$
Proof: Since $I \subset J$, $u^{(n)}(I) \geq u^{(n)}(J)$ and $u_{(n)}(I) \leq u_{(n)}(J)$. Also $util(J, Obj)$ is bounded by $u_{(n)}(J)$ and $u^{(n)}(J)$, and hence the result.

It can be observed that for an OOA frequent itemset I, the constraint $u_{(n)}(I) \geq mu$ is monotone and the constraint $u^{(n)}(I) < mu$ is anti-monotone.

Example 6 Suppose minimum support is 12.5%. There are 16 records in DB, therefore $n = 12.5\% \times 16 = 2$. Let $I = \{\text{tmt} = 5\}$. The top-*n* utility and bottom-*n* utility of I are $u^{(2)}(I) = \frac{1.4 + 1.4}{2} = 1.4$ and $u_{(2)}(I) = \frac{1.4 + 0.6}{2} = 1$ respectively. To demonstrate how we can use the anti-monotone constraint to prune itemsets, let us consider a minimum utility of 1.6. From the above calculations, we know that the utility of any OOA rules generated from supersets of I is in the range [1, 1.4], therefore I can be pruned because no supersets of I can result in a rule that has a utility higher than 1.6.

4. Mining top-*K* utility frequent closed patterns

4.1. OOApriori top-*K* closed algorithm

Let $ms\%$, $mc\%$ and K be a user specified minimum support, minimum confidence and number of OOA rules respectively. Define L to be the set of top-K utilities in $\{u \mid I \rightarrow Obj(s\%, c\%, u)$ is an OOA rule$\}$, u is given by Eq. (7); AR to be the set of top-K OOA rules with high utility; and τ be a variable to store minimum utility.

Initialize $L = \varnothing$, $AR = \varnothing$. For each $k \geq 1$, C_k is used to store OOA frequent closed itemsets in level k. A temporary variable to store minimum utility is given by
$$\tau = \begin{cases} \min\{u_{(n)}(I), \forall I \in C_k\} & \text{if } |L| < K \\ K^{\text{th}} \text{ best in } L & \text{if } |L| \geq K \end{cases} \quad (12)$$

Conceptually speaking, if we have not found K OOA rules yet, we set the temporary minimum utility τ to be the minimum value of the utility lower bound for all $I \in C_k$. This ensures that we are not missing out any rules generated by the supersets of I that may have higher utilities than I. If we have already found K OOA rules, we set the temporary minimum utility τ to be the Kth highest utility value in L. Finding K OOA rules effectively raises the minimum utility and hence the user does not need to explicitly set a minimum utility.

For each OOA frequent closed pattern $I \in C_k$, $I \rightarrow Obj(s\%, c\%, u)$ is an OOA rule if $c\% \geq mc\%$ and $u \geq \tau$. When this condition is satisfied, we put the OOA rule $I \rightarrow Obj(s\%, c\%, u)$ into AR, and the utility value u into L. If there are more than K items in AR (or L), i.e. $|AR| > K$ or $|L| > K$, we take away the OOA rule with the smallest utility from AR and the smallest utility value from L.

After all the OOA frequent closed patterns and OOA rules in level k are generated, an enhanced Apriori algorithm (called Apriori Closed and described in Section 4.2) is then used to generate new frequent closed itemsets in level $k + 1$.

The pseudo-code for mining the top-K utility OOA rules is shown below (Algorithm 1). For an OOA itemset $I = \{I_1, ..., I_m\}$ we use $I.count_1$ to store $count(I, DB)$, $I.count_2$ to store $count(I \cup \{Obj\}, DB)$, and $I.utility$ to store the utility defined by Eq. (7).

Algorithm 1 (OOApriori top-K closed)
Input: $ms\%$, $mc\%$, K, Obj and DB.
Output: FP, the set of OOA frequent closed itemsets; and
          AR, the set of top-K utility OOA rules.
function OOAprioriTopKClosed($ms\%$, $mc\%$, K, Obj, DB)
(1) $FP = AR = L = \varnothing$; $k = 1$;
(2) $G_k = G_1 = \{I \mid I$ is an OOA 1-itemset in $DB\}$;
(3) $C_k = C_1 = $ set of closed itemsets generated from G_1;
(4)   Obtain $I.count_1$, $I.count_2$, $I.utility$ for each $I \in C_k$;
(5)   **for each** $I \in C_k$ // Check for OOA rules (AR)
(6)   **if** $s\% = \frac{I.count_2}{|DB|} \times 100\% \geq ms\%$ **then begin**
(7)   **if** $|L| < K$ **then** $\tau = \min\{u_{(n)}(I), \forall I \in C_k\}$
            else $\tau = K^{\text{th}}$ best in L;
(8) $c\% = \frac{I.count_2}{I.count_1} \times 100\%$; $u = \frac{I.utility}{I.count_1}$;
(9)   **if** $c\% \geq mc\%$ and $u \geq \tau$ **then begin**
(10) $L = $ List of top-K utilities in $L \cup \{u\}$;
(11) $AR = $ List of top-K utility OOA rules in
              $AR \cup \{I \rightarrow Obj(s\%, c\%, u)\}$;
(12)   **end**
(13)   **end**
(14)   **if** $|L| < K$ **then** $\tau = \min\{u_{(n)}(I), \forall I \in C_k\}$
        else $\tau = K^{\text{th}}$ best in L;
(15)   **if** $k = 1$ **then** // Prune G_1 using utility upper bound
(16)   **for each** $I \in G_k$
(17)   **if** $u^{(n)}(I) < \tau$ **then** $G_k = G_k - \{I\}$;
(18)   **if** $G_k \neq \varnothing$ **then begin** // Generate C_k
(19) $k++$; $(C_k, G_k) = $ AprioriClosedGen(G_{k-1}); **goto** (4);
(20)   **end**
(21)   **return** $FP = \bigcup_i C_i$ and K OOA rules in AR
end

Example 7 To trace through Algorithm 1, suppose minimum support is 12.5%, minimum confidence is 60%, and we want to find the top-2 OOA rules (i.e. $K = 2$). The construction and pruning of G_1 and C_1 (lines 2 and 3 of Algorithm 1) are shown in Figure 1. Since L is still empty at this point, i.e. $|L| = 0$, in line 7,
$$\tau = \min\{u_{(n)}(I), \forall I \in C_1\} = -1.5$$
Lines 10 and 11 populate L and AR,
$$L = \{1.2, 0.8\}$$
and $AR = \{$tmt $= 5 \rightarrow Obj(18.75\%, 75\%, 1.2)$,
      tmt $= 4$, med $= 2 \rightarrow Obj(18.75\%, 75\%, 0.8)\}$
L is now filled with two utility values, and τ can now be raised to 0.8 (line 14). Since this is the first iteration (i.e. k

$= 1$), lines 16 and 17 are executed to prune the set of generators G_1 with $\tau = 0.8$. Nothing is pruned in this example.

OOA 1-itemset	$s\%$		OOA 1-itemset (G_1)	$s\%$	$u^{(n)}(I)$
tmt = 1	0%		tmt = 2	12.5%	0.8
tmt = 2	12.5%		tmt = 3	12.5%	0.8
tmt = 3	12.5%	prune	tmt = 4	18.75%	0.9
tmt = 4	18.75%	$\rightarrow$	tmt = 5	18.75%	1.4
tmt = 5	18.75%		med = 1	25%	1.1
med = 1	25%		med = 2	37.5%	1.4
med = 2	37.5%				

	Closure (C_1)	$s\%$	$c\%$	u	$u_{(n)}(I)$
generate closed itemsets from G_1 $\rightarrow$	tmt = 2, med = 1	12.5%	50%	−0.25	−1.3
	tmt = 3	12.5%	66.67%	−0.067	−0.5
	tmt = 4, med = 2	18.75%	75%	0.8	0.7
	tmt = 5	18.75%	75%	1.2	1
	med = 1	25%	50%	0.025	−1.5
	med = 2	37.5%	75%	0.625	−0.6

Figure 1.   Generation of G_1 and C_1.

4.2. Apriori closed algorithm

In [9] Pasquier, et al. propose a new algorithm, called A-Close, to find frequent closed itemsets based on the Apriori mining algorithm. The OOA mining presented in [13] is an extension of the Apriori algorithm to generate OOA frequent patterns. In this section we are going to present an algorithm that adapts the A-Close algorithm to the enhanced Apriori algorithm in order to mine the top-K utility frequent closed patterns.

Let G_k be the set of k-itemsets (called k-generators) used to obtain a set of $(k + 1)$-generators G_{k+1}. For a generator I, denote $I.closure$ as a closed itemset generated by I. The Apriori Closed algorithm works as follows. Each pair of k-generators in G_k with the same first $k - 1$ items in the form of $\{I_1, ..., I_{k-1}, I_k\}$ and $\{I_1, ..., I_{k-1}, I_{k+1}\}$ are joined together to form a new potential $(k + 1)$-generator $\{I_1, ..., I_{k+1}\}$. These potential $(k + 1)$-generators may produce infrequent closed itemsets or frequent closed itemsets that have already been produced, therefore pruning from G_{k+1} is required and described in the following.

Strategy 1 Similar to the Apriori algorithm pruning strategy, for every $(k + 1)$-generator I in G_{k+1}, if there exists a k-sub-itemset $J \subset I$ such that $J \notin G_k$, I is pruned from G_{k+1}. This strategy prunes all supersets of infrequent generators because G_k only contains frequent generators. It also prunes all generators having the same support as one of their sub-itemset. This is a by-product of pruning strategy 4 (presented below).

Strategy 2 For all the remaining $(k + 1)$-generators in G_{k+1}, we prune those generators that do not satisfy the user specified minimum support constraint. This strategy removes all infrequent generators. These infrequent generators cannot produce frequent closed itemsets because of the anti-monotone property of the support constraint.

Strategy 3 For the rest of the frequent $(k+1)$-generators in G_{k+1}, we prune those generators that has a top-n utility (utility upper bound) less than τ, the temporary K^{th} highest utility value during computation, which is defined in Eq. (12). This strategy applies the anti-monotone property of the utility upper bound constraint and removes all generators that cannot produce closed itemsets with a utility high enough to be in the top-K list.

Strategy 4 For every remaining $(k+1)$-generators I in G_{k+1}, if there exists a k-sub-itemset $J \subset I$ such that I and J have the same support, I is pruned from G_{k+1}. This strategy removes redundant generators since the closed itemset from I has already been generated by J previously.

Now we have to generate the closed itemsets from all the remaining $(k+1)$-generators in G_{k+1}. One database scan of DB is required to generate the closed itemsets from the generators. For each database record r of DB and for each generator I in G_{k+1}, the corresponding closed itemset $I.closure$ is updated. The update is performed as follows. If r is the first record that contains I, $I.closure$ is empty so we put all non-objective items into $I.closure$. If r is not the first record that contains I, $I.closure$ is non-empty so we perform an intersection between $I.closure$ and r (i.e. $I.closure \cap r$) and put the resulting itemset back to $I.closure$. At the end of the database scan, $I.closure$ will contain a closed itemset generated from generator I.

The outputs of the algorithm are C_{k+1} and G_{k+1}. G_{k+1} is fed back into the AprioriClosedGen function recursively.

Algorithm 2 (Apriori closed)
Input: G_k, the set of k-generators.
Output: C_{k+1}, the set of OOA frequent closed itemsets in
             level $k + 1$; and
             G_{k+1}, the set of frequent $(k+1)$-generators.
function AprioriClosedGen(G_k)
(1) $C_{k+1} = G_{k+1} = \varnothing$;
(2)   **for each** pair of itemsets in G_k of the form
        $\{I_1, ..., I_{k-1}, I_k\}$ and $\{I_1, ..., I_{k-1}, I_{k+1}\}$
(3) $G_{k+1} = G_{k+1} \cup \{\{I_1, ..., I_{k+1}\}\}$;
(4)   Apply prune strategies $1 - 4$ to itemsets in G_{k+1};
(5)   Scan DB and obtain $I.closure$ for each $I \in G_{k+1}$;
(6)   **for each** $I \in G_{k+1}$
(7) $C_{k+1} = C_{k+1} \cup I.closure$;
(8)   **return** C_{k+1} and G_{k+1};
end

Example 8 To trace through Algorithm 2, let us continue the example in Example 7. The set of 2-generators are constructed and shown in Figure 2(a). Prune strategy 1 states that if there exists a 1-sub-itemset that is not in G_1, that 2-generator should be removed. So if {tmt = 1, med = 1} was one of the 2-generators, it would have been pruned by strategy 1. In this example, nothing is pruned by strategy 1. Prune strategy 2 removes all infrequent generators, therefore all 2-generators with support less than 12.5% are removed, and the result is shown in Figure 2(b). Prune strategy 3 removes all 2-generators that do not satisfy the

utility upper bound constraint. Since $|L| = 2$, therefore $\tau = 2^{nd}$ best in $L = 0.8$. The result of prune strategy 3 is shown in Figure 2(c). Prune strategy 4 removes redundant 2-generators that have been generated in previous iteration by looking at the support. {tmt = 2, med = 1} and {tmt = 4, med = 2} are removed since their supports are the same as that of {tmt = 2} and {tmt = 4} respectively. The result is shown in Figure 2(d). Closed itemsets C_2 is generated from G_2 and shown in Figure 2(e). After obtaining G_2 and C_2, we go back to line 4 of Algorithm 1 and get

$$L = \{1.4, 1.2\}$$
$$AR = \{tmt = 5, med = 2 \rightarrow Obj(12.5\%, 100\%, 1.4),$$
$$tmt = 5 \rightarrow Obj(18.75\%, 75\%, 1.2)\}$$

2-generator (G_2)	s%
tmt = 2, med = 1	12.5%
tmt = 2, med = 2	0%
tmt = 3, med = 1	6.25%
tmt = 3, med = 2	6.25%
tmt = 4, med = 1	0%
tmt = 4, med = 2	18.75%
tmt = 5, med = 1	6.25%
tmt = 5, med = 2	12.5%

(a)

prune strategy 2 →

2-generator (G_2)	s%
tmt = 2, med = 1	12.5%
tmt = 4, med = 2	18.75%
tmt = 5, med = 2	12.5%

(b)

prune strategy 3 →

2-generator (G_2)	s%	$u^{(n)}(I)$
tmt = 2, med = 1	12.5%	0.8
tmt = 4, med = 2	18.75%	0.9
tmt = 5, med = 2	12.5%	1.4

(c)

prune strategy 4 →

2-generator (G_2)
tmt = 5, med = 2

(d)

Closure (C_2)	s%	c%	u
tmt = 5, med = 2	12.5%	100%	1.4

(e)

Figure 2. Generation of G_2 and C_2.

5. Experimental evaluation

Experiments are performed to test the effectiveness of our algorithm in obtaining the high utility rules. We also investigate the effect of increasing K, the number of OOA rules required. Finally we show the effect of pruning strategies $1 - 4$ mentioned in Section 4.2.

Two different datasets are used in our experiments. They are the widely used *German Credit* dataset (ftp://ftp.ics.uci.edu/pub/machine-learning-databases/statlog/german/) and *Heart Disease* dataset (ftp://ftp.ics.uci.edu/pub/machine-learning-databases/statlog/heart) from the UCI Machine Learning Archive. These two datasets consist of 1000 customer records with 21 attributes and 270 patient records with 14 attributes respectively. The reasons that we use these datasets in our experiments are because they are already in a format that can be directly employed by our algorithms without further manipulation.

Figure 3 shows the running time of our OOApriori Top-K Closed algorithm compare with the OOApriori algorithm for the two datasets. In the German Credit dataset, K is fixed at 100 and minimum support ranges from 1.9% to 4.1%. We observe that the running time of our algo-

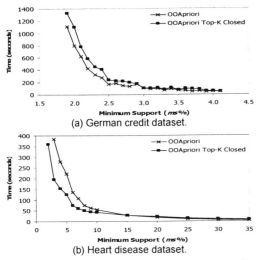

(a) German credit dataset.

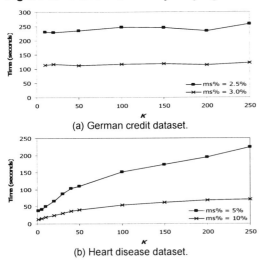

(b) Heart disease dataset.

Figure 3. Performances by varying *ms*%.

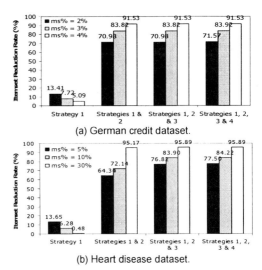

(a) German credit dataset.

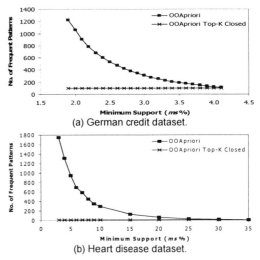

(b) Heart disease dataset.

Figure 5. Effect of prune strategies 1 to 4.

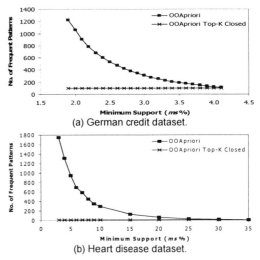

Figure 4. Performances by varying *K*.

Figure 6. Number of frequent patterns.

rithm is only slightly higher than that of the OOApriori algorithm with low minimum support and there is not much difference in running time with minimum support greater than 3%. In the Heart Disease dataset, *K* is fixed at 10 and minimum support ranges from 2% to 35%. For low minimum support, the OOApriori Top-*K* Closed algorithm is slightly faster than the OOApriori algorithm, and as the minimum support increases the difference gets smaller. A quick browse of the two datasets reveals that the German Credit dataset is composed of mainly closed patterns whereas the Heart Disease dataset consists of a lot of unclosed patterns. Because of the large number of unclosed patterns in the Heart Disease dataset, our OOApriori Top-*K* Closed algorithm can prune a lot of itemsets in the low minimum support region. Hence it is a little bit faster than the OOApriori algorithm. In the high minimum support region, there is not much difference in

performance because most itemsets have already been pruned by the support constraint.

Figure 4 shows the running time of our algorithm by varying *K*. The graph shows that the running time remains stable over the range of *K* for the German Credit dataset and increases as *K* increases for the Heart Disease dataset. The value of *K* relates to how fast we can raise the minimum utility internally. The smaller the value of *K*, the faster the minimum utility can be raised. The observation shows that our algorithm can prune the search space efficiently for datasets with a lot of unclosed patterns.

We also investigate the effect of applying the four pruning strategies mentioned in Section 4.2. The percentage of itemsets pruned by applying one, two, three, or all four strategies with different minimum supports is shown in Figure 5. For the German Credit dataset, it can be observed that most of the itemsets have already been pruned by strategies 1 and 2, which leaves very few itemsets to be pruned by strategies 3 and 4. On the other hand, strategies 3 and 4 can still prune a significant percentage of itemsets from the Heart Disease dataset because of the large number of unclosed patterns in this dataset.

Finally, we look at the number of frequent patterns produced by the OOApriori algorithm. Figure 6 shows that the OOApriori algorithm generates a large number of frequent patterns especially in the low minimum support region, whereas the OOApriori Top-K Closed algorithm only outputs K frequent closed patterns.

6. Conclusions

We have developed a new approach to modeling association mining. OOA mining discovers patterns that are explicitly relating to a given user defined objective. The OOA rules so discovered are not only frequent rules, but they are also rules with high utilities, thus providing useful and meaningful answers.

We developed an algorithm to mine the OOA frequent closed patterns and the top-K utility OOA rules. The algorithm is based on the Apriori algorithm with specific mechanisms for handling utility and generating closed patterns. Since the utility constraint is neither monotone nor anti-monotone, the standard Apriori pruning strategy no longer works. We found a weaker but anti-monotonic condition based on utility that helped us to prune the search space. Furthermore, specifying a minimum utility explicitly is not practical since the user cannot know in advance what minimum utility value should be used. To overcome this, our algorithm only requires the user to specify K, the number of OOA rules that he/she wants, and it will return the K most useful OOA rules.

Our experimental study shows that our algorithm can produce the desired results without too much overhead. It has the added advantage that frequent closed patterns are mined and we do not need to specify a minimum utility.

This study shows that OOA mining with the top-K utility frequent closed patterns is feasible with extensions to the Apriori algorithm. Future study includes the possibility of having a utility constraint pushed deep into the FP-tree algorithm or other frequent pattern mining algorithms.

7. References

[1] R. Agrawal, T. Imielinski, and A. Swami, "Mining association rules between sets of items in large datasets", *Proc. of the 1993 ACM SIGMOD Int. Conf. on Management of Data*, Washington, D.C., USA, May 1993.

[2] R. Agrawal and R. Srikant, "Fast algorithm for mining association rules", *Proc. of the 20th Int. Conf. on Very Large Databases*, Santiago, Chile, Sep 1994.

[3] R. Bayardo, R. Agrawal, and D. Gounopolos, "Constraint-based rule mining in large, dense databases", *Proc. of the 15th Int. Conf. on Data Engineering*, Sydney, Australia, Mar 1999.

[4] J. Dougherty, R. Kohavi, and M. Sahami, "Supervised and unsupervised discretization of continuous features", *Proc. of the 12th Int. Conf. on Machine Learning*, Tahoe City, California, USA, Jul 1995.

[5] J. Han, J. Pei, and Y. Yin, "Mining frequent patterns without candidate generation", *Proc. of the 2000 ACM SIGMOD Int. Conf. on Management of Data*, Dallas, Texas, USA, May 2000.

[6] J. Han, J. Wang, Y. Lu, and P. Tzvetkov, "Mining top-k frequent closed patterns without minimum support", *Proc. of the IEEE Int. Conf. on Data Mining*, Japan, Dec 2002.

[7] B. Liu, W. Hsu, S. Chen, and Y. Ma, "Analyzing the subjective interestingness of association rules", *IEEE Intelligent Systems*, 15(5):47–55, 2000.

[8] R. Ng, L. Lakshmanan, J. Han, and A. Pang, "Exploratory mining and pruning optimizations of constrained association rules", *Proc. ACM SIGMOD Int. Conf. on Management of Data*, Seattle, Washington, USA, Jun 1998.

[9] N. Pasquier, Y. Bastide, R. Taouil, and L. Lakhal, "Discovering frequent closed itemsets for association rules", *Proc. of the 7th Int. Conf. on Database Theory*, Jerusalem, Israel, Jan 1999.

[10] J. Pei and J. Han, "Can we push more constraints into frequent pattern mining?" *Proc. of the 6th ACM SIGKDD Int. Conf. on Knowledge Discovery and Data Mining*, Boston, MA, USA, Aug 2000.

[11] J. Pei, J. Han, and R. Mao, "CLOSET: An efficient algorithm for mining frequent closed itemsets", *ACM SIGMOD Workshop on Research Issues in Data Mining and Knowledge Discovery*, Dallas, Texas, USA, May 2000.

[12] J. Sese and S. Morishita, "Answering the most correlated N association rules efficiently", *Principles of Data Mining and Knowledge Discovery, 6th European Conference*, Helsinki, Finland, Aug 2002.

[13] Y.D. Shen, Q. Yang, and Z. Zhang, "Objective-oriented utility-based association mining", *Proc. of the IEEE Int. Conf. on Data Mining*, Japan, Dec 2002.

[14] A. Silberschatz and A. Tuzhilin, "What makes patterns interesting in knowledge discovery system", *IEEE Trans. on Knowledge and Data Engineering*, 8(6):970–974, 1996.

[15] R. Srikant, Q. Vu, and R. Agrawal, "Mining association rules with item constraints", *Proc. of the 3rd Int. Conf. on Knowledge Discovery and Data Mining*, Newport Beach, California, USA, Aug 1997.

[16] G. Webb, "Efficient search for association rules", *Proc. of the 6th ACM SIGKDD Int. Conf. on Knowledge Discovery and Data Mining*, Boston, MA, USA, Aug 2000.

[17] S. Wrobel, "An algorithm for multi-relational discovery of subgroups", *Principles of Data Mining and Knowledge Discovery, 1st European Symposium*, Trondheim, Norway, Jun 1997.

[18] M. Zaki and C.J. Hsiao, "CHARM: An efficient algorithm for closed itemset mining", *Second SIAM Int. Conf. on Data Mining*, Arlington, Virginia, USA, Apr 2002.

Zigzag: a new algorithm for mining large inclusion dependencies in databases

Fabien De Marchi, Jean-Marc Petit
Laboratoire LIMOS, UMR CNRS 6158
Université Blaise Pascal - Clermont-Ferrand II,
24 avenue des Landais 63 177 Aubière cedex, France
{demarchi,jmpetit}@math.univ-bpclermont.fr

Abstract

In the relational model, inclusion dependencies (INDs) convey many information on data semantics. They generalize foreign keys, which are very popular constraints in practice. However, one seldom knows the set of satisfied INDs in a database. The IND discovery problem in existing databases can be formulated as a data-mining problem. We underline in this article that the exploration of IND expressions from most general (smallest) INDs to most specific (largest) INDs does not succeed whenever large INDs have to be discovered. To cope with this problem, we introduce a new algorithm, called $Zigzag$, which combines the strength of levelwise algorithms (to find out some smallest INDs) with an optimistic criteria to jump more or less to largest INDs. Preliminary tests, on synthetic databases, are presented and commented on. It is worth noting that the main result of this paper is general enough to be applied to other data-mining problems, such as maximal frequent itemsets mining.

1. Introduction

In the relational model, inclusion dependencies (INDs) convey many information on the data structure and data semantics, and generalize in particular foreign keys [10].

Their utility is recognized for many tasks such as semantic query optimization [18, 12], logical and physical database design and tuning [26, 11, 23, 14] or data integration [28]. In practice, the implementation of these technics is generally made impossible by the ignorance of satisfied INDs in the database. One can then be interested in the problem of discovering INDs satisfied in a database [20]. In [13], we proposed an approach which, given a database, finds out most specific satisfied INDs, referred to as the *positive border of satisfied INDs* in the sequel. An original proposal for unary IND discovery is given, together with a levelwise algorithm which walks through the IND search space

from most general (smallest) INDs to most specific (largest) INDs. We qualify this approach of "pessimistic", since the positive border to be discovered is supposed not to be too far away from the most general INDs. In other words, most INDs to be tested appear to be not satisfied in the database. Not surprisingly, experiments show that this approach does not succeed whenever large INDs have to be discovered.

Of course, the same observation has been already made in similar contexts, typically for *large frequent itemsets* discovery [24, 5, 17, 2]: when the positive border to reach is made up of large candidates, levelwise methods do not scale up. Works related to large frequent itemsets discovery can be classified as follows:

- those which use the properties of frequent itemsets in order to avoid data accesses, one can quote [5, 30, 4, 9, 8].

- those which conjecture that there exist large itemsets [24, 17]. We will qualify these approaches of *optimistic*, since they benefit from the assumption that the majority of the tests to be carried out against the database are expected to be true.

Note also that an analogy between frequent itemsets and satisfied INDs can me made: if one guesses one of them of size n, then approximately $O(2^n)$ tests against data can be saved. Nevertheless, the problem arising for optimistic IND discovery is distinct from optimistic frequent itemsets discovery due to the nature of INDs:

- There does not exist, to our knowledge, properties making it possible to undoubtedly deduce satisfied large INDs without accessing the data (except properties given by IND inference rules).

- The search space exploration can be made only from INDs of small size to INDs of high size: let us consider without loss of generality two relations R and S having N attributes all of the same type: we have $O(N^2)$

candidate INDs of size 1 and more than $N!$ candidate INDs of size N. Note that this is false for the itemsets: consider a transaction database with N items, the number of candidate itemsets of size i is equal to that of size $N - i$, for $i \in \{0, N\}$. That means that the levelwise discovery of frequent itemsets in a bottom-up fashion is only justified by the hope to have a positive border composed of elements of small size.

- To our knowledge, there is not theoretical justification making it possible to be optimistic with frequent itemsets whereas we will see that such a justification exists for INDs: we will show how an axiom of interaction between INDs and Functional Dependencies (FDs) can be used to justify the following intuition: "The more large is the size of known satisfied INDs, the more chance candidate INDs of higher size are satisfied."

Contribution. For IND discovery in a database, we propose a new algorithm called $Zigzag$ combining a pessimistic approach for small INDs with an optimistic approach for large INDs. The main result of this paper gives a characterization of the *optimistic positive border* of the satisfied INDs according to the known unsatisfied INDs. This characterization is different from that given in a similar context [24, 17]. In order to guide the search, a key factor of $Zigzag$ is to estimate the distance between the optimistic positive border and the positive border to be discovered.

Experimental results of this approach are described on synthetic databases. Let us note that the majority of the propositions apply to all search spaces provided with a specialization relation in which a monotonous property is required (as for frequent itemsets).

Related works. To our knowledge, only few contributions address a subset of the initial problem of IND discovery: problem declaration [20], unary IND discovery [6], or theoretical frameworks in which the problem of IND discovery could be solved [19, 27]. During the writing of this article, we were informed of an interesting contribution which addresses the problem of large IND discovery [21]; the idea is to build an optimistic positive border starting from a set of known satisfied INDs, by introducing the concept of maximal hyperclique of a regular hypergraph. The authors do not mention theoretical justification for the use of an optimistic approach, and they do not integrate the distance with the positive border in the event of unsatisfied large INDs, to guide the algorithm during the search of the positive border. Moreover, their generation of hyperclique is based on an adaptation of heuristics known for the maximal clique problem which do not seem to be very efficient.

In [19], the authors propose an algorithm "Dualize and Advance" for search spaces provided with a relation of spe-

cialization. In their approach, the positive border in construction is always a subset of the positive border to be discovered. At each step, from some elements of the positive border, they generate the so-called negative border, i.e. elements which should not be satisfied in the database. If one of them appears to be satisfied, they generate a specialization of it which belongs to the positive border and they reiterate the process until each element of the negative border is indeed not satisfied. A difference with our algorithm is that the same strategy is always made to explore the candidates, it can not be guided by an estimation of the distance to the positive border. Another point is that it starts from an empty positive border, while a levelwise strategy initializes the negative border in our algorithm.

Paper organization. Section 2 points out some concepts of the relational model, and specifies the theoretical framework of IND discovery. Section 3 presents the proposed approach: a result linking the generation of large candidates to the computation of minimal transversals of an hypergraph is proposed (Section 3.1), with several justifications for the use of an hybrid approach combining optimism and pessimism (Section 3.2). An exploitation of the error made on the large INDs is also proposed to help in the orientation of the search. An algorithm is given in Section 3.3, and some practical considerations in Section 3.4. Section 3.5 presents preliminary experimental results, and we conclude in Section 4 giving some prospects.

2. Preliminaries

2.1. Relational model and inclusion dependencies

Some concepts of the relational databases, essential to the comprehension of the article, are briefly recalled (see for example [1, 22] for more details).

Let R be a finite set of *attributes*. For each attribute $A \in R$, the set of all its possible values is called the *domain of A* and denoted by $Dom(A)$. A *tuple* over R is a mapping $t : R \rightarrow \cup_{A \in R} Dom(A)$, where $t(A) \in Dom(A), \forall A \in R$. A *relation* is a set of tuples. The cardinality of a set X is denoted by $|X|$. We say that r is a relation *over R* and R is the *relation schema* of r. If $X \subseteq R$ is an attribute set[1] and t is a tuple, we denote by $t[X]$ the restriction of t to X. The projection of a relation r onto X, denoted as $\pi_X(r)$, is defined by $\pi_X(r) = \{t[X] \mid t \in r\}$.

A *database schema* **R** is a finite set of *relation schemas* R_i. A *relational database instance* **d** (or *database*) over **R** corresponds to a set of relations r_i over each R_i of **R**. Given a database **d** over **R**, the set of distinct domains (e.g. int, string ...) is denoted by $Dom(\mathbf{d})$.

---

[1]Letters from the beginning of the alphabet introduce single attributes whereas letters from the end introduce attribute sets.

An attribute sequence (e.g. $X = <A, B, C>$ or simply ABC) is an ordered set of attributes. When it is clear from context, we do not distinguish a sequence from its underlying set.

Two attributes A and B are said to be *compatible* if $Dom(A) = Dom(B)$. Two distinct attribute sequences X and Y are *compatible* if $|X| = |Y| = m$ and if for $j = [1, m]$, $Dom(X[j]) = Dom(Y[j])$.

An *inclusion dependency* (IND) over a database schema **R** is a statement of the form $R_i[X] \subseteq R_j[Y]$, where $R_i, R_j \in$ **R**, $X \subseteq R_i, Y \subseteq R_j$, X and Y are compatible sequences[2].

The size (or arity) of an IND $i = R[X] \subseteq R[Y]$, noted $|i|$ is such that $|i| = |X| = |Y|$. We call *unary inclusion dependency* an IND of size 1.

Let **d** be a database over a database schema **R**, where $r_i, r_j \in$ **d** are relations over $R_i, R_j \in$ **R** respectively. An inclusion dependency $R_i[X] \subseteq R_j[Y]$ is *satisfied* in a database **d** over **R**, denoted by **d** $\models R_i[X] \subseteq R_j[Y]$, if and only if $\forall u \in r_i, \exists v \in r_j$ such that $u[X] = v[Y]$ (or equivalently $\pi_X(r_i) \subseteq \pi_Y(r_j)$).

Let I_1 and I_2 be two sets of inclusion dependencies, I_1 is a *cover* of I_2 if $I_1 \models I_2$ (this notation means that each dependency in I_2 holds in any database satisfying all the dependencies in I_1) and $I_2 \models I_1$.

A sound and complete axiomatization for INDs was given in [29]. If I is a set of INDs, we have:

1. (reflexivity) $I \models R[A_1, ..., A_n] \subseteq R[A_1, ..., A_n]$

2. (projection and permutation) if $I \models R[A_1, ..., A_n] \subseteq S[B_1, ..., B_n]$ then
   $I \models R[A_{\sigma 1}, ..., A_{\sigma m}] \subseteq S[B_{\sigma 1}, ..., B_{\sigma m}]$ for each sequence $\sigma 1, ..., \sigma m$ of distinct integers from $\{1, ..., n\}$

3. (transitivity) if $I \models R[A_1, ..., A_n] \subseteq S[B_1, ..., B_n]$ et $I \models S[B_1, ..., B_n] \subseteq T[C_1, ..., C_n]$ then $I \models R[A_1, ..., A_n] \subseteq T[C_1, ..., C_n]$

4. (attribute equality) if $I \models R[AB] \subseteq S[CC]$, then A and B can be substituted to each other in all satisfied IND expressions.

5. (redundancy) if $I \models R[X] \subseteq S[Y]$, then $I \models R[XU] \subseteq S[YV]$, where $R[U] \subseteq S[V]$ can be obtained from $R[X] \subseteq S[Y]$ using second inference rule.

2.2. A framework for IND discovery

The problem of IND discovery can be formulated as follows: "Let **d** be a database, find a cover of all satisfied INDs

---

[2]Usually, the IND definition excludes repeated attributes in the sequences on left and right-hand sides. In this paper, we prefer to adopt a less restrictive framework in order to simplify the presentation of the principal result of this paper (cf Section 3.1) ; the exclusion of the repeated attributes is considered after the presentation of the algorithm (cf. Section 3.4).

in **d**". The number of potentially satisfied INDs, which constitutes the basic search space, is more than factorial in the number of attributes. We point out it here, and add some notations used in the sequel.

Definition 1 *Let* **R** *be a database schema. The search space of INDs over* **R** *, denoted by* C, *is defined by:*

$$C = \{R[<A_1...A_n>] \subseteq S[<B_1...B_n>] \mid R, S \in \mathbf{R}$$

$$and \ \forall 1 \leq i < j \leq n, (A_i < A_j) \vee (A_i = A_j \wedge B_i < B_j)\}$$

Thus, C contains IND expressions defined over **R** whose sequences are sorted in order to naturally restrict the search space to only one permutation of each IND expression (according to the second inference rule of INDs). In the sequel, let **d** be a database over a schema R, and C the corresponding IND search space.

Definition 2 *Let* i *and* j *be two IND expressions, we say that* i generalizes j *(or* j specializes i*), noted* $i \preceq j$, *if* i *can be obtained by projection on* j.

For example, $R[AC] \subseteq S[DF] \preceq R[ABC] \subseteq S[DEF]$. We note $i \prec j$ for $i \preceq j$ and $i \neq j$.

The satisfaction property of an IND in a database **d** is anti-monotonous with respect to the relation $'\preceq'$:

Property 1 *Let* $i, j \in C$ *such that* $j \preceq i$. *We have:* **d** $\not\models j \Rightarrow$ **d** $\not\models i$.

Thus, any set of INDs can be represented by its most specialized elements, i.e. its positive border:

Definition 3 *Let* $I \subseteq C$. *The positive border of* I, *noted* $\mathcal{B}d^+(I)$, *is defined by:* $\mathcal{B}d^+(I) = \{i \in I \mid \nexists j \in I, i \prec j\}$.

A set I of INDs can also be represented by the most general elements which it does not contain, i.e. its negative border:

Definition 4 *Let* $I \subseteq C$. *The negative border of* I, *noted* $\mathcal{B}d^-(I)$, *is defined by:* $\mathcal{B}d^-(I) = \{i \in C \setminus I \mid \nexists j \in C \setminus I, j \prec i\}$.

Note that when I is the set of the satisfied INDs in **d** , $\mathcal{B}d^+(I)$ answers the IND discovery problem. In [27], an levelwise approach is suggested to discover $\mathcal{B}d^+(I)$. The algorithm $MIND$ [13] in based on this idea, using an $AprioriGen$ like candidate generation [3]. Such an approach will be qualified in the sequel of *pessimistic*, because its effectiveness is based on the presence on each level of many unsatisfied INDs, in order to prune a great part of the remaining space. The experiments conducted in [13] show that such an approach is scalable according to the number of tuples and attributes: the greatest database had 90000 tuples and 200 attributes, the IND positive border of the database was composed of four unary IND and one IND of size 6.

Nevertheless, such a pessimistic approach is not adapted when large INDs have to be discovered; indeed, to discover an IND i of size n, it is necessary to have discovered the 2^n INDs which generalize i.

3. An hybrid approach for IND discovery

The principle of the method is to combine pessimistic and optimistic approaches. We first give some definitions and results which will make it possible to carry out "optimistic jumps" in the search space.

3.1. The optimistic positive border

The simple remark on which this work is founded is the following: a set of unsatisfied INDs makes it possible to prune a certain number of candidates by anti-monotony, and thus to define an *optimistic set of satisfied INDs*.

Definition 5 *Let C be the IND search space associated to a database d and $NI \subseteq C$ be a set such that $\forall i \in NI, d \not\models i$. The* optimistic set of INDs *with respect to NI, denoted by $I_{opt}(NI)$, is defined by: $I_{opt}(NI) = \{i \in C \mid \not\exists j \in NI, j \preceq i\}$.*

Moreover, the *optimistic positive border*, denoted by $\mathcal{B}d^+(I_{opt}(NI))$, is the set of most specific INDs in $I_{opt}(NI)$. When clear from context, we will note $\mathcal{B}d^+(I_{opt})$ instead of $\mathcal{B}d^+(I_{opt}(NI))$.

Remark that $\mathcal{B}d^+(I_{opt})$ corresponding to a set NI is exactly equal to $\mathcal{B}d^+(I_{opt})$ corresponding to the most general elements of NI.

We shall see that the optimistic positive border can be calculated by using the concept of minimal transversals of an hypergraph. As in [19], we need a representation as sets of INDs, given in the following definition:

Definition 6 *Let I_1 be the set of unary INDs in C. Each IND i in C can be associated with a set of unary INDs, thanks to the function $ens : C \longrightarrow 2^{I_1}$ defined by: $ens(i) = \{j \in I_1 \mid j \preceq i\}$.*

Example 1 *Consider the three unary INDs: $i_1 = R[A] \subseteq S[E]$, $i_2 = R[B] \subseteq S[F]$ and $i_3 = R[C] \subseteq S[G]$. The set representation of $i = R[ABC] \subseteq S[EFG]$ is $ens(i) = \{i_1, i_2, i_3\}$.*

The function ens is bijective, and thus imply a function ens^{-1} which associates to any IND of C one element of 2^{I_1}.

The following proposal follows from the representation as set of INDs and the definition of the relation $' \preceq'$:

Property 2 *If i and j are two IND expressions, $i \preceq j \Leftrightarrow ens(i) \subseteq ens(j)$.*

Thanks to this representation as set of INDs we can define an hypergraph associated with a set of INDs:

Definition 7 *Let I be a subset of C. The hypergraph (V, E) associated with I, denoted by $\mathcal{H}(I)$, is defined by: $V = \{i \in C \mid |i| = 1\}$ and $E = \{ens(i) \mid i \in I\}$.*

From this representation of INDs, we obtain a relationship between a set of unsatisfied INDs and the corresponding optimistic positive border.

Theorem 1 *Let $NI \subseteq C$ be a set of unsatisfied INDs in d and I_1 the set of unary INDs in C. The positive border w.r.t. NI is such that:*

$$\mathcal{B}d^+(I_{opt}) = \{i \in C \mid \overline{ens(i)} \in \mathcal{T}r(\mathcal{H}(NI))\}$$

where $\overline{ens(i)}$ is the complement of $ens(i)$ in I_1 and $\mathcal{T}r(\mathcal{H}(NI))$ the set of minimal transversals[3] of $\mathcal{H}(NI)$.

Proof *Let $i \in C$ be an IND expression.*
First, we show that $i \in I_{opt} \Leftrightarrow \overline{ens(i)}$ is a transversal of $\mathcal{H}(NI)$:
$i \in I_{opt}$
$\Leftrightarrow \forall j \in NI, j \not\preceq i$
$\Leftrightarrow \forall j \in NI, ens(j) \not\subseteq ens(i)$
$\Leftrightarrow \forall j \in NI, ens(j) \cap \overline{ens(i)} \neq \emptyset$
$\Leftrightarrow \overline{ens(i)}$ is a transversal of $\mathcal{H}(NI)$.
Then we show that i is maximal in $I_{opt} \Leftrightarrow \overline{ens(i)}$ is a minimal transversal of $\mathcal{H}(NI)$:
Let $i \in \mathcal{B}d^+(I_{opt})$. Since $i \in I_{opt}$, $\overline{ens(i)}$ is a transversal of $\mathcal{H}(NI)$. Suppose $\overline{ens(i)}$ is not minimal: $\exists X \in 2^{I_1}$, X transversal of $\mathcal{H}(NI)$ and $X \subset \overline{ens(i)}$, and thus $ens(i) \subset \overline{X}$. Then $ens^{-1}(\overline{X}) \in I_{opt}$ and $i \prec ens^{-1}(\overline{X})$ from proposition 2, which contradict the fact that $i \in \mathcal{B}d^+(I_{opt})$.
Now, let $X \in \mathcal{T}r(\mathcal{H}(NI))$. X is a transversal, then $ens^{-1}(\overline{X}) \in I_{opt}$. Suppose that $ens^{-1}(\overline{X})$ is not maximal: $\exists j \in I_{opt} \mid ens^{-1}(\overline{X}) \prec j$. Then $\overline{ens(j)}$ is a transversal of $\mathcal{H}(NI)$ with $\overline{X} \subseteq ens(j)$, and thus $\overline{ens(j)} \subseteq X$, which contradict the fact that X is a minimal transversal.

3.2. Principles of the algorithm

The proposed method can be decomposed into two main steps: a pessimistic exploration of the most general INDs until a given level, and then a "zigzag" between the negative border in construction and the corresponding optimistic positive border. Before entering into some details, some properties of INDs are studied to give some confidence in our optimistic criteria.

Why to be pessimistic ? Several factors justify to be pessimistic for the candidate INDs of small size. The first one

---

[3]A minimal transversal of an hypergraph (V, E) is a set of elements of V such that (1) it has an non empty intersection with every element of E and (2) it is minimal w.r.t. this property.

is that the first level contains the lowest number of candidates in all the search space, and thus is the best *entry point* of any exploration of C.

The second one is that in practice, a great proportion of unary IND candidates are not satisfied. Thus a significant part of the search space is disqualified by anti-monotony, justifying a pessimistic approach for this level.

Lastly, an efficient method was proposed in [13] for unary IND discovery, based on a data reorganization. The salient feature of this approach is not to make as many database passes as candidates exist (as it is the case in general for dependence discovery [27]), but only one database pass for all the candidates (as it is for example the case for frequent itemsets). To the best of our knowledge, from the level 2, no other method than generating and testing candidates one by one exists. Continuing a pessimistic approach is likely to succeed only if the majority of the candidates turns out to be false.

Why to be optimistic ? A justification for an optimistic approach can be expressed as follows: if all generalizations of size k of a candidate IND i are satisfied, then i has more chances to be satisfied when k increases. This result is justified by an inference rule[4] of Functional Dependencies (FDs) and INDs given by:

Proposition 1 *Let $\{r, s\}$ be a database, C the corresponding IND search space, and $I_k = \{i \in C, |i| = k \mid \{r, s\} \models i\}, k \geq 2$. Let $i = R[X] \subseteq S[Y], i \in C, |i| = n, n > k$ such that $\forall j \in C, |j| = k, j \prec i$, we have $j \in I_k$.*
If $\exists Y_1 \subseteq Y$ such that $|Y_1| = k - 1$ and $s \models Y_1 \to Y \setminus Y_1$, then $\{r, s\} \models i$

Proof *Let $\boldsymbol{d} = \{r, s\}$ be a database and C the corresponding IND search space. Let $i = R[X] \subseteq S[Y] \in C$ an IND expression of arity $n \geq 3$, and an integer $k < n$. Suppose that all INDs which generalize i, of size lower or equal to k, are satisfied. And let $Y_1 \subseteq Y$ be such that $|Y_1| = k - 1$ and $s \models Y_1 \to Y \setminus Y_1$.*
Let us put $Y \setminus Y_1 = B_1...B_{n-k+1}$. We note X_1 the sub-sequence of X in which the position of elements in X correspond to the position of elements of Y_1 in Y, and $A_1, ..., A_{n-k+1}$ the elements of X in which the position of elements in X correspond to the position respectively of $B_1, ..., B_{n-k+1}$ in Y.
Let $t \in r$. We have $\boldsymbol{d} \models R[X_1 A_1] \subseteq S[Y_1 B_1]$, since this IND is of arity k. Thus $\exists u_1 \in s$ such that $u_1[Y_1 B_1] = t[X_1 A_1]$. In the same way, $\boldsymbol{d} \models R[X_1 A_2] \subseteq S[Y_1 B_2]$, then $\exists u_2 \in s$ such that $u_2[Y_1 B_2] = t[X_1 A_2]$. We know that $s \models Y_1 \to B_2$ and thus $u_1[B_2] = u_2[B_2]$ since

$u_1[Y_1] = u_2[Y_1]$. *Thus, $u_1[Y_1 B_1 B_2] = t[X_1 A_1 A_2]$. We can repeat $n - k + 1$ times the same reasoning, to show that $u_1[Y_1 B_1 B_2...B_{n_k+1}] = t[X_1 A_1 A_2...A_{n_k+1}]$, and then $u_1[Y] = t[X]$. This is true for all tuple in r, and we have $\boldsymbol{d} \models R[X] \subseteq S[Y]$.*

Example 2 *Consider the IND $i = R[ABCDEF] \subseteq S[GHIJKL]$. Suppose that the 20 INDs of size 3 which generalize i are satisfied; then if there exists two attributes of $GHIJKL$ that determine the others, for example $GH \to IJKL$, we have $\boldsymbol{d} \models i$.*

Thus, the principle justified by this rule is, starting from an explored level k, to build the highest IND expressions for which all sub-INDs of size k are true. Notice that the larger k is, the more there are chances that sets of attributes of size $k - 1$ determine the others, meeting the conditions of the proposition 1.

However, when a suspected large IND i of size n is detected as false, it is necessary to choose between two alternatives: turn back to the level $k + 1$ "to consolidate" basic knowledge, or maintain an optimistic attitude by testing the INDs of the level $n - 1$ which generalize i. The following paragraph treats choice between these two alternatives.

Estimating the distance from positive border. Each time a candidate generated by an optimistic approach is detected to be false against the database, we try "to estimate" the distance between this element and the positive border of satisfied INDs. The idea is to count the number of tuples which does not satisfy the IND; we propose for that to use the error measure g'_3 [25] given by:

$$g'_3(R[X] \subseteq S[Y], \mathbf{d}) =$$
$$1 -$$
$$\frac{max\{|\pi_X(r')| \mid r' \subseteq r, (\mathbf{d} - \{r\}) \cup \{r'\} \models R[X] \subseteq S[Y]\}}{|\pi_X(r)|}$$

Intuitively, g'_3 is the proportion of distinct values one has to remove from X to obtain a database $\mathbf{d}'$ such that $\mathbf{d}' \models R[X] \subseteq S[Y]$. Such a computation can be implemented with SQL queries on top of RDBMS. Clearly, if $j \preceq i$, then $g'_3(j) \leq g'_3(i)$. Thus, when an IND i of the optimistic positive border is false, but with a very small error, one can reasonably hope to find a satisfied IND among its nearest generalizations. Thus we consider the generalizations of i from more specific ones to most general ones, i.e. implementing a top-down approach. Inversely when the error is large, i.e. a great number of values contradicts the IND, we start again the search in a bottom-up fashion.

3.3. The algorithm $Zigzag$

The principle of the algorithm 1 is to mix top-down and bottom-up approaches for eliciting the positive border of

---

[4]The inference rule stated by the proposition 1 does not form part of the Mitchell system [29], but of course is inferred by this system which is sound and complete. The demonstration suggested here seemed more comprehensible and shorter.

satisfied INDs. Initially (line 1) a purely pessimistic approach is performed from an adaptation of the levelwise algorithm $MIND$ [13], until the level k fixed by the user is reached. We then know I_k and NI_k, the set of the most specialized satisfied INDs and the set of the most general unsatisfied INDs (resp.) of size smaller or equal to k. I_k thus corresponds to an initialization of $\mathcal{B}d^+(I)$ and NI_k to an initialization of $\mathcal{B}d^-(I)$. The optimistic positive border $\mathcal{B}d^+(I_{opt})$ is then computed from $\mathcal{B}d^-(I)$ thanks to the theorem 1 (line 3)[5]. The algorithm terminates when every element of $\mathcal{B}d^+(I_{opt})$ has already been tested as true in previous passes, i.e. $\mathcal{B}d^+(I_{opt}) \setminus \mathcal{B}d^+(I)$ is empty (line 4). Otherwise, INDs of $\mathcal{B}d^+(I_{opt}) \setminus \mathcal{B}d^+(I)$ are evaluated against the database: Those satisfied are added to $\mathcal{B}d^+(I)$, the others are divided into two groups according to the committed error: the "almost true" ones in the optimistic set $optDI$ and the others in the pessimistic set $pessDI$. The INDs which generalize the INDs of $optDI$ are traversed in a top-down fashion, from the most specific to the more general; $\mathcal{B}d^+(I)$ and $\mathcal{B}d^-(I)$ are updated accordingly (lines 14 to 21). Lastly, INDs of size $k+1$ which generalize the INDs of $pessDI$ are tested, $\mathcal{B}d^+(I)$ and $\mathcal{B}d^-(I)$ are also updated (lines 23 to 26). $\mathcal{B}d^+(I_{opt})$ is then updated for the next iteration (line 28).

3.4. Practical aspects and optimizations

Unsatisfied unary INDs. In algorithm 1, line 2, the most general unsatisfied INDs are added in the initialization of $\mathcal{B}d^-(I)$. In practice, we do not add unsatisfied unary INDs to $\mathcal{B}d^-(I)$. It is enough not to take them into account during the computation of the complements of minimal transversal of the hypergraph associated with $\mathcal{B}d^-(I)$.

Dealing with repeated attributes in INDs. The usual IND definition rejects the repeated attributes in the left-hand side or the right-hand side, which reduces of course in a significant way the size of the search space; it is thus important to remove candidates with duplicate attributes in the optimistic positive border. For that, it is enough to introduce into the negative border, during its initialization (line 2 of algorithm 1) the set of INDs of size 2 with repeated attributes made up of two satisfied unary INDs. Indeed, consider an IND i having at least one repeated attribute on the left-hand side[6], i.e. $i = R[X_1AAX_2] \subseteq S[Y_1BCY_2]$. Thus there exist at least one IND of size 2, here $j = R[AA] \subseteq S[BC]$, which generalizes i. If j belong to the negative border, then i cannot belong to the corresponding optimistic positive border, according to definition 5.

---

[5]The optimistic positive border generation is not detailed here. We use an adaptation of the algorithm proposed in [15].

[6]The same justification still holds for right-hand side.

Algorithm 1 Zigzag : IND cover discovery

Require: a database $\mathbf{d}$, an integer k;
Ensure: $\mathcal{B}d^+(I)$ cover of the satisfied INDs in $\mathbf{d}$.
1: Compute I_k and NI_k by a pessimistic aproach.
2: $\mathcal{B}d^+(I) = I_k; \mathcal{B}d^-(I) = NI_k$;
3: Compute $\mathcal{B}d^+(I_{opt})$ from $\mathcal{B}d^-(I)$:
4: **while** $\mathcal{B}d^+(I_{opt}) \setminus \mathcal{B}d^+(I) \neq \emptyset$ **do**
5: $\quad optDI = pessDI = \emptyset$;
6: $\quad$ **for all** $i \in \mathcal{B}d^+(I_{opt}) \setminus \mathcal{B}d^+(I)$ **do**
7: $\quad\quad$ **if** $(g'_3(i, \mathbf{d}) = 0)$ **then** $\mathcal{B}d^+(I) = \mathcal{B}d^+(I) \cup \{i\} \setminus \{j \in \mathcal{B}d^+(I) \mid j \prec i\}$;
8: $\quad\quad$ **else**
9: $\quad\quad\quad \mathcal{B}d^-(I) = \mathcal{B}d^-(I) \cup i$;
10: $\quad\quad\quad$ **if** $(g'_3(i, \mathbf{d}) \leq \epsilon$ and $|i| > k + 1)$
11: $\quad\quad\quad$ **then** $optDI = optDI \cup \{i\}$;
12: $\quad\quad\quad$ **else** $pessDI = pessDI \cup \{i\}$;
13: $\quad$ **end for**
14: $\quad$ **while** $optDI \neq \emptyset$ **do**
15: $\quad\quad candidats = \cup_{i \in optDI}\{j \mid j \preceq i, |j| = |i| - 1$ and $|j| > k\}$;
16: $\quad\quad$ **for all** $i \in candidats$ **do**
17: $\quad\quad\quad$ **if** $(\mathbf{d} \models i)$ **then** $\mathcal{B}d^+(I) = \mathcal{B}d^+(I) \cup \{i\} \setminus \{j \in \mathcal{B}d^+(I) \mid j \prec i\}$; $candidats = candidats \setminus \{i\}$;
18: $\quad\quad\quad$ **else** $\mathcal{B}d^-(I) = \mathcal{B}d^-(I) \cup \{i\} \setminus \{j \in \mathcal{B}d^-(I) \mid i \prec j\}$;
19: $\quad\quad$ **end for**
20: $\quad\quad optDI = candidats$;
21: $\quad$ **end while**
22: $\quad C_{k+1} = \cup_{i \in pessDI}\{j \mid j \prec i, |j| = k + 1\}$;
23: $\quad$ **for all** $i \in C_{k+1}$ **do**
24: $\quad\quad$ **if** $(\mathcal{B}d^+(I) \models i$ or $\mathbf{d} \models i)$ **then** $\mathcal{B}d^+(I) = \mathcal{B}d^+(I) \cup \{i\} \setminus \{j \in \mathcal{B}d^+(I) \mid j \prec i\}$;
25: $\quad\quad$ **else** $\mathcal{B}d^-(I) = \mathcal{B}d^-(I) \cup \{i\} \setminus \{j \in \mathcal{B}d^-(I) \mid i \prec j\}$;
26: $\quad$ **end for**
27: $\quad k = k + 1$;
28: $\quad$ Compute $\mathcal{B}d^+(I_{opt})$ from $\mathcal{B}d^-(I)$:
29: **end while**
30: Return $\mathcal{B}d^+(I)$.

Parallelization of $Zigzag$. An interesting property of the IND search space can be given, making it possible to break up our exploration method into several independent courses.

Property 3 Let $\mathbf{d}$ be a database over a schema $\mathbf{R}$ and I the set of satisfied INDs in $\mathbf{d}$. Then $\mathcal{B}d^+(I) = \bigcup_{(R,S) \in \mathbf{d}^2} \mathcal{B}d^+(I_{R \to S})$ where $I_{R \to S}$ denotes INDs from R to S.

Thus, the IND discovery can be made through independent tasks, one for each couple of relations in the database. In addition to the natural parallelization of the algorithm, this decomposition also makes it possible to decrease the size of the negative border in each iteration, and thus to improve the performances of the optimistic positive border generation. The current implementation of the algorithm considers the couples of relation one by one, except for unary IND discovery, which as mentioned, does not consist of a candidate enumeration, but of a global data reorganization [13].

Optimistic positive border generation. In addition to the number of tested INDs, which remains factorial in worst cases, $Zigzag$ complexity comes from the optimistic positive border computation, which induces the calculation of minimal transversals of the hypergraph corresponding to the negative border in construction. The computation of minimal transversals of an hypergraph is a well-known problem studied in the literature (see e.g. [16] for a comprehensive survey). The exact complexity is, up to our knowledge, an open problem. The existence of incremental algorithms w.r.t the edges of the hypergraph is very interesting in our case [7, 15, 16]. Indeed, the first calculation occurs at the level k and then, new edges are considered for updating the set of minimal transversals.

An optimization can also be brought to the calculation of $\mathcal{B}d^+(I_{opt})$. Indeed, at each iteration, this set contains at the same time the largest "guessed" INDs, but also some satisfied INDs of smaller size which were already discovered. The idea is thus to characterize more finely the elements of $\mathcal{B}d^+(I_{opt})$: those which are to be discovered, and those already explored. The following results just follows from the theorem 1.

Proposition 2 *Let I_k be the set of satisfied INDs of size less or equal to k, NI the set of unsatisfied INDs, and n the number of unary INDs. We have:*
$$i \in (\mathcal{B}d^+(I_{opt}) \setminus I_k) \iff \overline{ens(i)} \in \mathcal{T}r(\mathcal{H}(NI))$$
and $|\overline{ens(i)}| \leq n - k$

In practice, this condition leads to optimize the generation of minimal transversals since candidates exceeding the size allowed can be safely removed.

3.5. Experimental results

Preliminary tests were carried out on synthetic databases. They were performed on an INTEL Pentium III 500 MHz, with 384 MB of main memory and running Windows 2000 Pro. The algorithms were implemented using C++/STL language. The test databases are stored under Oracle 9i, and data accesses were carried out via ODBC drivers. The tests were conducted on three databases having 2 relations, with 25 attributes and 90000 tuples in each relation. The databases differ on the constitution of the positive border of satisfied INDs to discover:

- database 1: 10 INDs, with arities of 2,5,6 and 7;

- database 2: 10 INDs, with arities of 3,5,6 and 11;

- database 3: 20 INDs, with arities of 6,8,13,17 and 18;

Table 1 gives execution times for IND discovery using algorithm $Zigzag$, with $k = 2$. Times are compared with those given by the levelwise algorithm $Mind$ [13]. The value for $Mind$ on the third database is an estimate: it multiplies the number of tests to be carried out with the average cost of a test.

Table 1. Experimental results

database	$Zigzag$	$Mind$
1	1 754 s.	2 790 s.
2	3 500 s.	25 626 s.
3	7 729 s.	≥ 1 year (estimate)

First of all, these results confirm the failure of levelwise approach for large IND discovery, and thus reinforce the interest of proposing alternatives. Moreover, algorithm $Zigzag$ makes it possible to reach INDs of size 18 in about only two hours (while $Mind$ would have take more than one year!), and thus shows the feasibility of the approach.

4. Conclusion

A new approach for the IND discovery in an existing database was proposed in this article. Since a levelwise approach does not work when INDs of size higher than 10 have to be discovered, we proposed an approach allowing to carry out *optimistic jumps* in the search space, performing "Zigzags" between the negative and positive borders in construction. This approach relies on a theoretical framework which could be apply to other search spaces. The principle of an optimistic attitude is justified by a structural property of the relational model. The proposed method exploits an error measure to guess how far the positive border of satisfied INDs is w.r.t. the optimistic positive border. Moreover, the characterization of a positive border according to a set of counterexamples is a general result: it can be applied to other data-mining tasks.

This work is integrated in a more general project devoted to DBA assistance and relational databases logical tuning, called "DBA Companion" [14]. We propose methods for discovering INDs, functional dependency and keys, and for computing small samples to represent data semantics (informative Armstrong databases).

We finish this article by mentioning some perspectives which could supplement this work:

- A complete study of $Zigzag$ complexity;

- The development of a more "probabilistic" approach, in order to estimate the value of k (the level from which optimist approach is likely to succeed) and the value of ϵ (to estimate the distance between positive optimistic border and positive border to be discovered);

- The adaptation and the implementation of this work for similar problems such as large frequent itemset discovery or functional dependency discovery.

References

[1] S. Abiteboul, R. Hull, and V. Vianu. *Foundations of Databases*. Addison-Wesley, Reading, Mass., 1995.

[2] C. C. Aggarwal. Towards long pattern generation in dense databases. *SIGKDD Explorations*, 3(1):20–26, 2001.

[3] R. Agrawal and R. Srikant. Fast algorithms for mining association rules in large databases. In J. B. Bocca, M. Jarke, and C. Zaniolo, editors, *International Conference on Very Large Data Bases (VLDB'94), Santiago de Chile, Chile*, pages 487–499. Morgan Kaufmann, 1994.

[4] Y. Bastide, R. Taouil, N. Pasquier, G. Stumme, and L. Lakhal. Mining frequent patterns with counting inference. *ACM SIGKDD Exploration*, 2(2):66–75, 2000.

[5] R. J. Bayardo. Efficiently mining long patterns from databases. In L. M. Haas and A. Tiwary, editors, *ACM SIGMOD International Conference on Management of Data, Seattle, USA*, pages 85–93. ACM Press, 1998.

[6] S. Bell and P. Brockhausen. Discovery of constraints and data dependencies in databases (extended abstract). In N. Lavrac and S. Wrobel, editors, *European Conference on Machine Learning (ECML'95), Crete, Greece*, pages 267–270, 1995.

[7] C. Berge. Hypergraphs. *North Holland Mathematic Library*, 45, 1989.

[8] J.-F. Boulicaut, A. Bykowski, and C. Rigotti. Free-sets: A condensed representation of boolean data for the approximation of frequency queries. *Data Mining and Knowledge Discovery*, 7(1):5–22, 2003.

[9] T. Calders and B. Goethals. Mining all non-derivable frequent itemsets. In *Principles of Data Mining and Knowledge Discovery*, volume 2431 of *Lecture Notes in Computer Science*. Springer, 2002.

[10] M. Casanova, R. Fagin, and C. Papadimitriou. Inclusion dependencies and their interaction with functional dependencies. *Journal of Computer and System Sciences*, 24(1):29–59, Feb. 1984.

[11] M. A. Casanova, L. Tucherman, and A. L. Furtado. Enforcing inclusion dependencies and referencial integrity. In F. Bancilhon and D. J. DeWitt, editors, *International Conference on Very Large Data Bases (VLDB'88), Los Angeles, California, USA*, pages 38–49. Morgan Kaufmann, 1988.

[12] Q. Cheng, J. Gryz, F. Koo, T. Y. C. Leung, L. Liu, X. Qian, and B. Schiefer. Implementation of two semantic query optimization techniques in DB2 universal database. In M. P. Atkinson, M. E. Orlowska, P. Valduriez, S. B. Zdonik, and M. L. Brodie, editors, *International Conference on Very Large Data Bases (VLDB'99), Edinburgh, Scotland, UK*, pages 687–698. Morgan Kaufmann, 1999.

[13] F. De Marchi, S. Lopes, and J.-M. Petit. Efficient algorithms for mining inclusion dependencies. In C. S. Jensen, K. G. Jeffery, J. Pokorný, S. Saltenis, E. Bertino, K. Böhm, and M. Jarke, editors, *International Conference on Extending Database Technology (EDBT'02), Prague, Czech Republic*, volume 2287 of *Lecture Notes in Computer Science*, pages 464–476. Springer, 2002.

[14] F. De Marchi, S. Lopes, J.-M. Petit, and F. Toumani. Analysis of existing databases at the logical level: the DBA companion project. *ACM Sigmod Record*, 32(1):47–52, 2003.

[15] J. Demetrovics and V. Thi. Some remarks on generating armstrong and inferring functional dependencies relation. *Acta Cybernetica*, 12(2):167–180, 1995.

[16] T. Eiter and G. Gottlob. Identifying the minimal transversals of a hypergraph and related problems. *SIAM Journal on Computing*, 24(6):1278–1304, 1995.

[17] K. Gouda and M. J. Zaki. Efficiently mining maximal frequent itemsets. In N. Cercone, T. Y. Lin, and X. Wu, editors, *International Conference on Data Mining, San Jose, USA*. IEEE Computer Society, 2001.

[18] J. Gryz. Query folding with inclusion dependencies. In *International Conference on Data Engineering (ICDE'98), Orlando, Florida, USA*, pages 126–133. IEEE Computer Society, 1998.

[19] D. Gunopulos, R. Khardon, H. Mannila, and H. Toivonen. Data mining, hypergraph transversals, and machine learning. In *Symposium on Principles of Database Systems (PODS'97), Tucson, Arizona*, pages 209–216. ACM Press, 1997.

[20] M. Kantola, H. Mannila, K. J. Räihä, and H. Siirtola. Discovering functional and inclusion dependencies in relational databases. *International Journal of Intelligent Systems*, 7:591–607, 1992.

[21] A. Koeller and E. A. Rundensteiner. Discovery of high-dimensional inclusion dependencies (poster). In *International Conference on Data Engineering*. IEEE Computer Society, 2003.

[22] M. Levene and G. Loizou. *A Guided Tour of Relational Databases and Beyond*. Springer, 1999.

[23] M. Levene and M. W. Vincent. Justification for inclusion dependency normal form. *IEEE Transactions on Knowledge and Data Engineering*, 12(2):281–291, 2000.

[24] D.-I. Lin and Z. M. Kedem. Pincer search: A new algorithm for discovering the maximum frequent set. In H.-J. Schek, F. Saltor, I. Ramos, and G. Alonso, editors, *Extending Database Technology, Valencia, Spain*, volume 1377 of *Lecture Notes in Computer Science*, pages 105–119. Springer, 1998.

[25] S. Lopes, J.-M. Petit, and F. Toumani. Discovering interesting inclusion dependencies: Application to logical database tuning. *Information System*, 17(1):1–19, 2002.

[26] H. Mannila and K.-J. Räihä. Inclusion dependencies in database design. In *International Conference on Data Engineering (ICDE'86), Los Angeles, California, USA*, pages 713–718. IEEE Computer Society, 1986.

[27] H. Mannila and H. Toivonen. Levelwise Search and Borders of Theories in Knowledge Discovery. *Data Mining and Knowledge Discovery*, 1(1):241–258, 1997.

[28] R. J. Miller, M. A. Hernández, L. M. Haas, L. Yan, C. T. H. Ho, R. Fagin, and L. Popa. The clio project: Managing heterogeneity. *ACM SIGMOD Record*, 30(1):78–83, 2001.

[29] J. C. Mitchell. The implication problem for functional and inclusion dependencies. *Information and Control*, 56(3):154–173, Mar. 1983.

[30] N. Pasquier, Y. Bastide, R. Taouil, and L. Lakhal. Efficient mining of association rules using closed itemset lattices. *Information Systems*, 24(1):25–46, 1999.

Frequent Sub-Structure-Based Approaches for Classifying Chemical Compounds*

Mukund Deshpande, Michihiro Kuramochi and George Karypis

University of Minnesota, Department of Computer Science/Army HPC Research Center
Minneapolis, MN 55455

{deshpand,kuram,karypis}@cs.umn.edu

Abstract

In this paper we study the problem of classifying chemical compound datasets. We present a sub-structure-based classification algorithm that decouples the sub-structure discovery process from the classification model construction and uses frequent subgraph discovery algorithms to find all topological and geometric sub-structures present in the dataset. The advantage of our approach is that during classification model construction, all relevant sub-structures are available allowing the classifier to intelligently select the most discriminating ones. The computational scalability is ensured by the use of highly efficient frequent subgraph discovery algorithms coupled with aggressive feature selection. Our experimental evaluation on eight different classification problems shows that our approach is computationally scalable and on the average, outperforms existing schemes by 10% to 35%.

1 Introduction

One of the key steps in the drug design process is to identify the chemical compounds (widely referred to as *"hit"* compounds) that display the desired and reproducible behavior against the disease [21] in a biological experiment. The standard technique to discover such compounds is to evaluate them with a biological experiment, known as an assay. The 1990s saw the widespread adoption of high-throughput screening (HTS), which uses highly automated techniques to conduct the biological assays and can be used to screen a large number of compounds. Though in principle, HTS techniques can be used to test each compound against every biological assay, it is never practically feasible for the following reasons. First, the number of chemical compounds that have been synthesized or can be synthesized using combinatorial chemistry techniques is extremely large. Second, not all biological assays can be converted to high throughput format. Third, in most cases it is hard to find all the desirable properties in a single compound and chemists are interested in not just identifying the hits but studying what part of the chemical compound leads to desirable behavior, so that new compounds can be rationally synthesized. The goal of this paper is to develop supervised learning techniques for identifying the hit compounds. These computational techniques can be used to replace or supplement the biological assay techniques.

In recent years two classes of techniques have been developed for solving the chemical compound classification problem. The first class builds a classification model using a set of physico-chemical properties derived from the compounds structure, called quantitative structure-activity relationships (QSAR) [10, 11, 1], whereas the second class operates directly on the structure of the chemical compound and tries to automatically identify a small number of chemical sub-structures that can be used to discriminate between the different classes [17, 2, 33, 13, 20, 4]. A number of comparative studies [31, 16] have shown that sub-structure-based techniques are superior to those based on QSAR properties and require limited user intervention and domain knowledge. However, despite their success, a key limitation of these techniques is that they rely on heuristic search methods and may lead to sub-optimal classifiers in cases in which the heuristic search failed to uncover sub-structures that are critical for the classification task.

In this paper we present a sub-structure-based classifier that overcomes the limitations associated with existing algorithms. One of the key ideas of our approach is to decouple the sub-structure discovery process from the classification model construction step and use frequent subgraph discovery algorithms to find all chemical sub-structures that occur a sufficiently large number of times. Once the complete set of these sub-structures has been identified, our algorithm then proceeds to build a classification model based on them. The advantage of such an approach is that during classification model construction, all relevant sub-structures are available allowing the classifier to intelligently select the most discriminating ones. We experimentally evaluated the performance of our algorithms on eight different problems derived from three publicly available datasets and compared their performance against that of traditional QSAR-based classifiers and existing sub-structure classifiers based on SUBDUE [3] and SubdueCL [9]. Our results show that our approach, on the average, outperforms QSAR-based schemes by 35% and

---

*This work was supported by NSF CCR-9972519, EIA-9986042, ACI-9982274, ACI-0133464, and by Army High Performance Computing Research Center contract number DAAD19-01-2-0014.

Figure 1: Chemical and Graphical representation of Flucytosine

(a) NSC 103025 Flucytosine   (b) Graph Representation

S: Single Bond
D: Double Bond

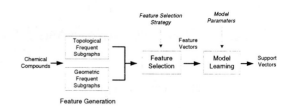

Figure 2: Frequent Subgraph Based Classification Framework

SUBDUE-based schemes by 10%.

The rest of the paper is organized as follows. Section 2 provides some background information related to chemical compounds, their activity, and their representation. Section 3 provides the details of our chemical compound classification approach. Section 4 experimentally evaluates its performance and compares it against other approaches. Finally, Section 5 provides some concluding remarks. An extended version of this paper is available at [6].

2 Background

A chemical compound consists of different atoms being held together via bonds adopting a well-defined geometric configuration. Figure 1(a) represents the chemical compound Flucytosine from the DTP AIDS repository [7] it consists of a central aromatic ring and other elements like N, O and F.

The activity of a compound largely depends on its chemical structure and the arrangement of different atoms in 3D space. As a result, effective classification algorithms must be able to directly take into account the structural nature of these datasets. In this paper we represent each compound as undirected graphs. The vertices of these graphs correspond to the various atoms, and the edges correspond to the bonds between the atoms. Each of the vertices and edges has a label associated with it. The labels on the vertices correspond to the type of atoms and the labels on the edges correspond to the type of bonds. As an example, Figure 1(b) shows the representation of Flucytosine in terms of this graph model. We will refer to this representation as the *topological graph* representation of a chemical compound. Note that such representations are quite commonly used by many chemical modeling software and are referred as the *connection table* for the chemical compound [22].

In addition, since chemical compounds have a physical three-dimensional structure, each vertex of the graph has a 3D-coordinate indicating the position of the corresponding atom in 3D space. However, there are two key issues that need to be considered when working with the compound's 3D structure. First, the number of experimentally determined molecular geometries is limited (about 270,000 X-ray structures in the Cambridge Crystallographic Database compared to 15 million known compounds). As a result, the 3D geometry of a compound needs to be computationally determined, which may introduce certain amount of error. To address this problem, we use the Corina [8] software package to compute the 3D coordinates for all the chemical compounds in our datasets. Second, each compound can have multiple low-energy conformations (*i.e.*, multiple 3D structures) that need to be taken into account in order to achieve the highest possible classification performance. However, due to time constraints, in this study we do not take into account these multiple conformations but instead use the single low-energy conformation that is returned by Corina's default settings. However, the presented approach for extracting geometric sub-structures can be easily extended to cases in which multiple conformations are considered as well. We will refer to this representation as the *geometric graph* representation of a chemical compound.

3 Classification Based on Frequent Subgraphs

The overall outline of our classification methodology is shown in Figure 2. It consists of three distinct steps: (i) feature generation, (ii) feature selection, and (iii) classification model construction. During the feature generation step, the chemical compounds are mined to discover the frequently occurring sub-structures that correspond to either topological or geometric subgraphs. These sub-structures are then used as the features by which the compounds are represented in the subsequent steps. During the second step, a small set of features is selected such that the selected features can correctly discriminate between the different classes found in the dataset. Finally, in the last step each chemical compound is represented using these set of features and a classification model is learned. The rest of this section describes these three steps in detail.

3.1 Feature Generation

Our classification algorithm finds sub-structures in a chemical compound database using two different methods. The first method uses the topological graph representation of each compound whereas the second method is based on the corresponding geometric graph representation (discussed in Section 2). In both of these methods, our algorithm uses the topological or geometric connected subgraphs that occur in at least σ% of the compounds to define the sub-structures.

Frequent Topological Subgraphs In our classification algorithm we find the frequently occurring subgraphs using the FSG algorithm. FSG takes as input a database D of graphs and a minimum support σ, and finds all connected subgraphs that occur in at least $\sigma\%$ of the transactions. FSG, initially presented in [18], with subsequent improvements presented in [20], uses a breadth-first approach to discover the lattice of frequent subgraphs. Despite the inherent complexity of the problem, FSG employs a number of sophisticated techniques to achieve high computational performance, and as the experiments presented in Section 4 show, it is able to scale to large datasets and low support values.

Frequent Geometric Subgraphs Topological substructures capture the connectivity of atoms in the chemical compound but they ignore the 3D shape (3D arrangement of atoms) of the sub-structures. For certain classification problems the 3D shape of the sub-structure might be essential for determining the chemical activity of a compound. For instance, the geometric configuration of atoms in a sub-structure is crucial for its ability to bind to a particular target [21]. For this reason we developed an algorithm that finds all frequent sub-structures whose topology as well as geometry is conserved.

There are two important aspects specific to the geometric subgraphs that need to be considered. First, since the coordinates of the vertices depend on a particular reference coordinate axes, we would like the discovered geometric subgraphs to be independent of these coordinate axes. Second, while determining if a geometric subgraph is contained in a bigger geometric graph we would like to allow some tolerance when we establish a match between coordinates. The amount of tolerance (r) should be a user specified parameter. The task of discovering such r-tolerant frequent geometric subgraphs dramatically changes the nature of the problem as there are many different geometric representations of the same pattern (all of which will be r-tolerant isomorphic to each other). Thus, the problem becomes not only that of finding a pattern and its support, but also finding the right representative for this pattern. These two aspects of geometric subgraphs makes the task of discovering the full fledged geometric subgraphs extremely hard [19].

To overcome this problem we use a property of a geometric graph called the ***average inter-atomic distance*** that is defined as the average Euclidean distance between all pairs of atoms in the molecule. The average inter-atomic distance can be thought of as a geometric signature of a topological subgraph. The geometric subgraph consists of two components, a topological subgraph and an interval of average inter-atomic distance associated with it. Note that this geometric representation is also translation and rotation invariant, and the width of the interval determines the tolerance displayed by the geometric subgraph. We are interested in discovering such geometric subgraphs that occur above $\sigma\%$ of the transactions and the interval of aver-

age inter-atomic distance is bound by r.

Since a geometric subgraph contains a topological subgraph, for the geometric subgraph to be frequent the corresponding topological subgraph has to be frequent, as well. This allows us to take advantage of the existing approach to discover topological subgraphs. We modify the frequency counting stage of the FSG algorithm as follows. If a subgraph g is contained in a transaction t then all possible embeddings of g in t are found and the average inter-atomic distance for each of these embeddings is computed. This list of average inter-atomic distances is added to the $g.aiadList$ such that at the end of the frequent subgraph discovery each topological subgraph has a list of average inter-atomic distances associated with it. Each one of the average inter-atomic distances corresponds to one of the embeddings *i.e.*, a geometric configuration of the topological subgraph.

The task of discovering geometric subgraphs now reduces to identifying those geometric configurations that are frequent enough, *i.e.*, to identify intervals of average inter-atomic distance such that each interval contains the minimum number geometric configurations (σ) and the width of the interval is less than the tolerance threshold (r). This task can be thought of as 1D clustering on the vector of average inter-atomic distances such that each cluster contains items above the minimum support and the spread of each cluster is bounded by the tolerance r. Note that not all items will belong to a valid cluster as some of them will be infrequent. In our experiments we set the value of r to be equal to half of the minimum distance between any two pairs of atoms in the compounds.

To find such clusters we perform agglomerative clustering on the vector of average inter-atomic distance values. To ensure that we get the largest possible clusters we use the maximum-link criterion function for deciding which two clusters should be merged [15]. The process of agglomeration is continued until the interval containing all the items in the cluster is below the tolerance threshold (r). When we reach a stage where further agglomeration would increase the spread of the cluster beyond the tolerance threshold, we check the number of items contained in the cluster. If the number of items is above the support threshold, then the interval associated with this cluster is considered as a geometric feature. Since we are clustering one-dimensional datasets, the clustering complexity is low.

Note that this algorithm for computing geometric subgraphs is approximate in nature for two reasons. First, the average inter-atomic distance may map two different geometric subgraphs to the same average inter-atomic distance value. Second, the clustering algorithm may not find the complete set of geometric subgraphs that satisfy the r tolerance. Nevertheless, as our experiments in Section 4 show the geometric subgraphs discovered by this approach improve the classification accuracy of the algorithm.

Additional Considerations Even though FSG provides the general functionality required to find all frequently occurring sub-structures in chemical datasets, there are a number of issues that need to be addressed before it can be applied as a black-box tool for feature discovery in the context of classification. One issue deals with selecting the right value for the σ, the support constraint used for discovering frequent sub-structures. The value of σ controls the number of subgraphs discovered by FSG. Choosing a good value of σ is especially important for the dataset containing classes of significantly different sizes. In such cases, in order to ensure that FSG is able to find features that are meaningful for all the classes, it must use a support that depends on the size of the smaller class.

For this reason we first partition the complete dataset, using the class label of the examples, into specific class specific datasets. We then run FSG on each of these *class datasets*. This partitioning of the dataset ensures that sufficient subgraphs are discovered for those class labels which occur rarely in the dataset. Next, we combine subgraphs discovered from each of the *class dataset*. After this step each subgraph has a vector that contains the frequency with which it occurs in each class.

3.2 Feature Selection

The frequent subgraph discovery algorithms described in Section 3.1 discovers all the sub-structures (topological or geometric) that occur above a certain support constraint (σ) in the dataset. Though the discovery algorithm is computationally efficient, the algorithm can generate a large number of features. A large number of features is detrimental for two reasons. First, it could increase the time required to build the model. But more importantly, a large number of features can increase the time required to classify a chemical compound (whose number can range in the millions), as we need to first identify which of the discovered features it contains before we can apply the classification model. Determining whether a compound contains a particular feature or not can be computationally expensive as it may require a subgraph isomorphism operation.

In order to develop an effective feature selection method, we use a scheme that first finds all frequent subgraphs and then selects among them a small set of discriminatory features. The advantage of this approach is that during feature selection all frequent subgraphs are considered irrespective of when they were generated and whether or not they contain less or more discriminatory subgraphs. The feature selection scheme is based on the ***sequential covering paradigm*** used to learn rule sets [25]. Specifically, we use the computationally efficient implementation of sequential covering known as CBA [24]. This algorithm proceeds by first sorting the features based on confidence and then applying the sequential covering algorithm on this sorted set of features. In addition, to obtain a better control over the number of selected features we use an extension of the sequential covering scheme known as (CMAR) [23].

In this scheme instead of removing the example after it is covered by the selected feature, the example is removed only if that example is covered by δ selected features. The value of δ is specified by the user and provides a means to the user to control the number of features used for classification.

3.3 Classification Model Construction

Given the frequent subgraphs discovered in the previous step, our algorithm treats each of these subgraphs as a feature and represents the chemical compound as a frequency vector. The ith entry of this vector is equal to the number of times (frequency) that feature occurs in the compound's graph. This mapping into the feature space of frequent subgraphs is performed both for the training and the test dataset.

Once the feature vectors for each chemical compound have been built, any one of the existing classification algorithms can potentially be used for classification. In our study we built the classification models using support vector machines (SVM) [32], as they are well-suited for operating in such sparse and high-dimensional datasets. Furthermore, an additional advantage of SVM is that it allows us to directly control the cost associated with the missclassification of examples from the different classes [26]. This allow us to associate a higher cost for the missclassification of positive instances; thus, biasing the classifier to learn a model that tries to increase the true-positive rate, at the expense of increasing the false positive rate.

4 Experimental Evaluation

We experimentally evaluated the performance of our classification algorithm and compared it against that achieved by earlier approaches on a variety of chemical compound datasets.

4.1 Datasets

We used three different publicly available datasets to derive a total of eight different classification problems. Some important characteristics of these datasets are summarized in Table 1.

The first dataset was initially used as a part of the Predictive Toxicology Evaluation Challenge [30] which was organized as a part of PKDD/ECML 2001 Conference. The goal being to estimate the carcinogenicity of different compounds on various rodents. There are four classification problems one corresponding to each of the rodents and will be referred as *P1*, *P2*, *P3*, and *P4*. The second dataset is obtained from the National Cancer Institute's DTP AIDS Anti-viral Screen program [7]. Each compound in the dataset is evaluated for evidence of anti-HIV activity, and they were assigned to three categories: confirmed active (CA), moderately active (CM), and confirmed inactive (CI). We have formulated three classification problems on this dataset, in the first problem we consider only CA and CM compounds and then build a clas-

	Toxic.	Aids	Anthrax	Class Dist. (% +ve class)	
N	417	42,687	34,836	**Toxicology**	
$\bar{N}_A$	25	46	25	P1: Male Mice	38.3%
$\bar{N}_B$	26	48	25	P2: Female Mice	40.9%
$\bar{L}_A$	40	82	25	P3: Male Rats	44.2%
$\bar{L}_B$	4	4	4	P4: Female Rats	34.4%
max N_A	106	438	41	**AIDS**	
min N_A	2	2	12	H1: CA/CM	28.1%
max N_B	1	276	44	H2: (CA+CM)/CI	3.5%
min N_B	85	1	12	H3: CA/CI	1.0%
				Anthrax	
				A1: active/inactive	35%

Table 1: The characteristics of the various datasets. N is the number of compounds in the database. $\bar{N}_A$ and $\bar{N}_B$ are the average number of atoms and bonds in each compound. $\bar{L}_A$ and $\bar{L}_B$ are the average number of atom- and bond-types in each dataset. max N_A/min N_A and max N_B/min N_B are the maximum/minimum number of atoms and bonds over all the compounds in each dataset.

sifier to separate these two compounds; this problem is referred as *H1*. For the second problem we combine CM and CA compounds to form one set of *active* compounds, we then build a classifier to separate these *active* and CI compounds; this problem is referred as *H2*. In the last problem we only use CA and CI compounds and build a classifier to categorize these two compounds; this problem is referred as *H3*. The third dataset was obtained from the Center of Computational Drug Discovery's anthrax project at the University of Oxford [29]. The goal of this project was to discover small molecules that would bind with the heptameric protective antigen component of the anthrax toxin, and prevent it from spreading its toxic effects. The classification problem for this dataset was given a chemical compound classify it in to one of these two classes, *i.e*, will the compound bind the anthrax toxin or not. This classification problem is referred as *A1*.

4.2 Experimental Methodology & Metrics

The classifications results were obtained by performing 5-way cross validation on the dataset, ensuring that the class distribution in each fold is identical to the original dataset. For the SVM classifier we used SVMLight library [14]. All the experiments were conducted on a 1500MHz Athlon MP processor having a 2GB of memory.

Since the size of the positive class is significantly smaller than the negative class, using *accuracy* to judge a classifier would be incorrect. To get a better understanding of the classifier performance for different cost settings we obtain the ROC curve [27] for each classifier. Two classifiers are compared in terms of the area under their respective ROC curves, a larger area under ROC curve indicating better performance. The area under the ROC curve will be referred by the parameter A.

4.3 Results

Varying Minimum Support To evaluate the sensitivity of the algorithm on the value of the minimum support we performed a set of experiments in which we varied σ

from 10% to 20% in 5% increments. The results of these experiments are shown in the left sub-table of Table 2 for both topological and geometric sub-structures. We can observe that as we increase σ, the classification performance for most datasets tends to degrade. However, in most cases this degradation is gradual and correlates well with the decrease on the number of discovered sub-structures. These results suggest that lower values of support are in general better as they lead to better classification performance. However, as the support decreases, the number of discovered sub-structures and the amount of time required also increases. Thus, depending on the dataset, some experimentation may be required to select the proper values of support that balances these conflicting requirements (*i.e.,* low support but reasonable number of sub-structures).

In our study we performed such experimentation. For each dataset we kept on decreasing the value of support down to the point after which the number of features that were generated was too large to be efficiently processed by the SVM library. The resulting support values, number of features, and associated classification performance are shown in the right sub-table of Table 2 under the table header "Optimized σ". Note that for each problem two different support values are displayed corresponding to the supports that were used to mine the positive and negative class, respectively. Also, the last column shows the amount of time required by FSG to find the frequent subgraphs and provides a good indication of the computational complexity at the feature discovery phase of our classification algorithm. Comparing the ROC values obtained in these experiments with those obtained for $\sigma = 10\%$, we can see that as before, the lower support values tend to improve the results, with measurable improvements for problems in which the number of discovered sub-structures increased substantially. In the rest of our experimental evaluation we will be using the frequent subgraphs that were generated using these values of support.

Varying Misclassification Costs Since for each classification problem instance the number of positive examples is in general much smaller than the number of negative examples, we performed a set of experiments in which the misclassification cost associated with each positive example was increased to match the number of negative examples. We refer to this value of β as the *"EqCost"* value. The classification performance achieved by our algorithm using either topological or geometric subgraphs for $\beta = 1.0$ and $\beta = EqCost$ is shown in Table 3. Note that the $\beta = 1.0$ results are the same with those presented in the right subtable of Table 2. From the results in this table we can see that, in general, increasing the misclassification cost so that it balances the size of positive and negative class tends to improve the classification accuracy. When $\beta = EqCost$, the classification performance improves for four and five problems for the topological and geometric subgraphs, respectively. Moreover, in the cases in which the performance decreased, that decrease was quite small,

Dset.	σ=10.0%				σ=15.0%				σ=20.0%				Optimized σ					
	Topo.		Geom.		Topo.		Geom.		Topo.		Geom.		Topo.		Geom.		Per class	$Time_p$
	A	N_f	A	N_f	A	N_f	A	N_f	A	N_f	A	N_f	A	N_f	A	N_f	σ	(sec)
P1	66.0	1211	65.5	1317	66.0	513	64.1	478	64.4	254	60.2	268	65.5	24510	65.0	23612	3.0, 3.0	211
P2	65.0	967	64.0	1165	65.1	380	63.3	395	64.2	217	63.1	235	67.3	7875	69.9	12673	3.0, 3.0	72
P3	60.5	597	60.7	808	59.4	248	61.3	302	59.9	168	60.9	204	62.6	7504	64.8	10857	3.0, 3.0	66
P4	54.3	275	55.4	394	56.2	173	57.4	240	57.3	84	58.3	104	63.4	25790	63.7	31402	3.0, 3.0	231
H1	81.0	27034	82.1	29554	77.4	13531	79.2	8247	78.4	7479	79.5	7700	81.0	27034	82.1	29554	10.0, 10.0	137
H2	70.1	1797	76.0	3739	63.6	307	62.2	953	59.0	139	58.1	493	76.5	18542	79.1	29024	10.0, 5.0	1016
H3	83.9	27019	89.5	30525	83.6	13557	88.8	11240	84.6	7482	87.7	7494	83.9	27019	89.5	30525	10.0, 10.0	392
A1	78.2	576	79.0	492	78.2	484	77.6	332	77.1	312	76.1	193	81.7	3054	82.6	3186	5.0, 3.0	145

Table 2: Varying minimum support threshold (σ). "A" denotes the area under the ROC curve and "N_f" denotes the number of discovered frequent subgraphs.

whereas the improvements achieved for some problem instances (*e.g.*, P4, H1, and H2) was significant. In the rest of our experiments we will focus only on the results obtained by setting $\beta = EqCost$.

Dataset	Topo		Geom	
	$\beta = 1.0$	$\beta = EqCost$	$\beta = 1.0$	$\beta = EqCost$
P1	65.5	65.3	65.0	66.7
P2	67.3	66.8	69.9	69.2
P3	62.6	62.6	64.8	64.6
P4	63.4	65.2	63.7	66.1
H1	81.0	79.2	82.1	81.1
H2	76.5	79.4	79.1	81.9
H3	83.9	90.8	89.5	94.0
A1	81.7	82.1	82.6	83.0

Table 3: The area under the ROC curve obtained by varying the misclassification cost.

Feature Selection We evaluated the performance of the feature selection scheme based on sequential covering (described in Section 3.2) by performing a set of experiments in which we varied the parameter δ that controls the number of times an example must be covered by a feature, before it is removed from the set of yet to be covered examples. Table 4 displays the results of these experiments. The results under the column labeled "Original" shows the performance of the classifier without any feature selection. These results are identical to those shown in Table 3 for $\beta = EqCost$ and are included here to make comparisons easier.

Two key observations can be made by studying the results in this table. First, as expected, the feature selection scheme is able to substantially reduce the number of features. In some cases the number of features that was selected decreased by almost two orders of magnitude. Also, as δ increases, the number of retained features increases; however, this increase is gradual. Second, the overall classification performance achieved by the feature selection scheme when $\delta \geq 5$ is quite comparable to that achieved with no feature selection. The actual performance depends on the problem instance and whether or not we use topological or geometric subgraphs. In particular, for the first four problems (P1, P2, P3, and P4) derived from the PTC dataset, the performance actually improves with feature selection. Such improvements are possible even in the context of SVM-based classifiers as models learned on lower dimensional spaces will tend to have better generalization ability [5]. Also note that for some datasets the number

Property	Dim.	Property	Dim.
Solvent accessible area	$\mathring{A}^2$	Moment of Inertia	*none*
Total accessible area	$\mathring{A}^2$	Total energy	$kcal/mol$
Total accessible volume	$\mathring{A}^3$	Bend energy	$kcal/mol$
Total Van der Waal's area	$\mathring{A}^2$	Hbond energy	$kcal/mol$
Total Van der Waal's volume	$\mathring{A}^3$	Stretch energy	$kcal/mol$
Dipole moment	*Debye*	Nonbond energy	$kcal/mol$
Dipole moment comp. (X, Y, Z)	*Debye*	Estatic energy	$kcal/mol$
Heat of formation	*Debye*	Torsion energy	$kcal/mol$
Multiplicity	*Kcal*	Quantum total charge	eV

Table 5: QSAR Properties.

of features decreases as δ increases. This is because the features that were selected have higher average support.

Topological versus Geometric Subgraphs The various results shown in Tables 2–4 also provide an indication on the relative performance of topological versus geometric subgraphs. In almost all cases, the classifier that is based on geometric subgraphs outperforms that based on topological subgraphs. For some problems, the performance advantage is marginal whereas for other problems, geometric subgraphs lead to measurable improvements in the area under the ROC curve. For example, if we consider the results shown in Table 3 for $\beta = EqCost$, we can see the geometric subgraphs lead to improvements that are at least 3% or higher for P2, P3, and H3, and the average improvement over all eight problems is 2.6%. As discussed in Section 3.1, these performance gains are due to the fact that conserved geometric structure is a better indicator of a chemical compounds activity than just its topology.

Comparison with QSAR For our study, we have chosen a set of 18 QSAR properties (shown in Table 5) that are good descriptors of the chemical activity of a compound and most of them have been previously used for classification purposes [1]. We used two different algorithms to build classification models based on these QSAR properties. The first is the C4.5 decision tree algorithm [28] that has been shown to produce good models for chemical compound classification based on QSAR properties [1], and the second is the SVM algorithm that was used to build the classification models in our frequent sub-structure-based approach. Since the range of values of the different QSAR properties can be significantly different, we first scaled them to be in the range of [0, 1] prior to building the SVM model. We found that this scaling resulted in some improvements in the overall classification results. Note that

Dataset.	Topological Features										Geometric Features									
	Original		$\delta=1$		$\delta=5$		$\delta=10$		$\delta=15$		Original		$\delta=1$		$\delta=5$		$\delta=10$		$\delta=15$	
	A	N_f	A	N_f	A	N_f	A	N_f	A	N_f	A	N_f	A	N_f	A	N_f	A	N_f	A	N_f
P1	65.3	24510	65.4	143	66.4	85	66.5	598	66.7	811	66.7	23612	68.3	161	68.1	381	67.4	613	68.7	267
P2	66.8	7875	69.5	160	69.6	436	68.0	718	67.5	927	69.2	12673	72.2	169	73.9	398	73.1	646	73.0	265
P3	62.6	7504	68.0	171	65.2	455	64.2	730	64.5	948	64.6	10857	71.1	175	70.0	456	71.0	241	66.7	951
P4	65.2	25790	66.3	156	66.0	379	64.5	580	64.1	775	66.1	31402	68.8	164	69.7	220	67.4	609	66.2	819
H1	79.2	27034	78.4	108	79.2	345	79.1	571	79.5	796	81.1	29554	80.8	128	81.6	396	81.9	650	82.1	885
H2	79.4	18542	77.1	370	78.0	1197	78.5	1904	78.5	2460	81.9	29024	80.0	525	80.4	1523	80.6	2467	81.2	3249
H3	90.8	27019	88.4	111	89.6	377	90.0	638	90.5	869	94.0	30525	91.3	177	92.2	496	93.1	831	93.2	1119
A1	82.1	3054	80.6	620	81.4	1395	81.5	1798	81.8	2065	83.0	3186	81.0	631	82.0	1411	82.4	1827	82.7	2106

Table 4: Results obtained using feature selection based on sequential rule covering.

C4.5 is not affected by such scaling.

Dataset	SVM	C4.5		Freq. Sub. Prec.	
	A	Precision	Recall	Topo	Geom
P1	60.2	0.4366	0.1419	0.6972	0.6348
P2	59.3	0.3603	0.0938	0.8913	0.8923
P3	55.0	0.6627	0.1275	0.7420	0.7427
P4	45.4	0.2045	0.0547	0.6750	0.8800
H1	64.5	0.5759	0.1375	0.7347	0.7316
H2	47.3	0.6282	0.4071	0.7960	0.7711
H3	61.7	0.5677	0.2722	0.7827	0.7630
A1	49.4	0.5564	0.3816	0.7676	0.7798

Table 6: Performance of the QSAR-based Classifier.

Table 6 shows the results obtained by the QSAR-based methods for the different datasets. The values shown for SVM correspond to the area under the ROC curve and can be directly compared with the corresponding values obtained by our approaches (Tables 2–4). The values shown for C4.5 correspond to the precision and recall of the positive class for the different datasets. To make the comparisons between C4.5 and our approach easier, we also computed the precision of our classifier at the same value of recall as that achieved by C4.5. These results are shown under the columns labeled "*Freq. Sub. Prec.*" for both topological and geometric features and were obtained from the results shown in Table 3 for $\beta = EqCost$. Note that the QSAR results for both SVM and C4.5 were obtained using the same cost-sensitive learning approach. Comparing both the SVM-based ROC results and the precision/recall values of C4.5 we can see that our approach substantially outperforms the QSAR-based classifier. In particular, our topological subgraph based algorithm does 35% better compared to SVM-based QSAR and 72% better in terms of the C4.5 precision at the same recall values. Similar results hold for the geometric subgraph based algorithm.

Comparison with SUBDUE & SubdueCL Finally, we performed a series of experiments in which we used the SUBDUE system to find the sub-structures and then used them for classification. Specifically, we performed two sets of experiments. In the first set, we obtain a set of sub-structures using the heuristic sub-structure discovery approach of SUBDUE [12]. In the second set, we used the sub-structures discovered by the more recent SubdueCL algorithm [9] that guides the heuristic beam search using a scheme that measures how well a subgraph describes the positive examples in the dataset without describing the negative examples.

Dataset	Subdue.			SubdueCL.		
	A	N_f	$Time_p$	A	N_f	$Time_p$
P1	61.9	1288	303sec	63.5	2103	301sec
P2	64.2	1374	310sec	63.3	2745	339sec
P3	57.4	1291	310sec	59.6	1772	301sec
P4	58.5	1248	310sec	60.8	2678	324sec
H1	74.2	1450	1,608sec	73.8	960	1002sec
H2	58.5	901	232,006sec	65.2	2999	476,426sec
H3	71.3	905	178,343sec	77.5	2151	440,416sec
A1	75.3	983	56,056sec	75.9	1094	31,177sec

Table 7: Performance of the SUBDUE and SubdueCL-based approaches.

Even though there are a number of parameters controlling SUBDUE's heuristic search algorithm, the most critical among them are the width of the beam search, the maximum size of the discovered subgraph, and the total number of subgraphs to be discovered. In our experiments, we spent a considerable amount of time experimenting with these parameters to ensure that SUBDUE was able to find a reasonable number of sub-structures. Specifically, we changed the width of the beam search from 4 to 50 and set the other two parameters to high numeric values. Note that in the case of the SubdueCL, in order to ensure that the subgraphs were discovered that described all the positive examples, the subgraph discovery process was repeated by increasing the value of beam-width at each iteration and removing the positive examples that were covered by subgraphs.

Table 7 shows the performance achieved by SUBDUE and SubdueCL on the eight different classification problems along with the number of subgraphs that it generated and the amount of time that it required to find these subgraphs. These results were obtained by using the subgraphs discovered by either SUBDUE or SubdueCL as features in an SVM-based classification model. To make the comparisons as fair as possible we used $\beta = EqCost$ as the misclassification cost. We also performed another set of experiments in which we used the rule-based classifier produced by SubdueCL. The results of this scheme was inferior to those produced by the SVM-based approach and we are not reporting them here.

Comparing SUBDUE against SubdueCL we can see that the latter achieves better classification performance. Comparing the SUBDUE and SubdueCL-based results with those obtained by our approach (Tables 2–4) we can see that in almost all cases both our topological and geometric frequent subgraph-based algorithms lead to substantially better performance. This is true both in the cases in which we performed no feature selection as well as in the cases in which we used the sequential covering based feature selection scheme. In particular, comparing the SubdueCL results against the results shown in Table 4 without any feature selection we can see that on the average, our topological and geometric subgraph based algorithms do 9.3% and 12.2% better, respectively. Moreover, even after feature selection with $\delta = 15$ that result in a scheme that have comparable number of features as those used by SubdueCL, our algorithms are still better by 9.7% and 13.7%, respectively. Finally, if we compare the amount of time required by either SUBDUE or SubdueCL to that required by the FSG algorithm to find all frequent subgraphs (last column of Table 2) we can see that despite the fact that we are finding the complete set of frequent subgraphs our approach requires substantially less time.

5 Conclusions

In this paper we presented a highly-effective algorithm for classifying chemical compounds based on frequent substructure discovery that can scale to large datasets. Our experimental evaluation showed that our algorithm leads to substantially better results than those obtained by existing QSAR- and sub-structure-based methods. Moreover, besides this improved classification performance, the sub-structure-based nature of this scheme provides to the chemists valuable information as to which sub-structures are most critical for the classification problem at hand (e.g., by analyzing the decision hyperplane produced by the SVM classifier). A chemist can then use this information to understand the models and potentially use it to design better compounds.

References

[1] A. An and Y. Wang. Comparisons of classification methods for screening potential compounds. In *ICDM*, 2001.

[2] Michael R. Berthold Christian Borgelt. Mining molecular fragments: Finding relevant substructures of molecules. In *Proc. of the (ICDM)*, 2002.

[3] D. J. Cook and L. B. Holder. Graph-based data mining. *IEEE Intelligent Systems*, 15(2):32–41, 2000.

[4] Mukund Deshpande and George Karypis. Automated approaches for classifying structure. In *Proc. of the 2nd ACM SIGKDD Workshop on Data Mining in Bioinformatics*, 2002.

[5] Mukund Deshpande and George Karypis. Using conjunction of attribute values for classification. In *Proc. of the eleventh CIKM*, pages 356–364. ACM Press, 2002.

[6] Mukund Deshpande, Michihiro Kuramochi, and George Karypis. Frequent sub-structure-based approach for classifying chemical compounds. Technical Report TR# 03-016, Dept. of Computer Science, University of Minnesota, 2003. Available at http://www.cs.umn.edu~karypis.

[7] dtp.nci.nih.gov. Dtp aids antiviral screen dataset.

[8] J. Gasteiger, C. Rudolph, and J. Sadowski. Automatic generation of 3d-atomic coordinates for organic molecules. *Tetrahedron Comp. Method*, 3:537–547, 1990.

[9] J. Gonzalez, L. Holder, and D. Cook. Application of graph based concept learning to the predictive toxicology domain. In *PTC, Workshop at the 5th PKDD*, 2001.

[10] C. Hansch, P. P. Maolney, T. Fujita, and R. M. Muir. Correlation of biological activity of phenoxyacetic acids with hammett substituent constants and partition coefficients. *Nature*, 194:178–180, 1962.

[11] C. Hansch, R. M. Muir, T. Fujita, C. F. Maloney, and Streich M. The correlation of biological activity of plant growth-regulators and chloromycetin derivatives with hammett constants and partition coefficients. *Journal of American Chemical Society*, 85:2817–1824, 1963.

[12] L. Holder, D. Cook, and S. Djoko. Substructure discovery in the subdue system. In *Proc. of the AAAI Workshop on Knowledge Discovery in Databases*, pages 169–180, 1994.

[13] Akihiro Inokuchi, Takashi Washio, and Hiroshi Motoda. An apriori-based algorithm for mining frequent substructures from graph data. In *Proc. of The 4th European Conf. on Principles and Practice of Knowledge Discovery in Databases*, pages 13–23, Lyon, France, September 2000.

[14] T. Joachims. *Advances in Kernel Methods: Support Vector Learning*, chapter Making large-Scale SVM Learning Practical. MIT-Press, 1999.

[15] George Karypis. CLUTO a clustering toolkit. Technical Report 02-017, Dept. of Computer Science, University of Minnesota, 2002. Available at http://www.cs.umn.edu/~cluto.

[16] Ross D. King, Stephen H. Muggleton, Ashwin Srinivasan, and Michael J. E. Sternberg. Structre-activity relationships derived by machine learning: The use of atoms and their bond connectivities to predict mutagenecity byd inductive logic programming. *PNAS*, 93:438–442, January 1996.

[17] S. Kramer, L. De Raedt, and C. Helma. Molecular feature mining in hiv data. In *7th International Conference on Knowledge Discovery and Data Mining*, 2001.

[18] Michihiro Kuramochi and George Karypis. Frequent subgraph discovery. In *IEEE International Conference on Data Mining*, 2001.

[19] Michihiro Kuramochi and George Karypis. Discovering geometric frequent subgraph. In *IEEE International Conference on Data Mining*, 2002.

[20] Michihiro Kuramochi and George Karypis. An efficient algorithm for discovering frequent subgraphs. *IEEE Transactions on Knowledge and Data Engineering*, (in press), 2003.

[21] Andrew R. Leach. *Molecular Modeling, Principles and Applications*. Prentice Hall, 2001.

[22] Andrew R. Leach. *Molecular Modeling: Principles and Applications*. Prentice Hall, Englewood Cliffs, NJ, 2001.

[23] Wenmin Li, Jiawei Han, and Jian Pei. Cmar: Accurate and efficient classification based on multiple class-association rules. In *IEEE International Conference on Data Mining*, 2001.

[24] Bing Liu, Wynne Hsu, and Yiming Ma. Integrating classification and association rule mining. In *4th Internation Conference on Knowledge Discovery and Data Mining*, 1998.

[25] Tom M. Mitchell. *Machine Learning*. Mc Graw Hill, 1997.

[26] K. Morik, P. Brockhausen, and T. Joachims. Combining statistical learning with a knowledge-based approach - a case study in intensive care monitoring. In *International Conference on Machine Learning*, 1999.

[27] F. Provost and T. Fawcett. Robust classification for imprecise environments. *Machine Learning*, 42(3), 2001.

[28] J. Ross Quinlan. *C4.5: Programs for machine learning*. Morgan Kaufmann, San Mateo, CA, 1993.

[29] Graham W. Richards. Virtual screening using grid computing: the screensaver project. *Nature Reviews: Drug Discovery*, 1:551–554, July 2002.

[30] A. Srinivasan, R. D. King, S. H. Muggleton, and M. Sternberg. The predictive toxicology evaluation challenge. In *Proc. of the Fifteenth International Joint Conference on Artificial Intelligence (IJCAI-97)*, pages 1–6. Morgan-Kaufmann, 1997.

[31] Ashwin Sriniviasan and Ross King. Feature construction with inductive logic programming: a study of quantitative predictions of biological activity aided by structural attributes. *Knowledge Discovery and Data Mining Journal*, 3:37–57, 1999.

[32] V. Vapnik. *Statistical Learning Theory*. John Wiley, New York, 1998.

[33] Xifeng Yan and Jiawei Han. gSpan: Graph-based substructure pattern mining. In *ICDM*, 2002.

Optimized Disjunctive Association Rules via Sampling

J. Elble [*]
Department of Economics
University of Rochester
Rochester, NY
Email: jelble@troi.cc.rochester.edu

C. Heeren[†]
Department of Computer Science
University of Illinois at Urbana-Champaign
Urbana, IL
Email: heeren@cs.uiuc.edu

L. Pitt [‡]
Department of Computer Science
University of Illinois at Urbana-Champaign
Urbana, IL
Email: pitt@uiuc.edu

Abstract

The problem of finding optimized support association rules for a single numerical attribute, where the optimized region is a union of k disjoint intervals from the range of the attribute, is investigated. The first polynomial time algorithm for the problem of finding such a region maximizing support and meeting a minimum cumulative confidence threshold is given. Because the algorithm is not practical, an ostensibly easier, more constrained version of the problem is considered. Experiments demonstrate that the best extant algorithm for the constrained version has significant performance degradation on both a synthetic model of patterned data and on real world data sets. Running the algorithm on a small random sample is proposed as a means of obtaining near optimal results with high probability. Theoretical bounds on sufficient sample size to achieve a given performance level are proved, and rapid convergence on synthetic and real-world data is validated experimentally.

1. Optimized Association Rules

The search for meaningful patterns in large datasets is one of the main foci of data mining research. A well-investigated type of pattern is the *association rule* (introduced in [1]) a rule of the form $X_1 X_2 \ldots X_s \rightarrow C$, meaning, in essence, that "when $X_1, \ldots, X_s$ all hold about a datum, then C tends to hold also". Often, data is so-called "market-basket" data, and X_i and C are boolean variables indicating the presence of some item in a customer's order. Such a rule is useful when it has sufficient *support* and *confidence*. The support of a rule is the number or percentage of records for which the antecedent $X_1 \ldots X_s$ holds. The confidence is a measure of the implication's validity – the percentage of time the consequent C holds given that the antecdent holds. The literature is rich with work on how to effectively find such rules and variants (survey in [5]).

The idea of *optimized* association rules was introduced by Fukuda et al. [4]. Consider a single large relation. The motivation is that in many settings, a user is interested in a specific attribute c of the data as a consequent in an association rule (e.g., c corresponds to "good credit risk"), as well as a collection of antecedent attributes X_i whose values are likely to be predictive of c. The goal is to find one or more instantiations of the attributes X_i that will result in rules satisfying constraints on support and confidence. For example, in a credit-history database, $X_1 \in \{$single, married, divorced$\}$ might represent marital status, X_2 and X_3 might be numeric attributes representing income and age, respectively, and $c \in \{0, 1\}$ might represent creditworthiness based on past history or by expert judgement. A discovered rule in the existing database such as $X_1 = $ married $\wedge X_2 > \$50K \wedge X_3 \in [30, 60] \rightarrow c = 1$ might be useful in making decisions about new cases.

Let D be a large relation. For any $S \subseteq D$, define

- The *support* of S, $\sup(S)$, is just $|S|$.
- The set $S^+ = \{s \in S : s.c = 1\}$.
- The *confidence* of S, $\mathrm{conf}(S)$, is $\sup(S^+)/\sup(S)$.
- If $S_1, \ldots, S_k$ are subsets of D, then the *cumulative support* and *cumulative confidence* of the sets are, respectively, the support and confidence of the union $\cup_{i=1}^k S_i$.

---

[*] Some of the work was performed at the National Center for Supercomputing Applications, supported in part by NSF grant ACI 96-19019.

[†] Supported in part by NSF grant IIS-9907483.

[‡] Supported in part by NSF grant IIS-9907483.

Results vary based on the form of the set S. Fukuda et al [4] first defined the problem, and considered the case that S is specified by a single numeric attribute, and later generalized the problem to that of two numeric attributes [4, 3]. Efficient algorithms were given for maximizing the cumulative support given a minimum confidence threshold, for the dual problem of maximizing the cumulative confidence given a minimum support threshold, and for maximizing the "gain" of a rule. Rastogi & Shim generalized the problem to allow unions of categorical attributes [7] and of one or two quantitative attributes [6]. Zelenko gave a polynomial time algorithm for unions of categorical attributes [12]. Wijsen and Meersman offer an investigation into the complexity of variants of the problem [10].

To better understand our results and their relationship to past work, we need just a couple more definitions. Let D be a data set of cardinality n, with each datum d containing a single real-valued attribute $d.r$ and a boolean "consequent" attribute $d.c$. Without loss of generality, assume that each value $d.r \in \{1, 2, \ldots, n\}$, reflecting the possibility of at most n distinct values. An interval I is just a pair (a, b) with $a \leq b$, and represents the set $D(a, b) = \{d \in D : a \leq d.r \leq b\}$.

Given a data set D as described above, a value minconf $\in [0, 1]$, and a positive integer k, the *max-support-min-cumulative-confidence* problem is to find a collection $\mathcal{I} = I_1, I_2, \ldots, I_k$ of k intervals with cumulative confidence conf$(\mathcal{I})$ is at least minconf, and so that the cumulative support sup$(\mathcal{I})$ is maximized. Alternatively, the *max-support-min-independent-confidence* problem is to find a collection $\mathcal{I}$ of k intervals so that each interval of $\mathcal{I}$ has confidence at least minconf and so that the cumulative support sup$(\mathcal{I})$ is maximized.

Our contributions are as follows:

- We provide the first polynomial time algorithm for the max-support-min-cumulative-confidence problem for a single numeric attribute.

- For the max-support-min-independent-confidence problem, we analyze the performance of an algorithm of Rastogi & Shim which was shown to scale well on random unpatterned data. We test the algorithm on several real-world data sets, and find that the algorithm does not scale as well, but rather behaves as it does on a proposed synthetic model of random *patterned* data.

- We propose sampling as a preprocessing phase for any algorithm addressing either the independent or the cumulative confidence problem, and derive theoretical bounds on the sample size sufficient to achieve near-optimal performance. Because the bounds are independent of the size of the original data set, dramatic speedups are possible.

- Experimental results demonstrate the utility of the sampling approach; a sample of size less than 500 was sufficient in all cases to obtain a solution within 5% of optimal on both real world and on synthetic data models.

2. Maximum support meeting minimum cumulative confidence

In [7] a reduction from the NP-hard (Weighted) Set Cover problem to the max-support-min-cumulative-confidence problem is given, showing that this latter problem is NP-hard. The reduction translates weights from the set cover problem directly into support and confidence values for the max-support problem, rather than creating a data set D that realizes these values. Because the NP-hardness relies on very large values of support and confidence that cannot be realized by a polynomially-sized database, it does not neccessarily apply to the problem in which a database is given as part of the input. But it is exactly this latter problem that is of interest to us; it is only natural to allow an algorithm for mining a database to at least scan the data, spending time polynomial in $n = |D|$ and k. The NP-hardness result of [7] does not preclude the existence of an algorithm that takes time poly(n, k). We give just such an algorithhm, admittedly impractical due to the degree of the polynomial.

Note that a trivial exhaustive algorithm solves the problem in time $O(n^{2k})$: The support and confidence for the $O\left(\binom{n}{2k}\right) = O(n^{2k})$ k-tuples can be computed and the optimal solution selected. However, we would like an algorithm that runs in time polynomial in k, not exponential. We describe a $O(n^5 k)$ algorithm, leaving its improvement as an open challenge.

We use dynamic programming in a manner similar to that of [6], taking advantage of a bound on confidence c as was done in [12]. For every interval $[i, j]$ on n data points, and every number of disjunctions l, the maximum support l-interval on $[i, j]$ exceeding minimum confidence has confidence tally c, where c is in the range $[1..n]$. For every possible confidence level c and for every interval $[i, j]$, and for every disjunct size l, store the largest support region exceeding minconf (θ), together with its support. Call that value $S([i, j], l, c)$. To solve the problem, we want $S([1, b], k, n\theta)$.

Consider $S([i, j], 1, c)$. From Fukuda et al. [4], these n^3 values can each be computed in $O(n)$ time. For the general case, subsequent values of l can be computed in terms of previous values, for each interval and confidence level. Specifically, notice that every solution for l intervals on $[i, j]$ of confidence c can be partitioned into a disjoint union of an optimal solution for 1 interval on $[i, m]$ with confidence c', and an optimal solution for $l-1$ intervals on $[m+1, j]$ with confidence $c-c'$, for some choice of m and c'. The task, then is to find the best choice of $m, c' \in [1 \ldots n]$. We know of no other way to do this than searching through all their possible values. Thus S([i,j],l,c) is the set of maximum support among the n^2 unions of the form

$$\{S([i, m], 1, c') \cup S([m + 1, j], l - 1, c - c')\},$$

where $1 \leq m, c' \leq n$.

The total running time of the algorithm is $O(n^5k)$, which corresponds to $O(n^2)$ update time for n^3k tabulated values.

3. Maximum support meeting minimum independent confidence

3.1. The RS Algorithm

Rastogi and Shim [6] attack a more tractable version of the problem, in which a disjoint union is found consisting entirely of intervals *each* meeting the minimum confidence constraint. Because of the additional constraint, they are able to obtain a relatively fast algorithm (denoted "RS"), whose performance will be of interest in our discussion of the efficacy of sampling.

The RS algorithm, like Fukuda et al's [4, 3] assumes initially that the data has been pre-bucketed, so that the input consists of n buckets $b_1, \ldots, b_n$, where each bucket corresponds to a particular discretized value of the quantitative attribute's range. The problem is to find k intervals each of which contains some contiguous collection of buckets. Each bucket may be thought of as an indivisible unit, corresponding to a weighted point with weight equal to the support of the bucket, and with "confidence" value c a real number in the *interval* $[0, 1]$, as opposed to the *set* $\{0, 1\}$. They assume also that the buckets have been sorted in order of increasing value of the attribute. The RS algorithm has three phases

1. Preprocess the data by merging all adjacent buckets that have confidence at least minconf. There is never any reason to include one of these without its sufficiently high confidence neighbors - they will all be in the same interval.

2. Find in linear time, all "partition points". A partition point is one that is not contained in any interval of confidence at least minconf. Note that no interval in the solution to the problem can contain any of these partition points.

3. Solve the k-interval problem separately on the subproblems between the partition points and merge the solutions to obtain a global choice of the k best intervals.

Suppose that the n original buckets are divided into m subgroups of $n_1, n_2, \ldots, n_m$ buckets separated by $m - 1$ or more partition points, with $\sum_i n_i = b$. Then if $b_{\max} = \max\{n_i\}$ is the number of buckets in the largest subproblem, algorithm RS takes time $O(b_{\max}^2 mk + mk^2)$. The first term is for solving the m subproblems, and the second term is the cost of combining the m local solutions into one global solution.

If there are many partition points, the data can splinter into a linear number of constant-sized sets. In this case, the run time will be dominated by the second term mk^2, and will grow only linearly with the size of the data set, as shown in [6]. On the other hand, if

there are few partition points, the data will not lend itself to the divide-and-conquer approach, since $b_{\max}$ will be large ($O(n)$). In this case the run time will be dominated by the first term, and will increase quadratically with the size of the data set.

The question is: "Where between these two extremes will the algorithm's performance fall *in practice*?"

In order to empirically test the utility of the preprocessing and divide and conquer approach, in [6] the algorithm was run on synthetic data. Binned data was created as follows: For each b_i, $1 \leq i \leq n$, a support value s_i and confidence value c_i were chosen to represent s_i data points, $c_i \cdot s_i$ of which corresponded to data points x satisfying the consequent requirement $x.c = 1$.

The values s_i were chosen uniformly in $[0, \frac{2}{n}]$, and then normalized so that the sum of all s_i was 1. The confidence values c_i were chosen uniformly in $[0, 1]$. As a consequence, there is no correlation between the confidence values in bucket b_i and b_{i+1}. The net result of using random data was that the partitioning algorithm performed very well, because, as noted by the authors, long stretches of high confidence were unlikely. The algorithm was able to handle problems with up to 100,000 initial buckets in less than 15 seconds. Even with this much data, $b_{\max}$ was no more than 20. In other words, linear growth was observed.

It can be shown that if minconf $> .5$, with probability approaching 1 exponentially quickly, the random data fragments into constant-sized chunks separated by partition points, explaining the dramatic improvement offered by the partitioning algorithm. On the other hand, if minconf $< .5 - \epsilon$, then with probability approaching 1 exponentially fast, the single interval encompassing all of the random data is an optimal solution, and, a constant time algorithm suffices (choose the entire data set!). It is only when minconf is close to $.5$ (the mean confidence) that the algorithm's performance degrades, as observed empirically in [6].

3.2. Our Data Models Described

While the RS algorithm was shown to provide dramatic speedups, this was only for a data model corresponding to uniform random data. It is reasonable to assert that real world data sets of interest would be less random than the artificial data generated in [6]. It is precisely the randomness of their data model that creates the fortuitous partitioning whose result is speedy run times.

The true utility of any method can only be demonstrated empirically by performance analysis on many different instances of real-world data. On the other hand, the availability of parameterized data models may be used to advantage to gain insight into how an algorithm's performance depends on various data characteristics. Toward this end, to better understand how the RS algorithm performs, we develop a model of random patterned data, and carefully examine the role played by various parameters controlling the data dis-

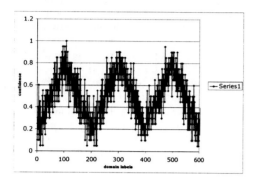

Figure 1. Example of patterned data

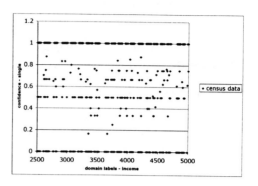

Figure 2. Census data

tribution and the effect on the run time of the algorithm. We also consider the behavior of the algorithm on real world data selected from a census database (prediction of marital status from income), and from forestry data (prediction of ground cover type from elevation). For the patterned synthetic data and for the real world data sets we find that the dramatic improvement observed on unpatterned random data is not typical, and that the behavior of the RS algorithm on the real world data more closely matches our patterned data model, for which quadratic runtime dominates. We conclude that such adverse data is not rare.[1]

Random patterned data

Our synthetic data was generated according to the following method. Each bucket received support as in [6]. We assumed, however, that confidence would be a function of the numeric attribute value (i.e., the bucket number), so that low confidence buckets would tend to cluster, as would high confidence buckets.

We generated a simple triangular wave-form with varying numbers of peaks and valleys. A typical peak had confidence values rising from .2 to .8, and then falling back to .2. Call this multipeak piecewise linear function function f. We randomly generated the confidence for bucket i to be a binomially distributed ratio with mean $f(i)$, and $N = 20$ trials. Figure 1 shows a typical example data set generated in this manner.

We do not mean to suggest that this synthetic model is "the right" one - indeed, we do not believe such a thing exists. The point is to consider how the algorithm performs when parameters such as the size and frequency of peaks change, empirically validating the

tradeoff suggested between the two terms in the complexity bounds for the divide and conquer algorithm.

We generated data with $n = 2000$, 4000, 8000, and 16000 buckets (distinct domain values for the quantitative attribute). This was done in two ways. For "fixed peaks" data, the number of peaks for these datasets were, respectively, $n/50$, $n/100$, $n/200$, and $n/400$, thus keeping the number of peaks constant at 40, and hence the peak width increasing from 50 to 400. For "fixed peak width" data, the number of peaks was set at $n/200$ for each data set, so that the peak width was fixed at 200, and the number of peaks varied from 10 to 80. Because each valley was likely to contain at least one partition point, and the neighborhood around each peak was unlikely to do so, this effectively allowed control of the parameters b_{max} (here, the peak width) and m (here, the number of peaks) in the RS algorithm.

Real-world data

In addition to the patterned synthetic data, we extracted a real world data set from the 1999 census data for the Los Angeles/Long Beach area. The total-family-income and marital-status attributes were projected from a database of 88443 households with positive income levels. The marital-status attribute was summarized by a boolean attribute whose values were 0 for a married head of household, and 1 otherwise. Finally, the data was bucketed according to the total-family-income, so that one record existed for every value in the income domain. A record consisted of an income level together with a tally of the number of households with that income, and a tally of the number of unmarried heads of household. The largest final data set consisted of 11990 records. This same procedure was followed on smaller census data sets to achieve smaller domains for our tests. Figure 2 shows a small portion of the census data set.

As a simple test point for scientific data in this con-

---

1   No special effort was made to find these data sets - they were selected due to their availability, their size, and the presence of a quantitative attribute with many possible values that was likely to be predictive of an associated categorical attribute.

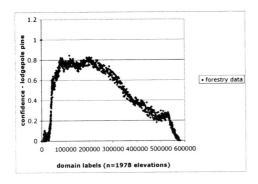

Figure 3. Forestry data

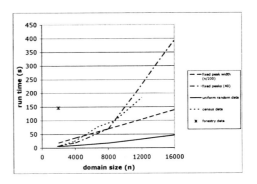

Figure 4. Size vs. run time (minconf = 0.65, k=5)

text, we tested the RS algorithm on the forestry data available from the UCI KDD archive at http://kdd.ics.uci.edu/. We used a similar procedure to that of the census data to extract the elevation and forest cover type for 581,012 soil samples. The elevation and cover type attributes were projected from the set of observations. The cover type attribute was condensed into a single boolean attribute whose value was 1 if the forest cover was "lodgepole pine", and 0 otherwise. Finally, the data was bucketed according to unique elevations. Each record in the final data set consisted of an elevation followed by a tally of the number of observations that were taken at that elevation and another tally of the number of samples at that elevation classified as cover type "lodgepole pine". The final data set had only 1978 elements (elevations). Figure 3 shows the entire forestry data set.

3.3. Results of RS algorithm on patterned and census data

We ran[2] the RS algorithm on each patterned data set for $k = 5$ intervals. We fix the value of k, since we are most interested in characteristics of the data, and how those characteristics affect running time. For each setting of the parameters, each experiment was run 30 times, and the average run times were recorded. As expected, because there were stretches of correlated confidence, within each peak there were sequences of buck-

---

2   The experiments presented in this paper were implemented in Perl and performed on an iBook laptop. The goal of our investigation was not to determine the maximum problem sizes that can be handled by the algorithm based on the limits of current technology, but rather to see how well the algorithm scales with various parameters. Our results are off by a fixed constant factor when compared to implementations with faster hardware and software. (Our run times are consistently 50 times slower than that of the implementation used by Rastogi & Shim.)

ets that neither merged together in the initial preprocessing phase, nor resulted in a partition point.

Figure 4 gives the running time for finding 5 intervals, as a function of the domain size. We expect the most salient parameter to be the peak width ($b_{\max}$). As discussed earlier, this value is a small constant for the uniform random data, so run time scales linearly with a small slope as the amount of data increases. For the fixed peak-width data ($n/200$), we also have a linear increase in running time, but with a larger coefficient as $b_{\max}$ is likely to be near 200. However, when the number of peaks is fixed, the number of buckets b_{max} within each peak grows with the amount of data, and the algorithm exhibits its characteristic quadratic increase in running time.

Also shown are the running times for the census datasets. Our admittedly subjective evaluation is that this data behaves more like fixed-peak data, hence exhibits quadratic running time. Also striking is the amount of time required for finding the best 5 intervals on the fewer than 2000 records of the forestry data set. Referring back to Figure 3 we see that the data has a single peak, and it appears that not much can be gained by partitioning the peak into five intervals so as to exclude some small amount of "unconfident" data. We suspect that the algorithm spends a lot of time fighting the law of diminishing returns. This view is supported by our sampling results in the next section, where most of the gain in support can be obtained by looking at relatively few records.

Another view is given in Figure 5, where for a fixed data size, runtime is plotted against the number of peaks in the synthetic data set. (The census and uniform random lines are plotted for comparison, and do not vary.) As the number of peaks increases for a fixed data size, the number of domain values within a peak decreases ($b_{\max}$), and the running time decreases quadratically, consistent with the complexity bounds

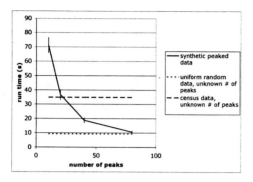

Figure 5. Shape vs. run time (n=4000, minconf=0.65, k=5)

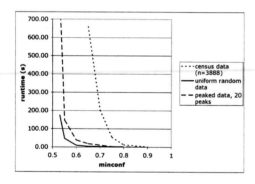

Figure 6. Minconf vs. run time (n=4000, k=3)

of the RS algorithm.

Finally, Figure 6 shows the effects of varying the demanded minimum confidence, while holding the other parameters fixed. Rastogi & Shim noted that as minconf approached the mean confidence (.5) for their uniform random data, the runtime increased dramatically. This phenomenon holds as well for our synthetic patterned data, as well as for the census data (which had mean .63, explaining why the curve is shifted). It seems reasonable that for any data set there would be many possible feasible intervals with confidence close to that of the mean, so setting minconf near the mean is inviting an algorithm to consider perhaps far more possibilities than is practical, with perhaps only nominal gain in support.

4. Sampling

We consider sampling as an alternative means for efficiently handling data with large domains and for which the divide and conquer algorithm offers no significant speed up.

While a worst-case quadratic (or any polynomial) time algorithm is theoretically acceptable, in data mining applications it is often impractical to implement an algorithm which requires more than a fixed number (one, say) of scans of the data. Absent a linear time exact algorithm, we turn to sampling to reduce the problem size, and, when we run the RS algorithm on a sample-driven coarsening of the data, thereby reduce the computation time.

Our data summarization technique is similar to that employed by Fukuda, et al. [4]. Let D denote the original data, $|D| = n$, and let B denote a coarsening of D. Create B as follows:

- Select a random sample of buckets, S, from D according to support ($|S| = s$). This can be done in linear time using the reservoir sampling of [9].

- If sample is unsorted, sort according to the numerical attribute of interest in time $O(s \log s)$.

- Partition the original data into a new set of buckets B, whose bucket boundaries are those in S. Thus, B consists of the buckets in S, together with a new bucket for every interval between sampled buckets, $|B| \leq 2s+1$. This requires time $O(n \log s)$ if the data is unsorted, $O(n)$ otherwise.

The burning question is, how many examples do we need to assure that the support of an optimal solution on our sample is likely to deviate only slightly from the support of an optimal solution on the whole data set?

We choose a dense enough sample so that, with high probability, any interval containing more than some small, user specified, amount of data is likely to be sampled, and thus, when the actual data is compiled into the new buckets, no interval's support deviates from its original support by more than this small amount. Then, this new set of bucketed data is used as input to algorithm RS. The choice of parameters gives the user a tradeoff between the error that she is willing to tolerate, and the amount of time required by the RS algorithm on the sample.

Definition 1 *An ϵ-significant interval, I, is an interval with $\sup(I) > \epsilon$.*

We choose a sample of sufficient size from D to assure, with high probability, that a bucket is sampled for every ϵ-significant interval in D. In so doing, we assure (whp) that the buckets representing the accumulation of data between sampled buckets have weight no more than ϵ. Call the resulting coarsened data B an ϵ-coarsening of D.

Lemma 2 *Given an independent uniform sample S of size s from a relation R containing n rows, if*

$$s \geq \max(\frac{4}{\epsilon} \log \frac{2}{\delta}, \frac{16}{\epsilon} \log \frac{13}{\epsilon})$$

then $Pr(\exists$ an ϵ-significant interval I with $I \bigcap S = \emptyset) < \delta$.

Proof: Follows from the fact that the VC-dimension of the class of intervals is 2, and the sufficient sample size bounds given by Blumer et al. [2]. □

Consider any interval I on the original data D and notice that the support of I can be estimated on the bucketed data B by selecting the largest interval I', $I' \subseteq I$, so that the endpoints of interval I' fall on bucket boundaries. Then, $\sup(I) - \sup(I') < 2\epsilon$, since the ϵ error can occur at each of the 2 endpoints. Now, let $I = \bigcup I_k$ be a k-interval, and let $I' = \bigcup I'_k$, where $I'_k \subseteq I_k$, are the intervals of largest support whose endpoints fall on sampled bucket boundaries, as in the single interval case. Then, because there are k intervals, $\sup(I) - \sup(I') < 2k\epsilon$. Thus we have:

Lemma 3 *Given a data set D, and B, an $\frac{\epsilon}{2k}$- coarsening of D, for any k-interval I on D, and I' on B with $I' = \arg\max_{i \subseteq I} \sup(i)$, $\sup(I) - \sup(I') < \epsilon$.*

We have assured that, with probability more than $(1 - \delta)$, the support of any k-interval can be computed on our coarsened data set with error no more than ϵ. That is, for association rule $F : A \in I \to C$, $\sup(A \in I)$ can be approximated by some interval I' on the set of buckets B so that $\sup(A \in I) - \sup(A \in I') < \epsilon$. Notice that the argument holds for the condition $A \in I \wedge C$ as well. That is, there exists an interval $I' \in B$ such that $\sup(A \in I \wedge C) - \sup(A \in I' \wedge C) < 2\epsilon$. This observation aids in analyzing the error in estimating confidence.

Finally, we are in a position to bound the error incurred by running the RS algorithm on our coarsened data set B. The optimal solution to the problem is a measure of support. There are two types of error in support we can incur. First, we may overlook small intervals. We have bounded the magnitude of this type of error by ϵ. Second, algorithm RS searches among intervals exceeding the minimum confidence threshold for the optimal solution. Danger lies in the case we fail to consider some sufficiently confident interval because we underestimate the confidence of that interval on the bucketed data. If an interval is actually confident, and we cannot detect it, we are at risk of tossing out large chunks of support. Instead of quantifying this neglected support, we create a new, slightly lower confidence bound that these deficient intervals will almost certainly meet, and so they will be considered by the algorithm for inclusion in the optimal solution to the problem. In the next lemma we show that any confident interval on the data set D can be approximated by an interval of slightly lower confidence on the coarsened data set B. Hence, the theoretical results show

that for a suitably smaller confidence threshold (which necessarily depends on the optimal support), with high probability only the first kind of error (where small intervals are overlooked) can occur.

Lemma 4 *For any k-interval I on D, let k-interval $I' \subseteq I$ be the largest subinterval of I on B. Suppose the minimum confidence threshold is θ, and that $\sup(I) - \sup(I') < \epsilon$. Then, with probability greater than $1 - \delta$,*

$$\operatorname{conf}(I) \geq \theta \to \operatorname{conf}(I') \geq \theta - \frac{\epsilon(1 - \theta)}{\sup(I')}.$$

The proof, which is largely algebraic, is available from the authors. Here's an intuitive explanation: The fact that the original region meets minimum confidence is an indication that the average confidence over the region is no less than the threshold. Since the sampled portion of the region is deficient, the unsampled region must have excess confidence. How deficient can the confidence of the sample be? At most, the unsampled region has $(1-\theta)\epsilon$ excess, where the $(1-\theta)$ arises because we are measuring excess above θ. This excess, in terms of average confidence for the sample, must be normalized by the support of the sample. In effect, we are redistributing the excess across a region of size $\sup(I')$.

The previous lemmas combine to give the following bounds demonstrating that small error (ϵ) in total support can be achieved on a sample if a suitably smaller value of confidence (depending on the support) is chosen. Our empirical results demonstrate, however, that this reduction in the minconf θ is not necessary in practice.

Theorem 5 *Let $RS(D, \theta)$ denote the maximum support k-interval exceeding confidence θ on data set D. Let $B = \{b_1, b_2, \ldots, b_m\}$ be an $\frac{\epsilon}{2k}$-coarsening of D. Then*

$$\sup(RS(D, \theta)) - \sup(RS(B, \theta - \frac{\epsilon(1 - \theta)}{\sup(RS(D, \theta))})) < \epsilon.$$

These analytic results imply a reasonable practical approach to sampling, with the only complication arising from the fact that the error in confidence depends on the support of the interval of interest. The sampling bounds are independent of the size of the domain, and thus, tradeoffs are simply between sample size and accuracy. In the next section we demonstrate that convergence to optimal solutions occur surprisingly quickly across different data sets.

The bounds we obtained are significantly different than those given by Toivonen [8], and Zaki et al. [11], for example. In both of these papers, a goal is to estimate the support of an itemset so as to determine with high probability whether or not it qualifies as "frequent" by meeting a minimum support threshold. In this context, dependence on the error parameter ϵ is quadratic (that is, there is a factor of $\frac{1}{\epsilon^2}$), whereas our bound improves this by relying only linearly on $\frac{1}{\epsilon}$. The key difference is that we are using sampling not to obtain uniformly good estimates of the support of intervals, but rather to select admissible endpoints of intervals. The *actual* support of these intervals are computed exactly by a linear scan of the original data. So, the error induced by sampling is not from inaccurate estimation of support, but rather solely from the necessity of representing an arbitrary interval using only "admissible" intervals (with endpoints in the sample).

RS Algorithm run on sampled data

Our sampling experiments were conducted as follows: for a data set D, and for sample size s and for 30 repetitions, a sample of s buckets was randomly selected from D and the optimized support set was found on the sample. The maximum support discovered among the 30 runs is compared to optimal.

We performed the following experiments using our synthetic and real world data models:

- fixed peak width ($n/200$), varied data size $n \in \{2000, 4000, 8000, 16000\}$;
- fixed data size ($n = 4000$), varied number of peaks $p \in \{n/400, n/200, n/100, n/50\}$;
- fixed number of peaks ($p = 40$), varied data size $n \in \{2000, 4000, 8000, 16000\}$.
- Census: varied $n \in \{1836, 3888, 6661, 11990\}$;
- Forestry: fixed $n = 1978$.

All of our experiments demonstrate that convergence to the optimal support is quite rapid for all data sizes and independent of the variability in our synthetic data. The results are remarkably consistent, with more than 95% convergence occurring for all sample sizes larger than 500. The same results are observed for the census data, as well as for the forest cover data. We show here a typical convergence graph from our experiments.

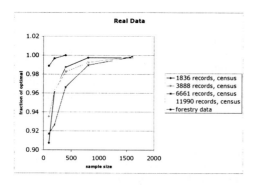

These experimental results are consistent with the theoretical results derived in the previous section. Indeed, the theory promises that convergence to optimal for a

particular level of minconf, θ, will occur, given a relaxation in θ. Our experiments indicate that such a relaxation is unnecessary.

When viewed together, the theoretical and experimental results demonstrated here offer sampling as a reasonable approach to data reduction in the case of optimized support association rule finding. The theoretical results suggest the appropriate tradeoffs between accuracy and sample size to be considered by the practitioner.

References

[1] R. Agrawal, T. Imielinski, and A. N. Swami. Mining association rules between sets of items in large databases. In P. Buneman and S. Jajodia, editors, *Proceedings of the 1993 ACM SIGMOD International Conference on Management of Data*, pages 207–216, Washington, D.C., 26–28 1993.

[2] A. Blumer, A. Ehrenfeucht, D. Haussler, and M. K. Warmuth. Learnability and the Vapnik-Chervonenkis dimension. *Journal of the ACM (JACM)*, 36(4):929–965, October 1989.

[3] T. Fukuda, Y. Morimoto, S. Morishita, and T. Tokuyama. Data mining using two-dimensional optimized association rules: scheme, algorithms, and visualization. In *Proceedings of the 1996 ACM SIGMOD international conference on Management of data*, pages 13–23. ACM Press, 1996.

[4] T. Fukuda, Y. Morimoto, S. Morishita, and T. Tokuyama. Mining optimized association rules for numeric attributes. In *Proceedings of the fifteenth ACM SIGACT-SIGMOD-SIGART symposium on Principles of database systems*, pages 182–191. ACM Press, 1996.

[5] J. Hipp, U. Güntzer, and G. Nakhaeizadeh. Algorithms for association rule mining – a general survey and comparison. *SIGKDD Explorations*, 2(1):58–64, July 2000.

[6] R. Rastogi and K. Shim. Mining optimized support rules for numeric attributes. *Information Systems*, 26(6):425–444, 2001.

[7] R. Rastogi and K. Shim. Mining optimized association rules with categorical and numeric attributes. *Knowledge and Data Engineering*, 14(1):29–50, 2002.

[8] H. Toivonen. Sampling large databases for association rules. In T. M. Vijayaraman, A. P. Buchmann, C. Mohan, and N. L. Sarda, editors, *In Proc. 1996 Int. Conf. Very Large Data Bases*, pages 134–145. Morgan Kaufman, 09 1996.

[9] J. S. Vitter. Random sampling with a reservoir. *ACM Transactions on Mathematical Software*, 11(1):37–57, Mar. 1985.

[10] J. Wijsen and R. Meersman. On the complexity of mining quantitative association rules. *Data Mining and Knowledge Discovery*, 2(3):263–281, 1998.

[11] M. J. Zaki, S. Parthasarathy, W. Li, and M. Ogihara. Evaluation of sampling for data mining of association rules. In *7th International Workshop on Research Issues in Data Engineering (RIDE'97)*, Birmingham, UK, Apr. 1997.

[12] D. Zelenko. Optimizing disjunctive association rules. In *Proe. of PKDD '99, Lecture Notes in Computer Science (LNAI 1704)*, pages 204–213. Springer-Verlag, 1999.

Is random model better? On its accuracy and efficiency

Wei Fan, Haixun Wang, Philip S. Yu, and Sheng Ma

IBM T.J.Watson Research

Hawthorne, New York 10532

{weifan,haixun,psyu,shengma}@us.ibm.com

Abstract

Inductive learning searches an optimal hypothesis that minimizes a given loss function. It is usually assumed that the simplest hypothesis that fits the data is the best approximate to an optimal hypothesis. Since finding the simplest hypothesis is NP-hard for most representations, we generally employ various heuristics to search its closest match. Computing these heuristics incurs significant cost, making learning inefficient and unscalable for large dataset. In the same time, it is still questionable if the simplest hypothesis is indeed the closest approximate to the optimal model. Recent success of combining multiple models, such as bagging, boosting and meta-learning, has greatly improved the accuracy of the simplest hypothesis, providing a strong argument against the optimality of the simplest hypothesis. However, computing these combined hypotheses incurs significantly higher cost. In this paper, we first advert that as long as the error of a hypothesis on each example is within a range dictated by a given loss function, it can still be optimal. Contrary to common beliefs, we propose a completely random decision tree algorithm that achieves much higher accuracy than the single best hypothesis and is comparable to boosted or bagged multiple best hypotheses. The advantage of multiple random tree is its training efficiency as well as minimal memory requirement.

1. Introduction

Inductive learning has wide applications in many different fields. Extensive research has been conducted in the past 2 decades to improve the accuracy of the model. We have found that most of the previously proposed inductive learning approaches, computing either the simplest model that fits the data or combining multiple hypotheses, may be way too complicated and too costly beyond necessity if minimizing a given loss function is the only purpose.

Optimal Model For a target function $t = F(\mathbf{x})$, given a training set of size n, $\{(\mathbf{x}_1, t_1), \ldots, (\mathbf{x}_n, t_n))\}$, an induc-

tive learner produces a model $y = f(\mathbf{x})$ to approximate the true function $F(\mathbf{x})$. Usually, there exists $\mathbf{x}$ such that $y \neq t$. In order to compare performance, we introduce a loss function. Given a loss function $L(t, y)$ where t is the true label and y is the predicted label, an optimal model is one that minimizes the average loss $L(t, y)$ for all examples, weighted by their probability. Typical examples of loss functions in data mining are 0-1 loss and cost-sensitive loss. For many problems, t is nondeterministic, i.e., if $\mathbf{x}$ is sampled repeatedly, different values of t may be given. The optimal decision y_* for $\mathbf{x}$ is the label that minimizes the expected loss $E_t(L(t, y_*))$ for a given example $\mathbf{x}$ when $\mathbf{x}$ is sampled repeatedly and different t's may be given. For 0-1 loss function, the optimal prediction is the most likely label or the label that appears the most often when $\mathbf{x}$ is sampled repeatedly. For cost-sensitive loss, the optimal prediction is the one that minimizes the empirical risk. In order to make the optimal decision, it is generally agreed that *a posterior* probability $P_t(y|\mathbf{x})$ for example $\mathbf{x}$ to be of class y is needed.

Simple Best Hypothesis There has been significant amount of work in machine learning and data mining to compute "an" (as distinguished from "the") optimal model. One major interest is on simple hypothesis. According to Occam's razor, we prefer the simplest hypothesis that fits the data (or " single best hypothesis"). For example, in decision tree construction [12, 4], a decision tree with fewer number of nodes that fits the data is usually preferred. For a chosen model representation and a formal definition of "simplicity," it is usually NP-hard to find the simplest hypothesis that fits the data. Most of the practical techniques is to use "greedy" to approximate the simplest model with various heuristics. For decision tree, typical heuristics include information gain [12], gini index [10], Kearns-Mansour criterion [9] among others. After the model is completely constructed, it is then further simplified via pruning with different techniques such as MDL-based pruning [11], reduced error pruning [12], cost-based pruning [2], among others.

Although no longer NP-hard, most of these techniques

still require significant amount of computation as well as storage. Most algorithms require multiple scans of the training data and require data to be held in main memory. For example, to compute information gain of every untested feature at each internal node of a decision tree, a brute force decision tree learner either has to group data items according to discrete feature value or sort them for continuous features. After a feature is chosen, the subset of data at the node has to be split into multiple subsets. There have been later proposals to improve the efficiency and scalability of decision tree learning [13, 10, 8]. However, these solutions employ rather sophisticated indexing and hashing data structures and do not completely solve the problems. In the same time, it is still questionable about the true accuracy of the simplest model; it is now a general consensus that the pruned decision tree is not necessarily better than the unpruned decision tree. One well cited example is the KDD-CUP'98 donation dataset; the pruned decision tree will not solicit to any people and consequently will not receive any donation [15].

Combining Multiple Hypotheses Apart from model comprehensibility and simplicity, it is doubtful whether the efforts to look for the simplest model that fits the data is indeed worthwhile just from accuracy point of view, given the fact that searching this model compromises learning efficiency and scalability. In [6], Domingos criticized one common notion of Occam's razor, "Simplicity leads to better accuracy." Empirical studies [14] have also shown that the simplest tree is not the best. The most evident supporting results are the success of bagging [3],boosting [7] and metalearning [5]. Besides improved accuracy, one biggest problem for the family of complicated hypotheses is the learning efficiency.

The Problem In summary, the observation we have found is that:

Most of the previously proposed inductive learning approaches, computing either the simplest model that fits the data or combining multiple hypotheses, may be way too complicated and too costly beyond necessity.

There exist multiple optimal models for a given loss function. To minimize a given loss function, in fact, it is not necessary to have the true probability $P_t(y|\mathbf{x})$ as long as the estimated probability $P(y|\mathbf{x})$ is within a tolerable error range of the true value. For a two-class problem, assume that the true probability for $\mathbf{x}$ to be of class y is 0.9. An inaccurate estimate of $p(y|\mathbf{x})$ to be 0.51 will have exactly the optimal prediction under 0-1 loss function.

The Solution We propose a multiple random decision tree algorithm. The algorithm works as follows. At each level of the tree, a non-tested feature is "randomly" chosen without using any training data. The tree construction stops as soon as the depth of the tree exceeds a predefined limit. The structure of the tree is only dependent on the order that the features are randomly chosen, and is completely independent from the training data. After the structure of the tree is built, we use the training data to update the statistics of each node. Each node records the number of examples of different classes that are "classified" through that node. The process is similar to classifying with a decision tree. Since each data item can be read once to update multiple random trees one by one, the update process requires only one complete scan of the data. To classify an example $\mathbf{x}$, the probability outputs from multiple random trees are averaged as an estimate to $P_t(y|\mathbf{x})$.

2. Random Decision Tree

The "strawman" version of random decision tree algorithm is summarized in Algorithm 1. It first builds the structure of N random decision trees without the data. It then updates the statistics of each node by scanning the training examples one by one. The feature set $\mathsf{X} = \{\mathcal{F}_1, \ldots, \mathcal{F}_k\}$ is provided to construct the structure of the tree. For discrete feature, $\mathcal{F}_i = \{d_1, \ldots, d_m\}$ is a list of valid values. For convenience, $\mathcal{F}_i(\mathbf{x})$ denotes the value of feature $\mathcal{F}_i$ of example $\mathbf{x}$. For continuous feature, we either use discretization or randomly pick a dividing point (i.e., $<$ and $\geq$ as the testing condition). For illustration purpose, we use discretization in the description of the algorithm. When classifying an example $\mathbf{x}$, the probability outputs from multiple random trees are averaged to estimate *a posteriori* probability. The loss function is required to make the decision.

To handle missing values in the training data, each example $\mathbf{x}$ is assigned an initial weight of $w = 1.0$. When missing feature value is encountered, the current weight of $\mathbf{x}$ is distributed across its children nodes. If the prior distribution of known values are given, the weight is distributed in proportion to this distribution. Otherwise, it is equally divided among the children nodes. The tree can grow up to the full number of features and the exact depth can be limited by a given parameter in tree growth. The structure of the tree can be simplified after training. We can remove all *empty* nodes (i.e., nodes with no examples) and their descendents without changing the logic of the tree. There may be practical reasons to keep these empty nodes. For example, if the same tree structure will be reused for new dataset such as streaming data, temporary empty nodes should be kept.

Single Feature Information Gain Bias of Decision Trees To the best of our knowledge, state-of-the-art decision algorithms (such as Ross Quinlan's C4.5 and Christian Borgelt's dti among others) use a "simple feature" information gain bias. The algorithm grows a tree *if and only if* there is at least one feature that has information gain. For the following example,

```
TRAIN(S, X, N)
Data       : training set S = {(x_1, t_1), ..., (x_n, t_n)}, set of
             features X = {F_1, ..., F_k}. F is a feature descrip-
             tor. N is the number of random decision trees.
Result     : N random trees {T_1, ..., T_N}
begin
    for i ∈ {1, ..., N} do
        BuildTreeStructure(T_i, X);
    end
    for (x, t) ∈ S do
        for i ∈ {1, ..., N} do
            UpdateStatistics(T_i, (x, t));
        end
    end
    return {T_1, ..., T_N}
end

BuildTreeStructure(T, X)
begin
    if X = ∅ then
        make the node as leaf;
    end
    else
        randomly choose feature F;
        F is the testing feature at current node;
        Feature F has m valid values, {d_i};
        construct m children nodes, n_j, for each valid value d_j;
        for j ∈ {1, ..., m} do
            BuildTreeStructure(n_j, X − {F});
        end
    end
end

UpdateStatistics(T, (x, t))
begin
    n[t] keeps the number of examples with class label t;
    n[t] ← n[t] + 1;
    if the node is a not a leaf then
        d is the value of the node's testing feature F, i.e., d =
        F(x);
        n is the corresponding child node for the feature value d;
        UpdateStatistics(n, (x, t));
    end
end

CLASSIFY({T_1, ..., T_N}, x)
begin
    For tree T_i, P_i(y|x) = n[y] / Σ_y n[y] where n[y] is the count at
    the leaf node that x finally reaches to;
    return 1/N Σ_{i=1}^{N} P_i(y|x) for all class labels y;
end
```

Algorithm 1: Random decision tree algorithm

f_1	f_2	label
0	0	**F**
0	1	**T**
1	0	**T**
1	1	**F**

Neither f_1 nor f_2 carries information gain *independently*. Only when they are examined *jointly*, they are predictive. State-of-the-art decision tree algorithms that only considers one feature at a time will compute a default model that always predicts either **T** or **F**. The empirical reason is that the computation of combined features involves combinatorial explosion and is intractable. The proposed random decision algorithm has the same "single feature information gain bias".

3. Analysis

We first discuss the heuristics to choose tree depth as well as the number of trees, then discuss the training cost and memory requirement.

Heuristics to choose tree depth The main reason for multiple random trees is to create diversity. However, when the random trees are too deep, the diversity may actually reduce. In the extreme case, there may be no diversity at all. When the random trees are generated to the depth of the complete feature set, it is very likely that they are equivalent to rote learning and every random tree is virtually the same. The simplest rote learning is to group data items with exactly the same feature values together and use the most frequent class as the prediction. If a fully-generated random tree have no empty nodes, in other words, all the nodes or feature tests in every path has supporting examples, it will degenerate into rote learning. Rote learning tests every feature of an example and a full depth tree with no empty nodes essentially does the same. When every feature is tested, the sequence of how they are tested are no longer significant.

We decide the depth of tree using combinatorics. Assume that there are k features in total and i is the number of feature tests. C_k^i is the number of unique ways to create i feature tests. $C_k^i = \frac{k!}{i! \cdot (k-1)!}$ is the number of unique combinations to sample i items with replacement from a population of k. Since each tested feature cannot be used again, we actually sample features with replacement. For example, when there are 4 features, there are $C_4^2 = 6$ unique ways to test 2 different features. C_k^i peaks at $i = \frac{k}{2}$. When we limit the random tree's depth to be $\frac{k}{2}$, i.e., the depth of tree is half of the number of features, we create the most diversity.

$$\text{Tree Depth: } \frac{k}{2} \tag{1}$$

Heuristics to choose the number of trees Since each tree is constructed randomly, it is in effect a random sample from a population of trees of a given depth. The averaging of multiple trees is to approximate the true mean of a large sample. When each feature is binary, the population size is $2^{\frac{k}{2}}$. We recast the random decision tree algorithm as a statistical sampling problem. The average probability is the sample mean using N trees. The problem is to decide if it is worthwhile to have larger samples, i.e., more random trees. Statistically, it is found that, quite surprisingly, a random sample as small as $N = 10$ gives very good result. When $N \geq 30$, the sample's mean (i.e., average probability in our case) usually has small error with at least 99.7% confidence. Because of the "error-tolerance" property in optimal decision making, $N = 10$ is probably sufficient for most applications.

We analyze the effect of the algorithm for the *worst case* scenario to derive the lower bound of the *confidence* that multiple random tree is the optimal model. The worst case is a dataset that has only one relevant feature. All remaining $k - 1$ features are irrelevant. This is the worst case because the single best tree will ignore all irrelevant feature and chooses the single relevant feature, resulting in an optimal model. However, the random tree may use all but the relevant feature. We derive the number of random trees (N) needed to ensure its optimality with confidence p. Please note that the example in Section 2 is not a worst case. When there is no "single" feature that has information gain independently, none of the state-of-the-art decision tree learner (eg. C4.5 and dti) that considers one feature at a time will be able to compute a correct model.

The *a posteriori* probability estimate by any number of irrelevant features approximates the default probability in the training data. If at least one random tree uses the only good feature to classify **x**, the averaged probability will be better than the default probability. The averaged probability may not be the same as the probability output of the single best tree. However, due to the error-tolerance property, it may not make a difference. Since every feature is chosen equally during tree construction, it has the same probability to appear in a decision path from the root to the leaf. Therefore, the probability for one feature to appear in a decision path is $p = \frac{1}{k}$. Considering all N random trees, the probability for at least one path to test the only relevant feature is at least

$$\text{Confidence Lower Bound: } p(k, N) = 1 - (1 - \frac{1}{k})^N \quad (2)$$

In other words, with confidence of at least $p(k, N)$, the random decision tree is optimal. This probability estimate is under the worst assumption that the decision path of different trees is completely independent. However they may be partially correlated due to the feature values of **x**. The actual probability will be higher than the above estimate. In practice, when there are a large number of features, the feature sets should be filtered to remove irrelevant features. Please note that Eq(2) does not contradict Eq(1). In the worst case assumption of Eq(2), the optimal decision is the prediction by the single relevant feature. Under this situation, tree depth is no longer important. This is because as long as the single relevant feature appears in a decision path of arbitrary length, a random tree will make the optimal decision.

Training Cost and Memory Requirement The training cost comes from updating the statistics in each node. This is similar to classifying a dataset. The main overhead comes from scanning the training data. The algorithm can be easily implemented to update multiple random trees from one complete data scan. For realistic problems, the multiple random trees can be held entirely in main memory, and all updates are done in main memory. Since there is no utility to keep a data record afterwards, we only need to keep the

multiple random trees and one data item at any given time. Since the random trees are iso-depth, one can construct one random tree from the data dictionary to measure its memory requirement and multiple by the total number of trees to compute the total memory requirement. In rare cases that the limited memory cannot hold multiple trees simultaneously, multiple trees can be computed from multiple scans. Learning a single best tree may not even be possible since it requires the entire data to be held in main memory.

4. Experiment

Since the random decision tree algorithm is contrary to common beliefs, the biggest concern is on its actual accuracy. We use both 0-1 loss and cost-sensitive loss functions to evaluate its performance. We compare its accuracy with the single best unpruned and pruned decision trees, bagging, boosting, meta-learning, MetaCost as well as decision trees with calibrated probability, i.e., Laplace smoothing, curtailment and their combination. We also study the effect of applying various calibrated probability methods to smooth the probability estimates of random trees. We varied both the number of random trees and the depth of each tree simultaneously to study the change in its performance. We recorded the size of each tree and the size of the training set. We also generated an artificial dataset with only one good feature and all $k - 1$ remaining features are irrelevant. We count the probability that the random trees are the optimal model as a function of the number of trees.

Data Sets We have carefully selected three datasets from real world applications. The first one is the famous donation dataset that first appeared in KDDCUP'98 competition. Suppose that the cost of requesting a charitable donation from an individual **x** is $0.68, and the best estimate of the amount that **x** will donate is $Y(\mathbf{x})$. Its benefit matrix (converse of loss function) is:

	predict *donate*	predict *¬donator*
actual *donate*	$Y(x)$ - $.0.68	0
actual *¬donate*	-$0.68	0

The accuracy is the total amount of received charity minus the cost of mailing. Assuming that $p(donate|\mathbf{x})$ is the estimated probability that **x** is a donor, we will solicit to **x** iff $p(donate|\mathbf{x}) \cdot Y(\mathbf{x}) > 0.68$. The data has already been divided into a training set and a test set. The training set consists of 95412 records for which it is known whether or not the person made a donation and how much the donation was. The test set contains 96367 records for which similar donation information was not published until after the KDD'98 competition. We used the standard training/test set splits to compare with previous results. The feature subsets (7 features in total) were based on the KDD'98 winning submission. To estimate the donation amount, we employed the multiple linear regression method. As suggested in [15], to avoid over estimation, we only used those contributions between $0 and $50.

The second data set is a credit card fraud detection problem. Assuming that there is an overhead $v \in \{\$60, \$70, \$80, \$90\}$ to dispute and investigate a fraud and $y(x)$ is the transaction amount, the following is the benefit matrix:

	predict $fraud$	predict $\neg fraud$
actual $fraud$	$y(x) - v$	0
actual $\neg fraud$	$-v$	0

The accuracy is the sum of recovered frauds minus investigation costs. If $p(fraud|\mathbf{x})$ is the probability that $\mathbf{x}$ is a fraud, $fraud$ is the optimal decision iff $p(fraud|\mathbf{x}) \cdot y(x) > v$. The dataset was sampled from a one year period and contains a total of .5M transaction records. The features (20 in total) record the time of the transaction, merchant type, merchant location, and past payment and transaction history summary. We use data of the last month as test data (40038 examples) and data of previous months as training data (406009 examples).

The third dataset is the adult dataset from UCI repository. We artificially associate a benefit of $1 \sim \$10$ to class label $\mathbf{F}$ and a fixed benefit of $1 to class label $\mathbf{N}$, as summarized below:

	predict $\mathbf{F}$	predict $\mathbf{N}$
actual $\mathbf{F}$	$1 \sim \$10$	0
actual $\mathbf{N}$	0	$1

We use the natural split of training and test sets, so the results can be easily duplicated. The training set contains 32561 entries and the test set contains 16281 records. The feature set contains 14 features that describe the education, gender, country of origin, martial status, capital gain among others.

Decision Tree Learner The experiments were based on C4.5 release 8 [12]. The single best tree is constructed by running C4.5 with all the default settings. It computes both the unpruned and pruned decision trees. The random decision tree algorithm is a modified version of C4.5 that does not compute information gain and constructs the structure of the tree prior to scanning the data.

Accuracy Comparison Since random decision tree may introduce large variation in accuracy, we run each test 5 times. For each test, up to 100 random trees are constructed. The results are plotted and summarized in Figures 1 to 3. We use the term accuracy to mean number of correctly predicted examples for 0-1 loss and total benefits for cost-sensitive loss.

The result for the donation dataset is shown in Figure 1. A pruned decision tree by C4.5 has only one default rule that says no one is a donor, and will not send any solicitation. Therefore, it will not receive any donation. In Figure 1, we plot the total benefits of all 5 test runs of random deci-

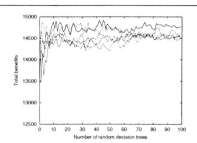

Model	Total Benefits
pruned	$0
unpruned	$12577.61
calibrated	$14424.9
10 random tree	$14567

Figure 1. Random Tree on Donation Dataset

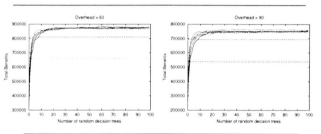

Model	Total Benefits			
	$60	$70	$80	$90
pruned	$810115	$760256	$728482	$694955
unpruned	$696596	$614644	$576634	$537903
calibrated	$801034	$761244	$731655	$691044
10 random tree	$830431	$779410	$751455	$712314

Figure 2. Random Tree on Credit Card

sion tree. We have also plotted two baselines in the same figure as a comparison. The first baseline, show as the straight line in the bottom, is the total benefits (=$12577.61) of the single unpruned decision tree. The second baseline, shown as the straight line at the top of the figure, is the total benefit (=$14424.9) of the best calibrated probability methods. We experimented with Laplace smoothing, curtailment as well as curtailment plus smoothing [15]. The best calibrated method for donation dataset is curtailment plus smoothing. The detailed numbers are summarized in the table of Figure 1. We compare the results of 10 random trees (averaged over 5 test runs) with the single-best unpruned tree, pruned tree as well as unpruned tree with calibrated probability output.

There are several important observations. First, when the number of random trees exceeds 10, the average total benefits of the random tree algorithm is more than that of the best method. The average total benefits of 10 random trees is $14567, but the best single decision tree method (un-

Model	Accuracy	
	c(F)=1	c(F)=10
pruned	13996	43277
unpruned	13733	41710
calibrated	13733	42127
10 random tree	13966.2	44137.8

Figure 3. Random Tree on Adult Dataset

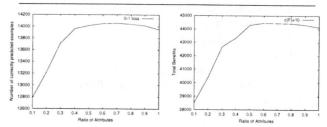

Figure 4. Tree Depth and Accuracy on Adult Dataset

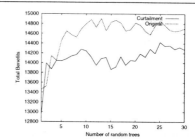

Figure 5. Curtailment on Random Trees - Donation Dataset

pruned decision tree with "curtailment plus smoothing") is $14424.9. Comparing the result of unpruned single best tree with random decision tree, the unpruned single best tree receives a donation of only $12577.61. The random method receives approximately $2000 more in donation. Another important observation is that the accuracy of the random trees increases significantly when the number of trees grows from 1 to 10 and starts to stabilize after 10. It starts to fluctuate after 10, but most of them are still higher than the best single decision tree method.

The results on credit card fraud dataset are shown in Figure 2. We plot the total benefits with increasing number of decision trees when the overhead is either $60 or $90. The plots for overhead $70 and $80 are similar. As a comparison baseline, we also plot the total benefits of the unpruned decision tree (the straight line in the bottom) and pruned decision tree (the one at the top). The phenomenon is similar to the donation dataset. The total benefits of 10 random trees significantly exceed the best of the single model methods. As a summary, the total benefits of the 10 random trees is about $20000 to $30000 or 2.5% to 3% higher than the corresponding best single classifier method. As shown in the table of Figure 2, the best single classifier method is either the pruned single decision tree or unpruned tree with calibrated probability. Similar to the donation dataset, when there are more than 10 random trees, the total benefits of multiple random trees stabilize. Computing more random trees doesn't produce a more accurate model.

The results on the adult dataset is shown in Figure 3. We only show the result for both 0-1 loss (or $c(F) = 1$) and cost-sensitive loss when $c(F) = 10$. The phenomenon for other loss functions, i.e., $c(F) = 2, \ldots, 9$, are similar. In summary, the random tree significantly improves the accuracy of the best single classifier method and its accuracy stabilizes when the number of trees is more than 10.

Depth of Random Decision Trees We have discussed in Section 3 that the optimal depth of random tree is half the number of features. We have varied the depth of the tree from 10% up to the full tree with 10% increment. The results on adult datasets are shown in Figure 4. The results closely confirms our theoretical analysis that when the tree depth is half of the features, the accuracy is the highest. As we can see from the plots, the accuracy starts to increase when the tree depth increases from 10% to 50% of the total number of features, peaks around 50% ~ 60% and be-

gins to drop afterwards.

Calibration on Random Trees Previous studies have shown that curtailment is the most effective probability calibration method. Curtailment stops searching down the tree if the number of examples in the current node is less than m. m is set as 100 in our experiments. Our results have shown that curtailment has no effect on the accuracy for random decision trees on adult and credit card dataset, but it is detrimental to donation dataset. The total benefits is reduced by about $100 ~ $800 for different number of random trees as shown in Figure 5.

Boosting, Bagging, Meta-learning and MetaCost As a study of accuracy, we compared multiple random decision trees to boosting, bagging, meta-learning as well as Meta-Cost. However, it is important to emphasize that none of boosting, bagging and MetaCost are scalable methods. The comparison with boosting, bagging and MetaCost is only limited to accuracy without efficiency and memory concerns. Meta-learning scans the complete training set approximately twice, but the proposed random tree scans the data subset exactly once.

We have applied boosting and bagging to both single best (pruned and unpruned) tree and single random decision tree. We applied the advanced version of AdaBoost that uses the numerical estimation and continuous predictive confidence. For meta-learning, we divided the training data into 8 sub-

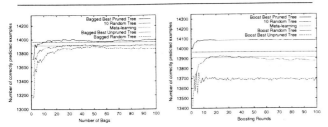

Figure 6. Boosting and Bagging on Adult Dataset (order of legends is the same as the curves)

DataSet	Training Size	Tree Size	Ratio
donation	2766942	2233	1239
credit card	27005476	18573	1454
adult	3466402	188945	18

Table 1. Memory Requirement

sets. Two base classifiers are combined in the same time, resulting tree of classifiers with depth equal to 3. We experimented on the adult dataset with 0-1 loss function. The results are plotted in Figure 6. The x-axis is the number of rounds and the y-axis is the number of correctly predicted examples. The y-axis starts from 13000 in order to "magnify" the trends. The left plot is the result of bagging and meta-learning. Only bagged best pruned tree after 10 round exceeds the accuracy of 10 random trees by only ±50 examples (out of 16281) . The other 3 bagged methods, i.e., bagged unpruned tree and bagged random tree, are less accurate than 10 random trees. The accuracy of meta-learning is slightly lower than the random tree (by ± 50 examples). The right plot is the result of boosting. Except for boost best pruned tree, all the other boosting methods, i.e., boost random tree and best best unpruned tree, are significantly less accurate than 10 random tree. Boost best pruned tree exceeds the accuracy of 10 random tree by about ±80 examples (out of 16281). It is important to emphasize that boosting and bagging best pruned tree are significantly more costly than computing 10 random trees.

As discussed in [15], MetaCost is significantly more costly for cost-sensitive learning than "empirical risk" based method. It uses multiple classifier bagging to estimate the *a posteriori* probability, intentionally changes the label of some examples to optimize the classification frontier and trains a best classifier at the end. We have applied MetaCost (using 10 round bagging to estimate *posteriori* probability and unpruned best decision tree) on the donation dataset. The total charity received is $11950 which is significantly less than both the multiple random tree ($14567) and single best unpruned tree ($12577.61).

Training Efficiency The total time to train the single best decision tree using C4.5 is 2 mins, 4 mins and 90 mins for adult, donation and credit card dataset (full training set) respectively. However, the training cost for random tree is 0.5 min, 0.6 min and 2 mins. If the training data cannot be held in main memory, the training time for the single best decision tree will be significantly longer due to memory swap.

Memory Requirement We measure the size of a decision tree from the size of its stored file in the file system. It is a good estimate for the tree kept in main memory. The data size is the file size of the training data stored in the file system. In Table 1, we list the size of the training data, the size of one single random tree (the depth is half of the number of features), and their ratio (closet smaller integer). For the credit card and donation dataset, the same amount of memory to hold the complete dataset can hold more than 1200 random trees. Computing multiple random trees has significantly less memory requirement but can achieve higher accuracy. For the adult data set, the same amount of memory to hold the training data can hold at least 18 random trees. Computing 10 random trees is sufficient. It still results in about 50% less memory requirement.

Artificial Dataset In Section 3, we theoretically derive the confidence probability $p = 1 - (1 - \frac{1}{k})^N$ that the multiple random tree is the optimal model under the pessimistic condition where there is only one good feature and all $k - 1$ remaining features are irrelevant. To verify this result, we have created an artificial dataset. The class label is binary, F and N. There are 50% F's and 50% N's in the training data. There is one good feature that is strictly correlated with the class label. In other words, using this feature alone can predict the true label with 100% accuracy. We then introduced 9 irrelevant features whose values are generated randomly. We compute $N = 1 \sim 30$ random trees. Tree depth ranges from 10% to 100% of the total number of features with 10% increment. (In each test, N trees of the same depth are used to classify an example.) One complete test generates 30×10 trees. We have completed the experiment 1000 times and measured the probability that the random tree has exactly the same accuracy (100%) as the single best tree. The result is plotted in Figure 7. As we can see the empirical results closely matches the theoretical analysis.

5. Related Work

One important distinction of the proposed random tree method from Amit and Geman's "randomized trees" [1] is as follows. In randomized trees, Amit and Geman randomly generates feature subset from the complete feature set; from each feature subset, they run a conventional decision tree learner to compute the single best tree with different kinds of heuristics such as information gain among others. However, in our proposed method, the random tree uses

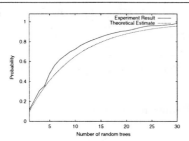

Figure 7. Probability that the random tree is the optimal model when there is only 1 useful feature. All remaining features are pure noise

the complete feature set. The structure of the tree is constructed by randomly picking an untested feature and splitting point. Our method does not use any heuristic, e.g., information gain, to choose a feature at any given step. The choice of feature at each step is completely stochastic. Our method scans the the training set exactly once. Amit and Geman's randomized trees scans the training set multiple times (each one with a different feature subset). Our proposed random tree and Amit and Geman's randomized tree are orthogonal methods.

6. Conclusion

Contrary to common beliefs, we propose a random decision tree algorithm that builds multiple iso-depth random decision trees. When classifying **x**, the probability outputs from multiple trees are averaged to estimate *a posteriori* probability. We discuss the heuristics to choose the depth of each random tree; when the tree depth is half of the number of features, the multiple random trees create the most diversity. We then discuss the minimal number of random trees to guarantee that the multiple random tree is an optimal model. We derive the lower bound of the confidence, as a function of the number of averaged random trees, that the multiple random tree is the optimal model. In practice, 10 trees are sufficient for most problems. We empirically evaluate the algorithm on both real world and artificial datasets. The empirical results have shown that the random decision tree algorithm achieves significantly higher accuracy than the single best hypothesis for both 0-1 loss and cost-sensitive problems. Comparing with more expensive combining techniques such as boosting, bagging, meta-learning and MetaCost, averaging random tree algorithm still achieves higher or comparable accuracy. The structure of a random tree is constructed completely independent of the training data. The training data is scanned exactly once to update the statistics in multiple random trees. The memory requirement is to store multiple random trees and one data item at any given time. With the necessary number of

random trees to ensure optimality, the memory requirement of the random tree algorithm is significantly less than learning a single best tree even if the very large training data could have been held entirely in main memory to compute the single best tree.

References

[1] Y. Amit and D. Geman. Shape quantization and recognition with randomized trees. *Neural Computation*, 9(7):1545–1588, 1997.

[2] J. P. Bradford, C. Kunz, R. Kohavi, C. Brunk, and C. E. Brodley. Pruning decision trees with misclassification costs. In *European Conference on Machine Learning*, pages 131–136, 1998.

[3] L. Breiman. Bagging predictors. *Machine Learning*, 24(2):123–140, 1996.

[4] W. Buntine. Learning classification trees. In D. J. Hand, editor, *Artificial Intelligence frontiers in statistics*, pages 182–201. Chapman & Hall,London, 1993.

[5] P. Chan. *An Extensible Meta-learning Approach for Scalable and Accurate Inductive Learning*. PhD thesis, Columbia University, Oct 1996.

[6] P. Domingos. Occam's two razors: The sharp and the blunt. In *Proceedings of the Fourth International Conference on Knowledge Discovery and Data Mining*. AAAI Press, 1998.

[7] Y. Freund and R. Schapire. A decision-theoretic generalization of on-line learning and an application to boosting. *Computer and System Sciences*, 55(1):119–139, 1997.

[8] J. Gehrke, V. Ganti, R. Ramakrishnan, and W.-Y. Loh. BOAT-optimistic decision tree construction. In *Proceedings of ACM SIGMOD International Conference on Management of Data (SIGMOD 1999)*, 1999.

[9] M. Kearns and Y. Mansour. On the boosting ability of top-down decision tree learning algorithms. In *Proceedings of the Annual ACM Symposium on the Theory of Computing*, pages 459–468, 1996.

[10] M. Mehta, R. Agrawal, and J. Rissanen. SLIQ: A fast scalable classifier for data mining. In *Extending Database Technology*, pages 18–32, 1996.

[11] M. Mehta, J. Rissanen, and R. Agrawal. MDL-based decision tree pruning. In *Proceedings of the First International Conference on Knowledge Discovery and Data Mining (KDD'95)*, pages 216–221, 1995.

[12] R. Quinlan. *C4.5: Programs for Machine Learning*. Morgan Kaufmann, 1993.

[13] J. Shafer, R. Agrawl, and M. Mehta. SPRINT: A scalable parallel classifier for data mining. In *Proceedings of Twenty-second International Conference on Very Large Databases (VLDB-96)*, pages 544–555, San Francisco, California, 1996. Morgan Kaufmann.

[14] J. Shawe-Taylor and N. Cristianini. Data-dependent structural risk minimisation for perceptron decision trees. In M. Jordan, M. Kearns, and S. Solla, editors, *Advances in Neural Information Processing Systems 10*, pages 336–342. MIT Press, 1998.

[15] B. Zadrozny and C. Elkan. Learning and making decisions when costs and probabilities are both unknown. In *Proceedings of the Seventh ACM International Conference on Knowledge Discovery and Data Mining (SIGKDD01)*, 2001.

Identifying Markov Blankets with Decision Tree Induction

Lewis Frey[1], Douglas Fisher

Dept. of Electrical Engineering and Computer Science, Box 1679 Station B, Nashville, TN 37235
Frey@vuse.vanderbilt.edu, DFisher@vuse.vanderbilt.edu

Ioannis Tsamardinos, Constantin F. Aliferis, Alexander Statnikov
[1]*Dept. of Biomedical Informatics, Vanderbilt University, 2209 Garland Avenue; Nashville, TN 37232*
Ioannis.Tsamardinos@, Constantin.Aliferis@, Alexander.Statnikov@vanderbilt.edu

Abstract

The Markov Blanket of a target variable is the minimum conditioning set of variables that makes the target independent of all other variables. Markov Blankets inform feature selection, aid in causal discovery and serve as a basis for scalable methods of constructing Bayesian networks. This paper applies decision tree induction to the task of Markov Blanket identification. Notably, we compare (a) C5.0, a widely used algorithm for decision rule induction, (b) C5C, which post-processes C5.0's rule set to retain the most frequently referenced variables and (c) PC, a standard method for Bayesian Network induction. C5C performs as well as or better than C5.0 and PC across a number of data sets. Our modest variation of an inexpensive, accurate, off-the-shelf induction engine mitigates the need for specialized procedures, and establishes baseline performance against which specialized algorithms can be compared.

1. Introduction

The Markov Blanket (MB) is the minimum conditioning set that makes all other features independent for a particular target. Tsamardinos & Aliferis [20] show that in faithful Bayesian Networks Markov Blankets consist of *strongly relevant* features as defined in relation to optimal classifiers [11]. The Markov Blanket is particularly useful for data sets with large numbers of features. For example, gene expression data has tens of thousands of features. Arnone [3] has estimated that on average, four to eight genes interact in higher organisms. Thus, an algorithm that finds the Markov Blanket of genes could reduce the data set by three orders of magnitude.

The Markov Blanket can be used for causal discovery under the condition of *faithfulness*, which is defined in Section 2. In essence, it can reduce the number of variables that need to be tested experimentally to discover direct causes of a target T.

Additionally, Markov Blanket discovery can be used for guiding Bayesian Network construction. The Markov Blanket for each variable is identified and used as a guide to construct the Bayesian Network for the domain. Margaritis and Thrun [15] use this approach for Bayesian Network structure learning.

Several algorithms have been developed or proposed for identifying Markov Blankets ([13], [15], [21], [22]). Because of the relationship between Markov Blankets and feature relevance, and because decision tree induction has been used to perform feature selection ([2], [7]), we evaluate the ability of C5.0 [19], an inexpensive, off-the-shelf induction engine, to identify Markov Blankets. Our evaluation motivates a modest post-processing step that demonstrably yields very accurate, low cost approximation of Markov Blankets. Our study thus forwards a scalable, accurate, and accessible algorithm for Markov Blanket identification. The observation that classification-motivated rule induction performs well at MB identification, also highlights the common principles of feature relevance that underlie induction of classifiers and Bayesian Networks [20].

The remainder of the paper reviews basic concepts of Bayesian Networks, describes C5.0, our variation called C5C, and the PC algorithm [18], a prototypical algorithm for Bayesian Network construction, which we use for comparison purposes. An experimental comparison of PC, C5C, and C5.0 evaluates how accurately each method finds the Markov Blankets for target variables in a variety of domains. The paper concludes with a discussion of the results.

2. Bayesian Networks

A *Bayesian Network*, $<V,G,J>$, consists of a set of variables V, a directed acyclic graph G and a joint probability distribution J over the variables V where the

Markov Conditions holds (i.e., a variable is independent from all variables other than its descendants when conditioned on its parents) [18].

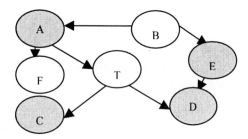

Figure 1. Example Bayesian Network Graph

The *Markov Blanket* (MB) of a target variable is the minimal set of variables X in V such that when a variable T in V is conditioned on X, any variable in $F \subseteq V\text{-}X\text{-}T$ is independent of T (i.e., $P(T|XUF)=P(T|X)$).

In Bayesian Networks (BN) the union of parents and children of T, and parents of children (spouses) of T is equivalent to the Markov Blanket [17]. In Figure 1, the Markov Blanket for T is $\{A, C, D, E\}$. This means that variables B and F are independent of T conditioned on $\{A, C, D, E\}$.

A Bayesian Network $N = <V, G, J>$ is *faithful* to joint probability distribution J over feature set V if and only if all dependencies entailed by G and the Markov Condition are also present in J. A data-generating process K is faithful to N, if K in the sample limit produces data with joint probability distribution P, and N is faithful to P. A data set is faithful to a BN N if in the sample limit the data was generated by a data generation process that is faithful to N.

Some algorithms work well in identifying the MB from faithful data. If the data set is faithful to the BN, then the MB of each variable is unique (proof in appendix) and the comparison of the algorithms' ability to find the unique MB is valid. If the data is unfaithful, then the MB is not unique. This can occur, for example, when deterministic relationships exist in the data [10]. Parity functions are examples of relationships that are not faithful. No current causal discovery methods can learn parity functions and most Bayesian methods assume faithfulness.

This paper focuses on the problem of inducing the Markov Blanket of the target concept in faithful distributions. For example, in the Bayesian Network depicted in Figure 1, the task of the algorithm is to predict A, C, D and E as the Markov Blanket and reject B and F as members of the Markov Blanket given a data set that is generated by the Bayesian Network. The algorithms for finding the Markov Blanket are discussed below.

3. Algorithms

This section describes the methods for Markov Blanket identification that we will compare. PC and C5.0 provide baseline performance to which C5C can be compared.

3.1 PC

The PC algorithm [18] starts with a fully connected, unoriented Bayesian Network graph and goes through three phases. In phase I, the algorithm eliminates edges by using the criterion that variable A has a direct edge to variable B if, and only if, for all subsets of features there is no subset S, such that A is independent of B conditioned on S. In phases II and III, the algorithm orients the edges by performing global constraint propagation. If the algorithm is not able to orient some edges, the output is actually a class of structurally equivalent BNs. The PC algorithm uses significance thresholds based on the G^2 statistic. In linear domains, Fisher's z-test is employed.

PC is intractable on densely connected data sets with a large number of variables. The algorithm has a complexity on the order of the number of variables raised to the maximal degree, d, for any node in the graph (i.e., $O(|V|^d)$). Consequently, it is exponentially bounded in the maximal degree. Similar complexity limitations hold for search and score Bayesian methods. The algorithm by Cheng et al. [9] improves the complexity (to $O(|V|^4)$) by introducing a distributional assumption ("monotone restriction") with properties currently being explored. In practice, these algorithms cannot run on more than a few hundred variables.

3.2 C5.0

A C5.0 decision tree is constructed using *GainRatio*. *GainRatio* is a measure incorporating entropy. Entropy ($E(S)$, Eq. 1) measures how unordered the data set is. It is denoted by the following equation when there are classes $C_1, ...,C_N$ in data set S where $P(S_c)$ is the probability of class C occurring in the data set S:

$$E(S) = -\sum_{c=1}^{N} P\!\left(S_c\right) * log_2 P\!\left(S_c\right) \tag{1}$$

Information Gain is a measure of the improvement in the amount of order.

$$Gain(S, V) = E(S) - \sum_{v \in values(V)} \frac{|S_v|}{|S|} * E(S_v) \qquad (2)$$

Gain has a bias towards variables with many values that partition the data set into smaller ordered sets. In order to reduce this bias, the entropy of each variable over its *m* variable values is calculated as *SplitInfo* (Eq. 3).

$$SplitInfo(S, V) = \sum_{i=1}^{m} -\frac{|S_i|}{|S|} * log_2 \frac{|Si|}{|S|} \qquad (3)$$

GainRatio (Eq. 4) is calculated by dividing *Gain* by *SplitInfo* so that the bias towards variables with large value sets is dampened.

$$GainRatio(S, V) = \frac{Gain(S, V)}{SplitInfo(S, V)} \qquad (4)$$

C5.0 builds a decision tree greedily by splitting the data on the variable that maximizes gain ratio. CF-pruning is set to 25% (the default setting for C5.0) in this paper.

A final decision tree is changed to a set of rules by converting the paths into conjunctive rules and pruning them to improve classification accuracy. When using C5.0 to predict the Markov Blanket, each variable involved in any rule output by C5.0 is predicted to be in the Markov Blanket of the target/class variable.

3.3 C5C

The working hypothesis is that frequently occurring features in C5.0 production rules provide a good approximation of the *MB(T)*. This hypothesis is encapsulated as a simple augmentation of C5.0 to count the number of variable occurrences in C5.0 rules and use the most frequent to predict the Markov Blanket. This is called the C5C algorithm and it uses the C5.0 rules output to order the variables from most likely MB variables to least likely.. The modification consists of a simple script that counts the occurrence of the variables in the C5.0 rules output (i.e., if variable occurs in rule, then increment the variable's frequency count) A frequency threshold is chosen to distinguish between Markov and non-Markov Blanket variables.

Three methods will be used to identify the MB given the C5C ranking of variables. First is choosing the best frequency threshold given knowledge of the true MB (this is used as a comparison in sections 6.1 and 6.2 and is intended as a best-case analysis). The second strategy finds the frequency threshold that gives the best accuracy

of C5.0 on a test set. The third strategy employs the G^2-test to test for independence.

4. Experimental Methods

The experiments involve generating data from six Bayesian Networks and comparing the prediction of Markov Blankets by C5.0, C5C and PC. The first five data sets are publicly available Bayesian Networks: Alarm [5], Hailfinder [1], Insurance [6], Mildew and Barley [12]. These data sets are generated using a logic sampling data-generating approach, implemented in the Hugin package [4], run to produce a data set of 20,000 discrete valued instances. The last data set is an Artificial Bayesian Network that is constructed to examine the effect of sample size on learning.

Using these generated data sets, C5.0, C5C and PC's abilities to reconstruct the Markov Blanket for each variable in the data sets are compared. Since the original networks are available, the predicted Markov Blankets can be compared against the actual Markov Blankets in terms of sensitivity and specificity. *Sensitivity* is the ratio of correctly predicted MB variables over true MB variables. *Specificity* is the ratio of correctly predicted (i.e., excluded) non-MB variables over true non-MB variables. Ratios for predicted Markov Blankets of different sizes and characteristics are compared.

In comparing C5.0 and C5C, a measure of closeness to the true MB is determined by calculating the distance (*dist*) of sensitivity (*sen*) and specificity (*spec*) of a predicted MB to that of the true MB (Eq. 5). Thus, the smaller the distance, the closer the predicted MB is to the true MB.

$$dist = \sqrt{(1 - sen)^2 + (1 - spec)^2} \qquad (5)$$

The area under the Receiver Operating Characteristic (ROC) curve is calculated and serves as a measure of how well C5C and PC output the Markov Blanket with different thresholds. For C5C, we vary the frequency threshold, and for PC we vary the significance threshold. A one hundred percent area under the ROC curve equates to exactly identifying the Markov Blanket and fifty percent area is guessing.

5. Data Sets

5.1 Generated data from Bayesian Networks

A data set generated from the Alarm Network, a medical monitoring network, is used to explore how well the algorithms find the Markov Blankets for all of the

61

variables in the network. The alarm network has 37 variables, each of which has its own Markov Blanket.

The data set generated from the Hailfinder Network has 56 variables, which are used for severe weather forecasting [1].

The Insurance network has 27 variables and is used for estimating expected claim costs for insurance policies [6].

The data set generated from the Mildew Network has 35 variables, which determine amounts of fungicides to use against attacks of mildew on wheat.

The Barley data has 48 variables, which help predict yield and quality parameters for growing barley without pesticides [12].

5.2 Artificial Bayesian Network

A data set generated from an artificial Bayesian Network is used to explore the effect of the number of variables and the sample size upon the algorithms' ability to find the Markov Blanket. For this data set, the Markov Blanket is found for only one variable. The Markov Blanket for this variable has three parents, two children and one parent of a child for a total of six variables. The Markov Blanket for this variable is kept constant over the conditions of increasing noisy-variables and reduced sample size.

The above data sets are examined because their true Markov Blankets are known. Because the predicted Markov Blankets of the methods are compared against the true Markov Blankets, this is necessary.

6. Results

6.1 Comparisons between C5C and C5.0

In Table 1, the average sensitivity, specificity and distance over target variables for C5.0 and the best thresholds for C5C are listed for the first five Bayesian Networks. Table 1 illustrates that C5C's average predicted MB is closest to the true MB. Examining the sensitivity and specificity values, it appears that C5C's distances are improved by the increase in specificity without the loss of sensitivity. Discarding low frequency variables from the MB usually causes non-MB variables to be discarded.

Table 1. Average over target variables of sensitivity (sen), specificity (spec) and distance (dist) for C5.0 and the best thresholds for C5C. Data sets have 20,000 instances. The asterisk (*) denotes the mean distance for C5C is significantly different from C5.0 by the paired Wilcoxon signed rank test of the equality of means (p<0.05).

DATA SET	C5.0			C5C		
	Sen	Spec	Dist	Sen	Spec	Dist
ALARM	0.83	0.84	0.32	0.82	0.99	0.18*
HAILFINDER	0.81	0.27	0.89	0.80	0.98	0.22*
INSURANCE	0.89	0.46	0.64	0.78	0.93	0.25*
MILDEW	0.94	0.11	0.95	0.80	0.90	0.26*
BARLEY	0.84	0.43	0.67	0.76	0.94	0.28*

Table 2 shows that for 156 variables (75% of the total variables) C5C's predicted MB is closer to the true MB than C5.0's predicted MB. C5C is equal to C5.0 for the remaining 47 variables.

Table 2. Number of target variables (var) out of the total for each data set that the distance of C5C's best predicted MB is closer to the true MB than C5.0.

DATA SET	FREQ THAT C5C IS CLOSER TO TRUE MB THAN C5.0	TOTAL VAR
ALARM	15	37
HAILFINDER	46	56
INSURANCE	22	27
MILDEW	34	35
BARLEY	39	48

Table 3 shows the improvement in average distance over the 156 variables where C5C is closer to the true MB than C5.0. It also shows the reduction in the average predicted MB size from C5.0 to the best C5C thresholds.

Table 3. Average Markov Blanket size and average distance to the true MB for C5.0 and best threshold for C5C. The asterisk (*) denotes significance by the paired Wilcoxon signed rank test of the equality of means (p<0.05) in comparing C5.0 and C5C distance.

DATA SET	AVG MB SIZE		DISTANCE	
	C5.0	C5C	C5.0	C5C
ALARM	16	3	0.40	0.05*
HAILFINDER	49	4	0.93	0.12*
INSURANCE	19	6	0.67	0.20*
MILDEW	31	6	0.98	0.27*
BARLEY	34	7	0.73	0.22*

Table 3 also demonstrates that C5C reduces the size of the predicted MB more than C5.0. The quality of the predicted MB is of interest. This also supports the hypothesis that the low frequency variables tend to be non-Markov Blanket variables. This is why there can be such a reduction in the predicted MB size while improving the average distance.

6.2 C5C Identifying Markov Blanket variables

The results in Tables 1-3 show that C5C tends to rank MB variables higher than non-MB variables. Two methods that use C5C ranking of variables are tested in their ability to identify the MB: method one uses decision tree test set accuracy and method two uses the G^2 test.

For method one, C5.0 decision tree test set accuracy is assumed to improve when only MB variables are used in the training set. The filtered variable set with the best accuracy should correspond to the Markov Blanket because the Markov Blanket is the complete set of strongly relevant features. Variables are added to the training set for the decision tree starting with the variable(s) with the highest C5C ranking and proceeding to the lowest via a wrapper method [8]. The accuracy of the classifier is recorded for each of these subsets of variables. The subset with the highest test accuracy is proposed as the MB. The results in Table 4 are for running C5.0 with training set with sample size 16,000 for the training set and 4,000 for the test set.

The second method uses the G^2-test [18], to test for independence between two variables given a conditioning set (p < 0.05). A weakness of the G^2-test is that its validity is sensitive to the amount of sample. The larger the Markov Blanket conditioning set the more sample needed (i.e., sample grows exponentially with conditioning set size). For this method all variables with zero C5C frequency counts are classified as non-Markov Blanket variables. Then the n top ranked variables of C5C are proposed as the conditioning set for the G^2-test. The top k ranked variables (where $k > n$) are then tested for independence from the target variable given the conditioning set. This is a heuristic approach to identify a larger MB than the sample size supports for the G^2-test. If the variables are not independent, they are included in the final MB. Each variable in the conditioning set is then tested for independence given the other features in the conditioning set. Those that are not independent are included in the final MB. In Table 4 $n=4$ and $k=10$ and the sample size is 20,000. The conditioning set is size 4 because with a sample of 20,000 the G^2-test tends to be valid for the data sets examined. This can be increased with larger sample size or reduced with smaller sample size.

One of the benefits of the ordered C5C output is that it provides a subset of the variables (i.e., k variables with high frequency counts) to be examined for Markov Blanket candidacy. For the examined data sets, the parameter k is arbitrarily set to 10. To minimize the exclusion of Markov Blanket variables, it is recommended that k is greater than the expected quantity of Markov Blanket variables. For example, in some biological data set, Arnone [3], there are on average less than eight interacting variables, so $k = 10$ is reasonable and $k = 15$ would be more conservative. Since the assumption of C5C is that variables in the C5.0 rules reflect the Markov Blanket, all variables with zero frequency counts (i.e., they do not occur in C5.0 rules) are not considered candidates for the Markov Blanket. For some data sets examined, many of the variables in the C5C output have zero frequency.

Table 4. Average over target variables of sensitivity (sen), specificity (spec) and distance (dist) for C5C with the C5.0 decision tree test set accuracy determining threshold and the G^2-test identifying the MB. For the test accuracy the training set is 16,000 instances and the test set is 4,000 instances. The G^2-test uses 20,000 instances. The asterisk (*) and plus (+) denote the mean distance for the method is significantly different from C5.0 (Table 1) by the paired Wilcoxon signed rank test of the equality of means at $p<.05$ and $p< 0.1$, respectively.

DATA SET	C5C – TEST ACC.			C5C – G^2		
	Sen	Spec	Dist	Sen	Spec	Dist
ALARM	0.79	0.97	0.23	0.83	0.97	0.20+
HAILFINDER	0.76	0.95	0.27*	0.79	0.88	0.29*
INSURANCE	0.74	0.80	0.42*	0.76	0.88	0.31*
MILDEW	0.75	0.85	0.38*	0.78	0.80	0.35*
BARLEY	0.71	0.91	0.36*	0.76	0.87	0.31*

Table 4 shows that the two methods improve the identification of the MB over the C5.0 algorithm (see Table 1 C5.0 dist column). For some data sets the distances are close to the "best distance" (Table 1 C5C dist column), but both methods are significantly different from the "best distance". In comparing the two methods against each other they are not significantly different (p <0.05) except for Hailfinder and Insurance. This means the two methods are comparable in their ability to identify the MB.

6.3 Comparisons between C5C and PC

C5C and PC are run on the Bayesian Network data for each variable. The average area under the ROC is then computed for the algorithms by plotting the sensitivity and specificity values for the thresholds.

Six thresholds are used with C5C. The first threshold proposes all variables in the C5.0 rules as the Markov Blanket for the target variable (0% of variables in rules are excluded). The second threshold excludes from the Markov Blanket variables in the C5.0 rules whose counts are infrequent (20% of the most frequent feature count for the given target variable). For example, if the most frequent variable in the rules occurred 100 times, then the second threshold would exclude any variable in the C5.0 rules that occurred fewer than 20 times. The thresholds occur in 20% increments (i.e., 20%, 40%, 60%, 80% and 100%). The area under the ROC curve drops if C5.0 rules don't contain Markov Blanket variables or if infrequent variables in the C5.0 rules are part of the Markov Blanket.

It is computationally cheap to get multiple thresholds from C5.0's output file, unlike PC that must be run for each threshold, so a finer granularity of thresholds (one hundred and one) are examined to see if better ROC area can be obtained. The thresholds are incremented by 1% of the maximum count variable in the C5.0 rules.

The six thresholds for the PC algorithm are 0.005, 0.01, 0.02, 0.05, 0.10 and 0.20. These thresholds are significance levels for the G^2 test used by the algorithm. The smaller the threshold, the higher the confidence level that the variables are independent. This means the smaller the threshold, the fewer the number of edges removed from the fully connected graph used by PC to determine Markov Blankets. PC must be run separately for each threshold confidence level.

Table 5 shows that both PC and C5C performed comparatively well in finding the Markov Blankets for Alarm, Hailfinder and Insurance data sets (i.e., not significantly different) across both sets of thresholds.

C5C does better than PC on both the Mildew and Barley data sets for both thresholds (Table 5). This is because these data sets have variables with large value sets (100 values). This condition makes it difficult for PC to eliminate edges from the fully connected graph.

Table 5. Average ROC over all variables in Network: PC & C5C with 6 thresholds (T'holds) and C5C with 101 thresholds. Data sets have 20,000 instances. The asterisk (*) denotes the mean ROC for C5C as significantly different from PC by the paired Wilcoxon signed rank test (p<0.05).

DATA SET	TOTAL TARGETS	PC	C5C	
# OF T'HOLDS		6	6	101
ALARM	37	96.3	91.1	91.4
HAILFINDER	56	91.7	87.5	88.9
INSURANCE	27	82.0	86.3	88.0
MILDEW	35	64.3	80.0*	88.0*
BARLEY	48	50.0	81.6*	85.9*

In summary, Table 5 shows that C5C is not significantly different from PC for three data sets and is significantly better for two data sets. C5C behaves similarly with 6 and 101 thresholds so the distinction will be dropped in further analysis. Importantly, C5C can be

run on data with many more variables than is reasonable with PC.

6.4 C5C over increasing noisy-variables and reduced sample size

Figure 2 shows that PC and C5C have similar performance across sample size and number of variables. C5C appears to do better at smaller sample size across the number of variables. C5C's greedy nature works in its favor while PC tends to get lower ROC for small sample size because it starts with a fully connected graph and needs enough evidence to remove edges. If there is not enough evidence to remove edges, then specificity is low.

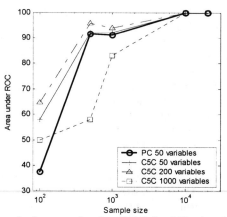

Figure 2. Area under the ROC for MB size 6 for PC with 50 variables and C5C with 50, 200 and 1,000 variables. The artificial Bayesian Network sample sizes are 100, 500, 1,000, 10,000 and 20,000 examples.

When there are a larger number of noisy variables (e.g., 1,000 variables), the C5C algorithm needs more data to distinguish the MB. Still, as Figure 2 demonstrates, C5C is able to find the Markov blanket for large sample and larger variable size.

C5C is also time-efficient. The largest computation (i.e., 1,000 variables for a sample size of 20,000) takes 30 seconds to perform on a 2.4GHz Xeon desktop machine for all thresholds.

7. Discussion

C5C is a simple modification to C5.0 that approximates the Markov Blanket as well as or better than C5.0 and PC in these experiments. Additionally, for the constructed Bayesian Network there is evidence that smaller sample sizes have good values of area under the ROC curve. This reduction in sample size could be due to the greedy nature of the algorithm. It chooses the best variables (usually Markov Blanket variables) given the small sample. The C5C algorithm is quick, in that it greedily hill climbs through the space of possible decision trees.

Note that the concept of causal structure within a data set is, in general, different than the goal of improving classification accuracy. C5.0 is designed to improve classification accuracy. Thus, there is no explicit bias encoded into the algorithm for finding causal structure. C5.0 outputs a decision tree and a set of rules with the goal of learning to classify the data set with highest accuracy.

7.1 Limitations

Due to this bias, the C5C algorithm is not able to find the Markov Blanket for target variables that occur a disproportionate number of times in one class. In such a case, C5.0 implementation uses default classification and assigns the variable to the majority class. This happens once in Insurance, twice in Barley and three times in Alarm. When a default classification occurs, no rules are formed so no variables can be part of the Markov Blanket. This cannot be remedied by changing the pruning level.

The C5C algorithm is not able to predict the Markov Blanket when one variable predicts the target variable without error, even though there are other variables in the Markov Blanket. The single variable becomes the only variable in the rules so all other variables are excluded from the Markov Blanket. Changing the pruning level does not affect the rules when one variable perfectly predicts the target variable. This happens for eight variables in Hailfinder. However, this is an unfaithful distribution because there are deterministic relationships in the data set.

A related approach is that of Li et al. [14] who use Genetic Algorithms and frequently occurring features in their classifiers to determine feature relevance in gene expression data. Their motivation is establishing a set of predictors that are robust to noise. C5C, even in non-noisy data, gives a good approximation of the MB.

7.2 Future Work

Recall that the task of feature selection is to find a subset that maintains the optimal classifier. Markov blankets have been mapped to the concept of strongly relevant features in feature selection [21]. Hence, this simple and scalable method for finding the Markov Blanket is widely applicable in the area of feature selection in machine learning and data mining.

The method of using the C5C ranking of features to identify the minimal feature subset for improvement in classification accuracy had some success (Table 4). The thresholds of C5C produce different filtered feature sets. These feature sets can be used as input into the C5.0 decision tree algorithm with cross-validated accuracy. The filtered feature set with the best accuracy should correspond to the Markov Blanket because the Markov Blanket is the complete set of strongly relevant features. G^2-test method generally performed better than the decision tree accuracy test. The MB from this test could also be used as a filtered feature set to improve classification accuracy.

Additional areas of future exploration are methods for selecting pruning levels and weighting the importance of features as opposed to straight counting. The weighting could include factors such as size of rule, accuracy of rule and its coverage.

8. Conclusion

It has been shown empirically that a simple post-processing step using the C5C algorithm performs at least as well as the PC algorithm when finding the Markov Blanket on the data sets compared. The method of using the ranked C5C variables in conjunction with performing G^2-tests (i.e., the cheapest of the two methods that we examined) can be used to identify the Markov Blanket variables. In addition, C5.0 scales up very well. Since C5.0 can be used to obtain the Markov Blanket right out of the box, applying this counting algorithm, C5C, for useful applications is a simple matter.

9. Acknowledgements

Support for this research was provided in part by NIH grant LM 007613-01.

10. Appendix

Denote d-separation of X and Y by Z in the graph of BN C, as $D_C(X ; Y | Z)$. Denote independent X and Y given Z in the probability distribution as $I(X;Y|Z)$. Denote the set of parents and children of T in the graph of BN C as $PC_C(T)$. Denote the set of the parents, children, and spouses of T in the graph of BN C as $MB_C(T)$.

Proposition 1: A faithful BN C is a perfect map of independencies and dependencies of the data. In other words, the d-separation criterion gives all the dependencies and independencies: $D_C(X;Y|Z) \Leftrightarrow I(X;Y|Z)$ [17].

Proposition 2: In a faithful BN C on variables V, X and T have a direct edge between them, if and only if $\forall S \subseteq V \backslash \{T,X\}, \neg I(X;T|S)$ [18].

Proposition 3: In any BN C on variables V, the set of parents, children, and spouses of T d-separates T from any other node in V [16].

Proposition 4: If BN N is faithful, then for every variable T, $MB(T)$ is unique and is the set of parents, children, and spouses of T [20].

Theorem 1. For any two BNs C and N, both faithful to the same distribution J on a variable set V, and for any variable T in that distribution, $PC_C(T) = PC_N(T)$ (i.e., the set $PC(T)$ is unique in all faithful BNs).

Proof: By Proposition 2 we get $X \in PC_C(T) \Leftrightarrow \forall S \subseteq V \backslash \{T, X\}, \neg I(X;T|S) \Leftrightarrow X \in PC_N(T)$.

Theorem 2: For any two BNs C and N, both faithful to the same distribution J on a variable set V, and for any variable T in that distribution, $MB_C(T) = MB_N(T)$ (i.e., the set $MB(T)$ is unique for all faithful BNs).

Proof: Let us denote the set of parents, children, and spouses of T in C with $MB'_C(T)$. By Proposition 4 we have that $MB'_C(T) = MB(T)$. By the same proposition we also have that $MB'_N(T) = MB(T)$. So, $MB'_C(T) = MB'_N(T)$.

11. References

[1] Abramson, B., Brown, J., Edwards, W., Murphy, A. and Winkler, R.L, Hailfinder: A Bayesian system for forecasting severe weather, *International Journal of Forecasting*, (1996), 12, 57-71.

[2] Aluallim, H., and Dietterich, T. G., Learning with many irrelevant features, *Proceedings, Ninth National Conference on Artificial Intelligence*, Anaheim, CA. AAAI Press/ The MIT Press, (1991), pp. 547-552.

[3] Arnone, M.I. and Davidson, E.H., The hardwiring of development: organization and function of genomic regulatory systems, *Development*, (1997), 12(4), pp. 1851-1864.

[4] Andersen, S.K., Olesen, K.G., Jensen, F. V. and Jensen, F., HUGIN - a shell for building bayesian belief universes for expert systems, in *Proceedings of the Eleventh International Joint Conference on Artificial Intelligence*, (1989), pp. 1080-1085.

[5] Beinlich, I., Suermondt, G., Chavez R. and Cooper G., The ALARM monitoring system: A case study with two probabilistic inference techniques for belief networks, *Proceedings of 2'nd European Conference on AI and Medicine*, Springer-Verlag, Berlin, (1989).

[6] Binder, J., Koller, D., Russell, S. and Kanazawa, K., Adaptive Probabilistic Networks with Hidden Variables, *Machine Learning*, (1997), 29, 213-244.

[7] Cardie, C., Using decision trees to improve case-based learning, in *Proceedings of the Tenth International Conference on Machine Learning*, (1993), pp. 25-32.

[8] Caruana, R. and D. Freitag, Greedy Attribute Selection, *in International Conference on Machine Learning*, (1994).

[9] Cheng, J., Greiner, R., Kelly, J., Bell D. and Liu, W., Learning Bayesian networks from data: an information-theory based approach, *Artificial Intelligence*, (2002), *137*, pp. 43-90.

[10] Glymour, C. & Cooper, G.F., *Computation, Causation and Discovery*, AAAI/The MIT Press, (1999) .

[11] Kohavi, R. and G.H. John, Wrappers for Feature Subset Selection, *Artificial Intelligence*, (1997), 97(1-2), pp. 273-324.

[12] Kristensen, K. and Rasmussen, I.A., The use of a Bayesian network in the design of a decision support system for growing malting barley without use of pesticides, *Computers and Electronics in Agriculture*, (2002), 33, pp. 197-217.

[13] Koller, D and M. Sahami, Toward Optimal Feature Selection, in *Thirteenth International Conference in Machine Learning*, (1996), pp. 284-292.

[14] Li, L., Pedersen, L.G., Darden, T.A. and Weinberg, C.R., Computational Analysis of Leukemia Micorarray Expression Data Using the GA/KNN Method, CAMDA'01, (2001).

[15] Margaritis, D. and Thrun, S., Bayesian Network Induction via Local Neighborhoods, Technical Report: CMU-CS-99-134, (1999).

[16] Neapolitan, R.E., *Probabilistic Reasoning in Expert Systems: Theory and Algorithms*, John Wiley and Sons (1990).

[17] Pearl, J., *Probabilistic Reasoning in Intelligent Systems*, San Mateo, CA: Morgan Kaufman, (1988).

[18] Spirtes, P., C. Glymour, and R. Scheines, *Causation, Prediction and Search*, Cambridge, MA: MIT Press, (2000).

[19] Quinlan, J.R., Induction of decision trees, *Machine Learning*, (1987), 1 pp. 81-106.

[20] Tsamardinos, I. and Aliferis, C.F., Towards Principled Feature Selection: Relevancy, Filters and Wrappers, in *Proceedings of the Ninth International Workshop on Artificial Intelligence and Statistics*, (2003).

[21] Tsamardinos, I., Aliferis, C.F. and Statnikov, A., Algorithms for Large Scale Markov Blanket Discovery to appear, in *Proceedings of the 16th International FLAIRS Conference*, (2003).

[22] Tsamardinos, I., Aliferis, C. F., and Statnikov A., Time and Sample Efficient Discovery of Markov Blankets and Direct Causal Relations, in *The Ninth ACM SIGKDD International Conference on Knowledge Discovery and Data Mining*, (2003).

Reliable Detection of Episodes in Event Sequences

Robert Gwadera [*]
Purdue University
Department of Computer Sciences
West Lafayette, Indiana
gwadera@cs.purdue.edu

Mikhail Atallah [†]
Purdue University
Department of Computer Sciences
West Lafayette, Indiana
mja@cs.purdue.edu

Wojciech Szpankowski [‡]
Purdue University
Department of Computer Sciences
West Lafayette, Indiana
spa@cs.purdue.edu

Abstract

Suppose one wants to detect "bad" or "suspicious" subsequences in event sequences. Whether an observed pattern of activity (in the form of a particular subsequence) is significant and should be a cause for alarm, depends on how likely it is to occur fortuitously. A long enough sequence of observed events will almost certainly contain any subsequence, and setting thresholds for alarm is an important issue in a monitoring system that seeks to avoid false alarms. Suppose a long sequence T of observed events contains a suspicious subsequence pattern S within it, where the suspicious subsequence S consists of m events and spans a window of size w within T. We address the fundamental problem: is a certain number of occurrences of a particular subsequence unlikely to be fortuitous (i.e., indicative of suspicious activity)? If the probability of fortuitous occurrences is high and an automated monitoring system flags it as suspicious anyway, then such a system will suffer from generating too many false alarms. This paper quantifies the probability of such an S occurring in T within a window of size w, the number of distinct windows containing S as a subsequence, the expected number of such occurrences, its variance, and establishes its limiting distribution that allows to set up an alarm threshold so that the probability of false alarms is very small. We report on experiments confirming the theory and showing that we can detect bad subsequences with low false alarm rate.

1. Introduction

Detecting subsequence patterns in event sequences is important in many applications, including intrusion detection, monitoring for suspicious activities, and molecular biology (e.g., see [10, 13, 18, 19]). Whether an observed pattern of activity is significant or not (i.e., whether it should be a cause for alarm) depends on how likely it is to occur fortuitously. A long enough sequence of observed events will almost certainly contain any subsequence, and setting thresholds for alarm is an important issue in a monitoring system that seeks to avoid false alarms.

The basic question is then: *when is a certain number of occurrences of a particular subsequence unlikely to be fortuitous (i.e., indicative of suspicious activity)?* A quantitative analysis of this question helps one to set a *threshold* so that real "intrusions" are detected and false alarms are avoided. Setting the threshold too low will lead to too many false alarms, whereas setting the threshold too high can result in failure to detect. By knowing the most likely number of occurrences and the probability of deviating from it, we can set a threshold such that the probability of missing real suspicious activities is small. Such a quantitative analysis can also help to choose the size of the sliding window of observation. Finally even in a court case one cannot consider certain observed "bad" activity as a convincing evidence against somebody if that activity is quite likely to

---

[*] The work of this author was supported by the NSF Grant CCR-0208709.

[†] Portions of this work were supported by Grants EIA-9903545, IIS-0325345, IIS-0219560, IIS-0312357, and IIS-0242421 from the National Science Foundation, Contract N00014-02-1-0364 from the Office of Naval Research, by sponsors of the Center for Education and Research in Information Assurance and Security, and by Purdue Discovery Park's e-enterprise Center.

[‡] The work of this author was supported by the NSF Grant CCR-0208709, and NIH grant R01 GM068959-01.

occur under given circumstances. Therefore it is very important to quantify such probabilities and present a universal and reliable framework for analyzing a variety of event sources.

Let T be an ordered sequence of events (time-ordered events in a computer system, transactions in a database, purchases made, web sites visited, phone calls made, or combinations of these). Systems designed to detect "bad things" in T usually do not look at the whole of T, they usually involve a sliding "window of observation" (of size, say, w) within which the analysis is confined. This is done for two reasons: (i) T is usually too long, and without a limited window approach it would involve having to save too much state, and (ii) T can be so long (e.g., in a continuously monitoring system) that *any* subsequence (bad or good) would likely occur within it. As an example of the need to confine the analysis to such a limited sliding window, note that three failed login attempts (with failure due to wrong password) are significant if they occur in rapid succession, but quite innocuous if they occur within a one-month interval. In this study we do not use the notion of real calendar time such as a "one month interval", instead we use the number of events as a proxy for time. This is why our interval length w is not the difference between two time stamps, but rather the size of a (contiguous) substring of T.

More formally consider an alphabet $\mathcal{A}$ of cardinality $|\mathcal{A}|$, an infinite event sequence $T = t_1 t_2 \ldots$ over $\mathcal{A}$ and an episode over $\mathcal{A}$ in one of the following forms: either a single pattern $S = s_1 s_2 \ldots s_m$ of length m, or a set of patterns $S_1, S_2, \ldots, S_d$, or the set of all distinct permutations of S; this last case captures situations where the ordering of the events within the window of observation does not matter, e.g., for the two events "bought a large amount of fertilizer" and "bought an assault rifle" it may not matter which one occurred first. We use a positive integer $w \geq m$ to represent the length of the window of observation. We assume that the pattern S is given while the event sequence is generated by a memoryless (Bernoulli) or Markov source. Our interest is in finding $\Omega^{\exists}(n, w, m)$ that represents the number of windows containing *at least one* occurrence of S when sliding the window along n consecutive events of T. Based on the observed value of $\Omega^{\exists}(n, w, m)$ our task is to decide whether a suspicious activity took place or not. In this conference paper we analyze only the Bernoulli model.

We study the probabilistic behavior of $\Omega^{\exists}(n, w, m)$. We first compute the expected value of $\Omega^{\exists}(n, w, m)$, its variance, and then show that, appropriately normalized $\Omega^{\exists}(n, w, m)$ converges in distribution to the standard normal distribution. This will allow us to set up a threshold $\tau(n, m, w)$ such that for a given confidence level β we assure that $P\{\Omega^{\exists}(n, w, m) > \tau(n, m, w)\} < \beta$. That is, if one observes more than $\tau(n, m, w)$ occurrences of windows with suspicious subsequences, it is highly unlikely that such a number is generated by randomness (i.e., its probability is smaller than β). We also design the window size w so that the suspicious subsequence does not occur almost surely in any window. This is necessary to reliably set up the threshold.

We verify our theoretical results by running an extensive series of experiments. One set of experiments is run on an on-line version of *War and Peace*, as an example of English text source. In another experiment we use web-logs obtained from http://www.cs.washington.edu/ai/adaptive-data/ that contains user accesses to the music machines web site (currently at http://machines.hyperreal.org) from 1/01/99 through 4/30/99. We first show that our formula for the probability approximates very well the experimental one. Then we insert randomly some sequences, defined as "suspicious", and detect them through our threshold mechanism.

Pattern matching has been used in a number of applications. In most applications, however, *substring* pattern matching was applied, in which an "occurrence" is when the pattern symbols occur contiguously in the text. Kumar and Spafford [10] applied subsequence pattern matching to intrusion detection. Atallah and Apostolico [2] designed a fast algorithm to detect subsequences in a text, while Flajolet *et al.* [7] presented a precise statistical analysis of the subsequence problem. In [11] Mannila *et al.* discussed the problem of episode matching and counted the number of windows containing episodes as a subsequence. The authors in [11] also showed the effect of the window width on the number of frequent episodes. Following [11] we consider and analyze the *windowed* version of the subsequence problem. Papers [4, 9] introduced the *Window-Accumulated Subsequence Matching Problem (WASP)* and counted all w-windows within which the pattern is a subsequence of event sequence. None of the above work provides probabilistic analysis that quantifies $\Omega^{\exists}(n, w, m)$.

The paper is organized as follows. In section 2 we present our main results containing theoretical foundation. Section 3 contains experimental results demonstrating the applicability of the derived formulas. In derivation of our results we used analytic tools of analysis of algorithms such as generating functions and complex asymptotic (cf. [16, 17]). However, because of space limitations, we skip most of the derivations and proofs. Interested readers can find them in [8].

2. Main Results

Given an alphabet $\mathcal{A} = \{a_1, a_2, \ldots, a_{|\mathcal{A}|}\}$ and a pattern $S = s_1 s_2 \ldots s_m$ of length m, we search for some occurrences of S as a subsequence within a window of size w in another sequence known as the event sequence

$T = t_1 t_2 \ldots$. A valid occurrence of S in T corresponds to a set of integers $i_1, i_2, \ldots, i_m$ such that the following conditions hold:

1. $1 \le i_1 < i_2 < \ldots < i_m$
2. $t_{i_1} = s_1, t_{i_2} = s_2, \ldots t_{i_m} = s_m$
3. $i_m - i_1 < w$.

The first two conditions above state that S is a subsequence of T, while the last condition guarantees that S is a subsequence of T within the window of length w.

It is of interest to estimate $\Omega^\exists(n, w, m, S, \mathcal{A})$ that represents the number of windows of length w containing *at least one* occurrence of S when sliding the window n consecutive events in the event sequence $T..$

Notation: Throughout the paper we drop S and $\mathcal{A}$ in the notation $\Omega^\exists(n, w, m, S, \mathcal{A})$ using $\Omega^\exists(n, w, m)$ instead (S and $\mathcal{A}$ are implied). We use the same rule for all other variables depending on w, m, S and $\mathcal{A}$. We also use $m - k$ instead of m, which means "dropping the last k symbols of S", e.g., $P^\exists(w, m - k)$ implies a pattern that is the prefix of S of length $m - k$.

Based on the observed value of $\Omega^\exists(n, w, m)$ our task is to decide whether a suspicious activities took place or not. We shall find a threshold $\tau(n, w, m)$ such that, for any given β (e.g., $\beta = 10^{-5}$) the following holds

$$P\{\Omega^\exists(n, w, m) > \tau(n, m, w)\} \quad < \quad \beta.$$

Another interesting problem is the selection of parameters of a monitoring system, in particular the size of the window so one can design properly the system (e.g., to make sure that a pattern does not occur almost surely in every window).

We answer these questions in this paper, by assuming that the event sequence is generated by a memoryless (Bernoulli) source, i.e., symbols are generated independently of each others with probability $P(a_i)$ for any $a_i \in \mathcal{A}$.

We need to analyze $\Omega^\exists(n, w, m)$ in order to find the above mentioned threshold. We will prove here that appropriately normalized $\Omega^\exists(n, w, m)$ is normally distributed. We also find the mean and the variance of $\Omega^\exists(n, w, m)$.

We start with computing the mean value $\mathbf{E}[\Omega^\exists(n, w, m)]$. Clearly, it is equal to

$$\mathbf{E}[\Omega^\exists(n, w, m)] \quad = \quad nP^\exists(w, m)$$

where $P^\exists(w, m)$ is the probability that a window of size w contains at least one occurrence of the episode S of size m as a subsequence.

2.1. Analysis of $P^\exists(w, m)$

The probability $P^\exists(w, m)$ satisfies the following recurrence

$$\begin{cases} P^\exists(w, m) &= (1 - p_m)P^\exists(w - 1, m) + \\ & \quad p_m P^\exists(w - 1, m - 1) \quad w > 0, m > 0 \\ P^\exists(w, 0) &= 1 \quad w > 0 \\ P^\exists(0, m) &= 0 \quad m > 0 \\ P^\exists(0, 0) &= 1. \end{cases}$$

Indeed, consider a window of size $w - 1$. Observe that either the last symbol of the pattern, s_m, does not occur at the w-th position of the window or it does occur. In the former situation S must occur within the window of size $w - 1$ leading to the term $(1 - p_m)P^\exists(w - 1, m)$ of the above recurrence. The latter situation provides the second term of the recurrence.

We used the method of generating functions to find the solution for $P^\exists(w, m)$. Then we applied Cauchy's residue theorem to obtain an asymptotic expansion of $P^\exists(w, m)$ for fixed m and large w. We summarized our results in the next theorem. A full proof is given in the full version of the paper [8]. In this paper we present only the proof of the asymptotic approximation.

Theorem 1 *Consider a memoryless source with p_i being the probability of generating the i-th symbol of S and $q_i = 1 - p_i$. Let also*

$$P(S) = \prod_{i=1}^{m} p_i$$

Then for all m and $w \ge m$ we have

$$P^\exists(w, m) \quad = \quad P(S) \sum_{i=0}^{w-m} \sum_{\sum_{k=0}^{m} n_k = i} \prod_{k=1}^{m} q_k^{n_k}.$$

Let now m be fixed and assume $i \ne j$ implies $p_i \ne p_j$. Then

$$P^\exists(w, m) \quad \sim \quad 1 - P(S) \sum_{i=1}^{m} \frac{(1 - p_i)^w}{p_i} \prod_{j \ne i}^{m} \frac{1}{p_j - p_i}$$

as $w \to \infty$.

Proof:
Let $W_m(x) = \sum_{w=0}^{\infty} P^\exists(w, m)x^w$. Then, using the above recurrence for $P^\exists(w, m)$ we have

$$\begin{cases} W_m(x) &= q_m \sum_{w=1} P^\exists(w - 1, m)x^w + \\ & \quad p_m \sum_{w=1} P^\exists(w - 1, m - 1)x^w \quad m > 0 \\ W_0(x) &= \sum_{w=0} P^\exists(w, 0)x^w. \end{cases}$$

From the above we derive, after some algebra,

$$W_m(z) = P(S)z^m \prod_{i=1}^{m} \frac{1}{(1 - q_i z)} \frac{1}{(1 - z)}.$$

Observe that the exact value of $P^\exists(w,m)$ is equal to the coefficient of $W_m(x)$ at x^w which we denote as $[x^w]W_m(x)$. By the Cauchy theorem (cf. [17]) we find

$$P^\exists(w,m) = [z^w]W_m(z) = \frac{1}{2\pi i}\oint W_m(z)z^{-w-1}dz$$
$$= -\sum_p Res[W_m(z)z^{-w-1}, z=p] + O(r^{-w})$$
$$= -Res[W_m(z)z^{-w-1}, z=1]-$$
$$\sum_{i=0}^m Res\left[W_m(z)z^{-w-1}, z=\frac{1}{q_i}\right]$$

where $Res[f(z), z=a]$ is the residue of $f(z)$ at $z=a$. In particular, standard analysis reveals ([17])

$$Res[W_m(z)z^{-w-1}, z=1] =$$
$$P(S)1^{m-w-1}\prod_{i=1}^m \frac{1}{(1-q_i)}(-1) = -1$$

and

$$Res\left[W_m(z)z^{-w-1}, z=\frac{1}{q_i}\right] =$$
$$(-1)\frac{1}{q_i}P(S)\left(\frac{1}{q_i}\right)^{m-w-1}\prod_{j\neq i}^m \frac{1}{\left(1-\frac{q_j}{q_i}\right)}\frac{1}{1-\frac{1}{q_i}}$$
$$= P(S)\frac{(1-p_i)^w}{p_i}\prod_{j\neq i}^m \frac{1}{p_j-p_i}.$$

Combining everything we finally obtain

$$P^\exists(w,m) \sim 1 - P(S)\sum_{i=1}^m \frac{(1-p_i)^w}{p_i}\prod_{j\neq i}^m \frac{1}{p_j-p_i}$$

for large w □.

We also propose a dynamic programming equation for computing $P^\exists(w,m)$. Let $Q^n(j)$ denote the product $\prod_{k=1}^j q_k^{n_k}$ such that $\sum_{k=1}^j n_k = n$ then

$$\begin{cases} Q^n(j) &= \sum_{k=1}^n Q^{n-k}(j-1)q_j^k & 1\le j\le m \\ Q^n(1) &= q_1^n & \\ Q^0(j) &= 1 & 1\le j\le m \\ P^\exists(w,m) &= P(S)\sum_{k=0}^{w-m} Q^k(m). \end{cases}$$

The time complexity of the algorithm is $O((w-m)*m)$ and is equal to the space required to build the table for $Q^{w-m}(m)$.

When establishing the above formulas for $P^\exists(w,m)$ we also solved two related combinatorial problems on strings that are of interest. Namely, given $\mathcal{A}$, w and S:

1. Construct the set $\mathcal{W}^\exists(w,m)$ of all windows as strings of length w over $\mathcal{A}$ containing all possible occurrences of S as a subsequence.

2. Find the cardinality of $\mathcal{W}^\exists(w,m)$, that we denote $C^\exists(w,m)$.

2.2. Analysis of $\mathcal{W}^\exists(w,m)$

Let $\mathcal{W}^\exists(w,m)$ be the *set* (enumeration) of all distinct windows of length w containing S as a subsequence. Let $\mathcal{W}^\exists(w,m)[i]$ be the i-th string of $\mathcal{W}^\exists(w,m)$ if

the strings were ordered lexicographically. Then we can express $P^\exists(w,m)$ as follows

$$P^\exists(w,m) = \sum_{i=1}^{|\mathcal{W}^\exists(w,m)|} P(\mathcal{W}^\exists(w,m)[i]).$$

The recursive formula for $\mathcal{W}^\exists(w,m)$ has the following form

$$\begin{cases} \mathcal{W}^\exists(w,m) &= (\mathcal{A}-\{s_m\})\times \mathcal{W}^\exists(w-1,m)\cup \\ & \quad \{s_m\}\times \mathcal{W}^\exists(w-1,m-1)\ w,m>0 \\ \mathcal{W}^\exists(w,0) &= \mathcal{A}^w \quad w>0 \\ \mathcal{W}^\exists(0,m) &= 0 \quad m>0 \\ \mathcal{W}^\exists(0,0) &= 1. \end{cases}$$

Indeed, this can be established by a combinatorial argument. We need to show that we enumerate all distinct elements of $\mathcal{W}^\exists(w,m)$. That we generate distinct elements at each level of the recursion is obvious since we partition $\mathcal{W}^\exists(w,m)$ into two subsets: strings having s_m as the last symbol and those that do not. Now we show that we generate all strings. Consider the enumeration of all $\binom{w}{m}$ positions of S as a subsequence in a window of length w. We enumerate the positions using *reverse lex* order, i.e., $(i_1,i_2,\ldots,i_m)$ is before $(i_1',i_2',\ldots,i_m')$ if for some j, $1<j\le m$, $(i_j,i_2,\ldots,i_m)=(i_j',i_2',\ldots,i_m')$ and $i_{j-1}<i_{j-1}'$.

Therefore $\mathcal{W}^\exists(w,m)$ can be split into two subsets:

1. Windows having s_m on the last position. But then if we remove the last symbol from this subset of $\mathcal{W}^\exists(w,m)$ we must create $\mathcal{W}^\exists(w-1,m-1)$.

2. Windows not having s_m on the last position. But then if we remove the last symbol from this subset we must create $\mathcal{W}^\exists(w-1,m)$.

Theorem 2 *The set of all distinct windows of length w containing S of length m as a subsequence can be enumerated as follows*

$$\mathcal{W}^\exists(w,m) = \bigcup_{\substack{\sum_{k=1}^{m+1} n_k = w-m}} (\mathcal{A}-s_1)^{n_1}\times\{s_1\}\times$$
$$(\mathcal{A}-s_2)^{n_2}\times\{s_2\}\times\ldots\times$$
$$(\mathcal{A}-s_m)^{n_m}\times\{s_m\}\times\mathcal{A}^{n_{m+1}}.$$

Using Theorem 2 we can compute $P^\exists(w,m)$ for Markov model of any order.

2.3. Analysis of $C^\exists(w,m)$

The recurrence for $C^\exists(w,m)$ follows directly form the one for $\mathcal{W}^\exists(w,m)$.

$$\begin{cases} C^\exists(w,m) &= (|\mathcal{A}|-1)C^\exists(w-1,m)+ \\ & \quad C^\exists(w-1,m-1) & w,m>0 \\ C^\exists(w,0) &= |\mathcal{A}|^w & w>0 \\ C^\exists(0,m) &= 0 & m>0 \\ C^\exists(0,0) &= 1. \end{cases}$$

Theorem 3 *The number of all windows of length w which contain at least one occurrence of a pattern of length m does not depend on the symbols of the pattern and is equal to:*

$$C^{\exists}(w,m) = \sum_{k=0}^{w-m} \binom{k+m-1}{k}(|\mathcal{A}|-1)^k |\mathcal{A}|^{w-m-k}.$$

2.4. Analysis of $\tau(n,w,m)$

Let us now come back to $\Omega^{\exists}(n,w,m)$ and establish its normal limiting distribution. Observe that

$$\Omega^{\exists}(n,w,m) = \sum_{i=1}^{n} X_i^{\exists}$$

where

$$X_i^{\exists} = \begin{cases} 1 & \text{if } S \text{ occurs at least once as a subsequence in} \\ & \text{the window of length } w \text{ ending at position } i \text{ in } T \\ 0 & \text{otherwise.} \end{cases}$$

and easily we have $\mathbf{E}[X_i^{\exists}] = P^{\exists}(w,m)$ and $\mathbf{Var}[X_i^{\exists}] = P^{\exists}(w,m) - (P^{\exists}(w,m))^2$.

Let $P^{\exists}_{(X_i^{\exists} \cap X_j^{\exists})}(w,m,k)$ be the probability that two overlapping windows at respective position i and j for $|i-j| = k < w$ have $X_i^{\exists} = 1$ and $X_j^{\exists} = 1$.

The variance can be expressed as follows

$$\mathbf{Var}[\Omega^{\exists}(n,w,m)] = n\mathbf{Var}[X_1^{\exists}] +$$
$$2\sum_{1 \leq i < j \leq n}^{n} \mathbf{Cov}[X_i^{\exists}, X_j^{\exists}] = n\mathbf{Var}[X_1^{\exists}] +$$
$$2(n-w+1)\sum_{k=1}^{w-1}\left[P^{\exists}_{(X_i^{\exists} \cap X_j^{\exists})}(w,m,k) - (P^{\exists}(w,m))^2 \right]$$
$$+2\sum_{k=1}^{w-2}\left[P^{\exists}_{(X_i^{\exists} \cap X_j^{\exists})}(w,m,k) - (P^{\exists}(w,m))^2 \right].$$

The two terms involving $P^{\exists}_{(X_i^{\exists} \cap X_j^{\exists})}(w,m,k)$ in the above formula represent correlation between windows (with $2(w-1)$ neighborhood). $P^{\exists}_{(X_i^{\exists} \cap X_j^{\exists})}(w,m,k)$ can be computed from Theorem 2. One concludes, however, that $\mathbf{Var}[\Omega^{\exists}(n,w,m)] \sim n\sigma$ for some $\sigma > 0$.

In view of the above, and using the fact that $\Omega^{\exists}(n,w,m)$ is the so called m-dependent sequence (i.e., $\Omega^{\exists}(n,w,m)$ depends on the last $w-1$ windows), we may apply Theorem 27.5 of [3] to establish the central limit theorem for $\Omega^{\exists}(n,w,m)$, as stated below.

Theorem 4 *The random variable $\Omega^{\exists}(n,w,m)$ obeys the Central Limit Theorem in the sense that its distribution is asymptotically normal, for $a,b = O(1)$ we have*

$$\lim_{n \to \infty} P\left\{ a < \frac{\Omega^{\exists}(n,w,m) - \mathbf{E}[\Omega^{\exists}(n,w,m)]}{\sqrt{\mathbf{Var}[\Omega^{\exists}(n,w,m)]}} < b \right\} =$$
$$\frac{1}{\sqrt{2\pi}}\int_a^b e^{\frac{-t^2}{2}}dt$$

for m and w fixed.

We convert the above to a more useful form representing it as follows

$$\begin{cases} P\left\{\Omega^{\exists}(n,w,m) > x(a)\right\} &= y(a) \\ x(a) &= a\sqrt{\mathbf{Var}[\Omega^{\exists}(n,w,m)]} + \\ & \quad \mathbf{E}[\Omega^{\exists}(n,w,m)] \\ y(a) &= \frac{1}{\sqrt{2\pi}}\int_a^\infty e^{\frac{-t^2}{2}}dt. \end{cases}$$

Knowing that the distribution of $\Omega^{\exists}(n,w,m)$ around the mean is normal within *finite* number of standard deviations $\sqrt{\mathbf{Var}[\Omega^{\exists}(n,w,m)]}$ we can compute the threshold $\tau(n,w,m) = x(a_0)$.

3. Experimental Results

The purpose of our experiments was to test the applicability of the analytical results we derived for sources that are apparently not memoryless, i.e., they do not satisfy the assumptions under which the formulas for memoryless source were derived. We of course do not need to test the formulas for memoryless sources, because we already know the equations hold in such cases. Therefore we ran the experiments for an English text source and also for web access data.

An English text is of course not memoryless. As an example consider string "th" which occurs more frequently than "tz" or "ts". So in this example the letter "h" will occur more likely if the previous letter was "t". However, English text can be modeled well by a Markov source.

The web accesses are also not memoryless not only because of hierarchical structure but also because of correlations between links. For example a person looking for a product in an on-line store will most likely visit all manufacturers of the search product.

We divided our sources into training sets and testing sets. Training sets are data sets, which we consider to constitute normal behavior for the environment from which the data were drawn. Once the training data has been characterized, which in our case means our probability model has been built, we can start monitoring unknown data called testing data. During the monitoring process the testing data are compared to expectations generated by the training data.

Thus, the main focus of our experiments was to test how well the formula for $P^{\exists}(w,m)$ works for apparently non memoryless sources, since it is the corner stone of our theory. To accomplish this we estimated the actual probability of existence based on the actual number of windows $\Omega^{\exists}(n,w,m)$ as $P_e^{\exists}(w,m) = \frac{\Omega^{\exists}(n,w,m)}{n}$ and compared its value to the computed $P^{\exists}(w,m)$ for different values of w. We used the following error metric d

$$d = \left[\frac{1}{r}\sum_{i=1}^{r}\frac{|P_e^{\exists}(w_i,m) - P^{\exists}(w_i,m)|}{P_e^{\exists}(w_i,m)}\right]100\%$$

where $w_1 < w_2 < \dots w_r$ are the tested window sizes.

We used an algorithm, based on dynamic programming, for finding windowed subsequences. We also implemented the dynamic programming solution to $P^\exists(w, m)$ given in chapter 2. We converted the sources appropriately to a special text file format that was used by the algorithm implemented in C++ and run under Linux.

3.1. English text source

The text source we used is an on-line version of *War and Peace* by Leo Tolstoy from www.friends-partners. org/newfriends/culture/literature/war_ and_peace/war-peace_intro.html. The work consists of 15 books. Each book has over 20 chapters each of which consists of over 5000 letters. We preprocessed the chapters in order to remove all symbols but 26 letters of the English alphabet without distinguishing between upper and lower case letters.

In this experiment we compared the analytically computed $P^\exists(w, m)$ (cf. Theorem 1) with its estimator $P_e^\exists(w, m) = \frac{\Omega^\exists(n,w,m)}{n}$. We used chapter 1-5 as a training set for estimation of $p_1, p_2, \dots p_m$ based on the symbol frequencies. We set $S = gwadera$ and for each w in the range $13 - 600$ we ran the algorithm for finding $\Omega^\exists(n, w, m)$ in chapter 6 as the testing source. Figures 1 and 2 illustrate the results showing two main facts: $P^\exists(w, m)$ approaches 1 as w goes to infinity and $P^\exists(w, m)$ very closely reflects the real $P_e^\exists(w, m)$ since the difference d between them equals 12%.

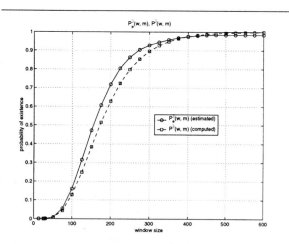

Figure 1. $P_e^\exists(w, m) = \frac{\Omega^\exists(n,w,m)}{n}$ and $P^\exists(w, m)$ for $S = gwadera$

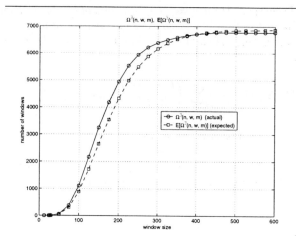

Figure 2. $\Omega^\exists(n, w, m)$ and $\mathbf{E}[\Omega^\exists(n, w, m)]$ for $S = gwadera$

In the next experiment we estimated variance of $\Omega^\exists(n, w, m)$ denoted $\widehat{\mathbf{Var}}[\Omega^\exists(n, w, m)]$. For this purpose we randomly chose 8 chapters and shortened them to the same length 8000 letters creating 8 training sources denoted $T_1, T_2, \dots, T_8$ and one testing source T_9. We used the following sample mean and variance estimators

$$\widehat{\mathbf{E}}[\Omega^\exists(n, w, m)] = \frac{\sum_{i=1}^{8} \Omega^\exists(n,w,m)_i}{8}$$

$$\sqrt{\widehat{\mathbf{Var}}[\Omega^\exists(n, w, m)]} = \sqrt{\frac{\sum_{i=1}^{8}(\Omega^\exists(n,w,m)_i - \widehat{\mathbf{E}}[\Omega^\exists(n,w,m)])^2}{7}}.$$

for $S = wojciech$ and $w = 100$. In particular, we set $\tau(n, w, m) = \mathbf{E}[\Omega^\exists(n, w, m)] + 5\sqrt{\widehat{\mathbf{Var}}[\Omega^\exists(n, w, m)]}$, that is, $a_0 = 5$.

Now we know what the normal behavior is in terms of $\Omega^\exists(n, w, m)$ given $S = wojciech$ and $w = 100$. We used such a trained model to monitor T_9 as the testing set. To verify our threshold experimentally we artificially kept injecting $S = wojciech$ as a subsequence into different places in T_9. After each insertion we ran the algorithm for finding $\Omega^\exists(n, w, m)$ and checked whether we exceeded $\tau(n, w, m)$. To make it more interesting we considered two values of gaps between inserted symbols of S: $gap = 0$ and $gap = 11$. In other words we injected S as $s_1 \#^{gap} s_2 \#^{gap} \dots \#^{gap} s_m$, where $\#$ means a do not care symbol. The results are shown in Figure 3, where $\tau(n, w, m) = 125$, $\widehat{\mathbf{E}}[\Omega^\exists(n, w, m)] = 27.88$ and $\sqrt{\widehat{Var}[\Omega^\exists(n, w, m)]} = 19.45$. The horizontal dash-dot line shows $\mathbf{E}[\Omega^\exists(n, w, m)] = 27.88$ for no insertions. We can see that if $gap = 0$, then we need only two patterns to exceed $\tau(n, w, m)$ versus three if $gap = 11$. This makes sense if we notice that if the pattern is stretched to the window boundaries ($gap = 11$) then it is more noise-like compared to the case when $gap = 0$, which suggests an intentional action (attack) and should be detected early. Furthermore notice that for the training set $\widehat{\mathbf{E}}[\Omega^{\exists}(n, w, m)] = 27.88$ and $\sqrt{\widehat{\mathbf{Var}}[\Omega^{\exists}(n, w, m)]} = 19.45$ so by injecting two episodes for ($gap = 11$) we really did not go beyond the normal behavior.

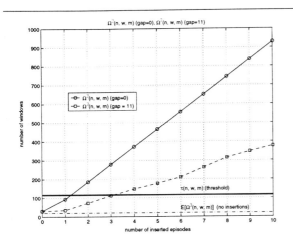

Figure 3. Detection of artificially inserted pattern *wojciech*

3.2. Web access data

We used logs of user accesses to the music machines web site (currently at `http://machines.hyperreal.org`), which record accesses from 1/01/99 through 4/30/99 . The logs have been anonymized with respect to originating machines. That is, in each hit, the IP address of the machine generating the server request has been converted to a random looking number. All hits from one machine on a particular day are labeled with the same number. In the experiments we focused on `http://machines.hyperreal.org/manufacturers/` web page containing links to manufacturers of music instruments. Each link corresponds to an alphabet symbol and the alphabet size was $|A| = 81$. The training and testing sequences were created by considering only unique accesses made by the same originating machine. If a given host made many accesses to the same manufacturer per session then we treated it as one access and considered the first access only.

In the first experiment we compared the computed $P^{\exists}(w, m)$ with its estimator $P_e^{\exists}(w, m) = \frac{\Omega^{\exists}(n, w, m)}{n}$. We created three sources T_1, T_2, T_3. The training set estab-

lished T_1, T_2 and the testing source was T_3. We set $S = \{Akai, ARP, Korg, Moog, Yamaha, Casio, Sequential\}$ and for each w in the range $25 - 500$ we ran the algorithm for finding $\Omega^{\exists}(n, w, m)$ on T_3. Figures 4 and 5 illustrate the results. $P^{\exists}(w, m)$ still provides a good approximation of $P_e^{\exists}(w, m)$ ($d = 18\%$). The reason the value of d is bigger than for the text source is the fact that the web accesses are a more memory dependent source than English text. Therefore the Markov model seems to be more suitable for the web access source.

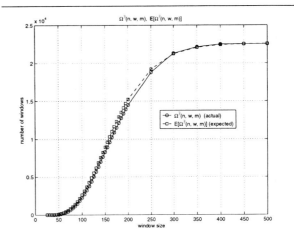

Figure 4. $\Omega^{\exists}(n, w, m)$ **and** $\mathrm{E}[\Omega^{\exists}(n, w, m)]$ **number of occurrences for the web access data**

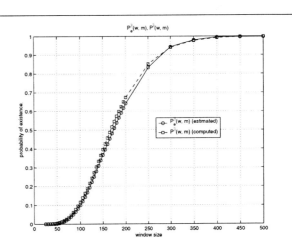

Figure 5. $P_e^{\exists}(w, m) = \frac{\Omega^{\exists}(n, w, m)}{n}$ **and computed** $P^{\exists}(w, m)$ **for the web access data**

4. Conclusion

We presented an exact formula for $P^\exists(w, m)$, the probability that an episode S of length m occurs in a window of length w in an event sequence T over alphabet $\mathcal{A}$ for the memoryless model. In addition we gave an asymptotic approximation of $P^\exists(w, m)$, which shows that, for appropriately large w, $P^\exists(w, m)$ goes to 1 as expected. By providing an efficient dynamic programming method for computing $P^\exists(w, m)$ we showed its applicability for real time monitoring systems. In the experiments we chose two apparently non memoryless sources (the English alphabet and the web access data) and showed that, even for these cases $P^\exists(w, m)$ closely approximated the estimated $P_e^\exists(w, m)$. This seems to be yet another one of those intriguing situation where an equation derived under a certain set of assumptions holds in practical examples for which those assumptions are clearly violated.

Based on the formula for $P^\exists(w, m)$ we proposed a reliable episode detection method, where as a measure of normal behavior we used $\Omega^\exists(n, w, m)$ the number of windows which contain at least one occurrence of a defined "bad" episode. Reliability of $\Omega^\exists(n, w, m)$ as a normal behavior measure stems from the fact that, for a given S and $\mathcal{A}$, we can analytically select the window length w to minimize false alarms. We proved that, $\Omega^\exists(n, w, m)$ has Gaussian distribution. Knowing $\mathbf{E}[\Omega^\exists(n, w, m)]$, $\mathbf{Var}[\Omega^\exists(n, w, m)]$ or their estimates, and for a given confidence level β, we showed how to set up a threshold $\tau(n, w, m)$. Contrary to $\mathbf{E}[\Omega^\exists(n, w, m)]$ which can be easily computed or estimated based on the training set, computing $\mathbf{Var}[\Omega^\exists(n, w, m)]$ efficiently for large w and $\mathcal{A}$ is a difficult problem. Therefore we used an estimator of the sample variance $\widehat{\mathbf{Var}}[\Omega^\exists(n, w, m)]$ in the experiments. We tested the threshold $\tau(n, w, m)$ by artificially injecting bad episodes into the testing source and observed that, $\tau(n, w, m)$ did indeed provide a sharp detection of intentional (bad) episodes. We also pointed out our approach can be extended to Markov source of any order.

References

[1] A. Aho and M. Corasick, Efficient String Matching: An Aid to Bibliographic Search *Programming Techniques*, 1975.

[2] A. Apostolico and M. Atallah, Compact Recognizers of Episode Sequences, *Information and Computation*, 174, 180-192, 2002.

[3] P. Billingsley, *Probability and measure*, John Wiley, New York, 1986.

[4] L. Boasson, P. Cegielski, I. Guessarian, and Y. Matiyasevich, Window-Accumulated Subsequence Matching Problem is Linear, *Proc. PODS*, 327-336, 1999.

[5] M. Crochemore and W. Rytter, *Text Algorithms*, Oxford University Press, New York, 1994.

[6] G. Das, R. Fleischer, L. G asieniec, D. Gunopulos, and J. Kärkkäinen, Episode Matching, In *Combinatorial Pattern Matching, 8th Annual Symposium, Lecture Notes in Computer Science* vol. 1264, 12–27, 1997.

[7] P. Flajolet, Y. Guivarc'h, W. Szpankowski, and B. Vallée, Hidden Pattern Statistics, ICALP 2001, Crete, Greece, LNCS 2076, 152-165, 2001.

[8] R. Gwadera, M. Atallah and W. Szpankowski, Reliable Detection of Episodes in Event Sequences, http://www.cs.purdue.edu/homes/spa/papers/gwadera.ps

[9] G. Kucherov, M. Rusinowitch Matching a Set of Strings with Variable Length Don't Cares, *Theoretical Computer Science* 178, 129–154, 1997.

[10] S. Kumar and E.H. Spafford, A Pattern-Matching Model for Intrusion Detection, *Proceedings of the National Computer Security Conference*, 11–21, 1994.

[11] H. Mannila, H. Toivonen, and A. Verkamo Discovery of frequent episodes in event sequences *Data Mining and Knowledge Discovery*, 1(3), 241-258, 1997.

[12] P. Nicodème, B. Salvy, and P. Flajolet, Motif Statistics, *European Symposium on Algorithms, Lecture Notes in Computer Science*, No. 1643, 194–211, 1999.

[13] P. Pevzner, *Computational Molecular Biology: An Algorithmic Approach*, MIT Press, 2000.

[14] M. Régnier and W. Szpankowski, On pattern frequency occurrences in a Markovian sequence *Algorithmica*, 22, 631-649, 1998.

[15] I. Rigoutsos, A. Floratos, L. Parida, Y. Gao and D. Platt, The Emergence of Pattern Discovery Techniques in Computational Biology, *Metabolic Engineering*, 2, 159-177, 2000.

[16] R. Sedgewick and P. Flajolet, *An Introduction to the Analysis of Algorithms*, Addison-Wesley, Reading, MA, 1995.

[17] W. Szpankowski, *Average Case Analysis of Algorithms on Sequence*, John Wiley, New York, 2001.

[18] M. Waterman, *Introduction to Computational Biology*, Chapman and Hall, London, 1995.

[19] A. Wespi, H. Debar, M. Dacier, and M. Nassehi, Fixed vs. Variable-Length Patterns For Detecting Suspicious Process Behavior, *J. Computer Security*, 8, 159-181, 2000.

[20] S. Wu and U. Manber, Fast Text Searching Allowing Errors, *Comm. ACM*, 35:10, 83–991, 1995.

A Dynamic Adaptive Self-Organising Hybrid Model for Text Clustering

Chihli Hung and Stefan Wermter
Centre for Hybrid Intelligent Systems
School of Computing and Technology, University of Sunderland, UK
[chihli.hung;stefan.wermter]@sunderland.ac.uk

Abstract

Clustering by document concepts is a powerful way of retrieving information from a large number of documents. This task in general does not make any assumption on the data distribution. In this paper, for this task we propose a new competitive Self-Organising (SOM) model, namely the Dynamic Adaptive Self-Organising Hybrid model (DASH). The features of DASH are a dynamic structure, hierarchical clustering, non-stationary data learning and parameter self-adjustment. All features are data-oriented: DASH adjusts its behaviour not only by modifying its parameters but also by an adaptive structure. The hierarchical growing architecture is a useful facility for such a competitive neural model which is designed for text clustering. In this paper, we have presented a new type of self-organising dynamic growing neural network which can deal with the non-uniform data distribution and the non-stationary data sets and represent the inner data structure by a hierarchical view.

1. Introduction

Clustering by document concepts is useful to reduce the search space for linking a query to relevant information. One well-known project is WebSOM [1], which employs a Self-Organising Map (SOM) for clustering documents and presents them on a 2-dimensional map. Documents with a similar concept are grouped into the same cluster and clusters with similar concepts are located nearby on a map. This is the main difference between neural clustering and traditional statistical cluster analysis, which only assigns objects to clusters but ignores the relationship between clusters. The Self-Organising Map (SOM) combines non-linear projection, vector quantization (VQ), and data clustering functions [2]. However, in terms of the clustering algorithm, a SOM suffers from the following problems:

- The network structure including the topology and the number of units has to be set before training. Different architectures lead to different results. The fixed architecture is not ideal for non-uniform distributions.

This constraint causes an unnecessarily large vector quantization error.

- Using a large single map with a huge data set is not ideal and so a hierarchical approach may be needed.
- A SOM is not ideal for non-stationary information environments. Real world knowledge, for example, news stories, is changing over time. An algorithm which handles non-stationary data sets will offer more flexibility for a web-based project, such as WebSOM.

In this paper, we focus on a text clustering task and propose an alternative model, the Dynamic Adaptive Self-organising Hybrid model (DASH), to address the above deficiencies. We use the new Reuters news Corpus, RCV1[1], as our main test-bed and evaluate DASH based on classification accuracy and average quantization error.

The remainder of this paper is organised as follows. In Section 2, we give a general review of current related competitive models. In section 3, we introduce the DASH approach. In section 4, we test the features of the DASH using two small data sets. Section 5 contains three experiments using the new Reuters Corpus given under different scenarios. Then a conclusion is presented in section 6.

2. Related Unsupervised Competitive Models

Several related unsupervised neural learning models have been proposed to enhance the practicability of the SOM. Different modifications of the SOM suggest different enhancements from different viewpoints. These models can be divided into four groups, which are static models, dynamic models, hierarchical models and non-stationary learning models.

Static models, such as the pure competitive learning (CL) [2,3] and Neural Gas (NG) [4], relax the constraint of a fixed topological structure, i.e. a grid, of SOM. Dynamic models, such as the Growing Grid (GG) [5] and Growing SOM (GSOM) [6], try to define a model with no need of prior knowledge for the number of output units by an incremental growing architecture. Hierarchical models,

---

[1]The new version of the Reuters news corpus can be found at http://about.reuters.com/researchandstandards/corpus/

such as the TreeGCS [7], Multilayered Self-Organising Feature Maps (M-SOM) [8] and Growing Hierarchical Self-Organizing Map (GHSOM) [9], offer a detailed view for a complicated clustering task. Non-stationary learning models, such as the Growing Cell Structure (GCS) [10], Growing Neural Gas (GNG) [11], Incremental Grid Growing (IGG) [12], Growing Neural Gas with Utility criterion (GNG-U) [13], Plastic Self Organising Map (PSOM) [14] and Grow When Required (GWR) [15], contain unit-growing and unit-pruning functions which are analogous to biological functions of remembering and forgetting under a dynamic environment.

We focus on models which are able to handle a data set with the nature of hierarchical relationships, non-uniform distributions, or non-stationary varieties. For a neural model to offer automatic hierarchical clustering, it may need a function to further prune the map by removing unsuitable units to form several partitions on a map. Hodge and Austin [7] use this technique to produce synonym clusters as an automatic thesaurus. However, this unit-pruning function seriously depends on a pre-defined constant threshold. Based on the unknown data distribution, this threshold is very difficult to determine. Second, the partition is formed because of the nature of the input data. One should not foresee that a hierarchy must be built by a competitive model with the unit-pruning function. A proper policy may build such a hierarchy by further developing a whole map from a unit with many input data mapped to this unit or with higher error information, e.g. [8] and [9]. We take advantage of both concepts to build DASH as an automatic hierarchical clustering model.

For the non-stationary data set, a trained unit or training unit should be updated by a unit which is trained with new input samples. This is performed by the unit-pruning or connection-trimming function. A model with the connection-trimming function should be based on a global aged consideration. The reason is that a local age variable of a connection does not grow when units of this connection is not activated. That is, the aged connection may be kept forever so that the capability of self-adjustment for a model to new stimuli is diminished. Thus, a model, such as the GNG and GWR, using the connection-trimming function based on a local aged consideration can be treated as an incomplete non-stationary model only.

On the other hand, the stop criterion of models should not be a time-dependent threshold, such as iteration or epoch. However, this stop criterion is used for the models in our survey. Moreover, an unsuitable constant unit-pruning or a connection-trimming threshold may make the model train forever but learn nothing. This constant value can be very small or very large, which is totally dependent on trial-and-error. Therefore, it is not a good idea to use such a constant threshold for a big data set. Unfortunately,

the GCS, GNG, IGG, GNG-U, PSOM and GWR apply a constant threshold for detection of unsuitable units. We argue that a unit-pruning or a connection-trimming threshold should be automatically adjusted to suit different data sets during training.

3. Dynamic Adaptive Self-organising Hybrid (DASH) Model

3.1. The Need for DASH

We start by inspecting the features of text clustering for a real-world task. First, the quantity of text information is continuously growing so the information is not static. Therefore, a text clustering model should allow the learning of growing knowledge. It implies that a clustering model which contains a time-based decaying learning function is not suitable for such a task. Second, text information usually has some relationship with time, for instance, news. Some specific events often occur during a specific period. Thus, in this period, several news articles with similar topics are presented repeatedly and the recent information is more important. Therefore, a clustering model should be able to handle dynamic knowledge acquisition during this period. Third, clustering should use a hierarchical concept to complement searching. A hierarchical structure for a large set of data is not only necessary to keep the elasticity of the query response but also to analyse the contents easily. Due to this reason, a text clustering model should explicitly offer hierarchical learning for a large and complicated text set. However, none of the existing models meet all the needs of the features required for a text clustering task. This leads to the development of the DASH.

3.2. Features of DASH

From the viewpoint of concept, the DASH is an integrated model of the GNG and GHSOM, and contains several unique features. The DASH is a growing self-organising model which has characteristics of a dynamic structure, hierarchical training, non-stationary data learning and parameter self-adaptation. Three main percentage-like parameters, which influence the style of the DASH architecture, have to be defined. The first one is τ, which has an impact on how well DASH represents the current data set and a link to the size of a map. The second one is S_{min}, a minimum number of input samples which a map represents. This parameter affects the depth of a DASH hierarchy. The third one is a connection-trimming variable, β, which functions as a unit-pruning threshold. However, the β variable is self-adjusted when the current model does not grow continuously to meet the requirement of a map quality, i.e. the AQE, which is defined as the average distance between every input vector and its Best Matching Unit (BMU) [16]. An example of the DASH structure is given in (Figure 1).

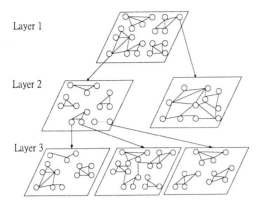

Figure 1. The hierarchical structure of DASH

The flowchart of DASH is shown in (Figure 2), which involves two main iterations and seven processes. The inner iteration is a GNG-like learning procedure for each map in a hierarchy. However, unlike the GNG, the DASH applies a global connection-trimming function instead of a local one to remove aged relationships between units and therefore, the isolated units are pruned globally. The GNG grows in every pre-defined cycle, which is determined by trial-and-error. In contrast, this cycle is a part of DASH, which is mutually decided by τ, S_{min} and the number of input samples in the current map (see Eq. 5 in Appendix). Furthermore, the connection-trimming and growing period are constants for GNG but they are self-adjusted variables for DASH.

The outer iteration is a GHSOM-like recursive training cycle. The GHSOM applies two constants, i.e. τ_1 and τ_2, to define the size and the depth of GHSOM architecture, respectively. The DASH uses τ, which is percentage-like parameter, to decide the size of map but use S_{min} to decide how detailed the data samples are represented by the DASH. For training kernel, the GHSOM directly employs the SOM training algorithm for each unit-growing procedure. For example, a GHSOM with 3x3 units in a map needs to employ 3 traditional SOM training cycles, i.e. one for a 2x2 structure, one for 2x3 (or 3x2) structure and one for 3x3 structure, using the same number of input data. However, only the training for the final map, i.e. the 3x3 map, is necessary. This behaviour may not be suitable for a real-world clustering task. The DASH applies a modification of GNG training procedure. For training a child map, the GHSOM applies a threshold based on the AQE in top level. However this threshold is dependent on the AQE in its direct parent level for DASH. This feature makes the DASH enforce a distributed learning which trains a whole input set by training several smaller input

sub-sets separately. Moreover, the GHSOM does not contain a unit-pruning function. Once units grow, they have no chance to be removed. Conversely, the DASH contains unit-pruning and unit-growing functions, which can deal with the non-stationary and non-uniform data set. The detailed DASH algorithm is shown in the Appendix.

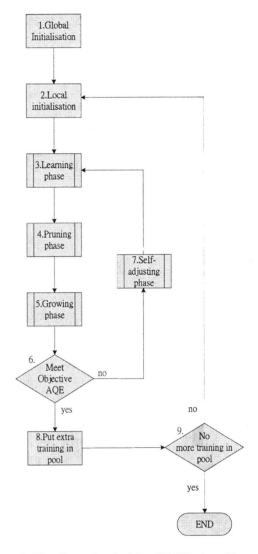

Figure 2. The flow chart of the DASH algorithm

4. Initial Experiments

We design two small experiments to present how DASH works. In the first experiment, we use a pre-arranged four-corner data set to test how the model deals with a non-uniform distribution. In the second experiment, we use a jumping-corner data set to show the capability of handling a non-stationary data set for the model.

4.1. Four Corners

A 4-corner data set is applied to test the ability of competitive models for learning a non-uniform data distribution. Each corner contains 30x30 2-D input vectors. The results of the SOM and DASH are presented and both models can faithfully represent the associated input vectors on 4 corners. However while the SOM contains many "dead units" and cannot represent data well at the borders of corners (Figure 3), DASH successfully removes the unsuitable connections to form 4 clusters during learning (Figure 4).

Figure 3. The convergence of SOM training at initial, 1,000 and 10,000 iterations

Figure 4. The convergence of DASH training at initial, 1,000 and 10,000 iterations

4.2. A Jumping Corner

A jumping-corner data set is used to mimic the non-stationary input data. A data set distributed in the bottom left corner at the beginning moves to the top right corner at iteration 5001. It can be seen that a new data set in the top right corner substitutes for the existing data set in the bottom left corner. The SOM learns well in the beginning because the data set is a uniform distribution (Figure 5). However, when the existing data set is replaced by the new data set, some units of the SOM cannot be re-trained since the learning rate is decayed. Thus, "dead units" are inevitable for a SOM to train a non-stationary data set. Conversely, DASH removes unsuitable existing units when new input stimuli happen (Figure 6).

Figure 5. The convergence of SOM training at initial, 6,000 and 10,000 iterations

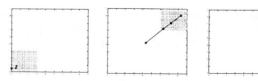

Figure 6. The convergence of DASH training at initial, 6,000 and 10,000 iterations

5. Experiments

5.1. Description of New Reuters Corpus and Data Set

We evaluate our model by the classification accuracy and AQE, which have also been used in the work of Kohonen et al. [17]. Based on the classification accuracy criterion, a pre-labelled corpus is necessary. We work with the new version of the Reuters corpus, RCV1, since this news corpus is a representative test for text classification, a common benchmark and a fairly recent comprehensive data source [18, 19]. This corpus is made up of 984 Mbytes of news. The number of total news articles is 806,791 which contain about two hundred million word occurrences. One hundred and twenty six topics are defined in this new corpus. Each news article is pre-classified to 3.17 topics on average but 10,186 of them are assigned to no topic.

In this paper, the 8 most dominant topics in the corpus are considered initially. Because a news article can be pre-classified as more than one topic, the multi-topic combination is treated as a new topic in this research. Thus, the 8 dominant topics are expanded into 40 combined topics for the first 10,000 news articles. Each full-text document is represented using vector space model (VSM) [20]. Due to the massive dimensionality of vectors, we remove the stop words, confine to words shown in WordNet [21] and lemmatise each word to its base form. WordNet is a net of words which only contains open-classed words, i.e. nouns, verbs, adjectives and adverbs. After this pre-processing, there are 16,122 different words in the master word list. The 1,000 most frequent words are picked from the master word list since this method is as good as most dimensionality reduction techniques [22].

5.2. Static Data Set

The first 10,000 full-text documents without title information is used as our test-bed. The pre-processing procedure mentioned in the previous section is used. We apply a normalised TFxIDF as the vector representation approach [23]. In this experiment, three different τ, i.e. 95%, 90% and 85% of DASH are applied. For convenience, they are termed DASH95, DASH90 and

DASH85 in this paper. The S_{min} is 1% and the initial β is 95%. Please note β is an adjustable parameter during training. These three parameters are the same for following experiments. We compare the results with six other models, i.e. the CL, SOM, NG, GG, GCS and GNG. We use 15x15 = 225 units for each model, but this number is only an estimate for dynamic models, i.e. the GG, GCS and GNG. All learning rates of models are initialised to 0.1. Such a learning rate is certainly decayed in some models, such as the CL, SOM and NG. SOM fine-tuning training starts with a 0.001 learning rate. Other models, such as the GG, GCS, GNG and DASH, also use an extra learning rate which is 0.001 for training runner-up units of BMU. Except the DASH, we train all models using 10,000 iterations. The DASH stop criterion is defined by objective AQE. According to the results in (Table 1), we notice that models with a sticker structures have higher AQEs. For example, the SOM and GG contain a grid-style topographic structure which may be difference from the relationships between data. Thus, their AQEs are higher than other models in this paper. The performance of DASH85 is worse than that of DASH90, which contains a smaller AQE and a higher accuracy. The reason is that a lower τ, i.e. 85%, introduces a bigger size of map which consists of 262 units in the first layer. That is, the average number of units mapped to a unit is only 38.17 ($10,000 \div 262 \cong 38.17$) which is much smaller than the stop criterion of S_{min} ($10,000 \times 1\% = 100$). Thus, only 3 maps are in the hierarchy of DASH85 but there are 21 maps in the DASH90. However, the total training time of the DASH85 is longer than that of the DASH90 training.

Table 1. A comparison of neural models for a static data set

	CL	SOM	NG	GG	GCS
AQE	0.836	0.930	0.837	0.881	0.820
accuracy	65.49%	69.16%	69.54%	68.82%	68.18%

	GNG	DASH95	DASH90	DASH85
AQE	0.823	0.818	0.790	0.802
Accuracy	68.60%	69.60%	70.42%	68.37%

5.3. Knowledge Acquisition

This section is to test the ability of models to handle the non-stationary data set. The pre-processing and vector representation approaches are the same as those in the previous section. We treat the new data set as new knowledge that complements the existing knowledge. The first 5,000 full-text documents are applied as an existing data set and the second 5,000 full-text documents as a new

data set. There are three scenarios, which evaluates the relationships of models and non-stationary data sets. The existing data set is used for all experiments in the beginning. The new data set is introduced in scenario 1 at iteration 10,000, scenario 2 at iteration 30,000 and scenario 3 at iteration 50,000. SOM rough-training is stopped at iteration 30,000 and its fine-tuning training is stopped at 50,000 iterations. The stop criterion of DASH is finding the objective AQE. According to our experiments, the SOM does not suffer from the new data set seriously, if the distribution of the new data set is similar to that of the existing data set (Table 2). In this case, the performance of the SOM is comparable to the non-stationary model, i.e., the DASH.

Table 2. A comparison of SOM and DASH for knowledge acquisition scenario

		10000iter	30000iter	50000iter
SOM	AQE	0.937	0.938	0.940
	accuracy	69.06%	68.44%	69.08%
DASH	AQE	0.771	0.780	0.802
	accuracy	72.23%	71.42%	70.39%

5.4. Knowledge Update

This section is to compare the performance of models under a non-stationary environment where the existing data set is treated as out-of-date knowledge and should be updated by the new knowledge, i.e. the new data set. The same pre-processing procedure mentioned above is used. To mimic the non-stationary data set, the first 10,000 full-text documents are transformed by using the normalized TFxIDF vector representation as our new data set but by using the non-normalized TFxIDF as the old data set. The averaged weights of the existing set are much higher than those of the new data set. Thus, the AQEs are also much higher when models deal with the existing data set. We also introduce the new data set at iteration 10,000 for the scenario 1, iteration 30,000 for the scenario 2 and iteration 50,000 for the scenario 3.

Some non-stationary competitive models such as GNG-U and GWR have been tried in these experiments. However, it is not possible to use their unit-pruning and connection-trimming constant thresholds for both data sets. When a proper threshold is set for the existing data set, this threshold is always too large for the new data set. Thus, models do not grow. Conversely, if a threshold is suitable for the new data set, this threshold is always too small for the existing data set. However, we should not set such a threshold by presuming the distribution of the new data set. Therefore, we only test our model and SOM in these experiments.

According to our experiments, the SOM clearly suffers from the decayed learning rate (Table 3). The new data samples are not learnt completely, so the accuracy drops while the AQE increases. On the other hand, DASH removes all unsuitable trained units very fast and adjusts its new objective AQE automatically. Thus, there is no large difference between the performance at each point when a new data set is introduced during training for DASH.

Table 3. A comparison of SOM and DASH for knowledge update scenario

		10000iter	30000iter	50000iter
SOM	AQE	0.948	1.352	2.513
	accuracy	64.37%	21.52%	25.75%
DASH	AQE	0.784	0.776	0.793
	accuracy	71.40%	72.25%	69.30%

6. Conclusion

Due to the features of a real-world text clustering task, a neural model which can handle both static and non-stationary datasets and represent the inner data structure by a hierarchical view is necessary. This paper has presented such a new type of self-organising dynamic growing neural network, i.e. DASH. In terms of concept, the DASH is a hybrid model of GHSOM and GNG but the DASH contains several unique features, such as the parameter self-adjustment, hierarchical training and continuous learning. Based on these features, a real-world document clustering task has been demonstrated in this paper. Those existing models which are designed for the non-stationary data sets may not be suitable for a real-world clustering task. The main reason is the difficulty of determining unit-pruning and connection-trimming parameters. Furthermore, those non-stationary models should not use a time-dependent stop criterion. For more complex data sets, such as a document collection, a hierarchical structure is preferable. The DASH is a hierarchical neural approach which functions as a non-stationary distributing learning facility.

7. Reference

[1] T. Honkela, S. Kaski, K. Lagus, and T. Kohonen, "Newsgroup exploration with WEBSOM method and browsing interface", *Report A32*, Helsinki University of Technology, 1996.

[2] T. Kohonen, *Self-organization and associative memory*, Springer-Verlag, Berlin, 1984.

[3] S. Grossberg, "Adaptive pattern classification and universal recoding: I. Parallel development and coding of neural feature detectors", *Biological Cybernetics*, vol. 23, 1976, pp. 121-131.

[4] T. Martinetz and K. Schulten, "A 'Neural-Gas' network learns topologies", *Artificial Neural Network*, vol. I, 1991, pp. 397-402.

[5] B. Fritzke, "Growing grid-a self-organizing network with constant neighborhood range and adaptation strength", *Neural Processing Letters*, vol. 2 no. 5, 1995, pp. 9-13.

[6] D. Alahakoon, S.K. Halgamuge and B. Srinivasan, "Dynamic self-organizing maps with controlled growth for knowledge discovery", *IEEE Tractions on Neural Networks*, vol. 11, no. 3, 2000, pp. 601-614.

[7] V. Hodge and J. Austin, "Hierarchical growing cell structures: TreeGCS", *Proceedings of the Fourth International Conference on Knowledge-Based Intelligent Engineering Systems*, 2000.

[8] H. Chen, C. Schuffels and R. Orwig, "Internet categorization and search: a self-organizing approach", *Journal of Visual Communication and Image Representation*, vol. 7, no. 1, March, 1996, pp. 88-102.

[9] A. Rauber, D. Merkl and M. Dittenbach, "The growing hierarchical self-organizing maps: exploratory analysis of high-dimensional data", *IEEE Transactions on Neural Networks*, vol. 13, no. 6, 2002, pp.1331-1341.

[10] B. Fritzke, "Growing cell structures – a self-organizing network for unsupervised and supervised learning", *Neural Networks*, vol. 7, no. 9, 1994, pp.1441-1460.

[11] B. Fritzke, "A growing neural gas network learns topologies", *Advances in Neural Information Processing Systems 7*, G. Tesauro, D.S. Touretzky, and T.K. Leen, eds., MIT Press, Cambridge MA, 1995, pp. 625-632.

[12] J. Blackmore and R. Miikkulainen, "Incremental grid growing: encoding high-dimensional structure into a two-dimensional feature map", *Proceedings of the IEEE International Conference on Neural Networks (ICNN'93)*, San Francisco, CA, USA, 1993.

[13] B. Fritzke, "A self-organizing network that can follow non-stationary distributions", *Proceedings of ICANN'97, International Conference on Artificial Neural Networks*, Springer, 1997, pp. 613-618.

[14] R. Lang and K. Warwick, "The plastic self organising map", *IEEE World Congress on Computational Intelligence*, 2002.

[15] S. Marsland, J. Shapiro and U. Nehmzow, "A self-organising network that grows when required", *Neural Networks*, vol. 15, 2002, pp. 1041-1058.

[16] T. Kohonen, *Self-organizing maps*, Springer-Verlag, 2001.

[17] T. Kohonen, S. Kaski, K. Lagus, J. Salojärvi, J. Honkela, V. Paatero and A. Saarela, "Self organization of a massive document collection", *IEEE Transactions on Neural Networks*, vol. 11, no. 3, 2000, pp. 574-585.

[18] S. Wermter and C. Hung, "Selforganising Classification on the Reuters News Corpus", *The 19th International Conference on Computational Linguistics (COLING2002)*, Taipei, Taiwan, 2002, pp.1086-1092.

[19] T.G. Rose, M. Stevenson and M. Whitehead, "The Reuters Corpus Volume 1 - from Yesterday's News to Tomorrow's Language Resources", *Proceedings of the Third International Conference on Language Resources and Evaluation*, Las Palmas de Gran Canaria, 2002, pp. 29-31.

[20] G. Salton, *Automatic Text Processing: the Transformation, Analysis, and Retrieval of Information by Computer*, Addison-Wesley, USA, 1989.

[21] G.A. Miller, "WordNet: a dictionary browser", *Proceedings of the First International Conference on Information in Data*, University of Waterloo, Waterloo, 1985.

[22] S. Chakrabarti, "Data mining for hypertext: a tutorial survey", *ACM SIGKDD Explorations*, vol. 1, no. 2, 2000, pp. 1-11.

[23] G. Salton, and C. Buckley, "Term-weighting approaches in automatic text retrieval", *Information Processing & Management*, vol. 24, no. 5, 1988, pp. 513-523.

8. Appendix – DASH Algorithm

For convenience, we describe the main structure of the model as follows. Let $A=\{L_1,L_2,...L_l\}$, where A is the set of sub-maps. Let $L=\{U_1,U_2,...U_u\}$, where U_i is the unit i in the map L. Each U_i has an error variable, err_i. Let C_{ij} be the binary connection between U_i and U_j. Each C_{ij} has a variable, age_{ij}, to store the connection age. Let the input distribution be $p(X)$ for the input set X. Let $X=\{x_1,x_2,...x_n\}$, where x_i is the input sample i in the input set X. We define the weight vectors for an input sample and for a unit as x_i and w_i respectively. Then the precise processes of the DASH algorithm are as below.

1) Global network initialisation
   1.1) Define a map quality index, τ, where $0 < \tau \leq 1$. τ decides the objective AQE for a child map. It controls the extent of the size for a single map and is also the stop criterion for the child map training. A smaller τ builds a bigger map, which means that a map contains a larger number of units. An assumption is made before training that there is a virtual map L_0 above the first map L_1. L_0 contains only one unit whose weight vector, w_0, is the mean value of the untrained input data set, X, which contains N input samples.

$$w_0 = \frac{1}{N}\sum_{i=1}^{N} x_i \qquad \text{(Eq. 1)}$$

Thus, the AQE of L_0 is:

$$AQE_0 = \frac{1}{N}\sum_{i=1}^{N} \|x_i - w_0\| \qquad \text{(Eq. 2)}$$

   1.2) Define learning rates α_b and α_s for the Best Matching Unit b, and its neighbours s, respectively, where $0 < \alpha_s < \alpha_b < 1$.

   1.3) Define an age threshold, β, for a connection C_{ij}, where $0 < \beta \leq 1$. The β cooperates with the current highest age of connection to decide whether a connection is too old. A β adjusting parameter, J_β, is defined as well, which is used to modulate β based on the current data samples.

   1.4) Define S_{min}, a minimum number of input samples which a map represents. The default value is two because the minimum number of units is two in a map. S_{min} can also be set as a proportion of the size of input data, where $0<S_{min}<1$. In this case, S_{min} will be found by $S_{min} \times N$. S_{min} influences the depth of a DASH hierarchy. A smaller S_{min} makes the DASH expand deeper down a hierarchy.

   1.5) Let O_l be a temporal maximum number of units in a map for the layer l. It is defined by (Eq. 3). The value of 3 is used as the minimum of O_l because a sub-map of DASH starts with 2 units, which allows the model with one spare unit to grow. The value of 100 is applied in (Eq. 3) for two reasons. The first is that the model is better if it can achieve the quality requirement using a smaller map. The model is forced to train properly rather than adding units to pursue a smaller AQE. The second reason is that a very large map is not preferred because it is hard to analyse or visualise. Besides the parameter, O_l, an γ adjusting parameter, J_γ, is also defined to modify O_l, where $0 < J_r \leq 1$. O_l will be modified in the self-adjusting phase, if a map contains O_l units but does not meet the map quality.

$$\begin{cases} O_l = \max(3, \min(100, \frac{S_{min}}{2})), \text{ where } l=1 \\ O_l = \max(3, \min(O_{l-1} \times \frac{\tau}{2}, \frac{S_{min}}{2})), \text{where } l>1 \end{cases} \quad \text{(Eq. 3)}$$

2) Local network initialisation
   2.1) Determine an objective AQE based on the AQE in the direct parent map.

$$\begin{cases} objective\ AQE_l = AQE_{l-1} \times \tau, where\ l=1 \\ objective\ AQE_l = AQE_{l-1} \times \tau^2, where\ l>1 \end{cases} \quad \text{(Eq. 4)}$$

   2.2) Based on O_l, define how often the unit grows as follows:

$$\text{IterGrow} = \frac{N_l}{O_l - 1},$$ (Eq. 5)

where N_l is the number of current input data.

2.3) Create two units and initialise weights randomly from $p(X)$.

2.4) Re-order the current data set randomly.

3) Learning Phase

3.1) Generate a data sample x_i for the model.

3.2) Calculate the Euclidean distance of each unit to x_i and decide the Best Matching Unit, b, and the Second Best Matching Unit, s, by

$$b = \arg\min_{n \in L} \|x_i - w_n\| \text{ and}$$ (Eq. 6)

$$s = \arg\min_{n \in l/\{b\}} \|x_i - w_n\|$$ (Eq. 7)

and connect them as C_{bs}, if it does not exist.

3.3) Update the weights to the BMU b, and other units n, with a connection from b:

$$w_b(t+1) = w_b(t) + \alpha_b \cdot (x_i - w_b) \text{ and}$$ (Eq. 8)

$$w_n(t+1) = w_n(t) + \alpha_s \cdot (x_i - w_n)$$ (Eq. 9)

3.4) Add 1 to the age variables for all connection C, but zero to C_{bs}.

$$\begin{cases} age = age + 1 \\ age_{bs} = 0 \end{cases}$$ (Eq. 10)

3.5) Increase the error to the BMU error variable, err_b:

$$err_b(t+1) = err_b(t) + \|x_i - w_b\|$$ (Eq. 11)

4) Pruning Phase: at each n IterGrow iteration, where n is ≥ 1.

4.1) Find the maximum age of connections currently.

$age_{max} = \arg\max(age)$ (Eq. 12)

4.2) Remove any connection whose age is larger than a portion of the maximum age of connections currently.

Remove C_{ij}, if $\dfrac{age_{ij}}{age_{max}} > \beta$ (Eq. 13)

This will be carried out if the number of units is more than two.

4.3) Prune any unit without any connection but still keep the minimum number of units, 2.

5) Growing Phase: at each IterGrow iteration, insert a new unit as follows:

5.1) Find the unit q with maximum accumulated error:

$$q = \arg\max_{u \in L}(err)$$ (Eq. 14)

5.2) Find the unit f, the unit with the highest accumulated error amongst the neighbours of q.

$$f = \arg\max_{u \in Neighbours_q}(err)$$ (Eq. 15)

5.3) Insert a new unit r to a map and initialise its weight by interpolating weight vectors q and f.

$$w_r = \frac{w_q + w_f}{2}$$ (Eq. 16)

5.4) Set up the err variables for units q, f and r.

$$err_q = \frac{err_q}{2}$$ (Eq. 17)

$$err_f = \frac{err_f}{2}$$ (Eq. 18)

$$err_r = \frac{err_q + err_f}{2}$$ (Eq. 19)

5.5) Connect unit r to unit q and f. Set up the age variable for these two connections, i.e. C_{rq} and C_{rf}.

$$age_{rq} = age_{rf} = age_{qf}$$ (Eq. 20)

5.6) Remove the connection between unit q and unit f.

6) Check the condition whether the map AQE meets the objective AQE at each IterGrow iteration.

6.1) Evaluate the AQE for a map l:

$$AQE_l = \frac{1}{N_l} \sum_{i=1}^{N_l} \|x_i - w_{b(i)}\|,$$ (Eq. 21)

where $w_{b(i)}$ is the weight vector of BMU for input sample i.

6.2) If $AQE_l \leq objective\ AQE_l$, then stop training for this map, or go to the self-adjusting phase.

7) Self-adjusting Phase: at some IterGrow iteration, modify some parameters to suit the object AQE_l.

7.1) Increase the age threshold, β by the adjusting parameter, J_β, if units are not growing.

$$\beta(t+1) = \beta(t) \times (2 - J_\beta),$$ (Eq. 22)

where $0.5 < J_\beta \leq 1$.

7.2) Decrease the age threshold, if the number of units reach O_l, which is the reference number of units in a map:

$$\beta(t+1) = \beta(t) \times J_\beta,$$ (Eq. 23)

7.3) Increase the reference number of units in a map, if the number is reached.

$$O_l(t+1) = O_l(t) \times (2 - J_r),$$ (Eq. 24)

where $0.5 < J_r < 1$.

8) Put all units whose AQEs are greater than the objective AQE in the same layer into the training pool if the number of their associated input vectors is greater than Smin.

9) Continue the hierarchical training until there are no training requirements in the training pool.

Mining Significant Pairs of Patterns from Graph Structures with Class Labels

Akihiro Inokuchi and Hisashi Kashima

Tokyo Research Laboratory, IBM Japan

1623-14, Shimotsuruma, Yamato, Kanagawa, 242-8502, Japan

{inokuchi,hkashima}@jp.ibm.com

Abstract

In recent years, the problem of mining association rules over frequent itemsets in transactional data has been frequently studied and yielded several algorithms that can find association rules within a limited amount of time. Also more complex patterns have been considered such as ordered trees, unordered trees, or labeled graphs. Although some approaches can efficiently derive all frequent subgraphs from a massive dataset of graphs, a subgraph or subtree that is mathematically defined is not necessarily a better knowledge representation. In this paper, we propose an efficient approach to discover significant rules to classify positive and negative graph examples by estimating a tight upper bound on the statistical metric. This approach abandons unimportant rules earlier in the computations, and thereby accelerates the overall performance. The performance has been evaluated using real world datasets, and the efficiency and effect of our approach has been confirmed with respect to the amount of data and the computation time.

1 Introduction

In recent years, the problem of mining association rules over frequent itemsets in transactional data has been thoroughly studied and led to several algorithms that can find association rules within a limited amount of time. Also more complex patterns have been considered, such as ordered trees, unordered trees, or labeled graphs. Modeling objects using such complex structures allows us to represent arbitrary relations among entities. Recently some approaches which can efficiently mine frequent substructures from a set of structured data such as graphs or trees have been proposed [6, 10, 19, 20, 1]. They mine frequent patterns stepwise in ascending order of their sizes beginning with frequent patterns of size 1, based on the anti-monotonic property of their support values. AGM [6, 8], TreeMiner [20], and FREQT [1] mine in a stepwise manner by expanding a

vertex, whereas FSG [10] and gSpan [19] are expanding an edge. From another perspective, AGM, FSG, and FREQT use breadth-first search whereas gSpan and TreeMiner are depth-first search algorithms. Although they are characterized by their strategies to traverse the search space and by their strategies to expand patterns, the discovered patterns that are contained in each graph or tree are frequent subgraphs which are mathematically defined in the graph theory domain.

However, a subgraph or subtree which is mathematically defined is not a necessarily better knowledge representation. Assume that the above algorithms are applied to chemical compounds where each atom, chemical bond, atom type, and bond type in a compound correspond to vertex, edge, vertex label, and edge label in a graph, respectively, and that chemical compounds which contained Figure 1(a-1) exhibit some specified activity[1]. In general, a carbon atom with 2 single bonds has 2 other single bonds or a double bond. When the algorithms are applied to discover patterns or rules to classify active and inactive compounds, the pattern P_1 shown in Figure 1(b-1) may not be found, because a pattern is defined as a subgraph and the pattern P_1 is also contained in compounds which have Figure 1(a-2), which may not contribute to activity. Therefore, a representation to mine the rules in Figure 1(a-1) is needed.

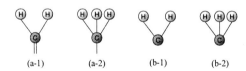

Figure 1. Examples of Patterns in Chemical Compounds

Some approaches have been applied to derive negative association rules and association rules which include negative elements in the conventional Basket Analysis. A negative association rule is represented as $A \Rightarrow \neg B$ where A and

---

[1]We assume that a fragment shown in Figure 1(a-2) is contained in both active and inactive compounds.

B are itemsets. The negative rule indicates that the presence of itemset A implies the absence of another itemset B in the same transaction. An association rule with negative factors is represented as $\{item_1, \neg item_2\} \Rightarrow \{item_3\}$. [18] suggests that decision making in many applications such as product placement and investment analysis often involves a number of factors, some of which play advantageous roles and others play disadvantageous roles, and that negative relationships play the same important role as positive relationship from experiences in science and engineering. We can represent a rule shown in Figure 1(a-1) as that chemical compounds which contain the pattern P_1 shown in Figure 1(b-1) and which do not contain the pattern P_2 shown in Figure 1(b-2) are associated with activity. We seek to discover rules with negative factors from the labeled graphs.

A straightforward approach to derive the rules is to first enumerate all of the patterns which are contained as subgraphs in the database and then to combine two patterns P_1 and P_2 whose subgraph is P_1 in postprocessing. It is inefficient because the set of potential patterns is too large and its combinations are intractable. To design a more efficient algorithm, we use the method of estimating a tight upper bound for the statistical metric. AprioriSMP which uses the upper bound can efficiently discover correlation rules maximizing a certain statistical measure from transactional database when an item corresponding to the right hand side of a rule is specified [12]. It can easily be integrated into graph mining algorithms to mine for the rules such as $P \Rightarrow active$ where P is a graph with no negative factors. Furthermore, it can be easily expanded to discover rules with negative factors from a transactional database. For example, the rule $\{item_1, \neg item_2\} \Rightarrow \{item_3\}$ can be derived by adding all $\neg item_i$s to a transaction without any $item_i$s, and applying AprioriSMP. Given a set of transactions and a complete set of items, the transformation of transactions is easily calculated. However, in the case that input dataset is a set of graphs or trees, the transformation is intractable, because it is difficult to define a graph which contains all of the graphs in a database.

In this paper, we propose an efficient approach to discover significant rules to classify positive and negative examples. The rest of this paper is organized as follows. We define the problem statement to derive patterns and rules in Section 2. We introduce our algorithm in Section 3. In Section 4, we explain the algorithm in detail and in section 5 present experimental results. Section 6 reviews related work and Section 7 concludes.

2 Problem Statement

A graph G consists of 4 sets, the set of vertices V, the set of edges E, the set of vertex labels L_V, and the set of edge labels L_E. When V, E, L_V and L_E are provided as

$$V = \{v_1, v_2, \ldots, v_k\},$$

$$E = \{e_h = (v_i, v_j) | v_i, v_j \in V\},$$

$$L_V = \{lb(v_i) | \forall v_i \in V\}, \; and$$

$$L_E = \{lb(e_h) | \forall e_h \in E\},$$

respectively, the graph G is mathematically defined as

$$G = (V, E, L_V, L_E),$$

where multiple vertices can have an identical label, and multiple edges also can have. For the convenience of description, the tuples of G are represented as $V(G)$, $E(G)$, $L_V(G)$ and $L_E(G)$ respectively. Each vertex $v \in V$ and edge $e \in E$ have labels $lb(v) \in L_v$ and $lb(e) \in L_E$, respectively[2]. Given a graph G, the subgraph G_s of G fulfills the following conditions.

$$\phi : V(G_s) \rightarrow V(G),$$

$$i \in V(G_s) \quad lb(i) = lb(\phi(i)),$$

$$i, j \in V(G_s) \quad lb(i, j) = lb(\phi(i), \phi(j)).$$

$G \sqsupseteq G_s$ means that G_s is a subgraph of G or G includes G_s.

A database is given as a set of examples $GD = \{(G_1, y_1), (G_2, y_2), \cdots, (G_N, y_N)\}$ where each example (G_i, y_i) is given as a pair of the graph G_i and the class $y_i \in \{+1, -1\}$ that the graph belongs to. Given a set GD of graph structured data, the support $\sigma(g)$ for a graph g is defined as the number of graphs including g in GD.

$$\sigma(g) = |\{g | G \in GD, g \sqsubseteq G\}|$$

We call a graph whose support is more than or equal to 1 a *pattern*. We denote that the supports for graph g on a positive dataset and a negative dataset are $\sigma_p(g)$ and $\sigma_n(g)$, respectively. The sum of $\sigma_p(g)$ and $\sigma_n(g)$ is equal to $\sigma(g)$.

The *expansion* of a pattern P is to add some vertices or some edges in order to generate a larger pattern P' (Figure 2). P is a subgraph of P'. For example, AGM, FSG, gSpan, and TreeMiner generate patterns of size k by joining two frequent patterns of size $k-1$ if and only if certain conditions are fulfilled[3]. FREQT expands patterns by adding a vertex and an edge to a vertex in the right most path of the tree pattern[4].

---

[2]The method presented in this paper can be integrate into AGM, FSG, and gSpan which can be applied to both undirected and directed graphs.

[3]In the cases of AGM and TreeMiner, the size is defined as the number of vertices in a graph. In other cases, it is the number of edges in a graph.

[4]In the case of Apriori, a itemset P_k and Q_k of size k are expanded to R_{k+1} of size $k+1$ by joining $P_k = \{item_1, item_2, \cdots, item_{k-1}, item_k\}$ and $Q_k = \{item_1, item_2, \cdots, item_{k-1}, item_{k+1}\}$ to generate $R_{k+1} = \{item_1, item_2, \cdots, item_{k+1}\}$.

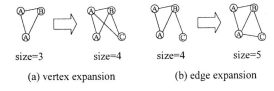

size=3   size=4   size=4   size=5

(a) vertex expansion   (b) edge expansion

Figure 2. Vertex and Edge Expansion

A rule discovered by our approach is denoted as

$$P \Rightarrow positive \ (or \ negative), \ or \qquad (1)$$

$$P_1 \wedge \overline{P_2} \Rightarrow positive \ (or \ negative) \qquad (2)$$

where P, P_1, and P_2 are patterns and $P_1 \sqsubset P_2$. The rule (2) means that data which contains pattern P_1 and does not contain pattern P_2 correlates with positive (or negative). Our approach discovers both types of rule (1) and rule (2) simultaneously. When a dataset which consists of a set of graphs is given as input, the problem is to discover a rule which maximizes a certain statistical metric or to list the N most significant rules with respect to the metric.

3 Statistical Measurement Property

Morishita et al. studied a method called AprioriSMP for efficiently computing significant association rules according to common statistical measures such as chi-square values or correlation coefficient [12, 14]. They introduced a method of estimating a tight upper bound on the statistical metric associated with any superset of an itemset, as well as a novel use of the resulting information about upper bounds to prune unproductive supersets while traversing the itemset lattices. We also use this method to estimate the upper bounds of the statistical indices and expand it for our problem. For the sake of simplicity in this paper, we use the chi-square value method.

Let GD be a dataset, and p and n be the number of positive and negative examples in the dataset GD, respectively. Let I be the left-hand side of the rule, i.e., $P_1 \wedge \overline{P_2}$ where $P_1 \sqsubset P_2$, and C be a positive class. Let O_{ij} where $(i,j) \in \{I, \overline{I}\} \times \{C, \overline{C}\}$ denotes the number of graphs that fulfill both i and j. Let O_i where $i \in \{I, \overline{I}, C, \overline{C}\}$ denote the number of graphs that fulfill i. $O_{I\overline{C}}$ represents the number of graphs that fulfill I, but which are not positive examples. O_I represents the number of graphs that fulfill I, which is equal to the sum of the values in the row $O_{IC} + O_{I\overline{C}}$.

We now consider how to estimate the upper bound of the chi-square value for $P_1 \wedge \overline{P_2} \Rightarrow Positive$. Let $\sigma_p(P_1)$ and $\sigma_p(P_2)$ be the number of positive examples which contain P_1 and P_2, respectively, and $\sigma_n(P_1)$ and $\sigma_n(P_2)$ be the number of negative examples which contain P_1 and

P_2, respectively. $O_{IC} = \sigma_p(P_1) - \sigma_p(P_2)$ and $O_{I\overline{C}} = \sigma_n(P_1) - \sigma_n(P_2)$, because graphs which contain P_2 also contain P_1 according to $P_1 \sqsubset P_2$. Table 1 is a contingency table summarizing the above definitions. For each pair $(i,j) \in \{I, \overline{I}\} \times \{C, \overline{C}\}$, we calculate an expectation under the assumption of independence: $E_{ij} = \frac{O_i O_j}{p+n}$. We denote the chi-square value as $\chi^2(P_1 \wedge \overline{P_2})$ or $chi(O_{IC}, O_{I\overline{C}})$. The chi-square value $\chi^2(P_1 \wedge \overline{P_2})$ is the normalized deviation of observation from expectation, namely,

$$\chi^2(P_1 \wedge \overline{P_2}) = chi(O_{IC}, O_{I\overline{C}}) = \sum_{i \in \{I, \overline{I}\}, j \in \{C, \overline{C}\}} \frac{(O_{ij} - E_{ij})^2}{E_{ij}}. \qquad (3)$$

In this definition, each O_{ij} must be non-negative; hence, $0 \le \sigma_p(P_2) \le \sigma_p(P_1) \le p$, and $0 \le \sigma_n(P_2) \le \sigma_n(P_1) \le n$. It is often helpful to explicitly state that O_{IC} and $O_{I\overline{C}}$ are determined by P_1 and P_2, and we define them as $O_{IC}(P_1 \wedge \overline{P_2})$ and $O_{I\overline{C}}(P_1 \wedge \overline{P_2})$.

It is known that any convex function is maximized at one of the vertices on the boundary of a convex polygon [5], and it has been proven that $chi(O_{IC}, O_{I\overline{C}})$ is a convex function [12]. The upper bound of the chi-square value is derived as follows.

Let P_1' be a pattern which is made by expanding P_1 and P_3 be a pattern which includes P_1', i.e., $P_3 \sqsupset P_1'$. It can be derived that

$$\chi^2(P_1' \wedge \overline{P_3}) \le max\{chi(\sigma_p(P_1), 0), chi(0, \sigma_n(P_1))\}, \qquad (4)$$

because

$$0 \le O_{IC}(P_1' \wedge \overline{P_3}) \le \sigma_p(P_1) \ and \ 0 \le O_{I\overline{C}}(P_1' \wedge \overline{P_3}) \le \sigma_n(P_1).$$

In other words, defining

$$u_1(P_1 \wedge \overline{P_2}) = max\{chi(\sigma_p(P_1), 0), chi(0, \sigma_n(P_1))\},$$

inequality (4) implies that when a pattern P_1 is expanded into P_1' to generate larger patterns, $\chi^2(P_1' \wedge \overline{P_3})$ is bounded by $u_1(P_1 \wedge \overline{P_2})$. Figure 3 shows that $(\sigma_p(P_1') - \sigma_p(P_3), \sigma_n(P_1') - \sigma_n(P_3))$ is mapped onto the gray rectangle whose vertices are $(0,0)$, $(\sigma_p(P_1), 0)$, $(0, \sigma_n(P_1))$ and $(\sigma_p(P_1), \sigma_n(P_1))$.

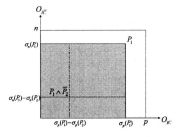

Figure 3. Mapped Space of $(O_{IC}(P_1' \wedge \overline{P_3}), O_{I\overline{C}}(P_1' \wedge \overline{P_3}))$

Table 1. Contingency Table for $P_1 \wedge \overline{P_2}$

	$C = Positive$	$\overline{C} = Negative$	$\sum row$
I	$O_{IC} = \sigma_p(P_1) - \sigma_p(P_2)$	$O_{I\overline{C}} = \sigma_n(P_1) - \sigma_n(P_2)$	$O_I = \sigma(P_1) - \sigma(P_2)$
$\overline{I}$	$O_{\overline{I}C}$	$O_{\overline{I}\,\overline{C}}$	$O_{\overline{I}}$
$\sum column$	$O_C = \sigma_y(null) = p$	$O_{\overline{C}} = \sigma_n(null) = n$	$p + n$

Moreover, let P_2' be a pattern which fullfils $P_2' \sqsupset P_2 \sqsupset P_1$. It can be derived that

$$\chi^2(P_1 \wedge P_2') \leq max\{chi(\sigma_p(P_1) - \sigma_p(P_2),$$

$$\sigma_n(P_1)), chi(\sigma_p(P_1), \sigma_n(P_1) - \sigma_n(P_2))\}, \quad (5)$$

because

$$\sigma_p(P_1) - \sigma_p(P_2) \leq O_{IC}(P_1 \wedge \overline{P_2'}) \leq \sigma_p(P_1), \; and$$

$$\sigma_n(P_1) - \sigma_n(P_2) \leq O_{I\overline{C}}(P_1 \wedge \overline{P_2'}) \leq \sigma_n(P_1).$$

In other words, defining

$$u_2(P_1 \wedge \overline{P_2}) = max\{chi(\sigma_p(P_1) - \sigma_p(P_2),$$

$$\sigma_n(P_1)), chi(\sigma_p(P_1), \sigma_n(P_1) - \sigma_n(P_2))\},$$

inequality (5) states that when a pattern P_2 is expanded into P_2' to generate larger patterns, $\chi^2(P_1 \wedge \overline{P_2'})$ is bounded by $u_1(P_1 \wedge \overline{P_2})$. Figure 4 shows that $(\sigma_p(P_1) - \sigma_p(P_2'), \sigma_n(P_1) - \sigma_n(P_2'))$ is mapped onto the gray rectangle whose vertices are $(\sigma_p(P_1) - \sigma_p(P_2), \sigma_n(P_1) - \sigma_n(P_2))$, $(\sigma_p(P_1), \sigma_n(P_1) - \sigma_n(P_2))$, $(\sigma_p(P_1) - \sigma_p(P_2), \sigma_n(P_1))$ and $(\sigma_p(P_1), \sigma_n(P_1))$.

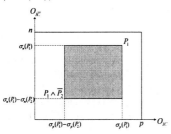

Figure 4. Mapped Space of $(O_{IC}(P_1 \wedge \overline{P_2'}), O_{I\overline{C}}(P_1 \wedge \overline{P_2'}))$

When the type of the discovered rule is $P \Rightarrow positive$, let P' be a pattern which contains P. Since $0 \leq O_{IC} \leq \sigma_p(P), 0 \leq O_{I\overline{C}} \leq \sigma_n(P)$,

$$\chi^2(P') \leq max\{chi(\sigma_p(P), 0), chi(0, \sigma_n(P))\}. \quad (6)$$

Inequality (6) is described as $\chi^2(P') \leq u_1(P)$.

Although AprioriSMP uses only inequality (6), we use inequalities (4) and (5) in addition to inequality (6).

4 Algorithm

We propose an algorithm to mine the significant rules in ascending order of their sizes. It gradually narrows down the space where $(O_{IC}, O_{I\overline{C}})$ is mapped by expanding the patterns. For the moment, for the sake of simplicity, we consider the case that the dataset consists of itemsets. However, it can easily be integrated into the existing frequent graph mining and tree mining algorithms. When we discuss frequent itemset mining, the lattice representation is often used to represent the search space as in Figure 5 (a). The lattice of itemsets is scanned beginning with smaller itemsets and continuing to larger ones. Figure 5 (b) shows our lattice for mining the significant rules when the dataset has three types of items, A, B, and C. Instead of an itemset for each node in the conventional representation, a pair of patterns is described for each node. We always retain the current maximum (or N-th largest) chi-square value among all the chi-square values calculated so far, and set it to the cutoff value. This discards unimportant rules earlier in the computations, and thereby accelerates the overall performance. We begin a rule with $P_1 = null$ and $P_2 = null$. It is expanded by recursively adding one item in each step. If $P_1 = P_2$, both P_1 and P_2 are expanded by adding the same item, or only P_2 is expanded with an item according to inequalities (4) and (6). Otherwise, P_2 is expanded by adding an item which P_1 does not have according to inequality (5). It is not possible that only P_1 is expanded, because it is not possible to narrows down the space where $(O_{IC}, O_{I\overline{C}})$ is mapped. Each node has 2 counters, one of them is for support on a positive dataset and the other is for a negative dataset. There are seven nodes that have $P_2 = ABC$ in Figure 5. Since it is redundant to scan the dataset seven times to count the support values of the itemset ABC, our algorithm is implemented to scan it once to count them. This is done by implementing the algorithm as though the nodes have pointers to one another. When the support value of one of them is counted, the value is propagated the others. In any node, if $u_1(P_1 \wedge \overline{P_2})$, $u_2(P_1 \wedge \overline{P_2})$, and $u_1(P_1)$ are all less than a cutoff value, the node is pruned from the lattice according to inequalities (4), (5), and (6). For instance, when traversing from a node with $P_1 = null$ and $P_2 = null$ to another node with $P_1 = AC$ and $P_2 = ABC$, the space where $(O_{IC}, O_{I\overline{C}})$ is mapped is gradually narrowed down as shown in Figure 6. Figure 7 presents our algorithm for mining the most significant rule.

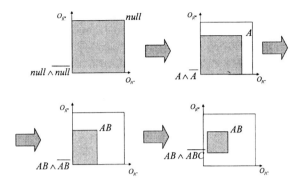

Figure 6. Transition of Mapped Space of $(O_{IC}, O_{I\overline{C}})$

5 Experiments

The proposed algorithm was integrated into AcGM (Apriori-based connected Graph Mining) algorithm which is an optimized version of AGM to mine only frequent *connected* subgraphs [7][5]. The method proposed in this paper was implemented using C++, and an IBM IntelliStation with Windows XP was used for the evaluation experiments, with a Xeon-2.4 GHz CPU and 2 GB of main memory installed. For testing, we used two read world datasets in chemistry. In our experiment, each atom, chemical bond, atom type, and bond type in a compound correspond to vertex, edge, vertex label, and edge label in a graph, respectively. The number of vertices in a graph is called the size of the graph.

5.1 Carcinogenic Data

First, the molecular structure data of carcinogenic compounds was analyzed. This data was provided by Predictive Toxicology Evaluation [13], and contains information on 337 chemical compounds. Each data entry is categorized into either active or inactive. A total of 182 compounds are categorized into active and 155 compounds are categorized as inactive. The number of types of the atoms which constitute chemical compounds is 24. The atomic bonds which correspond to edges in a graph have 4 types. The average size of the graph data is around 27, and the maximum size is 214.

---

[5]Our method can also be integrated into other algorithms such as gSpan, FSG, TreeMiner, and FREQT.

Figure 8 shows the result of the distribution of chi-square values for the discovered rules when the 100 most significant rules were mined by using AcGM with the proposed method and AcGM without it. Although AcGM without the proposed method can mine the only type of rules $P \Rightarrow positive$, AcGM with the method can mine both types of rules $P \Rightarrow positive$ and $P_1 \wedge \overline{P_2} \Rightarrow positive$. The figure shows that our proposed method can discover more significant rules than the existing frequent graph mining algorithms.

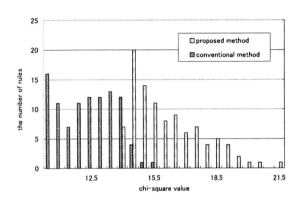

Figure 8. Distribution of Chi-square Values of Discovered Rules

5.2 HIV Data

Next, we used Developmental Therapeutics Program's AIDS Antiviral Screening Database. This project has checked tens of thousands of compounds for evidence of anti-HIV activity [4, 9]. The dataset contains 42,687 chemical compound structures and their screening data. Each data entry is categorized into either active (CA), moderately active (CM), or inactive (CI). We used the entries which are categorized to CA and CI. A total of 422 compounds are categorized into CA and 40,891 compounds are categorized as CI. The chemical compounds were formed from 69 atom types in the database, but hydrogen atoms are omitted and atoms with aromatic bonds are distinguished from atoms with no aromatic bonds in our experiment. The atomic bonds have 4 types. The average number of vertices in graph data is around 25.6, and the maximum number of vertices is 222.

The AcGM algorithm which integrated with the proposed method applied to the dataset. Figures 9 and 10 show the discovered rules. It took about 6 hours. P_1 in Figure 9 is contained in 64 compounds whose classes are CA and 16

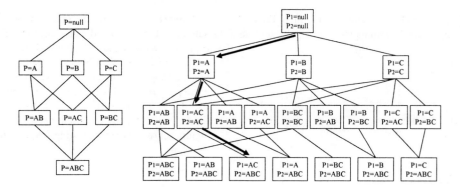

(a) Lattice for conventional method   (b) Lattice for our new approach

Figure 5. Lattice Representations of Search Space for Significant Rule Mining

```
    // GD is a database consisting of graph structured data.
    // A_k, B_k is a set of pairs of patterns, where the size of P_2 is k.
    // τ is a cut-off value.
0)  Main(GD){
1)     A_1 ← {all pairs of patterns P_1 and P_2 whose sizes are 1};
2)     τ ← 0;
3)     k ← 1;
4)     while(A_k ≠ ∅) {
5)        Scan GD to compute χ²(P_1 ∧ P_2̄), χ²(P_1), u_1(P_1), u_1(P_1 ∧ P_2̄),
              and u_2(P_1 ∧ P_2̄) for each pair (P_1, P_2) ∈ A_k;
6)        τ ← max(τ, max{χ²(P_1 ∧ P_2̄)|(P_1, P_2) ∈ A_k}, max{χ²(P_1)|(P_1, P_2) ∈ A_k});
7)        B_k ← {(P_1, P_2) ∈ A_k|u_1(P_1) ≥ τ, u_1(P_1 ∧ P_2̄) ≥ τ, or u_2(P_1 ∧ P_2̄) ≥ τ};
8)        A_{k+1} = Expand(B_k); // process to expand patterns
9)        k ← k + 1;
10)    }
11)    return τ with its corresponding pair of patterns;
12) }
```

Figure 7. Outline of Algorithm

compounds whose classes are CI and P_2 in Figure 9 is contained in 6 compounds whose classes are CI. The value of $\chi^2(P_1 \wedge \overline{P_2})$ is about 5,355.8[6]. Hence, although a compound which contains P_1 in the figure and does not contain P_2 in the figure correlates with active, the difference between P_1 and P_2 may reduce the physiological activity. Similarly, Figure 10 also shows another discovered rule. The value of $\chi^2(P_1 \wedge \overline{P_2})$ is about 5,142.5. If a benzene ring is attached to the position of the figure as in the previous example, the physiological activity as an anti-HIV medicine may be reduced.

Figure 11 shows the result of computation time for various minimum support threshold, when all frequent subgraph are derived by using the conventional AcGM algorithm. We can discover the rules shown in Figures 9 and 10 by first enumerating all of the frequent patterns with the AcGM and then combining two patterns in postprocessing.

However, the support values of the patterns P_2 in the figures are very low, so the existing frequent graph mining algorithms can not mine the patterns because of the computation complexity shown in Figure 11. Our system could efficiently discover characteristic rules with statistical significance and they are candidates for developing new anti-HIV medicines.

[figure: chemical structures for P_1 and P_2]

P_1
Active=64, Inactive=16

P_2
Active=0, Inactive=6

Figure 9. Discoverd Pair of Patterns (1)

---

[6]The value of $\chi^2(P_1)$ for P_1 in Figure 9 is about 4945.2.

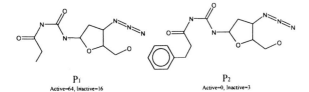

P₁
Active=64, Inactive=16

P₂
Active=0, Inactive=3

Figure 10. Discoverd Pair of Patterns (2)

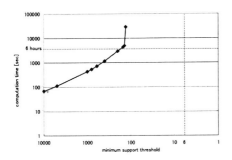

Figure 11. Computation Time of conventional AcGM Algorithm

6 Discussion and Related Work

Some approaches which can efficiently mine frequent substructures from a set of structured data such as graphs or trees have been proposed [6, 10, 19, 20, 1]. The discovered patterns that are contained in each graph or tree are frequent subgraphs which are mathematically defined in the graph theory domain. However, our approach can efficiently discover more significant and complex rules than those which the existing algorithms discover.

Some approaches have been applied to derive negative association rules and association rules which include negative elements in the conventional Basket Analysis. However, the existing graph mining approaches can not be applied to graphs for practical purposes, because of representation of the negative factors and combinatorial explosion of patterns.

Liu et al. proposed a method to discover interesting rules from transactional database based on statistical significance [11]. They introduced Direction Setting rules. The directions of the discovered rules $\{A\} \Rightarrow \{B\}$ are categorized into either "1", "-1", or "0". The direction "1" means that itemsets A and B are correlative, and $\sigma(A, B)/(\sigma(A)\sigma(A)) > 1$. The direction "-1" means that itemsets A and B are correlative, and $\sigma(A, B)/(\sigma(A)\sigma(A)) < -1$. The direction "0" means that itemsets A and B are independent. Assuming that itemsets

A is divided into A_1 and A_2, the method discovers the interesting rules $\{A\} \Rightarrow \{B\}$, where directions of the rules $\{A_1\} \Rightarrow \{B\}$, $\{A_2\} \Rightarrow \{B\}$ and $\{A\} \Rightarrow \{B\}$ are either (0,0,1), (-1,-1,1), (-1,0,1), or (-1,1,1). Although our approach is similar to their method if we focused on a pair of rules $\{A_1\} \Rightarrow \{B\}$ and $\{A\} \Rightarrow \{B\}$ whose directions are different, their method first enumerates all frequent patterns from a database and then to discovers direction setting rules. On the other hand, our approach abandons unimportant rules earlier in the computations, and thereby accelerates the overall performance. Suzuki introduced a method to discover exception rules which are represented as a pair of rules $\{A\} \Rightarrow \{x\}$ and $\{AB\} \Rightarrow \{\overline{x}\}$ where A and B are itemsets and x is an item [15, 16, 17]. Our approach is similar to their method. However, we can not apply the method to graph structures because the method is based on multidimensional normal distributions of vectors.

In this paper, we focused a combination $P_1 \wedge \overline{P_2}$ of two patterns, assuming $P_1 \sqsubset P_2$. However, there are various combinations of two patterns other than $P_1 \wedge \overline{P_2}$. Table 2 summarizes chi-square values for the combinations of patterns. The number of graphs which contain patterns both P_1 and P_2 is equal to the number of graphs which contain P_2, because graph which contain P_2 also contains P_1 according to $P_1 \sqsubset P_2$. Hence, the first row of the table mentions that to discover a type of the rule $P_1 \wedge P_2 \Rightarrow positive$ (or $negative$) corresponds to discover a type of the rule $P_2 \Rightarrow positive$ (or $negative$). The fourth and fifth rows means that no graph which fulfills the conditions $\overline{P_1} \wedge P_2$, and graphs which fulfill the conditions $P_1 \oplus P_2$ are equal to graphs which fulfill $P_1 \wedge \overline{P_2}$. In the sixth to tenth rows, $\chi^2(P)$ is equal to $\chi^2(\overline{P})$ according to Equation (3). Therefore, to mine a rule $\overline{P} \Rightarrow positive$ from a value $\chi^2(\overline{P})$ corresponds to mine a rule $P \Rightarrow negative$ from $\chi^2(P)$. Although we focused the only combination $P_1 \wedge \overline{P_2}$ of two patterns, it is denoted that all combinations of two patterns and complex combinations of more patterns than two can be derived by using our proposed method.

7 Conclusion

In this paper, we proposed an efficient approach to discover significant rules to classify positive and negative graphs by estimating a tight upper bound on the statistical metric. It abandons unimportant rules earlier in computation, and thereby accelerates the overall performance. The performance has been evaluated using real world datasets, and the efficiency and effect of our approach has been confirmed with respect to the amount of data and the computation time. In our future work, we plan to use the discovered pairs of patterns as features of machine learning algorithms to develop a classifier, and to compare to other relational supervised learners such as SubdueCL[3] or ILP systems.

Table 2. All Combinations of Two Patterns P_1 and P_2 where $P_1 \sqsubseteq P_2$

	Conbination of Patterns
1	$\chi^2(P_1 \wedge P_2) = \chi^2(P_2)$
2	$\chi^2(P_1 \vee P_2) = \chi^2(P_1)$
3	$\chi^2(P_1 \wedge \overline{P_2})$
4	$\chi^2(\overline{P_1} \wedge P_2) = 0$
5	$\chi^2(P_1 \ominus P_2) = \chi^2(P_1 \wedge \overline{P_2})$
6	$\chi^2(\overline{P_1} \vee \overline{P_2}) = \chi^2(\overline{P_1 \wedge P_2}) = \chi^2(\overline{P_2}) = \chi^2(P_2)$
7	$\chi^2(\overline{P_1} \wedge \overline{P_2}) = \chi^2(\overline{P_1 \vee P_2}) = \chi^2(\overline{P_1}) = \chi^2(P_1)$
8	$\chi^2(\overline{P_1} \vee P_2) = \chi^2(\overline{P_1 \wedge \overline{P_2}}) = \chi^2(P_1 \wedge \overline{P_2})$
9	$\chi^2(P_1 \vee \overline{P_2}) = \chi^2(\overline{\overline{P_1} \wedge P_2}) = \chi^2(\overline{P_1} \wedge P_2) = 0$
10	$\chi^2(\overline{P_1 \ominus P_2}) = \chi^2(P_1 \ominus P_2) = \chi^2(P_1 \wedge \overline{P_2})$

References

[1] Asai, T., Abe, K., Kawasoe, S., Arimura, H., Sakamoto, H, & Arikawa, S. Efficient Substructure Discovery from Large Semi-structured Data, *Proc. of the 2nd SIAM International Conference on Data Mining* (SDM-2002), pp.158-174, 2002.

[2] De Raedt, L., & Kramer, S. The Levelwise Version Space Algorithm and its Application to Molecular Fragment Finding. *Proc. of the 17th International Joint Conference on Artificial Intelligence* (IJCAI-2001), pp. 853–859, 2001.

[3] Gonzalez, J., Holder, L., & Cook, D. Graph-Based Relational Concept Learning. *Proc. of the 19th International Conference on Machine Learning* (ICML-2002), pp. 219-226, 2002.

[4] AIDS Antiviral Screen, http://dtp.nci.nih.gov/docs/aids/aids_data.html

[5] Horst, R. and Tuy, H. *Global Optimization Deterministic Approaches.* Springer, 1996.

[6] Inokuchi, A., Washio, T., & Motoda, H. An Apriori-based Algorithm for Mining Frequent Substructures from Graph Data. *Proc. of the 4th European Conference on Principles and Practice of Knowledge Discovery in Databases* (PKDD-2000), pp. 13–23, 2000.

[7] Inokuchi, A., Washio, T., Nishimura, Y., & Motoda, H. A Fast Algorithm for Mining Frequent Connected Subgraphs. *IBM Research Report*, RT0448 February, 2002.

[8] Inokuchi, A., Washio, T. & Motoda, H. Complete Mining of Frequent Patterns from Graphs: Mining Graph Data, *Machine Learning*, 50 (3): 321-354, March, 2003,

[9] Kramer, S., De Raedt, L., & Helma, C. Molecular Feature Mining in HIV Data. *Proc. of the 17th International Conference on Knowledge Discovery and Data Mining* (KDD-2001), pp. 136–143, 2001.

[10] Kuramochi, M., & Karypis, G. Frequent Subgraph Discovery. *Proc. of the 1st International Conference on Data Mining* (ICDM-2001), pp.313–320, 2001.

[11] Liu, B., Hsu, W. & Ma, Y. Pruning and Summarizing the Discovered Associations *Proc. of the 5th International Conference on Knowledge Discovery and Data Mining* (KDD-99), pp.125–134, 1999.

[12] Motishita, S. and Sese, J. Traversing Lattice Itemset with Statistical Metric Pruning. *Proc. of Symposium on Principles of Database Systems* (PODS-2000), pp.226–236, 2000.

[13] PTE, http://oldwww.comlab.ox.ac.uk/oucl/groups/machlearn/PTE

[14] Sese, J. and Morishita, S. Answering the Most Correlated N Association Rules Efficiently. *Proc. of 6th European Conference on Principles and Practice of Knowledge Discovery in Databases* (PKDD-02), pp.410–422, 2002.

[15] Suzuki, E. Discovering Unexpected Exceptions: A Stochastic Approach. *Proc. of the 4th International Workshop on Rough Sets, Fuzzy Sets, and Machine Discovery* (RSFD-96), pp. 225–232, 1996.

[16] Suzuki, E. & Kodratoff, Y. Discovery of Surprising Exception Rules based on Intensity of Implication. *Proc of Principles of Data Mining and Knowledge Discovery* (PKDD-98), pp. 10–18, 1998.

[17] Suzuki, E & Zytkow, J. M. Unified Algorithm for Undirected Discovery of Exception Rules. *Proc. of Principles of Data Mining and Knowledge Discovery* (PKDD-2000), pp. 169-180, 2000.

[18] Wu, X., Zhang, C., & Zhang, S. Mining Both Positive and Negative Association Rules. *Proc. of the 19th International Conference on Machine Learning*, pp. 658–665, 2002.

[19] Yan, X. & Han, J. gSpan: Graph-Based Substructure Pattern Mining. *Proc. of the 3rd International Conference on Data Mining*, (ICDM-2002), pp.721–724, 2002.

[20] Zaki, M. Efficiently Mining Frequent Trees in a Forest. *Proc. of the 8th International Conference on Knowledge Discovery and Data Mining* (KDD-2002), pp. 71–80, 2002.

Scalable Model-based Clustering by Working on Data Summaries [1]

Huidong Jin[‡ˣ],   Man-Leung Wong[‡],
[‡]Department of Information Systems
Lingnan University
Tuen Mun, N.T., Hong Kong
hdjin@ieee.org,   mlwong@ln.edu.hk,

Kwong-Sak Leung[ˣ]
[ˣ]Department of Computer Sci. & Eng.
The Chinese University of Hong Kong
Shatin, N.T., Hong Kong
ksleung@cse.cuhk.edu.hk

Abstract

The scalability problem in data mining involves the development of methods for handling large databases with limited computational resources. In this paper, we present a two-phase scalable model-based clustering framework: First, a large data set is summed up into sub-clusters; Then, clusters are directly generated from the summary statistics of sub-clusters by a specifically designed Expectation-Maximization (EM) algorithm. Taking example for Gaussian mixture models, we establish a provably convergent EM algorithm, EMADS, which embodies cardinality, mean, and covariance information of each sub-cluster explicitly. Combining with different data summarization procedures, EMADS is used to construct two clustering systems: gEMADS and bEMADS. The experimental results demonstrate that they run several orders of magnitude faster than the classic EM algorithm with little loss of accuracy. They generate significantly better results than other model-based clustering systems using similar computational resources.

1. Introduction

With the explosive growth of data amassed from business and scientific disciplines, scalable data mining systems become more and more important. They bridge the gap between the limited computational resources and large databases. Their running time grows linearly or sub-linearly with data size, given computational resources such as main memory [1, 7]. Model-based clustering techniques can identify clusters of various shapes and handle complicated databases with different kinds of attributes [3, 4]. Furthermore, they have solid mathematical foundations from the statistics community [9]. These techniques have successfully been applied to numerous real-life applications

[2, 3, 6, 9, 14]. Thus, the research on scalable model-based cluster analysis is significant.

The Expectation-Maximization (EM) algorithm is an iterative procedure for finding maximum likelihood estimates of parameters in a mixture model. EM normally generates more accurate results than hierarchical model-based clustering [6, 10]. Though some attempts have been made to speed up EM [9, 11], EM and its extensions are still computationally expensive for large databases. The lazy EM algorithm [15] evaluates the significance of data items and then operates only on the significant ones. Comparing with EM, its speedup factor is less than three. The scalable EM algorithm [1] uses a heuristically extended EM algorithm to identify compressible regions of data. Then it retains their sufficient statistics in order to load another batch of data, and invokes EM again. Its speedup factor is up to ten [1, 7].

In this paper, we will present our scalable model-based clustering systems which can run several orders of magnitude faster than the classical EM algorithm on large databases. Moreover, there is no or little loss of accuracy. They also can generate much more accurate results than other scalable model-based clustering systems. The basic idea is to categorize a data set into sub-clusters first and then generate a mixture model from their summary statistics directly by a specifically designed EM algorithm. This new EM algorithm works on the summary statistics of the sub-clusters, and it is associated with a pseudo mixture model that is developed to approximate the aggregate behavior of each sub-cluster of data items under the original mixture model. Thus, the new EM algorithm can efficiently generate a good estimate of the original mixture model. For example, for the California housing data plotted in a scaled Latitude-Longitude space in Figure 1(a), our clustering systems generate two mixtures, respectively, from 551 and 780 data summaries of 20,640 data items. The two mixture models clearly describe the housing structure in California, as illustrated in Figures 1(b) and 1(c), where a data summary is indicated by '*', and a Gaussian distribution is indicated by an 'o' and its associated ellipse.

[1]The work is partially supported by Hong Kong RGC Grant CUHK 4212/01E and Lingnan University direct research grant (RES-021/200). We would like to thank the referees for their constructive suggestions.

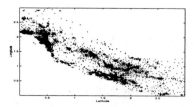

(a) California housing data.

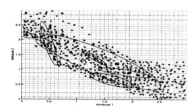

(b) Clusters generated by gEMADS.

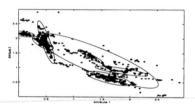

(c) Clusters generated by bEMADS.

Figure 1. Gaussian mixture models generated for the California housing data by two model-based clustering systems.

In the next section, we describe our model-based clustering framework and then apply it to a Gaussian mixture model. Two possible data summarization procedures are described in Section 3. A pseudo mixture model and its associated EM algorithm are developed for the Gaussian mixture model in Section 4. In Section 5, comprehensive experiment results are given on both synthetic and real-life data sets. The conclusive comments come in the last section.

2 Scalable Model-based Clustering

Given a data set $X = \{\mathbf{x}_1, \cdots, \mathbf{x}_N\}$, the model-based clustering techniques assume that each data item $\mathbf{x}_i = [x_{1i}, \cdots, x_{Di}]^T$ is drawn from a K-component mixture model Φ with probability $p(\mathbf{x}_i|\Phi) = \sum_{k=1}^{K} p_k \phi(\mathbf{x}_i|\theta_k)$. Here p_k is

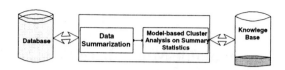

Figure 2. A scalable clustering framework.

the mixing proportion for the kth cluster ($0 < p_k < 1$ for $k = 1, \cdots, K$, and $\sum_{k=1}^{K} p_k = 1$); $\phi(\mathbf{x}_i|\theta_k)$ is a *component density function* with parameter θ_k. Given Φ, one may get a crisp clustering by assigning the data items $\mathbf{x}_i$ to cluster k where $k = \arg\max_l \{p_l \phi(\mathbf{x}_i|\theta_l)\}$. Thus, a mixture model Φ can be viewed as a clustering solution. Expectation-Maximization (EM) is a widely used algorithm for finding maximum likelihood estimates of Φ iteratively. In each iteration, EM needs to scan the whole set, which prohibits EM from large databases.

There are three approaches to scale-up classic clustering algorithms such as EM. Random sampling is easy to implement, but often brings about inaccuracy [5]. The weighted sampling uses a weighted (pseudo) sample to represent a group of data item [5, 13], and requires slight modification on the classical clustering techniques. However, as shown in Section 5, its performance also depends heavily on the sampling procedures. The third strategy is to construct summary statistics of the large data set on which to base the desired analysis [1, 16].

Our scalable model-based clustering framework falls into the last category. It is motivated by the following observation. In a scalable system, a group of similar data items usually needs to be handled as an object in order to save computational resources. In model-based cluster analysis, a component density function essentially determines clustering results. Thus, for each group of similar data items, a new component density function can be defined in order to remedy the possible loss of clustering accuracy caused by the trivially homogeneous treatment of these data items. For example, a pseudo component density function for their summary statistics can be developed to approximate their aggregate behavior under the original component density function. Finally, its associated clustering algorithm, e.g., an algorithm derived from the general EM algorithm [9], can effectively generate a good mixture model from these summary statistics directly. Thus, as illustrated in Figure 2, our framework has two phases: *data summarization*, which partitions similar data items into exclusive sub-clusters and generates their summary statistics, and *in-memory model-based clustering analysis*, which generates mixture models using the new EM algorithm associated with the pseudo mixture model.

In principle, the framework is applicable to many mixture models, but we focus on Gaussian mixture models in the paper because of their wide applications [1, 3, 6, 14]. In a Gaussian mixture model, each component is a multivariate Gaussian distribution:

$$\phi(\mathbf{x}_i|\theta_k) = \frac{\exp\left\{-\frac{1}{2}(\mathbf{x}_i - \mu_k)^T \Sigma_k^{-1}(\mathbf{x}_i - \mu_k)\right\}}{(2\pi)^{\frac{D}{2}} |\Sigma_k|^{\frac{1}{2}}}. \quad (1)$$

The parameter θ_k consists of a mean vector μ_k and a covariance matrix Σ_k. The classical EM algorithm estimates the parameters to maximize log-likelihood $L(\Phi) = \log\left[\prod_{i=1}^{N} p(\mathbf{x}_i|\Phi)\right]$ iteratively. It alternates between the following two steps.

1. **E-Step**: Given the mixture model parameters, compute the membership probability $t_{ik}^{(j)} = \frac{p_k^{(j)} \phi(\mathbf{x}_i|u_k^{(j)}, \Sigma_k^{(j)})}{\sum_{l=1}^{K} p_l^{(j)} \phi(\mathbf{x}_i|u_l^{(j)}, \Sigma_l^{(j)})}$.

2. **M-step**: Given $t_{ik}^{(j)}$, update the mixture model parameters from the total N data items for $k = 1, \cdots, K$:

$$p_k^{(j+1)} = \frac{1}{N} \sum_{i=1}^{N} t_{ik}^{(j)} \quad (2)$$

$$\mu_k^{(j+1)} = \frac{\sum_{i=1}^{N} t_{ik}^{(j)} \mathbf{x}_i}{\sum_{i=1}^{N} t_{ik}^{(j)}} = \frac{\sum_{i=1}^{N} t_{ik}^{(j)} \mathbf{x}_i}{N \cdot p_k^{(j+1)}} \quad (3)$$

$$\Sigma_k^{(j+1)} = \frac{\sum_{i=1}^{N} t_{ik}^{(j)} (\mathbf{x}_i - \mu_k^{(j+1)})(\mathbf{x}_i - \mu_k^{(j+1)})^T}{N \cdot p_k^{(j+1)}} \quad (4)$$

As the summary statistics of sub-clusters are the only information passed from the first phase onto the second one, they play an important role in clustering accuracy. They had better reflect the data distribution within the sub-clusters. For example, a Gaussian distribution embodies a covariance matrix, thus the covariance information should be included in the summary statistics for Gaussian mixture models. Thus, we define the following data summary as the summary statistics of a sub-cluster.

Definition 1 *For the mth sub-cluster, the **data summary** is defined as a triple: $DS_m = \{n_m, \nu_m, \Gamma_m\} (m = 1, \cdots, M$, where M is the number of sub-clusters). Here, n_m is the number of data items in the mth sub-cluster; $\nu_m = \frac{1}{n_m} \sum_{the\ m^{th} sub-cluster} \mathbf{x}_i$ is the mean of the data in the mth sub-cluster; and $\Gamma_m = \frac{1}{n_m} \sum_{the\ m^{th} sub-cluster} \mathbf{x}_i \mathbf{x}_i^T$ is the average of the outer products of the n_m data items.*

The data summary DS_m comprises the zeroth, first, and second moments of the mth sub-cluster of data items. It

contains sufficient statistics when the data items within the sub-cluster follow a Gaussian distribution. Taking the data summary as summary statistics for a sub-cluster, a new pseudo mixture model and its associated EM algorithm, EMADS, will be derived in Section 4. Two scalable clustering systems can be developed by cooperating with the two data summarization procedures presented in the next section.

3 Data Summarization Procedures

Our data summarization procedures sum up similar data items into data summaries. The grid-based data summarization procedure partitions a data set by imposing a multidimensional grid structure in the data space, and then incrementally sums up the data items within a cell into its data summaries. That is, the data items within a cell form a sub-cluster. For simplicity, each attribute is partitioned into several equidistant segments by grids. Thus, each cell has the same width in each attribute and has the same volume. For example, for the California housing data in Figure 1(a), we partition each attribute into 40 segments and obtain 551 non-empty sub-clusters, as shown in Figure 1(b). Thus, the cell widths specify the grid structure and the total number of sub-clusters.

To operate within the given main memory, we only store data summaries for the non-empty cells in a data summary array: DS-array. This DS-array has a fixed number of entries, M, according to the given amount of main memory. When a new data item is read, we calculate which cell it is located in. Then we efficiently search for its associated entry in the DS-array by using a hash function. If a corresponding entry is found, its data summary is updated to absorb the data item. Otherwise, a new entry will be allocated to store the data summary of the cell.

The grid-based data summarization procedure adaptively determines the cell width to better use the given main memory. At the beginning, the cell widths are initialized to reasonably small values. If the cell widths are quite small, then the number of non-empty cells may be greater than the number of entries in the DS-array. When the entries in the DS-array are used up, the cell width are increased and the DS-array is rebuilt. The grid-based data summarization procedure merges every two adjacent cells into a larger one along the dimension with the smallest width. Thus, a new data summary is calculated from two old ones without rereading the data.

If the Euclidean distance is used to define the similarity between two data items within sub-clusters, we may employ existing scalable distance-based clustering techniques [12, 13], such as BIRCH [16], to generate sub-clusters. BIRCH scans the data set to build an initial in-memory CF(Clustering Features)-tree, which can be viewed as a multilevel compression of the data set that tries to preserve its inherent clustering structure. Different from clustering features, data summaries contain covariance information. Hence, in our experiments, BIRCH is modified to generate data summaries. The generated 780 data summaries for the California housing data are illustrated in Figure 1(c).

Both the BIRCH's and the grid-based data summarization procedures attempt to generate data summaries using restricted computational resources. They both read the data set only once. However, the former uses a tree indexing, while the later employs a hash indexing. The former makes better use of memory, while the later is simpler to implement and manipulate [8].

4 EMADS

Our in-memory model-based clustering algorithm directly generates a Gaussian mixture model from data summaries. Our design method is first to introduce a pseudo component density function on the data summaries. The pseudo density function can approximate the aggregate behavior of each sub-cluster of data items under the Gaussian distribution. We then define a pseudo mixture model and derive its associated EM algorithm — EM Algorithm for Data Summaries (EMADS) — according to the general EM algorithm [9].

In order to embody the covariance information in our pseudo component density function to better approximate the aggregate behavior, we simplify the data summary $DS_m = \{n_m, \nu_m, \Gamma_m\}$ into a **simplified data summary** $\mathbf{s}_m = \{n_m, \nu_m, \delta_m\}$. δ_m is the product of the square root of the largest eigenvalue of the covariance matrix $(\Gamma_m - \nu_m \nu_m^T)$ and its corresponding component vector. According to Theorem 6.1 in [8, p.120], δ_m is a good choice because its outer product best approximates the matrix. Now we introduce a new density function based on the sub-cluster to which a data item $\mathbf{x}_i$ belongs.

Definition 2 *For a single data item* $\mathbf{x}_i$ *within the* m^{th} *sub-cluster, its probability under the* **pseudo component density function** ψ *is*

$$
\begin{aligned}
\psi(\mathbf{x}_i &\in \text{the } m^{th} \text{ sub-cluster} | \theta_k) \triangleq \psi(\mathbf{s}_m | \theta_k) \\
&= \frac{\exp\left\{-\frac{1}{2}\left[\delta_m^T \Sigma_k^{-1}\delta_m + (\nu_m - \mu_k)^T \Sigma_k^{-1}(\nu_m - \mu_k)\right]\right\}}{(2\pi)^{\frac{D}{2}}|\Sigma_k|^{\frac{1}{2}}},
\end{aligned} \quad (5)
$$

where $\theta_k = (\mu_k, \Sigma_k)$ *is the parameter for the* k^{th} *component of the* **pseudo mixture model** Ψ.

If $\delta_m = 0$, the density function in Eq.(5) is equivalent to a Gaussian density function. In general, however, it is not a genuine density function because its integral over the whole data space is often less than 1. Roughly speaking, if the sub-cluster variance $n_m\left(\Gamma_m - \nu_m\nu_m^T\right)$ is small, say, in

1-D case, then the item $\delta_m^T \Sigma_m^{-1}\delta_m$ is also small. In other words, this density function has a higher probability for a data item in a dense area, which accords with the Gaussian density function. Furthermore, its associated EM algorithm, EMADS, can well approximate the aggregate behavior of each sub-cluster of data items, as explained in [8]. Hence, the pseudo component density function is practicable.

With Eq.(5), we get a density function under the pseudo mixture model Ψ for $\mathbf{x}_i$ within the mth sub-cluster,

$$
p(\mathbf{x}_i|\Psi) \triangleq p(\mathbf{s}_m|\Psi) = \sum_{k=1}^{K} p_k \psi(\mathbf{s}_m|\mu_k, \Sigma_k).
$$

The pseudo mixture model Ψ has the same parameters as the Gaussian mixture model Φ. In addition, the pseudo component density function approximates the aggregate behavior of each sub-cluster of data items under the Gaussian distribution. Thus, we can find a good Gaussian mixture model Φ by finding a maximum likelihood estimate of Ψ. Given the number of clusters K, we derive a new EM algorithm according to the general EM algorithm [9]. It efficiently gets an estimate of Ψ by maximizing the log-likelihood $L(\Psi) = \sum_{m=1}^{M} n_m \log\left(\sum_{k=1}^{K} p_k \psi(\mathbf{s}_m|\mu_k, \Sigma_k)\right)$ iteratively as follows.

Algorithm 3 EMADS

1. **Initialization**: *Set the current iteration* $j = 0$ *and initialize the parameters,* $p_k^{(j)}, \mu_k^{(j)}$ *and* $\Sigma_k^{(j)}$, *such that* $\sum_{k=1}^{K} p_k^{(j)} = 1$, *and* $\Sigma_k^{(j)}$ *is symmetric and positive definite.*

2. **E-step**: *Given the mixture model* $\Psi^{(j)}$, *compute the membership probability* $r_{mk}^{(j)}$ *for all* $\mathbf{s}_m$,

$$
r_{mk}^{(j)} = \frac{p_k^{(j)} \psi(\mathbf{s}_m|u_k^{(j)}, \Sigma_k^{(j)})}{\sum_{i=1}^{K} p_i^{(j)} \psi(\mathbf{s}_m|u_i^{(j)}, \Sigma_i^{(j)})}. \quad (6)
$$

3. **M-step**: *Given* $r_{mk}^{(j)}$, *update the model parameters using* $\mathbf{s}_m$ *for all* k,

$$
p_k^{(j+1)} = \frac{1}{N}\sum_{m=1}^{M} n_m r_{mk}^{(j)}, \quad (7)
$$

$$
\mu_k^{(j+1)} = \frac{\sum\limits_{m=1}^{M} n_m r_{mk}^{(j)} \nu_m^{(j)}}{\sum\limits_{m=1}^{M} n_m r_{mk}^{(j)}} = \frac{\sum\limits_{m=1}^{M} n_m r_{mk}^{(j)} \nu_m^{(j)}}{N \cdot p_k^{(j+1)}}, \quad (8)
$$

$$
\Sigma_k^{(j+1)} = \frac{\sum\limits_{m=1}^{M} n_m r_{mk}^{(j)}\left[\delta_m \delta_m^T + (\nu_m - \mu_k^{(j)})(\nu_m - \mu_k^{(j)})^T\right]}{N \cdot p_k^{(j+1)}}. \quad (9)
$$

4. **Termination:** *If* $\left|L(\Psi^{(j+1)}) - L(\Psi^{(j)})\right| \geq \epsilon \left|L(\Psi^{(j)})\right|$, *set* j *to* $j + 1$ *and go to step 2.*

Different from the Extended EM algorithm in [1] and the classical EM algorithm for Gaussian mixture models, EMADS embodies the covariance information explicitly in both E-step and M-step. Thus, more accurate results can be expected. EMADS is also easy to implement because it involves only several equations (Eqs.(6)-(9)). Furthermore, EMADS can surely terminate according to the following theorem.

Theorem 4 *If the matrix $[\nu_1, \nu_2, \cdots, \nu_M]$ is full rank, then the log-likelihood $L(\Psi)$ for EMADS converges monotonically to a log-likelihood value $L^* = L(\Psi^*)$ for a stationary mixture model Ψ^*.*

A proof can be found in [8]. The computational complexity of EMADS is $O(MKD^2I)$, where I is the number of iterations. It is linear with the number of data summaries. The total memory requirement of EMADS is $2MD + MK + KD^2 + KD + K + M$ floating point numbers. Thus, given a large data set, we can choose an appropriate number of sub-clusters, M, to sum up the data set into the given main memory and then generate Gaussian mixture models.

EMADS may be simplified into Weighted Expectation Maximization (WEM) when the component density function ψ is replaced by a Gaussian density function ϕ. Thus, WEM handles each data item in the same way as its corresponding sub-cluster mean vector, and the weights are the cardinality of the sub-clusters.

5 Performance of EMADS

5.1 Methodology and Synthetic Data

Working on the data summaries generated by the grid-based and the BIRCH's data summarization procedures, EMADS is used to construct two clustering systems. We call them gEMADS and bEMADS, respectively. The gEMADS system is mainly specified to examine the sensitivity of EMADS to different data summaries. To highlight their performance, we compare them with several model-based clustering systems designed according to the other scaling-up strategies. They are

The EM algorithm: It is the classical EM algorithm for Gaussian mixture models.

The sampling EM algorithm: It is EM working on 5% random samples. It is referred to as sampEM hereafter.

The gWEM and the bWEM systems: They are WEM working on the data summaries generated by two data summarization procedures, respectively. These two systems may be viewed as density-biased sampling clustering techniques [13].

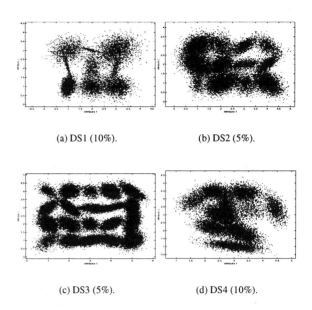

(a) DS1 (10%).

(b) DS2 (5%).

(c) DS3 (5%).

(d) DS4 (10%).

Figure 3. Data samples of four data sets.

All these systems are coded in MATLAB and experiments are conducted on a Sun Enterprise E4500 server. EMADS, WEM and EM are initialized with the cluster centers generated by K-means from M random samples. They terminate if the successive log-likelihood modification is within 10^{-5} of current value as used in [10, 15]. All experimental results reported are averaged on 10 independent runs. The data summarization procedures are set to generate at most 4,000 data summaries and use about 8 megabytes main memory. In contrast, there is no restriction on the amount of the main memory used for both EM and sampEM in our experiments.

Since all systems finally generate Gaussian mixture models, the natural evaluation metric is their log-likelihood value. For convenience, we average the log-likelihood over the samples. We also use *the clustering accuracy* to measure the generated mixture models for the synthetic data sets. The clustering accuracy is defined as the proportion of samples which are correctly clustered [10].

We generate three groups of synthetic data sets based on random mixture models. The first group has three data sets, and their mean vectors of Gaussian components are located on 2-D grid, as illustrated in Figures 3(a), 3(b), and 3(c), respectively. In the second group of four data sets, two mean vectors of a mixture model are generated together to ensure that their Euclidean distance is 1.0. Hence, these two clusters are close and not well separated. A typical data set is illustrated in Figure 3(d). The parameters of these seven data set are listed in Table 1, where N, D, K, and

M indicate the number of data items, the data dimensionality, the number of clusters, and the number of sub-clusters, respectively. The third group of 8 data sets is generated according to a 10-component Gaussian mixture model in 4-dimensional space. They differ only in their data sizes, which increase exponentially from 6,250 to 800,000.

5.2 Sensitivity

The data set (DS1) shown in Figure 3(a) is taken to examine the sensitivity of gEMADS to different data summaries. Figure 4 summaries the clustering accuracy of three clustering systems. The data summarization results are determined by different grid structures. For example, for the first 56*56 grid structure, we partition two attributes into 56 segments respectively and obtain 3,136 cells. These sub-clusters usually do not follow a Gaussian distribution. Here, sampEM(M) refers to sampEM working on M random samples where M is the number of sub-clusters.

For the first 7 grid structures, the segment numbers for each attribute are 56, 48, 40, 32, 24, 16, and 12, respectively. The cell granularity increases gradually. As shown in Figure 4, although the clustering accuracy of the three systems decreases, the accuracy of gEMADS decreases slowly and is normally higher than its two counterparts. Especially, it ranges from 95.4% to 91.4% for the first five grid structures, and the generated mixture models are very close to the original one. The last three grid structures in Figure 4 are used to generate very skew sub-clusters. For example, in the 12*86 grid structure, the cell width is 7.2 times longer than the cell height. Although the clustering accuracy of gEMADS system decreases from 92.0% to 83.6% for the last three grid structures, the decrease is much slower than that of gWEM. The one-tailed paired Student's t-Test for the 10 grid structures indicates that gEMADS significantly outperforms gWEM and sampEM at the 0.01 level. The performance of gEMADS is not so sensitive to the data summarization procedures, and acceptable when the sub-clusters are not too skew and large.

Table 1. The parameters of seven synthetic data sets.

DataSet	N (1000)	D	K	M
DS1	108	2	9	2986
DS2	500	2	12	2499
DS3	1100	2	20	3818
DS4	200	2	10	2279
DS5	200	3	10	3227
DS6	240	4	12	3982
DS7	280	5	14	2391

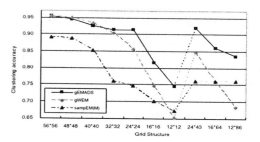

Figure 4. The clustering accuracy of three clustering systems for different data summarization or sampling procedures.

5.3 Scalability and Accuracy

The second set of experiments is conducted on the third group of data sets in order to analyze the scalability of bEMADS. Figure 5(a) illustrates the execution time of bEMADS, EM, bWEM, and sampEM.

It can be observed from Figure 5(a) that the execution time of bEMADS increases very slowly with the number of data items. It takes 673.8 seconds for the data set with 6,250 data items, and takes 1,106.2 seconds for the data set with 800,000 data items. The execution time of bEMADS mainly spends on the mixture model generation. For example, the data summarization procedure takes about 255.2 seconds and EMADS takes 851.0 seconds for the largest data set.

The execution time of EM increases from 2,344.4 seconds for the data set with 6,250 data items to 359,966.7 seconds for the largest data set. It increases almost linearly with the data size, as plotted in Figure 5(a). This is because that the amount of main memory used is not restricted during the execution. For the 8 data sets, the speedup factors of bEMADS to EM range from 3.5 to 339.0. Thus, bEMADS can run several orders of magnitude faster than EM. In addition, as indicated in Figure 5(b), bEMADS can generate slightly more accurate clustering results than EM on four data sets. The average clustering accuracy of bEMADS is 93.5%. This is a little bit higher than the value of 92.7% for EM. The execution time of sampEM ranges from 125.2 seconds to 12,071.0 seconds. The ratio of the execution time of sampEM to bEMADS is 10.9:1 for the largest data sets. Although bEMADS does not run as fast as sampEM for those small data sets, it generates much better results than sampEM. As plotted in Figure 5(b), the average clustering accuracy of bEMADS is 5.5% higher than the value of 88.0% for sampEM, which is statistically significant at the 0.05 level.

The bWEM system, similar to bEMADS, is scalable too.

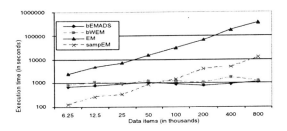

(a) Execution time.

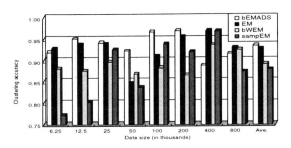

(b) Clustering accuracy.

Figure 5. Performance of four clustering systems for eight 4-dimensional data sets.

As plotted in Figure 5(b), bEMADS generates more accurate results than bWEM for almost all eight data sets. The average clustering accuracy of bWEM is 89.2%, which is significantly lower than that of bEMADS at the 0.05 level.

Similar comparison results can be found in the third set of experiments for different mixture models. Figure 6 illustrates the clustering accuracy of bEMADS, EM, bWEM, and sampEM for the seven data sets in Table 1. For the seven data sets, bEMADS generates the most accurate results on the second and the third data sets. On average, the clustering accuracy values of bEMADS, EM, bWEM, and sampEM are 89.6%, 90.6%, 84.7%, and 86.3%, respectively. Though EM generates slightly more accurate clustering results than bEMADS does, the one-tailed paired t-Test does not indicate that it is significantly different at the 0.05 level. However, the average clustering accuracy of bEMADS is significantly better than that of bWEM and sampEM at the 0.05 level.

5.4 Application on Two Real-life Data Sets

For the two real-life data sets, the average log-likelihood serves as the accuracy metric of the generated mixture models. The larger the average log-likelihood is, the better a

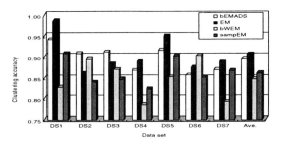

Figure 6. Clustering accuracy for the seven synthetic data sets.

mixture model matches a data set. Table 2 summarizes the experimental results, including the standard deviations of log-likelihood and execution time.

The first real-life data set is the California housing data, downloaded from www.spatial-statistics.com. It has 20,640 data items. We use a 7-component Gaussian mixture model to describe the data set. The data summarization procedure of BIRCH generates 2,907 data summaries. Figure 1(a) illustrates the data set in the scaled Latitude-Longitude space. For this 8-dimensional data set, bEMADS takes about 3,232.4 seconds to generate the mixture models with the average log-likelihood of 7.517. EM spends about 5.1 times longer. Though the accuracy of bEMADS is slightly lower than the value of 7.682 for EM, the one-tailed t-Test indicate that the difference is not statistically significant at the 0.05 level. For this moderate data set, sampEM runs faster than bEMADS. However, the average log-likelihood of sampEM is as low as 6.776, significantly lower than that of bEMADS. The log-likelihood of bWEM is also significantly lower than that of bEMADS, though both spend similar execution time.

The second real-life data set, the Forest CoverType Data, is from the UCI KDD Archive (kdd.ics.uci.edu). The data set has 581,012 data items and five attributes are used in our experiments. We use a Gaussian mixture model with 15 components to describe the data set. The BIRCH's data

Table 2. The performance of bEMADS on the two real-life data sets.

Housing	bEMADS	bWEM	EM	sampEM
log-likelihood	7.517 ± 0.191	6.882 ± 0.153	**7.682** ± 0.159	6.776 ± 0.239
time(Sec.)	3232.4 ± 525.8	3488.6 ± 317.7	16405.5 ± 2906.2	1433.9 ± 514.7
Forest	bEMADS	bWEM	sampEM(15%)	sampEM
log-likelihood	-3.083 ± 0.011	-3.278 ± 0.053	**-3.078** ± 0.017	-3.086 ± 0.018
time(Sec.)	7985.5 ± 3635.2	6039.7 ± 1313.5	173672.5 ± 80054.2	49745.8 ± 10328.9

summarization procedure generates 3,186 sub-clusters.

Because EM cannot generate a mixture model after running for 200 hours, we use sampEM(15%) for comparison. In fact, even it takes about 173,672.5 seconds. On average, bEMADS takes about 7,985.5 seconds. It runs 21.7 times faster than sampEM(15%), and 6.2 times faster than sampEM. The average log-likelihood value of bEMADS is -3.083. It is slightly larger than the value of -3.086 for sampEM, and slightly smaller than the value of -3.078 for sampEM(15%). However, the one-tailed t-Test indicate that no significant difference exists among them. The bWEM system runs a bit faster than bEMADS. However, it generates the worst mixture models among the four systems with the average log-likelihood value of -3.278. The one-tailed t-Test indicates that the log-likelihood value of bWEM is significantly worse than its three counterparts at the 0.05 level.

6 Conclusion

Through working on summary statistics, we have given a two-phase scalable model-based clustering framework: First, a large data set is categorized into mutually exclusive sub-clusters; Second, a new model-based clustering algorithm is used to directly generate clusters from the summary statistics of the sub-clusters. The new algorithm is designed for a pseudo mixture model that approximates the aggregate behavior of each sub-cluster of data items under the original mixture model.

To exemplify this framework, we have established two model-based clustering systems for the Gaussian mixture model. The main novelties are the pseudo component density function for data summaries and its associated iterative algorithm — EMADS (Expectation-Maximization Algorithm for Data Summaries). EMADS, derived from the general EM algorithm, can embody the cardinality, mean, and covariance information of each sub-cluster into both E-step and M-step to generate accurate Gaussian mixtures. We have also shown that EMADS converges to local maxima, which renders it the first mathematically sound algorithm to generate mixture models directly from data summaries. We have illustrated the insensitivity of EMADS to different data summary granularities by combining EMADS with the grid-based data summarization procedure. By combining EMADS with the BIRCH's data summarization procedures, we have established the scalable clustering system, bEMADS. The comprehensive experimental results on both the synthetic and real-life data sets have shown that bEMADS can run several orders of magnitude faster than the classical EM algorithm with little or no loss of accuracy. It runs faster and generates higher quality results than the random sampling EM algorithm for large data sets. It, using comparable computational resources, has generated statistically significantly more accurate results than the density-biased-sampling clustering system.

For future work, we will apply the scalable model-based clustering framework to heterogeneous, or other more complicated, data sets. We will also develop some effective approaches to automatically determine the number of clusters for large databases.

References

[1] P. Bradley, U. Fayyad, and C. Reina. Clustering very large databases using EM mixture models. In *ICPR'00*, volume 2, pages 76–80, 2000.

[2] I. Cadez, S. Gaffney, and P. Smyth. A general probabilistic framework for clustering individuals. In *KDD-2000*, pages 140–149, 2000.

[3] P. Cheeseman and J. Stutz. Bayesian classification (AutoClass): Theory and results. In U. M. Fayyad and *et al.*, editors, *Advances in Knowledge Discovery and Data Mining*, pages 153–180, 1996.

[4] T. Chiu, D. Fang, J. Chen, Y. Wang, and C. Jeris. A robust and scalable clustering algorithm for mixed type attributes in large database environment. In *KDD-2001*, pages 263–268, 2001.

[5] W. DuMouchel, C. Volinsky, T. Johnson, C. Cortes, and D. Pregibon. Squashing flat files flatter. In *KDD-1999*, pages 6–15, 1999.

[6] C. Fraley. Algorithms for model-based Gaussian hierarchical clustering. *SIAM Journal on Scientific Computing*, 20(1):270–281, Jan. 1999.

[7] J. Han and M. Kamber. *Data Mining: Concepts and Techniques*. Morgan Kaufmann Publishers, 2001.

[8] H.-D. Jin. *Scalable Model-based Clustering Algorithms for Large Databases and Their Applications*. Ph.D. thesis, the Chinese University of Hong Kong, Hong Kong, Aug. 2002.

[9] G. J. McLachlan and T. Krishnan. *The EM Algorithm and Extensions*. John Wiley & Sons, Inc., New York, 1997.

[10] M. Meilă and D. Heckerman. An experimental comparison of model-based clustering methods. *Machine Learning*, 42(1/2):9–29, 2001.

[11] A. Moore. Very fast EM-based mixture model clustering using multiresolution KD-trees. In *NIPS'99*, pages 543–549, 1999.

[12] R. T. Ng and J. Han. Efficient and effective clustering methods for spatial data mining. In *VLDB'94*, pages 144–155, 1994.

[13] C. R. Palmer and C. Faloutsos. Density biased sampling: An improved method for data mining and clustering. In *SIGMOD-2000*, pages 82–92, 2000.

[14] J. Shanmugasundaram, U. Fayyad, and P. S. Bradley. Compressed data cubes for OLAP aggregate query approximation on continuous dimensions. In *KDD-1999*, pages 223–232, 1999.

[15] B. Thiesson, C. Meek, and D. Heckerman. Accelerating EM for large databases. *Machine Learning*, 45:279–299, 2001.

[16] T. Zhang, R. Ramakrishnan, and M. Livny. BIRCH: A new data clustering algorithm and its applications. *Data Mining and Knowledge Discovery*, 1(2):141–182, 1997.

On the Privacy Preserving Properties of Random Data Perturbation Techniques

Hillol Kargupta and Souptik Datta
Computer Science and
Electrical Engineering Department
University of Maryland Baltimore County
Baltimore, Maryland 21250, USA
{hillol, souptik1}@cs.umbc.edu

Qi Wang and Krishnamoorthy Sivakumar
School of Electrical Engineering
and Computer Science
Washington State University
Pullman, Washington 99164-2752, USA
{qwang, siva}@eecs.wsu.edu

Abstract

Privacy is becoming an increasingly important issue in many data mining applications. This has triggered the development of many privacy-preserving data mining techniques. A large fraction of them use randomized data distortion techniques to mask the data for preserving the privacy of sensitive data. This methodology attempts to hide the sensitive data by randomly modifying the data values often using additive noise. This paper questions the utility of the random value distortion technique in privacy preservation. The paper notes that random objects (particularly random matrices) have "predictable" structures in the spectral domain and it develops a random matrix-based spectral filtering technique to retrieve original data from the dataset distorted by adding random values. The paper presents the theoretical foundation of this filtering method and extensive experimental results to demonstrate that in many cases random data distortion preserve very little data privacy. The paper also points out possible avenues for the development of new privacy-preserving data mining techniques like exploiting multiplicative and colored noise for preserving privacy in data mining applications.

1. Introduction

Many data mining applications deal with privacy-sensitive data. Financial transactions, health-care records, and network communication traffic are some examples. Data mining in such privacy-sensitive domains is facing growing concerns. Therefore, we need to develop data mining techniques that are sensitive to the privacy issue. This has fostered the development of a class of data mining algorithms [2, 9] that try to extract the data patterns without directly accessing the original data and guarantees that the mining process does not get sufficient information to reconstruct the original data.

This paper considers a class of techniques for privacy-preserving data mining by randomly perturbing the data while preserving the underlying probabilistic properties. It explores the random value perturbation-based approach [2], a well-known technique for masking the data using random noise. This approach tries to preserve data privacy by adding random noise, while making sure that the random noise still preserves the "signal" from the data so that the patterns can still be accurately estimated. This paper questions the privacy-preserving capability of the random value perturbation-based approach. It shows that in many cases, the original data (sometimes called "signal" in this paper) can be accurately estimated from the perturbed data using a spectral filter that exploits some theoretical properties of random matrices. It presents the theoretical foundation and provides experimental results to support this claim.

Section 2 offers an overview of the related literature on privacy preserving data mining. Section 3 presents the motivation behind the framework presented in this paper. Section 4 describes the random data perturbation method proposed in [2]. Section 5 presents a discussion on the eigenvalues of random matrices. Section 6 presents the intuition behind the thoery to separate out random component from a mixture of non-random and random component. Section 7 describes the proposed random matrix-based filtering technique . Section 8 applies the proposed technique and reports its performance for various data sets. Finally, Section 9 concludes this paper.

2. Related Work

There exists a growing body of literature on privacy-sensitive data mining. These algorithms can be divided into several different groups. One approach adopts a distributed framework. This approach supports computation of data mining models and extraction of "patterns" at a given node by exchanging only the minimal necessary information among the participating nodes without transmitting the

99

raw data. Privacy preserving association rule mining from homogeneous [9] and heterogeneous [19] distributed data sets are few examples. The second approach is based on data-swapping which works by swapping data values within same feature [3].

There is also an approach which works by adding random noise to the data in such a way that the individual data values are distorted preserving the underlying distribution properties at a macroscopic level. The algorithms belonging to this group works by first perturbing the data using randomized techniques. The perturbed data is then used to extract the patterns and models. The randomized value distortion technique for learning decision trees [2] and association rule learning [6] are examples of this approach. Additional work on randomized masking of data can be found elsewhere [18].

This paper explores the third approach [2]. It points out that in many cases the noise can be separated from the perturbed data by studying the spectral properties of the data and as a result its privacy can be seriously compromised. Agrawal and Aggarwal [1] have also considered the approach in [2] and have provided a expectation-maximization (EM) algorithm for reconstructing the distribution of the original data from perturbed observations. They also provide information theoretic measures (mutual information) to quantify the amount of privacy provided by a randomization approach. Agrawal and Aggarwal [1] remark that the method suggested in [2] does not take into account the distribution of the original data (which could be used to guess the data value to a higher level of accuracy). However, [1] provides no explicit procedure to reconstruct the original data values. Evfimievski et al. [5, 4] and Rizvi [15] have also considered the approach in [2] in the context of association rule mining and suggest techniques for limiting privacy breaches. Our primary contribution is to provide an explicit filtering procedure, based on random matrix theory, that can be used to estimate the original data values.

3. Motivation

As noted in the previous section, a growing body of privacy preserving data mining techniques are adopting randomization as a primary tool to "hide" information. While randomization is an important tool, it must be used very carefully in a privacy-preserving application.

Randomness may not necessarily imply uncertainty. Random events can often be analyzed and their properties can be explained using probabilistic frameworks. Statistics, randomized computation, and many other related fields are full of theorems, laws, and algorithms that rely on probabilistic characterization of random processes that often work quite accurately. The signal processing literature [12] offers many filters to remove white noise from data and they often work reasonably well. Randomly generated structures like graphs demonstrate interesting properties [7]. In short, randomness does seem to have "structure" and this structure may be used to compromise privacy issues unless we pay careful attention. The rest of this paper illustrates this challenge in the context of a well-known privacy preserving technique that works using random additive noise.

4. Random Value Perturbation Technique: A Brief Review

For the sake of completeness, we now briefly review the random data perturbation method suggested in [2] for hiding the data (i.e. guaranteeing protection against the reconstruction of the data) while still being able to estimate the underlying distribution.

4.1. Perturbing the Data

The random value perturbation method attempts to preserve privacy of the data by modifying values of the sensitive attributes using a randomized process [2]. The authors explore two possible approaches — Value-Class Membership and Value Distortion — and emphasize the Value Distortion approach. In this approach, the owner of a dataset returns a value $u_i + v$, where u_i is the original data, and v is a random value drawn from a certain distribution. Most commonly used distributions are the uniform distribution over an interval $[-\alpha, \alpha]$ and Gaussian distribution with mean $\mu = 0$ and standard deviation σ. The n original data values $u_1, u_2, \ldots, u_n$ are viewed as realizations of n independent and identically distributed (i.i.d.) random variables U_i, $i = 1, 2, \ldots, n$, each with the same distribution as that of a random variable U. In order to perturb the data, n independent samples $v_1, v_2, \ldots, v_n$, are drawn from a distribution V. The owner of the data provides the perturbed values $u_1 + v_1, u_2 + v_2, \ldots, u_n + v_n$ and the cumulative distribution function $F_V(r)$ of V. The reconstruction problem is to estimate the distribution $F_U(x)$ of the original data, from the perturbed data.

4.2. Estimation of Distribution Function from the Perturbed Dataset

The authors [2] suggest the following method to estimate the distribution $F_U(u)$ of U, given n independent samples $w_i = u_i + v_i$, $i = 1, 2, \ldots, n$ and $F_V(v)$. Using Bayes' rule, the posterior distribution function $F'_U(u)$ of U, given that $U + V = w$, can be written as

$$F'_U(u) = \frac{\int_{-\infty}^{u} f_V(w - z) f_U(z) dz}{\int_{-\infty}^{\infty} f_V(w - z) f_U(z) dz},$$

which upon differentiation with respect to u yields the density function

$$f'_U(u) = \frac{f_V(w-u)f_U(u)}{\int_{-\infty}^{\infty} f_V(w-z)f_U(z)dz},$$

where $f_U(.)$, $f_V(.)$ denote the probability density function of U and V respectively. If we have n independent samples $u_i + v_i = w_i$, $i = 1, 2, \ldots, n$, the corresponding posterior distribution can be obtained by averaging:

$$f'_U(u) = \frac{1}{n}\sum_{i=1}^{n}\frac{f_V(w_i-u)f_U(u)}{\int_{-\infty}^{\infty} f_V(w_i-z)f_U(z)dz}. \quad (1)$$

For sufficiently large number of samples n, we expect the above density function to be close to the real density function $f_U(u)$. In practice, since the true density $f_U(u)$ is unknown, we need to modify the right-hand side of equation 1. The authors suggest an iterative procedure where at each step $j = 1, 2, \ldots$, the posterior density $f_U^{j-1}(u)$ estimated at step $j-1$ is used in the right-hand side of equation 1. The uniform density is used to initialize the iterations. The iterations are carried out until the difference between successive estimates becomes small. In order to speed up computations, the authors also discuss approximations to the above procedure using partitioning of the domain of data values.

5. Randomness and Patterns

The random perturbation technique "apparently" distorts the sensitive attribute values and still allows estimation of the underlying distribution information. However, does this apparent distortion fundamentally prohibit us from extracting the hidden information? This section presents a discussion on the properties of random matrices and presents some results that will be used later in this paper.

Random matrices [13] exhibit many interesting properties that are often exploited in high energy physics [13], signal processing [16], and even data mining [10]. The random noise added to the data can be viewed as a random matrix and therefore its properties can be understood by studying the properties of random matrices. In this paper we shall develop a spectral filter designed based on random matrix theory for extracting the hidden data from the data perturbed by random noise.

For our approach, we are mainly concerned about distribution of eigenvalues of the sample covariance matrix obtained from a random matrix. Let V be a random $m \times n$ matrix whose entries are V_{ij}, $i = 1, \ldots, m$, $j = 1, \ldots, n$, are i.i.d. random variables with zero mean and variance σ^2. The covariance matrix of X is given by $Y = \frac{1}{m}V'V$. Clearly, Y is an $n \times n$ matrix. Let $\lambda_1 \leq \lambda_2 \leq \cdots \leq \lambda_n$ be the eigenvalues of Y. Let

$$F_n(x) = \frac{1}{n}\sum_{i=1}^{n} U(x-\lambda_i),$$

be the empirical cumulative distribution function (c.d.f.) of the eigenvalues λ_i, $(1 \leq i \leq n)$, where

$$U(x) = \begin{cases} 1 & x \geq 0 \\ 0 & x < 0 \end{cases}$$

is the unit step function. In order to consider the asymptotic properties of the c.d.f. $F_n(x)$, we will consider the dimensions $m = m(N)$ and $n = n(N)$ of matrix X to be functions of a variable N. We will consider asymptotics such that in the limit as $N \to \infty$, we have $m(N) \to \infty$, $n(N) \to \infty$, and $\frac{m(N)}{n(N)} \to Q$, where $Q \geq 1$. Under these assumptions, it can be shown that [8] the empirical c.d.f. $F_n(x)$ converges in probability to a continuous distribution function $F_Q(x)$ for every x, whose probability density function (p.d.f.) is given by

$$f_Q(x) = \begin{cases} \frac{Q\sqrt{(x-\lambda_{\min})(\lambda_{\max}-x)}}{2\pi\sigma^2 x} & \lambda_{\min} < x < \lambda_{\max} \\ 0 & \text{otherwise,} \end{cases}$$
$$(2)$$

where $\lambda_{\min}$ and $\lambda_{\max}$ are as follows:

$$\lambda_{\min} = \sigma^2(1-1/\sqrt{Q})^2.$$
$$\lambda_{\max} = \sigma^2(1+1/\sqrt{Q})^2. \quad (3)$$

Further refinements of this result and other discussions can be found in [16].

6. Separating the Data from the Noise

Consider an $m \times n$ data matrix U and a noise matrix V with same dimensions. The random value perturbation technique generates a modified data matrix $U_p = U + V$. Our objective is to extract U from U_p. Although the noise matrix V may introduce seemingly significant difference between U and U_p, it may not be successful in hiding the data.

Consider the covariance matrix of U_p:

$$\begin{aligned} U_p^T U_p &= (U+V)^T(U+V) \\ &= U^T U + V^T U + U^T V + V^T V. \end{aligned} \quad (4)$$

Now note that when the signal random vector (rows of U) and noise random vector (rows of V) are uncorrelated, we have $E[U^T V] = E[V^T U] = 0$. The uncorrelated assumption is valid in practice since the noise V that is added to the data U is generated by a statistically independent process. Recall that the random value perturbation technique discussed in the previous section introduces uncorrelated noise to hide the signal or the data. If the number of observations is sufficiently large, we have that $U^T V \sim 0$ and $V^T U \sim 0$. Equation 4 can now be simplified as follows:

$$U_p^T U_p = U^T U + V^T V \qquad (5)$$

Since the correlation matrices $U^T U$, $U_p^T U_p$, and $V^T V$ are symmetric and positive semi-definite, let

$$\begin{aligned} U^T U &= Q_u \Lambda_u Q_u^T, \\ U_p^T U_p &= Q_p \Lambda_p Q_p^T, \text{ and} \\ V^T V &= Q_v \Lambda_v Q_v^T, \end{aligned} \qquad (6)$$

where Q_u, Q_p, Q_v are orthogonal matrices whose column vectors are eigenvectors of $U^T U$, $U_p^T U_p$, $V^T V$, respectively, and $\Lambda_u, \Lambda_p, \Lambda_v$ are diagonal matrices with the corresponding eigenvalues on their diagonals.

The following result from matrix perturbation theory [20] gives a relationship between Λ_u, Λ_v, and Λ_v.

Theorem 1 [20] Suppose $\lambda_{1,(a)} \geq \lambda_{2,(a)} \geq \dots \lambda_{n,(a)} \geq 0$, $a \in \{u, p, v\}$ are the eigenvalues of $U^T U$, $U_p^T U_p$, and $V^T V$, respectively. Then, for $i = 1, \dots, n$,

$$\lambda_{i,(p)} \in [\lambda_{i,(u)} + \lambda_{n,(v)}, \lambda_{i,(u)} + \lambda_{1,(v)}].$$

This theorem provides us a bound on the change in the eigenvalues of the data correlation matrix $U^T U$ in terms of the minimum and maximum eigenvalues of the noise correlation matrix $V^T V$. Now let us take a step further and explore the properties of the eigenvalues of the perturbed data matrix U_p for large values of m.

Lemma 1 Let data matrix U and noise matrix V be of size $m \times n$ and $U_p = U + V$. Let Q_u, Q_p, Q_v be orthogonal matrices and $\Lambda_u, \Lambda_p, \Lambda_v$ be diagonal matrices as defined in 6. If $m/n \to \infty$ then $\Lambda_p = \Delta \Lambda_u \Delta^T + \Lambda_v$ where $\Delta = Q_p^T Q_u$.

Proof:
Using Equations 5 and 6 we can write,

$$\begin{aligned} Q_p \Lambda_p Q_p^T &= Q_u \Lambda_u Q_u^T + Q_v \Lambda_v Q_v^T \\ \Rightarrow \Lambda_p &= Q_p^T Q_u \Lambda_u Q_u^T Q_p + Q_p^T Q_v \Lambda_v Q_v^T Q_p \\ &= \Delta \Lambda_u \Delta^T + Q_p^T Q_v \Lambda_v Q_v^T Q_p \end{aligned} \qquad (7)$$

Let the minimum and maximum eigenvalues of V be $\lambda_{\min,(v)}$ and $\lambda_{\max,(v)}$ respectively. It follows from equation 2 that $m/n \to \infty$ all the eigenvalues in Λ_v become identical since $\lim_{m/n=Q \to \infty} \lambda_{\max,(v)} = \lim_{m/n=Q \to \infty} \lambda_{\min,(v)} = \sigma^2$ (say). This implies that, as $m/n \to \infty$, $\Lambda_v \to \sigma^2 I$, where I is the $n \times n$ identity matrix. Therefore, if the number of observations m is large enough (note that, in practice, number of features n is fixed), $V^T V = Q_v \Lambda_v Q_v^T = \sigma^2 Q_v Q_V^T = \sigma^2 I$. Therefore Equation 7 becomes

$$\begin{aligned} \Lambda_p &= \Delta \Lambda_u \Delta^T + Q_p^T Q_p \Lambda_v Q_p^T Q_p \\ \Lambda_p &= \Delta \Lambda_u \Delta^T + \Lambda_v. \end{aligned} \qquad (8)$$

∎

If the norm of the perturbation matrix V is small, the eigenvectors Q_p of $U_p^T U_p$ would be close to the eigenvectors $Q_u^T Q_u$ of $U^T U$. Indeed, matrix perturbation theory provides precise bounds on the angle between eigenvectors (and invariant subspaces) of a matrix U and that of its perturbation $U_p = U + V$, in terms of the norms of the perturbation matrix V. For example, let (x_u, λ_u) be an eigenvector-eigenvalue pair for matrix $U^T U$ and $\epsilon = \|V^T V\|_2 = \sigma_{\max}(V^T V)$ be the two-norm of the perturbation, where $\sigma_{\max}(V^T V)$ is the largest singular value of $V^T V$. Then there exists an eigenvalue-eigenvector pair (x_p, λ_p) of $U_p^T U_p$ satisfying [20, 17]

$$\tan(\angle(x_u, x_p)) < 2\frac{\epsilon}{\delta - \epsilon},$$

where δ is the distance between λ_u and the closest eigenvalue of $U^T U$, provided $\epsilon < \delta$. This shows that the eigenvalues of $U^T U$ and $U_P^T U_P$ are in general close, for small perturbations. Moreover,

$$|\lambda_u - x^* U_p x_u| < 2\frac{\epsilon^2}{\delta - \epsilon},$$

where x^* is the conjugate-transpose of x. Consequently, the product $\Delta = Q_p^T Q_u$, which is the matrix of inner products between the eigenvectors of $U^T U$ and $U_p^T U_p$ would be close to an identity matrix; i.e., $\Delta = Q_p^T Q_u \approx I$. Thus equation 8 becomes

$$\Lambda_p \approx \Lambda_u + \Lambda_v. \qquad (9)$$

Suppose the signal covariance matrix has only a few dominant eigenvalues, say $\lambda_{1,(u)} \geq \dots \geq \lambda_{k,(u)}$, with $\lambda_{i,(u)} \leq \epsilon$ for some small value ϵ and $i = k + 1, \dots, n$. This condition is true for many real-world signals. Suppose $\lambda_{k,(u)} > \lambda_{1,(v)}$, the largest eigenvalue of the noise covariance matrix. It is then clear that we can separate the signal and noise eigenvalues Λ_u, Λ_v from the eigenvalues Λ_p of the observed data by a simple thresholding at $\lambda_{1,(v)}$.

Note that equation 9 is only an approximation. However, in practice, one can design a filter based on this approximation to filter out the perturbation from the data. Experimental results presented in the following sections indicate that this provides a good recovery of the data.

7. Random Matrix-Based Data Filtering

This section describes the proposed filter for extracting the original data from the noisy perturbed data. Suppose actual data U is perturbed by a randomly generated noise matrix V in order to produce $U_p = U + V$. Let $u_{p,i} = \mathbf{u}_i + \mathbf{v}_i$,

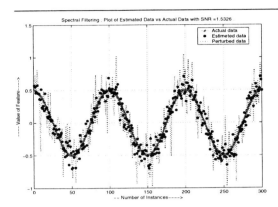

Figure 1. Estimation of original sinusoidal data with known random noise variance.

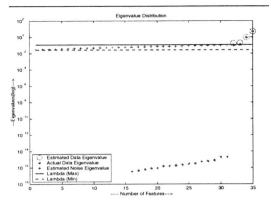

Figure 2. Distribution of eigenvalues of actual data, and estimated eigenvalues of random noise and actual data.

$i = 1, 2, \ldots, m$, be m (perturbed) data points, each being a vector of n features.

When the noise distribution $F_V(v)$ of V is completely known (as required by the random value perturbation technique [2]), the noise variance σ^2 is first calculated from the given distribution. Equation 2 is then used to calculate λ_{max} and λ_{min} which provide the theoretical bounds of the eigenvalues corresponding to noise matrix V. From the perturbed data, we compute the eigenvalues of its covariance matrix Y, say $\lambda_1 \leq \lambda_2 \leq \cdots \leq \lambda_n$. Then we identify the noisy eigenstates $\lambda_i \leq \lambda_{i+1} \leq \cdots \leq \lambda_j$ such that $\lambda_i \geq \lambda_{min}$ and $\lambda_j \leq \lambda_{max}$. The remaining eigenstates are the eigenstates corresponding to actual data. Let, $\Lambda_v = \text{diag}(\lambda_i, \lambda_{i+1}, \ldots, \lambda_j)$ be the diagonal matrix with all noise-related eigenvalues, and A_v be the matrix whose columns are the corresponding eigenvectors. Similarly, let Λ_u be the eigenvalue matrix for the actual data part and A_u be the corresponding eigenvector matrix which is an $n \times k$ matrix ($k \leq n$). Based on these matrices, we decompose the covariance matrix Y into two parts, Y_s and Y_r with $Y = Y_s + Y_r$, where $Y_r = A_v \Lambda_r A_v^T$, is the covariance matrix corresponding to random noise part, and $Y_s = A_u \Lambda_u A_u^T$, is the covariance matrix corresponding to actual data part. An estimate $\hat{U}$ of the actual data U is obtained by projecting the data U_p on to the subspace spanned by the columns of A_u. In other words, $\hat{U} = U_p A_u A_u^T$.

8. Experimental Results

In this section, we present results of our experiments with the proposed spectral filtering technique. This section also includes discussion on the effect of noise variance on the performance of the spectral filtering method.

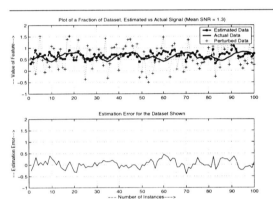

Figure 3. Spectral filtering used to estimate real world audio data. Waveform of a audio signal is closely estimated from its perturbed version.

8.1. Estimation with Known Perturbing Distribution

We tested our privacy breaching technique using several datasets of different sizes. We considered both artificially generated and real data sets. Towards that end, we generated a dataset with 35 features and 300 instances. Each feature has a specific trend like sinusoidal, square, and triangular shape, however there is no dependency between any two features. The actual dataset is perturbed by adding Gaussian noise (with zero mean and known variance), and our proposed technique is applied to recover the actual data from the perturbed data. Figure 1 shows the result of our spectral filtering for one such feature where the actual data has a sinusoidal trend. The filtering technique appears to provide an accurate estimate of the individual values of the actual data. Figure 2 shows the distribution of eigenvalues of the actual and perturbed data. It also identifies the estimated noise eigenvalues and the theoretical bounds λ_{max} and λ_{min}. As we see, the filtering method accurately distinguishes between noisy eigenvalues and eigenvalues corresponding to actual data. Note that the estimated eigenvalues of actual data is very close to eigenvalues of actual data and almost overlap with them above λ_{max}. The eigenvalues of actual data below λ_{min} are practically negligible. Thus, the estimated eigenvalues of the actual data capture most of the information and discard the additive noise.

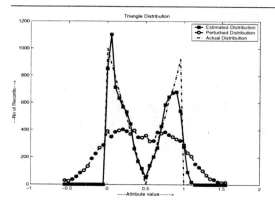

Figure 5. Reconstruction of the 'Triangular' distribution. Perturbed data distribution does not look like a triangular distribution, but reconstructed distribution using spectral filtering resembles the original distribution closely.

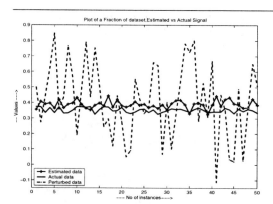

Figure 4. Plot of the individual values of a fraction of the dataset with 'Triangular' distribution. Spectral filtering gives close estimation of individual values.

The random matrix-based filtering technique can also be extended to datasets with a single feature, i.e when the dataset is a single column vector. The data vector is perturbed with a noise vector with the same dimension. The perturbed data vector is then split into a fixed number of vectors with equal length and all of these vectors are appended to form a matrix. The spectral filtering technique is then applied to this matrix to estimate the original data. After the data matrix is estimated, its columns are concatenated to form a single vector.

We used a real world single feature data set to verify the performance of the spectral filtering. The dataset used is the scaled amplitude of the waveform of an audio tune recorded using a fixed sampling frequency. The tune recorded is fairly noise free with 10000 sample points. We perturbed this data with additive Gaussian noise.

We define the term *Signal-to-Noise Ratio* (SNR) to quantify the relative amount of noise added to actual data to perturb it:

$$\text{SNR} = \frac{\text{Variance of Actual Data}}{\text{Noise Variance}}. \quad (10)$$

In this experiment, the noise variance was chosen to yield a signal-to-noise ratio of 1.3. We split this vector of perturbed data into 40 columns, each containing 250 points and applied the spectral filtering technique to recover the actual data. The result is shown in Figure 3. For the sake of clarity, only a fraction of dataset is shown, and estimation error is plotted for that fraction. As shown in Figure 3, the perturbed data is very different from the actual data, whereas the estimated data is a close approximation of the actual data. The estimation performance is similar to that for a multi-featured data (see Figure 1).

8.2. Comparison With Results in [2]

The proposed spectral filtering technique can estimate values of individual data-points from the perturbed dataset. This point-wise estimation can then be used to reconstruct the distribution of actual data as well. The methods suggested by [2, 1] can only reconstruct the distribution of the original data from the data perturbed by random value distortion; but it does not consider estimation of the individual values of the data-points. The spectral filtering technique, on the other hand, is explicitly designed to reconstruct the individual data-points and hence, also the distribution of the actual dataset.

We tried to replicate the experiment reported in [2] using our method to recover the triangular distribution. We used a vector data of 10000 values having a triangular distribution as shown in Figure 2 in [2]. The individual values of actual data are within 0 and 1 and are independent of each other. We added Gaussian random noise with mean 0 and standard deviation $\sigma = 0.25$ to this data and split the data vector into 50 columns, each having 200 values. We then applied our spectral filter to recover the actual data from the perturbed data. Figure 4 shows a portion of the actual data, their values after distortion, and their estimated values. Note that the estimated values are very close to the actual values, compared to the perturbed values. Using the estimate of individual data-points, we reconstruct the distribution of the actual data. Figure 5 shows estimation of the distribution from the estimated value of individual data-points. The distribution of the perturbed data is very different than the actual triangular distribution, but the estimated distribution looks very similar to the original distribution. This shows that our method recovers the original distribution along with individual data-points, similar to the result reported in [2]. The estimation accuracy is greater than 80% for all datapoints. Since spectral filtering can filter out the individual values of actual data and its distribution from a perturbed representation, it breaches the privacy preserving protection of the randomized data perturbation technique [2].

8.3. Effect of Perturbation Variance and the Inherent Random Component of the Actual Data

Quality of the data recovery depends upon the relative noise content in the perturbed data. We use the SNR (see equation (10)) to quantify the relative amount of noise added to actual data to perturb it. As the noise added to the actual value increases, the SNR decreases. Our experiments show that the proposed filtering method predicts the actual data reasonably well up to a SNR value of 1.0 (i.e. 100% noise). The results shown in Figure 1 corresponds to an SNR value nearly 2, i.e. noise content is about 50%. Figure 4 shows a data-block where the SNR is 1.9. As the SNR goes below 1, the estimation becomes too erroneous. Figure 6 shows the difference in estimation accuracy as the SNR increases from 1. The dataset used here has a sinusoidal trend in its values. The top graph corresponds to 23% noise (SNR = 4.3), whereas the bottom graph corresponds to 100% noise (SNR = 1.0).

Another important factor that affects the quality of recovery of the actual data is the inherent noise in the actual dataset (apart from the perturbation noise added intentionally). If the actual dataset has a random component in it, and random noise is added to perturb it, spectral filtering method does not filter the actual data accurately. Our experiments with some inherently noisy real life dataset show that the eigenvalues of signal and noise no longer remains clearly separable since the their eigenvalues may not be distributed over two non-overlapping regimes any longer.

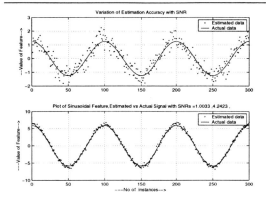

Figure 6. A higher noise content (low SNR)leads to less accurate estimation. SNR in the upper figure is 1, while that for the lower figure is 4.3.

We have performed experiments with artificial dataset with specific trend in its value as well as real world dataset containing a random component. Figure 1 in fact shows that our method gives a close estimation of actual data when the dataset has some specific trend (sinusoid). We also applied our method to "Ionosphere data" available from [14], which is inherently noisy. We perturbed the original data with random noise such that mean SNR is same as the artificial dataset, i.e. 1.1. Figure 7 shows that recovery quality is poor compared to datasets having definite trend.

However, this opens up a different question: Is the random component of the original data set really important as far as data mining is concerned? One may argue that most data mining techniques exploit only the non-random structured patterns of the data. Therefore, losing the inherent random component of the original data may not be important in a privacy preserving data mining application.

9. Conclusion and Future Work

Preserving privacy in data mining activities is a very important issue in many applications. Randomization-based techniques are likely to play an important role in this domain. However, this paper illustrates some of the challenges that these techniques face in preserving the data privacy. It showed that under certain conditions it is relatively easy to breach the privacy protection offered by the random perturbation based techniques. It provided extensive experimental results with different types of data and showed that this is really a concern that we must address. In addition to raising this concern the paper offers a random-matrix based data filtering technique that may find wider application in developing a new perspective toward developing better privacy-preserving data mining algorithms.

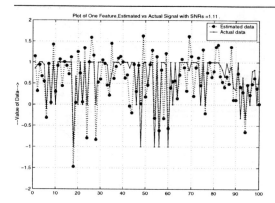

Figure 7. Spectral filtering performs poorly on a dataset with a random component in its actual value. However, it is not clear if loosing the random component of the data is a concern for data mining applications.

Since the problem mainly originates from the usage of additive, independent "white" noise for privacy preservation, we should explore "colored" noise for this application. We have already started exploring multiplicative noise matrices in this context. If U be the data matrix and V be an appropriately sized random noise matrix then we are interested in the properties of the perturbed data $U_p = UV$ for privacy-preserving data mining applications. If V is a square matrix then we may be able to extract signal using techniques like independent component analysis. However, projection matrices that satisfy certain conditions may be more appealing for such applications. More details about this possibility can be found elsewhere [11].

Acknowledgments

The authors acknowledge supports from the United States National Science Foundation CAREER award IIS-0093353, NASA (NRA) NAS2-37143, and TEDCO, Maryland Technology Development Center.

References

[1] D. Agrawal and C. C. Aggawal. On the design and quantification of privacy preserving data mining algorothms. In *Proceedings of the 20th ACM SIMOD Symposium on Principles of Database Systems*, pages 247–255, Santa Barbara, May 2001.

[2] R. Agrawal and R. Srikant. Privacy-preserving data mining. In *Proceeding of the ACM SIGMOD Conference on Management of Data*, pages 439–450, Dallas, Texas, May 2000. ACM Press.

[3] V. Estivill-Castro and L. Brankovic. Data swaping: Balancing privacy against precision in mining for logic rules. In *Proceedings of the first Conference on Data Warehousing and Knowledge Discovery (DaWaK-99)*, pages 389 – 398, Florence, Italy, 1999. Springer Verlag.

[4] A. Evfimevski, J. Gehrke, and R. Srikant. Limiting privacy breaches in privacy preserving data mining. In *Proceedings of the ACM SIMOD/PODS Conference*, San Diego, CA, June 2003.

[5] A. Evfimevski, R. Srikant, R. Agrawal, and J. Gehrke. Privacy preserving mining of association rules. In *Proceedings of the ACM SIKDD Conference*, Edmonton, Canada, 2002.

[6] S. Evfimievski. Randomization techniques for privacy preserving association rule mining. In *SIGKDD Explorations*, volume 4(2), Dec 2002.

[7] S. Janson, T. L. , and A. Rucinski. *Random Graphs*. Wiley Publishers, 1 edition, 2000.

[8] D. Jonsson. Some limit theorems for the eigenvalues of a sample covariance matrix. *Journal of Multivariate Analysis*, 12:1–38, 1982.

[9] M. Kantarcioglu and C. Clifton. Privacy-preserving distributed mining of association rules on horizontally partitioned data. In *SIGMOD Workshop on DMKD*, Madison, WI, June 2002.

[10] H. Kargupta, K. Sivakumar, and S. Ghosh. Dependency detection in mobimine and random matrices. In *Proceedings of the 6th European Conference on Principles and Practice of Knowledge Discovery in Databases*, pages 250–262. Springer, 2002.

[11] K. Liu, H. Kargupta, and J. Ryan. Random projection and privacy preserving correlation computation from distributed data. Technical report, University of Maryland Baltimore County, Computer Science and Electrical Engineering Department, Technical Report TR-CS-03-24, 2003.

[12] D. G. Manolakis, V. K. Ingle, and S. M. Kogon. *Statistical and Adaptive Signal Processing*. McGraw Hill, 2000.

[13] M. L. Mehta. *Random Matrices*. Academic Press, London, 2 edition, 1991.

[14] U. M. L. Repository. http://www.ics.uci.edu/ mlearn/mlsummary.html.

[15] S. J. Rizvi and J. R. Haritsa. Maintaining data privacy in association rule mining. In *Proceedings of the 28th VLDB Conference*, Hong Kong, China, 2002.

[16] J. W. Silverstein and P. L. Combettes. Signal detection via spectral theory of large dimensional random matrices. *IEEE Transactions on Signal Processing*, 40(8):2100–2105, 1992.

[17] G. W. Stewart. Error and perturbation bounds for subspaces associated with certain eigenvalue problems. *SIAM Review*, 15(4):727–764, October 1973.

[18] J. F. Traub, Y. Yemini, and H. Woz'niakowski. The statistical security of a statistical database. *ACM Transactions on Database Systems (TODS)*, 9(4):672–679, 1984.

[19] J. Vaidya and C. Clifton. Privacy preserving association rule mining in vertically partitioned data. In *The Eighth ACM SIGKDD International conference on Knowledge Discovery and Data Mining*, Edmonton, Alberta, CA, July 2002.

[20] H. Weyl. Inequalities between the two kinds of eigenvalues of a linear transformation. In *Proceedings of the National Academy of Sciences*, volume 35, pages 408–411, 1949.

Semantic Log Analysis Based on a User Query Behavior Model

KAWAMAE Noriaki, MUKAIGAITO Takeya, HANAKI Miyoshi
NTT Information Sharing Platform Laboratories
3-9-11,Midori-cho Musashino-shi Tokyo 180-8585 Japan
{kawamae.noriaki, mukaigaito.takeya,hanaki.miyoshi}@lab.ntt.co.jp

Abstract

We propose a novel log analysis method to capture the semantic relations among words appearing in Web search logs. Our method focuses on the reciprocal relations among a user's intentions, stages of information need, and query behavior in seeking information via a search engine. The approach works because it is based on the assumption that a user's intentions in each query can be derived as a model on the basis of his stage of information need and query behavior, through multiple empirical observations of search logs. The user's intentions drive user to change the words in each successive queries and can thus be used to clarify the semantic relations among words. As a result, this method has the advantage of capturing the semantic relations among words without requiring either manual or natural language processing. Our experimental results indicate that semantic relations could successfully be derived from search logs, confirming that an ontology and thesaurus could be constructed automatically.

1. Introduction

Currently, with the spread of personal computers and growth of the World Wide Web, it has become easier and more convenient for us to obtain data and documents electronically than ever before. However, it is often difficult to extract useful information from the voluminous data and documents available on the Web. Search engines are currently the most popular and important tool for searching the Web. Existing search engines are inconvenient for most users, because they are largely based on database systems, so they can't really be used to understand the contents of data and documents on the World Wide Web. As a result, most users change words in their queries in order to find sites that will meet their needs. To make this process easier for users, existing search engines should be modified to deal with semantic relations on the Web.

The Semantic Web is an approach proposed by Berners [1] to address this problem. The Semantic Web requires metadata that provide resource descriptions for instance class definitions and describe how they are semantically interlinked by their properties. Individual users can freely describe the metadata, but to facilitate this, schema must be prepared.

Ontologies and thesauruses are expected to play important roles both in searching and for the Semantic Web. Therefore, we must develop a method for constructing these automatically in each domain of information. This requires capturing the semantic relations between words automatically.

We hence propose a novel log analysis method to capture the semantic relations among words appearing in Web search logs. The main idea of our analysis is to utilize search logs and a user query behavior model. The advantage of our method is its ability to capture semantic relations without manual or natural language processing. Throughout this paper, we use the phrase "user's intention" to denote the intention that drives a user to change the words in each successive queries. Because we assume that these intentions can be derived as a model based on the user's stage of information need and query behavior, through multiple empirical observations of search logs, our method focuses on the reciprocal relations among the user's intentions, stages of information need, and query behavior in seeking information As a result, our method could be used to capture the semantic relations among words. We thus applied our log analysis to a real search log and confirmed its effectiveness experimentally.

2. SURVEY OF PREVIOUS WORKS

2.1. User's Stages of Information Need

We consider the user's stage of information need to analyze search logs, because our method utilizes not only the logs generated by one user but also those generated by many users. Taylor [21] formulated a four-stage model of how a user's need for information unfolds:

Q1: the actual but unexpressed need for information (visceral need)

Q2: the conscious, within-brain description of the need (the conscious need)

Q3: the formal statement of the need (formalized need)

Q4: the question presented to an intermediary or information system (compromised need)

We can say that a user's stages of information need affect the relations among words in each user's successive queries. Even if a user can formulate a query, the query may not necessarily be efficient. There are two reasons for this. First, using inappropriate words in the query will produce search results that are too extensive for the user to browse through and find relevant documents. Second, the search results may not contain the required documents due to lexical disagreement [17]. This refers to the situation in which different users use different words to indicate a single meaning. These are reasons why even a user with a formalized information need may change words in each query behavior. Therefore, ontologies and thesauruses are needed for information retrieval.

2.2. Ontology and Thesaurus Construction

There are two different ways to construct an ontology and a thesaurus automatically: the symbolic approach, and the statistical approach. In the symbolic approach, the main idea is to extract the semantic identity of a word by using a syntactic pattern in the form of a regular expression. Pattern-based approaches like this that utilize regular expressions to extract information are heuristic methods [6], [7].In one such method, words are extracted from documents based on the relative degrees of relevance between words occurring simultaneously [15].In other methods [16], [19], words are extracted from search logs, and the only target words for extraction are synonyms. The problem with these approaches is that the semantic relation among words is restricted.

In the statistical approach, the main idea is that the semantic identity of a word is reflected in its distribution over different contexts, so that its meaning can be represented in terms of the words occurring with it and the frequencies of co-occurrence. The distribution of a word is used to generate clusters of organizing words, which consist of groups whose members have similar distributions [9], [14], [17].The problem with thess approaches is that the extracted relations between words vary.

2.3. Log Analysis

Log analysis focuses on learning a user's query behavior while user navigates a search site. Understanding the user's navigational preferences is expected to improve query behavior. In fact, the knowledge of the most likely user access patterns allows service providers to customize and adapt their sites' interfaces for individual users [8], as well as to improve the sites' static structures within the wider hypertext system [9]. These previous works analyzed not semantic relations but preference patterns Studies on user navigation activity based on logs spanning long periods of time. Ramakrishnan [18]focused on site visitors' behaviors and proposed an algorithm to automatically find pages whose locations differ from what visitors expect. Cooley [4]used a timeout value to divide an individual user's access to pages into separate sessions. Catledge [3]focused on user behavior and applied the same timeout concept. Lawrence [11]reported on the coverage of various search-engine services, while Huberman [8] analyzed users' patterns of Web surfing. Silverstein [20] gathered statistics from a large corpus of raw log data. Lau [10] analyzed logs from a single search engine in order to assign query-refinement classes and estimate users' informational goals. Goker [5] reported the results of the same method for another search engine. These approaches all considered not the semantic relations but the changes in users' intentions. Note that the approaches introduced here have not focused on the stages of information need and the user's intentions in changing the words in each successive queries.

3. APPLYING USER QUERY BEHAVIOR TO SEMANTIC ANALYSIS OF WORDS

3.1. Search Logs and Semantic Relations

We propose a novel log analysis method to capture the semantic relations among words appearing in Web search logs. We use search logs because we assume that they contain information about the semantic relations, and that we could capture the relations from them with a smaller number of simpler model than other methods. As the model capturing these relations, we propose a user query behavior model based on a formula utilizing multiple observations of search logs. Here, "multiple observations" means observed numerical relation such as time interval between words, order of word appearance, position interval between words in each user's successive queries, and number of words' pair. The essential idea of this model is to focus on the reciprocal relation among a user's intentions, stage of information need, and query behavior in seeking information. We show an example of this relation in Figure 1. In this figure, the users' intentions and stages of information need are invisible, but their behaviors are clearly visible. A user's intention not only drives user to change the words but also could explain the semantic relations among the words appearing in each user's successive queries.

On the other hand, multiple observations of search logs

could also be used to clarify a user's intentions and stages of information need. Consequently, the process of clarifying intentions based on the stage of information need and multiple observations enables us to capture the semantic relations among the words used in search logs. The starting points of our analysis method are the search logs, which provide the data, and the user behavior model for query formulation, which provides the processing framework. We describe our log analysis method in the following subsections.

3.2. Search Logs and Search Sequences

Our method uses search logs generated by the servers used for Internet search engines. These logs consist of records for many individual sessions. Most of sessions, contain both multiple- and single-word queries. In addition to the words used in each query, the time the query was submitted and the source IP address are also recorded. One such server log is shown in Figure 2.

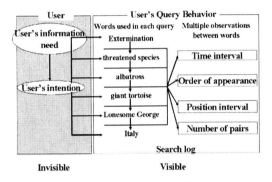

Fig. 1: The reciprocal relation among a user's intentions, stage of information need, the words in each query, and multiple observations of a search log.

Because our analysis focuses on the words appearing in each user's successive query behavior, we assemble the log entries for each search session and analyze the relations among words in each query. Note that when some words are used together in one query, we treat them as a set. We refer to the assembled log entries as a search sequence. The search sequence generated from the log example in Figure 2 is shown in Figure 3.

In Figure 3, the UID denotes a unique identifier assigned to each search sequence. From the search sequence, we create a group in which each word is placed with all the other words in the same sequence, providing an index entry or key to the other words. We call this an associated group of

```
***.***.***.*** - - [01/Sep/1999:00:00:11 +0900] "GET
      /?kw=extermination HTTP/1.0" 200 - "http:
**.***.***.*** - - [01/Sep/1999:00:01:05 +0900] "GET
      /?kw=threatened species HTTP/1.0" 200 - "http:
**.***.***.*** - - [01/Sep/1999:00:02:18 +0900] "GET
      /?kw=albatross HTTP/1.0" 200 - "http:
**.***.***.*** - - [01/Sep/1999:00:03:42 +0900] "GET
      /?kw=giant tortoise HTTP/1.0" 200 - "http:
**.***.***.*** - - [01/Sep/1999:00:06:29 +0900] "GET
      /?kw= Lonesome George HTTP/1.0" 200 - "http:
**.***.***.*** - - [01/Sep/1999:00:10:11 +0900] "GET
      /?kw=Italy HTTP/1.0" 200 - "http:
```

Fig. 2: Search log

{UID}={extermination, threatened species, albatross, giant tortoise, Lonesome George, Italy}

Fig. 3: A search sequence

words. For example, the associated groups of words generated from the search sequence of Figure 3 are listed in Table 1. An associated group of words is drawn from not a specific search sequence but all sequences. In other words, we create the associated groups of words by analyzing every search sequence. When a new word in a sequence has not yet been included in any associated group of words, we add it to the appropriate groups. Also, if the word has not yet been used as the key of an associated group of words, we create a new group with it as the key. Otherwise, we do nothing.

3.3. Modeling User Query Behavior

In this section, we explain user query behavior, taking the user's intentions and stages of information need into consideration. Knowledge of a user's intention in changing query words can be applied to capture the semantic relations among these words. Our classification of these changes differs from that of Lau [10] in that we eliminate the refinement class, integrate one pair of classes, and divide another class. First, we place "specialization" and "request for additional results" in a single "specialization" class. Second, we divide the "reformulation" class into "paraphrase" and "alternative" classes. The resulting classifications of a user's intentions in changing query words are as follows, with examples taken from Figure 1.

Paraphrase : A word used as a substitute for a previously used word, with the same intended topic. The substitution of "threatened species" for "extermination" is of this type.

Table 1: Associated groups of words generated from the search sequence shown in Figure 3

Key	Associated groups of words indexed by key
extermination	threatened species, albatross, giant tortoise, Lonesome George, Italy
threatened species	extermination, albatross, giant tortoise, Lonesome George, Italy
albatross	extermination, threatened species, giant tortoise, Lonesome George, Italy
giant tortoise	extermination, threatened species, albatross, Lonesome George, Italy
Lonesome George	extermination, threatened species, albatross, giant tortoise, Italy
Italy	extermination, threatened species, albatross, giant tortoise, Lonesome George

Specialization: A word used to narrow the topic in a series of queries. The substitution of "albatross" for "threatened species" is of this type.

Generalization: A word used to broaden the topic in a series of queries. The substitution of "threatened species" for "albatross" is of this type.

Alternative: A word that does not change the general topic of the queries, but that seeks entries containing a word of a different type from the previously used word. The substitution of "Lonesome George" for "albatross" as a specialization of "threatened species" is of this type. (Note: "Lonesome George" is the name of the world's last remaining Galapagos giant tortoise.)

Interruption: A word that changes the topic in a series of queries. The substitution of "Italy" for "Lonesome George" is of this type.

Broder [2] classifies user query behavior as navigational, informational, or transactional. We consider the paraphrase and alternative classes to correspond to navigational behavior; the specialization and generalization classes, to informational behavior; and the interruption class, to transactional behavior. Our log analysis utilizes the numerical relations in search sequences generated from search logs, as follows.

the time intervals between words in search sequence
the order of word appearance in search sequence
the position intervals between words in search sequence
the number of search sequence containing words

Multiple observations thus provide us with much useful information for inferring user query behavior. First, the more strongly formalized the user's information stage is in the query, the more quickly the user can submit other words. Hence, the time interval between words indicates the stage of information need. Second, the later a word is used in a search sequence, the more strongly it expresses the user's refined information need. The order of word appearance thus indicates the degree of refinement of the words in each search sequence. Third, the similarity among words in a query increases with the formalization of the information need, so the position interval between words indicates

their similarity as used to express the information need. For example, the value of the position interval for "threatened species" and "Lonesome George" in Figure 3 is two. Fourth, the more the number of a user use a word in each query, the more frequently the word is appeared in the log. Hence, the number of pairs of words appearing together enables us to infer the user's tendencies in searching certain topics.

With these parameters explained, we can now define user query behavior model. We assume that the stage of user's information need and the observing numerical relations in search sequences from a user's search log could be used as descriptors for the semantic relations among the words in search logs. We then classify the user query behavior according to his or her intention in changing words, as reflected by the stage of information need and the multiple observations. In Table 2, we list the correspondences between the user's intention, the stage of information need, and the numerical relations in search sequences shown in Figure 2. Each column represents a change of the user's intention, the corresponding stage of information need, the example of words change in each query, and the numerical relations in search sequences generated from search logs.

In our approach, we do not have to classify the stage of information need as precisely as in Taylor's scheme [21]. We treat a user at Taylor's stage Q3 and Q4 as formalized and users at Q1 and Q2 as non-formalized. For example, the entry in the table for "paraphrase" indicates that the user is at the formalized stage. Only a user at this stage is able to select appropriate paraphrases, generalizations, and alternatives to a previously used word. We know, of course, that many users at non-formalized stages will attempt to take these behaviors, but users at the formalized stage are much more likely to behave effectively. We thus assume that the words used by a user with a non-formalized information need do not reflect the semantic relations we want to capture. As suggested by this example, we identify the changes "paraphrase", "specialization", "generalization", and "alternative" as representing behaviors of users at the formalized stage. On the other hand, we do not specify a stage of information need for users who take behavior of "interruption."

Table 2: Multiple observations of search logs with the user query behavior model

User's intention	Stage of information need	Example of words change	Time interval	Order of appearance	Position interval	Number of pairs
Paraphrase	Formalized	extermination → threatened species	short		short	
Specialization	Various	threatened species → albatross	short	later		many
Generalization	Formalized	albatross → threatened species	short			
Alternative	Formalized	giant tortoise → Lonesome George	short		short	
Interruption	Various	Lonesome George → Italy				many

We assume, rather, that users at both the formalized and non-formalized stages may take this behavior. Therefore, we identify these changes as representing various stages of information need. The change from "extermination" to "threatened species" is given as an example of a paraphrase. This semantic relation between these words clearly matches the user's intention in changing words in user query.

The last four columns show the numerical relations between words in all search sequences. Note that the features given in the cells are defined relative feature to other users' intentions. The time interval is related to the stage of information need, as noted earlier; that is, it becomes shorter as a user's information need becomes more formalized. The order of appearance of words is related to their relative suitability within a single topic area. More specialized words thus tend to appear later in each sequence. The position interval is related to the similarity between words within a single topic. In fact, words of a paraphrase or an alternative tend to appear successively. Finally, the largest numbers of pairs are generated by topic changes, so the number of pairs expresses the overall activity level of the user.

4. EXPERIMENTS

4.1. Experimental Concept

Nevertheless the evaluation of ontology and thesaurus construction is a challenging task, no standard evaluation measure, like precision and recall or accuracy, is available to assess performance [13]. Therefore, we assessed our proposed method in terms of search log analysis. Our aim was to evaluate whether our method could be used to identify intentions in user queries and thus capture the semantic relations among words. For this evaluation, we processed search logs by first assembling them to generate search sequences. We then converted all the search sequences into associated groups of words.

4.2. Basic Data

The search log used in this experiment was generated by an Internet search engine over a 24-hour period on September 1, 1999. The log consisted of 952,666 lines, with each line corresponding to one transaction. The transactions were grouped into search sequences by checking the IP addresses and time intervals between successive lines with the same address. When the time interval between these lines was greater than 20 minutes, we didn't treat these lines as representing the behavior of a single user [22]. This processing generated 144,886 search sequences. We found 128,211 unique words and 120,677 unique URLs in this log, and we generated 128,211 associated groups of words.

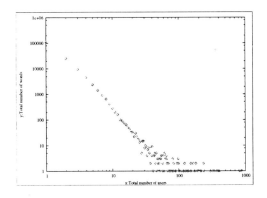

Fig. 4: Log-log plot of the total number of users(X) vs. the total number of words(Y).

Figure 4 shows a log-log plot of the total number of words with respect to the same total number of users. We can see that the plot is very close to a straight line. Figure 5 shows a log-log plot of the total number of users with

111

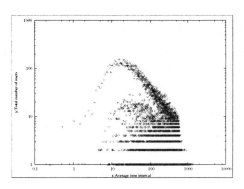

Fig. 5: Log-log plot of the average time interval(X) vs. the total number of users(Y).

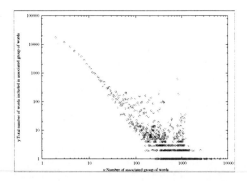

Fig. 6: Log-log plot of the number of associated group of words(X) vs. the total number of words included in an associated group of words(Y).

respect to the same average time interval for each user's queries. Notice that the most of plot is very close to two different parallel straight lines. We consider that this character shows that a user's query behavior has forked about time. Figure 6 shows a log-log plot of the total number of words included in an associated group of words with the same number of associated group of words. We can see that the plot is very close to a straight line. These data also follow Lotka's Law [12]. These results suggest that the user's query behavior followed Lotka's Law like many other social phenomena.

4.3. Semantic Relations Based on User Query Behavior Model

The aim of this evaluation was to determine whether our proposed user query behavior model could effectively cap-ture the semantic relations among words. Table 3 lists all the formulas that can be constituted with multiple observations. We assume that the correspondences between user intentions and the formulas are as follows: $Infbyf$ reflects specialization and the inverse of generalization; Fre reflects interruption; and, after filtering by the time interval, $Avemp$ reflects paraphrase and alternative.

We assessed the performance of our method in the following manner. For each 10 words "key" selected arbitrarily, we additionally selected and ordered 10 words "word" according to the value of the formula for each "key". We then judged whether the assigned semantic relation between "key"and "word" as measured by the formula coincided with the semantic relation (i.e., the "correct" relation), and calculated the percentage of correct semantic relations to all relations. As described above, the possible semantic relations between "key"and "word" were paraphrase, specialization, generalization, alternative, and interruption. We selected "word" with large values for the formulas based on number of appearances, such as Fre, $AFre$, $BFre$, $InFre$, $AinFre$, $BinFre$, $Infbyf$, $Ainfbyf$, and $Binfbyf$, but with small values for those based on interval, such as $Avemp$, $Aveap$, and $Avebp$.

In Table 4, the columns denote the formula used in measuring the words, while the rows denote the semantic relations between words, with two filtering methods used to create the associated groups of words. The aim of filtering is to distinguish those users with a formalized information need from the other users. One filtering method is based on each user's average time interval between words in each search sequence. We defined 60s as the threshold value and used search sequences of users below this value.The other is based on the kinds of words used by each user. We defined 5 words as the threshold value and used search sequences of users above this value. Each cell gives the percentage of the corresponding semantic relation for each formula and time. The sum of the cells within each column is thus 100.0 (e.g., for Filtering = None and $Infbyf$, 3 + 37 + 3 + 5 + 52 = 100).

The results in Table 4 indicate the following. For filtering, the percentage of words selected as interruption was most large for each formula regardless of filtering. Among all formulas, the percentage of Fre was the highest with interruption. This means that we can identify interruption by applying Fre. On the other hand, the filtering based on time decreased the percentage of interruption and increased the percentages for the other behaviors with formalized information need. This means that the time-based filtering is effective in distinguishing users at the formalized stage of information need. For specialization, $Infbyf$ had the highest percentage. After time-based filtering, its value increased from 37 to 45. The reason for this increase was that the filtering succeeded in distinguishing users taking behavior of

Table 3: All formulas constituted from multiple observations of search logs

Number of appearances in search log		
Ignoring order	$Fre\{word\}$	Number of search sequences including "word"
Considering order	$AFre\{word\}$	Number of search sequences including "word" appearing after "key"
Considering order	$BFre\{word\}$	Number of search sequences including "word" appearing before "key"
Number of appearances of "key" and "word" pair in search sequence		
Ignoring order	$InFre\{key\}\{word\}$	Number of search sequences including both "key" and "word"
Considering order	$AinFre\{key\}\{word\}$	Number of search sequences including both "key" and "word" appearing after "key"
Considering order	$BinFre\{key\}\{word\}$	Number of search sequences including both "key" and "word" appearing before "key"
Average position interval between "key" and "word" in search sequence		
Ignoring order	$Avemp\{key\}\{word\} = Ma\{key\}\{word\}/ InFre\{key\}\{word\}$	Average position interval between "key" and "word" in search sequence (Ma$\{key\}\{word\}$: total position interval between "key" and "word" in search sequence)
Considering order	$Aveap\{key\}\{word\} = Aa\{key\}\{word\}/ AinFre\{key\}\{word\}$	Average appearance interval between "key" and "word" appearing after "key" in search sequence (Aa$\{key\}\{word\}$: total position interval between "key" and "word" appearing after "key" in search sequence)
Considering order	$Avebp\{key\}\{word\} = Ba\{key\}\{word\}/ BinFre\{key\}\{word\}$	Average position interval between "key" and "word" appearing after "key" in search sequence (Ba$\{key\}\{word\}$: total position interval between "key" and "word" appearing before "key" in search sequence)
Ration		
Ignoring order	$Infbyf\{key\}\{word\} = InFre\{key\}\{word\}/ Fre\{word\}$	Ratio of number of search sequences including both "key" and "word" to number of search sequences including "word"
Considering order	$AInfbyf\{key\}\{word\} = AInFre\{key\}\{word\}/ Fre\{word\}$	Ratio of number of search sequences including both "key" and "word" appearing after "key" to number of search sequences including "word"
Considering order	$BInfbyf\{key\}\{word\} = BInFre\{key\}\{word\}/ Fre\{word\}$	Ratio of number of search sequences including both "key" and "word" appearing before "key" to number of search sequences including "word"

specialization from the other users. This again confirms that the time-based filtering is effective in distinguishing users with a formalized information need. The process of generalization can essentially be regarded as the inverse of specialization. Therefore, identifying the relation between any two words as specialization also simultaneously identifies a semantic relation of generalization between these words. This means that we can also identify specialization and generalization by applying $Infbyf$. The reason $AInfbyf$ and $BInfbyf$ are inferior measures compared to $Infbyf$ is that not all users take behavior of only specialization or generalization in each query. For paraphrases and alternatives, the percentages were too small. Therefore, we could not completely confirm the effectiveness of the proposed model in this experiment. The reason is the following. The search log we used included many users with different information needs. But, the number of users taking behavior of paraphrase and alternative was too small. It was thus too difficult to identify these users' intentions of paraphrase and alternative. Comparing the values for all formulas, we can see which models performed more correctly and effectively in capturing the corresponding semantic relations.

5. CONCLUSIONS

We have proposed a novel log analysis method that can capture the semantic relations among words by utilizing search logs and modeling user query behavior. Our experimental results indicate that this method could successfully capture semantic relations that previous log analysis methods could not, and at a lower cost than other methods based on manual or natural language processing. Our future work will focus on helping users to increase their efficiency in seeking information, and also on constructing ontologies and thesauruses.

Table 4: Percentages of semantic relations for all formulas

Filter	Semantic relation	Fre	$AFre$	$BFre$	InF	$AInF$	$BInF$	$Infbyf$	$AInfbyf$	$BInfbyf$	$Avebp$	$Aveap$	$Avemp$
None	Paraphrase	0	0	0	1	1	0	3	3	2	2	2	4
	Specialization	0	1	0	4	4	2	37	25	12	30	13	8
	Generalization	0	2	0	1	1	0	3	5	0	3	3	2
	Alternative	5	3	6	4	3	4	5	5	6	8	4	6
	Interruption	95	94	94	90	91	94	52	62	80	57	78	80
Time	Paraphrase	1	1	0	2	5	1	5	4	3	3	3	4
	Specialization	9	7	8	18	7	12	45	24	36	36	24	31
	Generalization	3	4	0	2	1	0	3	4	0	3	0	0
	Alternative	7	3	2	6	1	2	5	1	5	1	1	6
	Interruption	80	85	90	70	86	85	42	67	56	57	72	59
Word	Paraphrase	0	0	1	1	2	0	2	1	2	2	1	2
	Specialization	0	2	2	3	3	1	17	7	25	18	3	16
	Generalization	0	0	0	0	0	0	1	2	1	0	1	1
	Alternative	4	6	1	4	2	2	6	4	4	2	2	1
	Interruption	96	92	96	92	93	97	74	86	68	78	93	80

References

[1] T. Berners. *Semantic Web Road Map*. http://www.w3.org/DesignIssues/Semantic.html, 1999.

[2] A. Broder. *A Taxonomy of Web Search, SIGIR Forum*. Vol. 36, No. 2, 2002.

[3] L. D. Catledge and J. E. Pitkow. *Characterizing Browsing Strategies in the World-Wide Web*. In Proceedings of the 3rd WWW Conference, 1995.

[4] R. Cooley, B. Mobasher, and J. Srivastava. *Data Preparation for Mining World Wide Web Browsing Patterns*. Knowledge and Information Systems 1(1):5-32, 1999.

[5] A. Goker and D. He. *Analysing Web search logs to determine session boundaries for user-oriented learning*. Adaptive Hypermedia and Adaptive Web-Based Systems International Conference (AH2000), 2000.

[6] M. Hearst. *Automatic Acquisition of Hyponyms from Large Text Corpora*. In Proceedings of the Fourteenth International Conference on Computational Linguistics, 1992.

[7] J. Hobbs. *The Generic Information Extraction System*. In Proceedings of the Fifth Message Understanding Conference (MUC-5), 1993.

[8] B. Huberman, P. L. T. Pirolli, J. E. Pitkow, and R. M. Lukose. *Strong regularities in World Wide Web surfing*. Science, Vol. 280(5360), 95-97, 1998.

[9] L. Kaufman and P. J. Rousseeuw. *Finding Groups in Data: An Introduction to Cluster Analysis*. John Wiley & Sons, 1990.

[10] T. Lau and E. Horvitz. *Patterns of Search: Analyzing and Modeling Web Query Refinement*. In Proceedings of the Seventh International Conference on User Modeling. ACM Press, 1998.

[11] S. Lawrence and C. L. Giles. *Searching the World Wide Web*. Web, Science, 280 (5360), 98-100, 1998.

[12] A. J. Lotka. *The Frequency Distribution of Scientific Productivity*. Journal of the Washington Academy of Sciences, 16 (12), 317-323, 1926.

[13] A. Maedche and R. Volz. *The Text-To-Ontology Extraction and Maintenance System*. ICDM-Workshop on Integrating Data Mining and Knowledge Management, 2001.

[14] C. Manning and H. Schuetze. *Foundations of Statistical Language Processing*. MIT Press, 1999.

[15] Y. Niwa. *Dynamic Co-occurrence Analysis for Interactive Document Retrieval*. IPSJ SIGNotes Natural Language Abstract No. 115-014, 1996.

[16] M. Ohkubo, M. Sugizaki, T. Inoue, and K. Tanaka. *Extracting Information Demand by Analyzing a WWW Search Log*. IPSJ Vol. 39, No. 07, 1998.

[17] F. Pereira, N. Tishby, and L. Lee. *Distributional Clustering of English Words*. In Proceedings of the 31st ACL, 1993.

[18] S. Ramakrishnan and Y. Yinghui. *Mining web logs to improve website organization*. In Proceedings of the Tenth International WWW Conference (WWW2001), 2001.

[19] S. Sato, M. Harada, and K. Kazama. *Some Results from an Analysis of Queries to a Search Engine*. IPSJ SIG Notes, 2000-FI-57-18, 1999.

[20] C. Silverstein, M. Henzinger, H. Marais, and M. Moricz. *Analysis of a Very Large AltaVista Query Log*. Technical Report 1998-014, Digital Systems Research Center, 1998.

[21] R. Taylor. *Question-negotiation and information seeking in libraries*. College Research Libraries, 29(3), 1968.

[22] M. Weintraub, Y. Aksu, S. Dharanipragada, S. Khudanpur, H. Ney, J. Prange, A. Stolcke, F. Jelinek, and E. Shriberg. *Lm95 project report: Fast training and portability*. Research Notes No. 1, Center for Language and Speech Processing, 1996.

Clustering of Time Series Subsequences is Meaningless: Implications for Previous and Future Research

Eamonn Keogh   Jessica Lin   Wagner Truppel

Computer Science & Engineering Department
University of California - Riverside
Riverside, CA 92521

{eamonn, jessica, wagner}@cs.ucr.edu

Abstract

Time series data is perhaps the most frequently encountered type of data examined by the data mining community. Clustering is perhaps the most frequently used data mining algorithm, being useful in it's own right as an exploratory technique, and also as a subroutine in more complex data mining algorithms such as rule discovery, indexing, summarization, anomaly detection, and classification. Given these two facts, it is hardly surprising that time series clustering has attracted much attention. The data to be clustered can be in one of two formats: many individual time series, or a single time series, from which individual time series are extracted with a sliding window. Given the recent explosion of interest in streaming data and online algorithms, the latter case has received much attention.

In this work we make an amazing claim. Clustering of streaming time series is completely meaningless. More concretely, clusters extracted from streaming time series are forced to obey a certain constraint that is pathologically unlikely to be satisfied by any dataset, and because of this, the clusters extracted by any clustering algorithm are essentially random. While this constraint can be intuitively demonstrated with a simple illustration and is simple to prove, it has never appeared in the literature.

We can justify calling our claim surprising, since it invalidates the contribution of dozens of previously published papers. We will justify our claim with a theorem, illustrative examples, and a comprehensive set of experiments on reimplementations of previous work.

Keywords

Time Series, Data Mining, Clustering, Rule Discovery

1. Introduction

Time series data is perhaps the most commonly encountered kind of data explored by data miners [26, 35]. Clustering is perhaps the most frequently used data mining algorithm [14], being useful in it's own right as an exploratory technique, and as a subroutine in more complex data mining algorithms [3, 5]. Given these two facts, it is hardly surprising that time series data mining has attracted an extraordinary amount of attention [3, 7, 8, 9, 11, 12, 15, 16, 17, 18, 20, 21, 24, 25, 27, 28, 29, 30, 31, 32, 33, 36, 38, 40, 42, 45]. The work in this area can be broadly classified into two categories:

- **Whole Clustering**: The notion of clustering here is similar to that of conventional clustering of discrete objects. Given a set of individual time series data, the objective is to group similar time series into the same cluster.

- **Subsequence Clustering**: Given a single time series, individual time series (subsequences) are extracted with a sliding window. Clustering is then performed on the extracted time series.

Subsequence clustering is commonly used as a subroutine in many other algorithms, including rule discovery [9, 11, 15, 16, 17, 20, 21, 30, 32, 36, 42, 45], indexing [27, 33], classification [7, 8], prediction [37, 40], and anomaly detection [45]. For clarity, we will refer to this type of clustering as STS (Subsequence Time Series) clustering.

In this work we make a surprising claim. Clustering streaming time series is meaningless! More concretely, clusters extracted from streaming time series are forced to obey a certain constraint that is pathologically unlikely to be satisfied by any dataset, and because of this, the clusters extracted by any clustering algorithm are essentially random.

Since we use the word "*meaningless*" many times in this paper, we will take the time to define this term. All useful algorithms (with the sole exception of random number generators) produce output that depends on the input. For example, a decision tree learner will yield very different outputs on, say, a credit worthiness domain, a drug classification domain, and a music domain. We call an algorithm "*meaningless*" if the output is independent of the input. As we prove in this paper, the output of STS clustering does not depend on input, and is therefore meaningless.

Our claim is surprising since it calls into question the contributions of dozens of papers. In fact, the existence of so much work based on STS clustering offers an obvious counter argument to our claim. It could be argued: "*Since many papers have been published which use time series subsequence clustering as a subroutine, and these papers produced successful results, time series subsequence clustering must be a meaningful operation.*"

We strongly feel that this is not the case. We believe that in all such cases the results are consistent with what one would expect from random cluster centers. We recognize that this is a strong assertion, so we will demonstrate our claim by reimplementing the most successful (i.e. the most referenced) examples of such work, and showing with exhaustive experiments that these contributions inherit the property of meaningless results from the STS clustering subroutine.

The rest of this paper is organized as follows. In Section 2 we will review the necessary background material on time series and clustering, then briefly review the body of research that uses STS clustering. In Section 3 we will show that STS clustering is meaningless with a series of simple intuitive experiments; then we will explain *why* STS clustering cannot produce useful results. In Section 4 we show that the many algorithms that use STS clustering as a subroutine produce results indistinguishable from random clusters.

2. Background Material

In order to frame our contribution in the proper context we begin with a review of the necessary background material.

2.1 Notation and Definitions

We begin with a definition of our data type of interest, time series:

> **Definition 1**. *Time Series*: A time series $T = t_1, ..., t_m$ is an ordered set of m real-valued variables.

Data miners are typically not interested in any of the global properties of a time series; rather, data miners confine their interest to subsections of the time series, called subsequences.

> **Definition 2**. *Subsequence*: Given a time series T of length m, a subsequence C_p of T is a sampling of length $w < m$ of contiguous positions from T, that is, $C = t_p, ..., t_{p-w-1}$ for $1 \le p \le m - w + 1$.

In this work we are interested in the case where all the subsequences are extracted, and then clustered. This is achieved by use of a sliding window.

> **Definition 3**. *Sliding Windows*: Given a time series T of length m, and a user-defined subsequence length of w, a matrix S of all possible subsequences can be built by "sliding a window" across T and placing subsequence C_p in the pth row of S. The size of matrix S is $(m - w + 1)$ by w.

Figure 1 summarizes all the above definitions and notations.

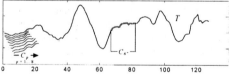

Figure 1. An illustration of the notation introduced in this section: a *time series* T of length 128, a *subsequence* of length w = 16, beginning at datapoint 67, and the first 8 subsequences extracted by a *sliding window*.

Note that while S contains exactly the same information as T, it requires significantly more storage space. This is typically not a problem, since, as we shall see in the next section, the limiting factor tends to be the CPU time for clustering.

2.2 Background on Clustering

One of the most widely used clustering approaches is hierarchical clustering, due to the great visualization power it offers [26, 29]. Hierarchical clustering produces a nested hierarchy of similar groups of objects, according to a pairwise distance matrix of the objects. One of the advantages of this method is its generality, since the user does not need to provide any parameters such as the number of clusters. However, its application is limited to only small datasets, due to its quadratic computational complexity. Table 1 outlines the basic hierarchical clustering algorithm.

Table 1: An outline of hierarchical clustering.

Algorithm Hierarchical Clustering	
1.	Calculate the distance between all objects. Store the results in a distance matrix.
2.	Search through the distance matrix and find the two most similar clusters/objects.
3.	Join the two clusters/objects to produce a cluster that now has at least 2 objects.
4.	Update the matrix by calculating the distances between this new cluster and all other clusters.
5.	Repeat step 2 until all cases are in one cluster.

A faster method to perform clustering is k-means [5]. The basic intuition behind k-means (and a more general class of clustering algorithms known as iterative refinement algorithms) is shown in Table 2:

Table 2: An outline of the k-means algorithm.

Algorithm *k-means*	
1.	Decide on a value for k.
2.	Initialize the k cluster centers (randomly, if necessary).
3.	Decide the class memberships of the N objects by assigning them to the nearest cluster center.
4.	Re-estimate the k cluster centers, by assuming the memberships found above are correct.
5.	If none of the N objects changed membership in the last iteration, exit. Otherwise goto 3.

The k-means algorithm for N objects has a complexity of $O(kNrD)$, with k the number of clusters specified by the user, r the number of iterations until convergence, and D the dimensionality of time series (in the case of STS clustering, D is the length of the sliding window, w). While the algorithm is perhaps the most commonly used clustering algorithm in the literature, it does have several shortcomings, including the fact that the number of clusters must be specified in advance [5, 14].

It is well understood that some types of high dimensional clustering may be meaningless. As noted by [1, 4], in high dimensions the very concept of nearest neighbor has little meaning, because the ratio of the distance to the nearest neighbor over the distance to the average neighbor rapidly approaches one as the dimensionality increases. However, time series, while often having high dimensionality, typically have a low intrinsic dimensionality [25], and can therefore be meaningful candidates for clustering.

2.3 Background on Time Series Data Mining

The last decade has seen an extraordinary interest in mining time series data, with at least one thousand papers on the subject [26]. Tasks addressed by the researchers include segmentation, indexing, clustering, classification, anomaly detection, rule discovery, and summarization.

Of the above, a significant fraction use streaming time series clustering as a subroutine. Below we will enumerate some representative examples.

- There has been much work on finding association rules in time series [9, 11, 15, 16, 20, 21, 30, 32, 26, 42, 45].

Virtually all work is based on the classic paper of Das et. al. that uses STS clustering to convert real valued time series into symbolic values, which can then be manipulated by classic rule finding algorithms [9].

- The problem of anomaly detection in time series has been generalized to include the detection of surprising or interesting patterns (which are not necessarily anomalies). There are many approaches to this problem, including several based on STS clustering [45].

- Indexing of time series is an important problem that has attracted the attention of dozens of researchers. Several of the proposed techniques make use of STS clustering [27, 33].

- Some techniques for classifying time series make use of STS clustering to preprocess the data before passing to a standard classification technique such as a decision tree [7, 8].

- Clustering of time series has also been proposed as a knowledge discovery tool in its own right. Researchers have suggested various techniques to speed up the clustering [11].

The above is just a small fraction of the work in the area, more extensive surveys may be found in [24, 35].

3. Demonstrations of the Meaninglessness of STS Clustering

In this section we will demonstrate the meaninglessness of STS clustering. In order to demonstrate that this meaninglessness is a product of the way the data is obtained by sliding windows, and not some quirk of the clustering algorithm, we will also do whole clustering as a control [12, 31].

3.1 K-means Clustering

Because k-means is a heuristic, hill-climbing algorithm, the cluster centers found may not be optimal [14]. That is, the algorithm is guaranteed to converge on a local, but not necessarily global optimum. The choices of the initial centers affect the quality of results. One technique to mitigate this problem is to do multiple restarts, and choose the best set of clusters [5]. An obvious question to ask is how much variability in the shapes of cluster centers we get between multiple runs. We can measure this variability with the following equation:

- Let $A = (\overline{a}_1, \overline{a}_2, ..., \overline{a}_k)$ be the cluster centers derived from one run of k-means.

- Let $B = (\overline{b}_1, \overline{b}_2, ..., \overline{b}_k)$ be the cluster centers derived from a different run of k-means.

- Let $dist(\overline{a}_i, \overline{a}_j)$ be the distance between two cluster centers, measured with Euclidean distance.

Then the distance between two sets of clusters can be defined as:

$$cluster\_distance(A, B) \equiv \sum_{i=1}^{k} \min \left[dist(\overline{a}_i, \overline{b}_j) \right] , 1 \leq j \leq k \quad (1)$$

The simple intuition behind the equation is that each individual cluster center in A should map on to its closest counterpart in B, and the sum of all such distances tells us how similar two sets of clusters are.

An important observation is that we can use this measure not only to compare two sets of clusters derived for the same dataset, but also two sets of clusters which have been derived from *different* data sources. Given this fact, we propose a simple experiment.

We performed 3 random restarts of k-means on a stock market data set, and saved the 3 resulting sets of cluster centers into set **X**. We also performed 3 random restarts on random walk dataset, saving the 3 resulting sets of cluster centers into set **Y**.

We then measured the average cluster distance (as defined in equation 1), between each set of cluster centers in **X**, to each other set of cluster centers in **X**. We call this number *within_set_X_distance*. We also measured the average cluster distance between each set of cluster centers in **X**, to cluster centers in **Y**; we call this number *between_set_X_and_Y_distance*.

We can use these two numbers to create a fraction:

$$clustering\,meaningfulness(X, Y) \equiv \frac{within\_set\_X\_distance}{between\_set\_X\_and\_Y\_distance} \quad (2)$$

We can justify calling this number "*clustering meaningfulness*" since it clearly measures just that. If the clustering algorithm is returning the same or similar sets of clusters despite different initial seeds, the numerator should be close to zero. In contrast, there is no reason why the clusters from two completely different, unrelated datasets to be similar. Therefore, we should expect the denominator to be relatively large. So overall we should expect that the value of *clustering meaningfulness*(**X**,**Y**) should be close to zero when **X** and **Y** are sets of cluster centers derived from different datasets.

As a control, we performed the exact same experiment, on the same data, but using subsequences that were randomly extracted, rather than extracted by a sliding window. We call this whole clustering.

Since it might be argued that any results obtained were the consequence of a particular combination of k and w, we tried the cross product of $k = \{3, 5, 7, 11\}$ and $w = \{8, 16, 32\}$. For every combination of parameters we repeated the entire process 100 times, and averaged the results. Figure 2 shows the results.

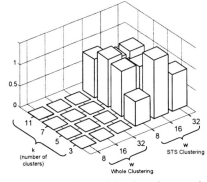

Figure 2. A comparison of the clustering meaningfulness for whole clustering, and STS clustering, using k-means with a variety of parameters. The two datasets used were Standard and Poor's 500 Index closing values and random walk data.

The results are astonishing. The cluster centers found by STS clustering on any particular run of k-means on stock market

117

dataset are not significantly more similar to each other than they are to cluster centers taken from random walk data! In other words, if we were asked to perform clustering on a particular stock market dataset, we could reuse an old clustering obtained from random walk data, and no one could tell the difference!

We reemphasize here that the difference in the results for STS clustering and whole clustering in this experiment (and all experiments in this work) are due exclusively to the feature extraction step. In particular, both are being tested on the same dataset, with the same parameters of w and k, using the same algorithm.

We also note that the exact definition of *clustering meaningfulness* is not important to our results. In our definition, each cluster center in A maps onto its closest match in B. It is possible therefore that two or more cluster centers from A map to one center in B, and some clusters in B have no match. However we tried other variants of this definition, including pairwise matching, minimum matching and maximum matching, together with dozens of other measurements of clustering quality suggested in the literature [14]; it simply makes no significant difference to the results.

3.2 Hierarchical Clustering

The previous section suggests that k-means clustering of STS time series does not produce meaningful results, at least for stock market data. An obvious question to ask is, is this true for STS with other clustering algorithms? We will answer the question for hierarchical clustering here.

Hierarchical clustering, unlike k-means, is a deterministic algorithm. So we can't reuse the experimental methodology from the previous section, however, we can do something similar.

First we note that hierarchical clustering can be converted into a partitional clustering, by cutting the first k links [29]. Figure 3 illustrates the idea. The resultant time series in each of the k subtrees can then be merged into single cluster prototypes. When performing hierarchical clustering, one has to make a choice about how to define the distance between two clusters, this choice is called the linkage method (cf. line 3 of Table 1).

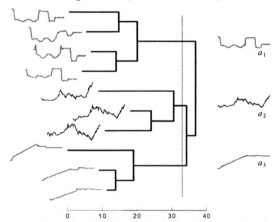

Figure 3. A hierarchical clustering of ten time series. The clustering can be converted to a k partitional clustering by "sliding" a cutting line until it intersects k lines of the dendrograms, then averaging the time series in the k subtrees to form k cluster centers (gray panel).

Three popular choices are complete linkage, average linkage and Ward's method [14]. We can use all three methods for the stock market dataset, and place the resulting cluster centers into set X. We can do the same for random walk data and place the resulting cluster centers into set Y. Having done this, we can extend the measure of clustering meaningfulness in Eq. 2 to hierarchical clustering, and run a similar experiment as in the last section, but using hierarchical clustering. The results of this experiment are shown in Figure 4.

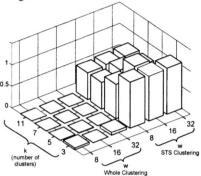

Figure 4. A comparison of the clustering meaningfulness for whole clustering and STS clustering using hierarchical clustering with a variety of parameters. The two datasets used were Standard and Poor's 500 Index closing values and random walk data.

Once again, the results are astonishing. While it is well understood that the choice of linkage method can have minor effects on the clustering found, the results above tell us that when doing STS clustering, the choice of linkage method has as much effect as the choice of dataset! Another way of looking at the results is as follows. If we were asked to perform hierarchical clustering on a particular dataset, but we did not have to report which linkage method we used, we could reuse an old random walk clustering and no one could tell the difference without rerunning the clustering for every possible linkage method.

3.3 Other Datasets and Algorithms

The results in the two previous sections are extraordinary, but are they the consequence of some properties of stock market data, or as we claim, a property of the sliding window feature extraction? The latter is the case, which we can simply demonstrate. We visually inspected the UCR archive of time series datasets for the two time series datasets that appear the least alike [23]. The best two candidates we discovered are shown in Figure 5.

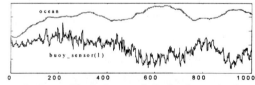

Figure 5. Two subjectively very dissimilar time series from the UCR archive. Only the first 1,000 datapoints are shown. The two time series have very different properties of stationarity, noise, periodicity, symmetry, autocorrelation etc.

We repeated the experiment of Section 3.2, using these two datasets in place of the stock market data and the random walk data. The results are shown in Figure 6.

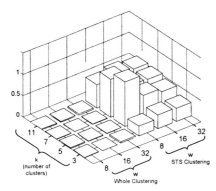

Figure 6. A comparison of the clustering meaningfulness for whole clustering, and STS clustering, using k-means with a variety of parameters. The two datasets used were buoy_sensor(1) and ocean.

In our view, this experiment sounds the death knell for clustering of STS time series. If we cannot easily differentiate between the clusters from these two extremely different time series, then how could we possibly find meaningful clusters in any data?

In fact, the experiments shown in this section are just a tiny subset of the experiments we performed. We tested other clustering algorithms, including EM and SOMs [43]. We tested on 42 different datasets [24, 26]. We experimented with other measures of clustering quality [14]. We tried other variants of k-means, including different seeding algorithms. Although Euclidean distance is the most commonly used distance measure for time series data mining, we also tried other distance measures from the literature, including Manhattan, L_∞, Mahalanobis distance and dynamic time warping distance [12, 24, 31]. We tried various normalization techniques, including Z-normalization, 0-1 normalization, amplitude only normalization, offset only normalization, no normalization etc. In every case we are forced to the inescapable conclusion: whole clustering of time series is usually a meaningful thing to do, but sliding window time series clustering is *never* meaningful.

3.4 Why is STS Clustering Meaningless?

Before explaining why STS clustering is meaningless, it will be instructive to visualize the cluster centers produced by both whole clustering and STS clustering. We will demonstrate on the classic Cylinder-Bell-Funnel data [26]. This dataset consists of random instantiations of the eponymous patterns, with Gaussian noise added. While each time series is of length 128, the onset and duration of the shape is subject to random variability. Figure 7 shows one instance from each of the three clusters.

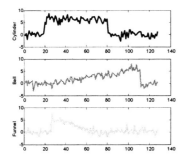

Figure 7. Examples of Cylinder, Bell, and Funnel patterns.

We generated a dataset of 30 instances of each pattern, and performed k-means clustering on it, with $k = 3$. The resulting cluster centers are show in Figure 8. As one might expect, all three clusters are successfully found. The final centers closely resemble the three different patterns in the dataset, although the sharp edges of the patterns have been somewhat "softened" by the averaging of many time series with some variability in the time axis.

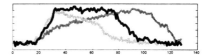

Figure 8. The three final centers found by k-means on the cylinder-bell-funnel dataset. The shapes of the centers are close approximation of the original patterns.

To compare the results of whole clustering to STS clustering, we took the 90 time series used above and concatenated them into one long time series. We then performed STS k-means clustering. To make it easy for the algorithm, we use the exact length of the patterns ($w = 128$) as the window length, and $k = 3$ as the number of desired clusters. The cluster centers are shown in Figure 9.

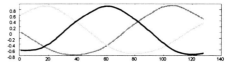

Figure 9. The three final centers found by subsequence clustering using the sliding window approach.

The results are extraordinarily unintuitive! The cluster centers look nothing like any of the patterns in the data; what's more, they appear to be perfect sine waves.

In fact, for $w << m$, we get approximate sine waves with STS clustering regardless of the clustering algorithm, the number of clusters, or the dataset used! Furthermore, although the sine waves are always exactly out of phase with each other by $1/k$ period, overall, their joint phase is arbitrary, and will change with every random restart of k-means.

This result completely explains the results from the last section. If sine waves appear as cluster centers for every dataset, then clearly it will be impossible to distinguish one dataset's clusters from another. Although we have now explained the inability of STS clustering to produce meaningful results, we have revealed a new question: why do we always get cluster centers with this special structure?

3.5 A Hidden Constraint

To explain the unintuitive results above, we must introduce a new fact.

> **Theorem 1**: For any time series dataset T with an overall trend of zero, if T is clustered using sliding windows, and $w << m$, then the mean of all the data (i.e. the special case of $k = 1$), will be an approximately constant vector.

In other words, if we run STS k-means on *any* dataset, with $k = 1$ (an unusual case, but perfectly legal), we will always end up with a horizontal line as the cluster center. The proof of this fact is straightforward but long, so we have elucidated it in a separate technical report [41]. Note that the requirement that the overall trend be zero can be removed, in which case, the $k = 1$ cluster center is still a straight line, but at some angle.

We content ourselves here with giving the intuition behind the proof, and offering a visual "proof" in Figure 10.

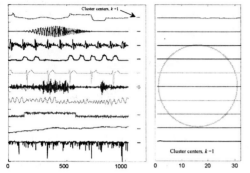

Figure 10: A visual "proof" of Theorem 1. Ten time series of vastly different properties of stationarity, noise, periodicity, symmetry, autocorrelation etc. The cluster centers for each time series, for $w = 32$, $k = 1$ are shown at right. Far right shows a zoom-in that shows just how close to a straight line the cluster centers are. While the objects have been shifted for clarity, they have *not* been rescaled in either axis; note the light gray circle in both graphs. The datasets used are, reading from top to bottom: Space Shuttle, Flutter, Speech, Power_Data, Koski_ecg, Earthquake, Chaotic, Cylinder, Random_Walk, and Balloon.

The intuition behind Theorem 1 is as follows. Imagine an arbitrary datapoint t_i somewhere in the time series T, such that $w \leq i \leq m - w + 1$. If the time series is much longer than the window size, then virtually all datapoints are of this type. What contribution does this datapoint make to the overall mean of the STS matrix S? As the sliding window passes by, the datapoint first appears as the rightmost value in the window, then it goes on to appear exactly once in *every* possible location within the sliding window. So the t_i datapoint contribution to the overall shape is the same everywhere and must be a horizontal line. Only those points at the very beginning and the very end of the time series avoid contributing their value to all w columns of S, but these are asymptotically irrelevant. The average of many horizontal lines is clearly just another horizontal line.

The implications of Theorem 1 become clearer when we consider the following well documented fact. For any dataset, the weighted (by cluster membership) average of k clusters must sum up to the global mean. The implication for STS clustering is profound. If we hope to discover k clusters in our dataset, we can only do so if the weighted average of these clusters happens to sum to a constant line! However, there is no reason why we should expect this to be true of *any* dataset, much less *every* dataset. This hidden constraint limits the utility of STS clustering to a vanishing small set of subspace of all datasets.

3.6 The Importance of Trivial Matches
There are further constraints on the types of datasets where STS clustering could possibly work. Consider a subsequence C_p that is a member of a cluster. If we examine the entire dataset for similar subsequences, we should typically expect to find the best matches to C_p to be the subsequences $...,C_{p-2}, C_{p-1}, C_{p-1}, C_{p-2},...$ In other words, the best matches to any subsequence tend to be just slightly shifted versions of the subsequence. Figure 11 illustrates the idea, and Definition 4 states it more formally.

Definition 4. *Trivial Match*: Given a subsequence C beginning at position p, a matching subsequence M beginning at q, and a distance R, we say that M is a *trivial match* to C of order R, if either $p = q$ or there does not exist a subsequence M' beginning at q' such that $D(C, M') > R$, and either $q < q' < p$ or $p < q' < q$.

The importance of trivial matches, in a different context, has been documented elsewhere [28]

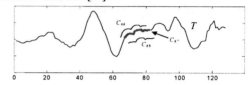

Figure 11: For almost any subsequence C in a time series, the closest matching subsequences are the subsequences immediately to the left and right of C.

An important observation is the fact that different subsequences can have vastly different numbers of trivial matches. In particular, smooth, slowly changing subsequences tend to have many trivial matches, whereas subsequences with rapidly changing features and/or noise tend to have very few trivial matches. Figure 12 illustrates the idea. The figure shows a time series that subjectively appears to have a cluster of 3 square waves. However, the bottom plot shows how many trivial matches each subsequence has. Note that the square waves have very few trivial matches, so all three taken together sit in a sparsely populated region of w-space. In contrast, consider the relatively smooth Gaussian bump centered at 125. The subsequences in the smooth ascent of this feature have more than 25 trivial matches, and thus sit in a dense region of w-space; the same is true for the subsequences in the descent from the peak. So if clustering this dataset with k-means, $k = 2$, the two cluster centers will be irresistibly drawn to these two "shapes", simple ascending and descending lines.

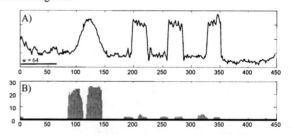

Figure 12: A) A time series T that subjectively appears to have a cluster of 3 noisy square waves. B) Here the ith value is the number of trivial matches for the subsequence C_i in T, where $R = 1$, $w = 64$.

The importance of this observation for STS clustering is obvious. Imagine we have a time series where we subjectively see two clusters: equal numbers of a smooth slowing changing pattern, and a noisier pattern with many features. In w-dimensional space, the smooth pattern is surrounded by many trivial matches. This dense volume will appear to any clustering algorithm an extremely promising cluster center. In contrast, the highly featured, noisy pattern has very few trivial matches, and thus sits in a relatively sparse space, all but ignored by the clustering algorithm. Note that it is not possible to simply remove or "factor out" the trivial matches since there is no way to know beforehand the true patterns.

In the 1920's "data miners" were excited to find that by preprocessing their data with repeated smoothing, they could discover trading cycles. Their joy was shattered by a theorem by Evgeny Slutsky (1880-1948), who demonstrated that any noisy time series will converge to a sine wave after repeated applications of moving window smoothing [22]. While STS clustering is not exactly the same as repeated moving window smoothing, it is clearly highly related. For brevity we will defer future discussion of this point to future work.

4. A Case Study on Existing Work

As we noted in the introduction, an obvious counter argument to our claim is the following. *"Since many papers have been published which use time series subsequence clustering as a subroutine, and these papers produce successful results, time series subsequence clustering must be a meaningful operation."* To counter this argument, we have reimplemented the most influential such work, the Time Series Rule Finding algorithm of Das et. al. [9] (the algorithm is not named in the original work, we will call it TSRF here for brevity and clarity).

4.1 (Not) Finding Rules in Time Series

The algorithm begins by performing STS clustering. The centers of these clusters are then used as primitives that are fed into a slightly modified version of a classic association rule algorithm [2]. Finally the rules are ranked by their J-measure, an entropy based measure of their significance.

The rule finding algorithm found the rules shown in Figure 13 using 19 months of NASDAQ data. The high values of support, confidence and J-measure are offered as evidence of the significance of the rules. The rules are to be interpreted as follows. In Figure 13 (b) we see that *"if stock rises then falls greatly, follow a smaller rise, **then** we can expect to see within 20 time units, a pattern of rapid decrease followed by a leveling out."* [9].

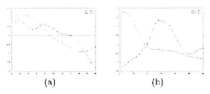

w	d	Rule	Sup %	Conf %	J-Mea.	Fig
20	5.5	$7 \Rightarrow^{15} 8$	8.3	73.0	0.0036	(a)
30	5.5	$18 \Rightarrow^{20} 21$	1.3	62.7	0.0039	(b)

Figure 13: Above, two examples of "significant" rules found by Das et. al. (This is a capture of Figure 4 from their paper). Below, a table of the parameters they used and results they found.

What would happen if we used the TSRF algorithm to try to find rules in random walk data, using exactly the same parameters? Since no such rules should exist by definition, we should get radically different results[1]. Figure 14 shows one such experiment; the support, confidence and J-measure values are essentially the same as in Figure 13!

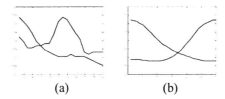
(a)   (b)

w	d	Rule	Sup %	Conf %	J-Mea	Fig
20	5.5	$11 \Rightarrow^{15} 3$	6.9	71.2	0.0042	(a)
30	5.5	$24 \Rightarrow^{20} 19$	2.1	74.7	0.0035	(b)

Figure 14: Above, two examples of "significant" rules found in *random walk* data using the techniques of Das et. al. Below, we used identical parameters and found near identical results.

For every result shown in the original paper we ran 100 recreations using different random walk datasets, using quantum mechanically generated numbers to insure randomness [44]. In every case the results published cannot be distinguished from our results on random walk data.

The above experiment is troublesome, but perhaps there are simply no rules to be found in stock market. We devised a simple experiment in a dataset that does contain known rules. In particular we tested the algorithm on a normal healthy electrocardiogram. Here, there is an obvious rule that one heartbeat follows another. Surprisingly, even with much tweaking of the parameters, the TSRF algorithm cannot find this rule.

The TSRF algorithm is based on the classic rule mining work of Agrawal et. al. [2]; the only difference is the STS step. Since the work of [2] has been carefully vindicated in 100's of experiments on both real and synthetic datasets, it seems reasonable to conclude that the STS clustering is at the heart of the problems with the TSRF algorithm.

These results may appear surprising, since they invalidate the claims of a highly referenced paper, and many of the dozens of extensions researchers have proposed [9, 11, 15, 16, 17, 20, 21, 30, 32, 36, 42, 45]. However, in retrospect, this result should not really be too surprising. Imagine that a researcher claims to have an algorithm that can differentiate between three types of Iris flowers (Setosa, Virginica and Versicolor) based on petal and sepal length and width [10]. This claim is not so extraordinary, given that it is well known that even amateur botanists and gardeners have this skill [6]. However, the paper in question is claiming to introduce an algorithm that can find rules in stock market time series. There is simply no evidence that any human can do this, in fact, the opposite is true: every indication suggests that the patterns much beloved by technical analysts such as the "calendar effect" are completely spurious [19, 39].

5. Conclusions

We have shown that a popular technique for data mining does not produce meaningful results. We have further explained the reasons why this is so[2].

Acknowledgments: We gratefully acknowledge the following people who looked at an early draft of this paper and made useful comments and suggestions: Christos Faloutsos, Michalis Vlachos, Frank Höppner, Howard Hamilton, Daniel Barbara, Magnus Lie Hetland, Hongyuan Zha,

---

[1] Note that the shapes of the patterns in Figures 13 and 14 are only very approximately sinusoidal. This is because the time series are relatively short compared to the window length. When the experiments are repeated with longer time series, the shapes converge to pure sine waves.

---

[2] We encourage the reader to read the expanded version of this paper. It is available at the authors website. There are several important extensions to this work.

Sergio Focardi, Xiaoming Jin, Shoji Hirano, Shusaku Tsumoto, Mark Last, and Zbigniew Struzik.

6. References

[1] Aggarwal, C., Hinneburg, A., & Keim, D. A. (2001). On the Surprising Behavior of Distance Metrics in High Dimensional Space. In *proceedings of the 8th Int'l Conference on Database Theory*. London, UK, Jan 4-6. pp 420-434.

[2] Agrawal, R., Imielinski, T. & Swami, A. (1993). Mining Association Rules Between Sets of Items in Large Databases. In *proceedings of the 1993 ACM SIGMOD International Conference on Management of Data*. Washington, D.C., May 26-28. pp. 207-216.

[3] Bar-Joseph, Z., Gerber, G., Gifford, D., Jaakkola, T. & Simon, I. (2002). A New Approach to Analyzing Gene Expression Time Series Data. In *proceedings of the 6th Annual Int'l Conference on Research in Computational Molecular Biology*. Washington, D.C. pp 39-48.

[4] Beyer, K., Goldstein, J., Ramakrishnan, R. & Shaft, U. (1999). When is Nearest Neighbor Meaningful? In *proceedings of the 7th Int'l Conference on Database Theory*. Jerusalem, Israel, pp. 217-235.

[5] Bradley, P. S. & Fayyad, U.M. (1998). Refining Initial Points for K--Means Clustering. In *proceedings of the 15th Int'l Conference on Machine Learning*. Madison, WI, July 24-27. pp. 91-99.

[6] British Iris Society, Species Group Staff. (1997). A Guide to Species Irises: Their Identification and Cultivation. *Cambridge University Press*.

[7] Cotofrei, P. (2002). Statistical Temporal Rules. In *proceedings of the 15th Conference on Computational Statistics* - Short Communications and Posters. Berlin, Germany, Aug 24-28.

[8] Cotofrei, P. & Stoffel, K (2002). Classification Rules + Time = Temporal Rules. In *proceedings of the 2002 Int'l Conference on Computational Science*. Amsterdan, Netherlands, pp 572-581.

[9] Das, G., Lin, K., Mannila, H., Renganathan, G. & Smyth, P. (1998). Rule Discovery from Time Series. In *proceedings of the 4th Int'l Conference on Knowledge Discovery and Data Mining*. New York, NY, Aug 27-31. pp 16-22.

[10] Fisher, R. A. (1936). The Use of Multiple Measures in Taxonomic Problems. *Annals of Eugenics*. Vol. 7, No. 2, pp 179-188.

[11] Fu, T. C., Chung, F. L., Ng, V. & Luk, R. (2001). Pattern Discovery from Stock Time Series Using Self-Organizing Maps. *Workshop Notes of KDD2001 Workshop on Temporal Data Mining*. San Francisco, CA, Aug 26-29. pp 27-37.

[12] Gavrilov, M., Anguelov, D., Indyk, P. & Motwani, R. (2000). Mining the Stock Market: Which Measure is Best? In *proceedings of the 6th ACM Int'l Conference on Knowledge Discovery and Data Mining*. Boston, MA, Aug 20-23. pp 487-496.

[13] Guha, S. Mishra, N. Motwani, R. & O'Callaghan, L (2000). Clustering Data Streams. In *Proceedings of the 41st Annual Symposium on Foundations of Computer Science*. Redondo Beach, CA. pp. 359-366.

[14] Halkidi, M., Batistakis, Y. & Vazirgiannis, M. (2001). On Clustering Validation Techniques. *Journal of Intelligent Information Systems* (JIIS), Vol. 17, No. 2-3. pp. 107-145.

[15] Harms, S. K., Deogun, J. & Tadesse, T. (2002). Discovering Sequential Association Rules with Constraints and Time Lags in Multiple Sequences. In *proceedings of the 13th Int'l Symposium on Methodologies for Intelligent Systems*. Lyon, France, pp 432-441.

[16] Harms, S. K., Reichenbach, S. Goddard, S. E., Tadesse, T. & Waltman, W. J. (2002). Data Mining in a Geospatial Decision Support system for Drought Risk Management. In *proceedings of the 1st National Conference on Digital Government*. Los Angeles, CA, pp. 9-16.

[17] Hetland, M. L. & Sætrom, P. (2002). Temporal Rules Discovery Using Genetic Programming and Specialized Hardware. In *proceedings of the 4th Int'l Conference on Recent Advances in Soft Computing*. Nottingham, UK.

[18] Honda, R., Wang, S., Kikuchi, T. & Konishi, O. (2002). Mining of Moving Objects from Time-Series Images and its Application to Satellite Weather Imagery. *The Journal of Intelligent Information Systems*, Vol. 19, No. 1, pp. 79-93.

[19] Jensen, D. (2000). Data Snooping, Dredging and Fishing: The dark Side of Data Mining. SIGKDD99 panel report. *ACM SIGKDD Explorations*, Vol. 1, No. 2.

[20] Jin, X., Lu, Y. & Shi, C. (2002). Distribution Discovery: Local Analysis of Temporal Rules. In *proceedings of the 6th Pacific-Asia Conference on Knowledge Discovery and Data Mining*. Taipei, Taiwan, pp 469-480.

[21] Jin, X., Wang, L., Lu, Y. & Shi, C. (2002). Indexing and Mining of the Local Patterns in Sequence Database. In *proceedings of the 3rd International Conference on Intelligent Data Engineering and Automated Learning*. Manchester, UK, Aug 12-14. pp 68-73.

[22] Kendall, M. (1976) Time-Series. 2nd Edition. Charles Griffin and Company, Ltd., London.

[23] Keogh, E. (2002). The UCR Time Series Data Mining Archive [http://www.cs.ucr.edu/~eamonn/TSDMA/index.html]. Riverside CA.

[24] Keogh, E. (2002). Exact Indexing of Dynamic Time Warping. *In proceedings of the 28th International Conference on Very Large Data Bases*. Hong Kong, Aug 20-23. pp 406-417.

[25] Keogh, E. Chakrabarti, K. Pazzani, M & Mehrotra, S. (2001). Dimensionality Reduction for Fast Similarity Search in Large Time Series Databases. KAIS. Vol. 3, No. 3, pp. 263-286.

[26] Keogh, E. & Kasetty, S. (2002). On the Need for Time Series Data Mining Benchmarks: A Survey and Empirical Demonstration. *In proceedings of the 8th ACM SIGKDD International Conference on Knowledge Discovery and Data Mining*, Alberta, Canada. pp 102-111.

[27] Li, C., Yu, P. S. & Castelli, V. (1998). MALM: A Framework for Mining Sequence Database at Multiple Abstraction Levels. In *proceedings of the 7th ACM CIKM Int'l Conference on Information and Knowledge Management*. Bethesda, MD, Nov 3-7. pp 267-272.

[28] Lin, J. Keogh, E. Patel, P. & Lonardi, S. (2002). Finding motifs in time series. In *the 2nd Workshop on Temporal Data Mining, at the 8th ACM SIGKDD International Conference on Knowledge Discovery and Data Mining*. July 23 - 26, 2002. Edmonton, Alberta, Canada.

[29] Mantegna., R. N. (1999). Hierarchical Structure in Financial Markets. *European. Physical Journal*. B11, pp. 193-197.

[30] Mori, T. & Uehara, K. (2001). Extraction of Primitive Motion and Discovery of Association Rules from Human Motion. In *proceedings of the 10th IEEE Int'l Workshop on Robot and Human Communication*, Bordeaux-Paris, France, Sept 18-21. pp 200-206.

[31] Oates, T. (1999). Identifying Distinctive Subsequences in Multivariate Time Series by Clustering. In *proceedings of the 5th International Conference on Knowledge Discovery and Data Mining*, pp 322-326.

[32] Osaki, R., Shimada, M. & Uehara, K. (2000). A Motion Recognition Method by Using Primitive Motions, Arisawa, H. and Catarci, T. (eds.) *Advances in Visual Information Management, Visual Database Systems*, Kluwer Academic Pub. pp 117-127.

[33] Radhakrishnan, N., Wilson, J. D. & Loizou, P. C. (2000). An Alternate Partitioning Technique to Quantify the Regularity of Complex Time Series. *International Journal of Bifurcation and Chaos*, Vol. 10, No. 7. World Scientific Publishing. pp 1773-1779.

[34] Reinert, G., Schbath, S. & Waterman, M. S. (2000). Probabilistic and statistical properties of words: An overview. J. *Comput. Bio.*, Vol. 7, pp 1-46.

[35] Roddick, J. F. & Spiliopoulou, M. (2002). A Survey of Temporal Knowledge Discovery Paradigms and Methods. *Transactions on Data Engineering*. Vol. 14, No. 4, pp 750-767.

[36] Sarker, B. K., Mori, T. & Uehara, K. (2002). Parallel Algorithms for Mining Association Rules in Time Series Data. TR-CS24-2002-1.

[37] Schittenkopf, C., Tino, P. & Dorffner, G. (2000). The Benefit of Information Reduction for Trading Strategies. *Report Series for Adaptive Information Systems and Management in Economics and Management Science*, July. Report #45.

[38] Steinback, M., Tan, P.N., Kumar, V., Klooster, S. & Potter, C. (2002). Temporal Data Mining for the Discovery and Analysis of Ocean Climate Indices. In the *2nd Workshop on Temporal Data Mining, at the 8th ACM SIGKDD International Conference on Knowledge Discovery and Data Mining*. Edmonton, Alberta, Canada. July 23.

[39] Timmermann, A., Sullivan, R. & White, H. (1998). The Dangers of Data-Driven Inference: The Case of Calendar Effects in Stock Returns. *FMG Discussion Papers dp0304*, Financial Markets Group and ESRC.

[40] Tino, P., Schittenkopf, C. & Dorffner, G. (2000). Temporal Pattern Recognition in Noisy Non-stationary Time Series Based on Quantization into Symbolic Streams: Lessons Learned from Financial Volatility Trading. *Report Series for Adaptive Information Systems and Management in Economics and Management Science*, July. Report #46.

[41] Truppel, Keogh, Lin (2003). A Hidden Constraint When Clustering Streaming Time Series. UCR Tech Report.

[42] Uehara, K. & Shimada, M. (2002). Extraction of Primitive Motion and Discovery of Association Rules from Human Motion Data. *Progress in Discovery Science 2002, Lecture Notes in Artificial Intelligence*, Vol. 2281. Springer-Verlag. pp 338-348.

[43] Van Laerhoven, K. (2001). Combining the Kohonen Self-Organizing Map and K-Means for On-line Classification of Sensor data. *Artificial Neural Networks*, Dorffner, G., Bischof, H. & Hornik, K. (Eds.), Vienna, Austria; Lecture Notes in Artificial Intelligence. Vol. 2130, Springer Verlag, pp.464-470.

[44] Walker, J. (2001). HotBits: Genuine Random Numbers Generated by Radioactive Decay. www.fournilab.ch/hotbits/

[45] Yairi, T., Kato, Y. & Hori, K. (2001). Fault Detection by Mining Association Rules in House-keeping Data. In *proceedings of the 6th International Symposium on Artificial Intelligence, Robotics and Automation in Space*. Montreal, Canada, June 18-21.

Dynamic Weighted Majority: A New Ensemble Method for Tracking Concept Drift

Jeremy Z. Kolter and Marcus A. Maloof
Department of Computer Science
Georgetown University
Washington, DC 20057-1232, USA
{jzk, maloof}@cs.georgetown.edu

Abstract

Algorithms for tracking concept drift are important for many applications. We present a general method based on the Weighted Majority algorithm for using any on-line learner for concept drift. Dynamic Weighted Majority (DWM) maintains an ensemble of base learners, predicts using a weighted-majority vote of these "experts", and dynamically creates and deletes experts in response to changes in performance. We empirically evaluated two experimental systems based on the method using incremental naive Bayes and Incremental Tree Inducer (ITI) as experts. For the sake of comparison, we also included Blum's implementation of Weighted Majority. On the STAGGER Concepts and on the SEA Concepts, results suggest that the ensemble method learns drifting concepts almost as well as the base algorithms learn each concept individually. Indeed, we report the best overall results for these problems to date.

1. Introduction

Learning algorithms that track *concept drift* [23] are important for many domains. Such algorithms must be applicable to a variety of problems, both large and small. They must be robust to noise. Finally, they must converge quickly to target concepts with high accuracy.

In this paper, we present an *ensemble method* that uses on-line learning algorithms to track drifting concepts. It is based on the Weighted Majority algorithm [15], but we added mechanisms to create and delete experts dynamically in response to changes in performance. Hence, we call this new method *Dynamic Weighted Majority* (DWM).

Using an incremental version of naive Bayes and Incremental Tree Inducer [25] as base algorithms, we evaluated the method using two synthetic problems involving concept drift: the STAGGER Concepts [23] and the "SEA Concepts", a problem recently proposed in the data mining commu-

nity [24]. For the sake of comparison, we also evaluated Blum's [3] implementation of Weighted Majority on the STAGGER Concepts. We did so because it is an obvious evaluation that to our knowledge has never been published. Our results suggest that DWM learns drifting concepts almost as well as the base algorithms learn each concept individually (i.e., with perfect forgetting).

We make three contributions. First, we present a general method for using any on-line learning algorithm for problems involving concept drift. Second, we conducted a thorough empirical study of the method, which included two incremental learners as base algorithms, two synthetic problems that have appeared in the literature, and five other methods for the sake of comparison. Third, because of our comprehensive evaluation, we firmly place our results in context with those reported previously. To the best of our knowledge, we present the best overall results for these problems to date.

2. Background and Related Work

The on-line learning task is to acquire a set of concept descriptions from labeled training data distributed over time. This type of learning is important for many applications, such as computer security, intelligent user interfaces, and market-basket analysis. An important class of problems for on-line learning involves target concepts that change over time [23]. For instance, customer preferences change as new products and services become available. Algorithms for coping with concept drift must converge quickly and accurately to new target concepts, while being efficient in time and space.

Researchers have proposed and evaluated several algorithms for coping with concept drift. STAGGER [23] was the first designed expressly for concept drift, as were many of the algorithms that followed, such as FLORA2 [26], AQ-PM [18], AQ11-PM [19], and AQ11-PM-WAH [17].

Although researchers have not yet established the degree to which these algorithms scale to large problems, some have been designed expressly for learning time-varying concepts from large data sets [11,24]. Other algorithms are amendable to such problems because of their formal properties, at least in theory [3, 14, 15]. One such algorithm in this category is Weighted Majority [15]. It is a method for weighting and combining the decisions of "experts", each of which is a learning method. For instance, Blum [3] used pairs and triples of features as experts, which returned the majority vote over the most recent k predictions.

The algorithm begins by creating a set of experts and assigning a weight to each. When a new instance arrives, the algorithm passes it to and receives a prediction from each expert. The algorithm predicts based on a weighted-majority vote of the expert predictions. If an expert incorrectly classifies the example, then the algorithm decreases its weight by a multiplicative constant. Winnow [14] is similar to Weighted Majority, except that experts may abstain, and thus have been called "specialists" [3].

Blum [3] evaluated variants of Weighted Majority and Winnow on a calendar-scheduling task and results suggested that the algorithms responded well to concept drift and executed fast enough to be useful for real-time applications. However, using pairs of features requires $\binom{n}{2}$ experts, where n is the number of relevant features (i.e., attribute-value pairs), which makes the direct application of these implementations impractical for most data mining problems. In one case, when learning the scheduling preferences of one user using 34 attributes, Weighted Majority and Winnow required 59,731 experts and specialists, respectively.

The advantage of Weighted Majority and Winnow is that they provide a general scheme for weighting any fixed collection of experts. However, since there are no mechanisms for dynamically adding or removing new experts or specialists, they are restricted to problems for which we can determine *a priori* the number required. We provide a remedy in the next section, and in Section 4.1, we show that by using more sophisticated base algorithms, we can reduce the number of experts.

Weighted Majority and Winnow are ensemble methods, and in an off-line setting, such methods create individual classifiers and combine the predictions of these classifiers into a single prediction. For example, bagging [4] involves sampling with replacement from a data set, building a classifier using each sample, and predicting the majority prediction of the individual classifiers. Boosting [9] likewise creates a series of classifiers, albeit with a different method, weighting each classifier based on its performance. Several empirical evaluations suggest that ensembles perform better than do single classifiers [1,5,9,21].

More recently, there has been work on ensemble methods for on-line learning tasks [8] and for concept drift [24].

Unfortunately, in an on-line setting, it is less clear how to apply ensemble methods directly. For instance, with bagging, when one new example arrives that is misclassified, it is too inefficient to resample the available data and learn new classifiers. One solution is to rely on the user to specify the number of examples from the input stream for each base learner [7], but this approach assumes we know a great deal about the structure of the data stream and is likely to be impractical for drifting concepts. There are on-line boosting algorithms that reweight classifiers [8], but these assume a fixed number of classifiers. Again, this could be a strong assumption when concepts change, but we are unaware of any on-line boosting approaches that have been applied to the problem of concept drift.

The Streaming Ensemble Algorithm (SEA) [24] copes with concept drift with an ensemble of C4.5 classifiers [22]. SEA reads a fixed amount of data and uses it to create a new classifier. If this new classifier improves the performance of the ensemble, then it is added. However, if the ensemble contains the maximum number of classifiers, then the algorithm replaces a poorly performing classifier with the new classifier. Performance is measured over the most recent predictions and is based on the performance of both the ensemble and the new classifier.

Unfortunately, there are problems with this approach. One is that members of the ensemble stop learning after being formed. This implies that a fixed period of time will be sufficient for learning all target concepts. In addition, if concepts drift during this fixed period of time, the learner may not be able to acquire the new target concepts. Finally, replacing the worst performing classifier in an unweighted ensemble may not yield the fastest convergence to new target concepts. In the next section, we describe a new ensemble method that copes with concept drift and addresses these problems.

3. DWM: A New Ensemble Method for Concept Drift

Dynamic Weighted Majority (DWM), shown in Figure 1, maintains as its concept description an ensemble of learning algorithms, each referred to as an expert and each with an associated weight. Given an instance, the performance element polls the experts, each returning a prediction for the instance. Using these predictions and expert weights, DWM returns as the global prediction the class label with the highest accumulated weight.

The learning element, given a new training example, first polls each expert in the manner described previously. If an expert predicts incorrectly, then its weight is reduced by the multiplicative constant β.

DWM then determines the global prediction. If it is incorrect, then the algorithm creates a new expert with a weight

Dynamic-Weighted-Majority ($\{\vec{x}, y\}_n^1$)

$\{\vec{x}, y\}_n^1$: training data, feature vector and class label
β : factor for decreasing weights, $0 \leq \beta < 1$
$c \in \mathbb{N}^*$: number of classes
$\{e, w\}_m^1$: set of experts and their weights
$\Lambda, \lambda \in \{1, \ldots, c\}$: global and local predictions
$\vec{\sigma} \in \mathbb{R}^c$: sum of weighted predictions for each class
θ: threshold for deleting experts
p: period between expert removal, creation, and
    weight update

for $i = 1, \ldots, n$
   $\vec{\sigma} \leftarrow 0$
   for $j = 1, \ldots, m$
      $\lambda = \text{Classify}(e_j, \vec{x}_i)$
      if ($\lambda \neq y_i$ **and** $i \bmod p = 0$)
         $w_j \leftarrow \beta w_j$
      $\sigma_\lambda \leftarrow \sigma_\lambda + w_j$
   end;
   $\Lambda = \text{argmax}_j \, \sigma_j$
   if ($i \bmod p = 0$)
      $w \leftarrow \text{Normalize-Weights}(w)$
      $\{e, w\} \leftarrow \text{Delete-Experts}(\{e, w\}, \theta)$
      if ($\Lambda \neq y_i$)
         $m \leftarrow m + 1$
         $e_m \leftarrow \text{Create-New-Expert}()$
         $w_m \leftarrow 1$
      end;
   end;
   for $j = 1, \ldots, m$
      $e_j \leftarrow \text{Train}(e_j, \vec{x}_i)$
   output Λ
  end;
end.

Figure 1. Algorithm for dynamic weighted majority (DWM).

of one. The algorithm normalizes expert weights by uniformly scaling them such that the highest weight will be equal to one. This prevents any newly added experts from dominating the decision making of existing ones. The algorithm also removes experts with weights less than the user-defined threshold θ. Finally, DWM passes the training example to each expert's learning element. Note that normalizing weights and incrementally training all experts gives the base learners an opportunity to recover from concept drift. Large and noisy problems required the parameter p, which governs the frequency that DWM creates experts, removes them, and updates their weights (i.e., reduction and normalization.)

We implemented DWM using two different base learners: an incremental version of naive Bayes and an incre-

mental decision-tree learner. For symbolic attributes, our incremental version of naive Bayes (NB) stores as its concept description counts for the number of examples of each class and for each attribute value given the class. Learning, therefore, entails incrementing the appropriate counts given the new instance. During performance, the algorithm uses the stored counts to compute the prior probability of each class, $P(C_i)$, and the conditional probability of each attribute value given the class, $P(v_j|C_i)$. Then, under the assumption that attributes are conditionally independent, it uses Bayes' rule to predict the most probable class, C, given by

$$C = \underset{C_i}{\text{argmax}} \, P(C_i) \prod_j P(v_j|C_i).$$

For continuous attributes, our implementation stores for each class the sum of the attribute values and the sum of the squared values. Learning simply entails adding an attribute's value and the square of that value to the appropriate sum. During performance, the implementation uses the example count and the sums to compute the mean (μ) and variance (σ^2). Then, assuming that the jth attribute's values are normally distributed, it computes

$$P(v_j|C_i) = \Delta v_j \frac{1}{\sqrt{2\pi\sigma^2}} e^{-(v_j-\mu)^2/2\sigma^2},$$

where Δv_j is the size of interval in which the random variable for the attribute lies. (See John and Langley [12] for details.) We will refer to the system with naive Bayes as DWM-NB.

The Incremental Tree Inducer (ITI) [25] is a complex algorithm, so we will be unable to describe it fully here. Briefly, ITI uses as its concept description a decision tree with only binary tests. In internal nodes, ITI stores frequency counts for symbolic attributes and a list of observed values for continuous attributes. In leaf nodes, it stores examples. ITI updates a tree by propagating a new example to a leaf node. During the descent, the algorithm updates the information at each node, and upon reaching a leaf node, determines if the tree should be extended by converting the leaf node to a decision node. A secondary process examines whether the tests at each node are most appropriate, and if not, restructures the tree accordingly. We will refer to the system with ITI as DWM-ITI.

4. Empirical Study and Results

In this section, we present experimental results for DWM-NB and DWM-ITI. We evaluated both systems on the STAGGER Concepts [23], a standard benchmark for evaluating how learners cope with drifting concepts. We also included Blum's implementation of Weighted Majority [3] for the sake of comparison. We know of no published results for this algorithm on the STAGGER Concepts. Finally, in an effort to determine how our method scales to larger problems involving concept drift, we also evaluated DWM-NB on the SEA Concepts [24], a problem recently proposed in the data mining community.

We did not include any UCI data sets [2] in our evaluation because naive Bayes, ITI, and ensemble methods in general, have been well studied on many of these tasks (e.g., [1,5,13,16,21,24,25]). Instead, we chose to evaluate the methods on problems involving concept drift, on which their performance is less understood.

4.1. The STAGGER Concepts

The STAGGER Concepts [23] comprise a standard benchmark for evaluating a learner's performance in the presence of concept drift. Each example consists of three attribute values: *color* ∈ {*green, blue, red*}, *shape* ∈ {*triangle, circle, rectangle*}, and *size* ∈ {*small, medium, large*}. The presentation of training examples lasts for 120 time steps, and at each time step, the learner receives one example. For the first 40 time steps, the target concept is *color = red* ∧ *size = small*. During the next 40 time steps, the target concept is *color = green* ∨ *shape = circle*. Finally, during the last 40 time steps, the target concept is *size = medium* ∨ *size = large*.

To evaluate the learner, at each time step, one randomly generates 100 examples of the current target concept, presents these to the performance element, and computes the percent correctly predicted. In our experiments, we repeated this procedure 50 times and averaged the accuracies over these runs. We also computed 95% confidence intervals.

We evaluated DWM-NB, DWM-ITI, and Blum's Weighted Majority [3] with pairs of features as experts on the STAGGER Concepts. All of the Weighted Majority algorithms halved an expert's weight when it made a mistake (i.e., $\beta = 0.5$). For Blum's Weighted Majority, each expert maintained a history of only its last prediction (i.e., $k = 1$), under the assumption that this setting would provide the most reactivity to concept drift. Finally, for DWM, we set it to update its weights and create and remove experts every time step (i.e., $p = 1$). The algorithm removed experts when their weights fell below 0.01 (i.e., $\theta = 0.01$). Pilot studies indicated that these were the optimal settings for p and k; Varying β affected performance little; The selected value for θ did not affect accuracy, but did reduce the number of experts considerably.

For the sake of comparison, in addition to these algorithms, we also evaluated naive Bayes, ITI, naive Bayes with perfect forgetting, and ITI with perfect forgetting. The "standard" or "traditional" implementations of naive Bayes and ITI provided a worst-case evaluation, since these sys-

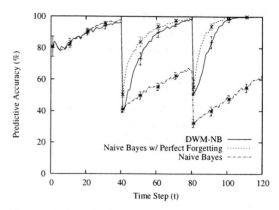

Figure 2. Predictive accuracy for DWM-NB **on the** STAGGER **Concepts.**

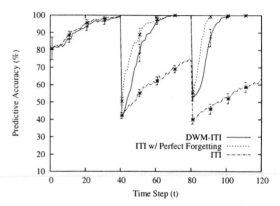

Figure 3. Predictive accuracy for DWM-ITI **on the** STAGGER **Concepts.**

tems have not been designed to cope with concept drift and learn from all examples in the stream regardless of the target concept. The implementations with perfect forgetting, which is the same as training the methods on each target concept individually, provided a best-case evaluation, since the systems were never burdened with examples or concept descriptions from previous target concepts.

Figure 2 shows the results for DWM-NB on the STAGGER Concepts. As expected, naive Bayes with perfect forgetting performed the best on all three concepts, while naive Bayes without forgetting performed the worst. DWM-NB performed almost as well as naive Bayes with perfect forgetting, which converged more quickly to the target concept. Nonetheless, by time step 40 for all three target concepts, DWM-NB performed almost as well as naive Bayes with perfect forgetting. (We place these results in context with related work in the next section.)

DWM-ITI performed similarly, as shown in Figure 3, achieving accuracies nearly as high as ITI with perfect forgetting. DWM-ITI converged more quickly than did DWM-NB to the second and third target concepts, but if we com-

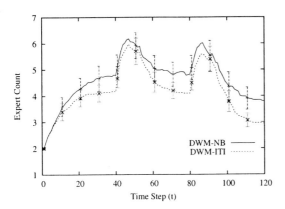

Figure 4. Number of experts maintained for DWM-NB **and** DWM-ITI **on the** STAGGER **Concepts.**

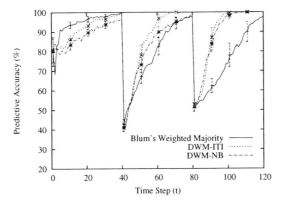

Figure 5. Predictive accuracy for DWM-ITI, DWM-NB, **and Blum's Weighted Majority on the** STAGGER **Concepts.**

pare the plots for naive Bayes and ITI with perfect forgetting, we see that ITI converged more quickly to these target concepts than did naive Bayes. Thus, the faster convergence is due to differences in the base learners rather than to something inherent to DWM.

In Figure 4, we present the average number of experts each system maintained over the fifty runs. On average, DWM-ITI maintained fewer experts than did DWM-NB, and we attribute this to the fact that ITI performed better on the individual concepts than did naive Bayes. Since naive Bayes made more mistakes than did ITI, DWM-NB created more experts than did DWM-ITI. We can also see in the figure that the rates of removing experts is roughly the same for both learners.

Finally, Figure 5 shows the results from the experiment involving Blum's implementation of Weighted Majority [3]. This learner outperformed DWM-NB and DWM-ITI on the first target concept, performed comparably on the second, and performed worse on the third. We evaluated Blum's

implementation of Weighted Majority that used pairs of features as experts. The STAGGER Concepts consist of three attributes, each taking one of three possible values. Therefore, this implementation of Weighted Majority maintained $\binom{9}{2} = 36$ experts throughout the presentation of examples, as compared to the maximum of six that DWM-NB maintained. Granted, pairs of features are much simpler than the decision trees that ITI produced, but our implementation of naive Bayes was quite efficient, maintaining twenty integers for each expert. There were occasions when Weighted Majority used less memory than did DWM-NB, but we anticipate that using more sophisticated classifiers, such as naive Bayes, instead of pairs of features, will lead to scalable algorithms, which is the topic of the next section.

4.2. Performance on a Large Data Set with Drift

To determine how well DWM-NB performs on larger problems involving concept drift, we evaluated it using a synthetic problem recently proposed in the data mining community [24]. This problem, which we call the "SEA Concepts", consists of three attributes, $x_i \in \mathbb{R}$ such that $0.0 \leq x_i \leq 10.0$. The target concept is $x_1 + x_2 \leq b$, where $b \in \{7, 8, 9, 9.5\}$. Thus, x_3 is an irrelevant attribute.

The presentation of training examples lasts for 50,000 time steps. For the first fourth (i.e., 12,500 time steps), the target concept is with $b = 8$. For the second, $b = 9$; the third, $b = 7$; and the fourth, $b = 9.5$. For each of these four periods, we randomly generated a training set consisting of 12,500 examples. In one experimental condition, we added 10% class noise; in another, we did not. We also randomly generated 2,500 examples for testing. At each time step, we presented each method with one example, tested the resulting concept descriptions using the examples in the test set, and computed the percent correct. We repeated this procedure ten times, averaging accuracy over these runs. We also computed 95% confidence intervals.

On this problem, we evaluated DWM-NB, naive Bayes, and naive Bayes with perfect forgetting. We set DWM-NB to halve the expert weights (i.e., $\beta = 0.5$) and to update these weights and to create and remove experts every fifty time steps (i.e., $p = 50$). We set the algorithm to remove experts with weights less than 0.01 (i.e., $\theta = 0.01$).

In Figure 6, we see the predictive accuracies for DWM-NB, naive Bayes, and naive Bayes with perfect forgetting on the SEA Concepts with 10% class noise. As with the STAGGER Concepts, naive Bayes performed the worst, since it had no method of removing outdated concept descriptions. Naive Bayes with perfect forgetting performed the best and represents the best possible performance for this implementation on this problem. DWM-NB achieved accuracies nearly equal to those achieved by naive Bayes with perfect forgetting.

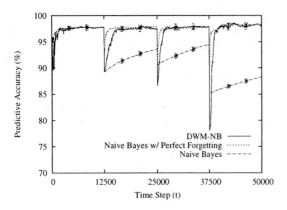

Figure 6. Predictive accuracy for DWM-NB **on the** SEA **Concepts with 10% class noise.**

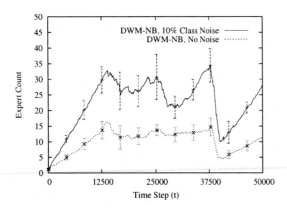

Figure 7. Number of experts maintained for DWM-NB **on the** SEA **Concepts.**

Finally, Figure 7 shows the number of experts that DWM-NB maintained during the runs with and without class noise. Recall that DWM creates an expert when it misclassifies an example. In the noisy condition, since 10% of the examples had been relabeled, DWM-NB made more mistakes and therefore created more experts than it did in the condition without noise. In the next section, we analyze these results and place them in context with related work.

5. Analysis and Discussion

In Section 4.1, we presented results for DWM-NB and DWM-ITI on the STAGGER Concepts. In this section, we focus discussion on DWM-ITI, since it performed better than did DWM-NB on this problem. Researchers have built several systems for coping with concept drift and have evaluated many of them on the STAGGER Concepts. For instance, on the first target concept, DWM-ITI did not perform as well as did FLORA2 [26]. However, on the second and third tar-

get concepts, it performed notably better than did FLORA2, not only in terms of asymptote, but also in terms of slope.

DWM-ITI and AQ-PM [18] performed identically on the first target concept, but DWM-ITI significantly outperformed AQ-PM on the second and third concepts, again in terms of asymptote and slope. AQ11 [20], although not designed to cope with concept drift, outperformed DWM-ITI in terms of asymptote on the first concept and in terms of slope on the third, but on the second concept, performed significantly worse than did DWM-ITI [19]. Finally, comparing to AQ11-PM [19] and AQ11-PM-WAH [17], DWM-ITI did not perform as well on the first target concept, performed comparably on the second, and converged more quickly on the third.

Overall, we concluded that DWM-ITI outperformed these other learners in terms of accuracy, both in slope and asymptote. In reaching this conclusion, we gave little weight to performance on the first concept, since most learners can acquire it easily and doing so requires no mechanisms for coping with drift. On the second and third concepts, with the exception of AQ11, DWM-ITI performed as well or better than did the other learners. And while AQ11 outperformed DWM-ITI in terms of slope on the third concept, this does not mitigate AQ11's poor performance on the second.

We attribute the performance of DWM-ITI to the training of multiple experts on different sequences of examples. (Weighting experts also contributed, and we will discuss this topic in detail shortly.) Assume a learner incrementally modifies its concept descriptions as new examples arrive. When the target concept changes, if the new one is disjoint, then the best policy to learn new descriptions from scratch, rather than modifying existing ones. This makes intuitive sense, since the learner does not have to first unlearn the old concept, and results from this and other empirical studies support this assertion [18, 19]. Unfortunately, target concepts are not always disjoint, it is difficult to determine precisely when concepts change, and it is challenging to identify which rules (or parts of rules) apply to new target concepts. DWM addresses these problems both by incrementally updating existing descriptions and by learning new concept descriptions from scratch.

Regarding our results for the SEA Concepts [24], which we reported in Section 4.2, DWM-NB outperformed SEA on all four target concepts. On the first concept, performance was similar in terms of slope, but not in terms of asymptote, and on subsequent concepts, DWM-NB converged more quickly to the target concepts and did so with higher accuracy. For example, on concepts 2–4, just prior to the point at which concepts changed, SEA achieved accuracies in the 90–94% range, while DWM-NB's were in the 96–98% range.

We suspect this is most likely due to SEA's unweighted voting procedure and its method of creating and removing new classifiers. Recall that the method trains a new classifier on a fixed number of examples. If the new classifier improves the global performance of the ensemble, then it is added, provided the ensemble does not contain a maximum number of classifiers; otherwise, SEA replaces a poorly performing classifier in the ensemble with the new classifier.

However, if every classifier in the ensemble has been trained on a given target concept, and the concept changes to one that is disjoint, then SEA will have to replace at least half of the classifiers in the ensemble before accuracy on the new target concept will surpass that on the old. For instance, if the ensemble consists of 20 classifiers, and each learns from a fixed set of 500 examples, then it would take at least 5000 additional training examples before the ensemble contained a majority number of classifiers trained on the new concept.

In contrast, DWM under similar circumstances requires only 1500 examples. Assume $p = 500$, the ensemble consists of 20 fully trained classifiers, all with a weight of one, and the new concept is disjoint from the previous one. When an example of this new concept arrives, all 20 classifiers will predict incorrectly, DWM will reduce their weights to 0.5—since the global prediction is also incorrect—and it will create a new classifier with a weight of one. It will then process the next 499 examples.

Assume another example arrives. The original 20 experts will again misclassify the example, and the new expert will predict correctly. Since the weighted prediction of the twenty will be greater than that of the one, the global prediction will be incorrect, the algorithm will reduce the weights of the twenty to 0.25, and it will again create a new expert with a weight of one. DWM will again process 499 examples.

Assume a similar sequence of events occurs: another example arrives, the original twenty misclassify it, and the two new ones predict correctly. The weighted-majority vote of the original twenty will still be greater than that of the new experts (i.e., $20(0.25) > 2(1)$), so DWM will decrease the weight of the original twenty to 0.125, create a new expert, and process the next 499 examples. However, at this point, the three new classifiers trained on the target concept will be able to overrule the predictions of the original twenty, since $3(1) > 20(0.125)$. Crucially, DWM will reach this state after processing only 1500 examples.

Granted, this analysis of SEA and DWM does not take into account the convergence of the base learners, and as such, it is a best-case analysis. The actual number of examples required for both to converge to a new target concept may be greater, but the relative proportion of examples will be similar. This analysis also holds if we assume that DWM replaces experts, rather than creating new ones. Generally, ensemble methods with weighting mechanisms, like those present in DWM, will converge more quickly to target concepts (i.e., require fewer examples) than will methods that replace unweighted learners in the ensemble.

DWM certainly has the potential for creating a large number of experts. We used a simple heuristic that added a new expert whenever the global prediction was incorrect, which intuitively, should be problematic for noisy domains. However, even though on the SEA Concepts DWM-NB maintained as many as 40 experts at, say, time step 37,500, it maintained only 22 experts on average over the ten runs, which is similar to the 20–25 that SEA reportedly stored [24]. If the number of experts were to reach impractical levels, then DWM could simply stop creating experts after obtaining acceptable accuracy; training would continue. Plus, we could also easily distribute the training of experts to processors on a network or in course-grained parallel machine.

One could argue that better performance of DWM-NB is due to differences between the base learners. SEA was an ensemble of C4.5 classifiers [22], while DWM-NB, of course, used naive Bayes as the base algorithm. We refuted this hypothesis by running both base learners on each of the four target concepts. Both achieved comparable accuracies on each concept. For example, on the first target concept, C4.5 achieved 99% accuracy and naive Bayes achieved 98%. Since these learners performed similarly, we concluded that our positive results on this problem were due not to the superiority of the base learner, but to the mechanisms that create, weight, and remove experts.

6. Concluding Remarks

Tracking concept drift is important for many applications. In this paper, we presented a new ensemble method based on the Weighted Majority algorithm [15]. Our method, Dynamic Weighted Majority, creates and removes base algorithms in response to changes in performance, which makes it well suited for problems involving concept drift. We described two implementations of DWM, one with naive Bayes as the base algorithm, the other with ITI [25]. Using the STAGGER Concepts, we evaluated both methods and Blum's implementation of Weighted Majority [3]. To determine performance on a larger problem, we evaluated DWM-NB on the SEA Concepts. Results on these problems, when compared to other methods, suggest that DWM maintained a comparable number of experts, but achieved higher predictive accuracies and converged to those accuracies more quickly. Indeed, to the best of our knowledge, these are the best overall results reported for these problems.

In future work, we plan to investigate more sophisticated heuristics for creating new experts: Rather than creating one when the global prediction is wrong, perhaps DWM should take into account the expert's age or its history of predictions. We would also like to investigate another decision-tree learner as a base algorithm, one that does not maintain encountered examples and that does not periodically restructure its tree; VFDT [6] is a likely candidate. Although removing experts of low weight yielded positive results for the problems we considered in this study, it would be beneficial to investigate mechanisms for explicitly handling noise, or for determining when examples are likely to be from a different target concept, such as those based on the Hoeffding bounds [10] present CVFDT [11]. We anticipate that these investigations will lead to general, robust, and scalable ensemble methods for tracking concept drift.

Acknowledgments

The authors thank William Headden and the anonymous reviewers for helpful comments on earlier drafts of the manuscript. We also thank Avrim Blum and Paul Utgoff for releasing their respective systems to the community. This research was conducted in the Department of Computer Science at Georgetown University. The work was supported in part by the National Institute of Standards and Technology under grant 60NANB2D0013 and by the Georgetown Undergraduate Research Opportunities Program.

References

[1] B. Bauer and R. Kohavi. An empirical comparison of voting classification algorithms: Bagging, boosting, and variants. *Machine Learning*, 36:105–139, 1999.

[2] C. Blake and C. Merz. UCI Repository of machine learning databases. Web site, http://www.ics.uci.edu/~mlearn/MLRepository.html, Department of Information and Computer Sciences, University of California, Irvine, 1998.

[3] A. Blum. Empirical support for Winnow and Weighted-Majority algorithms: Results on a calendar scheduling domain. *Machine Learning*, 26:5–23, 1997.

[4] L. Breiman. Bagging predictors. *Machine Learning*, 24:123–140, 1996.

[5] T. Dietterich. An experimental comparison of three methods for constructing ensembles of decision trees: Bagging, boosting, and randomization. *Machine Learning*, 40:139–158, 2000.

[6] P. Domingos and G. Hulten. Mining high-speed data streams. In *Proceedings of the 6th ACM International Conference on Knowledge Discovery and Data Mining*, pages 71–80, ACM Press, New York, NY, 2000.

[7] W. Fan, S. Stolfo, and J. Zhang. The application of AdaBoost for distributed, scalable and on-line learning. In *Proceedings of the 5th ACM International Conference on Knowledge Discovery and Data Mining*, pages 362–366, ACM Press, New York, NY, 1999.

[8] A. Fern and R. Givan. Online ensemble learning: An empirical study. *Machine Learning*, 53, 2003.

[9] Y. Freund and R. Schapire. Experiments with a new boosting algorithm. In *Proceedings of the 13th International Conference on Machine Learning*, pages 148–156, Morgan Kaufmann, San Francisco, CA, 1996.

[10] W. Hoeffding. Probability inequalities for sums of bounded random variables. *Journal of the American Statistical Association*, 58(301):13–30, 1963.

[11] G. Hulten, L. Spencer, and P. Domingos. Mining time-changing data streams. In *Proceedings of the 7th ACM International Conference on Knowledge Discovery and Data Mining*, pages 97–106, ACM Press, New York, NY, 2001.

[12] G. John and P. Langley. Estimating continuous distributions in Bayesian classifiers. In *Proceedings of the 11th Conference on Uncertainty in Artificial Intelligence*, pages 338–345, Morgan Kaufmann, San Francisco, CA, 1995.

[13] R. Kohavi. Scaling up the accuracy of naive-Bayes classifiers: A decision-tree hybrid. In *Proceedings of the 2nd International Conference on Knowledge Discovery and Data Mining*, pages 202–207, AAAI Press, Menlo Park, CA, 1996.

[14] N. Littlestone. Learning quickly when irrelevant attributes abound: A new linear-threshold algorithm. *Machine Learning*, 2:285–318, 1988.

[15] N. Littlestone and M. Warmuth. The Weighted Majority algorithm. *Information and Computation*, 108:212–261, 1994.

[16] R. Maclin and D. Opitz. An empirical evaluation of bagging and boosting. In *Proceedings of the 4th National Conference on Artificial Intelligence*, pages 546–551, AAAI Press, Menlo Park, CA, 1997.

[17] M. Maloof. Incremental rule learning with partial instance memory for changing concepts. In *Proceedings of the International Joint Conference on Neural Networks*, pages 2764–2769, IEEE Press, Los Alamitos, CA, 2003.

[18] M. Maloof and R. Michalski. Selecting examples for partial memory learning. *Machine Learning*, 41:27–52, 2000.

[19] M. Maloof and R. Michalski. Incremental learning with partial instance memory. *Artificial Intelligence*, to appear.

[20] R. Michalski and J. Larson. Incremental generation of VL_1 hypotheses: The underlying methodology and the description of program AQ11. Technical Report UIUCDCS-F-83-905, Department of Computer Science, University of Illinois, Urbana, 1983.

[21] D. Opitz and R. Maclin. Popular ensemble methods: An empirical study. *Journal of Artificial Intelligence Research*, 11:169–198, 1999.

[22] J. Quinlan. *C4.5: Programs for machine learning*. Morgan Kaufmann, San Francisco, CA, 1993.

[23] J. Schlimmer and R. Granger. Beyond incremental processing: Tracking concept drift. In *Proceedings of the 5th National Conference on Artificial Intelligence*, pages 502–507, AAAI Press, Menlo Park, CA, 1986.

[24] W. Street and Y. Kim. A streaming ensemble algorithm (SEA) for large-scale classification. In *Proceedings of the 7th ACM International Conference on Knowledge Discovery and Data Mining*, pages 377–382, ACM Press, New York, NY, 2001.

[25] P. Utgoff, N. Berkman, and J. Clouse. Decision tree induction based on efficient tree restructuring. *Machine Learning*, 29:5–44, 1997.

[26] G. Widmer and M. Kubat. Learning in the presence of concept drift and hidden contexts. *Machine Learning*, 23:69–101, 1996.

Probabilistic Noise Identification and Data Cleaning

Jeremy Kubica
Carnegie Mellon University
Robotics Institute
Pittsburgh, PA 15213
jkubica@ri.cmu.edu

Andrew Moore
Carnegie Mellon University
School of Computer Science
Pittsburgh, PA 15213
awm@cs.cmu.edu

Abstract

Real world data is never as perfect as we would like it to be and can often suffer from corruptions that may impact interpretations of the data, models created from the data, and decisions made based on the data. One approach to this problem is to identify and remove records that contain corruptions. Unfortunately, if only certain fields in a record have been corrupted then usable, uncorrupted data will be lost. In this paper we present LENS, an approach for identifying corrupted fields and using the remaining non-corrupted fields for subsequent modeling and analysis. Our approach uses the data to learn a probabilistic model containing three components: a generative model of the clean records, a generative model of the noise values, and a probabilistic model of the corruption process. We provide an algorithm for the unsupervised discovery of such models and empirically evaluate both its performance at detecting corrupted fields and, as one example application, the resulting improvement this gives to a classifier.

1 Introduction

Real world data is never as perfect as we would like it to be and can often suffer from corruptions that may impact interpretations of the data, models created from the data, and decisions made based on the data. In this paper we present LENS (Learning Explicit Noise Systems), an approach for identifying corrupted fields and using the remaining non-corrupted fields for subsequent modeling and analysis. We consider the case where a corruption completely replaces the original data value. Such errors could be the result of: partial sensor failure, environmental conditions, transcription error, or data storage corruption. By identifying noisy values it may be possible to increase classification accuracy, improve models, or make better decisions.

We present an approach that uses the data to learn a probabilistic model of the complete data generation pro-cess. We explicitly model both the noise and the data corruption process giving several possible advantages. First, explicitly modeling the noise and the data corruption process may increase the accuracy and robustness of the noise identification. For example, attribute corruptions may not be independent. Noise in a camera image may affect multiple pieces of information extracted from the image. Second, a model of the corruption process may be used to improve the data collection process. For example, in the case of robotic planning an explicit model of sensor failure can show that one or more sensors have an abnormally high noise rate. This information could then be used to plan better experiments or to choose the best (and presumably reduced) weights given to those sensors.

The input is assumed to consist N records with D real, categorical, or mixed attributes. Formally, each *record* is an entry in the data and corresponds to a single observation, item, or data point. Each *attribute* corresponds to a single field in the record. A *cell* refers to a single attribute of a single record. Thus the entire data set contains $N * D$ cells, certain fraction of which have been corrupted by noise. It is important to appreciate that we are interested in cases where corruptions occur on the level of the individual cells and not entire records or attributes. We wish to label only the corrupted portions of the records as such and to use all of the data to obtain better estimates of both the underlying model and the corruption process itself.

Figure 1 provides a motivating example. Although the record marked with an X has a corrupted attribute, the remaining uncorrupted attribute can be used in estimating the x-coordinate of the mean. Further, the record marked with a triangle is a second outlier that has been corrupted the same way, but could have plausibly resulted from corruptions in either or both attributes. By modeling the corruption process we may be able to use knowledge of the first record's corruption to more accurately determine which corruptions are present in the second record. Both of these advantages are more significant as the number of corrupted records and attributes increase.

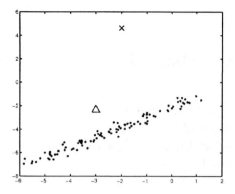

Figure 1. Example of two records each with a single corrupted attribute.

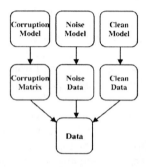

Figure 2. Model of data generation.

2 Model Learning and Noise Identificiation

The ultimate task is to both identify the corrupted cells and learn accurate models of the generative process. The information gained can then be used to calculate "clean" values for the corrupted cells. We approach this task by defining a probabilistic generative model and presenting an iterative approach for maximizing the model's log-likelihood.

2.1 Generative Model

We assume that records are generated independently by the model shown in Figure 2. Consequently we currently do not consider the case of time dependent data or noise. Records are generated using three distinct models: the clean model, the noise model, and the corruption model. Record generation can be viewed as a two-stage process. In the generation stage, (noise free) records are generated according to an underlying "clean" probabilistic model. The data is then corrupted. Which cells are corrupted is determined by an underlying corruption probability model and the new values for the corrupted cells are generated according to an underlying noise model.

We define the elements of our model as:

- *Clean Model* (M_C): The generative model for the uncorrupted records.

- *Noise Model* (M_N): The generative model for the noise values.

- *Corruption Model* (M_R): The probabilistic model for which attributes are corrupted by noise.

We call the combination of the corruption model and the noise model our *noise system* and the combination of all three models the *generative model*. Further, we refer to the Boolean matrix marking whether or not a cell has been corrupted as the *corruption matrix* (CM) and the correspond Boolean vector for a record a *corruption vector*.

It is important to appreciate that we do not restrict ourselves to specific classes of probability models. This is done intentionally to provide flexibility and allow the algorithm to work on a wide range of underlying models. Further, the use of an arbitrary corruption model allows us the possibility to account for dependent corruptions.

2.2 Iterative Identification of Noisy Values

We want to learn the underlying models for which the data and learned corruption matrix are most likely. Thus, the problem reduces to:

$$\underset{M_C, M_N, M_R, CM}{argmax} P(Data, CM | M_C, M_N, M_R) \qquad (1)$$

where:

$$P(Data, CM | M_C, M_N, M_R) = \\ P(Data | M_C, M_N, CM) P(CM | M_R) \qquad (2)$$

because CM is conditionally independent of M_C and M_N given M_R. This optimization can be interpreted two ways. First, the corruption matrix itself is a piece of hidden data and we are trying to find the models for which all of the data is most likely. Second, the corruption matrix is part of the set of models we are trying to learn, but we are constraining it to be probable with respect to the corruption model. Thus the hope is the corruption matrix will not be arbitrarily complex, but rather will contain some underlying structure.

Due to the large number, $O(2^{N*D})$, of corruption matrices it is computationally infeasible to exhaustively search for the best corruption matrix. Instead we propose an iterative approach that consists of alternating between learning the underlying generative models and learning the corruption matrix. We turn the optimization into a hill-climbing problem. Using the model given above, we can break our task into two steps:

132

1. For a fixed corruption matrix, learn the models:

$$\underset{M_C,M_N,M_R}{argmax} P(Data, CM|M_C, M_N, M_R) \qquad (3)$$

2. For fixed generative models, estimate the corruption matrix.

$$\underset{CM}{argmax} P(Data|M_C, M_N, CM)P(CM|M_R) \qquad (4)$$

Step 1 reduces the problem to that of learning models from data with missing values. The clean model can be learned by treating marked cells in the corruption matrix as missing. Depending on the models used, this can effectively be done using an EM based approach such as the one described in [7] for Gaussian mixture models with missing data. Similarly the noise model can also be learned from the records, this time using the complement of the corruption matrix to mark which cells are missing. Finally, learning the corruption model simply consists of learning a probability distribution over Boolean vectors.

Step 2 consists of finding a corruption matrix or "surprising" cells given fixed probabilistic models. Since the records are assumed to be independent, we can find the corrupted cells for one record at a time. Below we discuss techniques to estimate the corruption vector of a record.

It should also be mentioned that it is possible to suggest an alternative approach that uses an EM method to learn the models while treating the corruption matrix as hidden data. Real valued entries could be stored in the corruption matrix to track the probability that a given cell is corrupted. Unfortunately, this approach quickly becomes computationally infeasible for many interesting models. For example, as an extreme case consider learning a full joint corruption model from a real valued corruption matrix. Simply accounting for a *single* record's corruption vector would take time $O(2^D)$. Further, this does not account for the cost of estimating the corruption matrix or learning the other two models.

2.3 Identification of Noisy Values

There are a variety of methods for estimating a record's corruption vector given the underlying generative models. From (1) we note that we would like to find:

$$\underset{R}{argmax} P(R, x|M) = \underset{R}{argmax} P(R|x, M) \qquad (5)$$

where R is the corruption vector for a given record x under consideration and M is the collection all of the models (M_C, M_N, and M_R).

Again it is possible to use an exhaustive approach to solve (5) by iterating over each of R's 2^D possible settings. Unfortunately, this approach is not computationally feasible for high dimensional data sets. Instead, one possible

solution is to approximately solve (5) using a hill climbing search over R.

We consider a greedy approach that limits the search to look at each attribute in turn, asking whether this attribute in this record is corrupt. Let R_d indicate the value of the dth attribute of this vector (where $R_d = 1$ indicates that the cell is corrupt and $R_d = 0$ indicates that it is not). The probability that the dth attribute is corrupted (that $R_d = 1$) given the record and models is:

$$P(R_d = 1|x, M) = \frac{\sum_{R s.t. R_d=1} P(x|R, M)P(R|M)}{\sum_R P(x|R, M)P(R|M)} \qquad (6)$$

Again these sums are over at least 2^{D-1} elements and may not be computationally feasible. Fortunately, we can quickly approximate this probability by assuming that the previous corruption vector holds for the other $D - 1$ attributes:

$$P(R_d = 1|x, M) = \frac{P(x, R_{(d=1)}|M)}{P(x, R_{(d=1)}|M) + P(x, R_{(d=0)}|M)} \qquad (7)$$

where the symbol $R_{(d=v)}$ denotes the vector R with the dth attribute set to v and the other elements set to their previous values.

We can mark the dth attribute of the record corrupt if $P(R_d = 1|x, M)$ exceeds some threshold or simply:

$$R_d = \begin{cases} 1 & if \ P(R_d = 1|x, M) \geq P(R_d = 0|x, M) \\ 0 & if \ P(R_d = 1|x, M) < P(R_d = 0|x, M) \end{cases} \qquad (8)$$

For each record we are effectively asking: "Given that I believe that this corruption vector holds, what is the probability that this attribute is corrupt?" Thus we are doing a hill-climbing search that does not blindly try neighbors, but rather uses information about the current corruption vector to direct the step to a neighboring corruption vector.

It is also possible to randomize the search to possibly aid optimization and escape local minima. Specifically, we can mark each cell as corrupt with probability $P(R_d = 1|x, M)$ as defined in (7). Including a small minimum probability of flipping a bit in the corruption vector may also help the algorithm escape local minima.

3 Noise Correction

The models above can be directly employed to correct the corrupted records. Specifically, given a record and corresponding corruption vector we can "correct" the record by using EM to determine the most likely values for the corrupted cells given the uncorrupted cells.

More importantly, this approach can be applied to previously unseen records. The above techniques can be used to estimate a record's corruption vector and correct the appropriate cells. Thus we can build the models on a small portion of the data and use them to clean the remainder of the data or to check for corruptions online.

4 Related Work

There is a significant interest in noise identification and data cleaning in the field of computer science. One technique that has seen a significant amount of work is to consider noise on the record/point scale and remove noisy records such as presented in [1, 4, 8, 6, 11] and others. For example, in Arning *et. al.* present a linear time method for detecting deviations in a database [1]. They assume that all records should be similar, which may not be true in unsupervised learning tasks, and that an entire record is either noisy or clean. Assuming entire records are noisy or clean is also common in outlier and novelty detection [9, 10]. A significant downside to looking at noise on the scale of records is that entire records are thrown out and useful, uncorrupted data may be lost. In data sets where almost all records have at least a few corrupted cells this may prove disastrous.

Several domain independent models have been presented which examine the case of noisy cells. Schwarm and Wolfman examined the use of Bayesian methods to clean data [16]. They also use a probabilistic approach, but it differs from this paper in several respects: we do not assume a subset of precleaned instances and we use an iterative approach that considers other corruptions that may be present in a record. Further, our model includes explicit models of both the noise and the corruption process allowing us to take advantages of dependencies in the corruption process and regularities in the noise. Teng presents a data cleaning method designed to improve accuracy on classification tasks [17]. This model only looks at records which have been misclassified and attempts to make corrections based in part on the predicted attribute value given the rest of the record (which itself may be noisy). Again there is no attempt to model the noise or the corruption process. Finally, Maletic and Marcus survey several methods for finding outlier cells including statistical methods, association rules, and pattern-based methods [12]. The methods they describe do not account for or utilize possible dependencies between the attributes and do not build a model of the corruption process.

Speech recognition and signal separation are other areas that have seen work in data cleaning and noise modeling, including [2, 14, 15] and others. While these methods have been shown effective, they often make limiting assumptions, such as time dependencies between points or pretrained models and classifiers. For example, Roweis presents a refiltering method designed to separate noise values from speech values in a signal, but requires the use of pretrained hidden Markov models for each speaker and data with time dependencies [15] .

There has been a significant amount of recent work in data cleaning the field of data warehousing and data/information quality management. [12, 13] and references there in present an overview of some of this work. Much of this work is concerned with solving problems that are different from ours, such as: identifying duplicate records, merging databases, and finding inconsistencies. Further, much of the work makes use of the fact that the databases have some known structure which can by utilized. For example, many of the errors in name attribute will be in terms of spelling or formatting errors.

Finally, the AutoClass system is also similar to LENS in that it performs unsupervised clustering while allowing different classes to use different models for their attributes [5]. Determining which models to use for a given class is done in a step similar to the one described in section 2.2. In contrast to LENS, AutoClass appears to generate all records from a given class from the models for that class. As a result it does not appear to consider noise on the level of cells, where a single cell may be generated by a different model than cells of the corresponding attribute for the other records from this class.

5 Evaluation

5.1 Naturally Corrupted Data Sets

As an initial test, we ran LENS on several real world data sets. These data sets contained "natural" corruptions that were not explicitly generated from the assumed models.

5.1.1 Leaf and Rock Data

The leaf and rock data, summarized in Table 1, consist of attributes extracted from a series of pictures of leaves and rocks respectively. The leaf data set contains 71 records from pictures of living and dead leaves. As expected, the living leaves were green in color while the dead leaves were brownish or yellow. The rock data set contains 56 records from pictures of slate and granite. The granite rocks contained sufficient feldspar to give them a slightly orange coloring. All pictures were taken against a white background with a single lamp providing primary lighting, but little was done to standardize lighting conditions. One record was then generated for each picture as the three number vector corresponding to the average of each pixel's RGB value. Two natural corruptions were introduced: some pictures were *red corrupted* by placing a red filter over the primary light source and some pictures were *black corrupted* by taking a picture without removing the lens cap (thereby producing a picture of black pixels).

Table 1. Leaf and Rock data sets.

	TOTAL	RED	BLACK
LIVING	35	4	1
DEAD	36	4	0
GRANITE	28	4	0
SLATE	28	4	1

5.1.2 Leaf/Rock Cleaning Results

The settings for both data sets were chosen heuristically. Both data sets were initially modeled using: a single 3-dimensional Gaussian as the clean model, uniform noise (with the same range as the observed data) as the noise model, and a joint Bayesian model as the corruption model.

The LENS algorithm was run on the leaf data set for 2,000 iterations using randomized greedy search and a minimum flip probability of 0.02. The resulting output found 12 corruptions including 7 of the 8 corruptions in the R values for the red-corrupted pictures, corruptions in the B and G values of the 8th red corrupted pictures, and corruptions in all three values of the black corrupted picture. Thus the results agreed almost exactly with those predicted from knowledge of the corruptions.

The LENS algorithm was run on the rock data set for 500 iterations using randomized exhaustive search, a joint corruption model, and a minimum flip probability of 0.01. The algorithm found 27 corruptions, marking all three values of the 9 corrupted records as corrupt. Since only entire records were labeled as corrupt, later experiments used a naive corruption model and a randomized greedy search with 5,000 iterations and a minimum flip probability of 0.05. These settings only identified one corrupt record, the picture taken with the lens cap on, but showed promise in aiding the classification task discussed below.

It should be appreciated that the corruptions in the above data are very simple and could be identified by hand. This allows us to compare the resulting corruptions found with a known ground truth. Further, since both the data and the corruptions are generated by a real world process, we do not force either to be generated from the assumed models.

5.1.3 Leaf/Rock Classification Results

Since the data sets above contain class information, we are able to test whether noise identification leads to an improvement on classification. Leave One Out Cross Validation tests were performed on both sets of data. Each test consisted of: removing a record from the training set, fully re-learning the models and corruption matrix from their default values, and classifying the removed record. The results are shown in Table 2. In addition to the randomized LENS algorithm, we also tested the following algorithms:

Table 2. Number of LOOCV errors for different noise identification methods.

SEARCH METHOD	LEAF ERROR	ROCK ERROR
ASSUME NOISELESS	17	11
RANDOMIZED GREEDY	6	6
GREEDY (1 ITR)	17	10
GREEDY (10 ITR)	17	10
GREEDY (500 ITR)	17	10
SIMPLE CELL	11	14
SIMPLE RECORD	6	10

- *Assume Noiseless* - assuming all records were noiseless:

$$R_d = 0 \ \forall d \qquad (9)$$

- *Greedy* - a pure greedy variation (no randomization) of the LENS algorithm run for 1, 10, and 500 iterations as given in (7) and (8);

- *Simple Cell* - a non-iterative approach that determines whether a cell was more likely to have been generated from the learned clean model or a uniform noise model:

$$R_d = \begin{cases} 1 & P(x_d|x, M_N) \geq P(x_d|x, M_C) \\ 0 & P(x_d|x, M_N) < P(x_d|x, M_C) \end{cases} \qquad (10)$$

This approach does not relearn the models given the corruption matrix; and

- *Simple Record* - a non-iterative approach that determines whether an entire record was more likely to have been generated from the learned clean model or a uniform noise model:

$$R = \begin{cases} (1, 1, \ldots) & P(x|M_N) \geq P(x|M_C) \\ (0, 0, \ldots) & P(x|M_N) < P(x|M_C) \end{cases} \qquad (11)$$

This approach does not relearn the models given the corruption matrix.

Assume Noiseless corresponds to the performance of the system if no noise identification had taken place. *Simple Cell* and *Simple Record* do not learn corruption or noise models. Thus *Simple Cell* is similar to the approach presented in [16] for a single iteration probabilistic noise identification and *Simple Record* is similar to some approaches used for full point noise identification.

The results in Table 2 indicate that accounting for corruptions and learning a model of the corruption process, as with the randomized greedy algorithm, can lead to an improvement in classification accuracy. Further, the randomized nature of the algorithm can help escape local minima and result in a better ultimate performance. It is important to appreciate that at no time does the optimization consider the classification task itself. The algorithm simply tries to learn clean models (one for each class), a noise model, and a corruption model that give the best log-likelihood.

5.2 Artificial Corruption

We also compared the algorithms by their ability to identify artificial corruptions. Three different test sets were used: a noise free version of the rock data described above, the UCI Iris data set, and the UCI Wine data set [3]. Noise was generated by choosing to corrupt each record with some probability p. For each record chosen, corruption and noise vectors were sampled from their respective models. The corruption model was a joint Bayesian model for the rock and iris data and naive Bayesian model for the wine data. Parameters for the corruption models were generated randomly at the start of each iteration.

The algorithm's success was measured using percent improvement:

$$Improvement = \frac{Errs_{\text{Before}} - Errs_{\text{After}}}{Errs_{\text{Before}}} \quad (12)$$

where the error in a corruption matrix is the Hamming distance between the learned corruption matrix (CM_L) and the actual one (CM_A):

$$Errs = \sum_{i=1}^{N} \sum_{j=1}^{D} | CM_A(i,j) - CM_L(i,j) | \quad (13)$$

This measure of performance was used for two reasons. First, since the records were corrupted randomly, the actual number of corruptions on a given trial varied. Secondly, this method penalizes any false positives. An improvement of 0 corresponds to the results if no noise detection was done (assume noiseless).

Figures 3, 4, and 5 show the improvement versus p on artificially corrupted rock, iris, and wine data respectively. The solid line shows the 95% confidence interval for the results of LENS using randomized greedy search with 2500, 2500, and 5000 optimization iterations for the rock, iris, and wine data respectively. The dashed line shows the 95% confidence interval for the results of the Simple Record algorithm describe above. As mentioned above this approach is similar to approaches used for full record noise identification. Finally, the dotted line shows the 95% confidence interval for the results of the Simple Cell algorithm describe above. Again as mentioned above this approach is similar to the approach presented in [16].

On the rock and iris data sets, the LENS algorithm consistently performs significantly better than either of the other algorithms on small to medium amounts of noise. As

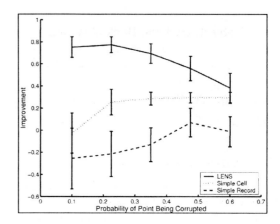

Figure 3. Percent improvement on artificially corrupted rock data.

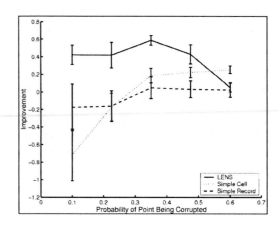

Figure 4. Percent improvement on artificially corrupted iris data.

expected, performance begins to decline as the amount of noise increases. In the tests using the wine data set the performance is superior to that of Simple Record, but on the later cases is not significantly better than that of Simple Cell. Here it is important to notice that since an axis aligned Gaussian and naive corruption model are being used, LENS is unable to take advantage of possible dependencies between the attributes. Despite this, these results demonstrate an advantage to learning a noise and corruption model and using them in the identification of noise. The figures also show a significant advantage to looking for corruptions on the scale of cells rather than records.

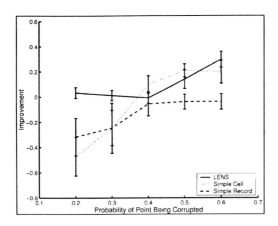

Figure 5. Percent improvement on artificially corrupted wine data.

Table 3. Error in parameter estimation from noisy data using various algorithms.

ESTIMATION METHOD	ERROR	
	DS1	DS2
ALL RECORDS	3.20	1.95
CLEANED (JOINT M_R)	0.71	0.65
CLEANED (NAIVE M_R)	1.86	2.14
SIMPLE CELL	3.25	0.82
SIMPLE RECORD	3.20	3.69
NOISELESS RECORDS	1.54	N/A

5.3 Model Accuracy

A final and important test is whether the learned clean model is accurate. In other words, we would like "cleaning" the data to result in a more accurate estimate of the model's parameters. To test this we examined corrupted data from two known clean distributions. In the first set (DS1) 50 records were artificially generated from a 4-dimensional Gaussian with the first 20 records corrupted in the 2nd and 3rd dimensions and the second 20 records corrupted in the 1st and 4th dimensions. In the second set (DS2) 80 records were artificially generated from a 4-dimensional Gaussian with each record corrupted (non-symmetrically) in exactly one attribute. Note that this means that 100% of the records were corrupted.

The LENS algorithm was then used to learn the parameters of the clean models. A Gaussian clean model, uniform noise model, and joint corruption model were assumed. For comparison, we also examined the performance in estimating the means after several other cleaning methods, including: no cleaning (assume noiseless), perfect record cleaning (all records containing any noise are removed), Simple Record from Section 5.1.3, Simple Cell from Section 5.1.3, and LENS with a naive corruption model. The estimation that removed all of the records containing at least one corruption did not use uncorrupted cells from corrupted records and thus produced results similar to those that would be obtained after perfectly filtering all outlier records.

Error was measured by the Euclidean distance of the estimated mean to the true mean that generated the data. The results are shown in Table 3. As shown, taking advantage of both dependencies in the corruptions and the uncorrupted cells in the corrupted records can result in a better performance at estimating the true underlying model. Also

of interest is the performance of Simple Cell, which performed very well when records had at most a single corruption (DS2) and poorly when records contained multiple corruptions (DS1).

5.4 Comments on Evaluation

The above tests reflect an inherent difficulty in algorithm evaluation. Specifically, in order to evaluate a data-cleaning algorithm either the actual corruptions must be known or less direct evaluation, such as classification error, must be used. For example, all of the above tests used either simple and readily identifiable corruptions or synthetic corruptions generated from a known model. This was done in order to compare the discovered corruptions with a known ground truth.

6 Data Cleaning as Anomaly Detection

The LENS algorithm can also be run on uncorrupted data. In this case, abnormal points (or even points that simply do not conform to the clean model) may be identified as corrupted. In this way the LENS algorithm serves as an anomaly detector. Again, since we are identifying corruptions at the level of attributes, we can mark specific attributes as anomalous and give an "explanation" as to why a point may contain anomalies.

The webpage data consists of site counter data: the number of page views and time spent, for two personal websites. Here the "corruptions" correspond to abnormal viewing patterns, such as spending a large amount of time looking at few pages. The records are shown in Figure 6. LENS was run on the data for 1000 iterations using randomized greedy search and a minimum flip probability of 0.01. The clean, noise and corruption models were assumed to be a mixture of 3 Gaussians, uniform noise, and a naive Bayesian model respectively. Since some values were repeated several times, a small amount of random noise [0.0,0.1] was added to all values to prevent singular covariance matrices.

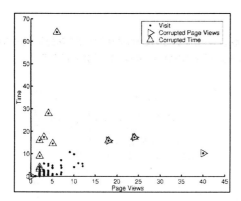

Figure 6. Web data with corruptions marked.

The results are also shown in Figure 6. Corrupted/Abnormal records are marked with one or two triangles that point along the axis in which the corruption was found. The results provide anomalies and explanations (direction of corruption) that correctly agree with intuition.

A word of caution should be added. The identified points may not truly fit the criterion of being anomalies; they might just be points that do not fit the clean model. For example, consider the case of four tight clusters that are modeled with 3 Gaussians. We would expect points from at least one cluster to be poorly accounted for by the Gaussians and thus be considered noise.

7 Conclusions

This paper presents an iterative and probabilistic approach to the problem of identifying, modeling, and cleaning data corruption. The strength of this approach is that it builds explicit models of the noise and the corruption process, which may be used to facilitate such tasks as data cleaning and planning the collection of future records. Further, it considers noise on the cell level, allowing it to use uncorrupted data from records with only a few corrupted attributes. We show that this approach can lead to benefits in classification, overall data accuracy, and model accuracy using both real world and artificial data.

Acknowledgements

Jeremy Kubica is supported by a grant from the Fannie and John Hertz Foundation. Andrew Moore supported by the National Science Foundation under Grant No. 0121671. The authors thank Dan Pelleg for his helpful comments and Theodore Kim for providing site counter data.

References

[1] A. Arning, R. Agrawal, and P. Raghavan. A linear method for deviation detection in large databases. In *Knowledge Discovery and Data Mining*, pages 164–169, 1996.

[2] H. Attias, L. Deng, A. Acero, and J. C. Platt. A new method for speech denoising and robust speech recognition using probabilistic models for clean speech and for noise. In *Proc. of the Eurospeech Conference*, 2001.

[3] C. Blake and C. Merz. UCI repository of machine learning databases. http://www.ics.uci.edu/~mlearn/mlrepository.html, 1998.

[4] C. E. Brodley and M. A. Friedl. Identifying and eliminating mislabeled training instances. In *AAAI/IAAI, Vol. 1*, pages 799–805, 1996.

[5] P. Cheeseman and J. Stutz. Bayesian classification (autoclass): Theory and results. In U. M. Fayyad, G. Piatetsky-Shapiro, P. Smyth, and R. Uthurusamy, editors, *Advances in Knowledge Discovery and Data Mining*. AAAI Press/MIT Press, 1996.

[6] D. Gamberger, N. Lavrač, and C. Grošelj. Experiments with noise filtering in a medical domain. In *Proc. 16th International Conf. on Machine Learning*, pages 143–151. Morgan Kaufmann, San Francisco, CA, 1999.

[7] Z. Ghahramani and M. I. Jordan. Supervised learning from incomplete data via an EM approach. In J. D. Cowan, G. Tesauro, and J. Alspector, editors, *Advances in Neural Information Processing Systems*, volume 6, pages 120–127. Morgan Kaufmann Publishers, Inc., 1994.

[8] I. Guyon, N. Matic, and V. Vapnik. Discovering informative patterns and data cleaning. In *Advances in Knowledge Discovery and Data Mining*, pages 181–203. 1996.

[9] F. R. Hampel, P. J. Rousseeuw, E. M. Ronchetti, and W. A. Stahel. *Robust Statistics: The Approach based on Influence Functions*. Wiley International, 1985.

[10] P. J. Huber. *Robust Statistics*. John Wiley and Sons, 1981.

[11] G. H. John. Robust decision trees: Removing outliers from databases. In *Knowledge Discovery and Data Mining*, pages 174–179, 1995.

[12] J. I. Maletic and A. Marcus. Data cleansing: Beyond integrity analysis. In *Proceedings of the Conference on Information Quality*, pages 200–209, 2000.

[13] V. T. Raisinghani. Cleaning methods in data warehousing. Seminar Report, 1999.

[14] B. Raj, M. L. Seltzer, and R. M. Stern. Reconstruction of damaged spectrographic features for robust speech recognition. In *Proceedings of the International Conference on Spoken Language Processing*, 2000.

[15] S. Roweis. One microphone source separation. In *Neural Information Processing Systems*, volume 13, pages 793–799, 2000.

[16] S. Schwarm and S. Wolfman. Cleaning data with bayesian methods. 2000.

[17] C. M. Teng. Correcting noisy data. In *Proc. 16th International Conf. on Machine Learning*, pages 239–248. Morgan Kaufmann, San Francisco, CA, 1999.

Localized Prediction of Continuous Target Variables
Using Hierarchical Clustering

Aleksandar Lazarevic[1], Ramdev Kanapady[2], Chandrika Kamath[3], Vipin Kumar[1], Kumar Tamma[2]

[1]Dept. of Computer Science, University of Minnesota, Minneapolis, MN 55455
[2]Dept. of Mechanical Engineering, University of Minnesota, Minneapolis MN 55455
[3]Center for Applied Scientific Computing, Lawrence Livermore National Laboratory, CA 94551
aleks@cs.umn.edu, ramdev@cs.umn.edu, kamath2@llnl.gov, kumar@cs.umn.edu, ktamma@tc.umn.edu

Abstract

In this paper, we propose a novel technique for the efficient prediction of multiple continuous target variables from high-dimensional and heterogeneous data sets using a hierarchical clustering approach. The proposed approach consists of three phases applied recursively: partitioning, localization and prediction. In the partitioning step, similar target variables are grouped together by a clustering algorithm. In the localization step, a classification model is used to predict which group of target variables is of particular interest. If the identified group of target variables still contains a large number of target variables, the partitioning and localization steps are repeated recursively and the identified group is further split into subgroups with more similar target variables. When the number of target variables per identified subgroup is sufficiently small, the third step predicts target variables using localized prediction models built from only those data records that correspond to the particular subgroup. Experiments performed on the problem of damage prediction in complex mechanical structures indicate that our proposed hierarchical approach is computationally more efficient and more accurate than straightforward methods of predicting each target variable individually or simultaneously using global prediction models.

1. Introduction

Many large-scale data analysis problems very often involve an investigation of high dimensional and heterogeneous databases, where different prediction models are responsible for different regions [7, 9]. In addition, these large data sets sometimes have extremely large numbers of target (output) variables (order of thousands or hundred of thousands of target variables) that need to be predicted and the task of predicting all of them may seem daunting. For instance, in a manufacturing process we may want to predict various quality aspects of a product from the parameter settings used in the manufacturing. In financial markets, given econometric variables as predictors, the goal may be to predict changes in the valuations of the stocks in large number of industry groups [2]. These scenarios are often characterized with the presence of strong correlation among target variables, and incorporating this knowledge into learning process may produce more efficient and accurate prediction models. Grouping highly correlated target variables naturally fits into the general problem of learning multiple target variables, which can be described through three prediction levels: 1) is there any change among target variables; 2) which target variables have been changed; and 3) how much these target variables have changed.

In this paper, we propose a novel technique for efficient prediction of multiple continuous target variables from high-dimensional and heterogeneous data sets using a hierarchical clustering approach. Instead of predicting target variables individually or simultaneously using global prediction models, which are built considering all data records, the proposed approach consists of three phases applied recursively: (1) partitioning of data set (2) localization of groups of interesting target variables, and (3) the prediction of target variables. In the partitioning step, similar data records are first grouped using clustering algorithm and then corresponding groups of similar target variables are identified. In the localization step, a classification model is used to predict which group of the target variables needs to be further investigated. If the identified group of target variables still contains large number of target variables, then the partitioning and localization steps are repeated recursively and the identified group is further split into subgroups with more similar target variables. When the number of target variables per identified subgroup is sufficiently small, the prediction phase takes place and the target variables are predicted using localized prediction models that are built not using all data records from entire data set, but using only those data records that correspond to the particular subgroup.

Significant research work has been done in the area of predicting multiple target variables. Some of these approaches include multitask learning [3], learning to learn

139

[1], curds and whey algorithm [2], clustering learning tasks [15] and learning internal representations [6]. A key feature that distinguishes our work from these existing algorithms is that our approach learns a very large number of target variables by exploring problem-specific interrelationships among them. In addition, it decomposes the complex problem of predicting multiple target variables from the global data set into many simpler ones where particular target variables are predicted using only relevant set of data records as well as relevant features.

The proposed hierarchical approach has two main advantages over existing techniques for predicting large numbers of target variables from high-dimensional and heterogeneous databases. First, it is computationally more efficient, since it uses less number of training records as well as a fewer number of features. Second, the clusters obtained at each partitioning level correspond only to small subsets of similar target variables and tend to be more homogeneous than the entire data set. Therefore, when predicting target variables, more accurate prediction models can be constructed more efficiently by using only the local data from corresponding clusters instead of the entire global data set.

The effectiveness of the proposed approach is demonstrated by applying it to scientific simulation data sets (Finite Element Analysis) for damage prediction in complex mechanical structures. Our experiments performed on the large-scale complex civilian structures indicate that the proposed method is computationally more effective and more accurate than straightforward approaches of predicting each target variable individually or simultaneously using global prediction models. An extended version of this paper is available in [8].

2. Problem description

Given a high-dimensional heterogeneous data set D with a large number of continuous target variables (Table 1), the problem consists of effectively and accurately predicting real value of all target variables. The typical data layout used in predicting multiple target variables is shown in Table 1, where data set D contains data records $d_1, d_2, \ldots, d_N, i = 1, \ldots, N$. Each data record d_i is described with the pair $\{\mathbf{f}, \mathbf{E}\}$, where $\mathbf{f} = \{f_1, f_2, \ldots, f_m\}$ is the feature set, while $\mathbf{E} = \{E_1, E_2, \ldots, E_n\}$ is the set of target variables. Each data record d_i in the data set D pertains to a specific state depending on domain knowledge.

One of the problems that exhibit these characteristics corresponds to damage detection in complex mechanical structures. This phenomenon includes localized softening or cracks in a certain neighborhood of a structural component due to high operational loads, or the presence of flaws due to manufacturing defects. In general, there are three levels of damage identification: 1. *Recognition* -

qualitative indication that damage might be present in the structure; 2. *Localization* - information about the probable position of the damage in the structure 3. *Assessment* - estimate of the extent of severity of the damage in the structure. Structural damages in mechanical structures usually result in static deformations and changes in dynamic characteristics such as natural frequencies and the mode shapes. In our work, structural damage is assumed to be associated with structural stiffness: a reduction in Young's modulus or modulus of elasticity (E) [14].

Table 1. A typical input to data mining model for damage detection in mechanical structures.

Data records	Features (Frequencies)				Target variables			
	f_1	f_2	$\ldots$	f_m	E_1	E_2	$\ldots$	E_n
d_1	72.833	151.67	$\ldots$	213.45	0.5E	E	$\ldots$	E
d_2	73.45	152.56	$\ldots$	213.65	0.6E	E	$\ldots$	E
$\ldots$	$\ldots$	$\ldots$	$\ldots$	$\ldots$	$\ldots$	$\ldots$	$\ldots$	$\ldots$
d_N	74.01	153.01	$\ldots$	214.21	E	E	$\ldots$	0.7E

Since mechanical structures may be represented with a certain number of structural elements, the problem of predicting multiple target variables in damage detection in mechanical structures is reduced to predicting the intensity of the damage in structural elements $\{E_1, E_2, \ldots, E_n\}$ (Table 1) using dynamic characteristics (e.g., natural frequencies, mode shapes) as features $\{f_1, f_2, \ldots, f_m\}$ (Table 1).

Standard analytical techniques for this problem employ mathematical models to approximate the relationships between specific damage conditions and changes in the structural response or dynamic properties [4]. Although recent research work [12, 14] has shown that neural networks may provide a potential solution for damage prediction, these studies are restricted to very small models with a small number of target variables (order of ten).

3. Methodology
3.1. Hierarchical Partitioning

To partition target variables, there is a need to define similarity between them using domain specific knowledge. Although in this paper we focus on spatial domains that incorporate extra constrains, the proposed method is general and may be applied to any domain. In spatial domains, variables may be similar if they are spatially close to each other or if they are symmetric according to some symmetry axis. Therefore, the simplest method for partitioning target variables into similar groups is to perform *manual partitioning* of target variables by incorporating heuristics describing spatial locality of target variables (e.g. locations of target variables). For example, Figure 1 illustrates manual partitioning of the airplane structure.

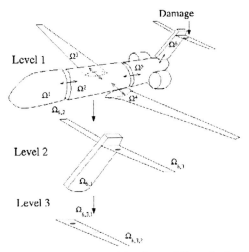

Figure 1. Manual partitioning of the airplane

However, the *manual partitioning* approach is restricted to using only visual characteristics of mechanical structures, and many hidden characteristics inherent for the problem may not be available for sub-structuring. Therefore, our alternative approach groups similar target variables $\{E_1, E_2, \ldots, E_n\}$ using features $\{f_1, f_2, \ldots, f_m\}$ that characterize them, since the features usually indirectly incorporate the information about spatial locality and symmetry of target variables, and may incorporate any other similarities. For example, in damage detection problem, frequencies provide information about locality and symmetry of structural elements, but they also provide information about the correlation among target variables, which is not available in the *manual partitioning*. Therefore, by using particular set of features, it is possible to group similar target variables that are either close or symmetric in 3D space. In such a way, data records with similar set of features belong to one group of target variables, while data records that have different features from a specific set of features correspond to different groups. When the identified group needs to be further partitioned, different and/or additional set of features that bring additional knowledge needs to be considered (e.g., higher frequencies in damage detection problem) in order to distinguish among similar target variables already identified.

The proposed hierarchical clustering based approach for partitioning groups of target variables and predicting their values is presented in Figure 2. As input arguments, the proposed algorithm takes entire data set D (Table 1) and m_1 features $\{f_1, f_2, \ldots, f_{m1}\}$ considered at that level of partitioning. The first step in the proposed algorithm involves applying the clustering algorithm with similar specified features $\{f_1, f_2, \ldots, f_{m1}\}$. One of the biggest challenges of applying a clustering algorithm is to select right set of features $\{f_1, f_2, \ldots, f_{m1}\}$ that will be used at particular level of clustering, but this choice depends on

specific domain and is typically determined using expert background knowledge. This grouping is performed using several clustering algorithms (k-way clustering algorithms with repeated bisections, direct k-way clustering, agglomerative clustering and a graph partitioning clustering approach) from the CLUTO clustering package [16]. Another challenge in clustering is to determine the optimal number of discovered clusters. The methodology that we employ here is to discover a relatively small number (between 3 and 10) of well-balanced clusters.

Algorithm *Partitioning*(D, m_1)
- Given: set with data records $D = \{d_1, d_2, \ldots, d_N\}$, where each $d_i = \{f_1, \ldots, f_m, E_1, \ldots, E_n\}$, $i = 1, \ldots, N$.
- Select the set of low natural frequencies $\{f_1, f_2, \ldots, f_{m1}\}$, where $m_1 \ll m$.
- Apply clustering algorithm on the following data set $\{f_1, f_2, \ldots, f_{m_1}\}$ and obtain k clusters $C_1, C_2, \ldots, C_k$, where the criterion for obtaining optimal clusters was identification of well balanced clusters.
- Identify k substructures $S_1, S_2, \ldots, S_k$ such that they correspond to identified clusters $C_1, C_2, \ldots, C_k$.
- For $i = 1, \ldots, k$
  ○ Predict the existence of damage in substructure S_i using classification model.
  ○ If there is the damage in the substructure S_i,
    ▪ If the substructure S_i is not sufficiently small:
      • Chose the set of low natural frequencies $\{f_{m_1}, f_{m_1+1}, \ldots, f_{m_2}\}$, where $m_1 < m_2 < m$.
      • Call algorithm *Partitioning* (C_i, m_2) to discover finer substructures in the substructure S_i.
    ▪ Else (the substructure S_i is sufficiently small)
      • Apply localized regression model to predict the intensity of the damage for all the elements within the identified substructure with the damage.

Figure 2. Partitioning algorithm for discovering groups of similar target variables, identifying the group of interest and predicting the values of target variables.

Identifying interesting groups of target variables. When the clusters of data records with similar features are identified, the next step is to identify their corresponding groups of similar target variables (e.g., to identify the structures of similar structural elements in damage detection problem). Although obtained clusters usually do not contain contiguous data records, for simplicity assume that obtained clusters are presented in Figure 3.

Clusters C_i, $i = 1, \ldots, k$ from Figure 3 contain particular data records as sets of particular features $\{f_1, f_2, \ldots, f_{m1}\}$. For example, cluster C_1 contains data records $d_{11}, \ldots, d_{1,n_1}$, where n_1 is the number of data records in the cluster C_1. Each data record from a particular cluster C_i determines which particular target variable is set or which particular target variable is of particular interest. For instance, if data record d_{11} that belongs to the cluster C_1 is the result of damage in the structure element E_l, it is apparent that this structural element may belong to the corresponding group of elements (structure) S_l. Therefore, all the damaged structural elements that are result of data records from the cluster C_l should belong to the group of target variables (elements) S_l. However, sometimes this method will create situations when a specific target variable may belong to more than one group of target variables. In such scenario, there is a need to determine what is the most appropriate group of target variables that the particular target variable should belong to. For example, in Figure 3, the target variable E_l is set for two data records from the cluster C_l and for one data record from the cluster C_k, and it is not clear whether the target variable E_l should belong to the corresponding group S_l or to the group S_k. In order to determine the most appropriate group of target variables that the specific target variable should belong to, we considered three approaches:

- *Maximum value* – For each target variable E_i, identify the cluster C_f that contains the maximum value of target variable E_i. The considered target variable E_i then belongs to the group of target variables S_f.
- *Weighted majority* – For each target variable E_i, sum the values of specific target variables within each cluster and identify the cluster C_f with the largest computed value. The considered target variable E_i then belongs to the group of target variables S_f.
- *Overlapping* – For each target variable E_i, identify all clusters C_f for which the target variable E_i is set. The considered target variable E_i then belongs to all groups of target variables S_f. In this approach one target variable may belong to more than one group.

Data records	Features					Target Variables				
	f_1	f_2	F_3	...	f_m	E_1	E_2	E_3	...	E_n
d_{11}						*				
d_{12}							*			
			Cluster C_1							
d_{1,n_1}						*				
...		...					...			
d_{k1}							*			
d_{k2}						*				
			Cluster C_k							*
d_{k,n_k}							*			

Figure 3. Typical data obtained by employing the clustering algorithm (* means that specific target variable has damage, e.g. for d_{11}, E_1 is damaged).

3.2. Localization of Interesting Target Variables

When the groups of similar target variables are identified, a classification model is used to identify the group of target variables that is of specific interest (e.g., in damage detection problem, a structure with damaged elements). If a data record $d_{i,j}$ that belongs to a cluster C_i has a target variable which is set within the subgroup S_i, the specific group of target variables S_i is assumed to be of particular interest for further analysis and the corresponding data record $d_{i,j}$ is assigned an "interesting class" label. Otherwise, if data record $d_{i,j}$ does not contain any target variables which are set within a corresponding group of target variables, the "non-interesting" class label is assigned to considered data record. For example, in damage detection, every structure that has damaged elements will have "interesting" class label, while structures that do not have damaged elements will be labelled as "non-interesting".

This procedure is repeated for all the data records within all clusters and corresponding groups of target variables. As a result, if there are k clusters and k corresponding groups of target variables, k data sets DS_i are also created, and each of them is used to build a classifier that will predict the presence of set target variables within the group S_i (e.g. the presence of damaged elements in the structure). As classification models, we have used multilayer (2-layered) feedforward neural network models with two output nodes representing both "non-interesting' and "interesting" classes, where the predicted class is from the output with the largest response. Our previous experimental work [9] has shown that this type of neural network is more accurate than a neural network with a single output node coding 0 as "non-interesting" and 1 as "interesting" class. The number of hidden neurons was equal to the number of input attributes. In order to reduce the number of input attributes considered in neural network model, dimensionality reduction through principal component analysis is also employed. Three learning algorithms were used: resilient propagation [11], conjugate gradient backpropagation with Powell-Beale restarts [10], and Levenberg-Marquardt [5].

3.3. Prediction of Target Variables

If sufficiently large number of target variables are available within identified group of particular interest, the entire procedure of partitioning the group of target variables and predicting new subgroups of interests, presented in Figure 2, is repeated recursively. Otherwise, if the group of target variables contains sufficiently small numbers of target variables, the localized regression models that are constructed using only those data records that correspond to the identified group are employed to predict the value of each belonging target variables (e.g., to predict the intensity of the damage of belonging structural elements). As local regression models, we have trained 2-layered feedforward neural network models with number of hidden neurons equal to the number of input attributes.

The proposed hierarchical approach can identify similar target variables that are either close or symmetric in 3-D space, unlike manual partitioning which only discovers similar target variables that are close in 3-D space. Therefore, identified clusters contain more similar data records and consequently correspond to more homogeneous regions than data subsets obtained with manual partitioning thus causing better prediction performance.

4. Experiments

Predicting damage in mechanical structures using data mining techniques requires feature construction and data generation steps. For more details about these steps, reader is referred to [8]. The electric transmission tower (Figure 4), studied in [13], has been chosen to demonstrate the effectiveness of our approach in damage detection. The dataset of 1,560 records, 700 natural frequencies (features) and 312 structure elements (target variables) is generated by failing a random single element by a random amount. This data set corresponds to the scenario of 5 failure states per element (312 elements x 5 = 1560). The training and testing data sets were obtained by randomly splitting generated data set into equal partitions.

We first performed manual partitioning of the electric transmission tower into four legs and a head (Figure 4). The results of applying the neural network classifiers for predicting the existence of the damage within the structures identified using manual sub-structuring approach is given in Table 2. The prediction performance of neural network classifiers is measured by computing the overall classification accuracy, as well as by computing the recall, precision and F-value for each class (since in damage detection problem target variable (element) of interest is damaged one, we consider "damage" class and. "non-damage" class). In order to alleviate the effect of neural network instability in our experiments, measures for pre-

diction accuracy for each substructure are averaged over 20 trials of the neural network learning algorithm.

From Table 2 it can be observed that the manual sub-structuring approach followed by building neural network classification models can be very accurate for predicting the presence of damage within the substructures at the first level of partitioning. The achieved accuracy was higher than 98% for four substructures, while for leg 2, the classification accuracy was slightly worse (95.8%).

When partitioning the electric transmission tower using the hierarchical clustering approach, one of major issues was to select right set of natural frequencies that will be used in clustering. Since natural frequencies that are easy to be measured in practice are usually less than 25Hz, the first step typically involves elimination of higher frequencies. The second step includes the selection of features for the first level of partitioning and according to the domain knowledge, usually considers 10-30% of the total number of features (frequencies). In order to identify the exact number of features for the first level, we use a heuristic approach that looks for the largest gap between two natural frequencies in the vicinity of some round natural frequency (e.g. the biggest gap around 0.5 Hz or 1Hz). Identifying the number of frequencies that needs to be considered at each additional level of partitioning is performed in the same manner. Thus, the first level of partitioning was performed employing the 252 lowest frequencies, since these frequencies were smaller than 0.5Hz.

All five clustering algorithms within the CLUTO package were investigated, but only the best results achieved with agglomerative approach are reported here. We have discovered 5 well balanced clusters C_i, $i = \overline{1,5}$ of

Table 2. The manual sub-structuring based approach employing neural networks for five sub-structures by partitioning electric transmission tower.

	Leg 1		Leg 2		Leg 3		Leg 4		Head	
Accuracy	98.2		95.8		98.3		98.5		99.5	
Classes	Non-damage	Damage	Non-damage	Damage	Non-damage	Damage	Non-damage	Damage	Non-damage	Damage
Recall	98.3	97.6	98.93	91.4	99.4	93.6	99.4	93.2	100	98.5
Precision	99.5	91.9	94.5	94.3	98.6	97.1	98.8	96.5	99.2	100
F-value	98.9	94.7	96.6	94.7	98.9	95.3	99.1	94.8	99.6	99.2

Table 3. Classification results for predicting the presence of the damage within the substructures of electric transmission tower identified at the first level of partitioning

	S1		S2		S3		S4		S5	
Accuracy	98.3		99.8		99.5		97.7		99.2	
Classes	Non-damage	Damage	Non-damage	Damage	Non-damage	Damage	Non-damage	Damage	Non-damage	Damage
Recall	98.5	97.5	100	97.9	99.4	100	98.0	96.9	99.3	99.2
Precision	99.6	91.7	99.7	100	100	97.2	99.0	93.9	99.6	98.4
F-value	99.1	94.5	99.9	98.9	99.7	98.6	98.5	95.4	99.4	98.8

size: 571, 167, 241, 278 and 303 data records. In identifying five substructures corresponding to the discovered five clusters, the *weighted majority* approach achieved the best results, and therefore only these results are reported here.

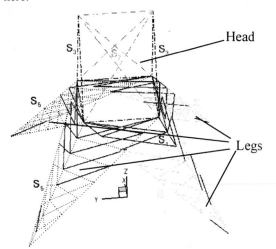

Figure 4. Illustrative five sub-structures at the first level of clustering employing the algorithm Partitioning. (Figure is best viewed in color)

Figure 4 shows five substructures S_i, $i = \overline{1,5}$, identified using the proposed approach, which sizes are 47, 40, 63, 76 and 86 structural elements respectively. From Figure 4 it is clear that the proposed algorithm *Partitioning* (Figure 2) is able to partition the mechanical structure into spatially close and symmetric sub-structures that are characterized by their low natural frequencies. The results of applying the neural network classifiers for predicting the existence of the damage within identified structures is given in Table 3. It is apparent from Table 3 that the proposed hierarchical partitioning approach achieved similar and even better prediction performance when identifying the presence of the damage within discovered substructures. For three substructures (S_1, S_2 and S_3) the achieved classification accuracies were slightly (S_1) or significantly better (S_2, S_3) for hierarchical clustering approach than for the manual partitioning approach, while for other two substructures (S_4, S_5), the achieved classification accuracies for hierarchical partitioning approach were slightly worse than for the manual partitioning approach. It is important to note that the neural network classifiers in both cases were constructed using only the features employed at the first level of partitioning (in this case first 252 frequencies), since other features (frequencies) are irrelevant for predicting the presence of the damage at the first level.

Although the number of elements per substructures identified at the first level of hierarchical partitioning is still large, we constructed local regression models R_j, j

$= \overline{1,312}$ for each element from substructures S_i, $i = \overline{1,5}$, using only data records from corresponding clusters C_i. We used these models then to predict the intensity of the damage of particular elements within the substructure S_i. To compare the predictive power of both manual and hierarchical partitioning, we also constructed local regression models M_j, $j = \overline{1,312}$, that are responsible for predicting each of the elements from substructures SM_i, $i = \overline{1,5}$, identified using manual approach. Finally, the global neural network regression models G_j, $j = \overline{1,312}$, were also built using all data records from entire data set.

For each of these models, the prediction performance was measured using the coefficient of determination defined as $R^2 = 1 - MSE/\sigma^2$, where σ is a standard deviation of the target variable. R^2 value is a measure of the explained variability of the target variable, where 1 corresponds to a perfect prediction, and 0 to a trivial mean predictor. The R^2 value for each element from substructures is again averaged over 10 trials of the neural network learning algorithm. The experimental results of predicting the intensity of damage in the elements within particular substructures are given in Table 4.

Table 4. Prediction of damage intensity (given in R^2 values) for those elements within structures for which hierarchical clustering approach achieves the worst and the best accuracy.

Structure	Element	Direct (global) approach	Manual partitioning	Hierarchical clustering approach
S_1	E_{15} (worst)	< 0	≈ 0	**0.154**
	E_{96} (best)	< 0	0.485	**0.814**
	average*	0.004	0.182	**0.447**
S_2	E_{241} (worst)	< 0	< 0	**0.140**
	E_{263} (best)	< 0	0.23	**0.411**
	average*	0.03	0.172	**0.245**
S_3	E_{312} (worst)	< 0	0.121	**0.148**
	E_{209} (best)	< 0	≈ 0	**0.469**
	average*	0.005	0.04	**0.172**
S_4	E_{102} (worst)	< 0	≈ 0	**≈ 0**
	E_2 (best)	0.243	≈ 0	**0.357**
	average*	0.02	0.04	**0.225**
S_5	E_{207} (worst)	< 0	≈ 0	**≈ 0**
	E_{195} (best)	< 0	0.218	**0.299**
	average*	0.007	0.08	**0.152**

Since the lack of space did not allow reporting prediction performance for all 312 elements, for each structure identified using the hierarchical approach, two elements were chosen such that they had the worst and the best prediction performance within the particular substructure. In addition, the average R^2-value of all the elements within particular structures is also reported. Since the R^2-

value of predicting particular elements may be less than 0 in many cases (e.g., –1 or –2 for extremely poor global regression models in the direct approach), the average R^2-value for substructures is computed such that the R^2-value of those models with negative R^2-value is assigned zero value. Thus, the exceptionally bad regression models will not negatively influence the accurate ones.

It is apparent from Table 4 that both partitioning approaches produce localized regression models that are more accurate as well as require less data records for training than the global regression models used in the direct approach. In addition, the localized regression models built using hierarchical clustering approach are in most cases more accurate then localized models obtained by manual partitioning. Only in approximately 5-10% of the total number of elements, are the models obtained from manual partitioning M_i more accurate than the models R_i constructed in the hierarchical clustering approach. For example, the prediction of element E_{145} that belongs to the structure S_5 is more accurate when using the localized models obtained through manual partitioning (R^2 = 0.245) than when using the models obtained in hierarchical clustering based approach (R^2 = 0.165).

The superior prediction performance of local regression models built through the proposed hierarchical approach compared to other regression models may be explained by the fact that local regression models R_j are constructed using more similar data records than models M_j from manual partitioning and global prediction models G_j. Specifically, the similarity of data records in clusters originates from elements that are both close and symmetric in 3-D space, while the similarity of data records in the data subsets used for building models M_j from manual partitioning arise only from elements that are close in space. Therefore, the heterogeneity of these data subsets is potentially higher than the heterogeneity of data clusters and thus, the corresponding localized models built on these data subsets are less accurate. On the other hand, a few scenarios where the models M_j built through manual partitioning are more accurate then the models R_j built through hierarchical clustering may be explained by imperfect quality of the obtained clusters. Imperfect clusters were probably achieved due to the hidden information in domain specific knowledge, which was incorporated into the clustering algorithm.

Since the number of elements per structures S_i, $i = \overline{1,5}$, identified at the first level is still large, we performed additional level of partitioning using algorithm *Partitioning*, (presented in Figure 2) in order to further reduce the number of elements per substructure. Each of the clusters C_i identified at the first partitioning level was further partitioned into clusters C_{ij} using additional 198 lowest frequencies (frequencies smaller than 1.5Hz). The clustering was performed using only these 198 frequencies (fre-

quencies f_{253} to f_{450}), since the lowest 252 frequencies used at the first level of partitioning are not useful for further identification of similar structure elements. The number of clusters identified at the second level varied between 3 and 5, and each of these clusters C_{ij} at the second level corresponded to particular substructures S_{ij}. The results of applying the neural network classifiers for predicting the existence of the damage within the substructures identified at the second level of partitioning using our proposed hierarchical clustering based approach are omitted due to lack of space. Although there was a slight decrease in overall classification accuracy when predicting the presence of the damage, especially for structures S_{12}, S_{13} and S_{43}. The achieved prediction performance for remaining substructures (using local neural network classifiers that are also constructed using only data records from corresponding clusters C_i) is still very high, larger than 97.5% as earlier for the first level of partitioning.

Our previous experimental results [13] have shown that the decrease in the classification performance at the second level of manual partitioning was significantly larger (20–30%) than the drop observed for the proposed hierarchical approach. The prediction of the modulus of elasticity for elements within the substructures is again performed using only the localized regression models built after the second level of hierarchical approach.

Table 5. Prediction of damage intensity (R^2 value) for those elements within structures for which hierarchical approach at the first level achieves the worst and the best accuracy

Structure	Element	Hierarchical clustering approach (the **first** level)	Hierarchical clustering approach (the **second** level)
S_1	E_{15}	0.154	**0.264**
	E_{96}	**0.814**	0.668
	average	**0.447**	0.424
S_2	E_{241}	0.140	**0.477**
	E_{263}	**0.411**	0.264
	average	0.245	**0.294**
S_3	E_{312}	0.148	**0.243**
	E_{209}	**0.469**	0.431
	average	0.172	**0.244**
S_4	E_{102}	≈ 0	**0.145**
	E_2	**0.357**	0.285
	average	0.225	**0.234**
S_5	E_{207}	≈ 0	≈ 0
	E_{195}	0.299	**0.334**
	average	0.152	**0.195**

Table 5 illustrates how the prediction of the modulus of elasticity for the same elements investigated within substructures at the first level has been changed when these substructures are further partitioned. It is apparent that for large number of elements, further localization and the building of more specific regression models results in an improved R^2 value, while for some other smaller number of elements additional localization hurt the prediction accuracy. There may be several reasons for such phenomenon. First, at the second level the number of data records that are relevant for the damage of the specific element may be smaller than the number of data records at the first level of partitioning thus causing a possible loss of valuable information or potential overfitting of neural network regression model. Second, this loss is inevitably caused by an imperfect clustering algorithm that does not necessarily assign all data records corresponding to the damage of specific element to a single cluster. On the other side, improvement in prediction performance at the second partitioning level is evidently due to the fact that are also fewer data records that are irrelevant to the damage of a particular element and therefore, localized regression models are more accurate.

5. Conclusions

The paper presented a novel general framework for the efficient prediction of multiple target variables from high dimensional and heterogeneous data sets using the hierarchical clustering approach. This approach is especially effective where there is a natural relationship among target variables. A key desirable feature of this scheme is that it achieves a reduction in both data records and the number of used features, which is of great importance in applications where it is difficult to find a large number of training records, or when learning a monolithic prediction model from very large data sets is prohibitively slow. The effectiveness of the approach was demonstrated on the problem of damage detection in very large and complex mechanical structures. Our experiments indicate that the proposed approach can be successfully used to predict the presence of damage within the structure, as well as the intensity of the damage in any of the several hundred structure elements that served as target variables. Furthermore, we have shown that the proposed approach is computationally more efficient, more accurate and requires less data records than the direct approach that was earlier used for damage detection, as well as the manual partitioning approach.

6. Acknowledgments

This work is partially supported by the Department of Energy LLNL B512340 and by the Army High Performance Computing Research Center (AHPCRC) under the auspices of the Department of the Army, Army Research Laboratory (ARL) under contract number DAAD19-01-2-0014. The content does not necessarily reflect the position or the policy of the government, and no official endorsement should be inferred. Additional thanks are also due to S. Sandhu and M. Steinbach for related technical discussions. Access to computing facilities was provided by the AHPCRC and the Minnesota Supercomputing Institute.

7. References

[1] J. Baxter, Theoretical Models of Learning to Learn, In T. Mitchell, S. Thrun, Eds, *Learning to Learn*. Kluwer, Boston, 1997.

[2] L. Breiman, J. Friedman, Predicting Multivariate Responses in Multiple Linear Regression, *Journal of the Royal Statistical Society*, Series B 59, 3—54, 1997.

[3] R. Caruana, Multitask Learning, *Machine Learning*, 28:41-75, 1997.

[4] H. Chen, N. Bicanoc, Assessment of Damage in Continuum Structures Based in Incomplete Modal Information, *Computers and Structures*, 74:559-570, 2000.

[5] M. Hagan, M. Menhaj, Training feedforward networks with the Marquardt algorithm, *IEEE Transactions on Neural Networks*, 5:989-993, 1994.

[6] N. Intrator, S. Edelman, How to Make a Low-dimensional Representation Suitable for Diverse Tasks, *Connection Science*, 8, 1996.

[7] Jordan, M. I., Jacobs, R. A., Hierarchical Mixtures of Experts and The EM Algorithm, *Neural Computation*, 6 (2), 181–214, 1994.

[8] A. Lazarevic, R. Kanapady, C. Kamath, V. Kumar, K. Tamma, Localized Prediction of Continuous Target Variables Using Hierarchical Clustering, *AHPCRC Technical Report* 2003-123, www.cs.umn.edu/~aleks/pub_list.htm

[9] A. Lazarevic, Z. Obradovic, Knowledge Discovery in Multiple Spatial Databases, *Journal of Neural Computing and Applications*,, Vol. 10, pp. 339-350, 2002.

[10] M. Powell, Nonconvex minimization calculations and the conjugate gradient method, In D. Griffths Ed., *Numerical Analysis, Lecture Notes in Mathematics*, Springer-Verlag, Berlin, 1066: 122-141, 1984.

[11] M. Riedmiller, T. Braun, A Direst Adaptive Method for Faster Backpropagation Learning: The RPROP Algorithm, *IEEE International Conference on Neural Networks*, San Francisco, 1993.

[12] G. J. Rix, Interpretation of Nondestructive Integrity tests using artificial neural networks, *Structure Congress 12, ASCE*, Reston VA, 1246-1351, 1994.

[13] S. Sandhu, R. Kanapady, K. Tamma, C. Kamath, V. Kumar, A sub-structuring approach via data mining for damage prediction and estimation in complex structures, SIAM International Conference on Data Mining, Arlington, VA, 2002.

[14] Z. Szewczyk, P. Hajela, Damage detection in structures based on feature sensitive neural networks, *Journal of Computation in Civil Engineering*, ASCE, 8(2):163-179, 1994.

[15] S. Thrun, J. O'Sullivan, Clustering Learning Tasks and the Selective Cross-task Transfer of Knowledge, *Technical Report* CMU-CS-95-209, Carnegie Mellon University, Pittsburgh, 1995.

[16] Y. Zhao and G. Karypis, Criterion Functions for Document Clustering Experiments and Analysis, *AHPCRC Technical Report* #01-40, 2000.

An Algebra for Inductive Query Evaluation

Sau Dan Lee   Luc De Raedt

Institut für Informatik
Albert-Ludwigs-Universität Freiburg
Georges-Köhler-Allee, Gebäude 079
D-79110 Freiburg im Breisgau
Germany
E-mail: {danlee,deraedt}@informatik.uni-freiburg.de

Abstract

Inductive queries are queries that generate pattern sets. This paper studies properties of boolean inductive queries, i.e. queries that are boolean expressions over monotonic and anti-monotonic constraints. More specifically, we introduce and study algebraic operations on the answer sets of such queries and show how these can be used for constructing and optimizing query plans. Special attention is devoted to the dimension of the queries, i.e. the minimum number of version spaces needed to represent the answer sets. The framework has been implemented for the pattern domain of strings and experimentally validated.

1. Introduction

Many data mining problems address the problem of finding a set of patterns that satisfy a constraint. Formally, this can be described as the task of finding the set of patterns $Th(Q, \mathcal{D}, \mathcal{L}) = \{\varphi \in \mathcal{L} \mid Q(\varphi, \mathcal{D})\}$, i.e. those patterns φ satisfying query Q on database $\mathcal{D}$. Here $\mathcal{L}$ is the language in which the patterns or rules are described and Q is a predicate or constraint that determines whether a pattern φ is a solution to the data mining task or not [14]. This framework allows us to view the predicate or the constraint Q as an *inductive query* to an *inductive database system* [6]. It is then the task of the inductive database management system to efficiently generate the answers to the query. This view of data mining as a declarative querying process is also appealing as the basis for a theory of data mining.

Relational algebra has proven to be useful for database theory because of a variety of reasons. First, there is the so-called closure property, which states that the result of a query is a relation. This allows the result of one query to be used in the next query. Secondly, relational algebra allows one to reason about query execution and optimization.

Thirdly, the relational algebra relies on a simple yet powerful set of mathematical primitives. These provide inspiration for developing inductive database theories. Because inductive databases aim at putting data mining on the same methodological grounds as databases, it should be useful to develop an algebra for manipulating pattern sets.

This paper contributes an algebraic framework for manipulating pattern sets and inductive queries. It extends the theoretical framework of De Raedt *et al.* [7], who have contributed a theory centered around the class of boolean inductive queries. Such queries are boolean expressions over monotonic and anti-monotonic predicates. The present paper is an extension as we consider algebraic set operations on pattern sets and study their properties. A central concept in this theory is the notion of version space [15]. A version space is a convex set, which can be represented by its border sets (of maximally general and maximally specific elements). The solution space corresponding to a conjunctive query is a version space. Furthermore, effective algorithms exist for computing these solution sets [8, 12, 7, 3]. In this context, De Raedt *et al.* have studied the dimension of pattern sets (and boolean queries), i.e. the minimum number of version spaces needed to represent the pattern set. This in turn is related to the number of calls to a conjunctive query answering algorithm needed to answer an inductive query. In the present paper, these results are extended in the light of the algebraic operations and we also show how these results can be employed when reasoning about query execution and optimization.

Version spaces have been introduced in the context of concept-learning by Tom Mitchell [15] and have been rather popular ever since. Hirsh [11, 10] has investigated various set operations on version spaces and has shown that version spaces are closed under intersection but not under union. From this perspective, our present results extend those by Hirsh in that we show that generalized version spaces (i.e. finite unions of version spaces) are closed under set operations and that we also deduce bounds on the dimensions of the resulting sets.

Finally, as an illustration of our general framework, we apply it to the pattern domain of strings. For this domain, we have designed a data structure, called the generalized version space tree, that is useful for computing and memorizing the solution space w.r.t. inductive queries. The pattern domain of strings is of interest because of the rapid generation of biological string databases.

This paper is organized as follows. Section 2 introduces boolean inductive queries, closely following [7]. Section 3 then studies the algebraic operations, which enable us to construct many equivalent query execution plans for a given query (Section 4) and seek the optimal one. We implemented our framework on the domain of string patterns (Section 5), and performed some experiments on two data sets (Section 6). Finally, we conclude in Section 7.

2. Boolean Inductive Queries

Let us first define boolean inductive queries. We closely follow De Raedt et al. [7].

A pattern language $\mathcal{L}$ is a formal language for specifying patterns. Each pattern $\varphi \in \mathcal{L}$ matches (or covers) a set of examples φ_e, which is a subset of the universe $\mathcal{U}$ of possible examples. One pattern φ is *more general* than a pattern ψ, written $\varphi \preceq \psi$, if and only if $\varphi_e \supseteq \psi_e$. For instance, for the domain of strings over an alphabet Σ, one could choose $\mathcal{L} = \mathcal{U} = \Sigma^*$ and have that a pattern or string is covered by all its substrings in $\mathcal{L}$.

A pattern *predicate* defines a primitive property of a pattern, usually relative to some data set $\mathcal{D}$ (a set of examples), and sometimes other parameters. For any given pattern, it evaluates to either *true* or *false*.

For illustration purposes, we introduce a number of pattern predicates inspired on MolFea [12].

- min_freq(φ, D, n) evaluates to true iff φ is a pattern that occurs in database $\mathcal{D}$ with frequency at least n, where the frequency of a pattern φ in a database $\mathcal{D}$ is the (absolute) number of data items in $\mathcal{D}$ covered by φ. Analogously, define max_freq$(\varphi, \mathcal{D}, n)$.

- more_gen(φ, ψ) is a predicate that evaluates to true iff pattern $\varphi \preceq \psi$. Dually, define more_spec.

These predicates have the form pred(φ, Π) or pred$(\varphi, \mathcal{D}, \Pi)$, where Π is a tuple of parameter values, $\mathcal{D}$ is a data set and φ is a pattern variable. We say that m is a *monotonic* predicate, if for all possible parameter values Π and all data sets $\mathcal{D}$:

$$\forall \varphi, \psi \in \mathcal{L} \text{ such that } \varphi \preceq \psi : \mathsf{m}(\varphi, \mathcal{D}, \Pi) \to \mathsf{m}(\psi, \mathcal{D}, \Pi)$$

The class of *anti-monotonic* predicates is defined dually. Thus, min_freq and more_gen are monotonic, their duals are anti-monotonic.

A pattern predicate pred$(\varphi, \mathcal{D}, \Pi)$ that can be applied to the patterns from a language $\mathcal{L}$ defines relative to $\mathcal{D}$ the *solution set* $Th(\mathsf{pred}(\varphi, \mathcal{D}, \Pi), \mathcal{L}) = \{\phi \in \mathcal{L} \mid \mathsf{pred}(\varphi, \mathcal{D}, \Pi) = true\}$. The definition of $Th(\mathsf{pred}(\varphi, \mathcal{D}, \Pi), \mathcal{L})$ is extended in the natural way to a definition of the solution set $Th(Q, \mathcal{L})$ for boolean combinations Q of pattern predicates over a unique pattern variable: $Th(\neg Q, \mathcal{L}) = \mathcal{L} \setminus Th(Q, \mathcal{L})$; $Th(Q_1 \vee Q_2, \mathcal{L}) = Th(Q_1, \mathcal{L}) \cup Th(Q_2, \mathcal{L})$; $Th(Q_1 \wedge Q_2, \mathcal{L}) = Th(Q_1, \mathcal{L}) \cap Th(Q_2, \mathcal{L})$. The predicates that appear in Q may reference one or more data sets $\mathcal{D}_1, \ldots, \mathcal{D}_n$.

We are interested in computing solution sets $Th(Q, \mathcal{D}, \mathcal{L})$ for boolean queries Q that are constructed from monotonic and anti-monotonic pattern predicates. This is the *boolean inductive query evaluation problem* :

Given

- a language $\mathcal{L}$ of patterns,
- a set of monotonic predicates $\mathcal{M} = \{\mathsf{m}_1(p, D_1, \Pi_1), \ldots, \mathsf{m}_n(p, D_j, \Pi_j)\}$ and a set of anti-monotonic predicates $\mathcal{A} = \{\mathsf{a}_1(p, D_1, \Pi_1), \ldots, \mathsf{a}_k(p, D_k, \Pi_k)\}$
- a query Q that is a boolean expression over the predicates in $\mathcal{M}$ and $\mathcal{A}$.

Find the set of patterns $Th(Q, \mathcal{D}, \mathcal{L})$, i.e. the solution set of the query Q in the language $\mathcal{L}$ with respect to the data subsets $D_1, \ldots, D_n \subseteq \mathcal{D}$.

De Raedt *et al.* have proposed a strategy for evaluating inductive queries and also a first step in the direction of query optimization. Their strategy consists of decomposing a boolean query Q into k sub-queries Q_i such that Q is equivalent to $Q_1 \vee \ldots \vee Q_k$, k is minimal and each of the Q_i is the conjunction of a monotonic and an anti-monotonic subquery $Q_{m,i} \wedge Q_{a,i}$. Notice that $Q_{m,i}$ and $Q_{a,i}$ may be boolean expressions themselves. Indeed, [7] show that $Q_{m,i}$ may be a DNF formula in which all the literals are monotonic, and similarly for $Q_{a,i}$. A DNF formula of the form $M_1 \vee \ldots \vee M_n$ where each of the M_i is a conjunction of monotonic predicates is monotonic. The reason is that the conjunction of monotonic predicates is monotonic (hence all of the M_i are), and also the disjunction of monotonic predicates is monotonic as well (and hence $Q_{m,i}$ is). The query evaluation strategy proposed by [7] first decomposes the query and then computes $Th(Q, \mathcal{D}, \mathcal{L})$ as $\cup_i Th(Q_i, \mathcal{D}, \mathcal{L})$. Because each of the sub-queries Q_i will be such that $Th(Q_i, \mathcal{D}, \mathcal{L})$ is a version space (also called a convex space), it can be efficiently computed for a wide class of pattern languages $\mathcal{L}$, and queries Q_i, cf. [12, 3]. Furthermore, the number of calls to such an algorithm is minimized because in the decomposition process, one minimizes the number k of subqueries. This is the so-called dimension of a query, which [7] introduced as follows:

Definition 1 *Let $\mathcal{L}$ be a pattern language, and $X \subseteq \mathcal{L}$. Then X is a version space of dimension 1, if $\forall \varphi, \varphi', \psi \in \mathcal{L} : \varphi \preceq \psi \preceq \varphi'$ and $\varphi, \varphi' \in X \implies \psi \in X$. The set of all version spaces of dimension 1 for $\mathcal{L}$ is denoted $\mathcal{VS}^1(\mathcal{L})$.*

Definition 2 *The subset of patterns in $\mathcal{L}$ that satisfy a boolean query Q, composed of monotonic or anti-monotonic predicates, is a generalized version space, denoted by $Th(Q, \mathcal{D}, \mathcal{L})$. The set of all generalized version spaces for $\mathcal{L}$ is denoted by $\mathcal{VS}^{\mathbb{Z}}(\mathcal{L})$. Note that $\mathcal{VS}^1(\mathcal{L}) \subseteq \mathcal{VS}^{\mathbb{Z}}(\mathcal{L})$.*

Definition 3 *The set $X \in \mathcal{VS}^{\mathbb{Z}}(\mathcal{L})$ has dimension k if it is the union of k sets in $\mathcal{VS}^1$, but not the union of $k-1$ sets in $\mathcal{VS}^1$. A query Q has dimension k (with respect to the pattern language $\mathcal{L}$) if k is the maximal dimension of any solution set $Th(Q, \mathcal{D}, \mathcal{L})$ of Q (where the maximum is taken w.r.t. all possible data sets $\mathcal{D}$ and w.r.t. the fixed language $\mathcal{L}$).*

If Q has dimension 1 w.r.t. $\mathcal{L}$, then $Th(Q, \mathcal{D}, \mathcal{L})$ is a version space [15] or a convex space [10]. Version spaces are particularly useful when they can be represented by boundary sets, i.e. by the sets $G(Q, \mathcal{D}, \mathcal{L})$ of their maximally general elements, and $S(Q, \mathcal{D}, \mathcal{L})$ of their minimally general elements.

With the following lemma, De Raedt *et al.* [7] provided an alternative characterization of dimension k sets.

Lemma 4 *Let $X \subseteq \mathcal{L}$. Call a chain $\varphi_1 \preceq \rho_1 \preceq \varphi_2 \preceq \rho_2 \preceq \cdots \preceq \varphi_{k-1} \preceq \rho_{k-1} \preceq \varphi_k$ an alternating chain (of length k) for X if $\varphi_i \in X$ ($i = 1, \ldots, k$) and $\rho_j \notin X$ ($j = 1, \ldots, k-1$). Then the dimension of X is equal to the maximal k for which there exists in $\mathcal{L}$ an alternating chain of length k (or a k-chain for short) for X.*

Example 5 *Consider the following queries:*

$$Q_3 = more\_gen(\varphi, abc) \wedge more\_spec(\varphi, a)$$
$$Q_4 = more\_gen(\varphi, c)$$
$$Q_5 = Q_3 \vee Q_4$$

Then c, bc, abc is an alternating chain of length 2 for $Th(Q_5, \mathcal{L}_\Sigma)$.

The dimension of an inductive query is an important concept because it corresponds to the minimum number of calls to an algorithm for computing a convex solution space.

3. Operations on Solution Spaces

Consider two generalized version spaces $V, W \in \mathcal{VS}^{\mathbb{Z}}$. We would like to know how we can combine them using the usual set operations. This is of interest because the solution set to an inductive query is, by definition, obtained as the result of applying set operations on solution set of simpler queries. At the same time, these operations promise to be useful when constructing query plans and in interactive querying sessions (cf. Section 4 for a detailed discussion).

We will analyze the operations: intersection ($\cap$), union ($\cup$), and complement ($'$) w.r.t. $\mathcal{L}$. Set difference can be treated as $V \setminus W \equiv V \cap W'$ whereas symmetric difference can be interpreted as $(V \setminus W) \cup (W \setminus V)$.

When $\dim(V) = \dim(W)$ are both 1, this reduces to traditional version spaces $\mathcal{VS}^1$. We know from the previous discussion that $V \cap W$ is in $\mathcal{VS}^1$. We have also shown above by a counter-example that the dimension of the union can be 2, although it may also be 1 (e.g. when $V \subseteq W$). So, traditional version spaces, i.e. $\mathcal{VS}^1$, are not closed under union (as shown by [11]).

Nevertheless, our extension $\mathcal{VS}^{\mathbb{Z}}$ is closed under the usual set operations. The following theorems thus generalize Hirsh's results to the case where solution sets are represented by a finite number of version spaces.

Theorem 6 *$\mathcal{VS}^{\mathbb{Z}}(\mathcal{L})$ is closed under the following set operations: intersection, union, complement, difference and symmetric difference.*

It suffices to analyze the first 3 of them, as the latter can be defined out of the first 3 operations. The proofs are given below together with bounds for the resulting dimensions.

Theorem 7 *Let $V, W \in \mathcal{VS}^{\mathbb{Z}}(\mathcal{L})$. Then, $U = V \cap W \in \mathcal{VS}^{\mathbb{Z}}(\mathcal{L})$ and $0 \leq \dim(U) \leq \dim(V) + \dim(W) - 1$.*

Proof: Let $v = \dim(V)$ and $w = \dim(W)$. By Definition 3, we can write $V = \bigcup_{i=1}^{v} X_i$ and $W = \bigcup_{k=1}^{w} Y_k$ for some $X_i, Y_k \in \mathcal{VS}^1(\mathcal{L})$. Then, we have $U = (\bigcup_{i=1}^{v} X_i) \bigcap (\bigcup_{k=1}^{w} Y_k) = \bigcup_{\substack{i=1,\ldots,v \\ k=1,\ldots,w}} Z_{i,k}$ where $Z_{i,k} = X_i \cap Y_k$. Since every $Z_{i,k} \in \mathcal{VS}^1(\mathcal{L})$, we have $U \in \mathcal{VS}^{\mathbb{Z}}(\mathcal{L})$.

For the bounds, in case V and W are disjoint, U is empty and hence, $\dim(U) = 0$, a lower bound. For the upper bound, we provide a proof by contradiction. Assume that $U = V \cup W$ has dimension at least $u = v + w$. Then, by Lemma 4, U has a u-chain, i.e.

$$\exists \varphi_i \in U (i = 1, \ldots, u) \, \exists \rho_j \in \mathcal{L} \setminus U (j = 1, \ldots, u-1)$$
$$\varphi_1 \preceq \rho_1 \preceq \varphi_2 \preceq \rho_2 \preceq \cdots \preceq \rho_{u-1} \preceq \varphi_u$$

Denote the sequence $\{\rho_j\}_{j=1}^{u-1}$ by R. Observe now that at most $v - 1$ members of R do not belong to V (Otherwise, if there would be at least v such members, one can use these to construct a $v + 1$ chain for V, which would imply $dim(V) \geq v + 1$, which contradicts our assumption.) This means that at least $(u - 1) - (v - 1) = w$ members of R must belong to V. They form a subsequence

$R_V = \{\rho_{p_r}\}_{r=1}^p$ of R, where $\{p_r\}_{r=1}^p$ is an increasing sequence on $\{0, \ldots, u-1\}$ and $p \geq w$.

By a similar argument, at least v members of R must belong to W. They form a subsequence $R_W = \{\rho_{q_s}\}_{s=1}^q$ of R. Now, R_V and R_W together have at least $v + w = u$ members, all coming from R. But R has only $u - 1$ members. By the pigeon hole principle, at least one member of R is shared by R_W and R_V. Let us call this element ρ'. According to the definition of R_W and R_V, $\rho' \in V \cap W = U$. But this contradicts with the fact that $\rho_j \in \mathcal{L} \setminus U$ for all j $\blacksquare$

Theorem 8 *Let $V, W \in \mathcal{VS}^{\mathbb{Z}}(\mathcal{L})$. Then, $U = V \cup W \in \mathcal{VS}^{\mathbb{Z}}(\mathcal{L})$ and $0 \leq \dim(U) \leq \dim(V) + \dim(W)$.*

Proof: Let $v = \dim(V)$ and $w = \dim(W)$. By Definition 3, we can write $V = \bigcup_{i=1}^v X_i$ and $W = \bigcup_{k=1}^w Y_k$ for some $X_i, Y_k \in \mathcal{VS}^1(\mathcal{L})$. Then, we have $U = (\bigcup_{i=1}^v X_i) \cup (\bigcup_{k=1}^w Y_k) = \bigcup_{l=1}^{v+w} Z_k$ where $Z_l = X_l$ for $l = 1, \ldots, v$ and $Z_{l-v} = Y_{l-v}$ for $l = v+1, \ldots, v+w$. Since each $Z_k \in \mathcal{VS}^1(\mathcal{L})$, we have $U \in \mathcal{VS}^{\mathbb{Z}}(\mathcal{L})$. Moreover, $\dim(U) \leq w + v$ by Definition 3. We cannot give a tighter lower bound other than 0, because of the following special case. Consider the case when both V and W are empty. This gives an empty U, and hence $\dim(U) = 0$. Therefore, $0 \leq \dim(U) \leq \dim(V) + \dim(W)$. $\blacksquare$

Theorem 9 *Let $V \in \mathcal{VS}^{\mathbb{Z}}(\mathcal{L})$ and $v = \dim(V)$. Then, $U = \mathcal{L} \setminus V \in \mathcal{VS}^{\mathbb{Z}}(\mathcal{L})$ and $u = \dim(U) = v - 1, v$ or $v + 1$.*

Proof: There is a special case: $V = \emptyset$. In this case $\dim(V) = 0$, and $\mathcal{L} \setminus V = \mathcal{L}$, which has dimension 1. So, the theorem holds.

For the general case, observe first that $u \geq v - 1$. Indeed, by Lemma 4, V has a v-chain. i.e.

$$\exists \varphi_i \in V (i = 1, \ldots, v) \, \exists \rho_j \in \mathcal{L} \setminus V (j = 1, \ldots, v-1)$$
$$\varphi_1 \preceq \rho_1 \preceq \varphi_2 \preceq \rho_2 \preceq \cdots \preceq \varphi_{v-1} \preceq \rho_{v-1} \preceq \varphi_v$$

Then, $\rho_1 \preceq \varphi_2 \preceq \rho_2 \preceq \cdots \preceq \varphi_{v-1} \preceq \rho_{v-1}$ constitutes a $(v-1)$-chain of $U = \mathcal{L} \setminus V$. Thus, with Lemma 4, we may conclude that $\dim(U) = u \geq v - 1$. Similarly, one can derive that $\dim(V) = v \geq u - 1$, or equivalently $u \leq v + 1$ Combining these results gives $v - 1 \leq u \leq v + 1$. The result then follows from the fact that u is an integer. $\blacksquare$

4. Query Plans and Algebraic Operations

By the definition of boolean inductive queries, the solution set $Th(Q, \mathcal{D}, \mathcal{L})$ of a query Q is obtained by applying algebraic operations on the solution sets w.r.t. the underlying queries. This can be formalized using the notion of a query plan.

Definition 10 *A query plan is a boolean formula with some of its subqueries marked using the symbol $\smile$. Furthermore, all marked subqueries are the conjunction of a monotonic and an anti-monotonic subquery.*

Example 11 *Consider the query $Q = (a_1 \wedge m_1) \vee (a_1 \wedge m_2) \vee (a_2 \wedge m_1) \vee (a_2 \wedge m_2)$ where the a_i and m_i are anti-monotonic (resp. monotonic) predicates. The solution set of this query can be obtained by first computing the solution sets to the queries $(a_1 \wedge m_1)$, $(a_1 \wedge m_2)$, $(a_2 \wedge m_1)$ and $(a_2 \wedge m_2)$ and then taking their union. This way of computing $Th(Q, \mathcal{D}, \mathcal{L})$ corresponds to the plan*

$$\underbrace{(a_1 \wedge m_1)} \vee \underbrace{(a_1 \wedge m_2)} \vee \underbrace{(a_2 \wedge m_1)} \vee \underbrace{(a_2 \wedge m_2)}$$

Alternatively, one could rewrite query Q into the form $\underbrace{(a_1 \vee a_2) \wedge (m_1 \vee m_2)}$ and obtain the result using one call to a conjunctive query solver (i.e. an algorithm or system that computes the set of all solutions to a conjunctive query). Intermediate forms are also possible.

For any inductive query Q, one can now construct a variety of different query plans by annotating queries that are logically equivalent to Q. The question then arises as to which query plan is optimal, in the sense that the resources (i.e. memory and cpu-time) needed for computing its solution set are as small as possible. A general approach to this problem would involve the use of cost estimates that for each call to a conjunctive solver and operation. One example of a cost function for a call to a conjunctive solver could be *Expected Number of Scans of Data $\times$ Size of Data Set*. Another one could be the *Expected Number of Covers Tests*. De Raedt *et al.* have studied (and solved) the query optimization problem under the assumption that each call to a conjunctive solver has unit cost and that the only set operation allowed is union. Under this assumption, decomposing a query Q into k subqueries of the form $Q_{a,i} \wedge Q_{m,i}$ with ($Q_{a,i}$ anti-monotonic and $Q_{m,i}$ monotonic) and $\dim(Q) = k$ is an optimal strategy. In this paper, we will leave open the challenging question as to which cost-estimates to use in practice. However, what should be clear is that given such cost-estimates, one could optimize inductive queries by constructing all possible query plans and then selecting the best one. This is effectively an optimization problem, not unlike the query optimization problem in relational databases.

The optimization problem becomes even more interesting in the light of interactive querying sessions [2], which should be quite common when working with inductive databases. In such sessions, one typically submits a rough query to get some insight in the domain, and when the results of this query are available, the user studies the results and refines the query. This often goes through a few iterations until the desired results are obtained.

These interactive sessions are again similar in spirit to those in traditional databases, where the results of intermediate queries are often cached for optimizing later queries. Indeed, consider that for the above example, we would already have the result of the query $(a_1 \vee a_2) \wedge m_1$. In this

150

case, one could actually employ the following query plan:

$$\underbrace{((a_1 \vee a_2) \wedge m_1)} \vee \underbrace{((a_1 \vee a_2) \wedge m_2)}$$

where $\cdots$ denotes a query for which the solution is readily available. This query plan employs a union and could save a lot of time when m_1 is a minimum frequency query in a large database.

Even when the refined query Q_1 is not related to the original one Q_0 via Boolean algebra, there is still a possibility for reusing the cached results $Th(Q_0, \mathcal{D}, \mathcal{L})$ to obtain the new solution $Th(Q_1, \mathcal{D}, \mathcal{L})$ efficiently. One such situation occurs with the minimum frequency constraints. For example, $Q_0 = \mathsf{min\_freq}(\varphi, \mathcal{D}, \theta_1)$ and $Q_1 = \mathsf{min\_freq}(\varphi, \mathcal{D}, \theta_2)$. When $\theta_2 \geq \theta_1$, then $Th(Q_1, \mathcal{D}, \mathcal{L}) \subseteq Th(Q_0, \mathcal{D}, \mathcal{L})$. So, we can find out the answer $Th(Q_1, \mathcal{D}, \mathcal{L})$ by simply performing a filtering operation on $Th(Q_0, \mathcal{D}, \mathcal{L})$. If the frequencies of all patterns in $Th(Q_0, \mathcal{D}, \mathcal{L})$ were stored with the results, we can even do this filtering without scanning the database! On the other hand, when $\theta_2 \leq \theta_1$, a simple filtering does not work. In this case, we can make use of an incremental update algorithm [4, 13], with adaptations, to efficiently compute $Th(Q_1, \mathcal{D}, \mathcal{L})$ by using the cached results of $Th(Q_0, \mathcal{D}, \mathcal{L})$.

The problem boils down to recognizing the parts of queries Q_0 and Q_1 which are related this way. For simple queries, such recognition is simple. However, for more complicated queries, it becomes challenging to recognize such related parts of the queries. Our algebraic framework allows one to break down a complicated query into a disjunctive normal form, making it easier to recognize such related parts for optimization. Moreover, it is possible to rewrite the queries Q_0 and Q_1 into many equivalent forms, and we can then devise algorithms to recognize the related parts in these forms. This provides further opportunities for optimizations in data mining.

5. Generalized Version Space Trees

We have extended our previous data structure "Version Space Trees" [7] for mining $\mathcal{VS}^1$ of strings to handle the general case of $\mathcal{VS}^{\mathbb{Z}}$. The extended data structure is called *Generalized Version Space Trees* (GVS Tree).

The GVS Tree maintains a set of strings which are patterns we are discovering from the database. Each such string is represented by a node in the tree. For any given node n, we denote the string pattern it represents by $s(n)$. The organization of the tree is based on suffix tries. A *suffix trie* is a trie with the following properties:

- For each node n in the trie, and for each suffix t of $s(n)$, there is also a node n' in the trie representing t, i.e. $t = s(n')$.

- Each node n has as a *suffix link*, $suffix(n) = n'$, such that $s(n')$ is obtained from $s(n)$ by dropping the first character. The root node is special because it represents ϵ, which has no suffixes. We define $suffix(root) = \Omega$, where Ω denotes a unique fake node.

Unlike the common approach in the literature on suffix trees [16, 17], we use suffix tries in two very different ways from the main stream. The first one is that instead of building a suffix tree on all the suffixes of a *single* string, we are indexing all the suffixes of a *set of strings patterns* for a string database $\mathcal{D}$. This means multiple strings are stored in the tree. Moreover, in parts of our algorithms, we even keep a count of occurrences of each such substring in the corresponding node.

We label each node n of the GVS Tree with either a "$\oplus$" or a "$\ominus$", according to whether or not the $s(n) \in Th(Q, \mathcal{D}, \Sigma^*) \in \mathcal{VS}^{\mathbb{Z}}(\Sigma^*)$. In our previous publication [7], the VS Tree had a restriction that there can be at most one sign change the root to any leaf. This is because VS Tree was designed to model sets in $\mathcal{VS}^1$ only. As a generalization in this current work, we have removed this restriction, allowing complete freedom on the assignment of the labels "$\oplus$" or a "$\ominus$" to any node. As a result, a GVS Tree can represent sets of string patterns in $\mathcal{VS}^{\mathbb{Z}}$. Observe that if $\dim(V) = n$, then there exists a path (exploiting both child and suffix links, and ignoring the link directions) in T with alternating signs so that the number of sign changes from $\ominus$ to $\oplus$ is n (Lemma 4).

Figure 1 shows a labelled GVS Tree for the set $Th(Q, \mathcal{D}, \Sigma^*)$ where $\Sigma = \{\mathsf{a}, \mathsf{b}, \mathsf{c}, \mathsf{d}\}$ and $Q(\varphi, \mathcal{D}) = (\mathsf{bc} \preceq \varphi \preceq \mathsf{abcd}) \vee (\mathsf{a} \preceq \varphi \preceq \mathsf{acd})$. The dashed, curved arrows show the suffix links. The suffix links of the nodes immediate below the root node all points back to the root node, and are omitted for clarity. The $\oplus$ nodes represent the seven members of the GVS, namely a, abc, abcd, ac, acd, bc and bcd. Note that Q above is already in a minimal disjunctive normal form. So, the GVS has a dimension of 2, and the path through the nodes representing ϵ, a, ab, abc with exactly 2 sign changes.

An important property of the GVS Tree is that checking for membership is very efficient. Given any string $\varphi \in \Sigma^*$, we just need to follow the symbols on φ and descend through the tree accordingly. We will then end up at a node n so that $s(n) = \varphi$. This node has an $\oplus$ mark if and only if φ is in the GVS. The time complexity is $O(|\varphi|)$. The space complexity of a GVS Tree and the time required to build it is the same of that of suffix tries—quadratic in the size of the input strings.

The TreeMerge algorithm is basically an algorithm for merging two ordinary trees. However, we have to combine the flags ($\ominus$ or $\oplus$) from both trees, too. The combining algorithm is presented in the pseudocode in Algorithm 1 as an abstract Boolean operation $\odot$. When the operation is "and",

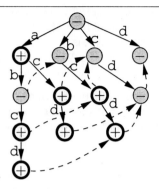

Figure 1. An example of GVS Tree

(a) Unix command database			(b) Yeast database	
Subset	no. of users	number of sequences	Subset	number of sequences
nov	55	5164	cat30	209
exp	36	3859	cat40	2256
non	25	1906	cat2	252
sci	52	7751		

Table 1. Summary statistics of the databases

there is no need to look at a corresponding branch in T_2.

the flags are combined using conjunction during the merging ($\ominus$ is interpreted as "false" while $\oplus$ is treated as "true"), and hence the TreeMerge algorithm will compute the intersection of the represented GVSes. When $\odot = \vee$, we get the union operation. When $x \odot y \equiv \neg(x \rightarrow y)$, we get the set difference operation.

In the algorithm, the function *root_or_negative*(T) returns the root node of a tree T if T is non-empty, or a node with label $\ominus$ and no children if T is empty. Function *child*(n, σ) returns the child node of n on the child link labelled σ, where $\sigma \in \Sigma$. If there is no such child, *NULL* is returned. The function *tree_with_root*(n) returns a GVS Tree whose root node is n, or T_{empty} if n is *NULL*. T_{empty} denotes an empty GVS Tree.

Algorithm 1 TreeMerge

Input: T_1, T_2: two GVS Trees
$\quad \odot$: a binary, boolean operator
Output: T' = The resulting of merging T_1 and T_2.
Body:
$\quad$**if** $T_1 = T_{\text{empty}} \wedge T_2 = T_{\text{empty}}$ **then**
$\quad\quad$**return** T_{empty}
$\quad r_1 \leftarrow root\_or\_negative(T_1)$; $r_2 \leftarrow root\_or\_negative(T_2)$
$\quad$Create new tree T' with root node r'.
$\quad label(r') \leftarrow label(r_1) \odot label(r_2)$
$\quad$**for all** $\sigma \in \Sigma$ **do**
$\quad\quad c_1 \leftarrow child(r_1, \sigma)$; $c_2 \leftarrow child(r_2, \sigma)$
$\quad\quad$**if** $c_1 \neq NULL \vee c_2 \neq NULL$ **then**
$\quad\quad\quad T_{c_1} \leftarrow tree\_with\_root(c_1)$
$\quad\quad\quad T_{c_2} \leftarrow tree\_with\_root(c_2)$
$\quad\quad\quad c' \leftarrow root\_or\_negative(\text{TreeMerge}(T_{c_1}, T_{c_2}, \odot))$
$\quad\quad\quad$add c' to r' as a child node along link σ
$\quad$**return** T'

It should be emphasized that Algorithm 1 is pseudo code. In practice, optimizations can be introduced by specializing the code for each particular Boolean operation. For instance, when $\odot = \wedge$ and a certain branch in T_1 is empty,

6. Preliminary Experiments

We have implemented the algorithm VST [7] that computes the results of conjunctive queries (with dimension 1) and a tree merging algorithm TreeMerge in C and performed some experiments on a PC computer with a Pentium-4 2.8GMHz processor, 2GB main memory, and running Linux operating system (kernel 2.4.19, glibc 2.2.5). The former is used as our conjunctive query solver (see Section 4) while the latter is for performing set operations on pattern sets. Our implementation supports as primitives the two predicates min_freq and max_freq as given in Section 2.

Two databases were used in the experiments. The first one is a command history collected from 168 Unix users over a period of time. [9] The users are divided into four groups: computer scientists, experienced programmers, novice programmers and non-programmers. The corresponding data subsets are denoted "sci", "exp", "nov" and "non", respectively. Each group has a number of users. When a user accesses the Unix system, he first logs in, then types in a sequence of commands, and finally logs out. Each command is taken as a symbol in the database, The sequence of commands from log in to log out constitutes a login session, which is mapped to a string in our experiment. The alphabet is the set of available commands. Each user contributes to many login sessions in the database. Table 1(a) gives some summary data on the database.

The second database is a collection of ORFs (open reading frames) of yeast, cf. [5]. The alphabet is the set of 20 amino acids. Out of these 20 symbols, every ORF (encoding for a protein) can be represented. Our database contains 6354 such sequences. Each sequence has a length between 8 and 4910. In addition, each sequence is associated with one or more functional categories (cat30: "Control of cellular organization", cat40: "Subcellular localisation", cat2: "Energy", etc.). As preprocessing, we have separated the sequences into groups according to their functional categories. When a sequence has more than one category, it appears in multiple groups. However, within each group, a sequence appears at most once. Three of these groups were used in the experiments. They are given in Table 1(b).

For both databases, we used a query of the following form and ran our programs to mine the patterns satisfying the constraints.

$$Q = (Q_1 \vee Q_2) \wedge Q_A \text{ where}$$
$$Q_1 = \text{min\_freq}(\varphi, D_1, |D_1| \times \theta_1) \wedge \text{len\_lb}(\varphi, 3)$$
$$Q_2 = \text{min\_freq}(\varphi, D_2, |D_2| \times \theta_2) \wedge \text{len\_lb}(\varphi, 2)$$

and Q_A is an anti-monotonic constraint. The monotonic predicate $\text{len\_lb}(\varphi, n)$ evaluates to true iff the length of φ is at least n. Here, D_1 and D_2 are subsets of the database being used, θ_1 and θ_2 are the corresponding minimum frequency thresholds, also set to 10%, and Q_A is an anti-monotonic constraint.

Note that Q is neither monotonic nor anti-monotonic. So, the solution set is in $\mathcal{VS}^{\mathbb{Z}}$. However, Q_1 and Q_2 are each a conjunction of an anti-monotonic constraint (minimum frequency) and a monotonic one (minimum length). So, $\dim(Q_1) = \dim(Q_2) = \dim(Q_A) = 1$. Thus, one (straight-forward) strategy to find the set of patterns satisfying Q is to use the query plan

$$\left(\underbrace{Q_1} \vee \underbrace{Q_2} \right) \wedge \underbrace{Q_A}$$

This involves 3 invocations of our frequent pattern miner VST. However, the VST algorithm (or any other frequent pattern discovery algorithm such as Apriori [1]) is the most time-consuming part of the whole processes. We would like to minimize this cost. This is possible now with our algebra on generalized version spaces and theorems on the dimension. By Theorem 8, we know that $\dim(Q_1 \vee Q_2) \leq \dim(Q_1) + \dim(Q_2) = 1 + 1 = 2$. Now, applying Theorem 7, we have $\dim(Q) \leq \dim(Q_1 \vee Q_2) + \dim(Q_A) - 1 \leq 2 + 1 - 1 = 2$. Thus, Q has a dimension of at most 2. Thus, one can express Q as the union of two version spaces.

Indeed, we can obtain a different query plan for Q, which we denote by Q':

$$Q' = \underbrace{Q_1'} \vee \underbrace{Q_2'} \text{ where}$$
$$Q_1' = Q_1 \wedge Q_A$$
$$Q_2' = Q_2 \wedge Q_A$$

This query plan involves only 2 invocations of algorithm VST. It is thus expected to be faster. Moreover, having pushed the anti-monotonic constraint Q_A deeper into the query evaluation, we expect the levelwise algorithm VST to prune more effectively.

To verify this, we have run experiments on the two databases with the values for D_1, D_2 and Q_A as shown in Table 2. On the unix command database, this query translates to "What sequences of unix commands are used often

	Unix command database	Yeast database
D_1	experienced programmers	cat30
D_2	computer scientists	cat40
θ_1	10%	20%
θ_2	10%	20%
Q_A	min_freq(φ, non, |non| × 10%) ∧ min_freq(φ, nov, |nov| × 10%)	min_freq(φ, cat2, |cat2| × 20%)

Table 2. Queries used for the experiments

Query	No. of patterns		Time (sec.)	
Strategy	Unix	Yeast	Unix	Yeast
Q (total)	41	404	2.15	4.03
Q_1	110	638	0.74	0.42
Q_2	212	122	1.18	3.34
Q_A	67	434	0.23	0.27
Q' (total)	41	404	1.60	3.65
Q_1'	16	403	0.65	0.55
Q_2'	40	38	0.95	3.10

Table 3. Experimental Results

by experienced programmers with a length of at least 3 or by computer scientists with a length of at least 2, and are also frequently used by the other two groups of users?". With our algebraic framework, it is possible to perform data mining with such complicated constraints. The query for the protein database translates to "What amino acid sequences occur frequently in function category 'cat30' with a length of at least 3 or in function category 'cat40' with a length of at least 2, and is at the same time frequent among the function category 'cat2'?".

The queries Q and Q' are evaluated as described above using our implementation of the VST and TreeMerge algorithms. For each database the resulting patterns for both queries are compared and found to be identical. This verifies the correctness of our theory and implementation.

The time taken are noted and given in Table 3. With the unix command database, it took 2.15 seconds to evaluate the query as Q and only 1.60 seconds to evaluate as Q'. With the yeast database, it took 4.03 and 3.65 seconds, respectively. It is thus 9–26% faster to use strategy Q' than Q to find out the set of patterns. The table also shows a breakdown of the time taken for evaluating the queries Q_1, Q_2, Q_A, Q_1' and Q_2'. The pattern sets for these are all in $\mathcal{VS}^1$, and are computed by the VST algorithm. It should be noted that the time taken for the TreeMerge algorithm is negligible (less than 1 ms). This confirms our claim that invoca-

Query	No. of patterns		Heap memory (bytes)	
Strategy	Unix	Yeast	Unix	Yeast
Q (total)	41	404	128619	119988
Q' (total)	41	404	66740	106476

Table 4. Memory usage

tions of algorithm VST is the most time-consuming part of the whole process.

Another important observation in Table 3 is the number of patterns found for each query strategy and subqueries. In query strategy Q', the constraint Q_A is pushed down to the subqueries Q'_1 and Q'_2, effectively pruning the number of patterns that needs to be processed by the programs. This accounts for the improved speed and memory usage.

Not only is time saved, but also is memory more efficiently used when we use strategy Q' instead of Q to compute the set of patterns in question. The amount of heap memory used by our programs were recorded. The maximum amount of heap memory usage is shown in Table 4. Using query evaluation strategy Q', we save 11–48% of memory. Thus, it saves both time and memory to evaluate the query using Q'.

7. Conclusions

We have generalized the notion of convex sets or version spaces to represent sets of higher dimensions. These generalized version spaces are useful for representing the solution sets to boolean inductive queries. Furthermore, we have studied the effect of algebraic operations on such generalized version spaces and shown that these generalized version spaces are closed under the set operations. This generalizes Hirsh's results on traditional version spaces (sets of dimension 1).

We have also shown how the resulting algebraic framework can be employed for query planning and optimization. The framework has been implemented for the pattern domain of strings and experimental results that illustrate the use of the framework have been presented.

Nevertheless, there are many remaining opportunities for further research. Most important is the development of effective and realistic cost functions for inductive query evaluation and their use in query optimization.

Acknowledgements This work was partly supported by the EU IST project cInQ (Consortium on Inductive Querying). The authors would also like to thank Manfred Jaeger and Heikki Mannila, with whom they developed the original theory of inductive querying [7] that is extended in the present paper, as well as Ross D. King and Amanda Clare for providing the yeast data.

References

[1] R. Agrawal and R. Srikant. Fast algorithms for mining association rules. In *Proc. 20th VLDB*, pages 487–499. Morgan Kaufmann, 1994.

[2] E. Baralis and G. Psaila. Incremental refinement of mining queries. In *Proc. 1st DaWaK*, LNCS 1676, pages 173–182, Florence, Italy, August 30–September 1 1999. Springer.

[3] C. Bucila, J. Gehrke, D. Kifer, and W. White. DualMiner: A dual-pruning algorithm for itemsets with constraints. In *Proc. 8th ACM SIGKDD*, Edmonton, Alberta, Canada, July 23–26 2002.

[4] D. W. L. Cheung, S. D. Lee, and B. Kao. A general incremental technique for maintaining discovered association rules. In *Proc. 5th DASFAA*, pages 185–194, Melbourne, Australia, 1–4 Apr. 1997.

[5] A. Clare and R. D. King. Machine learning of functional class from phenotype data. *Bioinformatics*, 18(1):160–166, 2002.

[6] L. De Raedt. A perspective on inductive databases. *SIGKDD Explorations*, 4(2):69–77, January 2003.

[7] L. De Raedt, M. Jaeger, S. D. Lee, and H. Mannila. A theory of inductive query answering (extended abstract). In *Proc. 2nd IEEE ICDM*, pages 123–130, Maebashi, Japan, December 9–12 2002.

[8] L. De Raedt and S. Kramer. The levelwise version space algorithm and its application to molecular fragment finding. In *Proc. 17th IJCAI*, August 4–10 2001.

[9] S. Greenberg. Using unix: Collected traces of 168 users. Research Report 88/333/45, Department of Computer Science, University of Calgary, Canada, 1988.

[10] H. Hirsh. Theoretical underpinnings of version spaces. In *Proc. 12th IJCAI*, pages 665–670. Morgan Kaufmann Publishers, 1991.

[11] H. Hirsh. Generalizing version spaces. *Machine Learning*, 17(1):5–46, 1994.

[12] S. Kramer, L. De Raedt, and C. Helma. Molecular feature mining in hiv data. In *Proc. 7th ACM SIGKDD*, Association for Computing Machinery, August 26–29 2001. ISBN: 158113391X.

[13] S. D. Lee and D. Cheung. *Maintenance of Discovered Association Rules*, volume 600 of *The Kluwer International Series in Engineering and Computer Science*, chapter 8. Kluwer Academic Publishers, Boston, November 2000. ISBN-0-7923-7243-3.

[14] H. Mannila and H. Toivonen. Levelwise search and borders of theories in knowledge discovery. *Data Mining and Knowledge Discovery*, 1(3):241–258, 1997.

[15] T. M. Mitchell. Generalization as search. *Artificial Intelligence*, 18(2):203–226, March 1982.

[16] E. Ukkonen. On-line construction of suffix trees. *Algorithmica*, 14(3):249–260, 1995.

[17] P. Weiner. Linear pattern matching algorithm. In *Proc. 14 IEEE Symposium on Switching and Automata Theory*, pages 1–11, 1973.

Direct Interesting Rule Generation

Jiuyong Li
Department of Mathematics and Computing
The University of Southern Queensland
Australia, 4350
jiuyong@usq.edu.au

Yanchun Zhang
School of Computer Science and Mathematics
Victoria University
Australia, 8001
yzhang@csm.vu.edu.au

Abstract

An association rule generation algorithm usually generates too many rules including a lot of uninteresting ones. Many interestingness criteria are proposed to prune those uninteresting rules. However, they work in post-pruning process and hence do not improve the rule generation efficiency. In this paper, we discuss properties of informative rule set and conclude that the informative rule set includes all interesting rules measured by many commonly used interestingness criteria, and that rules excluded by the informative rule set are forwardly prunable, i.e. they can be removed in the rule generation process instead of post pruning. Based on these properties, we propose a Direct Interesting rule Generation algorithm, DIG, to directly generate interesting rules defined by any of 12 interestingness criteria discussed in this paper. We further show experimentally that DIG is faster and uses less memory than Apriori.

1 Introduction

Data mining is a growing research area due to the increasing popularity of dealing with a large number of data in various fields. We can obtain benefits when understanding data in a meaningful form rather than a collection of tedious alphanumeric symbols.

Association rule discovery has been a central issue in data mining, because of the simplicity of the problem statement and the efficiency of pruning by support. However, an association rule generation algorithm may generate too many rules and selecting interesting rules is a big task.

Many interesting criteria are proposed to select user-interesting rules. However, they are usually used in the post pruning process hence do not improve the efficiency of rule generation.

In this paper, we prove that the informative rule set includes all interesting rules according to 12 interestingness criteria. We further propose a direct algorithm to generate

interesting rules, and show experimentally that the proposed algorithm is faster and uses less memory than Apriori. DIG improves interesting rule discovery efficiency without more memory consumption and works on both transactional and relational data sets.

2 Informative rule set and its properties

An association rule set [1] is defined by the minimum support and the minimum confidence constraints. A lot of rules satisfying these constraints are not interesting. One major reason is that many rules are redundant. For example, $a \Rightarrow z$, $ab \Rightarrow z$ and $abc \Rightarrow z$ carry the similar message. Why do we need those complex ones having long antecedents? A complex rule covers a subset of instances covered by its simple form rules, so it has to provide something more than the simple form rules to be interesting. This extra provided by the complex rules is to be measured by an interestingness criterion. In the context of classic association rules, we expect that they have higher confidence than their simple form rules. Based on these observations, we define the informative rule set as follows.

Given a set of items $I = \{i_1, i_2, \ldots, i_m\}$, and a collection of transactions $D = \{T_1, T_2, \ldots, T_n\}$, where $T_i \subset I|_{i \le n}$. D is called a transactional data set. An itemset is a subset of I, and is called a l-itemset if it contains l items. The support for itemset S is its occurrence probability in D, denoted by $P(S)$. $S \Rightarrow q$ is called a rule if $P(Sq) > \sigma$ [1] and $P(q|S) > P(q)$, where σ is called the minimum support and $P(q|S) = \frac{P(Sq)}{P(S)}$ is called the confidence of the rule. Given two rules $S \rightarrow i_q$ and $V \rightarrow i_q$ where $S \subset V$, we say the latter is more specific than the former or the former is more general than the latter.

---

[1]For simplicity, in the rest of this paper we use upper case letters, e.g. S, V, Z, to stand for itemsets, and lower case letters, e.g. a, b, c, p, q, to stand for items. We abbreviate $S \cup q$ as Sq.

Definition 1 We call a rule set the informative rule set if it satisfies the following two conditions: 1) it contains all rules that satisfy the minimum support; and 2) it excludes all more specific rules with no greater confidence than one of its more general form rule.

In the above definition, we did not specify the minimum confidence constraint. We suppose that a user may impose another minimum interestingness threshold since the discussion in this paper is to generate general interesting rules.

The informative rule set was defined in our previous work, and we concluded that it is the smallest subset of an association rule set having the same predictive power as the association rule set based on a confidence priority predictive model [12, 14]. In this paper, we reveal its general practical implication.

Theorem 1 *Rules excluded by the informative rule set are uninteresting measured by many interestingness criteria, namely odd ratio, lift (interest or strength), gain, added-value, Klosgen, conviction, p-s, Laplace, estimate accuracy, cosine, certainty factor and Jaccard.*

Proof In this proof, we use $AX \Rightarrow c$ to stand for a more specific form rule of $A \Rightarrow c$. $AX \Rightarrow c$ is excluded by the informative rule set because of $P(c|AX) \leq P(c|A)$. We will prove that by all criteria listed above, rule $AX \Rightarrow c$ is ranked lower than rule $A \Rightarrow c$ and hence is uninteresting. When two rules have the same value by an interesting metric, the shorter rule is ranked higher. We also know that $P(A) \geq P(AX)$.

Odds ratio is a classic statistical metric to measure the association between events. odd-ratio $(A \Rightarrow c) = \frac{P(Ac)P(\neg A \neg c)}{P((\neg A)c)P(A\neg c)}$ (the definition of $\neg c$ can be referred to the paragraph before Lemma 1 in this section). We rewrite the odd ratio by support and confidence as follow: odd-ratio $(A \Rightarrow c) = \frac{P(c|A)}{1-P(c|A)} / \frac{P(c|\neg A)}{1-P(c|\neg A)}$.

Since $P(c|A) \geq P(c|AX)$, $\frac{P(c|A)}{1-P(c|A)} \geq \frac{P(c|AX)}{1-P(c|AX)}$. Now we need to prove that $\frac{P(c|\neg A)}{1-P(c|\neg A)} \leq \frac{P(c|\neg(AX))}{1-P(c|\neg(AX))}$ to get odd-ratio$(A \Rightarrow c) \geq$ odd-ratio$(AX \Rightarrow c)$. To reach this goal, we need to prove that $P(c|\neg A) \leq P(c|\neg(AX))$ given $P(c|A) \geq P(c|AX)$.

$P(c|\neg A) = \frac{P((\neg A)c)}{P(\neg A)} = \frac{P(c)-P(Ac)}{1-P(A)} = \frac{P(c)/P(A)-P(c|A)}{1/P(A)-1} \leq \frac{P(c)/P(A)-P(c|AX)}{1/P(A)-1}$. Consider function $f(x) = \frac{\alpha x - \beta}{x-1}$ (β is a constant) monotonically increases with x when $\beta > \alpha$. We know that $\frac{1}{P(A)} \leq \frac{1}{P(AX)}$ and $P(c|AX) > P(c)$, so $\frac{P(c)/P(A)-P(c|AX)}{1/P(A)-1} \leq \frac{P(c)/P(AX)-P(c|AX)}{1/P(AX)-1} = P(c|\neg(AX))$. As a result, $P(c|\neg A) \leq P(c|\neg(AX))$.

Hence, odd-ratio$(A \Rightarrow c) \geq$ odd-ratio$(AX \Rightarrow c)$, and rule $A \Rightarrow c$ is ranked higher than rule $AX \Rightarrow c$ by odds ratio.

Lift [22], also known as interest [6] or strength [9], is a widely used metric to rank the interestingness of association rules. It has been used in IBM Intelligent Miner. lift$(A \Rightarrow c) = \frac{P(Ac)}{P(A)P(c)} = \frac{P(c|A)}{P(c)}$. Consider $P(c|AX) \leq P(c|A)$. We have lift$(A \Rightarrow c) = \frac{P(c|A)}{P(c)} \geq \frac{P(c|AX)}{P(c)} =$ lift$(AX \Rightarrow c)$. Hence, rule $A \Rightarrow c$ is ranked higher than rule $AX \Rightarrow c$ by the lift.

Gain [10] is an alternative for confidence. gain $(A \Rightarrow c) = P(Ac) - \theta \times P(A)$ where θ is a fractional constant between 0 and 1, and only rules obtaining positive gain are interesting. We rewrite gain as the following: gain$(A \Rightarrow c) = P(A)(P(c|A) - \theta)$. Consider $P(A) \geq P(AX)$ and $P(c|A) \geq P(c|AX) \geq \theta$ (otherwise both rules are uninteresting or answer is clear). We have gain$(A \Rightarrow c) \geq$ gain$(AX \Rightarrow c)$. Hence, rule $A \Rightarrow c$ is ranked higher than rule $AX \Rightarrow c$ by gain.

Two other similar metrics of gain are added-value and Klosgen. added-value $(A \Rightarrow c) = P(c|A) - P(c)$. Klosgen $(A \Rightarrow c) = \sqrt{P(Ac)}(P(c|A) - P(c))$. We go through the similar proof procedure and draw the same conclusion. Rule $A \Rightarrow c$ is ranked higher than rule $AX \Rightarrow c$ by added value and Klosgen metrics.

Conviction [6] is used to measure deviations from the independence by considering outside negation. conviction $(A \Rightarrow c) = \frac{P(A)P(\neg c)}{P(A \neg c)}$. We simplify the conviction as $(A \Rightarrow c) = \frac{1-P(c)}{1-P(c|A)}$. Consider $P(c|A) \geq P(c|AX)$. We have conviction$(A \Rightarrow c) \geq$ conviction$(AX \Rightarrow c)$. Hence, rule $A \Rightarrow c$ is ranked higher than rule $AX \Rightarrow c$ by the conviction.

P-s metric [18] is a classic interesting criterion for rules and is proposed by Piatesky-Shaprio. p-s$(A \Rightarrow c) = P(Ac) - P(A)P(c)$. We rewrite it as the following: p-s$(A \Rightarrow c) = P(A)(P(c|A) - P(c))$. Consider $P(c|A) \geq P(c|AX)$ and $P(A) \geq P(AX)$. We have p-s$(A \Rightarrow c) \geq$ p-s$(AX \Rightarrow c)$. Hence, rule $A \Rightarrow c$ is ranked higher than rule $AX \Rightarrow c$ by the p-s metric.

Laplace [7, 21] accuracy is a metric for classification rules. Strictly speaking, it is not an interestingness metric for association rules. However, association rules have been used to solve classification problems. So we consider it still. Laplace$(A \Rightarrow c) = \frac{P(Ac)|D|+1}{P(A)|D|+k}$, where $|D|$ is the number of transactions in D and k is the number of classes. We rewrite it as follows: Laplace$(A \Rightarrow c) = \frac{P(c|A)|D|+1/P(A)}{|D|+k/P(A)}$. Consider $P(c|A) \geq P(c|AX)$. We have Laplace$(A \Rightarrow c) \geq \frac{P(c|AX)|D|+1/P(A)}{|D|+k/P(A)}$. Function $f(x) = \frac{\alpha|D|+x}{|D|+kx}$ (α is a constant) monotonically decreases with x when $\alpha \times k > 1$. Usually, for classification rules the minimum confidence is set to be greater than 0.5 and $k \geq 2$. Hence $\alpha \times k > 1$ is satisfied. Consider $\frac{1}{P(A)} \leq$

$\frac{1}{P(AX)}$. We have Laplace$(A \Rightarrow c) \geq \frac{P(c|AX)|D|+1/P(A)}{|D|+k/P(A)} \geq \frac{P(c|AX)|D|+1/P(AX)}{|D|+k/P(AX)} = $ Laplace$(AX \Rightarrow c)$. Hence, rule $A \Rightarrow c$ is ranked higher than rule $AX \Rightarrow c$ by laplace accuracy.

Estimate true accuracy [16] is used in [13] to suppress rules with a slight confidence improvement but a big support loss over their simple form rules. Accuracy $(A \Rightarrow c) = P(c|A) - z_N \sqrt{\frac{P(c|A)(1-P(c|A))}{P(Ac)|D|}}$, where $|D|$ is the number of transactions in D and z_N is a constant related with a statistical confidence interval. In classification, the minimum confidence of a rule is usually set to be greater than 0.5. In this case, accuracy$(A \Rightarrow c) \geq$ accuracy$(AX \Rightarrow c)$ given $P(c|A) \geq P(c|AX)$ and $P(A) \geq P(AX)$. Hence, rule $A \Rightarrow c$ is ranked higher than rule $AX \Rightarrow c$ by the estimate accuracy.

We consider some other metrics discussed in [20].

Cosine$(A \Rightarrow c) = \frac{P(Ac)}{\sqrt{P(A)P(c)}}$. We rewrite it as cosine$(A \Rightarrow c) = \frac{\sqrt{P(A)P(c|A)}}{\sqrt{P(c)}}$. Consider that $P(AX) \leq P(A)$ and $P(c|AX) \leq P(c|A)$. We have cosine$(A \Rightarrow c) \geq$ cosine$(AX \Rightarrow c)$. Hence, rule $A \Rightarrow c$ is ranked higher than rule $AX \Rightarrow c$ by cosine.

Certainty-factor $(A \Rightarrow c) = \frac{P(c|A)-P(c)}{1-P(c)}$. Consider $P(c|A) \geq P(c|AX)$. We have certainty-factor$(A \Rightarrow c) \geq$ certainty-factor$(AX \Rightarrow c)$. Hence, rule $A \Rightarrow c$ is ranked higher than rule $AX \Rightarrow c$ by certainty factor.

Jaccard$(A \Rightarrow c) = \frac{P(Ac)}{P(A)+P(c)-P(Ac)}$. We rewrite it as Jaccard$(A \Rightarrow c) = \frac{P(c|A)}{1+P(c)/P(A)-P(c|A)}$. Consider $P(A) \geq P(AX)$. Jaccard$(A \Rightarrow c) \geq \frac{P(c|A)}{1+P(c)/P(AX)-P(c|A)}$. Function $f(x) = \frac{x}{\alpha-x}$ (α is a constant.) monotonically increases with x when $\alpha > 0$. Consider $P(c|A) \geq P(c|AX)$ and $1 + P(c)/P(AX) > 0$. We have Jaccard$(A \Rightarrow c) \geq \frac{P(c|A)}{1+P(c)/P(AX)-P(c|A)} \geq \frac{P(c|AX)}{1+P(c)/P(AX)-P(c|AX)} = $ Jaccard$(AX \Rightarrow c)$. Hence, rule $A \Rightarrow c$ is ranked higher than rule $AX \Rightarrow c$ by Jaccard.

The theorem is proved. $\square$

Now we will present two properties of informative rule set to facilitate the design of an efficient rule generation algorithm. We do not provide proofs here, and please refer to [14] for details.

We introduce a special item $\neg q$, which appears in all transactions where q does not occur. Itemset $\neg(ab)$ means both a and b do not occur in a transaction, and hence $\neg(ab) = \neg a \neg b$. One obvious usefulness of this special item is to separate the support of an itemset into two parts, e.g. $P(S) = P(S\neg q) + P(Sq)$ and $P(S\neg q) = P(S) - P(Sq)$, or $P(q) = P(\neg Sq) + P(Sq)$ and $P(\neg Sq) = P(q) - P(Sq)$.

In the following lemma, we use $Sp \Rightarrow q$ to denote a more specific form rule of $S \Rightarrow q$. All more specific form rule of $Sp \Rightarrow q$ is $SZp \Rightarrow q$ for $Z \neq \emptyset, p, q \notin Z$ and $S \neq Z$.

Lemma 1 *If $P(S\neg q) = P(Sp\neg q)$, then for any item q rule $Sp \Rightarrow q$ and all its more specific form rules do not occur in the informative rule set.*

The meaning of this lemma is very clear. If a more specific rule r does not reduce negative instances from one of its more general form rule, then all more specific rules of r will not reduce negative instance from at least one of its more general form rules. Hence they are all excluded from the informative rule set. For example, if $P(a\neg q) = P(ab\neg q)$, then $P(q|ab) \leq P(q|a)$, further we also have $P(q|abX) \leq P(q|aX)$. $abX \Rightarrow q$ will not occur in the informative rule set because $aX \Rightarrow q$ is more general.

We have a look why this property is similar to the one that support has. Given itemset S is infrequent. SZ is infrequent because of upwards closure property of infrequent itemsets. This enables us to totally ignore all super itemsets of S in rule generation process. Given SZq is frequent. We usually have to test all rules from $S \Rightarrow q$ to $SZ \Rightarrow q$ where Z can be any itemset. However, if we observe that $P(S\neg q) = P(V\neg q)$ where V is a $(|S| - 1)$-itemset and $V \subset S$, then to generate interesting rules we need not to test all rules from $S \Rightarrow q$ to $SZ \Rightarrow q$ according to the lemma.

Now we have a look at a useful corollary.

Corollary 1 *If $P(S) = P(Sp)$, then rule $Sp \Rightarrow q$ for any q and all its more specific form rules do not occur in the informative rule set.*

Both lemma and corollary are very useful for efficient algorithm design.

3 Direct interesting rule generation

An association rule generation algorithm prunes infrequent itemsets forwardly. An itemset is frequent if its support is greater than the minimum support. An itemset is potentially frequent only if all its subsets are frequent, and this property is used to limit the number of itemsets to be searched. This is called *upwards closure* property of infrequent itemset and is useful for forward pruning.

In the process of the association rule generation, confidence plays no role for the efficiency. It only controls the number of rules. It is well-known that an association rule generation algorithm produces too many uninteresting rules. According to the previous analysis, we know that those rules excluded by the informative rule set are uninteresting. In addition, we have upwards closure properties to forwardly prune those uninteresting rules. These enable us to design efficient algorithm to directly generate interesting rules.

157

3.1 Candidate representation

To facilitate the implementation of forward pruning by the lemma and the corollary, we define a rule candidate as a pair of (itemset, target-set), denoted by (S, C). The target-set C is a set of items that are possible consequences of rules. Initially, we set $S = C$. We call (S_1, C_1) as a sub candidate of (S_2, C_2) if $S_1 \subset S_2$. Equivalently, (S_2, C_2) is a super candidate of (S_1, C_1).

Target-set C is a sub or equal set of S and a candidate represents a number of potential rules. For example, candidate (abc, abc) indicates three potential rules $ab \Rightarrow c$, $ac \Rightarrow b$ and $bc \Rightarrow a$, and candidate (abc, ab) indicates two potential rules $ac \Rightarrow b$ and $bc \Rightarrow a$. Please note that we generate interesting single target rules as defined in the previous section.

The removal of items from target-set C is determined by the lemma, and we will show this in Subsection 3.3.

Usually, candidate $(S, \emptyset)$ is a legal candidate. We build a super candidate from its sub candidates. Though there is no potential rule for candidate $(abc, \emptyset)$, but there may be rule $abc \Rightarrow d$. Constructing candidate $(abcd, d)$ needs candidate $(abc, \emptyset)$.

Candidate $(S, \emptyset)$ is useless when no non-empty target-set super candidate can be built from it. Formally, given a set of items $I = \{i_1, i_2, \ldots, i_m\}$, itemset S and V where $V \neq S$. The target-set of candidate $(S, \emptyset)$ is permanently empty if there is no possibility to form rule $SV \Rightarrow p$, for all p and V where $p \in I \wedge p \notin SV$, to be in the informative rule set. This means that itemset S and all its super itemsets could not be the antecedent of an interesting rule.

The existence of a candidate depends on two conditions: (1) itemset S is frequent, and (2) target-set C is not permanently empty.

The determination of frequent S is straightforward, and hence we discuss how to determine of a permanently empty target-set.

The first criterion follows the corollary.

Criterion 1 *If $P(Sp) = P(S)$, then the target-set of candidate $(SZp, \emptyset)$ is permanently empty.*

We know that rule $Sp \Rightarrow q$ and all its more general form rules do not occur in the informative rule set according to the corollary. We note that q can be any item, so we need not to test rules from supersets of Sp.

This criterion is associated with a 100% confidence rule. If $P(Sp) = P(S)$, then $P(p|S) = 1$. When we know S always implies p, it is redundant to have $SZp \Rightarrow q$ since $SZ \Rightarrow q$ is more general.

For example, candidate $(abc, \emptyset)$ means rule $ab \Rightarrow c$, $ac \Rightarrow b$, $bc \Rightarrow a$ and their more specific rules are not in the informative rule set. For more details please refer to Subsection 3.3. However, for any $q \notin \{abc\}$ rule $abc \Rightarrow q$

and its more specific form rules may still be in the informative rule set and this is the reason for us to keep this candidate. If we know $sup(abc) = sup(ab)$, then according to the corollary rule $abc \Rightarrow q$ and all its more specific form rules are not in the informative rule set. Hence $(abc, \emptyset)$ is permanently empty.

We will present another criterion after presenting the candidate generation function.

3.2 Candidate generator

For easy understanding and comparison, we present Candidate-generator for the informative rule set discovery in the similar way of Apriori-gen. We call a candidate l-candidate if its itemset is a l-itemset. A l-candidate set includes all l-candidates. In the following discussions, we assume all items in an itemset are in the alphabetic order.

Function Candidate-generator
    // Combining
1)   for each pair of candidates $(S_{l-1}p, C_p)$ and $(S_{l-1}q, C_q)$
        in l-candidate set
2)   insert candidate (S_{l+1}, C)
            where $S_{l+1} = S_{l-1}pq$ and $C = (C_p q) \cap (C_q p)$
            in the $(l + 1)$-candidate set
    // Pruning
3)   for all $S_l \subset S_{l+1}$
4)   let $r = S_{l+1} \setminus S_l$
5)   if candidate (S_l, C_l) does not exist
6)   then remove candidate (S_{l+1}, C) and return
7)   else $C = C \cap (C_l r)$
8)   If the target-set of (S_{l+1}, C) is permanently empty
9)   then remove the candidate

We first explain lines 1 and 2. Suppose that we have two candidates (abc, a) and (abd, ad). When we extend itemset $\{abc\}$ to itemset $\{abcd\}$, we should add item d to the target-set of candidate (abc, a) because it is new to itemset (abc). For the same reason, we add item c to the target-set of candidate (abd, ad). We then intersect two extended target-sets, $\{ad\}$ and $\{acd\}$, and put the intersection as the target-set of the new candidate. The new candidate is $(abcd, ad)$. The intersection of target-sets here and in line 7 is to ensure that removed items from the target-set of a candidate never appear in the target-set of its super candidates. The correctness is guaranteed by the lemma since any item removal in the target-set is determined by the lemma as shown in Subsection 3.3.

Then we explain line 3 to 9. Suppose that we have new candidate $(abcd, ad)$. It is the combination of (abc, a) and (abd, ad). We need to check if candidates identified by itemsets $\{acd\}$ and $\{bcd\}$ exist. Suppose that they do exist and are (acd, cd) and (bcd, b). Because item a

could not be the consequence of a rule including itemset $\{acd\}$, and item d could not be the consequence of a rule including itemset $\{bcd\}$, the new candidate looks like $(abcd, \emptyset)$. This is achieved by line 7, e.g. when $S_l = \{acd\}$, $C = \{ad\} \cap (\{cd\} \cup \{b\}) = \{d\}$, and when $S_1 = \{bcd\}$, $C = \{d\} \cap (\{b\} \cup \{a\}) = \emptyset$.

Last, we need to determine if a target-set is permanently empty. We presented Criterion 1 before, and here present another criterion.

Criterion 2 *Consider candidate $(Sp, \emptyset)$. If for every candidate (Sq, C_q) there is $q \notin C_q$, then the target-set of $(Sp, \emptyset)$ is permanently empty.*

We £rst examine the next level candidate. Based on line 2 in Candidate-generator, the new candidate must be $(Spq, \emptyset)$. We note "for all" condition in the criterion. We can obtain $(SZp, \emptyset)$ in a recursive way. Hence the target-set of $(Sp, \emptyset)$ is permanently empty.

Here is an example to show how Criterion 2 works. Suppose that there are only three candidates $(abc, \emptyset)$, (abd, a) and (abe, a) beginning with $\{ab\}$ in 3-candidate set. Since item d is not in the target-set of (abd, a) and item e is not in the target-set of (abe, a), $(abc, \emptyset)$ has a permanently empty target-set according to Criterion 2 and hence is removed. Consequently, all its super candidates will not be generated.

3.3 More pruning

We have a pruning process in candidate generation, and will have another pruning process after counting the support of candidates. This is a key issue to make use of the con£dence for pruning and to have an ef£cient algorithm. In the following algorithm, σ is the minimum support, and $\{S \setminus c\}$ means set S less $\{c\}$.

Function Prune($l + 1$)
// $l + 1$ is the new level where candidates are counted.
1) for each candidate (S, C) in $(l + 1)$-candidate set
2)   if $P(S) \leq \sigma$ then remove candidate (S, C)
3)   else for each $c \in C$
        // test the satisfaction of the lemma
4)   if there is a sub candidate (S', C')
            in l-candidate set such that
              $c \in C'$ and $P(\{S \setminus c\} \neg c) = P(\{S' \setminus c\} \neg c)$
5)   then remove c from C
6)   if C is permanently empty then remove (S, C)

We prune a rule candidate from two aspects, the infrequency of the itemset and the permanently empty set of the target-set. In line 2 a candidate with infrequent itemset is removed. From line 3 to 6, we limit possible targets in the target-set of a candidate (a possible target is equivalent to a potential rule) by the lemma. In line 7 we consider removing a candidate when its target-set is empty.

For example, consider a candidate (abc, abc) in 3-candidate set. It includes three potential rules $ab \Rightarrow c$, $ac \Rightarrow b$ and $bc \Rightarrow a$. How can we omit some items from the target-set? The removal of an item in the target-set means that a potential rule and all its more speci£c rules are permanently removed. We do this according to the lemma. If we observe $P(ab \neg c) = P(a \neg c)$, then by the lemma rule $ab \Rightarrow c$ and all its more speci£c form rules are not in the informative rule set. As a result we remove item c from the target-set. The candidate should look like (abc, ab), and includes two potential rules, $bc \Rightarrow a$ and $ac \Rightarrow b$. The Candidate-generator ensures that item c never appears in target-sets of all super candidates of (abc, ab).

The determination of a permanently empty target-set has been introduced in the previous subsection, and hence we do not repeat them here. In our implementation, for convenience of applying Criterion 1, we call a candidate as *restricted* candidate if the support of its itemset equals to that of one of its sub itemsets. This restricted status is inheritable because $P(Sp) = P(S) \Longrightarrow P(SZp) = P(SZ)$. A super candidate inherits this status from any sub candidates. According to criterion 1, the target-set of a restricted candidate is permanently empty if it is empty. In addition, a restricted candidate also inherits the target-set from its sub candidate. According to the corollary we could not form any rules to be in the informative rule set if their righthand side items are not in the target-set of the candidate where the restricted status is from. Therefore, there is no need to extend the target-set of a restricted candidate.

3.4 DIG algorithm

Now we are able to present our algorithm for the informative rule set generation.

Algorithm DIG: Direct Interesting rule Generation
Input: data set D, the minimum support σ and the minimum interestingness threshold θ.
Output: an interesting rule set R

1) Set $R = \emptyset$
2) Count support of 1-itemsets and 2-itemsets by arrays
3) build 1 and 2-candidate sets
4) Prune 1 and 2- candidate sets
5) Select interesting rules to R
6) Generate 3-candidate set
7) While new candidate set is not empty
8)   Count support of itemsets for new candidates
9)   Prune candidates in the new candidate set
10)   Select interesting rules to R
11)   Generate next level candidate set
12)   Return rule set R

The minimum interestingness threshold θ can be set by any of 12 interestingness criteria discussed in Section 2. Two main functions are discussed in the previous subsections.

In the above algorithm, we use rule $\emptyset \Rightarrow c$ to prune 1-candidates. For example, if 80% customers buy bread when they shop in a supermarket, then rule, egg $\Rightarrow$ bread, with 75% con£dence states nothing new. Hence the rule is uninteresting. Rule $\emptyset \Rightarrow$ bread can prune those uninteresting rules. One may argue that that rule egg $\Rightarrow$ bread is interesting if it has very low con£dence, say 20%. In this case, we may formulate the rule as egg $\Rightarrow \neg$ bread, and call the rule as a negative rule. Interestingness of negative rules is beyond the discussions of this paper.

The correctness of this algorithm is guaranteed by the completeness of enumerating all itemsets by the £rst two lines of Candidate-generator and accurate forward pruning uninteresting rules by Lemma 1 and Corollary 1. Its time complexity is determined by the number of candidates, and so is its memory usage.

Please note line 9 in function Candidate-generator and line 6 in function Prune, not only are all super candidates of a candidate with the infrequent itemset removed, but also all super candidates of a candidate with a permanently empty target-set. Accordingly, DIG does not generate all frequent itemsets.

DIG is more ef£ciency than an association rule generation algorithm and its memory usage is smaller because it uses con£dence to prune uninteresting rules in addition to the support pruning.

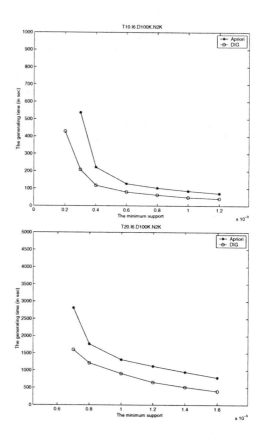

Figure 1. The comparison of time ef£ciency

4 Experimental results

In this section, we show the ef£ciency of DIG in the comparison with a well-known association rule generation algorithm, Apriori [1]. Though some association rules algorithms [11, 19, 24] are faster than Apriori, they usually use more memory to trade for faster speed. We note that in most applications, an association rule generation algorithm fails because it runs out of the computer memory. So we stick with Apriori, and will compare memory usage with Apriori.

Two test transactional data sets, T10.I6.D100K.N2K and T20.I6.D100K.N2K, are generated by the synthetic data generator from QUEST of IBM Almaden research center. Two data sets contain 1000 items and 100,000 transactions each. Our experiments were conducted on a Dell computer with 2G memory and a 2.4GHZ Intel processor running Red Hat Linux 7.3. Apriori is implemented with the storage structure of pre£x tree and so is DIG.

We £rst examine the time ef£ciency of DIG. It was compared against Apriori. The rule generation time of DIG and Apriori are listed in Figure 1. We can see that DIG is faster than Apriori and the ef£ciency improvement is more signif-icant when the support is low.

To demonstrate DIG improve ef£ciency without any additional memory consumption, we list the number of total candidates for different rule sets in Figure 2. We can see that DIG uses less memory than Apriori does. We also note that the time ef£ciency improvement is consistent with the candidate reduction. DIG searches less candidates for interesting rues. This is a major reason for ef£ciency improvement.

When we apply DIG to relational data sets, the ef£ciency improvement is much more signi£cant than to transactional data sets. This is because a relational data set is denser than a transactional data set and the lemma and corollary are more ef£cient in forward pruning. Importantly, DIG enables us to generate interesting rules in relational data with lower support than Apriori does.

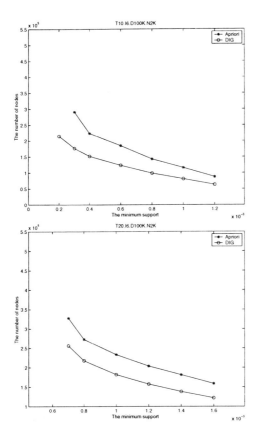

Figure 2. The comparison of memory eff-ciency

5 Related work

Association mining [1] has been studied for many years. Most research work has been on how to mine frequent itemsets efficiently since it is the base for association rule forming. Apriori [2] is a widely accepted approach. There are many other, like [17, 11, 19, 24]. Most of them use more memory to trade for faster speed. A comparison research was conducted in [25].

Many association rule generation algorithms undergo two stages. They first generate all frequent itemsets and then form rules among them. At the second stage, a large amount of rules are generated, and many of them are uninteresting. Much research focuses on how to select interesting rules, and many interestingness criteria are proposed, such as lift [22] (interest [6] or strength [9]), gain [10], conviction [6], p-s [18], and Laplace [7, 21]. A recent study on interestingness criteria is reported in [20]. Actually, all interestingness criteria only decrease the number of rules but do not increase the efficiency of rule mining.

Direct interesting rule generation algorithms, which do not generate all frequent itemsets first, can improve efficiency of association rule mining. A direct algorithm usually utilizes additional forward pruning besides support pruning. Closed itemset property, Chi-square and confidence (or laplace accuracy) have been used for such pruning.

Non-redundant association rule set generation [23], presented by M. Zaki, utilizes closed itemset properties for forward pruning. This pruning alone is not very efficient for rule generation on transactional data. Its effect is similar to the corollary in this paper, and we characterized the relationship between the non-redundant association rule set and the informative rule set in [14].

Upward closure property of chi-square was used to generate correlated association rule set [5] by S. Brin et al. This rule set is very meaningful and reveals correlation betweens items. However, both complexity and inaccuracy of chi-square test increase when the number of cells in a contingency table grows. In [8], a simplified chi-squared criterion is used, but generated rules are restricted to those with 1-itemset antecedents.

Confidence based pruning is used by R. Bayardo et al for generating constraint rule set [4] and optimality rule sets [3]. However, practical implication of these rule sets needs further clarification. Further, the presented rule generation algorithms are unsuitable for applications without constraint targets or with a large number of targets since they focus only on one fixed consequence at one time.

OPUS algorithms proposed by G. Webb to systematically search for rule sets also utilize a variant confidence, Laplace accuracy, for pruning[21]. These "optimal rule sets" are quite different from association rule based optimal rule sets since rules in an OPUS based rule set are generated in a AQ-like covering algorithm [15]. An OPUS algorithm scans a data set at least as many times as the number of rules. A modified OPUS algorithm [22] to generate association rules scans a data set as many times as the number of different antecedents in the generated rule set. As a result, it may not be efficient when a data set cannot be retained in the main memory.

This work is very similar to the above two studies in terms of confidence based pruning. However, the well-defined informative rule set has clear practical implication. The presented algorithm generates all rules with respect to all possible consequences once, and scans a data set only as many times as the length of the longest rule in the generated rule set. The algorithm presented in this paper works on both transactional and relational data sets, whereas algorithms of above two studies handle only relational data sets.

6 Conclusions

In this paper, we discussed properties of the informative rule set. We proved that all rules excluded by the informative rule set are uninteresting by 12 interestingness criteria and that excluded rules are forwardly prunable. These properties enabled us to design an ef£cient algorithm, DIG, to directly generate interesting rules. We showed experimentally that DIG is faster and uses less memory than Apriori. DIG avoids time consuming post pruning that an algorithm to generate interesting rules through an association rule set has to undergo.

References

[1] R. Agrawal, T. Imielinski, and A. Swami. Mining associations between sets of items in massive databases. In *Proc. of the ACM SIGMOD Int'l Conference on Management of Data*, pages 207–216, 1993.

[2] R. Agrawal and R. Srikant. Fast algorithms for mining association rules in large databases. In *Proceedings of the Twentieth International Conference on Very Large Databases*, pages 487–499, Santiago, Chile, 1994.

[3] R. Bayardo and R. Agrawal. Mining the most interesting rules. In *Proceedings of the Fifth ACM SIGKDD International Conference on Knowledge Discovery and Data Mining*, pages 145–154, N.Y., 1999. ACM Press.

[4] R. Bayardo, R. Agrawal, and D. Gunopulos. Constraint-based rule mining in large, dense database. In *Proc. of the 15th Int'l Conf. on Data Engineering*, pages 188–197, 1999.

[5] S. Brin, R. Motwani, and C. Silverstein. Beyond market baskets: Generalizing association rules to correlations. *SIGMOD Record (ACM Special Interest Group on Management of Data)*, 26(2):265, 1997.

[6] S. Brin, R. Motwani, J. D. Ullman, and S. Tsur. Dynamic itemset counting and implication rules for market basket data. In *Proceedings, ACM SIGMOD International Conference on Management of Data: SIGMOD 1997: May 13–15, 1997, Tucson, Arizona, USA*, volume 26(2), pages 255–264, NY, USA, 1997. ACM Press.

[7] P. Clark and R. Boswell. Rule induction with CN2: Some recent improvements. In *Machine Learning - EWSL-91*, pages 151–163, 1991.

[8] E. Cohen, M. Datar, S. Fujiwara, A. Gionis, P. Indyk, R. Motwani, J. Ullman, and C. Yang. Finding interesting associations without support pruning. In *16th International Conference on Data Engineering (ICDE' 00)*, pages 489–500, Washington - Brussels - Tokyo, 2000. IEEE.

[9] V. Dhar and A. Tuzhilin. Abstract-driven pattern discovery in databases. *IEEE Transactions on Knowledge and Data Engineering*, 5(6), 1993.

[10] T. Fukuda, Y. Morimoto, S. Morishita, and T. Tokuyama. Data mining using two-dimensional optimized association rules: scheme, algorithms, and visualization. In *Proceedings of the 1996 ACM SIGMOD International Conference on Management of Data, Montreal, Quebec, Canada, June 4–6, 1996*, pages 13–23, New York, 1996. ACM Press.

[11] J. Han, J. Pei, and Y. Yin. Mining frequent patterns without candidate generation. In *Proc. 2000 ACM-SIGMOD Int. Conf. on Management of Data (SIGMOD'00)*, pages 1–12, May, 2000.

[12] J. Li, H. Shen, and R. Topor. Mining the smallest association rule set for prediction. In *Proceedings of 2001 IEEE International Conference on Data Mining (ICDM 2001)*, pages 361–368. IEEE Computer Society Press, 2001.

[13] J. Li, H. Shen, and R. Topor. Mining the optimal class association rule set. *Knowledge-Based System*, 15(7):399–405, 2002.

[14] J. Li, H. Shen, and R. Topor. Mining informative rule set for prediction. *Journal of intelligent information systems*, in press.

[15] R. Michalski, I. Mozetic, J. Hong, and N. Lavrac. The AQ15 inductive learning system: an overview and experiments. In *Proceedings of IMAL 1986*, Orsay, 1986. Université de Paris-Sud.

[16] T. M. Mitchell. *Machine Learning*. McGraw-Hill, 1997.

[17] J. S. Park, M. Chen, and P. S. Yu. An effective hash based algorithm for mining association rules. In *ACM SIGMOD Intl. Conf. Management of Data*, 1995.

[18] G. Piatetsky-Shapiro. Discovery, analysis and presentation of strong rules. In G. Piatetsky-Shapiro, editor, *Knowledge Discovery in Databases*, pages 229–248. AAAI Press / The MIT Press, Menlo Park, California, 1991.

[19] P. Shenoy, J. R. Haritsa, S. Sudarshan, G. Bhalotia, M. Bawa, and D. Shah. Turbo-charging vertical mining of large databases. In *Proceedings of the ACM SIGMOD International Conference on Management of Data (SIGMOD-99)*, ACM SIGMOD Record 29(2), pages 22–33, Dallas, Texas, 1999. ACM Press.

[20] P. Tan, V. Kumar, and J. Srivastava. Selecting the right interestingness measure for association patterns. In *Proceedings of the eighth ACMKDD international conference on knowledge discovery and data mining*, pages 32 – 41, Edmonton, Canada, 2002. ACM press.

[21] G. I. Webb. OPUS: An ef£cient admissible algorithm for unordered search. In *Journal of Arti£cial Intelligence Research*, volume 3, pages 431–465, 1995.

[22] G. I. Webb. Ef£cient search for association rules. In *Proceedinmgs of the 6th ACM SIGKDD International Conference on Knowledge Discovery and Data Mining (KDD-00)*, pages 99–107, N. Y., 2000. ACM Press.

[23] M. J. Zaki. Generating non-redundant association rules. In *6th ACM SIGKDD International Conference on Knowledge Discovery and Data Mining*, pages 34–43, August 2000.

[24] M. J. Zaki, S. Parthasarathy, M. Ogihara, and W. Li. New algorithms for fast discovery of association rules. In *Proceedings of the Third International Conference on Knowledge Discovery and Data Mining (KDD-97)*, page 283. AAAI Press, 1997.

[25] Z. Zheng, R. Kohavi, and L. Mason. Real world performance of association rule algorithms. In *Proceedings of the seventh International Conference on Knowledge Discovery and Data Mining (SIGKDD-01)*, 2001.

Spatial Interest Pixels (SIPs): Useful Low-Level Features of Visual Media Data

Qi Li
Department of CIS
University of Delaware
qili@cis.udel.edu

Jieping Ye
Department of CS
University of Minnesota
jieping@cs.umn.edu

Chandra Kambhamettu
Department of CIS
University of Delaware
chandra@cis.udel.edu

Abstract

Visual media data such as an image is the raw data representation for many important applications. The biggest challenge in using visual media data comes from the extremely high dimensionality. We present a comparative study on spatial interest pixels (SIPs), including eight-way (a novel SIP miner), Harris, and Lucas-Kanade, whose extraction is considered as an important step in reducing the dimensionality of visual media data. With extensive case studies, we have shown the usefulness of SIPs as the low-level features of visual media data. A class-preserving dimension reduction algorithm (using GSVD) is applied to further reduce the dimension of feature vectors based on SIPs. The experiments showed its superiority over PCA.

1 Introduction

Visual media data such as an image is the raw data representation for many important applications, such as facial expression recognition [18, 29], face recognition [27, 20, 24], video classification [13], etc. The biggest challenge in using the visual media data comes from its extremely high dimensionality.

To reduce the dimensionality of visual media data, the first step is usually to extract the *low-level features*[1]. Color, texture, shape/contour are three types of low-level features frequently used [26, 3, 25, 7]. The use of interest pixels [2] (say corners, salient image points) has attracted attention [23, 15] because of their *repeatability* (an interest pixel found in one image can be found again in another if these two images are spatially similar to each other). Interested readers can further refer to [16, 12].

We study spatial interest pixels (SIPs) in this paper. Intuitively, a SIP is a pixel that has stronger interest strength than most of other pixels in an image. The interest strength is basically measured by the change in pixel values along different 2D directions (say horizontal, vertical, etc). We study three miners of SIPs, eight-way, Harris, and Lucas-Kanade. The latter two are commonly used in computer vision community [9, 17] (Harris is attracting more attention in image retrieval community [23]). Both Harris and Lucas-Kanade utilize the local change of pixel values along only two directions (left-to-right and top-to-bottom), and non-maximum suppression is applied to suppress the pixels that do not have the strongest interest strength within their neighborhood. Eight-way is a novel SIP miner that utilizes the local change of pixel values along eight directions (uniformly distributed from 0 to 360 degrees). The distributions of SIPs (over the regular grid of image plane) is then used as feature vectors for classification task.

The dimensionality of SIP distributions is still pretty high (it ranges from several hundreds to several thousands). A class-preserving dimension reduction algorithm is thus introduced to further reduce their dimensionality. The class-preserving dimension reduction algorithm is based on the generalized discriminant analysis. The difference between generalized discriminant analysis and classic linear discriminant analysis (LDA), also called Fisher discriminant analysis (FDA) [6], is the use of the trace optimization in the former. GSVD provides a convenient tool for generalized discriminant analysis.

To show the usefulness of SIPs as low-level features for visual media data, we present our results on universal facial expression recognition [5] and face recognition. We tested one facial expression dataset Jaffe[3][18], four face datasets, including Jaffe, Yale[4][2], AR1[5][19], and Stirling[6][8]. Our results are very encouraging (see Section 7). The classifier used in this paper is nearest neighbor [1].

---

[1]We will strictly distinct the term feature from the term feature vector in the context of media-based classification applications. The former means color, texture, shape and pixel, whereas the latter means the representation of an image/video instance that are ready to feed into some classifier.

[2]In the context of image retrieval or 3D computer vision, they are called *interest points*. Renaming them as interest pixels in the context of data mining is to avoid confusion between the image point and data point (i.e., feature vector).

[3]http://www.mis.atr.co.jp/~mlyons/jaffe.html
[4]http://cvc.yale.edu/projects/yalefaces/yalefaces.html
[5]http://rvl1.ecn.purdue.edu/~aleix/aleix_face_DB.html
[6]http://pics.psych.stir.ac.uk/

The rest of the paper is organized as follows: Section 2 presents the related work. Section 3 reviews Harris and Lucas-Kanade detectors, and presents a novel SIP miner. Section 4 is on SIP distributions. A class-preserving dimension reduction algorithm is presented in Section 5. Nearest neighbor as the unique classifier is briefly reviewed in Section 6. Section 7 presents three case studies on SIP feature vectors. Finally, we conclude our study on SIP and give a future work in Section 8.

2 Related work

[23] gave a survey on several interest pixel detectors. To evaluate the performance of an interest pixel detector, two criteria are used. One is the repeatability, and the other is entropy. The criterion of repeatability is important in our work, mostly for the usefulness of SIP distribution. We did not give quantitative measure of the repeatability of SIP in this paper (but the classification accuracy in case studies gives a qualitative measure of repeatability). Interested readers can find more details in [23]. [15] presented a wavelet based salient pixel detector. Their motivation comes from the multiresolution property of wavelet coefficients.

Principal component analysis (PCA) is a widely used dimension reduction [11]. PCA does not utilize the class label information of training data. The limitation of PCA can be overcome by introducing linear/Fisher discriminant analysis (LDA/FDA) [6] where within-class scatter and between-class scatter are used to refine the single global covariance matrix in PCA. The classic LDA involves the inverse computation of one scatter matrix. If that matrix is singular, classic LDA will fail. We consider the generalized discriminant analysis whose criterion is to minimize the ratio of the traces of within-class scatter to between-class scatter. Using generalized singular value decomposition (GSVD), we can derive a simple algorithm to solve the trace ratio minimization problem and thus achieve class-preserving dimension reduction. [22] have the similar work on GSVD-based discriminant analysis, but they did not explicitly define any global objective function.

Static universal facial expression recognition is still a hard problem. [29] obtained the accuracy of around 90% using 10-fold cross validation [7], Gabor wavelet coefficients at 34 manually extracted fiducial points as the feature vectors, neural network as the classifier, and Jaffe as the test dataset. With the same Gabor feature and same evaluation method used in [29], [18] applied LDA to Jaffe dataset and obtained the accuracy of 92%. The disadvantage of their method is that the feature vectors are essentially manually extracted.

---

[7]In 10-fold cross validation, an entire dataset will first be split into 10 pieces. Then the test will be run 10 times. In each time, 9 pieces are used as training data, and remaining one piece is used as test data. The final accuracy estimation is the mean estimation.

Intensive research on face recognition has been done in the past 30 years [27, 4, 20, 24]. It is beyond our ability to give an even relatively comprehensive view on the problem. Two surveys on face recognition [4, 30] can be excellent sources for the interested readers. The most recent work on the comparison between PCA and LDA can be found in [20] that used pixel values of face regions as feature vectors, nearest neighbor (in L_2-norm) as classifier, AR as the test dataset (AR is further split into several datasets). With different further split datasets, the accuracies range from 60% to 90%.

3 SIP miners

In this section, we will first review the Harris and Lucas-Kanade detectors, including the basic concept, algorithm implementation, and parameter setting. Based on another natural perspective in interpreting a spatial interest pixel, we then present the eight-way miner.

3.1 Harris and Lucas-Kanade

Given an image I and a pixel p, assume $I_x(p)$ and $I_y(p)$ are the derivatives at p along x and y axis. Both Harris detector and Lucas-Kanade detector are based on the gradient correction matrix of p defined as the following formula:

$$C(p) = \begin{pmatrix} \sum_{q \in O_p} w_q I_x^2(q) & \sum_{q \in O_p} w_q I_x(q) I_y(q) \\ \sum_{q \in O_p} w_q I_x(q) I_y(q) & \sum_{q \in O_p} w_q I_y^2(q) \end{pmatrix},$$
(3.1)

where O_p is a square neighborhood of p, and $(w_q)_{q \in O_p}$ is a 2D-smoothing filter used to weight the derivatives.

In Harris detector, the interest strength of pixel p is defined to be the summation of the eigenvalues of $C(p)$. To save the computational time, the following equivalent form is more commonly used in practice [23]:

$$\text{strengh}(p) = \det(C(p)) - \alpha \text{trace}^2(C(p)),$$
(3.2)

where α is a discriminant factor that is usually set to be 0.6 [23]. In Lucas-Kanade detector, the interest strength of p is defined to be the minimal eigenvalue of $C(p)$. After the interest strength of each pixel in an image is computed, all pixels will be sorted according to their strength, and the h pixels with highest interest strength will be chosen as the SIPs. To spread out the SIPs, *non-maximum suppression* is applied. More specifically, for each pixel p, we compare its interest strength and the interest strength of its neighboring pixels (usually defined to be those pixels in a small square window (say 3×3) centered by p; if it is not the maximum, then its strength is reset to be zero (i.e., be suppressed).

Note that using the gradient correlation matrix of the derivatives rather than the derivatives themselves to decide the interest strength of a pixel is to earn the invariance to image orientation.

Even though the algorithm implementation of Harris detector and Lucas-Kanade detector is simple, their parameter setting plays more important roles. There are two versions on the parameter setting of Harris detector (more details can be found in [23]). In the standard Harris, the derivative I_x or I_y is computed by convolution with the mask [-2,-1,0,1,2], and the filter used in weighting the derivatives is a Gaussian ($\sigma = 2$). In an improved version of Harris [23], I_x or I_y are computed by replacing the [-2,-1,0,1,2] mask by derivatives of a Gaussian ($\sigma = 1$). The improved version of Harris detector is found to mine the interest pixels with highest repeatability in the comparative study in [23] In our case studies, we will use the improved version of Harris. We now summarize the Harris and Lucas-Kanade detectors as Algorithm 1:

Algorithm 1 Harris/Lucas-Kanade SIP miner

Input: An image

Output: SIPs

1. Compute the image gradient
2. For each pixel p
    2.1. Form matrix $C(p)$ by formula (3.1)
    2.2. (Harris) Strength is assigned according to formula (3.2)
    2.2′. (Lucas-Kanade) Strength is assigned by the smaller eigenvalue of $C(p)$
3. Non-maximum suppression
4. Choose the first n pixels of largest strength

3.2 Eight-way

Intuitively, if a pixel is spatially interesting, its rich information may not be sufficiently covered by the derivatives along two directions. Fig. 1 demos three typical and simplified cases that a SIP may look like. The changes of pixel values significantly across the edge/boundary, but changes slightly within a same region. A long (short) arrow shows the large (small) derivative magnitude along the direction of the arrow. The common ground of these three cases is that these pixels (expected to be SIPs) have a majority of long arrows (i.e., the numbers of long arrows are always more than 4). This observation gives us a new interpretation of SIP: *if the number of strong derivative is larger than 4, then the pixel is a good candidate of SIP and will be assigned a derivative-related value as interest strength; otherwise it will be assigned zero strength.* To distinguish between a large derivative and a small derivative, we first compute the mean of eight derivatives and then claim those above the mean to be large ones. The relatively challenging part in the above definition of SIP is the assignment of interest strength. Apparently, we at least have two options: one is maximal derivative, and the other is the mean derivative. We currently choose the first option based on the visual evaluation of the distribution of SIPs in several experiments of face images.

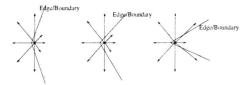

Figure 1. Three typical cases showing the asymmetry of SIPs

Figure 2. The symmetry of pixels near an edge/boundary.

Fig. 2 shows that the eight-way SIP miner has strong ability in discriminating an edgel from a SIP because an edgel has equal number of long arrows and short arrows. So non-maximum suppression is not necessary for eight-way miner. It is good for SIP mining because non-maximum suppression involves local uncertainty. Algorithm 2 summarizes eight-way SIP miner.

Algorithm 2 Eight-way SIP miner

Input: An image

Output: SIPs

1. For each pixel p
    1.1. For each of eight directions
        1.1.1. Compute the change of along that direction (by convolving a Gaussian first derivative)
    1.2. Compute the mean change
    1.3. Count the number of changes above mean change
    1.4. If the count is larger than 4
        strength is assigned to be the largest change
        otherwise
        strength is set to 0
2. Choose the first h pixels of largest strength

3.3 SIP Examples

Fig. 3 shows the 300 SIPs found by applying the three SIP miners, eight-way miner, improved version of Harris detector (for convenience, we will still call it Harris in the rest of the paper), and Lucas-Kanade detector, on two different face images (namely, KA and KL that are taken from Jaffe dataset).

Let us first consider the SIPs on KA (in the first row).

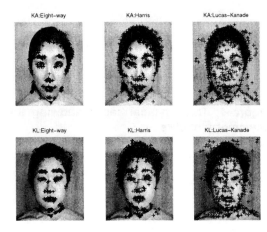

Figure 3. SIPs found by applying eight-way, Harris, and Lucas-Kanade detector on two different faces, namely KA and KL.

The SIPs found by eight-way are mostly located near the facial features (say eye, mouth, etc) of KA's face. Among the SIPs found by Harris, there are many located along some edges/boundaries (of large brightness contrast). Among the SIPs found by Lucas-Kanade, there are many of them located at "non-intent" regions, say not only at the edge/boundary, but also at the regions that have small brightness contrast. However, we should not be too disappointed by the visual performance of Lucas-Kanade detector. Even though it is not competitive enough against eight-way or Harris when it is individually used in case studies, it has been found to be helpful in improving the classification accuracies when the SIPs found by Lucas-Kanade are combined with eight-way or Harris, or both (by concatenating their distributions).

We can observe that the SIPs (of KA and KL) found by eight-way or Harris are mostly distributed around the facial features (say eye, nose, etc). Comparing the SIPs distributions in columns (between different classes), we will have the expectation that the first two pairs are more discriminant than the third pair (contributed by Lucas-Kanade).

4 Distribution of SIPs

A SIP distribution (of an image) represents the number of occurrence of SIPs in each fixed small block of an image. Using regular (rectangle) grids is a simple method to split an image region in multiple blocks.

There are two important parameters in order to build a good SIP distribution. One parameter is the number of SIPs to be used, and the other is the size of rectangle grids. For a general view on distribution construction, more SIPs leads to more accurate distribution. But in practice, we may need some compromise between the accuracy and computation

cost. In our study, we found that 300 SIPs of an image are usually sufficient to build a "good" distribution representation (500 SIPs can contribute slightly better representation).

Another important parameter is the size of rectangle grids. A basic principle in deciding the size of rectangle grids is that: *it should be small enough to accurately characterize the local information.* We use 4×8 as the size of rectangle grids (except for Yale dataset where 16×16 is used). Remind that an image plane is usually a rectangle. The distribution representation is not invariant to image translation/video temporal shift. However, if the visual media data is aligned, SIP distribution can then faithfully represent its essential content/information. The face images in many datasets are aligned, thus can be used directly as our case studies.

We now complete the discussion of SIP distribution with its algorithm implementation:

Algorithm 3 Distribution of SIPs: get_dist()

Input: SIPs of one image (obtained from some SIP miner)
Output: SIP distribution: dist
1. Initialize the grid size (g_1, g_2)
2. For each SIP $p = (p_x, p_y)$
   2.1 dist($[p_x/g_1], [p_y/g_2]$)++
3. Align the dist from a matrix to a vector

Fig. 4 shows the feature vectors of the face images of KA and KL (given in Fig. 3). Consistently with the visual measurement, the SIP distribution contributed by eight-way has richer "structure", whereas, the structure of Lucas-Kanade is the flattest one.

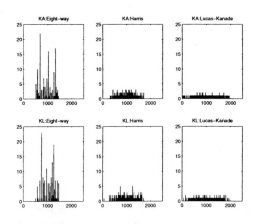

Figure 4. The SIP distributions of eight-way, Harris, and Lucas-Kanade of the face images, KA and KL.

5 Class-preserving dimension reduction

A general dimension reduction problem is formulated as follows: Given a data matrix $A \in R^{m \times n}$, where each column corresponds to a data point, to find a linear transformation $G^T \in R^{\ell \times m}$ that maps each column a_i, for $1 \leq i \leq n$, of A in the m dimensional space to a column y_i in the ℓ dimension space:

$$G^T : a_i \in R^{m \times 1} \to y_i \in R^{\ell \times 1}. \qquad (5.3)$$

In this section, we will study the class-preserving dimension reduction. The class information is known and the data matrix A is formulated by: $A = [A_1 \quad A_2 \quad \cdots \quad A_k]$, where k is the number of classes, and $\sum_{i=1}^{k} n_i = n$, and $A_i \in R^{m \times n_i}$, is collection of data points in i-th class. We will first have a brief review on classic LDA, and then formulate an objective/energy function for reduction transformation G^T using the ratio of the traces of within-class scatter, and between-class scatter in low dimension space. Similar work has been done in [22], where no explicit global objective function is defined.

5.1 Classic LDA

In classic LDA, two scatter matrices, within-class scatter matrix S_w, and between-class scatter matrix S_b are defined to quantify the quality of the classes, as follows,

$$S_w = H_w H_w^T, \quad S_b = H_b H_b^T. \qquad (5.4)$$

where

$$\begin{aligned} H_w &= [A_1 - c^{(1)}(e^{(1)})^T, \cdots, A_k - c^{(k)}(e^{(k)})^T] \in R^{m \times n}, \\ H_b &= [\sqrt{n_1}(c^{(1)} - c), \cdots, \sqrt{n_k}(c^{(k)} - c)] \in R^{m \times k}, \qquad (5.5) \end{aligned}$$

and the centroid $c^{(i)}$ of the ith class is defined as $c^{(i)} = \frac{1}{n_i} A_i e^{(i)}$ where $e^{(i)} = (1, 1, \cdots, 1)^T \in R^{n_i \times 1}$, and the global centroid c is defined as $c = \frac{1}{n} A e$ where $e = (1, 1, \cdots, 1)^T \in R^{n \times 1}$.

Classic LDA finds transformation G^T as eigenvectors (associated with the smallest eigenvalues) of matrix $S_b^{-1} S_w$, which requires S_b to be nonsingular.

5.2 Dimension reduction by optimizing trace ratio

A way to overcome the requirement of nonsingular scatters in classic LDA is using the trace ratio. Assume N_i be the set of column indices that belong to the ith class. Let us first have a look at what are the traces of within-class and between-class scatter matrices of original data:

$$\begin{aligned} \text{trace}(S_w) &= \sum_{i=1}^{k} \sum_{j \in N_i} (a_j - c^{(i)})^T (a_j - c^{(i)}) \\ &= \sum_{i=1}^{k} \sum_{j \in N_i} ||a_j - c^{(i)}||^2 \qquad (5.6) \\ \text{trace}(S_b) &= \sum_{i=1}^{k} n_i (c^{(i)} - c)^T (c^{(i)} - c) \\ &= \sum_{i=1}^{k} n_i ||c^{(i)} - c||^2. \qquad (5.7) \end{aligned}$$

So $\text{trace}(S_w)$ and $\text{trace}(S_b)$ characterize the closeness of the points within a class, and the separation between classes separately. Thus, small $\text{trace}(S_w)$ and large $\text{trace}(S_b)$ are desirable in order to achieve good classification rates in real applications.

Denote $S_w^L = (G^T H_w)(G^T H_w)^T = G^T H_w H_w^T G = G^T S_w G$. Similarly, we have the between-class covariance matrices $S_b^L = G^T S_b G$. The goal of a class-preserving dimension reduction is thus to find a reduction transformation G^T to minimize the ratio of the traces of scatter matrices S_w^L and S_b^L, i.e.,

$$\min F(G) = \frac{\text{trace}(S_w^L)}{\text{trace}(S_b^L)}. \qquad (5.8)$$

We can solve the trace optimization problem (5.8) using the generalized singular value decomposition (GSVD) [14]. Denote $K = [H_b, H_w]$. The GSVD on the matrix pair (H_b^T, H_w^T), will give orthogonal matrices $U \in R^{k \times k}$, $V \in R^{n \times n}$, and a nonsingular matrix $X \in R^{m \times m}$, such that

$$\begin{bmatrix} U & 0 \\ 0 & V \end{bmatrix}^T K X = \begin{bmatrix} \Sigma_1 & 0 \\ \Sigma_2 & 0 \end{bmatrix}. \qquad (5.9)$$

where $\Sigma_1 = \begin{bmatrix} I_b & 0 & 0 \\ 0 & D_b & 0 \\ 0 & 0 & 0_b \end{bmatrix}$, and $\Sigma_2 = \begin{bmatrix} 0_w & 0 & 0 \\ 0 & D_w & 0 \\ 0 & 0 & I_w \end{bmatrix}$.

Here $I_b \in R^{r \times r}$ is an identity matrix with $r = \text{rank}(K) - \text{rank}(H_b^T)$, $D_b = \text{diag}(\alpha_{r+1}, \cdots, \alpha_{r+s})$, and $D_w = \text{diag}(\beta_{r+1}, \cdots, \beta_{r+s}) \in R^{s \times s}$, are diagonal matrices with $s = \text{rank}(H_b) + \text{rank}(H_w) - \text{rank}(K)$, satisfying $1 > \alpha_{r+1} \geq, \cdots, \geq \alpha_{r+s} > 0, 0 < \beta_{r+1} \leq, \cdots, \leq \beta_{r+s} < 1$, and $\alpha_i^2 + \beta_i^2 = 1$ for $i = r + 1, \cdots, r + s$.

Denote u_{ii} is the ii-th term of the matrix $X^{-1} G G^T X^T$. Trace optimization problem (5.8) can be re-formulated as the following problem:

$$\text{minimize} \quad \text{trace}(S_w^L) = \sum_{i=1}^{t} u_{ii} - 1$$

$$\text{subject to} \quad \text{trace}(S_b^L) = \sum_{i=1}^{r} u_{ii} + \sum_{i=r+1}^{r+s} \alpha_i^2 u_{ii} = 1. \qquad (5.10)$$

We now present a novel result in Thm 5.1. Limited by the space, we refer the readers to our technical report [28] for the details of proof. A simple algorithm to compute GSVD can be found in [22], based on [21]. GSVD is also provided in Matlab software. Our class-preserving dimension reduction algorithm is summarized in Algorithm 4. The time/space complexity of PCA and LDA/GSVD is essentially the same to each other, as shown in Table 1. More details can be found in [28].

Theorem 5.1 *If $\{u_{ii}^{\star}\}_{i=1}^{m}$ is an optimal solution of the optimization problem (5.10), then $u_{ii}^{\star} \geq u_{jj}^{\star}$, for $1 \leq i \leq j \leq r + s$.*

Algorithm 4 GSVD based dimension reduction

Input: High dimension feature vectors of training data

Ouput: Reduction transformation G^T

Main variables:

H_b- between-class covariance matrix

H_w- within-class covariance matrix

G^T- reduction transformation

1. Construct the matrices H_b and H_w as defined in (5.5)
2. Compute GSVD on the matrix pair (H_b^T, H_w^T), and get the matrix X as in (5.9).
3. Compute rank(H_b) and assign it to u
4. Let X_u^T be the first u columns of X
5. Assign transformation matrix $G^T = X_u^T$

Methods	Time Complexity	Space Complexity
PCA	$O(m^2 n)$	$O(nm)$
LDA/GSVD	$O((m+k)^2 n)$	$O(nm)$

Table 1. Complexity comparison: n is the number of training data points, m is the number of the dimensions, and k is the number of classes.

6 Classifier: nearest neighbor

Nearest neighbor classifier is used in our case studies, which is quite simple. Given a set of training data points (that are labeled) and a query data point, we compute the distance (or similarity) between the query data point to each training points. The query data point is annotated as the same class label as the one which has the shortest distance to the query point.

Given two data points, $q = (q_1, q_2, \cdots, q_d)$ and a point $q = (q_1', q_2', \cdots, q_d')$ in R^d, their distance can be measured by the L_p-norm, i.e., $L_p(q, q') = \left[\sum_{i=1}^d |q_i - q_i'|^m \right]^{1/p}$. L_2-norm (i.e., Euclidean distance) is the most widely used metric because of its convenient analytic properties (note that the GSVD-based class-preserving dimension reduction assumes Euclidean distance because of the trace optimization). However the robust statistic literature shows that L_2 overly penalizes outliers [10]. So in our case studies, we will try different L_p-norms on the space of SIP distributions, whereas apply L_2-norm in the Eigenspace or Fisherspace[8]. Our experiments will show that $p < 1$ does outperform Euclidean distance. Using the sub-sample pixel values of images as feature vector, [24] also observed the superiority of $p < 1$ in face recognition task.

7 Case studies

In this section, we present two case studies on the visual media data based classification using SIP feature vectors. They are static facial expression recognition, and face

[8]Eigenspace and Fisherspace refers to the reduced spaces via PCA and LDA (either classic or generalized) respectively.

recognition. 10-fold cross validation method is used to estimate the classification accuracy.

The results on one dataset are presented in one table. To present the results compactly, we will use the following simplified notations: e = eight-way SIP distribution, shortly e = eight-way; Similarly, h = Harris; l = Lucas-Kanade; e+h = eight-way concatenated by Harris; e+l = eight-way concatenated by Lucas-Kanade; h+l = Harris concatenated by Lucas-Kanade; all = the concatenation of three distributions. The values appearing in the first row of tables are the norm index for nearest neighbor classifier. The first column of the result tables will be indexed by these simplified notations. The last two columns are the classification accuracy (in percentage) based on the high-level features extracted by the PCA dimension reduction and our class-preserving dimension reduction. They are used only in Euclidean space because trace optimization is based on L_2-norm. With the left three columns, we can analyze what norm is good at measuring SIP distributions. With the right two columns, we can analyze how well the dimension reduction techniques work.

Each table will present the answers for the following four questions:

1. What is the best SIP miner (by comparing the best accuracies that they can reach in individual use)?
2. Which L_p-norm performs the best?
3. What is the best accuracy?
4. How well do PCA and the class-preserving dimension reduction (denoted by C-P) work?

For the convenience of reading, we highlight/underline the answers for the first three questions in each table. The overall conclusion on all experiments will be given the next section.

7.1 Datasets

We have one dataset for universal facial expression recognition, and four datasets for face recognition. Jaffe was originally built for the study of static facial expression recognition [18], but will also be used for face recognition in our case study. There are little variation in translation, pose, occlusion and lighting. Jaffe contains 10 female faces, 7 universal facial expressions, and all together 210 image instances. So when it is used as a dataset for facial expression recognition, each class has 30 instances; when it is used as a dataset for face recognition, each class has 21 instances. In either application context, there are always some image instances visually very similar to each other, which objectively creates the opportunity of achieving high accuracy on this dataset.

The images in Yale face dataset have the variations in facial expressions (as well as Jaffe) in addition to illumination. The publicly available Yale face dataset is aligned to some degree but not perfectly. Yale dataset contains 15

Figure 5. Yale, Stirling, AR1 each have two samples

classes/faces and each face has 11 instances. The major variation in Stirling face images is pose and color. Stirling contains 659 face images. We use the first 100 images (of 10 classes) in our case studies. The last face dataset we will test is named AR whose images contains the variations in occlusion and facial expressions. AR is a huge dataset of face images. We use the first 100 images (of 9 classes)in our case studies.

Fig. 5 shows some examples of the face image datasets, Yale, Stirling and AR1. The dimensions of the SIP feature vectors of these four datasets are 2048, 336, 1100 and 3577 respectively. Note that LDA (either classic or generalized) always reduces the original dimensionality to the number of classes minus 1. Thus The reduced dimensions in our case studies are 9, 14, 9, and 8 respectively.

7.2 Case study 1: Static universal facial expression recognition

Tab.2 shows the classification accuracies on Jaffe as a facial expression dataset. Without using the class information of training data, PCA was found to severely degrade the accuracies by using the SIP distributions, whereas C-P can approximate the accuracies very well.

7.3 Case study 2: Face recognition

Tab. 3, 4, 5 and 6 show the classification accuracies on Jaffe, Yale, Stirling and AR1 dataset respectively. PCA usually degrades the accuracy downfrom 15% to 25%, whereas the class-preserving dimension reduction preserves (either slightly degrades or slightly increases) the accuracies by using SIP distributions.

8 Conclusion and future work

In this paper, we present a comparative study on the spatial interest pixels (SIPs). With extensive experiments, we

SIPs	1/2	3/4	**1**	2	2 PCA	2 C-P
e	81.2	81.6	82.0	81.2	60.2	79.5
h	78.0	79.5	78.3	77.4	54.6	77.6
l	67.2	68.0	68.2	67.0	47.3	65.2
e+h	89.1	90.6	91.5	89.1	66.2	86.2
e+l	81.5	82.3	83.0	82.3	61.4	80.5
h+l	88.5	90.2	91.5	89.1	66.2	86.2
all	89.2	91.4	**91.9**	90.0	66.7	87.6

Table 2. Classification accuracy on Jaffe as a facial expression recognition dataset.

SIPs	**1/2**	**3/4**	**1**	**2**	2 PCA	2 C-P
e	99.5	99.5	98.1	94.8	78.3	98.6
h	96.2	99.5	99.5	99.5	84.2	99.1
l	99.1	99.1	98.6	98.6	81.6	98.1
e+h	99.5	99.5	99.5	96.7	79.2	99.1
e+l	99.5	99.5	99.1	96.2	80.5	99.5
h+l	99.5	99.5	99.5	99.5	82.3	98.6
all	**99.5**	**99.5**	**99.5**	**99.5**	83.8	99.1

Table 3. Classification accuracy on Jaffe as face recognition dataset.

SIPs	1/2	**3/4**	1	2	2 PCA	2 C-P
e	88.7	90.0	90.7	85.3	82.5	82.0
h	90.7	91.3	91.3	88.6	86.0	90.0
l	85.3	85.3	87.3	89.0	85.3	83.3
e+h	94.7	94.8	94.7	89.0	86.0	91.3
e+l	94.0	95.3	95.3	89.3	88.7	92.7
h+l	94.7	94.7	94.1	92.7	90.7	91.3
all	95.3	**96.0**	94.7	90.0	88.0	93.3

Table 4. Classification accuracy on YALE dataset as face recognition.

SIPs	1/2	**3/4**	**1**	2	2 PCA	2 C-P
e	93.8	95.0	93.8	86.3	78.2	86.3
h	88.8	87.5	85.0	83.8	75.2	92.5
l	60.0	62.5	61.2	56.2	48.5	61.2
e+h	93.8	95.0	95.0	93.8	85.0	95.0
e+l	93.8	95.0	93.8	86.3	79.2	93.8
h+l	81.3	81.3	82.5	82.5	74.8	86.2
all	93.8	**95.0**	**95.0**	93.8	85.0	95.0

Table 5. Classification accuracy on Stirling sub dataset (first 100 images 10 classes).

SIPs	**1/2**	**3/4**	1	2	2 PCA	2 C-P
e	92.0	95.0	92.0	87.0	69.0	93.0
h	90.0	93.0	93.0	93.0	72.0	92.0
l	86.0	88.0	87.0	83.0	65.0	85.0
e+h	94.0	94.0	95.0	95.0	74.0	95.0
e+l	94.0	95.0	96.0	89.0	68.0	93.0
h+l	96.0	96.0	96.0	93.0	72.0	95.0
all	**98.0**	**98.0**	96.0	96.0	70.0	95.0

Table 6. Classification accuracy on AR1 (first 100 instances, 8 classes).

have shown that SIPs are useful low-level features for visual media data. The best classification accuracies on these applications we can achieve are either higher than or close to those in the literature.

With the comparative study on different applications, we have the following overall conclusions on the use of SIP features (mainly on SIP distributions):

- Eight-way SIP miner is statistically the best. Among the 5 experiments/Tables, eight-way wins 3 times, ties one time (with Harris), and loses one time

- SIP distributions contributed by different SIP miner can be concatenated together into longer feature vectors that are more useful for different applications.

- The best distance measure in SIP feature vector space is L_p-norm with $p < 1$, In static facial expression recognition and face recognition, $p = 0.75$ are usually the "best" (among the four options provided in this paper).

- The GSVD-based dimension reduction can essentially preserve the classification accuracy on SIP feature vectors. It distinctly outperforms PCA dimension reduction.

In the future, we will study spatial-temporal interest pixel to reduce the dimensionality of video data.

References

[1] S. Arya. Nearest neighbor searching and applications. In *Ph. D. Thesis, University of Maryland, College Park, MD*, 1995.

[2] P. Belhumeur, J. Hespanha, and D. Kriegman. Eigenfaces vs. fisherfaces: Recognition using class specific linear projection. *IEEE TPAMI*, 19(7):711–720, 1997.

[3] J. Bergen and M. Landy. Computational modeling of visual texture segregation. In *Computational Models of Visual Perception*, pages 253–271. MIT Press, Cambridge MA, 1991., 1991.

[4] R. Chellappa, C. Wilson, and S. Sirohey. Human and machine recognition of faces: A survey. *Proceedings of the IEEE*, 83(5):705–740, 1995.

[5] P. Ekman and W. Friesen. Pictures of facial affect. In *Consulting psychologist, Palo Alto, CA*, 1976.

[6] R. Fisher. The use of multiple measurements in taxonomic problems. In *Annals of Eugenics 7*, pages 179–188, 1936.

[7] T. Gevers and A. W. M. Smeulders. Image indexing using composite color and shape invariant features. In *ICCV*, pages 576–581.

[8] P. Hancock, A. Burton, and V. Bruce. Face processing : Human perception and principal components analysis. In *Memory Cognition, 24*, pages 26–40, 1996.

[9] C. Harris and M. Stephens. A combined corner and edge detector. In *Proc. 4th Alvey Vision Conference, Manchester*, pages 147–151, 1988.

[10] P. Huber. *Robust Statistics*. Wiley, 1981.

[11] I. Jolliffe. Principle component analysis. *Journal of Educational Psychology*, 24:417–441, 1986.

[12] D. Joyce, P. lewis, R. Tansley, M. Dobie, and W. Hall. Semiotics and agents for integrating and navigating through multimedia representations of concepts. In *Proceedings of SPIE Vol. 3972, Storage and Retrieval for Media Databases 2000*, pages 132–143, 2000.

[13] W.-H. Lin and A. Hauptmann. News video classification using svm-based multimodal classifiers and combination strategies. In *ACM Multimedia, Juan-les-Pins, France*, 2002.

[14] C. V. Loan. Generalizing the singular value decomposition. *SIAM Journal on Numerical Analysis*, 13(1):76–83, 1976.

[15] E. Loupias and N. Sebe. Wavelet-based salient points for image retrieval. In *RR 99.11, Laboratoire Reconnaissance de Formes et Vision, INSA Lyon*, November 1999.

[16] Y. Lu, C. Hu, X. Zhu, H. Zhang, and Q. Yang. A unified framework for semantics and feature based relevance feedback in image retrieval systems. In *ACM Multimedia*, pages 31–37, 2000.

[17] B. D. Lucas and T. Kanade. An iterative image registration technique with an application to stereo vision. In *International Joint Conference on Artificial Intelligence*, pages 674–679, 1981.

[18] M. Lyons, J. Budynek, and S. Akamatsu. Automatic classification of single facial images. *IEEE transcations on PAMI*, 21(12):1357–1362, 1999.

[19] A. Martinez and R. Benavente. The ar face database. Technical Report CVC Tech. Report No. 24, 1998.

[20] A. Martinez and A. Kak. PCA versus LDA. *IEEE TPAMI*, 23(2):228–233, 2001.

[21] C. Paige and M.A.Saunders. Towards a generalized singular value decomposition. *SIAM Journal on Numerical Analysis*, 18:398–405, 1981.

[22] H. Park, P. Howland, and M. Jeon. Cluster structure preserving dimension reduction based on the generalized singular value decomposition. *SIAM Journal on Matrix Analysis and Applications*, to appear.

[23] C. Schmid, R. Mohr, and C. Bauckhage. Evaluation of interest point detectors. *International Journal of Computer Vision*, 37(2):151–172, 2000.

[24] T. Sim, R. Sukthankar, M. Mullin, and S. Baluja. Memory-based face recognition for visitor identification. In *Proc. 4th Intl. Conf. on FG'00*, pages 214–220.

[25] J. Smith. Integrated spatial and feature image systems: Retrieval and compression. In *PhD thesis, Graduate School of Arts and Sciences, Columbia University, New York, NY*, 1997.

[26] M. Swain and D. Ballard. Color indexing. *Int. J. computer vision*, 7:11–32, 1991.

[27] M. Turk and A. Pentland. Eigenfaces for recognition. *Journal of Cognitive Neuroscience*, 3(1):71–86, 1991.

[28] J. Ye, R. Janardan, C. park, and H. Park. A new optimization criterion for generalized discriminant analysis on undersampled problems. Technical Report TR-026-03, 2003.

[29] Z. Zhang. Feature-based facial expression recognition: experiments with a multi-layer perceptron. *Int.l Journal of Pattern Recognition and Artificial Intelligence*, 13(6):893–911, 1999.

[30] W. Zhao, R. Chellappa, A. Rosenfeld, and P. Phillips. Face recognition: A literature survey. Technical Report CAR-TR-948, 2000.

Unsupervised Link Discovery in Multi-relational Data via Rarity Analysis

Shou-de Lin
Computer Science Department
University of Southern California
sdlin@isi.edu

Hans Chalupsky
Information Sciences Institute
University of Southern California
hans@isi.edu

Abstract

A significant portion of knowledge discovery and data mining research focuses on finding patterns of interest in data. Once a pattern is found, it can be used to recognize satisfying instances. The new area of link discovery requires a complementary approach, since patterns of interest might not yet be known or might have too few examples to be learnable. This paper presents an unsupervised link discovery method aimed at discovering unusual, interestingly linked entities in multi-relational datasets. Various notions of rarity are introduced to measure the "interestingness" of sets of paths and entities. These measurements have been implemented and applied to a real-world bibliographic dataset where they give very promising results.

1. Introduction

Link discovery is a relatively new form of data mining with the goal of automatically identifying abnormal or threatening activities in large and heterogeneous data sets. Mooney et al. [10] describe it as the task of "identifying known, complex, multi-relational patterns that indicate potentially threatening activities in large amounts of relational data." Under this view of link discovery, once a pattern of interest is known or has been learned, a sophisticated pattern matcher can use it to detect satisfying instances in the data. The match process is usually difficult given the scale, heterogeneity, distribution, incompleteness and corruption of the data. Its biggest limitation is, however, that it can only detect instances of known patterns and cannot cope with previously unknown or evolving patterns of interest. Senator [17] describes link discovery more broadly as the process of looking for "evidence of known patterns and, perhaps more important, for unexplainable connections that may indicate previously unknown but significant connections, representing, for example, a new group, threat, or capability." It is this requirement for being able to discover novel, previously unknown kinds of links that motivated the work presented in this paper. We will call

this requirement the *novel link discovery* (NLD) problem to distinguish it from the overall or more traditional pattern-based link discovery problem (LD).

In the following we describe an unsupervised link discovery approach based on rarity analysis to address the NLD problem. Unsupervised link discovery is different from traditional link discovery from an input/output perspective. A traditional LD program takes multi-relational evidence data and a set of learned patterns as inputs and produces (usually partial) instantiations of the patterns as results. For example, given some police evidence database and a pattern description of contract murders, the program will try to detect and report instances of such murder events. An unsupervised link discovery program takes the same evidence data as input but does not use any pattern information. Instead of pattern instantiations, the results are any interesting connections found in the evidence data based on some model of "interestingness". For example, given the same evidence database the result might be a list of interesting connections between certain criminals or gangs.

Traditionally, knowledge discovery and data mining research focuses on discovering and extracting previously unknown, valid, novel, potentially useful and understandable patterns from lower-level data [20]. Such patterns can be represented as association rules, classification rules, clusters, sequential patterns, time series, contingency tables, etc [9]. Identifying "interesting" information in large, multi-relational data sets without using a pattern, on the other hand, has not received much attention at all. We argue, however, that patterns and rules are not the only things that should be mined from data sets, and that some version of unsupervised, pattern-free link discovery is necessary to handle the NLD problem.

The next section describes the problem and underlying assumptions in more detail. Section 3 defines different rarity measures and how they can be applied to NLD problems. Section 4 describes experiments performed to validate the proposed rarity measures, Section 5 describes related work and in the last section we conclude with a discussion and future work.

2. The problem

In this paper we focus on discovering "interesting" paths and nodes from data that can be represented as sets of entities connected by a set of binary relations. In other words, each object in the data set is treated as a separate entity and there are different types of binary relations connecting these entities. This kind of data can naturally be represented by a labeled graph such as the one shown in Figure 1 where nodes stand for entities and links for binary relations. For example, social network data [16] or Web-pages with proper classification on hyperlinks can be represented in this way. We also assume that the data employs a rich vocabulary of relations where different link types represent different semantic relationships. For example, we have different links representing that "X wrote a letter to Y" or that "X is the brother of Y". Therefore, different graphs with identical structure will usually have very different meanings depending on the types of links involved.

Given these assumptions, we define the following three classes of NLD problems addressed by our approach:

(1) *Novel path discovery:* given an arbitrary pair of entities in a graph, find the most interesting or novel paths between them.

(2) *Novel loop discovery:* given an arbitrary entity in a graph, find the most interesting or novel loops starting and ending at it.

(3) *Significant node discovery:* given an arbitrary entity in a graph, find other entities that are most significantly connected to it. For example, given some person A, find the set of people that A is most significantly connected to.

2.1 Challenges in novel link discovery

The first challenge of the NLD problem is that the term "novelty" or "interestingness" is user dependent. Each person might view data from different angles and, thus, which connections interest them varies. A good NLD program should therefore take users preferences into consideration while still doing most of the work automatically. Balancing this trade-off is a challenging design issue.

The second challenge is that "interestingness" is domain specific, that is, it depends on the characteristics of the particular domain described by the data. For example, for the novel path discovery problem most people would probably think that the link "A killed B" is more interesting than "A wrote a letter to B". The justification for this is that, empirically, the event "killing" happens less frequently than the event "writing a letter". This, however, is only true if the mined data set describes the behavior of the general population. If instead we were looking at a police murder database containing primarily murder events, the reverse would be the case. This is because in this data set everybody is

more or less involved in some "killing" event while "writing a letter" is considerably more rare or unusual. In other words, when investigating this data set, users will expect to find data related to "killing" but not necessarily to "writing a letter". Information-theoretically, we can say that "killing" conveys less information in this context. Therefore, the evidence "writing a letter" might surprise a user and trigger him or her to consult additional sources for further information. This explains why it is not sufficient to tackle the NLD problem simply by analyzing individual semantics of the relations, but that it is very important to consider the domain and context the data is in.

A typical supervised learning approach for this problem would be to learn a weight of interestingness for each relation or series of relations in a data set and then apply a shortest path algorithm accumulating these weights to look for solutions. This, however, is not practical due to the difficulty of generating unbiased training data. Take the novel path discovery problem for example. To obtain unbiased training data we have to rank the novelty of training paths manually with consistency. In other words, we have to develop a "standard operating procedure" about how to quantify interestingness of paths in a specific domain. The third challenge arises from this "chicken and egg" dilemma: if we could develop a standard evaluation criterion to judge the interestingness of paths or nodes, then we could apply it directly as our novel link finder and would not have to learn it. But since we do not have such a criterion, we also cannot generate labeled training examples to learn it. This limits the applicability of a supervised learning approach to solve the NLD problem and shows that we are really dealing with a *discovery* and not a learning problem.

There is a significant body of work in data mining that deals with measuring the interestingness of discovered association or classification rules [4, 8, 9]; however, these interestingness measures are not appropriate for the NLD problem. The reasons are twofold. First, most of these methods assume the data is in the form of a feature-vector (a single relational table), while for the NLD problem we have to be able to handle multi-relational data with potentially large vocabularies of relations. The second and more serious problem is that one has to first learn a pattern or rule before its interestingness can be measured. This, however, is only possible if there are enough supporting cases in the data to warrant the discovery of a particular rule. If a pattern of interest occurs only once, no rule or pattern would be available to be evaluated with one of these measures. These measures are therefore not directly applicable for novel link discovery.

3. Novel link discovery via rarity analysis

In this section we propose a set of *rarity* measures to capture the notion of "interestingness". These measures form the foundation on which all our novel path, novel loop and significant node discovery algorithms are based.

3.1 Novel path discovery

Besides the challenges described in the previous section, another problem for novel path discovery is that the interestingness of a path is non-linearly related to the interestingness of its individual links. That is, each individual link of a path might not be interesting at all but it is the combination of them that represents something special. This non-linearity characteristic limits the effectiveness of a shortest-path like algorithm that might simply accumulate statically assigned link interestingness to compute path interestingness.

To deal with novel path discovery problems, we observe that to some extent **rarity** carries the information of **interestingness.** That is, an event that occurs infrequently compared to other events has the potential to be interesting and, thus, worth being reported. Using rarity as a measure for interestingness fulfills the need of capturing domain specificity: the same event can be rare in one domain but not in the other. For example, the event "A cites B's paper" could be interesting in a criminal database because it occurs rarely, despite the fact that people might think it to be uninteresting, since in general this citation behavior is not rare. Rarity is also flexible enough to handle different points of view. For example "A cites B's paper" can be rare from A's point of view but not from B's point of view due to the fact that A rarely cites others but B is commonly cited by many other people.

To apply these ideas to the novel path discovery problem, we have to define rarity measurements for paths in the network. Note that in a multi-relational network as shown in Figure 1, every path occurs exactly once, thus all of them are equally rare. We therefore need a more relaxed definition to measure path rarity. We do this by defining the rarity of a path as the reciprocal of the number of **similar** paths to it. We accommodate view dependency by defining four different measures based on different views of similarity.

An *n*-step path can in general be defined as a combination of *n*+1 entities (or nodes) e_i and *n* relations (or links) r_i between them:

$$e_0 \xrightarrow{r_0} e_1 \xrightarrow{r_1} e_2 \ldots \ldots \xrightarrow{r_{n-1}} e_n$$

Note that in the novel path discovery problem we do not consider paths that contain loops (in other words all *n* entities in a path must be distinct).

We define the **type** of a path as the ordered sequences of relations $[r_0 \ldots r_{n-1}]$ of that path. For example, the path "A writes a paper that cites a paper published at time t1" and the path "B writes a paper that cites a paper published at time t2" are of the same type [writes, cites, published_at].

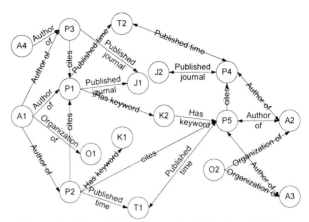

Figure 1: Example bibliography dataset containing 16 nodes and 21 links

The first path rarity measurement considers two paths as similar if they have the same type as well as identical source and target nodes. Then the rarity of a path *P* can be defined as 1/N1, where N1 is the total number of paths in the dataset that are similar to *P* in this sense. For example, in Figure 1 the path p_1 "A1 is the author of P2 and P2 cites P1" (between A1 and P1) has rarity 1/2 since there exists only one other similar path "A1 is the author of P3 and P3 cites P1". For convenience we call N1 "spindle fan-out value" since according to the constraints the path emanates from the source and terminates to the target just like a spindle.

The second path rarity measurement considers two paths as similar if they have the same type and emanate from the same source node. The rarity of a path *P* can then be defined as 1/N2, where N2 is the total number paths in the dataset that are similar to *P* in this sense. According to this rarity measure, the path p_1 described above has rarity 1/3, since there is one more path "A1 is the author of P2 and P2 cites P5" that matches the similarity criteria. We call N2 the "source fan-out value", since similar paths fans out from the source.

The third measure 1/N3 is similar to the previous one but with identical target instead of source. The rarity of path p_1 in this sense is 1/3, since besides the paths that satisfy N1 rarity, there is one more path "A4 is the author of P3 and P3 cites P1" that matches the criteria. N3 is called "target fan-out value", since similar paths fan out from the same target.

The fourth path rarity measure considers two paths with the same type as being similar. This rarity measure is defined as 1/N4 where N4 equals the total number of paths of the same type in the dataset. According to this measure, the rarity of p_1 is 1/5 since there are five paths in Figure 1 of the type "*X* is the author of *Y* and *Y* cites *Z*". We call N4 the "global fan-out value", since it represents how rare this type of path is in general.

Equipped with these measures, we can now answer novel path discovery questions for the graph displayed in

Figure 1. For example: Is the path "A1 writes P2 and P2 cites P1" more interesting than the path "A1 writes P3, P3 is published in journal J1 and J1 also contains P1"? This query will have different answers for different points of view (spindle, source, target, global fan out), and which view is chosen will depend on the user's focus. For example, if the user is the author of P1, he/she might be interested in viewing things from P1 and using 1/N3 as the rarity measure. Therefore, he/she could discover that the first path is more interesting than the second given that not a lot of people in the dataset cite the paper, but many of them have papers published in the same journal. In general, 1/N2 can be used when the user cares more about the source than the target and 1/N3 is used vice versa. 1/N1 is used when the user focuses on both the source and the target. 1/N4 is used when the user is concerned more about the general rarity of the path-type (or pattern) without focusing on any individual nodes. Sometimes the query itself determines the view as well. For example, it is reasonable to use the target fan-out value when being asked whether "K1 is the keyword of paper P1 and P1's author belongs Organization O1" is more interesting than "A1 belongs to O1", since both paths ends at the same node.

With these rarity measures, we have a systematic way to answer a query such as "what is the most interesting path between nodes X and Y?" We simply enumerate all paths between X and Y and return the one with the highest rarity value. By using rarity to determine the most interesting path, we not only take the domain specificity and user views into consideration, but also avoid being misled by the apparent meaning of the links.

3.2 Novel loop discovery

The novel loop discovery problem aims at finding interesting loops in the dataset. It is a variation of novel path discovery, since a loop can be treated as a special type of a path that has identical source and target. The rarity of a loop such as this one going from e_0 to e_0

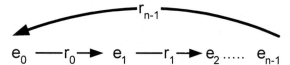

can be measured similarly to path rarity. But since in a loop the source node is identical to the target, the N1, N2, N3 value will be the same. Thus, there are only two different loop rarity measurements: 1/N1 measures how rare a specific loop is to the source and 1/N4 determines how rare this type of loop is in general.

3.3 Significant node discovery

The significant node discovery problem aims at finding the entities most significantly connected to a given node.

Our intuition is that whether two nodes are significantly connected or not depends not only on the quantity but also on the quality of paths that connect them. In other words, two nodes are significantly connected with each other if there are many interesting or rare paths between them. We therefore claim that the significance between two nodes can be measured by aggregating the rarity of paths between them. Equation 1 shows how we compute the significance of connection between two nodes A and B by accumulating the path rarity of all paths connecting them.

$$node\_significance(A, B) = \sum_{\substack{P_i \in paths \\ between\,(A,B)}} path\_rarity(P_i)$$

Equation 1: Computing the connection significance value between two nodes A and B.

Again, which path rarity measure needs to be applied in Equation 1 depends on different points of view. Equation 2 shows how we determine the node that is the most significantly connected with node A. Note that in this case the source fan-out value N2 is used for path rarity since we have to adopt A's point of view to judge the rarity.

$$\underset{X}{\mathrm{argmax}}(\sum_{\substack{P_i \in paths \\ between\,(A,X)}} path\_rarity(P_i)) = \underset{X}{\mathrm{argmax}}(\sum_{\substack{P_i \in paths \\ between\,(A,X)}} \frac{1}{N2(P_i)})$$

Equation 2: Determining the node that is most significantly connected to a given node A.

For a specific **type** of path, the N1 value represents the total number of times it occurs between source and target. The N2 value stands for the total number of times the path occurs between the source and somebody else (this is the source fan-out value). Since 1/N2 stands for how rare a path is from the source's point of view and N1 stands for how many times the path occurs between source and target, it is easy to show that the node significance value defined in Equation 1 is equivalent to the accumulation of N1/N2 for all different types of paths. Therefore, we call the N1/N2 value of a particular path type its **contribution** to the overall significance value.

According to our definition, finding an entity that is significantly connected with the source entity A is not equivalent to finding an entity that is tightly connected with A. For example, entities A and B might have much more connections between each other than entities A and C, but entity C can still be more significant to A given that there are more rare paths between A and C.

4. Experiments

Below we describe a set of experiments aimed to illustrate the validity and usefulness of our approach. The experiments are performed on the "High Energy Physics - Theory" bibliographic database (or HEP-Th), which is a natural dataset that was used as the experimental dataset for the KDD Cup 2003[1].

The HEP-Th dataset contains a total of 29016 papers with 1.7Gbytes of associated data. Each paper in the dataset is described by a unique ID, its authors, their e-mail addresses, paper title, the journal it appeared in, publication date, abstract and a set of other papers cited by it. The source text of each paper is also available which we ignore.

To model the data we used five different types of nodes and ten different types of links. Nodes represent paper IDs (29016), author names (12755), journal names (267), organization names (753) and publication times encoded as year/season pairs (60). Numbers in parentheses indicate the number of different entities for each type in the dataset. Organizations are not given directly but inferred from author's e-mail addresses. Different spellings of author names were not consolidated and resulted in multiple nodes.

We defined the following types of links to connect nodes:

author_of(a, p) : connects author a to his/her paper p.
date_published(p, d) : connects paper p to its publication date d.
affiliation(a, o) : connects person p to an organization o he/she belongs to.
published_in(p, j) : connects paper p to journal j it is in.
cites(p, r): connects paper p to a paper r it cites.

All of these links are viewed to be directional with an implicit inverse link, thus there are a total of 5*2 link types.

In sum there are 42871 different nodes and 461932 links in the graph representing the data. We then applied our rarity measures to identify interesting paths, loops and significant nodes in this graph.

4.1 Significant node discovery

In our first experiment we attempted to evaluate our significant node discovery method. That is, given some source node S we wanted to find other nodes of various types that were significantly connected to S. Since the nodes represent real-world entities such as people, we can then manually "verify" the computed results by investigating whether they reflected real-world, significant connections visible on the World-Wide Web. For the experiment we picked C.N. Pope as the source node S, since in this dataset he is the one with the highest number of publications (130 in total), which provides us with a rich number of connections through this node.

Table 1 lists the top three interesting nodes connected to C.N. Pope for various different node types with their significance scores relative to Pope.

[1] http://www.cs.cornell.edu/projects/kddcup/datasets.html

Table 1: Nodes significantly connected to C.N. Pope

Node Type	Top-Three Scoring Nodes (sum of path rarity)		
Person	H. Lu (4.1)	M. Cvetic (2.60)	K.S. Stelle (0.98)
Organization	UTexas (3.42)	UMich (1.80)	UPenn (1.18)
Journal	Nucl.Phys (1.33)	Phys.Lett (0.30)	Phys.Rev (0.27)
Time	Spring 2000 (0.40)	Summer 2002 (0.37)	Winter1995 (0.37)

The results show that among the 12755 people in this dataset, the one that is the most significantly connected to Pope is H. Lu, while M. Cvetic is the second and K.S. Stelle is the third. To get some further insight why these people were picked as the most significant ones, we can look at what path types contributed the most to the overall significance value. The most significant path for person entities connected to C.N. Pope is that of co-authorship. This type of path emanates from Pope a total of 332 times and ends up at H. Lu 117 times, i.e., Lu contributes 35% of them while the runners up Cvetic and Stelle contribute 42 times (12.6%) and 21 times (6.3%), respectively. The second-most significant path represents a chain of co-authorship (i.e., Person1 writes with Person2 and Person2 writes with Person3 on different papers). This path is not really rare from Pope's point of view (it occurs 34473 times). However, Cvetic was involved in it 5376 times, thus, for her this type of relation still contributes 15.6% to the overall score. It shows that a significant path is not necessarily a rare path; it could be a non-rare one but occurs frequently for a specific target. The third-most significant path represents a citation relationship. Pope cites Lu's papers much more often than those of others. Looking for organizations that are interestingly connected with Mr. Pope, we found that U. Texas A&M is the most important surpassing the second U. Michigan and third U. Pennsylvania significantly.

Next we tried to verify whether the discovered relationships actually represent important real-world relationships visible through other means. After investigating through the World-Wide Web, we found that Dr. Pope is a professor at U. Texas A&M and he was Dr. Lu's thesis advisor (1988-1994) and that Dr. Lu is currently a post-doc at U. Michigan. Dr. Cvetic is a professor at U. Pennsylvania, has similar research interests to Pope and works closely with him. Dr. Stelle is a professor of Imperial College London who has ties with Pope not only academically but also personally. For example, Dr. Pope's homepage shows a picture showing him, Dr. Stelle, and others traveling together in Afghanistan.

While this "verification" is anecdotal, it does indicate that our unsupervised method, which did not know any semantics of the entities and links in this domain, is capable of returning significant relationships that are relevant in the real world.

The rest of Table 1 describes journals and time periods significantly connected to Pope. The results show that the journal Nucl.Phys. has the highest score followed by Phys.Lett. and Phys.Rev. We checked the three types of paths that contribute the most to each of these rarity values. The most important relationship discovered and taken into account by our program is frequency of publication, which intuitively makes sense. Pope published a total of 110 journal papers and 52 of them are in Nucl.Phys. He did not publish that many papers in Phys.Lett., but a significant portion of his colleagues' papers are published there. For his connection with Phys.Rev. the program discovered that the papers cited by Mr. Pope's papers are also frequently cited by papers published in Phys.Rev. As to the time periods, Spring 2000 followed by Summer 2002 and Winter 1995 connect significantly to Mr. Pope, because various types of paths such as, for example, the publication time for his papers and the publication time for his colleagues' papers, contribute relatively highly from these nodes to Pope.

4.2 Novel path discovery

We also experimented with novel path discovery questions such as, for example, which path is the most interesting (or rarest) between two people. To determine rare paths between two known nodes, we applied $1/N1$ as our rarity measure where $N1$ is the spindle fan-out described in Section 3.1. Looking at all paths between Pope and Lu we find the path "Pope belongs to organization O that has another member P who writes a paper together with Lu" to be the rarest according to this measure. This indicates that not many of Pope's colleagues at his university write papers with Lu, which is consistent with Lu's role as Pope's student. However, this type of path is not the rarest between Pope and Cvetic, instead "Pope co-authors a paper with Cvetic" is rarer, since Cvetic seems to write more with Pope's colleagues than with him. The examples show that our novel path discovery method can take point-of-view into account, since the computed interestingness of paths changes when the view shifts (e.g. from Lu to Cvetic in this case).

In this domain rarity of individual paths does not convey such strong semantic relationships as node significance and is harder to evaluate. In this sense the relationship between path rarity and node significance resembles the relationship between a probability density function and its corresponding probability distribution function, since the integrated probability usually carries more real-world meaning than the density function itself.

4.3 Novel loop discovery

For experiments on novel loop discovery, we calculated loop rarity via $1/N4'$ where $N4'$ is a variation of global fan-out (see Section 3.1) with the additional requirement that source and target have to be the same node. Said differently, for each possible path type leading from a node to itself we count how often that path occurs in the dataset. The rarest, least frequent loops are listed in the top portion of Table 2, the most common loops are listed at the bottom.

Table 2: The rarest and the most common loops

Top 6 loops with highest rarity value
PaperX cites PaperX
PaperX cites Paper1→Paper1 cites PaperX
PaperX cites Paper1→Paper1 cites Paper2 → Paper2 cites PaperX
PaperX cites Paper1→Paper1 cites Paper2 → Paper2 cites Paper3 →Paper3 cites PaperX
PaperX cites (or cited by) Paper1 → Paper 1 published at Time1→ At Time1, PaperX also published.
PaperX is written by Person1 → Person 1 has another Paper1→ Paper1 published at the same time as PaperX
Bottom 3 loops with lowest rarity value
PaperX cites PaperY → PaperY is being cited by PaperZ → PaperZ is being cited by PaperX
PaperX cites PaperY → PaperY published in the same journal as PaperZ→ PaperZ cites PaperX
PaperX is cited by Paper Y → Paper Y published in same season as PaperZ → PaperZ cites Paper X

The rarest loops are papers citing themselves directly, which only occurs 28 times in the whole dataset. We do not have a real world explanation for this and can only attribute it to errors in the dataset. The second, third and fourth loops are also citation loops of different length. The explanation behind this finding is that for a paper to cite another, the cited paper needs to be published earlier. In this sense a citation loop such as "P1 cites P2 cites P3 cites P1" is really a temporal contradiction and should not occur at all. One explanation for such "contradictions" is that sometimes an author (or close colleague) might cite one of his/her own submitted but not yet published papers P2 (which has already cited P1) in a paper P1. The other explanation is that one journal might have a very long revising period and during that period other people can access the previous version. For both explanations we have found supporting instances from the dataset. The fifth path shows a similar concept where it is rare for a paper to cite another paper that was published during the same time period. This type of loop could also be an indicator for authors that work closely with each other. Finally, the last path shows that people seldom publish multiple papers at the same time.

The bottom portion of the table shows the most frequently occurring loops as a contrast to the rare loops described above. For example, the most frequent loops are two papers published at the same time period that both cite X. They are loops that intuitively should occur very frequently. Note that "A cites B cites C" is a very common path, thus, we did not expect it to be interesting as a loop and were surprised by the results.

The experiments demonstrate that our approach is capable of uncovering interesting instances masked inside thousands of uninteresting facts. Furthermore, the instances found by novel loop discovery lead us to the discovery of interesting hypotheses or patterns, e.g., that citation loops are an indicator for authors who work closely with each other or for journals that have a long revision cycle.

4.4 Discussion

The experiments show that our program can find interesting connections in a network without having to learn the patterns of interestingness. For the bibliography dataset, which does not have too many different types of relations, one might be able to write a rule-based system or supervised learning program to answer similar queries as we did. However, it is time consuming to do this, since different rules or training data are required for different queries (e.g. the rules to identify the people that are interestingly connect to a keyword are different from the ones required to determine the organizations that are interestingly connected to a person). The advantage of our method is that it does everything in an unsupervised manner and eliminates the necessity to regenerate new rules or new training data for different queries or even when the whole domain is changed. It also eliminates the risk of being biased by the apparent meaning of link types.

Another advantage of our approach is that it can focus the user's attention on events that are otherwise hard to be noticed. The inspirations triggered by such evidences can sometimes lead to the discovery of pattern/knowledge. For example, without being made aware of those rare loops, we might not ever look into the issue of citation loops at all, since there are thousands of different loops in the dataset that mask this phenomenon. They also prompt us to discover other related knowledge when we try to explain them, for example, that citation loops can be an indicator of authors adding additional citations during a revision of a journal submission.

5. Related work

To our knowledge there is no other work that addresses the NLD problem in multi-relational data via an unsupervised approach. One focus of current link discovery research is on learning patterns from complex multi-relational data. For example, inductive logic programming has been applied to learn relational patterns [11] . Additionally, graph-based methods such as [6] have been used to learn subgraph categories and isomorphisms. These approaches either require training examples or learn things at the structure/schema level, while for the NLD problem it is necessary to perform discovery at the instance level by using unsupervised methods. Kovalerchuk and Vityaev's hybrid evidence correlation technique [1] first identifies common patterns via standard data mining techniques and then hypothesizes interesting or unusual patterns by negating some of the statistically significant patterns found. It is conceptually similar to our approach but requires the occurrence of very common patterns in the data.

Other analysis algorithms such as PageRank compute the importance of links through the connections between nodes in an unsupervised manner [12, 13]. In that framework, however, all relations are treated to be identical (that is, "A kills B" is not different from "A writes to B"), therefore, this approach is not suitable for the multi-relational NLD problem.

The area of outlier detection in data mining and statistics aims at detecting points that are considerably dissimilar or inconsistent with the remainder of the data [2, 3, 7, 14, 15]. This is conceptually related to our use of rarity analysis to solve the NLD problem. Current research on outlier detection, however, analyzes primarily numerical entity-attribute data instead of multi-relational social network data. In threat detection each individual event is usually not an outlier; nevertheless, combinations of seemingly harmless events can suddenly become threatening when they occur in a particular context. Outlier computations that do not take such combinations into account will fail to detect such threats. Our path rarity analysis is designed to search for these kinds of unusual connections in a multi-relational dataset.

The area of social network analysis has investigated multi-relational social behavior using graph and matrix-theoretic representations [16]. The concept of "centrality" is applied widely to determine important nodes in a network from a global point of view, while our significant node discovery tries to tackle the problem locally by answering "which node is important to a chosen node". Moreover, centrality analysis uses only the connectivity (the number of paths) to judge the significance while our algorithm considers not only the quantity but also the quality (rarity) of the paths.

Valdes-Perez [21] characterizes discovery in science as the generation of novel, interesting, plausible and intelligible knowledge about the objects of study. In this sense the novel link discovery problem is similar to literature-based discovery introduced by Swanson [18, 19], since they both intend to find interesting facts and connections in large amounts of data. Since 1986 Swanson has triggered interesting discoveries in biomedicine strictly by looking for mediators that connect otherwise unconnected corpora of scientific literature. Literature-based discovering systems are primarily aimed at finding one-step connections between independent corpora instead of ranking the interestingness of the multi-step paths in a multi-relational network, and are therefore different from our approach.

6. Conclusion

We presented an unsupervised link discovery method aimed at detecting interesting paths or interestingly connected nodes in multi-relational datasets. Interestingness is modeled via different measures of rarity that are based on computing how often similar paths occur in the data. The method does not rely on any pre-existing or learnable pattern information and can detect novel, interesting connections that do not need to be conceived prior to the analysis. Our approach is a general-purpose method and can be applied to arbitrary multi-relational datasets. Potential applications are in law enforcement, threat detection, data cleaning [5] and scientific discovery. The experiment shows that our approach can capture interesting connections that are representative of meaningful real-world relationships. Future work will include more extensive evaluation with different data sets, handling of temporal information, negation and better handling of noise and corruption.

7. Acknowledgements

This research was supported by the Defense Advance Research Projects Agency under Air Force Research Laboratory contract F30602-01-2-0583.

8. References

[1] B. Kovalerchuk, E. Vityaev. *Correlation of complex evidences and link discovery. The Fifth International Conference on Forensic Statistics.* 2002. Venice, Italy.

[2] C. Aggarwal, P.Yu. *Outlier detection for high dimensional data. ACM SIGMOD Conference.* 2001.

[3] E.M. Knorr, R.T. Ng. *Algorithms for Mining Distance-Based Outliers in Large Datasets. Proc. of VLDB Conf.* 1998.

[4] A. A. Freitas, *On rule interestingness measures. Knowledge-Based Systems.* 1999.

[5] R.Kimball, *Dealing with Dirty Data, DBMS Magazine.* 1996.

[6] L. B. Holder, D. J Cook, *Graph-based data mining.* IEEE Intelligent Systems 15, 2000.

[7] M.M. Breunig, H.P. Kriegel, R. T. Ng, and J. Sander. *Optics-of: Identifying local outliers. Proc. of PKDD '99.*

[8] P.N. Tan, V. Kumar. *Interestingness measures for association patterns: A perspective. KDD.* 2000.

[9] R. Hilderman , H. Hamilton, *Knowledge discovery and interestingness measures: A survey.* 1999, Technical Report, University of Regina:

[10] R. J. Mooney, P. Melville, L. P. Rupert Tang, J. Shavlik, I.d. Dutra, D. Page, V. S. Costa. *Relational Data Mining with Inductive Logic Programming for Link Discovery. Proceedings of the National Science Foundation Workshop on Next Generation Data Mining.* 2002.

[11] R.J. Mooney, P.Melville, L. P. Rupert Tang, J. Shavlik, I.d. Dutra, D. Page, V. S. Costa. *Relational Data Mining with Inductive Logic Programming for Link Discovery. Proceedings of the National Science Foundation Workshop on Next Generation Data Mining.* 2002.

[12] S. Brin, L. Page. *The anatomy of a large-scale hypertextual Web search engine. Proceedings of the 7th International World Wide Web Conference.* 1998.

[13] S. Candan, W.S. Li, *Reasoning for Web Document Associations and Its Applications in Site Map Construction.* International Journal of Data and Knowledge Engineering, 2002: p.121-150.

[14] S. Ramaswamy, R. Rastogi, K. Shim. *Efficient algorithms for mining outliers from large data sets. Proceedings of the ACM SIGMOD Conference.* 2000.

[15] S. Shekhar, C.T. Lu, P. Zhang. *Detecting Graph-based Spatial Outliers: Algorithms and Applications. The Seventh ACM SIGKDD* 2001.

[16] S. Wasserman, K. Faust, *Social Network Analysis: Methods & Applications.* 1994: Cambridge, UK: Cambridge University Press.

[17] T. Senator, *Evidence Extraction and Link Discovery Program.* 2002, DARPATech 2002: http://www.darpa.mil/DARPATech2002/presentations/iao_pdf/speeches/SENATOR.pdf

[18] D. R. Swanson, *Fish Oil, Raynaud's syndrome and undiscovered public knowledge.* Perspectives in Biology and Medicine, 1986.

[19] D. R. Swanson, *Somatomedin C and arginine: Implicit connections between mutually isolated literatures.* Perspectives in Biology and Medicine, 1990.

[20] U. Fayyad, G. Piatetsky-Shapiro, P. Smyth, *The KDD Process for Extracting Useful Knowledge from Volumes of Data.* Communications of the ACM, 1996. p.27-34.

[21] R. E. Valdes-Perez, *Principles of human-computer collaboration for knowledge discovery in science.* Artificial Intelligence, 1999.

Building Text Classifiers Using Positive and Unlabeled Examples

Bing Liu
Department of Computer Science
University of Illinois at Chicago {liub@cs.uic.edu}

Yang Dai
Department of Bioengineering
University of Illinois at Chicago {yangdai@uic.edu}

Xiaoli Li, Wee Sun Lee
School of Computing, National University of Singapore/Singapore-MIT Alliance
{lixl, leews}@comp.nus.edu.sg

Philip S. Yu
IBM T. J. Watson Research Center, Yorktown Heights, NY 10598, USA

This paper studies the problem of building text classifiers using positive and unlabeled examples. The key feature of this problem is that there is no negative example for learning. Recently, a few techniques for solving this problem were proposed in the literature. These techniques are based on the same idea, which builds a classifier in two steps. Each existing technique uses a different method for each step. In this paper, we first introduce some new methods for the two steps, and perform a comprehensive evaluation of all possible combinations of methods of the two steps. We then propose a more principled approach to solving the problem based on a biased formulation of SVM, and show experimentally that it is more accurate than the existing techniques.

1. Introduction

Text classification is the process of assigning pre-defined category labels to new documents based on the classifier learnt from training examples. In traditional classification, training examples are labeled with the same set of pre-defined category or class labels and labeling is often done manually. Many text classification techniques have been proposed by researchers so far, e.g., the Rocchio algorithm [29], the naive Bayesian method (NB) [17][22], support vector machines (SVM) [32][12] and many others (see [33]).

The main problem with this classic approach is that a large number of labeled training examples of every class are needed for accurate learning. Since labeling is typically done manually, it is labor intensive and time consuming. In recent years, researchers investigated the idea of using a small labeled set of every class and a large unlabeled set to help learning [26]. This reduces the manual labeling effort.

This paper studies the problem of building two-class classifiers with only positive and unlabeled examples, but no negative examples. Recently, a few algorithms were proposed to solve the problem. One class of algorithms is based on a two-step strategy. These algorithms include S-EM [20], PEBL [34], and Roc-SVM [18].

Step 1: Identifying a set of reliable negative documents from the unlabeled set. In this step, S-EM uses a Spy technique, PEBL uses a technique called 1-DNF, and Roc-SVM uses the Rocchio algorithm [29].

Step 2: Building a set of classifiers by iteratively applying a classification algorithm and then selecting a good classifier from the set. In this step, S-EM uses the Expectation Maximization (EM) algorithm [7] with a NB classifier, while PEBL and Roc-SVM use SVM. Both S-EM and Roc-SVM have some methods for selecting the final classifier. PEBL simply uses the last classifier at convergence, which can be poor.

These two steps together can be seen as an iterative method of increasing the number of unlabeled examples that are classified as negative while maintaining the positive examples correctly classified. It was shown theoretically in [20] that if the sample size is large enough, maximizing the number of unlabeled examples classified as negative while constraining the positive examples to be correctly classified will give a good classifier.

In this paper, we first introduce another method for Step 1, i.e., the NB method, and another method for Step 2, i.e., SVM alone, and perform an evaluation of all 16 possible combinations of methods of Step 1 and Step 2. This also results in a benchmark system, called LPU (Learning from Positive and Unlabeled data), which is available on the first author's Web page. We then propose a more principled approach to solving this problem based on a biased formulation of SVM. Experimental results show that the new method is superior to all the existing two-step techniques.

2. Related Work

Traditional text classification techniques require labeled training examples of all classes to build a classifier [33]. They are thus not suitable for building classifiers using only positive and unlabeled examples.

A theoretical study of Probably Approximately Correct (PAC) learning from positive and unlabeled data was first conducted in [8]. [24] presents a theoretical study in the Bayesian framework. Sample complexity results for learning by maximizing the number of unlabeled examples labeled as negative while constraining the classifier to label all the positive examples correctly were presented in [20].

The S-EM technique is reported in [20]. The PEBL technique is reported in [34]. The Roc-SVM technique is reported in [18]. We will discuss them in detail later. Unlike these techniques which are based on the two-step strategy, [16] reports a logistic regression technique to solve the problem.

Besides maximizing the number of unlabeled examples labeled as negative, other methods for learning from positive and unlabeled examples are possible. A NB based method (called PNB) that tries to statistically remove the effect of positive data in the unlabeled set is proposed in [9]. The main shortcoming of the method is that it requires the user to give the positive class probability, which is hard for the user to provide in practice. It is also possible to discard the unlabeled data and learn only from the positive data. This was done in the one-class SVM [31][21], which tries to learn the support of the positive distribution. Our results show that its performance is poorer than learning methods that take advantage of the unlabeled data.

Finally, our work is related to learning using a small labeled set and a large unlabeled set [2][3][4][5][10] [11][25][26][28][35]. In these works, a small set of labeled examples of every class and a large unlabeled set are used for classifier building. It was shown that the unlabeled data helps learning. These works are different from ours as we have no negative example.

3. Techniques for Step 1

In this section, we first introduce the naïve Bayesian technique (NB) as a new method for Step 1 to identify a set RN of reliable negative documents from the unlabeled set U (we use P to denote the positive example set). We then describe the Rocchio technique used in Roc-SVM, the Spy technique used in S-EM, and the 1-DNF technique used in PEBL to facilitate our later evaluation.

3.1 The Naïve Bayesian classifier

The naïve Bayesian technique is a popular method for classification. Given a set of training documents D, each document is considered an ordered list of words. We use $x_{d_i,k}$ to denote the word x_t in position k of document d_i, where x_t is a word in the vocabulary $V = \{x_1, \ldots, x_{|V|}\}$. The vocabulary is the set of all words considered for classification. Let $C = \{c_1, c_2, \ldots, c_{|C|}\}$ be a set of pre-defined classes (in this paper we only consider two classes, thus $C = \{c_1, c_2\}$). To perform classification, we compute the posterior probability, $Pr(c_j|d_i)$, where c_j is a class and d_i is a document. Based on the Bayesian probability and the multinomial model [22][26], we have

$$Pr(c_j) = \frac{\sum_{i=1}^{|D|} Pr(c_j \mid d_i)}{|D|}, \qquad (1)$$

and with additive (Lidstone) smoothing [19]

$$Pr(x_t \mid c_j) = \frac{\lambda + \sum_{i=1}^{|D|} N(x_t, d_i) Pr(c_j \mid d_i)}{\lambda |V| + \sum_{s=1}^{|V|} \sum_{i=1}^{|D|} N(x_s, d_i) Pr(c_j \mid d_i)}, \quad (2)$$

where λ is the smoothing factor, $N(x_t, d_i)$ is the number of times that word x_t occurs in document d_i and $Pr(c_j|d_i) \in \{0, 1\}$ depending on the class of the document. Experimental results in [1] show that $\lambda = 0.1$ performs well for text data. $\lambda = 1$ is the commonly used Laplacian smoothing. However, $\lambda = 1$ is significantly inferior to $\lambda = 0.1$ [1]. We used $\lambda = 0.1$ in all our experiments.

Finally, assuming that the probabilities of the words are independent given the class, we obtain the NB classifier:

$$Pr(c_j \mid d_i) = \frac{Pr(c_j) \prod_{k=1}^{|d_i|} Pr(x_{d_i,k} \mid c_j)}{\sum_{r=1}^{|C|} Pr(c_r) \prod_{k=1}^{|d_i|} Pr(x_{d_i,k} \mid c_r)}. \quad (3)$$

In classifying a document d_i, the class with the highest $Pr(c_j|d_i)$ is assigned as the class of the document.

Identifying a set RN of reliable negative documents from the unlabeled set U is done as follows (Figure 1):

1. Assign each document in P the class label 1;
2. Assign each document in U the class label -1;
3. Build a NB classifier using P and U;
4. Use the classifier to classify U. Those documents in U that are classified as negative form the reliable negative set RN.

Figure 1: The NB method for Step 1

3.2 The Rocchio technique

Rocchio is an early text classification method [29]. In this method, each document is represented as a vector, and each feature value in the vector is computed using the classic *tf-idf* scheme [30]. Let D be the whole set of training documents, and C_j be the set of training documents in class c_j. Building a Rocchio classifier is achieved by constructing a prototype vector $\vec{c}_j$ for each class c_j.

$$\vec{c}_j = \alpha \frac{1}{|C_j|} \sum_{\vec{d} \in C_j} \frac{\vec{d}}{\|\vec{d}\|} - \beta \frac{1}{|D - C_j|} \sum_{\vec{d} \in D - C_j} \frac{\vec{d}}{\|\vec{d}\|}.$$

α and β are parameters that adjust the relative impact of relevant and irrelevant training examples. [6] recommends $\alpha = 16$ and $\beta = 4$. In classification, for each test document td, it uses the cosine similarity measure [30] to compute the similarity of td with each prototype vector. The class whose prototype vector is more similar to td is assigned to td.

The algorithm that uses Rocchio to identify a set RN of reliable negative documents from U is the same as that in Figure 1 except that we replace NB with Rocchio.

3.3 The Spy technique in S-EM

The Spy technique in S-EM is given in Figure 2. It first randomly selects a set S of positive documents from P and put them in U (lines 2 and 3). The default value for $s\%$ is 15% in S-EM. Documents in S act as "spy" documents from the positive set to the unlabeled set U. The spies behave similarly to the unknown positive documents in U. Hence, they allow the algorithm to infer the behavior of the unknown positive documents in U. It then runs I-EM algorithm using the set P–S as positive and the set $U \cup S$ as negative (lines 3-7). I-EM basically runs NB twice (see the EM algorithm below). After I-EM completes, the resulting classifier uses the probabilities assigned to the documents in S to decide a probability threshold th to identify possible negative documents in U to produce the set RN. See [20] for details.

3.4 The 1-DNF technique in PEBL

The 1-DNF method (Figure 3) first builds a positive feature set PF which contains words that occur in the positive set P more frequently than in the unlabeled set U (lines 1-5). In lines 6-9, it tries to filter out possible positive documents from U. A document in U that does

1. $RN = NULL$;
2. $S = Sample(P, s\%)$;
3. $Us = U \cup S$;
4. $Ps = P - S$;
5. Assign each document in Ps the class label 1;
6. Assign each document in Us the class label -1;
7. I-EM(Us, Ps);   // This produces a NB classifier.
8. Classify each document in Us using the NB classifier;
9. Determine a probability threshold th using S;
10. **for** each document $d \in Us$
11.   **if** its probability $Pr(1|d) < th$ **then**
12. $RN = RN \cup \{d\}$;

Figure 2: The Spy technique in S-EM.

not have any positive feature in PF is regarded as a strong negative document.

1. Assume the word feature set be $\{x_1, ..., x_n\}$, $x_i \in U \cup P$;
2. Let positive feature set PF = null;
3. **for** $i = 1$ to n
4.   **if** ($freq(x_i, P)/|P| > freq(x_i, U)/|U|$) **then**
5. $PF = PF \cup \{x_i\}$;
6. $RN = U$;
7. **for** each document $d \in U$
8.   **if** $\exists x_j$ $freq(x_j, d) > 0$ and $x_j \in PF$ **then**
9. $RN = RN - \{d\}$;

Figure 3: The 1-DNF technique in PEBL.

4. Techniques for Step 2

Four techniques are given here for the second step:

1. Run SVM only once using sets P and RN after Step 1. This method is not used before.
2. Run EM. This method is used in S-EM.
3. Run SVM iteratively. This method is used in PEBL.
4. Run SVM iteratively and then select a final classifier. This method is used in Roc-SVM.

We now discuss the 4 methods in turn.

4.1 Support Vector Machines (SVM)

Support vector machines (SVM) are linear functions of the form $f(\mathbf{x}) = \mathbf{w}^T\mathbf{x} + b$, where $\mathbf{w}^T\mathbf{x}$ is the inner product between the weight vector $\mathbf{w}$ and the input vector $\mathbf{x}$. SVM is used as a classifier by setting the class to 1 if $f(\mathbf{x}) > 0$ and to -1 otherwise. The main idea of SVM is to select a hyperplane that separates the positive and negative examples while maximizing the smallest margin. Let a set of training examples be $\{(\mathbf{x}_1, y_1), (\mathbf{x}_2, y_2), ..., (\mathbf{x}_n, y_n)\}$, where $\mathbf{x}_i$ is an input vector and y_i is its class label, $y_i \in \{1, -1\}$. The problem of finding the hyperplane can be stated as the following optimization problem:

Minimize: $\dfrac{1}{2} \mathbf{w}^T \mathbf{w}$

Subject to: $y_i(\mathbf{w}^T \mathbf{x}_i + b) \geq 1, \quad i = 1, 2, ..., n$

To deal with cases where there may be no separating hyperplane due to noisy labels of both positive and negative training examples, the soft margin SVM is proposed [12], which is formulated as:

Minimize: $\dfrac{1}{2} \mathbf{w}^T \mathbf{w} + C \sum_{i=1}^{n} \xi_i$

Subject to: $y_i(\mathbf{w}^T \mathbf{x}_i + b) \geq 1 - \xi_i, \quad i = 1, 2, ..., n$

where $C \geq 0$ is a parameter that controls the amount of training errors allowed.

4.2 The EM algorithm in S-EM

The Expectation-Maximization (EM) algorithm is a popular iterative algorithm for maximum likelihood estimation in problems with missing data [7]. The EM algorithm consists of two steps, the *Expectation* step, and the *Maximization* step. The *Expectation* step basically fills in the missing data. In our case, it produces and revises the probabilistic labels of the documents in *U-RN* (see below). The parameters are estimated in the *Maximization* step after the missing data are filled. This leads to the next iteration of the algorithm. EM converges when its parameters stabilize. Using NB in each iteration, EM employs the same equations as those used in building a NB classifier (equations (1) and (2) for the *Expectation* step, and equation (3) for the *Maximization* step) [26] [20]. The class probability given to each document now takes the value in [1, 0] instead of {1, 0}. The algorithm is given in Figure 4.

1. Each document in *P* is assigned the class label 1;
2. Each document in *RN* is assigned the class label -1;
3. Each document $d \in Q (= U - RN)$ is not assigned any label initially. At the end of the first iteration of EM, it will be assigned a probabilistic label, $Pr(1|d)$. In subsequent iterations, the set *Q* will participate in EM with its newly assigned probabilistic classes.
4. Run the EM algorithm using the document sets, *P*, *RN* and *Q* until it converges.

Figure 4: The EM algorithm with the NB classifier.

Basically, EM iteratively runs NB to revise the probabilistic label of each document in set $Q = U - RN$. Since each iteration of EM produces a NB classifier, S-EM also has a mechanism to select a good classifier [20].

4.3 Iterative SVM in PEBL

PEBL uses *P*, *RN* and *U-RN* to run SVM iteratively (Figure 5). The basic idea is to use each iteration of SVM to extract more possible negative data from *U-RN* and put

1. Every document in *P* is assigned the class label 1;
2. Every document in *RN* is assigned the class label −1;
3. *i* = 1;
4. **Loop**
5.   Use *P* and *RN* to train a SVM classifier S_i;
6.   Classify *Q* using S_i;
7.   Let the set of documents in *Q* that are classified as negative be *W*;
8.   **if** $W = \{\}$ **then** *exit-loop*
9.   **else** $Q = Q - W$;
10. $RN = RN \cup W$;
11. $i = i + 1$;

Figure 5: Running SVM iteratively.

them in *RN* because PEBL's first step is only able to identify a very small set of negative documents. Let *Q* be the set of remaining unlabeled documents, $Q = U - RN$. The iteration converges when no document in *Q* is classified as negative. The final classifier is the result.

4.4 Iterative SVM with Classifier Selection in Roc-SVM

This method is similar to the method in Section 4.3 except that it also decides which classifier to use after the algorithm in Figure 5 converges because each SVM iteration builds a different SVM classifier, and the last classifier may not be a good classifier. After iterative SVM converges, we add the following four lines:

1. Use the last SVM classifier S_{last} to classify *P*;
2. **if** > 8% positive are classified as negative **then**
3.   use S_1 as the final classifier;
4. **else** use S_{last} as the final classifier;

Figure 6: Classifier selection.

The reason for selecting a classifier is that there is a danger in running SVM repetitively. Since SVM is sensitive to noise, if some iteration of SVM extracts many positive documents from *Q* and put them in *RN*, then the last SVM classifier will be poor. This is the problem with PEBL. In this algorithm, we decide whether to use the first SVM classifier or the last one. Basically, we use the SVM classifier at convergence (called S_{last} in line 1) to classify *P*. If too many (> 8%) positive documents in *P* are classified as negative, it indicates that SVM has gone wrong. We then use the first classifier (S_1). Otherwise, we use S_{last} as the final classifier. 8% is used as the threshold because we want to be very conservative so that we will not select a very weak last SVM classifier at convergence.

The above method will not work if both the first and the last SVM classifiers are poor. This is often the case for PEBL because its Step 1 extracts too few negative documents from *U* and thus results in a weak first classifier. PEBL's last classifier may be weak also because one of the iterative SVMs may go wrong. If we use Spy or Rocchio in Step 1, the first SVM is often quite strong, although it may not be the best. Note that neither the first nor the last SVM may be the best classifier. In many cases, a SVM classifier somewhere in the middle is the best. However, it is hard to catch the best classifier.

5. The Proposed Biased SVM

We now present the proposed biased SVM formulation of the problem. Let the set of training examples be $\{(x_1, y_1), (x_2, y_2), ..., (x_n, y_n)\}$, where x_i is an input vector and y_i is its class label, $y_i \in \{1, -1\}$. Assume that the first *k*-1 examples are positive examples (labeled 1), while the rest are unlabeled examples, which we label negative (-1). It was shown in [20] that if the sample size is large enough, minimizing the number of unlabeled examples classified as positive while constraining the positive examples to be correctly classified will give a good classifier. In the noiseless case, this results in the following SVM formulation (no error for positive examples but only for unlabeled examples).

$$\text{Minimize: } \frac{1}{2}\mathbf{w}^T\mathbf{w} + C\sum_{i=k}^{n}\xi_i$$

$$\text{Subject to: } \mathbf{w}^T\mathbf{x}_i + b \geq 1, \quad i = 1, 2, ..., k-1$$

$$-1(\mathbf{w}^T\mathbf{x}_i + b) \geq 1 - \xi_i, \quad i = k, k+1,..., n$$

$$\xi_i \geq 0, i = k, k+1..., n$$

To distinguish this formulation with the classic SVM we call it *Biased-SVM*. If we also allow noise (or error) in positive examples, we have the following soft margin version of the Biased-SVM formulation which uses two parameters C_+ and C_- to weight positive errors and negative errors differently.

$$\text{Minimize: } \frac{1}{2}\mathbf{w}^T\mathbf{w} + C_+\sum_{i=1}^{k-1}\xi_i + C_-\sum_{i=k}^{n}\xi_i$$

$$\text{Subject to: } y_i(\mathbf{w}^T\mathbf{x}_i + b) \geq 1 - \xi_i, \quad i = 1, 2, ..., n$$

$$\xi_i \geq 0, i = 1, 2, ..., n$$

We can vary C_+ and C_- to achieve our objective. Intuitively, we give a big value for C_+ and a small value for C_- because the unlabeled set, which is assumed to be negative, also contains positive data. Note that this asymmetric cost formulation has been used to solve unbalance data problem in [23] (one class of data is very small, while the other class is very large). Our formulation, however, is based on a different motivation.

To choose C_+ and C_-, the common practice is to use a separate validation set to verify the performance of the resulting classifier with the selected values for C_+ and C_-. Since the need to learn from positive and unlabeled examples often arises in retrieval situations, we employ the commonly used F score as the performance measure, F = $2pr/(p+r)$, where p is the *precision* and r is the *recall*.

Unfortunately it is not clear how to estimate the F score without negative examples. In [16], a performance criteria for comparing different classifiers is proposed, which can be estimated directly from the validation set without the need of negative examples.

Let X be the random variable representing the input vector, Y be the actual label. The criteria is $pr/\Pr[Y = 1]$, where $\Pr[Y = 1]$ is the probability of actual positive documents. In [16], it is shown that $pr/\Pr[Y = 1] = r^2/\Pr[f(X) = 1]$, where $\Pr[f(X) = 1]$ is the probability that a document is classified as positive. r can be estimated using the positive examples in the validation set and $\Pr[f(X) = 1)$ can be estimated from the whole validation set. This criteria works because it behaves similarly to the

F score in the sense that it is large when both p and r are large and is small if either p or r is small.

6. Empirical Evaluation

We now evaluate all the techniques of the two-step approach and the new biased-SVM problem formulation.

6.1 Experimental Setup

Datasets: We used two popular text collections in our experiments. The first one is the Reuters-21578[1], which has 21578 documents collected from the Reuters newswire. Of the 135 categories, only the most populous 10 are used. Each category is employed as the positive class, and the rest as the negative class. This gives us 10 datasets. The second collection is the Usenet articles[2] collected by Lang [15] from 20 different newsgroups. Each group has approximately 1000 articles. We use each newsgroup as the positive set and the rest of the 19 groups as the negative set, which creates 20 datasets. In data pre-processing, we applied *stopword* removal, but no feature selection or *stemming* were done. For Rocchio and SVM, *tf-idf* values are used in the feature vectors.

For each dataset, 30% of the documents are randomly selected as test documents. The rest (70%) are used to create training sets as follows: γ percent of the documents from the positive class is first selected as the positive set P. The rest of the positive documents and negative documents are used as unlabeled set U. We range γ from 10%-90% (0.1-0.9) to create a wide range of scenarios.

Experimental systems: Experiments on S-EM and Roc-SVM were conducted using our own systems. Since PEBL is not publicly available, we implemented it based on [34]. For SVM, we used the SVMlight system with linear kernel [14]. All the other methods are implemented by us.

Evaluation measure: In our experiments, we use the popular F score on the positive class as the evaluation measure. F score takes into account of both recall (r) and precision (p), F = $2pr/(p+r)$. We also have accuracy results. However, due to space limitations, we do not list them here. Accuracies behave similarly to F scores.

6.2 Results of the two-step strategy

Below we first summarize all the methods studied in this paper for the two-step approach.

Step 1:
1. Spy: This is the method used in S-EM.
2. 1-DNF: This is the method used in PEBL.
3. Rocchio: This method used in Roc-SVM.

---

[1] http://www.research.att.com/~lewis/reuters21578.html
[2] http://www.cs.cmu.edu/afs/cs/project/theo-11/www/naive-bayes/20_newsgroups.tar.gz

4. NB: This method is proposed in this paper.

Step 2:

1. EM: This is the method used S-EM
2. SVM: This method is proposed in this paper. It runs SVM only once after Step 1.
3. SVM-I: This method is used in PEBL. It runs SVM iteratively. The last classifier at convergence is the final classifier evaluated on the test data.
4. SVM-IS: This method is used in Roc-SVM. It runs SVM iteratively with classifier selection, i.e., after iterative SVM converges, it selects either the first or the last classifier as the final classifier.

Clearly, each technique for Step 1 can be combined with each technique for Step 2. We will empirically evaluate all the 16 possible combinations[3].

Table 1 shows the macro-averaged F score of the 10 Reuters datasets for each γ setting. Due to space limitations, we are unable to list all the detailed results. All the F scores are obtained from unseen test sets.

Columns 1 to 16 show the F scores of all 16 combinations of methods in Steps 1 and 2. PEBL is 1-DNF combined with SVM-I, S-EM is Spy combined with EM, and Roc-SVM is Rochio+SVM-IS. Column 17 gives the results of NB alone for each γ setting. In this case, NB simply treats all the documents in the unlabeled set as negative examples. Its results allow us to see whether all the sophisticated techniques work (more on this later).

Table 2 shows the macro-averaged F scores of the 20 20Newsgroup datasets for each γ setting. From the results in Tables 1 and 2, we draw the following conclusions.

1. S-EM: Its performance is stable over a wide range of conditions. However, it is only comparable with others when the positive set is very small (γ = 0.1-0.3). When the positive set is large, it is worse than some other combinations. These observations are also true for columns 9 and 13. The reasons are that EM uses NB, which is a weaker classifier than SVM [13][33], and that these data sets are not suitable for NB and EM. See the detailed discussion for point 7 below.
2. PEBL: Its performance is poor when the number of positive examples is small. The reason is that PEBL's second step can go wrong without a large number of positive documents. When the positive set is large, it becomes more stable. Its results are comparable with others for Reuters datasets. However, for 20Newsgroup datasets, it is worse than many others e.g., Spy+SVM, Roc-SVM, and NB+SVM.

_____

[3] The PNB system in [9] is not compared as it requires the user to input the positive class probability, which is hard for the user to supply in practice. Furthermore, as we will see, NB based techniques (PNB is based on NB) are inferior to SVM based techniques. We plan to compare with the logistic regression based approach in [16] in the near future.

3. Spy+SVM: It underperforms a few other combinations when the positive set is very small (γ = 0.1-0.2). The reason is that when the positive set is small the number of spies put in the unlabeled set will be too small and thus the resulting RN set will not be very reliable. However, it is the best method as long as the positive set is not too small. NB+SVM also gives good results in such cases, although it is slightly inferior to Spy+SVM. We believe that in practice most positive sets are reasonably large because the user is aware that without a sufficiently large and/or representative positive set, he/she will not obtain a good result. These two methods are also very efficient because they run SVM only once.
4. Roc-SVM and Rocchio+SVM-I: They are also good techniques for large positive sets.
5. 1-DNF, Spy, Rocchio, and NB for Step 1: 1-DNF is weaker for Step 1. It is only good for Reuters data with large positive sets. Spy and Rocchio are more robust. NB is slightly weaker than them.
6. SVM vs EM (NB) for Step 2: It is clear that SVM-based methods for Step 2 (SVM, SVM-I and SVM-IS) significantly outperform EM-based methods when the positive set is reasonably large. It is well-known that SVM is a stronger classifier than NB (EM uses NB).
7. NB alone: It is interesting to observe that a single NB (column 17 of both tables) slightly outperforms S-EM (column 5) and Rocchio+EM (column 9) and NB+EM (column 13). It is known that NB is able to tolerate some noise. Running EM actually makes the results worse. The reason is that EM has a weakness due to the assumptions of NB (our EM runs NB multiple times). In devising the NB classifier, two assumptions are made [22][26]: (1) words are independent given a class, and (2) text documents are generated by a mixture model and there is a one-to-one mapping between mixture components and classes (which means that each class contains only documents of one topic or category). This is not true for our situations because each of our negative class contains documents from many diverse topic categories. Thus, the more we run NB, the worse the results get. This phenomenon is also mentioned in [26]. In [20], it is shown that S-EM outperforms NB because most of its datasets contain only documents of two topics. Then, the above assumption (2) is satisfied. However, we believe that in practice, the negative class typically contains documents from many topics. We noticed in our experiments that the results become worse and worse with each iteration of EM. However, EM in S-EM has a classifier selection mechanism which is able to select the first classifier almost all the time. This means that EM is simply NB for Step 2.

Note that there are a few other methods that can be used alone just like NB, e.g., Rocchio, SVM, and one-

Table 1: Average F scores on Reuters collection

	1	2	3	4	5	6	7	8	9	10	11	12	13	14	15	16	17
Step1	1-DNF	1-DNF		1-DNF		Spy	Spy	Spy	Rocchio	Rocchio	Rocchio		NB	NB	NB	NB	
Step2	EM	SVM	PEBL	SVM-IS	S-EM	SVM	SVM-I	SVM-IS	EM	SVM	SVM-I	Roc-SVM	EM	SVM	SVM-I	SVM-IS	NB
0.1	0.187	0.423	0.001	0.423	0.547	0.329	0.006	0.328	0.644	0.589	0.001	0.589	0.547	0.115	0.006	0.115	0.514
0.2	0.177	0.242	0.071	0.242	0.674	0.507	0.047	0.507	0.631	0.737	0.124	0.737	0.693	0.428	0.077	0.428	0.681
0.3	0.182	0.269	0.250	0.268	0.659	0.733	0.235	0.733	0.623	0.780	0.242	0.780	0.695	0.664	0.235	0.664	0.699
0.4	0.178	0.190	0.582	0.228	0.661	0.782	0.549	0.780	0.617	0.805	0.561	0.784	0.693	0.784	0.557	0.782	0.708
0.5	0.179	0.196	0.742	0.358	0.673	0.807	0.715	0.799	0.614	0.790	0.737	0.799	0.685	0.797	0.721	0.789	0.707
0.6	0.180	0.211	0.810	0.573	0.669	0.833	0.804	0.820	0.597	0.793	0.813	0.811	0.670	0.832	0.808	0.824	0.694
0.7	0.175	0.179	0.824	0.425	0.667	0.843	0.821	0.842	0.585	0.793	0.823	0.834	0.664	0.845	0.822	0.843	0.687
0.8	0.175	0.178	0.868	0.650	0.649	0.861	0.865	0.858	0.575	0.787	0.867	0.864	0.651	0.859	0.865	0.858	0.677
0.9	0.172	0.190	0.860	0.716	0.658	0.859	0.859	0.853	0.580	0.776	0.861	0.861	0.651	0.846	0.858	0.845	0.674

Table 2: Average F scores on 20Newsgroup collection

	1	2	3	4	5	6	7	8	9	10	11	12	13	14	15	16	17
Step1	1-DNF	1-DNF		1-DNF		Spy	Spy	Spy	Rocchio	Rocchio	Rocchio		NB	NB	NB	NB	
Step2	EM	SVM	PEBL	SVM-IS	S-EM	SVM	SVM-I	SVM-IS	EM	SVM	SVM-I	Roc-SVM	EM	SVM	SVM-I	SVM-IS	NB
0.1	0.145	0.545	0.039	0.545	0.460	0.097	0.003	0.097	0.557	0.295	0.003	0.295	0.368	0.020	0.003	0.020	0.333
0.2	0.125	0.371	0.074	0.371	0.640	0.408	0.014	0.408	0.670	0.546	0.014	0.546	0.649	0.232	0.013	0.232	0.611
0.3	0.123	0.288	0.201	0.288	0.665	0.625	0.154	0.625	0.673	0.644	0.121	0.644	0.689	0.469	0.120	0.469	0.674
0.4	0.122	0.260	0.342	0.258	0.683	0.684	0.354	0.684	0.671	0.690	0.385	0.682	0.705	0.610	0.354	0.603	0.704
0.5	0.121	0.248	0.563	0.306	0.685	0.715	0.560	0.707	0.663	0.716	0.565	0.708	0.702	0.680	0.554	0.672	0.707
0.6	0.123	0.209	0.646	0.419	0.689	0.758	0.674	0.746	0.663	0.747	0.683	0.738	0.701	0.737	0.670	0.724	0.715
0.7	0.119	0.196	0.715	0.563	0.681	0.774	0.731	0.757	0.660	0.754	0.731	0.746	0.699	0.763	0.728	0.749	0.717
0.8	0.124	0.189	0.689	0.508	0.680	0.789	0.760	0.783	0.654	0.761	0.763	0.766	0.688	0.780	0.758	0.774	0.707
0.9	0.123	0.177	0.716	0.577	0.684	0.807	0.797	0.798	0.654	0.775	0.798	0.790	0.691	0.806	0.797	0.798	0.714

class SVM. In fact, we experimented each of them. However, their results are poor and thus are not listed here. For example, the F score for one-class SVM is around 0.3-0.5 for most datasets.

8. Pure NB and pure SVM: We also obtain the F scores (see the table below) in the pure case with original (70%) training data, i.e., no positive examples are added to the negative set to form the unlabeled set.

	Reuters (F)	20Newsgroup (F)
NB	0.670	0.709
SVM	0.870	0.792

Comparing the results here with the results in Tables 1 and 2, we observe that when the positive set is large, the F scores of a few SVM based methods are very close to the pure case (sometime better than the pure case). However, when the number of positive documents is not that large, there is still room for further improvements.

6.3 Results of Biased-SVM

In this set of experiments, we again used the SVMlight package, which allows control of C_- and C_- through the parameters c and j, where c is C_- and $j = C_-/C_-$. In our experiments, we varied c from 0.01, 0.03, 0.05, ..., 0.61 and j from 10, 20, 30, ..., 200. We use 30% of the training documents as the validation set in each experiment. The classifier selection criterion $pr/Pr[Y = 1]$ is used to select the best c and j parameters based on the validation set. The final test results are obtained by using the original training set after the parameter c and j have

been selected. Note that we need to run SVM a large number of times. However, some heuristics have been designed to reduce the number of runs, which will be described in the full version of the paper.

We have performed experiments with $\gamma = 0.3$ and 0.7. The averaged results given in Table 3 show that Biased-SVM performs better than the (previous) best of all methods in Tables 1 and 2. We observe that when the positive set is small, the improvement is more significant. This is especially true for the 20Newsgroup collection, which is a harder collection.

Table 3: Average F scores on the two collections

	γ	Average F score of Biased-SVM	Previous best F score
Reuters	0.3	0.785	0.78
	0.7	0.856	0.845
20Newsgroup	0.3	0.742	0.689
	0.7	0.805	0.774

7. Conclusions

In this paper, we discussed the two-step strategy for learning a classifier from positive and unlabeled data. Two new methods were added to the existing techniques. A comprehensive evaluation of all the combinations of methods was conducted to compare their performances, which enables us to draw some important conclusions. We also proposed a more principled approach to solving the problem based on a biased formulation of SVM. Our results show that in general Biased-SVM outperforms all the existing two-step techniques.

References

[1]. Agrawal, R., Bayardo Jr., R. & Srikant, R. (2000) "Athena: Mining-based interactive management of text databases." *EDBT-00*.

[2]. Basu, S., Banerjee, A., & Mooney, R. (2002) "Semi-supervised clustering by seeding." *ICML-02*.

[3]. Bennett, K., and Demiriz. (1998) "A Semi-supervised support vector machines." *Advances in Neural information processing systems* 11.

[4]. Blum, A., Mitchell, T. (1998) "Combining labeled and unlabeled data with co-training," *COLT-98*.

[5]. Bockhorst, J., and Craven, M. (2002) "Exploiting relations among concepts to acquire weakly labeled training data." *ICML-02*.

[6]. Buckley, C., Salton G., and Allan J. (1994) "The effect of adding relevance information in a relevance feedback environment," *SIGIR-94*.

[7]. Dempster, A., Laird, N. M. & Rubin. D. (1997) "Maximum likelihood from incomplete data via the EM algorithm." *Journal of the Royal Statistical Society*, B:39, 1-38.

[8]. Denis, F. "PAC learning from positive statistical queries." *ALT-98*.

[9]. Denis, F. Gilleron, R and Tommasi, M. (2002). "Text classification from positive and unlabeled examples." *IPMU*, 2002.

[10]. Ghani, R. (2002) "Combining labeled and unlabeled data for multiclass text categorization." *ICML-2002*.

[11]. Goldman, S. and Zhou, Y. (2000) "Enhancing supervised learning with unlabeled data." *ICML-00*.

[12]. Guyon, I., Boser, B. and Vapnik, V. (1993). "Automatic capacity tuning of very large VC-dimension classifiers." *Advances in Neural Information Processing Systems*, Vol. 5.

[13]. Joachims, T. (1998) "Text categorization with support vector machines: Learning with many relevant features." *ECML-98*.

[14]. Joachims, T. (1999). "Making large-scale SVM learning practical." *Advances in Kernel Methods - Support Vector Learning*, B. Schölkopf and C. Burges and A. Smola (ed.).

[15]. Lang, K. (1995). "Newsweeder: Learning to filter netnews." *ICML-95*.

[16]. Lee, W. S, and Liu, B. (2003) "Learning with positive and unlabeled examples using weighted logistic regression." *ICML-2003*.

[17]. Lewis, D., and Gale, W. (1994). "A sequential algorithm for training text classifiers." *SIGIR-94*.

[18]. Li, X., and Liu, B. (2003). "Learning to classify text using positive and unlabeled data." *IJCAI-03*.

[19]. Lidstone, G. (1920). "Note on the general case of the Bayes-Laplace formula for inductive or a posteriori probabilities." *Transactions of the Faculty of Actuaries*, 8:182-192.

[20]. Liu, B., Lee, W. S., Yu, P., and Li, X. (2002). "Partially supervised classification of text documents." *ICML-02*.

[21]. Manevitz, L & Yousef, M. (2001). "One-class SVMs for document classification." *J. of Machine Learning research*, 2.

[22]. McCallum, A., Nigam, K. (1998) "A comparison of event models for naïve Bayes text classification." *AAAI-98 Workshop on Learning for Text Categorization*. 1998.

[23]. Morik, K., Brockhausen, P. and Joachims, T. (1999) "*Combining statistical learning with a knowledge-based approach - A case study in intensive care monitoring.*" *ICML-99*, 1999.

[24]. Muggleton, S. (2001). "Learning from the positive data." *Machine Learning*, Accepted.

[25]. Muslea, I., Minton, S., and Knoblock, C. A. (2002). "Active + semi-supervised learning = robust multi-view learning." *ICML-02*.

[26]. Nigam, K., McCallum, A., Thrun, S. and & Mitchell, T. (2000). "Text classification from labeled and unlabeled documents using EM." *Machine Learning*, 39.

[27]. Osuna, E., R. Freund, and F. Girosi (1997). Support vector machines: Training and applications. AI Memo 1602, Massachusetts Institute of Technology.

[28]. Rakutti, B. Ferra, H. Kowalczyk, A. (2002). "Using unlabeled data for text classification through addition of cluster parameters." *ICML-02*.

[29]. Rocchio, J. (1971). "Relevant feedback in information retrieval." In G. Salton (ed.). *The smart retrieval system- experiments in automatic document processing*, Englewood Cliffs, NJ.

[30]. Salton, G. and McGill, M. (1983). *Introduction to Modern Information Retrieval*. McGraw-Hill.

[31]. Scholkopf, S. Platt, J. Shawe, J. Smola, A. & Williamson, R. (1999). "Estimating the support of a high-dimensional distribution." *Technical Report MSR-TR-99-87*, Microsoft Research.

[32]. Vapnik, V. (1995). *The nature of statistical learning theory*, Springer-Verlag, NY, USA, 1995

[33]. Yang, Y. and Liu, X. (1999). "A re-examination of text categorization methods." *SIGIR-99*.

[34]. Yu, H., Han, J. & Chang, K. (2002). "PEBL: Positive example based learning for Web page classification using SVM." *KDD-02*.

[35]. Zhang, T. (2000). "The value of unlabeled data for classification problems," *ICML-00*.

OP-Cluster: Clustering by Tendency in High Dimensional Space

Jinze Liu and Wei Wang
Computer Science Department
University of North Carolina
Chapel Hill, NC, 27599
{liuj, weiwang }@cs.unc.edu

Abstract

Clustering is the process of grouping a set of objects into classes of similar objects. Because of unknownness of the hidden patterns in the data sets, the definition of similarity is very subtle. Until recently, similarity measures are typically based on distances, e.g Euclidean distance and cosine distance. In this paper, we propose a flexible yet powerful clustering model, namely OP-Cluster (Order Preserving Cluster). Under this new model, two objects are similar on a subset of dimensions if the values of these two objects induce the same relative order of those dimensions. Such a cluster might arise when the expression levels of (co-regulated) genes can rise or fall synchronously in response to a sequence of environment stimuli. Hence, discovery of OP-Cluster is essential in revealing significant gene regulatory networks. A deterministic algorithm is designed and implemented to discover all the significant OP-Clusters. A set of extensive experiments has been done on several real biological data sets to demonstrate its effectiveness and efficiency in detecting co-regulated patterns.

1 Introduction

As a fundamental tool to analyze large databases, clustering has been studied extensively in many areas including statistics, machine learning and pattern recognition. Most clustering models, including those proposed for subspace clustering, define similarities among objects via some distance functions. Some well-known distance functions include Euclidean distance, Manhattan distance, and cosine distance. However, distance functions are not always adequate in capturing correlations among objects. In fact, strong correlations may still exist among a set of objects even if they are far apart from each other in distance.

In light of this observation, the δ-pCluster model [17] was introduced to discover clusters by pattern similarity (rather than distance) from raw data sets. A major limitation of the δ-pCluster model is that it only considers either strict shifting patterns or strict scaling patterns[1], which is

insufficient in many cases.

In this paper, we propose a flexible clustering model, order preserving cluster (OP-Cluster), which is able to capture the general tendency of objects across a subset of dimensions in a high dimensional space.

Figure 1 a) shows a set of 3 objects with 10 attributes. In this raw data, no obvious pattern is visible. However, if we pick the set of attributes $\{b, c, e, g, l\}$ as in Figure 1 b) for these 3 objects, we can observe the following fact: *The ranks for each of these attributes are the same for all the three objects.* If we rearrange the columns in the ascending order of their ranks: $< g, c, l, e, b >$, in Figure 1 c), the consistency of *escalation* along the ordered list of attributes can be seen much clearer.

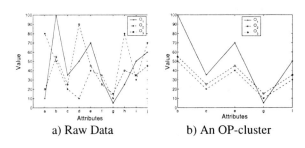

a) Raw Data   b) An OP-cluster

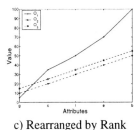

c) Rearranged by Rank

Figure 1. An Example of OP-cluster

1.1 Applications

- *DNA microarray analysis.* Microarray is one of the latest breakthroughs in experimental molecular biology.

---

[1]The scaling patterns can be transformed into shifting patterns by applying a logarithmic function on the raw data.

Investigators show that more often than not, if several genes contribute to a disease, it is possible to identify a subset of conditions, under which these genes show a coherent tendency. Since a gene's expression level may vary substantially due to its sensitivity to systematic settings, the direction of movement (up or down) in response to condition change is often considered more credible than its actual value. Discovering clusters of genes sharing coherent tendency is essential in revealing the significant connections in gene regulatory networks[9].

- *E-commerce*. In recommendation systems and target marketing, the tendency of people's affinities plays a more important role than the absolute value. Revealing sets of customers/clients with similar behavior can help the companies to predict customers' interest and make proper recommendation for future marketing.

1.2   Challenges and Our Contributions

To discover the general tendency in a cluster, the major challenge is the huge number of potential rankings. If we have n attributes, there are $N!$ different permutations of (subsets of) attributes. Each permutation corresponds to one unique ordering for this set of attributes, which is embedded in a subset of objects. Moreover, it is possible that similar ranking only occur in a subset of the N attributes. So totally, the number of potential candidates for OP-Clusters with at least nc attributes is

$$\sum_{nc \le i \le N} \frac{N!}{(N-i)!} \qquad (1)$$

Data sets in DNA array analysis or collaborative filtering can have hundreds of attributes. This results in a huge number of candidates of various lengths. To tackle this problem, we introduce OPC-Tree to guide the enumeration of potential candidates. The following are our contributions.

- We propose a new clustering model, namely OP-Cluster, to capture general tendencies exhibited by the objects. The OP-Cluster model is a generalization of existing subspace clustering models. It has a wide variety of applications, including DNA array analysis and collaborative filtering, where tendency along a set of attributes carries significant meaning.

- We design a compact tree structure OPC-Tree to mine OP-Cluster effectively. Compared with one of fastest sequential pattern mining algorithms, prefixSpan(modified to serve our purpose), the OPC-Tree based algorithm delivers a shorter response time in most cases, especially when the data is pattern-rich.

- We apply the model of OP-Cluster to two real data sets and discover interesting patterns that tend to be overlooked by previous models.

1.3   Paper Layout

The remainder of the paper is organized as follows. Section 2 discusses some related work. Section 3 defines the model of OP-Cluster. Section 4 presents the algorithm to mine OP-Cluster in detail. An extensive performance study is reported in Section 5. Section 6 concludes the paper.

2   Related Work

2.1   Subspace Clustering

Clustering in high dimensional space is often problematic as theoretical results [8] questioned the meaning of closest matching in high dimensional spaces. Recent research work [18, 19, 3, 4, 6, 9, 12] has focused on discovering clusters embedded in the subspaces of a high dimensional data set. This problem is known as subspace clustering. Based on the measure of similarity, there are two categories of clustering model. The first category is distance based. In this category, one of the well known subspace clustering algorithms is CLIQUE [6]. CLIQUE is a density and grid based clustering method. The PROCLUS [3] and the ORCLUS [4] algorithms find projected clusters based on representative cluster centers in a set of cluster dimensions. Another interesting approach, Fascicles [12], finds subsets of data that share similar values in a subset of dimensions.

The second category is pattern-based. The first algorithm proposed in this category is the bicluster model [10] by Cheng et al. The algorithm tries to measure the coherence of the genes and the conditions in a sub-matrix of a DNA array. Recently, δ-pCluster is introduced by Wang et al [17] to cluster objects exhibiting shifting or scaling patterns in a data set in a very efficient way. In many applications, only allowing shifting or scaling patterns is too restrictive. To include more generic pattern in a cluster, the threshold has to be relaxed. This, in turn, can result in unavoidable noise inside a cluster.

The concept of OPSM(order preserving submatrix) was first introduced in [7] to represent a subset of genes identically ordered among a subset of the conditions in microarray analysis. The OPSM problem is proven to be NP-hard. A model-based statistical algorithm was also given in [7] to discover OPSMs. There are some drawbacks in this pioneering work. First, only one cluster can be found at a time. And the quality of the resulted cluster is very sensitive to some given parameters and the initial selection of partial models. Secondly, OPSM algorithm favors clusters with a large row support, which as a result, can obstruct the discovery of the small but significant ones.

In our work, we generalize the OPSM model by allowing grouping. Based on the new model, we propose a deterministic subspace clustering algorithm, namely OPC-Tree, to capture all the general tendencies exhibited by a subset of objects along a subset of dimensions in one run.

2.2 Sequential Pattern Mining

Since it was first introduced in [5], sequential pattern mining has been studied extensively. Conventional sequential pattern mining finds frequent subsequences in the database based on exact match. There are two classes of algorithms. On one hand, the breadth-first search methods (e.g., GSP [15] and SPADE [21]) are based on the Apriori principle [5] and conduct level-by-level candidate-generation-and-tests. On the other hand, the depth-first search methods (e.g., PrefixSpan [14] and SPAM [1]) grow long patterns from short ones by constructing projected databases.

In our paper, we are facing a similar but more complicated problem than sequential pattern mining. Rows in matrix will be treated as a sequence to find sequential patterns. However, in order to finally determine OP-Cluster, the ID associated with each sequence has to be kept during the mining process. A depth-first traversal of the tree is carried out to generate frequent subsequences by recursively concatenating legible suffixes with the existing frequent prefixes.

3 Model

In this section, we define the OP-Cluster model for mining objects that exhibit tendency on a set of attributes.

3.1 Notations

$\mathcal{D}$	A set of objects
$\mathcal{A}$	A set of attributes of the objects in $\mathcal{D}$
$(\mathcal{O}, \mathcal{T})$	A sub-matrix of the data set, where $\mathcal{O} \subseteq \mathcal{D}, \mathcal{T} \subseteq \mathcal{A}$
$x, y, \dots$	Objects in $\mathcal{D}$
$a, b, \dots$	Attributes in $\mathcal{A}$
d_{xa}	Value of object x on attribute a
δ	User-specified grouping threshold
δ^p	User-specified shifting threshold
nc, nr	User-specified minimum # of columns and minimum # of rows of a model

3.2 Definitions and Problem Statement

Let $\mathcal{D}$ be a set of objects, where each object is associated with a set of attributes $\mathcal{A}$. We are interested in subsets of objects that exhibit a coherent tendency on a subset of attributes of $\mathcal{A}$.

Definition 3.1 *Let o be an object in the database, $\langle d_{o1}, d_{o2}, \dots, d_{on} \rangle$ be the attribute values in a non-decreasing order, n be the number of attributes and δ be the user specified threshold. We say that o is **similar** on attributes i, $i + 1$, ..., $i + j$, $(0 < i \le n, 0 < j \le n)$, if*

$$(d_{o(i+j)} - d_{oi}) < \mathcal{G}(\delta, d_{oi}) \tag{2}$$

where $\mathcal{G}(\delta, d_{oi})$ is a grouping function that defines the equivalent class. We call the set of attributes $\langle i, i+1, ..., i+$

$j\rangle$ a **group** *for object o. Attribute d_{oi} is called a **pivot point** of this group.*

The intuition behind this definition is that, if the difference between the values of two attributes is not significant, we regard them to be "equivalent" and do not order them. For example, in gene expression data, each tissue(condition) might belong to a class of tissues corresponding to a stage or time point in the progression of a disease, or a type of genetic abnormality. Hence, within the same class, no restrict order would be placed on the expression levels.

There are multiple ways to define the grouping function $\mathcal{G}(\delta, d_{oi})$. One way is to define it as the average difference between every pair of attributes whose values are closest.

$$\mathcal{G}(\delta, d_{oi}) = \mathcal{G}(\delta) = \delta \times \sum_{0 < i < n} (d_{o(i+1)} - d_{oi}) \tag{3}$$

This definition is independent of d_{oi} and is usually used when each attribute has a finite domain and its value is evenly distributed within its domain. The previous example on movie rating belongs to this case. When the value of each attribute may follow a skew distribution as the gene expression data, Equation 4 is a better choice. For the sake of simplicity in explanation, we use Equation 4 in the remainder of this paper, unless otherwise specified.

$$\mathcal{G}(\delta, d_{oi}) = \delta \times d_{oi} \tag{4}$$

For example, a viewer rates five movies (A, B, C, D, E) as $(1, 4, 4.5, 8, 10)$. If $\delta = 0.2$, 4 and 4.5 will be grouped together and the corresponding attributes B and C will be considered equivalent. The rating is divided into four groups $\{\{A\}, \{B, C\}, \{D\}, \{E\}\}$.

Definition 3.2 *Let o be an object in the database, and $(g_{o1}) (g_{o2})...(g_{ok})$ be a sequence of similar groups of o by Equation 2 and in non-descending order of their values. o shows an '**UP pattern** ' on an ordered list of attributes $a_1, a_2, ..., a_j$ if $a_1, a_2, ..., a_j$ is a subsequence of $(g_{o1})(g_{o2})...(g_{ok})$.*

In the above example, $(1, 4, 4.5, 8, 10)$ is the rating for movies (A, B, C, D, E). After we apply the similar group, we are able to transform the original rating to the sequence $A(BC)DE$. The subsequence $ABDE$, AE, and $(BC)E$, for example, show 'UP' patterns.

Definition 3.3 *Let $\mathcal{O}$ be a subset of objects in the database, $\mathcal{O} \subseteq \mathcal{D}$. Let $\mathcal{T}$ be a subset of attributes $\mathcal{A}$. $(\mathcal{O}, \mathcal{T})$ forms an **OP-Cluster(Order Preserving Cluster)** if there exists a permutation of attributes in $\mathcal{T}$, on which every object in $\mathcal{O}$ shows the "UP" pattern.*

Suppose that we have two movie ratings o_1 and o_2 for movies (A, B, C, D, E). The ratings are $(1, 4, 4.5, 8, 10)$ and $(2, 5, 7, 4.5, 9)$, respectively. According to Definition 3.3, the corresponding sequence of groups for o_1 is $A(BC)DE$, and for o_2 is $A(DB)CE$. Since $ABCE$ is a common subsequence of them, we say that o_1 and o_2 form an OP-Cluster on the attribute set of $ABCE$.

Essentially, OP-Cluster captures the consistent tendency exhibited by a subset of objects in a subspace. Compared with δ-pCluster, which is restricted to either shifting or scaling pattern, OP-Cluster is more flexible. It includes δ-pCluster as a special case. The following lemmas address the relationship between these two models.

Lemma 3.1 *Let $(\mathcal{O}^p, \mathcal{T}^p)$ be a δ-pCluster, and δ^p is maximum skew factor allowed by this δ-pCluster. $(\mathcal{O}^p, \mathcal{T}^p)$ can be identified as an OP-Cluster if the absolute difference between any two attributes a, b, $a, b \subseteq \mathcal{T}^p$ of any object o, $o \in \mathcal{O}^p$ is at least $\frac{\delta^p}{2}$.*

Please refer to [13] for the detailed proof.

When the condition in Lemma 3.1 cannot be met in real data sets, the grouping threshold δ in OP-Cluster can be set higher to accommodate any δ-pCluster with a maximum skew factor δ^p and to include it as a special case of an OP-Cluster. For example, for any δ-pCluster with threshold δ^p, we can set the grouping threshold to be δ^p. By this means, the order between two attributes with the difference less than δ^p will be put in alphabetical order. If another object has the same set of attributes grouped together, these two objects and the two attributes will form an OP-Cluster. This will be summarized in Lemma 3.2.

Lemma 3.2 *Let $(\mathcal{O}^p, \mathcal{T}^p)$ be a δ-pCluster, and δ^p is maximum skew factor allowed by this δ-pCluster. $(\mathcal{O}^p, \mathcal{T}^p)$ can be identified as an OP-Cluster, if the grouping threshold $\delta \geq \delta^p$.*

Please refer to [13] for the detailed proof.

In the following sections, since the input data is a matrix, we refer to objects as rows and attributes as columns.

Problem Statement Given a grouping threshold δ, a minimal number of columns nc, and a minimal number of rows nr, the goal is to find all (maximum) submatrices $(\mathcal{O}, \mathcal{T})$ such that $(\mathcal{O}, \mathcal{T})$ is an OP-Cluster according to Definition 3.3, and $|\mathcal{O}| \geq nr$, $|\mathcal{T}| \geq nc$.

4 Algorithm

In this section, we present the algorithm to generate OP-Clusters. It consists of two steps: (1) preprocess each row in the matrix into a sequence of groups by Defintion 3.1; (2) mine the sets of rows containing frequent subsequences in the sequences generated in step(1).

In this paper, we propose a novel compact structure OPC-Tree to organize the sequences and to guide the pattern generation. Compared with prefixSpan, OPC-Tree can group sequences sharing the same prefixes together to eliminate multiple projections in the future. Meanwhile, single path subtree can be identified to avoid any usefulless projections at all.

4.1 Preprocessing

To preprocess the data, first, we sort all the entry values in non-decreasing order for each row. Secondly, each sorted row will be organized into a sequence of groups based on their similarity. The resulted sequences of column labels will be taken as the input to the second step— mining OP-Cluster. This process is illustrated in the following example. In the raw data present in Table 1, if the grouping threshold δ is set to be 0.1, for the row 1, the sorted order of attributes for row 1 is $[228 : d, 284 : b, 4108 : c, 4392 : a]$. a and c can be grouped together since $4392 - 4108 < 4108 \times 0.1$. By processing the rest of rows in the same way, the sequences are generated as shown in the last column of row 1. Attributes in each "()"are in the same group. Without loss of generality, they are put in the alphabetical order.

rID	a	b	c	d	seq
1	4392	284	4108	228	$db(ac)$
2	401	281	120	298	$c(bd)a$
3	401	292	109	238	$cdba$
4	280	318	37	215	$cdab$
5	2857	285	2576	226	$dbca$
6	48	290	224	228	$a(cd)b$

Table 1. Example Data Set

4.2 OPC-Tree

In the above subsection, each row in the matrix has been converted into a sequence of column labels. The goal in the next step is to discover all the frequent subsequences hidden in the generated sequences. This problem seems to be a sequential pattern mining problem. However, it is different from a conventional sequential pattern mining problem in the following two aspects. First, the identities of the rows associated with each frequent subsequence have to be recorded in order to determine the rows involved in an OP-Cluster. Conventional sequential mining algorithms only keep the number of appearance of frequent subsequences but not their identities. To discover the set of rows associated with them, one possible approach is to scan database to collect the related rows during postprocessing. However, this method is very time consuming and is not scalable to the size of the database. Secondly, our data sets are special in the sense that the number of appearance of each item(column) is the same since each item appears once and exactly once in each sequence. As a result, no pruning can actually happen in the first round of operation by using either apriori-based or projection-based algorithm. Based on the above observation, we develop the following algorithm.

Our algorithm uses a compact tree structure to store the crucial information used in mining OP-Clusters. The discovery of frequent subsequences and the association of rows with frequent subsequences occur simultaneously. Sequences sharing the same prefixes will be gathered and recorded in the same location. Hence, further operations along the shared prefixes will be performed only once for all the rows sharing them. Pruning techniques can also be applied easily in the OPC-Tree structure.

Before we define the OPC-Tree formally, we first give the following example.

Example 4.1 *For the sequences in Table 1, with nc =* 3, *nr = 3, the OPC-Tree algorithm makes a pre-order depth-first traversal of the tree and works in the following steps.*

Step 1: *Create root -1(NULL) and insert all the sequences into the tree.* This is shown in Figure 2 (A). Notice that all rows sharing the same prefix fall on the same prefix of the tree. The sequence ID is stored in the leaves. This is the *initial* OPC-Tree on which a recursive procedure depicted in Step 2-5 is performed to fully develop the tree.

Step 2: *For each child of the root, insert suffixes in its subtree to the root's child that has a matching label.* In Figure 2 (B), *c* is a child of the root −1. In this subtree, the suffix subtree starting at *d* (for the sequences 3, 4) is inserted into the root −1's child *d*. If the same subtree exists in the destination node, the sequence IDs associated with the suffixes are combined with existing IDs in the destination node. Otherwise a new subtree will be created in the destination node. In the case where a suffix is too short to satisfy *current depth + length of the suffix > nc*, the suffix will not be inserted. For example, *ba* in sequence 3 is also a suffix, it is not to be inserted because the *depth 0 + length of ba < nc.*

Step3: *Prune current root's children.* If the number of rows that fall in a subtree is smaller than *nr*, the subtree will be deleted because no further development can generate a cluster with more than *nr* rows. For example, the subtree leading from −1*b* in Figure 2 (B) is deleted in Figure 2 (C) since there are only two sequences falling in this subtree.

Step4: *Repeat Step2-Step5 on the root's first child and its subtree recursively.* For example, *c* is the first child of root −1. Therefore, the same procedure in Step2 is applied to *c* first. The suffixes of *c*'s subtree *d*, such as *ba* and *ab* are inserted into *c*'s subtree *b* and *a* respectively. Since there are less than three sequences falling on *c*'s subtrees *a* and *b*, the branches −1*ca*− and −1*cb*− are deleted. Following the same procedure, we develop *c*'s only subtree −1*cd*−, which is shown in Figure 2(D).

Step5: *Follow the sibling link from the first child and repeat Step2-Step5 on each sibling node recursively.* For example, after finishing −1*c*−'s subtree development, the next subtree to develop is −1*c*−'s sibling −1*d*−.

Definition 4.1 OPC-tree (Order Preserving Clustering tree). *An OPC-Tree is a tree structure defined below.*
1. It consists of one root labeled as "-1", a set of subtrees as the children of the root;
2. Each node in the subtrees consists of four entries: entry value, a link to its first children node, a link to its next sibling node, and a list of all the rows that share the same path leading from root to this node but do not have longer common subsequences passing this node. In another word,

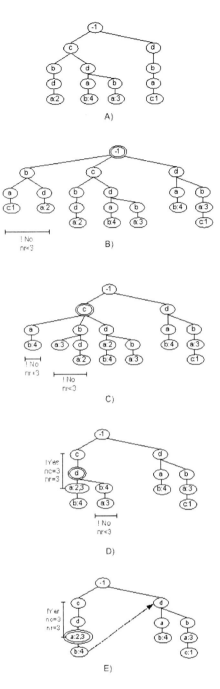

Figure 2. OPC-Tree for Table 1. The label in the oval shape represents the column name. The number following ':' represents the row ID. The node with double oval means the active node in the depth first traversal. '!No' means that the subtree must be pruned. 'Yes' means that subtree is an OP-Cluster. A). Initiate the tree with all the rows B). Active node -1, Insert the suffix of -1's subtrees to node -1. C). Active node -1c, Insert and Prune the subtree (*nr* < 3). D). Active node -1cd-. Identify the first OP-Cluster E). Finish growing the -1's first subtree-1c, the next subtree is -1d.

191

the sequence IDs are only recorded at the nodes that mark the end of a commom subsequence.

Algorithm *growTree*(T,nc,nr,depth)
Input: T: the root of the initiated tree, nc and nr
Output: OP-Cluster existed in T
(* Grow patterns based on original T *)
1. **if** $T = $ **nil**
2. 　　　　**return**;
3. 　$T_{child} \leftarrow T$'s first child;
4. **for** any sub-tree $subT$ of T
5. 　　**do** insertSubTree($subT$, T);
6. 　pruneTreeNode(T);
7. 　growTree(T_{child}, nc, nr, $depth + 1$);
8. 　growTree(T's next sibling, nc, nr, $depth$);
9. **return**.

Analysis of OPC-Tree construction Only one scan of the entire data matrix is needed during the construction of the OPC-Tree. Each row is converted into a sequence of column labels. The sequences are then inserted into the OPC-Tree. With OPC-Tree structure, sequences that have the same prefix naturally fall onto the same path from root to the node corresponding to the end of prefix. To save memory, the row IDs associated with each path are only recorded at the node marking the end of the longest common prefix shared by these rows. To find the OP-Cluster using the OPC-Tree, the common subsequences are developed by adding suffixes of each sub-tree as the tree's children, via a pre-order traversal of the OPC-Tree.

Lemma 4.1 *Given a matrix M, a grouping threshold, the initial OPC-Tree contains all the information of matrix M.*

Rationale: Based on the OPC-Tree construction process, each row in the matrix is mapped onto one path in the OPC-Tree. The row IDs and the order of the columns are completely stored in the initial OPC-Tree.

4.2.1 Mining OP-Cluster Using OPC-Tree

Lemma 4.2 *The developed OPC-Tree on a set of sequences contains all subsequences hidden in the initial OPC-Tree.*

Rationale: Given any sequence $S = x_1 x_2 x_3 x_4 \ldots x_n$, we want to show that all of the subsequences of S can be found in a path starting from root. Through the initiation of OPC-Tree, we know that S will exist in the OPC-Tree. Then given any subsequence $SS = x_i x_j \ldots x_s, (1 \leq i, s \leq n)$, we can obtain SS by the following steps. First, at node x_i, insert suffix $x_i x_{i+1} \ldots x_n$. Now in the subtree of x_i, node x_j can be found because it should be along the path $x_i x_{i+1} \ldots x_n$ that is inserted in the first step. Similarly, we insert the suffix $x_j \ldots x_n$. As a result, we get the path $x_i x_j x_{j+1} \ldots x_n$. By repeating the same procedure until we insert the suffix starting with x_s, we get the path $x_i x_j \ldots x_s$. Because all the suffixes are inserted in the OPC-Tree, the OPC-Tree contains all the subsequences presented in the original OPC-Tree.

Rows in an OP-Cluster share the same rank of a set of columns, which corresponds to the same path in the OPC-Tree. We can conclude that the OPC-Tree contains all the clusters. This leads to the following lemma.

Lemma 4.3 *The developed OPC-Tree on a set of sequences contains all potential OP-Clusters. The columns in these clusters are on the paths leading from the root to any tree node with depth no less than nc and row support count in its subtree no less than nr .*

4.2.2 Pruning OPC-Tree

Without any pruning, the whole OPC-Tree fits well into memory when we have a small to medium sized matrix (15 columns by 3000 rows). However, for large matrices, some pruning strategies have to be employed to minimize the size of the OPC-Tree. There are two pruning techniques used in our implementation. One strategy is to prune the suffixes to be inserted that are shorter than nc; the other is to prune the subtrees where the row support count is below nr.

Lemma 4.4 *For a node N in the OPC-Tree with depth d, and for a suffix S with length l in its sub-tree, if $d + l < nc$ (the minimum columns required for a cluster), this suffix S will not be useful in forming any OP-Cluster cluster.*

Rationale: The length of the path L we can get by combining the path from root to N and S is $d + l$. Based on Lemma 4.3, L will not form any cluster. Therefore, suffix S need not to be inserted. In our implementation, we check depth of the node at which the end of the suffix is inserted. If the depth is smaller than nc, the row IDs recorded in this node will be deleted.

The major cost of OPC-Tree development is suffix concatenation. To minimize the storage cost of the suffixes, the single-path subtree can be collapsed into one node. The detailed data structure and algorithm can be found in technical report [13]

5 Experiments

We experimented our OP-Cluster algorithm, OPC-Tree by collapsing nodes on two real data sets. The program was implemented in C and executed on a Linux machine with a 700 MHz CPU and 2G main memory. We also implemented an optimized version of prefixSpan algorithm for comparison. The following tests are organized into three categories. First, we show promising patterns found in real data sets, which failed to be discovered by other models. Secondly, we study the sensitivity of OP-Cluster to various parameters. At last, we evaluate the performance of OPC-Tree and compare it with the optimized prefixSpan algorithm.

5.1 Data Sets

The following two real data sets are used in our experiments.

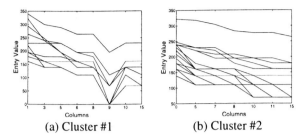

(a) Cluster #1   (b) Cluster #2

Figure 3. Cluster Analysis: Two examples of OP-Clusters in yeast data

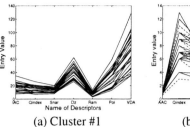

(a) Cluster #1   (b) Cluster #2

Figure 4. Cluster Analysis: Two examples of OP-Clusters in drug activity data

Gene Expression Data

Gene expression data are generated by DNA chips and other microarray techniques. The yeast microarray contains expression levels of 2,884 genes under 17 conditions [16]. The data set is presented as a matrix. Each row corresponds to a gene and each column represents a condition under which the gene is developed. Each entry represents the relative abundance of the mRNA of a gene under a specific condition. The entry value, derived by scaling and logarithm from the original relative abundance, is in the range of 0 and 600. Biologists are interested in finding a subset of genes showing strikingly similar up-regulation or down-regulation under a subset of conditions [10].

Drug Activity Data

Drug activity data is also a matrix with 10000 rows and 30 columns. Each row corresponds to a chemical compound and each column represents a descriptor/feature of the compound. The value of each entry varies from 0 to 1000.

5.2 Results from Real Data

We apply the OP-Cluster algorithm to the two data sets. With parameter $\delta = 0.1$, Some interesting clusters are reported in both of the data sets. As showed in Figure 3, the two patterns generated from yeast dataset [10] present the coherent tendency along the columns. In Figure 3(a), Figure 3 (b) shows another interesting cluster which presents with a descending tendency itself. In both of the figures, we can observe that each of the four example OP-Clusters contains the curves with sharp slopes and the curves with potentially long distances to the rest.

5.3 Scalability

We evaluate the performance of the OP-Cluster algorithm with the drug activity data which has a larger size. Figure 5 shows the performance data. As we know, the columns and the rows of the matrix carry the same significance in the OP-Cluster model, which is symmetrically defined in Formula 2. Although the algorithm is not entirely

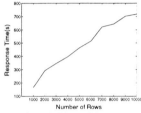 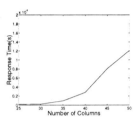

(a) Scalability with respect to number of rows   (b) Scalability with respect to number of columns

Figure 5. Performance Study: Response time V.S. number of columns and number of rows

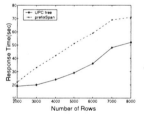

Figure 6. Performance comparison of prefixS-pan and UPC-tree

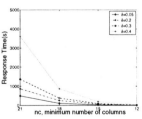 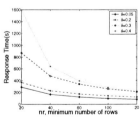

(a) Response time varying similarity threshold and nc (b) Response time varying similarity threshold and nr

Figure 7. Performance Study: Response time V.S. similarity threshold , nc and nr

symmetric in the sense that it chooses to project column-pairs first, the curves in Figure 5 demonstrate similar trends.

Data sets used in Figure 5 are taken from the drug activity data. For experiments in Figure 5(a), the total number of columns is fixed at 30. The mining program is invoked with $\delta = 0.2$, $nc = 9$, and $nr = 0.01N$, where N is the total number of rows. For the experiemnts in Figure 5(b), the total number of rows is fixed at 1000. The mining algorithm is invoked with $\delta = 0.2$, $nc = 0.66C$, and $nr = 30$, where C is the total number of columns. The response time of the OPC-Tree is mostly determined by the size of the tree. As the number of rows and number of columns increase, the size of developed OPC-Tree will get deeper and broader. Hence, the response time will unavoidably become longer.

Figure 6 presents the performance comparison between the prefixSpan algorithm and the OPC-Tree algorithm. The parameter setting for this set of experiment is the following: $nc = 9$, $nr = 0.01N$, $\delta = 0.2$. The number of columns is 20. We can observe that the OPC-Tree algorithm can constantly outperform the prefixSpan algorithm and the advantage becomes more substantial with larger data set.

Next, we study the impact of the parameters (δ, nc, and nr) towards the response time. The results are shown in Figure 7. The data set used in this experiment is the yeast data. When nc and nr are fixed, the response time gets shorter as the group threshold δ relaxes. The reason is that as more columns are grouped together, the number of rows sharing the same path in the OPC-Tree is increasing. Hence, the OPC-Tree is shorter, which results in less overall response time. As nc or nr decreases, the response time prolonged. This is showed in Figure 7. According to the pruning techniques discussed in Lemma 4.4, fewer number of subsequences can be eliminated when nc is smaller. As a result, a larger tree is constructed, which consumes more time. A similar effect can be observed with respect to nr from Figure 7(b).

6   Conclusions

In many applications including collaborative filtering and DNA array analysis, although the distance (e.g., measured by Euclidean distance or cosine distance) among the objects may not be close, they can still manifest consistent patterns on a subset of dimensions. In this paper, we proposed a new model called OP-Cluster to capture the consistent tendency exhibited by a subset of objects in a subset of dimensions in high dimensional space. We proposed a compact tree structure, namely OPC-Tree, and devised a depth-first algorithm that can efficiently and effectively discover all the closed OP-Clusters with a user-specified threshold.

References

[1] J. Ayres, J. E. Gehrke, T. Yiu, and J. Flannick. Sequential PAttern Mining Using Bitmaps. In *SIGKDD*, July 2002.

[2] R. C. Agarwal, C. C. Aggarwal, and V. Parsad. Depth first generation of long patterns. In *SIGKDD*, 2000.

[3] C. C. Aggarwal, C. Procopiuc, J. Wolf, P. S. Yu, and J. S. Park. Fast algorithms for projected clustering. In *SIGMOD*, 1999.

[4] C. C. Aggarwal and P. S. Yu. Finding generalized projected clusters in high dimensional spaces. In *SIGMOD*, pages 70-81, 2000.

[5] R. Agrawal and R. Srikant. Mining sequential patterns. In *ICDE*, 3-14, Mar. 1995.

[6] R. Agrawal, J. Gehrke, D. Gunopulos, and P. Raghavan. Authomatic subspace clustering of high dimensional data for data mining applications. In *SIGMOD*, 1998.

[7] A. Ben-Dor, B. Chor, R.Karp, and Z.Yakhini. Discovering Local Structure in Gene Expression Data: The Order-Preserving Submatrix Problem. In *RECOMB* 2002.

[8] K. Beyer, J. Goldstein, R. Ramakrishnan, and U. Shaft. When is nearest neighbors meaningful. In *Proc. of the Int. Conf. Database Theories*, pages 217-235, 1999.

[9] C. H. Cheng, A. W. Fu, and Y. Zhang. Entropy-based subspace clustering for mining numerical data. In *SIGKDD*, pages 84-93, 1999.

[10] Y. Cheng and G. Church. Biclustering of expression data. In *Proc. of 8th International Conference on Intelligent System for Molecular Biology*, 2000.

[11] M. Ester, H. Kriegel, J. Sander, and X. Xu. A density-bsed algorithm for discovering clusters in large spatial databases with noise. In *SIGKDD*, pages 226-231, 1996.

[12] H.V.Jagadish, J.Madar, and R. Ng. Semantic compression and pttern extraction with fasicicles. In *VLDB*, pages 186-196, 1999.

[13] J.Liu and W.Wang. Flexible clustering by tendency in high dimensional spaces. Technical Report TR03-009, Computer Science Department, UNC-CH, 2003.

[14] J. Pei, J. Han, B. Mortazavi-Asl, H. Pinto, Q. Chen U. Dayal, and M.-C. Hsu. PrefixSpan mining sequential patterns e.ciently by prefix projected pattern growth. In *ICDE* 2001, pages 215-226, Apr. 2001.

[15] R.Srikant and R.Agrawal. Mining sequential patterns: Generalizations and performance improvements. In *EDBT'96*, pages 3-17, Mar. 1996.

[16] S. Tavazoie, J. Hughes, M. Campbell, R. Cho, and G. Church. Yeast micro data set. In *http://arep.med.harvard.edu/biclustering/yeast.matrix*, 2000.

[17] H. Wang, W. Wang, J. Yang, and P. Yu. Clustering by pattern similarity in large data sets, in *SIGMOD*, pp. 394-405, 2002.

[18] J. Yang, W. Wang, H. Wang, and P. S. Yu. δ-clusters: Capturing subspace correlation in a large data set. In *ICDE*, pages 517-528, 2002.

[19] J. Yang, W. Wang, P. Yu, and J. Han. Mining long sequential patterns in a noisy environment. In *SIGMOD*,pp.406-417, 2002.

[20] T. Zhang, R. Ramakrishnan, and M. Livny. Birch: An efficient data clustering method for very large databases. In *SIGMOD*, pages 103114, 1996.

[21] M. J. Zaki, S. Parthasarathy, M.Orihara, and W. Li. Parallel algorithm for discovery of association rules. In *DMKD*, 343-374, 1997.

Parsing Without a Grammar: Making Sense of Unknown File Formats

Levon Lloyd and Steven Skiena
Department of Computer Science
State University of New York at Stony Brook
Stony Brook, NY 11794-4400
{lloyd, skiena}@cs.sunysb.edu

Abstract

The thousands of specialized structured file formats in use today present a substantial barrier to freely exchanging information between applications programs. We consider the problem of deducing such basic features as the whitespace characters, bracketing delimiter symbols, and self-delimiter characters of a given file format from one or more example files. We demonstrate that for sufficiently large example files, we can typically identify the basic features of interest.

1. Introduction

Literally thousands of specialized structured file formats are used by modern computer systems. Applications programs for word processing, spreadsheets, and databases are typically built around incompatible proprietary file formats. Markup languages such as XML, HTML, and latex annotate texts using distinct notations. Dozens of programming and scripting languages are in wide use, each defining a different syntax and semantics. Document interchange formats such as PostScript and PDF are sufficiently complex as to be capable of universal computation [6]. Image formats such as TIFF and gif differ greatly in richness and representation.

This Tower of Babel presents a substantial barrier to freely exchanging information between applications programs. Although parsers can be written for any particular file format (given a complete description of the format) and conversion programs written to transform A files to B files for every pair of formats A and B, such approaches quickly become intractable as the number of distinct formats becomes large.

In this paper, we introduce a different approach to the problem. Given one or more files written in a specific unknown file format, we seek to analyze these examples to deduce basic features of the format:

- What symbols serve as *whitespace* or separation characters? Blanks, tabs, and line feeds serve as whitespace characters in many file formats, but not all of them (consider comma-separated formats such as .csv files).

- Which pairs of characters nest together as *delimiters*? Left/right parentheses, brackets, and angle-brackets are common nesting pairs of delimiters, but not all such pairs have meaning in all formats. For example, left/right angle brackets nest in HTML but not in latex documents, where they denote less-than and greater-than respectively.

- Which single characters act in pairs as *self-delimiters*? The single (') or double quote (") symbols often serve in such roles in natural language text or in programming languages to demarcate character strings. In latex, the dollar sign symbol ($) self-delimits mathematics notation from other text.

- Which larger symbols nest together as *tags*? Examples include *begin* and *end* in many programming and markup languages.

Recognizing such features from a set of example files is a very challenging task, which becomes even harder when limited to a single example file. However, a program which could accurately extract plain text from formatted files would have many important data mining applications:

- *Super Google* – Search engines such as Google build indices on plain text extracted from a relatively small number of file formats in wide use (e.g. HTML, Word, and pdf) for which they have built specialized parsers. However, a host of other informative file formats such as Mathematica notebooks and UNIX tar files remain unindexed.

The scale of the problem is reflected by the website www.filext.com, which maintains a searchable database of file extensions matched with the

195

names of applications/systems that typically generate the format/extension. They currently have over 14, 000 records in their database! This diversity of file formats is indeed currently reflected by the web. We identified over 4,000 distinct file extensions (which correlate highly with distinct format types) during a modest web crawl reported in Section 2.

- *Reverse Engineering Proprietary File Formats* – Many companies are not forthcoming concerning the details of their proprietary file formats. The difficulty of extracting the details of such formats limits the interoperability of software systems. Further, file formats evolve over time, and finding parsers for even popular old formats is a challenging task. For example, current versions of Microsoft Word do not support the oldest Word file formats, which presents a serious problem in digital library applications [7].

- *Interpreting Legacy Files* – In certain legacy applications, *all* documentation of the file specification may have disappeared. We have heard anecdotes to the effect that some of the earliest satellite data from outer space is now uninterpretable for such reasons.

Lorie [5] considers the related problem of preserving the data of today to ensure it may be accessed by the systems of tomorrow. He proposes the creation of a parsing program written in a Universal Virtual Computer (UVC) for every significant file format. At a later date, a user could run the parser on a UVC emulator to access the content of the file. Although this is an interesting solution for future file archiving, it requires the support of companies in making such UVC programs freely available for their proprietary formats. Further, it does not help in legacy applications when format specifications are unavailable.

In this paper, we give algorithms for identifying the meaning of symbols in a particular file format, and provide both theoretical and experimental results on their performance. We believe our work to be the first substantial study of this natural class of problems.

Our paper is organized as follows. In Section 2, we present the results of a brief web crawl to document the rich variety of file formats currently in use. In Section 3.1, we present some theoretical results on identifying well-parenthesized parts of strings, and build upon them in Section 3.2 to construct programs for matching symbol identification. In Section 4.1 we discuss our algorithms and experiences in whitespace and self-delimiter character recognition.

Our results are encouraging. We demonstrate that for sufficiently large example files, we can typically identify the

Extension	Frequency Counts		Corresponding File Types
	Relative	Absolute	
htm*	64.39%	4, 936, 161	HyperText Markup Language
asp*	10.13%	776, 747	Active Server Page Source
php*	6.72%	515, 069	php script
cgi	3.80%	290, 959	CGI script
cfm	3.05%	233, 955	Cold Fusion Template File
jpg	1.86%	142, 473	JPEG image
pdf	1.50%	114, 114	Adobe Acrobat
pl	1.40%	106, 269	Perl script
jsp	0.76%	57, 992	Java Server Page
txt	0.44%	34, 060	ASCII text
gif	0.41%	31, 309	GIF image
zip	0.35%	26, 953	ZIP compressed file
exe	0.34%	26, 150	Window's executable
mv	0.33%	25, 517	Miva script
dll	0.32%	24, 782	Windows DLL
mid	0.24%	18, 087	MIDI file
ram	0.22%	17, 069	Real Audio Media
adp	0.19%	14, 558	AOL Server Dynamic Page
gz	0.18%	14, 147	Gnu Zip compressed file
mp3	0.14%	11, 051	mp3 audio
doc	0.14%	10, 643	Microsoft Word
ps	0.11%	8, 421	Postscript
guest	0.09%	7, 055	HTML Gear guestbook
dbm	0.08%	6, 366	ColdFusion
wav	0.08%	6, 036	Waveform Audio

Table 1. Top 25 file extensions in our crawl of 7, 666, 486 **web documents in October, 2002**

basic features of interest. This suggests several directions for future research, briefly discussed in Section 5.

2. Analysis of File Types

In order to better understand the diversity of file formats in use today, we performed a modest web crawling experiment which touched on 7, 666, 486 different files using the Yunits crawler [4]. We discovered that over 4,000 different extensions occurred at least once on our crawl, and of these 302 occurred at least 100 times each. Table 1 presents the 25 file extensions occurring most frequently on our crawl. While a few popular extensions like html, cgi, and php comprise the bulk of our hits, we observe that proprietary file types like ColdFusion, Miva, and Microsoft Word also occur surprisingly often.

We do not assert that these frequencies necessarily reflect the distribution of file extensions on the entire web, due to search locality and temporal changes in the web (our crawl was performed in October 2002). Still, these results confirm our intuition that it is impractical to write format-specific parsers for all formats currently in use. Thus a tool which attempts to interpret the structure in a file of unknown type should facilitate a variety of data mining applications.

3. Recognizing Well-Formed Formulae

A string S over the two-character alphabet "(" and ")" is said to be a *well-formed formula* (WFF) if S is the empty string, or $S = (S_1)S_2$ where S_1 and S_2 are themselves well-formed formulae. More generally, a string S over a larger alphabet Σ is well-formed with *respect* to a given pair of symbols if the subsequence of S defined on these symbols is well-formed.

Since many interesting features of structured file formats are distinguished using such bracketing commands, we seek to identify interesting pairs of nesting symbols. For example, given a large enough HTML file, we would like to discover that the symbols `<i>` and `<\i>` nest, or even better that the parameterized symbols `<a href=''...''>` and `<\a>` nest.

Pairs of symbols serving as complementary bracketing symbols observe two properties:

1. They occur the exact same number of times, and

2. The substring induced by these two strings must be well formed.

That two symbols from a large alphabet in a modest-sized text occur with equal frequency is fairly weak evidence of nesting. What is more surprising is that the proper nesting of two symbols has little significance unless the symbols occur very frequently:

Lemma 1 *Let S be a random string of length $2n$ on 2 letters such that each occurs n times. The probability that S is well-formed is $\frac{1}{n+1}$.*

Proof: Let $P(n)$ denote the probability that a random string of n left parentheses and n right parenthesis forms a valid parenthesization. Then $P(n)$ equals the number of valid parenthesizations over the number of possible parenthesizations.

Counting the possible subsets of left-parenthesis positions implies that there are $\binom{2n}{n}$ possible parenthesizations. The number of valid parenthesizations is counted the nth Catalan number [1], where

$$C_n = \sum_{k=0}^{n-1} C_k C_{n-1-k} = \binom{2n}{n}\frac{1}{n+1}$$

The ratio of these terms yields $P(n) = 1/(n+1)$. ∎

Complicating matters further are that random strings of equally or almost equally frequent symbols have very long subsequences which are well-formed. Figure 1 presents the results of computational experiments which shows that approximately $n - c\sqrt{n}$ pairs of symbols nest in random sequences out of a maximum possible n pairs, where $c \approx 1$.

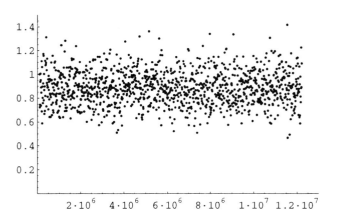

Figure 1. The results of generating 10 random strings of n left and n right parenthesis, finding the length of the longest sub-WFF and averaging. The X-axis shows n and the Y-axis shows $\frac{n - longestsub-WFF(n)}{\sqrt{n}}$

These results demonstrate that we must insist on frequently occurring, perfectly nesting, equal cardinality symbols to declare a match. Accurate determination of lower frequency pairs will only be possible if these symbols nest within larger formulae (such `[ ]` nesting properly within `( )`).

3.1. Recognition Algorithms for Nested Symbols

In this section, we will present some basic algorithmic results on nested symbol recognition. First, we give efficient algorithms to identify pairs of symbols which nest within a given string. Then we demonstrate that it is much harder (indeed, NP-complete) to identify large sets of mutually pairing characters.

Lemma 2 *Given a string s on an alphabet $\Sigma, |\Sigma| = \sigma$, and a pair of symbols $x, y \in \Sigma$, then we can determine whether s is a WFF with respect to x and y in linear time. Furthermore, we can find all pairs in Σ that make s a WFF in $O(\sigma n)$ time.*

Proof: The first problem can be solved by the following simple stack algorithm. When you encounter a left parenthesis, push it onto the stack, and when you encounter a right parenthesis, pop from the stack. At the end, if the stack is empty, and at no time did you try and pop an empty stack, then the string is a WFF.

For the second problem the following algorithm works:

1. Initialize a $\sigma \times \sigma$ matrix of stacks. (One for each ordered pair (x, y))

2. For each letter in the string, pop off each stack for which it is the right parenthesis and push on to each stack for which it is a left parenthesis.

3. The (x, y) stacks which are empty at this stage and from which you never tried to pop them when they were empty are the (x, y) pairs which induce a WFF from s.

∎

The longest sub-well-formed formula (sub-WFF) of s is the longest sub-sequence x of s such that x is a WFF.

Lemma 3 *Given a string s on an alphabet Σ and two symbols $x, y \in \Sigma$, we can determine the length of the longest sub-WFF of s in linear time.*

Proof: The algorithm is based on the stack algorithm of Lemma 2, but when we come across a right parenthesis and the stack is empty we throw it away and we throw away any left parenthesis that are on the stack when there are no more right parenthesis.

We prove correctness by contradiction. Assume the above algorithm is correct until reading the $(i-1)$st right parenthesis, and then matches the ith right parenthesis with a non-optimal left parenthesis. There are four cases:

- Case 1: *Both the left and right parenthesis should go unmatched in an optimal matching.*

  Assuming that the above algorithm is optimal until the current step, we have that all left and right parenthesis in between the pair in question are either matched with each other or will not be matched in an optimal matching. This means that in any optimal matching all the parenthesis to the left and right of the parenthesis in question will match with each other. Thus matching the left and right parenthesis in question will not decrease the number of parenthesis in the final matching, but increase it by 1.

- Case 2: *The right parenthesis should go unmatched and the left parenthesis should match another right parenthesis in an optimal matching.*

  From the above assumption we see that the left parenthesis can only match another right parenthesis that is to the right of the one in question. Since everything in between the left and right parentheses in question is matched, matching the left parentheses in question with a right parentheses that is further right will not be any better.

- Case 3: *Both the left and right parenthesis should match different parenthesis in an optimal matching.*

We assumed that the above algorithm was optimal until the current step. This means that any right parenthesis that we match to the left parenthesis in question is to the right of the right parenthesis in question and, similarly any left parenthesis that we match with the right parenthesis in question will be to the left of the left parenthesis in question. Any matching that does both things will not find a well nested matching of parenthesis. Thus this case is not possible.

- Case 4: *The left parenthesis should go unmatched and the right parenthesis should match another left parenthesis in an optimal matching.*

  This case is symmetric with case 2.

∎

A string U on an 4-character alphabet $\{$ (,), [,] $\}$ is a WFF if U is the empty string or $U = U_1(U_2)U_3$ or $U = U_1[U_2]U_3$ and U_1, U_2, U_3 are all WFF's. Finally, a string T on an arbitrary alphabet Σ is a WFF with respect to some matching M on Σ if for each pair of pairs in the matching, T is a WFF with respect to the pair.

Let M be a matching between certain pairs of symbols in a subset $\Sigma' \subset \Sigma$. A string S is well-formed with respect to M iff, for the string S' induced from S by Σ', the string induced from S' by all pairs of matching pairs $(a, b), (c, d) \in M$ is well formed. The *maximum matching sub-WFF* problem takes as input a string S on an alphabet Σ and an integer m. The question is whether there exists a way of pairing symbols from Σ so that there is a subsequence T of S that is a WFF and $|T| = m$.

Lemma 4 *The maximum matching sub-WFF problem is NP-complete.*

Proof: We show that the maximum matching sub-WFF problem is NP-hard by reducing 3-SAT to it. Given an instance of 3-SAT with variables V and clauses C on V, where $|V| = n, |C| = m$, we will reduce it as follows:

- Define a fixed "super parenthesis" matching pair by including the sequence $s_0 = (^{3n+4m})^{3n+4m}$ into the target string. Any possible solution to our sub-WFF problem will have to match (and) because the super parenthesis portion will be half the total length of our constructed string, and our query will demand a sub-WFF of more than half the size of the string.

- For each variable v_i create a variable gadget $s_{v_i} = (a_i b_i c_i d_i)$. Now each variable gadget can only pair up in one of two ways, either $a_i \to b_i$ and $c_i \to d_i$ or $a_i \to d_i$ and $b_i \to c_i$. We will adopt the convention that $a_i \to b_i$ and $c_i \to d_i$ is the same as selecting $v_i = true$.

- For each clause $c_i = (u_i, u_j, u_k), u_i \in \{v_i, \bar{v}_i\}$ create a clause gadget $s_{c_i} = (a_i a_j a_k x_i x_j x_k)$ where $x_i = b_i$ if $u_i = v_i$ and $x_i = d_i$ if $u_i = \bar{v}_i$. Each s_{c_i} will contribute exactly one pair of parenthesis to a WFF sub-sequence iff it is satisfied by the chosen truth assignment.

If you set S to the concatenation of s_0, s_{v_i}, and s_{c_i}, then the instance of 3-SAT is satisfiable iff S has a WFF sub-sequence of size $6n + 8m + 6n + 4m$. The $6n + 8m$ is from the super parenthesis, the $6n$ is from the n variable gadgets that must match completely, and the $4m$ is from the clause gadgets that must match the super parenthesis and one of the interior variables. ■

Example: Say you are given the following 3-SAT instance.

$$V = \{v_1, v_2, v_3, v_4\}, \quad C = \{\{v_1, v_2, v_3\}, \{\overline{v_1}, v_2, \overline{v_4}\}, \{v_2, \overline{v_3}, v_4\}\}$$

Then this reduction will give
$$s_0 = (((((((((((((((((((((((())))))))))))))))))))))))),$$
$$s_{v_i} = (a_i b_i c_i d_i),$$
$$s_{c_1} = (a_1 a_2 a_3 b_1 b_2 b_3),$$
$$s_{c_2} = (a_1 a_2 a_4 d_1 b_2 d_4),$$
$$s_{c_3} = (a_2 a_3 a_4 b_2 d_3 b_4).$$
for a final sequence S of

$$(((((((((((((((((((((((()))))))))))))))))))))))(a_1 b_1 c_1 d_1)(a_2 b_2 c_2 d_2)$$
$$(a_3 b_3 c_3 d_3)(a_4 b_4 c_4 d_4)(a_1 a_2 a_3 b_1 b_2 b_3)(a_1 a_2 a_4 d_1 b_2 d_4)(a_2 a_3 a_4 b_2 d_3 b_4)$$

Since the matching $\{(\rightarrow), a_2 \rightarrow b_2, a_1 \rightarrow b_1, a_3 \rightarrow d_3, a_4 \rightarrow b_4\}$ gives S a sub-WFF of size $48 + 24 + 12 = 84$, the input 3-SAT instance is satisfied by setting $v_1 = $ true, $v_2 = $ true, $v_3 = $ false, $v_4 = $ true.

3.2. Practical Nested Pair Identification

Finding such nesting substrings in practice is complicated by several factors:

- *The Goal of Context Independence* – The style of nesting substrings is often specific to a particular file format. For example, HTML commands are always enclosed with angle brackets, while latex commands begin with backslash. However, our goal of context independence means we cannot use such prior knowledge or clues to identify nesting symbols.

- *Arbitrary Length Bracketing Commands* – Although single character pairs such as (), {}, and [] often nest, bracketing symbols may be of arbitrary length. Latex equations are bracketed by \begin{theorem} and \end{theorem}, for example. However, any long substrings of these symbols such as \begin{theorem and \end{theorem are also likely to nest. Thus we seek maximal length strings as delimiters, although such strings may have lower frequencies than shorter substrings.

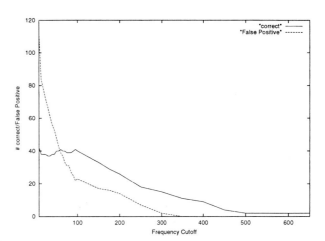

Figure 2. The accuracy of our parenthesis-finding program as a function of the number-of-occurrences cut-off parameter.

- *Parameterized Substrings* – Many languages use parameterized substrings as brackets, such as `<img src=''...''  height=''...'' width=''...''>` in HTML. Since these substrings appear with slight variation in each occurrence, they will not be discovered by any strategy that only considers exact matches.

We applied our parenthesis-finding program for each of eight different types of file formats. Four of our file formats were source code for popular programming languages (C, C++, Java, and Pascal), with the remainder split between markup languages (HTML, latex) and page-display formats (PostScript and pdf). For each format class, we identified 10 representative files; the same files were used in each of our experiments.

Table 2 shows the results of our system with two different levels of permissiveness, modulating between false positives and false negatives. We do a pretty good job of recognizing the most significant bracketing symbol of each file type. Although we fail to identify all matching symbols in all files, this is readily explainable because several of our test files are too short to provide confident identification under the restrictions of Lemma 1. Figure 2 shows the tradeoffs between the number of false positive and negative matching-symbol identifications as we modulate the frequency that a string must occur to be evaluated. For these tests, we eliminate any string from consideration as a bracketing command if it contains any whitespace characters, where we assume that whitespace characters are identified by the C library function `isspace`.

	High Threshold		Low Threshold	
File Type	Correct	False +	Correct	False +
c	3((,), [,])	0	8((,),[,])	2(0, scr+i)
c++	1((,))	0	4((,))	4(m,on)
Java	0	1(i,r)	7((,))	1(o,f)
html	5(<,>)	0	7(<,>)	1(g,u)
Pascal	0	1(s,de)	5((,))	5(R,p)
pdf	0	0	0	1 (6,')
Postscript	6((,))	0	9((,))	1(at,th)
TEX	0	0	1(,)	7(nt,b)
Total	15	2	41	22

Table 2. Parenthesis recognition applied to different file types at each of two different thresholds (10 files per type).

File Type	Interesting Cluster	Cnt
c	`j=0; j<length; j++`	4
	`ptr==NULL`	4
c++	`m==11->size()`	7
	FALSE	16
Java	`metx[n] >= 0`	3
	`int i = 0; i < num; i`	3
html	a href="..."	14
	img src="..."	5
pascal	`X <= 0.0`	4
	map y to y`	4
Postscript	conclusion\	55
	\(199*\)	9
TEX	verbatim	18
	\relax	10

Table 3. Interesting Clusters Found on Various File Types

To determine what substrings of a file provide formatting information instead of content, we seek to find a maximal set of maximal-length substrings such that the file is a WFF with respect to it.

Our implementation uses suffix trees [2], a very powerful data structure for facilitating efficient substring operations on texts. The edge labels of each internal node of the suffix tree represents some substring that occurs more than once. We annotate each node of the suffix tree with the number of leaves in the subtree – equivalent to the number of occurrences of the string. Finally, each node of the suffix tree also holds the information about the position of the occurrences.

To efficiently find all the maximal length repeated substrings of the file, we build a suffix tree and then do a depth first search on this tree in order to retrieve the information that we need. One problem is that every suffix of string S occurs at least as frequently as S. Suppose the string "abcd" occurs multiple times. Then not only will "abcd" be an edge label, but also "bcd" because there are suffices that start with "bcd". To efficiently remove superseded suffixes, we sort the strings found in the DFS by their reversal, traverse the list, and eliminate a string if its predecessor in the list is a superstring that occurs the same number of times.

In order to find a maximal matching on these frequently occurring substrings, we try all pairs of substrings and keep track of all pairs which the file is a WFF with respect to. For each pair (x, y) that occurs m times, we also keep score of the probability it occurs: $P = (256^{|x|+|y|} * 256^m * m)^{-1}$, where $|x|$ and $|y|$ are the lengths of the left and right bracketing symbols, respectively. For numerical stability we take the log of the inverse for a score of $(|x| + |y|) * m * \log m$. We sort all of the pairs we have by this score for our next step. In order to form our maximal matching, we iteratively add strings in order of score to the matching. Each time we add a string, we first make sure that the file will still be a WFF with respect to the new matching.

3.2.1 Parameterized Input

To handle parameterized commands like `\includegraphics[angle=''INT'']` in latex or `<a href=''URL''>` in html, we identify all of the strings that lie between the delimiters and cluster them. We use furthest neighbor clustering [3] with string edit distance as our metric and accept any significant clusters as parameterized commands.

The results of the clustering portion of our program are shown in Table 3. Interesting clusters include the metaphor for the `for` loop in C and Java, and the `verbatim` argument of latex. The clustering algorithm successfully detects that `<a href=''...''>` is a delimiter in html.

The results of our parenthesis recognition program are shown in Table 2. Our program does a good job of identifying the main single character delimiters of formats like <, > in html and (,) in postscript, but does not do as well at finding multiple character delimiters like begin / end in Pascal. At the high threshold, very few false positives are detected.

4. White Space and Self-Delimiter Identification

4.1. White Space Recognition

Whitespace characters are used to separate tokens. Although such whitespace characters as tab, space, and newline are commonly used in file formats, they are not uni-

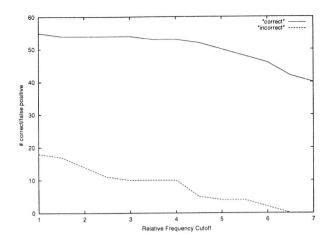

Figure 3. The results of running our whitespace finding program with the suffix tree constant set to 2 and varying the occurs constant.

File Type	Correct	False +	False -
c	4(space)	0	0
c++	4(space)	0	3(space)
Java	9(space, tab)	0	0
html	5(space)	0	0
Pascal	7(space)	0	0
pdf	1(space)	0	1(space)
Postscript	3(space)	0	0
TEX	9(space)	0	0
Total	42	0	4

Table 4. Results of our Whitespace Recognizer on Various File Types. Run on 10 Test Files of Each Type.

File Type	Correct	Incorrect
c	1(')	1(e)
c++	3(', ")	3(w,!)
Java	3(")	1(M)
html	1(')	0
Pascal	1(')	2(X,*)
pdf	0	3
Postscript	0	0
TEX	2($)	1([)
Total	11	11

Table 5. Results of our Self-Delimiter Recognizer on Various File Types. Run on 10 Files of Each Type.

versal — consider comma-separated formats such as .csv files. De novo recognition of whitespace symbols proved more difficult than we anticipated. We tried the following sequence of ideas/algorithms:

1. We anticipated that whitespace would usually be the most frequently occurring character in the file. However, this consistently fails on Microsoft Word files, where often 50% of Word format files consist of the hexadecimal bytes 00 and FF!

2. We anticipated that whitespace symbols also occur at fairly regular intervals, i.e. the distance between consecutive occurrences of the character should have a low variance. This is because tokens (such as words in natural language text) are generally short and have a fairly uniform size. However many formats (again including Microsoft Word) appear to consist of variable regions/segments which throws off this analysis.

3. Finally, we anticipated that the frequency of the occurrences of the character at the end of suffix-tree edge labels would be revealing. Whitespace characters should be over-represented at the end of edge labels of the suffix-tree of the string because repeated tokens will appear as edge labels in the suffix tree. The separating whitespace symbol should always follow the token, so it will be the last character on the edge. Unfortunately, this strategy often uncovered structures in the text unrelated to the whitespace-ness of a character.

However, we were able to combine all of these ideas to create a successful whitespace-finding program that uses two phases. In the first phase, it parses the file to find all of the characters that occur frequently and calculates the variance of the gap between consecutive occurrences of them. It accepts as whitespace candidates all the characters that are undominated in the sense that no other character has both more occurrences and a lower variance. In the second phase, we build a suffix tree on the file. We then traverse the tree, keeping count of frequency each character occurs as the last character in an edge label. The program ultimately accepts all characters that pass both phases.

Table 4 shows the correctness of our program when it is run on files of various types. The results show that we rarely misidentify a character as being whitespace, but miss whitespace characters when they do not occur frequently in a file. Our worst performance is on PostScript and pdf files, however, these computer-generated files by definition do not necessarily respect whitespace conventions (particularly pdf).

4.2. Self-Delimitering Symbols

A self-delimiter character is a symbol that is used to both begin and end a structure, like $ in latex or the quotation mark in English. These characters are difficult to identify because any character that appears an even number of times is potentially a self-delimiting character.

We conjectured that the distance between consecutive occurrences of any self-delimiting character will have a strongly bimodal distribution, i.e. quotations are small but separations between quotations are large. Thus this distribution will be very periodic, alternating long and short sequences.

Our self-delimiter identifying program attempts to find characters that satisfies these criteria. To test if the distribution of a character c is bimodal, we find the distances between consecutive occurrences of c. We then sort these values and find the average of the second and third quartiles. We score each character by the ratio of the third quartile average to the second quartile average, eliminating the first and last quartiles for robustness. We accept a frequently-occurring character if it has a score greater than 3. To test the periodicity of the distances between occurrences of c, we find the sequence of differences between neighboring distances. In the ideal case this will alternate between positive and negative numbers. We divide the number of sign changes in this sequence by the length of the sequence to get a score, and accept a character as a self-delimiter if this ratio is at least 0.9.

The results of our recognition program are shown in Table 5. We correctly distinguish between context-specific self-delimiters in all sufficiently rich input files.

5. Conclusions

We have presented several techniques for analyzing files of unknown type and determining major structural components of its file format. We have shown that such structures can be recognized fairly robustly, at least for sufficiently large/rich example files.

Several research directions remain. One is to improve the accuracy of our predictions by analyzing multiple files of a given type and accepting structures which reflect the collected input. Such analysis could greatly reduce the frequency of symbol occurrence needed for accurate matching pair recognition, since each file would represent an independent "trial" for a putative symbol pair. Another interesting direction would be to incorporate these algorithms into a general file analysis tool. In particular, the UNIX utility `strings` extracts printable strings from an arbitrary file; our algorithms could lead to a utility which extracts the plaintext from an arbitrary formatted file. Finally, certain interesting algorithmic issues remain open, most no-

tably the complexity of well-formed symbol pairing when all symbols in the string must match.

6. Acknowledgments

We thank Maxim Lifantsev for performing our web crawl using his Yuntis system and Alberto Apostolico for interesting discussions on this topic.

References

[1] R. Graham, D. Knuth, and O. Patashnik. *Concrete Mathematics.* Addison-Wesley, second edition, 1994.

[2] D. Gusfield. *Algorithms on Strings, Trees, and Sequences: Computer Science and Computational Biology.* Cambridge University Press, 1997.

[3] A. Jain and R. Dubes. *Algorithms for Clustering Data.* Prentice-Hall, Englewood Cliffs NJ, 1988.

[4] M. Lifantsev. Yuntis: Collaborative web resource categorization and ranking project. http://www.ecsl.cs.sunysb.edu/yuntis/.

[5] R. Lorie. Long term preservation of digital information. In *Proceedings of the First ACM/IEEE-CS Joint Conference on Digital Libraries*, pages 346–352, Roanoke, Virginia, United States, January 2001.

[6] C. Nevill-Manning, T. Reed, and I. Witten. Extracting text from postscript. *Software Practice and Experience*, pages 481–491, 1998.

[7] I. Witten. Browsing around a digital library. In *Proceedings of the ACM-SIAM Symposium on Discrete Algorithms*, Baltimore, Maryland, United States, January 2003.

Probabilistic User Behavior Models

Eren Manavoglu
Pennsylvania State University
001 Thomas Building
University Park, PA 16802
manavogl@cse.psu.edu

Dmitry Pavlov*
Yahoo Inc.
701 First Avenue
Sunnyvale, California 94089
dpavlov@yahoo-inc.com

C. Lee Giles
Pennsylvania State University
001 Thomas Building
University Park, PA 16802
giles@ist.psu.edu

Abstract

We present a mixture model based approach for learning individualized behavior models for the Web users. We investigate the use of maximum entropy and Markov mixture models for generating probabilistic behavior models. We first build a global behavior model for the entire population and then personalize this global model for the existing users by assigning each user individual component weights for the mixture model. We then use these individual weights to group the users into behavior model clusters. We show that the clusters generated in this manner are interpretable and able to represent dominant behavior patterns. We conduct offline experiments on around two months worth of data from CiteSeer, an online digital library for computer science research papers currently storing more than 470,000 documents. We show that both maximum entropy and Markov based personal user behavior models are strong predictive models. We also show that maximum entropy based mixture model outperforms Markov mixture models in recognizing complex user behavior patterns.

1. Introduction and Related Work

Whether the underlying reason is to detect fraud or malicious visitors, to improve the organization of a Web site to better serve customers or to identify hidden patterns and new trends in consumer behavior for improving profit, massive amounts of Web data are being collected and stored everyday. Understanding user behavior and discovering the valuable information within such huge databases involves several phases: *data cleaning and preprocessing*, where typically noise is removed, log files are broken into sessions and users are identified; *data transformation*, where useful features are selected to represent the data and/or dimension reduction techniques are used to reduce the size of the data;

applying data mining techniques to identify interesting patterns, statistical or predictive models or correlations among parts of data; *interpretation of the results*, which includes visualization of the discovered knowledge and transforming them into user friendly formats.

The focus of this paper is the data mining and interpretation phases of this process. We investigate the use of maximum entropy mixture models and mixture of Markov models for inferring individualized behavior models of Web users, where a behavior model is a probabilistic model describing which actions the user will perform in the future. Mixture models also provide a means to cluster the data. The interpretation of clusters obtained in our experiments allows us to conclude that maximum entropy and Markov mixture models have both descriptive and predictive power.

A variety of data mining techniques have been used for the purpose of Web data analysis. Association rule extraction, collaborative filtering, clustering, classification, dependency modeling, and sequential pattern analysis are the most common and noticeable of these methods. Association rule extraction has been used to identify sets of items that are accessed together [15]. Collaborative filtering algorithms [21, 18] have been used to first find similar users based on the overlap between their requested items, and then recommend the given user items accessed by the like-minded users. Clustering, in the context of Web data, can either be used to group together similar items or users with similar usage patterns [2]. Probabilistic graphical models are used to discover and represent dependencies among different variables such as, for instance, the effect of gender on the shopping behavior. Dependency [12] and Bayesian networks [11] are examples of such techniques. Sequential pattern analysis algorithms use time-ordered sessions or episodes and attempt to discover patterns such that the current history of items/actions is evidence to the following item/action.

One of the most motivating reasons for Web usage analysis is its potential to provide customized services. Successful applications of personalization based on Web usage

---

*Work done at NEC Laboratories America.

mining include adaptive Web-sites, where the structure of the Web-site is optimized for each individual's taste [19]; extracting usage patterns for deriving intelligent marketing strategies [5, 1]; personalized recommendations [16] and individualized predictive profile generation [3].

In this paper, we use personalized probabilistic sequential models to represent user behavior. User behavior can be viewed as a probabilistic model $P(A^{next}|H(U))$, where A^{next} is the next action taken by the user U, $H(U)$ is the action history for the user U in the present session, and P can be any probabilistic function. In our previous work on sequence modeling [17] and recommender systems [6] we explored mixture of maximum entropy (maxent) and Markov models in the context of sequential analysis problems. Here, we use mixture models to capture the diversity in individual behaviors. Each component of a mixture model represents a dominant pattern in the data and each sequence (user sessions in our case) is modeled as a weighted combination of these components. By grouping each session into the highest weighted component, we are also able to cluster the user sessions. Personalization is achieved by optimizing the weights for each individual user, as suggested by Cadez et al [3]. We are able to eliminate one of the biggest problems of personalization, the lack of sufficient information about each individual, by starting with a global model and optimizing the weights for each individual with respect to the amount of data we have about him/her.

We use web-server logs of CiteSeer (a.k.a. ResearchIndex) [1], an online digital library of computer science papers, as our test bed. The site automatically locates computer science papers found on the Web, indexes their full text, allows browsing via the literature citation graph, and isolates the text around citations, among other services [14]. The archive contains over 470,000 documents including the full text of each document, citation links between documents and receives thousands of user accesses per hour. Users of CiteSeer can search both the documents and citations, view and download documents, follow the recommendations, upload documents or correct document information.

We show how the mixture model can be learned directly from the available data. Although maxent learning has high computational cost, the dimension of the action space is inside the limits of feasible computation.

The contributions of this paper can be summarized as:

1. proposed to represent the user behavior as a sequential model;

2. introduced a maxent-based mixture model framework for user behavior modeling;

3. adapted a personalized mechanism which overcomes the insufficient data problem by individual optimiza-

tion proportional to the amount of data available for each user;

4. evaluated the proposed models and showed that personalization outperforms global models and mixture of maxent models are able to capture complex patterns in user behavior.

The rest of the paper is organized as follows. In Section 2 we give a definition of the problem and describe the general notation. We introduce our model in Section 3. Section 4 describes our visualization method. We give an overview of our data set and preprocessing steps in Section 5. Experimental results and comparisons are given in Section 6. In Section 7 we present our conclusions and ponder future work.

2. General Notation and Problem Definition

We assume that we are given a data set consisting of ordered sequences in some alphabet and that each sequence is labeled with a user id U. For the purposes of this paper we refer to individual items in the alphabet as actions and each sequence represents a user session.

For each action in a user session, the history $H(U)$ is defined as the so-far observed ordered sequence of actions. Our behavior model for individual U is a model, e.g. maxent or Markov, that predicts the next action A^{next} given the history $H(U)$. Therefore the problem is to infer this model, $P(A^{next}|H(U), Data)$, for each individual given the training data.

A serious drawback of personalization algorithms for the Web domain is the insufficient data problem. For many transaction data sets most user ids are seen only in one or two sessions, which makes it impossible to learn reliable predictive profiles for those users. If the Web site does not require registration and the user ids are set with temporary cookies, the situation gets even worse. Log files will have lots of users with only a few sessions, most of which won't be seen in the future transactions at all and most of the users seen in run-time will be new users, unknown to the system.

This is the primary reason why a straightforward approach to personalization, that consists of learning the model for each user only from that user's past transactions, fails for the personalization task with the Web data. Specifically, even after being learned on a wealth of training data for a user, the system could suffer from over-fitting and "cold-start" problem for new visitors the Web site.

The approach that we advocate is to use a global mixture model to capture specific patterns of general behavior of the users, and once the global model is learned, we optimize the weight of each component for each known user individually, hence combining the global patterns with individual irregularities.

---

[1]http://www.researchindex.com

3. Mixture of Maxent and Markov Models

In this section we describe the global and individualized maxent and Markov mixture models.

3.1. Global Mixture Models

The use of mixture models to represent the behavior of an individual can be viewed as assuming that the ordered sequence of actions of a visitor U at the Web site, is assigned to cluster k with a probability α_k, ($k = 1, \ldots, N_c$), and each cluster assigns a probability to the sequence via a distribution specific to that cluster. The formal definition of a N_c-component mixture model is as follows:

$$P(A^{next}|H(U), Data) = \sum_{k=1}^{N_c} \alpha_k P(A^{next}|H(U), Data, k)$$

where $\sum_{k=1}^{N_c} \alpha_k = 1$. α_k is the prior probability of cluster k, and $P(A^{next}|H(U), Data, k)$ is the distribution for the k-th component. For the global model α_k's take the same values across all the users. Based on the results of our previous research [17, 6] we decided to use first order Markov model and maxent to model cluster-specific distributions. Both models are explained in the following sections.

3.1.1 Markov Model

In the first order Markov model, the current action depends on the history $H(U)$ only through the last observed action, A^{prev}. The definition of a Markov model for the distribution of the k-th cluster is therefore

$$P(A^{next}|H(U), Data, k) \propto \theta_{0,k} \prod_{h=1}^{|H(U)|} \theta_{h \rightarrow (h+1),k}$$

where $\theta_{0,k}$ is the probability of observing $H(U)_0$ as the first action in the history, and $\theta_{(h \rightarrow h+1),k}$ is the probability of observing a transition from action number h to action number $h+1$ in the history. For $h = |H(U)|$, action with index $h+1$ is A^{next}. The number of parameters is quadratic in the number of actions. Note that the regular Markov model only depends on the so-called *bigrams* or first order Markov terms, i.e. the frequencies of pairs of consecutive actions.

3.1.2 Maximum Entropy Model

It's also possible to model the component distribution $P(A^{next}|H(U), Data, k)$ as a maximum entropy model. Maximum entropy provides a framework to combine information from different knowledge sources. Each knowledge source imposes a set of constraints on the combined model. The intersection of all the constraints contains a set of probability functions, satisfying all the conditions. Maximum entropy principle chooses among these functions the one

with the highest information entropy, i.e. the most flat function. We are motivated to use maximum entropy approach in order to combine first order Markov model features with other properties of the data. More specifically, we believe that the most recent action, A^{prev}, has the most influence on the current action taken by the user. However, we also believe that actions other than A^{prev} seen in the history $H(U)$ are also effective. Higher order Markov models may seem to be solving this problem, but it is not feasible to build them for high-dimensional data due to the curse of dimensionality. Furthermore, higher order Markov models use a strict order of the action sequence. Maxent, on the other hand, can be set up with much milder restrictions.

We selected two flavors of low-order statistics or features, as they are typically referred to in the maximum entropy literature, for estimation [13]. Bigrams, or first order Markov terms, were one type. In order to introduce long term dependence of A^{next} on the actions that occurred in the history of the user session, we include triggers, position-specific or non-position-specific, in addition to bigrams. A non position-specific trigger is defined as a pair of actions (a, b) in a given cluster such that $P(A^{next} = b|a \in H(U))$ is substantially different from $P(A^{next} = b)$. If we restrict the action pairs to be exactly $|H(U)|$ actions apart from each other, the resulting trigger would be position-specific. We use both types of triggers in our experiments. To measure the quality of triggers and in order to rank them we computed mutual information between events $E_1 = \{A^{next} = b\}$ and $E_2 = \{a \in H(U)\}$. We then discarded low scoring triggers but retained all bigrams. Note that the quantity and quality of selected triggers depend on the length of $H(U)$. Since the majority of the user sessions is shorter than 5 actions, we chose 5 to be the maximum length of the history.

The set of features, bigrams and triggers in our case, together with maximum entropy as an objective function, can be shown to lead to the following form of the conditional maximum entropy model

$$P(A^{next}|H(U), Data) =$$
$$\frac{1}{Z_\lambda(H(U))} exp[\sum_{s=1}^{S} \lambda_s F_s(A^{next}, H(U))]$$

where $Z(H(U))$ is a normalization constant ensuring that the distribution sums to 1 and F_s are the features. The set of parameters $\{\lambda\}$ needs to be found from the following set of equations that restrict the distribution $P(A^{next}|H(U), Data)$ to have the same expected value for each feature as seen in the training data:

$$\sum_H \sum_A P(A|H, Data)F_s(A, H) =$$
$$\sum_{H(U)} F_s(A(H(U)), H(U)), \quad s = 1, \ldots, S$$

where the left hand side represents the expectation (up to a normalization factor) of the feature $F_s(A, H)$ with respect to the distribution $P(A|H, Data)$ and the right hand side is the expected value (up to the same normalization factor) of this feature in the training data.

There exist efficient algorithms for finding the parameters $\{\lambda\}$ (e.g. generalized [7], improved [20] and sequential conditional [10] iterative scaling algorithms) that are known to converge if the constraints imposed on P are consistent. The pseudocode of the algorithm and a detailed discussion on the ways of speeding it up can be found, for example in [13, 9, 10].

Under fairly general assumptions, maximum entropy model can also be shown to be a maximum likelihood model [20]. Employing a Gaussian prior with a zero mean on parameters λ yields a maximum aposteriori solution that has been shown to be more accurate than the related maximum likelihood solution and other smoothing techniques for maximum entropy models [4]. We use Gaussian smoothing in our experiments for a maxent model.

3.2. Personalized Mixture Model

We personalize the mixture model by using individual cluster probabilities, $\alpha_{U,k}$'s, for each user. The resulting model is therefore specific to each user U:

$$P_U(A^{next}|H(U), Data) = \sum_{k=1}^{N_c} \alpha_{U,k} P(A^{next}|H(U), Data, k)$$

where $\sum_{k=1}^{N_c} \alpha_{U,k} = 1$. The component distribution, $P(A^{next}|H(U), Data, k)$, is the same as in global mixture model: either maximum entropy or Markov model, which is fixed across all users. The N_c component distributions can also be viewed as N_c dimensions of the whole population's behavior space. $\alpha_{U,k}$'s specify where the user U stands in this population. This formulation allows the use of the whole population's experience for each individual's own use, thus avoiding the over-fitting problem. Unknown user problem is resolved naturally as well, by using the global α_k's for new users.

3.3. Parameter Estimation

We assume that the action sequences are drawn independently from a fixed distribution. Thus, the likelihood of the data can be formulated as the product of the individual likelihoods:

$$P(Data|\Theta) = \prod_{k=1}^{N_u} P(Data_U|\Theta)$$

where Θ stands for the full set of parameters of the model and N_u is the number of users.

By the chain rule:

$$P(Data_U|\Theta) = \prod_{s=1}^{N_s} \prod_{j=1}^{N_s a} P(A^j|H(U), \Theta)$$

where N_s is the number of sesions user U has and $N_s a$ is the number of actions taken by user U in session s.

Unknown parameters for the global model include α_k's and λ_k's of the maxent or θ_k's of the Markov model. Parameters can be learned by using the Expectation-Maximization (EM) algorithm as described in [3, 8].

For learning the personalized model, two different approaches can be taken. Our goal is to learn individual $\alpha_{U,k}$'s, therefore we can fix the component distribution model's parameters (i.e. λ_k's of the maxent model or θ_k's of the Markov model) to the values of the global model, and perform the optimization on the $\alpha_{U,k}$'s only. Or we can vary the component distribution's parameters as well. For both cases the optimization is carried out for each user individually, i.e. personal models are trained on each user's data set separately.

If the first approach is taken and the component distribution model parameters are fixed, EM algorithm is run on each individual's own data set to find $\alpha_{U,k}$'s, which are initialized with the global α_k values. If the second approach is chosen instead, EM algorithm is used to learn both $\alpha_{U,k}$'s and component distribution model parameters, which are again initialized with the values learned for the global model. Steps of the parameter estimation process can be summarized as follows:

- Run EM on the whole data set to learn global α_k's and component distribution model parameters;

- Group the sessions by individuals;

- Do either

  - Fix component distribution parameters to the global values and initialize $\alpha_{U,k}$'s with global α_k values;

  - Run EM on the individual data sets to learn $\alpha_{U,k}$'s.

  Or

  - Initialize $\alpha_{U,k}$'s and component distribution parameters with global values;

  - Run EM on the individual data sets to learn all the parameters.

According to this framework, for the new users in the test set, user specific α values will be the initialization values, which are the global α_k's, since there will be no user data to change it.

Notice that even if the component distribution parameters are optimized for the personal model, these values won't be user specific values. Cadez et al. [3] mention that the final values of the parameters of the multinomial model are close to the initial estimates, however, we found that for maxent and Markov models this is not true. Optimizing the λ_k's of the maxent model or θ_k's of the Markov model for the second time causes the model to over-fit the known users' behavior. We recomend using the initial global model for the unknown users if this approach is taken for parameter estimation. Since the difference between the recommended method and fixed component distribution parameter method is negligible and optimizing the λ_k's for maxent is too time consuming, we chose fixing these parameters to conduct our experiments.

4. Visualization and Interpretation

As mentioned earlier, each component of a mixture model can be viewed as a cluster, representing a certain pattern present in the data. The resulting model represents each session as a weighted combination of these clusters. Given the observed session S_U of user U, the probability distribution over the cluster variable k can be computed by the Bayesian rule:

$$P(k|S_U, Data) = \frac{\alpha_k P_U(S_U|Data, k)}{\sum_{k'=1}^{N_c} \alpha_{k'} P_U(S_U|Data, k')}$$

where

$$P_U(S_U|Data, k) = \prod_{j=1}^{|S_U|} P_U(A^j|H(U), Data, k)$$

Once $P(k|S_U, Data)$'s, which are aldo referred to as membership probabilities, are computed we assign session S_U to the cluster with highest probability. Instead of this *hard* assignment strategy we could also do *soft* clustering and assign the session to a set of clusters.

Interpreting the key behaviors exhibited by the users in each cluster is important for a number of tasks, such as managing the site, targeted advertising, identifying malicious visitors. It also helps understanding the navigation patterns of different user groups and therefore helps in organizing the site to better suit the users. Visualizing the users' behavior also makes it possible to identify and provide customized services, like customized help and recommendations.

5. Data Description and Preprocessing

Our data set consists of CiteSeer log files covering a period of approximately two months. The log files are a series of transaction in the form <time, action, user id, action related information>. The complete list of user actions that were available in CiteSeer during the period of our experiments can be found in Table 1. Some of these actions are not being used in CiteSeer anymore.

When a user accesses CiteSeer, a temporary cookie is set on the client side, if a cookie enabled browser is being used. CiteSeer uses this cookie to identify returning users. If no cookie is found, a new user id is given to the user. Each

Table 1. CiteSeer user actions and their descriptions.

Active Bibliography	Active bibliography of a document
Bibtex	Bibtex entry page of the active document
Same Site Documents	The page of documents residing on the same site
Related Documents	Related documents page
Users Who Viewed	Documents viewed by the viewers of active document
Text Related	Page with the list of text based similar documents
Author Homepage	Homepage of the active document's author
Source URL	Original URL of the document
Add Documents	Document upload request
Submit Documents	Document upload submission
Correct Document Title	Request to correct a document's title
Submit Document Title Correction	Title correction submission
Correct Document Abstract	Request to correct a document's abstract
Submit Document Abstract Correction	Abstract correction submission
Check Citations	Citations referring to the active document
Cached Page	Cached page image of the active document
Download	Download a document
Update Cache	Update the cached copy of the active document
Add Comment	Submit comments about the active document
Rate	Rate the active document
Citation Query	Submit a citation query
Document Query	Submit a document query
Document Details	Document's details page
Context	Document's citation context information page
Context Summary	Document's citation context summary page
Homepage	CiteSeer homepage
Help	CiteSeer help page

access is recorded on the server side with a unique user id and time stamp.

First step of preprocessing the data is aggregating the transactions by user id and breaking them into sessions. We use time oriented heuristics to recognize new sessions. For a fixed user id, we define a session as a sequence of actions with no two consecutive actions more than 300 seconds apart. If a user is inactive for more than 300 seconds his/her next action is considered as the start of a new session.

Next, we identify robots and discard sessions belonging to them. We examine the histogram of number of accesses in one session to recognize robots. Users who access the archive more than some threshold in one session, are labeled as robots. After removing the robot sessions we collapse the same consecutive actions into a single instance of that action, and discard sessions which contain only one action.

We chronologically partitioned the data into 1,720,512 training sessions and 430,128 test sessions. The total number of actions in the training data is 12,200,965 and in test data this number is 3,853,108. The average number of sessions per user is 7 in the training data and 9 in the test data. The preprocessed data is represented as a collection of ordered sequences of user actions, where each sequence is labeled with a user id. Test data includes 54,429 users out of which only 8139 of the users were seen in the training data also. Since the model proposed in this paper uses the global model for the unknown users, the effects of personalization won't be seen clearly in the results for all the users. We therefore report the results on the revisiting users, and give the results for the whole data if there are any major differences between the two cases.

6. Experimental Results and Comparisons

We evaluated the user behavior models based on the accuracy of their predictions and visualized the user behavior clusters to demonstrate the descriptive ability of the models. Prediction accuracy is evaluated by scanning the user sessions and for each action in the session predicting the identity of the following action.

In our experiments we compare mixtures of position specific (PS) maximum entropy models, mixtures of non position specific (non-PS) maximum entropy models and mixtures of Markov models. For maximum entropy models, the length of the history was set to 5. Our main criteria for prediction evaluation is the *hit ratio*, which is the ratio of the correct predictions to the total number of predictions made. The predictions made by the mixture models are actually lists of ranked actions, where the ranking is done by ordering the actions by their probability values. If the system were to predict only one action, the first action on the ranked list would be chosen. However, the quality of the remaining predictions is also an indication of the success of the model. Therefore we take the first N predictions on the list and evaluate the performance of the models based on the success of these N predictions, for $N = 1, ..., 5, 10$. In this case, a hit occurs if the true action is predicted in any of these N guesses.

We also report the likelihoods of the models on the test data, since it's our optimization criteria and is another indication of how well the model represents the data.

Table 2. Hit ratio results on known users for 3 component mixture model.

	Bin 1	Bin 2	Bin 3	Bin 4	Bin 5	Bin 10
Global Markov	0.5849	0.7826	0.8502	0.8982	0.9229	0.9816
Personal Markov	0.5872	0.7858	**0.8578**	**0.9061**	**0.9291**	**0.9825**
Global PS Maxent	0.6127	0.7863	0.8388	0.8820	0.9081	0.9794
Personal PS Maxent	0.6153	0.7874	0.8430	0.8862	0.9153	0.9810
Global NonPS Maxent	0.6122	0.7813	0.8337	0.8715	0.9059	0.9787
Personal NonPS Maxent	**0.6154**	**0.7879**	0.8402	0.8765	0.9100	0.9806

In Table 2, we present hit ratio results for $N = 1, ..., 5, 10$ on the known users for 3-component mixture model, and in Table 3 hit ratios for 10-component mixture

Table 3. Hit ratio results on known users for 10 component mixture model.

	Bin 1	Bin 2	Bin 3	Bin 4	Bin 5	Bin 10
Global Markov	0.6073	0.7967	0.8639	0.9083	0.9361	0.9842
Personal Markov	**0.6245**	**0.8054**	**0.8824**	**0.9232**	**0.9472**	**0.9867**
Global PS Maxent	0.6139	0.7835	0.8450	0.8856	0.9115	0.9797
Personal PS Maxent	0.6209	0.7953	0.8555	0.8963	0.9247	0.9823
Global NonPS Maxent	0.6113	0.7829	0.8393	0.8785	0.9097	0.9799
Personal NonPS Maxent	0.6226	0.7970	0.8556	0.8941	0.9256	0.9834

models are presented. Regardless of the number of components and the length of the prediction list, personalized models outperformed the corresponding global models. PS and non-PS specific maxent models' hit ratios are very close to each other, but non-PS model performed better than the PS in the 10-component mixture model and for $N \leq 2$ in 3-component mixture model. An interesting point about the non-PS maxent model is the altitude of the effect of personalization on it. Although the PS model is better in all test cases for the global models, personalization improves the non-PS model more, such that it's able to beat the PS model.

As follows from the tables, personalized Markov mixture model has the highest hit ratio for the known users. However non-PS maxent was able to perform better for $N \leq 2$ in the 3-component model. This result may seem surprising considering the fact that first order Markov models are making use of only bigrams, whereas maxent models are using triggers in addition to bigrams, but it's not. The goal of maximum entropy is to choose the most general model within the set of functions satisfying the constraints. Markov models, on the other hand, do not have this property, and thus may fit the training data better. The advantage of maxent models can be seen more clearly when looked at the results for all users. Table 4 and Table 5 present the hit ratios of the personal models for 3-component and 10-component mixture models, respectively. Non-PS maxent outperforms Markov model for all prediction list lengths, but 4 in 3-component mixture model, and it performs worse only for $N = 3, 4, 5$ in the 10-component mixture model.

In Table 6, we report the likelihood of the personalized models for the test data. Best likelihood is achieved by Markov mixture model and non-PS maxent mixture follows it. PS maxent mixture performs even worse when the number of components is increased.

As discussed in Section 4 we are also interested in the interpretation of the user behavior clusters. Each user session is grouped into the cluster for which it has the highest $\alpha_{U,k}$

Table 4. Hit ratio results of personalized mixture models on all users for 3 components.

	Bin 1	Bin 2	Bin 3	Bin 4	Bin 5	Bin 10
Personal Markov	0.5699	0.7372	0.8014	**0.8714**	0.8941	0.9525
Personal PS Maxent	0.5872	0.7542	0.8095	0.8506	0.8773	0.9357
Personal Non-PS Maxent	**0.5948**	**0.7615**	**0.8126**	0.8636	**0.8943**	**0.9557**

Table 5. Hit ratio results of personalized mixture models on all users for 10 components.

	Bin 1	Bin 2	Bin 3	Bin 4	Bin 5	Bin 10
Personal Markov	0.5830	0.7680	**0.8520**	**0.8891**	**0.9132**	0.9567
Personal PS Maxent	0.5865	0.7492	0.8208	0.8595	0.8857	0.9416
Personal Non-PS Maxent	**0.6081**	**0.7713**	0.8336	0.8679	0.8982	**0.9614**

Table 6. Test data likelihoods for the personalized models.

	PS Maxent	Non-PS Maxent	Markov Model
3 Component	-2.10191	-2.03604	-2.04539
10 Component	-2.19488	-2.00861	-1.93454

Figure 2. User Clusters Generated by the 10-Component Non-PS Maximum Entropy Mixture Model.

value. For cluster visualization we chose 100 sample user sessions randomly from each cluster. Each unique action is represented by a unique color (action-color mapping is also shown in the figure). Hence, each user session is represented as a row of colored squares, where each squares corresponds to an action.

Figure 1. User Clusters Generated by the 10-Component Markov Mixture Model.

This visualization technique has enabled us to actually identify different behavior models among CiteSeer users. Users identified as belonging to Cluster 8 by the Markov model (Figure Figure 1), for example, go to CiteSeer homepage, submit citation queries, view document details and

context or download the document. Cluster 9 users, on the other hand, view details of a document and download, with hardly taking any other actions. The interesting point about Cluster 9 is that these users go to the details of a document directly, without submitting a query. This is probably an indication of browsing CiteSeer via another search engine. Following Figure 1, it's also clearly seen that Cluster 6 represents the users who after viewing the context or details of a document try to correct the title and then download it. Maximum entropy model (Figure 2) is able to capture the mentioned behavior models, as well as more complex ones. Cluster 4 of maxent model represents users who probably browse CiteSeer through another engine. At first sight Cluster 6 may seem to be presenting the same pattern, however there's a huge difference between the two. Users of Cluster 6 do submit a document query before the document details - download cycle, suggesting that after viewing document details or downloading they go back to the query results page to browse the rest of the results. Although some session in Cluster 1 of Markov model show a similar pattern, it's not as clear. Maximum entropy model was also able to identify a cluster of users, Cluster 3, who check the recommendations after viewing the document information. These users also happen to correct document abstracts or titles.

Overall, we conclude that personalized mixture of maximum entropy and Markov models provide a decent predictive model for representing user behaviors, and a useful mechanism for identifying and interpreting user behavior patterns for the Web data.

7. Conclusions and Future Work

We described a mixture model based approach to generating and visualizing individual behavior models for CiteSeer users. We represented the Web data as a collection of ordered action sequences for each user. We introduced a maximum entropy based approach for modeling the user behavior, motivated by its ability to model long term dependencies in data sequences. In addition to maxent model, we also investigated the use of first order Markov mixture models. We demonstrated that both methods are able to generate strong predictive models with different strengths and weaknesses. Markov model performed better for predicting the behavior of the known users, whereas maximum entropy model was better at modeling the global behavior model, and therefore the unknown users also. We used a simple method to achieve personalization, yet managed to avoid the insufficient data problem of traditional personalization techniques. By using mixture model based clustering we were able to identify and visualize specific behavior patterns of CiteSeer users, where it was demonstrated that maximum entropy model's computational cost pays off at recognizing complex dominant patterns of user behavior.

We plan to expand our work on identifying specific user behavior patterns and provide customized services, for instance customized recommendations, for each of the behavior model groups. We are also interested in naming these groups of users. We intend to perform real-time experiments on CiteSeer with our maximum entropy based predictive model. We are also planning to apply our personalization algorithm to mixtures of hidden Markov models and compare it with the maxent model proposed in this paper.

8. Acknowledgements

This work has been partially supported by a grant from Lockheed Martin. We would like to thank Steve Lawrence for making the CiteSeer log data available to us.

References

[1] A. G. Buchner and M. D. Mulvenna. Discovering internet marketing intelligence through online analytical web usage mining. *SIGMOD Record*, 27(4):54–61, 1998.

[2] I. V. Cadez, D. Heckerman, C. Meek, P. Smyth, and S. White. Visualization of navigation patterns on a web site using model-based clustering. In *Knowledge Discovery and Data Mining*, pages 280–284, 2000.

[3] I. V. Cadez, P. Smyth, E. Ip, and H. Mannila. Predictive profiles for transaction data using finite mixture models. Technical Report UCI-ICS 01-67, UC Irvine, 2001.

[4] S. Chen and R. Rosenfeld. A gaussian prior for smoothing maximum entropy models. Technical Report CMUCS -99-108, Carnegie Mellon University, 1999.

[5] R. Cooley, B. Mobasher, and J. Srivastava. Data preparation for mining world wide web browsing patterns. *Knowledge and Information Systems*, 1(1):5–32, 1999.

[6] D. P. D. Pavlov, E. Manavoglu and C. L. Giles. Collaborative filtering with maximum entropy. Technical Report 2003-L001, NEC Labs, 2003.

[7] J. N. Darroch and D. Ratcliff. Generalized iterative scaling for log-linear models. *Annals of Mathematical Statistics*, 43:1470–1480, 1972.

[8] A. P. Dempster, N. M. Laird, and D. B. Rubin. Maximum likelihood from incomplete data via the EM algorithm. *Journal of the Royal Statistical Society*, B-39:1–38, 1977.

[9] J. Goodman. Classes for fast maximum entropy training. In *Proceedings of IEEE International Conference on Acoustics, Speech, and Signal Processing*, 2001.

[10] J. Goodman. Sequential conditional generalized iterative scaling. In *Proceedings of ACL*, 2002.

[11] D. Heckerman. Bayesian networks for data mining. *Data Mining and Knowledge Discovery*, 1(1):79–119, 1997.

[12] D. Heckerman, D. Chickering, C. Meek, R. Rounthwaite, and C. Kadie. Dependency networks for density estimation, collaborative filtering, and data visualization. *Journal of Machine Learning Research*, 1:49—75, 2000.

[13] F. Jelinek. *Statistical Methods for Speech Recognition*. Cambridge. MA:MIT Press, 1998.

[14] S. Lawrence, C. L. Giles, and K. Bollacker. Digital libraries and Autonomous Citation Indexing. *IEEE Computer*, 32(6):67–71, 1999.

[15] B. Liu, W. Hsu, and Y. Ma. Integrating classification and association rule mining. In *Proceedings of the Fourth International Conference on Knowledge Discovery and Data Mining*, pages 80–96, 1998.

[16] B. Mobasher, R. Cooley, and J. Srivastava. Automatic personalization based on Web usage mining. *Communications of the ACM*, 43(8):142–151, 2000.

[17] D. Pavlov. Sequence modeling with mixtures of conditional maximum entropy distributions. In *Proceedings of the Third IEEE Conference on Data Mining (ICDM'03)*, 2003.

[18] D. Pavlov and D. Pennock. A maximum entropy approach to collaborative filtering in dynamic, sparse, high-dimensional domains. In *Proceedings of Neural Information Processing Systems*, 2002.

[19] M. Perkowitz and O. Etzioni. Adaptive web sites: Automatically synthesizing web pages. In *Proceedings of the Fifteenth National Conference on Artificial Intelligence*, pages 727—732, 1998.

[20] S. D. Pietra, V. D. Pietra, and J. Lafferty. Inducing features of random fields. *IEEE Transactions on Pattern Analysis and Machine Intelligence*, 19(4):380–393, April 1997.

[21] P. Resnick, N. Iacovou, M. Suchak, P. Bergstorm, and J. Riedl. GroupLens: An Open Architecture for Collaborative Filtering of Netnews. In *Proceedings of ACM 1994 Conference on Computer Supported Cooperative Work*, pages 175–186, Chapel Hill, North Carolina, 1994. ACM.

Privacy-preserving Distributed Clustering using Generative Models

Srujana Merugu and Joydeep Ghosh
Electrical and Computer Engineering
University of Texas at Austin
Austin, TX 78712
{merugu, ghosh}@ece.utexas.edu

Abstract

We present a framework for clustering distributed data in unsupervised and semi-supervised scenarios, taking into account privacy requirements and communication costs. Rather than sharing parts of the original or perturbed data, we instead transmit the parameters of suitable generative models built at each local data site to a central location. We mathematically show that the best representative of all the data is a certain " mean" model, and empirically show that this model can be approximated quite well by generating artificial samples from the underlying distributions using Markov Chain Monte Carlo techniques, and then fitting a combined global model with a chosen parametric form to these samples. We also propose a new measure that quantifies privacy based on information theoretic concepts, and show that decreasing privacy leads to a higher quality of the combined model and vice versa. We provide empirical results on different data types to highlight the generality of our framework. The results show that high quality distributed clustering can be achieved with little privacy loss and low communication cost.

1. Introduction

Extracting useful knowledge from large, distributed data repositories can be a very difficult task when such data cannot be directly centralized or unified as a single file or database either due to legal, proprietary or technical restrictions. This has led to the emergence of distributed data mining techniques that try to obtain high quality information from distributed sources with minimal interactions among the data sources. Most of the techniques developed so far have focused on classification or on association rules [1, 2, 8, 13]. There has also been some work on distributed clustering for *vertically partitioned data* (different sites contain different attributes/features of a common set of records/objects) [12, 18], and on parallelizing clustering al-

gorithms for *horizontally partitioned data* (i.e. the objects are distributed amongst the sites, which record the same set of features for each object) [7]. These techniques, however, do not specifically address privacy issues.

In this paper, we focus on the little explored problems of clustering horizontally distributed data in unsupervised and semi-supervised settings, taking into account various privacy restrictions. The prototypical application scenario is one in which there are multiple parties with confidential databases of the same schema. The goal is to characterize *via* clustering or classification, the entire distributed data, without actually pooling this data. For example, the parties can be a group of banks, with their own sets of customers, who would like to have a better insight into the behavior of the entire customer population without compromising the privacy of their individual customers. A fundamental assumption is that there is an (unknown) underlying distribution that represents the different datasets and it is possible to learn this unknown distribution by combining high-level information from the different sources instead of sharing individual records.

In this paper we make three main contributions. First, we introduce a privacy preserving framework for distributed clustering in unsupervised and semi-supervised scenarios that is applicable to a wide variety of data types and learning algorithms, so long as they can provide a generative model [11]. In this framework, the parties owning the individual data sources independently train generative models on the local data and send the model parameters to a central combiner that integrates the models. This limits the amount of interactions between the data sources and the combiner and enables us to formulate the distributed clustering problem in a general as well as tractable form. Second, we present the idea that it is possible to obtain efficient solutions to optimization problems based on generative models by formulating approximate versions of the problems using sampling techniques, which can then be solved using existing learning algorithms. We apply this idea to the specific problem of distributed clustering in unsupervised and semi-supervised sce-

211

narios to develop EM based algorithms that are guaranteed to asymptotically converge to a global model that is locally optimal as the sample size used to obtain the global model goes to ∞. Finally, we propose a measure for quantifying privacy based on ideas from information theory. This allows us to formalize the problem of obtaining a local model given the privacy constraints and demonstrate that there is an asymptotic relation between the average logarithm of privacy of the local models and the KL-divergence quality cost of the optimal model.

A word about the notation: Sets such as $\{z_1, \cdots, z_n\}$ are enumerated as $\{z_i\}_{i=1}^n$. Probability density functions of a model λ is denoted by p_λ. Expectation of functions of a random variable z following a distribution p are denoted by $\mathbf{E}_{z \sim p}[\cdot]$. x is used to denote objects and takes values over the domain of data while y is used to denote class labels and z is used when a statement holds for both (x, y) and x.

2. Problem definition

Consider a situation wherein there are multiple data sources containing unlabeled or partially labeled data and our aim is to obtain a combined global clustering or classification model subject to privacy and communication restrictions. We will approach this distributed clustering problem by first dividing it into two sub-problems — (i) choosing local models based on privacy and communication restrictions, and (ii) combining the local models effectively to obtain a "good" global model. In our current work, we formalize the first problem by quantifying privacy and communication costs and mainly focus on solving the second problem, assuming that the first problem is solved. This separation of concerns obviates the need for optimizing a complicated objective function that simultaneously captures the quality of clustering, privacy and communication costs. This approach also allows the individual parties to use proprietary algorithms and domain knowledge, and enables reuse of legacy clusterings [18].

Let $\{\mathcal{X}_i\}_{i=1}^n$ be n horizontally partitioned data sources generated by a common underlying model, λ^0 and let $\{\lambda_i\}_{i=1}^n$ be the local models obtained by applying clustering or classification algorithms to these data sources. Then, the objective of the first sub-problem is to obtain the local models $\{\lambda_i\}_{i=1}^n$, such that the constraints on the privacy and communication costs are satisfied, i.e., $\forall i, 1 \le i \le n$, $\mathcal{P}(\lambda_i) \ge \rho_i$ and $\mathcal{C}(\lambda_i) \le c_i$, where $\mathcal{P}(\cdot)$ and $\mathcal{C}(\cdot)$ are the privacy and communication cost functions discussed later in section 5, and $\{\rho_i\}_{i=1}^n$ and $\{c_i\}_{i=1}^n$ are the lowest allowed privacy and highest allowed communication costs for the local models.

For the second sub-problem, the aim is to obtain a high quality global model that is also highly interpretable. Quality can be easily quantified in terms of how representative the model is of the true distribution, while interpretability, i.e., ease of understanding or describing the model, is difficult to quantify. Hence, to make the problem tractable, we require that the global model be specified as a mixture model based on a given parametric family (e.g., mixture of Gaussians). We call the resulting search problem of finding the highest quality global model within this family of models the **Distributed Model-based Clustering** (DMC) problem and state it more formally below.

Let $\{\nu_i\}_{i=1}^n$ be non-negative weights associated with the local models based on their importance or on the size of the corresponding data sources. The objective of the DMC problem is to obtain the optimal global clustering model λ_c^* belonging to a given family of models $\mathcal{F}$, i.e.,

$$\lambda_c^* = \operatorname*{argmin}_{\lambda_c \in \mathcal{F}} \mathcal{Q}(\lambda_c),$$

where $\mathcal{Q}(\cdot)$ is the model quality cost function defined in terms of the local models and their weights.

2.1. Model representation

We represent both classification and clustering models in terms of density functions. This common representation enables us to define cost functions for both types of models in a uniform manner and also leads to a systematic approach for combining classification and clustering models. In our scheme, a **classification model**, i.e., a generative model λ, produced by a classification algorithm is specified in terms of the joint density on the data objects x and the class labels y, $p_\lambda(x, y) = \sum_{h=1}^k I[y = h]\pi_\lambda^h p_\lambda(x|h)$, where $\{\pi_\lambda^h\}_{h=1}^k$ are the class priors, $\{p_\lambda(x|h)\}_{h=1}^k$ are the class conditional densities, k is the number of classes and $I[\cdot]$ is the indicator function. On the other hand, a **clustering** model, i.e., a generative model λ, produced by a clustering algorithm is specified in terms of probability density $p_\lambda(x)$ on the data objects x alone and is given by, $p_\lambda(x) = \sum_{h=1}^k \pi_\lambda^h p_\lambda(x|h)$, where $\{\pi_\lambda^h\}_{h=1}^k$ are the cluster priors, $\{p_\lambda(x|h)\}_{h=1}^k$ are the cluster densities and k is the number of clusters.

2.2. Model quality

A natural definition for the quality cost, $\mathcal{Q}_I(\cdot)$, for a global model, is just the "distance" from the underlying true model λ^0, i.e., $\mathcal{Q}_I(\lambda_c) = D(\lambda^0, \lambda_c)$, where $D(\cdot, \cdot)$ is a suitable distance measure for models. Since λ^0 is not known, we instead, consider the different local models $\{\lambda_i\}_{i=1}^n$ as estimators of λ^0 with weights $\{\nu_i\}_{i=1}^n$ and define the quality cost function in terms of the average distance from the local models, i.e., $\mathcal{Q}(\lambda_c) = \sum_{i=1}^n \nu_i D(\lambda_i, \lambda_c)$, where $\sum_{i=1}^n \nu_i = 1$.

Metrics based on the norms of density functions such as the L_1 distance and the squared L_2 distance and KL-divergence are the commonly used distance measures for comparing a pair of generative models. For classification models, another suitable measure is the mismatch in the labelings, which reduces to the misclassification error when one of the models being compared is the true model. Of all these, KL-divergence is the most natural comparison measure since it is linearly related to the average log-likelihood of the data generated by one model with respect to the other. It is also a well-behaved differentiable function of the model parameters unlike the other measures.

Hence, we try to optimize the quality cost function based only on the KL-divergence measure and use other measures only for secondary evaluation of the experimental results. For clustering models, we consider the KL-divergence between the density functions of just the data values, i.e.,

$$
\begin{aligned}
D_{KL}^{\text{clus}}(\lambda_1, \lambda_2) &= KL(p_{\lambda_1}(x)\|p_{\lambda_2}(x)) \\
&= \int_{\Omega_x} p_{\lambda_1}(x) \log\left(\frac{p_{\lambda_1}(x)}{p_{\lambda_2}(x)}\right) dx,
\end{aligned}
$$

where Ω_x is the domain of x, and for classification models, we consider the KL-divergence between the joint densities $p_{\lambda_1}(x, y)$ and $p_{\lambda_2}(x, y)$, i.e., $D_{KL}^{\text{class}}(\lambda_1, \lambda_2) = KL(p_{\lambda_1}(x, y)\|p_{\lambda_2}(x, y))$.

3. Unsupervised distributed clustering

In this section, we pose the DMC problem for an unsupervised scenario as an optimization problem and propose a practical algorithm that asymptotically converges to a locally optimal solution. The objective of the DMC problem for an unsupervised scenario is to obtain a global model λ_c belonging to a particular parametric family $\mathcal{F}$ such that the quality cost function $\mathcal{Q}(\cdot)$ based on KL-divergence is minimized, i.e.,

$$
\lambda_c^* = \underset{\lambda_c \in \mathcal{F}}{\operatorname{argmin}} \, \mathcal{Q}(\lambda_c) = \underset{\lambda_c \in \mathcal{F}}{\operatorname{argmin}} \sum_{i=1}^n \nu_i D_{KL}^{\text{clus}}(\lambda_i, \lambda_c), \quad (1)
$$

where $\{\lambda_i\}_{i=1}^n$ are the local clustering models based on different unlabeled data sources with weights $\{\nu_i\}_{i=1}^n$ summing to 1. This problem can be simplified using the following result.

Theorem 1 [1] *Given a set of models $\{\lambda_i\}_{i=1}^n$ with weights $\{\nu_i\}_{i=1}^n$ summing to 1, then for any model λ_c,*

$$
\begin{aligned}
\sum_{i=1}^n \nu_i KL(p_{\lambda_i}(z)\|p_{\lambda_c}(z)) = & \sum_{i=1}^n \nu_i KL(p_{\lambda_i}(z)\|p_{\bar{\lambda}}(z)) \\
& + KL(p_{\bar{\lambda}}(z)\|p_{\lambda_c}(z)),
\end{aligned}
$$

where $\bar{\lambda}$ is such that $p_{\bar{\lambda}}(z) = \sum_{i=1}^n \nu_i p_{\lambda_i}(z)$.

Applying the above theorem for clustering models, we can see that the cost function in (1) is equal to $\sum_{i=1}^n \nu_i D_{KL}^{\text{clus}}(\lambda_i, \bar{\lambda}) + D_{KL}^{\text{clus}}(\bar{\lambda}, \lambda_c)$. The first term is independent of λ_c and hence, optimizing the cost function in (1) is equivalent to minimizing KL-divergence with respect to the mean model $\bar{\lambda}$. In the absence of constraints, the optimal solution is just the mean model $\bar{\lambda}$, as KL-divergence is always non-negative and zero only when both the arguments are equal.

The mean model also has the following nice property, which follows from Jensen's inequality.

Theorem 2 *Given a set of models $\{\lambda_i\}_{i=1}^n$ with weights $\{\nu_i\}_{i=1}^n$ summing to 1 and the true model λ^0,*

$$
D(\lambda^0, \bar{\lambda}) \le \sum_{i=1}^n \nu_i D(\lambda^0, \lambda_i),
$$

where $\bar{\lambda}$ is such that $p_{\bar{\lambda}}(z) = \sum_{i=1}^n \nu_i p_{\lambda_i}(z)$ and $D(\cdot, \cdot)$ is any distance function [2] that is convex in the density function of the second model.

Since the true model λ^0 is unknown, it is not possible to find out which of the models $\{\lambda_i\}_{i=1}^n$ is more accurate in terms of the ideal quality cost function $\mathcal{Q}_I(\cdot)$. However, from the above lemma, one can guarantee that the mean model will always provides an improvement over the average quality of the available models. When the individual models have independent errors, the expected improvement can be considerably higher. The mean model is thus a good choice in terms of both $\mathcal{Q}(\cdot)$ and $\mathcal{Q}_I(\cdot)$, but it might not be a very interpretable model as it will in general have a large number of overlapping components. Instead, it is desirable to require the combined model to belong to a specified parametric family $\mathcal{F}$. Therefore, we find the model in $\mathcal{F}$ that is closest to the mean model in terms of KL-divergence. From Theorem 1, this is also the exact solution to the DMC problem (1).

$$
\lambda_c^* = \underset{\lambda_c \in \mathcal{F}}{\operatorname{argmin}} \, D_{KL}^{\text{clus}}(\bar{\lambda}, \lambda_c) \quad (2)
$$

The new optimization problem (2) is difficult to solve directly using gradient descent techniques. Therefore, we pose an approximate version of the above problem and solve it *via* Expectation-Maximization [6]. Let $\bar{\mathcal{X}} = \{x_j\}_{j=1}^m$ be a dataset obtained by sampling from the mean model. Consider the problem of finding the model $\lambda_c^a \in \mathcal{F}$ that maximizes the average log-likelihood of the dataset $\bar{\mathcal{X}}$, i.e.,

$$
\max_{\lambda_c \in \mathcal{F}} L(\bar{\mathcal{X}}, \lambda_c) = \max_{\lambda_c \in \mathcal{F}} \frac{1}{m} \sum_{j=1}^m \log(p_{\lambda_c}(x_j)), \quad (3)
$$

---

[1] This result is true for a class of functions called Bregman divergences [3] of which KL-divergence and squared L_2 distance are particular cases.

[2] Examples of distance functions that are convex in the density function of the second argument include KL-divergence, L_1 distance and squared L_2 distance.

Algorithm 1 Unsupervised Distributed Clustering

Input: Set of models $\{\lambda_i\}_{i=1}^n$ with weights $\{\nu_i\}_{i=1}^n$ summing to 1, Mixture model family $\mathcal{F}$.

Output: $\lambda_c^a \simeq \underset{\lambda_c \in \mathcal{F}}{\operatorname{argmin}} \sum_{i=1}^n \nu_i D_{KL}^{\mathrm{clus}}(\lambda_i, \lambda_c)$

Method:

1. Obtain mean model $\bar{\lambda}$ such that

$$p_{\bar{\lambda}}(x) = \sum_{i=1}^n \nu_i p_{\lambda_i}(x).$$

2. Generate $\bar{\mathcal{X}} = \{x_j\}_{j=1}^m$ from mean model, $\bar{\lambda}$ using MCMC sampling.

3. Apply EM algorithm to obtain the optimal model, λ_c^a, such that

$$\lambda_c^a = \underset{\lambda_c \in \mathcal{F}}{\operatorname{argmax}} L(\bar{\mathcal{X}}, \lambda_c) = \underset{\lambda_c \in \mathcal{F}}{\operatorname{argmax}} \frac{1}{m} \sum_{j=1}^m \log(p_{\lambda_c}(x_j)).$$

where $L(\bar{\mathcal{X}}, \lambda_c)$ is the average log-likelihood of $\bar{\mathcal{X}}$ with respect to λ_c. As the size of the dataset $\bar{\mathcal{X}}$ goes to ∞, the average log-likelihood converges to the cross entropy between the densities $p_{\bar{\lambda}}$ and p_{λ_c}, i.e., $\underset{m \to \infty}{\mathrm{Lt}} L(\bar{\mathcal{X}}, \lambda_c) = \underset{m \to \infty}{\mathrm{Lt}} \mathbf{E}_{x \in \bar{\mathcal{X}}}[\log(p_{\lambda_c}(x))] = \mathbf{E}_{x \sim p_{\bar{\lambda}}}[\log(p_{\lambda_c}(x))]$. Now, the cross entropy between any two densities is linearly related to the KL-divergence between them, i.e., $\mathbf{E}_{x \sim p_{\bar{\lambda}}}[\log(p_{\lambda_c}(x))] = \mathbf{E}_{x \sim p_{\bar{\lambda}}}[\log(p_{\bar{\lambda}}(x)) - \log\left(\frac{p_{\bar{\lambda}}(x)}{p_{\lambda_c}(x)}\right)] = H(\bar{\lambda}) - D_{KL}^{\mathrm{clus}}(\bar{\lambda}, \lambda_c)$, where $H(\bar{\lambda})$ is the entropy of the mean model and is independent of λ_c. Hence, maximizing the cross entropy with respect to the mean model is equivalent to minimizing the KL-divergence with respect to the mean model. The approximate problem (3), therefore converges to the unsupervised DMC problem (2) as the size of $\bar{\mathcal{X}}$ goes to ∞.

Viewing (3) as a maximum-likelihood parameter estimation problem leads to Algorithm 1. The main idea is to first generate a dataset $\bar{\mathcal{X}}$ following the mean model $\bar{\lambda}$, using Markov Chain Monte Carlo (MCMC) sampling techniques [14] and then, apply the EM algorithm to this dataset to obtain the clustering model $\lambda_c^a \in \mathcal{F}$ that maximizes its likelihood of being observed. The resulting model λ_c^a is a local minimizer of the approximate problem and not necessarily the same as the solution λ_c^* of the original unsupervised DMC problem (1). However, it is guaranteed to asymptotically converge to a locally optimal solution as the size of $\bar{\mathcal{X}}$ goes to ∞. In practice, one can use multiple runs of the EM algorithm and pick the best solution among these so that the obtained model is reasonably close to the globally optimal model.

4. Semi-supervised distributed clustering

In this section, we consider the DMC problem for a semi-supervised setting of which the unsupervised and completely supervised scenarios are special cases. Then, as in the unsupervised case, we pose it as an optimization problem and present an efficient EM based algorithm to solve it.

Consider a situation where only some of the data sources have labeled data. In this case, the objective is to use the local classification models $\{\lambda_{Ai}\}_{i=1}^{n_A}$ based on labeled sources and local clustering models $\{\lambda_{Bi}\}_{i=1}^{n_B}$ based on the unlabeled data sources to obtain a global model whose components correspond to the different classes. As in the previous case, we minimize the KL-divergence of the global model from the local models leading to the optimization problem,

$$\min_{\lambda_c \in \mathcal{F}} \left\{ \sum_{i=1}^{n_A} \nu_{Ai} D_{KL}^{\mathrm{class}}(\lambda_{Ai}, \lambda_c) + \sum_{i=1}^{n_B} \nu_{Bi} D_{KL}^{\mathrm{clus}}(\lambda_{Bi}, \lambda_c) \right\},$$
(4)

where $\mathcal{F}$ is a mixture model family and $\{\nu_{Ai}\}_{i=1}^{n_A}$, $\{\nu_{Bi}\}_{i=1}^{n_B}$ are the weights of the classification and clustering models respectively that together sum to 1. Applying Theorem 1 for the clustering and classification models, it is easy to see that the semi-supervised DMC problem (4) is exactly equivalent to a simpler problem,

$$\min_{\lambda_c \in \mathcal{F}} \{ \nu_A D_{KL}^{\mathrm{class}}(\bar{\lambda}_A, \lambda_c) + \nu_B D_{KL}^{\mathrm{clus}}(\bar{\lambda}_B, \lambda_c) \}, \quad (5)$$

where $\nu_A = \sum_{i=1}^{n_A} \nu_{Ai}$, $\nu_B = \sum_{i=1}^{n_B} \nu_{Bi}$ and the models $\bar{\lambda}_A$ and $\bar{\lambda}_B$ are such that $p_{\bar{\lambda}_A}(x, y) = \frac{1}{\nu_A} \sum_{i=1}^{n_A} \nu_{Ai} p_{\lambda_{Ai}}(x, y)$ and $p_{\bar{\lambda}_B}(x) = \frac{1}{\nu_B} \sum_{i=1}^{n_B} \nu_{Bi} p_{\lambda_{Bi}}(x)$. When $\nu_A = 0$, i.e., there are no classification models, this problem reduces to the unsupervised DMC problem (2) and when $\nu_B = 0$, i.e., there are no clustering models, it reduces to a supervised distributed classification problem. For the supervised case, this formulation is different from the usual formulation based on the misclassification error. However, it turns out that empirically, the most effective solution [4] for minimizing the misclassification error given a set of classification models is to obtain a combined classifier based on the mean posterior probabilities, which is exactly the same as the mean classification model $\bar{\lambda}_A$ under the assumption that the data densities $p_{\lambda_i}(x)$ for the different classification models are the same. This assumption is not restrictive and is in fact usually true for distributed classification scenarios, e.g., bagged predictors, for which the mean posterior classifier performs well.

We now address the simplified semi-supervised DMC problem (5) using the following approximate version. Let $\bar{\mathcal{X}}_A = \{(x_{Aj}, y_{Aj})\}_{j=1}^{m_A}$ be a labeled dataset sampled from the mean classification model $\bar{\lambda}_A$ and $\bar{\mathcal{X}}_B = \{x_{Bj}\}_{j=1}^{m_B}$ be an unlabeled dataset sampled from the mean clustering

Algorithm 2 Semi-supervised Distributed Clustering

Input: Set of classification models $\{\lambda_{Ai}\}_{i=1}^{n_A}$ and clustering models $\{\lambda_{Bi}\}_{i=1}^{n_B}$ with weights $\{\nu_{Ai}\}_{i=1}^{n_A}$ and $\{\nu_{Bi}\}_{i=1}^{n_B}$ respectively that together sum to 1, Mixture model family $\mathcal{F}$.

Output: $\lambda_c^a \simeq \underset{\lambda_c \in \mathcal{F}}{\operatorname{argmin}} \{\sum_{i=1}^{n_A} \nu_{Ai} D_{KL}^{\text{class}}(\lambda_{Ai}, \lambda_c) + \sum_{i=1}^{n_B} \nu_{Bi} D_{KL}^{\text{clus}}(\lambda_{Bi}, \lambda_c)\}$

Method:
1. Obtain mean classification model $\bar{\lambda}_A$ and mean clustering model $\bar{\lambda}_B$ such that

$$p_{\bar{\lambda}_A}(x,y) = \frac{1}{\nu_A} \sum_{i=1}^{n_A} \nu_{Ai} p_{\lambda_{Ai}}(x,y)$$

and

$$p_{\bar{\lambda}_B}(x) = \frac{1}{\nu_B} \sum_{i=1}^{n_B} \nu_{Bi} p_{\lambda_{Bi}}(x),$$

where $\sum_{i=1}^{n_A} \nu_{Ai} = \nu_A$ and $\sum_{i=1}^{n_B} \nu_{Bi} = \nu_B$.

2. Generate $\bar{\mathcal{X}}_A = \{(x_{Aj}, y_{Aj})\}_{j=1}^{m_A}$ and $\bar{\mathcal{X}}_B = \{x_{Bj}\}_{j=1}^{m_B}$ from the mean models, $\bar{\lambda}_A$ and $\bar{\lambda}_B$ respectively so that $\frac{m_A}{m_B} = \frac{\nu_A}{\nu_B}$ using MCMC sampling.

3. Apply the modified EM algorithm to obtain the optimal model, λ_c^a that is the solution of

$$\underset{\lambda_c \in \mathcal{F}}{\operatorname{argmax}} L(\bar{\mathcal{X}}, \lambda_c) = \underset{\lambda_c \in \mathcal{F}}{\operatorname{argmax}} \{\nu_A L(\bar{\mathcal{X}}_A, \lambda_c) + \nu_B L(\bar{\mathcal{X}}_B, \lambda_c)\}.$$

---

model $\bar{\lambda}_B$ such that the sizes of the datasets, m_A and m_B are proportional to the weights ν_A and ν_B and $m_A + m_B = m$. Now consider the problem of finding a mixture model $\lambda_c^a \in \mathcal{F}$ that maximizes the average log-likelihood of the combined dataset $\bar{\mathcal{X}} = \bar{\mathcal{X}}_A \cup \bar{\mathcal{X}}_B$, i.e.,

$$\max_{\lambda_c \in \mathcal{F}} L(\bar{\mathcal{X}}, \lambda_c) = \max_{\lambda_c \in \mathcal{F}} \{\nu_A L(\bar{\mathcal{X}}_A, \lambda_c) + \nu_B L(\bar{\mathcal{X}}_B, \lambda_c)\} \tag{6}$$

where $L(\cdot, \lambda_c)$ is the average log-likelihood function with respect to λ_c. Using the same relations between the log-likelihood, cross entropy and the KL-divergence as for unsupervised DMC, it is easy to show that the solution to the approximate problem converges to the solution of the original problem (5) as the size of the dataset $\bar{\mathcal{X}}$ goes to ∞.

The approximate problem is again a maximum likelihood parameter estimation problem where we need to learn the parameters for the mixture model that maximizes the likelihood of the combined dataset $\bar{X} = \bar{\mathcal{X}}_A \cup \bar{\mathcal{X}}_B$. This can be easily solved using the EM framework, by assuming that the missing data is the posterior probabilities of the mixture components for only the objects in $\bar{\mathcal{X}}_B$, i.e., the unlabeled data objects [15]. Because of this, we only need to update the posterior probabilities of the unlabeled data objects in the expectation step. The maximization step remains unchanged. This results in a modified EM algorithm that can be used as part of the overall semi-supervised distributed clustering algorithm (Algorithm 2).

5. Privacy and communication costs

In this section, we quantify the privacy and communication costs using ideas from information theory and also show that there is an inverse relation between the privacy of the local models and the quality of the mean model.

Privacy. In order to quantify privacy, we need a measure that indicates the uncertainty in predicting the original dataset from the model. The work in [1] proposes a privacy measure based on the differential entropy of the generating distribution given by $h(\lambda) = -\int_{\Omega_z} p_\lambda(z) \log_2(p_\lambda(z)) dz$, where Ω_z is the domain of z. This quantity indicates the uncertainty in predicting the data given the model λ [5], but does not consider the privacy of a particular dataset with respect to a model. For example, a model with an extremely peaked distribution will have very low entropy, but if the peaks do not correspond to the actual objects in the dataset, then there is not much privacy lost. This motivates us to define a slightly different measure that considers the privacy of the model with respect to the actual objects in the dataset. We propose that the privacy, $\mathcal{P}(z, \lambda)$ of an object z given a model λ be defined in terms of the probability of generating the data object from the model. The higher the probability, the lower the privacy. More specifically, noting that the reciprocal of the probability is related to uncertainty [5], we have $\mathcal{P}(z, \lambda) = (p_\lambda(z))^{-1}$.

For vector data, $\mathcal{P}(z, \lambda) = 1$ implies that z can be predicted with the same accuracy as a random variable with a uniform distribution on a ball of unit volume. We can now define the privacy, $\mathcal{P}(\mathcal{Z}, \lambda)$ of a dataset $\mathcal{Z}$ with respect to the model as some function of the privacy of the individual data objects. The geometric mean has a nice interpretation as the reciprocal of the average likelihood of the dataset being generated by the model, assuming that the individual samples are i.i.d., i.e., $\mathcal{P}(\mathcal{Z}, \lambda) = \left(\prod_{z \in \mathcal{Z}} p_\lambda(z)\right)^{\frac{-1}{|\mathcal{Z}|}} = 2^{\left(-\frac{1}{|\mathcal{Z}|} \sum_{z \in \mathcal{Z}} \log_2 p_\lambda(z)\right)}$.

A higher likelihood of generating the dataset from the model implies a lower amount of privacy. For example, let us consider vector space data being modeled by a mixture of Gaussians. A highly detailed model with Gaussians of vanishing variance, centered at each of the data objects gives away the entire dataset and has no privacy. This is to be expected as the probability density $p_\lambda(z)$ goes to ∞, for all data objects $z \in \mathcal{Z}$ making the privacy measure go to 0^+. On the other hand, a very coarse model, say with a single Gaussian with high variance has a low likelihood of generating the data and hence, has a high privacy.

Intuitively, if the local models are more detailed, the combined model can be improved at the cost of decreased privacy. In particular, using the weak law of large numbers and Chebyshev inequality [16], it can be shown that the average log-privacy of the local models converges to their average cross-entropy with a high probability when the sizes of the individual datasets are large enough. Since the average cross entropy is linearly related to the KL-divergence between the mean model and the true model, there exists an asymptotic linear relation between the average log-privacy and ideal quality cost of the mean model, i.e., $\sum_{i=1}^{n} \nu_i \log(\mathcal{P}(\mathcal{Z}_i, \lambda_i)) + H(\lambda^0) \simeq KL(p_{\lambda^0}(z) \| p_{\bar{\lambda}}(z)) = \mathcal{Q}_I(\bar{\lambda})$, where $\bar{\lambda}$ is the mean model. As the privacy of the local models increases, the ideal quality cost of the mean model, which is the optimal model with no constraints, also goes up.

Communication cost. To quantify the communication cost $\mathcal{C}(\lambda)$, we consider the number of bits or words required to unambiguously specify the model to the central combiner. When the generative model family is already known to the central combiner, then one needs to only consider the cost of specifying the values of the parameters. A more formal definition would be to consider the Kolmogorov complexity [5] or the minimum description length of the local model, i.e., $\mathcal{C}(\lambda) = K_v(\lambda)$.

6 Experimental evaluation

In this section, we provide empirical evidence that for a reasonable global sample size and privacy level and a few runs of the EM algorithm, the global model obtained through our approach is as good as or better than the best local model for different types of data not only in terms of KL-divergence but also for other distance measures. We also present results that show how the privacy, communication and quality costs vary with the resolution of local models.

We performed experiments on the four different types of data shown in Table 1. Artificial data was preferred since the true generative models is known, unlike in the case of real data, and one can perform controlled experiments to better understand algorithmic properties. In order to generate the data, we chose, for each run of the experiment, a mixture model with a fixed number (=5) of components and used it to create a collection of datasets of equal size by sampling independently using MCMC techniques. These datasets and models can be downloaded from http://www.lans.ece.utexas.edu/~srujana /gencl/data.

We empirically found that our approach is more beneficial when the number of clusters as well as the learning algorithms applied to the individual data sites are different, as this creates diversity in the models. However, since in this work our emphasis is not on the model selection problem, we present results obtained by applying the same learning algorithm to all the sites. For the unlabeled datasets, we used EM algorithms based on mixture models of the appropriate type. For the labeled datasets, we estimated the parameters of the class conditional distributions using maximum likelihood estimation (MLE) methods. The EM algorithms at

Table 1. Details of generative models and datasets for different data types.

Data Type	Model Type	#Dim/Seq. Length	Total Data Size (N)	#Sites	#Runs
Vector	Gaussian Full-covariance	8	5000	5	10
Directional	von Mises-Fisher	100	5000	5	10
Discrete sequence	Discrete HMM 5 states 4 symbols	30	1000	5	5
Continuous sequence	Cont. HMM 5 states 4 mixtures	30	600	3	5

both the local and global level were run multiple times and the best solution was chosen in order to reduce the probability of getting stuck in local minima.

For each setting, we computed the privacy and communication costs of the local models and the ideal quality cost functions based on the various distance measures listed in section 2. Distance measures that are integrals were estimated by averaging over 10,000 samples drawn from the appropriate distributions. The centralized model obtained using the union of all the datasets was used as the reference for each experiment.

6.1 Results and discussion

We applied our algorithm to different types of data in both unsupervised and semi-supervised settings choosing the global MCMC sample size to be equal to the combined size of all the data sources and the local model resolution to be the same as that of the true model. We also studied how the quality of the global model varies with the global sample size, the resolution of the local models and the percentage of labeled data by performing experiments on the Euclidean vector datasets.

Quality of global model. Figure 1 shows the quality of the different models for all four data types, in a *fully unsupervised* setting. The rows 1-4 correspond to the results on Gaussian, directional, discrete and continuous sequence data respectively. The black bar represents the average value and the white bar represents the standard deviation. In all the cases, the global model performs better than the best local model. Moreover, the global model quality is in general closer to the quality of the centralized model than the average quality of the local models. Figure 2 shows the quality of the different models in a *semi-supervised* setting.

The mean model in this setting is the mean classification model obtained by combining only the local classification models. Once again, the global model provides better quality than any of the local classification models. Sometimes, it is even better than that of the mean classification model,

216

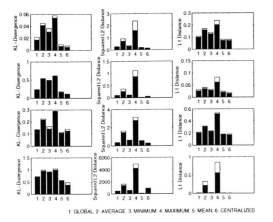

1: GLOBAL, 2: AVERAGE, 3: MINIMUM, 4: MAXIMUM, 5: MEAN, 6: CENTRALIZED

Figure 1. Global model quality for different types of data in an unsupervised setting.

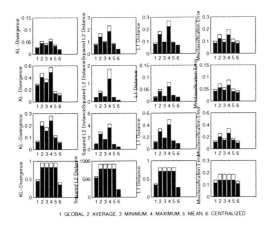

1: GLOBAL, 2: AVERAGE, 3: MINIMUM, 4: MAXIMUM, 5: MEAN, 6: CENTRALIZED

Figure 2. Global model quality for different types of data in a semi-supervised setting.

underscoring the effectiveness of using unlabeled data for improving the performance of classification models.

Variation of global model quality with sample size. For a fair comparison, we chose the global sample size to be equal to the combined size of all the data sources for the previous experiments. However, theoretical results indicate that we can obtain a better quality model with a higher sample size. In order to test this hypothesis, we ran our algorithm multiple times on the Euclidean vector datasets changing only the global sample size. Figure 3 shows how the quality of the different models vary with the sample size in an unsupervised setting. As one may expect, the quality of the global model improves with the number of artificially generated samples, with diminishing returns after a point. The behavior is similar for semi-supervised settings as well.

Variation of privacy, communication and quality cost with model resolution. An important aspect of the our clustering framework is the trade-off between privacy, commu-

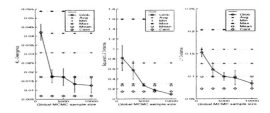

Figure 3. Variation of global model quality with sample size.

nication restrictions and the quality of the combined model obtained. This trade-off can be controlled by picking a suitable model resolution, e.g., number of clusters/classes. Figure 4 shows the variation of the average log-privacy, communication and quality cost with the number of clusters in the local models for Euclidean vector datasets. The behavior is similar for semi-supervised settings as well. From the plots, we note that the average log-privacy as well as the quality costs decrease as the number of clusters increases, while the communication cost goes up. At a thousand clus-

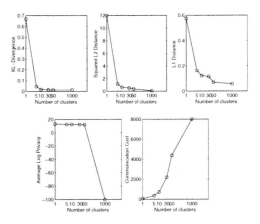

Figure 4. Variation of privacy, cluster quality and communication cost with respect to base model resolution.

ters/location (i.e. one cluster per point) there is maximum loss of privacy, but because of the natural clusters in the data, comparable cluster quality can be obtained much before this limiting value, i.e., at a much lesser privacy cost.

Variation in model quality with percentage of labeled data. Figure 5 shows the quality of the models obtained using different number of local classification models on Euclidean vector data, i.e., different percentages of labeled data. From the figure, we note that the quality costs of the mean classification model as well as global model decrease as the number of classification models increases. Another interesting trend is that the global model performs better than the mean classification model when the percentage of labeled data is less but becomes relatively worse as the per-

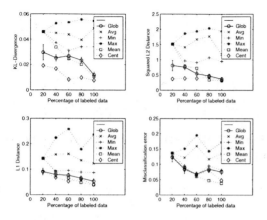

Figure 5. Variation in the model quality with percentage of labeled data.

centage of labeled data increases. This shows that it might be beneficial to use unlabeled data for improving classification models when there is very little labeled data. On the other hand, there is little utility in using unlabeled data when there is significant amount of labeled data.

7 Related work

Our distributed clustering technique relies on combining multiple parametric models. Other works of similar flavor applied to different settings include stacking for density estimation [17], distributed cooperative Bayesian learning [19]. However, in all these cases the emphasis is on quality and robustness rather than interpretability or privacy.

A simple example of integrating multiple generative models for clustering is the combining of the sets of means obtained through multiple k-means solutions. This has been studied in a variety of settings [9, 10], all of which are restricted to vector data. In contrast, our framework applies to arbitrary generative clustering models, hence covering a wide range of complex data types encountered in data mining.

In works that focus on privacy-preserving data mining, often individual records or attributes are subjected to a "privacy preserving" transformation and the goal is to obtain useful information from such transformed data. Classification and association rule techniques for this scenario have been proposed in [1, 2, 8]. These approaches are also restricted to vector data because of an add operator requirement. Another setting is an inter-enterprise data mining scenario such as the one considered in this paper, where multiple parties with confidential databases want to apply data mining algorithms to the union of their databases. There is very little literature in this area, a notable exception being the cryptographic method for enabling a secure two party computation for performing the ID3 decision tree algorithm

in [13].

Acknowledgments This work was supported in part by NSF grants IDM-0307792 and ITR-0312471. We would also like to thank Arindam Banerjee and Ravi Koku for their helpful suggestions.

References

[1] D. Agrawal and C. C. Aggarwal. On the design and quantification of privacy preserving data mining algorithms. In *Symposium on Principles of Database Systems*, 2001.

[2] R. Agrawal and R. Srikant. Privacy-preserving data mining. In *ACM SIGMOD*, pages 439–450, 2000.

[3] K. S. Azoury and M. K. Warmuth. Relative loss bounds for on-line density estimation with the exponential family of distributions. *Machine Learning*, 43(3):211–246, 2001.

[4] L. Breiman. Bagging predictors. *Machine Learning*, 24(2):123–140, 1996.

[5] T. M. Cover and J. A. Thomas. *Elements of Information Theory*. Wiley, 1991.

[6] A. P. Dempster, N. M. Laird, and D. B. Rubin. Maximum likelihood from incomplete data via the EM algorithm. *J. Royal Statistical Society. Series B (Methodological)*, 39(1):1–38, 1977.

[7] I. S. Dhillon and D. S. Modha. A data-clustering algorithm on distributed memory multiprocessors. In *ACM SIGKDD*, 1999.

[8] A. Evfimievski, R. Srikant, R. Agrawal, and J. Gehrke. Privacy preserving mining of association rules. In *KDD*, 2002.

[9] U. M. Fayyad, C. Reina, and P. S. Bradley. Initialization of iterative refinement clustering algorithms. In *ICML*, pages 194–198, 1998.

[10] A. L. N. Fred and A. K. Jain. Data clustering using evidence accumulation. In *ICPR*, pages IV:276–280, 2002.

[11] J. Ghosh. Scalable clustering methods for data mining. In N. Ye, editor, *Handbook of Data Mining*, pages 247–277. Lawrence Erlbaum, 2003.

[12] E. Johnson and H. Kargupta. Collective, hierarchical clustering from distributed, heterogeneous data. In M. Zaki and C. Ho, editors, *Large-Scale Parallel KDD Systems*, volume 1759 of *LNCS*, pages 221–244. Springer-Verlag, 1999.

[13] Y. Lindell and B. Pinkas. Privacy preserving data mining. *LNCS*, 1880:36–77, 2000.

[14] R. M. Neal. Probabilistic inference using Markov Chain Monte Carlo methods. Technical Report CRG-TR-93-1, Dept. of Computer Science, University of Toronto, 1993.

[15] K. Nigam, A. K. Mccallum, S. Thrun, and T. Mitchell. Text classification from labeled and unlabeled documents using EM. *Machine Learning*, 39(2/3):103–134, 2000.

[16] A. Papoulis. *Probability, Random Variables, and Stochastic Processes*. McGraw-Hill, New York, 1984.

[17] P. Smyth and D. Wolpert. An evaluation of linearly combining density estimators via stacking. *Machine Learning*, 36(1/2):53–89, July 1999.

[18] A. Strehl and J. Ghosh. Cluster ensembles – a knowledge reuse framework for combining partitionings. *JMLR*, pages 3:583–617, 2002.

[19] K. Yamanishi. Distributed cooperative Bayesian learning strategies. *Information and Computation*, 150:22–56, 1998.

Change Profiles

Taneli Mielikäinen
HIIT Basic Research Unit
Department of Computer Science
University of Helsinki, Finland
Taneli.Mielikainen@cs.Helsinki.fi

Abstract

In this paper we introduce a generalization of association rules: change profiles. We analyze their properties, describe their relationship to other structures in pattern discovery and sketch their possible applications. We study how the frequent patterns can be clustered based on their change profiles and propose methods for approximating the frequencies of the patterns from the approximate change profiles and bounding the intervals where the frequencies of the patterns are guaranteed to be. We evaluate empirically the methods for estimating the frequencies and the stability of their frequency estimates under different kinds of noise.

1 Introduction

Pattern discovery is a central task in data mining [19, 27]. Finding frequently occurring patterns from data has been one of the most actively studied problems in the field, and many kinds of frequent patterns can be found efficiently, see e.g. [1, 16, 26, 29, 38]. However, the fundamental problem in pattern discovery is how to benefit from the found patterns.

In this paper we study the global structure of the pattern collection from the local point of view of patterns. This is pursued by a new representation for pattern collections: *change profiles*. A change profile of a pattern describes what are the ratios between the frequency of the pattern and the frequencies of its sub- and superpatterns in the pattern collection, i.e., the patterns comparable with it w.r.t. a given partial order relation. To simplify the considerations, we divide the change profile ch^p of a pattern p into two parts (adapting the terminology of [28, 33]): the specializing change profile ch_s^p describes the changes to the superpatterns of p, and the generalizing change profile ch_g^p describes the changes to the subpatterns of p.

As a concrete example, let us consider the set collection $\{A, B, C, AB, BC, AC, ABC\}$ with frequencies $fr(A) =$ $3/4$, $fr(B) = 1/2$, $fr(C) = 3/4$, $fr(AB) = 1/4$, $fr(AC) = 1/2$, $fr(BC) = 1/2$ and $fr(ABC) = 1/4$. For these frequencies, the specializing change profiles of the (singleton) sets A, B and C are mappings $ch_s^A = \{B \mapsto fr(AB)/fr(A) = 1/3, C \mapsto fr(AC)/fr(A) = 2/3, BC \mapsto fr(ABC)/fr(A) = 1/3\}$, $ch_s^B = \{A \mapsto fr(AB)/fr(B) = 1/2, C \mapsto fr(BC)/fr(B) = 1, AC \mapsto fr(ABC)/fr(B) = 1/2\}$ and $ch_s^C = \{A \mapsto fr(AC)/fr(C) = 2/3, B \mapsto fr(BC)/fr(C) = 2/3, AB \mapsto fr(ABC)/fr(C) = 1/3\}$.

The change profiles attempt to reach from the local description of the data, a collection of patterns, to more global view of the relationships between the patterns. As an application to more classical pattern analysis, the change profiles can be used to define (dis)similarity measures between the patterns. Also, the patterns can be scored with help of their change profiles.

In addition of being a potentially useful tool in data analysis, the change profiles can be used to construct condensed representations of pattern collections [5, 6, 7, 8, 9, 25, 30, 32, 34, 35]. Many known condensed representations can be adapted to the change profiles but the change profiles suggest also some novel approaches to frequency estimation.

In this paper we introduce the concept of a change profile, a new representation for pattern collections that attempts to bridge the gap between local and global description of data. We describe several variations of change profiles and examine their properties. As the change profiles have more complex structure than the frequencies of the frequent patterns, they can be used to define dissimilarity measures between the frequent patterns. We consider different approaches to cluster the change profiles and show that many of the clustering problems are NP-hard and inapproximable for a wide variety of natural dissimilarity measures for change profiles. As an application to the condensed representations, we propose methods for approximating frequencies of the frequent patterns from their approximate change profiles and evaluate the methods empirically.

The rest of the paper is organized as follows. The concept of the change profile and its refinements are introduced in Section 2. The clustering of change profiles is studied in Section 3. In Section 4 a few approaches to estimate frequencies of a pattern collection from approximate change profiles are described. In Section 5 the frequency estimation methods are evaluated empirically. Section 6 consists of a short conclusion.

In the remaining sections we describe everything using frequent sets but the discussion generalizes readily to arbitrary pattern collections with a partial order.

2 Association Rules and Change Profiles

The *frequent set mining problem* is, given a sequence $d = d_1 \ldots d_n$ of subsets of a finite set R and a threshold value $\sigma \in [0, 1]$, find all subsets X of R such that the frequency of X,

$$fr(X, d) = \frac{|\{i : X \subseteq d_i, 1 \le i \le n\}|}{n},$$

is at least σ. These sets are called σ-*frequent sets* in d and they are denoted by $\mathcal{F}(\sigma, d)$. The frequency of X can be interpreted as the empirical probability $\mathbb{P}(X)$ of the event "the event contains X as its subset".

A classical set R is the collection of items sold in a supermarket. Then the most popular sequence d of subsets of R is sequence of market baskets of the customers. In addition to the market baskets of the customers, there are several other interesting sequences of subsets of the items: for the logistics division of a company, an interesting sequence d could rather be the sequence of packages arriving from the logistics center.

The frequent set mining is computationally feasible as there are several methods for mining frequent sets (output) efficiently [1, 3, 17, 18, 21, 22, 37]. Although each frequent set contains useful information about the data set, also the relationships between different frequent sets might be valuable. These relationships has been exploited by association rules.

An *association rule* $X \Rightarrow Y$ is a rule that associates a set $X \subseteq R$ to a set $Y \subseteq R$. An association rule $X \Rightarrow Y$ is called *simple* if Y is a singleton. The accuracy of the association rule $X \Rightarrow Y$ is

$$acc(X \Rightarrow Y, d) = \frac{fr(X \cup Y, d)}{fr(X, d)}.$$

The frequency of the rule $X \Rightarrow Y$ is defined to be $fr(X \Rightarrow Y, d) = fr(X \cup Y, d)$. The accuracy of the association rule $X \Rightarrow Y$ can be interpreted as a conditional probability $\mathbb{P}(Y|X)$. Thus each association rule $X \Rightarrow Y$ describes one relationship of the set X. (Empirical conditional probabilities with different kinds of events has been studied in data mining under the name of *cubegrades* [23].)

A more global view to relationships between the frequent set X and other frequent sets can be obtained by combining the association rules $X \Rightarrow Y$ into a mapping from the frequent sets to the interval $[0, 1]$. We call this mapping a *specializing change profile*:

Definition 1 (Specializing change profile) *A specializing change profile of a frequent set X is a mapping*

$$ch_s^X : \{Y : X \cup Y \in \mathcal{F}(\sigma, d)\} \to [0, 1]$$

consisting of the accuracies of frequent rules $X \Rightarrow Y$, i.e.,

$$ch_s^X(Y) = \frac{fr(X \cup Y, d)}{fr(X, d)}$$

where $X \cup Y \in \mathcal{F}(\sigma, d)$.

A specializing change profile ch_s^X can be interpreted as a conditional probability distribution $\mathbb{P}(\mathbf{Y}|X)$ where $\mathbf{Y}$ is a random variable.

Similarly to the specializing change profiles, we can define a *generalizing change profile*:

Definition 2 (Generalizing change profile) *A specializing change profile of a frequent set X is a mapping*

$$ch_g^X : \mathcal{F}(\sigma, d) \to [1, 1/\sigma)$$

consisting of the inverse accuracies of the frequent rules $acc(X \setminus Y \Rightarrow X)$, i.e.,

$$ch_g^X(Y) = \frac{fr(X \setminus Y, d)}{fr(X, d)}.$$

We denote change profiles by ch^X when we do not want to fix the type of the change profile. $ch^X(Y)$ is called a *change* of X on Y. The generalizing change profile of X corresponds to $1/\mathbb{P}(X|X \setminus \mathbf{Y})$.

Each specializing and generalizing change profile ch_s^X and ch_g^X describe "upper" and "lower" neighborhoods $N_s(X)$ and $N_g(X)$ of the frequent set X in the collection of frequent sets, respectively. The neighborhood $N(X) = N_s(X) \cup N_g(X)$ of X consists of the frequent sets $Y \in N_s(X)$ that contain X and the frequent sets $Y \in N_g(X)$ that are contained in X, i.e., the frequent sets that are comparable with X.

The change profiles, as we have defined them, are highly redundant due to the following simple properties of sets:

- $X \cup Y = X \cup (Y \setminus X)$ and

- $X \setminus Y = X \setminus (Y \cap X)$.

By exploiting these properties, we can reduce (without loss of information) the number of defined values of the change profile by factor $2^{|X|}$ in the case of a specializing change profile ch_s^X, and by factor $2^{|R \setminus X|}$ in the case of a generalizing change profile ch_g^X. We call this kind of change profiles with reduced redundancy the *concise change profiles*:

Definition 3 (Concise specializing change profile) *A concise specializing change profile cch_s^X is a restriction of ch_s^X to elements Y such that $Y \cap X = \emptyset$ and $X \cup Y \in \mathcal{F}(\sigma, d)$.*

Definition 4 (Concise generalizing change profile) *A concise generalizing change profile cch_g^X is a restriction of ch_g^X to elements Y such that $Y \subseteq X$.*

The concise change profiles can be interpreted as affine axis-parallel subspaces of $\mathbb{R}^{|\mathcal{F}(\sigma,d)|}$ that are indexed by Y s.t. $Y \cap X = \emptyset, X \cup Y \in \mathcal{F}(\sigma, d)$ in the specializing case, and Y s.t. $Y \subseteq X$ in the generalizing case. The concise change profiles for $\mathcal{F}(\sigma, d)$ can be computed output-optimally by a careful implementation of the following algorithm:

CHANGE-PROFILES($\mathcal{F}(\sigma, d), fr$)
1   **for each** X **in** $\mathcal{F}(\sigma, d)$
2   **do for each** $Y, Y \subseteq X$
3   **do** $cch_s^{X \setminus Y}(Y) \leftarrow fr(X) / fr(X \setminus Y)$
4         $cch_g^X(Y) \leftarrow fr(X \setminus Y) / fr(X)$
5   **return** (cch_s, cch_g)

The neighborhoods of even the concise change profiles can be too large: For example, if $X \in \mathcal{F}(\sigma, d)$, then $|cch_s^{\emptyset}| \geq 2^{|X|}$ and $|cch_g^X| \geq 2^{|X|}$. Thus, following the definitions of association rules, we define *simple specializing change profiles* and *simple generalizing change profiles*:

Definition 5 (Simple change profile) *A simple specializing (generalizing) change profile sch_s^X (sch_g^X) is a restriction of ch_s^X (of ch_s^X) to singletons Y.*

The number of bits needed for a simple change profile is at most $|R| \log |d|$: Each change profile can be expressed as a vector of length $|R|$ and each value of the change profile can be describe using at most $\log |d|$ bits. Especially for the generalizing change profiles, this upper bound can be quite loose when R is large as the number of sets in $\mathcal{F}(\sigma, d)$ is $\Omega(2^{|X|})$ where X is the largest set in $\mathcal{F}(\sigma, d)$.

3   Clustering the Change Profiles

In order to be able to find groups of similar change profiles, it would be useful to be able to somehow measure the (similarity or) dissimilarity between the change profiles. The dissimilarity between change profiles ch^X and ch^Y can be defined to be their distance in the common domain $Dom(ch^X) \cap Dom(ch^Y)$ w.r.t. some distance function. (We assume the dissimilarity function δ to be such that $\delta(ch^X, ch^Y) = 0 \iff ch^X(Z) = ch^Y(Z)$ holds for all $Z \in Dom(ch^X) \cap Dom(ch^Y)$.) A complementary approach would be to focus on the differences in the structure of the pattern collection, e.g., to measure the difference

between two change profiles by computing the symmetric difference of their domains. This kind of dissimilarity function concentrates wholly on the structure of the pattern collection and thus neglects the frequencies. A sophisticated dissimilarity function should probably consist both points of view. We shall focus on the first one. We further assume that for the distance function δ holds:

There are several ways to define what is a good clustering (and each approach has its own strengths and weaknesses [13, 24]). A simple way to group change profiles based on a dissimilarity function defined in their (pairwise) common domains, is to allow two change profiles ch^X and ch^Y to be in the same group only if $\delta(ch^X, ch^Y) = 0$. The task is, given a collection Ch of change profiles, to find a partition $Ch_1, \ldots, Ch_k$ of Ch such that for each $ch^X, ch^Y \in Ch_i, 1 \leq i \leq k$, holds: $\delta(ch^X, ch^Y) = 0$. Let us call this problem the *change profile packing problem*. Unfortunately, the problem seems to be very difficult:

Theorem 1 *The change profile packing problem for specializing change profiles is at least as hard as the minimum graph coloring problem*

Proof. The *minimum graph coloring problem* is, given a graph $G = (V, E)$, to find a labeling $l : V \to \mathbb{N}$ of vertices with the smallest number of different labels $l(u)$ such that if $u, v \in V$ are adjacent then $l(u) \neq l(v)$ [2].

Let $v_1, \ldots, v_n$ be an (arbitrary) ordering of the vertices in V and $e_1, \ldots, e_m$ an ordering of the edges in E. We first construct an instance (σ, d) of frequent set mining problem and then show that the specializing change profiles Ch computed from the frequent sets $\mathcal{F}(\sigma, d)$ can be partitioned into k sets $Ch_1, \ldots, Ch_k$ if and only if the graph G is k-colorable. To simplify the description we shall consider, w.l.o.g., simple change profiles instead of change profiles.

The set R consists of the elements in $V \cup E$. For each v_i there are $3n$ sets $d_{i,1}, \ldots, d_{i,3n}$. Each set $d_{i,j}$ contains v_i. We put the edge $\{v_i, v_j\} \in E$ into $d_{i,3(j-1)+1}$ and $d_{i,3(j-1)+2}$ if $i < j$, and otherwise into $d_{i,3j}$. We set $\sigma = 1/(3n^2)$ and compute the collection $\mathcal{F}(\sigma, d)$ of frequent sets.

The collection $\mathcal{F}(\sigma, d)$ consists of the empty set $\emptyset$, singletons $\{v_1\}, \ldots, \{v_n\}, \{e_1,\}, \ldots, \{e_m\}$ and pairs $\{v_i, e\} \subset V \times E$ where $v_i \in e$. Thus the cardinality of $\mathcal{F}(\sigma, d)$ is polynomial in the size of G.

The simple change profiles of $\mathcal{F}(\sigma, d)$ are the following:

$$
\begin{aligned}
sch_s^{\emptyset}(x) &= \begin{cases} 1/n & \text{if } x \in V \\ 1/n^2 & \text{if } x \in E \end{cases} \\
sch_s^e(v) &= 1 & \text{if } v \in e \\
sch_s^{v_i}(\{v_i, v_j\}) &= \begin{cases} 2/(3n) & \text{if } i < j \\ 1/(3n) & \text{if } i > j \end{cases}
\end{aligned}
$$

Clearly, $\delta(sch^{\emptyset}, sch^v) > 0$, $\delta(sch^{\emptyset}, sch^e) > 0$ and $\delta(sch^v, sch^e) > 0$. Thus no two of sch^v, sch^e and $sch^{\emptyset}$

for any $v \in V$ and $e \in E$ can be in same group. On the other hand, all the sch_s^e can be packed into one set Ch_{k+1} and $sch_s^\emptyset$ will always have its own set Ch_{k+2}.

Now we only have show that the simple specializing change profiles $sch_s^v(e)$, can be partitioned into k sets $Ch_1, \ldots, Ch_k$ if and only if the graph G is k-colorable: No two simple specializing change profiles $sch_s^{v_i}$ and $sch_s^{v_j}$ can be in the same group if $\{v_i, v_j\} \in E$ since $sch_s^{v_i}(\{v_i, v_j\}) \neq sch_s^{v_j}(\{v_i, v_j\})$. If $\{v_i, v_j\} \notin E$ then $Dom\left(sch_s^{v_i}\right) \cap Dom\left(sch_s^{v_j}\right) = \emptyset$ they can be in the same group.

As the minimum graph coloring problem can be mapped to the change profile packing problem for specializing change profiles, the latter is at least as hard as the minimum graph coloring problem. □

The minimum graph coloring problem is hard to approximate within $|V|^{1-\epsilon}$ for any $\epsilon > 0$ unless $NP = ZPP$ [15]. Assuming that the graph is connected we get from the above mapping from graphs to change profiles the following rough upper bound: $|Ch| = 1 + |V| + 2|E| \leq 1 + |V| + 2\left|\binom{|V|}{2}\right| = \mathcal{O}\left(|V|^2\right)$. Therefore, the change profile packing problem is hard to approximate within $\Omega\left(|Ch|^{(1/2)-\epsilon}\right)$ for any $\epsilon > 0$.

Although the inapproximability results seem to be devastating, there are efficient heuristics, such as the first-fit and the best-fit heuristics [10], that might be able find sufficiently good partitions efficiently. However, the usefulness of the heuristics should be evaluated carefully for different data sets and pattern collections.

The requirement that two change profiles ch^X and ch^Y can be in the same group Ch_i only if $\delta\left(ch^X, ch^Y\right) = 0$, might be too strict. A simple approach to relax this is to discretize the frequencies of frequent sets or the changes in the change profiles. Discretizations minimizing several different loss functions can be found efficiently, see e.g. [31].

Instead of minimizing the number of clusters, one could minimize the error for fixed number of clusters. This kind of clustering is called k-*clustering*, it is well-studied and good approximation algorithms are known if the dissimilarity function is a metric [11, 12, 14].

Unfortunately, it turns out that distance function defined to be the dissimilarity between change profiles in their common domain cannot be a metric as it cannot satisfy even the triangle inequality:

Theorem 2 *Let d be a function that measures the distance between the change profiles ch^X and ch^Y in their common domain domain $Dom\left(ch^X\right) \cap Dom\left(ch^Y\right)$. Then d does not satisfy the triangle inequality.*

Proof. Let ch^X, ch^Y and ch^Z be three change profiles such that $Dom\left(ch^X\right) \cap Dom\left(ch^Y\right) = Dom\left(ch^Y\right) \cap Dom\left(ch^Z\right) = \emptyset$ and $\delta\left(ch^X, ch^Y\right) > 0$. (Thus

$Dom\left(ch^X\right) \cap Dom\left(ch^Z\right) \neq \emptyset$.) Clearly, these change profiles do not satisfy the triangle inequality since $\delta\left(ch^X, ch^Z\right) > 0 = \delta\left(ch^X, ch^Y\right) + \delta\left(ch^Y, ch^Z\right)$. □

It turns out that the k-clustering of specializing change profile is even worse than the change profile packing problem as by combining Theorem 1 and Theorem 2 we get:

Theorem 3 *k-clustering of specializing change profiles cannot be approximated within any ratio.*

Proof. If we could approximate k-clustering of specializing change profiles, then we could, by Theorems 1 and 2, solve the minimum graph coloring problem exactly. □

A major goal in the clustering of the change profiles is to further understand the relationships between the frequent sets. As the nature of data mining is exploratory, defining a maximum number for clusters or a maximum dissimilarity threshold might be difficult and unnecessary. These parameters can be avoided by searching for hierarchical clustering instead [20]. A hierarchical clustering of Ch is a recursive partition of the elements to $2, 3, \ldots, |Ch|$ clusters. It has the enormous benefit from the exploratory data analysis point of view that all the clusterings can be visualized in the same time by a tree.

There are two main categories of hierarchical clustering: agglomerative and divisive. The first begins with $|Ch|$ clusters and recursively merges them and the latter recursively partites the set Ch. Both are optimal in a certain sense: each agglomerative (divisive) hierarchical clustering of Ch into k groups is optimal w.r.t. the clustering into $k+1$ groups (into $k-1$ groups) determined the same agglomerative (divisive) hierarchical clustering.

Divisive strategy seems to be more suitable for clustering the change profiles as the dissimilarity functions we consider are defined to be distances between change profiles in their (pairwise) common domains: The agglomerative clustering groups first change profiles with disjoint domains more or less arbitrary. The choices of groups made in the first few merges can cause huge differences in the clusterings into smaller number of clusters, although the groups of change profiles with disjoint domains are probably quite unimportant for the whole hierarchical clustering. On the other hand, the divisive clustering concentrates first on the nonzero distances and thus the change profiles with disjoint domains do not bias the whole hierarchical clustering.

4 Frequency Estimation from Change Profiles

The change profiles can be used as a basis of condensed representations and several known condensed representations can be adapted to the change profiles. One interesting approach to condense the change profiles is to choose a small set of representative change profiles (by using e.g. divisive clustering), replace the original change profiles by the chosen representatives, and then estimate the frequencies from the approximate change profiles. This can be seen as a condensed representation of the frequent sets as the approximate change profiles can fit (potentially) into smaller space than the exact change profiles or even the frequent sets. Also, the condensed representations can be applied to further condense the approximate change profiles. In addition to that frequencies can be estimated from the approximate change profiles, the change profiles can benefit from the estimation: the quality of the approximate change profiles can be assessed by evaluating how well the frequencies can be approximated from them.

For the rest of the section we consider only the case where no change profile is missing but they are corrupted. However, the methods can be generalized to handle missing change profiles and missing change profile values.

Thus, given approximations of change profiles for a frequent set collection $\mathcal{F}(\sigma, d)$, it is possible to estimate (approximations of) the frequencies of the sets in $\mathcal{F}(\sigma, d)$ from the approximative change profiles. This estimation can be done in many ways and which approach is the best depends on how the change profiles are approximated. Here we describe an approach that is based on the estimates given by different paths from the empty set $\emptyset$ to the set X of which frequency is being estimated. Especially, we concentrate on computing the average of the frequencies given by the paths from $\emptyset$ to X. (We describe the methods using simple specializing change profiles but the adaptation to simple generalizing change profiles is straightforward.)

The number of paths equals to the number of permutations of elements in X which is $|X|!$. If $\mathcal{F}(\sigma, d)$ consists of X and all of its subsets, then $|X| = \log |\mathcal{F}(\sigma, d)|$ and the number of paths is superpolynomial in $|\mathcal{F}(\sigma, d)|$. (This example is the worst case.) However, the average frequency estimate over all paths can be computed much faster by observing that the average frequency of X is the average of the average frequencies of $Y \subseteq X, |Y| = |X| - 1$, scaled by $ch_s^Y (X \setminus Y)$'s, i.e.,

$$fr(X) = \frac{1}{|X|} \sum_{Y \subset X, |Y| = |X| - 1} fr(Y) \, sch_s^Y (X \setminus Y).$$

From this observation we can derive a dynamic programming solution for the problem:
DP-FROM-SCHS(X, sch_s)
1   $fr(\emptyset) \leftarrow 1$
2   for $i = 1$ to $|X|$
3   do for each $Y \subseteq X, |Y| = i$
4   do $fr(Y) \leftarrow 0$
5   for each $Z \subset Y, |Z| = |Y| - 1$
6   do $fr(Y) \leftarrow fr(Y) + fr(Z) \, sch_s^Z (Y \setminus Z)$
7            $fr(Y) \leftarrow fr(Y) / |Y|$

8   **return** $fr(X)$

The time complexity of the algorithm is $\mathcal{O}\left(|X| 2^{|X|}\right) = \mathcal{O}\left(|\mathcal{F}(\sigma, d)| \log |\mathcal{F}(\sigma, d)|\right)$ where k is the number of paths sampled. Even this can be too much. We can further speed up the estimation by simply sampling uniformly from the paths from $\emptyset$ to X:
SAMPLER-FROM-SCHS(X, sch_s, k)
1   $fr(\emptyset) \leftarrow 1$
2   $fr(X) \leftarrow 0$
3   for $j = 1$ to k
4   do $Y \leftarrow \emptyset$
5   for $i = 1$ to $|X| - 1$
6   do $A \leftarrow$ RANDOM-ELEMENT $(X \setminus Y)$
7               $fr(Y \cup \{A\}) \leftarrow fr(Y) \, sch_s^Y (\{A\})$
8               $Y \leftarrow Y \cup \{A\}$
9         $fr(X) \leftarrow fr(X) + fr(Y) \, sch_s^Y (X \setminus Y)$
10 $fr(X) \leftarrow fr(X) / k$
11 **return** $fr(X)$

The time complexity of the algorithm is $\mathcal{O}(k|X|)$. The algorithm can be easily modified to an any-time algorithm. This is very useful for interactive data mining (and for resource bounded computation in general).

We can apply the same algorithms to other kinds of estimates, too. Especially, if we have upper and lower bounds for $sch_s^Y (Z)$ for all $Y \subset X, Z \in X \setminus Y$, then we can compute upper and lower bounds for $fr(X)$: the frequency of $fr(X)$ is at most (at least) the maximum of the minimum estimates (the minimum of the maximum estimates) given by the paths from $\emptyset$ to X.

5 Empirical Evaluation of the Frequency Estimation

In this section we experimentally evaluate the stability of the (noisified) simple (specializing) change profiles in frequency approximation. More specifically, we want to find out how the frequency estimation from change profiles tolerates different kinds of noise and how the number of sampled paths affects the quality of approximation compared to the dynamic programming solution of the problem.

Our primary data were two data sets from UCI KDD Repository:[1] Internet Usage data set consisting of 10104 rows and 10674 attributes, and IPUMS Census data set consisting of 88443 rows and 39954 attributes.

The noisified simple change profiles were constructed as follows: We computed the frequent sets with different minimum frequency thresholds from the above mentioned data sets using Christian Borgelt's implementation of the Apriori algorithm [4]. From the frequent sets, we computed the

[1]http://kdd.ics.uci.edu

223

simple change profiles.

In order to study how estimation methods tolerate different kinds of noise, the change profiles were noisified in three different ways:

- randomly perturbing the values of the change profiles by $\pm\epsilon$,

- adding uniform noise from the interval $[-\epsilon, \epsilon]$ to the values of the change profiles, and

- adding zero-mean Gaussian noise with standard deviation ϵ to the values of the change profiles.

We truncated the noisified changes to the interval $[0, 1]$ as, by the definition of specializing change profile, the changes in a generalizing change profile must be in that interval.

We tested the dependency of the approximation on the number of sampled paths by evaluating the absolute difference between the correct and the estimated frequencies for the dynamic programming solution corresponding to the average over all paths, and the sampling solution corresponding to the average over different number of paths. We experimented with different number of paths, minimum frequency thresholds σ and noise levels ϵ. Also multiplicative variants of the noising schemes were tested. The results were similar to the representative results shown in Figure 1 and Figure 2. Clearly, quite small number of paths suffices to give approximations close to the dynamic programming solution.

6 Conclusions

In this paper we have introduced the concept of change profiles, a new representation for a pattern collection that attempts to reach for a more global view to data without losing the benefits of the local view. We have studied their basic properties and applications. Approaches to cluster change profiles has been suggested and several change profile clustering problems has been shown to be computationally hard for wide variety of natural dissimilarity measures. Also, we have shown how the collection of frequent sets can be approximated from a collection of their approximate change profiles.

There are several interesting open problems for further research:

- The connection between change profiles and local search should be explored systematically. For example, the change profiles could be interpreted through the research on combinatorial landscapes [36].

- The applicability of clustering methods to cluster change profiles should be evaluated. Although the theoretical results about the change profile clustering

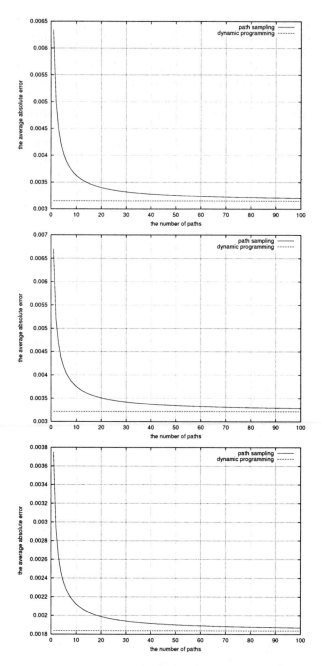

Figure 1. The error of the frequency estimation of the 0.20-frequent sets in Internet Usage data from the change profiles noisified by additive Gaussian zero-mean noise with standard deviation 0.01 (up), perturbed by ± 0.01 (middle), and noisified by additive uniform noise from the interval $[-0.01, 0.01]$ (down). The curves are averages of 1000 random experiments.

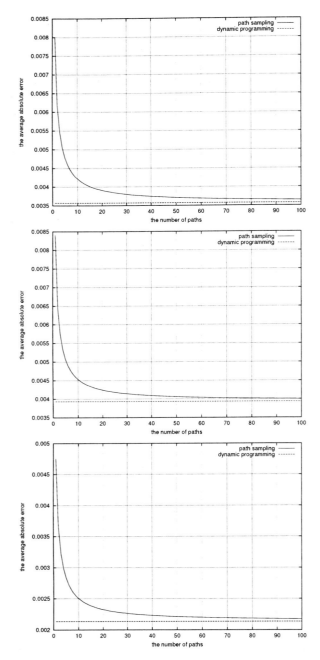

Figure 2. The error of the frequency estimation of the 0.30**-frequent sets in IPUMS Census data from the change profiles noisified by additive Gaussian zero-mean noise with standard deviation** 0.01 **(up), perturbed by** ± 0.01 **(middle), and noisified by additive uniform noise from the interval** $[-0.01, 0.01]$ **(down). The curves are averages of 200 random experiments.**

are somewhat negative, some clustering methods still seem to be useful for the change profile clustering. Also, distance functions suitable for comparing change profiles should be examined rigorously.

- The condensed representations based on change profiles should be studied further. For example, exploring the possible rule systems (see e.g. [8]) to find ones that are well-suited for condensing collections of change profiles could be useful. The frequency estimation from change profiles seems to generalize nicely to outside the frequent sets. Thus the possibilities to use change profiles to estimate the joint probability distribution from the change profiles of frequent sets should be investigated.

Acknowledgments. I wish to thank Floris Geerts and Heikki Mannila for constructive comments and encouragement.

References

[1] R. Agrawal, H. Mannila, R. Srikant, H. Toivonen, and A. I. Verkamo. Fast discovery of association rules. In U. M. Fayyad, G. Piatetsky-Shapiro, P. Smyth, and R. Uthurusamy, editors, *Advances in Knowledge Discovery and Data Mining*, chapter 12, pages 307–328. AAAI/MIT Press, 1996.

[2] G. Ausiello, P. Crescenzi, V. Kann, A. Marchetti-Spaccamela, and M. Protasi. *Complexity and Approximation: Combinatorial Optimization Problems and Their Approximability Properties*. Springer-Verlag, 1999.

[3] Y. Bastide, R. Taouil, N. Pasquier, G. Stumme, and L. Lakhai. Mining frequent patterns with counting inference. *SIGKDD Explorations*, 2(2):66–75, 2000.

[4] C. Borgelt and R. Kruse. Induction of association rules: Apriori implementation. In W. Härdle and B. Rönz, editors, *15th Conference on Computational Statistics (Compstat 2002)*, pages 395–400. Physika Verlag, 2002.

[5] J.-F. Boulicaut and A. Bykowski. Frequent closures as a concise representation for binary data mining. In T. Terano, H. Liu, and A. L. P. Chen, editors, *Knowledge Discovery and Data Mining*, volume 1805 of *Lecture Notes in Artificial Intelligence*, pages 62–73. Springer-Verlag, 2000.

[6] J.-F. Boulicaut, A. Bykowski, and C. Rigotti. Free-sets: a condensed representation of Boolean data for the approximation of frequency queries. *Data Mining and Knowledge Discovery*, 7(1):5–22, 2003.

[7] A. Bykowski and C. Rigotti. A condensed representation to find frequent patterns. In *Proceedings of the Twentieth ACM SIGACT-SIGMOD-SIGART Symposium on Principles of Database Systems*. ACM, 2001.

[8] T. Calders and B. Goethals. Mining all non-derivable frequent itemsets. In T. Elomaa, H. Mannila, and H. Toivonen, editors, *Principles of Data Mining and Knowledge Discovery*, volume 2431 of *Lecture Notes in Artificial Intelligence*, pages 74–865. Springer-Verlag, 2002.

[9] T. Calders and B. Goethals. Minimal k-free representations of frequent sets. In N. Lavrac, D. Gamberger, L. Todorovski, and H. Blockeel, editors, *Knowledge Discovery in Databases: PKDD 2003*, volume 2838 of *Lecture Notes in Artificial Intelligence*. Springer-Verlag, 2003.

[10] E. G. Coffman Jr., C. Courcoubetis, M. R. Garey, D. S. Johnson, P. W. Shor, R. R. Weber, and M. Yannakakis. Perfect packing theorems and the average-case behaviour of optimal and online bin packing. *SIAM Review*, 44(1):95–108, 2002.

[11] S. Dasgupta. Performance guarantees for hierarchical clustering. In J. Kivinen and R. H. Sloan, editors, *Computational Learning Theory*, volume 2375 of *Lecture Notes in Artificial Intelligence*, pages 351–363. Springer-Verlag, 2002.

[12] W. F. de la Vega, M. Karpinski, C. Kenyon, and Y. Rabani. Approximation schemes for clustering problems. In *Proceedings on 35th Annual ACM Symposium on Theory of Computing*. ACM, 2003.

[13] V. Estivill-Castro. Why so many clustering algorithms – a position paper. *SIGKDD Explorations*, 4(1):65–75, 2002.

[14] T. Feder and D. H. Greene. Optimal algorithms for approximate clustering. In *Proceedings of the twentieth annual ACM Symposium on Theory of Computing, Chicago, Illinois, May 2–4, 1988*, pages 434–444. ACM, 1988.

[15] U. Feige and J. Kilian. Zero knowledge and the chromatic number. *Journal of Computer and Systems Science*, 57(2):187–199, 1998.

[16] M. Garofalakis, R. Rastogi, and K. Shim. Mining sequential patterns with regular expression constraints. *IEEE Transactions on Knowledge and Data Engineering*, 14(3):530–552, 2002.

[17] F. Geerts, B. Goethals, and J. Van den Bussche. A tight upper bound on the number of candidate patterns. In N. Cercone, T. Y. Lin, and X. Wu, editors, *Proceedings of the 2001 IEEE International Conference on Data Mining (ICDM 2001)*, pages 155–162. IEEE Computer Society, 2001.

[18] J. Han, J. Pei, and Y. Yin. Mining frequent patterns without candidate generation. In W. Chen, J. F. Naughton, and P. A. Bernstein, editors, *Proceedings of the 2000 ACM SIGMOD International Conference on Management of Data*, pages 1–12. ACM, 2000.

[19] D. J. Hand. Pattern detection and discovery. In D. Hand, N. Adams, and R. Bolton, editors, *Pattern Detection and Discovery*, volume 2447 of *Lecture Notes in Artificial Intelligence*, pages 1–12. Springer-Verlag, 2002.

[20] T. Hastie, R. Tibshirani, and J. Friedman. *The Elements of Statistical Learning: Data Mining, Inference, and Prediction*. Springer Series in Statistics. Springer-Verlag, 2001.

[21] J. Hipp, U. Güntzer, and G. Nakhaeizadeh. Algorithms for association rule mining – a general survey and comparison. *SIGKDD Explorations*, 1(2):58–64, 2000.

[22] J. D. Holt and S. M. Chung. Mining association rules using inverted hashing and pruning. *Information Processing Letters*, 82:211–220, 2002.

[23] T. Imieliński, L. Khachiyan, and A. Abdulghani. Cubegrades: Generalizing association rules. *Data Mining and Knowledge Discovery*, 6(3):219–257, 2002.

[24] J. Kleinberg. An impossibility theorem for clustering. In *Advances in Neural Information Processing Systems (NIPS)*, volume 15, 2002.

[25] M. Kryszkiewicz. Concise representation of frequent patterns based on disjunction-free generators. In N. Cercone, T. Y. Lin, and X. Wu, editors, *Proceedings of the 2001 IEEE International Conference on Data Mining*, pages 305–312. IEEE Computer Society, 2001.

[26] M. Kurakochi and G. Karypis. Discovering frequent geometric subgraphs. In *Proceedings of the 2002 IEEE International Conference on Data Mining*. IEEE Computer Society, 2002.

[27] H. Mannila. Local and global methods in data mining: Basic techniques and open problems. In P. Widmayer, F. Triguero, R. Morales, M. Hennessy, S. Eidenbenz, and R. Conejo, editors, *Automata, Languages and Programming*, volume 2380 of *Lecture Notes in Computer Science*, pages 57–68. Springer-Verlag, 2002.

[28] H. Mannila and H. Toivonen. Levelwise search and borders of theories in knowledge discovery. *Data Mining and Knowledge Discovery*, 1(3):241–258, 1997.

[29] H. Mannila, H. Toivonen, and A. I. Verkamo. Discovery of frequent episodes in event sequences. *Data Mining and Knowledge Discovery*, 1(3):259–289, 1997.

[30] T. Mielikäinen. Chaining patterns. In G. Grieser, Y. Tanaka, and A. Yamamoto, editors, *Discovery Science*, volume 2843 of *Lecture Notes in Artificial Intelligence*, pages 232–243. Springer-Verlag, 2003.

[31] T. Mielikäinen. Frequency-based views to pattern collections. In *IFIP/SIAM Workshop on Discrete Mathematics and Data Mining*, 2003.

[32] T. Mielikäinen and H. Mannila. The pattern ordering problem. In N. Lavrac, D. Gamberger, L. Todorovski, and H. Blockeel, editors, *Knowledge Discovery in Databases: PKDD 2003*, volume 2838 of *Lecture Notes in Artificial Intelligence*. Springer-Verlag, 2003.

[33] T. M. Mitchell. Generalization as search. *Artificial Intelligence*, 18(2):203–226, 1982.

[34] N. Pasquier, Y. Bastide, R. Taouil, and L. Lakhal. Discovering frequent closed itemsets for association rules. In C. Beeri and P. Buneman, editors, *Database Theory - ICDT'99*, volume 1540 of *Lecture Notes in Computer Science*, pages 398–416. Springer-Verlag, 1999.

[35] J. Pei, G. Dong, W. Zou, and J. Han. On computing condensed pattern bases. In *Proceedings of the 2002 IEEE International Conference on Data Mining (ICDM 2002)*, pages 378–385. IEEE Computer Society, 2002.

[36] C. M. Reidys and P. F. Stadler. Combinatorial landscapes. *SIAM Review*, 44(1):3–54, 2002.

[37] M. J. Zaki. Scalable algorithms for association mining. *IEEE Transactions on Knowledge and Data Engineering*, 12(3):372–390, 2000.

[38] M. J. Zaki. Efficiently mining frequent trees in a forest. In D. Hand, D. Keim, and R. Ng, editors, *Proceedings of the Eight International Conference on Knowledge Discovery and Data Mining (KDD-2002)*. ACM, 2002.

Complex Spatial Relationships

Robert Munro and Sanjay Chawla and Pei Sun
School of Information Technologies
University of Sydney
{rmunro, chawla, psun2712}@it.usyd.edu.au

Abstract

This paper describes the need for mining complex relationships in spatial data. Complex relationships are defined as those involving two or more of: multi-feature colocation, self-colocation, one-to-many relationships, self-exclusion and multi-feature exclusion. We demonstrate that even in the mining of simple relationships, knowledge of complex relationships is necessary to accurately calculate the significance of results. We implement a representation of spatial data such that it contains known 'weak-monotonic' properties, which are exploited for the efficient mining of complex relationships, and discuss the strengths and limitations of this representation.

1. Introduction

A relationship in spatial data is a relationship between features in a Euclidean space, defined in terms of the colocational trends of two or more features over that space. An example is determining the confidence of the *'where there's smoke there's fire'* with respect to a set of coordinates, each representing the feature smoke or fire. The task here would be to determine whether fire occurs in the neighborhood of smoke more than is randomly likely.

Neighborhoods are defined in terms of cliques (also known as neighbor-sets). A clique is defined as any set of items such that *all* items in that set colocate, for example, in Figure 1 and Table 1, the colocational pattern {A,D} occurs three times in four cliques, iv, v/vi & ix. Two features are typically said to colocate if they are positioned within a distance d of one another. As has been assumed in Figure 1, d is usually constant, but it may also be defined as varying locally within the space or with respect to a given feature.

Typically, the mining of information in a spatial domain involves representing the cliques as transactions, and undertaking association rule mining upon these transactions. While association rule mining is a well-developed field [5], the mining of confident cliques as transactions fails to cap-

ture many spatial phenomena of interest, due to most association mining techniques being optimized for 'market-basket' data. Spatial data is fundamentally different from market-basket data, both in its basic nature and distributional tendencies.

One factor unique to spatial data is that the number of transactions a single item may participate in is potentially unbounded, while in a market-basket this is limited to one (obviously, two people may purchase the same toothpaste product, but not the same exact tube). Self-colocation is also more likely in spatial data. The upper limit in a market-basket is multiple purchases of only one product, which is less likely than an equivalent spatial situation of an area of monoculture forest. Similarly, there may be direct relationships between features that don't colocate, as between animals displaying territorial behavior, making such relationships intrinsically more interesting in spatial data. A complex relationship is simply any combination of these different relationships. It is important to note that while the relationships are defined as complex, the phenomena they represent are often very simple [8].

Perhaps the most fundamental difference between spatial and other data in a transactional representation is the notion of significance. A colocation is considered significant if it occurs more than is randomly likely. In transactions representing market-baskets, the transactions, by definition, represent the complete space of the data (there are no empty baskets). In such cases, the significance of the data may be represented by frequency of the features in relation to the number of transactions, such as the interest measure proposed in [4]. In spatial data, however, the random likelihood of a colocation depends on the volume of the space from which it was taken. This is discussed in more detail in section 6.1.

1.1 Our contribution

We describe the need for mining complex relationships in spatial data. To the authors' best knowledge, this problem has not previously been addressed:

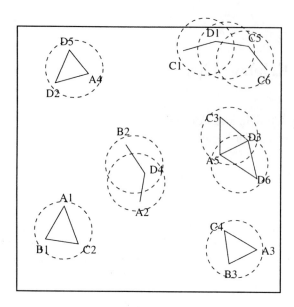

Figure 1. An example of spatial colocational patterns of the features A,B,C and D

No	Clique
i.	C_1, D_1
ii.	C_5, D_1
iii.	C_5, C_6
iv.	A_4, D_2, D_5
v.	A_5, C_3, D_3
vi.	A_5, D_3, D_6
vii.	A_1, B_1, C_2
viii.	B_2, D_4
ix.	A_2, D_4
x.	A_3, B_3, C_4

Table 1. Cliques in Figure 1

1. We demonstrate that complex relationships are more numerous than simple ones and discuss why they are desirable to mine in the spatial domain.

2. We demonstrate that a representation and mining strategy for spatial data is possible such that it facilitates the efficient mining of complex relationships.

3. Most significantly, we demonstrate that it is necessary to mine complex relationships to accurately calculate the significance of results, even when the goal is only the mining of simple relationships.

1.2 Outline

In sections 2 and 3 we give the problem definition and a discussion of related work. In section 4 we describe and discuss the use of a participation threshold, rather than a support threshold, in the mining of spatial colocations. It should be noted that we are not redefining / refining any association rule algorithms; rather than throwing out the baby with the bathwater, we explore new applications and interpretations of existing ones. In section 5 we define and give examples of the various types of relationships in spatial data, including complex relationships. In section 6 we demonstrate that the knowledge of complex relationships in spatial data is necessary, even when the goal is the mining of only simple relationships. In section 7 we implement a transactional representation of spatial data such that

it contains weak-monotonic properties, which are exploited by the maxPI algorithm [6] for the efficient mining of complex relationships, and discuss the strengths and limitations of this representation. In section 8 we conclude and discuss possible future directions.

2 Problem Definition

Given: a set of items, $S = s_1, ...s_n$, each representing some entity with one or more features at a given coordinate and a rule confidence threshold, c

Find: all complex spatial relationships with confidence greater than c.

Constraints: The discovery of all rules of a given confidence is an intractable problem, so any method that can improve the efficiency of mining these rules is paramount. The data must be represented in a way that facilitates the mining of complex rules. (a transactional representation, as in Table 1, is the most commonly used in mining spatial data, as it allows the inclusion and the discovery of the interrelation of non-spatial features)

For mining colocations, this is a 3-step process: generate a set of the cliques in a representation that facilitates the mining of colocations; apply a mining algorithm to the cliques, returning a set of colocations and their confidences, the constituency of which is determined by given pruning and confidence thresholds; and calculate the significance of the mined colocations.

The first two steps are typically combined, so as to not to generate cliques already known to be below the given thresholds. In this paper, we assume that the first step has already taken place.

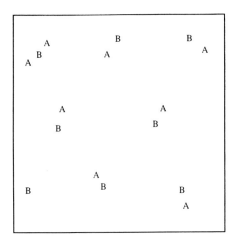

Figure 2. A positive relationship $A \to B$

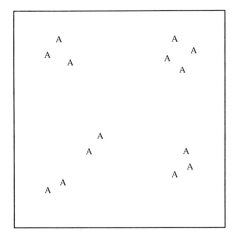

Figure 3. A self-colocating relationship $A \to A$

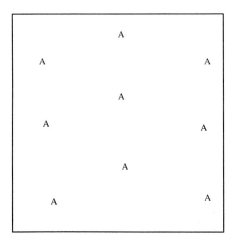

Figure 4. Self-exclusion, low confidence for $A \to A$

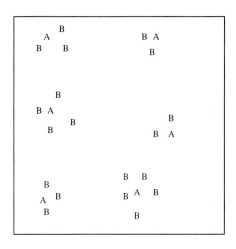

Figure 5. A one-to-many relationship $A \to B+$

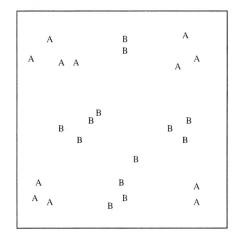

Figure 6. A multi-feature exclusive relationship $A \to -B$

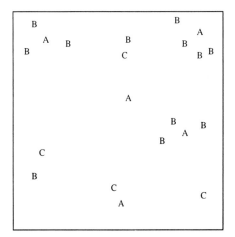

Figure 7. A complex relationship $A, -C \to B+$

229

3   Related Work

The first extension of the Apriori paradigm to spatial data was in [7]. However in their method they materialized all the possible spatial relationships that they intended to mine. This is equivalent to determining the universe of candidate interesting relationships. Thus, in some ways, their technique was 'hypothesis driven' rather than 'hypothesis generating.'

An efficient algorithm to mine a kind of spatial colocations was presented in [11]. The concepts of neighborhood, participation ratio and participation index were defined. Instead of support, the participation index was used as a pruning measure in the conventional Apriori-like technique.

The drawback of above method is that some confident colocation rules with low support are also pruned. In order to solve this problem, [6] proposed the concept of maximal participation index and it was used as pruning measure to replace the participation index . We will discuss these measures in detail in the next section, as they are central to our approach.

In [12], an algorithm was used to mine both positive and negative association rules. Negative rules are generated from infrequent item sets and interest is used as a further pruning measure. Their algorithm involves no spatial component.

4   Maximal Participation Ratio

In this section we will briefly describe the notion of Maximal Participation Index (maxPI) as described in [6] where more details can be found.

4.1   Participation ratio

Given a colocation pattern L and a feature $f \in L$, the participation ratio of f, $pr(L, f)$, can be defined as the support of L divided by the support of f. For example, in Figure 1, the support of $\{A, B, C\}$ is 2 and the support of C is 6, so $pr(\{A, B, C\}, C) = 2/6$.

4.2   Maximal participation index

Given a co-location pattern L, the maximal participation index of L, $maxPI(L)$ can be define as the maximal participation ratio of all the features in L, that is:

$$maxPI(L) = max_{f \in L}(pr(L, f)). \qquad (1)$$

For example, in Figure 1, $maxPI(\{A, B, C\})$ $=$ $max(pr(\{A, B, C\}, A),$ $pr(\{A, B, C\}, B),$ $pr(\{A, B, C\}, C)) = max(2/5, 2/3, 2/6) = 2/3$. A high maximal participation index indicates that at least

one spatial feature strongly implies the pattern. By using maxPI, low frequency confident rules can be found which would be pruned by a support threshold [6].

4.3   The weak monotonic property of maxPI

Maximal participation index is not monotonic with respect to the pattern containment relations. For example, in the Figure 1, $(maxPI(A, C) = 3/5) < (maxPI(A, B, C) = 2/3)$. Interestingly, as pointed out in [6] the maximal participation index does have the following weak monotonic property: If P is a k-colocation pattern, then there exists at most one $(k - 1)$ subpatterns P' of P such that $maxPI(P') < maxPI(P)$. Relying on this weak monotonic property, the Apriori-like algorithm can be modified to mine confident patterns by using a maxPI threshold.

5   Relationship Definitions

5.1   Notation used

Feature: In this paper, a feature is represented as a capital letter, for example A.

Item: An instance of a feature (one item) is represented as the feature followed by an id number unique for that feature, for example A_2.

Absence: The absence of an item is represented by negation, for example $-A$. (Note: this is not the equivalent of the set-theory, $\neg A$, meaning the presence of any item other than A).

Self-colocation: Multiple instances of a feature (multiple items) are represented by a '+' following the feature, for example $A+$.

5.2   Types of Spatial Relationships

Here we define the different types of spatial relationships that are desirable to mine:

Positive (Simple) Relationships: This is the most common type of relationship mined, describing, for example, the fraction of A's that colocate with a B. eg: $A \to B$

   Definition 1: A positive relationship (multi-feature colocation) in spatial data is a set of features that colocate at a ratio greater than some predefined threshold.

Self-colocation / Self-exclusion: This is the measure of which a feature tends to colocate with itself. Formally, it is the average cardinality of an item in a clique with respect to the expected cardinality of a random distribution. Extreme self-exclusion will be a perfectly uniform distribution with respect to the data space. eg: $A \rightarrow A+$

Definition 2: A feature is defined as self-colocating in spatial data if the items representing that feature colocate with each other at a ratio greater than some predefined threshold.

Definition 3: A feature is defined as self-excluding in spatial data if the items representing that feature colocate with each other at a ratio less than some predefined threshold.

One-to-Many relationships: This explicitly captures the cardinality of a relationship between two features. eg: $B+ \rightarrow A$.

Definition 4: Two features are defined as having a one-to-many relationship in spatial data if one feature occurs multiple times in the presence of the other feature, greater than some pre-defined threshold. Included within this definition are two-way one-to-many (many-to-many) relationships.

Multi-feature exclusive relationships: These are exclusive relationships with respect to two or more features. In terms of a transactional representation, they are negative rules, which are explored in [12]. eg: $A \rightarrow -B$

Definition 5: A multi-feature exclusive relationship in spatial data is defined as where a feature is absent from a given colocation at a ratio greater than a predefined threshold.

Complex relationships: These are any combination of two or more spatial relationship types.

Definition 6: A complex relation in spatial data is any relationship containing two or more of the properties defined in definitions 1-5. The independent application of the above rules may produce complex relationships such as $A+ \rightarrow B$ *and* $A \rightarrow -C$, but will not produce complex relationships such as $\{A+, -C\} \rightarrow B+$.

5.3 Sparse data and the mining of absence

A participation index directly addresses the problem that a certain item may have low support resulting in it being absent from very many cliques, and hence having a high negative support, in that it with therefore have a low participation ratio for each of those cliques. For example, if D is an infrequent feature, then the rule $A \rightarrow -D$ will most likely be confident. However, the participation ratio of $-D$ in $\{A, -D\}$ will be very low, as $-D$ will occur in many cliques. In other words the participation ratio of $-D$ in $\{A, -D\}$ will only be high if D is *atypically* absent from

cliques containing A. Therefore, when using a participation ratio for sparse data, there is, in fact, a gain in efficiency. The results in section 7 confirm this.

6 Statistical Applications of Complex Relationships

Complex relationships are not restricted to mining complex rules. Complex relationships can be used to provide stronger definitions and more accurate significance testing for simple relationships.

6.1 Significance as a Complex relationship

In terms of confidence, the significance of a rule is given by the extent to which the observed confidence of a rule differs from the expected confidence given by a random distribution.

Lemma 1: The significance of a confidence rule of the form $A \rightarrow B$, is independent of the self-colocation/exclusion of A, but is dependent on the self-colocation/exclusion of B.

Proof Outline: In general, given that A occurs with frequency $F(A)$, and B with frequency $F(B)$, in a two dimensional space with dimensions x and y, with cliques formed by a distance d the random chance of $A \rightarrow B$ can be given by the product of the fraction of the total volume that each features occupies:

$$\frac{F(A)\pi d^2}{xy} \frac{F(B)\pi d^2}{xy} = \frac{F(A)F(B)\pi^2 d^4}{x^2 y^2} \quad (2)$$

The problem with the above, however, is that B may not be exclusively distributed with respect to itself.

Note that the random chance will not change with respect to the self-colocation/exclusion of A. The two extreme cases are: A self-excludes such that no A's are in the same clique (the equation given above); and A self-colocates such that all A's co-occur in one clique. In the second case all A's occupy an effective total space of πd^2, giving $F(A)$ an effective value of 1. However, if a B exists in that clique, then all A's in that clique colocate with it, so the equation must be multiplied by the number of A's in the clique - in this case $F(A)$. The equation is, therefore the equivalent of where A self-excludes.

The random chance will, however, change with respect to the self-colocation/exclusion of B. Assume the two extreme cases: B self-excludes such that no B's are in the same clique (again, this is the equation given above); and B self-colocates such that all B's co-occur

231

in one clique. In the second case, all B's occupy an effective total space of πd^2, giving $F(B)$ an effective value of 1. If one A exists in that clique, the number of B's in that clique has no effect on the confidence as, by definition 1, only one unique A colocates with a B. The expected value of $A \to B$ is therefore given by:

$$\frac{F(A)1\pi^2 d^4}{x^2 y^2} \qquad (3)$$

As the two extreme cases demonstrate, the expected value of $A \to B$ exists in a range with boundaries differing by a factor of $F(B)$. The consequence of this is that an accurate measure of the significance of a rule $A \to B$ must also include the measure of B's self-colocation/exclusion. The importance of this becomes obvious when, in spatial data, $F(B)$ may literally be the number of stars in the sky. Therefore, by definition 6, in order to measure the significance of a simple relationship $A \to B$, it is necessary to know a complex relationship.

An approximation of self-exclusion may be given by the ratio of the number of cliques containing B to the total number of B's. Assuming B occurs in $cf(B)$ cliques. This can underestimate the random chance, as it doesn't take into account the intersection of cliques in the data space where two or more B's are greater than distance d but less than distance $2d$ apart, or over-estimate, as it doesn't take into account the distance between items within a clique.

Alternatively, a calculation of deviance from expected behaviour can be found by observing the original coordinate distributions with a metric such as Ripley's K-function [2]. This will not necessarily give a more accurate measure, as it relates to global distributions not cliques, but it's relationship with colocation mining and clique representations is, in itself, an interesting area deserving further investigation.

Perhaps the most intuitive reason for above is because in the spatial domain, the rule $A \to B$ cannot be divorced from it's spatial properties. Even when A and B represent coordinates, *A must be thought of as coordinates and B must be thought of as (potentially overlapping) volumes*. This is a general truism for spatial data and will hold whether a constant or variable d is used, and when a simpler clique definition is given, such as the division of the feature space into 'grids', or a more complicated definition, such as the result of a clustering algorithm.

Lemma 2: The potential range of confidence rules of the form $A \to B$, will depend on the self-colocation/exclusion of both A and B.

Proof Outline: While the self-colocation/exclusion of A does not affect the significance of a confidence rule,

it can limit the possible range of the observed confidence. Assuming that all A's and B's self-exclude, then, as in market-basket data, the maximum possible confidence for $A \to B$ is simply given by:

$$min\left[\frac{F(B)}{F(A)}, 1\right] \qquad (4)$$

Where $F(A) > F(B)$, this will obviously be less than 1. However, if A self-colocates such that $cf(A) \leq F(B)$ than the maximum possible confidence will be 1.

Similarly, if B self-colocates, then the maximum possible confidence may be lower. The exact measure for the maximum possible observed confidence is:

$$min\left[\frac{cf(B)}{cf(A)}, 1\right] \qquad (5)$$

A further factor that is not discussed here is where the potential size of some cliques extend beyond the boundaries of the measured space. Again, the random likelihood of this will relate to the ratio between d and the dimensions of the space. Here, it is simply assumed that it is very low.

6.2 Exclusion and maxPI

As a support threshold can prune confident rules with low frequency, a maxPI threshold can prune confident rules with low participation. While maxPI will return the complete set of items that satisfy both thresholds of maxPI and the minimum confidence, there may be the case such that a high confidence rule will not have a high corresponding maximal participation index.

An improved measure of participation includes the atypical exclusion of an item. We posit that by including the absence of items (negative items), we may discover a more robust measure for a participation index measure.

7 A Representation of Spatial Data for Mining Complex Relationships

In this section we propose and test one simple representation of spatial data that facilitates the efficient mining of complex relationships.

7.1 Mining complex relationships using the maximal participation index

In terms of the steps in the problem definition, the steps taken are: Generate all positive cliques in a transactional representation adding features representing the absence of

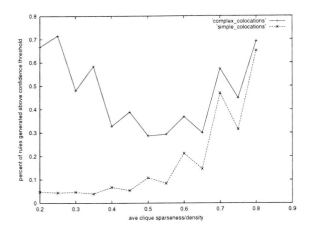

Figure 8. comparison of efficiency from sparse to dense data

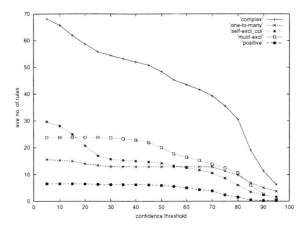

Figure 9. comparison of relationship type frequencies

features and the presence of multiple features; apply the maxPI algorithm to the transactions, as described in section 4, automatically pruning trivial/nonsensical collocations such as $A \rightarrow -A$. (For an analysis of the efficiency and application across different spatial data sets, see [6]) and return a set of colocations and their confidences; and calculate the significance of the confidences of the mined relationships, with respect to their significance, as described in section 6.1.

7.2 Test Sets

Synthetic data sets were created similar to those described in [1], but with the specific properties of spatial data, such as the occurrence of a single item in many cliques and the occurrence of many items representing a single feature in one clique. Set constituency was varied according to sparseness, the number of features, and the number of items. The mining of relationships was varied according to the participation and confidence thresholds. A comprehensive set of tests corresponding was completed across approximately 100,000 different set/parameter combinations. A summary of results is given below.

Testing was undertaken to compare the efficiency of mining complex relationships to the mining of simple relationships with maxPI, and to investigate the relative frequencies of the different relationship types.

7.3 Results: Efficiency

As Figure 8 shows, the ratio of rules generated to confident rules found is typically more efficient for the mining of

complex rules, especially when the data is sparse. Although it was never the case here, we do not rule out the possibility of the existence of a set such that the mining of simple relationships is more efficient than the mining of complex relationships. The results in Figure 8 are the average ratios for approximately 10,000 randomly generated data sets, which were varied according to sparseness/density: the average probability of a feature occurring in a given clique. The maxPI and confidence were held constant at 0.6 and 0.8, respectively. Varying the maximal participation index had little impact on the respective ratios. Varying the confidence threshold varied the scale of the ratio, but did not affect the scale of the two distributions with respect to each other.

A constant maintained across the generation of all sets were the inclusion of skews in the data such as: 'the probability of C appearing in a clique increases by 0.15 if A and B are present'. These were originally generated randomly, then maintained as averages about which all random sets were created. It is the interaction of such skews with the various thresholds that cause the unevenness in distributions in Figure 8.

7.4 Results: Frequency of relationship types

The results in Figure 9 are averages for approximately 1000 separate data sets, each with 10 features. The number of features is the most sensitive variable in the relative frequencies, due to the fact that there is the possibility of exponentially more exclusive and therefore complex sets with respect to the number of features in a clique, as discussed in section 5.3.

233

Typically, the number of complex relationships found was greater than but correlated with the number of other relationship types found. As Figure 9 shows, the number of complex relationships at a given confidence threshold was sensitive to the variance in the number of the other relationship types. Self-exclusion and self-colocation were modeled together in Figure 9 emphasize the complementary relationship between the two, as described in section 5.2. This is revealed in the corresponding steepness of gradient for self-exclusion/colocation at confidence < 0.3 and confidence > 0.7.

7.5 Limitations/Strengths of the representation

While there are representational issues with any type of data, appropiate representation is particularly important in the spatial domain [9].

Limitations. In one-to-many relationships, this model doesn't capture interesting ranges or distributions in the 'many', which is a task better suited for mixture modelling, or the techniques described in [3]. As pointed out in [10], the cost of fully transcribing spatial data into a transactional representation can, in some cases, be more expensive than the mining of the colocations, but as a full representation is necessary to accurately add the features representing absent and multiple items, a solution to this in the current representation may be problematic.

Strengths. The most obvious strength of this representation is that, currently, it is the only model that allows the mining of complex relationships in spatial data. A major strength of a transactional representation of spatial data not explored here is that it may be combined with non-spatial data, and so the addition of non-spatial data to the representation described here would be uncomplicated.

8 Conclusions / Future Work

We have defined the concept of complex relationships in spatial data.

We have described how, even in transactional representations, spatial data is fundamentally different from other forms of data, making the need to mine complex relationships of inherent interest.

We have demonstrated that even when simple relationships are the goal of mining spatial data, the mining of complex relationships is necessary for determining the significance of those relationships.

We have implemented and demonstrated a transactional representation of spatial data that allows the efficient mining

of complex relationships, and discussed its limitations and strengths.

8.1 Future Work:

Apart from investigating improvements to the representation to address the limitations mentioned in 7.5, there are several future directions evident, such as the application to other types of data with a spatial component, such as spatio-temporal data and to a lesser extent natural language and biological systems.

One important step would be the combination of spatial coordinate features with spatial volume features (this is especially important in Geographic Information Systems, where a volume may represent the area of a lake, valley etc.). As we have demonstrated that with a purely coordinate system B in $A \rightarrow B$ must be treated as a volume, the inclusion of features that explicitly represent volumes should prove interesting.

References

[1] R. Agrawal and R. Srikant. Fast algorithms for mining association rules. In J. B. Bocca, M. Jarke, and C. Zaniolo, editors, *Proc. 20th Int. Conf. Very Large Data Bases, VLDB*, pages 487–499. Morgan Kaufmann, 12–15 1994.

[2] T. C. Bailey and A. T. Gatrell. *Interactive spatial data analysis*. Longman Scientific & Technical, 1995.

[3] S. Brin, R. Rastogi, and K. Shim. Mining optimized gain rules for numeric attributes. *IEEE transactions on knowledge and data engineering*, 15, 2003.

[4] G. Piatetsky-Shapiro. *Discovery, analysis and presentation of strong rules*. AAAI/MIT Press, 1991.

[5] J. Han, J. Pei, and Y. Yin. Mining frequent patterns without candidate generation. In W. Chen, J. Naughton, and P. A. Bernstein, editors, *2000 ACM SIGMOD Intl. Conference on Management of Data*, pages 1–12. ACM Press, 05 2000.

[6] Y. Huang, H. Xiong, and S. Shekhar. Mining confident co-location rules without a support threshold. In *Proc. 18th ACM Symposium on Applied Computing (ACM SAC)*, 2003.

[7] K. Koperski and J. Han. Discovery of spatial association rules in geographic information databases. In M. J. Egenhofer and J. R. Herring, editors, *Proc. 4th Int. Symp. Advances in Spatial Databases, SSD*, volume 951, pages 47–66. Springer-Verlag, 6–9 1995.

[8] R. Munro, S. Chawla, and P. Sun. Complex spatial relationships. *University of Sydney, School of Information Technologies Technical Report 539*, 2003.

[9] D. J. Peuquet. *Representations of space and time*. Guilford Press, 2002.

[10] S. Shekhar and S. Chawla. *Spatial Databases, A Tour*. 2002.

[11] S. Shekhar and Y. Huang. Discovering spatial co-location patterns: A summary of results. *Lecture Notes in Computer Science*, 2121, 2001.

[12] X. Wu, C. Zhang, and S. Zhang. Mining both positive and negative association rules. In *19th International Conference on Machine Learning (ICML-2002)*, 2002.

TECNO-STREAMS: Tracking Evolving Clusters in Noisy Data Streams with a Scalable Immune System Learning Model

Olfa Nasraoui, Cesar Cardona Uribe, Carlos Rojas Coronel
Department of Electrical and Computer Engineering
The University of Memphis
206 Engineering Science Bldg., Memphis, TN 38152
{onasraou,ccardona,crojas}@memphis.edu

Fabio Gonzalez
Department of Systems and Industrial Engineering
National University of Colombia
Bogota, Colombia
email: fgonza@ing.unal.edu.co

Abstract

Artificial Immune System (AIS) models hold many promises in the field of unsupervised learning. However, existing models are not scalable, which makes them of limited use in data mining. We propose a new AIS based clustering approach (TECNO-STREAMS) that addresses the weaknesses of current AIS models. Compared to existing AIS based techniques, our approach exhibits superior learning abilities, while at the same time, requiring low memory and computational costs. Like the natural immune system, the strongest advantage of immune based learning compared to other approaches is expected to be its ease of adaptation to the dynamic environment that characterizes several applications, particularly in mining data streams. We illustrate the ability of the proposed approach in detecting clusters in noisy data sets, and in mining evolving user profiles from Web clickstream data in a single pass. TECNO-STREAMS adheres to all the requirements of clustering data streams: compactness of representation, fast incremental processing of new data points, and clear and fast identification of outliers.

1 Introduction

Natural organisms exhibit powerful learning and processing abilities that allow them to survive and proliferate generation after generation in ever changing and challenging environments. The natural immune system is a powerful defense system that exhibits many signs of cognitive learning and intelligence [5]. In particular the acquired or adaptive immune system is comprised mainly of lymphocytes which are special types of white blood cells (*B-cells*) that detect and destroy pathogens, such as viruses and bacteria. Identification of a particular pathogen is enabled by soluble proteins on the cell surface, called *antigens*. Special *proteins receptors* on the B-cell surface, called *antibodies* are specialized to react to a particular antigen by binding to this antigen. Furthermore, lymphocytes bind only approximately to pathogens, to allow the recognition of a large repertoire of antigens. Lymphocytes are only activated when the bond exceeds a minimum strength that may be different for different lymphocytes. A stronger binding with an antigen induces a lymphocytes to clone more copies of itself, hence providing reinforcement. Moreover, to diversify their repertoire, lymphocytes undergo somatic hypermutation (10^9 times compared to evolutionary mutation in other cells). Mature lymphocytes form the long term memory of the immune system, and help recognize and fight similar antigens that may be encountered in the future. Therefore, the immune system can perform pattern recognition and associative memory in a continuous and decentralized manner. Of particular relevence to our work, is the Artificial Immune Network (AIN) model. In their attempt to apply immune system metaphors to machine learning, Hunt and Cooke based their model [10] on Jerne's Immune Network theory [11]. The system consisted of a network of B cells used to create antibody strings that can be used for DNA classification. The resource limited AIN (AINE) model [15] brought some improvements for more general data analysis. It consisted of a set of ARBs (Artificial Recognition Balls), each consisting of several identical B cells, a set of antigen training data, links between ARBs, and cloning operations as before. Each ARB represents a single $n-$dimensional data item that could be matched by Euclidean distance to an antigen or to another ARB in the network. A link was created if the affinity (distance) between 2 ARBs was below a Network Affinity Threshold parameter, *NAT*, defined as the average distance between all data items in the training set. Each member of the antigen training set is matched against each ARB based on Euclidean distance. This affects ARB_i's stimulation level which is inversely related to its average distance from the antigen set. In [12], a new immune system model was presented that achieved improved quality and less complexity for unsupervised robust clustering. However, the model required several iterations over the data set, and the data had to fit into main memory.

In existing AIS models [10, 15], it is common for the ARB population to grow at a prolific rate and to converge rather prematurely to a state where a few ARBs matching a small number of antigens overtake the entire population. In order to contemplate using artificial immune system based techniques for data mining, we have to seriously consider their *scalability*. The most radical way to achieve scalability is to reduce the size of the repertoire of B-Cells, while still maintaining *a high quality approximation* of the antigen space (data). High quality is achieved with a repertoire of B-cells that is at the same time, *diverse* or specialized, accurate, and complete.

Recently, data mining has put even higher demands on clustering algorithms. They now must handle very large data sets, leading to some scalable clustering techniques. For example, BIRCH [16] and the scalable K-Means (SKM) [3] assume that clusters are clean of noise, hyper-spherical, similar in size, and span the whole data space. *Robust* clustering techniques have recently been proposed to handle noisy data. Another limitation of most clustering algorithms is that they assume that the number of clusters is known. However, in practice, the number of clusters may not be known. This problem is called *unsupervised clustering*. A recent explosion of applications generating and analyzing *data streams* has added new unprecedented challenges for clustering algorithms if they are to be able to track changing clusters in noisy data streams using only the new data points because storing past data is not even an option [2, 1, 4, 7].

In this paper, we propose a new AIS learning approach for clustering noisy multi-dimensional stream data, called TECNO-STREAMS (Tracking Evolving Clusters in NOisy Streams), that addresses the shortcomings of current AIS models. Our approach exhibits improved learning abilities, while also achieving *scalability, robustness, and automatic scale estimation*.

The rest of the paper is organized as follows. In Section 2, we present a new dynamic AIS model based on a robust and dynamic D-W-B-Cell model and learning algorithm designed to address the challenges of stream data mining. In Section 3, we present a new approach to tackle the immune network complexity and the TECNO-STREAMS algorithm. In Section 4, we formally prove the robustness properties of the newly proposed immune cell model with respect to outliers and the ability to evolve with changing data. In Section 5, we compare our approach to some existing scalable clustering algorithms. In Section 6, we illustrate using the proposed Dynamic AIS model for robust cluster detection and for mining Web clickstream data. Finally, in Section 7, we present our conclusions.

2. A Dynamic Weighted B-Cell Model based on Robust Weights: The D-W-B-Cell Model

In a dynamic environment, the antigens from a data stream $\mathbf{X}_a$ are presented to the immune network one at a time, with the stimulation and scale measures re-updated with each presentation. It is more convenient to think of the antigen index, j, as monotonically increasing with time. That is, the antigens are presented in the following chronological order: $\mathbf{x}_1, \mathbf{x}_2, \cdots, \mathbf{x}_N$. The Dynamic Weighted B-Cell (*D-W-B-cell*) represents an influence zone over the domain of discourse consisting of the training data set. However, since data is dynamic in nature, and has a temporal aspect, data that is more current will have higher influence compared to data that is less current. Quantitatively, the influence zone is defined in terms of a weight function that decreases not only with distance from the antigen/data location to the D-W-B-cell prototype, but also with the time since the antigen has been presented to the immune network. It is convenient to think of time as an additional dimension that is added to the D-W-B-Cell compared to the classical B-Cell, traditionally statically defined in antigen space only

[12].

Definition 1: (Robust Weight/Activation Function) For the ith D-W-B-cell, DWB_i, $i = 1, \cdots, N_B$, we define the activation caused by the jth antigen data point as

$$w_{ij} = w_i \left(d_{ij}^2 \right) = e^{-\left(\frac{d_{ij}^2}{2\sigma_{i,j}^2} + \frac{j}{\tau} \right)} \quad (1)$$

where τ controls the time decay rate of the contribution from old antigens, and hence how much emphasis is placed on the currency of the immune network compared to the sequence of antigens encountered so far. d_{ij}^2 is the distance from antigen $\mathbf{x}_j$ (which is the jth antigen encountered by the immune network) to D-W-B-cell, DWB_i. $\sigma_{i,j}^2$ is a scale parameter that controls the decay rate of the weights along the spatial dimensions, and hence defines the size of an influence zone around a cluster prototype. Data samples falling far from this zone are considered outliers. The weight functions decrease exponentially with the order of presentation of an antigen, j, and therefore, will favor more current data in the learning process.

Definition 2: (Influence Zone) The ith D-W-B-cell represents a soft influence zone, $\mathbf{IZ}_i$, that can be interpreted as a robust zone of influence.

$$\mathbf{IZ}_i = \{\mathbf{x}_j \in \mathbf{X}_a | w_{ij} \geq w_{min}\}, \quad (2)$$

Each D-W-B-cell is allowed to have is own zone of influence with radial size proportional to σ_i^2, that is dynamically estimated. Hence, outliers are easily detected as data points falling outside the influence zone of all D-W-B-cells or through their weak activations ($w_{ij} < w_{min}, \quad \forall i$).

Definition 3: (Pure Stimulation) The stimulation level, after J antigens have been presented to DWB_i, is defined as the density of the *antigen* population around DWB_i:

$$s_{ai,J} = \frac{\sum_{j=1}^{J} w_{ij}}{\sigma_{i,J}^2}, \quad (3)$$

Lemma 1: (Optimal Scale Update) The equations for optimal scale updates are given by

$$\sigma_{i,J}^2 = \frac{\sum_{j=1}^{J} w_{ij} d_{ij}^2}{2 \sum_{j=1}^{J} w_{ij}}. \quad (4)$$

Idea of the Proof: Since the time dependency has been absorbed into the weight function, and assuming that the previous values, $\sigma_{i,J-1}^2$, are constant, the equations for scale updates are found by solving $\frac{\partial s_{ai,j}}{\partial \sigma_{i,j}^2} = 0$.

For the purpose of computational efficiency, however, we convert the above equations to incremental counterparts as follows.

Lemma 2: (Incremental Update of Pure Stimulation and Optimal Scale) After J antigens have been presented to DWB_i, pure stimulation and optimal scale can be updated using the following approximate incremental equations, respectively,

$$s_{ai,J} = \frac{e^{-\frac{1}{\tau}} W_{i,J-1} + w_{iJ}}{\sigma_{i,J}^2}, \quad (5)$$

$$\sigma_{i,J}^2 = \frac{e^{-\frac{1}{\tau}} \sigma_{i,J-1}^2 W_{i,J-1} + w_{iJ} d_{iJ}^2}{2 \left(e^{-\frac{1}{\tau}} W_{i,J-1} + w_{iJ} \right)}. \quad (6)$$

where $W_{i,J-1} = \sum_{j=1}^{J-1} w_{ij}$ is the sum of the contributions from previous antigens, $\mathbf{x}_1, \mathbf{x}_2, \cdots, \mathbf{x}_{J-1}$, to D-W-B-Cell i.

Idea of the Proof: Each term that takes part in the computation of the above measures (Equations (3) and (4) above) is updated individually with the arrival of each new antigen using the old values of each term in the numerator and each term in the denominator, and adding the contribution of the new antigen/data item to each one of these terms.

2.1 Dynamic Stimulation and Suppression

We propose incorporating a dynamic stimulation factor, $\alpha(t)$, in the computation of the D-W-B-cell stimulation level by adding a compensation term that depends on other D-W-B-cells in the network [10, 15]. In other words, a group of co-stimulated D-W-B-cells can self-sustain themselves in the immune network, even after the antigen that caused their creation disappears from the environment. However, we need to put a limit on the time span of this memory to forget truly outdated patterns. This is done by allowing D-W-B-cells to have their own stimulation coefficient, and to have this stimulation coefficient decrease with their age: $\alpha(t) = \frac{1}{1+\frac{t}{\tau_\alpha}}$. In the absence of a recent antigen that succeeds in stimulating a given subnet, the age (t) of the D-W-B-cell increases by 1 with each antigen presented to the immune system. However, if a new antigen succeeds in stimulating a given cell, then its age is refreshed back to zero. This makes extremely old D-W-B-cells die gradually, if not re-stimulated by more recent relevent antigens.

Incorporating a dynamic suppression factor, $\beta(t)$, in the computation of the D-W-B-cell stimulation level is also a more sensible way to take into account internal interactions. The suppression factor is not related to memory management, but rather as a way to control the proliferation and redundancy of the D-W-B-cell population. This adaptive way to control the amount of redundancy to achieve the right balance between the needed memory and the useless redundancy can be achieved by allowing D-W-B-cells to have their own suppression coefficient, and using an annealing schedule similar to stimulation, i.e., $\beta(t) = \frac{1}{1+\frac{t}{\tau_\beta}}$

In order to understand the combined effect of the proposed stimulation and suppression mechanism, we consider the following two extreme cases: (i) Positive suppression (competition), but no stimulation results in good population control and avoids redundancy. However, there is no memory, and the immune network will forget past encounters. (ii) When there is positive stimulation, but no suppression, there is good memory but no competition. This will cause the proliferation of the D-W-B-cell population or maximum redundancy. Hence, there is a natural tradeoff between redundancy/memory and competition/reduced costs. Hence the total stimulation for DWB_i should take into account dynamic interactive co-stimulation and co-suppression from other B-cells, in addition to antigen (pure) stimulation:

$$s_i = s_{a_i,J} + \alpha(t) \frac{\sum_{l=1}^{N_B} w_{il}}{\sigma_{i,J}^2} - \beta(t) \frac{\sum_{l=1}^{N_B} w_{il}}{\sigma_{i,J}^2}, \qquad (7)$$

3. Bridging the Scalability Gap: Organization and Compression of the Immune Network

A divide and conquer strategy can have significant impact on the number of interactions that need to be processed in the immune network. We define *external interactions* as those occuring between an antigen (external agent) and the D-W-B-cell in the immune network

(giving rise to the first term in (7)). We define *internal interactions* as those occuring between one D-W-B-cell and all other D-W-B-cells in the immune network(giving rise to the second and third terms in (7)). Note that the number of possible internal interactions can be a serious bottleneck in the face of all existing immune network based learning techniques [10, 15]. Suppose that the immune network is compressed by clustering the D-W-B-cells using a linear complexity approach such as K Means. Then the immune network can be divided into K *subnetworks* that form a parsimonious view of the entire network. For global low resolution interactions, such as the ones between D-W-B-cells that are very different, only the *inter-subnetwork interactions* are germane. For higher resolution interactions such as the ones between similar D-W-B-cells, we can drill down inside the corresponding subnetwork and afford to consider all the *intra-subnetwork interactions*.

Lemma 3: (Effect of Network Compression on Scalability) The proposed AIS based clustering model can achieve scalability at a finite compression rate.

Proof: Since the AIS model is updated incrementally for each data sample, there is no need to store the data samples. What needs to be stored and manipulated is the immune network itself. Hence, the most expensive computation and storage overhead stems from calculating and storing all the internal network interactions (quadratic complexity with respect to the network size). However, if the network is divided into roughly K equal sized subnetworks, then the number of internal interactions in an immune network of N_B D-W-B-cells, can drop from N_B^2 in the uncompressed network, to $\left(\frac{N_B}{K}\right)^2$ *intra-subnetwork interactions* and $K - 1$ *inter-subnetwork interactions* in the compressed immune network. This clearly can approach linear complexity as $K \to \sqrt{N_B}$. Similarly the number of external interactions relative to each antigen can drop from N_B in the uncompressed network to K in the compressed network. Furthermore, the compression rate can be modulated by choosing the appropriate number of clusters, $K \approx \sqrt{N_B}$, when clustering the D-W-B-cell population, to maintain linear complexity, $O(N_B)$. Sufficient summary statistics for each subnetwork of D-W-B-cells are computed, and can later be used as approximations in lieu of repeating the computation of the entire suppression/stimulation sum. The summary statistics are in the form of average dissimilarity within the group, cardinality of the group (number of D-W-B-cells in the group), and density of the group. This approach can be seen as forming sub-networks of the immune network with sufficient summary statistics to be used in evolving the entire immune network.

3.1 Effect of the Network Compression on Interaction Terms

Instead of taking into account all possible $(N_B)^2$ interactions between all N_B cells in the immune network, only the intra-subnetwork interactions with the N_B^i D-W-B-cells inside the parent subnetwork (the closest subnetwork to which this B cell is assigned) are taken into account. In case K-Means is used, this representative as well as the organization of the network into subnetworks is a by-product. For more complex data structures, a reasonable best representative/prototype (such as a medoid) can be chosen. Taking these modifications into account, the stimulation and scale values that take advantage of the compressed network are given by

$$s_i = s_{ai,J} + \alpha(t) \frac{\sum_{l=1}^{N_B^i} w_{il}}{\sigma_{i,J}^2} - \beta(t) \frac{\sum_{l=1}^{N_B^i} w_{il}}{\sigma_{i,J}^2}, \qquad (8)$$

where $s_{ai,J}$ is the pure antigen stimulation after encountering J antigens, given by (5) for D-W-B-cell$_i$; and N_B^i is the number of B-cells in the subnetwork that is closest to the ith DWB-cell. This will modify the D-W-B-cell scale update equations to become

$$\sigma_{i,J}^2 = \frac{1}{2} \frac{D_{i,J}^2 + \alpha(t) \sum_{l=1}^{N_B^i} w_{il} d_{il}^2 - \beta(t) \sum_{l=1}^{N_B^i} w_{il} d_{il}^2}{W_{i,J} + \alpha(t) \sum_{l=1}^{N_B^i} w_{il} - \beta(t) \sum_{l=1}^{N_B^i} w_{il}}, \qquad (9)$$

where $D_{i,J}^2 = e^{-\frac{1}{\tau}} \sigma_{i,J-1}^2 W_{i,J-1} + w_{iJ} d_{iJ}^2$ and $W_{i,J} = e^{-\frac{1}{\tau}} W_{i,J-1} + w_{iJ}$

3.2 Cloning in the Dynamic Immune System

The D-W-B-cells are cloned in proportion to their stimulation levels relative to the average network stimulation. However, to avoid preliminary proliferation of D-W-B-Cells, and to encourage a diverse repertoire, new D-W-B-Cells do not clone before they are mature (their age, t_i exceeds a lower limit t_{min}). Similarly, D-W-B-cells with age $t_i > t_{max}$ are frozen, or prevented from cloning, to give a fair chance to newer D-W-B-Cells. This means that $N_{clones_i} = K_{clone} \frac{s_i}{\sum_{k=1}^{N_B} s_k}$ if $t_{min} \leq t_i \leq t_{max}$. When the B-cell population size (N_B) exceeds a prespecified maximum (N_{Bmax}), the B-cells are sorted in ascending order of their stimulation levels, and the top ($N_B - N_{Bmax}$) B-cells (with lowest stimulation) are killed. New B-cells ($t_i < t_{min}$) are compensated to be able to compete with more mature cells in the immune network by temporarily (for the purpose of sorting) scaling their stimulation level to the network's average stimulation level.

3.3 Learning New Antigens and Relation to Outlier Detection

Somatic hypermutation is a powerfull natural exploration mechanism in the immune system, that allows it to learn how to respond to new antigens that have never been seen before. However, from a *computational* point of view, this is a very costly and inefficient operation since its complexity is exponential in the number of features. Therefore, we model this operation in the artificial immune system model by an instant antigen duplication whenever an antigen is encountered that fails to activate the entire immune network. A new antigen, $\mathbf{x}_j$ is said to activate the ith B-Cell, if it falls within its Influence Zone, $\mathbf{IZ}_i$, essentially meaning that its activation of this D-W-B-Cell, w_{ij} exceeds a minimum threshold w_{min}.
Definition 4: (Potential Outlier) A *Potential outlier* is an antigen that fails to activate the entire immune network, i.e., $w_{ij} < w_{min}$, $\forall i = 1, \cdots, N_B$.

To further take advantage of the compressed immune network, only the $N_B^{(j^*)}$ D-W-B-cells within the closest subnetwork (say the $(j^*)^{th}$ subnetwork) to the current (j^{th}) antigen are considered. This results in activation iff. $w_{ij} < w_{min}$, $\forall i = 1, \cdots, N_B^{(j^*)}$. The outlier is termed *potential* because, initially, it may either be an outlier or a new emerging pattern. It is only through the continuous learning process that lies ahead, that the fate of this outlier will be decided. If it is indeed a true outlier, then it will form no mature DWB-Cells in the immune network.

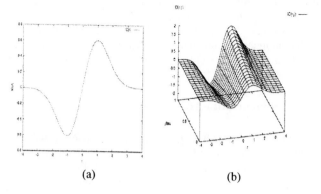

| (a) | (b) |

Figure 1. D-W-B-cell's ψ −function (showing influence of outliers): (a) $\psi(r_j)$. (b) $\psi(r_j, j/\tau)$

3.4 TECNO-STREAMS: Tracking Evolving Clusters in Noisy Data Streams with a Scalable Immune System Learning Model

---

TECNO-STREAMS Algorithm:
(optional steps are enclosed in [ ])

Fix the maximal population size, N_{Bmax};
Initialize D-W-B-cell population and $\sigma_i^2 = \sigma_{init}$ using the first N_{Bmax} input antigens;
Compress immune network into K subnets using 2 iterations of K Means;
Repeat for each incoming antigen $\mathbf{x}_j$ {
  Present antigen to each subnet centroid, $\mathbf{C}_k, k = 1, \cdots, K$ in network : Compute distance, activation weight, w_{kj} and update σ_k^2 incrementally using (6);
  Determine the most activated subnet (the one with maximum w_{kj});
  IF All B-cells in most activated subnet have $w_{ij} < w_{min}$ (antigen does not sufficiently activate subnet) THEN{
    Create by duplication a new D-W-B-cell = $\mathbf{x}_j$ and $\sigma_i^2 = \sigma_{init}$;
  }
  ELSE {
  Repeat for each D-W-B-cell$_i$ in most activated subnet {
    IF $w_{ij} > w_{min}$ (antigen activates D-W-B-cell$_i$) THEN
    Refresh age ($t = 0$) for D-W-B-cell$_i$;
    ELSE
    Increment age (t) for D-W-B-cell$_i$;
    Compute distance from antigen $\mathbf{x}_j$ to D-W-B-cell$_i$;
    Compute D-W-B-cell$_i$'s stimulation level using (8);
    Update D-W-B-cell$_i$'s σ_i^2 using (9);
  }
  }
  Clone and mutate D-W-B-cells;
  IF population size $> N_{Bmax}$ Then {
    IF (Age of B-cell $< t_{min}$) THEN
    Temporarily scale D-W-B-cell's stimulation level to the network average stimulation;
    Sort D-W-B-cells in ascending order of their stimulation level;
    Kill worst excess (top ($N_B - N_{Bmax}$) according to previous sorting) D-W-B-cells;
    [or move oldest/mature D-W-B-Cells to secondary (long term) storage];
  }
  Compress immune network periodically (after every T antigens), into K subnets using 2 iterations of K Means with the previous centroids as initial centroids;
}

---

4 Theoretical Resistance Properties of the Proposed D-W-B-Cell Model as a Robust Statistical Estimator

Lemma 4: (Robustness via the Influence Curve Approach) It can be shown based on robust statistical theory [8] that the Influence Function is bounded when the model is mapped to a *robust* statistical estimator, and that the scale update method also results in a *robust* scale estimator.

Proof: The D-W-B-cell model estimates the location and scale parameter by optimizing the following stimulation/inverse loss function, if the time/sequence information, j, is ignored for data: $\rho(r_j)\left(1/\sigma^2\right) = r_j^2 e^{\left(-r_j^2/2\right)}$, where, r_j is the jth normalized residual. Thus, it can be considered an M-estimator with the ψ−function, $\psi(r) = \frac{\partial \rho(r)}{\partial r} = \left(-2r/\sigma^2\right)e^{\left(-\frac{r^2}{2}\right)}$, displayed in Fig. 1(a). The Influence curve (IC) [8] has the same shape as the ψ-function, displayed in Fig. 1 (a). IC tells us how an infinitesimal proportion of contamination affects the estimate in large samples, and hence summarizes the influence of data points with given residuals on the resulting estimate. It can be inferred from IC that the influence is asymptotically zero at locations corresponding to infinite residuals, meaning that *gross outliers have almost no effect on the estimate*. Also, most importantly, at any point, *the influence is bounded*. This constitutes the most important *resistance* property of any robust estimator. Taking the sequential information of the data into account, the following stimulation/inverse loss function, results: $\rho(r_j, j/\tau)\left(1/\sigma^2\right) = r_j^2 e^{\left(-(r_j^2 + j/\tau)/2\right)}$, where, r_j is the jth normalized residual. Thus, it can be considered an M-estimator with the ψ−function, $\psi(r,, j/\tau) = \frac{\partial \rho(r, j/\tau)}{\partial r} = \left(-2r/\sigma^2\right)e^{\left(-(r^2 + j/\tau)/2\right)}$, displayed in Fig. 1(b), showing a decreasing influence both with the distance and age of the samples.

Lemma 5: (Winsor's Principle and Gaussian Efficiency) The D-W-B-cell model is expected to have good efficiency at the Gaussian distribution

Proof: The D-W-B-cell model's ψ−function satisfies the linearity in the middle criterion, since its slope approaches a constant for very small residuals. This is because $\psi'(r)$ satisfies $\lim_{r \to 0} \psi'(r) = \lim_{r \to 0}(2/\sigma^2)e^{\left(-\frac{r^2}{2}\right)}\left(r^2 - 1\right) = -2$. This means that the D-W-B-cell model is expected to have good efficiency at the Gaussian distribution. This important property is motivated by the fact that most distributions are normal in the middle (i.e. for small residuals).

Lemma 6: (Unbiased Estimates) Since the D-W-B-cell model is a robust M-estimator with an odd ψ−function, its location estimate is *unbiased*.

5. Comparison to Other Clustering Techniques

Because of paucity of space, we review only some related methods, as summarized in Table 1. We note that all immune based techniques, as well as most evolutionary type clustering techniques are expected to benefit from insensitivity to initial conditions (*reliability*) by virtue of being population based. Also, some techniques require a memory buffer for storage of a compression of the data set in main memory which imposes an unwanted constraint on stream data mining. Moreover, most techniques achieve their scalability by using a special indexing structure which requires an additional preliminary scan of the data which may not be acceptable in the

context of data streams. Finally, unlike most other clustering techniques that are Distance and Partitioning based (such as K Means and its variants, as well as most older immune based techniques), Density type methods, such as the proposed approach, directly seek dense areas of the data space, and can find more good clusters, while being robust to noise. This tends to be very beneficial especially in high dimensional and sparse data sets such as web usage, text, and transactional data.

Table 1. Comparison of proposed Scalable Immune Clustering Approach with Other Algorithms

Approach →	TECNO-STREAMS	SKM [3]	DBSCAN [6]	DENCLUE [9]	BIRCH [16]
Reliability/Insensitivity to initialization	yes	no	yes	no	no
Robustness to noise	yes	no	yes	yes	no
Requires Pre-Clustering scan/ Spatial Data Structure	no	yes (integrated)	yes (R^*-tree)	yes (B^+-tree)	yes (CF-tree)
Time Complexity: $O(\ )$	N	N	$N\log(N)$	$\log(N)$	N
Requires Buffer for Data	no	yes	yes	yes	yes
Requires No. of Clusters	no	yes	no	yes	no
Handles evolving clusters	yes	no	no	no	no
Robust Automatic Scale Estimation	yes	no	no	no	no
Cluster Model	network	centroids	medoids	centroids	centroids
Handles Arbitrary Dissimilarity Measures	yes	no	yes	no	no
Density/Partition based?	Density	Partition	Density	Density	Partition

6 Experimental Results

6.1 Single-Pass Location of Dense Cluster Representatives in Noisy 2-D Data

First, we show the results on 2-D data sets because the results can be inspected visually and easily. Clean and noisy 2-dimensional sets, with roughly 1000 to 3200 points, and between 3 and 5 clusters, are used to illustrate the performance of TECNO-STREAMS in detecting an appropriate number of clusters. The implementation parameters used for all experiments were as follow: The initial value for the scale was $\sigma_{init} = 0.0025$ (an upper radial bound based on the range of normalized values in $[0, 1]$). D-W-B-cells were only allowed to clone past the age of $t_{min} = 2$, $K_{clone} = 0.97$, $N_{Bmax} = 30$ to 50, mutation rate of 0.01, $\tau = 6$, $w_{min} = 0.2$, and compression rate, K between 1 and 7, with the upper limit roughly corresponding to making the immune network complexity linear. The network compression was performed after every $T = 40$ antigens have been processed.

The evolution of the D-W-B-cell population, limited to a maximum size of 30 cells, with $K = 1$, for 3 noisy clusters, when the antigens are presented in random order, is shown in Figure 2, superimposed on the original data set. Only the data points processed thus far are shown on each figure. Each vertical line is centered on a B-cell location, and its length represents the diameter of its Influence Zone ($\approx 3\sigma_i$). We emphasize that the final results after all antigens have been processed is equivalent to a *single* pass, with a small immune network size of only 30 D-W-B-cells. The results for the same data set, but with antigens presented in the order of the clusters is shown in Figure 3. This scenario is the most difficult (worst) case for single-pass learning, as it truly tests the ability of the system to memorize the old patterns, adapt to new patterns, and still avoid excessive proliferation.

Similar experiments are shown for a noisy data set of five clusters in Figure 4 and Figure 5. These results illustrate the ability of the immune network to track the clusters. Since this is an unsupervised clustering problem, it is not important that a cluster is modeled by one or several D-W-B-cells. The effect of the compression of the immune network if illustrated by showing the final D-W-B-cell population for different compression rates corresponding to $K = 3, 5, 7$ on the data set with 5 clusters, in Fig. 6. Linear complexity is reached for the case of $K = 7$. The antigens were presented in the most challenging order (one cluster at a time), and in a single pass. Notice that depending on the order of presentation of the data, some of the noise presented at the very end of the run may not be labeled as outliers with full certainty. It is temporarily treated like a possible emerging pattern until future data can resolve its fate with certainty. Other than the natural uncertainty arising from last minute noise points, the quality of the final immune network or cluster model is practically insensitive to the order of presentation of the data and to the compression rate, and it shows an ability to model clusters with arbitrary shape since multiple B-cells can represent a single cluster. Finally Fig. 7 shows with different shades the core points and outliers as easily recognized by our approach (outliers have negligible activations to the entire final immune network, i.e., $w_{ij} < 0.001, \forall i$). Notice that in the absence of knowledge about future data, noise presented at the very end of the run may be temporarily treated as a possible emerging pattern. This explains why a few noise points that happen to be presented last are shown in black at the end of the run. Naturally, because of the different order of presentation of the samples (first to last cluster, last to first cluster, and random), these last undecided noise points may differ from one image to another in Fig. 7 (a), (b), and (c), respectively. The spaces that are void of data contain the first points (unplotted) used to initialize the immune network.

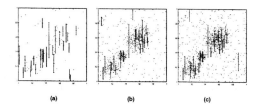

(a)　　　　(b)　　　　(c)

Figure 2. Single Pass Results on a Noisy dataset presented one at a time in random order: Location of D-W-B-cells and estimated scales for data set with 3 clusters after processing (a) 100 samples, (b) 700 samples, and (c) all 1133 samples

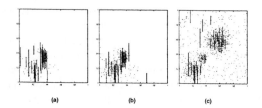

(a)　　　　(b)　　　　(c)

Figure 3. Single Pass Results on a Noisy dataset presented one at a time in the same order as clusters: Location of D-W-B-cells and estimated scales for data set with 3 clusters after processing (a) 100 samples, (b) 300 samples, and (c) all 1133 samples

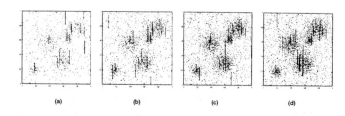

(a)　　　　(b)　　　　(c)　　　　(d)

Figure 4. Single Pass Results on a noisy dataset presented one at a time in random order with $K = 7$: Location of D-W-B-cells and estimated scales after processing (a) 875 samples, (b) 1750 samples, and (c) 2625 samples, (d) all 3200 samples

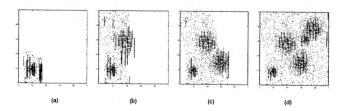

(a)　　　　(b)　　　　(c)　　　　(d)

Figure 5. Single Pass Results on a noisy dataset presented one at a time in the same order as clusters with $K = 7$: Location of D-W-B-cells and estimated scales for data set after processing (a) 350 samples, (b) 1225 samples, and (c) 1925 samples, (d) all 3200 samples

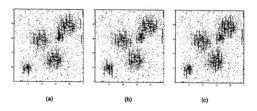

(a)　　　　(b)　　　　(c)

Figure 6. Effect of Compression rate on Immune Network: Location of D-W-B-cells and estimated scales for noisy data set presented in random order(a) $K = 3$, (b) $K = 5$, (c) $K = 7$ (linear complexity)

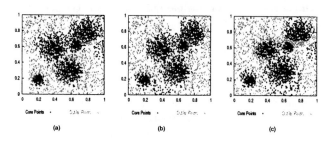

(a)　　　　(b)　　　　(c)

Figure 7. Ability to distinguish between core and outlier points ($w_{ij} < 0.001, \forall i$) for noisy data set presented in the following order: (a) cluster 1 to cluster 5 (b) cluster 5 to cluster 1 (c) random order

6.2　Single-Pass Mining of User Profiles from Real Web Clickstream Data

Profiles were mined from the 12-day clickstream data (from 1998) with 1704 sessions and 343 URLs from the website of the department of Computer Engineering and Computer Science at the University of Missouri. This is a benchmark data set used in [13, 14]. The profiles that were discovered using TECNO-STREAMS in a single pass are comparable to the ones previously obtained using a variety of less scalable techniques [13, 14]. The maximum population size was 100, the control parameter for compression was varied between $K = 1$ and 50, and periodical compression every $T = 40$ sessions. The activation threshold was $w_{min} = 0.6$, and $\tau = 20$. We illustrate the *continuous* learning ability of the proposed technique using the following simulations:

scenario 1: We partition the Web sessions into 20 distinct sets of sessions, each one assigned to the closest of 20 profiles previously discovered using Hierarchical Unsupervised Niche Clustering (HUNC) [14], and listed in Table 2. Then we presented these sessions to TECNO-STREAMS one profile at a time: sessions assigned to trend 0, then sessions assigned to profile 1, ···, etc.

scenario 2: We used the same session partition as scenario 1, but presented the profiles in reverse order: sessions assigned to trend 19, then sessions assigned to trend 18, ···, etc, ending with trend 0.

scenario 3: The Web sessions are presented in their natural chronological order exactly as received in real time by the web server.

We track the number of B cells that succeed in learning each one of the 20 ground truth profiles after each session is presented, by counting the number of B-cells within 0.4 radius of each ground truth profile (distance is computed as the square of 1 - cosine similarity). This provides an evolving number of hits per profile as shown in Figures 8, 9, and 10, for the three above scenarios respectively. The y-axis is split into 20 intervals, with each interval devoted to the trend/profile number indicated by the lower value (from 0 to 19). A hit for the ith profile for session No. t is shown in these figures at location (t, i). The proposed immune clustering algorithm can learn the user profiles in a single pass. A single pass over all 1704 Web user sessions (with non-optimized Java code) took less than 7 seconds on a 2 GHz Pentium 4 PC running on Linux. With an average of *4 milliseconds per user session*, the proposed profile mining system is suitable for use in a real time personalization system to constantly and continuously provide a fresh and current list of an unknown number of evolving user profiles. Old profiles can be handled in a variety of ways. They may either be discarded, moved to secondary storage, or cached for possible re-emergence. Even if discarded, older profiles that re-emerge later, would be re-learned from scratch just like new profiles. Hence the logistics of maintaining old profiles are less crucial compared to existing techniques.

Figure 8 exhibits an expected staircase pattern showing the gradual learning of emergent usage trends as these are experienced by the immune network in the order from trend 0 to 19. The plot shows some peculiarities, for example at trend 15 since it records a short lived hit at the same time as trend 2. Table 2 shows that trends 2 and 15 do indeed share many similarities. Typical cross reactions between similar patterns are actually desired and illustrate a certain tolerance for inexact matching. Figure 9 shows an interesting inversed staircase pattern due to the reverse presentation order.

Finally Figure 10 shows the B-cell hits when the sessions are presented in their original chronological order corresponding to scenario 3. Figure 11 shows the distribution of the original input sessions, but with all the noise sessions excluded. It shows that the session data is quite noisy, and the arrival sequence and pattern of sessions belonging to the same usage trend may vary in a way that makes incremental tracking and discovery of the profiles even more challenging than in a batch style approach, where the sessions can be stored in memory, and a standard iterative approach is used to mine the profiles. It also shows how some of the usage trends (e.g: No. 13, 14, 15) are not synchronized with others, and how some of the trends are weak and noisy. Such weak profiles can be even more elusive to discover in a real time system. While Figure 10 shows the B-cell distribution with time, Figure 11 shows the distribution of the input data with time. The fact that both figures show some similarity and the emergence patterns of the trends, attests to the

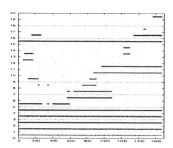

Figure 8. Hits per usage trend versus session number when sessions are presented in order of trend 0 to trend 19. $K = 10, \tau = 20$

fact that the immune network is able to form a reasonable dynamic synopsis of the usage data. It is interesting to note that the *memory span* of the network is affected by the parameter τ which affects the rate of forgetting in the immune network. A low value will favor faster forgetting, and therefore a more current set of profiles that reflect the most recent activity on a website, while a higher value will tend to keep older profiles in the network for longer periods. Figure 12 shows the number of discovered profiles versus the network compression rate K, indicating between 12 and 17 stable profiles.

Table 2. Summary of some usage trends previously discovered using Hierarchical Unsupervised Niche Clustering (only URLs with top 3 to 4 relevance weights shown in each profile)

i	P_{T_i}	P_{T_i}
0	106	{0.99 - /people_index.html}, {0.98 - /people.html}, {0.97 - /faculty.html}
1	104	{0.99 - /}, {1.00 - /cecs_computer.class}
2	177	{0.90 - /courses_index.html}, {0.88 - /courses100.html}, {0.87 - /courses.html}, {0.81 - /}
3	61	{0.80 - /}, {0.48 - /degrees.html}, {0.23 - /degrees_grad.html}
4	58	{0.97 - /degrees_undergrad.html}, {0.97 - /bsce.html}, {0.95 - /degrees_index.html}
5	50	{0.56 - /faculty/springer.html}, {0.38 - /faculty/palani.html}
6	116	{0.91 - /˜saab/cecs333/private}, {0.78 - /˜saab/cecs333}
12	74	{0.57 - /˜shi/cecs345}, {0.45 - /˜shi/cecs345/java_examples}, {0.46 - /˜shi/cecs345/Lectures/07.html}
13	38	{0.82 - /˜shi/cecs345}, {0.47 - /˜shi}, {0.34 - /˜shi/cecs345/references.html}
14	33	{0.55 - /˜shi/cecs345}, {0.55 - /˜shi/cecs345/java_examples}, {0.33 - /˜shi/cecs345/Projects/1.html}
15	51	{0.92 - /courses_index.html}, {0.90 - /courses100.html}, {0.86 - /courses.html}, {0.78 - /courses200.html}
16	77	{0.78 - /˜yshang/CECS341.html}, {0.56 - /˜yshang/W98CECS341.html}, {0.29 - /˜yshang}
19	120	{0.27 - /access}, {0.23 - /access/details.html}

7 Conclusion

We presented a robust and scalable algorithm (TECNO-STREAMS) for detecting an unknown number of evolving clusters in a noisy data stream. Other than the natural uncertainty arising from very recent noise points, the quality of the final cluster model is practically insensitive to the order of presentation of the data and to the compression rate, and it can model clusters with arbitrary shape since multiple B-cells can represent a single cluster. The main factor behind the ability of the proposed method to learn in a single pass lies in the richness of the immune network structure that forms a dynamic synopsis of the data. Such complex network structures have the reputation of being huge, thus hard and time

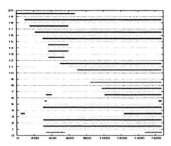

Figure 9. Hits per usage trend versus session number when sessions are presented in reverse order from trend 19 to trend 0, $K = 10$, $\tau = 20$

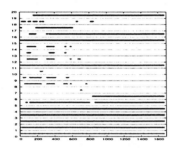

Figure 10. Hits per usage trend versus session number when all sessions are presented in natural chronological order: $K = 25$, $\tau = 20$

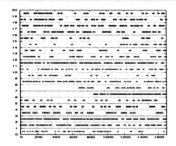

Figure 11. Distribution of input sessions over usage trend versus session number when only non-noisy ($w_{ij} > 0.6$) sessions are presented in natural chronological order: Trends 5, 9, 13, 14, 15, and 19 appear to be weaker and noisier. Also trends 6 and 7 emerge late in the 12-day access log, while trend 0 weakens in the last days.

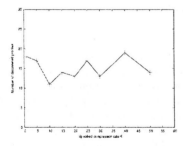

Figure 12. Number of discovered profiles versus specifed compression rate K, when sessions are presented in natural chronological order

consuming to manipulate. The proposed compression mechanism and new B-cell model make this network manageable, and continuous learning possible. Finally, we note that TECNO-STREAMS adheres to the requirements of clustering data streams formulated in [2]: *compactness of representation*, *fast incremental processing of new data points*, and *clear and fast identification of outliers*.

8 Acknowledgments

This work is supported by National Science Foundation CAREER Award IIS-0133948 to O. Nasraoui, and by a grant from the Southeastern Consortium for Electrical Engineering Education. F. Gonzalez is supported by the National University of Colombia.

References

[1] S. Babu and J. Widom. Continuous queries over data streams. In *SIGMOD Record'01*, pages 109–120, 2001.

[2] D. Barbara. Requirements for clustering data streams. *ACM SIGKDD Explorations Newsletter*, 3(2):23–27, 2002.

[3] P. Bradley, U. Fayyad, and C. Reina. Scaling clustering algorithms to large databases. In *Proceedings of the 4th international conf. on Knowledge Discovery and Data Mining (KDD98)*, 1998.

[4] Y. Chen, G. Dong, J. Han, B. W. Wah, and J. Wang. Multi-dimensional regression analysis of time-series data streams. In *2002 Int. Conf. on Very Large Data Bases (VLDB'02)*, Hong Kong, China, 2002.

[5] I. Cohen. *Tending Adam's Garden*. Springer Verlag, 2000.

[6] M. Ester, H. P. Kriegel, J. Sander, and X. Xu. A density-based algorithm for discovering clusters in large spatial databases with noise. In *Proceedings of the 2nd international conf. on Knowledge Discovery and Data Mining (KDD96)*, Portland Oregon, 1996.

[7] S. Guha, N. Mishra, R. Motwani, and L. O'Callaghan. Clustering data streams. In *IEEE Symposium on Foundations of Computer Science (FOCS'00)*, Redondo Beach, CA, 2000.

[8] F. R. Hampel, E. M. Ronchetti, P. J. Rousseeuw, and W. A. Stahel. *Robust Statistics the Approach Based on Influence Functions*. John Wiley & Sons, New York, 1986.

[9] A. Hinneburg and D. A. Keim. An efficient approach to clustering in large multimedia databases with noise. In *Knowledge Discovery and Data Mining*, pages 58–65, 1998.

[10] J. Hunt and D. Cooke. An adaptative, distributed learning system, based on immune system. In *IEEE International Conference on Systems, Man and Cybernetics*, pages 2494–2499, Los Alamitos, CA, 1995.

[11] N. K. Jerne. The immune system. *Scientific American*, 229(1):52–60, 1973.

[12] O. Nasraoui, D. Dasgupta, and F. Gonzalez. An artificial immune system approach to robust data mining. In *Genetic and Evolutionary Computation Conference (GECCO)*, pages 356–363, New York, NY, 2002.

[13] O. Nasraoui, H. Frigui, R. Krishnapuram, and A. Joshi. Mining web access logs using relational competitive fuzzy clustering. In *Eighth International Fuzzy Systems Association Congress*, Hsinchu, Taiwan, Aug. 1999.

[14] O. Nasraoui and R. Krishnapuram. One step evolutionary mining of context sensitive associations and web navigation patterns. In *SIAM conference on Data Mining*, pages 531–547, Arlington, VA, 2002.

[15] J. Timmis, M. Neal, and J. Hunt. An artificial immune system for data analysis. *Biosystems*, 55(1).

[16] T. Zhang, R. Ramakrishnan, and M. Livny. Birch: An efficient data clustering method for large databases. In *ACM SIGMOD International Conference on Management of Data*, pages 103–114, New York, NY, 1996. ACM Press.

Efficient Nonlinear Dimension Reduction
for Clustered Data Using Kernel Functions

Cheong Hee Park   Haesun Park*

Dept. of Computer Science and Engineering
University of Minnesota
Minneapolis, MN 55455
chpark@cs.umn.edu   hpark@cs.umn.edu

Abstract

In this paper, we propose a nonlinear feature extraction method which is based on centroids and kernel functions. The dimension reducing nonlinear transformation is obtained by implicitly mapping the input data into a feature space using a kernel function, and then finding a linear mapping based on an orthonormal basis of centroids in the feature space that maximally separates the between-class relationship. The proposed method utilizes an efficient algorithm to compute an orthonormal basis of centroids in the feature space transformed by a kernel function and achieves dramatic computational savings. The experimental results demonstrate that our method is capable of extracting nonlinear features effectively so that competitive performance of classification can be obtained in the reduced dimensional space.

1. Introduction

Dimension reduction in data analysis is an important preprocessing step for speeding up the main tasks and reducing the effect of noise. As the amount of data grows larger, extracting the right features is not only a useful preprocess step but becomes necessary for efficient and effective processing, especially for high dimensional data. The Principal Component Analysis (PCA) and the Linear Discriminant Analysis (LDA) are two of the most commonly used dimension reduction methods [1, 2]. However, these methods have a limitation for the data which are not linearly separable since it is difficult to capture a nonlinear relationship with a linear mapping. In order to overcome such a limitation, nonlinear extensions of these methods have been proposed. One way for a nonlinear extension is to transform the input space to a higher dimensional feature space by a nonlinear mapping and then to find a linear dimension reduction in the feature space. It is well known that kernel functions allow such nonlinear extensions without explicitly forming a nonlinear mapping or a feature space, as long as the problem formulation involves only the *inner products* between the data points and never the data points themselves [3, 4]. The kernel Principal Component Analysis (kernel PCA) [5] and the generalized Discriminant Analysis [6, 7, 8, 9] have recently been introduced as nonlinear generalizations of the PCA and the LDA by kernel functions, respectively.

The PCA aims at representing data in a lower dimensional space minimizing information loss but it does not reflect well the clustered structure of data in the dimension reduced space. While the goal of the LDA is dimension reduction for classification in the reduced dimensional space maximizing the class separability, the LDA requires a solution from generalized eigenvalue problem which is expensive. When the input space is mapped to a feature space through a kernel function, the dimension of the feature space becomes much larger (possibly infinite) than that of the original sample space. As a result, the scatter matrices used in the optimization criteria for the LDA become singular. In the KFD analysis [6], Mika et al. used regularization parameters to make the within-class scatter matrix nonsingular. In generalized Discriminant Analysis (GDA) [7], centering in the feature space is performed by shifting each feature vector by the global average, and then the kernel matrix is computed. This kernel matrix is assumed to be nonsingular. However, even when the kernel function is symmetric positive definite, the kernel matrix becomes singular after centering in the feature space and this makes the theoretical development of GDA difficult. In this paper, we focus on a nonlinear dimension reduction method

---

*This work was supported in part by the National Science Foundation grants CCR-0204109 and ACI-0305543. Any opinions, findings and conclusions or recommendations expressed in this material are those of the authors and do not necessarily reflect the views of the National Science Foundation (NSF).

243

which can efficiently extract optimal features for classification, utilizing the clustered structure in the input training data and kernel methods. Throughout the paper, we assume that the dataset we need to handle has already been clustered, as in the case of LDA.

The centroid of a class minimizes the sum of the squared distances to vectors within the class and it yields a rank one approximation of the class. In the Orthogonal Centroid method [10] the centroids are taken as representatives of each class and the vectors of the input space are transformed by an orthonormal basis of the space spanned by the centroids. This method provides a dimension reducing linear transformation which preserves the clustering structure in the given data. However, when the data is not linearly separable, structure preserving dimension reduction may not be optimal for a classification problem. By considering that nonlinear mappings by kernel functions can transform original data to a linearly separable structure in a higher dimensional space, we aim to obtain both computational efficiency and high classification accuracy.

We apply the centroid-based orthogonal transformation to the data transformed by a nonlinear mapping through kernel method and show that it can extract nonlinear features effectively, thus reducing the data dimension down to the number of classes and saving the computational cost. In Section 2, we briefly review the Orthogonal Centroid method which is a dimension reduction method based on an orthonormal basis for the centroids. In Section 3, we derive the new Kernel Orthogonal Centroid method extending the Orthogonal Centroid method using kernel functions to handle nonlinear feature extraction and analyze the computational complexity of our new method. Our experimental results presented in Section 4 demonstrate that the new Kernel Orthogonal Centroid method is capable of extracting nonlinear features effectively so that competitive classification performance can be obtained with linear classifiers after nonlinear dimension reduction. In addition, it is shown that once we obtain a lower dimensional representation, a *linear* soft margin Support Vector Machine (SVM) is able to achieve high classification accuracy with much less number of support vectors, thus reducing prediction costs as well.

2. Orthogonal Centroid Method

Given a vector space representation of the data matrix A with r classes,

$$A = [a_1, \cdots, a_n] = [A_1, A_2, \cdots, A_r] \in \mathbb{R}^{m \times n} \quad (1)$$

where each class A_i consists of n_i column vectors and $\sum_{i=1}^r n_i = n$, dimension reduction by linear transformation is to find $G^T \in \mathbb{R}^{l \times m}$ that maps a vector x to a vector

---

Algorithm 1 Orthogonal Centroid method

Given a data matrix $A \in \mathbb{R}^{m \times n}$ with r classes and a data point $x \in \mathbb{R}^{m \times 1}$, it computes a matrix $Q_r \in \mathbb{R}^{m \times r}$ and gives a r-dimensional representation $\hat{x} = Q_r^T x \in \mathbb{R}^{r \times 1}$.

1. Compute the centroid c_i of the ith class for $1 \leq i \leq r$ and set the centroid matrix $C = [c_1, c_2, \cdots, c_r]$.

2. Compute an orthogonal decomposition of C, which is $C = Q_r R$.

3. $\hat{x} = Q_r^T x$ gives a r-dimensional representation of x.

$\hat{x}$ for some $l < m$:

$$G^T : x \in \mathbb{R}^{m \times 1} \to \hat{x} \in \mathbb{R}^{l \times 1} \quad i.e. \quad G^T x = \hat{x}. \quad (2)$$

In particular, we seek for a linear transformation G^T with which the cluster structure existing in the given data A is preserved in the reduced dimensional space.

The centroid c_i of each class A_i is the average of the columns in A_i, i.e., $c_i = \frac{1}{n_i} A_i e_i$ where $e_i = [1, \ldots, 1]^T \in \mathbb{R}^{n_i \times 1}$ and the global centroid c is defined as $c = \frac{1}{n} \sum_{j=1}^n a_j$. The centroid of each class is the vector that minimizes the sum of squared distances to vectors within the class. Taking the centroids as representatives of the classes, we find an orthonormal basis of the space spanned by the centroids by computing an orthogonal decomposition

$$C = Q \begin{bmatrix} R \\ 0 \end{bmatrix} = [Q_r, Q_{m-r}] \begin{bmatrix} R \\ 0 \end{bmatrix} \quad (3)$$

of the centroid matrix $C = [c_1, \cdots, c_r]$, where $Q = [q_1, \cdots, q_m] \in \mathbb{R}^{m \times m}$ is an orthogonal matrix and $R \in \mathbb{R}^{r \times r}$ is an upper triangular matrix. Taking the first r columns of Q, we obtain

$$C = Q_r R \quad \text{with} \quad Q_r = [q_1, \cdots, q_r], \quad (4)$$

where the columns of Q_r is an orthonormal basis for $Range(C)$ spanned by the columns of C when the columns of C are linearly independent. The algorithm can easily be modified when the columns of C are not linearly independent. The matrix Q_r^T gives a dimension reducing linear transformation preserving the clustering structure in the sense that the relationship between any data item and a centroid measured using L_2-norm or cosine in the full dimensional space is completely preserved in the reduced dimensional space [10]. This method is called the Orthogonal Centroid method (OCM) and is summarized in Algorithm 1.

The linear transformation obtained in the Orthogonal Centroid method solves a trace optimization problem, providing a link between the methods of linear discriminant analysis and those based on centroids [11]. Dimension reduction by the Linear Discriminant Analysis searches for a linear transformation which maximizes the between-class scatter and minimizes the within-class scatter. The between-class scatter matrix is defined as

$$S_b = \sum_{i=1}^{r} n_i (c_i - c)(c_i - c)^T \quad \text{and} \qquad (5)$$

$$\text{trace}(S_b) = \sum_{i=1}^{r} n_i \|c_i - c\|_2^2.$$

Let's consider a criterion that involves only the between-class scatter matrix, i.e., to find a dimension reducing transformation $G^T \in \mathbb{R}^{l \times m}$ such that the columns of G are orthonormal and $\text{trace}(G^T S_b G)$ is maximized. Note that $\text{rank}(S_b)$ can not exceed $r - 1$. Accordingly,

$$\text{trace}(S_b) = \lambda_1 + \cdots + \lambda_{r-1} \qquad (6)$$

where λ_i's, $1 \le i \le r - 1$, are the $r - 1$ largest eigenvalues of S_b. Denoting the corresponding eigenvectors as u_i's, for any $l \ge r - 1$ and $U_l = [u_1, \cdots, u_l]$, we have

$$\text{trace}(U_l^T S_b U_l) = \lambda_1 + \cdots + \lambda_l = \lambda_1 + \cdots + \lambda_{r-1}. \quad (7)$$

In addition, for any $G \in \mathbb{R}^{m \times l}$ which has orthonormal columns, $\text{trace}(G^T S_b G) \le \text{trace}(S_b)$. Hence $\text{trace}(G^T S_b G)$ is maximized when G is chosen as U_l for any $l \ge r - 1$ and $\text{trace}(U_l^T S_b U_l) = \text{trace}(S_b)$, according to Eqns. (6) and (7).

By the orthogonal decomposition (3) and (4),

$$\left\| \sum_{i=1}^{r} \alpha_i c_i \right\|_2 = \left\| Q^T \left(\sum_{i=1}^{r} \alpha_i c_i \right) \right\|_2 \qquad (8)$$

$$= \left\| \begin{bmatrix} Q_r^T \\ Q_{m-r}^T \end{bmatrix} \left(\sum_{i=1}^{r} \alpha_i c_i \right) \right\|_2$$

$$= \left\| \begin{bmatrix} Q_r^T \sum_{i=1}^{r} \alpha_i c_i \\ 0 \end{bmatrix} \right\|_2 = \left\| Q_r^T \left(\sum_{i=1}^{r} \alpha_i c_i \right) \right\|_2$$

for any $\alpha_i \in \mathbb{R}$. Eqn. (8) implies that the transformation by Orthogonal Centroid Method (OCM) preserves the subspace spanned by centroids in L_2-norm sense. In particular, distances among centroids and the global centroid are preserved in the transformed space, and all the other items are projected to the subspace spanned by centroids, maintaining the relative distance relationship with centroids. Hence

$$\text{trace}(S_b) = \sum_{i=1}^{r} n_i \|c_i - c\|_2^2 \qquad (9)$$

$$= \sum_{i=1}^{r} n_i \|Q_r^T c_i - Q_r^T c\|_2^2 = \text{trace}(Q_r^T S_b Q_r).$$

Therefore, by computing an orthogonal decomposition of the centroid matrix we obtain a solution that maximizes $\text{trace}(G^T S_b G)$ over all G with orthonormal columns. Instead of computing the eigenvectors u_i's, $i = 1, \cdots, r - 1$, we simply need to compute Q_r, which is much less costly.

If the within-class scatter is isotropic, the eigenvectors in LDA are the eigenvectors of S_b [1]. Hence, OCM produces the same solution as LDA. Especially when the data dimension is higher than the number of items as in text data, the data is sparse in the space and tends to be linearly separable. The extensive experiments show that OCM can obtain competitive performance compared with other expensive dimension reduction methods [12], especially when the within-class scatter matrix is close to identity.

3. Kernel Orthogonal Centroid Method

Although a linear hyperplane is a natural choice as a boundary to separate classes it has limitations for nonlinearly structured data. To overcome this limitation we map input data to a feature space (possibly an infinite dimensional space) through a nonlinear feature mapping

$$\Phi : \mathcal{S} \subset \mathbb{R}^{m \times n} \to \mathcal{F} \subset \mathbb{R}^{N \times n} \qquad (10)$$

which transforms input data into linearly separable structure. Without knowing the feature mapping Φ or the feature space $\mathcal{F}$ explicitly, we can work on the feature space $\mathcal{F}$ through kernel functions, as long as the problem formulation depends only on the inner products between data points in $\mathcal{F}$ and not on the data points themselves. For any kernel function κ satisfying Mercer's condition, there exists a reproducing kernel Hilbert space H and a feature map Φ such that $\kappa(x, y) = < \Phi(x), \Phi(y) >$ where $< , >$ is an inner product in H [4, 13]. As positive definite kernel functions satisfying Mercer's condition, polynomial kernel

$$\kappa(x, y) = (\gamma_1 (x \cdot y) + \gamma_2)^d, d > 0 \text{ and } \gamma_1, \gamma_2 \in \mathbb{R} \quad (11)$$

and Gaussian kernel

$$\kappa(x, y) = \exp(-\|x - y\|^2 / \sigma), \sigma \in \mathbb{R} \qquad (12)$$

are in wide use.

Fig. 1 illustrates an example of a nonlinear mapping

$$\Phi(x) = [x_1^2, \sqrt{2} x_1 x_2, x_2^2]^T \text{ for } x = [x_1, x_2]^T \in \mathbb{R}^2$$

by a polynomial kernel, $\kappa(x, y) = (x \cdot y)^2$ [14]. The nonlinearly separable input data $[-1, 1] \times [-1, 1]$ in the left figure was transformed to the linearly separable structure in the right figure by a mapping Φ.

Next we show how the Orthogonal Centroid algorithm can be combined with the kernel function to produce a nonlinear dimension reduction method which does not require

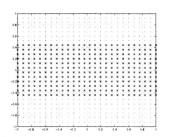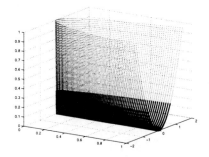

Figure 1. An example of a nonlinear mapping Φ by a polynomial kernel κ of degree 2. Data points represented with $\cdot$ and $\times$ belong to two different classes.

the feature mapping Φ or the feature space $\mathcal{F}$ explicitly. Let Φ be a feature mapping and $\mathcal{C}$ be the centroid matrix of $\Phi(A)$, where the input data matrix A is represented as in (1). Consider the orthogonal decomposition

$$\mathcal{C} = \mathcal{Q}_r \mathcal{R} \qquad (13)$$

of $\mathcal{C}$ where $\mathcal{Q}_r \in \mathbb{R}^{N \times r}$ has orthonormal columns and $\mathcal{R} \in \mathbb{R}^{r \times r}$ is a nonsingular matrix [15]. We apply the Orthogonal Centroid algorithm to $\Phi(A)$ to reduce the data dimension to r, the number of classes in the input data. Then for any data point $x \in \mathbb{R}^{m \times 1}$, the dimension reduced representation of x in a r-dimensional space will be given by $\mathcal{Q}_r^T \Phi(x)$.

We now show how we can calculate $\mathcal{Q}_r^T \Phi(x)$ without knowing Φ explicitly, i.e., without knowing $\mathcal{C}$ explicitly. The centroid matrix $\mathcal{C}$ in the feature space is

$$\mathcal{C} = \left[\frac{1}{n_1} \sum_{i \in N_1} \Phi(a_i), \cdots, \frac{1}{n_r} \sum_{i \in N_r} \Phi(a_i) \right] \in \mathbb{R}^{N \times r} \quad (14)$$

where N_i denotes the index set for items which belong to the i-th class. Hence $\mathcal{C}^T \mathcal{C} = M^T K M$, where $K \in \mathbb{R}^{n \times n}$ is the kernel matrix with

$$K(i,j) = \kappa(a_i, a_j) = < \Phi(a_i), \Phi(a_j) > \qquad (15)$$

and $M^T \in \mathbb{R}^{r \times n}$ is defined as

$$\left[\begin{array}{ccccccccc} \frac{1}{n_1} & \cdots & \frac{1}{n_1} & 0 & & \cdots & & & 0 \\ 0 & \cdots & 0 & \frac{1}{n_2} & \cdots & \frac{1}{n_2} & 0 & & \cdots & 0 \\ & & & & \ddots & & & & \\ 0 & & & \cdots & & & 0 & \frac{1}{n_r} & \cdots & \frac{1}{n_r} \end{array} \right].$$

Due to the assumption that the kernel function κ is symmetric positive definite, the kernel matrix K is symmetric positive definite. Since the matrix M has linearly independent columns, $\mathcal{C}^T \mathcal{C}$ is also symmetric positive definite. The Cholesky decomposition of $\mathcal{C}^T \mathcal{C}$ gives a nonsingular matrix $\mathcal{R}$ such that

$$\mathcal{C}^T \mathcal{C} = \mathcal{R}^T \mathcal{R}. \qquad (16)$$

Since $\mathcal{Q}_r = \mathcal{C} \mathcal{R}^{-1}$ from (13), we have

$$\mathcal{Q}_r^T \Phi(x) = (\mathcal{R}^{-1})^T \mathcal{C}^T \Phi(x) \qquad (17)$$

$$= (\mathcal{R}^{-1})^T \left[\begin{array}{c} \frac{1}{n_1} \sum_{i \in N_1} \kappa(a_i, x) \\ \vdots \\ \frac{1}{n_r} \sum_{i \in N_r} \kappa(a_i, x) \end{array} \right].$$

We summarize our algorithm in Algorithm 2 the Kernel Orthogonal Centroid (KOC) method.

We now briefly discuss the computational complexity of the KOC algorithm where one flop (floating point operation) represents roughly what is required to do one addition (or subtraction) and one multiplication (or division) [15]. Evaluating kernel functions $\kappa(a_i, a_j)$ is needed for the composition of the kernel matrix K. In both polynomial kernels and Gaussian kernels, the main computation in $\kappa(a_i, a_j)$ is an inner product of two data items in m-dimensional space, which takes $O(m)$. Hence the total cost for the composition of kernel matrix is $O(mn^2)$. However, we do not include the cost for evaluating the kernel functions $\kappa(a_i, a_j)$ in the comparison of computational complexity since this is required in any kernel-based methods. In Algorithm 2, the computation of $\mathcal{C}^T \mathcal{C} = M^T K M$ requires $n^2 + rn$ flops taking advantage of the special structure of the matrix M. Cholesky decomposition of $\mathcal{C}^T \mathcal{C}$ for obtaining the upper triangular matrix $\mathcal{R}$ in (16) takes $O(\frac{r^3}{6})$ flops since $\mathcal{C}^T \mathcal{C}$ is $r \times r$ where r is the number of clusters. Once we obtain the upper triangular matrix $\mathcal{R}$, then the lower dimensional representation $\hat{x} = \mathcal{Q}_r^T \Phi(x)$ of a specific input x can be computed without computing $\mathcal{R}^{-1}$, but from solving a linear system

$$\mathcal{R}^T \hat{x} = \left[\begin{array}{c} \frac{1}{n_1} \sum_{i \in N_1} \kappa(a_i, x) \\ \vdots \\ \frac{1}{n_r} \sum_{i \in N_r} \kappa(a_i, x) \end{array} \right], \qquad (18)$$

which requires $O(\frac{r^2}{2} + n)$ flops. Typically the number of classes is much smaller than the total number of training

Algorithm 2 Kernel Orthogonal Centroid Method

Given a data matrix $A \in \mathbb{R}^{m \times n}$ with r classes and index sets N_i, $i = 1, \cdots, r$ which denote the set of the column indices of the data in the class i, and a kernel function κ, this algorithm computes nonlinear dimension reduced representation $\hat{x} = Q_r^T \Phi(x) \in \mathbb{R}^{r \times 1}$ for any input vector $x \in \mathbb{R}^{m \times 1}$.

1. Formulate the kernel matrix K based on the kernel function κ as

$$K(i,j) = \kappa(a_i, a_j), 1 \leq i, j \leq n.$$

2. Compute $C^T C = M^T K M$ where

$$M(i,j) = \left\{ \begin{array}{ll} 1/n_j & \text{if } i \in N_j \\ 0 & \text{otherwise} \end{array} \right. , 1 \leq i \leq n, 1 \leq j \leq r.$$

3. Compute the Cholesky factor $\mathcal{R}$ of $C^T C$:
$C^T C = \mathcal{R}^T \mathcal{R}$.

4. The solution $\hat{x}$ for the linear system

$$\mathcal{R}^T \hat{x} = \left[\begin{array}{c} \frac{1}{n_1} \sum_{i \in N_1} \kappa(a_i, x) \\ \vdots \\ \frac{1}{n_r} \sum_{i \in N_r} \kappa(a_i, x) \end{array} \right]$$

gives r-dimensional representation of x.

---

samples n. Therefore, the complexity in nonlinear dimensional reduction by the Kernel Orthogonal Centroid method presented in Algorithm 2 is $O(n^2)$. However, the kernel-based LDA or PCA needs to handle an eigenvalue problem of size $n \times n$ where n is the number of training samples, which is more expensive to compute [5, 6, 7, 15].

Our proposed method can achieve dramatic computational savings by optimizing the between-class relationship, finding much cheaper algorithm and taking advantage of linear separability in a high dimensional feature space transformed by kernel functions. While linear or nonlinear Discriminant Analysis can consider the minimization of the within-class scatter as well as the maximization of the between-class distances, they have some disadvantages. The nonsingularity of scatter matrices should be appropriately taken care of. The eigenvalue decomposition requires high computational complexity and memory requirement. Making an optimal balance between within-class and between-class scatteredness can make model selection for kernel functions difficult, since it is impossible to maximize between-class scatter and minimize within-class scatter at the same time. In the next section, we present the numerical test results that compare the effectiveness of our proposed method to other existing methods. We also visualize data distribution in the reduced dimensional space using various dimension reduction methods.

4. Computational Test Results

The Kernel Orthogonal Centroid method has been implemented in C on IBM SP at the University of Minnesota Supercomputing Institute in order to investigate its computational performance. The prediction accuracy of classification of the test data whose dimension was reduced to the number of classes by our KOC method was compared to other existing linear and nonlinear feature extraction methods. We used two of the most commonly used kernels, polynomial and Gaussian kernels shown in (11) and (12) for our KOC method. Our experimental results illustrate that when the Orthogonal Centroid method is combined with a nonlinear mapping, as in the KOC algorithm, with an appropriate kernel function, the linear separability of the data is increased in the reduced dimensional space.

4.1. Performance in Classification

In our first test, the purpose was to compare the effectiveness of dimension reduction from our KOC method in classification. For this purpose, we compared the accuracy of binary classification results where the dimension of the data items are reduced by our KOC method as well as by the kernel Fisher discriminant (KFD) method of Mika et al. [6]. The test results presented in Table 1 are for binary classifications for comparisons to KFD which can handle two-class cases only. For more details on the test data generation and results, see [6], where the authors presented the kernel Fisher Discriminant(KFD) method for the binary-class with substantial test results comparing their method to other classifiers.

In Table 1, we present the implementation results on five data sets which Mika et al. have used in their tests[1] [6]. The data sets which are not already clustered or with more than two classes were reorganized so that the results have only two classes. Each data set has 100 pairs of training and test data items which were generated from one pool of data items. For each data set, the average accuracy is calculated by running these 100 cases. Parameters for the best candidate for the kernel function and SVM are determined based on a 5 fold cross-validation using the first five training sets. We repeat their results in the first five columns of Table 1 which show the prediction accuracies in percentage (%) from the RBF classifier(RBF), AdaBoost(AB), regularized AdaBoost, SVM and KFD. For more details, see [6].

---

[1] The breast cancer data set was obtained from the University Medical Center, Inst. of Oncology, Ljubljana, Yugoslavia. Thanks to M. Zwitter and M. Soklic for the data.

	Data dimension	Results from [6]					KOC	
		RBF	AB	AB_R	SVM	KFD	Gaussian (σ)	poly. d=3
B.cancer	9	72.4	69.6	73.5	74.0	**74.2**	75.0 (5.0)	**76.4**
German	20	75.3	72.5	75.7	**76.4**	76.3	**76.3** (6.0)	74.6
Heart	13	82.4	79.7	83.5	**84.0**	83.9	83.9 (49.0)	**84.9**
Thyroid	5	95.5	95.6	95.4	95.2	**95.8**	95.5 (1.8)	88.9
Twonorm	20	97.1	97.0	97.3	97.0	**97.4**	**97.6** (38.0)	97.6

Table 1. The prediction accuracies (%) are shown. The first part (RBF to KFD) is from [6]. The last two columns are from the proposed Kernel Orthogonal Centroid method. For each test, the best prediction accuracy result is shown in boldface.

The results shown in the column for KOC are obtained from the *linear* soft margin SVM classification using the software svm^{light} [16] after dimension reduction by KOC. Since the number of classes is two, KOC reduces the dimension to 2, while the reduced dimension is one in KFD. The test results with the polynomial kernel with degree 3 and the Gaussian kernel with an optimal σ value for each data set are presented in Table 1. The results show that our method obtained comparable accuracy to other methods in all the tests we performed. Using our KOC algorithm, we were able to achieve substantial computational savings not only due to the lower computational complexity of our algorithm, but from using a *linear* SVM. Since no kernel function (or *identity* kernel function) is involved in the classification process by a linear SVM, the parameter w in the representation of the optimal separating hyperplane $f(x) = w^T x + b$ can be computed explicitly, saving substantial computation time in the testing stage. In addition, due to the dimension reduction, kernel function values are computed with inner products between much shorter vectors.

Our second test is to show the performance of KOC method on high dimensional data. We obtained datasets with high dimensionality from UCI repository [17]. Each dataset was split to the training data and test data of equal size. In order to avoid the possible bias, we repeated experiments 5 times by splitting the dataset randomly and report mean and standard deviation of prediction accuracy. For this test, we used kNN classifier in the reduced dimensional space obtained by linear and nonlinear dimension reduction methods as well as in the original dimensional space. For all the dimension reduction methods used, the reduced dimension was the number of classes. Table 2 compares the prediction accuracies showing the effectiveness of KOC method.

4.2. Performance of the Support Vector Machines

Using an artificial data, we compared the performance of classification on the soft-margin SVMs using the origi-

nal data as well as using the data of which the dimension is reduced by our KOC. The artificial data we generated has three classes. Each class consists of 200 data points uniformly distributed in the cubic region with height 1.4, width 4 and length 18.5. The three classes intersect each other as shown in the first figure of Figure 3, for the total of 600 given data points. The test data are generated following the same rules as the training data, but independently from the training data.

In order to apply the SVMs to solve a three-class problem with classes C_1, C_2 and C_3, we used the method where after a binary classification of C_1 vs. not C_1 ($C_1/\sim C_1$) is determined, data classified not to be in the class C_1 is further classified to be in C_2 or C_3 (C_2/C_3). There are three different ways to organize the binary classifiers for a three-class problem depending on which classifier $C_i/\sim C_i$, $i = 1, 2, 3$, is considered in the first step. One may run all three cases to achieve better prediction accuracy. We present the results obtained from $C_1/\sim C_1$ and C_2/C_3, since all three ways produced comparable results in our tests.

In Figure 3, the prediction accuracy and the number of support vectors for the generated artificial data are shown when the nonlinear soft margin SVM is applied in the original dimension and the *linear* soft margin SVM is applied in the reduced dimension obtained from our KOC algorithm. In both cases, Gaussian kernels with various σ values were used. While the best prediction accuracy among various σ values is similar in both cases, it is interesting to note that the number of support vectors is much less in the case of the linear soft margin SVM with data in the reduced space. In addition, the performance and the number of support vectors are less sensitive to the value of σ after dimension reduction by the KOC algorithm.

The test results confirm that the KOC algorithm is an effective method in extracting important nonlinear features. Once the features are extracted, the computation of finding the optimal separating hyperplane and classification of new data become much more efficient. An added benefit we

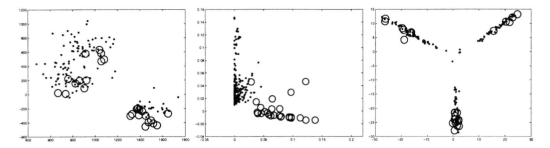

Figure 2. Musk data represented in a 2-dimensional space. The first figure is obtained by the Orthogonal Centroid Method. The second and third figure are by KOC and Kernel PCA with Gaussian kernels where $\sigma = 10^5$ (the second) and $6 * 10^5$ (the third), respectively.

Dataset			kNN	Original	OCM	KOC	Kernel PCA
Musk			k = 1	94.6 (0.3)	87.2 (0.2)	95.7 (0.4)	87.8 (0.6)
dim.	class	total	15	94.9 (0.2)	88.5 (0.3)	96.0 (0.1)	89.2 (0.5)
167	2	6599	29	94.0 (0.2)	88.5 (0.4)	96.1 (0.1)	88.5 (0.8)
Isolet5			1	76.4 (1.8)	82.3 (1.9)	86.5 (1.9)	74.6 (1.8)
dim.	class	total	15	78.5 (1.9)	82.5 (2.4)	84.9 (1.9)	75.1 (1.7)
617	26	1559	29	75.8 (1.2)	81.5 (1.7)	83.8 (1.6)	72.7 (1.6)

Table 2. Performance on high dimensional datasets. Mean and standard deviation of prediction accuracies (%) from 5 runnings.

observed in all our tests is that after the kernel-based nonlinear feature extraction by the KOC algorithm, the simple linear SVM can be effectively used achieving further efficiency in computation. A merit of the KOC method is that after its dramatic dimension reduction, in the classification stage the comparison between the vectors by any similarity measure such as Euclidean distance (L_2 norm) or cosine becomes much more efficient, since we now compare the vectors with r components each, rather than m components each.

5. Conclusion

We have presented a new method for nonlinear feature extraction called the Kernel Orthogonal Centroid (KOC). The KOC method reduces the dimension of the input data down to the number of classes. The dimension reducing nonlinear transformation is a composite of two mappings; the first implicitly maps the data into a feature space by using a kernel function, and the second mapping with orthonormal vectors in the feature space is found so that the data items belonging to different clusters are maximally separated. One of the major advantages of our KOC method is its computational efficiency, compared to other kernel-based methods such as kernel PCA [5] or KFD [6, 18]

and GDA [7]. The efficiency compared to other nonlinear feature extraction method utilizing discriminant analysis is achieved by only considering the between-class scatter relationship and by developing an algorithm which achieves this purpose from finding an orthonormal basis of the centroids, which is far cheaper than computing the eigenvectors.

The experimental results illustrate that the KOC algorithm achieves an effective lower dimensional representation of the input data which are not linearly separable, when combined with the right kernel function. With the proposed feature extraction method, we were able to achieve comparable or better prediction accuracy to other existing classification methods in our tests. In addition, when it is used with the SVM, in all our tests the linear SVM performed as well and with far less number of support vectors, further reducing the computational costs in the test stage.

Acknowledgements

The authors would like to thank the University of Minnesota Supercomputing Institute (MSI) for providing the computing facilities. We also would like to thank Dr. S. Mika for valuable information.

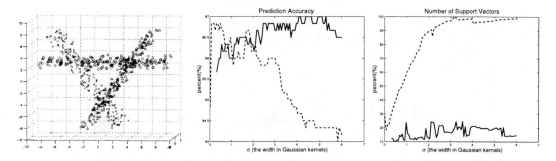

Figure 3. The left graph shows the training data. The second figure shows the prediction accuracy in the full input space by a SVM with a Gaussian kernel (dashed line), and that in the reduced dimensional space obtained by our KOC method with a Gaussian kernel and a linear SVM (solid line). The last graph compares the number of support vectors generated in the training process.

References

[1] R.O. Duda, P.E. Hart, and D.G. Stork. *Pattern Classification.* Wiley-interscience, New York, 2001.

[2] K. Fukunaga. *Introduction to Statistical Pattern Recognition.* Acadamic Press, second edition, 1990.

[3] S. Saitoh. *Theory of Reproducing Kernels and its Applications.* Longman Scientific & Technical, Harlow, England, 1988.

[4] B. Schölkopf, S. Mika, C.J.C. Burges, P. Knirsch, K.-R. Müller, G. Rätsch, and A.J. Smola. Input space versus feature space in kernel-based methods. *IEEE transactions on neural networks,* 10(5):1000–1017, September 1999.

[5] B. Schölkopf, A.J. Smola, and K.-R. Müller. Nonlinear component analysis as a kernel eigenvalue problem. *Neural computation,* 10:1299–1319, 1998.

[6] S. Mika, G. Rätsch, J. Weston, B. Schölkopf, and K.-R. Müller. Fisher discriminant analysis with kernels. In E.Wilson J.Larsen and S.Douglas, editors, *Neural networks for signal processing IX,* pages 41–48. IEEE, 1999.

[7] G. Baudat and F. Anouar. Generalized discriminant analysis using a kernel approach. *Neural computation,* 12:2385–2404, 2000.

[8] V. Roth and V. Steinhage. Nonlinear discriminant analysis using kernel functions. *Advances in neural information processing systems,* 12:568–574, 2000.

[9] S.A. Billings and K.L. Lee. Nonlinear fisher discriminant analysis using a minimum squared error cost function and the orthogonal least squares algorithm. *Neural networks,* 15(2):263–270, 2002.

[10] H. Park, M. Jeon, and J.B. Rosen. Lower dimensional representation of text data based on centroids and least squares. *BIT Numerical Mathematics,* 43(2):1–22, 2003.

[11] P. Howland and H. Park. Generalizing discriminant analysis using the generalized singular value decomposition. Technical Reports 03-013, Department of Computer Science and Engineering, University of Minnesosta, Twin Cities.

[12] J. Ye, R. Janardan, C.H. Park, and H. Park. A new optimization criterion for generalized discriminant analysis on undersampled problems. To appear in the Proceedings of the third IEEE International Conference on Data Mining.

[13] N. Cristianini and J. Shawe-Taylor. *An Introduction to Support Vector Machines and other kernel-based learning methods.* Cambridge, 2000.

[14] C.J.C. Burges. A tutorial on support vector machines for pattern recognition. *Data Mining and Knowledge Discovery,* 2(2):121–167, 1998.

[15] G.H. Golub and C.F. Van Loan. *Matrix Computations.* Johns Hopkins University Press, first edition, 1983.

[16] T.Joachims. Making large-scale svm learning practical. LS8-Report 24, Universität Dortmund, LS VIII-Report, 1998.

[17] http://www.ics.uci.edu/~mlearn/MLRepository.html

[18] S. Mika, G. Rätsch, J. Weston, B. Schölkopf, A.J. Smola, and K.-R. Müller. Invariant feature extraction and classification in kernel spaces. *Advances in neural information processing systems,* 12:526–532, 2000.

Sequence Modeling with Mixtures of Conditional Maximum Entropy Distributions

Dmitry Pavlov *
Yahoo Inc.
701 First Avenue
Sunnyvale, California 94089
dpavlov@yahoo-inc.com

Abstract

We present a novel approach to modeling sequences using mixtures of conditional maximum entropy (maxent) distributions. Our method generalizes the mixture of first-order Markov models by including the "long-term" dependencies in model components. The "long-term" dependencies are represented by the frequently used in the natural language processing (NLP) domain probabilistic triggers or rules (such as "A occurred k positions back" $\implies$ "the current symbol is B" with probability P). The maxent framework is then used to create a coherent global probabilistic model from all selected triggers. In this paper, we enhance this formalism by using probabilistic mixtures with maxent models as components, thus representing hidden or unobserved effects in the data. We demonstrate how our mixture of conditional maxent models can be learned from data using the generalized EM algorithm that scales linearly in the dimensions of the data and the number of mixture components. We present empirical results on the simulated and real-world data sets and demonstrate that the proposed approach enables us to create better quality models than the mixtures of first-order Markov models and resist overfitting and curse of dimensionality that would inevitably present themselves for the higher order Markov models.

1 Introduction

Analyzing protein families or DNA sequences, understanding behavior of a Web user on a Web site, preventing intrusions on a UNIX system, recommending books to the customers of the Internet bookstore—all these and many other tasks can be reduced to a sequence modeling problem.

Consider the following probabilistic statement of a discrete sequence modeling problem. Given a set of sequences $S = \{S_1, \ldots, S_N\}$ in the alphabet A, find a probability model P best approximating the "true" distribution that generated the data.[1]

Arguably, this is one of the central problems in knowledge discovery and data mining, and it is not surprising that there exist a number of methods to solve it. The popular choices include mixtures of zeroth and first order Markov models. In these models, a probability of a sequence S is first factorized using the chain rule $P(S) = \prod_k P(D_k|H_k)$, where D_k is the k-th item in S, and H_k is the history of the k-th item in S, i.e. all (ordered) items preceding D_k. The chain rule thus reduces a problem of modeling $P(S)$ to the problem of modeling conditional distributions $P(D|H)$ for the item D and its history H. To learn a distribution $P(D|H)$, we can model H as either unordered sequence ("bag-of-items") in the zeroth order model or as a single previous item (D_{-1}) in the first order model. When these models are used in a mixture, they are capable of not only handling vast amounts of high-dimensional data but also produce acceptable quality models as reported by a number of papers in the past [4, 3, 19].

Improvements to these models can be sought in two major directions: assuming a richer latent structure in the data, as is done in hidden Markov models (HMMs) [23], or increasing the order of the model, i.e. allowing D to depend on $k > 1$ previous symbols in H. In this paper, we do not pursue the former venue in the current paper leaving the comparisons of our methodology with HMMs for future. The proposed increase in the order of the model is also often problematic because of the curse of dimensionality and related overfitting issues. Indeed, the memory complexity for the k-th order Markov model is exponential in k, $O(|A|^{k+1})$. Notice, however, that one could extract a much larger number of low-order statistics from H than is

---

* Work done at NEC Laboratories America.

[1] In what follows, we work in the (commonly used) i.i.d. assumption, i.e. we assume that the sequences were generated independently of one another by a fixed stationary distribution.

done by the first-order Markov model. The latter essentially discards all of H but the last observed item D_{-1}. In particular, we may have grounds to believe that an item D_{-k}, $k > 1$, observed farther in H than D_{-1}, bears some information of what the current item D should be. Or, we can limit H to at most k items preceding D and use events of the type $\{D = b | a \in H\}$, for various $a, b \in A$. In what follows we will refer to events of the type $\{D = b | a \in H\}$ as non-position-specific (non-PS) triggers and to events of the type $D = b | D_{-k} = a)$ as position-specific (PS) triggers. Importantly, we can not only efficiently extract triggers from data, but also rank them according to their potential predictive power. More precisely, we can measure the quality of triggers by computing mutual information between events $E = \{D = b\}$ and either $E_1 = \{a \in H\}$ or $E_2 = \{D_{-k} = a\}$ and discard low scoring triggers.

How can the possibly overlapping sparse low-order information about D be used to create a global coherent probabilistic model $P(D|H)$? The maxent framework provides such an ability. Maxent modeling has a long history, beginning as a concept in physics and later working its way into the foundations of information theory and Bayesian statistics [11]. In recent years, advances in computing and the growth of available data contributed to increased popularity of maxent modeling, leading to a number of successful applications, including NLP [1], language modeling [5], part of speech tagging [22], database querying [21], and protein modeling [2], to name a few.

The maxent approach has several attractive properties that have contributed to its popularity:

1. The approach guarantees that the obtained distribution is as close as possible to the uniform, which makes it as "flat" as possible, subject to specific constraints given (triggers in our case). Note that unlike in Markov mixtures, the maxent modeling allows us to create a model from any number of constraints. In particular, we may use only a fraction of first-order Markov statistics. As we show in our experiments, this could be advantageous for sparse high-dimensional data.

2. The method is semi-parametric, meaning that the learned distribution can take on any form that adheres to the constraints. In this way, maxent modeling is able to combine sparse local information encoded in the constraints into a coherent global probabilistic model, without a priori assuming any particular distributional form.

3. The method is capable of combining heterogeneous and overlapping sources of information, and finally, under fairly general assumptions, maxent modeling has been shown to be equivalent to maximum-likelihood modeling of distributions from the exponential family [7].

Maxent modeling in the context of protein family modeling and the triggers was previously explored in [14, 2]. Present work extends this setting by adding the important ability to handle latent information. This paper also extends our recent work [20], where we considered *mixtures of maxent models* for classification, to handle sequential data. The latent maxent principle was also introduced in a general setting by Wang et. al. [24]. In particular, they gave a motivation for generalizing the standard Jaynes maxent principle [11] to include latent variables and formulated a convergence theorem of the associated EM algorithm.

We come from the assumption that many data sets with seemingly complex distributional structures can be seen as generated by several simpler latent distributions that are not directly observable. Consider, for instance, the case when the access to the Web from a home computer is performed by several family members who have different but possibly overlapping interests, and as a result browse different sites. On the server side, we observe the sequences of accesses to Web pages, but do not know who they belong to. It is reasonable to expect that we could come up with a simpler and better quality model if we attempted to model the observed data as a mixture of components, one for each of the family members. Other types of hidden information include gender, group age, marital status, income and so on, all potentially indicative of user browsing behavior on the Web. *Mixture models* [16] are designed to handle just such a case. In a sense, discovering the underlying structure in a data set can be thought of as an unsupervised learning subtask within a larger supervised learning problem. In cases where data can be decomposed into latent clusters, our framework leverages this extra structural information to produce models with higher out-of-sample log-likelihood.

Note that modeling latent structure won't enable us to tell with certainty whether a user behind the screen is, for instance, a single millionaire or a married graduate student. However, once the components are learned we can attempt interpreting them as was done, for instance, by Cadez et.al., who analyzed the market basket data fit with a mixture of multinomial models in [4] and Web browsing patterns on the *msnbc.com* site in [3]. A more recent example of such analysis in the context of maxent mixtures can be found in [13].

Similar to the case of the mixture of Markov models, in maxent mixture modeling each sequence is assigned a vector of probability labels, reflecting the degree with which it belongs to each of the clusters k. Thus, another attractive property of the proposed method is that it defines a "soft" clustering over all sequences.

The main contributions of this paper are as follows:

1. proposed a probabilistic framework to efficiently model long term dependencies in discrete sequential data;

2. introducing the mixture modeling in the context of exponential family models learned with maxent from the triggers;

3. derivation of the generalized EM algorithm [8] for learning such mixture models;

4. experimental evaluation of the proposed model showing improvements over the standard maxent and the mixture of Markov models.

The rest of the paper is organized as follows. In Section 2 we briefly describe the mixture of Markov models that is commonly used for modeling sequential data. Section 3 introduces the maxent framework for sequence modeling, and shows how it can be integrated into the mixture modeling framework. In Section 4, we present the experimental evaluation of the proposed methodology and Section 5 concludes the paper by summarizing the contributions and outlining the directions of future work.

2 Markov Mixture Model

In the first order Markov model, the main assumption is that the current item depends on the history H only through the last observed item in H, i.e. D_{-1}. The equations defining the *mixture of Markov models* are as follows:

$$P(D|H) = \sum_{k=1}^{N_c} \alpha_k \left[\theta_{0,k} \prod_{h=1}^{|H|} \theta_{(h \to h+1),k} \right] \tag{1}$$

where the first equation is just a standard equation for the mixture, while the second equation uncovers how each component is modeled; $\theta_{0,k}$ is the probability of observing H_0 as a first item in the history, and $\theta_{(h \to h+1),k}$ is the probability of observing a transition from item number h to item number $h + 1$ in the history. For $h = |H|$, item with index $h + 1$ is D. This model can be learned by using the EM algorithm. The number of parameters is quadratic in the number of items and linear in the number of components.

3 MaxEnt Framework

3.1 Trigger Maximum Entropy Model

As we mentioned above, the higher order Markov models cannot be reliably learned and used because of the curse of dimensionality. Thus, we have to restrict ourselves to models that can be reliably estimated from the low-order statistics but still model the whole history H. This leads

us to consider triggers as low-order statistics and the maxent framework as a way to combine the low-order information into a coherent global probabilistic model as was done in [12].

For the purposes of this paper, a *non-position-specific* (non-PS) trigger is a probabilistic rule involving a pair of items (a, b) and a fixed natural number k such that $a \in H_k \implies D = b$ with probability $p = P(D = b | a \in H_k)$, where H_k is the history H of item D truncated to include only k most recent items preceding D. A *position-specific* (PS) trigger is defined similarly except it involves events $D_{-k} = a \implies D = b$. To measure the quality of triggers and in order to filter them, one can compute mutual information between events $E = \{D = b\}$ and $E_1 = \{a \in H_k\}$ (or $E_2 = \{D_{-k} = b\}$) and discard low scoring triggers.

We define a set of features used for maxent modeling as indicator functions $F_s(D, H)$, $s = 1, \ldots, S$, based on the individual items as well as bigrams and triggers with high mutual information scores. For example, a feature number s corresponding to a bigram $\{D = a, D_{-1} = b\}$ is defined as

$$F_s(D, H) = \begin{cases} 1 & \text{, if } D = a, D_{-1} = b \\ 0 & \text{, otherwise.} \end{cases}$$

Features corresponding to individual items and triggers are defined similarly.

The set of features together with maxent as an objective function, leads to the following form of the conditional maxent model [12]:

$$P(D|H) = \frac{1}{Z_\lambda(H)} \exp\left[\sum_{s=1}^{S} \lambda_s F_s(D, H) \right], \tag{2}$$

where $Z_\lambda(H)$ is a normalization constant ensuring that the distribution sums to 1. The set of parameters $\{\lambda\}$ is found from the following set of equations that restrict the distribution $P(D|H)$ to have the same expected value for each feature as observed in the training data:

$$\sum_H \sum_D P(D|H) F_s(D, H) = \sum_H F_s(D(H), H), \tag{3}$$

where $D(H)$ is the item following H in the training data and $s = 1, \ldots, S$. The left-hand side of Equation 3 represents the expectation of the feature $F_s(D, H)$ with respect to the distribution $P(D|H)$ and the right-hand side is the frequency of this feature in the training data (both up to the same normalization factor). There exist efficient algorithms for finding the parameters $\{\lambda\}$ (e.g. generalized [6], improved [7] and sequential conditional [10] iterative scaling algorithms) that are known to converge iff the constraints imposed on P are consistent. Several good sources [12, 9, 10] provide pseudocode for the algorithm and discuss in detail ways of speeding up learning.

Under fairly general assumptions, the maxent model can also be shown to be a maximum likelihood model [7]. Employing a Gaussian prior with a zero mean on parameters λ yields a maximum aposteriori solution that has been shown to be more accurate than the related maximum likelihood solution and other smoothing techniques for maxent models [5].

Note that in this paper we focus on the "proof of concept", i.e. on showing that the proposed approach is valuable for sequence modeling and prediction, rather than on the feature selection issues[2]. It might very well be possible that features other than the ones we consider here, such as sequence length, or, for biological sequences, symbols surrounding the current one, may be useful for modeling. An important advantage of the maxent modeling is that it allows to consistently combine diverse features into a consistent probabilistic model.

3.2 Mixture of Conditional Maxent Models

As we pointed out in the introduction, the primary motivation for considering the mixture of maxent models comes from the desire to model unobserved, hidden effects, with a potential to get a better fit to the data. In a mixture model setting, we assume that the data points are generated from a set of K clusters, with each cluster described by its own distribution:

$$P(S_p) = \sum_{k=1}^{K} P(S_p|k)\alpha_k, \qquad (4)$$

where $\alpha_k = P(k)$ is a prior probability of cluster k, $\sum_k \alpha_k = 1$ and for each $k = 1, \ldots, K$, $P(S_p|k)$ has a maxent form

$$P(S_p|k) = \prod_{l=1}^{|S_p|} P(D_{pl}|H_{pl}, k)$$

$$= \prod_{l=1}^{|S_p|} \frac{1}{Z_{plk\lambda}} exp[\sum_{s=1}^{S} \lambda_{sk} F_s(D_{pl}, H_{pl})]. (5)$$

The derivation of the generalized EM algorithm for finding parameters λ and α can be found in longer version of this paper [18]. In what follows, we present the update equations for the maximum likelihood estimates of parameter values.

In the E-step, we find the posterior distribution over the clusters, given the training sequences S_p and current values

---

[2]A comprehensive treatment of feature selection issues can be found, for instance, in [12, 15]

of parameters:

$$P_{kp} \triangleq P(cluster = k|S_p) = \frac{P(S_p|k)\alpha_k}{\sum_{k=1}^{K} P(S_p|k)\alpha_k}. (6)$$

In the M-step, we maximize the likelihood by finding the new values of parameters using the cluster memberships obtained in the E-step:

$$\alpha_k^{new} = \frac{1}{N} \sum_{p=1}^{N} P(cluster = k|S_p);$$

$$\delta_{s'k'} = \sum_{p=1}^{N} P_{k'p} \sum_{l=1}^{|S_p|} F_{s'}(D_{pl}, H_{pl})$$

$$- \sum_{p=1}^{N} P_{k'p} \sum_{l=1}^{|S_p|} \sum_{D \in A} P(D|H_{pl}, k') F_{s'}(D, H_{pl});$$

$$\lambda_{s'k'}^{new} = \lambda_{s'k'}^{old} + \epsilon \delta_{s'k'},$$

where ϵ is a small step in the direction of the gradient of the log-likelihood, ensuring that the likelihood increases, N is the total number of sequences, $|S_p|$ is the length of the p-th sequence. Finding exact values of parameters λ that maximize the likelihood is difficult since it requires solving the system of non-linear equations. However, for the GEM algorithm to converge, it is sufficient that the likelihood only increases in the M-step [17]. We employ this form of the generalized EM algorithm and do a single step of the gradient ascent for parameters λ in the M-step.

We also employ a quasi-Newton method that finds a critical point of the likelihood without computing the second order derivatives, once a good approximation to the optimum of the likelihood is found. We empirically observed that often convergence of the gradient descent may be extremely slow, and quasi-Newton methods provide a much more efficient alternative.

4 Experimental Results

We ran experiments on both simulated and real-world data sets. The main objective of experiments was to show that for a range of data sets the mixture of maxent models is capable of outperforming the mixture of Markov models at the expense of longer model-fitting times. Note that the main bottleneck in using the mixture of maxent as opposed to the mixture of Markov models is the time complexity of the algorithm. Even though it scales linearly in both the number of components and the number of constraints/features, empirically we observe that convergence is quite slow, in particular, due to the necessity to perform gradient ascent in the M-step.

Due to a strict positiveness of maxent model for any assignment to the variables, Markov and maxent mixtures are mathematically different, even when learned from the same initial information (for instance, a one-component mixture of maxent models learned from bigrams does not in general reduce to the mixture of Markov models). Thus, it makes sense to compare the models even on the data sets simulated from the simplest Markov models.

4.1 Experiments on Simulated Data

We ran two experiments on the simulated data. In the first experiment, the data was simulated from Markov mixture and our main goal was to show that maxent mixture provides the same quality of fit to the data as Markov mixture. In the second experiment, the current item D was dependent on the random item in the history H, and not necessarily on D_{-1}. In this experiment, our main goal was to show that maxent mixture is capable of delivering a consistent improvement over Markov mixture. We purposefully chose to work with low-dimensional data to make description and findings transparent. The experimental settings for both these cases are as follows.

In the first experiment, we generated the simulated data from a two-component mixture of Markov models on 3 variables. The weights of components were the same, each equal to .5. The initial distribution for each component was uniform. The transition matrices for the first and second components were

$$T^{(1)} = \begin{pmatrix} 0.1 & 0.8 & 0.1 \\ 0.1 & 0.1 & 0.8 \\ 0.8 & 0.1 & 0.1 \end{pmatrix}, T^{(2)} = \begin{pmatrix} 0.8 & 0.1 & 0.1 \\ 0.1 & 0.8 & 0.1 \\ 0.1 & 0.1 & 0.8 \end{pmatrix}.$$

We used the model to simulate 1000 sequences for each of the training and test data sets. The length of the sequence was 30 plus a random number uniformly distributed in the range $[0, 9]$. We also assumed the best number of components (2) was known in advance, and only explored the question of which of the models provided the better fit to the data. Maxent did not use triggers in this experiment.

In order to compare the models we generated 100 random data sets from the model and plotted the average test set loglikelihood (LL) (normalized per sequence symbol) in Figure 1. The bisecting line is the line of equal LL. This experiment confirmed our expectations that maxent mixture shows similar performance to Markov mixture. In particular, the average LL across 100 runs is -0.9747 for maxent and -0.9744 for Markov mixture.

In the second set of experiments, we again generated 100 data sets using the same components, but this time the next generated symbol was dependent on a random symbol in the history, and not necessarily on the previous one as before. We refer to this model as non-Markov mixture. Three mixture models were used to fit the data sampled from the non-Markov mixture: Markov, maxent with non-PS triggers and maxent with PS triggers. For all models a single run of

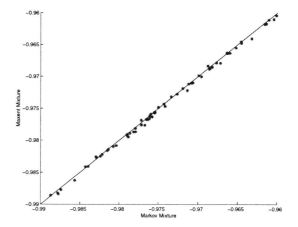

Figure 1. Test set loglikelihood (LL) for Markov (x-axis) versus maxent (y-axis) mixtures.

EM algorithm was made, with a stopping criterion set to 10^{-6} on the relative change in LL between two consecutive iterations. Figure 2 shows how the average across 100 sampled data sets test set LL delivered by the competing mixture models depends on the number of components. Again, in line with our expectations maxent mixture consistently outperformed Markov mixture. The same relationship was verified on the individual runs. We thus claim that maxent mixture provides a better fit to the data, and should be preferred to Markov mixture.

4.2 Experiments on Real World Data

We ran experiments on a number of data sets, including the data collected from $msnbc.com$[3] and used in [3], UNIX user[4] and hemoglobins[5] data sets.

For all data sets, we performed cross-validation by sampling 15 sets of training, holdout and test data from the full set of sequences in the proportion 2 : 1 : 1. The training of both Markov and maxent mixtures was stopped when either the relative increase in the train LL was less than 10^{-4} or when the LL on the holdout data started increasing. The history length in maxent mixtures was chosen to equal 5. For both Markov and maxent mixtures we experimented with $1, \ldots, 5$ component models.

We compared the models with respect to the test set LL, which is a commonly used performance measure for sequential data. The results were averaged across cross-validation trials.

---

[3]http://www.msnbc.com
[4]http://kdd.ics.uci.edu
[5]http://www.ics.uci.edu/~icadez/projects/proteins

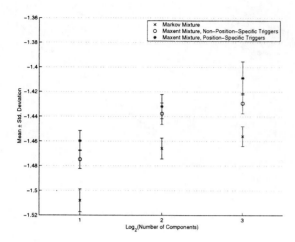

Figure 2. Error bar plots of mean test set LL (± std. dev.) delivered by the competing mixture models as a function of the number of components.

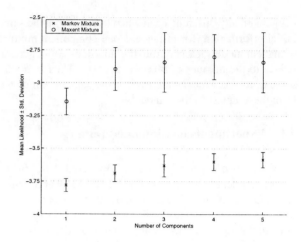

Figure 3. *Hemoglobins data.* **Error bar plots of mean test set LL (± std. dev.) delivered by Markov and maxent mixtures across 15 cross-validation runs.**

4.2.1 Hemoglobins Data

The hemoglobins data consisted of 585 hemoglobin protein sequences in the alphabet containing a total 23 characters (aminoacids and stop-deletion characters). For hemoglobins data, we worked with 50% top bigrams and 50% top PS triggers, so that the actual number of parameters in maxent model was roughly 3 times greater than in Markov model. These parameters (as well as parameters of the models on the other data sets) were set after some experimentation and before the full cross-validation was run.

Figure 3 illustrates how the average across runs test set LL measured in bits per item depends on the number of mixture components.

Note that for all number of components, the trigger maxent mixture outperforms Markov mixture. The advantage of maxent models is slightly less than 1 bit per symbol on average. Note also that 1 component maxent mixture outpeforms 3 component Markov mixture by about 0.5 bit per symbol and has roughly the same number of parameters. In a separate run (not presented on the plot) we confirmed that even for 25, 50, 75 and 100-component Markov mixtures the average LL of the Markov model was never greater than -3.5. The mixture modeling also helps both Markov and maxent models improve their performance as compared to single component models.

We also measured the increase in predictive accuracy with the increase in the number of components. To measure predictive accuracy, we divided the number of times the predicted (highest probability) aminoacid actually appeared next in the sequence by the total number of predic-

tions on the test data. Prediction accuracy increased from 16.5% for 1 component Markov mixture to 19.17% for a 5 component mixture on average across cross-validation runs. As to the maxent mixture, the corresponding numbers are 38.85% and 48.62%, essentially meaning that for a 5 component mixture we can correctly predict the next aminoacid 50% of the time.

The time taken to train a 1 component maxent mixture on the hemoglobins data set was about 404 seconds per 48 iterations, which corresponds to about 8.5 seconds per iteration of EM per mixture component. This is quite a bit longer than 0.16 seconds per iteration of EM per parameter in Markov mixtures. Note however, that maxent had 3 times more parameters, so effectively we should compare 2.83 seconds to 0.16 seconds, which suggests that maxent times are still manageable. As our experiments suggest, uncovering potential mixture structure and obtaining the improvement in model fit, could well be worth spending the extra time. Furthermore, one could try employing recent advances in speeding up maxent learning [10] to alleviate the complexity associated with the learning time and we plan to study this possibility in the future.

We conclude by emphasizing that the highly encouraging predictive modeling results on the protein data are attributed to modeling long-term sequence dependencies and could improve further with appropriate feature selection. But even the present evidence suggests that advantages of the maxent mixture over a single-component maxent model and the Markov mixture could be quite significant.

4.2.2 UNIX User Data

The UNIX user data was collected over several years from UNIX users at Purdue University. The data for a specific user we considered (number 6) consisted of roughly 250 different commands with an order of 2500 total sequences available. For UNIX user data, we worked with 25% top bigrams and 25% top PS triggers, so that the actual number of parameters (per component) in maxent model was only 24. This explains why maxent mixture avoided overfitting.

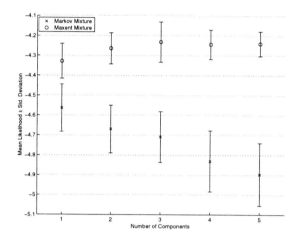

Figure 4. *UNIX user data.* **Error bar plots of mean test set LL (± std. dev.) delivered by Markov and maxent mixtures across 15 cross-validation runs.**

On the other hand, Markov mixture had 1876 parameters, i.e. almost 80 times greater than maxent, and its likelihood Markov mixture, as can be seen in Figure 4, decreased as the number of components increased. This happened despite of employing Dirichlet priors for the parameters of the Markov mixture.

Thus, unlike Markov mixtures, maxent mixtures allowed us to choose the number of features supplied to the model and thus be more flexible in parsimony-accuracy tradeoff. This feature selection in maxent can be used along or instead of choosing prior distributions on the parameters for high-dimensional sparse data sets, or for data sets with only few data points.

4.2.3 Msnbc Data

The *msnbc.com* data was represented by sequences of topics corresponding to user accesses to pages on the *msnbc.com* Web site during a single day in September 28, 1999. There is a total of 14 categories, including sports, news, etc. Each time a page was requested, its category was recorded in the log file. We preprocessed this data by collapsing every two consecutive categories into a single one, and then followed by removing all single category requests. We worked with a random set of 50,000 sequences in our experiments with this data.

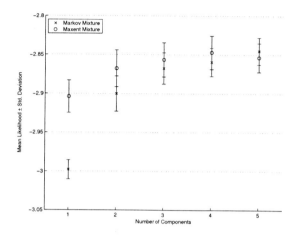

Figure 5. *MSNBC data.* **Error bar plots of mean test set LL (± std. dev.) delivered by Markov and maxent mixtures across 15 cross-validation runs.**

For *msnbc.com* data, we worked with all bigrams and 50% top PS triggers, so that the actual number of parameters (per component) in maxent mixture was roughly twice higher than in Markov mixture. Figure 5 shows the average test set LL plots for Markov and maxent mixtures versus the number of components. Note that even though maxent shows some advantage over Markov for 1 component mixtures, the models show roughly same performance for greater number of components.

Note that each sequence recorded in the data represents a single day worth of accesses to *msnbc.com* per user. This could make two consecutive accesses far apart in time, and, as a result, misrepresent the influence of one access on another.

For this data set and within the scope of experiments we ran, we conclude that position specific triggers provide little to no additional improvement beyond the Markov mixture.

In the future, we plan to undertake a more detailed study of two mixtures for the Web data, in particular having recommendation (prediction) and visualization tasks in mind.

5   Conclusions and Future Work

We presented a methodology for modeling sequential data that exploits the latent structure in the data using a mixture of maxent models. We defined a mixture of maxent models and derived a generalized EM algorithm for solving the corresponding optimization problem. Our experiments on both simulated and real-world data sets suggest that the mixture of maxent models can provide a significant improvement over the widely used mixtures of first-order Markov models. The idea of employing the mixture of maxent models to uncover and exploit the latent structure in the data can be generalized to such applications as chemical naming, Internet user disambiguation, online recommending and others.

The major algorithmical challenge that remains open is how to make the model scalable to high-dimensional data. In the previous work [19], we used clustering and maxent models for recommending documents to Citeseer users. The two modeling steps were decoupled, i.e. clustering of the documents was performed first and then maxent was used to model user access sequences projected onto clusters, and thus could lead to a suboptimal performance. Even though in this paper we have shown a practical value to coupling the clustering procedure (done by the mixture) with maxent modeling, still in the present form the method remains prohibitively slow for use with high dimensional data sets.

In the future, we also plan to study how the maxent mixture can be used for prediction and data visualization as well as perform comparisons with HMMs, a more powerful rival than Markov mixtures.

6   Acknowledgements

We would like to thank David Heckerman and *msnbc.com* for providing the data for experiments. We also thank David Pennock, Alexandrin Popescul, Lyle Ungar, Andrew Schein, Darya Chudova and Eren Manavoglu for many productive discussions and support.

References

[1] A. Berger, S. Della Pietra, and V. Della Pietra. A maximum entropy approach to natural language processing. *Computational Linguistics*, 22(1):39–72, 1996.

[2] E. C. Buehler and L. H. Ungar. Maximum entropy methods for biological sequence modeling. In *BIOKDD*, pages 60–64, 2001.

[3] I. Cadez, D. Heckerman, C. Meek, P. Smyth, and S. White. Visualization of navigation patterns on a web site using model-based clustering. In *Knowledge Discovery and Data Mining*, pages 280–284, 2000.

[4] I. Cadez, P. Smyth, E. Ip, and H. Mannila. Predictive profiles for transaction data using finite mixture models. Technical Report UCI-ICS 01-67, UC Irvine, 2001.

[5] S. Chen and R. Rosenfeld. A Gaussian prior for smoothing maximum entropy models. Technical Report CMUCS-99-108, Carnegie Mellon University, 1999.

[6] J. N. Darroch and D. Ratcliff. Generalized iterative scaling for log-linear models. *Annals of Mathematical Statistics*, 43:1470–1480, 1972.

[7] S. Della Pietra, V. Della Pietra, and J. Lafferty. Inducing features of random fields. *IEEE Transactions on Pattern Analysis and Machine Intelligence*, 19(4):380–393, April 1997.

[8] A. P. Dempster, N. M. Laird, and D. B. Rubin. Maximum likelihood from incomplete data via the em algorithm. *Journal of the Royal Statistical Society*, B-39:1–38, 1977.

[9] J. Goodman. Classes for fast maximum entropy training. In *Proceedings of IEEE International Conference on Acoustics, Speech, and Signal Processing*, 2001.

[10] J. Goodman. Sequential conditional generalized iterative scaling. In *Association for Computational Linguistics Annual Meeting*, 2002.

[11] E. T. Jaynes. Where do we stand on maximum entropy? In *The Maximum Entropy Formalism*, pages 15—118, Cambridge MA, 1979. MIT Press.

[12] F. Jelinek. *Statistical Methods for Speech Recognition*. Cambridge. MA:MIT Press, 1998.

[13] E. Manavoglu, D. Pavlov, and C. L. Giles. Probabilstic user behavior models. In *Proceedings of the Third IEEE International Conference on Data Mining (ICDM'03)*, 2003.

[14] H. Mannila, D. Pavlov, and P. Smyth. Predictions with local patterns using cross-entropy. In *Proc. of Fifth ACM SIGKDD International Conference on Knowledge Discovery and Data Mining*, pages 357—361. New York, NY: ACM Press, 1999.

[15] A. McCallum. Efficiently inducing features of conditional ramdom fields. In *Proceedings of the 19th Conference on Uncertainty in Artficial Intelligence (UAI'03)*, 2003.

[16] G. McLachlan and K. Basford. *Mixture Models*. Marcel Dekker, New York, 1988.

[17] G. McLachlan and T. Krishnan. *The EM Algorithm and Extensions*. John Wiley and Sons, New York, 1997.

[18] D. Pavlov. Sequence modeling with mixtures of conditional maximum entropy distributions. Technical Report NEC Laboratories TR, NEC Laboratories America, 2002.

[19] D. Pavlov and D. Pennock. A maximum entropy approach to collaborative filtering in dynamic, sparse, high-dimensional domains. In *Proceedings of Neural Information Processing Systems (NIPS-2002)*, 2002.

[20] D. Pavlov, A. Popescul, D. Pennock, and L. Ungar. Mixtures of conditional maximum entropy models. In *International Conference on Machine Learning (ICML-2003)*, 2003.

[21] D. Pavlov and P. Smyth. Probabilistic query models for transaction data. In *Proceedings of Seventh ACM SIGKDD International Conference on Knowledge Discovery and Data Mining*, pages 164–173. New York, NY: ACM Press, 2001.

[22] A. Ratnaparkhi. A maximum entropy model for part-of-speech tagging. In *Proceedings of the Conference on Empirical Methods in Natural Language Processing*, pages 133–142. ACL, 1996.

[23] P. Smyth. Clustering sequences with hidden markov models. In M. C. Mozer, M. I. Jordan, and T. Petsche, editors, *Advances in Neural Information Processing Systems*, volume 9, page 648. The MIT Press, 1997.

[24] S. Wang, R. Rosenfeld, Y. Zhao, and D. Shuurmans. The latent maximum entropy principle. In *IEEE International Symposium on Information Theory (ISIT)*, 2002.

MaPle: A Fast Algorithm for Maximal Pattern-based Clustering[*]

Jian Pei   Xiaoling Zhang   Moonjung Cho   Haixun Wang   Philip S. Yu

State University of New York at Buffalo
{jianpei, xzhang7, mcho}@cse.buffalo.edu

IBM T.J. Watson Research Center
{haixun, psyu}@us.ibm.com

Abstract

Pattern-based clustering is important in many applications, such as DNA micro-array data analysis, automatic recommendation systems and target marketing systems. However, pattern-based clustering in large databases is challenging. On the one hand, there can be a huge number of clusters and many of them can be redundant and thus make the pattern-based clustering ineffective. On the other hand, the previous proposed methods may not be efficient or scalable in mining large databases.

In this paper, we study the problem of maximal pattern-based clustering. *Redundant clusters are avoided completely by mining only the maximal pattern-based clusters. MaPle, an efficient and scalable mining algorithm is developed. It conducts a depth-first, divide-and-conquer search and prunes unnecessary branches smartly. Our extensive performance study on both synthetic data sets and real data sets shows that maximal pattern-based clustering is effective. It reduces the number of clusters substantially. Moreover, MaPle is more efficient and scalable than the previously proposed pattern-based clustering methods in mining large databases.*

1 Introduction

Clustering large databases is a challenging data mining task with many important applications. Most of the previously proposed methods are based on similarity measures defined globally on a (sub)set of attributes/dimensions. However, in some applications, it is hard or even infeasible to define a good similarity measure on a global subset of attributes to serve the clustering.

To appreciate the problem, let us consider clustering the 5 objects in Figure 1(a). There are 5 dimensions. No patterns among the 5 objects are visibly explicit. However, as elaborated in Figure 1(b) and (c), respectively, objects 1, 2 and 3 follow the same pattern in dimensions a, c and d, while objects 1, 4 and 5 share another similar pattern in di-

mensions b, c, d and e. If we use the patterns as features, they form two *pattern-based clusters*.

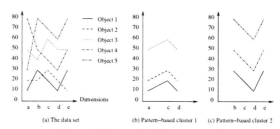

(a) The data set   (b) Pattern-based cluster 1   (c) Pattern-based cluster 2

Figure 1. A motivating example.

Some recent researches (e.g., [12]) indicate that pattern-based clustering is useful in many applications. In general, given a set of data objects, a subset of objects form a pattern-based clusters if these objects follow a similar pattern in a subset of dimensions. Comparing to the conventional clustering, pattern-based clustering is a more general model and has two distinct features. On the one hand, *it does not require a globally defined similarity measure*. Different clusters can follow different patterns on different subsets of dimensions. On the other hand, *the clusters are not necessary exclusive*. That is, an object can appear in more than one cluster.

The generality and flexibility of pattern-based clustering may provide interesting and important insights in some applications where conventional clustering methods may meet difficulties. For example, in DNA micro-array data analysis, the gene expression data are organized as matrices, where rows represent genes and columns represent samples/conditions. The number in each cell records the expression level of the particular gene under the particular condition. The matrices are often large, containing thousands of genes and hundreds of conditions. It is important to identify subsets of genes whose expression levels change coherently under a subset of conditions. Such information is critical in revealing the significant connections in gene regulatory networks. As another example, in the applications of automatic recommendation and target marketing, it is essential to identify sets of customers/clients with similar behavior/interest. As a concrete example, suppose that the ranks of movies given by customers are collected. To identify customer groups, it is essential to find the subsets

[*]This research is partially supported by NSF Grant IIS-0308001. Any opinions, findings, and conclusions or recommendations expressed in this publication are those of the authors and do not necessarily reflect the views of NSF.

of customers who rank subsets of movies similarly. In the above two examples, pattern-based clustering is the major data mining task.

Although the pattern-based clustering problem is proposed and a mining algorithm is developed by Wang et al. [12], some important problems remain not thoroughly explored. In particular, we address the following two fundamental issues and make corresponding contributions in this paper.

First, *what is the effective representation of pattern-based clusters?* As can be imagined, there can exist many pattern-based clusters in a large database. Given a pattern-based cluster C, any non-empty subset of the objects in the cluster is trivially a pattern-based cluster on any non-empty subset of dimensions. Mining and analyzing a huge number of pattern-based clusters may become the bottleneck of effective analysis. *Can we devise a non-redundant representation of the pattern-based clusters?*

Our contributions. In this paper, we propose the mining of *maximal pattern-based clusters*. The idea is to report only those non-redundant pattern-based clusters, and skip their trivial sub-clusters. We show that, by mining maximal pattern-based clusters, the number of clusters can be reduced substantially. Moreover, many unnecessary searches for sub-clusters can be pruned and thus the mining efficiency can be improved dramatically as well.

Second, *how to mine the maximal pattern-based clusters efficiently?* Our experimental results indicate that the algorithm *p-Clustering* developed in [12] may not be satisfactorily efficient or scalable in large databases. The major bottleneck is that it has to search many possible combinations of objects and dimensions.

Our contributions. In this paper, we develop a novel mining algorithm, *MaPle* (for Maximal Pattern-based Clustering). It conducts a depth-first, progressively refining search to mine maximal pattern-based clusters. We propose techniques to guarantee the completeness of the search and also prune unpromising search branches. An extensive performance study on both synthetic data sets and real data sets is reported. The results show that *MaPle* is significantly more efficient and more scalable in mining large databases than method *p-Clustering* in [12].

The remainder of the paper is organized as follows. Section 2 defines the problem of mining maximal pattern-based clusters and reviews related work. In Section 3, we develop algorithm *MaPle*. An extensive performance study is reported in Section 4. Section 5 concludes the paper.

2 Problem Definition and Related Work

Given a set of objects, where each object is described by a set of attributes. A pattern-based cluster (R, D) is a subset of objects R that exhibit a coherent pattern on a subset of attributes D. To formulate the problem, it is essential to describe, given a subset of objects R and a subset of attributes D, how coherent the objects are on the attributes. The measure $pScore$ serves this purpose.

Definition 2.1 (pScore) Let $DB = \{r_1, \ldots, r_n\}$ be a database with n *objects*. Each object has m *attributes* $A = \{a_1, \ldots, a_m\}$. We assume that each attribute is in the domain of real numbers. The value of object r_j on attribute a_i is denoted as $r_j.a_i$. For any objects $r_x, r_y \in DB$ and any attributes $a_u, a_v \in A$, the $pScore$ is defined as $pScore\left(\begin{bmatrix} r_x.a_u & r_x.a_v \\ r_y.a_u & r_y.a_v \end{bmatrix}\right) = \|(r_x.a_u - r_y.a_u) - (r_x.a_v - r_y.a_v)\|$.

Clearly, the $pScore$ describes the similarity between two objects on two attributes. The smaller the $pScore$ value, the more similar are the two objects on the two dimensions. Pattern-based clusters can be defined as follows.

Definition 2.2 (Pattern-based cluster) Let $R \subseteq DB$ be a subset of objects in the database and $D \subseteq A$ be a subset of attributes. (R, D) is said a δ-pCluster (for pattern-based cluster) if for any objects $r_x, r_y \in R$ and any attributes $a_u, a_v \in D$, $pScore\left(\begin{bmatrix} r_x.a_u & r_x.a_v \\ r_y.a_u & r_y.a_v \end{bmatrix}\right) \leq \delta$, where $\delta \geq 0$.

In a large database with many attributes, there can be many coincident, statistically insignificant pattern-based clusters. A cluster may be considered *statistically insignificant* if it contains a small number of objects, or a small number of attributes. Thus, a user may want to impose constraints on the minimum numbers of objects and attributes in a pattern-based cluster.

In general, given (1) a cluster threshold δ, (2) an *attribute threshold* min_a (i.e., the minimum number of attributes), and (3) an *object threshold* min_o (i.e., the minimum number of objects), the task of *mining δ-pClusters* is to find the complete set of δ-pClusters (R, D) such that $(\|R\| \geq min_o)$ and $(\|D\| \geq min_a)$. A δ-pCluster satisfying the above requirement is called *significant*.

Although the attribute and object thresholds are used to filter out insignificant pClusters, there still can be some "*redundant*" significant pClusters. For example, consider the objects in Figure 1. Let $\delta = 5$, $min_a = 3$ and $min_o = 3$. Then, we have 6 significant pClusters: $C_1 = (\{1, 2, 3\}, \{a, c, d\})$, $C_2 = (\{1, 4, 5\}, \{b, c, d\})$, $C_3 = (\{1, 4, 5\}, \{b, c, e\})$, $C_4 = (\{1, 4, 5\}, \{b, d, e\})$, $C_5 = (\{1, 4, 5\}, \{c, d, e\})$, and $C_6 = (\{1, 4, 5\}, \{b, c, d, e\})$. Among them, C_2, C_3, C_4 and C_5 are subsumed by C_6, i.e., the objects and attributes in the four clusters, C_2-C_5, are subsets of the ones in C_6.

In general, a pCluster $C_1 = (R_1, D_1)$ is called a *subcluster* of $C_2 = (R_2, D_2)$ provided $(R_1 \subseteq R_2) \wedge (D_1 \subseteq D_2)$. Moreover, C_1 is called a *proper sub-cluster* of C_2 if either $R_1 \subset R_2$ or $D_1 \subset D_2$. Pattern-based clusters have the following property.

Lemma 2.1 (Closure of sub-clusters) *Let $C = (R, D)$ be a δ-pCluster. Then, every sub-cluster (R', D') is a δ-pCluster.*

Mining the redundant sub-clusters is tedious and ineffective for analysis. Therefore, it is natural to mine only the "maximal clusters", i.e., the pClusters that are not sub-cluster of any other pClusters.

Definition 2.3 (maximal pCluster) A δ-pCluster C is said *maximal* (or called a δ-MPC in short) if there exists no δ-pCluster C' such that C is a proper sub-cluster of C'.

Problem Statement (mining maximal δ-pClusters). Given (1) a cluster threshold δ, (2) an attribute threshold min_a, and (3) an object threshold min_o, the task of *mining maximal δ-pClusters* is to find the complete set of maximal δ-pClusters with respect to min_a and min_o.

2.1 Related Work

The problem of pattern-based clustering and an algorithm, *p-Clustering*[1], are proposed in [12]. According to the extensive performance study reported in the paper, *p-Clustering* outperforms all previous methods.

The study of pattern-based clustering is related to previous work on subspace clustering and frequent itemset mining.

The meaning of clustering in high dimensional data sets is often unreliable [6]. Some recent studies (e.g. [3, 1, 2, 7]) focus on mining clusters embedded in some subspaces. For example, CLIQUE [3] is a density and grid based method. It divides the data into hyper-rectangular cells and uses the dense cells to construct subspace clusters.

Subspace clustering can be used to semantically compress data. An interesting study in [10] employs a randomized algorithm to find fascicles, the subsets of data that share similar values in some attributes. While their method is effective for compression, it does not guarantee the completeness of mining the clusters.

In some applications, global similarity-based clustering may not be effective. Still, strong correlations may exist among a set of objects even if they are far away from each other as measured by distance functions (such as Euclidean) used frequently in traditional clustering algorithms. Many scientific projects collect data in the form of Figure 1(a), and it is essential to identify clusters of objects that manifest coherent patterns. A variety of applications, including DNA microarray analysis, collaborative filtering, will benefit from fast algorithms that can capture such patterns.

Cheng and Church propose the biclustering model [8], which captures the coherence of genes and conditions in a sub-matrix of a DNA micro-array. Yang et al. [13] develop a move-based algorithm to find biclusters more efficiently.

On the other hand, a transaction database can be modelled as a binary matrix, where columns and rows stand for items and transactions, respectively. A cell $r_{i,j}$ is set to 1 if item j is contained in transaction i. Then, the problem of

mining frequent itemsets [4] is to find subsets of rows and columns such that the sub-matrix is all 1's, and the number of rows is more than a given support threshold. If a minimum length constraint min_a is imposed to find only frequent itemsets of no less than min_a items, then it becomes a problem of mining 0-pClusters on binary data. Although there are many efficient methods for frequent itemset mining, such as [5, 9], they cannot be extended to handle the general pattern-based clustering problem since they can only handle the binary data.

3 Algorithm *MaPle*

3.1 Overview

Essentially, *MaPle* enumerates all the maximal pClusters systematically. It guarantees both the completeness and the non-redundancy of the search, i.e., every maximal pCluster will be found, and each combination of attributes and objects will be tested at most once.

MaPle enumerates every combination of attributes systematically in a dictionary order according to an order of attributes. For each subset of attributes D, *MaPle* finds the maximal subsets of objects R such that (R, D) is a δ-pCluster. If (R, D) is not a sub-cluster of another pCluster (R', D) such that $R \subset R'$, then (R, D) is a maximal δ-pCluster. This *"attribute-first-object-later"* search is illustrated in Figure 2.

Figure 2. Attribute-first-object-later search.

There can be a huge number of combinations of attributes. *MaPle* prunes many combinations unpromising for δ-pClusters. Following Lemma 2.1, for subset of attributes D, if there exists no subset of objects R such that (R, D) is a significant pCluster, then we do not need to search any superset of D. On the other hand, when searching under a subset of attributes D, *MaPle* only checks those subsets of objects R such that (R, D') is a pCluster for every $D' \subset D$. Clearly, only subsets $R' \subseteq R$ may achieve δ-pCluster (R', D). Such pruning techniques are applied recursively. Thus, *MaPle* progressively refines the search step by step.

Moreover, *MaPle* also prunes searches that are unpromising to find maximal pClusters. It detects the attributes and objects that can be used to assemble a larger pCluster from the current pCluster. If *MaPle* finds that the current subsets of attributes and objects as well as all possible attributes and objects together turn out to be a sub-

---

[1]Wang et al. did not give a specific name to their algorithm in [12]. We call it *p-Clustering* since the main function in the algorithm is *pCluster()* and we want to distinguish the algorithm from the pclusters.

cluster of a pCluster having been found before, then the recursive searches rooted at the current node are pruned, since it cannot lead to a maximal pCluster.

Why does MaPle *enumerate attributes first and then objects later, but not in the reverse way?* In real databases, the number of objects is often much larger than the number of attributes. In other words, the number of combinations of objects is often dramatically larger than the number of combinations of attributes. In the pruning using maximal pClusters discussed above, if the attribute-first-object-later approach is adopted, once a set of attributes and its descendants are pruned, all searches of related subsets of objects are pruned as well. Heuristically, the attribute-first-object-later search may bring a better chance to prune a more bushy search sub-tree.[2]

Essentially, we rely on MDSs, the maximal δ-MPC containing only two objects or two attributes, to determine whether a subset of objects and a subset of attributes together form a pCluster. Therefore, as a preprocessing, we materialize all non-redundant MDSs.

Based on the above discussion, we have the framework of *MaPle* as shown in Figure 3.

Input: database DB, cluster threshold δ, attribute threshold
min_a and object threshold min_o;
Output: the complete set of maximal δ-pClusters;
Method:
(1)   compute and prune attribute-pair MDSs and object-pair
       MDSs; // Section 3.2
(2)   progressively refining, depth-first search for maximal
       δ-pClusters; // Section 3.3

Figure 3. Algorithm *MaPle*.

Comparing to *p-Clustering*, *MaPle* has several advantages. First, in the third step of *p-Clustering*, for each node in the prefix tree, the combinations of the objects registered in the node will be explored to find pClusters. This can be expensive if there are many objects in a node. In *MaPle*, the information of pClusters is inherited from the "parent node" in the depth-first search and the possible combinations of objects can be reduced substantially. Moreover, once a subset of attributes D is determined hopeless for pClusters, the searches of any superset of D will be pruned. Second, *MaPle* prunes non-maximal pClusters. Many unpromising searches can be pruned in their early stages. Third, new pruning techniques are adopted in the computing and pruning MDSs. That also speeds up the mining.

In the remainder of this section, we will explain the two steps of *MaPle* in detail.

---

[2]However, there is no theoretical guarantee that the attribute-first-object-later search is optimal. There exist counter examples that object-first-attribute-later search wins. Limited by space, we omit the details here.

3.2 Computing and Pruning MDSs

A pCluster must have at least two objects and two attributes. Intuitively, we can use those pClusters containing only two objects or two attributes to construct larger pClusters having more objects and attributes. Given a database DB and a cluster threshold δ. A δ-pCluster $C_1 = (\{o_1, o_2\}, D)$ is called an *object-pair MDS* (for **m**aximal **d**imension **s**et) if there exists no δ-pCluster $C_1' = (\{o_1, o_2\}, D')$ such that $D \subset D'$. On the other hand, a δ-pCluster $C_2 = (R, \{a_1, a_2\})$ is called an *attribute-pair MDS* if there exists no δ-pCluster $C_2' = (R', \{a_1, a_2\})$ such that $R \subset R'$.

MaPle computes all attribute-pair MDSs as *p-Clustering* does. The method is illustrated in Figure 4(b). Limited by space, we omit the detailed algorithm here and only show the following example.

Example 1 (Finding attribute-pair MDSs) Figure 4(a) shows the object values of two attributes, x and y. The last row shows the differences of the object values.

Attribute	Objects							
	a	b	c	d	e	f	g	h
x	13	11	9	7	9	13	2	15
y	7	4	10	1	12	3	4	7
$x - y$	6	7	−1	6	−3	10	−2	8

(a) The object values of two attributes x and y.

| −3 | −2 | −1 | 6 | 6 | 7 | 8 | 10 |

e   g   c   a   d   b   h   f

(b) Finding MDS

Figure 4. Finding MDS for two attributes.

To compute the attribute-pair MDS, *p-Clustering* sorts the objects in the difference ascending order, as shown in Figure 4(b). Suppose $\delta = 2$. *P-Clustering* runs through the sorted list using a sliding window of variable width. The objects in the sliding window form a δ-pCluster provided the difference between the rightmost element and the leftmost one is no more than δ. For example, *p-Clustering* firstly sets the left edge of the sliding window at the left end of the sorted list, and moves rightward until it sees the first 6. The objects in between, $\{e, g, c\}$, is the set of objects of an attribute-pair MDS. Then, *p-Clustering* moves the left edge of the sliding window to object g, and repeats the process until the left end of the window runs through all elements in the list. In total, three MDSs can be found, i.e., $(\{x, y\}, \{e, g, c\})$, $(\{x, y\}, \{a, d, b, h\})$ and $(\{x, y\}, \{h, f\})$. A similar method can be used to find the object-pair MDSs.

As our running example, consider mining maximal pattern-based clusters in a database DB as shown in Figure 5(a). Suppose $min_a = 3$, $min_o = 3$ and $\delta = 1$. For each pair of attributes, we calculate the attribute pair MDSs. The attribute-pair MDSs returned are shown in Figure 5(b).

We can also generate all the object-pair MDSs similarly. However, we can speed up the calculation of object-pair

Object	a_1	a_2	a_3	a_4	a_5
o_1	5	6	7	7	1
o_2	4	4	5	6	10
o_3	5	5	6	1	30
o_4	7	7	15	2	60
o_5	2	0	6	8	10
o_6	3	4	5	5	1

(a) The database

Objects	Attribute-pair
$\{o_1, o_2, o_3, o_4, o_6\}$	$\{a_1, a_2\}$
$\{o_1, o_2, o_3, o_6\}$	$\{a_1, a_3\}$
$\{o_1, o_2, o_6\}$	$\{a_1, a_4\}$
$\{o_1, o_2, o_3, o_6\}$	$\{a_2, a_3\}$
$\{o_1, o_2, o_6\}$	$\{a_2, a_4\}$
$\{o_1, o_2, o_6\}$	$\{a_3, a_4\}$

(b) The attribute-pair MDSs

Figure 5. The running example.

Object-pair	Attributes
$\{o_1, o_2\}$	$\{a_1, a_2, a_3, a_4\}$
$\{o_1, o_3\}$	$\{a_1, a_2, a_3\}$
$\{o_1, o_6\}$	$\{a_1, a_2, a_3, a_4\}$
$\{o_2, o_3\}$	$\{a_1, a_2, a_3\}$
$\{o_2, o_6\}$	$\{a_1, a_2, a_3, a_4\}$
$\{o_3, o_6\}$	$\{a_1, a_2, a_3\}$

(a) Object-pair MDSs in *MaPle*.

Object-pair	Attributes
$\{o_1, o_2\}$	$\{a_1, a_2, a_3, a_4\}$
$\{o_1, o_3\}$	$\{a_1, a_2, a_3\}$
$\{o_1, o_6\}$	$\{a_1, a_2, a_3, a_4\}$
$\{o_2, o_3\}$	$\{a_1, a_2, a_3\}$
$\{o_2, o_6\}$	$\{a_1, a_2, a_3, a_4\}$
$\{o_3, o_4\}$	$\{a_1, a_2, a_4\}$
$\{o_3, o_6\}$	$\{a_1, a_2, a_3\}$

(b) Object-pair MDSs in method *p-Clustering*

Figure 6. Pruning using Lemma 3.1.

MDSs by utilizing the information on the number of occurrences of objects and attributes in the attribute-pair MDSs.

Lemma 3.1 (Pruning MDSs) *Given a database DB and a cluster threshold δ, object threshold min_o and attribute threshold min_a. (1) An attribute a cannot appear in any significant δ-pCluster if a appears in less than $\frac{min_o \cdot (min_o - 1)}{2}$ object-pair MDSs, or appears in less than $(min_a - 1)$ attribute-pair MDSs; (2) An object o cannot appear in any significant δ-pCluster if o appears in less than $\frac{min_a \cdot (min_a - 1)}{2}$ attribute-pair MDSs, or appears in less than $(min_o - 1)$ object-pair MDSs.*

Example 2 (Pruning using Lemma 3.1) Let us check the attribute-pair MDSs in Figure 5(b). Object o_5 does not appear in any attribute-pair MDS, and object o_4 appears in only 1 attribute-pair MDS. According to Lemma 3.1, o_4 and o_5 cannot appear in any significant δ-pCluster. Therefore, object-pairs containing o_4 or o_5 can be pruned.

There are 6 objects in the database. Without this pruning, we have to check $\frac{6 \times 5}{2} = 15$ pairs of objects. With this pruning, only four objects, o_1, o_2, o_3 and o_6 survive. Thus, we only need to check $\frac{4 \times 3}{2} = 6$ pairs of objects. 60% of the original searches are pruned.

Moreover, since attribute a_5 does not appear in any attribute-pair MDS, it cannot appear in any significant δ-pCluster. The attribute can be pruned, i.e., a_5 can be removed from any object-pair MDS.

In summary, after the pruning, only attributes a_1, a_2, a_3 and a_4, and objects o_1, o_2, o_3 and o_6 survive. We use these attributes and objects to generate object-pair MDSs. The result is shown in Figure 6(a). In method *p-Clustering*, it uses all attributes and objects to generate object-pair MDSs. The result is shown in Figure 6(b). As can be seen, not only the computation cost in *MaPle* is less, the number of object-pair MDSs in *MaPle* is also one less than that in method *p-Clustering*.

Once we get the initial object-pair MDSs and attribute-pair MDSs, we can conduct a mutual pruning between the object-pair MDSs and the attribute-pair MDSs, as method *p-Clustering* does. Furthermore, Lemma 3.1 can be applied in each round to get extra pruning. The pruning algorithm is shown in Figure 7.

---

(1) REPEAT
(2)   count the number of occurrences of objects and attributes in the attribute-pair MDSs;
(3)   apply Lemma 3.1 to prune objects and attributes;
(4)   remove object-pair MDSs containing less than min_a attributes;
(5)   count the number of occurrences of objects and attributes in the object-pair MDSs;
(6)   apply Lemma 3.1 to prune objects and attributes;
(7)   remove attribute-pair MDSs containing less than min_o objects;
(8) UNTIL no pruning takes place

Figure 7. The algorithm of pruning MDSs.

3.3 Progressively Refining, Depth-first Search of Maximal pClusters

The algorithm of the progressively refining, depth-first search of maximal pClusters is shown in Figure 8. We explain the algorithm step by step in this subsection.

3.3.1 Dividing Search Space

By a list of attributes, we can enumerate all combinations of attributes systematically. The idea is shown in the following example.

Example 3 (Enumeration of combinations of attributes) In our running example, there are four attributes surviving from the pruning: a_1, a_2, a_3 and a_4. We list any subset of attributes in the order of a_1-a_2-a_3-a_4. Suppose that $min_a = 3$, i.e., every maximal δ-pCluster should have at

(1) let n be the number of attributes;
     make up an attribute list $AL = a_1 \text{-} \cdots \text{-} a_n$;
(2) FOR $i = 1$ TO $n - min_a + 1$ DO
(3)   FOR $j = i + 1$ TO $n - min_a + 2$ DO
(4)   find row-maximal pClusters $(R, \{a_i, a_j\})$;
         //Section 3.3.2
(5)   FOR EACH row-maximal pCluster $(R, \{a_i, a_j\})$ DO
(6)   call $search(R, \{a_i, a_j\})$;
(7)   END FOR EACH
(8)   END FOR
(9) END FOR
(10)
(11) FUNCTION $search(R, D)$;
     // (R, D) is a row-maximal pCluster.
(12) compute PD, the set of possible attributes;
     //Optimization 1 in Section 3.3.3
(13) apply optimizations in Section 3.3.3 to prune, if possible;
(14) FOR EACH attribute $a \in PD$ DO
(15)   find row-maximal pClusters $(R', D \cup \{a\})$;
       //Section 3.3.2
(16)   FOR EACH row-maximal pCluster $(R', D \cup \{a\})$ DO
(17)   call $search(R', D \cup \{a\})$;
(18)   END FOR EACH
(19) END FOR EACH
(20) IF (R, D) is not a subcluster of some maximal pCluster
     having been found
(21) THEN output (R, D);
(22) END FUNCTION

Figure 8. Projection-based search.

least 3 attributes. We divide the complete set of maximal pClusters into 3 exclusive subsets according to the first two attributes in the pClusters: (1) the ones having attributes a_1 and a_2, (2) the ones having attributes a_1 and a_3 but no a_2, and (3) the ones having attributes a_2 and a_3 but no a_1.

In general, the set of maximal pClusters can be divided into exclusive subsets by a list of attributes. Heuristically, for an attribute a, if there are many distinct objects appearing in the attribute-pair MDSs containing a, then it is likely that a may appear in a maximal pCluster of large size (i.e., a maximal pCluster containing many objects and attributes). Such attributes should be considered first in our search. Based on the heuristic, given a database DB, the *rank* of an attribute a is the number of distinct objects in the attribute-pair MDSs containing a. That is, $rank(a) = \| \bigcup_{(R,D)|a \in D} R \|$, where (R, D) is an attribute-pair MDS. The list of all attributes in the database in rank descending order is called the *attribute-list* of DB. Attributes having an identical rank can be sorted arbitrarily.

For example, from the attribute-pair MDSs in Figure 5(b), we can compute the ranks of the attributes. The ranks of a_1, a_2, a_3 and a_4 are 4, 4, 4 and 3, respectively. Thus, we make up the attribute-list as $a_1\text{-}a_2\text{-}a_3\text{-}a_4$. We will use this list to search for maximal δ-pClusters in our running example.

Since a pCluster has at least 2 attributes, *MaPle* first partitions the complete set of maximal pClusters into exclusive subsets according to the first two attributes, then searches the subsets one by one in the depth-first manner. For each subset, *MaPle* further divides the pClusters in the subset into smaller exclusive sub-subsets according to the third attributes in the pClusters, and searches the sub-subsets. Such a process proceeds recursively until all the maximal pClusters are found. This is implemented by line (1)-(3) and (14) in Figure 8.

3.3.2 Finding Row-maximal pClusters

Now, the problem becomes how to find the maximal δ-pClusters on the subsets of attributes. For each subset of attributes D, we will find the maximal subsets of objects R such that (R, D) is a pCluster. Such a pCluster is a maximal pCluster if it is not a sub-cluster of some others.

Given a set of attributes D such that $(\|D\| \geq 2)$. A pCluster (R, D) is called a *row-maximal δ-pCluster* if there exists no any δ-pCluster (R', D) such that $R \subset R'$. In other words, a row-maximal pCluster is maximal in the sense that no more objects can be included so that the objects are still coherent on the same subset of attributes. For example, in the database shown in Figure 5(a), $(\{o_1, o_2, o_3, o_6\}, \{a_1, a_2\})$ is a row-maximal pCluster for subset of attributes $\{a_1, a_2\}$. Clearly, a maximal pCluster must be a row-maximal pCluster, but not vice versa.

Given a subset of attributes D, how can we find all row-maximal pClusters efficiently? There are two cases.

If D has only two attributes, then the row-maximal pClusters are the attribute-pair MDSs for D. Since the MDSs are computed and stored before the search, they can be retrieved immediately.

Now, let us consider the case where $(\|D\| \geq 3)$. Suppose $D = \{a_{i_1}, \ldots, a_{i_k}\}$ where the attributes in D are listed in the order of attribute-list AL. Intuitively, (R, D) is a pCluster if R is shared by attribute-pair MDSs from any two attributes from D. (R, D) is a row-maximal pCluster if R is a maximal set of objects.

One tricky thing here is that, in general, there can be more than one attribute-pair MDS for given attributes a_u, a_v. Thus, there can be more than one row-maximal pCluster on a subset of attributes D. Technically, (R, D) is a row-maximal pCluster if for each pair of attributes $\{a_u, a_v\} \subset D$, there exists an attribute-pair MDS $(\{a_u, a_v\}, R_{uv})$, such that $R = \bigcap_{\{a_u, a_v\} \subset D} R_{uv}$.

Recall that *MaPle* searches the combinations of attributes in the depth-first manner, all row-maximal pClusters for subset of attributes $D - \{a_{i_k}\}$ is found before we search for D. Therefore, we only need to find the subset of objects in a row-maximal pCluster of $D - \{a_{i_k}\}$ that are shared by attribute-pair MDSs of a_{i_j}, a_{i_k} $(j < k)$.

3.3.3 Pruning and Optimizations

Several optimizations can be used to prune the search so that the mining can be more efficient.

Optimization 1: Only *possible attributes* should be considered to get larger pClusters.

Suppose that (R, D) is a row-maximal pCluster. *For every attribute a such that a is after all attributes in D in the attribute-list, under what condition can we find a significant pCluster $(R', D \cup \{a\})$ such that $R' \subseteq R$?*

If $(R', D \cup \{a\})$ is significant, i.e., has at least min_o objects, then a must appear in at least $\frac{min_o(min_o-1)}{2}$ object-pair MDSs $(\{o_i, o_j\}, D_{ij})$ such that $\{o_i, o_j\} \subseteq R'$. In other words, for an attribute a that appears in less than $\frac{min_o(min_o-1)}{2}$ object-pair MDSs of objects in R, there exists no row-maximal pCluster with respect to $D \cup \{a\}$.

Based on the above observation, an attribute a is called a *possible attribute* with respect to row-maximal pCluster (R, D) if a appears in $\frac{min_o(min_o-1)}{2}$ object-pair MDSs $(\{o_i, o_j\}, D_{ij})$ such that $\{o_i, o_j\} \subseteq R$. In line (12) of Figure 8, we compute possible attributes and only those attributes are used to extend the set of attributes in pClusters.

Optimization 2: Pruning local maxiaml pClusters having insufficient possible attributes.

Suppose that (R, D) is a row-maximal pCluster. Let PD be the set of possible attributes with respect to (R, D). Clearly, if $\|D \cup PD\| < min_a$, then it is impossible to find any maximal pCluster of a subset of R. Thus, such a row-maximal pCluster should be discarded and all the recursive search can be pruned.

Optimization 3: Extracting common attributes from possible attribute set directly.

Suppose that (R, D) is a row-maximal pCluster with respect to D, and D' is the corresponding set of possible attributes. If there exists an attribute $a \in D'$ such that for every pair of objects $\{o_i, o_j\}$, $\{a\} \cup D$ appears in an object pair MDS of $\{o_i, o_j\}$, then we immediately know that $(R, D \cup \{a\})$ must be a row-maximal pCluster with respect to $D \cup \{a\}$. Such an attribute is called a *common attribute* and should be extracted directly.

Example 4 (Extracting common attributes) In our running example, $(\{o_1, o_2, o_3, o_6\}, \{a_1, a_2\})$ is a row-maximal pCluster with respect to $\{a_1, a_2\}$. Interestingly, as shown in Figure 6(a), for every object pair $\{o_i, o_j\} \subset \{o_1, o_2, o_3, o_6\}$, the object-pair MDS contains attribute a_3. Therefore, we immediately know that $(\{o_1, o_2, o_3, o_6\}, \{a_1, a_2, a_3\})$ is a row-maximal pCluster.

Optimization 4: Prune non-maximal pClusters.

Our goal is to find maximal pClusters. Once we know that the recursive search on a row-maximal pCluster cannot lead to a maximal pCluster, the recursive search thus can be pruned. The earlier we detect the impossibility, the more search efforts can be saved. We can use the *dominant attributes* to detect the impossibility. We illustrate the idea in the following example.

Example 5 (Detect non-maximal pClusters) In our running example, let us try to find the maximal pClusters whose first two attributes are a_1 and a_3. Following the above discussion, we identify a row-maximal pCluster $(\{o_1, o_2, o_3, o_6\}, \{a_1, a_3\})$.

One interesting observation from the object-pair MDSs on objects in $\{o_1, o_2, o_3, o_6\}$ (Figure 6(a)): attribute a_2 appears in every object pair. We called a_2 a *dominant attribute*. That means $\{o_1, o_2, o_3, o_6\}$ also coherent on attribute a_2. In other words, we cannot have a maximal pCluster whose first two attributes are a_1 and a_3, since a_2 must also be in the same maximal pCluster. Thus, the search of maximal pClusters whose first two attributes are a_1 and a_3 can be pruned.

The idea in Example 5 can be generalized. Suppose (R, D) is a row-maximal pCluster. If there exists an attribute a such that a is before the last attribute in D according to the attribute-list, and $\{a\} \cup D$ appears in an object-pair MDS $(\{o_i, o_j\}, D_{ij})$ for every $(\{o_i, o_j\} \subseteq R)$, then the search from (R, D) can be pruned, since there cannot be a maximal pCluster having attribute set D but no a. Attribute a is called a *dominant attribute* with respect to (R, D).

4 Empirical Evaluation

We test both *MaPle* and *p-Clustering* extensively on both synthetic and real life data sets. In this section, we report the results.

MaPle is implemented using C/C++. We obtained the executable of *p-Clustering* from the authors of [12]. Please note that the authors of *p-Clustering* improved their algorithm dramatically after their publication in SIGMOD'02. All the experiments are conducted on a PC with a P4 1.2 GHz CPU and 384 M main memory running a Microsoft Windows XP operating system.

The algorithms are tested against both synthetic and real life data sets. Synthetic data sets are generated by a synthetic data generator reported in [12]. Limited by space, we only report the results on a real data set, the Yeast microarray data set [11]. This data set contains the expression levels of $2,884$ genes under 17 conditions.

Results on Yeast Data Set

The results on Yeast data set are shown in Figure 9. We can obtain the following two interesting observations.

δ	min_a	min_o	# of MPC	# of pClusters
0	9	30	5	5520
0	8	40	5	2.05×10^9
0	7	50	11	3.37×10^{15}

Figure 9. Test results on Yeast raw data set.

On the one hand, there are significant pClusters existing in real data. For example, we can find pure pCluster (i.e., $\delta = 0$) containing more than 30 genes and 9 attributes in Yeast data set. That shows the effectiveness and utilization of mining maximal pClusters in bioinformatics applications.

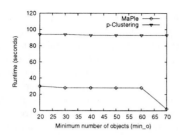 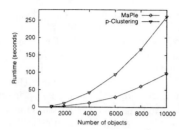 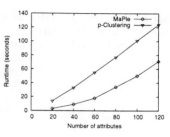

(a) Runtime vs. minimum number of objects in pClusters.

(b) Scalability with respect to the number of objects in the data sets.

(c) Scalability with respect to the number of attributes in the data sets.

Figure 10. Results on synthetic data sets.

On the other hand, while the number of maximal pClusters is often small, the number of all pClusters can be huge, since there are many different combinations of objects and attributes as sub-clusters to the maximal pClusters. This shows the effectiveness of the notation of maximal pClusters.

Results on Synthetic Data Sets

We test the scalability of the algorithms on the two parameters, the minimum number of objects min_o and the minimum number of attributes min_a in pClusters. In Figure 10(a), the runtime of the algorithms versus min_o is shown. The data set has 6000 objects and 30 attributes.

Both algorithms are in general insensitive to parameter min_o, but *MaPle* is faster than *p-Clustering*. The major reason is that the number of pClusters in the synthetic data set does not change dramatically as min_o decreases and thus the overhead of the search does not increase substantially. Please note that we do observe the slight increases of runtime in both algorithms as min_o goes down. One interesting observation here is that, when $min_o > 60$, the runtime of *MaPle* is significantly shorter. That is because there is no pCluster in such a setting. *MaPle* can detect this in an early stage and thus can stop early.

We observe the similar trends on the runtime versus parameter min_a. The reasoning similar to that on min_o holds here. Limited by space, we omit the details here.

We test the scalability of both algorithms on the number of objects in the data sets. The result is shown in Figure 10(b). The data set contains 30 attributes, where there are 30 embedded clusters. We fix $min_a = 5$ and set $min_o = n_{obj} \cdot 1\%$, where n_{obj} is the number of objects in the data set. $\delta = 1$. The result clearly shows that both *MaPle* and *p-Clustering* are scalable with respect to the number of objects in the data sets. *MaPle* performs substantially better than *p-Clustering* in mining large data sets.

We also test the scalability of both algorithms on the number of attributes. The result is shown in Figure 10(c). The number of objects is fixed to $3,000$ and there are 30 embedded pClusters. We set $min_o = 30$ and $min_a = n_{attr} \cdot 20\%$, where n_{attr} is the number of attributes in the data set. Both *MaPle* and *p-Clustering* are approximately linearly scalable with respect to the number of attributes,

and *MaPle* performs consistently better than *p-Clustering*.

In summary, from the tests on synthetic data sets, we can see that *MaPle* clearly outperforms *p-Clustering*. *MaPle* is efficient and scalable in mining large data sets.

5 Conclusions

In this paper, we propose *MaPle*, an efficient and scalable algorithm for mining maximal pattern-based clusters in large databases. We test the algorithm on both real life data sets and synthetic data sets. The results show that *MaPle* outperforms the best method previously proposed.

References

[1] C.C. Aggarwal et al. Fast algorithms for projected clustering. In *SIGMOD'99*.

[2] C.C. Aggarwal and P.S. Yu. Finding generalized projected clusters in high dimensional spaces. In *SIGMOD'00*.

[3] R. Agrawal et al. Automatic subspace clustering of high dimensional data for data mining applications. In *SIGMOD'98*.

[4] R. Agrawal et al. Mining association rules between sets of items in large databases. In *SIGMOD'93*.

[5] R. Agrawal and R. Srikant. Fast algorithms for mining association rules. In *VLDB'94*.

[6] K. S. Beyer et al. When is "nearest neighbor" meaningful? In *ICDT'99*.

[7] C. H. Cheng et al. Entropy-based subspace clustering for mining numerical data. In *KDD'99*.

[8] Y. Cheng and G.M. Church. Biclustering of expression data. In *Proc. of the 8th Int'l Conf on Intelligent System for Molecular Biology*.

[9] J. Han et al. Mining frequent patterns without candidate generation. In *SIGMOD'00*.

[10] H. V. Jagadish et al. Semantic compression and pattern extraction with fascicles. In *VLDB'99*.

[11] S. Tavazoie et al. Yeast micro data set. In *http://arep.med.harvard.edu/biclustering/yeast.matrix*, 2000.

[12] H. Wang et al. Clustering by pattern similarity in large data sets. In *SIGMOD'02*.

[13] J. Yang et al. δ-cluster: Capturing subspace correlation in a large data set. In *ICDE'02*.

Exploiting Unlabeled Data for Improving Accuracy of Predictive Data Mining

Kang Peng, Slobodan Vucetic, Bo Han, Hongbo Xie, Zoran Obradovic

Center for Information Science and Technology, Temple University, Philadelphia, PA 19122, USA
{kangpeng, vucetic, hanbo, hongbox, zoran}@ist.temple.edu

Abstract

Predictive data mining typically relies on labeled data without exploiting a much larger amount of available unlabeled data. The goal of this paper is to show that using unlabeled data can be beneficial in a range of important prediction problems and therefore should be an integral part of the learning process. Given an unlabeled dataset representative of the underlying distribution and a K-class labeled sample that might be biased, our approach is to learn K contrast classifiers each trained to discriminate a certain class of labeled data from the unlabeled population. We illustrate that contrast classifiers can be useful in one-class classification, outlier detection, density estimation, and learning from biased data. The advantages of the proposed approach are demonstrated by an extensive evaluation on synthetic data followed by real-life bioinformatics applications for (1) ranking PubMed articles by their relevance to protein disorder and (2) cost-effective enlargement of a disordered protein database.

1. Introduction

A common assumption in supervised learning is that labeled data conforms to the same distribution as the data to which the predictor will be applied. However, due to various reasons such as sampling bias or prohibitive labeling costs, labeled datasets are often small and/or biased, which makes them unrepresentative of the underlying distribution. A predictor learned from such data may not generalize well on out-of-sample examples. On the other hand, it is typically easier to collect large amounts of unlabeled data at a significantly lower cost. Moreover, unlabeled samples are less likely to be biased and could therefore often be considered as representatives of the underlying data distribution. This property of unlabeled data makes it an attractive tool for improving accuracy of predictive data mining [17].

As a natural approach to handling unlabeled data, the Expectation Maximization (EM) algorithm [6] can be used to iteratively estimate the model parameters and assign soft labels to unlabeled examples by treating the unknown labels as missing data and assuming generative model such as mixture of Gaussians. EM has been widely used in areas such as text document classification [10], image retrieval [22] and multispectral data classification [18]. Co-training [2] provides another popular strategy for incorporating unlabeled data if the data can be described in two different sufficient views, or sets of attributes. The transduction approach [20] assigns labels to a given set of unlabeled data by maximizing the classification margins on both labeled and unlabeled data. However, it is often observed that these techniques could also degrade performance due to violated model assumption or convergence to local maxima [17].

Another line of research deals with learning problems characterized by extreme bias in labeled data. In one-class classification problems [19] only labeled examples from a single class are available and the goal is to predict out-of-sample examples either as belonging to the class or as outliers. A possible approach to address this problem is to apply kernel density estimation (KDE) for learning the probability density of labeled data. Another approach is the support vector data description (SVDD) method which learns from the positive examples and artificially generated outliers [19] to separate the positive class from the rest. However, these approaches are ignoring unlabeled data that might be readily available. Partially supervised classification [9] provides a notable solution to one-class classification problems that utilizes unlabeled data; it initially assumes that all unlabeled examples come from the negative class, and then applies the EM algorithm to refine the assumption.

In this study, we propose a novel approach for utilizing unlabeled data in data mining. It is based on constructing a *contrast classifier* that discriminates between labeled and unlabeled examples. The name contrast classifier comes from the meaning of its output - it represents a measure of difference, or contrast, in density of a given data point between labeled and unlabeled data. Given this property, it is apparent that contrast classifiers could be used in a wide range of important data mining applications such as outlier detection, one-class classification, density estimation, and learning from biased data. In Section 2, we provide a description of contrast classifiers and a range of their applications. In Section 3 we compare our approach to alternative methods on a challenging 3-class synthetic dataset. In

Section 4, we illustrate the usefulness of the contrast classifiers on two real-life bioinformatics problems of (1) re-ranking of PubMed articles based on their relevance to protein disorder and (2) cost-effective enlargement of a dataset of disordered proteins.

2. Methodology

2.1. Contrast classifiers

By $g(\mathbf{x})$ we denote the probability density function (pdf) of unlabeled data $\mathbf{U} = \{\mathbf{x}_i, i = 1, \ldots, N_U\}$, and we assume that it corresponds to the underlying distribution. In a K-class classification problem, $g(\mathbf{x})$ can be represented as a mixture of K class-conditional pdfs, or $g(\mathbf{x}) = \Sigma_j p_j g_j(\mathbf{x})$, where p_j is prior probability of class j and $g_j(\mathbf{x})$ is class-conditional pdf of data from class j. In a number of applications, the available unlabeled dataset $\mathbf{U}$ is large and could be used to derive a quite accurate estimate of $g(\mathbf{x})$. By $h(\mathbf{x})$ we denote the probability density function of labeled data $\mathbf{L} = \{(\mathbf{x}_i, c_i), i = 1, \ldots, N_L, c_i \in \{1, 2, \ldots, K\}\}$. It can also be represented as a mixture of class-conditional pdfs, or $h(\mathbf{x}) = \Sigma_j q_j h_j(\mathbf{x})$, where q_j is prior probability of class j and $h_j(\mathbf{x})$ is class-conditional pdf of data from class j. Since $\mathbf{L}$ could be obtained through biased sampling, $h_j(\mathbf{x})$ may not equal $g_j(\mathbf{x})$ and thus $h(\mathbf{x})$ may not equal $g(\mathbf{x})$.

We define a *contrast classifier* $cc(\mathbf{x})$ as a classifier trained to discriminate between labeled data (class 0) and unlabeled data (class 1). Given an input $\mathbf{x}$, the optimal contrast classifier able to approximate posterior class probability would output

$$cc(\mathbf{x}) = \frac{r \cdot g(\mathbf{x})}{(1-r) \cdot h(\mathbf{x}) + r \cdot g(\mathbf{x})}, \quad (1)$$

where r is the fraction of unlabeled data in the training set. In the following subsection we will discuss the proper choice of r in practical applications. It is evident that if unlabeled and labeled data are drawn from the identical distribution, i.e., $g(\mathbf{x}) = h(\mathbf{x})$, the optimal $cc(\mathbf{x})$ would be a constant equal to r.

Assuming that the pdf of unlabeled data $g(\mathbf{x})$ is known, the optimal $cc(\mathbf{x})$ can be used to estimate $h(\mathbf{x})$ as

$$h(\mathbf{x}) = \frac{1-cc(\mathbf{x})}{cc(\mathbf{x})} \cdot \frac{r}{1-r} \cdot g(\mathbf{x}). \quad (2)$$

To measure the difference in density of labeled and unlabeled data, we define the *contrast* as ratio $h(\mathbf{x})/g(\mathbf{x})$ and from equation (2) we have

$$contrast(\mathbf{x}) = h(\mathbf{x}) / g(\mathbf{x}) = \frac{1-cc(\mathbf{x})}{cc(\mathbf{x})} \cdot \frac{r}{1-r}. \quad (3)$$

As we will illustrate later, the contrast measure can be extremely useful in a number of applications such as one-class classification, outlier detection and learning from biased data. Since $contrast(\mathbf{x})$ is a monotonically

decreasing function of $cc(\mathbf{x})$, contrast classifiers could be used directly to rank examples by their contrast measure.

If labeled data consist of K classes, K *class-specific* contrast classifiers $cc_j(\mathbf{x})$, $j=1, 2, \ldots, K$, could be constructed where $cc_j(\mathbf{x})$ is trained to discriminate between unlabeled data and class j of labeled data. The class-specific contrast classifiers can then be used to construct the *maximum a posteriori* (MAP) classifier. Using (2), posterior probability $p(c = j | \mathbf{x})$ of class j can be expressed as

$$p(c = j | \mathbf{x}) = \frac{h_j(\mathbf{x}) \cdot q_j}{\sum_i h_i(\mathbf{x}) \cdot q_i} = \frac{q_j \cdot (1 - cc_j(\mathbf{x}))/cc_j(\mathbf{x})}{\sum_i q_i \cdot (1 - cc_i(\mathbf{x}))/cc_i(\mathbf{x})}, \quad (4)$$

where, for simplicity, r was set to 0.5 in all $cc_j(\mathbf{x})$, $j = 1, \ldots, K$. Often, we have some knowledge about prior class probabilities in unlabeled data and about the misclassification costs, which should be used to select more appropriate priors in (4) instead of q_j. Based on (4), the decision rule using contrast classifiers as a MAP classifier can be expressed as

$$\hat{c} = \arg\max_j \frac{(1 - cc_j(\mathbf{x}))}{cc_j(\mathbf{x})} \cdot q_j. \quad (5)$$

An important result is that knowledge of $g(\mathbf{x})$ is not needed to construct the MAP classifier from class-specific contrast classifiers. Therefore, as seen from (5), if labeled data are an unbiased sample, contrast classifiers can be directly used to provide an optimal solution for multi-class problems.

2.2. Construction of contrast classifiers

In practice, unlabeled dataset could be much larger than labeled dataset. Learning on such imbalanced data would result in a low-quality contrast classifier, while learning time could be prohibitively long. Moreover, the quantity $(1-cc(\mathbf{x}))/cc(\mathbf{x}) \cdot r/(1-r)$, which provides a measure of contrast in labeled data, is numerically less stable for imbalanced training data with large r. Learning on imbalanced data has received a lot of attention in the data mining community, and most successful strategies are based on balanced training data [8]. In our approach, we train an *ensemble* of classifiers on *balanced* training sets consisting of equal number of labeled and unlabeled examples randomly sampled from the available labeled and unlabeled data. Similar to bagging [5] we construct a contrast classifier by aggregating the predictions of these classifiers through averaging. With the proposed method we are effectively using information available from the large unlabeled data, thus allowing construction of more accurate contrast classifiers.

Classification algorithms able to approximate posterior class probability are suitable choices for contrast classifiers. These algorithms include logistic regression, feed-forward neural networks with sigmoid activation functions [15], or even decision trees [14]. Additionally, there are several types of binary classifiers (e.g. support vector machines; naive Bayes) producing output scores that can be interpreted as prediction strength. It has been shown that these scores could be successfully calibrated to posterior class probability in case of support vector machine (SVM) [12] and naive Bayes [24] classifiers. The results indicate that the output from such classifiers can be interpreted as a monotonically increasing function of the posterior class probabilities. It follows that $h(\mathbf{x})/g(\mathbf{x})$ can be represented as $F(cc(\mathbf{x}))$, where $F(\cdot)$ is a monotonically decreasing function. In section 4 we will illustrate that this property allows successful use of classifiers such as SVM as contrast classifiers in some important applications.

While contrast classifiers could be used to produce a MAP classifier, it is evident that $(1-cc(\mathbf{x}))/cc(\mathbf{x})$ term in (4) could cause prediction instability for inputs $\mathbf{x}$ with small $cc(\mathbf{x})$. In practice, this should not be an issue since unlabeled data can be considered to be a mixture of distributions with one or more mixture components corresponding to the unlabeled data. Therefore, contrast classifiers are not likely to produce values near zero. Exceptions could be extreme scenarios where labeled data are outliers obtained by highly biased sampling and covering a highly limited portion of a feature space. The property of unlabeled data that allows construction of well-behaved contrast classifiers in most realistic cases is essential for the success of the proposed methodology.

2.3. Contrast classifiers for density estimation

As seen from equation (2), contrast classifiers could be used for class-conditional density estimation. Since unlabeled dataset could be very large, relatively accurate estimation of $g(\mathbf{x})$ should be feasible using some of the standard nonparametric methodologies such as mixture modeling or kernel density estimation. Therefore, if a contrast classifier able to approximate posterior class probability is used, it should be possible to obtain a fairly accurate estimate of labeled data pdf from (2). However, in this paper we will not pursue this direction any further.

2.4. Contrast classifiers for one-class classification and outlier detection

In one-class classification, labeled dataset contains examples from only one class, called *positive* class. The goal is to build a model able to recognize whether a new example is from positive class. Complementary, the task can be detection of outlying examples that are distributionally underrepresented in labeled data. Therefore, *contrast*(**x**) from equation (3) is very suitable for both tasks: given an appropriate threshold, all examples with *contrast*(**x**) above (below) the threshold

can be classified as positive (outliers). Since *contrast*(**x**) is a monotonically decreasing function of $cc(\mathbf{x})$, a threshold can be applied directly on contrast classifier outputs.

A choice of an appropriate threshold for one-class classification could be difficult since the output range of contrast classifiers depends on the dataset. To alleviate this problem, in our approach we introduce the threshold θ^p such that condition $cc(\mathbf{x}) > \theta^p$ is satisfied for a user-specified $p\%$ of labeled examples. Therefore, p represents an upper bound on the false negative rate (percent of rejected positive examples), and a user should select it in order to achieve the optimal trade-off between false positive and false negative rates in one-class classification.

2.5. Contrast classifiers for learning from biased data and generalized outlier detection

As seen from equation (4), contrast classifiers could in theory be used to substitute standard multi-class classification algorithms. Therefore, in scenarios where labeled data is an unbiased sample with $h(\mathbf{x}) = g(\mathbf{x})$ both approaches should achieve the similar classification accuracy. However, in the more general setup where labeled data is a biased sample with $h(\mathbf{x}) \neq g(\mathbf{x})$, the benefits of contrast classifiers become apparent. They follow from the ability of contrast classifiers to detect examples underrepresented in labeled data while achieving near-optimal classification on the others.

For a given example $\mathbf{x}$, let $cc_j(\mathbf{x})$, $j = 1, 2, \ldots, K$, denote the outputs of K class-specific contrast classifiers. If all K outputs are large, $\mathbf{x}$ is likely to be an outlier or an example underrepresented in the labeled data. In such a case, the best policy could be not to provide classification; this would result in an increased overall accuracy at the cost of somewhat decreased coverage. Similar to the use of contrast classifiers in one-class classification, in our approach a user-specified constant p is used to determine K thresholds θ_j^p, $j = 1, 2, \ldots, K$, such that $p\%$ of positive training examples satisfy $cc_j(\mathbf{x}) > \theta_j^p$, for each $j = 1, 2, \ldots, K$. Classification is not provided for examples with $cc_j(\mathbf{x}) > \theta_j^p$ for all $j = 1, 2, \ldots, K$. Otherwise, equation (4) is used for classification.

It is evident that the procedure for classification on biased data includes detection of outliers that we denote as *generalized outlier detection* since it detects examples underrepresented in each of the K classes available in labeled data.

3. Experiments on waveform data

In this section we use the well-known waveform dataset [4] to illustrate the effectiveness of our approach on one-class classification in the presence of unlabeled data, as well as on multi-class classification on unbiased and biased data. In this 3-class dataset, there are 21 attributes defined as a linear combination of two out of 3 basic waveforms with randomly generated coefficients. Its noisy version includes 20 additional irrelevant attributes with Gaussian distribution. Learning on the waveform dataset is generally considered a difficult task with reported accuracy of 86.8% using a Bayes optimal classifier.

3.1. One-class classification

We first compared contrast classifier (CC) with two alternatives for one-class classification: kernel density estimation (KDE) and support vector data description (SVDD) [19]. While both KDE and SVDD learn exclusively from labeled data to directly or indirectly estimate $h(\mathbf{x})$, the contrast classifier utilizes unlabeled data to estimate $h(\mathbf{x})/g(\mathbf{x})$.

Kernel density estimators directly estimate $h(\mathbf{x})$ from labeled data as

$$h(\mathbf{x}) = \frac{1}{n} \sum_{i=1}^{n} G(\mathbf{w}; \mathbf{x} - \mathbf{x}_i) \qquad (6)$$

where G is the *Gaussian* kernel with bandwidth $\mathbf{w}$ and n is the number of labeled examples. If a new example has $h(\mathbf{x})$ below a certain threshold it is considered an outlier. The threshold can be determined as described in Section 2.4. The optimal bandwidth w is the value that maximizes the data likelihood.

Instead of estimating the $h(\mathbf{x})$ directly, the SVDD method uses artificially generated outliers [19] along with the positive examples to construct a hyperspherical decision boundary of minimal possible volume that separates the positive class examples from others. To construct more flexible decision boundaries, kernel functions are introduced to map the data into a higher dimensional space. For SVDD experiments we used the data description toolbox (*dd_tools*) from *http://ida.first.gmd.de/~davidt/*.

The contrast classifier was implemented as an ensemble of feed-forward neural networks. Each network had 10 hidden and 1 output sigmoid neurons. The number of component neural networks was determined empirically. To train a single network, a balanced dataset was formed from N examples taken randomly with replacement from the labeled data and another N from the unlabeled data. As discussed in Section 2.4, we used contrast classifier output $cc(\mathbf{x})$ instead of *contrast*$(\mathbf{x})$ for classification.

Two sets of waveform data were generated: N (<< 150,000) labeled examples from class 1 and 150,000 unlabeled examples, 50,000 from each of the 3 classes. To examine the effect of labeled data size and irrelevant attributes, experiments were performed under four scenarios: 1) N = 200, 2) N = 200 noisy, 3) N = 2000, 4) N = 2000 noisy. Here "noisy" refers to the noisy version

of waveform data with 20 irrelevant attributes. The accuracy of one-class classification was measured as the true positive rate when the false positive rate was 20%. For CC and KDE, the desired false positive rate was obtained by selecting appropriate thresholds. For SVDD, it was obtained from the ROC curve generated by the *dd_tools* software.

In Figure 1 we show that the accuracy of contrast classifiers improved with the number of component neural networks but then saturated at around 20. Therefore, in the remaining experiments in Section 3 we used an ensemble of 20 neural networks as the contrast classifier. Table 1 compares the accuracies of the three methods. In all four scenarios, contrast classifier was superior to the other two methods showing that unlabeled data could greatly improve the accuracy of one-class classification. It is worth noting that the performance of the KDE method degraded as irrelevant attributes were introduced, while CC and SVDD appeared to be robust to noise.

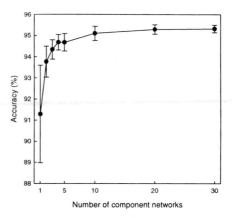

Figure 1. The effect of the number of component neural networks on accuracy for N = 2000 noisy scenario

3.2. Classification with unbiased data

As shown in Section 2.1, if labeled data is unbiased, class-specific contrast classifiers could be used to construct a MAP classifier. In this section, we compare it with a standard 3-class neural network classifier, which is an ensemble of 20 3-output neural networks each trained on a bootstrap replicated sample of the labeled data. The 3 class-specific contrast classifiers were trained with a balanced set consisting of labeled examples from a given class and unlabeled examples. For this experiment, a total of 1500 labeled examples and 150,000 unlabeled examples were generated with different class proportions.

In Table 2 we report their accuracies obtained in experiments with 3 different class proportions. The overall accuracy was calculated as average of individual class accuracies weighted by class proportions. It is evident that the contrast classifier approach achieved accuracy comparable to the best multi-class classifiers when labeled data is unbiased. As will be seen in the next subsection, the true strength of contrast classifiers becomes apparent when labeled data is biased.

Table 1. Comparison of three methods in one-class classification

Dataset	Method	Accuracy (%)
N = 200	CC	94.9
	KDE	63.8
	SVDD	67.7
N = 200 noisy	CC	92.7
	KDE	54.3
	SVDD	68.6
N = 2000	CC	96.1
	KDE	65.2
	SVDD	68.1
N = 2000 noisy	CC	95.1
	KDE	56.9
	SVDD	65.3

CC - contrast classifier, KDE - kernel density estimation, SVDD - support vector data description

Table 2. Comparison of a MAP based on class-specific contrast classifier and a standard 3-class neural network in classification with unbiased labeled data

Class Proportion	Method	Class 1 (%)	Class 2 (%)	Class 3 (%)	Overall (%)
1:1:1	CC	81.9	88.1	88.4	86.1
	NN	80.9	87.1	89.4	85.8
1:4.5:4.5	CC	54.9	94.4	94.2	90.4
	NN	65.2	91.1	94.7	90.1
1:1:8	CC	62.9	75.0	99.5	93.4
	NN	69.7	78.6	98.5	93.6

CC - the MAP classifier based on 3 class-specific contrast classifiers
NN - an ensemble of 20 neural network with 3 outputs

3.3. Classification with biased data

We consider a biased data scenario where examples from class 3 are completely missing from the labeled data. In such a case, the desired classifier should have high classification accuracy on examples from classes 1 and 2, while it should be able to recognize class 3 examples as underrepresented in labeled data and thus refuse to predict on them. We examined the performances of contrast classifier (CC) and kernel density estimation (KDE) approaches on this challenging problem.

For the CC approach, two contrast classifiers specific for classes 1 and 2 were constructed and combined to detect underrepresented examples as described in Section 2.5. For the KDE approach, the class-conditional densities $h(\mathbf{x}|c=1)$ and $h(\mathbf{x}|c=2)$ were estimated from the labeled data. If $h(\mathbf{x}|c=j) < \theta_j^p$ for both $j=1, 2$, $\mathbf{x}$ was characterized as an outlier and classification was not provided. The thresholds θ_j^p were determined such that $p\%$ of class j examples satisfy $h(\mathbf{x}|c=j) < \theta_j^p$. Otherwise, classification was provided using the Bayes rule: if $h(\mathbf{x}|c=1) > h(\mathbf{x}|c=2)$,

$\mathbf{x}$ was labeled with class 1 and vice versa.

We generated labeled data with N examples from classes 1 and 2. The unlabeled data consisted of 50,000 examples for each of the 3 classes. Two experiments were performed: (a) $N = 500$ with 20 noisy attributes, (b) $N = 5000$ without noisy attributes. For a range of choices of parameter p with both CC and KDE approaches we measured (1) classification accuracy of classes 1 and 2, (2) prediction coverage of classes 1 and 2, and (3) prediction coverage of class 3. An ideal predictor should have a 100% accuracy and 100% coverage of classes 1 and 2, but 0% coverage of class 3.

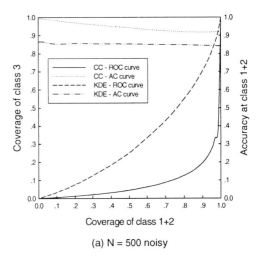

(a) N = 500 noisy

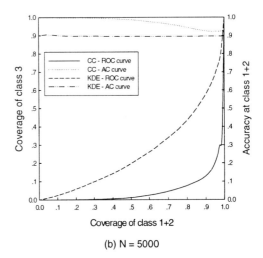

(b) N = 5000

Figure 2. ROC and AC curves for classification with biased data

In Figure 2 we report the performance of both approaches as: (1) ROC curve - class 3 coverage vs. class 1+2 coverage (2) AC curve - accuracy vs. class 1+2 coverage. Clearly, CC achieves both better accuracy and lower class 3 coverage than KDE for a whole range of class 1+2 coverage. As in Figure 2(b), while retaining 95% coverage on classes 1+2, CC approach reduced class 3 coverage to about 20% vs. 70% by KDE, thus was more effective in detecting outliers. An interesting result is that slight increase in accuracy was achieved with decrease in class 1+2 coverage in both scenarios with both models. Consistent with results reported in Section 3.1, contrast classifiers proved to be very robust to noisy attributes and small labeled data size. These results show that unlabeled data can be extremely useful in classification of biased labeled samples and should be an integral part of learning process whenever available.

4. Bioinformatics application: analysis of protein disorder

Disordered proteins are characterized by long regions of amino acids that do not have a stable three-dimensional conformation under normal physiological conditions. Recent results indicate that, despite the traditional view, disordered proteins are common in nature and are responsible for a spectrum of important biological functions [7]. However, due to the historical overlooking of this property, the knowledge about protein disorder is scattered across literature and described with non-unified terminology. Important data mining challenges include allowing cost-effective extraction of knowledge about protein disorder from literature, as well as assisting in better understanding available information about protein disorder. In this section we illustrate that contrast classifiers are appropriate tools for addressing these challenges.

4.1. Ranking of PubMed articles

In a search for biological papers describing properties of uncharacterized disordered proteins, we started from a set of 178 articles describing properties of 90 known disordered proteins collected through intensive literature search by several experts [7]. By querying PubMed (*http://www.ncbi.nlm.nih.gov/entrez/query.fcgi?db=PubMed*), an open access web-based archive of biomedical literature, with names of the 90 disordered proteins, we found that 67 of these proteins had more than 100 PubMed citations, 35 had more than 1,000 citations, and 12 had more than 10,000 citations. Out of the 178 articles only 13% (28%) were returned as the top 5 (10) PubMed retrievals. Our goal was to improve this fraction by ranking the abstracts retrieved by PubMed based on their relevance to properties of disordered proteins extracted automatically from the relevant articles.

In this one-class classification scenario, the labeled (positive) set P contained 166 abstracts stored at PubMed, while the unlabeled set contained 18,499 abstracts from PubMed obtained by querying with the 90 disordered

protein names. After removing infrequent and stop words, remaining words were preprocessed into terms by eliminating suffixes using Porter stemmer [13]. Frequencies of terms were computed over C and P sets and terms were ranked based on the difference in their frequency in C and P. The most discriminative K terms, called keywords, were used to represent each PubMed abstract as a vector of TF-IDF weights [16] calculated as a ratio between the term frequency and the inverse document frequency. Following the approach outlined in Section 2.2, we then trained the contrast classifier as a linear SVM to rank the unlabeled abstracts based on its output.

Using the top 200 keywords (K = 200), significant improvement was achieved in ranking as compared to PubMed default output: the fraction of citations ranked in the top 5 (top 10) was increased from 13% (28%) to 50% (71%). These results suggest that labor involved in finding relevant literature can be reduced many times through the proposed re-rankings by contrast. We note that while the illustrated use of unlabeled data in text mining is not novel, the value of our work is in describing this approach through the statistically appealing framework of contrast classifiers.

4.2. Contrast classifiers for study of protein disorder

Here the problem was to discover and understand proteins that are underrepresented in a labeled database of known ordered and disordered proteins. By using contrast classifiers we showed that the outlying proteins are numerous and have specific properties that may provide a novel insight into structural and functional properties of proteins.

4.2.1. Contrast classifiers for ordered and disordered proteins prediction. The labeled dataset we used consisted of 152 proteins containing disordered regions longer than 30 consecutive residues and 290 completely ordered proteins [21]. Every pair of the labeled sequences had less than 30% sequence identity. The unlabeled data was constructed from the October 2001 release 40 of *SWISS-PROT* database [3] containing 101,602 proteins. The ProtoMap database [23] was used to group these proteins into 17,676 clusters based on their sequence similarities [21]. One representative protein was then selected from each cluster, resulting in an unlabeled dataset of 17,676 proteins.

In our previous work it was found that order/disorder properties of a given sequence position could be predicted fairly accurately based on sequence properties within a symmetric input window centered on that position. Our currently best disorder predictor VL3 [11], an ensemble of 10 neural networks, uses 20 window-based attributes including 18 relative frequencies of 18 out of the 20 amino acids within an input window of length 41, the flexibility index averaged over the window, and the K2-entropy. Its overall accuracy is 83.9%, with 76.3%/91.4% accuracy on disorder/order class.

In a more recent study [21] two class-specific autoassociator neural networks were constructed to detect underrepresented proteins. The two resulting models were effective in discovering important classes of under-represented proteins. However, the overall accuracy of a disorder predictor based on the two models was only 69.8%, more than 10% worse than that of VL3, indicating that more accurate outlier detection is possible.

In this study, we built two class-specific contrast classifiers $cc_{disorder}$ and cc_{order} as ensembles of 50 neural networks using the same attributes as VL3. A MAP disordered predictor was then constructed according to equation (5) where both priors were set to 0.5. Its overall accuracy was 84.0%, with 75.6%/92.3% on disorder/order class, which were practically identical to those of VL3. This result suggests the effectiveness of contrast classifiers in the selection and analysis of underrepresented proteins.

4.2.2. Application of contrast classifiers to selection and analysis of underrepresented proteins.

We first filtered the 17,676 unlabeled proteins by applying one round of *blastp* algorithm [1] with E-value threshold 1 to remove proteins similar to the labeled proteins. Then we retained only those with lengths between 200 and 500 amino acids, which resulted in the *SWISS* set with 6,964 proteins.

After applying the two contrast classifiers on a protein of length L, two L-dimensional vectors of position-by-position predictions are obtained. To allow detection of proteins that are overall the most different from the labeled ordered and disordered proteins, we summarized each protein with cc_avg_{order} and $cc\_avg_{disorder}$, representing the average predictions of the contrast classifiers. Similar to the approach described in Section 2.5, we determined thresholds $\theta_{order}{}^p$ and $\theta_{disorder}{}^p$, such that p% of *SWISS* proteins satisfy $cc\_avg_{order} > \theta_{order}{}^p$ and $cc\_avg_{disorder} > \theta_{disorder}{}^p$, respectively. In Figure 3 we show the proportions of selected outliers from *SWISS* set and the labeled proteins for different p. As could be seen, the proportion of outliers in *SWISS* set is significantly higher than the labeled proteins for a whole range of choices for p. This shows that a significant portion of proteins from *SWISS-PROT* have properties different from the known ordered and disordered proteins.

Using $p = 50$ we selected 1,259 outliers from *SWISS* proteins and denoted this set as *OutAvg*. To properly evaluate *OutAvg* proteins, we constructed two additional datasets: *OrdHom* with 539 *SWISS-PROT* homologues of 290 ordered proteins, and *DisHom* with 356 *SWISS-PROT*

homologues of 152 disordered proteins. Similar to our previous approach [21], for each dataset we calculated the frequencies of 840 keywords listed in *SWISS-PROT* that summarize the structural and functional properties of a given protein. Table 3 shows a summary for the 3 most interesting keywords selected according to their frequencies, which correspond to a large family of membrane proteins known to have specific structural and functional characteristics. It can be seen that they are highly underrepresented among our labeled ordered and disordered proteins as compared to *SWISS*, while they are very common in the identified set of outliers *OutAvg*. Thus, it is likely that most of the bias in our labeled data comes from membrane proteins. It is the matter of further research to determine the full significance of these and other detected underrepresented functional groups and their impact on our study of protein disorder.

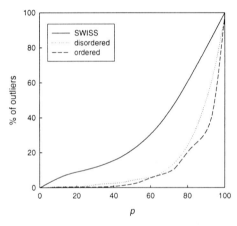

Figure 3. The proportion of selected outliers from *SWISS* set, disordered and ordered proteins for different p.

Table 3. Comparison of frequencies of the 3 most interesting keywords associated with proteins in 4 datasets.

Keyword	SWISS	OrdHom	DisHom	OutAvg
Inner Membrane	2.1	2.2	2.1	6.5
Membrane	21.1	13.4	13.2	57.6
Transmembrane	17.7	9.3	8.9	55.7

5. Conclusions

We proposed a framework for exploiting large amount of available unlabeled data in order to improve accuracies of various predictive data mining tasks such as one-class classification, outlier detection, and learning with biased data.

As the crucial part of our approach, the contrast

classifiers are trained to characterize the contrast or difference between the possibly biased labeled data and unlabeled data. Performance of contrast classifiers was similar to standard classifiers when labeled sample is unbiased. However, the true strength of contrast classifier comes from its ability to effectively detect outlying examples with statistical properties contrasting those of labeled data. While the extensive experiments on synthetic data provided a useful characterization of the proposed framework compared to a range of standard alternatives, the two successful applications in biology domain showed that contrast classifiers could be very useful in solving important practical problems.

The conclusion is that unlabeled data, if available in large amount should be considered as an integral part of data mining process and, therefore, should not be ignored. The results indicate that the appropriate use of unlabeled data could be greatly beneficial to improvement of predictive data mining quality.

Acknowledgements

This study was supported in part by NSF grant IIS-0219736 to Z. Obradović and S. Vucetic and NSF grant CSE-IIS-0196237 to Z. Obradovic and A.K. Dunker.

References

[1] S.F. Altschul, T.L. Madden, A.A. Schiffer, J. Zhang, Z. Zhang, W. Miller and D.J. Lipman, "Gapped BLAST and PSI-BLAST: a new generation of protein database search programs", *Nucleic Acids Res.*, 1997, vol. 25, pp. 3389-3402.

[2] A. Blum and T. Mitchell, "Combining labeled and unlabeled data with co-training", In *Proc. of COLT'98*, 1998, pp. 92-100.

[3] B. Boeckmann, A. Bairoch, R. Apweiler, M. C. Blatter, A. Estreicher, E. Gasteiger, M. J. Martin, K. Michoud, C. O'Donovan, I. Phan, S. Pilbout and M. Schneider, "The SWISS-PROT protein knowledgebase and its supplement TrEMBL in 2003", *Nucleic Acids Res.*, 2003, vol. 31, pp. 365-370.

[4] L. Breiman, J. H. Friedman, R. A. Olshen, and C. J. Stone, *Classification and regression trees*, Wadsworth Inc., 1984, pp. 43-49.

[5] L. Breiman, "Bias, variance, and arcing classifiers", Technical Report 460, UC-Berkeley, 1996.

[6] A. P. Dempster, N. M. Laird and D. B. Rubin, "Maximum likelihood from incomplete data via the EM algorithm", *J. Roy. Statistical Society (B)*, 1977, vol. 39, pp. 1-38.

[7] A. K. Dunker, C. J. Brown, J. D. Lawson, L. M. Iakoucheva and Z. Obradovic, "Intrinsic disorder and protein function", *Biochemistry*, 2002, vol. 41(21), pp. 6573-6582.

[8] N. Japkowicz, "The class imbalance problem: significance and strategies", In *Proc. of IC-AI'00*, 2000.

[9] B. Liu, W. S. Lee, P. S. Yu and X. Li, "Partially supervised classification of text documents", In *Proc. of ICML'02*,

2002, pp. 387-394.

[10] K. Nigam, A. McCallum, S. Thrun and T. Mitchell, "Text classification from labeled and unlabeled documents using EM", *Mach. Learning*, 2000, vol. 39(2/3), pp. 103-134.

[11] Z. Obradovic, K. Peng, S. Vucetic, P. Radivojac, C. J. Brown and A. K. Dunker, "Predicting intrinsic disorder from amino acid sequence", *Proteins, Special Issue on CASP5*, in press.

[12] J. C. Platt, "Probabilistic outputs for support vector machines and comparison to regularized likelihood methods", In *Advances in Large Margin Classifiers*, A. J. Smola, P. Bartlett, B. Scholkopf, D. Schuurmans (eds.): MIT Press, 1999, pp. 61-74.

[13] M. F. Porter, "An algorithm for suffix stripping", *Program*, 1980, vol. 14(3), pp. 130-137.

[14] F. Provost and P. Domingos, "Well-trained PETs: Improving probability estimation trees", CeDER Working Paper #IS-0004, Stern School of Business, New York University, 2000.

[15] M. D. Richard and R. P. Lippmann, "Neural network classifiers estimate Bayesian a posteriori probabilities", *Neural Comput.*, 1991, vol. 3, pp. 461-483.

[16] G. Salton and C. Buckley, "Term-weighting approaches in automatic text retrieval", *Inf. Process. Manage.*, 1988, vol. 24(5), pp. 513-523.

[17] M. Seeger, "Learning with labeled and unlabeled data", Technical Report, Institute for Adaptive and Neural Computation, University of Edinburgh, 2001.

[18] B. Shahshahani and D. Landgrebe, "The effect of unlabeled samples in reducing the small sample size problem and mitigating the Hughes phenomenon", *IEEE Trans. Geosci. Remote Sens.*, 1994, vol. 32(5), pp. 1087-1095.

[19] D. M. J. Tax and R. P. W. Duin, "Uniform Object Generation for Optimizing One-class Classifiers", *J. Mach. Learn. Res., Special Issue on Kernel Methods*, 2002, vol. 2(2), pp. 155-173.

[20] V. N. Vapnik, *Statistical Learning Theory*, Wiley, 1998.

[21] S. Vucetic, D. Pokrajac, H. Xie and Z. Obradovic, "Detection of underrepresented biological sequences using class-conditional distribution models", In *Proc. of SIAM SDM'03*, 2003, pp. 279-283.

[22] Y. Wu, Q. Tian and T. S. Huang, "Integrating unlabeled images for image retrieval based on relevance feedback", In *Proc. of ICPR'00*, 2000.

[23] G. Yona, N. Linial and M. Linial, "ProtoMap: Automatic classification of protein sequences, a hierarchy of protein families, and local maps of the protein space", *Proteins*, 1999, vol. 37, pp. 360-378.

[24] B. Zadrozny and C. Elkan, "Transforming classifier scores into accurate multiclass probability estimates", In *Proc. of KDD'02*, 2002, pp. 694-699.

Statistical Relational Learning for Document Mining

Alexandrin Popescul
Computer and Information Science
University of Pennsylvania
Philadelphia, PA 19104 USA
popescul@cis.upenn.edu

Lyle H. Ungar
Computer and Information Science
University of Pennsylvania
Philadelphia, PA 19104 USA
ungar@cis.upenn.edu

Steve Lawrence*
Google
2400 Bayshore Parkway
Mountain View, CA 94043 USA
lawrence@google.com

David M. Pennock*
Overture Services, Inc.
74 N. Pasadena Ave., 3rd floor
Pasadena, CA 91103 USA
david.pennock@overture.com

Abstract

A major obstacle to fully integrated deployment of many data mining algorithms is the assumption that data sits in a single table, even though most real-world databases have complex relational structures. We propose an integrated approach to statistical modeling from relational databases. We structure the search space based on "refinement graphs", which are widely used in inductive logic programming for learning logic descriptions. The use of statistics allows us to extend the search space to include richer set of features, including many which are not boolean. Search and model selection are integrated into a single process, allowing information criteria native to the statistical model, for example logistic regression, to make feature selection decisions in a step-wise manner. We present experimental results for the task of predicting where scientific papers will be published based on relational data taken from CiteSeer. Our approach results in classification accuracies superior to those achieved when using classical "flat" features. The resulting classifier can be used to recommend where to publish articles.

1. Introduction

Statistical learning techniques play an important role in data mining, however, their standard formulation is almost exclusively limited to a one table domain representation. Such algorithms are presented with a set of candidate features, and a model selection process then makes decisions

regarding their inclusion into a model. Thus, the process of feature generation is decoupled from modeling, often being performed manually. This stands as a major obstacle to the fully integrated application of such modeling techniques in real-world practice where data is most often stored in relational form. It is often not obvious which features will be relevant, and the human effort to fully explore the richness of a domain is often too costly. Thus, it is crucial to provide statistical modeling techniques with an integrated functionality to navigate richer data structures to discover potentially new and complex sources of relevant evidence.

We present a form of statistical relational learning which integrates regression with feature generation from relational data. In this paper we use logistic regression, giving a method we call Structural Logistic Regression (SLR). SLR combines the strengths of classical statistical modeling with the high expressivity of features, both boolean and real-valued, automatically generated from a relational database. SLR falls into a family of models proposed in Inductive Logic Programming (ILP) called "upgrades" [23]. Upgrades extend propositional learners to handle relational representation. An upgrade implies that modeling and relational structure search are integrated into a single process dynamically driven by the assumptions and model selection criteria of a propositional learner used. This contrasts with another approach proposed in ILP called "propositionalization" [21]. Propositionalization generally implies a decoupling of relational feature construction and modeling. It has certain disadvantages compared to upgrading, as it is difficult to decide a priori what features will be useful. Upgrading techniques let their learning algorithms select their own features with their own criteria. In large problems it is impossible to "exhaustively" propositionalize, and the fea-

---
* Work conducted at NEC Laboratories America, Inc., 4 Independence Way, Princeton, NJ 08540 USA.

275

ture construction should be driven dynamically at the time of learning. An extreme form of propositionalization is generating the full join of a database. This is both impractical and incorrect—the size of the resulting table is prohibitive, and the notion of a training instance is lost, now being represented by multiple rows. Moreover, the entries in the full join table will be atomic attribute values, rather than richer features resulting from complex queries.

We apply SLR to document mining in (hyper)-linked domains. Linked document collections, such as the Web, patent databases or scientific publications are inherently relational, noisy and sparse. The characteristics of such domains form a good match with our method: i) links between documents suggest relational representation and ask for techniques being able to navigate such structures; "flat" file domain representation is inadequate in such domains; ii) the noise in available data sources suggests statistical rather than deterministic approaches, and iii) often extreme sparsity in such domains requires a focused feature generation and their careful selection with a discriminative model, which allows modeling of complex, possibly deep, but local regularities rather than attempting to build a full probabilistic model of the entire domain.

SLR integrates logistic regression with relational feature generation. We formulate the feature generation process as search in the space of relational database queries, based on the top-down search of refinement graphs widely used in ILP [10]. The use of statistics allows modeling of real-valued features, and instead of treating each node of the graph as a logic formula, we treat it as a database query resulting in a table of all satisfying solutions and the introduction of aggregate operators resulting in a richer set of features. We use statistical information criteria during the search to dynamically determine which features are to be included into the model. The language of non-recursive first-order logic formulas has a direct mapping to SQL and relational algebra, which can be used as well for the purposes of our discussion, e.g. as we do in [29]. In large applications SQL should be preferred for efficiency and database connectivity reasons.

We use the data from CiteSeer, an online digital library of computer science papers [24]. CiteSeer contains a rich set of relational data, including citation information, the text of titles, abstracts and documents, author names and affiliations, and conference or journal names, which we represent in relational form (Section 2). We report results for the task of paper classification into conference/journal classes.

The next section introduces the CiteSeer relational domain and defines the learning tasks. The methodology is presented in Section 3. Section 4 presents the experimental results demonstrating that relational features significantly improve classification accuracies. We provide an extended discussion of related work in Section 5. Section 6 concludes the paper with discussion and future work directions.

2. Task and Data

The experimental task explored here is the classification of scientific papers into categories defined by the conference or journal in which they appear. Publication venues vary in size and topic coverage, possibly overlapping, but do focus around a particular scientific endeavor, broader or narrower. This task can be viewed as a variant of community classification. Communities are not only defined by topical commonalities through document content but also by interaction between community members in the form of citations, co-authorship, and publishing in the same venues.

The data for our experiments was taken from CiteSeer [24]. CiteSeer catalogs scientific publications available in full-text on the web in PostScript and PDF formats. It extracts and matches citations to produce a browsable citation graph. Documents in CiteSeer were matched with the DBLP database (http://dblp.uni-trier.de/) to extract their publication venues. The domain contains rich sources of information which we represent in relational form. The following schema is used, where capitalized words indicate the type of a corresponding attribute:

$published\_in(Document, Venue)$,
$cites(Document, Document)$,
$word\_count(Document, Word, Count)$,
$title\_word(Document, Word)$,
$author\_of(Document, Person)$.

We define a number of separate binary classification tasks. The choice of binary rather than multi-class tasks is dictated in this paper by the use of (two-class) logistic regression which comes with readily available model selection functionality. A multi-class classifier, if equipped with model selection, can be used for more general multi-class tasks. For each classification task here, we:

- Select a pair of conferences or journals.

- Split the documents of two classes 50/50 into training and test core sets.

- Include documents that are cited by or cite the core documents (citation graph neighborhood).

- Extract relation *cites* for all core and just added documents in the citation graph neighborhood.

- Exclude from the training background knowledge any reference to the test set core documents.

- For all documents extract the remaining background knowledge: *word_count*, *title_word*, *author_of*, and *published_in*. Since, in the case of core class documents, the last relation is the actual answer, we allow it to be used only when relating to the venues of linked documents (Section 4).[1]

3. Methodology

SLR couples two main processes: generation of features from relational data and their selection with statistical model selection criteria. Figure 1 highlights the main components of our learning setting. Relational feature generation is a search problem. It requires formulation of the search in the space of relational database queries. Our structuring of the search space is based on the formulation widely used in inductive logic programming for learning logic descriptions, and extended to include other types of queries as the use of statistics relaxes the necessity of limiting the search space to only boolean values. The process results in a statistical model where each selected feature is the evaluation of a database query encoding a predictive data pattern in a given domain.

Logistic regression is a discriminative model, that is, it models conditional class probabilities without attempting to model marginal distributions of features. Model parameters are learned by maximizing a conditional likelihood function. Regression coefficients linearly combine features in a "logit" transformation resulting in values in the [0,1] interval, interpreted as probabilities of a positive class. More complex models will results in higher likelihood values, but at some point will likely overfit the data, resulting in poor generalization. A number of criteria aiming at striking the balance between optimizing the likelihood of training data and model complexity have been proposed. Among the more widely used are the Akaike Information Criterion (AIC) [1] and the Bayesian Information Criterion (BIC) [33]. These statistics work by penalizing the likelihood by a term that depends on model complexity (i.e. the number of selected features). AIC and BIC differ in this penalty term, which is larger for BIC in all but very small data sets of only several examples, and resulting in smaller models and better generalization performance. A model selection process selects a subset of available predictors with the goal of learning a more generalizable model.

Relational feature generation is a search problem. We use top-down search of refinement graphs [34, 10], and introduce aggregate operators into the search to extend the feature space. The extension is possible when using a statistical modeling which allows modeling of real-valued features in addition to only boolean values used in logic.

The top-down search of refinement graphs starts with the most general rule and specializes it producing more specific ones. The search space is constrained by specifying a language of legal clauses, for example by disallowing nega-

tions and recursive definitions, and is structured by imposing a partial ordering on such clauses through the syntactic notion of generality. This defines the refinement graph as a directed acyclic graph, where each node is a clause. The nodes are expanded from the most general to more specific clauses by applying a refinement operator. The refinement operator is a mapping from a clause to a set of its most general specializations. This is achieved by applying two syntactic operations: i) a single variable substitution, or ii) an addition of a new relation to the body of the clause, involving one or more of variables already present, and possibly introducing new variables. We make typing control with meta-schema, that is, we disallow bindings of variables of different types (e.g. $Document$ is never attempted to match with $Word$). Figure 2 presents a fragment of the search space in our domain.

We extend the search space by treating bodies of clauses not as $true/false$ values, but rather as queries resulting in a table of all satisfying solutions. These tables are aggregated to produce scalar numeric values to be used as features in statistical learners. The use of refinement graphs to search over database queries rather than over the first-order formulas retains richer information. In our approach, numeric attributes are always left unbound (substitutions for numeric attributes are disallowed). This avoids certain numeric reasoning limitations known to exist when learning first-order logic rules. Consider a refinement graph node referring to a learning example d:

$$word\_count(d, logistic, C).$$

Its evaluation will produce a one cell table for each d. Evaluation for all such training examples produces a column of counts of the word "logistic". The query

$$cites(d, D), word\_count(D, logistic, C)$$

will produce, for each training example d, a table of pairs of cited document IDs with their counts of the word "logistic". Averaging the column of counts produces the average count of the word "logistic" in cited documents.

An algebra for aggregations is necessary. Although there is no limit to the number of aggregate operators one may try, for example square root of the sum of column values, logarithm of their product etc., we find a few of them to be particularly useful. We propose the aggregate operators typically used in SQL: $size$, ave, min, max, and $empty$. Aggregations can be applied to a whole table or to individual columns, as appropriate given type restrictions. We use the following notation to denote aggregate query results: $function_{Var}[query]$, where $function$ is an aggregate operator, its subscript Var is a variable in the query specifying the aggregated column. If an aggregate operator applies to the whole table rather than an individual column, the subscript is omitted.

---

[1] Word counts are extracted from the first 5k of document text. The words are normalized with the Porter stemmer. Stop words are removed.

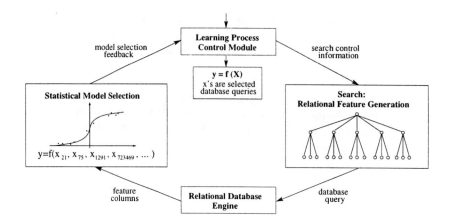

Figure 1. The search in the space of database queries involving one or more relations produces feature candidates one at a time to be considered by the statistical model selection component.

For example, the number of times a training example d is cited is $size[cites(D, d)]$. The average count of the word "learning" in documents cited from d is:

$$ave_C [cites(d, D), word\_count(D, learning, C)].$$

Once the search space is structured, a search strategy should be chosen. Here we use breadth-first search. This will not always be feasible in larger domains, and intelligent search heuristics will be needed. Incorporating statistical modeling into the search, as we do, opens a number of attractive options such as sampling, providing a well understood statistical interpretation of feature usefulness.

4. Results

We demonstrate the use of Structural Logistic Regression (SLR) by predicting publication venues of articles from CiteSeer. We select five binary classification tasks. Four tasks are composed by pairing both KDD and WWW with their two closest conferences in the immediate citation graph neighborhood as measured by the total number of citations connecting the two conferences. SIGMOD and VLDB rank the top two for both KDD and WWW. The fifth task is a pair of AI and ML Journals (Artificial Intelligence, Elsevier Science and Machine Learning, Kluwer respectively). Table 1 contains the sizes of classes and their immediate citation graph neighborhoods. The number of papers analyzed is subject to availability in both CiteSeer and DBLP.

The results reported here are produced by searching the subspace of the search graph over the queries involving one or two relations, where in the latter case one relation is *cites*. At present, we avoid subspaces resulting in a quadratic (or larger) number of features, such as co-authorship or word co-occurrences in a document. The exploration of such larger subspaces as an important future

Table 1. Sizes of classes and their citation graph neighborhoods.

CLASS	# CORE DOCS	# NEIGHBORS
ARTIF. INTELLIGENCE	431	9,309
KDD	256	7,157
MACHINE LEARNING	284	5,872
SIGMOD	402	7,416
VLDB	484	3,882
WWW	184	1,824

direction (e.g. sampling can be used). We do not consider queries involving the incoming citations to the learning core class documents as we assume that this knowledge is missing for the test examples. Since the relation *published_in* duplicates the response class labels, we allow it to participate in the search only as part of more complex queries relating to the venues of cited documents.

Model selection is performed in two phases: preselection and final model selection. We allow the first phase to be more inclusive and make more rigorous model selection at the final phase. First, the features generated during the search are checked for addition into the model by the AIC. This phase performs a forward-only step-wise selection. A feature is preselected if it improves the AIC by at least 1%. After every 500 search nodes, the model is refreshed. All preselected features participate in the final selection phase with a forward-backward stepwise procedure. A more restrictive BIC statistic is used at this phase. The preselection phase is currently used to remove the ordering bias, which may favor shallow features.

We compare the performance of the resulting models to those trained using only "flat" features. Flat features only involve the data available immediately in a learning exam-

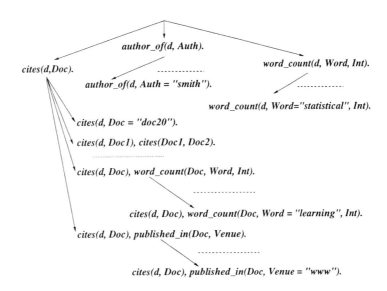

Figure 2. Fragment of the search space. Each node is a database query about a learning example d evaluated to a table of satisfying bindings. Aggregate operators are used to produce scalar features.

ple, that is authorship, text and title words. They do not involve data referring to or contained in other documents. We refer the reader to [30] for evidence supporting logistic regression in comparisons to pure or propositionalized FOIL modeling in this domain. We do not compare to other "flat" components; they can also be used within our approach, if supplied with a model selection mechanism. We focus instead on demonstrating the usefulness of more complex relational features as part of a common feature generation framework. Comparing logistic regression to other propositional models would be attempting to answer a different question. A common conclusion made in large-scale comparison studies, e.g. [25], is that there is no single best algorithm across all different datasets. However, logistic regression is often quite successful.

The models we found had average test set accuracies of 83.5% and 80.2% for relational and flat representations respectively. The 3.3 percentage points improvement is significant at the 99% confidence level based on the standard t-test. The improvement from relational features was achieved in all tasks. Table 2 details the performance in each task. Table 3 summarizes for each task the final number of selected features, the number of preselected features, and the total number of features considered. The total number of features considered is a function of vocabulary selection and of the density of citation graph neighborhoods. We store in the database word counts greater than two for a given document. Authors of only one paper in a data set are not recorded, nor are the non-core class documents linked to the rest of the collection by only one citation.

Table 4 gives examples of some of the highly significant

Table 2. Training and test sets accuracy (selection with BIC).

TASK	TRAIN		TEST	
	REL.	FLAT	REL.	FLAT
WWW - SIGMOD	95.2	90.3	**79.3**	77.5
WWW - VLDB	93.5	90.6	**85.1**	83.2
KDD - SIGMOD	99.1	90.4	**83.3**	79.8
KDD - VLDB	97.8	91.2	**87.7**	83.7
AI - ML	93.8	86.5	**82.2**	76.7

relational features learned. Not all types of relational features were equally useful in terms of how often they were selected into the models. Commonly selected features are based on word counts in cited documents and cited publication venues. Authorship or features involving citations to concrete documents were selected relatively infrequently; their utility would increase when other sources of features are unavailable, for example, when the words are not available or in multi-lingual environments.

5. Related Work and Discussion

A number of approaches "upgrading" propositional learners to relational representations have been proposed in the inductive logic programming (ILP) community. Often, these approaches upgrade learners most suitable to binary attributes, for example, decision trees and association rules [4, 9]. The upgrade of classification and regression trees is proposed in [22]. Reinforcement learning was extended to relational representations [11]. Upgrading usu-

Table 3. Number of selected and generated features.

TASK	IN FINAL MODEL (BIC)		PRESELECTED		TOTAL CONSIDERED	
	REL.	FLAT	REL.	FLAT	REL.	FLAT
WWW - SIGMOD	17	18	588	138	79,878	16,230
WWW - VLDB	15	19	498	105	85,381	16,852
KDD - SIGMOD	20	13	591	122	83,548	16,931
KDD - VLDB	22	15	529	111	76,751	15,685
AI - ML	21	19	657	130	85,260	17,402

Table 4. Examples of selected relational features (p-values are less than 0.05; using BIC).

TASK	FEATURE	SUPPORTS CLASS
WWW - SIGMOD	$not\_empty\,[cites(d,\,D),\,published\_in(D,\,icde)]$	SIGMOD
	$size\,[cites(d,\,D),\,word\_count(D,\,page,\,C)]$	WWW
	$not\_empty\,[cites(d,\,D),\,word\_count(D,\,memori,\,C)]$	SIGMOD
WWW - VLDB	$size\,[cites(d,\,D),\,title\_word(D,\,join)]$	VLDB
	$not\_empty\,[cites(d,\,D),\,published\_in(D,\,www)]$	WWW
	$size\,[cites(d,\,D),\,word\_count(D,\,relat,\,C)]$	VLDB
KDD - SIGMOD	$ave_C\,[cites(d,\,D),\,word\_count(D,\,mine,\,C)]$	KDD
	$not\_empty\,[cites(d,D),\,word\_count(D,\,dbm,\,C)]$	SIGMOD
	$not\_empty\,[cites(d,D),\,cites(doc81863,\,D)]$	KDD
KDD - VLDB	$ave_C\,[cites(d,\,D),\,word\_count(D,\,learn,\,C)]$	KDD
	$not\_empty\,[cites(d,\,D),\,published\_in(D,\,icml)]$	KDD
	$not\_empty\,[cites(d,\,D),\,published\_in(D,\,kdd)]$	KDD
AI - ML	$not\_empty\,[cites(d,\,D),\,author\_of(D,\,schapire)]$	ML
	$ave_C\,[cites(d,\,D),\,word\_count(D,\,exampl,\,C)]$	ML
	$not\_empty\,[cites(d,\,D),\,published\_in(D,\,ijcai)]$	AI

ally implies that generation of relational features and their modeling are tightly coupled and driven by propositional learner's model selection criteria. SLR falls into the category of upgrading methods. Perhaps the approach most similar in spirit to ours is that taken in MACCENT system [8], which uses expected entropy gain from adding binary features to a maximum entropy classifier to direct a beam search over first-order clauses. They determine when to stop adding variables by testing the classifier on a held-out data set. A detailed discussion of upgrading is presented in [23]. ILP provides one way to structure the search space; others can be used [31].

Another approach is "propositionalization" [21], in which, as the term is usually used, features are first constructed from relational representation and then presented to a propositional algorithm. Feature generation is thus fully decoupled from the model used to make predictions. One form of propositionalization is to learn a logic theory with an ILP rule learner and then use it as binary features in a propositional learner. For example, linear regression is used to model features constructed with ILP to build predictive models in a chemical domain [35]. Aggregate operators are an attractive way of extending the set of propositionalized features. For example, aggregates can be used to construct a single table involving aggregate summaries and then using a standard propositional learner on this table [20]. Aggre-

gation in relational learning is discussed in detail in [28].

Decoupling feature construction from modeling, as in propositionalization, however, retains the inductive bias of the technique used to construct features, that is, better models potentially could be built if one allowed the propositional learner itself to select its own features based on its own criteria. First Order Regression System [18] more closely integrates feature construction into regression, but does so using a FOIL-like covering approach for feature construction. Additive models, such as logistic regression, have different criteria for feature usefulness; integrating feature generation and selection into a single loop is advocated in this context in [3, 30]. Coupling feature generation and model selection can also significantly reduce computational cost. By fully integrating a rich set of aggregate operators into the generation and search of the refinement graph, SLR avoids costly generation of features which will not be tested for inclusion in the model.

A number of models have been proposed which combine the expressivity of first-order logic with probabilistic semantics [2, 14, 19, 26, 32, 36]. For example, Stochastic Logic Programs [26] model uncertainty from within the ILP framework by providing logic theories with a probability distribution; Probabilistic Relational Models (PRMs) [14] are a relational upgrade of Bayesian networks. The marriage of richer representations and probability theory yields extremely powerful formalisms, and inevitably a number of equivalences among them can be observed. In addition to the question of semantic and representational equivalence, it is useful to also consider the differences in how models are built, that is, what objective function is optimized, what algorithm is used to optimize that function, what is done to avoid over-fitting, what simplifying assumptions are made.

A conflict exists between the two goals: i) probabilistically characterizing the entire domain and ii) building a model that addresses a specific question, such as classification or regression modeling of a single response variable. This distinction typically leads to two philosophies: "generative" and "discriminative" modeling. Generative models attempt to model feature distributions, while discriminative models, like SLR, only model the distribution of the response variable conditional on the features, thus vastly reducing the number of parameters which must be estimated. For this reason, our method allows inclusion of arbitrarily complex features without estimating their distribution, which is impossible in large and sparse environments.

PRMs, for example, are generative models of joint probability distribution capturing probabilistic influences between entities and their attributes in a relational domain. PRMs can provide answers to a large number of possible questions about the domain. An important limitation, however, of generative modeling is that often there is not enough data to reliably estimate the entire model. Generative modeling does not allow focusing the search for complex features arbitrarily deep. One can achieve superior performance by focusing only on a particular question, for example, class label prediction, and training models discriminatively to answer that question. Relational Markov Networks (RMNs) [36] address this problem since they are trained discriminatively. In RMNs, however, the structure of a learning domain, which determines which direct interactions are explored, is prespecified by a relational template, which precludes the discovery of deeper and more complex regularities advocated in this paper.

Learning from relational data brings new challenges. Relational correlations invalidate independence assumptions. This can be addressed explicitly by quantifying such relational correlations and learning to control for them [17], or for example, by using random effects structures to model relational dependencies [16]. Here, we address the problem of relational correlations implicitly by generating more complex features automatically. In the presence of a large number of feature candidates, selecting the right features can eliminate the independence violation by making the observations conditionally independent given these features.

Various techniques have been applied to learning hypertext classifiers. For example, predicted labels of neighboring documents can be used to reinforce classification decisions for a given document [5]. An iterative technique based on a Bayesian classifier that uses high confidence inferences to improve class inferences for linked objects at later iterations is proposed in [27]. A technique called Statistical Predicate Invention [7] which combines statistical and relational learning by using Naive Bayes classifications as predicates in FOIL has been applied to hypertext classification. Joint probabilistic models of document content and connectivity have also been used for document classification [6]. The text surrounding hyperlinks pointing to a given document was found to greatly improve text classification accuracy [13], and the so-called "extended anchortext" in citing documents has been used for classification and document description [15].

6. Conclusions and Future Work

We presented Structural Logistic Regression (SLR), an approach for statistical relational learning. It allows learning accurate predictive models from large relational databases. Modeling and feature selection is integrated into the search over the space of database queries generating feature candidates involving complex interactions among objects in a given database.

SLR falls into the category of upgrade methods proposed in inductive logic programming. Upgrades integrate a propositional learner into a search of relational features, where propositional learners feature selection criteria dynamically drive the process. We demonstrate the advantages of coupling a rich SQL-based extension of Horn clauses with classical statistical modeling for document classification. SLR extends beyond standard ILP approaches, allowing generation of richer features, better control of search of the feature space, and more accurate modeling in the presence of noise. On the other hand, SLR differs from relational probabilistic network models, such as PRMs and RMNs, because these network models, while being good at handling uncertainly, have not been used successfully to learn complex new relationships. Our approach is easily extended to other regression models.

Our experimental results show the utility of SLR for document classification in the CiteSeer domain, which includes citation structure, textual evidence, paper authorship and publication venues. Relational features improved classification accuracy in all tasks. The average improvement of 3.3 percentage points over already high accuracies achieved by models using only flat features is statistically significant at the 99% confidence level.

Our approach is designed to scale to large data sets, and thus generates features by searching SQL queries rather than Horn clauses, and uses statistical rather than ad hoc methods for deciding which features to include into the model. SQL encourages the use of a much richer feature space, including many aggregates which produce real values, rather than the more limited boolean features produced by Horn clauses. SQL is preferable to Prolog for efficiency reasons, as it incorporates many optimizations necessary for scaling to large problems. Also, statistical feature selection allows rigorous determination of what information about current regression models should be used to select the subspaces of the query space to explore. Further information such as sampling from feature subspaces to determine their promise and use of database meta-information will help scale SLR to truly large problems.

We are also working on using clustering to extend the set of relations generating new features. Clusters improve modeling of sparse data, improve scalability, and produce richer representations [12]. New cluster relations can be derived using attributes in other relations. As the schema is expanded, the search space grows rapidly, and intelligent search and feature selection become even more critical.

References

[1] H. Akaike. Information theory and an extension of the maximum likelihood principle. In *2nd Int'l Symposium on Information Theory*, 1973.

[2] C. Anderson, P. Domingos, and D. Weld. Relational Markov models and their application to adaptive web navigation. In *KDD*, 2002.

[3] H. Blockeel and L. Dehaspe. Cumulativity as inductive bias. In *Workshops: Data Mining, Decision Support, Meta-Learning and ILP at PKDD*, 2000.

[4] H. Blockeel and L. D. Raedt. Top-down induction of logical decision trees. *Artificial Intelligence*, 101(1-2), 1998.

[5] S. Chakrabarti, B. E. Dom, and P. Indyk. Enhanced hypertext categorization using hyperlinks. In *SIGMOD*, 1998.

[6] D. Cohn and T. Hofmann. The missing link - A probabilistic model of document content and hypertext connectivity. In *NIPS*, volume 13. MIT Press, 2001.

[7] M. Craven and S. Slattery. Relational learning with statistical predicate invention: Better models for hypertext. *Machine Learning*, 43(1/2), 2001.

[8] L. Dehaspe. Maximum entropy modeling with clausal constraints. In *ILP*, 1997.

[9] L. Dehaspe and H. Toivonen. Discovery of frequent datalog patterns. *Data Mining and Knowledge Discovery*, 3(1), 1999.

[10] S. Dzeroski and N. Lavrac. An introduction to inductive logic programming. In S. Dzeroski and N. Lavrac, editors, *Relational Data Mining*. Springer-Verlag, 2001.

[11] S. Dzeroski, L. D. Raedt, and H. Blockeel. Relational reinforcement learning. In *ICML*, 1998.

[12] D. Foster and L. Ungar. A proposal for learning by ontological leaps. In *Snowbird Learning Conference*, 2002.

[13] J. Furnkranz. Exploiting structural information for text classification on the WWW. *Intelligent Data Analysis*, 1999.

[14] L. Getoor, N. Friedman, D. Koller, and A. Pfeffer. Learning probabilistic relational models. In S. Dzeroski and N. Lavrac, editors, *Relational Data Mining*. Springer-Verlag, 2001.

[15] E. J. Glover, K. Tsioutsiouliklis, S. Lawrence, D. M. Pennock, and G. Flake. Using web structure for classifying and describing web pages. In *Int'l WWW Conference*, 2002.

[16] P. Hoff. Random effects models for network data. In *National Academy of Sciences: Symposium on Social Network Analysis for National Security*, 2003.

[17] D. Jensen and J. Neville. Linkage and autocorrelation cause feature selection bias in relational learning. In *ICML*, 2002.

[18] A. Karalic and I. Bratko. First order regression. *Machine Learning*, 26, 1997.

[19] K. Kersting and L. D. Raedt. Towards combining inductive logic programming and Bayesian networks. In *ILP*, 2001.

[20] A. J. Knobbe, M. D. Haas, and A. Siebes. Propositionalisation and aggregates. In *PKDD*. 2001.

[21] S. Kramer, N. Lavrac, and P. Flach. Propositionalization approaches to relational data mining. In S. Dzeroski and N. Lavrac, editors, *Relational Data Mining*. Springer-Verlag, 2001.

[22] S. Kramer and G. Widmer. Inducing classification and regression trees in first order logic. In S. Dzeroski and N. Lavrac, editors, *Relational Data Mining*. Springer-Verlag, 2001.

[23] W. V. Laer and L. D. Raedt. How to upgrade propositional learners to first order logic: A case study. In S. Dzeroski and N. Lavrac, editors, *Relational Data Mining*. Springer-Verlag, 2001.

[24] S. Lawrence, C. L. Giles, and K. Bollacker. Digital libraries and autonomous citation indexing. *IEEE Computer*, 32(6), 1999.

[25] T.-S. Lim, W.-Y. Loh, and Y.-S. Shih. A comparison of prediction accuracy, complexity, and training time of thirty-three old and new classification algorithms. *Machine Learning*, 40, 2000.

[26] S. Muggleton. Stochastic logic programs. In *ILP*, 1995.

[27] J. Neville and D. Jensen. Iterative classification in relational data. In *AAAI Workshop on Learning Statistical Models from Relational Data*, 2000.

[28] C. Perlich and F. Provost. Aggregation-based feature invention and relational concept classes. In *KDD*, 2003.

[29] A. Popescul and L. H. Ungar. Statistical relational learning for link prediction. In *IJCAI Workshop on Learning Statistical Models from Relational Data*, 2003.

[30] A. Popescul, L. H. Ungar, S. Lawrence, and D. M. Pennock. Towards structural logistic regression: Combining relational and statistical learning. In *KDD Workshop on Multi-Relational Data Mining*, 2002.

[31] D. Roth and W. Yih. Relational learning via propositional algorithms. In *IJCAI*, 2001.

[32] T. Sato. A statistical learning method for logic programs with distribution semantics. In *ICLP*, 1995.

[33] G. Schwartz. Estimating the dimension of a model. *The Annals of Statistics*, 6(2), 1979.

[34] E. Shapiro. *Algorithmic Program Debugging*. MIT, 1983.

[35] A. Srinivasan and R. King. Feature construction with inductive logic programming: A study of quantitative predictions of biological activity aided by structural attributes. *Data Mining and Knowledge Discovery*, 3(1), 1999.

[36] B. Taskar, P. Abbeel, and D. Koller. Discriminative probabilistic models for relational data. In *UAI*, 2002.

Integrating Customer Value Considerations into Predictive Modeling

Saharon Rosset, Einat Neumann

Amdocs Ltd

{saharonr, einatn}@amdocs.com

Abstract

The success of prediction models for business purposes should not be measured by their accuracy only. Their evaluation should also take into account the higher importance of precise prediction for "valuable" customers. We illustrate this idea through the example of churn modeling in telecommunications, where it is obviously much more important to identify potential churn among valuable customers. We discuss, both theoretically and empirically, the optimal use of "customer value" data in the model training, model evaluation and scoring stages. Our main conclusion is that a non-trivial approach of using "decayed" value-weights for training is usually preferable to the two obvious approaches of either using non-decayed customer values as weights or ignoring them.

1. Introduction

Successful analysis and modeling of data can contribute greatly to the success of businesses. A key ingredient in fulfilling this promise is to integrate an understanding of the true goals, processes and criteria for success of the business into the data analysis process. In previous papers we have tackled the problems of correct consideration of business goals in model evaluation [10] and of calculating and utilizing customer lifetime value [11]. In this paper we present another key issue in successful modeling for business purposes: consideration and inclusion of customer-value information in all phases of the data analysis process: insight discovery, predictive modeling, model evaluation and scoring. As a concrete example, consider the problem of churn analysis in wireless telephony. The prediction task is clearly a binary one, namely to predict whether or not a customer will disconnect and switch to a competitor. However the loss incurred by incorrect prediction depends on the individual customer value: wrongly predicting the behavior of a low value customer should not worry the telecommunication company at all, while making a mistake on a premium customer can lead to grave consequences.

Calculating a customer's current value is usually a straight forward calculation based on the customer's current or recent information: usage, price plan, payments, collection efforts, call center contacts, etc. An example for the customer value can be 'The financial value of a customer to the organization'. This value can be calculated from 'received payments' minus the 'cost of supplying products and services' to the customer.

Let us assume, therefore, that we know how to calculate customer value from available data. In this case, although the customer value is a *known* quantity, it still plays an important role in evaluating the performance of prediction models for *unknown* quantities such as a churn indicator. The key statistical question is what is the correct use of these customer values in the modeling stage, to create models that are most useful for the "weighted" loss. We tackle this problem theoretically in section 3 and experimentally in section 6. We consider the two naive extreme approaches:

1. Ignore customer values in the modeling stage i.e. treat the problem as a "standard" modeling problem
2. Optimize customer-value weighted loss on the training data

We show that these are both generally sub-optimal and that an intermediate approach of using decayed customer-value weights for training is usually preferable to both.

Additional stages in the modeling and scoring process where customer values should be considered are:

- Presenting knowledge discovery results (e.g. patterns) to a user. We advocate presenting both the customer-value weighted and non-weighted results to complement each other. An example can be seen in section 5.

- Model evaluation. Model evaluation on unseen ("test") data should clearly take into account the specific way in which "future" loss is defined. Thus it should use the customer values to weigh the loss in the same way as the business would. See section 4.

- Scoring for prediction. This is the "deployment" stage of the model. The way in which the scoring process should use the customer values depends on the way in which the resulting scores are to be used. For example, if the scores are going to be used for choosing a segment to run a retention campaign on, then the individual customer churn scores should be multiplied by customer values and then sorted to find the optimal campaign population.

In section 6 we give a detailed example of the use of customer value in the various data analysis stages within the Amdocs CRM Analytics module. It illustrates the importance and usefulness of correctly using customer value. Our formulation of the learning problem can be interpreted as a cost-sensitive learning task where the costs differ by instance rather than by class. [13] mentions it as one of the under-researched types of cost-sensitive learning. Several authors have presented and discussed similar problems in this context. For example, [8] attribute costs to fraud cases in telecommunication, while [2] considers donation amounts as "customer values" in a donation solicitation direct marketing campaign. Our discussion adds to previous work in two main points: Rather than concentrating on the specific stages, we track the use of customer value throughout the knowledge discovery process in a churn analysis system. In the modeling stage, we present our novel approach of using "decayed" customer values as weights in model training. This approach is justified both theoretically and empirically.

2. The role of customer value

When building prediction models, we usually have in mind a "loss function" which describes the measure of accuracy we are going to apply to our prediction model. In the churn analysis example this loss function may consider the cost of losing a customer because the model did not classify him/her as a "churner" (i.e. a "false negative"); and the cost of making a needless retention effort on a "loyal" customer because the model classified her/him as a "churner" (i.e. a "false positive"). Denote the former cost by c_1 and the latter cost by c_2. A naive modeling effort would target finding a model, which minimizes the loss when applied to future, unseen data, i.e. minimize

$$P(\text{false negative}) \cdot c_1 + P(\text{false positive}) \cdot c_2$$

over the population distribution. A more sophisticated view would consider customer value as a relevant quantity in determining the loss. In particular, a reasonable modeling goal is to minimize *expected customer-value weighted loss*, i.e. look for a model, which minimizes:

$$E\{V [I(\text{false negative}) \cdot c_1 + I(\text{false positive}) \cdot c_2]\}$$

where V is a random variable describing the customer's value, and I is the indicator function.

More generally, we could consider having a "non-weighted" loss function L, which depends on the observed responses and the predicted ones, where our real goal is to minimize the customer-value weighted expected loss, i.e. we want to find a model $f(x)$ that minimizes

$$E [V L(Y, f(X))] \qquad (1)$$

Situations where such a value-weighted loss would be natural for the problem are actually quite prevalent in various areas, such as credit card fraud [1], loan approval data [9], survey analysis [3] and more. The modeling tasks involved could be classification, regression or even non-predictive parameter estimation.

3. The use of customer values in modeling

We now concentrate on investigating the correct use of customer values (or more generally observation importance weights) when building prediction models, from a theoretical perspective. The general framework is: We have data $(x_i, y_i)i=1^n$ and we also have observation value information $(v_i)i=1^n$. These data come from a joint distribution on (X, Y, V). Our goal is to build a model, which minimizes some expected loss L, weighted by observation value, i.e. we want our model f to minimize $E_{XYV} V L (Y, f(X))$.

The main question we want to answer, is how should we use the training observation values vi in order to build "good" models. More specifically, we consider minimizing a weighted loss function on our training data of the following form:

$$\sum_{i=1}^{n} v_i^p L(y_i, f(x_i)) \qquad (2)$$

Taking $p=1$ amounts to weighting the empirical loss by the customer values, while taking $p=0$ means we are ignoring the values completely in building our model. We could certainly consider other families of transformations for the customer values, other than the power transformation used here, but for clarity and brevity we limit this discussion to this family only. As candidates for f we will consider the family of linear models in our predictors $f(x) = \beta'x$. Our results will have broader implications than for what is usually called "linear models" only, since many "non-linear" modeling techniques can be described as linear models in some alternative domain: kernel support vector machines [4], boosting [12] and logistic regression are a few examples.

We will start by analyzing linear regression, i.e. the loss is squared error loss. For that case we can derive rigorous results about the effects of weighting on the prediction error of our model. The results and insights we gain from this analysis will serve us as intuition for understanding and interpreting the experimental results we get for less "mathematically-friendly" situations.

3.1. Theoretical analysis of linear regression

Consider the simple case of linear regression, using squared error loss:

$$L(y, \hat{f}(x)) = (y - \hat{f}(x))^2$$

The family of models we are considering is linear models:

$$\hat{f}(x) = \hat{\beta}'x$$

Our goal is to minimize the expected value-weighted "future" squared error loss:

$$E_{XYV}[V(Y - \beta^t X)^2]$$

As in (2), we estimate β by minimizing weighted squared error loss on our training data, with the weights being decayed versions of the actual observation weights:

$$\hat{\beta}^{(p)} = \arg\min_{\beta} \sum_{i=1}^{n} v_i^p (y_i - \beta^t x_i)^2, \qquad p \in [0,1]$$

Finding $\hat{\beta}^{(p)}$ is straightforward. If we denote by Z the data matrix whose rows are the x_i observations and denote by $W(p)$ a diagonal $n*n$ matrix, with the diagonal elements being v_i^p, then it is easy to obtain that

$$\hat{\beta}^{(p)} = (Z'W(p)Z)^{-1} Z'W(p)\mathbf{y}$$

Note that although this estimator is the same as the standard "weighted least squares" estimator (e.g. [14]), the underlying statistical theory is different, as in our case increased weight does <u>not</u> correspond to decreased variance. This affects our results in theorems 1 and 2 below, which do not hold for weighted least squares.

Let us now add a couple of additional assumptions for the purpose of our statistical analysis:

1. Our true model is of the form $Y = f(x) + \varepsilon$, where $f(x)=E(Y|x)$ is the best "oracle" prediction at this x, and ε has mean 0 and variance σ^2.

2. We are interested only in the predictions at the given "training" set of x_i and v_i values. In other words, the only randomness we are considering is in the distribution of the response. This is an extension of the "fixed-x" assumption usually made to facilitate easier analysis of linear models. This extension is somewhat problematic as the stochasticity of the customer value plays an important role in our discussion. However the insights we gain from our results will remain valid even when we allow random customer values (see discussion below).

The key to our analysis will be the decomposition of the expected squared error loss into three components: irreducible error, squared bias and variance. For a derivation of this decomposition, see for example [4]. In our case, we apply this decomposition to the weighted squared error loss in the "fixed x and v" case to get (denote by $\hat{f}(x)$ the prediction $\hat{\beta}^{(p)t} x$):

$$\sum_{i=1}^{n} v_i E(Y_i - \hat{f}(x_i))^2 = \sum_{i=1}^{n} v_i \sigma^2 +$$

$$\sum_{i=1}^{n} v_i (f(x_i) - E\hat{f}(x_i))^2 + \sum_{i=1}^{n} v_i E(\hat{f}(x_i) - E\hat{f}(x_i))^2 \quad (3)$$

Where all the expectations are over the distribution of both the sample y_i's and the future y_i's.

The first term is the "irreducible" error, which an ideal prediction would incur because of the inherent variability in the response. The second term is the value-weighted squared bias, sometimes referred to as approximation error. The third term is the variance of the prediction, or estimation error, since:

$$E(\hat{f}(x) - E\hat{f}(x))^2 = Var(\hat{f}(x))$$

The main idea behind this decomposition is that the two "reducible" additive components usually trade-off as a function of model complexity. Making the model more complex (for example, adding dimensions to the x predictor vector) decreases the bias by giving our model more flexibility to represent the "real" function f, but increases the variance since we are estimating a more complex model.

In our current context it turns out that the "decay" parameter p also serves to trade-off bias and variance. Setting $p=1$, i.e. using the non-decayed customer values in training, minimizes the value-weighted bias. Setting $p=0$ and ignoring the customer values in training, minimizes the variance. These two concepts are captured in the following theorems, whose proofs can be found in [9].

Theorem 1:
The variance of the fit is minimized when p=0:

$$\forall p, x, \quad Var(\hat{\beta}^{(0)t} x) \leq Var(\hat{\beta}^{(p)t} x)$$

This theorem shows that the variance term in (3) is uniformly minimized by ignoring the customer values completely. In other words, ignoring the values makes "most efficient" use of the training sample to estimate the coefficient vector β.

Theorem 2:
The average value-weighted squared bias is minimized when p=1:

$$\forall p, \quad \sum_{i=1}^{n} v_i (f(x_i) - (E\hat{\beta}^{(1)})^t x_i)^2 \leq \sum_{i=1}^{n} v_i (f(x_i) - (E\hat{\beta}^{(p)})^t x_i)^2$$

This theorem shows that the bias term in (3) is minimized by using the non-decayed customer values. In other words, using the values makes "most representative" use of the training sample to estimate the coefficient vector β.

Combining theorems 1 and 2 gives us some intuition about the bias-variance tradeoff involved in customer-value weighted analysis. We see that the variance is uniformly minimized when we take $p=0$, while the average value-weighted bias is minimized when we take $p=1$. The optimal power $p*$ will thus be determined by the balance between these two effects. In general, if the reducible error is dominated by variance (in particular if the model is unbiased), we can expect to get $p* \cong 0$, while if the bias effect is much bigger (in particular if we have a large training sample and not many parameters) then we can expect to get $p* \cong 1$.

It is important to note, though, that the bias results were based on the notion that the values remain the same on the ``future'' copy of the data. This assumption strongly biases our results towards favoring value weighting. For example, imagine that in reality the customer values of unseen customers are all i.i.d from some V-distribution, independent of the values of (X, Y). In that case, theorem 2 is completely irrelevant (since we cannot infer any useful information from the training customer value) and we can easily show that we can do no better than the solution with $p=0$ in terms of value weighted prediction error. However, if the unseen customer values are correlated with the training set values (as would generally be the case in real-life data), theorem 2 still has merit as an indicator that use of the training set values is likely to decrease future value-weighted bias.

3.2. Interpretation and discussion

If our loss is not squared error loss, in particular if the prediction task at hand is a classification task, then the terms "bias" and "variance" don't have a clear mathematical definition. However the conceptual ideas of "approximation error" and "estimation error" still describe the sources of error in our model. Approximation error tells us how good of a model our method could build if it had infinite data, while "estimation error" indicates how far from this best model are we can expect to be in our finite-sample case. And it stands to reason that the trade-off we observed in the squared error loss case would still be in effect, i.e.: using customer values as observation weights in the modeling stage improves "approximation" because it gives us a more reliable description of what our "future" loss looks like. Ignoring customer values in the modeling stage improves "estimation" because it gives us more "effective" observations to estimate the model with. This intuition is confirmed empirically in [9], as well as in our experiments with logistic regression in section 6.

4. The use of customer values in model evaluation and deployment

Our formulation of the prediction problem's true loss (1) as expected value-weighted loss implies that evaluation of our prediction models - whether using cross validation, a test-set, or real-life performance - should use value-weighted average loss as its performance measure:

$$\frac{1}{n}\sum_{i=1}^{n} v_i \, L(y_i, f(x_i))$$

Note that $f(x)$ is still a model for y, and the way in which we build the model (discussed in the previous section) affects only the way we estimate $f(x)$ but not the basic fact that it models the response y. Thus, the observation importance weights still need to be accounted for explicitly in the evaluation stage.

In many cases the situation is not as straight forward as the formulation we have described so far. In particular, the "true" loss may not have the form (1), and may not even be clearly defined when we build the model. This takes us back to the issue of correct "business oriented" evaluation of prediction models, with the added complication that we also need to take customer value into account. The intuitive way to overcome this complication is to use the same evaluation measure one would choose for the problem if all customer values were equal, and then modify it to take customer values into account and perform "value-weighted" evaluation. For example, consider using evaluation measures related to the lift or the ROC curve (see [10] for definition of the methods and discussion of their equivalence and [7] for a discussion of the desirable properties of the ROC). These measures require calculating scores for all test-set observations, sorting them and calculating ratios of coverage of "responders" and "non-responders" at a pre-determined cutoff point. If we want to calculate these measures with regard to a customer-value weighted objective, we should re-calibrate the "scores" by multiplying them by individual customer values. In the example of churn analysis, the *value-lift at percentile x* would then correspond to: *percentage of churn customer value in the top x% of sorted list / percentage of total customer value in the top x% of the sorted* list.

We discuss this model evaluation approach in more detail in section 5.3, and give an illustrated example in section 6. In the model deployment (or scoring) stage, when the model we have built is actually used for supporting and guiding business or marketing decisions, we should similarly consider customer value in any scoring process. In particular, customer propensity scores should be multiplied by customer value to give "expected value loss" scores. Such value-weighted scores should also guide selection of campaign populations.

5. Value weighted analysis in Amdocs CRM Analytics module

The Business Insight Professional Services unit of the CRM division at Amdocs tailors analytical solutions to the business problems of Amdocs' customers in the telecommunication industry. Among the solutions are Churn and retention analysis, Fraud detection [5], Lifetime Value modeling [11], Bad Debt analysis, Product analysis and more. For the purpose of churn management and analysis, we use the CRM Analytics module, which allows the users to perform all stages of the churn management process within one system. Customer value considerations come into play in many different stages of its workflow:
- Rule Discovery

- Segmentation and Analysis session
- Modeling
- Model Evaluation
- Scoring

We will now describe the main system components and the way in which customer value features in each one of them. The Knowledge Discovery process starts with data collection, cleaning, pre-processing and transforming to get a "flat file" which is the input to the analysis. In our context we need to make sure that customer value variables are included in the input data, in particular that a "customer value" calculated field has been added. Analytics offers a flexible value calculation interface, based on the information in the customer data-mart.

5.1. Rule discovery, segmentation and analysis

The first analytic step in Analytics is rule discovery. The algorithms used are decision tree and rule induction. Its output is a collection of rules (a.k.a. patterns) describing customer segments with strong tendency towards churn or loyalty. These rules are presented to the analyst, who can view and interpret them, modify them and add new rules that represent business knowledge not captured by the automated discovery. Figure 1 gives an example of a rule as viewed in the application. It contains the conditions defining the segment – in this case: at least 2 call center contacts and specific handsets (which are old and unsophisticated). It also displays various graphic and numeric illustrations of its statistics. For example, the "coverage" field tells us what population size this segment covers - it covers 252 customers in the sample, which are 8.4% of the total customer sample. The expected hit denotes the estimated churn probability, which is 72.2%. All of these statistics ignore customer value, i.e. are based on counting customers regardless of their value.

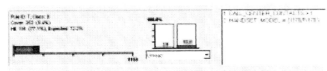

Figure 1. Rule view "by number"

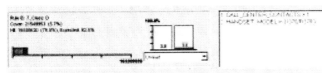

Figure 2. Rule view "by value"

However to give the analyst a reliable picture of the monetary impact of this segment's churn behavior it seems interesting to give a view of the segment's statistics calculated "by value" rather than "by number". Figure 2

shows the same segment as figure 1 but using the "by value" view instead of the "by number" view. Consider the "coverage" field in figure 2. It tells us that the combined "customer value" of all customers in this segment is 215,499.53, which is actually 5.7% of the total customer value in our customer sample. We see that this segment covers 8.4% of the customer population but only 5.7% of the total customer value. Also of interest is the difference in the "accuracy" field between the two panels. It tells us that 72.2% of the customers in this segment are churners, but that these represent 62.5% of the total customer value for all customers in the segment. To summarize our conclusions about this segment of customers that have unsophisticated handsets and have contacted the call center at least twice in the past month from this dual view:
- Their average customer value is 50% less than that of the general population
- Within this segment, the non-churn customers tend to have higher customer value than the churners (incidentally, that difference is about 50% as well – an easy calculation based on the numbers above).

This example illustrates the merit in combining a standard customer-based view and customer-value based view, which together allow us to understand the churn behavior of our customers and how it relates to revenue movement. The final output of the analysis stage is a set of useful and accurate segments that are used as inputs to the actual model building stage.

5.2. Model building

The main modeling tool in Analytics is logistic regression, which takes as input both the original variables and binary "features" representing the rules generated in the analysis stage. As we discussed in section 3, the main statistical focus of this paper is how to correctly transform the customer values into observation weights in the model training stage.

To understand how logistic regression can be modified to take observation weights, consider the generic formulation (2). Since logistic regression seeks to maximize the binomial log likelihood of the data, we can formulate is as a "loss minimization" problem using minus binomial log-likelihood as our loss. The weighted criterion analogy to (2) for logistic regression would thus be to minimize (4):

$$\sum_{i=1}^{n} w_i [y_i \log(\hat{p}_i) + (1 - y_i) \log(1 - \hat{p}_i)]$$

where $w_i = v_i^p$, $\hat{p}_i = \text{logit}^{-1}(\hat{\beta}^{(p)t} x_i)$, and β is the vector of coefficients which we aim to estimate.

Not surprisingly, this formulation is equivalent to having w_i identical copies of observation i in our training data, which also gives us an idea how we could estimate β using methods that are essentially identical to those used for non-weighted data (described in [6]). It should be emphasized that the output of logistic regression with this "weighted" criterion is still a model, which assigns a churn probability to each customer. All we have changed is the way in which these probabilities are estimated.

The logistic regression component in Analytics uses the weighting rule $w = v^{\frac{1}{2}}$ for building prediction models. This "rule of thumb" is a result of extensive experiments on various data sets and represents a "bias-variance" compromise, which tends, in general, to perform reasonably. An alternative approach could be to make the power p a user selected tuning parameter, which is problematic due to the difficulty in interpreting it. Another alternative would be to add p as another parameter to the model optimization process, which is difficult computationally and may present algorithmic difficulties.

5.3. Model evaluation and scoring

The typical use of a churn prediction model is not for classification but rather for two quite different tasks:

- Selection of populations for pro-active retention campaigns. This entails selecting a small part of the total population (typically a few percents) to make a concerted retention effort on. The selection criterion can be by population segment or it may just ask for a list of customers who represent the most "value at risk" on whom the retention effort is most warranted (we will concentrate on the second option).
- Maintenance of an individual "churn propensity" score for all customers, but in particular the important and valuable customers. These scores may or may not correspond to actual probabilities (in many cases they are just in the form of qualitative "levels" of risk), although getting good probability estimates is certainly advantageous in any case.

For the first task a "lift at $x\%$" measure would be appropriate if the desired cutoff point is known in advance, otherwise a global lift measure like "area under lift curve" may be warranted. For the second task, it seems like a likelihood measure may actually be the most appropriate one, although misclassification rate and the total area under the lift curve may be a reasonable surrogates. Model evaluation in Analytics uses the lift measure, displaying numerically the model's lift at a large number of cutoff points, displaying the resulting lift curve and the area under the curve. Customer value considerations are integrated into the evaluation as described in section 4. The test set scores are calculated as a product of propensity to churn given by the model and the (known) customer values:

$$Score_i = v_i * p_i \qquad (5)$$

They are then sorted in descending order and the "value-lift" at $x\%$ is calculated as:

$$\frac{\sum_{i \in I_x} v_i I\{\text{Customer i is a churner}\} / \sum_{i=1}^{n} v_i I\{\text{Customer i is a churner}\}}{\sum_{i \in I_x} v_i / \sum_{i=1}^{n} v_i}$$

where I_x is the set of test-set observations whose scores are in the top $x\%$ of scores.

The model evaluation component in Analytics supports both standard lift and value-lift evaluation. As we observed in the analysis stage, the different views can give distinctly different results in this stage too.

Figure 3 shows a pair of lift curves, for the same model on the same test data. One is a regular lift curve and the other is a value-lift curve. The two curves are very different and represent the essential difference in the two evaluation methods. See also the case study in section 6.

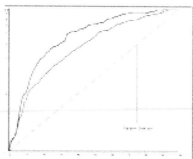

Figure 3. Regular lift (on bottom) and value lift (on top)

A similar two-views approach is taken by the application in the scoring component, which is used for prediction once the model is deployed. Customer churn propensities are estimated using the model and "value propensity" scores are calculated from them as in (5) (recall that customer value is a function of the predictors and is therefore known even for real prediction tasks). The business user can ask for propensity scores, value-propensity scores or both, and can use either one to select populations for retention campaigns or other campaigns.

6. Case study

We now describe a case study of churn analysis performed with customer value considerations on real data, using the Amdocs CRM Analytics. The data source is a telecommunication service provider and the data consists of around 400 predictors. The data was split to a training sample set containing 1500 churn observations and 1500 loyal observations and to a test sample set containing 750 churn observations and 750 loyal observations. The customer value formula was defined in Analytics, using several fields available in the data.

The first stage was to perform knowledge discovery by running the rule discovery mechanism described in section 5.1. Figure 1 (in that section) displays one of the rules automatically discovered by the application. The total number of rules discovered was 21. The next stage was to construct logistic regression models using a combination of binary variables representing these 21 rules and 50 of the original variables as predictors.

Following our approach of using decayed customer values as observation weights for modeling, we proceeded to build several weighted logistic regression models for this data.. The value transformations we used were:

1. Non-decayed weights: using the training customer values v_i as weights for the logistic regression
2. Square root decay: using $v_i^{0.5}$ as weights for the logistic regression training. This is the default approach of Analytics, as discussed in section 5.2
3. Strong decay: using the quadruple roots $v_i^{0.25}$ as weights for logistic regression training.
4. Ignoring customer values completely in the modeling stage (i.e. each observation has "weight" 1).

The same training data set, as described above, was used for building all models. The models were evaluated on a leave-out test sample from the same population. The evaluation measure used was the lift, and we calculated its value at a range of cutoff points. We calculated both the value-lift as described in section 5.3 and the standard, non-value-weighted lift. Table 1 and figure 4 show the results for the value-lift evaluation and table 2 and figure 5 show the results for the standard lift evaluation.

We observe that for the value-lift calculations, the model using non-decayed values is best for very low cutoff points, but for the vast majority of cutoff points

considered, the two decayed models (2 and 3 above) seem to do significantly better than the two extreme models.

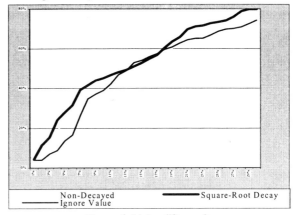

Figure 4. Value-lift results

In the two tables we can also see 95% confidence intervals for the various value-lift values at the various cutoff points, calculated using the hyper-geometric approximation described in [10]. We see that the decayed models seem to do significantly better than the two extreme ones in many cutoff points. For the standard lift calculations our results in section 3 would lead us to expect the non-weighted model (model 4) to be the best modeling approach. The actual differences we observe in table 2 and figure 5 are less striking than those for the value weighted evaluation. We observe that the strongly decayed model and the non-weighted model (models 3,4) generally perform best, although the differences for much of the range are not big. The non-decayed model 1, which is supposed to be least appropriate for this evaluation, does give significantly worse lift than models 3,4 for the higher cutoff points considered, as we can see in table 2.

Table 1. Value-lift results

Percentile	Non-Decayed	Square-Root Decay	Strong Decay	Ignore Value
2%	14.9% (12.6,17.3)	11.4% (9.3,13.5)	12.5% (10.3,14.8)	3.9% (2.5, 5.3)
4%	19.2% (16.7,21.8)	24.0% (21.4,26.7)	26.6% (23.9,29.3)	8.7% (6.8,10.6)
10%	36.9% (34.2,39.7)	45.1% (42.5,47.7)	47.5% (44.9,50.1)	38.9% (36.2,41.6)
20%	61.4% (59.3,63.6)	65.8% (63.8,67.7)	67.3% (65.4,69.2)	62.7% (60.6,64.8)
30%	74.2% (72.6,75.8)	79.8% (78.5,81.1)	77.7% (76.3,79.1)	74.1% (72.5,75.7)

Table 2. Standard lift results

Percentile	Non-Decayed	Square-Root Decay	Strong Decay	Ignore Value
2%	11.1% (9.0,13.2)	9.8% (7.8,11.8)	8.7% (6.8,10.6)	8.8% (6.9,10.7)
4%	16.4% (14.0,18.8)	15.5% (13.1,17.9)	17.3% (14.8,19.8)	15.1% (12.7,17.5)
10%	36.6% (33.9,39.3)	39.1% (36.4,41.8)	39.4% (36.7,42.1)	36.7% (34.0,39.4)
20%	54.0% (51.6,56.4)	55.5% (53.1,57.9)	60.1% (57.9,62.3)	59.6% (57.4,61.8)
30%	69.6% (67.8,71.4)	75.2% (73.7,76.7)	74.0% (72.4,75.6)	73.6% (72.0,75.2)

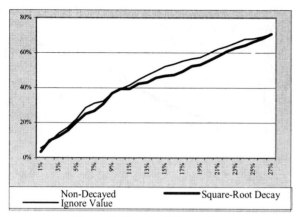

Figure 5. Standard lift results

We can emphasize the difference between value-lift and standard lift results by observing these points:
1. The model built using non-weighted data (model 4) is not better than either of the two decayed models for practically every cutoff point considered in the value-lift evaluation (Table 1). For the standard lift evaluation model 4 is at the very least competitive, sometimes better than both model 2 and model 3.
2. Comparing model 1 and model 4's performance for the two evaluations show us that on the value-lift evaluation they behave quite similarly and tend to do worse that the decayed models. However on the standard lift evaluation, model 1 is clearly much less appropriate than model 4. This is what we would expect theoretically, and what we observe.

Looking at our results, it seems a bigger test set may have been useful in better differentiating the various models. While the differences in their performance may be a few percents only, consider that these models are to be deployed on customer databases containing millions of customers, among them tens of thousands of churners each month. Simple ROI calculations show that a rise of 3% in value-lift typically corresponds to $50k difference monthly in the profits of retention efforts, considering both the effect of missing valuable churners and wasting retention efforts on non-valuable customers.

This case study confirms our main points:
1. Decay of training customer values is beneficial for value-weighted prediction
2. Value-weighted presentation and evaluation of results is important for building better prediction models for business purposes

7. Summary

In this paper we have tackled the practical use of customer values throughout the data analysis process, in particular for churn analysis in telecommunications. We have illustrated that in the modeling stage it is beneficial to choose a transformation of the training data customer values as weights for learning, and discussed the correct use of customer values in evaluation, scoring and insight discovery. We have shown how these concepts are applied in practice in the Amdocs CRM Analytics and illustrated their performance on real-life churn data.

There are many additional interesting and relevant questions that come up when considering data with observation importance weights, such as:
- What are good modeling approaches (or algorithms) for building value-weighted prediction models?
- How can we adjust "standard" modeling tools to take value into consideration (this problem has been widely addressed in the machine learning literature)
- What can we do when customer values are not certain but we have approximate values? What can we do when they are known only "in the future"?

8. References

[1] Chan, P. K., and Stolfo, S. J. (1998) Toward Scalable Learning with Non-uniform Class and Cost Distributions: A Case Study in Credit Card Fraud Detection, *KDD-98*.

[2] Elkan, C. (2000) Cost-Sensitive Learning and Decision-Making when Costs Are Unknown. *WCSL at ICML-2000*.

[3] Korn, E.L., Graubard, B.I. (1995) Examples of Differing Weighted and Unweighted Estimates from a Sample Survey. *The American Statistician*, 49:291-295.

[4] Hastie, T., Tibshirani, R., Friedman J. (2001). *The Elements of Statistical Learning*. Springer.

[5] Murad, U., Pinkas, G. (1999). Unsupervised Profiling for Identifying Superimposed Fraud. *PKDD-99*: 251-261

[6] McCullagh, P., Nelder, J.A. (1989). *Generalized Linear Models*. Chapman & Hall, second edition, 1989

[7] Provost, F.; Fawcett, T. (1997). Analysis and Visualization of Classifier Performance: Comparison under Imprecise Class and Cost Distribution. *KDD-97*.

[8] Provost, F., Fawcett, T. (1998). Adaptive fraud detection. *Data Mining and Knowledge Discovery*, 1 (3).

[9] Rosset, S. (2003). Building prediction models for data with observation importance weights. In preparation. www-stat.stanford.edu/~saharon/papers/vwpaper.ps

[10] Rosset, S., Neumann, E., Eick, U., Vatnik, N., Idan, I.(2001). Evaluation of prediction models for marketing campaigns. *KDD-2001*: 456-461

[11] Rosset, S., Neumann, E., Eick, U., Vatnik, N., Idan, I.(2002).Customer lifetime value modeling and its use for customer retention planning. *KDD-2002*.

[12] Rosset, S., Zhu, J., Hastie, T. (2002). Boosting as a regularized path to a maximum margin classifier. *Technical report, Dept. of Statistics, Stanford Univ.*

[13] Turney, P.D. (2000). Types of cost in inductive concept learning. *WCSL at ICML-2000*.

[14] Weisberg, S. (1985). *Applied Linear Regression*, John Wiley and Sons, Inc.

A High-Performance Distributed Algorithm for Mining Association Rules*

Assaf Schuster, Ran Wolff, and Dan Trock
Technion – Israel Institute of Technology
Email: {assaf,ranw,dtrock}@cs.technion.ac.il

Abstract

We present a new distributed association rule mining (D-ARM) algorithm that demonstrates superlinear speedup with the number of computing nodes. The algorithm is the first D-ARM algorithm to perform a single scan over the database. As such, its performance is unmatched by any previous algorithm. Scale-up experiments over standard synthetic benchmarks demonstrate stable run time regardless of the number of computers. Theoretical analysis reveals a tighter bound on error probability than the one shown in the corresponding sequential algorithm.

1 Introduction

The economic value of data mining is today well established. Most large organizations regularly practice data mining techniques. One of the most popular techniques is association rule mining (ARM), which is the automatic discovery of pairs of element sets that tend to appear together in a common context. An example would be to discover that the purchase of certain items (say tomatoes and lettuce) in a supermarket transaction usually implies that another set of items (salad dressing) is also bought in that same transaction.

Like other data mining techniques that must process enormous databases, ARM is inherently disk-I/O intensive. These I/O costs can be reduced in two ways: by reducing the number of times the database needs to be scanned, or through parallelization, by partitioning the database between several machines which then perform a distributed ARM (D-ARM) algorithm. In recent years much progress has been made in both directions.

The main task of every ARM algorithm is to discover the sets of items that frequently appear together – the frequent itemsets. The number of database scans required for the task has been reduced from a number equal to the size of the largest itemset in Apriori [3], to typically just a single scan in modern ARM algorithms such as Sampling and DIC [17, 5].

Much progress has also been made in parallelized algorithms. With these, the architecture of the parallel system plays a key role. For instance, many algorithms were proposed which take advantage of the fast interconnect, or the shared memory, of parallel computers. The latest development with these is [18], in which each process makes just two passes over its portion of the database.

Parallel computers are, however, very costly. Hence, although these algorithms were shown to scale up to 128 processors, few organizations can afford to spend such resources on data mining. The alternative is distributed algorithms, which can be run on cheap clusters of standard, off-the-shelf PCs. Algorithms suitable for such systems include the CD and FDM algorithms [2, 6], both parallelized versions of Apriori, which were published shortly after it was described. However, while clusters may easily and cheaply be scaled to hundreds of machines, these algorithms were shown not to scale well [15]. The DDM algorithm [15], which overcomes this scalability problem, was recently described. Unfortunately, all the D-ARM algorithms for share-nothing machines scan the database as many times as Apriori. Since many business databases contain large frequent itemsets (long patterns), these algorithms are not competitive with DIC and Sampling.

In this work we present a parallelized version of the Sampling algorithm, called D-Sampling. The algorithm is intended for clusters of share-nothing machines. The main obstacle of this parallelization, that of achieving a coherent view of the distributed sample at reasonable communication costs, was overcome using ideas taken from DDM. Our distributed algorithm scans the database once, just like the Sampling algorithm, and is thus more efficient than any D-ARM algorithm known today. Not only does this algorithm divide the disk-I/O costs of the single scan by partitioning the database among several machines, but also uses the combined memory to linearly increase the size of the sample. This increase further improves the performance of the algorithm because the safety margin required in Sam-

---

*This work was supported in part by Microsoft Academic Foundation and by THE ISRAEL SCIENCE FOUNDATION founded by the Israel Academy of Sciences and Humanities.

pling decreases when the (global) sample size increases.

Extensive experiments on standard synthetic benchmarks show that D-Sampling is superior to previous algorithms in every way. When compared to Sampling – one of the best sequential algorithms known today – it offers superlinear speedup. When compared to FDM, it improves runtime by orders of magnitude. Finally, on scalability tests, an increase in both the number of computing nodes and the size of the database does not degrade D-Sampling performance. FDM, on the other hand, suffers performance degradation in these tests.

The rest of this paper is structured as follows: We conclude this section with some notations and a formal definition of the D-ARM problem. In the next section we present relevant previous work. Section 3 describes the D-Sampling algorithm, and section 4 provides the required statistical background. Section 5 describes the experiments we conducted to verify D-Sampling performance. We conclude with some open research problems in section 6.

1.1 Notation and Problem Definition

Let $I = \{i_1, i_2, ..., i_m\}$ be the items in a certain domain. An *itemset* is a subset of I. A *transaction* t is also a subset of I which is associated with a unique transaction identifier – TID. A database DB is a list of such transactions. Let $\overline{DB} = \{DB^1, DB^2, ..., DB^n\}$ be a partition of DB into n parts. Let S be a list of transactions which were sampled uniformly from DB, and let $\overline{S} = \{S^1, S^2, ..., S^n\}$ be the partition of S induced by $\overline{DB}$. For any itemset X and any group of transactions A, $Support(X, A)$ is the number of transactions in A which contain all the items of X and $Freq(X, A) = \frac{Support(X, A)}{|A|}$. We call $Freq(X, DB^i)$ the *local frequency* of X in partition i and $Freq(X, DB)$ its *global frequency*; likewise, we call $Freq(X, S^i)$ the *estimated local frequency* of X in partition i and $Freq(X, S)$ its *estimated global frequency*.

For some frequency threshold $0 \leq MinFreq \leq 1$, we say that an itemset X is *frequent* in A if $Freq(X, A) \geq MinFreq$ and infrequent otherwise. If A is a sample, we say that X is *estimated frequent* or *estimated infrequent*. If A is a partition, we say that X is *locally frequent*, and if A is the whole database, then X is *globally frequent*. Hence an itemset may be estimated locally frequent in the kth partition, globally infrequent, etc. The group of all itemsets with frequency above or equal to fr in A is called $\mathcal{F}_{fr}[A]$. The *negative border* of $\mathcal{F}_{fr}[A]$ is all those itemsets which are not themselves in $\mathcal{F}_{fr}[A]$ but have all their subsets in $\mathcal{F}_{fr}[A]$. Finally, for a pair of globally frequent itemsets X and Y such that $X \cap Y = \emptyset$, and some confidence threshold $0 < MinConf \leq 1$, we say the rule $X \Rightarrow Y$ is *confident* if and only if $Freq(X \cup Y, DB) \geq MinConf \cdot Freq(X, DB)$.

Definition 1 *Given a partitioned database $\overline{DB}$, and given $MinFreq$ and $MinConf$, the D-ARM problem is to find all the confident rules between frequent itemsets in $\overline{DB}$.*

2 Previous Work

Since its introduction in 1993 [1], the ARM problem has been studied intensively. Many algorithms, representing several different approaches, were suggested. Some algorithms, such as Apriori, Partition, DHP, DIC, and FP-growth [3, 14, 11, 5, 8], are bottom-up, starting from itemsets of size 1 and working up. Others, like Pincer-Search [10], use a hybrid approach, trying to guess large itemsets at an early stage. Most algorithms, including those cited above, adhere to the original problem definition, while others search for different kinds of rules [5, 16, 13].

Algorithms for the D-ARM problem usually can be seen as parallelizations of sequential ARM algorithms. The CD, FDM, and DDM [2, 6, 15] algorithms parallelize Apriori [3], and PDM [12] parallelizes DHP [11]. The major difference between parallel algorithms is in the architecture of the parallel machine. This may be shared memory as in the case of [18], distributed shared memory as in [9], or shared nothing as in [2, 6, 15].

One of the best sequential ARM algorithms – Sampling – was presented in 1996 by Toivonen [17]. The idea behind Sampling is simple. A random sample of the database is used to predict all the frequent itemsets, which are then validated in a single database scan. Because this approach is probabilistic, and therefore fallible, not only the frequent itemsets are counted in the scan but also their negative border. If the scan reveals that itemsets that were predicted to belong to the negative border are frequent then a second scan is performed to discover whether any superset of these itemsets is also frequent. To further reduce the chance of failure, Toivonen suggests that mining be performed using some $low\_fr < MinFreq$, and the results reported only if they pass the original $MinFreq$ threshold. He also gives a heuristic which can be used to determine low_fr. The cost of using low_fr is an increase in the number of candidates. The Sampling algorithm and the DIC algorithm (Brin 1997 [5]) are the only single-scan ARM algorithms known today. The performance of the two is thus unrivaled by any other sequential ARM algorithm.

The algorithm presented here combines ideas from several groups of algorithms. It first mines a sample of the database and then validates the result and can, thus, be seen as a parallelization of the Sampling algorithm [17]. The sample is stored in a vertical trie structure that resembles the one in [14, 4], and it is mined using modifications of the DDM [15] algorithm, which is Apriori-based.

3 D-Sampling Algorithm

All distributed ARM algorithms that have been presented until now are Apriori based and thus require multiple database scans. The reason why no distributed form of Sampling was suggested in the six years since its presentation may lie in the communication complexity of the problem. As we have seen, the communication complexity of D-ARM algorithms is highly dependent on the number of candidates and on the noise level in the partitioned database. When Sampling reduces the database through sampling and lowers the $MinFreq$ threshold, it greatly increases both the number of candidates and the noise level. This may render a distributed algorithm useless.

This is the reason that the reduced communication complexity of DDM seems to offer an opportunity. The main idea of D-Sampling is to utilize DDM to mine a distributed sample using low_fr instead of $MinFreq$. After $\mathcal{F}_{low\_fr}\left[S\right]$ has been identified, the partitioned database is scanned once in parallel to find the actual frequencies of $\mathcal{F}_{low\_fr}\left[S\right]$ and its negative border. Those frequencies can then be collected and rules can be generated from itemsets more frequent than $MinFreq$.

We added three modifications to this scheme. First, although the given DDM is levelwise, here it is executed on a memory resident sample. Thus we could modify DDM to develop new itemsets on-the-fly and calculate their estimated frequency with no disk-I/O. Second, a new method for the reduction of $MinFreq$ to low_fr yielded two additional benefits: it is not heuristic, i.e., our error bound is rigorous, and it produces many less candidates than the rigorous method suggested previously. Third, after scanning the database, it would not be wise to just collect the frequencies of all candidates. Since these candidates were calculated according to the lowered threshold, few of them are expected to have frequencies above the original $MinFreq$. Instead, we run DDM once more to decide which candidates are frequent and which are not. We call the modified algorithm D-Sampling (Algorithm 1).

3.1 Algorithm

D-Sampling begins by loading a sample into memory. The sample is stored in a trie – a lexicographic tree. This trie is the main data structure of D-Sampling and is accessed by all its subroutines. Each node of the trie stores, in addition to structural information (parents, descendants etc.), the list of $TIDs$ of those transactions that include the itemset associated with this node. These lists are initialized from the sample for the first level of the trie; when a new trie node – and itemset – are developed, the TID lists of two of the parent nodes are intersected to create the TID list of the new node.

The first step of D-Sampling is to run a modification of DDM on the distributed sample. Then, in order to set low_fr, the algorithm enters a loop; in each cycle through the loop it calls another DDM derivative called M-Max to mine the next M estimated-frequent itemsets. M is a tunable parameter we set to about 100. After it finds those additional itemsets, D-Sampling reduces low_fr to the estimated frequency of the least frequent one and re-estimates the error probability using a formula described in section 4. When this probability drops below the required error probability, the loop ends. Then D-Sampling creates the final candidate set C by adding to $\mathcal{F}_{low\_fr}\left[S\right]$ its negative border.

Algorithm 1 D-Sampling

For node i out of n
Input:
$MinFreq, MinConf, DB^i, s, M, \delta$
Output:
The set of confident associations between globally frequent itemsets
Main:
Set $p\_error \leftarrow 1, low\_fr \leftarrow MinFreq$
Load a sample S^i of size s from DB^i into memory
Initialize the trie with all the size-1 itemsets and calculate their TID lists
$\mathcal{F}_{low\_fr}\left[S\right] \leftarrow MDDM\left(MinFreq\right)$
While $p\_error > \delta$

1. $\mathcal{F}_{low\_fr}\left[S\right] \leftarrow \mathcal{F}_{low\_fr}\left[S\right] \cup M\_Max\left(M\right)$

2. Set low_fr to the frequency of the least frequent itemset in $\mathcal{F}_{low\_fr}\left[S\right]$

3. Set p_error to the new error bound according to $MinFreq, low\_fr$ and $\mathcal{F}_{low\_fr}\left[S\right]$

Let C be $\mathcal{F}_{low\_fr}\left[S\right] \cup Negative\_Border\left(\mathcal{F}_{low\_fr}\left[S\right]\right)$
Scan the database and compute $Freq\left(c, DB^i\right)$ for each $c \in C$. Update the frequencies in the trie to the computed ones
Compute $\mathcal{F}_{MinFreq}\left[DB\right]$ by running $MDDM\left(MinFreq\right)$, this time with the actual frequencies
If exists $c \in \mathcal{F}_{MinFreq}\left[DB\right]$ such that $c \notin \mathcal{F}_{low\_fr}\left[S\right]$ (i.e., from negative border) report failure
$Gen\_Rules\left(\mathcal{F}_{MinFreq}\left[DB\right], MinConf\right)$

Once the candidate set is established, each partition of the database is scanned exactly once and in parallel, and the actual frequencies of each candidate are calculated. With these frequencies D-Sampling performs yet another round of the modified DDM. In this round the original $MinFreq$ is used; thus, unless there is a failure, this round should never develop a candidate which is outside the negative border. If indeed no failure occurs, then all frequent itemsets will be evaluated according to the actual frequencies which were found in the database scan. Hence, after this round it is known which of the candidates in C are globally frequent and which are not. In this case, rules are generated from $\mathcal{F}_{MinFreq}\left[DB\right]$ using the known global frequencies.

If an itemset belonging to the negative border of $\mathcal{F}_{low\_fr}\left[S\right]$ does turn out to be frequent, this means that D-Sampling has failed: a superset of that candidate, which was not counted, might also turn out to be frequent. In this case we suggest the same solution offered by Toivonen: to create a group of additional candidates that includes all combinations of anticipated and unanticipated frequent itemsets, and then perform an additional scan. The size of this group is limited by the number of anticipated frequent itemsets times the number of possible combinations of unanticipated frequent itemsets. Since failures are very rare events, and the probability of multiple failure is exponentially small, the additional scan will incur costs that are of the same scale as the first scan.

3.2 MDDM – A Modified Distributed Decision Miner

The original DDM algorithm, as described in [15], is levelwise. When the database is small enough to fit into memory, the levelwise structure of the algorithm becomes superfluous. Modified Distributed Decision Miner, or MDDM (Algorithm 2), therefore starts by developing all the locally frequent candidates, regardless of their size. It then continues to develop candidates whenever they are required, i.e., when all their subsets are assumed frequent (according to the local hypothesis - P) or when another node refers to the associated itemset.

The remaining steps in MDDM are the same as in DDM. Each party looks for itemsets for which the global hypothesis and local hypothesis disagree and communicate their local counts to the rest of the parties. When no such itemset exists, the party passes (it can return to activity if new information arrives). If all of the parties pass, the algorithm terminates and the itemsets which are predicted to be frequent according to the public hypothesis H are the estimated globally frequent ones. If a message is received for an itemset which has not yet been developed, it is developed on-the-fly and its local frequency is calculated.

3.3 M-Max Algorithm

The modified DDM algorithm identifies all itemsets with frequency above $MinFreq$. D-Sampling, however, requires a further decrease in the frequency of itemsets which are included in the database scan. The reason for this, as we shall see in section 4, is that three parameters affect the

---

Algorithm 2 Modified Distributed Decision Miner

For node i out of n
Input:
fr – the target frequency
Output:
$\mathcal{F}_{fr}\left[S\right]$
Definitions:

$$P\left(X,S^i\right) = \sum_{j\in G(X)} \frac{\left|S^j\right|Freq\left(X,S^j\right)}{|S|} +$$

$$\sum_{j\notin G(X)} \frac{\left|S^j\right|Freq\left(X,S^i\right)}{|S|}$$

$$H\left(X\right) = \begin{cases} \dfrac{\sum_{j\in G(X)}\left|S^j\right|Freq\left(X,S^j\right)}{\sum_{j\in G(X)}\left|S^j\right|} & G\left(X\right)\neq\emptyset \\ 0 & otherwise \end{cases}$$

Main:
Develop all the candidates which are more frequent than fr according to P
Do

- Choose a candidate X that was not yet chosen and for which either $H\left(X\right) < fr \leq P\left(X,S^i\right)$ or $P\left(X,S^i\right) < fr \leq H\left(X\right)$

- Broadcast $m = \langle id\left(X\right), Freq\left(X,S^i\right)\rangle$

- If no such itemset exists broadcast $\langle pass\rangle$

Until $|Passed| = N$
$R \leftarrow$ all X with $H\left(X\right) \geq fr$
Return R
When node i receives a message m from party j:

1. If $m = \langle pass\rangle$ insert j into $Passed$

2. Else $m = \langle id\left(X\right), Freq\left(X,S^j\right)\rangle$

   If $j \in Passed$ remove j from $Passed$

   If X was not developed then: develop it, set $G\left(X\right) = \emptyset$, Calculate $X.tid\_list$ by intersecting the TID lists of two of X's immediate subsets and set $Freq\left(X,S^i\right) = \frac{|X.tid\_list|}{|S^i|}$

   Insert j to $G\left(X\right)$

   Recalculate $H\left(X\right)$ and $P\left(X,S^i\right)$

---

chances for failure. These are the size of the sample N, the size of the negative border, and the estimated frequency of the least frequent candidate. The first parameter is given, the second is a rather arbitrary value which we can calculate or bound, and the last parameter is the one we can control.

The frequency of the least frequent candidate can be controlled by reducing low_fr. However, this must be done with care: lowering the frequency threshold increases the number of candidates. This increase depends on the distribution of itemsets in the database and is therefore nondeterministic. The larger number of candidates affects the scan time: the more candidates you have, the more comparisons must be made per transaction. In a distributed setting, the number of candidates is also strongly tied to the communication complexity of the algorithm.

To better control the reduction of low_fr, we propose another version of DDM called M-Max (Algorithm 3). M-Max increases the number of frequent itemsets by a given factor rather than decreasing the threshold value by an arbitrary value. Although worst case analysis shows that an increase of even one frequent itemset may require that any number of additional candidates be considered, the number of such candidates tends to remain small and roughly proportional to the number of additional frequent itemsets. We complement this algorithm with a new bound for the error (presented in section 4). The combined scheme is both rigorous and economical in the number of candidates.

The M-Max algorithm is based on the inference that changing the $MinFreq$ threshold to the H-value of the M-largest itemset[1] every time an itemset is developed or a hypothesis value is changed will result in all parties agreeing on the M most frequent itemsets when DDM terminates. This is easy to prove. Take any final state of the modified algorithm. The H value of each itemset is equal in all parties; hence, the final $MinFreq$ is equal in all parties as well. Now compare this state to the corresponding state under DDM, with the static $MinFreq$ value set to the one finally agreed upon. The state attained by M-Max is also a valid final state for this DDM. Thus, by virtue of DDM correctness, all parties must be in agreement on the same set of frequent itemsets.

As a stand-alone ARM algorithm, M-Max may be impractical because a node may be required to refer to itemsets it has not yet developed. If the database is large, this would require an additional disk scan whenever new candidates are developed. Nevertheless, at the low_fr correction stage of D-Sampling, the database is the memory-resident sample. It is thus possible to evaluate the frequency of arbitrary itemsets with no disk-I/O.

Algorithm 3 M-Max

For node i out of n
Input:
low_fr
Output:
The M most frequent itemsets not yet in $\mathcal{F}_{low\_fr}\left[S\right]$
Definitions: same as for algorithm 3.2
Let B denote the initial size of $\mathcal{F}_{low\_fr}\left[S\right]$, $fr = low\_fr$
Main:
Do

1. call set_fr

2. Choose X that was not yet chosen and for which either $H(X) < fr \leq P(X, S^i)$ or $P(X, S^i) < fr \leq H(X)$

   Broadcast $m = \langle id(X), Freq(X, S^i)\rangle$

3. If no such itemset exists broadcast $\langle pass\rangle$

Until $|Passed| = N$
$R \leftarrow$ all X in the trie with $H(X) \geq fr$ which are not in $\mathcal{F}_{low\_fr}\left[S\right]$
Return R
When node i receives a message m from party j:

1. If $m = \langle pass\rangle$ insert j into $Passed$

2. Else $m = \langle id(X), Freq(X, S^j)\rangle$

   If $j \in Passed$ remove j from $Passed$

   If X was not developed then: develop it, set $G(X) = \emptyset$, Calculate $X.tid\_list$ by intersecting the TID lists of two of X's immediate subsets and set $Freq(X, S^i) = \frac{|X.tid\_list|}{|S^i|}$

   Insert j to $G(X)$

   Recalculate $H(X)$ and $P(X, S^i)$

   call set_fr

procedure set_fr:
Do M times:

- Select the next most frequent itemset outside $\mathcal{F}_{low\_fr}\left[S\right]$ and develop its descendants if they have not been developed yet

Set fr to the H value of the last itemset selected. For itemsets with $H = 0$ consider P instead.

---

[1] P is used when the M largest H is zero.

4 Statistical Analysis

The M-Max subroutine requires that we estimate the probability of an error – i.e., an itemset which is actually frequent but appears with frequency of less than the lowered frequency threshold in the sample. An over estimation may result in an unnecassary decrease in low_fr which would result in a larger than required number of candidates. Here we describe the probability bound we have used in our implementation which outperforms the naive Chernoff bound discussed in the original paper which described the Sampling algorithm.

Let $0 < fr < 1$ be the frequency of some arbitrary itemset X in DB. Consider a random sample S of size N from DB. We will assume that transactions in the sample are independent. Hence, the number of rows in S which contain X can be seen as a random variable, $x \sim Bin(N, fr)$.

The frequency of X in N transactions, $s\_fr = x/N$, is an estimate for fr, which improves as N increases. The best-known way to bound the chance that s_fr will deviate from fr is with the Chernoff bound. We use a tighter bound for the case of binomial distributions (see Hagerup and Rub [7]):

$$Pr\left(|fr - s\_fr| > \varepsilon\right) \leq \left[\left(\frac{1-fr}{1-s\_fr}\right)^{1-s\_fr} \left(\frac{fr}{s\_fr}\right)^{s\_fr}\right]^N$$

Lemma 1 *Given a random uniform sample S of N transactions from DB, a frequency threshold $MinFreq$, the lowered frequency threshold low_fr, and the negative border of $\mathcal{F}_{low\_fr}[S]$, denoted NB, the probability $p_{failure}$ that any $X \in NB$ will have frequency larger than or equal to $MinFreq$ (hence causing failure) is bounded by:*

$$|NB| \cdot \left[\left(\frac{1-MinFreq}{1-low\_fr}\right)^{1-low\_fr} \left(\frac{MinFreq}{low\_fr}\right)^{low\_fr}\right]^N$$

For any specific itemset in NB, the probability that this itemset will cause failure is the probability that its estimated frequency is below low_fr while its actual frequency is above $MinFreq$. Substituting $MinFreq$ for fr and low_fr for s_fr, the bound gives us:

$$Pr\left(|Freq\left(X, DB\right) - Freq\left(X, S\right)| > \epsilon\right) \leq$$

$$\left[\left(\frac{1-MinFreq}{1-low\_fr}\right)^{1-low\_fr} \left(\frac{MinFreq}{low\_fr}\right)^{low\_fr}\right]^N$$

As for the entire NB:

$$Pr\left(\exists X \in NB : X\ fails\right) \leq \sum_{X \in NB} Pr\left(X\ fails\right) \leq$$

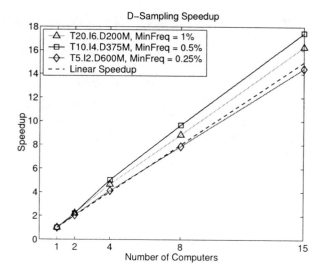

Figure 1. D-Sampling speedup.

$$|NB| \left[\left(\frac{1-MinFreq}{1-low\_fr}\right)^{1-low\_fr} \left(\frac{MinFreq}{low\_fr}\right)^{low\_fr}\right]^N$$

Since calculating the negative border is in itself a costly process, we choose to relax this bound by substituting $|I| \, |\mathcal{F}_{low\_fr}[S]|$ for $|NB|$. Obviously, any itemset in $\mathcal{F}_{low\_fr}[S]$ can only be extended by at most $|I|$ items, and thus this relaxed bound holds.

Corollary 1 *(Toivonen 1996) If none of the itemsets in the negative border caused failure, then no other itemset can cause failure.*

Any other itemset X outside $\mathcal{F}_{low\_fr}[S]$ and NB must include a subset from NB. Hence its frequency must be less than or equal to the frequency of this subset. It follows that if the frequency of each itemset in NB is below $MinFreq$, so is the frequency of X.

5 Experiments

We carried out three sets of experiments. The first set tested D-Sampling to see how much faster it is to run the algorithm with the database split among n machines than to run it on a single node. The second set compared D-Sampling, DDM and FDM on a range of $MinFreq$ values. The last one checked scale-up: the change in runtime when the number of machines is increased together with the size of the database.

We ran our experiments on two clusters: the first cluster, which was used for the first, second and fourth sets of experiments, consisted of 15 Pentium computers with dual 1.7GHz processors. Each of the computers had at least 1

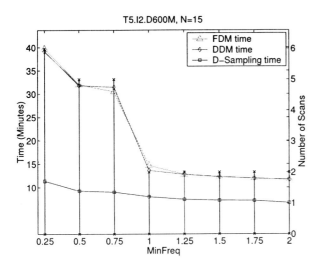

Figure 2. Runtime of D-Sampling, DDM, and FDM for varying MinFreq.

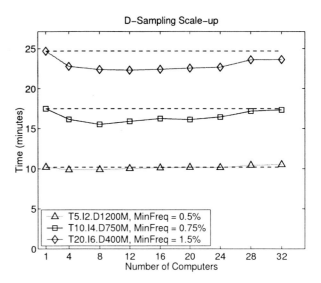

Figure 3. D-Sampling scale-up.

gigabyte of main memory. The computers were connected via an Ethernet-100 network. The second cluster, which we used for the scale-up experiments, was composed of 32 Pentium computers with a dual 500MHz processor. Each computer had 256 megabytes of memory. The second cluster was also connected via an Ethernet-100 network.

All of the experiments were performed with synthetic databases produced by the standard gen tool $available from http ://www.almaden.ibm.com/cs/quest$. The databases were built with the same parameters which were used by Toivonen in [17]. The only change we made was to enlarge the databases to about 18 gigabytes each; had we used the original sizes, the whole database would fit, when partitioned, into the memory of the computers. The database T5.I2.D600M has 600M transactions, each containing an average of five items, and patterns of length two. T10.I4.D375M and T20.I6.D200M follow the same encoding. When the database was to be partitioned, we divided it arbitrarily by writing transaction number TID into the $TID\%n$ partition.

5.1 Speedup Results

The speedup experiments were designed to demonstrate that parallelization works well for Sampling. We thus ran D-Sampling with $n = 1$ (with $n = 1$, D-Sampling reverts to Sampling) on a large database. Then we tested how splitting the database between n computers affects the algorithm's performance.

As figure 1 shows, the basic speedup of D-Sampling is slightly sublinear. However, when the number of candidates

is large, the speed-up becomes superlinear. This is because the global sample size increases with the number of computers. This larger sample size translates into a higher low_fr value and thus to a smaller number of candidates than with $n = 1$.

5.2 Dependency on $MinFreq$

The second set of experiments (figure 2) demonstrates the dependency of D-Sampling performance on $MinFreq$, which determines the number and size of the candidates. We compared the D-Sampling runtime to that of both DDM and FDM. D-Sampling turned out to be insensitive to the reduction in $MinFreq$; its runtime increased by no more than 50% across the whole range. On the other hand, the runtime of DDM and FDM increased rapidly as $MinFreq$ is decreased. This is because of the additional scans required as increasingly larger itemsets become frequent. Because it performs just one database scan, D-Sampling is expected to be superior to any levelwise D-ARM algorithm, just as Sampling is superior to all levelwise ARM algorithms.

5.3 Scale-up

The third set of tests was aimed at testing the scalability of D-Sampling. Here the partition size was fixed. We used a database of about 1.5 gigabytes on each computer. A scalable algorithm should have the same runtime regardless of the number of computers.

D-Sampling creates the same communication load per candidate as DDM. However, because it generates more candidates, it uses more communication. As can be seen from the graphs in figure 3, D-Sampling is scalable in two of the tests. In fact, for mid-range numbers of computers, D-Sampling runs even faster than with $n = 1$; this is due to the superlinear speed-up discussed earlier. The mild slowdown seen in figure 3c is due to the smaller average pattern size and the smaller number of candidates in T5.I2.D1200M. The larger the number of candidates, the greater the saving in candidates when the number of computers increases. If there are enough large patterns, this saving will compensate for the increasing communication overhead. Such is not the case, however, with T5.I2.D1200M.

6 Conclusions and Future Research

We presented a new D-ARM algorithm that uses the communication efficiency of the DDM algorithm to parallelize the single-scan Sampling algorithm. Experiments prove that the new algorithm has superlinear speedup and outperforms both FDM and DDM with any $MinFreq$ value. The exact improvement in relation to previous algorithms depends on the number of database scans they require. Experiments demonstrate good scalability, provided the database scan is the major bottleneck of the algorithm.

Some open questions still remain. First, it would be interesting to continue partitioning the database until every partition becomes memory resident. This approach may lead to a D-ARM algorithm that mines a database by loading it into the memory of large number of computers and then runs with no disk-I/O at all. Second, it would be interesting to have a parallelized version of the other single-scan ARM algorithm – DIC – on a share-nothing cluster, or of the two-scans partition algorithm. Finally, we feel that the full potential of the M-Max algorithm has not yet been realized; we intend to research additional applications for this algorithm.

References

[1] R. Agrawal, T. Imielinski, and A. N. Swami. Mining association rules between sets of items in large databases. In *Proc. of the 1993 ACM SIGMOD Int'l. Conference on Management of Data*, pages 207–216, Washington, D.C., June 1993.

[2] R. Agrawal and J. Shafer. Parallel mining of association rules. *IEEE Transactions on Knowledge and Data Engineering*, 8(6):962 – 969, 1996.

[3] R. Agrawal and R. Srikant. Fast algorithms for mining association rules. In *Proc. of the 20th Int'l. Conference on Very Large Databases (VLDB'94)*, pages 487 – 499, Santiago, Chile, September 1994.

[4] V. S. Ananthanarayana, D. K. Subramanian, and M. N. Murty. Scalable, distributed and dynamic mining of association rules. In *Proceedings of HiPC'00*, pages 559–566, Bangalore, India, 2000.

[5] S. Brin, R. Motwani, J. Ullman, and S. Tsur. Dynamic itemset counting and implication rules for market basket data. *SIGMOD Record*, 6(2):255–264, June 1997.

[6] D. Cheung, J. Han, V. Ng, A. Fu, and Y. Fu. A fast distributed algorithm for mining association rules. In *Proc. of 1996 Int'l. Conf. on Parallel and Distributed Information Systems*, pages 31 – 44, Miami Beach, Florida, December 1996.

[7] T. Hagerup and C. Rub. A guided tour of Chernoff bounds. *Information Processing Letters*, 33:305 – 308, 1989/90.

[8] J. Han, J. Pei, and Y. Yin. Mining frequent patterns without candidate generation. Technical Report 99-12, Simon Fraser University, October 1999.

[9] Z. Jarai, A. Virmani, and L. Iftode. Towards a cost-effective parallel data mining approach. Workshop on High Performance Data Mining (held in conjunction with IPPS'98), March 1998.

[10] D.-I. Lin and Z. M. Kedem. Pincer search: A new algorithm for discovering the maximum frequent set. In *Extending Database Technology*, pages 105–119, 1998.

[11] J. S. Park, M.-S. Chen, and P. S. Yu. An effective hash-based algorithm for mining association rules. In *Proc. of ACM SIGMOD Int'l. Conference on Management of Data*, pages 175 – 186, San Jose, California, May 1995.

[12] J. S. Park, M.-S. Chen, and P. S. Yu. Efficient parallel data mining for association rules. In *Proc. of ACM Int'l. Conference on Information and Knowledge Management*, pages 31 – 36, Baltimore, MD, November 1995.

[13] J. Pei and J. Han. Can we push more constraints into frequent pattern mining? In *Proc. of the ACM SIGKDD Conf. on Knowledge Discovery and Data Mining*, pages 350–354, Boston, MA, 2000.

[14] A. Savasere, E. Omiecinski, and S. B. Navathe. An efficient algorithm for mining association rules in large databases. *The VLDB Journal*, pages 432–444, 1995.

[15] A. Schuster and R. Wolff. Communication-efficient distributed mining of association rules. In *Proc. of the 2001 ACM SIGMOD Int'l. Conference on Management of Data*, pages 473 – 484, Santa Barbara, California, May 2001.

[16] R. Srikant and R. Agrawal. Mining generalized association rules. In *Proc. of the 20th Int'l. Conference on Very Large Databases (VLDB'94)*, pages 407 – 419, Santiago, Chile, September 1994.

[17] H. Toivonen. Sampling large databases for association rules. In *The VLDB Journal*, pages 134–145, 1996.

[18] O. R. Zaiane, M. El-Hajj, and P. Lu. Fast parallel association rules mining without candidacy generation. In *IEEE 2001 International Conference on Data Mining (ICDM'2001)*, pages 665–668, 2001.

Introducing Uncertainty into Pattern Discovery in Temporal Event Sequences

Xingzhi Sun, Maria E. Orlowska, and Xue Li
School of Information Technology and Electrical Engineering
The University of Queensland, Australia
{sun, maria, xueli}@itee.uq.edu.au

Abstract

Pattern discovery in temporal event sequences is of great importance in many application domains, such as telecommunication network fault analysis. In reality, not every type of event has an accurate timestamp. Some of them, defined as inaccurate events in this paper, may only have an interval as possible time of occurrence. The existence of inaccurate events may cause uncertainty in event ordering. The traditional support model cannot deal with this uncertainty, which would cause some interesting patterns to be missing. In this paper, a new concept, precise support, is introduced to evaluate the probability of a pattern contained in a sequence. Based on this new metric, we define the uncertainty model and present an algorithm to discover interesting patterns in the sequence database that has one type of inaccurate event. In our model, the number of types of inaccurate events can be extended to k readily, however, at a cost of increasing computational complexity.

1 Introduction

In reality, a large number of events are recorded with temporal information (e.g., a timestamp). We call a sequence of such events a temporal event sequence. In some application domains, not every type of event has an accurate timestamp. Some types of events may only have an interval indicating the possible happening time. Compared with *accurate events*, of which the temporal information is a timestamp, we define events, of which the temporal information is an interval (due to inaccurate recorded time), as *inaccurate events*. The existence of inaccurate events may cause ambiguity in the temporal order between two events, which could affect the accuracy of traditional sequential mining [2]. This paper will investigate such a problem originated from a real application: the telecommunication network fault analysis.

A telecommunication network can be viewed as a hierarchical network, with switches, exchanges and transmission equipment. Various devices and software are used in the network to monitor the network continuously, generating a large number of different types of events. One type of such event, trouble report (*TR*), is of particular importance. A *TR* is recorded by a consultant after a customer's complaint on some service difficulties, such as noisy lines, no dial tones or abnormal busy tones. All *TR*s must be investigated by the company, often involving sending engineers to check various parts of the network including the customer's place. The total cost for handling a large number of *TR*s is very high for the telecommunication company. With a database of extensive historical event data and a comprehensive monitoring network, it is highly desirable to find patterns leading *TR*s within one or a few sensible time intervals. Such patterns, when combined with real-time event data, can help to predict the fault in the telecommunication network. Thus, the company can improve customer services by a pro-active behaviour. For example, the company can take precautions before faults happens or contact customers in a possibly affected area before they lodge complaints.

In [9], we have studied finding interesting patterns for such an application. The basic idea is as follows. For each *TR*, we apply a time window with a sensible size to find a sequence of events happening before it. A set of sequences is generated in this way as the *mining dataset*, from which we can find patterns (including sequential patterns) that potentially lead to *TR*s. After that, we prune the pattern set based on our definition of *confidence*.

In the process of discovering sequential patterns from the mining dataset, we assume that each event has an accurate timestamp. However, there is one type of alarm e collected every δ period of time. It indicates that although the recorded time of this type of alarm is t, we can only claim that this alarm occurs sometime in the interval $[t - \delta, t]$. We regard events of type e as inaccurate events because we cannot find the accurate timestamp for them. Note that, given an inaccurate event u with interval $[t - \delta, t]$, for any accurate event v occurring in $(t - \delta, t)$, the order between u and v is uncertain. Traditional sequential mining approaches [2, 8, 5] are based on a support model. They only work for accurate events and do not consider the uncertainty on the event order. Unfortunately, in some applications (such as ours), if this kind of uncertainty is ignored, some frequent patterns could be missed out and some infrequent patterns may turn to be frequent.

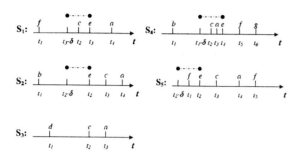

Figure 1. A mining dataset

Example 1.1: A mining dataset with 5 sequences is shown in Fig.1. Remember that events of type e may cause the uncertainty on the event order. Let the minimum support number be 3. Considering a sequential pattern $P = \langle e, c, a \rangle$, if we ignore the uncertainty (i.e., just consider the recorded time of e-type events), only S_2 and S_5 contain P. The support number of P is 2, which is less than the threshold. Therefore, P is infrequent pattern and will not be shown in the mining result. However, the fact is: in addition to S_2 and S_5, S_1 and S_4 may also have some probabilities to contain P. If we take these probabilities into account, P could be frequent.

More importantly, this problem can also be extended to data analysis for events with different granularity of time scales. In some applications, there is a need to investigate the order among selected types of events from different domains. Accordingly, the time scales for events from different domains may be different. Let us consider a temporal event sequence formed by integrating data sets from several application domains according to the timestamp of each event. In such a sequence, for example, some types of events have the timestamp with the accuracy to a minute, while others are with the timestamp accurate to an hour. Apparently, the temporal order between events with different granularity of time scales may be uncertain. If we adopt the timestamp scale with fine granularity as the time unit, events with rough granularity of time scale can be regarded as inaccurate events.

In this paper, we generalise such a problem as discovering sequential patterns in a database with uncertainty. To solve the problem, we build a data model to accommodate the uncertainty and propose a new metric, called *precise support*, to evaluate the significance of a pattern. In our uncertainty model, given a pattern P and a sequence S, the precise support of P in S is defined as the probabil-

ity that S contains P. Compared with the traditional concept of support, the value domain of precise support is $[0, 1]$ rather than $\{0, 1\}$. For example, in Fig. 1, the probability of S_1 containing $P = \langle e, c, a \rangle$ equals to the probability that e happens before c. If the density function of inaccurate event is given as $d(e, t)$, the precise support of P in S_1 is $\int_{t_3-\delta}^{t_2} d(e, t) \cdot dt$, where δ is the length of the interval and t_2 and t_3 are recorded timestamps of the events.

Now, we give assumptions in this paper for the problem of mining sequential patterns in a sequence database containing inaccurate events.

- There is only one type of event with an inaccurate timestamp, which is the case in our considered application. The problem can be extended to k types of inaccurate events, as will be discussed later.

- The length of a inaccurate interval is much smaller than the duration of the sequence. Otherwise, introducing inaccurate events becomes meaningless.

- The density function of the inaccurate event in the interval is given by domain experts; if not, we assume that it is uniformly distributed.

- For the simplicity of presentation, we only consider the total order between events (i.e., there does not exist two events with exactly the same temporal information). Discussions can be extended to the partial order easily (see discussions in [2, 8]).

The first assumption seems a bit restrict. However, it is the general case for data analysis for events with different granularity of time scales. Let us first consider that there are two time scales. According to the timestamp, events can be classified as fine granularity events and rough granularity events. We mentioned before that the time scale of fine granularity events should be defined as time unit and the rough granularity events are considered as inaccurate events. Note that the order between rough granularity events is certain, i.e., there is no overlap between the time intervals of any two inaccurate events. Thus, although rough granularity events can belong to different event types, the nature of the problem is the same as that of one inaccurate event type. If there are more than two time scales required in the application, we believe this is the rare case because it is not meaningful to investigate the total order between events with significantly different time scales.

The remainder of this paper is organized as follows. Related work on sequential mining and uncertainty issues is discussed in Section 2. Section 3 gives a model of uncertainty in sequential pattern mining. In Section 4, we propose an algorithm called *U_Apriori* to find a complete set of patterns from a sequence database containing uncertainty. The experiment results are shown in Section 5. Finally, we conclude this paper in Section 6.

2 Related Work

The problem of sequential pattern mining is first introduced by Agrawal and Srikant in [2]. Since then, substantial work has been done in sequential pattern discovery [8, 5, 12] and periodicity detection [10, 4, 11]. In most previous work, a sequence is regarded as a list of symbols without temporal information. In [8], Srikant and Agrawal have considered the timestamp for the transaction. To relax the the rigid definition of supermarket transactions, they dynamically combine transactions that happen inside a marginal interval (i.e., ignore their orders). However, in many other domains, one may not want to ignore the order of such events. Work in [5] by Mannila *et al.* is to find episodes from telecommunication event sequences. Despite in the application domain similar to ours, they only consider events with an accurate timestamp. The algorithms for sequential mining can be classified as *Apriori-based* algorithms [2, 8] and *project-based* algorithms [3, 6]. Our algorithm extends work [8] by providing a novel approach for precise support counting.

Because real data tend to contain noise, data mining in a noisy environment has become an important research area recently. In the sequential mining, we can regard inaccurate events as data with noise because they may make the order between events uncertain. Yang *et al.* in [12] have proposed a metric called *match* for defining the probability that a sequence matches a pattern. Their idea is similar to ours, but the uncertainty in their problem consists in the representation of a symbol rather than the order of events. In [10], to deal with the disturbance on the periodicity detection, Yang *et al.* has allowed a marginal shift on the starting position of a periodical pattern. Work in [7] by Pei *et al.* introduces flexibility into the format of association rules for finding more general fault-tolerant patterns. An example of their mining result could be "a customer who buys any 2 out of the products beer, cheese and juice is likely to buy cake as well". From our understanding, almost all work in this area is to relax the strict requirement, either in data modelling or in rule formats, for adapting uncleaned data in reality.

3 A Model of Uncertainty

In this section, we describe a mathematic model for discovering sequential patterns from a sequential database with one type of inaccurate event.

Definition 3.1 (Event): Let us consider k *event types* $E = \{e_i | i = 1..k\}$. In addition, let event type $e \in E$ be *inaccurate event type*. An *inaccurate event* is a triplet (a, t_s, t_e), where $a = e$ and $[t_s, t_e]$ indicates the possible happening period of the event. An *accurate event* is a pair (a, t) such that $a \in E \wedge a \neq e$ and t is the *timestamp* of the event.

Since we consider only one inaccurate event type, we assume that, in a sequence, any two intervals of inaccurate events are non-overlapped. In our application, a type of signal is collected every δ hours. It means that the order between any two inaccurate events in a sequence is certain. This is also the case for any two accurate events. Hence, the uncertainty on event order only exists between an accurate event and an inaccurate event.

Definition 3.2 (Event order): Given an accurate event (a_i, t_i) and an inaccurate event (a_j, t_{j_s}, t_{j_e}), the *order* between them is *uncertain* iff $t_i \in (t_{j_s}, t_{j_e})$; otherwise, it is *certain*.

Example 3.1: Considering S_1 in Fig. 1, the event of type e is an inaccurate event represented as $(e, t_3 - \delta, t_3)$. Others events, such as (f, t_1) and (c, t_2), are accurate events. The order between $(e, t_3 - \delta, t_3)$ and (c, t_2) is uncertain.

Definition 3.3 (Sequence): A *sequence* S is a list of events based on the definition of event order. The *length* of an sequence is the number of events it consists of. For any inaccurate event (e, t_s, t_e) in S, $w = (t_s, t_e)$ is called an *uncertain interval* of S iff there exists at least one event (a, t), such that $t \in (t_s, t_e)$ (i.e., the order between (e, t_s, t_e) and (a, t) is uncertain). A sequence is defined as a *fix-order sequence* if it has no uncertain intervals; otherwise, it is a *flexible-order sequence*. A *sequence database* is a set of tuples in the form of $\langle sid, S \rangle$, where sid is the ID of sequence S. Given a sequence S, S' is a *subsequence* of S, denoted as $S' \subseteq S$ if 1) S' is comprised of the events in S and 2) for any two events in S', the temporal relationship between them remains.

In the representation of a sequence, without loss of generality, for the inaccurate event (e, t_s, t_e), we refer to t_e in the ordering process. Also, a symbol [ ] is used in the sequence to delimit uncertain intervals explicitly. We also use these uncertain intervals to segment S into $S^1 \cdot S^2 \cdot \ldots \cdot S^m$, such that 1) S^i is a segment of S and 2) all events in S^i are either inside or outside an uncertain interval of S. We call S^i a *sequence segment*.

Example 3.2: In Fig.1, as the sequence S_4 has the uncertain interval $(t_4 - \delta, t_4)$, it is a flexible-order sequence denoted as $\langle (b, t_1), [(c, t_2), (a, t_3), (e, t_4 - \delta, t_4)], (f, t_5), (g, t_6) \rangle$. It is also represented as $S_4^1 \cdot S_4^2 \cdot S_4^3$, where $S_4^1 = \langle (b, t_1) \rangle$, $S_4^2 = \langle [(c, t_2), (a, t_3), (e, t_4 - \delta, t_4)] \rangle$, and $S_4^3 = \langle (f, t_5), (g, t_6) \rangle$. Considering the sequence S_2, note that $(t_2 - \delta, t_2)$ is not an uncertain interval of S_2 because there are no other events happening in this interval. Therefore, S_2 is a fix-order sequence represented as $\langle (b, t_1), (e, t_2 - \delta, t_2), (c, t_3), (a, t_4) \rangle$. The subsequence of S_4 could be obtained by dropping some events form S_4, such as $\langle (c, t_2), (a, t_3), (f, t_5) \rangle$ and $\langle (b, t_1), [(a, t_3), (e, t_4 - \delta, t_4)], (f, t_5) \rangle$.

Definition 3.4 (Pattern): A *pattern* P is a list of event types. It is represented as $\langle a_1, a_2, \ldots, a_l \rangle$ where $a_i \in E$. A pattern of *length* l is also referred as a l-pattern. Given two patterns $P = \langle a_1, a_2, \ldots, a_l \rangle$ and $P' = \langle a_1', a_2', \ldots, a_{l'}' \rangle$, where $l \geq l'$, P' is a *subpattern* of P, denoted as $P' \subseteq P$, if there exists a list of integers $1 \leq i_1 \leq i_2 \leq \cdots \leq i_{l'} \leq l$ such that $a_j' = a_{i_j}$ for $1 \leq j \leq l'$. Given two patterns P_1 and P_2, we define $P_1 = P_2$ iff $P_1 \subseteq P_2 \wedge P_2 \subseteq P_1$.

After introducing the concept of sequence and pattern in the uncertainty model, we now define the relationship between them. We consider that fix-order sequence is a special case of flexible-order sequence under the condition that the number of uncertain interval is 0. So, a fix-order sequence only has one sequence segment, i.e., itself. Now, we introduce an operator on sequence segment.

Definition 3.5 (Project): *Project* ∇ is an operator on sequence segment S^i, of which the operation is to drop the temporal information from events. ∇S^i is a pattern if S^i is outside any uncertain interval. For a S^i inside an uncertain interval, ∇S^i becomes a discrete random variable x whose value domain is the longest pattern that S^i probably contains. the probabilities of x is determined by the temporal information of the inaccurate event and the events inside the interval.

x	$\langle e, f, g \rangle$	$\langle f, e, g \rangle$	$\langle f, g, e \rangle$
$p(x)$	$\int_{t_{6_s}}^{t_4} d(e,t) \cdot dt$	$\int_{t_4}^{t_5} d(e,t) \cdot dt$	$\int_{t_5}^{t_{6_e}} d(e,t) \cdot dt$

Table 1. Random variable x

Example 3.3: Let us consider sequence segments $S^1 = \langle (a, t_1), (e, t_{2_s}, t_{2_e}), (c, t_3) \rangle$ and $S^2 = \langle [(f, t_4), (g, t_5), (e, t_{6_s}, t_{6_e})] \rangle$. $\nabla S^1 = \langle a, e, c \rangle$ and ∇S^2 is a random variable x, which is specified in Table 1. In the formula, $d(e, t)$ is the density function of the inaccurate events. The probability that $\nabla S^2 = \langle f, e, g \rangle$ equals the probability that e happens between f and g. Others are computed similarly.

Now we consider the precise support of a pattern in a sequence. Given a sequence S of length l_s and a pattern P of length l_p, where $l_s \geq l_p$, S may have more than one way to support P (because one type of event can occur multiple times in a sequence). Each way corresponds to a subsequence whose length is l_p. We will first define the precise support of a pattern in a same-length sequence and extend it to the condition of $l_s > l_p$.

Definition 3.6 (Contain rate): Given a sequence S' of length $l_{s'}$ and a pattern P of length l_p, where $l_{s'} = l_p$, using uncertain intervals, S' can be segmented as $S'^1 \cdot S'^2 \cdots S'^m$. Accordingly, the pattern P can have same segmentation $P^1 \cdot P^2 \cdots P^m$. The *contain rate* between sequence segment S'^i and corresponding *pattern segment* P^i is defined as $C(P^i, S'^i) = prob(\nabla S'^i = P^i)$.

If S'^i is outside uncertain interval, $\nabla S'^i$ is a pattern. Based on the formula, only if $\nabla S'^i = P^i$, $C(P^i, S'^i) = 1$. Otherwise, $C(P^i, S'^i) = 0$. If S'^i is inside uncertain interval, $\nabla S'^i$ is a random variable. We can calculate the contain rate by using probability theory, as shown in Example 3.3.

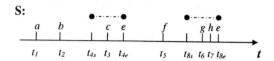

Figure 2. Flexible-order sequence

Example 3.4: Considering the sequence S in Fig. 2, we have $S^1 = \langle (a, t_1), (b, t_2) \rangle$, $S^2 = \langle [(c, t_3), (e, t_{4_s}, t_{4_e})] \rangle$, $S^3 = \langle (f, t_5) \rangle$, and $S^4 = \langle [(g, t_6), (h, t_7), (e, t_{8_s}, t_{8_e})] \rangle$. Given a pattern $P = \langle b, a, e, c, f, g, e, h \rangle$, it can be segmented as $P^1 \cdot P^2 \cdot P^3 \cdot P^4 = \langle b, a \rangle \cdot \langle e, c \rangle \cdot \langle f \rangle \cdot \langle g, e, h \rangle$. The contain rates between S^i and P^i ($i = 1 \ldots 4$) are $C(P^1, S^1) = 0$, $C(P^2, S^2) = \int_{t_{4_s}}^{t_3} d(e,t) \cdot dt$, $C(P^3, S^3) = 1$, $C(P^4, S^4) = \int_{t_6}^{t_7} d(e,t) \cdot dt$.

Definition 3.7 (Precise support w.r.t. subsequence): Given a sequence S' of length $l_{s'}$ and a pattern P of length l_p ($l_{s'} = l_p$), segmented as $S' = S'^1 \cdot S'^2 \cdots S'^m$ and $P^1 \cdot P^2 \cdots P^m$ respectively, the *precise support of P in S'* is defined as $P\_supp(P, S') = \prod_{1 \leq i \leq m} C(P^i, S'^i)$. The assumption behind this definition is that events are generated independently. Naturally, we say S contains P if $P\_supp(P, S) > 0$.

Example 3.5: Let us consider the pattern P and the sequence S in Example 3.4. The precise support $P\_supp(P, S) = 0$ because $C(P^1, S^1) = 0$. If we consider the pattern $P' = \langle a, b, e, c, f, g, e, h \rangle$, $P\_supp(P, S) = \int_{t_{4_s}}^{t_3} d(e,t) \cdot dt * \int_{t_6}^{t_7} d(e,t) \cdot dt$.

Definition 3.8 (Precise support w.r.t. sequence): Given a sequence S of length l_s and a pattern P of length l_p, where $l_s \geq l_p$, the *precise support of P in S* is defined as the *maximal* precise support of P in any l_p-length subsequence. Formally, $P\_supp(P, S) = Max_{S' \subseteq S} P\_supp(P, S')$ where S' is a subsequence of length l_p.

Example 3.6: Considering the sequence S in Fig. 2 and a pattern $P = \langle c, e \rangle$, only two subpatterns of S, $S_1' = \langle [(c, t_3), (e, t_{3_s}, t_{3_e})] \rangle$ and $S_2' = \langle (c, t_3), (e, t_{8_s}, t_{8_e}) \rangle$, contain pattern P. The precise support of P in S equals to $Max\{P\_supp(P, S_1'), P\_supp(P, S_2')\} = Max\left\{\int_{t_3}^{t_{4_e}} d(e,t) \cdot dt, 1\right\} = 1$.

In the fix-order sequence S, as there is no uncertain interval, the only sequence segment of S is itself and ∇S is a pattern. Based on our definitions, $P\_supp(P, S) = 1$ if $\nabla S \supseteq P$. Otherwise, $P\_supp(P, S) = 0$. This is identical to the traditional concept of support.

302

Definition 3.9 (Precise support w.r.t. sequence database): Given a pattern P and a sequence database D, the *precise support of P in D* is defined as $P\_supp(P, D) = \frac{\sum_{1 \le i \le N} P\_supp(P, S_i)}{N}$, where $N = |D|$.

Problem statement: After proposing the mathematic model, we give the formal definition of our problem as follows: given a sequence database D, one type of inaccurate event with its intervals and density function $d(e, t)$, and a threshold s_0, find any sequential pattern P such that $P\_supp(P, D) \ge s_0$.

4 Searching Interesting Patterns: *U_Apriori*

Most sequential pattern discovery algorithms are based on the Apriori property [1]. As an extension of the traditional sequential mining, our problem also holds the Apriori property.

Algorithm: U_Apriori
Input: a sequence database D, e type events with density function $d(e, t)$, and a threshold s_0
Output: patterns with precise support no less than s_0
Method:
    $F_1 = \{$frequent 1-patterns$\}$;
    Pre-compute uncertain intervals; /* see Section 4.1 */
    for$(k = 2; F_{k-1} \ne \phi; k++)$ **do**
        Generate candidate pattern set C_k from F_{k-1};
        for all sequence S_i in D **do**
            for all $P_j \in C_k$ **do**
                /* count the precise support, see Section 4.2 */
                $P_j.P\_supp+ = Max\_match(P_j, S_i)$;
        $F_k = \{P_j | P_j \in C_k \wedge \frac{P_j.P\_supp}{|D|} \ge s_0\}$;
    Frequent pattern set$= \bigcup_k F_k$;

Figure 3. U_Apriori Algorithm

Claim 4.1 (Apriori property): The precise support of a pattern P in a sequence S is no more than the precise support of any subpattern of P in S.

We do not give the proof here due space limitation. Because of Claim 4.1, we design the main algorithm called *U_Apriori*, which follows the structure of Apriori-based algorithms. U_Apriori searches for frequent patterns in a two-step process: candidate generation and precise support counting. The algorithm is demonstrated in Fig. 3. Compared with traditional sequential mining algorithm [2, 8], the challenge of U_Apriori lies in the precise support counting. In this paper, we propose an algorithm called *Max_match* to calculate the precise support of P in S, i.e, $P\_supp(P, S)$. To make precise support counting more efficient, a process is designed to pre-compute uncertain intervals, if any, from each sequence. In the following part of this section, we focus on the unique parts of U_Apriori,

namely, the pre-computing process and Max_match algorithm.

4.1 Pre-computing Uncertain Intervals

The goal of pre-computing uncertain intervals is twofold. First, not every sequence has uncertain intervals. We can identify those sequences in the pre-computing process and only do normal support counting in future passes. In addition, for those sequences that have uncertain intervals, we can record an uncertain interval list for future uses.

In this section, the definition of uncertain interval is slightly different with our previous definition. First, assume $\langle e \rangle$ is a frequent 1-pattern. Given an inaccurate event (e, t_s, t_e), the interval (t_s, t_e) is an uncertain interval iff there exists at least one event (a, t) such that 1) $t \in (t_s, t_e)$ and 2) $\langle a \rangle \in F_1$. Here we require the event type of the event inside (t_s, t_e) must be a frequent 1-pattern because events of infrequent event types are useless for further mining. Secondly, given uncertain interval (t_s, t_e), we use $[s\_i, e\_i]$ to represent it where s_i is the index of the first frequent-type event inside (t_s, t_e) and e_i is the index of the inaccurate event. For each sequence S, an *uncertain interval list* $l\_interval$ is used to represent uncertain intervals, if any, in S.

We can scan the sequence database once to find the uncertain interval list, if any, for each sequence. After pre-computing, a sequence is represented as a triplet $(sid, S, l\_interval)$.

4.2 Max_Match Algorithm

Compared with traditional support counting, the challenges of calculating precise support are as follows:

1. A sequence can have multiple ways to contain a pattern. Each way corresponds to a subsequence with the same length as that of the pattern. These subsequences may contain the pattern with different support values. Because the precise support is defined as the maximal value, in theory, we need to compute the support value for every such subsequence.

2. Unlike the traditional support counting, temporal information of events is needed for computing the precise support.

In the Max_Match Algorithm, we apply the greedy testing and recursive counting to find the precise support efficiently. Before looking at the algorithm, we first discuss when we need to consider the precise support of pattern P in sequence S.

Claim 4.2: Only if sequence S contains at least one uncertain interval and pattern P is a superpattern of $\langle e \rangle$, S may "partially" support P, i.e., $0 < P\_supp(P, S) < 1$.

Algorithm: Max_match
Input: a sequence S and a pattern P
Output: the precise support $P\_supp(P, S)$
Method:
    if ($P == Nil$) **then return** 1;
    if ($S == Nil$) **then return** 0;
    if ($S.l\_interval$ is null $\| P \not\supseteq e$) **then**
        /* do not consider uncertainty */
        if ($P \subseteq \nabla S$) **then return** 1;
        else return 0;
    else /* consider uncertainty */
        /* see Section 4.2.1 */
        if (Greedy testing succeeds) **then return** 1;
        if (back-point list l_back is not null) **then**
            /* see Section 4.2.2 */
            Create start-point list l_start;
            /* see Section 4.2.3 */
            for all $\alpha_i \in l\_start$ **do**
                Create subsequence S_i and subpattern P_i;
                $V_i = \alpha_i.value * Max\_Match(P_i, S_i)$;
            return $Max_i(V_i)$;
        return 0;

Figure 4. Max_match Algorithm

The high-level structure of the Max_match algorithm is given in Fig. 4. According to Claim 4.2, we can use the subpattern testing method to share some workload. When considering the uncertainty on the event order, we first use a greedy testing approach to find whether sequence S can *fully* support pattern P or not (i.e.,whether $P\_supp(P, S) = 1$). To do that, we skip the event, which matches the current element of pattern but introduces uncertainty on the event order. However, the position of such uncertain match is recorded in a structure called *back-point*. We can regard that each back-point indicates where the uncertain match happens. If the greedy testing succeeds, i.e., we can find a fix-order subsequence fully support the pattern, the precise support is 1. Otherwise, if there are no back-points recorded during the greedy scan, the precise support is 0 because S does not have any chance to contain P. If back-point list is not empty, for each back-point in it, we need to compute the contain rate between the uncertain part of S and any possible part of P. The information regarding such uncertain match is stored in a structure called *start-point*. For each case of such uncertain matches (corresponding to a start-point), we create subsequence S_i and subpattern P_i which are the unmatch parts of S and P respectively. The support value is calculated by calling $Max\_match(P_i, S_i)$ recursively. After the process of recursive counting, according to the definition of precise support, we select the maximal value from all support values as the precise support. Detailed explanations with examples can be found in the full version of this paper.

4.2.1 Greedy Testing

Definition 4.1: A *back-point* β of P in S is a pair $(intv, p\_index)$ where $intv$ is an uncertain interval of S and p_index is the index of P, from where the match starts to be uncertain.

We do greedy testing by interleaved scanning S and P. The testing terminates if S is scanned to the end. Suppose that given an element p_i of P, a procedure exists to find the first event that match p_i in S after a given event. In the greedy testing process, we need to set a back-point under two situations.

1. If 1) the current pattern element $p_i \neq e$, 2) the event that matches p_i is inside an uncertain interval I and 3) $p_{i+1} = e$, we set *the first class back-point* β_1 where $\beta_1.intv = I$ and $\beta_1.p\_index = j$. Here, j is the index of P such that p_j is the first element whose matched event is inside I.

2. If 1) the current pattern element $p_i = e$, 2) the event that matches p_i is inside an uncertain interval I and 3) inside I, there exists an events that can match p_{i+1}, we set *the second class back-point* β_2 where $\beta_2.intv = I$ and $\beta_2.p\_index = i$.

After setting the back-point, we skip the current matched event for p_{i+1} and continue searching S from the first event outside the uncertain interval I (Note that we do not consider the pattern element p_{i+2} at this moment). If we can find a certain matched event for the last element of P, the greedy testing succeeds and the precise support is 1. Otherwise, a list of back-points is returned.

4.2.2 Creating Start-Point List

After greedy testing fails, we acquire a list of back-points. Given a back-point $\beta(intv, p\_index)$, the uncertain part of sequence S is the sequence segment S^i that is inside $\beta.intv$, while the pattern segment P^i, which is possibly involved in uncertain matching, could be any pattern segment starting from $\beta.p\_index$. In this process, we need calculate the probability that S^i contains any possible P^i. We store this probability, as well as the next start matching positions of S and P, into a structure called *start-point*.

Definition 4.2: A *start-point* α is a triplet $(value, p\_i, s\_i)$. $value$ is a probability of sequence segment containing pattern segment. p_i and sq_i are the index of pattern and sequence respectively, indicating from where the further matching starts.

The procedure of creating start-point list is illustrated in Fig. 5. Note that P^i is initialized in terms of the class of back-point. For the first class back-point, P^i is the pattern segment of P starting from the element with index

Creating start-point list:

    for all $\beta_i \in l\_back$ **do**

        S^i =sequence segment of S inside $\beta_i.intv$;

        Set P^i according to $\beta_i.p\_index$;

        while (S^i contains P^i) **do**

            Create start point α;

            Add α to start_list l_start;

            P^i grows by adding the next element of P;

Figure 5. Creating start-point list

Recursive counting:

    Sort l_start;

    result=0;

    for ($i = 0; i < l\_start.length; i++$) **do**

        if ($result \geq a_i.value$) **then return** result;

        Compute P_i' and S_i'

        $V_i = a_i.value * Max\_match(P_i', S_i')$;

        if ($V_i > result$) **then** $result = V_i$;

    return result;

Figure 6. Recursive counting

$\beta_i.p\_index$ and ending with the next appeared e element in P. For the second class back-point, P^i is the pattern segment of P starting from the element with index $\beta_i.p\_index$ and ending with the element with index $\beta_i.p\_index + 1$. when creating a start-point α, according to Definition 4.2, $\alpha.p\_i$ should be the index of the element after P^i and $\alpha.sq\_i$ is the index of the first event after uncertain interval $\beta_i.intv$. Now we discuss how to compute $\alpha.value$, which is the probability that S^i contains P^i. Because S^i and P^i may have different length, in terms of the definition of contain rate, $\alpha.value$ should be defined as $Max_{S^{i'} \subseteq S^i} C(P^i, S^{i'})$ where the length of $S^{i'}$ equals to the length of P^i. Note that the maximum here requires us to find a subsequence of S^i which makes the integral interval largest (details in Example 3.3).

4.2.3 Recursive Counting

In this part, for each start-point, we calculate its support value by recursively calling Max_match and then select the maximal one as the precise support.

Given a start-point $\alpha_i (value, p\_i, s\_i)$ in l_start, we set P_i' as the subpattern of P starting from index $\alpha_i.p\_i$ and S_i' as the subsequence of S starting from index $\alpha_i.s\_i$. Note that P_i' and S_i' are the un-matched part of P and S respectively. Based on the definition of precise support, the *support value* V_i of α_i is computed as $\alpha_i.value * Max\_match(P_i', S_i')$. If $\alpha_i.p\_i = l_p$ or $\alpha_i.s\_i = l_s$, P_i' or S_i' will be Nil. Naturally, we define $Max\_match(Nil, S) = Max\_match(Nil, Nil) = 1$ and $Max\_match(P, Nil) = 0$, as is given in Fig. 4.

In theory, we need compute the support value for all start-points because the precise support is defined as the maximal probability (as demonstrated in Fig. 4). However, according the following property, we can find the maximal support value without computing for every start point.

Claim 4.3: Given two start-points α_i and α_j, let V_i and V_j be the support value of α_i and α_j respectively. If $V_i \geq \alpha_j.value$, $V_i \geq V_j$.

Proof: According to Definition 3.8, for any P and S, $0 \leq Max\_match(P, S) \leq 1$. $\square$

Because of Claim 4.3, we can sort the start-point list

l_start on $\alpha_i.value$ in a descending order. If the support value V_i of the current start-point α_i is no less than $\alpha_{i+1}.value$, we stop computing for the rest start-points. The details are given in Fig 6.

5 Empirical Results

In this section, we show the effectiveness and the efficiency of our algorithm by comparing it with the traditional sequential mining algorithm GSP [8].

The experiments are performed on a PC with an Intel Pentium III 500MHz CPU and 256M main memory, running Microsoft Windows 2000.

All sequence databases in the experiments are derived from a telecommunication event dataset which consists of 2,003,440 events of 190 types. Each event has a timestamp as its time of occurrence. However, a type of event is collected every 6 hours. We refer to this type of event as the inaccurate event. For any such type of event (e, t), we represent it as $(e, t-6, t)$. As no information is given for the distribution of inaccurate events, we assume that every inaccurate event is uniformly distributed in the 6-hour-length interval.

In the experiment, we have created a sequence database for each type of trouble report (TR) (details in [9]). For any sequence database D_i, we apply U_Apriori (considering uncertainty) and GSP (ignoring uncertainty) to find frequent patterns respectively.

Sequence database	$|R|$	$|R'|$	$|R' - R|$	$\frac{|R'-R|}{|R'|}$
D_1	170	158	8	5.06%
D_2	288	267	20	7.50%
D_3	117	114	6	5.26%

Table 2. Mining results

First, we study sequential patterns discovered by the two algorithms. Given a sequential database, let R be the set of patterns discovered by GSP and R' be the one discovered by U_Apriori. $|R' - R|$ is the number of the patterns that are ignored in traditional sequential mining. R' should be the expected mining result because it is more accurate than R.

Introducing uncertainty into our application helps us to find $\frac{|R'-R|}{|R'|}$ percent new patterns. Table 2 lists some experiment results. D_1, D_2 and D_3 are three sequence databases, each of which relates to a type of TR. The minimum (precise) support is set as 5% and the maximal duration of the sequence in each database is 48 hours. From the experiment, we find that, generally, we can achieve 5%-9% new patterns as the reward of considering the uncertainty.

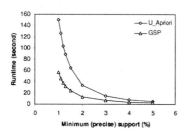

Figure 7. Performance comparison

The efficiency of our algorithm is studied in terms of response time. The test is carried out on different (precise) support thresholds in a database that consists of 10,261 sequences. Fig. 7 shows the performance curves of U_Apriori and GSP. We can see that GSP outperforms U-Apriori especially when the threshold of (precise) support is low. This is because the Max_match algorithm is much more complex than the subsequence testing. We conclude that in U_Apriori, we trade the system computation time for a better accuracy.

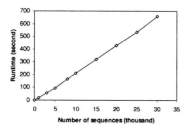

Figure 8. Scalability of U_Apriori

Further, we look at the scalability of U_Apriori. Fig. 8 shows the response time with respect to the number of sequences. The precise support threshold is set as 0.5%. We can see that U_Apriori is linearly scalable.

6 Conclusions and Discussions

In this paper, we have studied the problem of sequential mining with uncertainty. Compared with the traditional sequential mining, one type of inaccurate event is introduced.

We have defined a model to accommodate the uncertain event order caused by inaccurate events. In this model, a new metric, precise support, is proposed to measure the significance of the pattern. Based on this metric, we designed an algorithm called U_Apriori to find frequent sequential patterns in a database containing one type of inaccurate event.

The number of inaccurate event types can be extended to k. If there is no overlap between any two intervals of the inaccurate events, our model is still applicable. Otherwise, the definition of uncertain interval is modified as the maximal part that is covered by these overlapped intervals. In any case, we may still use the uncertain interval as the unit of probability counting. However, within an uncertain interval, the computational complexity for matching increases.

In general, introducing uncertainty into pattern discovery in temporal event sequences will risk for the computational complexity problem. This paper has provided an effective and yet efficient solution.

References

[1] R. Agrawal and R. Srikant. Fast algorithms for mining association rules. In *Proc. 20th VLDB*, pages 487–499, 1994.
[2] R. Agrawal and R. Srikant. Mining sequential patterns. In *Proc. 11th ICDE*, pages 3–14, 1995.
[3] J. Han, J. Pei, B. Mortazavi-Asl, Q. Chen, U. Dayal, and M. Hsu. Freespan: Frequent pattern-projected sequential pattern mining. In *Proc. 6th ACM SIGKDD*, pages 355–359, 2000.
[4] S. Ma and J. L. Hellerstein. Mining partially periodic event patterns with unknown periods. In *Proc. 17th ICDE*, pages 205–214, 2001.
[5] H. Mannila, H. Toivonen, and A. I. Verkamo. Discovery of frequent episodes in event sequences. *Data Mining and Knowledge Discovery*, 1(3):259–289, 1997.
[6] J. Pei, J. Han, B. Mortazavi-Asl, H. Pinto, Q. Chen, U. Dayal, and M.-C. Hsu. PrefixSpan mining sequential patterns efficiently by prefix projected pattern growth. In *Proc. 17th ICDE*, pages 215–226, 2001.
[7] J. Pei, A. K. H. Tung, and J. Han. Fault-tolerant frequent pattern mining: Problems and challenges. In *DMKD*, 2001.
[8] R. Srikant and R. Agrawal. Mining sequential patterns: Generalizations and performance improvements. In *Proc. 5th EDBT*, pages 3–17, 1996.
[9] X. Sun, M. E. Orlowska, and X. Zhou. Finding event-oriented patterns in long temporal sequences. In *Proc. 7th PAKDD*, 2003.
[10] J. Yang, W. Wang, and P. S. Yu. Mining asynchronous periodic patterns in time series data. In *Knowledge Discovery and Data Mining*, pages 275–279, 2000.
[11] J. Yang, W. Wang, and P. S. Yu. Infominer: mining surprising periodic patterns. In *Knowledge Discovery and Data Mining*, pages 395–400, 2001.
[12] J. Yang, W. Wang, P. S. Yu, and J. Han. Mining long sequential patterns in a noisy environment. In *SIGMOD Conference*, pages 406–417, 2002.

Evolutionary Gabor Filter Optimization with Application to Vehicle Detection

Zehang Sun[1], George Bebis[1] and Ronald Miller[2]

[1]Computer Vision Lab. Department of Computer Science, University of Nevada, Reno

[2]Vehicle Design R&A Department, Ford Motor Company, Dearborn, MI

(zehang,bebis)@cs.unr.edu, rmille47@ford.com

Abstract—Despite the considerable amount of research work on the application of Gabor filters in pattern classification, their design and selection have been mostly done on a trial and error basis. Existing techniques are either only suitable for a small number of filters or less problem-oriented. A systematic and general evolutionary Gabor filter optimization (EGFO) approach that yields a more optimal, problem-specific, set of filters is proposed in this study. The EGFO approach unifies filter design with filter selection by integrating Genetic Algorithms (GAs) with an incremental clustering approach. Specifically, filter design is performed using GAs, a global optimization approach that encodes the parameters of the Gabor filters in a chromosome and uses genetic operators to optimize them. Filter selection is performed by grouping together filters having similar characteristics (i.e., similar parameters) using incremental clustering in the parameter space. Each group of filters is represented by a single filter whose parameters correspond to the average parameters of the filters in the group. This step eliminates redundant filters, leading to a compact, optimized set of filters. The average filters are evaluated using an application-oriented fitness criterion based on Support Vector Machines (SVMs). To demonstrate the effectiveness of the proposed framework, we have considered the challenging problem of vehicle detection from gray-scale images. Our experimental results illustrate that the set of Gabor filters, specifically optimized for the problem of vehicle detection, yield better performance than using traditional filter banks.

I. INTRODUCTION

Motivated by biological findings on the similarity of 2-D Gabor filters and receptive fields of neurons in the visual cortex [1], there has been increased interest in deploying Gabor filters in various computer vision applications. An important property of Gabor filters that has contributed to this is that they have optimal joint localization both in the spatial and frequency domains [1]. Gabor filters have been successfully applied to various image analysis applications including edge detection [2], image coding[1], texture analysis [3][4][5], handwritten number recognition [6], face recognition [7], vehicle detection [8], and image retrieval [9]. Despite the considerable amount of research work on the application of Gabor filters to computer vision problems, their design is mostly performed on a trial and error basis. A filter design method is needed for selecting filter parameters to maximize the discriminating power of the filters. Previous efforts in designing Gabor filters follow two directions: the

"Filter-design approach" and the "Filter-bank approach" [10], [3].

In the "filter-design approach" the filter parameters are chosen by considering the data available, that is, the parameters are appropriate for the problem at hand only. In one of the pioneering studies on the design of Gabor filters conducted by Bovik et al. [11], the peak detection technique was used. In this approach, the center frequency of each filter corresponds to a peak of the power spectrum of the input image. Slightly different from [11], Okombi-Diba et al. [12] implemented a multi-iteration peak detection method for a texture segmentation problem. Dunn et al. [13] investigated an exhaustive search to find the center frequency. The search was guided by a "filter-quality measurement" (i.e., Rician statistical model) that was determined by the sample mean and sample variance of the values of an averaged windowed Fourier transform. This work was based on a bipartite (two-texture) image segmentation problem and required heuristics to find a proper bandwidth. The "filter-quality measurement" was the image-segmentation error and the filter with the lowest error was selected. Due to the exhaustive search, this method is quite time-consuming. A more computationally efficient method was described in [10], [3], using a segmentation-error criterion similar to [13]. The efficiency was gained using a method to calculate the filter output power for all Gabor filters at certain center frequencies simultaneously. It is worth mentioning that this method does not increase the efficiency of designing a single filter.

In the "filter-bank approach" the filter parameters are chosen in a data independent way. Then, a subset of filters is selected for a particular application. Turner [14] used 32 filters(4 frequencies $\times$ 4 orientations $\times$ 2 phase pairs) in a texture discrimination problem. Based on the observation that a constant bandwidth on the logarithmic scale assures the width of the filters to be inversely proportional to their radial frequencies, Jain et al. [4] chose the filter parameters such that the radial frequencies were one octave apart. To reduce the computational burden, a greedy filter selection method was employed using a selection

307

criterion based on the error between the original image and the one reconstructed by adding together a subset of the filtered images. To reduce the redundancy in the Gabor feature representation, Manjunath et al. [9] proposed a design method to ensure that the half-peak magnitude support of the filter responses in the frequency domain touch each other. For fast image browsing, they implemented an "adaptive filter selection algorithm", where spectrum difference information was used to select filters with better performance. In the context of handwritten number recognition, Hamamoto et al. [6] optimized the filters by checking the error rate for all possible combinations of filter parameters and then choosing those minimizing the error rates.

Although good performance has been reported in the literature, certain limitations still exist. "Filter-design approaches", for example, divide the design process into two stages: pre-filter and post-filter. Several pre-filter design approaches have been investigated, however, an explicit methodology for selecting an appropriate post-filter step for a given pre-filter step has not been suggested. Moreover the selection of the bandwidth parameter is done mostly heuristically. The design stage in the "filter-bank approach" is mostly problem-independent. Different pattern classification problems, however, might require selecting an optimum set of features and, consequently, an optimum set of Gabor filters. We would not expect, for example, that a set of Gabor filters optimized for a vehicle classification application (compact car v.s. truck) would work well in a vehicle detection application (vehicle v.s. non-vehicle), since more detailed information is required in the former case than in the later. Many researchers have realized that this is a serious problem and have suggested filter selection schemes to deal with it, however, filters are selected from an original small pool of filters that might not be suitable for the problem at hand (e.g., Hamamoto et al. [6] performed filter selection using a pool of 100 predefined filters). The main issue here is that we are not certain whether or not the optimum set of filters are included in the predefined pool of filters.

A systematic and general evolutionary filter optimization approach that yields a more optimal, problem-specific, set of filters is proposed in this paper. We believe that filter design and selection are not two independent problems and should not be treated separately. In this study, GAs have been integrated with an incremental clustering algorithm in the parameter space to enable Gabor filter optimization. GAs allow searching the space of filter parameters efficiently while clustering removes filters having a high degree of redundancy. The final set of filters is both compact and optimized. To customize the filters for a given problem, an application-oriented fitness criterion is used based on Support Vector Machines (SVMs).

The EGFO approach is suitable for optimizing any number of filters for a given application. It encapsulates the main characteristics of both of the previous two approaches. The search space of our method is much larger than that of the filter-bank approaches, providing a higher likelihood of getting close to the optimal solution as in the case of filter design approaches. Moreover, we represent filter optimization as a closed-loop learning problem. The search for an optimal solution is guided by the performance of a SVM classifier on features extracted from the responses of the Gabor filters.

The rest of the paper is organized as follows: In Section II, we define the Gabor filter optimization problem. Section III presents our evolutionary Gabor filter optimization approach in detail. The statistical Gabor filter feature extraction method and the learning engine used in our experiments are described in Section IV. The proposed framework is tested in Section VI on the challenging problem of vehicle detection. The analysis of our experimental results is given in Section VII. Finally, Section VIII summarizes the main results of the paper and presents possible directions for future work.

II. PROBLEM STATEMENT

We begin with a brief review of Gabor filters. One can refer to Daugman's seminal paper [1] for more details. The general functional of the two-dimensional Gabor filter family can be represented as a Gaussian function modulated by a complex sinusoidal signal. Specifically, a two dimensional Gabor filter $g(x, y)$ can be formulated as:

$$g(x,y) = \frac{1}{2\pi\sigma_x\sigma_y} \exp[-\frac{1}{2}(\frac{\tilde{x}^2}{\sigma_x^2} + \frac{\tilde{y}^2}{\sigma_y^2})] \exp[2\pi jW\tilde{x}] \quad (1)$$

$$\begin{cases} \tilde{x} = x\cos\theta + y sin\theta \\ \tilde{y} = -x\sin\theta + y cos\theta \end{cases} \quad (2)$$

where σ_x and σ_y are the scaling parameters of the filter and determine the effective size of the neighborhood of a pixel in which the weighted summation takes place. $\theta(\theta \in [0, \pi))$ specifies the orientation of the Gabor filters. W is the radial frequency of the sinusoid. A filter will respond stronger to a bar or an edge with a normal parallel to the orientation θ of the sinusoid.

The Fourier transform of the Gabor function in Eq. 1 is given by:

$$G(u,v) = \exp[-\frac{1}{2}(\frac{(u-W)^2}{\sigma_u^2} + \frac{v^2}{\sigma_v^2})] \quad (3)$$

where $\sigma_u = \frac{1}{2}\pi\sigma_x$, $\sigma_v = \frac{1}{2}\pi\sigma_y$. The Fourier domain representation in Eq. 3 specifies the amount by which the filter modifies each frequency component of the input image.

Gabor filter optimization corresponds to selecting the proper values for each of the four parameters in the parameter set

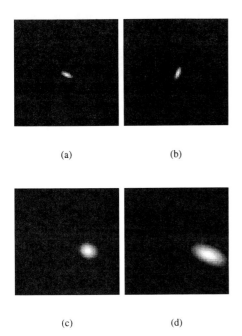

(a)   (b)

(c)   (d)

Fig. 1. The Gabor filter with different parameter $\Phi = \{\theta, W, \sigma_x, \sigma_y\}$ in frequency domain(the Fourier transform of the Gabor functions with different parameters) . (a) $\Phi_a = \{0^o, 0.0961, 0.0204, 0.01219\}$, (b) $\Phi_b = \{0^o, 0.3129, 0.06, 0.359\}$, (c) $\Phi_b = \{90^o, 0.3129, 0.06, 0.359\}$, (d) $\Phi_c = \{90^o, 0.3921, 0.0503, 0.3066\}$

$\Phi = \{\theta, W, \sigma_x, \sigma_y\}$. Gabor filters act as local bandpass filters. Fig. 1 shows four Gabor filters with different parameter settings in frequency domain. The light areas of the power spectrum indicate frequencies and wave orientations. It is obvious from Fig.1 that different parameter settings will lead to quite different filter responses, an important issue in pattern classification problems. Each filter is fully determined by choosing the four parameters in Φ. Therefore, choosing a filter for a particular application involves optimizing these four parameters. Assuming that N filters are needed in an application, $4N$ parameters need to be optimized. Solving this high dimensional multivariate optimization problem is very difficult in general. In contrast to previous filter design methods, a global optimization approach using GAs is investigated here to deal with this problem.

III. EVOLUTIONARY GABOR FILTER OPTIMIZATION

In this section, we describe the proposed evolutionary Gabor filter optimization approach.

A. A brief review of GAs

GAs are a class of optimization procedures inspired by the natural selection mechanisms[15]. GAs operate iteratively on a population of structures, each of which represents a candidate solution to the problem, encoded as a string of symbols (chro-

mosome). A randomly generated set of such strings forms the initial population from which the GA starts its search. Three basic genetic operators guide this search: selection, crossover and mutation.

B. Encoding and decoding

Using a binary encoding scheme, each Gabor filter is represented by M bits that encode its four parameters. To design N filters, we use a chromosome of length MN bits. Each of the four parameters in Φ is encoded using $n = M/4$ bits as illustrated in Fig. 2.

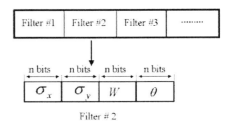

Fig. 2. Encoding scheme

It is worth mentioning that:
- The encoding scheme is quite flexible, and allows us to encode any number of filters by simply varying the length of the chromosome;
- The numbers of bits associated with each parameter need not to be the same, we can make the search for a particular parameter finer of coarser by simply adding or removing bits for this parameter;
- If we need to fix certain parameter(s) using prior knowledge, we can remove the parameter(s) from the chromosome. In this case, the GA will optimize the remaining parameters;

Each of the parameters in Φ has its own constraints and ranges. The encoding/decoding scheme was designed to ensure that the generated filters satisfy these requirements.

The orientation parameter θ should satisfy: $\theta \in [0, \pi)$. If D_θ denotes the decimal number corresponding to the chunk of bits associated with θ (see Fig.2) then the value of θ is computed by

$$\theta = D_\theta * \pi/2^n. \tag{4}$$

which always satisfies the range requirement.

W is the radial frequency of the Gabor filter, which is application dependent. Using some prior knowledge, we can limit the range of W into $[W_{min}, W_{max}]$. Then the decoding formula is given by

$$W = W_{min} + (W_{max} - W_{min}) * D_W/2^n \tag{5}$$

where D_W is the decimal number corresponding to the chunk of bits associated with W. In this study, we have used $W_{min} = 0$ and $W_{max} = 0.5$.

σ_x, and σ_y are essentially the effective sizes of the Gaussian functions and are within the range $[\sigma_{min}, \sigma_{max}]$. The upper limit σ_{max} is determined by the mask width w [16]. A relation between σ_{max} and the mask size w can be obtained by imposing that w subtends most of the energy of the Gaussian. An adequate choice is $\sigma_{max} < w/5$, which subtends 98.76% of the energy of the Gaussian filter. The lower limit can be derived using the *Sampling Theorem*. If the pixel width is taken as our unit step, we cannot reconstruct completely a signal containing frequencies higher than 0.5pixel^{-1} from its samples, which means that any frequency component at $|\omega| > \omega_c = 2\pi(0.5) = \pi$ is distorted. The ω_c is determined by the pixelization, not by the signal. To avoid aliasing, the best we can do is to keep most of the energy of the Gaussian function within the interval $[-\pi, \pi]$. Applying the "98.86% of the energy" criterion, we find $\sigma_{min} > 0.796$. To meet the range constraint ($[\sigma_{min}, \sigma_{max}]$), our decoding scheme follows:

$$\sigma_x = \sigma_{min} + (\sigma_{max} - \sigma_{min}) * D_{\sigma_x}/2^n \qquad (6)$$

for σ_x and

$$\sigma_y = \sigma_{min} + (\sigma_{max} - \sigma_{min}) * D_{\sigma_y}/2^n \qquad (7)$$

for σ_y. D_{σ_x} and D_{σ_y} are again the decimal numbers corresponding to the chunk of bits associated with σ_x and σ_y correspondingly.

C. Filter Selection

During parameter optimization, some of the Gabor filters encoded in a chromosome might end up being very similar to each other or even identical. These filters will result in similar/identical responses, therefore, introducing great redundancy and increasing time requirements. To eliminate redundant filters, we perform filter selection, implemented through filter clustering in the parameter space. An incremental clustering algorithm [17] has been adopted in this paper for its simplicity. A high level description of the clustering algorithm is given below:
1. Assign the first Gabor filter to a cluster.
2. Compute the distance of the next Gabor filter from the centroid of each cluster.
3. Find the smallest distance.
4. If the distance is less than a threshold, assign the filter to the corresponding cluster; otherwise, assign the filter to a new cluster.
5. Repeat step 2-4 for each of the remaining filters.
6. Represent the filters in each cluster by a single filter whose parameters correspond to the cluster's centroid.

The optimized filters are evaluated using the fitness function defined in Section III-E.

In our implementation, clustering is carried out in the parameter domain. Representing the parameters of a Gabor filter with $\{\theta^n, W^n, \sigma_x^n, \sigma_y^n\}$ and the centroids of the clusters with $\{\theta^i, W^i, \sigma_x^i, \sigma_y^i\}$ with $i \in [1\ N]$, where N is the number of currently existing clusters, we assign the filter to the ith cluster only if all of the following conditions are satisfied:

$$\theta^i - \frac{1}{2} \times Thre_\theta \leq \theta^n \leq \theta^i + \frac{1}{2} \times Thre_\theta \qquad (8)$$

$$W^i - \frac{1}{2} \times Thre_W \leq W^n \leq W^i + \frac{1}{2} \times Thre_W \qquad (9)$$

$$\sigma_x^i - \frac{1}{2} \times Thre_\sigma \leq \sigma_x^n \leq \sigma_x^i + \frac{1}{2} \times Thre_\sigma \qquad (10)$$

$$\sigma_y^i - \frac{1}{2} \times Thre_\sigma \leq \sigma_y^n \leq \sigma_y^i + \frac{1}{2} \times Thre_\sigma \qquad (11)$$

Otherwise, the filter is assigned to a new cluster. The above conditions are quite strict to make sure that filters falling in the same cluster are very similar to each other. We can always relax the criterion by increasing the predefined thresholds. The following thresholds were used in our experiments:

$\Phi = \{\theta, W, \sigma_x, \sigma_y\}$ are $Thre_\theta = \pi/K$, $Thre_W = (W_{max} - W_{min})/K$, and $Thre_{\sigma_x} = Thre_{\sigma_y} = Thre_\sigma = (\sigma_{max} - \sigma_{min})/K$. Depending on different applications and desired trade-off between model compactness and accuracy, K can be set to different values.

D. Selection, Mutation and Crossover

Mutation is a very low probability operator and just flips a specific bit. It plays the role of restoring lost genetic material. Our selection strategy was cross generational. Assuming a population of size N, the offspring double the size of the population and we select the best N individuals from the combined parent-offspring population. Uniform crossover is used here.

E. Fitness evaluation

Each individual's fitness will determine whether or not it will survive in subsequent generations. The fitness value used here is the performance of a SVM classifier on a validation set using features extracted from the responses of the selected Gabor filters. In this way, the Gabor filter optimization design is implemented as a closed-loop learning scheme, which is more powerful, more problem-specific, and less heuristic than in previous approaches.

IV. Feature extraction and classification

Designing an optimal set of Gabor filters is the first step in building a pattern classification algorithm. Then, we need to extract features using the responses of the selected filters and train a classifier using those features. To demonstrate the proposed filter design approach, redundant statistical Gabor features and SVMs are utilized.

A. Gabor Filter Features

Given an input image $I(x, y)$, Gabor feature extraction is performed by convolving $I(x, y)$ with a set of Gabor filters:

$$r(x, y) = \int \int I(\xi, \eta) g(x - \xi, y - \eta) d\xi d\eta \quad (12)$$

Although the raw responses of the Gabor filters could be used directly as features, some kind of post-processing is usually applied (e.g., Gabor-energy features, thresholded Gabor features, and moments based on Gabor features [18]). In this study, we use moments derived from Gabor filter outputs on subwindows defined on subimages extracted from the whole input image.

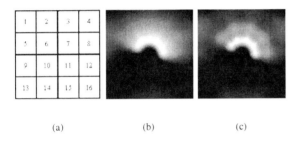

(a)   (b)   (c)

Fig. 3. (a) feature extraction patches; (b) Gabor filter bank with 4 scales and 6 orientations; (c) Gabor filter bank with 3 scales and 5 orientations;

First, each subimage is scaled to a fixed size of 32×32. Then, it is divided into 9 overlapping 16×16 subwindows. Each subimage consists of 16 8×8 patches as shown in Figure 3(a), patches 1,2,5,and 6 comprise the first 16×16 subwindow, 2,3,6 and 7 the second, 5, 6, 9, and 10 the fourth, and so forth. The Gabor filters are then applied on each subwindow separately. The motivation for extracting -possibly redundant - Gabor features from several overlapping subwindows is to compensate for the error due to the subwindow extraction step (e.g. subimages containing partially extracted objects or background information), making feature extraction more robust.

The magnitudes of the Gabor filter responses are collected from each subwindow and represented by three moments: the mean μ_{ij}, the standard deviation σ_{ij}, and the skewness κ_{ij} where i corresponds to the i-th filter and j corresponds to the j-th subwindow. Using moments implies that only the statistical properties of a group of pixels is taken into consideration,

while position information is discarded. This is particularly useful to compensate for errors in the extraction of the subimages. Suppose we are using $N = 6$ filters. Applying the filter bank on each of the 9 subwindows, yields a feature vector of size 162, having the following form:

$$[\mu_{11}\sigma_{11}\kappa_{11}, \mu_{12}\sigma_{12}\kappa_{12} \cdots \mu_{69}\sigma_{69}\kappa_{69}] \quad (13)$$

B. SVM classifier

SVMs are primarily two-class classifiers that have been shown to be an attractive and more systematic approach to learning linear or non-linear decision boundaries [19] [20]. Given a set of points, which belong to either one of the two classes, *SVM* finds the hyperplane leaving the largest possible fraction of points of the same class on the same side, while maximizing the distance of either class from the hyperplane. This is equivalent to performing structural risk minimization to achieve good generalization [19] [20]. Given l examples from two classes

$$(x_1, y_1)(x_2, y_2)...(x_l, y_l), \quad x_i \in R^N, y_i \in \{-1, +1\} \quad (14)$$

finding the optimal hyper-plane implies solving a constrained optimization problem using quadratic programming. The optimization criterion is the width of the margin between the classes. The discriminating hyperplane is defined as:

$$f(x) = \sum_{i=1}^{l} y_i a_i k(x, x_i) + b \quad (15)$$

where $k(x, x_i)$ is a kernel function and the sign of $f(x)$ indicates the membership of x. Constructing the optimal hyperplane is equivalent to finding all the nonzero a_i. Any data point x_i corresponding to a nonzero a_i is a support vector of the optimal hyperplane.

Kernel functions, which satisfy the Mercer's condition, can be expressed as a dot product in some space [19]. By using different kernels, *SVMs* implement a variety of learning machines (e.g., a sigmoidal kernel corresponds to a two-layer sigmoidal neural network while a Gaussian kernel corresponds to a radial basis function (*RBF*) neural network). The Gaussian radial basis kernel, which is used in this study, is given by

$$k(x, x_i) = \exp(-\frac{\| x - x_i \|^2}{2\delta^2}) \quad (16)$$

Our experiments with different kernels have shown that the Gaussian kernel outperforms the others in the context of our application.

V. Vehicle detection using optimized Gabor filters

In this section, we consider the problem of vehicle detection from gray-scale images. The first step in vehicle detection is usually hypothesizing the vehicle locations in an image.

Then, verification is applied to test the hypotheses. Both steps are equally important and challenging. Approaches to generate the hypothetical locations of vehicles in images include using motion, symmetry, shadows, and vertical/horizontal edges. Our emphasis here is on improving the performance of the verification step by optimizing the Gabor filters.

A. Vehicle Data

The images used in our experiments were collected in Dearborn, Michigan in two different sessions, one in the Summer of 2001 and one in the Fall of 2001. To ensure a good variety of data in each session, the images were captured at different times of different days and on five different highways. The training set contains subimages of rear vehicle views and non-vehicles, which were extracted manually from the Fall 2001 data set. A total of 1051 vehicle and 1051 non-vehicle subimages were extracted manually(see Figure 4). In [21], the subimages were aligned by warping the bumpers to approximately the same position. However we have not attempted to align the data since alignment requires detecting certain features on the vehicle accurately. Moreover, we believe that some variability in the extraction of the subimages can actually improve performance. Each subimage in the training and test sets was scaled to a size of 32×32 and preprocessed to account for different lighting conditions and contrast using the method suggested in [22].

To evaluate the performance of the proposed approach, the error rates (*ER*) are recorded using a three-fold cross-validation procedure. Specifically, we sample the training dataset randomly three times (*Set1*, *Set2* and *Set3*) by keeping 280 of the vehicle subimages and 280 of the non-vehicle subimages for training. 300 subimages (150 vehicle subimages and 150 non-vehicle subimages) are used for validation during the filter optimization design. For testing, we used a fixed set of 231 vehicle and non-vehicle subimages which were extracted from the Summer 2001 data set.

Fig. 4. Examples of vehicle and nonvehicle images used for training.

VI. EXPERIMENTAL RESULTS

For comparison purposes, we also report the detection error rates using two different Gabor filter banks without optimization: one with 4 scales and 6 orientations Fig.3(b), the other with 3 scales and 5 orientations Fig.3(c). These filter banks were designed by following the method proposed in [9].

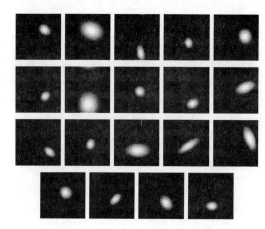

Fig. 5. 19 optimized Gabor filters for the vehicle detection problem with $K = 3$

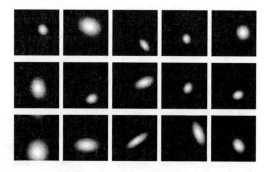

Fig. 6. 15 Gabor filters for the vehicle detection problem with $K = 2$

A. Results

We have performed a number of experiments and comparisons to demonstrate the proposed Gabor filter optimization approach in the context of vehicle detection. First, a Gabor filter bank with 3 scales and 5 orientations was tested using SVMs for classification. Using the feature extraction method described in Section IV-A, the size of each Gabor feature vector was 405 in this experiment. The average error rate was found to be 10.38%, (see Table I). Then, we tested a Gabor filter bank with 4 scales and 6 orientations which yielded features vectors of size 648. The error rate in this case was 9.09% which is slightly better than before.

Second, we used the EGFO approach to customize a group of filters, up to 24, for the vehicle detection problem. We limited the number of filters to 24 to make the comparison with the traditional filter bank design methods fair. The GA parameters used were as follows: population size: 700, number of generations: 100, crossover rate: 0.66 and mutation rate: 0.03. In all the experiments, the GA converged in less than 100 generations. Each parameter in $\Phi = \{\theta, W, \sigma_x, \sigma_y\}$ was encoded using 4 bits. The total length of the chromosome was 384($4 \times 4 \times 24$), which corresponds to a huge search space (i.e., 2^{384}). The threshold factor K for the clustering was set to 3 in our experiments. The average error rate in this case was 6.36%, and the average number of customized filters was 19.3. The optimized 19 filters generated for data *Set3* are shown in Fig.5. The individual results from the three data sets are shown in Table I. Fig. 7(a) shows the average detection error rates for all methods.

We also ran the filter optimization method without clustering on the same data sets, using the same parameters. The average error rate was 6.19%, slightly better than that yielded by the method with clustering. Obviously, clustering has the advantage of producing a more compact set of filters (i.e., 19 v.s. 24).

To get an idea regarding the effectiveness of the clustering subcomponent, we performed more experiments using different threshold settings for the factor $k = 2$. The average error rate was 8.23%, and the average number of customized filter was 14.7. The 15 filters generated for data *Set3* are shown in Fig.6.

TABLE I

VEHICLE DETECTION ERROR RATES USING DIFFERENT FILTERS. THE NUMBERS IN THE PARENTHESES INDICATE THE NUMBER OF OPTIMIZED FILTERS

	3×5	4×6	EGFO
Data Set1	10.82%	9.09%	6.93%(21)
Data Set2	11.69%	11.26%	7.79%(18)
Data Set3	8.66%	6.93%	4.33%(19)
Average	10.38%	9.09%	6.36%(19.3)

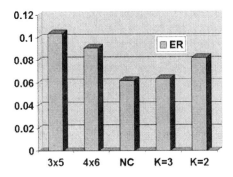

Fig. 7. Vehicle detection error rate. 3×5: the Gabor filter bank with 3 scales and 5 orientations; 4×6: 4 scales and 6 orientations; NC: EGFO method without clustering; K=3: EGFO method with K=3; and K=2: EGFO with K=2.

VII. DISCUSSION

To get a better idea about the filter parameters chosen by the EGFO approach, we computed a histogram for each of the parameters(Fig. 8), showing the average distribution of its values over the three data sets. In each graph, the x-axis corresponds

to a parameter from $\Phi = \{\theta, W, \sigma_x, \sigma_y\}$, and has been divided into 10 bins to compute the histogram. The y-axis corresponds to the average number of Gabor filters whose parameters are within a given interval. For example, Fig. 8.a shows the average distribution of θ, where the width of each bin is 18°, given $\theta \in [0 \ 180^o)$. The bar associated with the first bin indicates that there were 4 filters (average number over the three training data sets) in the optimized Gabor filter set, whose orientation parameter satisfies: $\theta \in [0 \ 18^o)$. The only difference for the rest parameters is the bin size, for instance, the ith bin in Fig. 8(b) corresponds to the interval $[(i - 1) * STEP_W \ i * STEP_W)$, where $STEP_W = (W_{max} - W_{min}/10)$.

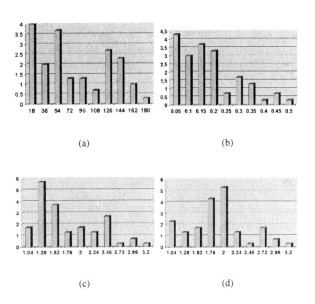

Fig. 8. Distributions of the Gabor filter parameters for vehicle Detection. (a) θ; (b) W ; (c) σ_x ; (d) σ_y

Several interesting comments can be made based on the experimental results presented in Section VI, the filters shown in Fig. 5, and the parameter distributions shown in Fig. 8:
• The Gabor filters customized using the proposed approach yielded better results in vehicle detection. The most important reason for this improvement is probably that the Gabor filters were designed specifically for the pattern classification problems at hand (i.e., the proposed method is more application-specific than existing filter design methods).
• The orientation parameters of the filters optimized by the GA were tuned to appreciate the implicit information available in vehicle data. Specifically, a Gabor filter is essentially a bar, edge, or grating detector, and will respond most strongly if the filter's orientation is consistent with the orientation of specific features in an image (i.e., bar, edge, etc.). We can see that horizontal, 45°, and 135° structures appear more often in a rear view of a vehicle image, which explains why most of the filter orientations

chosen were close to 0°, 45°, and 135° (see Fig. 8(a)).

• The radial frequency parameters (W) of the filters found by the GA approach were also tuned to encode the implicit information present in vehicle images. Generally speaking, we have more filters with lower radial frequencies than with higher radial frequencies (see Fig. 8(b)). This is reasonable given that vehicle images contain large structures (windows, bumper, etc.), requiring filters with lower radial frequencies.

• The parameters σ_x, σ_y were also tuned to respond to the basic structures of a vehicle. Fig. 8(c) and Fig. 8(d) show that the σ_y parameter has bigger values than the σ_x parameter. Bigger σ_y values implies a wider Gaussian mask in the y direction. This is consistent with the observation that horizontal structures in vehicle images spread more widely than structures in vertical direction.

• By setting the threshold factor to 2, we ended up with 14.7 filters on average. The error rate went up to 8.23% from 6.36%, which is still better than using the traditional Gabor filter bank with 3 sales and 5 orientations. When we build a pattern classification system, among other factors, we need to find the best balance point between model compactness and performance accuracy. Under some scenarios, we prefer the best performance, no matter what the cost might be. Under different situations, we might favor speed over accuracy, as long as the accuracy is within a satisfactory range. The EGFO approach provides a good base for compromising between model compactness and performance accuracy.

VIII. CONCLUSION AND FUTURE WORK

A systematic evolutionary filter optimization method was proposed in this paper. Specifically, Gabor filter parameters were optimized using GAs, followed by further filter clustering in the parameter domain to eliminate redundancy. The proposed approach provides a simple, general, and powerful framework for optimizing the parameters of a family of filters such as Gabor filters or steerable filters [23]. We have tested the proposed method on the challenging problem of vehicle detection. The filters customized by our method yielded better performance than using traditional filter banks. For future work, we plan to evaluate this framework using different data sets, and different types of filters. We also plan to test different filter selection schemes by encoding selection in the chromosome explicitly.

Acknowledgements: This research was supported by Ford Motor Company under grant No.2001332R, the University of Nevada, Reno under an Applied Research Initiative (ARI) grant, and in part by NSF under CRCD grant No.0088086.

REFERENCES

[1] J. Daugman, "Complete discrete 2-d gabor transforms by neural network for image analysis and compression," *IEEE Transactions on Acoustics, Speech, and Signal Processing*, vol. 36, no. 7, pp. 1169–1179, 1988.

[2] R. Mehrotra, K. Namuduri, and N. Ranganathan, "Gabor filter-based edge detection," *Pattern Recognition*, vol. 25, pp. 1479–1493, 1992.

[3] T. Weldon, W. Higgins and D. Dunn, "Efficient gabor filter design for texture segmentation," *Pattern Recognition*, vol. 29, no. 12, pp. 2005–2015, 1996.

[4] A. Jain and F. Farrokhnia, "Unsupervised texture segementation using gabor filters," *Pattern Recognition*, vol. 23, pp. 1167–1186, 1991.

[5] T. Hofmann, J. Puzicha, and J. Buhmann, "Unsupervised texture segmentation in a deterministic annealing framework," *IEEE Transactions on Pattern Analysis and Machine Intelligence*, vol. 20, pp. 803–818, 1998.

[6] Y. Hamamoto, S. Uchimura, M. Watanabe, T. Yasuda, Y. Mitani, and S. Tomota, "A gabor filter-based method for recognizing handwritten numerals," *Pattern Recognition*, vol. 31, no.4, pp. 395–400, 1998.

[7] K. Chung, S. Kee, and S. Kim, "Face recognition using independent component analysis og gabor filter responses," *IAPR Workshop on machine vision applications*, pp. 331–334, 2000.

[8] Z. Sun, G. Bebis, and R. Miller, "Improving the performance of on-road vehicle detection by combining gabor and wavelet features," *The IEEE Fifth International Conference on Intelligent Transportation Systems* , September, 2002, Singapore.

[9] B. Manjunath and W. Ma, "Texture features for browsing and retrieval of image data," *IEEE Transactions on Pattern Analysis and Machine Intelligence*, vol. 18, no. 8, pp. 837–842, 1996.

[10] T. Weldon, W. Higgins and D. Dunn, "Gabor filter desing for multiple texture segmentation," *Optical Engineering*, vol. 35, pp. 2852–2863, 1996.

[11] A. Bovik, M. Clark, and W. Geisler, "Multichannel texture analysis using localized spatial filters," *IEEE Transactions on Pattern Analysis and Machine Intelligence*, vol. 12, pp. 55–73, 1990.

[12] B. Okombi-Diba, J. Miyamichi, and K. Shoji, "Edge-based segmentation of textured images uing otimally selected gabor filters," *IAPR Workshop on machine vision applications*, pp. 267–270, 2000.

[13] D. Dunn, and W. Higgins, "Optimal gabor filters for texture segementation," *IEEE Transactions on Image Processing*, vol. 4, pp. 947–964, 1995.

[14] M. Turner, "Texture discrimination by gabor functions," *Biological Cybernetics*, vol. 55, pp. 71–82, 1986.

[15] D. Goldberg, *Genetic Algorithms in Search, Optimization, and Machine Learning*. Addison Wesley, 1989.

[16] E. Trucco, and A. Verri, *Introductory Techniques for 3-D Computer Vision*. Prentice Hall, 1998.

[17] A. Jain, M. Murty and P. Flynn, "Data clustering: A review," *ACM Computing Surveys*, vol. 31, pp. 265–323, 1999.

[18] P. Kuizinga, N. Petkov and S. Grigorescu, "Comparison of texture features based on gabor filters," *Proceedings of the 10th International Conference on Image Analysis and Processing*, pp. 142–147, 1999.

[19] V. Vapnik, *The Nature of Statistical Learning Theory*. Springer Verlag, 1995.

[20] C. Burges, "Tutorial on support vector machines for pattern recognition," *Data Mining and Knowledge Discovery*, vol. 2, no. 2, pp. 955–974, 1998.

[21] C. Papageorgiou and T. Poggio, "A trainable system for object detection," *International Journal of Computer Vision*, vol. 38, no. 1, pp. 15–33, 2000.

[22] G. Bebis, S. Uthiram, and M. Georgiopoulos, "Face detection and verification using genetic search," *International Journal on Artificial Intelligence Tools*, vol. 9, no. 2, pp. 225–246, 2000.

[23] W. T. Freeman and E. H. Adelson, "The design and use of steerable filters," *IEEE Transactions on Pattern Analysis and Machine Intelligence*, vol. 13, pp. 891–906, 1991.

Detecting Interesting Exceptions from Medical Test Data with Visual Summarization

Einoshin Suzuki[1]   Takeshi Watanabe[1]
Division of Electrical and Computer Engineering,
Yokohama National University, Japan
suzuki@ynu.ac.jp, nabekun@slab.dnj.ynu.ac.jp

Hideto Yokoi[2]   Katsuhiko Takabayashi[2]
2. Chiba University Hospital, Japan
yokoih@telemed.ho.chiba-u.ac.jp, takaba@ho.chiba-u.ac.jp

Abstract

In this paper, we propose a method which visualizes irregular multi-dimensional time-series data as a sequence of probabilistic prototypes for detecting exceptions from medical test data. Conventional visualization methods often require iterative analysis and considerable skill thus are not totally supported by a wide range of medical experts. Our PrototypeLines displays summarized information based on a probabilistic mixture model by using hue only thus is considered to exhibit novelty. The effectiveness of the summarization is pursued mainly through use of a novel information criterion. We report our endeavor with chronic hepatitis data, especially discoveries of interesting exceptions by a non-expert and an untrained expert.

1 Introduction

In computer science, it has been said that 20 % of exceptions cause 80 % of labors. History of science has evolved mainly by explaining exceptions which violate theories by a new theory. In Knowledge Discovery in Databases (KDD), several researchers believe that exceptions are important and can bring new discoveries which are interesting [7, 9, 11, 14, 15].

In KDD, exception discovery is important at least from three reasons. First, exceptions are often useful since they differ from people's common activities. For instance, suppose a species of poisonous mushrooms some of which are exceptionally edible. The exceptions are highly beneficial since it enables exclusive possession of the edible mushrooms. Second, as Silberschatz and Tuzhilin commented [11], exceptions are often related to actionability. Con-

sider exceptions which represent uncured patients in spite of effective antibiotics, and other exceptions which represent cured patients against a mortal disease. Investigation on the former and the latter can suggest precaution to the antibiotics and treatment to the mortal disease respectively. Third, "good" exceptions are typically few in number and are thus easy to be inspected in discovery results. Several researchers [9, 11, 14, 15] have shown this in a persuasive manner by comparing discovery of exception rules such as "seat belt and child → danger" with discovery of typical rules such as "seat belt → safe". These reasons also apply to KDD in a medical domain where exceptions discovery is expected to bring important results.

In exception discovery in a medical domain, however, the following three aspects might bring serious difficulties. First, interesting exceptions can be discovered by medical experts only and not by a data miner. One of the author has witnessed discovery of interesting exceptions by a medical expert with domain knowledge though the discovered patterns are not statistically significant [13]. Second, a typical medical expert is reluctant to master a data mining tool especially when the methods behind the tool require detailed specifications and iterative analysis. We attribute this reason to the fact that a typical medical expert is highly occupied with medical treatments and might stick to an analysis tool such as a statistical package. Third, exceptions appear in various levels in a medical domain and it is typically difficult to know the levels in advance. It is common that a medical expert cannot state the kinds of exceptions which the expert would like to discover beforehand. It should be noted that the third aspect necessitates interactive analysis against which the first two aspects are.

Due to intuitive comprehensibility of its results, information visualization is highly effective in application domains where user-interaction is required, and is gaining importance in data mining [2, 5]. Medical test data, which are collected from patients, pose various challenges including high dimensionality, irregular measurements, difference of individuals, and bias in measurements to the data mining community [17]. For instance, chronic hepatitis data, which is situated as a target data in Active Mining project [8], exhibit all these difficulties and have been employed in an international workshop [1]. The objective of this paper is to detect interesting exceptions in various levels with visualization from medical test data.

Methods in information visualization can be classified into pattern visualization and data visualization. The latter is more likely to be related to our objective than the former (e.g. decision-tree visualizer of MineSet [19]). An object in the data visualization approach can be classified into raw data, transformed data, and agglomerated data. Methods in the first category visualize each value and include parallel coordinates [2], LifeLines [2], and InfoZoom [12]. Methods in the second category transform raw values into a different format and include projection pursuit [10], multidimensional scaling [10], and VisDB [2]. Methods in the third category visualizes high level data such as objects or examples and include FilmFinder [2] and dendrograms [10]. Methods in the first category are inadequate for quickly recognizing a huge amount of data, and methods in the third category may fail to display exceptions in lower levels. On the other hand, methods in the second category are likely to overcome these difficulties but effectiveness of transformation and display is crucial. As far as we know, there is no visualization method which satisfactorily resolves the aforementioned three problems inherent in exception discovery in a medical domain.

In order to ameliorate this situation, we propose a novel visualization method which we call PrototypeLines. PrototypeLines transforms medical test results based on statistical prototypes [18] and displays them with colors which are assigned with a novel information criterion. This paper demonstrates several examples in which interesting exceptions were discovered by one of the authors who is a non-expert in medicine and by a medical expert who is inexperienced with PrototypeLines.

2 Visualizing Medical Test Data for Detecting Exceptions

2.1 Definition of the Problem

As we stated in the previous section, detecting exceptions is important in a medical domain. Discovered exceptions would prevent various danger, improve medical systems, and deepen domain knowledge. Here we formalize our problem of visualizing medical test data for exception detection. Medical test data D consist of data

$d_1, d_2, \cdots, d_n$ each of which is measured from n patients $1, 2, \cdots, n$ respectively i.e. $D = \{d_1, d_2, \cdots, d_n\}$. Data d_i consist of $l(i)$ medical test results $t_{i1}, t_{i2}, \cdots, t_{il(i)}$ i.e. $d_i = \{t_{i1}, t_{i2}, \cdots, t_{il(i)}\}$. In this paper, we assume that a medical test result t_{ij} is a set of (a medical test, a value).

Typically, medical test data are organized according to each medical test, and are displayed as a collection of time-series data with graphs. Figure 1 shows time-series data of medical tests GPT, CHE, T-BIL, and PLT of patients 404, 702, 763, and 629 from the chronic hepatitis data. In the figure, the unit of a horizontal axis represents a day, and a 0 in the axis represents the date of the first biopsy[1]. Medical test values are categorized for each medical test, and a horizontal dashed line separates different categories. A typical problem in the chronic hepatitis data involves several hundreds of patients and more than ten attributes. The format in figure 1 permits us to show only a few patients on a 21-inch screen thus prohibits effective analysis.

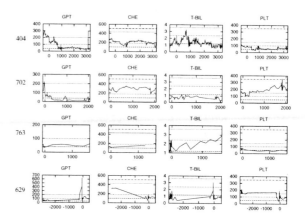

Figure 1. Part of the chronic hepatitis data, where each column and row represents an example and an attribute respectively.

As we stated in the previous section, exceptions appear in various levels in a medical domain, and a medical expert is mandatory in detecting interesting exceptions. We define our problem in a rather general manner due to these aspects. Medical test data D are transformed into a display result D' by a visualization method and D' is shown to a medical expert Ω, who discovers a set of exceptions Λ by visual inspection. An element of Λ represents a discovered exception which typically concerns various levels or characteristics of D including a set of patients, a patient, a time period, a set of medical test results, a set of values, and intervals of medical tests.

The patients in figure 1 belong to the same group of F4[2]

---

[1]We will explain a biopsy in section 4.1.
[2]We will explain F0, F1, $\cdots$, F4 in section 4.1.

and tell us difficulty of the problem intuitively. They differ in several aspects including intervals of medical tests and ranges of values, thus look different in their shapes of time-series data. Careful inspection of graphs in several tens of sheets of paper enabled one of the author Suzuki, who is a non-expert in medicine, to conclude that the patient 702 is exceptionally good as F4 and the patient 629 shows an exceptionally bad period just before the first biopsy. These exceptions seem to exhibit interestingness, but a medical expert would be reluctant to accept the labor and would rather request another format of visualization.

2.2 Problems of Conventional Visualization Methods

As we described in section 1, data visualization methods are more relevant to exception discovery from medical test data than pattern visualization methods. Data which are visualized in the former methods can be classified into raw data, transformed data, and agglomerated data.

Among the raw data visualization methods, LifeLines[3] [2], which displays events on a time axis for each patient, would be most relevant to our objective. We admit that adequate use of LifeLines would allow its user to discover interesting exceptions. It is, however, difficult to display even several patients on a screen. Therefore, it would necessitate a user to investigate a large number of display results in order to discover interesting exceptions.

Among the transformed data visualization methods, VisDB[4] [2], which transforms data into colored pixels according to the query of the user and displays each example as a square, would be most relevant. Actually, our method which will be presented in the next section transforms data into colored rectangles in order to discover interesting exceptions. However, VisDB, by its nature, is more appropriate to interactive analysis where the user successively refines the conditions of visualization. Moreover, VisDB assumes a table-formatted data set as its input thus modification is required for handling time-series data such as medical test data.

Among the agglomerated data visualization methods, FilmFinder[5] [2], which is specialized to movie data, seems promising. We admit that by modifying its display result to fit time-series data, its user would discover interesting exceptions in a level such as a patient level. A serious deficiency of this approach is its lack of ability in displaying exceptions in different levels on a screen.

When visualizing a large amount of data on a screen, a typical visualization method employs either data transformation (e.g. FilmFinder [2]), focus (e.g. table lens [2]), or projection (e.g. projection pursuit [10]). Typically, these methods allow specifications of various parameters by the user. Since the specification is by its nature interactive, it would be laborious even for a trained user. As we described in section 1, we believe that a visualization method should display satisfactory results even if the number of the specifications is small, and none of the conventional methods is totally supported by a wide range of medical experts.

3 PrototypeLines

3.1 Motivations and Example of Visualization

Figure 2. Example of display with Prototype-Lines for patients in chronic hepatitis data. A colored online version is available at [16].

Based on the discussions in previous sections, we propose a novel visualization method which allows detection of interesting exceptions from medical test data with a small

[3]A demo display can be found in http://www.cs.umd.edu/hcil/lifelines/ (current June 9, 2003).

[4]A hand-out with demo displays is available from http://dbvis.fmi.uni-konstanz.de/research /projects/VisDB/visdb.html (current June 9, 2003).

[5]A demo display is available from http://www.csl.sony.co.jp/person /masui/Visualization/FilmFinder/ (current June 9, 2003).

amount of labor and skill. From sections 1 and 2.2, we adopt the approach of visualizing transformed data. This enables us to display a large amount of data on a screen, and opens the possibility for detecting interesting exceptions by inspecting a few screens.

As we described in section 1, effectiveness of transformation and display is highly important in this approach, and we try to realize it as follows. First, an effective data transformation should be based on a method which enables easy detection of interesting exceptions with at most few parameters. A probabilistic mixture model allows us to represent data as a linear sum of prototypes and is frequently used in statistics. Since it summarizes results of a large number of medical tests with a small number of prototypes (i.e. base models), we believe that it facilitates discrimination of typical data and exceptional data[6]. Therefore, we adopt a method which obtains prototypes from data based on the EM method [4] and transforms each medical test result into a linear sum of the prototypes. Next, a comprehensive display result should represent medical test data naturally and be based on a small number of information media. Medical test data exhibit a hierarchy which consists of patients and medical test results. Color can be regarded as the most effective information media that is acquired by human beings. We adopt a method in which a patient is represented as a line on a time axis, and a medical test result is represented as a colored rectangle on the line.

In designing our display result, our primary objective was to arrange a large number of patients in order to clarify their temporal tendency, while displaying detailed information and avoiding occlusion were considered less important. Since patients exhibit a wide range of time periods, the width of a line for each patient was fixed and we varied their time scales. We also displayed results of biopsies and interferon (IFN)[7]. We show, in figure 2, an example of display result of our PrototypeLines for patients in the chronic hepatitis data. Details of computation will be given in the subsequent sections. In the example, we have summarized results for 17 medical tests with 7 prototypes. The 17 medical tests represent GOT, GPT, · · ·, MCV and are shown at the top of the figure. The subsequent rectangles in purple, blue, · · ·, red represent the 7 prototypes, which intuitively become worse from cold colors to warm colors[8]. The probability of each prototype is represented in the subsequent ratio graph. For instance, the best prototype which is in purple occupies approximately 30 % of medical test results. The rest of the figure represents data of each patient with

_____

[6]For instance, the sudden change around the date 0 of the patient 629 in figure 1 shows that medical test values are likely to be related each other. Actually, such relations exist probabilistically, and a dimension reduction method which agglomerates medical test results can be safely considered as effective.

[7]Intuitively, IFN is a drug for killing viruses.

[8]A number in parentheses after a prototype ID is currently not used.

results of biopsy (bio), the time period of IFN (ifn) treatment, and its result (Re or ?) if any. We visualized at most 500 days before biopsy and 500 days after it in the figure, but PrototypeLines makes no assumption on a length of display. A 2-digit figure on a time axis represents a beginning of a year.

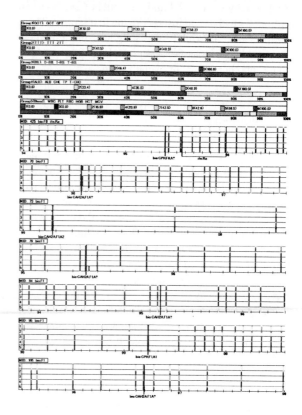

Figure 3. Example of display with multi-PrototypeLines for patients in chronic hepatitis data. A colored online version is available at [16].

While summarizing 17 medical tests allows us to display a large number of patients on a screen, there exist demands for detailed investigation of data by grouping related medical tests. In order to fulfill this requirement, we have developed multi-PrototypeLines which employs a set of prototypes for each group of medical tests. Figure 3 shows an example of its display result, which can be interpreted similarly. The upper half of the figure shows that the 17 medical tests are grouped into 2, 2, 3, 4, 6 and are summarized into 5, 4, 3, 5, 8 prototypes respectively. The figures 1, 2, 3, 4, 5 shown at the leftmost of each patient correspond to the groups of medical tests.

3.2 Estimation of Prototypes

In this section, we explain our method for obtaining the prototypes from medical test data and transforming each medical test result into a linear sum of the prototypes. We adopt a maximum likelihood method for a relatively simple discrete model for obtaining the prototypes.

We represent a medical test result of a patient in a day as an instance t_i[9]. The set which contains all instances will be represented by T. A prototype c_j is an element of a prototype set C i.e. $c_j \in C = \{c_1, c_2, \cdots, c_{|C|}\}$, and estimated parameters are represented by θ. The probability of obtaining the instance t_i is

$$P(t_i|\theta) = \sum_{j=1}^{|C|} P(c_j|\theta) P(t_i|c_j; \theta). \quad (1)$$

Let the value of a medical test k for a patient t_i be $v_{t,k}$, then assuming that each medical test value is mutually independent, we obtain

$$P(t_i|c_j; \theta) = \prod_k P(v_{t,k}|c_j; \theta). \quad (2)$$

Each prototype c_j consists of two kinds of parameters, one of which corresponds to the probability $\theta_{w_{kl}|c_j} = P(w_{kl}|c_j; \theta)$ of obtaining the category w_{kl} for a medical test k. Let V and w_k be the set of medical tests and the set of categories for k respectively, then $k = \{1, 2, \cdots, |V|\}$, $l = \{1, 2, \cdots, |w_k|\}$. The other kind of parameters corresponds to a priori probability $\theta_{c_j} = P(c_j|\theta)$ for each prototype c_j.

Our algorithm gives an estimate $\hat{\theta}$ of θ from T. Let ϵ represent a sufficiently small positive value, then

$$\hat{\theta}_{w_{kl}|c_j} = \frac{\sum_{i=1}^{|T|} N(w_{kl}, t_i) P(c_j|t_i)}{\sum_{l=1}^{|w_k|} \sum_{k=1}^{|V|} \sum_{i=1}^{|T|} N(w_{kl}, t_i) P(c_j|t_i)} \quad (3)$$

where $N(w_{kl}, t_i) = \epsilon$ if $v_{t,k} \neq w_{kl}$ and $N(w_{kl}, t_i) = 1$ otherwise. It should be noted that this is similar to Laplace correction [3]. A prior probability is estimated by

$$\hat{\theta}_{c_j} = \frac{\sum_{i=1}^{|T|} P(c_j|t_i)}{|T|}. \quad (4)$$

The estimated parameters $\hat{\theta}$ enable us to calculate the probability $P(c_j|t_i; \hat{\theta})$ that a medical test result t_i belongs to a prototype c_j. By Bayes rule, we obtain

$$
\begin{aligned}
P(c_j|t_i; \hat{\theta}) &= \frac{P(c_j|\hat{\theta}) P(t_i|c_j; \hat{\theta})}{P(t_i|\hat{\theta})} \\
&= \frac{P(c_j|\hat{\theta}) \prod_{k=1}^{|V|} P(v_{t,k}|c_j; \theta)}{\sum_{r=1}^{|C|} P(c_r|\hat{\theta}) \prod_{k=1}^{|V|} P(v_{t,k}|c_j; \theta)}. \quad (5)
\end{aligned}
$$

[9]In the data [1], a set of transactions with an equivalent patient ID and date. In section 2.1, we described this as t_{ij} since we took a patient ID and a medical test result as suffices, but we simplify it here.

Here the probability $P(T|\theta)$ of obtaining T is

$$P(T|\theta) = \prod_i \sum_{j=1}^{|C|} P(c_j|\theta) P(t_i|c_j; \theta). \quad (6)$$

Bayes rule states $P(\theta|T) = P(T|\theta) P(\theta) / P(T)$, and $P(\theta)$ is assumed to be a constant in the maximum likelihood method. Therefore, the log-likelihood $\log P(\theta|T)$ is given as follows.

$$\log P(\theta|T) = (\text{const}) + \sum_i \log \sum_{j=1}^{|C|} P(c_j|\theta) P(t_i|c_j; \theta) \quad (7)$$

The EM method [4] tries to give a maximum likelihood estimate of θ by hill climbing. A step of the hill climbing consists of an E-step and an M-step, and the evaluation function is the log-likelihood given in (7). Let the initial value of θ and its value in the s-th step be $\theta^{(0)}$ and $\theta^{(s)}$ respectively, then an E-step obtains $\hat{\theta}_{w_{kl}|c_j}^{(s+1)}$ by (3) while an M-step obtains $\hat{\theta}_{c_j}^{(s+1)}$ by (4)[10]. We have also developed an option which reduces influence of patients with a large number of medical test results.

The obtained set of prototypes $C = \{c_1, c_2, \cdots, c_{|C|}\}$ enables us to transform a medical test result t_i into a one-dimensional vector $(P(t_i|c_1; \hat{\theta}), P(t_i|c_2; \hat{\theta}), \cdots, P(t_i|c_{|C|}; \hat{\theta}))$. Since the number $|C|$ of prototypes is much smaller than the number $|V|$ of medical tests, this transformation would facilitate detection of interesting exceptions due to the reasons in section 3.1.

It should be noted that a similar data transformation method succeeded in detecting interesting exceptions in our previous work [18]. Most of the obtained prototypes were admitted as valid and comprehensive by medical experts. Moreover the medical experts commented that the method is useful in recognizing the state of a patient as well as detecting exceptional patients[11]. For instance, we have discovered an exceptional patient who suffered heavily, admitted to a hospital in emergency, then passed away soon. We, however, had not developed a visualization tool at that time, and the detection was laborious.

3.3 Hue Allocation to Prototypes

A typical visualization method employs various information media including colors, shapes, sizes [2, 5]. Such a method allows various assignments of medical tests to information media and is subject to the problems in section 2.2. Moreover, a display result of such a method typically becomes comprehensive through repeated trials and

[10]Recall that these give the maximum likelihood estimates in step $s + 1$.
[11]Due to the objective of this paper, the goodness of a mixture model should be evaluated from the last point.

acquired skill, and is also subject to overlooking of important information.

The HSV color space is a representation for colors based on perception of humans, and employs hue, saturation, and value as attributes. Hue describes color perception denoted by blue, green, yellow, red, purple, etc. [20], or its position in the color spectrum. Based on the previous discussions, each prototype is represented by using hue only in PrototypeLines. Prototypes are sorted according to the badness of the medical test results and each prototype is assigned a hue from purple to red. Since a warm color is easier to be perceived than a cold color, prototypes are assigned either of red (0 degree), orange (30 degree), yellow (60 degree), yellowish green (90 degree), green (120 degree), greenish blue (150 degree), blue (210 degree), purple (240 degree) from bad to good. We selected the angles based on easiness in discriminating colors. If the number of prototypes is less than eight, we omit colors appropriately.

In order to sort prototypes in terms of their degrees of goodness, we need an evaluation criterion. In the chronic hepatitis data, as we have described, medical test values can be classified into categories, among which N (normal) is the best one. A category is better than another if it is closer to N, e.g. L (low) is better than VL (very low). In chronic hepatitis data, a medical test result for GOT is more likely to become H or VH than that for T-BIL, and this signifies that each category of a medical test differs in importance.

In order to provide a generic solution, we propose an information criterion which measures the degree of deviation of a prototype from the corresponding average. In this criterion, the importance of a category w_{kl} is represented by its amount of information $-\log_2 P(w_{kl})$. In our experiments, the probability that a category occurs decreases as the category, if it is not N, moves to one of the two extremes from N. Our information criterion $I(c_j)$ represents the degree of badness of a prototype c_j.

$$I(c_j) = \sum_{k=1}^{|V|} \sum_{l=1, w_{kl} \neq N}^{|w_k|} -P(w_{kl}|c_j) \log_2 P(w_{kl}) \quad (8)$$

We skip a category N in $I(c_j)$ since N is normal and is thus neglected, and the probability that N occurs can be smaller than those of H or L.

4 Visualization of Chronic Hepatitis Data

4.1 Conditions of Visualization

Chronic hepatitis represents a disease in which liver cells become inflamed and harmed by virus infection. If the inflammation lasts a long period, the disease comes to an end which is called a liver cirrhosis. During the process to a liver cirrhosis, the degree of fibrosis represents an index of the progress, and the degree of fibrosis consists of five stages ranging from F0 (no fiber) to F4 (liver cirrhosis). The degree of fibrosis can be inspected by biopsy which picks liver tissue by inserting an instrument directly into a liver. A biopsy, however, cannot be frequently performed since it requires an admission to a hospital and involves danger such as hemorrhage. Therefore, the results of medical tests are closely investigated around the date of a biopsy.

Due to the nature of the disease, the degree of fibrosis is considered as stable before 500 days and after 500 days of a biopsy. We have derived a set of prototypes based on the method in section 3.2 from the data of patients with degrees of biopsy. In the data, a category is either of extremely high (UH), very high (VH), high (H), normal (N), low (L), very low (VL) or extremely low (UL). The number of random restarts in the EM method was settled to 100[12]. As we described in section 3.1, we obtained two sets of prototypes by first using all of the attributes then grouping them into 5. The number of prototypes were settled based on the diversity of prototypes and the probability that each prototype occurs. Since this number was the only tunable parameter, the process was fairly easy.

4.2 Display Results

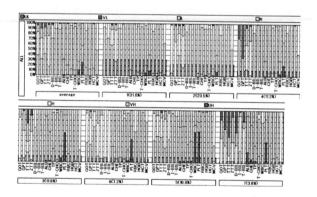

Figure 4. Prototypes discovered from data with 17 medical tests before 500 days and after 500 days from biopsy. A colored online version is available at [16].

Figure 4 shows the average value of each category (average) and the obtained prototypes (1, 2, 4, · · ·, 7) from the data without grouping medical tests. The seven prototypes are aligned from good ones to bad ones from left to right, and the prototype 4 in the up-right is better than the prototype 3 in the bottom-left. In the figure, each of the average and prototypes consists of 17 medical tests, and results for

---

[12]We show the best result among the 100 trials and leave investigation on stability of the solutions for future work.

each medical test is represented by a vertical ratio graph. A ratio in parentheses subsequent to the number of prototype represents the probability of the prototype. From the figure, we see that categories N and H of GOT both occur approximately 40 % in the whole data while approximately 90 % and 10 % respectively in prototype 1. Note that we have colored N (normal) in green while higher and lower categories are assigned warm and cold colors respectively.

From the average, we see that a value of GOT, GPT, TTT, ZTT, PLT, and MCV is likely to become abnormal, thus is regarded as less important in our information criterion than a value of other medical tests. Careful inspection shows that our information criterion in (8) seems to sort prototypes in appropriate order at least from the viewpoint of information theory. We have also derived prototypes by grouping the medical tests into five [16].

From several display results, we have found that detecting exceptions including those in section 2.1 is fairly easy. Further inspection for peculiar patients confirmed that PrototypeLines visualizes medical test data by an overall evaluation of categories.

4.3 Discovery with PrototypeLines

In this section, we show three examples of discovery with PrototypeLines. The first two were achieved by one of the authors Watanabe who is a non-expert in medicine and the discovery was confirmed by another author Yokoi who is a medical expert. The last one was achieved by a medical expert who listened to our explanation of PrototypeLines for a few minutes.

The first example concerns an exceptional patient discovered by effect of INF, and this discovery might have allowed us detection of possibility of a disease absent in the data. From figure 5, we see that the IFN treatment for patient 104 resulted in good (Re), and improved results of medical tests GOT and GPT in group 1. However, results of medical tests TTT and ZTT in group 2 were aggravated by the treatment, and this patient was recognized as an exception by Watanabe. This inference was justified since Yokoi concluded that the patient is likely to have another disease by inspecting raw data[13].

Figure 5. Multi-PrototypeLines of patient 104. A colored online version is available at [16].

---

[13]We believe that a discovered exception should be confirmed by an expert who inspects its original data.

The second example concerns an exceptional patient discovered from the biopsy data, and have enabled us to point out a disease absent in the data. Although patient 105 belongs ot F1, the display result of PrototypeLines without the attribute grouping shows that its status is extremely bad. Watanabe investigated its display result of multi-PrototypeLines in figure 6, and found that the results of group 3 related to Bilirubin (BIL) are the reason. Yokoi concluded that this patient is highly likely to suffer from constitutional jaundice although only chronic hepatitis is described in the data.

Figure 6. Multi-PrototypeLines of patient 105. A colored online version is available at [16].

The last example concerns an exceptional condition of a patient and shows that it is easy for a typical medical expert to understand the display results of our PrototypeLines. When we explained our method to medical experts for a few minutes, one of them pointed out that patient 285 vomited blood and became anemic at the end of the period in figure 7. He noticed this since the results of the group 5 concerning blood mass index were aggravated at the period. Before explaining our PrototypeLines, we have discussed more than one hour about another data mining method, thus we do not attribute this discovery to high concentration.

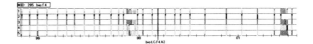

Figure 7. Multi-PrototypeLines of patient 285. A colored online version is available at [16].

Other examples and inspection revealed that PrototypeLines is also useful in detecting overlooked aspects by prejudice and carelessness as well as similar patients who are apparently different. The medical experts prefer a data mining method which is directly related to treatment, but consider that our method is useful in education and research. According to them, current medical education is weak in teaching chronological inference, and PrototypeLines seems to be an effective tool against this problem.

5 Conclusions

The proverb "seeing is believing" seems to represent some truth, but the amount of information which can be perceived by a human is limited. In information visualization, we believe that an approach which adequately abstracts information is more promising than an approach which visualizes all information through various information media. Conventional methods have relied on various information media or techniques such as zooming in order to display a large amount of data. Our PrototypeLines restricts its objective to discovery of interesting exceptions[14], and copes with this problem by summarizing data with prototypes. Its design philosophy is to display essential information by using hue only in order to reduce cognitive load of the user.

In data mining, the degree of abstraction of a pattern can be considered as representing the degree of omitting information of an instance. Intuitively, the higher the degree of a pattern is the more instances are described by the pattern. For instance, the degree of abstraction exhibited by a rule increases as the number of attributes in its premise decreases. One of the authors, through his work in instance discovery [13], noticed that a domain expert is likely to prefer a pattern which exhibits a lower degree of abstraction than a rule. Moreover, in our analysis of the chronic hepatitis data, we have observed that medical experts tend to prefer comprehensive representation such as a graph to a rule. PrototypeLines, which shows lower and higher degrees of abstraction than a rule and a graph respectively, can visualize information related to a large number of patients in a comprehensible format. Future work includes visualization which employs domain knowledge[15], quantitative evaluation of visualization methods, and application of PrototypeLines to other domains.

Acknowledgments

This work was partially supported by the grant-in-aid for scientific research on priority area "Active Mining" from the Japanese Ministry of Education, Culture, Sports, Science and Technology.

References

[1] P. Berka. ECML/PKDD 2002 discovery challenge, download data about hepatitis. http://lisp.vse.cz/challenge/ecmlpkdd2002/, 2002. (current September 28th, 2002).

[2] S. K. Card, J. D. Makinlay, and B. Shneiderman, editors. *Readings in Information Visualization*, San Francisco, 1999. Morgan Kaufmann.

[3] P. Clark and T. Niblett. The CN2 induction algorithm. *Machine Learning*, 3(4):261–283, 1989.

[4] A. P. Dempster, N. M. Laird, and D. B. Rubin. Maximum likelihood from incomplete data via the EM algorithm. *Journal of the Royal Statistical Society B*, 39(1):1–38, 1977.

[5] U. Fayyad, G. G. Grinstein, and A. Wierse, editors. *Information Visualization in Data Mining and Knowledge Discovery*, San Francisco, 2002. Morgan Kaufmann.

[6] I. J. Haimowitz and I. S. Kohane. Automated trend detection with alternate temporal hypotheses. In *Proc. Thirteenth International Joint Conference on Artificial Intelligence (IJCAI)*, pages 146–151. 1993.

[7] E. M. Knorr, R. T. Ng, and V. Tucakov. Distance-based outliers: Algorithms and applications. *VLDB Journal*, 8(3-4):237–253, 2000.

[8] H. Motoda, editor. *Active Mining*, Amsterdam, 2002. IOS Press.

[9] B. Padmanabhan and A. Tuzhilin. A belief-driven method for discovering unexpected patterns. In *Proc. Fourth Int'l Conf. Knowledge Discovery and Data Mining (KDD)*, pages 94–100. 1998.

[10] B. D. Ripley. *Pattern Recognition and Neural Networks*. Cambridge Univ. Press, Cambridge, U.K., 1996.

[11] A. Silberschatz and A. Tuzhilin. What makes patterns interesting in knowledge discovery systems. *IEEE Trans. Knowledge and Data Eng.*, 8(6):970–974, 1996.

[12] M. Spenke. Visualization and interactive analysis of blood parameters with infozoom. *Artificial Intelligence in Medicine*, 22(2):159–172, 2001.

[13] S. Sugaya, E. Suzuki, and S. Tsumoto. Instance selection based on support vector machine for knowledge discovery in medical database. In *Instance Selection and Construction for Data Mining*, pages 395–412. Kluwer, Norwell, Mass., 2001.

[14] E. Suzuki. Autonomous discovery of reliable exception rules. In *Proc. Third Int'l Conf. on Knowledge Discovery and Data Mining (KDD)*, pages 259–262. 1997.

[15] E. Suzuki. Undirected discovery of interesting exception rules. *International Journal of Pattern Recognition and Artificial Intelligence*, 16(8):1065–1086, 2002.

[16] E. Suzuki. Color figures in detecting exceptions from medical test data with visual summarization. http://www.slab.dnj.ynu.ac.jp/paper/20030910/figs.pdf, 2003. (current September 10th, 2003).

[17] S. Tsumoto. Rule discovery in large time-series medical databases. In *Principles of Data Mining and Knowledge Discovery (PKDD)* LNAI 1704, pages 561–567. 1999.

[18] T. Watanabe, E. Suzuki, H. Yokoi, and K. Takabayashi. Prototyping medical test results in chronic hepatitis data with the EM algorithm on multi-dice models. In *Proc. International Workshop on Active Mining (AM)*, pages 45–51. 2002.

[19] C. Westphal and T. Blaxton. *Data Mining Solutions*. John Wiley and Sons, New York, 2000.

[20] G. Wyszecki and W. S. Stiles. *Color Science*. John Wiley and Sons, New York, 1998.

---

[14]We believe that PrototypeLines is also useful in grasping the patient status as a whole in general.

[15]PrototypeLines would also serve as establishing domain knowledge such as those used in [6]

Learning Bayesian Networks from Incomplete Data Based on EMI Method

Fengzhan Tian
Department of Computer
Science & Technology
Tsinghua University
Beijing 100084 P.R.China
tfz99@mails.tsinghua.edu.cn

Hongwei Zhang
Department of Computer
Science & Technology
Tsinghua University
Beijing 100084 P.R.China
zhw99@mails.tsinghua.edu.cn

Yuchang Lu
Department of Computer
Science & Technology
Tsinghua University
Beijing 100084 P.R.China
lyc@tsinghua.edu.cn

Abstract

Currently, there are few efficient methods in practice for learning Bayesian networks from incomplete data, which affects their use in real world data mining applications. This paper presents a general-duty method that estimates the (Conditional) Mutual Information directly from incomplete datasets, EMI. EMI starts by computing the interval estimates of a joint probability of a variable set, which are obtained from the possible completions of the incomplete dataset. And then computes a point estimate via a convex combination of the extreme points, with weights depending on the assumed pattern of missing data. Finally, based on these point estimates, EMI gets the estimated (conditional) Mutual Information. This paper also applies EMI to the dependency analysis based learning algorithm by J. Cheng so as to efficiently learn BNs with incomplete data. The experimental results on Asia and Alarm networks show that EMI based algorithm is much more efficient than two search& scoring based algorithms, SEM and EM-EA algorithms. In terms of accuracy, EMI based algorithm is more accurate than SEM algorithm, and comparable with EM-EA algorithm.

1. Introduction

Bayesian network (BN) is a powerful knowledge representation and reasoning tool under uncertain conditions, which is a directed acyclic graph (DAG) with a conditional probability distribution for each node. The DAG structures of such networks contain nodes representing domain variables, and arcs between nodes representing probabilistic dependencies. In the past decade, the hardship to elicit BNs from expert knowledge makes researchers turn to learning BNs from data. Many current methods are successful in learning both structures and parameters of BNs from complete data[1, 3, 6, 8, 9]. Unfortunately, there are few effec-

tive and efficient methods for learning the network structures from incomplete data.

One earlier research on structure learning from incomplete data was made by Chickering[4], which deals with missing data by Gibbs sampling method. While in the application of Gibbs sampling, convergence detection is an open issue. Furthermore, the method is slow to converge and computationally expensive.

Arguably the most significant advance in the area of structure learning from incomplete data has been the SEM algorithm [7]. Roughly speaking, this method turns the structure learning problem with incomplete data into the easy solving structure learning problem with complete data using EM algorithm, and then searches the best network structure using greedy search algorithm. Friedman's innovation was to save computation by using EM parameter estimates for the current structure to evaluate candidates for the next structure, and to run EM again only for the structure actually chosen. However, when the search space is very large and multimodal landscape, the greedy search algorithm will stop at the local optimal model. In order to solve this problem, in practice, one can restart the algorithm with new randomly generated structures. But this will increase the calculation load.

Another research on structure learning from incomplete data was made by Myers[10]. [10] complete the incomplete data using generic operations, and evolve the network structures and missing data at the same time. Although it can avoid getting into the local maximum, one of its disadvantages is that the completion of incomplete data achieved by the generic operators is strongly stochastic, and could not reflect the characteristics of the probability distribution that the missing data actually follow. So when the number of missing data is big, the convergence of the algorithm could be very slow and the efficiency of the algorithm is very low.

In 2001, we put forward EM-EA algorithm for learning Bayesian network structures from incomplete data[15]. Using the research of Friedman and Myers for reference, EM-

EA transforms the incomplete data to complete data using EM algorithm and then evolves network structures using an evolutionary algorithm (EA) with the complete data. To much degree, EM-EA algorithm alleviated the problems of getting into local maximum of SEM algorithm and of low efficiency and convergence of Myers' algorithm. Additionally, EM-EA algorithm could not only learn BNs with hidden variables, but add hidden variables to network structure on as-needed basis.

All the above learning approaches could be called search & scoring based algorithms. There exists another kind of BN learning methods, dependency analysis based algorithms, which use dependencies between variables to infer the structure. Generally speaking, they are more efficient than search & scoring based methods owing to no need of searching the space of BNs, especially for the spare networks. While till now, the report has not been seen using the dependency analysis based learning algorithms to deal with incomplete data. The method by J. Cheng [2, 3] is the representatives of this kind of algorithms and enjoys many advantages compared with other dependency analysis based algorithms. The advantages of J. Cheng's algorithm motivate us to extend it to the conditions present of incomplete data. For this purpose, we must compute the approximate Mutual Information (MI) with incomplete dataset, and use them to complete Conditional Independency (CI) tests.

In this paper, we present a method of estimating (conditional) Mutual Information directly from incomplete datasets, EMI. Enlightened by the underlying principle of BC method [13], EMI starts by computing the interval estimates of a joint probability of a variable set with possible completions of the incomplete dataset. And then, EMI computes a point estimate via a convex combination of the extreme points. Finally, based on these point estimates, EMI gets the approximate (conditional) Mutual Information. Additionally, we apply EMI to the algorithm by J. Cheng to learn BNs with incomplete data and conduct experimental analysis on Asia and Alarm networks with respect to the EMI based algorithm and two search & scoring based algorithms, SEM and EM-EA algorithms.

The rest of this paper is organized as follows. In Section 2, we will start by establishing some notations and then briefly review J. Cheng's algorithm. In Section 3, we will describe EMI approach in detail and extend J. Cheng's algorithm to deal with incomplete datasets. The experimental analysis and conclusions will be given in Section 4 and Section 5 respectively.

2. Background

In this section, we will first describe the notations used throughout the paper, and then briefly review J. Cheng's algorithm. We assume readers are familiar with the basics about BNs.

We denote a variable by an upper-case letter (e.g. X, Y, X_i) and the state or value of a corresponding variable by the same letter in lower-case (e.g. x, y, x_i). We denote a set of variables by a bold-face upper-case letter (e.g. $\mathbf{X}, \mathbf{Y}, \mathbf{X_i}$). We use a corresponding bold-face lower-case letter (e.g. $\mathbf{x}, \mathbf{y}, \mathbf{x_i}$) to denote an assignment of state or value to each variable in a given set. We use $P(\mathbf{X} = \mathbf{x}|\xi)$ (or $P(\mathbf{x}|\xi)$ as a shorthand) to denote the probability that $\mathbf{X} = \mathbf{x}$ with state of prior information ξ. We also use $P(\mathbf{x}|\xi)$ to denote the probability distribution for $\mathbf{X}$. The distinction will be clear from the context.

J. Cheng's Algorithm[2, 3] does CI tests by mutual information calculations, and based on that, constructs a BN. His Algorithm has three phases: **drafting**, **thickening** and **thinning**. In the first phase, the algorithm computes mutual information of each pair of nodes as a measure of closeness, and creates a draft based on this information. The draft is a singly connected graph (a graph without loops). In a special case when the BN is a tree or polytree, this phase can construct the network correctly and the second and third phase will not change anything. So, Chow and Liu's algorithm[5] and Rebane and Pearl's algorithm[12] can be viewed as special cases of J. Cheng's algorithm.

In the second phase, the algorithm examines all pairs of nodes that have mutual information greater than ε and are not directly connected. Then the algorithm adds edges when the pairs of nodes can not be *d-separated*. The result of **Phase II** has the structure of an *Independency Map (I-map)* of the underlying dependency model given the underlying model is *normal DAG-Faithful*.

In the third phase, each edge of the *I-map* is examined using CI tests and will be removed if the two nodes of the edge can be *d-separated*. The result of **Phase III** has the structure of a *perfect map* when the underlying model is *normal DAG-Faithful*. At the end of the third phase, J. Cheng's algorithm also carries out a procedure to orient the edges of the graph if the node ordering is not known.

The concepts of *d-separated*, *I-map* and *perfect map* mentioned above are defined formally in [11]. The meaning of *normal DAG-Faithful* is depicted in detail in [2]. Also, J. Cheng provided proofs for the correctness of his algorithm in [2]. We do not say more than is needed here for space. Just as what we have said, J. Cheng's Algorithm is based on (conditional) mutual information calculations, which are used for CI tests. In BNs, mutual information can be used to measure the amount of information flow between two nodes when no node is instantiated, and conditional mutual information can be used to do so when some other nodes are instantiated. In J. Cheng's algorithm, the mutual information between two nodes is calculated as follows:

$$I(X, Y) = \sum_{x,y} P(x, y) \lg \frac{P(x, y)}{P(x)P(y)} \qquad (1)$$

	X1	X2
Case1	true	true
Case2	?	true
Case3	false	?
Case4	?	?

N(X1=true)=1	N*(X1=true)=2
N(X1=false)=1	N*(X1=false)=2
N(X2=true)=2	N*(X2=true)=2
N(X2=false)=0	N*(X2=false)=2
N(X1=true, X2=true)=1	N*(X1=true, X2=true)=2
N(X1=true, X2=false)=0	N*(X1=true, X2=false)=1
N(X1=false, X2=true)=0	N*(X1=false, X2=true)=3
N(X1=false, X2=false)=0	N*(X1=false, X2=false)=2

Figure 1. Compute the frequencies and artificial frequencies from an oversimplified incomplete dataset.

And given a nodes set $\mathbf{C}$, the conditional mutual information is calculated as follows:

$$I(X, Y|\mathbf{C}) = \sum_{x,y,\mathbf{c}} P(x, y, \mathbf{c}) \lg \frac{P(x, y|\mathbf{c})}{P(x|\mathbf{c})P(y|\mathbf{c})} \quad (2)$$

When $I(X, Y)$ is smaller than a certain threshold ε, it is said that X, Y are marginally independent. When $I(X, Y|\mathbf{C})$ is smaller than ε, it is said that $I(X, Y)$ are conditionally independent given $\mathbf{C}$.

Compared with other CI test based learning algorithms, J. Cheng's algorithm enjoys many advantages. First of all, it is more efficient. J. Cheng's algorithm uses mutual information calculation as the quantitative CI test and avoids the exponential complexity on CI tests. Secondly, it is reliable. Under the assumption *normal DAG-faithfulness* to the underlying probabilistic model, which is reasonable to most real world cases, it can construct the correct network of the underlying model. Therefore, we will extend J. Cheng's algorithm to the conditions present of incomplete data.

3. Learn Bayesian Networks from Incomplete Data Based on EMI Method

In order to extend J. Cheng's algorithm to the conditions present of incomplete data, we must estimate the (conditional) mutual information used to do CI tests from incomplete data. For this purpose, we present a method called EMI, which can efficiently estimate the mutual information directly from data with missing values. EMI is mainly composed of three steps: **Interval Estimation, Point estimation** and **(Conditional) Mutual Information Estimation**. They will be depicted in detail in the following subsections. At the end of this section, we will apply EMI method to J. Cheng's algorithm so as to efficiently learn BNs from incomplete data.

3.1. Interval Estimation

Interval estimation computes, for each parameter, a probability interval whose extreme points are the minimal and the maximal Bayes estimate that would have been inferred from all possible completions of the incomplete dataset.

Let $\mathbf{X}$ be a variable set, having r possible states $x_1, x_2, \ldots, x_r$, and the parameter vector $\theta = \theta_1, \theta_2, \ldots, \theta_r$, which satisfies the assumption of having a prior Dirichlet distribution, be associated to the probability $P(\mathbf{X} = x_i), i = 1, 2, \ldots, r$, so that $\sum_i \theta_i = 1$. Hence the prior distribution of θ:

$$P(\theta|\xi) = Dir(\theta|a_1, a_2, \ldots, a_r) = \frac{\Gamma(a)}{\prod_{k=1}^{r} \Gamma(a_k)} \prod_{k=1}^{r} \theta_k^{a_k - 1}$$

where $a_k(k = 1, 2, \ldots, r)$ are super parameters and $a = \sum_{k=1}^{r} a_k$.

Let $N(\mathbf{x}_i)$ be the frequency of complete cases with $\mathbf{X} = \mathbf{x}_i$ in the dataset and $N^*(\mathbf{x}_i)$ be the **artificial frequency** of incomplete cases with $\mathbf{X} = \mathbf{x}_i$, which can be obtained by completing incomplete cases of the variables set $\mathbf{X}$. An illustration of how to compute the frequencies of complete cases and artificial frequencies of incomplete cases is given in Figure 1. In Figure 1, as for variable X_1, there are two missing values in the four cases. Both of them can be completed as *true* or *false*. So the possible maximal numbers of the artificially completed cases corresponding to the two values are all 2. Therefore the **artificial frequencies** of variable X_1 are also all 2, i.e. $N^*(X_1 = true) = 2$ and $N^*(X_1 = false) = 2$. So are the **artificial frequencies** of variable X_2. As for variable set $\mathbf{X} = \{X_1, X_2\}$, there are 3 incomplete cases all together. The possible maximal numbers of the artificially completed cases corresponding to the four values, (*true,true*),(*true,false*),(*false,true*) and (*false,false*) are 2, 1, 3 and 2 respectively. Hence, we can get $N^*(X_1 = true, X_2 = true) = 2$, $N^*(X_1 = true, X_2 =$

$false) = 1, N^*(X_1 = false, X_2 = true) = 3$ and $N^*(X_1 = false, X_2 = false) = 2$, as shown in Figure 1. Following the same way, we can calculate the frequencies $N(\mathbf{x}_i)$ of complete cases corresponding to various values $\mathbf{x}_i$.

Assume that we have completed the dataset by filling all possible incomplete cases of $\mathbf{X}$ with value $\mathbf{x}_i$, and denote the completed dataset as D_X^i. Then given D_X^i, the prior distribution of θ is updated into the posterior distribution using Bayes' theorem:

$$P_i(\theta|D_X^i, \xi) = Dir(\theta|a_1', a_2', \ldots, a_r'), i = 1, 2, \ldots, r \quad (3)$$

where $a_i' = a_i + N(\mathbf{x}_i) + N^*(\mathbf{x}_i)$ and $a_k' = a_k + N(\mathbf{x}_k)$ for all $k \neq i$. From Equation (3), we obtain the maximal Bayes estimate of $P(\mathbf{X} = \mathbf{x}_i)$:

$$P^*(\mathbf{X} = \mathbf{x}_i) = \mathbf{E}(\theta_i) = \frac{a_i + N(\mathbf{x}_i) + N^*(\mathbf{x}_i)}{a + N^*(\mathbf{x}_i) + \sum_{k=1}^r N(\mathbf{x}_k)} \quad (4)$$

In fact, Equation (3) also identifies a unique probability for other states of $\mathbf{X}$:

$$P_{i*}(\mathbf{X} = \mathbf{x}_l) = \mathbf{E}(\theta_l) = \frac{a_l + N(\mathbf{x}_l)}{a + N^*(\mathbf{x}_i) + \sum_{k=1}^r N(\mathbf{x}_k)} \quad (5)$$

where $l = 1, 2, \ldots, r$ and $l \neq i$. Now we can define the minimal Bayes estimate of $P(\mathbf{X} = \mathbf{x}_i)$ as follows:

$$P_*(\mathbf{X} = \mathbf{x}_i) = Min_k(P_{k*}(\mathbf{X} = \mathbf{x}_i))$$

$$= \frac{a_i + N(\mathbf{x}_i)}{a + Max_{l \neq i} N^*(\mathbf{x}_l) + \sum_{k=1}^r N(\mathbf{x}_k)}, i = 1, 2, \ldots, r \quad (6)$$

Note that when the dataset is complete, we will have

$$P^*(\mathbf{X} = \mathbf{x}_i) = P_*(\mathbf{X} = \mathbf{x}_i) = \frac{a_i + N(\mathbf{x}_i)}{a + \sum_{k=1}^r N(\mathbf{x}_k)},$$

$i = 1, 2, \ldots, r$, which is the Bayes estimate of $P(\mathbf{X} = \mathbf{x}_i)$ that can be obtained from the complete dataset.

The minimal and maximal Bayes estimates of $P(\mathbf{X} = \mathbf{x}_i)$ comprise the lower and upper bounds of its interval estimates. The above calculation does not rely on any assumption on the distribution of the missing data because it does not try to infer them: the available information can only give rise to constraints on the possible estimates that could be learned from the dataset. Furthermore, it provides a new measure of information: the width of the interval accounts for the amount of information available in the dataset about the parameter to be estimated and represents a measure of the quality of the probabilistic information conveyed by the dataset about a parameter. In this way, intervals provide an explicit representation of the reliability of the estimates which can be taken into account when the extracted BN is used to perform a particular task.

3.2. Point Estimation

Next we will discuss how to compute the point estimates from these interval estimates using a convex combination of the lower and upper bounds of this interval. Suppose that some information on the pattern of missing data is available, which allows the user to formulate a probability distribution describing, for each incomplete case, the probability of a completion as:

$$P(\mathbf{X} = \mathbf{x}_i|\mathbf{X} = ?, D_{inc}) = \lambda_i, i = 1, 2, \ldots, r \quad (7)$$

where D_{inc} denotes the original incomplete dataset, ? denotes the incomplete values in D_{inc}, and $\sum_{i=1}^r \lambda_i = 1$. Such information can be used to summarize the interval estimate into a point estimate via a convex combination of the extreme probabilities:

$$P'(\mathbf{X} = \mathbf{x}_i) = \lambda_i P^*(\mathbf{X} = \mathbf{x}_i) + \sum_{k \neq i} \lambda_k P_{k*}(\mathbf{X} = \mathbf{x}_i) \quad (8)$$

where $i = 1, 2, \ldots, r$. This point estimate is the expected Bayes estimate that would be obtained from the complete dataset, when the mechanism generating the missing data in the dataset is described by Equation (7). Note that the estimates so found define a probability distribution since

$$\sum_{i=1}^r P'(\mathbf{X} = \mathbf{x}_i) = 1$$

The intuition behind Equation (8) is that the lower bound of the estimate of $P(\mathbf{X} = \mathbf{x}_i)$ is achieved when all the incomplete cases are assigned to $\mathbf{X} = \mathbf{x}_k, k \neq i$ and the upper case is achieved when all the incomplete cases are completed as $\mathbf{X} = \mathbf{x}_i$. Thus if the user specifies that

$$\lambda_i = P(\mathbf{X} = \mathbf{x}_i|\mathbf{X} = ?, D_{inc}) = 1$$

for a particular state $\mathbf{x}_i$, then Equation (8) will return the upper bound of the interval probabilities as estimate of $P(\mathbf{X} = \mathbf{x}_i)$. This case corresponds to the assumption that data is **Systematically Missing** [14] in the dataset. On the other hand, when no information on the mechanism generating missing data is available and therefore any pattern of missing data is equally likely, then

$$\lambda_i = \frac{1}{r}, i = 1, 2, \ldots, r \quad (9)$$

This case corresponds to the assumption that data is **Missing Completely at Random** (MCAR) [14]. When data is **Missing at Random** (MAR) [14], we will have:

$$\lambda_i = \frac{a_i + N(\mathbf{x}_i)}{a + \sum_{k=1}^r N(\mathbf{x}_k)}, i = 1, 2, \ldots, r \quad (10)$$

3.3. Mutual Information Estimation

Suppose now that we have obtained the Bayes point estimates of the joint probabilities interested from Equation (8). Then the (conditional) mutual information defined for complete datasets by Equation (1) and (2) can be estimated as follows:

$$I'(X,Y) = \sum_{x,y} P'(x,y) \lg \frac{P'(x,y)}{P'(x)P'(y)} \qquad (11)$$

$$I'(X,Y|\mathbf{C}) = \sum_{x,y,\mathbf{c}} P'(x,y,\mathbf{c}) \lg \frac{P'(x,y,\mathbf{c})P'(\mathbf{c})}{P'(x,\mathbf{c})P'(y,\mathbf{c})} \qquad (12)$$

The computation of the approximate (conditional) mutual information defined by Equation (11) and (12) depends only on the frequencies of complete entries and artificial frequencies of incomplete entries in the dataset, both of which can be obtained after only one dataset scan. Assume that we have obtained these frequencies, from Equation (11) and (12) we can see that the computation of the estimate of (conditional) mutual information requires at most $\bigcirc(r^2)$ basic operations (such as logarithm, multiplication, division), where r equals the number of the possible states of the variable set of $\{X,Y\}$ or $\{X,Y\} \cup \mathbf{C}$.

3.4. EMI Based Learning Algorithm

Once we have estimated all the needed (conditional) mutual information, we can construct BNs using the extension of J. Cheng's algorithm. The extension of J. Cheng's algorithm[3] can be simply achieved just by replacing the exact computation of (conditional) mutual information with our EMI calculation. The EMI Based Learning algorithm is as follows:

Phase I: (Drafting)

1. Initiate a graph $G = (V,E)$, where $V = \{$all the nodes where each corresponds an attribute of a dataset$\}$, $E = \{\}$. Initiate an empty list L.

2. For each pair of nodes (V_i, V_j), where $V_i, V_j \in V$, compute approximate mutual information $I'(V_i, V_j)$ by EMI method. For all the pairs of nodes that have mutual information greater than a certain small value ε, sort them by their mutual information and put these pairs of nodes into list L from large to small.

3. Create a pointer P that points to the first pair of nodes in L.

4. Get the pair of nodes from L at the position of the pointer P. If there is no adjacency path between the two nodes, add the corresponding edge to E and remove this pair of nodes from L.

5. Move the pointer P to the next pair of nodes and go back to Step 4 unless P is pointing to the end of L or G contains $n-1$ edges. (n is the number of nodes in G.)

Phase II: (Thickening)

6. Move the pointer P to the first pair of node in L.

7. If P is pointing to the end of L, then go to Step 10; otherwise, go to next step.

8. Get the pair of nodes from L at the position of the pointer P. Check if this pair of nodes can be d-separated in current graph. If so, go to next step; otherwise, connect the pair of nodes by adding a corresponding edge to E.

9. Move the pointer P to the next pair of nodes and go back to Step 7.

Phase III: (Thinning)

10. For each edge in E, if there are other paths besides this edge between the two nodes, remove this edge from E temporarily and then check if the two nodes are d-separated. If so, remove the edge permanently; otherwise add this edge back to E.

11. Assign the orientation of the edges in the graph if the node ordering is not known.

4. Experiments

The main aim of the experiments in this section is to evaluate our EMI based learning algorithm. For this aim, not only did we evaluate the relative error of the estimated (conditional) Mutual Information with respect to different percentage of missing data, but compared EMI based algorithm with SEM and EM-EA algorithms in terms of accuracy and efficiency with respect to different samples and different percentage of missing data.

4.1. Materials and Methods

For the convenience of comparison, SEM, EM-EA and EMI based algorithm have been implemented in a Java based system, and all of them run given the variable order. The criterion for evaluating the three algorithms is to make comparison between the numbers of the missing edges and extra edges of the learned networks from the experimental datasets by the three algorithms contrasted with the true networks.

In our experiments, we considered two well-known BNs: Asia network, which has 8 nodes and 8 arcs, and Alarm network, which has 37 nodes and 46 arcs. For each network, using Netica System (which is available at http://www.norsys .com) and setting various percentages, we generated random samples with different cases and different percentage of missing data. The incomplete datasets obtained in this way follow the assumption that data is **Missing at Random**. This means that we can compute the weights λ_i by Equation (10).

In the experiments, greedy search strategy and BDe score are used by SEM algorithm. The other experimental parameters are set as follows. The mutation and crossover probabilities in the EM-EA algorithm are set as 0.05 and 0.5 respectively; the group size during the evolution is set as 40; the stopping criterion for EM-EA algorithm is set at 500 generations. The threshold of Mutual Information in EMI based algorithm is set as 0.01.

All the experiments were conducted on a Pentium 500 MHz PC with 128MB of RAM running under Windows 2000. The datasets are stored in an SQL Server database. The experimental outcome is the average of the results run 10 times for each level of missing data.

4.2. Experiments on Asia Network.

In this subsection, we present our experimental results on Asia Network with different sample sizes and percentage of missing data. Figure 2 illustrates the relationship between

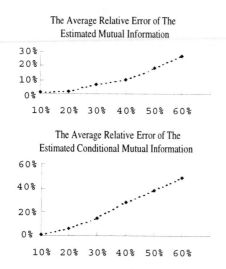

Figure 2. The average relative error of the estimated (conditional) Mutual Information for node pairs in Asia Network against percentage of missing data. The sample size is 1000.

the average relative error of the estimated (conditional) Mutual Information and the percentage of missing entries. The

average relative error of the estimated (conditional) Mutual Information is computed as follows:

$$\frac{1}{n(n-1)} \sum_{(X_i, X_j)} \frac{|I'(X_i, X_j) - I(X_i, X_j)|}{I(X_i, X_j)},$$

$$\frac{1}{n(n-1)} \sum_{(X_i, X_j)} \frac{|I'(X_i, X_j|\mathbf{C}) - I(X_i, X_j|\mathbf{C})|}{I(X_i, X_j|\mathbf{C})},$$

Where $i, j = 1, 2, \ldots, n$ and $i \neq j$; n is the number of attributes in the dataset; $I(X_i, X_j)$ and $I(X_i, X_j|\mathbf{C})$ can be calculated from the complete dataset by Equation (1) and (2) respectively; $I'(X_i, X_j)$ and $I'(X_i, X_j|\mathbf{C})$ from the incomplete dataset by Equation (11) and (12) respectively.

From Figure 2 we can see that both the estimated Mutual Information and the estimated conditional Mutual Information by EMI based algorithm are quite accurate until 20% missing data. However, as the percentage of missing data increases, the average relative errors of both kind of estimated Mutual Information become larger. While the one of the estimated conditional MI increases faster than that of the estimated MI probably because the computation estimating conditional MI usually involves more variables and can be more unreliable.

Figure 3 shows the experimental results of SEM, EM-EA and EMI based algorithms in terms of learning accuracy with respect to the Asia network given different percentage of missing data and sample size. Where the "A+B" in the Figure represents there are A missing edges and B extra edges in the networks learned from the datasets by the three algorithms compared with the true network. From this figure, we can see that the general trend for all the three algorithms is that the larger the datasets and the lower the percentage of missing data are, the fewer the errors. Furthermore, the experimental results by EM-EA and EMI based algorithms are much more accurate than that of SEM algorithm with respect to all the percentage of missing data and all the sample size. Especially when the percentage of missing data reaches 30% and 40%, the accuracy of SEM algorithm deteriorated significantly, while the EM-EA and EMI based algorithm could learn quite accurate networks if provided relative bigger sample sets. Another finding is that although it looks that EM-EA algorithm can achieve better accuracy than EMI based algorithm, there are no significant differences between them. The bad performance of SEM algorithm is because the increase of missing data leads to more local maxima in the search space of network structures so that greedy search used by SEM algorithm tends to "get stuck" on a local maximum. Also, the nature of EM procedure tending to converge to a parametric local maximum decreases the accuracy of SEM algorithm to some extent.

Figure 4 shows the relationship between running time of the three algorithms and the percentages of missing data fix-

Sample Size	Algorithms	Complete Data	10% Missing	20% Missing	30% Missing	40% Missing
500	EMI based	1+0	1+1	2+3	2+4	3+3
	SEM	1+3	0+6	1+5	1+7	2+6
	EM-EA	1+0	0+2	2+2	2+3	2+3
1,000	EMI based	1+0	1+0	2+2	2+2	1+4
	SEM	1+0	1+4	2+4	1+9	1+7
	EM-EA	0+0	1+0	2+1	2+2	1+3
2,000	EMI based	1+0	1+0	2+1	2+1	2+1
	SEM	0+0	1+4	1+5	1+8	2+6
	EM-EA	0+0	0+0	1+1	1+2	1+2
4,000	EMI based	1+0	1+0	1+0	2+1	2+1
	SEM	0+0	1+2	1+6	2+8	1+9
	EM-EA	0+0	0+0	1+0	2+0	1+1

Figure 3. The experimental results of SEM, EM-EA and EMI based algorithms in terms of learning accuracy with respect to the Asia network, given different percentage of missing data and sample size.

Algorithms	Complete Data	10% Missing	20% Missing	30% Missing	40% Missing
EMI based	1.02	1.12	1.01	1.04	1.05
SEM	5.76	152.12	194.62	214.40	320.36
EM-EA	12.64	176.49	203.32	213.42	328.53

Algorithms	500 Samples	1,000 Samples	2,000 Samples	4,000 Samples
EMI based	0.54	0.72	1.01	1.73
SEM	51.45	73.70	194.62	401.94
EM-EA	42.86	68.51	203.32	428.35

Figure 4. Relationship between the running time (seconds) consumed by SEM, EM-EA and EMI based algorithms and percentage of missing data, given sample size is fixed to 2,000.

Figure 5. Relationship between the running time (seconds) of SEM, EM-EA and EMI based algorithms and sample sizes, given that 20% data is missing in all datasets.

ing the sample size to 2000. From figure 4, the running time of EMI based algorithm is independent of the percentage of missing data on the whole, while that of SEM and EM-EA algorithms increases steadily with the increase of the missing data. And the more important is the running time of SEM and EM-EA algorithms is two orders higher than that of EMI based algorithm for all percentage of missing data. Besides the reason that it is of low efficiency for SEM and EM-EA algorithms having to search the space of possible Bayesian networks, the fact that SEM and EM-EA algorithms complete the incomplete datasets using Bayesian inference technique also causes high computational cost.

Figure 5 illustrates the relationship between running time of the three algorithms and different sample sizes fixing the percentage of missing data to 20%. We can see from Figure 5 that the running time of EMI based algorithm is roughly linear to the size of the dataset given the percentage of miss-

ing data, while the ones of SEM and EM-EA algorithms increase much more quickly, and also is two orders higher than that of EMI based algorithm for all sample sizes. This shows that EMI based algorithm can efficiently deal with much larger incomplete datasets.

4.3. Experiments on Alarm Network.

We also evaluated EMI based algorithm on Alarm network. Figure 6 shows the experimental results of EMI based algorithm in terms of learning accuracy with respect to the Alarm network. We can find from the Figure that even for such large network as Alarm, with such high percentage of missing data as 30%, networks with high accuracy also can be obtained by EMI based algorithm if provided larger sample sets. The time consumed of once run of EMI based algorithm in this experiment is about a few minutes. For instance, it is 329 seconds with respect to 40,000 samples and 10% missing data. While at the above conditions, it takes

SEM and EM-EA algorithms more than twenty hours and the experimental results by SEM and EM-EA algorithms are "2+1" and "1+1" respectively, which are not better than that of EMI based algorithm. Because of the reason of time, we have not completed the experiments in the Figure 6 by SEM and EM-EA algorithms. This also shows that EMI based algorithm has significant advantage over SEM and EM-EA algorithms with respect to large sample size with high percentage of missing data.

Sample Size	Complete Data	10% Missing	20% Missing	30% Missing
10,000	3+2	4+4	5+4	7+3
20,000	2+1	2+2	2+2	3+3
30.000	0+2	0+2	0+2	2+2
40,000	0+2	0+2	0+2	2+1

Figure 6. Experimental results on Alarm Network with different sample sizes and percentages of missing data by EMI algorithm.

5. Conclusions

In this paper, we first introduce a method that estimates the (Conditional) Mutual Information directly from incomplete datasets, EMI. And then we apply EMI to J. Cheng's algorithm to learn BNs with incomplete data. Finally, we evaluate EMI based algorithm by experimental comparison with two search & scoring based algorithms, SEM and EM-EA algorithms. The experimental results show that EMI based algorithm is much more efficient than SEM and EM-EA algorithms. In terms of accuracy, EMI based algorithm is more accurate than SEM algorithm, and comparable with EM-EA algorithm.

Additionally, it is worth noting that although EMI method is originally designed for CI tests in BNs structure learning algorithms, it is a general method to estimate (conditional) Mutual Information and can be applied to any other tasks based on information theory.

Considering that the search & scoring approaches work with a wider range of probabilistic models than the dependency analysis based approaches, next we will evaluate EMI based algorithm by further experimental analysis on wider range of networks.

6. Acknowledgments

This work is supported by NSF of China grant 79990584 and National 973 Fundamental Research Program grant G1998030414. Thank anonymous readers for helpful comments.

References

[1] W. Buntine. A guide to the literature on learning probabilistic networks from data. *IEEE Transactions on Knowledge and Data Engineering*, 8(2):195–210, 1996.

[2] J. Cheng, D. Bell, and W. Liu. Learning belief networks from data: An information theory based approach. *Proceeding of the sixth ACM International Conference on Information and Knowledge Management*, 1997.

[3] J. Cheng, R. Greiner, J. Kelly, D. Bell, and W. Liu. Learning bayesian networks from data: an information-theory based approach. *The Artificial Intelligence Journal*, 137:43–90, 2002.

[4] D. M. Chickering and D. Heckerman. Efficient approximations for the marginal likelihood of bayesian networks with hidden variables. *Machine Learning*, 29(2-3):181–212, 1997.

[5] C. Chow and C. Liu. Approximating discrete probability distributions with dependence trees. *IEEE Transactions on Information Theory*, 14:462–467, November 1968.

[6] G. Cooper and E. Herskovits. A bayesian method for the induction of probabilistic networks from data. *Machine Learning*, 9:309–347, 1992.

[7] N. Friedman. The bayesian structural em algorithm. *Fourteenth Conf. on Uncertainty in Artificial Intelligence*, 1998.

[8] D. Heckerman, D. Geiger, and D. Chickering. Learning bayesian networks: The combination of knowledge and statistical data. *Machine Learning*, 20:197–243, 1995.

[9] W. Lam and F. Bacchus. Learning bayesian belief networks: An approach based on the mdl principle. *Computational Intelligence*, 10:269–293, 1994.

[10] J. W. Myers, K. B. Laskey, and K. A. DeJong. Learning bayesian networks from incomplete data using evolutionary algorithms. *GECCO'99*, 1999.

[11] J. Pearl. Probabilistic reasoning in intelligent systems: Networks of plausible inference. *Morgan Kaufmann, Inc., San Mateo,CA*, 1988.

[12] G. Rebane and J. Pearl. The recovery of causal poly-trees from statistical data. *Third Annual Conf. on Uncertainty in Artificial Intelligence*, pages 175–182, 1987.

[13] P. Sebastiani and M. Ramoni. Bayesian inference with missing data using bound and collapse. *Journal of Computational and Graphical Statistics*, 9(4):779–800, DECEMBER 2000.

[14] M. Singh. Learning bayesian networks from incomplete data. *The 14th National Conf. on Artificial Intelligence*, July 1997.

[15] F. Tian, Y. Lu, and C. Shi. Learning bayesian networks with hidden variables using the combination of em and evolutionary algorithm. *PAKDD 2001, Hong Kong, China, Aril 2001 Proceeding*, pages 568–574, 2001.

Combining Multiple Weak Clusterings

Alexander Topchy, Anil K. Jain, and William Punch
Computer Science Department, Michigan State University,
East Lansing, MI, 48824, USA
{topchyal, jain, punch}@cse.msu.edu

Abstract

A data set can be clustered in many ways depending on the clustering algorithm employed, parameter settings used and other factors. Can multiple clusterings be combined so that the final partitioning of data provides better clustering? The answer depends on the quality of clusterings to be combined as well as the properties of the fusion method. First, we introduce a unified representation for multiple clusterings and formulate the corresponding categorical clustering problem. As a result, we show that the consensus function is related to the classical intra-class variance criterion using the generalized mutual information definition. Second, we show the efficacy of combining partitions generated by weak clustering algorithms that use data projections and random data splits. A simple explanatory model is offered for the behavior of combinations of such weak clustering components. We analyze the combination accuracy as a function of parameters controlling the power and resolution of component partitions as well as the learning dynamics vs. the number of clusterings involved. Finally, some empirical studies compare the effectiveness of several consensus functions.

1. Introduction

In contrast to supervised classification, clustering is an inherently ill-posed problem, whose solution violates at least one of the common assumptions about scale-invariance, richness, and cluster consistency [1]. Exploratory nature of the problem forces us to seek generic and robust clustering algorithms when explicit model-based approaches prove to be ineffective.

One of the methods used to increase the robustness of the clustering solution is to combine outputs of several clustering algorithms. Combination of clusterings using multiple sources of data or features is important in distributed data mining. Several recent studies on clustering combination [2,3,4] have pioneered a new area in the conventional taxonomy of clustering algorithms [5,6]. The problem of clustering fusion can be defined generally as follows: given multiple clusterings of the data set, find a combined clustering with better quality. We offer a representation of multiple clusterings as a set of

new attributes characterizing the data items. Such a view directly leads to a formulation of the combination problem as a categorical clustering problem in the space of these attributes, or, in other terms, a median partition problem. We show how median partition is related to the classical intra-class variance criterion when generalized mutual information is used as the evaluation function.

While the problem of clustering combination bears some traits of a classical clustering, it also has three major issues which are specific to combination design:

1. Consensus function: How to combine different clusterings? How to resolve the label correspondence problem? How to ensure symmetrical and unbiased consensus with respect to all the component partitions?

2. Diversity of clustering: How to generate different partitions? What is the source of diversity in the components?

3. Strength of constituents/components: How "weak" could each input partition be? What is the minimal complexity of component clusterings to ensure a successful combination?

Similar questions have already been addressed in the framework of multiple classifier systems [7]. However, it is not possible to mechanically apply the combination algorithms from classification (supervised) to clustering (unsupervised). Indeed, no labeled training data is available in clustering; therefore the ground truth feedback necessary for boosting the overall accuracy cannot be used. In addition, different clusterings may produce incompatible data labelings, resulting in intractable correspondence problems, especially when the numbers of clusters are different.

From the supervised case we also learn that the proper combination of weak classifiers [8,9] may achieve arbitrarily low error rates on training data, as well as reduce the predictive error. One of the goals of our work is to adopt weak clustering algorithms and combine their outputs. Vaguely defined, a weak clustering algorithm produces a partition, which is only slightly better than a random one. We propose two different weak clustering algorithms as the components of the combination:

1. Clustering of random 1-dimensional projections of multidimensional data. This can be generalized to clustering in any random subspace of the original data space.

2. Clustering by splitting the data using a number of random hyperplanes. For example, if only one hyperplane is used then data is split into two groups.

One can expect that using many simple, but computationally inexpensive components will be preferred to combining clusterings obtained by sophisticated, but computationally involved algorithms.

The second goal of this paper is to compare the performance of different consensus functions. A consensus function maps multiple clusterings to a final partitioning of the data. We study a family of consensus functions based on categorical clustering including the co-association based hierarchical methods [4], hypergraph algorithms [3] and a new simple centroid-based heuristic consensus function. Combination accuracy is analyzed as a function of the number and the resolution of the clustering components.

Previous research on clustering ensembles has addressed both how the component clusterings are obtained as well as method by which they are combined. Consensus functions using co-association values were explored in [2,4] with multiple k-means partitions. Hypergraph algorithms for consensus were analyzed in [3]. Other related work can be found in [10,11,12,13]

2. Problem of consensus clustering

Let X be a set of N data points (objects) in d-dimensional space. No assumptions are needed at the moment about the data input: it could be represented in a non-metric space or as an $N \times N$ dissimilarity matrix. Suppose we are given a set of H partitions $\Pi = \{\pi_1, \ldots, \pi_H\}$ of objects in X. Each component partition in Π is a set of disjoint, exhaustive and nonempty clusters $\pi_i = \{L^i_1, L^i_2, \ldots, L^i_{K(i)}\}$, $X = L^i_1 \cup \ldots \cup L^i_{K(i)}$, $\forall \pi_i$, and $K(i)$ is the number of clusters in the i-th partition. The problem of consensus clustering is to find a new partition $\sigma = \{C_1, \ldots, C_K\}$ of data X given the partitions in Π, such that the objects in a cluster of σ are more similar to each other than to objects in different clusters of σ. This statement of the problem is virtually the same as for a conventional clustering except that it uses information contained in already existing partitions $\{\pi_1, \ldots, \pi_H\}$. Other variants of this definition could be obtained by putting some extra requirements on the target partition σ, such as fixing the number of clusters in σ, or allowing fuzzy membership values for data points. In general, one could use information from two available sources: the partitions in Π and/or the original attributes of objects in X.

It is convenient to characterize consensus clustering as clustering in a space of new features induced by the set Π. Indeed, each component partition π_i represents a feature with categorical values. The values assumed by the i-th new feature are simply the cluster labels from partition π_i.

Therefore, membership of each object in different partitions is treated as a new feature vector, an H-tuple, given H different partitions in Π. Combined clustering becomes equivalent to a problem of clustering of H-tuples if we ignore the original d attributes.

3. Consensus functions

A consensus function maps a given set of partitions $\Pi = \{\pi_1, \ldots, \pi_H\}$ to a target partition σ. A family of hierarchical clustering consensus functions immediately follows from the similarity between two objects x and y:

$$s(x, y) = \sum_{i=1}^{H} \delta(\pi_i(x), \pi_i(y)), \quad \delta(a,b) = \begin{cases} 1, & \text{if } a = b \\ 0, & \text{if } a \neq b \end{cases} \quad (1)$$

Similarity between a pair of objects simply counts the number of clusters shared by these objects in the partitions $\{\pi_1, \ldots, \pi_H\}$. This is the same as the co-association value introduced in [2]. One can use a co-association matrix for subsequent clustering by single-link algorithm [4] or any other type of agglomerative procedure to obtain a target consensus clustering σ.

Another candidate consensus function is based on the notion of median partition. A median partition σ is the best summary of existing partitions in Π. In contrast to the co-association approach, median partition is derived from estimates of similarities between attributes (i.e., partitions in Π), rather then from similarities between objects. A well-known example of this approach is implemented in the COBWEB algorithm in the context of conceptual clustering [14]. The category utility function $U(\sigma, \pi_i)$ evaluates the quality of a candidate median partition $\sigma = \{C_1, \ldots, C_K\}$ against some other partition $\pi_i = \{L^i_1, \ldots, L^i_{K(i)}\}$, with labels L^i_j for j-th cluster [15]:

$$U(\sigma, \pi_i) = \sum_{r=1}^{K} p(C_r) \sum_{j=1}^{K(i)} p(L^i_j \mid C_r)^2 - \sum_{j=1}^{K(i)} p(L^i_j)^2, \quad (2)$$

with the following notations: $p(C_r) = |C_r|/N$, $p(L^i_j) = |L^i_j|/N$, and $p(L^i_j \mid C_r) = |L^i_j \cap C_r|/|C_r|$.

The function $U(\sigma, \pi_i)$ assesses the agreement between two partitions as the difference between the expected number of labels of partition π_i that can be correctly predicted both with the knowledge of clustering σ and without it. The overall utility of the partition σ with respect to all the partitions in Π can be measured as the sum of pair-wise agreements:

$$U(\sigma, \Pi) = \sum_{i=1}^{H} U(\sigma, \pi_i) \quad (3)$$

Therefore, the best median partition should maximize the value of overall utility:

$$\sigma_{best} = \arg\max_{\sigma} U(\sigma, \Pi) \quad (4)$$

Mirkin [16] has proved that maximization of partition utility (3) is equivalent to minimization of the square-error clustering criterion if the number of clusters K in target partition σ is fixed. This is somewhat suprising in that the partition utility function (4) uses only the between-attribute similarity measure (2), while the square-error criterion makes use of distances between objects and prototypes. Simple standardization of categorical labels in $\{\pi_1,...,\pi_H\}$ effectively transforms them to quantitative features [16]. This transformation replaces the i-th partition π_i assuming $K(i)$ values by $K(i)$ binary features, and standardizes each binary feature to a zero mean. In other words, for each object x we can compute the values of the new features $y_{ij}(x)$, for j=1...$K(i)$, i=1...H, as following:

$$y_{ij}(x) = \delta(L_j^i, \pi_i(x)) - p(L_j^i), \qquad (5)$$

Hence, the solution of median partition problem (4) can be approached by the k-means clustering algorithm operating in the space of features y_{ij} if the number of target clusters is predetermined. We use this heuristic as a part of empirical study of consensus functions.

In information-theoretic framework, the quality of the consensus partition σ is determined by the amount of information, $I(\sigma,\Pi)$, it shares with the given partitions in Π. Strehl and Ghosh [3] suggest an objective function that is based on the classical mutual information:

$$\sigma_{best} = \arg\max_{\sigma} I(\sigma,\Pi), \qquad (6)$$

where $I(\sigma,\Pi) = \sum_{i=1}^{H} I(\sigma,\pi_i)$,

$$I(\sigma,\pi_i) = \sum_{r=1}^{K}\sum_{j=1}^{K(i)} p(C_r,L_j^i)\log\left(\frac{p(C_r,L_j^i)}{p(C_r)p(L_j^i)}\right) \qquad (7)$$

Again, an optimal median partition can be found by solving this optimization problem. However, it is not clear how to use these equations to search for consensus.

We show that another information-theoretic definition of entropy will reduce the mutual information criterion to the category utility function discussed before. We proceed from the generalized entropy of degree s for a discrete probability distribution $P=(p_1,...,p_n)$:

$$H^s(P) = (2^{1-s}-1)^{-1}\left(\sum_{i=1}^{n} p_i^s - 1\right), \quad s > 0, \ s \neq 1 \qquad (8)$$

Shannon's entropy is the limit form of (8) when $s{\to}1$. Generalized mutual information between σ and π can be defined as:

$$I^s(\sigma,\pi) = H^s(\pi) - H^s(\pi \mid \sigma) \qquad (9)$$

Quadratic entropy (s=2) is of particular interest, since it is known to be closely related to classification error. When s=2, generalized mutual information $I^s(\sigma,\pi_i)$ becomes:

$$I^2(\sigma,\pi_i) = -2\left(\sum_{j=1}^{K(i)} p(L_j^i)^2 - 1\right) + \\ + 2\sum_{r=1}^{K} p(C_r)\left(\sum_{j=1}^{K(i)} p(L_j^i \mid C_r)^2 - 1\right) = 2U(\sigma,\pi_i) \qquad (10)$$

Therefore, generalized mutual information gives the same consensus clustering criterion as category utility function (3). The gini-index measure for attribute selection used by Breiman et al. [17] also follows from (2) and (10). In light of Mirkin's result, all these criteria are equivalent to within-cluster variance minimization, after simple label transformation.

Other interesting consensus functions can be obtained as solutions to the hypergraph minimum cut problem. The details can be found in [3], where three different hypergraph algorithms were investigated. These algorithms are also used in our comparative empirical study.

4. Combination of weak clusterings

We now turn to the issue of generating different clusterings for the combination. Do we use the partitions produced by numerous existing clustering algorithms? We argue that it is possible to generate the partitions using weak, but less expensive, clustering algorithms and still achieve comparable or better performance. Certainly, the key motivation is that the synergy of many such components will compensate for their weaknesses. We consider two simple clustering algorithms:

1. Clustering of the data projected to a random subspace of lower dimension. In the simplest case, the data is projected on 1-dimensional subspace, a random line. The k-means algorithm clusters the projected data and gives a partition for the combination.

2. Random splitting of data by hyperplanes. For example, a single random hyperplane would create rather trivial clustering of d-dimensional data by cutting the hypervolume into two regions.

4.1. Splitting by random hyperplanes

Direct clustering by use of a random hyperplane illustrates how a reliable consensus emerges from low-informative components. The random splits approach pushes the notion of weak clustering almost to an extreme. The data set is cut by random hyperplanes dissecting the original volume of d-dimensional space containing the points. Points separated by the hyperplanes are declared to be in different clusters. In this situation, a co-association consensus function is appropriate since the only information needed is whether the patterns are in the same cluster or not. Thus the contribution of a hyperplane partition to the co-association value for any pair of objects can be either 0 or 1. Finer resolutions of distance are possible by counting the number of hyperplanes separating the objects, but for simplicity we do not use it here. Consider a random line dissecting the classic 2-spiral data shown in Fig. 1(a). While any single partition does little to reveal the true underlying clusters, analysis of the hyperplane generating mechanism shows how multiple partitions can discover the true clusters.

Consider first the case of one-dimensional data. Splitting objects in 1-dimensional space is done by a random threshold in R^1. In general, if r points are randomly selected, then $(r+1)$ clusters are formed. It is easy to derive that in 1-dimensional space the probability of separating two points whose inter-point distance is x is exactly:

$$P(\text{split}) = 1 - (1 - x/L)^r, \qquad (11)$$

where L is the length of the interval containing the objects, and r points are drawn at random from uniform distribution on this interval. Fig. 1(b) illustrates the dependence for $L=1$ and $r =1,2,3,4$. If a co-association matrix is used to combine H different partitions, then the expected value of co-association between two objects is $H(1 - P(\text{split}))$, that follows from the binomial distribution of the number of splits in H attempts. Therefore, the co-association values found after combining many random split partitions are generally expected to be a non-linear and a monotonic function of respective distances. The situation is similar for multidimensional data, however, the generation of random hyperplanes is a bit more complex. To generate a random hyperplane in d dimensions, we should first draw a random point in the multidimensional region that will serve as a point of origin. Then we randomly choose a unit normal vector u that defines the hyperplane. The two objects characterized by vectors p and q will be in the same cluster if $(up)(uq)>0$ and will be separated otherwise (here ab denotes a scalar product). If r hyperplanes are generated, then the total probability that two objects remain in the same cluster is just the product of probabilities that each of hyperplanes does not split the objects. Thus we can expect that the law governing the co-association values is close to what is obtained in one-dimensional space in (11).

Let us compare the actual dependence of co-association values with the function in (11). Fig. 2 shows the results of experiments with 1000 different partitions by random splits of the Iris data set. The Iris data is 4-dimensional and contains 150 points. There are $(150 \cdot 149)/2$ pair-wise distances between the data items. For all the possible pairs of points, each plot in fig. 2 shows the number of times a pair was split. The observed dependence of the inter-point "distances" derived from the

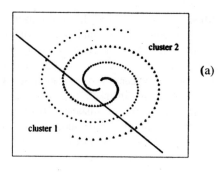

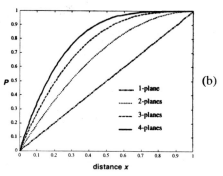

Figure 1. (a) An example of splitting 2-spiral data set by a random line. Points on the same side of the line are in the same cluster. (b) Probability of splitting two objects for different number of random thresholds as a function of distance between objects.

co-association values vs. the true Euclidean distance, indeed, can be described by the function in (11).

Clearly, the inter-point distances dictate the behavior of respective co-association values. The probability of a cut between any two given objects does not depend on the other objects in the data set. Therefore, we can conclude that any clustering algorithm that works well with the original inter-point distances is also expected to work well with co-association values obtained from a combination of multiple partitions by random splits. However, this result is more of theoretical value when true distances are available, since they can be used directly instead of co-association values. It illustrates the main idea of the approach, namely that the synergy of multiple weak clusterings can be very effective.

4.2. Combination in random subspaces

The weak projections approach combines multiple views of sample data. Each projection is much weaker, contains less information, then the data in the original space. However, combined partitions of projections become at least as powerful as clustering using the original data representation and may help to reveal data structure unattainable by any single clustering algorithm. Subspaces are not necessarily obtained by taking some of

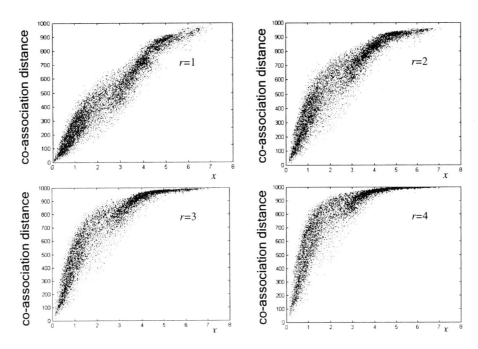

Figure 2. Dependence of distances derived from the co-association values vs. the actual Euclidean distance x for each possible pair of objects in Iris data. Co-association matrices were computed for several number of hyper planes $r =1,2,3,4$.

the original features (dimensions) as a whole, but could be created by projections, even random ones. Random subspaces are an excellent source of clustering diversity that provides different views of the data.

Each random subspace can be of very low dimension and it is by itself not very informative. On the other hand, clustering in 1-dimensional space is computationally cheap and can be effectively performed by k-means algorithm. The main subroutine of k-means algorithm – distance computation – becomes d times faster in 1-dimensional space. The cost of projection is linear with respect to the sample size and number of dimensions $O(Nd)$, and is less than the cost of one k-means iteration.

The main idea of our approach is to generate multiple partitions by projecting the data on a random line. A fast and simple algorithm such as k-means clusters the projected data, and the resulting partition becomes a component in the combination. Afterwards, a chosen consensus function is applied to the components. We discuss and compare several consensus functions in the experimental section.

It is instructive to consider a simple 2-dimensional data and one of its projections, as illustrated in Fig. 3(a). There are two natural clusters in the data. This data looks the same in any 1-dimensional projection, but the actual distribution of points is different in different clusters in the projected subspace. For example, Fig. 3(b) shows one possible histogram distribution of points in 1-dimensional projection of this data. There are three identifiable modes, each having a clear majority of points from one of the

classes. One can expect that clustering by k-means algorithm will reliably separate at least a portion of the points from class 2. It is easy to imagine that projection of the data in Fig. 3(a) on another random line would result in different distribution of points and different label assignment, but for this particular data set it will always appear as a mixture of three bell-shaped components. Most probably, these modes will be identified as clusters by k-means algorithm. Thus each new 1-dimensional view correctly helps to group some data points. Accumulation of multiple views eventually should result in a correct combined clustering.

The important parameter is the number of clusters in the component partition π_i returned by k-means algorithm at each iteration, i.e. the value of k. If the value of k is too large then the partitions $\{\pi_i\}$ will overfit the data set which in turn may cause unreliable co-association values. Small number of clusters in $\{\pi_i\}$ may not be sufficient to capture the true structure of data set. In addition, if the number of clusterings in the combination is too small then the effective sample size for the estimates of distances from co-association values is also insufficient, resulting in a larger variance of the estimates. That is why the consensus functions based on the co-association values are more sensitive to the number of partitions in the combination (value of H) than consensus functions based on hypergraph algorithms.

5. Experimental Results and Discussion

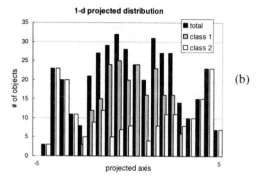

1-d projected distribution

Figure 3. (a) A sample data with two identifiable natural clusters and a line randomly selected for projection. (b) Histogram of the distribution of points that resulted from data projection onto a random line.

The experiments were performed with several data sets, including three classic problems, the "2 spirals" and "half-rings", the Iris dataset from UCI benchmarks repository and large real-world dataset of galaxies and stars described in [18]. All consensus functions were provided with the true known number of clusters in the data. By providing this information, we can use the misassignment rate (error) of the consensus partition as a measure of performance of clustering combination. Thus the optimal solution of the correspondence problem between the labels of known and derived clusters is easily found using Hungarian method for minimal weight bipartite matching problem

We study the consensus accuracy as a function of the resolution of partitions (value of k) as well as its dependence on the number of components for seven consensus functions:

1. Consensus functions operated on the co-association matrix, but with three different hierarchical clustering algorithms for obtaining the final partition, namely single-linkage, average-linkage, and complete-linkage.

2. Consensus function based on k-means clustering in the space of standardized features defined in (5), that is equivalent to maximization of partition utility criterion in (3).

3. Three consensus functions based on hypergraph algorithms [3]. We used a set of programs

'ClusterEnsemble' implemented by Strehl and available at http://www.strehl.com/.

Three fundamental parameters affect the quality of the target consensus partition: H – the number of combined clusterings that directly influences the reliability and resolution of the co-association values; k – the number of clusters in the component clusterings $\{\pi_1,...,\pi_H\}$ produced by k-means algorithm on one-dimensional projections; r – the number of hyperplanes used for obtaining clusterings $\{\pi_1,..., \pi_H\}$ by random splitting algorithm. The value of k was varied in the interval [2,10], r in [2,5] and H in [5,1000]. Note that we report the average error rate for 20 independent runs. We omit the detailed tables due to space limitations and refer the readers to complete experimental reports at http://www.cse.msu.edu/prip/. Some characteristics of the datasets are:

	Number of features	Number of classes	Number of points/class	Total number of patterns
Iris	4	3	50-50-50	150
Galaxy	14	2	2082-2110	4192
2-spirals	2	2	100-100	200
Half-rings	2	2	100-300	400

Let us start by demonstrating how the combination of clusterings in projected 1-dimensional subspaces outperforms the combination of clusterings in the original multidimensional space. Fig. 4(a) shows the learning dynamics for Iris data and $k=4$, using average-link consensus function based on co-association values. Note that the number of clusters in each of the components $\{\pi_1,..., \pi_H\}$ is set to $k=4$, and is different from the true number of clusters (=3). Clearly, each individual clustering in full multidimensional space is much stronger than any 1-dim partition, and therefore with only a small number of partitions ($H<50$) the combination of weaker partitions is no yet effective. However, for larger numbers of combined partitions ($H>50$), 1-dimensional projections taken together better reveal the true structure of the data. It is quite unexpected, since the k-means algorithm with $k=3$ makes, on average, 19 mistakes in original 4-dimensional space and 25 mistakes in 1-dimensional random subspace. Moreover, clustering in the projected subspace is d times faster than in multidimensional space. Although, the cost of computing a consensus partition σ is the same in both cases.

The results regarding the impact of value of k are reported in Fig. 4(b), which shows that there is a critical value of k for the Iris data set. This occurs when the average-linkage of co-association distances is used as a consensus function. In this case the value $k=2$ is not sufficient to separate the true clusters.

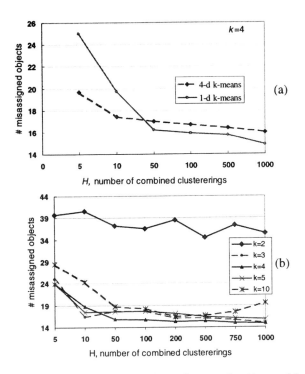

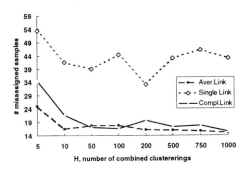

Figure 5. Dependence of performance of the projection algorithm on the type of consensus function for Iris data set. $k=3$.

Figure 4. Performance of random subspaces algorithm on Iris data. (a) Number of errors by the combination of k-means partitions ($k=4$) in multidimensional space and projected 1-d subspaces. Average-link consensus function was used. (b) Error of projection algorithm as a function of the number of components and the number of clusters k in each component.

The role of the consensus function is illustrated in Fig.5. Three consensus functions are compared on the Iris data set. They all use similarities from the co-association matrix but cluster the objects using three different criterion functions, namely, single link, average link and complete link. It is clear that the combination using single-link performs significantly worse than the other two consensus functions. This is expected since the three classes in Iris data have hyperellipsoidal shape.

More results were obtained on two data sets, which are traditionally difficult for any partitional centroid-based algorithm: "half-rings" data set and "2 spirals" data in Fig. 1(a). The single-link consensus function performed the best and was able to identify both the 'half-rings' clusters as well as spirals. In contrast to the results for Iris data, average-link and complete-link consensus were not suitable for these data sets. In general, one can expect that average-link (single-link) consensus will be appropriate if standard average-link (single-link) agglomerative clustering works well for the data and vice versa. Moreover, none of the three hypergraph consensus functions could find a correct combined partition. This is somewhat surprising given that the hypergraph algorithms performed well on the Iris data. However, the Iris data is far less problematic because one of the clusters is linearly separable, and the other classes are well described as a mixture of two multivariate normal distributions. Perfect separation of natural clusters was achieved with a large number of partitions in clustering combination ($H > 200$) and for values of $k > 3$ for "half-rings" and "2 spirals". It indicates that for each problem there is a critical value of resolution of component partitions that guarantees good clustering combination. This further supports the work of Fred and Jain [4] who showed that a random number of clusters in each partition ensures a greater diversity of components. We see that the minimal required value of resolution for the Iris data is $k=3$, for "half-rings" it is $k=2$ and for "2 spirals" it is $k=4$. In general, the value of k should be larger than the true number of clusters.

The number of partitions affects the relative performance of the consensus functions. With large values of H (>100), co-association consensus becomes stronger, while with small values of H it is preferable to use hypergraph algorithms or k-means median partition algorithm.

It is interesting to compare the combined clustering accuracy with the accuracy of some of the classical clustering algorithms. For example, for Iris data the EM algorithm has the best average error rate of 6.17%. In our experiments, the best performers for Iris data were the hypergraph methods, with an error as low as 3%, with $H > 200$ and $k > 5$. For the "half-rings" data, the best standard result is 5.25% error by the average-link algorithm, while the combined clustering using the single-link co-association algorithm achieved a 0% error with $H > 200$. Also, for the "2 spirals" data the clustering combination achieves 0% error, the same as by regular single-link clustering. Hence, with an appropriate choice of consensus function, clustering combination outperforms many standard algorithms. However, the choice of good consensus function is similar to the problem of choice of proper conventional clustering algorithm. Perhaps the good alternative to guessing the right consensus function, is simply to run all the available consensus functions and then pick the final consensus partition according to the partition utility criteria in (4) or (6).

Table 1. Summary of the best results

Dataset	Best consensus function(s)	Lowest error obtained	Prefered values of parameters
Galaxy	Median partition k-means	< 13%	$H > 10, k > 3$
Iris	Hypergraph methods	< 3%	$H > 100, k > 4$
2 spirals	Co-association SL	0%	$H > 200, k > 3$
Half-rings	Co-association SL	0%	$H > 200, k > 4$

Quadratic computational complexity effectively prohibits co-association based consensus functions from being used on large data sets, since $O(N^2)$ factor arises when co-association matrix is built for all the N objects. Even though computation of component partitions is d times faster due to projecting, the overall computational effort can be dominated by the complexity of computing the consensus partition. Therefore for large datasets it is problematic to use three hierarchical agglomerative methods as well as the CSPA hypergraph algorithm [3]. The k-means algorithm for median partition is most attractive in terms of speed with the complexity $O(kNH)$. For "galaxy" data we limited the number of components in combination to $H=20$ because of large data size. The results show that k-means algorithm for median partition has the best performance. On "galaxy" data HGPA did not work well due to its bias toward balanced cluster sizes, as it also happened in the case of the "half-rings" data set. Again the accuracy improved when the number of partitions and the number of clusters increases.

The same set of experiments was also performed with clustering combination via splits by random hyperplanes. The results in many details are close to what has been obtained by using random subspaces, with a slightly worse performance.

6. Conclusion

This study extended previous research on clustering ensembles in several respects. First, we have introduced a unified representation for multiple clusterings and formulated the corresponding categorical clustering problem. It is shown that the consensus function is related to classical intra-class variance criterion using the generalized mutual information definition. Second, we have considered combining weak clustering algorithms that use data projections and random data splits. A simple explanatory model is offered for the behavior of combination of such weak components. We have analyzed combination accuracy as a function of parameters, which control the power and resolution of component partitions. Empirical study compared effectiveness of several consensus functions.

Acknowledgements. This research was supported in part by ONR grant # N00014-01-1-0266 (A.K.J.) and by research award from Center for Biological Modeling at Michigan State University (A.T.)

7. References

[1] J. Kleinberg. "An Impossibility Theorem for Clustering", *Proc. of Adv. in Neural Information Processing Sys.* (NIPS 15), 2002.

[2] A.L.N. Fred, "Finding Consistent Clusters in Data Partitions". In *Proc. 3d Int. Workshop on Multiple Classifier Systems*. Eds. F. Roli, J. Kittler, LNCS 2364,2002, pp. 309-318.

[3] A. Strehl and J. Ghosh, "Cluster ensembles - a knowledge reuse framework for combining multiple partitions. *Journal of Machine Learning Research*, 3, 2002, pp. 583-617.

[4] A.L.N. Fred and A.K. Jain, "Data Clustering Using Evidence Accumulation", In *Proc. of the 16th International Conference on Pattern Recognition*, ICPR 2002 ,Quebec City, 2002, pp. 276-280.

[5] A. Jain, M. N. Murty, and P. Flynn, "Data clustering: A review. *ACM Computing Surveys"*, 31(3), 1999, pp. 264–323.

[6] A.K. Jain and R.C. Dubes, *Algorithms for Clustering Data*. Prentice-Hall Inc., New Jersey, 1988.

[7] J. R. Quinlan, "Bagging, boosting, and C4.5", In *Proc. of the 13th AAAI Conference on Artificial Intelligence*, AAAI Press, Menlo Park, CA, 1996, pp. 725-30.

[8] E.M. Kleinberg, "Stochastic Discrimination", *Annals of Mathematics and Artificial Intelligence*, 1, 1990, pp. 207-239.

[9] Y. Freund, R.E. Schapire, "Experiments with a New Boosting Algorithm", in *Proc. of the Thirteenth International Conference on Machine Learning*, Morgan Kaufmann, 1996, pp. 148-156.

[10] P. Kellam, X. Liu, N.J. Martin, C. Orengo, S. Swift and A. Tucker, "Comparing, contrasting and combining clusters in viral gene expression data", Proc. of 6th Workshop on Intelligent Data Analysis in Medicine and Pharmacology, 2001, pp. 56-62.

[11] F. Leisch, "Bagged clustering", Working Papers SFB "Adaptive Information Systems and Modelling in Economics and Management Science", 51, Institut für Informationsverarbeitung, Abt. Produktionsmanagement, Wien, 1999.

[12] E. Dimitriadou, A. Weingessel and K. Hornik, "Voting-merging: An ensemble method for clustering", In *Proc. Int. Conf. on Artificial Neural Networks*, Vienna, 2001, pp. 217-224

[13] E. Johnson and H. Kargupta, "Collective, hierarchical clustering from distributed, heterogeneous data", In *Large-Scale Parallel KDD Systems,* Eds. Zaki M. and Ho C., LNCS 1759, Springer-Verlag, 1999, pp. 221–244.

[14] D. H. Fisher, "Knowledge acquisition via incremental conceptual clustering", *Machine Learning*, 2, 1987, pp. 139-172.

[15] M.A. Gluck and J.E. Corter, "Information, uncertainty, and the utility of categories", In *Proc. of the Seventh Annual Conference of the Cognitive Science Society*, Hillsdale, NJ: Lawrence Erlbaum, 1985, pp. 283-287.

[16] B. Mirkin, "Reinterpreting the Category Utility Function", *Machine Learning*, 45(2), 2001, pp. 219-228.

[17] L. Breiman, J. Friedman, R. Olshen, C. Stone, *Classification and Regression Trees*. Wadsworth, Monterrey, Ca, 1984.

[18] S.C. Odewahn, E.B. Stockwell, R.L. Pennington, R.M. Humphreys and W.A. Zumach, "Automated Star/Galaxy Discrimination with Neural Networks", *Astronomical Journal*, 103: 1992, pp. 308-331.

Visualization of Rule's Similarity using Multidimensional Scaling

Shusaku Tsumoto and Shoji Hirano
Department of Medical Informatics,
Shimane University, School of Medicine,
Enya-cho Izumo City, Shimane 693-8501 Japan
tsumoto@computer.org, hirano@ieee.org

Abstract

One of the most important problems with rule induction methods is that it is very difficult for domain experts to check millions of rules generated from large datasets. The discovery from these rules requires deep interpretation from domain knowledge. Although several solutions have been proposed in the studies on data mining and knowledge discovery, these studies are not focused on similarities between rules obtained. When one rule r_1 has reasonable features and the other rule r_2 with high similarity to r_1 includes unexpected factors, the relations between these rules will become a trigger to the discovery of knowledge. In this paper, we propose a visualization approach to show the similar relations between rules based on multidimensional scaling, which assign a two-dimensional cartesian coordinate to each data point from the information about similiaries between this data and others data. We evaluated this method on two medical data sets, whose experimental results show that knowledge useful for domain experts could be found.

1. Introduction

One of the most important problems with rule induction methods is that it is very difficult for domain experts to check millions of rules generated from large datasets. Moreover, since the data collection is deeply dependent on domain knowledge, rules derived by datasets need deep interpretation made by domain experts. For example, Tsumoto and Ziarko reported the following case in analysis of a dataset on meningitis.

Even though the dataset is small, the number of records is 198, they obtained 136 rules with high confidence (more than 0.75) and support (more than 20). Here are the examples which are unexpected to domain experts.

```
1. [WBC  12000] & [Gender=Female]
              & [CSFcell  1000]
           => Virus meningitis
   (Accuracy: 0.97, Coverage: 0.55)

2. [Age > 40] & [WBC > 8000]
           => Bacterial meningitis
   (Accuracy: 0.80, Coverage: 0.58)

3. [WBC > 8000] & [Gender=Male]
           => Bacterial menigits
   (Accuracy: 0.78, Coverage: 0.58)

4. [Gender=Male] & [CSFcell>1000]
           => Bacterial meningitis
   (Accuracy: 0.77, Coverage: 0.73)
```

The factors in these rules unexpected to domain experts are gender and aga, which have not been pointed out in the literature on meningitis[1].

Since these detected patterns may strongly depends on the characteristics of data, Tsumoto and Ziarko searched for the hidden factors. For this analysis, several grouping of attributes are processed into the dataset.

The results obtained from the secondary analysis of processed show that both $[Gender = male]$ and $[Age > 40]$ are closely related with chronic diseases, which is a risk factor of bacterial meningitis. The first attribute-value pair, $[Gender = male]$ is supported by 70 cases in total 198 records: 48 cases are bacterial meningitis, all of which suffered from chronic diseases (25 cases: diabetes mellitus, 17 cases: liver cirrhosis and 6 cases: chronic sinusitis.) On the other hand, $[Age > 40]$ is supported by 121 cases: 59 cases are bacterial meningitis, 45 cases of which suffered from chronic diseases (25 cases: diabetes mellitus, 17 cases: liver cirrhosis and 3 cases: chronic sinusitis.) Domain explanation was given as follows: chronic diseases, especially diabetes mellitus and liver cirrhosis degrade the host-defence to microorganisms as immunological deficiency and chronic sinusitis influences the membrane of brain through the cranial bone. Epidemiological studies show that women before 50 having mensturation suffer from such chronic diseases less than men.

This example illustrates that deep interpretation based on data and domain knowledge is very important for discovery of new knowledge. Especially, the above example shows the importance of similarities between rules. When one rule r_i has reasonable features and the other rule r_j with high similarity to r_i includes unexpected factors, the relations between these rules will become a trigger to the discovery of knowledge.

In this paper, we propose a visualization approach to show the similar relations between rules based on multidimensional scaling, which assign a two-dimensional cartisian coordinate to each data point from the information about similiaries between this data and others data. We evaluated this method on three medical data sets, whose experimental results show that several knowledge useful for domain experts could be found.

2. Preliminaries

2.1. Assumed Discovery Process

Many discussions have been made on discovery process in the field on scientific discovery[6] and active data mining[7]. The example in Section 1 gives one simple model for such discovery process as follows:

1. Induce rules from a given dataset.

2. Compare rules of a given concept and group similar rules.

3. Detect unexpected factors in a group of similar rules.

4. Return to the dataset with unexpected patterns (If needed, data will be processed for the next data mining steps)

5. Apply data mining steps if possible

These process will be a part of KDD process[5], interactions among mining, post-processing and data selection.

In this paper, we assume the above discovery process and focus on the second and third steps. For this, we first define the three kinds of similarities among attribute-value pairs in the next session.

2.2. Defintions from Rough Sets

2.2.1. Preliminaries In the following sections, the following notations introduced by Grzymala-Busse and Skowron[9], are used which are based on rough set theory[8]. These notations are illustrated by a small database shown in Table 1, collecting the patients who complained of headache.

Let U denote a nonempty, finite set called the universe and A denote a nonempty, finite set of attributes, i.e., $a : U \rightarrow V_a$ for $a \in A$, where V_a is called the domain of a, respectively. Then, a decision table is defined as an information system, $A = (U, A \cup \{d\})$. For example, Table 1 is an information system with $U = \{1, 2, 3, 4, 5, 6\}$ and $A = \{age, location, nature, prodrome, nausea, M1\}$ and $d = class$. For $location \in A$, $V_{location}$ is defined as $\{occular, lateral, whole\}$.

The atomic formulae over $B \subseteq A \cup \{d\}$ and V are expressions of the form $[a = v]$, called descriptors over B, where $a \in B$ and $v \in V_a$. The set $F(B, V)$ of formulas over B is the least set containing all atomic formulas over B and closed with respect to disjunction, conjunction and negation. For example, $[location = occular]$ is a descriptor of B.

For each $f \in F(B, V)$, f_A denote the meaning of f in A, i.e., the set of all objects in U with property f, defined inductively as follows.

1. If f is of the form $[a = v]$ then, $f_A = \{s \in U | a(s) = v\}$
2. $(f \wedge g)_A = f_A \cap g_A$; $(f \vee g)_A = f_A \vee g_A$; $(\neg f)_A = U - f_a$

For example, $f = [location = occular]$ and $f_A = \{1, 5, 6, 7\}$. As an example of a conjunctive formula, $g = [location = occular] \wedge [nausea = no]$ is a descriptor of U and g_A is equal to $\{1, 5\}$.

By the use of the framework above, classification accuracy and coverage, or true positive rate is defined as follows.

Definition 1
Let R and D denote a formula in $F(B, V)$ and a set of objects whose decision class is d. Classification accuracy and coverage(true positive rate) for $R \rightarrow d$ is defined as:

$$\alpha_R(D) = \frac{|R_A \cap D|}{|R_A|} (= P(D|R)), \text{ and}$$

$$\kappa_R(D) = \frac{|R_A \cap D|}{|D|} (= P(R|D)),$$

where $|S|$, $\alpha_R(D)$, $\kappa_R(D)$ and P(S) denote the cardinality of a set S, a classification accuracy of R as to classification of D and coverage (a true positive rate of R to D), and probability of S, respectively.

In the above example, when R and D are set to $[nau = 1]$ and $[class = common]$, $\alpha_R(D) = 2/5 = 0.4$ and $\kappa_R(D) = 2/2 = 1.0$.

Finally, we define the partial order of formulae as follows:

Definition 2 *Let R_i and R_j be the formulae in $F(B, V)$ and let $A(R_i)$ denote a set whose elements are the attribute-value pairs of the form $[a, v]$ included in R_i. If $A(R_i) \subseteq A(R_j)$, then we represent this relation as:*

$$R_i \preceq R_j.$$

No.	loc	nat	his	prod	jolt	nau	M1	M2	class
1	occular	per	per	0	0	0	1	1	m.c.h.
2	whole	per	per	0	0	0	1	1	m.c.h.
3	lateral	thr	par	0	1	1	0	0	common.
4	lateral	thr	par	1	1	1	0	0	classic.
5	occular	per	per	0	0	0	1	1	psycho.
6	occular	per	subacute	0	1	1	0	0	i.m.l.
7	occular	per	acute	0	1	1	0	0	psycho.
8	whole	per	chronic	0	0	0	0	0	i.m.l.
9	lateral	thr	per	0	1	1	0	0	common.
10	whole	per	per	0	0	0	1	1	m.c.h.

Definition. loc: location, nat: nature, his:history,
Definition. prod: prodrome, nau: nausea, jolt: Jolt headache,
M1, M2: tenderness of M1 and M2, 1: Yes, 0: No, per: persistent,
thr: throbbing, par: paroxysmal, m.c.h.: muscle contraction headache,
psycho.: psychogenic pain, i.m.l.: intracranial mass lesion, common.:
common migraine, and classic.: classical migraine.

Table 1. A small example of a database

2.2.2. Probabilistic Rules According to the definitions, probabilistic rules with high accuracy and coverage are defined as:

$$R \overset{\alpha,\kappa}{\to} d \ s.t. \quad R = \vee_i R_i = \vee \wedge_j [a_j = v_k],$$
$$\alpha_{R_i}(D) \geq \delta_\alpha \text{ and } \kappa_{R_i}(D) \geq \delta_\kappa,$$

where δ_α and δ_κ denote given thresholds for accuracy and coverage, respectively. For the above example shown in Table 1, several probabilistic rules for m.c.h. are given as follows:

$$[M1 = yes] \rightarrow m.c.h. \quad \alpha = 3/4 = 0.75, \kappa = 1.0,$$
$$[nau = no] \rightarrow m.c.h. \quad \alpha = 3/5 = 0.6, \kappa = 1.0,$$

where δ_α and δ_κ are set to 0.75 and 0.5, respectively.

3. Similarity of Rules

Let $sim(a, b)$ denote a similarity between objects a and b. Formally, similarity relation should hold the following relations:

1. An object a is similar to oneself: $sim(a, a)$.

2. If $sim(a, b)$, then $sim(b, a)$. (Symmetry)

Iti is notable that the second property is the principal axiom for the similarity measure. In this section, we define three types of similarity measures for rules which hold the above relations. As shown in the subsection 2.2.2, rules are composed of (1) relation between attribute-value pairs (proposition) and (2) values of probabilistic indices (and its supporting sets). Let us call the former components **syntactic** part and the latter ones **semantic** part. The first two similarities are based on the characcgteristics fn these parts.

3.1. Syntactic Similarity

Syntatic similarity is defined as the similarity between conditional parts of the same target concept. In the example shown in Section 1, the following two rules have similar conditional parts:

```
R2. [Age > 40] & [WBC > 8000]
               => Bacterial meningitis
    (Accuracy: 0.80, Coverage: 0.58)

R3. [WBC > 8000] & [Gender=Male]
               => Bacterial menigits
    (Accuracy: 0.78, Coverage: 0.58)
```

The difference between these two rules are $[Age > 40]$ and $[Gender = Male]$. To measure the similarity between these two rules, we can apply several indices of two-way contigency tables. Table 2 gives a contingency table for two rules, $Rule_i$ and $Rule_j$. The first cell a (the intersection of the first row and column) shows the number of matched attribute-value pairs. From this table, several kinds of sim-

		$Rule_j$		
		Observed	Not Observed	Total
$Rule_i$	Observed	a	b	$a+b$
	Not Observed	c	d	$c+d$
	Total	$a+c$	$b+d$	$a+b$ $+c+d$

Table 2. Contingency Table for Similarity

ilarity measures can be defined. The best similarity measures in the statistical literature are four measures shown in

Table 3[4]. It is notable that these indices satisfies the property on symmetry shown in the beginning of this section.

(1)	Matching Number	a
(2)	Jaccard's coefficient	$a/(a+b+c)$
(3)	χ^2-statistic	$N(ad-bc)^2/M$
(4)	point correlation coefficient	$(ad-bc)/\sqrt{M}$

$N = a+b+c+d, M = (a+b)(b+c)(c+d)(d+a)$

Table 3. Definition of Similarity Measures

For example, the table for the above two rules is given as Table 4. From this table, the similarity measures are

		$Rule_3$		
		$Observed$	$Not\ Observed$	$Total$
$Rule_2$	$Observed$	1	1	2
	$Not\ observed$	1	1	2
	$Total$	2	2	4

Table 4. Example for Syntactic Similarity

given as: (1) matching number: 1, (2) Jaccard's coefficient: $1/(1+1+1) = 1/3$, (3) χ^2-statistic: 0 and (4) point correlation coefficient: 0.

In the case of rules shown in the subsection 2.2.2, the syntactic similarities between $[M1 = yes]$ and $[nau = 0]$ are (1) matching number: 0, (2) Jaccard's coefficient: $0/(0+1+1) = 0$, (3) χ^2-statistic: $2*(-1)^2/(1*1*1*1) = 2$ and (4) point correlation coefficient: $\sqrt{(2)} \sim 1.41$.

3.2. Semantic Similarity: Covering

The other similarity which can be defined from the definition of the rule is based on the *meaning* of the relations between formulae f_i and f_j from the viewpoint of set-theoretical point of view. Let us assume that we have two rules:

$$f_i \rightarrow D \quad (\alpha_{f_i}(D), \kappa_{f_i}(D))$$
$$f_j \rightarrow D \quad (\alpha_{f_j}(D), \kappa_{f_j}(D))$$

As shown in the last subsection, syntactic similarity is defined as $sim(f_i, f_j)$ from the viewpoint of syntactic representations. Since f_i and f_j have meanings (supporting sets), f_{iA} and f_{jA}, respectively, where A denotes the given attribute space. Then, we can define $sim(f_{iA}, f_{jA})$ by using a contingency table: Table 2. While this table is used in the last subsection as the number of matched number of attribute-value pairs,

For example, let us consider two attribute-value pairs $[M1 = yes]$ and $[nau = no]$ in Table 1. Since the supporting sets of $[M1 = yes]$ and $[nau = no]$ are $\{1,2,5,10\}$ and $\{1,2,5,8,10\}$, the contingency table for these two attribute-value pairs is given as Table 5. From this table,

		$[nau = 0]$		
		$Observed$	$Not\ Observed$	$Total$
$[M1 = yes]$	$Observed$	4	0	4
	$Not\ observed$	1	5	6
	$Total$	5	5	10

Table 5. Example for Semantic Similarity

the similarity measures are given as: (1) matching number: 4, (2) Jaccard's coefficient: $4/(4+1) = 4/5 = 0.8$, (3) χ^2-statistic: $10 * (20 - 0)^2/(4*6*5*5) = 20/3 \sim 6.667$ and (4) point correlation coefficient: $\sqrt{20/3} \sim 2.581$.

Compared with syntatic similarities, thsese values are much stronger, which means that $[M1 = yes]$ and $[nau = 0]$ are semantically similar, though syntactically different.

3.3. Semantic Similarity: accuracy and coverage

The similarity defined in the last subsection is based on the supporting sets of two formulas.

However, to calculate these similarities, we should go back to the dataset, which may be time-consuming for huge datasets. In such cases, we can use the combination of accuracy and coverage to measure the similarity between two rules. Let us return the definition of accuracy and coverage. From the viewpoint of a two-way contingency table, accuracy and coverage are defined as follows. Let R_1 and R_2 denote a formula in $F(B, V)$. A contingency tables is a table of a set of the meaning of the following formulas: $|[R_1 = 0]_A|, |[R_1 = 1]_A|, |[R_2 = 0]_A|, |[R_1 = 1]_A|, |[R_1 = 0 \wedge R_2 = 0]_A|, |[R_1 = 0 \wedge R_2 = 1]_A|, |[R_1 = 1 \wedge R_2 = 0]_A|, |[R_1 = 1 \wedge R_2 = 1]_A|, |[R_1 = 0 \vee R_1 = 1]_A|(= |U|)$. This table is arranged into the form shown in Table 1. From

	$R_1 = 0$	$R_1 = 1$	
$R_2 = 0$	a	b	$a+b$
$R_2 = 1$	c	d	$c+d$
	$a+c$	$b+d$	$a+b+c+d$ $(= |U| = N)$

Table 6. Two way Contingency Table

this table, accuracy and coverage for $[R_1 = 0] \rightarrow [R_2 = 0]$

are defined as:

$$\alpha_{[R_1=0]}([R_2=0]) = \frac{|[R_1=0 \wedge R_2=0]_A|}{|[R_1=0]_A|} = \frac{a}{a+c}, and$$

$$\kappa_{[R_1=0]}([R_2=0]) = \frac{|[R_1=0 \wedge R_2=0]_A|}{|[R_2=0]_A|} = \frac{a}{a+b}.$$

It is easy to show that accuracy and coverage do not hold the symmetric relation, that is, $\alpha_{[R_1=0]}([R_2 = 0]) \neq \alpha_{[R_2=0]}([R_1 = 0])$ nor $\kappa_{[R_1=0]}([R_2 = 0]) \neq \kappa_{[R_2=0]}([R_1 = 0])$.

However, combinations of these two indices give several types of similarity indices[2], as shown in Table 7. Since

(5)	Kulczynski	$\frac{1}{2}\left(\frac{a}{a+b} + \frac{a}{a+c}\right)$
(6)	Ochiai	$\frac{a}{\sqrt{(a+b)(a+c)}}$
(7)	Simpson	$\frac{a}{min\{(a+b).(a+c)\}}$

Table 7. Definition of Similarity Measures (2)

$a/(a+b)$ and $a/(a+c)$ are accuracy and coverage, they are transformed into the following formulae:

$$Kulczynski \quad \frac{1}{2}(\alpha_R(D) + \kappa_R(D)),$$
$$Ochiai \quad \sqrt{\alpha_R(D)\kappa_R(D)},$$
$$Simpson \quad min(\alpha_R(D), \kappa_R(D)),$$

where R and D denotes $[R1 = 0 \ or \ 1]$ and $[D = 0 \ or \ 1]$, respectively. For example, let us consider two attribute-value pairs $[M1 = yes]$ and $[nau = no]$ in Table 1. Since the accuary for both rules shown in the subsection 2.2.2 are 0.75 and 0.6, and the coverage are 1.0 and 1.0, respectively, Similarity measures between $[M2 = 1]$ or $[nau = 0]$ and $m.c.h.$ are obtained as shown in Table 8.

	$[M1 = yes]$	$[nau = 0]$
Kulczynski	0.875	0.8
Ochiai	0.867	0.774
Simpson	0.75	0.6

Table 8. Similarity Measure based on Accuracy and Coverage of $m.c.h.$

From these values, we should extract the similarity between $[M1 = yes]$ and $[nau = 0]$. The easiest way is to calculate the average, square root of the product or to select

the minimum one.[1] Then, the similarity between $[M1 = 1]$ and $[nau = 0]$ can be obtained as: (1) Kulczynski: 0.8375, 0.8367 or 0.8, (2) Ochiai: 0.8205, 0.8191 or 0.774, (3) Simpson: 0.675, 0.67082, 0.6, respectively.

4. Multidimensional Scaling

4.1. Problems with Clustering

After calculating the similarity relations among rules and deriving similarity matrix, patterns with respect to similarities will be investigated. Usually, data miners apply clustering methods to the similarity matrix obtained from a given datasets[4]. However, clustering have several problems: most of clustering methods, hierarchical or nearnest neighbor based methods, forces grouping given examples, attributes or classes into one or several classses, with one dimension. This limitation is already given as a formal form of similarity function, $sim(a, b)$. As a mapping, similarity function is given as $O \times O \rightarrow R$, where O and R denotes a set of objects and real number,respectively.

Since each objects may have many properties, one dimensional analysis may not be sufficient for detecting the similarity between two objects. In these cases, to increase the dimensionality is one of the extentions of reasoning about similarities. Multidimensional scaling (MDS) is one solution for dimensionality, which uses two-dimensional plane to visualize the similarity relations between objects.

4.2. How MDS works

4.2.1. Metric MDS The most important function of MDS is to recover cartesian coordinates (usually, two-dimensional) from a given similarity matrix. For recovery, we assume that a similarity is given as a inner product of two vectors for objects. Although we need three points to recover coordinates, but one point is fixed as the origin of the plane.

Let us assume that the coordinates of two objects x_i and x_j are given as: $(x_{i1}, x_{i2}, \cdots, x_{ip})$ and $(x_{j1}, x_{j2}, \cdots, x_{jp})$, where p is the number of dimension of the plane. Let k denote the origin of the plane $(0, 0, \cdots, 0)$. Then, here, we assume that the distance betweeen x_i and x_j d_{ij} is given as the formula of distance, such as Eucledian, Minkowski, and so on. MDS based on this assumption is called *metric MDS*. Then, the similarity between i and j s_{ij} is given

---

1 As shown in Section 2, similarity relaions do not hold the transitivity relation. Thus, we should take care of the usage of transitivity for the similarity relations. In this case, since the supporting set for a target concept, values of similarity between two formulae will hold transitivity. Due to the limitation of space, we will not get into the details.

as:

$$s_{ij} = d_{ik}d_{jk}\cos\theta = \sum_{m=1}^{p} x_{im}x_{jm}$$

From the triangle ijk, the following formula holds:

$$d_{ij}^2 = d_{ik}^2 + d_{jk}^2 - 2d_{ik}d_{jk}\cos\theta.$$

Therefore, similarity should hold the following formula.

$$s_{ij} = \frac{d_{ik}^2 + d_{jk}^2 - d_{ij}^2}{2}$$

Since s_{ij} is given as $\sum_{m=1}^{p} x_{im}x_{jm}$, the similarity matrix for s_{ij} is given as:

$$\mathbf{Z} = \mathbf{X}\mathbf{X}^{\mathbf{T}},$$

where $\mathbf{X}^{\mathbf{T}}$ denotes the transposition matrix of $\mathbf{X}$. To obtain $\mathbf{X}$, we consider the minimization of an objective function Q defined as:

$$Q = \sum_i \sum_j \left(z_{ij} - \sum_{m=1}^{p} x_{im}x_{jm} \right)^2.$$

For this purpose, we apply $EckartandYoung$ decomposition [3] in the following way. first, we calculate eigenvalues, denoted by $\lambda_1, \cdots, \lambda_p$, and eigenvectors of $\mathbf{Z}$, denoted by $\mathbf{v}^1, \cdots, \mathbf{v}^P$. Then by using a diagnoal matrix of eigenvalues, denoted by $\mathbf{\Lambda}$ and a matrix with eigenvectors, denoted by $\mathbf{Y}$, we obtain the following formula:

$$\mathbf{X} = \mathbf{Y}\mathbf{\Lambda}\mathbf{Y}^{\mathbf{T}},$$

where

$$\mathbf{\Lambda} = \begin{pmatrix} \lambda_1 & 0 & \ldots\ldots\ldots & 0 \\ 0 & \lambda_2 & 0\ldots & \ldots & 0 \\ \ldots\ldots & & \lambda_i & \ldots\ldots & \\ 0 & 0 & \ldots & \lambda_{p-1} & 0 \\ 0 & 0 & \ldots & 0 & \lambda_p \end{pmatrix},$$

and

$$\mathbf{Y} = \left(\mathbf{v}^1, \mathbf{v}^2, \cdots, \mathbf{v}^P \right).$$

From this decomposition, we obtain $\mathbf{X}$ as

$$\mathbf{X} = \mathbf{Y}\mathbf{\Lambda}^{1/2}.$$

4.2.2. Nonmetric MDS The above metric MDS can be applied to the case only when the difference between similarities have the meaning. In other words, the similarity index holds the property of interval calculus (interval scale).

If the similarity index holds the property of order, we should not apply the above calculus to the similarity matrix, but we should apply nonmetric MDS method. Here, we will introduce Kruskal method, which is one of the most well-known nonmetric MDS method[2]. First, we calculate given similarities s_{ij} into distance data d_{ij}^* (dissimilarity).

Next, we estimate the coordinates of x_i and x_j from the minimization of *Stress* function, defined as:

$$S = \sqrt{\frac{\sum\sum_{i<j}(d_{ij} - d_{ji}^*)^2}{\sum\sum d_{ij}^2}},$$

where the distance d_{ij} is defined as a Minkowski distance:

$$d_{ij} = \left(\sum_{m=1}^{P} |x_{im} - x_{jm}|^t \right)^{1/t},$$

where t denotes the Minkowski constant. For the minimization of S, optimization methods, such as gradient method are applied and the dimensionality and t will be estimated.

Since the similarity measures given above do not hold the property of distance (transitivity), we adopt nonmetric MDS method to visualize similarity relations.

4.3. Example

Let us apply nonmetric MDS to the data shown in Table 1. We use $m.c.h.$ as a target concept and apply Jaccard's coefficient as a similarity index. For simplicity, we assume that each rule have only one attribute-value pairs. Then, since all the syntactic similarities between two rules are 0, we can focus on the semantic similarity. From the table, the similarity matrix for m.c.h., is given as Figure 1 Since the Jaccard's coefficient takes the value from 0 to 1 and the dissimilarity of this coefficient can be defined as 1 - coefficient. That is, each element of the dissimilarity matrix is obtained from 1 minus the corresponding element of similarity matrix as shown in Figure 2. Finally, we apply the Kruskal method (nonmetric MDS) to the dissimilarity matrix and obtain the coordinate for each attribute. Table 9 shows the results of arrangements, and Figure 3 shows the results of plotting these points. This results corresponding to the following results: (1) $location$ have the different meaning, compared with other attributes: corresponding to the value of coverage. While other attributes have full coverage, these two attributes do not. (2) The other attributes seems to be classified into two groups: one is higher accuracy and the other is rather lower accuracy. From the coordinates, the features of $M1$ are the same as that of $M2$, and the features of $[jolt = 0]$ are the same as that of $[nau = 0]$, from the viewpoint of classification of $m.c.h.$

5. Experimental Results

We applied the combination of rule induction and nonmetric MDS to two medical databases on differential diagnosis of headache and cerebrovascular diseases (CVD), whose precise information is given in Table 10. In these experiments, rule induction based on rough sets[10] is applied,

	loc=occular	loc= whole	nat=per	his=per	jolt=0	nau=0	M1=1	M2=1
loc=occular	1	0	4/7	2/7	2/7	2/7	2/6	2/6
loc=whole	-	1	3/7	3/6	3/5	3/5	3/5	3/5
nat=per	-	-	1	4/8	5/7	5/7	4/7	4/7
his=per	-	-	-	1	4/6	4/6	4/5	4/5
jolt=0	-	-	-	-	1	1	4/5	4/5
nau=0	-	-	-	-	-	1	4/5	4/5
M1=1	-	-	-	-	-	-	1	1
M2=1	-	-	-	-	-	-	-	1

Figure 1. Similarity Matrix for $m.c.h.$

	loc=occular	loc= whole	nat=per	his=per	jolt=0	nau=0	M1=1	M2=1
loc=occular	0	1	3/7	5/7	5/7	5/7	4/6	4/6
loc=whole	-	0	4/7	3/6	2/5	2/5	2/5	2/5
nat=per	-	-	0	4/8	2/7	2/7	3/7	3/7
his=per	-	-	-	0	2/6	2/6	1/5	1/5
jolt=0	-	-	-	-	0	0	1/5	1/5
nau=0	-	-	-	-	-	0	1/5	1/5
M1=1	-	-	-	-	-	-	0	0
M2=1	-	-	-	-	-	-	-	0

Figure 2. Dissimilarity Matrix for $m.c.h.$

Attribute	x-axis	y-axis
loc=occular	2.672	-0.2755
loc=whole	1.2761	0.3504
nat=per	-0.6436	-1.5436
his=per	-0.6954	1.0926
jolt=0	-0.7689	-0.3441
nau=0	-0.7689	-0.3441
M1=1	-0.5356	0.5321
M2=1	-0.5356	0.5321

Table 9. Coordinates derived by MDS

Domain	Samples	Classes	Attributes
Headache	52119	45	73
CVD	7620	22	124

Table 10. Information about Databases

where δ_α and δ_κ were set to 0.75 and 0.5 for rule induction, respectively. For similarity measures, we adopt Kulczynski's similarity and calculate similarity measures from accuracy and coverage of rules obtained from data.

Due to the limitation of space, we focus on the most interesting visualized patterns for each datasets. First, Figure 4 shows the pattern of semantic similarity of rules for

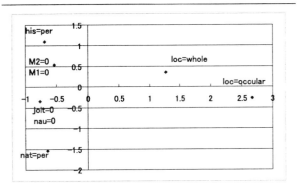

Figure 3. MDS Results

headache $m.c.h.$. The figure suggests three groups of the features of attributes. While the attributes in the right upper region are those which are regularly used for the differential diagnosis of headache, the left group and right lower group shows the attributes used for special types of $m.c.h.$, which we call emotional-evoked $m.c.h.$ and occupational $m.c.h.$. Thus, these patterns match with expert's knowledge.

Next, Figure 5 show the pattern of semantic similarity of rules for thalamic hemorrahge. While the left side group shows the symptoms of sensory disturbance, the right side group shows those of motor disturbance. Since the distance between points shows the dissimilarity between symptoms,

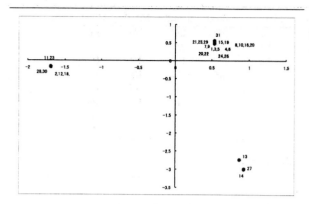

Figure 4. Patterns of Similar Rules for $m.c.h.$
(Semantic Similarity: Headache)

these results suggest that sensory disturbance are varied in each patient of thalamic hemorrhage, though motor disturbance are not so varied.

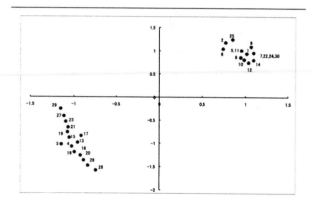

Figure 5. Pattern of Rules for Thalamic Hemorrahge (Semantic Similarity: CVD)

6. Conclusion

In this paper, we propose a visualization approach to show the similar relations between rules based on multidimensional scaling, which assign a two-dimensional cartesian coordinate to each data point from the information about similiaries between this data and others data. As similarity for rules, we define three types of similarities: syntactic, semantic (covering based) and semantic (indice based). Syntactic similarity shows the difference in attribute-value pairs, semantic similarity gives the similarity of rules from the viewpoint of supporting sets. MDS assigns each rule into the point of two-dimensional plane with distance information, which is useful to capture the intuitive dissimilarities between rules. Since the indices for these measures may not hold the property of distance (transitivity), we adopt nonmetric MDS, which is based on the stress function.

Finally, we evaluated this method on a medical data set, whose experimental results show that several knowledge useful for domain experts could be found. This study is a preliminary study on the visualization of rules' similarity based on MDS. Further analysis of this method, such as studies on computational complexity, scalability will be made and reported in the near future.

7. Acknowledgement

This work was supported by the Grant-in-Aid for Scientific Research (13131208) on Priority Areas (No.759) "Implementation of Active Mining in the Era of Information Flood" by the Ministry of Education, Science, Culture, Sports, Science and Technology of Japan.

References

[1] R. Adams and M. Victor. *Principles of Neurology 5th Edition.* McGraw-Hill, New York, 1993.

[2] T. Cox and M. Cox. *Multidimensional Scaling.* Chapman & Hall/CRC, Boca Raton, 2nd edition, 2000.

[3] C. Eckart and G. Young. Approximation of one matrix by another of lower rank. *Psychometrika*, 1:211–218, 1936.

[4] B. Everitt. *Cluster Analysis.* John Wiley & Son, London, 3rd edition, 1996.

[5] U. Fayyad, G. Piatetsky-Shapiro, and P. Smyth. The kdd process for extracting useful knowledge from volumes of data. *CACM*, 29:27–34, 1996.

[6] P. Langley, H. Simon, G. Bradshow, and J. Zytkow. *Scientific Discovery: Computational Explorations of the Creative Processes.* MIT Press, Cambridge, MA, 1987.

[7] H. Motoda, editor. *Active Mining.* Number 79 in Frontiers in Artificial Intelligence and Applications. IOS Press, Amsterdam, 2002.

[8] Z. Pawlak. *Rough Sets.* Kluwer Academic Publishers, Dordrecht, 1991.

[9] A. Skowron and J. Grzymala-Busse. From rough set theory to evidence theory. In R. Yager, M. Fedrizzi, and J. Kacprzyk, editors, *Advances in the Dempster-Shafer Theory of Evidence*, pages 193–236. John Wiley & Sons, New York, 1994.

[10] S. Tsumoto. Automated induction of medical expert system rules from clinical databases based on rough set theory. *Information Sciences*, 112:67–84, 1998.

TSP: Mining Top-K Closed Sequential Patterns *

Petre Tzvetkov   Xifeng Yan   Jiawei Han

Department of Computer Science

University of Illinois at Urbana-Champaign, Illinois, U.S.A.

{tzvetkov, xyan, hanj}@cs.uiuc.edu

Abstract

Sequential pattern mining has been studied extensively in data mining community. Most previous studies require the specification of a minimum support threshold to perform the mining. However, it is difficult for users to provide an appropriate threshold in practice. To overcome this difficulty, we propose an alternative task: mining top-k frequent closed sequential patterns of length no less than min_ℓ, where k is the desired number of closed sequential patterns to be mined, and min_ℓ is the minimum length of each pattern. We mine closed patterns since they are compact representations of frequent patterns.

We developed an efficient algorithm, called TSP, *which makes use of the length constraint and the properties of top-k closed sequential patterns to perform dynamic support-raising and projected database-pruning. Our extensive performance study shows that* TSP *outperforms the closed sequential pattern mining algorithm even when the latter is running with the best tuned minimum support threshold.*

1 Introduction

Sequential pattern mining is an important data mining task that has been studied extensively [1, 5, 3, 7, 11, 2]. It was first introduced by Agrawal and Srikant in [1]: *Given a set of sequences, where each sequence consists of a list of itemsets, and given a user-specified minimum support threshold (min_support), sequential pattern mining is to find all frequent subsequences whose frequency is no less than min_support.* This mining task leads to the following two problems that may hinder its popular use.

First, sequential pattern mining often generates an ex-

ponential number of patterns, which is unavoidable when the database consists of long frequent sequences. The similar phenomena also exists in itemset and graph patterns when the patterns are large. For example, assume the database contains a frequent sequence $\langle(a_1)(a_2)\ldots(a_{64})\rangle$ $(\forall i \neq j, a_i \neq a_j)$, it will generate $2^{64} - 1$ frequent subsequences. It is very likely some subsequences share the exact same support with this long sequence, which are essentially redundant patterns.

Second, setting *min_support* is a subtle task: *A too small value may lead to the generation of thousands of patterns, whereas a too big one may lead to no answer found.* To come up with an appropriate *min_support*, one needs to have prior knowledge about the mining query and the task-specific data, and be able to estimate beforehand how many patterns will be generated with a particular threshold.

A solution to the first problem was proposed recently by Yan, et al. [10]. Their algorithm, called CloSpan, can mine *closed sequential patterns*. A sequential pattern s is *closed* if there exists no superpattern of s with the same support in the database. Mining closed patterns may significantly reduce the number of patterns generated and is *information lossless* because it can be used to derive the complete set of sequential patterns.

As to the second problem, a similar situation occurs in frequent itemset mining. As proposed in [4], a good solution is to change the task of mining frequent patterns to *mining top-k frequent closed patterns of minimum length min_ℓ*, where k is the number of closed patterns to be mined, top-k refers to the k most frequent patterns, and $min_ℓ$ is the minimum length of the closed patterns. This setting is also desirable in the context of sequential pattern mining. Unfortunately, most of the techniques developed in [4] cannot be directly applied in sequence mining. This is because subsequence testing requires order matching which is more difficult than subset testing. Moreover, the search space of sequences is much larger than that of itemsets. Nevertheless, some ideas developed in [4] are still influential in our algorithm design.

* The work was supported in part by National Science Foundation under Grant No. 02-09199, the Univ. of Illinois, and Microsoft Research. Any opinions, findings, and conclusions or recommendations expressed in this material are those of the author(s) and do not necessarily reflect the views of the funding agencies.

In this paper, we introduce a new multi-pass search space traversal algorithm that finds the most frequent patterns early in the mining process and allows dynamic raising of $min\_support$ which is then used to prune unpromising branches in the search space. Also, we propose an efficient closed pattern verification method which guarantees that during the mining process the candidate result set consists of the desired number of closed sequential patterns. The efficiency of our mining algorithm is further improved by applying the minimum length constraint in the mining and by employing the early termination conditions developed in CloSpan [10].

The performance study shows that in most cases our algorithm TSP has comparable or better performance than CloSpan, currently the most efficient algorithm for mining closed sequential patterns, even when CloSpan is running with the best tuned $min\_support$.

The rest of the paper is organized as follows. In Section 2, the basic concepts of sequential pattern mining are introduced and the problem of mining the top-k closed sequential patterns without minimum support is formally defined. Section 3 presents the algorithm for mining top-k frequent closed sequential patterns. A performance study is reported in Section 4. Section 5 gives an overview of the related work on sequential pattern mining and top-k frequent pattern mining. We conclude this study in Section 6.

2 Problem Definition

This section defines the basic concepts in sequential pattern mining, and then formally introduces the problem of mining the top-k closed sequential patterns. We adopt the notations used in [10].

Let $I = \{i_1, i_2, \ldots, i_k\}$ be a set of items. A subset of I is called an *itemset*. A *sequence* $s = \langle t_1, t_2, \ldots, t_m \rangle$ ($t_i \subseteq I$) is an ordered list. We assume there exists a linear order in I and items in each itemset are sorted. The length of s, $l(s)$, is the total number of items in s. A sequence $\alpha = \langle a_1, a_2, \ldots, a_m \rangle$ is a *sub-sequence* of another sequence $\beta = \langle b_1, b_2, \ldots, b_n \rangle$, denoted by $\alpha \sqsubseteq \beta$, if and only if $\exists i_1, i_2, \ldots, i_m$, such that $1 \leqslant i_1 < i_2 < \ldots < i_m \leqslant n$ and $a_1 \subseteq b_{i_1}, a_2 \subseteq b_{i_2}, \ldots,$ and $a_m \subseteq b_{i_m}$. We also call β a *super-sequence* of α.

A sequence database, $D = \{s_1, s_2, \ldots, s_n\}$, is a set of sequences. The (absolute) *support* of a sequence α in a sequence database D is the number of sequences in D which contain α, $support(\alpha) = |\{s | s \in D \text{ and } \alpha \sqsubseteq s\}|$.

Definition 2.1 (top-k closed sequential pattern) A sequence s is a **frequent sequential pattern** in a sequence database D if its support (i.e., occurrence frequency) in D is no less than $min\_support$. A sequential pattern s is a **closed sequential pattern** if there exists no sequential pattern s' such that (1)$s \sqsubset s'$, and (2) $support(s) =$ $support(s')$. A closed sequential pattern s is a **top-k closed sequential pattern of minimum length** min_ℓ if there exist[1] no more than $(k-1)$ closed sequential patterns whose length is at least min_ℓ and whose support is higher than that of s. ∎

Our task is to *mine the top-k closed sequential patterns of minimum length min_ℓ efficiently in a sequence database.*

Example 1 Table 1 shows a sample sequence database. We refer to this databases as D and will use it as a running example in the paper. Suppose our task is to find the top-2 closed sequential patterns with $min\_\ell = 2$ in D. The output should be: $\langle (a)(e) \rangle : 4, \langle (ac)(e) \rangle : 3$. Although there are two more patterns with support equal to 3: $\langle (ac) \rangle : 3, \langle (c)(e) \rangle : 3$, they are not in the result set because they are not closed and both of them are absorbed by $\langle (ac)(e) \rangle : 3$. ∎

Seq ID.	Sequence
0	$\langle (ac)(d)(e) \rangle$
1	$\langle (e)(abcf)(e) \rangle$
2	$\langle (a)(e)(b) \rangle$
3	$\langle (d)(ac)(e) \rangle$

Table 1. Sample Sequence Database D

3 Method Development

Our method of mining is developed in this section. First, the concept of projection-based sequential pattern mining, PrefixSpan[7], is introduced, which provides the background for the development of our method. Next, we present a novel multi-pass search space traversal algorithm for mining the most frequent patterns and an efficient method for closed pattern verification and the minimum support raising during the mining process. Finally, two additional optimization techniques are proposed to further improve the efficiency of the algorithm.

3.1 Projection-based Sequential Pattern Mining

Definition 3.1 *Given two sequences, $s = \langle t_1, \ldots, t_m \rangle$ and $p = \langle t'_1, \ldots, t'_n \rangle$, $s \diamond p$ means s concatenates with p. It can be **itemset-extension**, $s \diamond_i p = \langle t_1, \ldots, t_m \cup t'_1, \ldots, t'_n \rangle$ if*

---

[1] Since there could be more than one sequential pattern having the same support in a sequence database, to ensure the result set is independent of the ordering of transactions, the proposed method will mine every closed sequential pattern whose support is no less than the support of the k-th frequent closed sequential pattern.

348

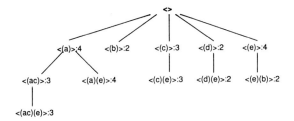

Figure 1. Lexicographic Sequence Tree

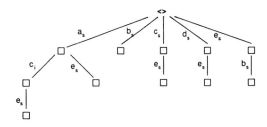

Figure 2. Prefix Search Tree

$\forall u \in t_m, v \in t'_1, u < v;$ *or* **sequence-extension**, $s \diamond_s p = \langle t_1, \ldots, t_m, t'_1, \ldots, t'_n \rangle$. *If* $s' = p \diamond s$, p *is a* **prefix** *of* s' *and* s *is a* **suffix** *of* s' *[10].* ∎

For example, $\langle (ae) \rangle$ is an itemset-extension of $\langle (a) \rangle$, whereas $\langle (a)(c) \rangle$ is a sequence-extension of $\langle (a) \rangle$. $\langle (ac) \rangle$ is a prefix of $\langle (ac)(d)(e) \rangle$ and $\langle (d)(e) \rangle$ is its suffix.

Definition 3.2 *An s-**projected** database is defined as* $D_s = \{ p \mid s' \in D, s' = r \diamond p, s.t., r \text{ is the minimum prefix (of } s') \text{ containing } s \text{ (i.e., } s \sqsubseteq r \text{ and } \nexists r', s \sqsubseteq r' \sqsubset r) \}.$ *Notice that* p *can be empty.* ∎

For Table 1, $D_{\langle (ac) \rangle} = \{ \langle (d)(e) \rangle, \langle (\_f)(e) \rangle, \langle (e) \rangle \}$, where $(\_f)$ in the second sequence means that item f and item c come from the same itemset $(abcf)$.

Sequence Lexicographic Order is given as follows: (i) if $s' = s \diamond p$, then $s < s'$; (ii) if $s = \alpha \diamond_i p$ and $s' = \alpha \diamond_s p'$, then $s < s'$; (iii) if $s = \alpha \diamond_i p$, $s' = \alpha \diamond_i p'$, and $p < p'$, then $s < s'$; (iv) if $s = \alpha \diamond_s p$, $s' = \alpha \diamond_s p'$, and $p < p'$ then $s < s'$; and (v) if $s = \langle (u) \rangle \diamond p$, $s' = \langle (v) \rangle \diamond p'$, and $u < v$, then $s < s'$ (u and v are the smallest item in the first itemset of s and s' respectively).

For example, $\langle (a, f) \rangle < \langle (b, f) \rangle$, $\langle (ab) \rangle < \langle (ab)(a) \rangle$ (i.e., a sequence is greater than its prefix), $\langle (ab) \rangle < \langle (a)(a) \rangle$ (i.e., a sequence-extended sequence is greater than an itemset-extended sequence if both of them share the same prefix).

A *Lexicographic Sequence Tree* is constructed as follows: Each node in the tree corresponds to a sequence; each node is either an itemset-extension or sequence-extension of its parent; and the left sibling is less than the right sibling in sequence lexicographic order.

Figure 1 shows a lexicographic sequence tree which records the frequent patterns of the sample database (Table 1) with $min\_support = 2$. The numbers in the figure represent the support of each frequent sequence. We define the *level of a node* by the number of edges from the root to this node. If we do pre-order transversal in the tree, we can build an operational picture of lexicographic sequence tree (Figure 2). It shows that the process extends a sequence by performing an itemset-extension or a sequence-extension.

PrefixSpan [7] provides a general framework for depth-first search in the prefix search tree. For each discovered sequence s and its projected database D_s, it performs itemset-extension and sequence-extension recursively until all the frequent sequences with prefix s are discovered.

3.2 Multi-Pass Mining and Support Threshold Raising

Since our task is to mine top-k closed sequential patterns without $min\_support$ threshold, the mining process should start with $min\_support = 1$, raise it progressively during the process, and then use the raised $min\_support$ to prune the search space. This can be done as follows: *as soon as at least k closed sequential patterns with length no less than min_ℓ are found, $min\_support$ can be set to the support of the least frequent pattern, and this $min\_support$-raising process continues throughout the mining process.*

This $min\_support$-raising technique is simple and can lead to efficient mining. However, there are two major problems that need to be addressed. The first is how to verify whether a newly found pattern is closed. This will be discussed in Section 3.3. The second is how to raise $min\_support$ as quickly as possible. When $min\_support$ is initiated or is very low, the search space will be huge and it is likely to find many patterns with pretty low support. This will lead to the slow raise of $min\_support$. As a result, many patterns with low support will be mined first but be discarded later when enough patterns with higher support are found. Moreover, since a user is only interested in patterns with length at least min_ℓ, many of the projected databases built at levels above min_ℓ may not produce any frequent patterns at level min_ℓ and below. Therefore, a naïve mining algorithm that traverses the search spaces in sequence lexicographic order will make the mining of the top-k closed sequential patterns very slow.

In this section we propose a heuristic search space traversal algorithm which in most cases mines the top-k frequent patterns as quickly as the currently fastest sequential pattern mining algorithm, even when the latter is tuned with the most appropriate $min\_support$ threshold.

3.2.1 Multi-pass mining and projected-database tree

Assuming that we have found the k most frequent closed sequential patterns for a given database, we call the support of the least frequent pattern $final\_support$. This is the maximum $min\_support$ that one can raise during the mining process. In Example 1, $final\_support = 3$.

Algorithm 3.1 TopSequencesTraversal
_____
Input: A sequence s, a projected DB D_s, min_ℓ,
      histograms H[$1..min\_\ell$], and constant factor θ
Output: The top-k frequent sequence set T.
1: **if** $support(s) < min\_support$ **then return**;
2: **if** $l(s) = min\_\ell$ **then**
3:     **Call** PrefixSpanWithSupportRaising(s, D_s,
        $min\_support$, T);
4:     **return**;
5: scan D_s once, find every frequent item α such that
    s can be extended to $s \diamond \alpha$;
    insert α in histogram H[$l(s) + 1$];
6: sort items in H[$l(s) + 1$] based on their support;
7: $next\_level\_top\_support \leftarrow$
        GetTopSupportFromHistogam (θ, H[$l(s) + 1$])
8: **for each** α, $support(\alpha) \geq next\_level\_top\_support$ **do**
9:     **Call** TopSequencesTraversal($s \diamond \alpha$, $D_{s \diamond \alpha}$, min_ℓ);
10: **return**;

Our goal is to develop an algorithm that builds as few prefix-projected databases with support less than $final\_support$ as possible. Actually, we can first search the most promising branches in the prefix search tree in Figure 2 and use the raised $min\_support$ to search the remaining branches. The algorithm is outlined as follows: (1) initially (during the first pass), build a small, limited number of projected databases for each prefix length, $l(l < min\_\ell)$, (2) then (in the succeeding passes) gradually relax the limitation on the number of projected databases that are built, and (3) repeat the mining again. Each time when we reach a projected database D_s, where $l(s) = min\_\ell - 1$, we mine D_s completely and use the mined sequences to raise $min\_support$. The stop condition for this multi-pass mining process is when all projected databases at level min_ℓ with support greater than $min\_support$ are mined completely. We limit the number of projected databases constructed at each level by setting different support thresholds for different levels. The reasoning behind this is that if we set a support threshold that is passed by a small number of projected databases at some higher level, in many cases this support will not be passed by any projected databases at lower levels and vice versa.

Algorithm 3.1 performs a single pass of TSP. Line 2-4

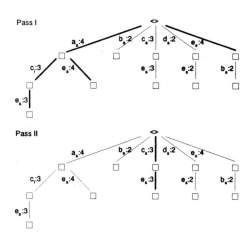

Figure 3. Multi-Pass Mining

calls PrefixSpan to find frequent patterns which have prefix s. Once there are at least k closed patterns discovered, it raises the minimum support threshold to the support of the least frequent one. We call this procedure PrefixSpan-WithSupportRaising. In order to find the complete result set we need to call Algorithm 3.1 multiple times to cover all potential branches. The limit on the number of projected databases that are built during each pass is enforced by function GetTopSupportFromHistogam, which uses histograms of the supports of the sequences found earlier in the same pass or in the previous passes and the factor θ which is set in the beginning of each pass. Figure 3 illustrates the multi-pass mining on the problem setting from Example 1, the bolded lines show the branches traversed in each pass. In this example, the mining is completed after the second pass because after this pass the support threshold is raised to 3 and there are no unvisited branches with support greater than or equal to 3.

In our current implementation the factor θ is a percentile in the histograms and the function GetTopSupportFromHistogam returns the value of the support at θ-th percentile in the histogram. The initial value of θ is calculated in the beginning of the mining process using the following formula: $\theta = (k*minl)/N_{Items}$, where N_{Items} is the number of distinct items in the database. In each of the following passes the value of θ is doubled. Our experiments show that the performance of the top-k mining algorithm does not change significantly for different initial values of θ as long as they are small enough to divide the mining process in several passes.

In order to efficiently implement the multi-pass mining process described above we use a tree structure that stores the projected databases built in the previous passes. We call this structure *Projected Database Tree* or PDB_Tree. PDB_Tree is a memory representation of the prefix search

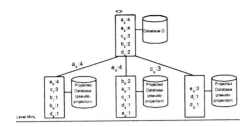

Figure 4. PDB_Tree: A tree of prefix-projected databases

tree and stores information about the partially mined projected databases during the multi-pass mining process. Since PDB_Tree consists of partially mined projected databases, once a projected database is completely mined, it can be removed from the PDB_Tree. Because of this property, PDB_Tree has a significantly smaller size than the whole prefix search tree traversed during the mining process. The maximum depth of PDB_Tree is always less than min_ℓ because TSP mines all projected databases at level min_ℓ and below completely. In order to further reduce the memory required to store PDB_Tree, we use pseudo-projected databases [7] at the nodes of PDB_Tree, i.e., we only store lists of pointers to the actual sequences in the original sequence database. Figure 4 shows an example of PDB_Tree, where each searched node is associated with a projected database.

3.3 Verification of Closed Patterns

Now we come back to the question raised earlier in this section: how can we guarantee that at least k *closed patterns* are found so that $min\_support$ can be raised in mining? Currently there is only one other algorithm, CloSpan, that mines closed sequential patterns. CloSpan stores candidates for closed patterns during the mining process and in its last step it finds and removes the non-closed ones. This approach is infeasible in top-k mining since it needs to know which pattern is closed and accumulates at least k closed patterns before it starts to raise the minimum support. Thus closed pattern verification cannot be delayed to the final stage.

In order to raise $min\_support$ correctly, we need to maintain a result set to ensure that there exists no pattern in the database that can absorb more than one pattern in the current result set. Otherwise, if such a pattern exists, it may reduce the number of patterns in the result set down to below k and make the final result incomplete or incorrect. For example, assume $k = 2, min\_\ell = 2$, and the patterns found so far are: $\{\langle (a), (b) \rangle : 5, \langle (a), (c) \rangle : 5\}$. If these

patterns are used to raise $min\_support$ to **5** but later a pattern $\langle (a), (b), (c) \rangle : 5$ is found, the latter will absorb the first two. Then the result set will consist of only one pattern instead of 2. Thus it is not correct to set $min\_support$ to 5. In this case the correctness and completeness of the final result can be jeopardized because during some part of the mining one might have used an invalid support threshold.

Here we present a technique that handles this problem efficiently.

Definition 3.3 *Given a sequence s, $s \in D$, the set of the sequence IDs of all sequences in the database D that contain s is called sequence ID list, denoted by $SIDList(s)$. The sum of $SIDList(s)$ is called sequence ID sum, denoted by $SIDSum(s)$.*

We have the following results:

Remark 3.1 *Given sequences s' and s'', if $s' \sqsubseteq s''$ and $support(s') = support(s'')$ then $SIDList(s') = SIDList(s'')$ and $SIDSum(s') = SIDSum(s'')$.*

Lemma 3.1 *Given sequences s' and s'', if $support(s') = support(s'')$, $SIDList(s') \neq SIDList(s'')$, then neither s' is subpattern of s'', nor s'' is a subpattern of s'.*

Remark 3.2 *If there exists a frequent item $u, u \in I$, such that $support(s \diamond_i \langle (u) \rangle) = support(s)$ or $support(s \diamond_s \langle (u) \rangle) = support(s)$, then s should not be added to the current top-k result set, because there exists a superpattern of s with the same support.*

Based on Remarks 3.1 and 3.2 and Lemma 3.1, we developed an efficient verification mechanism to determine whether a pattern should be added to the top-k set and whether it should be used to raise the support threshold.

A prefix tree, called $TopK\_Tree$, is developed to store the current top-k result set in memory. Also, in order to improve the efficiency of the closed pattern verification, a hash table, called $SIDSum\_Hash$, is maintained that maps sequence id sums to the nodes in $TopK\_Tree$.

In our top-k mining algorithm when a new pattern is found the algorithm takes one of the following three actions: (1) *add_and_raise*: the pattern is added to the top-k result set and is used to raise the support threshold, (2) *add_but_no_raise*: the pattern is added to the top-k result set but is not used to raise the support threshold, and (3) *no_add*: the pattern is not added to the top-k result set.

Algorithm 3.3 implements closed pattern verification. Notice that Algorithm 3.3 returns add_but_no_raise for patterns that have the same SIDList as some other patterns that are already in the top-k result set. Such patterns are stored separately and are not used to raise the support threshold $min\_support$. This eliminates the problem mentioned earlier: If two patterns in the top-k result set are absorbed by a single new pattern, it may lead to less than k

---

Algorithm 3.2 Closed Pattern Verification

Input: A sequential pattern s

Output: One of the following three operations:

      add_and_raise, add_but_no_raise, and no_add.

1: **if** $\exists$ an item u, such that $support(s \diamond_i \langle(u)\rangle) = support(s)$ or $support(s \diamond_s \langle(u)\rangle) = support(s)$ **then**

      return(no_add);

2: **if** $SIDSum(s)$ is not in $SIDSum\_Hash$ **then**

      return(add_and_raise);

3: **for each** s' such that $SIDSum(s') = SIDSum(s)$ and $support(s') = support(s)$ **do**

4:     **if** $s \sqsubset s'$ **then return**(no_add);

5:     **if** $s' \sqsubset s$ **then**

6:       replace s' with s;

7:       **return**(add_but_no_raise);

8:     **if** $SIDList(s') = SIDList(s)$ **then**

10:       **return**(add_but_no_raise);

11: **return**(add_and_raise);

---

patterns in the result set. In summary, our strategy is to maintain top-k patterns in the result set where no two patterns can be absorbed by a single new pattern.

3.4 Applying the Minimum Length Constraint

Now we discuss how to reduce the search space using the minimum length constraint min_ℓ.

Remark 3.3 *(Minimum Length Constraint) For any sequence $s' \in D_s$ such that $l(s') + l(s) < min\_\ell$, the sequence s' will not contribute to a frequent sequential pattern of minimum length min_ℓ, and it can be removed from the projected database D_s.*

Based on Remark 3.3, when our algorithm builds a projected database, it checks each projected sequence to see whether it is shorter than $min\_\ell - l(s)$ before adding it to the projected database.

Notice that the minimum length constraint can be used to reduce the size of a projected database D_s only when $l(s) < min\_\ell - 1$. Thus when the prefix s is longer than $min\_\ell - 2$, the program does not need to check the length of the projected sequences.

3.5 Early Termination by Equivalence

Early termination by equivalence is a search space reduction technique developed in CloSpan [10]. Let $\mathcal{I}(D)$ represent the total number of items in D, defined as

$$\mathcal{I}(D) = \sum_{i=1}^{n} l(s_i).$$

We call $\mathcal{I}(D)$ the *size of the database*. For the sample dataset in Table 1, $\mathcal{I}(D) = 17$. The property of early termination by equivalence shows if two sequences $s \sqsubseteq s'$ and $\mathcal{I}(D_s) = \mathcal{I}(D_{s'})$, then $\forall \gamma, support(s \diamond \gamma) = support(s' \diamond \gamma)$. It means the descendants of s in the lexicographical sequence tree must not be closed. Furthermore, the descendants of s and s' are exactly the same. CloSpan uses this property to quickly prune the search space of s.

To facilitate early termination by equivalence in the top-k mining, we explore both the partially mined projected database tree, PDB_Tree, and the result set tree, $TopK\_Tree$. Two hash tables are maintained: one, called PDB_Hash, mapping databases sizes to nodes in PDB_Tree and the other, called $TopK\_Hash$, mapping databases sizes to nodes in $TopK\_Tree$.

For each new projected database D_s that is built, we search the two hash tables using $\mathcal{I}(D_s)$ as a key and check the following conditions:

- If there exists a sequence $s', s' \in PDB\_Tree$, such that $\mathcal{I}(D_s) = \mathcal{I}(D_{s'})$ and $s \sqsubseteq s'$ then stop the search of the branch of s.

- If there exists a sequence $s', s' \in PDB\_Tree$, such that $\mathcal{I}(D_s) = \mathcal{I}(D_{s'})$ and $s' \sqsubseteq s$ then remove s' from PDB_Tree and continue the mining of the branch of s.

- If there exists a sequence $s', s' \in TopK\_Tree$ and $s' \notin PDB\_Tree$, such that $\mathcal{I}(D_s) = \mathcal{I}(D_{s'})$ and $s \sqsubseteq s'$ then stop the search of the branch of s.

With this adoption of early termination in TSP, the performance of TSP is improved significantly.

4 Experimental Evaluation

This section reports the performance testing of TSP in large data sets. In particular, we compare the performance of TSP with CloSpan. The comparison is based on assigning the optimal $min\_support$ to CloSpan so that it generates the same set of top-k closed patterns as TSP for specified values of k and min_ℓ. The optimal $min\_support$ is found by first running TSP under each experimental condition. Since this optimal $min\_support$ is hard to speculate without mining, even if TSP achieves the similar performance with CloSpan, TSP is still more valuable since it is much easier for a user to work out a k value for top-k patterns than a specific $min\_support$ value.

The datasets used in this study are generated by a synthetic data generator provided by IBM. It can be obtained at http://www.almaden.ibm.com/cs/quest. Table 2 shows the major parameters that can be specified in this data generator, more details are available in [1].

abbr.	meaning
D	Number of sequences in 000s
C	Average itemsets per sequence
T	Average items per itemset
N	Number of different items in 000s
S	Average itemsets in maximal patterns
I	Average items in maximal patterns

Table 2. Synthetic Data Parameters

All experiments were performed on a 1.8GHz Intel Pentium-4 PC with 512MB main memory, running Windows XP Professional. Both algorithms are written in C++ using STL and compiled with Visual Studio .Net 2002.

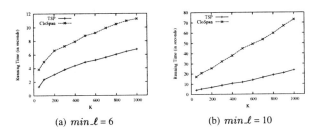

(a) $min\_\ell = 6$ (b) $min\_\ell = 10$

Figure 5. Dataset D100C5T2.5N10S4I2.5

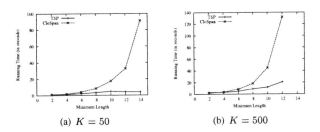

(a) $K = 50$ (b) $K = 500$

Figure 6. Dataset D100C5T2.5N10S4I2.5

The performance of the two algorithms has been compared by varying min_ℓ and k. When k is fixed, its value is set to either 50 or 500 which covers the range of typical values for this parameter. Figures 5 and 6 show performance results for dataset D100C5T2.5N10S4I2.5. This dataset consists of relatively short sequences, each sequence contains 5 itemsets on average and the itemsets have 2.5 items on average. The experimental results show that TSP mines this dataset very efficiently and in most cases runs several times faster than CloSpan. The difference between the running time of the two algorithms is more significant when longer patterns are mined (larger min_ℓ). There are two major reasons for the better performance of TSP in this dataset. First, it uses the min_ℓ constraint to prune short

sequences during the mining process which in some cases significantly reduces the search space and improves the performance. Second, TSP has more efficient closed pattern verification scheme and stores a result set that contains only a small number of closed patterns, while CloSpan keeps a larger number of candidate patterns that could not be closed and removes the non-closed ones at the end of the mining processes.

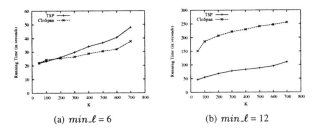

(a) $min\_\ell = 6$ (b) $min\_\ell = 12$

Figure 7. Dataset D100C10T10N10S6I5

Figures 7 and 8 show the experiments on dataset D100C10T10N10S4I5 which consists of longer patterns compared to the previous one. The average number of itemsets per sequence in this dataset is increased from 5 to 10. For this dataset the two algorithms have comparable performance. The reasons for the similar performance of the two algorithms are that the benefit of applying the min_ℓ constraint is smaller because the sequences in the dataset are longer, and also the major cost for mining this dataset is the construction of prefix-projected databases which has similar implementation in both algorithms.

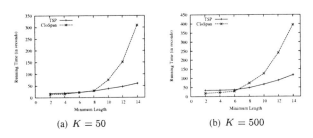

(a) $K = 50$ (b) $K = 500$

Figure 8. Dataset D100C10T10N10S6I5

As we can see, min_ℓ plays an important role in improving the performance of TSP. If we ignore the performance gain caused by min_ℓ, TSP can achieve the competitive performance with well tuned CloSpan. We may wonder why minimum support-raising cannot boost the performance like what min_ℓ does. The rule of thumb is that the support of upper level nodes should be greater than lower level nodes (the support of short sequences should be greater than that of long sequences). Then, few nodes in the upper level can be pruned by the minimum support. Since we cannot access the long patterns without accessing the short patterns, we have to search most of upper level nodes in the prefix search tree. As we know, the projected database of the upper level nodes is very big and expensive to compute. Thus, if we cannot reduce checking the upper level nodes' projected databases, it is unlikely we can benefit from support-raising technique a lot. However, the support-raising technique can free us from setting minimum support without sacrificing the performance.

5 Related Work

Agrawal and Srikant [1] introduced the sequential pattern mining problem. Efficient algorithms like GSP [8], SPADE [11], PrefixSpan [7], and SPAM [2] were developed. Because the number of frequent patterns is too huge, recently several algorithms were proposed for closed pattern mining: CLOSET [6] and CHARM [12] for closed itemset mining, CloSpan [10] for closed sequence mining, and CloseGraph [9] for closed graph mining. All of these algorithms can deliver much less patterns than frequent pattern mining, but do not lose any information. Top-k closed pattern mining intends to reduce the number of patterns further by only mining the most frequent ones.

As to top-k closed sequential pattern mining, CloSpan [10] and TFP [4] are the most related work. CloSpan mines frequent closed sequential patterns while TFP discovers top-k closed itemsets. The algorithm proposed in the present paper adopts the problem definition of TFP and provides an efficient solution to this problem in the more challenging setting of mining frequent closed sequential patterns in sequence databases.

6 Conclusions

In this paper, we have studied the problem of mining top-k (frequent) closed sequential patterns with length no less than min_ℓ and proposed an efficient mining algorithm TSP, with the following distinct features: (1) it adopts a novel, multi-pass search space traversal strategy that allows mining of the most frequent patterns early in the mining process and fast raising of the minimum support threshold $min\_support$ dynamically, which is then used to prune the search space, (2) it performs efficient closed pattern verification during the mining process that ensures accurate raising of $min\_support$ and derives correct and complete results, and (3) it develops several additional optimization techniques, including applying the minimum length constraint, min_ℓ, and incorporating the early termination proposed in CloSpan.

Our experimental study shows that the proposed algorithm delivers competitive performance and in many cases outperforms CloSpan, currently the most efficient algorithm for (closed) sequential pattern mining, even when

CloSpan is running with the best tuned $min\_support$. Through this study, we conclude that mining top-k closed sequential patterns without $min\_support$ is practical and in many cases more preferable than the traditional minimum support threshold based sequential pattern mining.

References

[1] R. Agrawal and R. Srikant. Mining sequential patterns. In *Proc. 1995 Int. Conf. Data Engineering (ICDE'95)*, pages 3–14, Taipei, Taiwan, Mar. 1995.

[2] J. Ayres, J. E. Gehrke, T. Yiu, and J. Flannick. Sequential pattern mining using bitmaps. In *Proc. 2002 ACM SIGKDD Int. Conf. Knowledge Discovery in Databases (KDD'02)*, pages 429–435, Edmonton, Canada, July 2002.

[3] S. Guha, R. Rastogi, and K. Shim. Rock: A robust clustering algorithm for categorical attributes. In *Proc. 1999 Int. Conf. Data Engineering (ICDE'99)*, pages 512–521, Sydney, Australia, Mar. 1999.

[4] J. Han, J. Wang, Y. Lu, and P. Tzvetkov. Mining top-k frequent closed patterns without minimum support. In *Proc. 2002 Int. Conf. on Data Mining (ICDM'02)*, pages 211–218, Maebashi, Japan, Dec. 2002.

[5] H. Mannila, H. Toivonen, and A. I. Verkamo. Discovering frequent episodes in sequences. In *Proc. 1995 Int. Conf. Knowledge Discovery and Data Mining (KDD'95)*, pages 210–215, Montreal, Canada, Aug. 1995.

[6] J. Pei, J. Han, and R. Mao. CLOSET: An efficient algorithm for mining frequent closed itemsets. In *Proc. 2000 ACM-SIGMOD Int. Workshop Data Mining and Knowledge Discovery (DMKD'00)*, pages 11–20, Dallas, TX, May 2000.

[7] J. Pei, J. Han, B. Mortazavi-Asl, H. Pinto, Q. Chen, U. Dayal, and M.-C. Hsu. PrefixSpan: Mining sequential patterns efficiently by prefix-projected pattern growth. In *Proc. 2001 Int. Conf. Data Engineering (ICDE'01)*, pages 215–224, Heidelberg, Germany, April 2001.

[8] R. Srikant and R. Agrawal. Mining sequential patterns: Generalizations and performance improvements. In *Proc. 5th Int. Conf. Extending Database Technology (EDBT'96)*, pages 3–17, Avignon, France, Mar. 1996.

[9] X. Yan and J. Han. CloseGraph: Mining closed frequent graph patterns. In *Proc. 2003 ACM SIGKDD Int. Conf. Knowledge Discovery and Data Mining (KDD'03)*, Washington, D.C., Aug. 2003.

[10] X. Yan, J. Han, and R. Afshar. CloSpan: Mining closed sequential patterns in large datasets. In *Proc. 2003 SIAM Int. Conf. Data Mining (SDM'03)*, pages 166–177, San Fransisco, CA, May 2003.

[11] M. Zaki. SPADE: An efficient algorithm for mining frequent sequences. *Machine Learning*, 40:31–60, 2001.

[12] M. J. Zaki and C. J. Hsiao. CHARM: An efficient algorithm for closed itemset mining. In *Proc. 2002 SIAM Int. Conf. Data Mining (SDM'02)*, pages 457–473, Arlington, VA, April 2002.

Interactive Visualization and Navigation in Large Data Collections using the Hyperbolic Space

Jörg Walter · Jörg Ontrup · Daniel Wessling · Helge Ritter

Neuroinformatics Group · Department of Computer Science
University of Bielefeld · D-33615 Bielefeld · Germany
E-mail: walter@techfak.uni-bielefeld.de

Abstract

We propose the combination of two recently introduced methods for the interactive visual data mining of large collections of data. Both, Hyperbolic Multi-Dimensional Scaling (HMDS) and Hyperbolic Self-Organizing Maps (HSOM) employ the extraordinary advantages of the hyperbolic plane (H2): (i) the underlying space grows exponentially with its radius around each point - ideal for embedding high-dimensional (or hierarchical) data; (ii) the Poincaré model of the $\mathbb{IH}^2$ exhibits a fish-eye perspective with a focus area and a context preserving surrounding; (iii) the mouse binding of focus-transfer allows intuitive interactive navigation.

The HMDS approach extends multi-dimensional scaling and generates a spatial embedding of the data representing their dissimilarity structure as faithfully as possible. It is very suitable for interactive browsing of data object collections, but calls for batch precomputation for larger collection sizes.

The HSOM is an extension of Kohonen's Self-Organizing Map and generates a partitioning of the data collection assigned to an $\mathbb{IH}^2$ tessellating grid. While the algorithm's complexity is linear in the collection size, the data browsing is rigidly bound to the underlying grid.

By integrating the two approaches we gain the synergetic effect of adding advantages of both. And the hybrid architecture uses consistently the $\mathbb{IH}^2$ visualization and navigation concept. We present the successfully application to a text mining example involving the Reuters-21578 text corpus.

1. Introduction

The demand for techniques handling large collections of data is rapidly growing. While the power of information systems increases – the amount of information a human user can directly digest does not. The challenge is to provide good clues for the right questions, which is the key to discoveries. The human expert possess not only valuable background knowledge, intuition and creativity – he is also vested with powerful pattern recognition and processing capabilities especially for the visual information channel. The design goals for an optimal user–data interaction strongly depend on the given exploration task but they certainly include an easy and intuitive navigation with strong support for the user's orientation.

Figure 1. Displaying larger collections of data with limited display area requires careful usage of space. The allocation of spatial representation for providing overview *and* detail is a challenge. After choosing the level of detail the data layout operated on the canvas ("layout space") before it is suitably projected onto the display area (e.g. after panning and zooming).

Visualizing large data collections has to provide means to effectively use a limited display space and give the user the overview as well as the details. Since most of available data display devices are two-dimensional – paper and screens – the following problem must be solved: finding a meaningful spatial mapping of data onto the display area. One limiting factor is the "restricted neighborhood" around a point in a Euclidean 2D surface. *Hyperbolic spaces* open an interesting loophole. The extraordinary property of exponential growth of neighborhood with increasing radius around all points enables us to build novel displays.

The *"hyperbolic tree viewer"*, developed at Xerox Parc [6], demonstrated the remarkably elegant interactive capabilities. The hyperbolic model appears as a continuously graded, focus+context mapping to the display. See [9, 10] for comparative studies with traditional display types.

Unfortunately, previous usage of direct hyperbolic visualization was limited to hierarchical, tree-like, or "quasigraph" data. Two reliefs were recently introduced, suggesting more general $\mathbb{IH}^2$-layout techniques: one generalizes Kohonen's SOM algorithm to the *Hyperbolic Self-Organizing Map algorithm* (HSOM) [11]; the other introduces *Hyperbolic Multi-Dimensional Scaling* (HMDS) [16] for a direct construction of a distance preserving embedding of high-dimensional data into the hyperbolic space.

In Sec. 2 and 3 we review the hyperbolic space and the three mentioned layout techniques for visualizing data in $I\!H^2$. Sec. 4 discusses a synthesis for a two step visualization architecture. Even though the look and feel of an interactive visualization and navigation cannot be really conveyed in a static format, we report in Sec. 5 several results and snapshots of an application to text mining. This approach allows to visualize, navigate and search in a space of documents appearing in the Reuters news stream.

2. The Hyperbolic Space $I\!H^2$

Historically, the hyperbolic space is a "recent" discovery in the 18th century. Lobachevsky, Bolyai, and Gauss independently discovered the non-Euclidean geometries by negating the "parallel axiom" which Euclid formulated 2300 years ago. Today we know three geometries with uniform curvature. Our daily experience is governed by the *flat* or *Euclidean* geometry with zero curvature. Still familiar is the *spherical geometry* with *positive* curvature – describing the surface of a sphere, like the earth or an orange. Its counterpart with constant *negative* curvature is known as the *hyperbolic plane* $I\!H^2$ (with analogous generalizations to higher dimensions) [2, 14]. Unfortunately, there is no "perfect" embedding of the $I\!H^2$ in $I\!R^3$, which makes it harder to grasp the unusual properties of the $I\!H^2$. Local patches resemble the situation at a saddle point, where the neighborhood grows faster than in flat space (see Fig. 2). Standard textbooks on Riemannian geometry (see, e.g. [7]) show that the circumference c and area a of a circle of radius ρ in $I\!H^2$ are given by

$$\text{area:} \quad a(\rho) \quad = \quad 4\pi \sinh^2(\rho/2) \quad (1)$$
$$\text{circumference:} \quad c(\rho) \quad = \quad 2\pi \sinh(\rho) . \quad (2)$$

This bears two remarkable asymptotic properties, *(i)* for small radius ρ the space "looks flat" since $a(\rho) \approx \pi\rho^2$ and $c(r) \approx 2\pi\rho$. *(ii)* For larger ρ both grow *exponentially* with the radius. As observed in [6, 5], this trait makes the hyperbolic space ideal for embedding hierarchical structures. Fig. 2 illustrates the spatial relations by embedding a small patch of the $I\!H^2$ in $I\!R^3$.

To use the visualization potential of the $I\!H^2$ we must solve the two problems displayed before in Fig. 1. Now we turn to the projection problem, which was solved for the $I\!H^2$ more than a century ago.

2.1. The Projection Solution for $I\!H^2$

The perfect projection into the flat display area should preserve length, area, and angles ($\approx$form). But it lays in the nature of a curvated space to resist the attempt to simultaneously achieve these goals. Consequently several projections

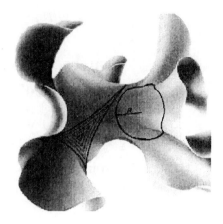

Figure 2. There is literally more room in hyperbolic space than in Euclidean space, as shown in this illustrated embedding of the hyperbolic plane into 3D Euclidean space (courtesy of Jeffrey Weeks). *(Right:)* Exponential growth (Eq. 1) of the circumference $c(\rho)$ and area $a(\rho)$ is experienced if a "circle" with radius ρ is drawn in the wrinkling structure. *(Left:)* The sum of angles in a triangle is smaller than $180°$.

or *maps* of the hyperbolic space were developed, four are especially well examined: *(i)* the *Minkowski*, *(ii)* the *upperhalf plane*, *(iii)* the *Klein-Beltrami*, and *(iv)* the *Poincaré* or *disk* mapping. See [2] for more details and geometric mappings to transform in-between *(i)*–*(iv)*.

The Poincaré projection is for our purpose the most suitable. Its main characteristics are:

Display compatibility: The infinite large area of the $I\!H^2$ is mapped entirely into a circle, the Poincaré disk *PD*. This infinity representation fascinated Maurits Escher and inspired him to several wood cuts [15].

Circle rim "$= \infty$": All remote points are close to the rim, without touching it.

Focus+Context: The *focus* can be moved to each location in $I\!H^2$, like a *"fovea"*. The zooming factor is 0.5 in the center and falls (exponentially) off with distance to the fovea. Therefore, the context appears very natural. As more remote things are, the less spatial representation is assigned in the current display.

Lines become circles: All $I\!H^2$-lines[1] appear as *circle* arc segments of centered straight lines in *PD*(both belong to the set of so-called "generalized circles"). There extensions cross the *PD*-rim always perpendicular on both ends.

Conformal mapping: Angles (and therefore form) relations are preserved in *PD*, area and length relations obviously not.

Regular tessellations with triangles offer richer possibilities than the $I\!R^2$. It turns out that there is an infinite set of choices to tessellate $I\!H^2$: for any integer $n \geq 7$, one can construct a regular tessellations in which n triangles meet at each vertex (in contrast to the plane with allows only

---

[1] A *line* is by definition the shortest path between two points

$n = 3, 4, 6$ and the sphere only $n = 3, 4, 5$). Fig. 3 depicts examples for $n = 7$ and $n = 10$.

One way to compute these tessellations algorithmically is by repeated application of a suitable set of generators of their symmetry group to a suitably sized "starting triangle" (see also Eq. 3 and [11]).

2.2. Moving the Focus

For changing the focus point in *PD* we need a translation operation which can be bound to mouse click and drag events. In the Poincaré disk model the *Möbius* transformation $T(z)$ is the appropriate solution. By describing the Poincaré disk *PD* as the unit circle in the complex plane, the isometric transformations for a point $z \in PD$ can be written

$$z' = T(z; c, \theta) = \frac{\theta z + c}{\bar{c}\theta z + 1}, \quad |\theta| = 1, \ |c| < 1. \quad (3)$$

Here the complex number θ describes a pure rotation of *PD* around the origin 0. The following translation by c maps the origin to c and $-c$ becomes the new center 0 (if $\theta = 1$). The *Möbius* transformations are also called the "circle automorphies" of the complex plane, since they describe the transformations from circles to (generalized) circles. Here they serve to translate $I\!H^2$ straight lines to lines – both *appearing* as generalized circles in the *PD* projection. For further details, see [5, 15].

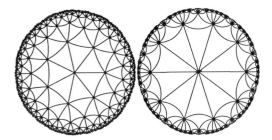

Figure 3. Regular $I\!H^2$ tessellation with congruent triangles. *(Left:)* Here, $n = 7$ triangles meet at each vertex. Due to the angular deficit of the triangle sum in $I\!H^2$-triangles, the minimal number to complete a circle is 7. *(Right:)* For $n = 10$ the triangle side length increases to perfectly fill the plane. Note, that all $I\!H^2$-lines appear as circle arcs, which extend perpendicular to the "∞-rim".

3. Layout Techniques in $I\!H^2$

In the following section we discuss three layout techniques for the $I\!H^2$.

3.1. Hyperbolic Tree Layout (HTL) for Tree-Like Graph Data

Now we turn to the question raised earlier: how to accommodate data in the hyperbolic space. A solution to this question for the case of acyclic, tree-like graph data was provided by Lamping and Rao [6, 5]. By using mainly successive applications of transformation Eq. 3 they developed (and patented) a method to find a suitable layout for this data type in $I\!H^2$. Each tree node receives a certain open space "pie segment", where the node chooses the locations of its siblings. For all its siblings i it calls recursively the layout-routine after applying the Möbius transformation Eq. 3 in order to center i.

Tamara Munzner developed another graph layout algorithm for the three-dimensional hyperbolic space [8]. While she gains much more space for the layout, the problem of more complex navigation (and viewport control) in 3D and, more serious, the problem of occlusion appears.

The next two layout techniques are freed from the requirement of hierarchical data.

3.2. Hyperbolic Self-Organizing Map (HSOM)

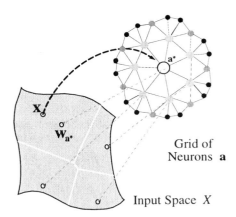

Figure 4. The "Self-Organizing Map" ("SOM") is formed by a grid of processing units, called formal *neurons*. Here the usual case, a two-dimensional grid is illustrated at the right side. Each neuron has a reference, or prototype vector $\mathbf{w}_a$ attached, which is a point in the embedding input space X. A presented input $\mathbf{x}$ will select that neuron with $\mathbf{w}_a$ closest to it. The HSOM uses a hyperbolic grid as displayed in Fig. 3 and the appropriate neighborhood function $h(\cdot)$.

The standard Self-Organizing Map (SOM) algorithm is used in many application for learning and visualization (Kohonen, e.g. [3]). Fig. 4 illustrated the basic operation. The feature map is built by a lattice of nodes (or formal neurons) $a \in A$, each with a reference vector or "prototype vector" $\mathbf{w}_a$ attached, projecting into the input space X. The response of a SOM to an input vector $\mathbf{x}$ is determined by the reference vector $\mathbf{w}_{a^*}$ of the discrete "best-match" node a^*, i.e. the node which has its prototype vector $\mathbf{w}_a$ closest to the given input

$$a^* = \underset{\forall a \in A}{\arg\min} \ \|\mathbf{w}_a - \mathbf{x}\|. \quad (4)$$

The distribution of the reference vectors $\mathbf{w}_a$, is iteratively adapted by a sequence of training vectors $\mathbf{x}$. After finding the best-match neuron a^* *all* reference vectors are updated $\mathbf{w}_a^{(new)} := \mathbf{w}_a^{(old)} + \Delta \mathbf{w}_a$ by the adaptation rule

$$\Delta \mathbf{w}_a = \epsilon \, h(a, a^*) \, (\mathbf{x} - \mathbf{w}_a). \quad \text{with} \quad (5)$$
$$h(a, a^*) = \exp\left[-(d_{a,a^*}/\lambda)^2\right] \quad (6)$$

Here $h(a, a^*)$ is a bell shaped Gaussian centered at the "winner" a^* and decaying with increasing distance $d_{a,a^*} = |\mathbf{g}_a - \mathbf{g}_a^*|$ in the neuron grid $\{\mathbf{g}_a\}$. Thus, each node or "neuron" in the neighborhood of the "winner" a^* participates in the current learning step (as indicated by the gray shading in Fig. 4.)

The network starts with a given node grid A and a random initialization of the reference vectors. During the course of learning, the width λ of the neighborhood bell function and the learning step size parameter ϵ is continuously decreased in order to allow more and more specialization and fine tuning of the (then increasingly) weakly coupled neurons.

This neighborhood cooperation in the adaptation algorithm has important advantages: *(i)* it is able to generate *topological order* between the $\mathbf{w}_a$ which means that similar inputs are mapped to neighboring nodes; *(ii)* As a result, the convergence of the algorithm can be *sped up* by involving a whole group of neighboring neurons in each learning step.

The structure of this neighborhood is essentially governed by the structure of $h(a, a^*) = h(d_{a,a^*})$ – therefore also called the *neighborhood* function. Most learning and visualization applications choose d_{a,a^*} as distances in a regular two and three-dimensional euclidian lattice.

SOMs in non-euclidian spaces were suggested by one of the authors [11]. The core idea of the Hyperbolic Self-Organizing Map (HSOM) is to employ a $I\!H^2$-grid of nodes. A particular convenient choice is to take the $\{\mathbf{g}_a\} \in PD$ of a finite patch of the triangular tessellation grid introduced in Sec. 2.1. The internode distance is computed in the appropriate the Poincaré metric as

$$d_{a,a^*} = 2 \operatorname{arctanh}\left(\frac{|\mathbf{g}_a - \mathbf{g}_{a^*}|}{|1 - \mathbf{g}_a \bar{\mathbf{g}}_{a^*}|}\right). \quad (7)$$

3.3. Hyperbolic Multidimensional Scaling (HMDS)

Multidimensional scaling refers to a class of algorithms for finding a suitable representation of *proximity* relations of N objects by distances between points in a low dimensional – usually Euclidean – space. In the following we represent proximity as *dissimilarity* values between pairs of objects, mathematically written as dissimilarity $\delta_{ij} \in \mathbb{R}_0^+$ between the i and j item. As usual we assume symmetry, i.e. $\delta_{ij} = \delta_{ji}$. Often the raw dissimilarity distribution is

not suitable for the low-dimensional embedding and an additional δ-processing step is applied. We model it here as a monotonic transformation $D(.)$ of dissimilarities δ_{ij} into *disparities* $D_{ij} = D(\delta_{ij})$.

The goal of the MDS algorithm is to find a spatial representation $\mathbf{x}_i$ of each object i in the L-dimensional space, where the pair distances $d_{ij} \equiv d(\mathbf{x}_i, \mathbf{x}_j)$ match the disparities D_{ij} as faithfully as possible $\forall_{i \neq j} D_{ij} \approx d_{ij}$. The pair distance is usually measured by the Euclidian distance:

$$d_{ij} = \|\mathbf{x}_i - \mathbf{x}_j\| \quad \text{with} \quad \mathbf{x}_i \in \mathbb{R}^L, \ i, j \in \{1, 2, ..N\} \quad (8)$$

One of the most widely known MDS algorithms was introduced by Sammon [12] in 1969. He formulates a minimization problem of a cost function which sums over the squares of disparities–distance misfits, here written as

$$E(\{\mathbf{x}_i\}) = \sum_{i=1}^{N} \sum_{j>i} w_{ij}(d_{ij} - D_{ij})^2. \quad (9)$$

The factors w_{ij} are introduced to weight the disparities individually and also to normalize the cost function E to be independent to the absolute scale of the disparities D_{ij}. Depending on the given analysis task the factors can be chosen to weight all the disparities equally – the *global* variant $(w_{ij}^{(g)} = const)$ – or to emphasize the *local* structure by reducing the influence of larger disparities $(w_{ij}^{(l)}$, which we are using in the following)

$$w_{ij}^{(g)} = \frac{1}{\sum_{k=1}^{N} \sum_{l>k} D_{kl}^2}, \quad w_{ij}^{(l)} = \frac{2}{N(N-1)} \frac{1}{D_{ij}^2}. \quad (10)$$

Note that the latter is undefined if any pair has zero disparity. In his original work [12] Sammon suggested an *intermediate* normalization $w_{ij}^{(m)} = (\sum_{k=1}^{N} \sum_{l>k} D_{kl})^{-1} D_{ij}^{-1}$. The set of $\mathbf{x}_i$ is found by a gradient descent procedure, minimizing iteratively the cost or stress function Eq. 9. The reader is referred to [12, 1] for further details on this and other MDS algorithms.

The recently introduced Hyperbolic Multi-Dimensional Scaling (HMDS) [16] combines the concept of MDS and hyperbolic geometry. The core idea turns out to be very simple: instead of finding a MDS solution in the low-dimensional Euclidean $\mathbb{R}^L$ and transferring it to the $I\!H^2$ (which can not work well), the MDS formalism operates in the hyperbolic space from the beginning. The key point is Eq. 8. The Euclidean distance in the target space is replaced by the appropriate distance metric for the Poincaré model (see, e.g. [7] and compare Eq. 7)

$$d_{ij} = 2 \operatorname{arctanh}\left(\frac{|\mathbf{x}_i - \mathbf{x}_j|}{|1 - \mathbf{x}_i \bar{\mathbf{x}}_j|}\right), \quad \mathbf{x}_i, \mathbf{x}_j \in PD. \quad (11)$$

While the gradients $\partial d_{ij,q}/\partial x_{i,q}$ required for the gradient descent are rather simple to compute for the Euclidean geometry, the case becomes complex for Eq. 11.[2] Details can be found in [16, 15].

Disparity preprocessing: Due to the non-linearity of Eq. 11, the preprocessing function D(.) (see Sec. 3.3) has more influence in $I\!H^2$. Consider, e.g., linear rescaling of the dissimilarities $D_{ij} = \alpha\delta_{ij}$: in the Euclidean case the visual structure is not affected – only magnified by α. In contrast in $I\!H^2$, α scales the distribution and with it the amount of curvature felt by the data. The optimal α depends on the given task, the dataset, and its dissimilarity structure. We set α manually and choose a compromise between visibility of the entire structure and space for navigation in the detail-rich areas.

4. Hyperbolic Data Viewer: Combining the advantages

Before we introduce a new hybrid architecture, we first compare the advantages and disadvantages of the three $I\!H^2$ layout methods with respect to several aspects.

Input data type: The HTL requires acyclic graph data and is therefore limited to hierarchically ordered data (preferably balanced with a branch count ≈ 4–12).

The HSOM processed only vectorial data representations – while the HMDS uses dissimilarity data. Since a suitable distance function can directly transform any data type into dissimilarly data (not vice versa) and handling of missing data is easy, this can considered the most general data type.

Scaling behavior for the number of objects N: Both, HTL and HSOM share the advantage of linear scaling with the number of objects. HSOM scales also linearly with the input space dimension and the number of nodes. HMDS does not scale well and requires to process $N(N-1)/2$ distance pairs. When N grows to several hundred objects, the layout generation becomes slow and the results less convincing. Then precomputation may help for undamped interactive exploration.

Layout result: the HTL returns the $I\!H^2$-location determined by the recursive space partitioning.

The HSOM returns the rigid grid, i.e., the triangular tessellation grid. Each object or document is mapped to the node with the best matching prototype vectors assigned (Eq. 4). Each node is associated with two sources of descriptive information: the collected set of assigned objects and the prototype vector representing the group. Those informations can be transformed in various kinds of graphical attribution and annotation.

In contrast to the former, the layout results of the HMDS directly carry information on the data level, since the spatial locations represent the similarity structure of the given pair distance data. Therefore, the map metaphor of closeness and proximity is here brought to the detail level.

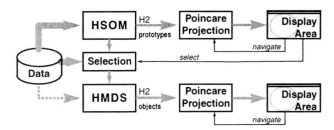

Figure 5. The proposed architecture combines the advantages of the two layout techniques: *(upper part)* the HSOM for obtaining a coarse map of a large data collection and *(lower part)* the HMDS for a mapping smaller data set to a spatially continuous representation of data relationships. The display concept is unified: both employ the extraordinary visualization and navigation features of the hyperbolic plane.

New objects: For the HTL a new object requires a new partial layout of the smallest subtree(s) containing the new objects.

The HSOM maps a new object to the best-matching node, i.e. a location in the map. The mapping time scales with the grid size since it involves number of node many comparisons. Furthermore the architecture many choose to implement online learning in order to adapt to new training data.

The HMDS requires a new minimization of the global cost function. For speedup, it can employ the previous object locations as start configuration.

New Hybrid Architecture: The previous discussion of advantages and disadvantages of the layout techniques motivates the here proposed synthesis of three core components: *(i)* the HSOM for building a coarse-grain theme map in a self-organized manner; *(ii)* HMDS for detailed inspection of data subsets where data similarities are continously reflected as spatial proximities; *(iii)* the display paradigm employs in both cases the hyperbolic plane in order to profit from its focus and context technique. Fig. 5 displays the basic architecture.

5. Application to Navigation in Unstructured Text

In times of exponential growth of digital information the semantic navigation in datasets – particularly for the case of unstructured text documents – is a major challenge. In this experiment we demonstrate the application of the proposed architecture to this situation.

As an example we use the "Reuters-21578"[3] collection

---

[2]Note, no complex gradient information is required in the HSOM approach.

[3]As compiled by David Lewis from the AT&T Research Lab in 1987. The data can be found at http://www.daviddlewis.com/resources/testcollections/reuters21578

of news articles that appeared on Reuters newswire between 1987/02/26 and 1987/10/20. Most of the documents were manually tagged with 135 different category names such as "earn", "trade" or "jobs". We employed the 9603 documents of the training set from the "ModApte" split to form the HSOM input vectors **x** using the standard bag-of-words model using the TFIDF scheme (term frequency times inverse document frequency) with a 5561 dimensional vector space (equals # derived word stems).

Distances and therewith dissimilarities of two documents are computed with the cosine metric

$$\delta_{ij} = 1 - \cos(\vec{f}_{t_i}, \vec{f}_{t_j}) = 1 - \vec{f}'_{t_i}\vec{f}'_{t_j}, \text{ with } \vec{f}' = \frac{\vec{f}}{||\vec{f}||} \quad (12)$$

and efficiently implemented by storing the normalized document feature vectors $\vec{f}'$.

5.1. Interactive Browsing of the Overview Map

Embedding the 2D Poincaré Model in 3D Euclidean space and placing at each node position a 3D glyph allows for the simultaneous visualization of several attributes at once. The glyph size, form, color or height above the PD ground plane might characterize the number of documents, the predominant category in the corresponding node or the number of new documents mapped.

Depending on the size of the text database to be mined, the number of nodes for the HSOM is chosen. In Figure 6 a HSOM with a total of 1306 nodes is shown. Since the HMDS approach can handle sizes of several hundred documents, such a map could easily contain a million articles.

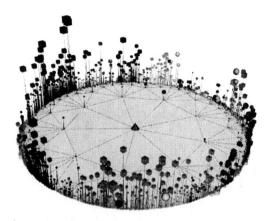

Figure 6. A HSOM projection of a large collection of newswire articles forms semantically related category clusters (shown as different glyphs).

In case of the Reuters-21578 collection we show results with a HSOM consisting of a tessellation with 3 "rings" and 8 neighbors per node, resulting in 161 prototype vectors as shown in Figure 7. By mapping the 12902 documents of the Reuters-21578 training and test collection we have a mean

of 80 documents per node, which are given to the HMDS module for further inspection. This number of documents can be handled in real time by HMDS and allows an on-line interactive text mining process.

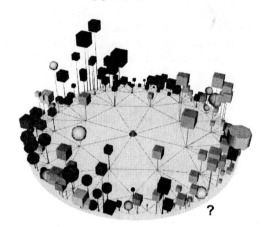

Figure 7. The Reuters-21578 corpus coarsly mapped with a HSOM containing 161 nodes. The glyph size corresponds to the number of documents before 1987/04/07, the height above ground plane the number of articles after 1987/04/07.

Figure 7 is the initial point for an interactive text mining session we describe in the following. The global hyperbolic overview map reveals several large clusters which mainly contain the top 10 topics. There is only one larger glyph (at the 3 o'clock position) indicating documents not belonging to the 10 top categories. The area marked with the question mark "?" contains an isolated yellow sphere which is surrounded by green cubes. In Figure 8 the user has adjusted the fovea of the hyperbolic map to inspect this selected region more closely. The figure shows that the relation of the nodes in this region can now be inspected more easily while the global context is still in view. By interactively selecting a node, the HSOM prototype vectors are used to automatically generate a key word list which annotate and semantically describe the selected glyph. To this end, the words corresponding to the ten largest components of the reference vector are selected. These describe the prototype document which resembles a non-linear superposition of the texts for which this node is the best-match node. In our example the most prominent words "strike", "union" and "port" indicate that this area of the map probably contains articles describing worker strikes in ports.

By mouse selection, all node-assigned-documents are send to the HMDS module. Fig. 9 displays the HMDS result. The presentation here is a lean 2D display with minimal occlusion and uses markers for category indication of each object. Several clusters can be easily recognized. The "A" marked group is a category mixture while the others are quite homogeneous.

By turning on the labels the document title become visible and the semantic homogeneity can be verified. Fig. 10 displays a screen shot after sweeping the navigation focus

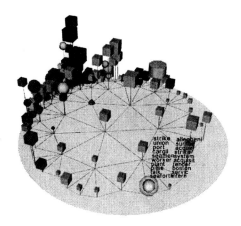

Figure 8. Inspection of a picked node by adjusting the fovea. The nodes' annotations were generated by evaluation of the corresponding prototype vectors. They indicate the nodes' contents and show the semantical relationship of adjacent nodes.

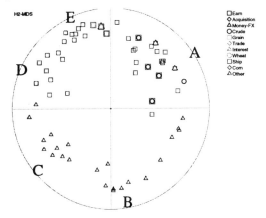

Figure 9. The screenshot of the HMDS visualizes all documents in the selected node #143 positioned in the $I\!H^2$. The legend at the right explains the marker type used for the top 10 categories each document can be labels with. The cross is for visual indication of a zero-point and markers A–E are an overlay for explanation.

to the cluster structure "C" in the previously lower left direction.

5.2. Similarity Search for Queries or New Documents

The hybrid approach can also be used to find similar documents to a query within a large collection. This is achieved by generating a query feature vector which is compared to all prototypes. The corresponding best match node is then visually highlighted, such that the user can adjust the focus of attention and "zoom" into that region. In order to demonstrate that context plays an important role, we formulate a query containing the word "strike" (which was the most important entry for the node inspected in Figure 8). Figure 11

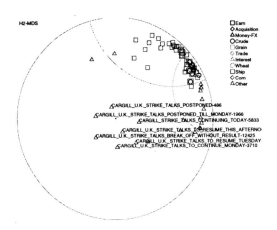

Figure 10. Navigation to the "C"-marked document cluster in Fig. 9. Now the cluster is focused and labels are turned on. All document are related to a strike at Cargill U.K. Ltd's oilseed processing plant at Seaforth in the beginning of 1987. Note how the quartering lines in Fig. 9 are transfered to other $I\!H^2$-lines(!) which appear as circle arc perpendicular to the rim.

shows a map where the focus is centered to the winning node of the query: *"USA leading the strike in a Gulf war against Iraq?"*.

Fig. 12 presents the drill-down with the HMDS and labels the neighboring documents to the new query. We find texts which deal with tensions in the gulf at that time and also mentions the word "strike" – but in another meaning than in the previously inspected node on a very distant HSOM node. A further query is a query from another news stream: CNN reported a very promising article "Bush: Ending Saddam's regime will bring stability to Mideast" (03/02/27[4]) which we find in the upper left corner in Fig. 12.

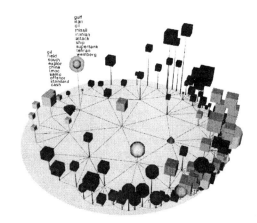

Figure 11. A query document was mapped to the HSOM and the fovea moved to the highlighted "best match" node. The automatic annotation scheme provides insightful informations about the semantic content in this area of the map.

---

[4] http://www.cnn.com/2003/WORLD/meast/02/27/sprj.irq.bush.speech/index.html

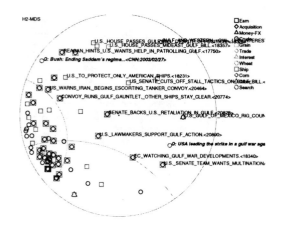

Figure 12. HMDS location of a manual query (4 o'clock) and another news document from these days (10 o'clock). The title reveal the successful mapping in a meaningful manner.

6. Discussion and Conclusion

Document visualization efforts like *ThemeScapes* [17] or the SOM based WebSOM [4] as well as Skupin's cartographic approach [13] have impressively demonstrated the usefulness of compressed, map-like 2D-representations of massive data collections, even if the data items contain extremely high-dimensional information such as text.

Recent work, such as [6, 11, 16] shows that the task of information visualization can significantly benefit from the use of hyperbolic space as a projection manifold. On the one hand it gains the exponentially growing space around each point which provides extra space for compressing semantic relationships. On the other hand the Poincaré model offers superb visualization and navigation properties, which were found to yield significant improvement in task time compared to traditional browsing methods [10]. By simple mouse interaction the focus can be transfered to any location of interest. The core area close to the center of the Poincaré disk magnifies the data with a zoom factor of 0.5 and decreases exponentially to the outer area. By this means a very natural visualization behavior is constructed: The fovea is an area with high resolution, while remote area are gradually compressed and still visible as context.

Another advantage is scalability. Due to the favorable linear scaling of $O(N)$ the HSOM can be used to form an initial overview map for very large data collections. This map then offers all strengths of the hyperbolic focus+context navigation, permitting the user to rapidly narrow down the to-be-investigated data to a much smaller subset which then can be interactively mapped to the individual level with the HMDS technique. Again, the same hyperbolic focus+context navigation is available.

Both approaches produce spatial representations of data similarity: The HSOM produces on a coarse level the "master map", providing the thematic overview. Additionally, the neurons of the HSOM can be regarded as data collect-

ing agents offering the potential to visualize temporal developments in data streams on the map. In the second stage the HMDS can represent the semantic closeness of the individual documents and is able to give a much more precise representation since is is decoupled from the rigid grid.

While the hybrid scheme may appear conceptually simple, we think that hybrid approaches to strike a flexible balance between scaling of computational demands and achievable precision can be crucial for making new methods applicable to massive data collections, an important goal towards which the present research is meant to be a modest but useful step.

References

[1] T. Cox and M. Cox. *Multidimensional Scaling*. Chapman and Hall, 1994.

[2] H.S.M. Coxeter. *Non-Euclidean Geometry*. University of Toronto Press, 1957.

[3] T. Kohonen. *Self-Organizing Maps*, volume 30 of *Springer Series in Information Sciences*. Springer, 1995.

[4] T. Kohonen et al. Organization of a massive document collection. *IEEE TNN Spec Issue Neural Networks for Data Mining and Knowledge Discovery*, 11(3):574–585, 2000.

[5] J. Lamping, R. Rao, and P. Pirolli. A focus+context technique based on hyperbolic geometry for viewing large hierarchies. In *ACM SIGCHI*, pages 401–408, 1995.

[6] J. Lamping and R. Rao. Laying out and visualizing large trees using a hyperbolic space. In *ACM Symp User Interface Software and Technology*, pages 13–14, 1994.

[7] F. Morgan. *Riemannian Geometry: A Beginner's Guide*. Jones and Bartlett Publishers, 1993.

[8] T. Munzner. H3: Laying out large directed graphs in 3d hyperbolic space. In *Proc IEEE Symp Info Vis*, pages 2–10, 1997.

[9] P. Pirolli, S. Card, and M. M. Van Der Wege. Visual information foraging in a focus + context visualization. In *CHI*, pages 506–513, 2001.

[10] K. Risden, M. Czerwinski, T. Munzner, and D. Cook. An initial examination of ease of use for 2d and 3d information visualizations of web content. *Int J Human Computer Studies*, 53(5):695–714, 2000.

[11] H. Ritter. Self-organizing maps on non-euclidean spaces. In *Kohonen Maps*, pages 97–110. Elsevier, 1999.

[12] J. W. Sammon, Jr. A non-linear mapping for data structure analysis. *IEEE Trans Computers*, 18:401–409, 1969.

[13] A. Skupin. A cartographic approach to visualizing conference abstracts. *IEEE Computer Graphics and Applications*, pages 50–58, 2002.

[14] J.A. Thorpe. *Elementary Topics in Differential Geometry*. Springer, 1979.

[15] J. Walter. H-MDS: a new approach for interactive visualization with multidimensional scaling in the hyperbolic space. *Information Systems*, (in print), 2003.

[16] J. Walter and H. Ritter. On interactive visualization of high-dimensional data using the hyperbolic plane. In *ACM SIGKDD Int Conf Knowledge Discovery and Data Mining*, pages 123–131. 2002.

[17] J. Wise. The ecological approach to text visualizationt. *J Am Soc Information Sci*, 50(13):1224–1233, 1999.

Association Rule Mining in Peer-to-Peer Systems*

Ran Wolff and Assaf Schuster
Technion – Israel Institute of Technology
Email: {ranw,assaf}@cs.technion.ac.il

Abstract

We extend the problem of association rule mining – a key data mining problem – to systems in which the database is partitioned among a very large number of computers that are dispersed over a wide area. Such computing systems include GRID computing platforms, federated database systems, and peer-to-peer computing environments. The scale of these systems poses several difficulties, such as the impracticality of global communications and global synchronization, dynamic topology changes of the network, on-the-fly data updates, the need to share resources with other applications, and the frequent failure and recovery of resources.

We present an algorithm by which every node in the system can reach the exact solution, as if it were given the combined database. The algorithm is entirely asynchronous, imposes very little communication overhead, transparently tolerates network topology changes and node failures, and quickly adjusts to changes in the data as they occur. Simulation of up to 10,000 nodes show that the algorithm is local: all rules, except for those whose confidence is about equal to the confidence threshold, are discovered using information gathered from a very small vicinity, whose size is independent of the size of the system.

1 Introduction

The problem of association rule mining (ARM) in large transactional databases was first introduced in 1993 [1]. The input to the ARM problem is a database in which objects are grouped by context. An example would be a list of items grouped by the transaction in which they were bought. The objective of ARM is to find sets of objects which tend to associate with one another. Given two distinct sets of objects, X and Y, we say Y is associated with X if the appearance of X in a certain context usually im-

plies that Y will appear in that context as well. The output of an ARM algorithm is a list of all the association rules that appear frequently in the database and for which the association is confident.

ARM has been the focus of great interest among data mining researchers and practitioners. It is today widely accepted to be one of the key problems in the data mining field. Over the years many variations were described for ARM, and a wide range of applications were developed. The overwhelming majority of these deal with sequential ARM algorithms. Distributed association rule mining (D-ARM) was defined in [2], not long after the definition of ARM, and was also the subject of much research (see, for example, [2, 5, 15, 7, 8]).

In recent years, database systems have undergone major changes. Databases are now detached from the computing servers and have become distributed in most cases. The natural extension of these two changes is the development of federated databases – systems which connect many different databases and present a single database image. The trend toward ever more distributed databases goes hand in hand with an ongoing trend in large organizations toward ever greater integration of data. For example, health maintenance organizations (HMOs) envision their medical records, which are stored in thousands of clinics, as one database. This integrated view of the data is imperative for essential data analysis applications ranging from epidemic control, ailment and treatment pattern discovery, and the detection of medical fraud or misconduct. Similar examples of this imperative are common in other fields, including credit card companies, large retail networks, and more.

An especially interesting example for large scale distributed databases are peer-to-peer systems. These systems include GRID computing environments such as Condor [10] (20,000 computers), specific area computing systems such as SETI@home [12] (1,800,000 computers) or UnitedDevices [14] (2,200,000 computers), general purpose peer-to-peer platforms such as Entropia [6] (60,000 peers), and file sharing networks such as Kazza (1.8 million peers). Like any other system, large scale distributed systems maintain and produce operational data. However,

---

*This work was supported in part by Microsoft Academic Foundation.

in contrast to other systems, that data is distributed so widely that it will usually not be feasible to collect it for central processing. It must be processed in place by distributed algorithms suitable to this kind of computing environment.

Consider, for example, mining user preferences over the Kazza file sharing network. The files shared through Kazza are usually rich media files such as songs and videos. participants in the network reveal the files they store on their computers to the system and gain access to files shared by their peers in return. Obviously, this database may contain interesting knowledge which is hard to come by using other means. It may be discovered, for instance, that people who download The Matrix also look for songs by Madonna. Such knowledge can then be exploited in a variety of ways, much like the well known data mining example stating that "customers who purchase diapers also buy beer".

The large-scale distributed association rule mining (LSD-ARM) problem is very different from the D-ARM problem, because a database that is composed of thousands of partitions is very different from a small scale distributed database. The scale of these systems introduces a plethora of new problems which have not yet been addressed by any ARM algorithm. The first such problem is that in a system that large there can be no global synchronization. This has two important consequences for any algorithm proposed for the problem: The first is that the nodes must act independently of one another; hence their progress is speculative, and intermediate results may be overturned as new data arrives. The second is that there is no point in time in which the algorithm is known to have finished; thus, nodes have no way of knowing that the information they possess is final and accurate. At each point in time, new information can arrive from a far-away branch of the system and overturn the node's picture of the correct result. The best that can be done in these circumstances is for each node to maintain an assumption of the correct result and update it whenever new data arrives. Algorithms that behave this way are called *anytime algorithms*.

Another problem is that global communication is costly in large scale distributed systems. This means that for all practical purposes the nodes should compute the result through local negotiation. Each node can only be familiar with a small set of other nodes – its immediate neighbors. It is by exchanging information with their immediate neighbors concerning their local databases that nodes investigate the combined, global database.

A further complication comes from the dynamic nature of large scale systems. If the mean time between failures of a single node is 20,000 hours[1], a system consisting of

100,000 nodes could easily fail five times per hour. Moreover, many such systems are purposely designed to support the dynamic departure of nodes. This is because a system that is based on utilizing free resources on non-dedicated machines should be able to withstand scheduled shutdowns for maintenance, accidental turnoffs, or an abrupt decrease in availability when the user comes back from lunch. The problem is that whenever a node departs, the database on that node may disappear with it, changing the global database and the result of the computation. A similar problem occurs when nodes join the system in mid-computation.

Obviously none of the distributed ARM algorithms developed for small-scale distributed systems can manage a system with the aforementioned features. These algorithms focus on achieving parallelization induced speed-ups. They use basic operators, such as broadcast, global synchronization, and a centralized coordinator, none of which can be managed in large-scale distributed systems. To the best of our knowledge, no D-ARM algorithm presented so far acknowledges the possibility of failure. Some relevant work was done in the context of incremental ARM, e.g., [13], and similar algorithms. In these works the set of rules is adjusted following changes in the database. However, we know of no parallelizations for those algorithms even for small-scale distributed systems.

In this paper we describe an algorithm which solves LSD-ARM. Our first contribution is the inference that the distributed association rule mining problem is reducible to the well-studied problem of distributed majority votes. Building on this inference, we develop an algorithm which combines sequential association rule mining, executed locally at each node, with a majority voting protocol to discover, at each node, all of the association rules that exist in the combined database. During the execution of the algorithm, which in a dynamic system may never actually terminate, each node maintains an ad hoc solution. If the system remains static, then the ad hoc solution of most nodes will quickly converge toward an exact solution. This is the same solution that would be reached by a sequential ARM algorithm had all the databases been collected and processed. If the static period is long enough, then all nodes will reach this solution. However, in a dynamic system, where nodes dynamically join or depart and the data changes over time, the changes are quickly and locally adjusted to, and the solution continues to converge. It is worth mentioning that no previous ARM algorithm was proposed which mines rules (not itemsets) on the fly. This contribution may affect other kinds of ARM algorithms, especially those intended for data streams [9].

The majority voting protocol, which is at the crux of our algorithm, is in itself a significant contribution. It requires no synchronization between the computing nodes.

Each node communicates only with its immediate neighbors. Moreover, the protocol is local: in the overwhelming majority of cases, each node computes the majority – i.e., identifies the correct rules – based upon information arriving from a very small surrounding environment. Locality implies that the algorithm is scalable to very large networks. Another outcome of the algorithm's locality is that the communication load it produces is small and roughly uniform, thus making it suitable for non-dedicated environments.

2 Problem Definition

The association rule mining (ARM) problem is traditionally defined as follows: Let $I = \{i_1, i_2, ..., i_m\}$ be the items in a certain domain. An itemset is some subset $X \subseteq I$. A transaction t is also a subset of I associated with a unique transaction identifier TID. A database DB is a list that contains $|DB|$ transactions. Given an itemset X and a database DB, $Support(X, DB)$ is the number of transactions in DB which contain all the items of X, and $Freq(X, DB) = Support(X, DB) / |DB|$. For some frequency threshold $0 \leq MinFreq \leq 1$, we say that an itemset X is frequent in a database DB if $Freq(X, DB) \geq MinFreq$ and infrequent otherwise. For two distinct frequent itemsets X and Y, and a confidence threshold $0 \leq MinConf \leq 1$, we say the rule $X \Rightarrow Y$ is confident in DB if $Freq(X \cup Y, DB) \geq MinConf \cdot Freq(X, DB)$. We will call confident rules between frequent itemsets correct and the remaining rules false. The solution for the ARM problem is $R[DB]$, the list of all the correct rules in the given database.

When the database is dynamically updated, that is, transactions are added to it or deleted from it over time, we denote DB_t the database at time t. Now consider that the database is also partitioned among an unknown number of share nothing machines (nodes); we denote the partition of node u at time t DB_t^u. Given an infrastructure through which those machines may communicate data, we denote $[u]_t$ the group of machines reachable from u at time t. We will assume symmetry, i.e., $v \in [u]_t \Leftrightarrow u \in [v]_t$. Nevertheless, $[u]_t$ may or may not include all of the machines. The solution to the large-scale distributed association rule mining (LSD-ARM) problem for node u at time t is the set of rules which are correct in the combined databases of the machines in $[u]_t$; we denote this solution $R[u]_t$.

Since both $[u]_t$ and DB_t^v of each $v \in [u]_t$ are free to vary with time – so does $R[u]_t$. It is thus imperative that u calculate not only the eventual solution but also approximated, ad hoc, solutions. We term $\tilde{R}[u]_t$ the ad hoc solution of node u at time t. It is common practice to measure the performance of an anytime algorithm according to its recall: $\frac{|R[u]_t \cap \tilde{R}[u]_t|}{|R[u]_t|}$, and its precision: $\frac{|R[u]_t \cap \tilde{R}[u]_t|}{|\tilde{R}[u]_t|}$.

We require that if both $[u]_t$ and DB_t^v of each $v \in [u]_t$ remain static long enough, then the approximated solution $\tilde{R}[u]_t$ will converge to $R[u]_t$. In other words, both the precision and the recall of u converge to a hundred percent.

Throughout this work we make some simplifying assumptions. We assume that node connectivity is a forest – for each u and v there could be either one route from u to v or none. Trees in the forest may split, join, grow, and shrink, as a result of node crash and recovery, or departure and join. We assume the failure model of computers is fail-stop, and that a node is informed of changes in the status of adjacent nodes.

3 An ARM Algorithm for Large-Scale Distributed Systems

As previously described, our algorithm is comprised of two rather independent components: Each node executes a sequential ARM algorithm which traverses the local database and maintains the current result. Additionally, each node participates in a distributed majority voting protocol which makes certain that all nodes that are reachable from one another converge toward the correct result according to their combined databases. We will begin by describing the protocol and then proceed to show how the full algorithm is derived from it.

3.1 LSD-Majority Protocol

It has been shown in [11] that a distributed ARM algorithm can be viewed as a decision problem in which the participating nodes must decide whether or not each itemset is frequent. However, the algorithm described in that work extensively uses broadcast and global synchronization; hence it is only suitable for small-scale distributed systems. We present here an entirely different majority voting protocol – LSD-Majority – which works well for large-scale distributed systems. In the interest of clarity we describe the protocol assuming the data at each node is a single bit. We will later show how the protocol can easily be generalized for frequency counts.

As in LSD-ARM, the purpose of LSD-Majority is to ensure that each node converges toward the correct majority. Since the majority problem is binary, we measure the recall as the proportion of nodes u whose ad hoc solution is one when the majority in $[u]_t$ is of set bits, or zero when the majority in $[u]_t$ is of unset bits. The protocol dictates how nodes react when the data changes, a message is received, or a neighboring node is reported to have detached or joined.

The nodes communicate by sending messages that contain two integers: *count*, which stands for the number of bits this message reports, and *sum* which is the number of those bits which are equal to one. Each node u will record, for every neighbor v, the last message it sent to v – $\{sum^{uv}, count^{uv}\}$ – and the last message it received from v – $\{sum^{vu}, count^{vu}\}$. Node u calculates the following two functions of these messages and its own local bit:

$$\Delta^u = s^u + \sum_{vu \in E^u} sum^{vu} - \lambda \left(c^u + \sum_{vu \in E^u} count^{vu} \right)$$

$$\Delta^{uv} = sum^{uv} + sum^{vu} - \lambda \left(count^{uv} + count^{vu} \right)$$

Here E^u is the set of edges colliding with u, s^u is the value of the local bit, and c^u is, for now, one. Δ^u measures the number of access set bits u has been informed of. Δ^{uv} measures the number of access set bits u and v have last reported to one another. Each time s^u changes, a message is received, or a node connects to v or disconnects from v, Δ^u is recalculated; Δ^{uv} is recalculated each time a message is sent to or received from v.

Algorithm 1 LSD-Majority

Input for node u: The set of edges that collide with it E^u, A bit s^u and the majority ratio λ.

Output: The algorithm never terminates. Nevertheless, at each point in time if $\Delta^u \geq 0$ then the output is 1, otherwise it is 0.

Definitions: $\Delta^u = s^u + \sum_{vu \in E^u} sum^{vu} - \lambda \left(c^u + \sum_{vu \in E^u} count^{vu} \right)$, $\Delta^{uv} = sum^{uv} + sum^{vu} - \lambda \left(count^{uv} + count^{vu} \right)$

Initialization: For each $vu \in E^u$ set $sum^{vu}, count^{vu}, sum^{uv}, count^{uv}$ to 0. Set $c^u = 1$.

On edge vu **recovery :** Add vu to E^u. Set $sum^{vu}, count^{vu}, sum^{uv}, count^{uv}$ to 0.

On failure of edge $vu \in E^u$: Remove vu from E^u.

On message $\{sum, count\}$ **received over edge** vu: Set $sum^{vu} = sum, count^{vu} = count$

On change in s^u, **edge failure or recovery, or the receiving of a message:**

For each $vu \in E^u$

If $count^{uv} + count^{vu} = 0$ and $\Delta^u \geq 0$
or $count^{uv} + count^{vu} > 0$ and either $\Delta^{uv} < 0$ and $\Delta^u > \Delta^{uv}$ or $\Delta^{uv} \geq 0$ and $\Delta^u < \Delta^{uv}$

Set $sum^{uv} = s^u + \sum_{wu \neq vu \in E^u} sum^{wu}$ and $count^{uv} = c^u + \sum_{wu \neq vu \in E^u} count^{wu}$

Send $\{sum^{uv}, count^{uv}\}$ over vu to v

Each node performs the protocol independently with each of its immediate neighbors. Node u coordinates its majority decision with node v by maintaining the same Δ^{uv} value (note that $\Delta^{uv} = \Delta^{vu}$) and making certain that Δ^{uv} will not mislead v into believing that the global majority is larger than it actually is. As long as $\Delta^u \geq \Delta^{uv} \geq 0$ and $\Delta^v \geq \Delta^{vu} \geq 0$, there is no need for u and v to exchange data. They both calculate the majority of the bits to be set; thus, the majority in their combined data must be of set bits. If, on the other hand, $\Delta^{uv} > \Delta^u$, then v might mistakenly calculate $\Delta^v \geq 0$ because it has not received the updated data from u. Thus, in this case the protocol dictates that u send v a message, $\left\{ s^u + \sum_{wu \neq vu \in E^u} sum^{wu}, c^u + \sum_{wu \neq vu \in E^u} count^{wu} \right\}$. Note that after this message is sent, $\Delta^{uv} = \Delta^u$.

The opposite case is almost the same. Again, if $0 > \Delta^{uv} \geq \Delta^u$ and $0 > \Delta^{vu} \geq \Delta^v$, then no messages are exchanged. However, when $\Delta^u > \Delta^{uv}$, the protocol dictates that u send v a message calculated the same way. The only difference is that when no messages were sent or received, v knows, by default, that $\Delta^u < 0$ and u knows that $\Delta^v < 0$. Thus, unless $\Delta^u \geq 0$, u does not send messages to v because the majority bits in their combined data cannot be set.

The pseudocode of the LSD-Majority protocol is given in Algorithm 1. It is easy to see that when the protocol dictates that no node needs to send any message, either $\Delta^v \geq 0$ for all nodes $v \in [u]_t$, or $\Delta^v < 0$ for all of them. If there is disagreement in $[u]_t$, then there must be disagreement between two immediate neighbors, in which case at least one node v must send data, which will cause $count^{uv} + count^{vu}$ to increase. This number is bounded by the size of $[u]_t$; hence, the protocol always reaches consensus in a static state. It is less trivial to show that the conclusion they arrive at is the correct one. This proof is too long to include in this context.

In order to generalize LSD-Majority for frequency counts, c^u need only be set to the size of the local database and s^u to the local support of an itemset. Then, if we substitute $MinFreq$ for λ, the resulting protocol will decide whether an itemset is frequent or infrequent in $[u]_t$. Deciding whether a rule $X \Rightarrow Y$ is confident is also straightforward using this protocol: c^u should now count in the local database the number of transactions that include X, s^u should count the number of these transactions that include both X and Y, and λ should be replaced with $MinConf$.

Deciding whether a rule is correct or false requires that each node run two instances of the protocol: one to decide whether the rule is frequent and the other to decide whether it is confident. Note, however, that for all rules of the form $A \Rightarrow B \setminus A$, only one instance of the protocol should be performed to decide whether B is frequent.

The strength of the protocol lies in its behavior when

the average of the bits over $[u]_t$ is somewhat different than the majority threshold λ. Defining the significance of the input as $\dfrac{\sum_{v \in [u]_t} s^v}{\lambda \cdot \sum_{v \in [u]_t} c^v} - 1$, we will show in section 4.1 that even a minor significance, on the scale of ± 0.1, is sufficient for making a correct decision using data from just a small number of nodes. In other words, even a minor significance is sufficient for the algorithm to become local. Another strength of the protocol is that during static periods, most of the nodes will make the correct majority decision very quickly. These two features make LSD-Majority especially well-suited for LSD-ARM, in which the overwhelming majority of the candidates are far from significant.

3.2 Majority-Rule Algorithm

LSD-Majority efficiently decides whether a candidate rule is correct or false. It remains to show how candidates are generated and how they are counted in the local database. The full algorithm must satisfy two requirements: First, each node must take into account not only the local data, but also data brought to it by LSD-Majority, as this data may indicate that additional rules are correct and thus further candidates should be generated. Second, unlike other algorithms, which produce rules after they have finished discovering all itemsets, an algorithm which never really finishes discovering all itemsets must generate rules on the fly. Therefore the candidates it uses must be rules, not itemsets. We now present an algorithm – Majority-Rule – which satisfies both requirements.

The first requirement is rather easy to satisfy. We simply increment the counters of each rule according to the data received. Additionally, we employ a candidate generation approach that is not levelwise: as in the DIC algorithm [4], we periodically consider all the correct rules, regardless of when they were discovered, and attempt to use them for generating new candidates.

The second requirement, mining rules directly rather than mining itemsets first and producing rules when the algorithm terminates, has not, to the best of our knowledge, been addressed in the literature. To satisfy this requirement we generalize the candidate generation procedure of Apriori [3]. Apriori generates candidate itemsets in two ways: Initially, it generates candidate itemsets of size 1: $\{i\}$ for every $i \in I$. Later, candidates of size $k + 1$ are generated by finding pairs of frequent itemsets of size k that differ by only the last item – $X \cup \{i_1\}$ and $X \cup \{i_2\}$ – and validating that all of the subsets of $X \cup \{i_1, i_2\}$ are also frequent before making that itemset a candidate. In this way, Apriori generates the minimal candidate set which must be generated by any deterministic algorithm.

In the case of Majority-Rule, the dynamic nature of the

Algorithm 2 Majority-Rule

Input for node u: The set of edges that collide with it E^u. The local database DB^u. $MinFreq, MinConf, M$

Initialization: Set $C \leftarrow \{\langle \emptyset \Rightarrow \{i\} \rangle \ for \ all \ i \in I\}$

For each $r \in C$ set $r.sum = r.count = 0$, and $r.\lambda = MinFreq$

For each $r \in C$ and every $vu \in E^u$ set $r.sum^{uv} = r.count^{uv} = r.sum^{vu} = r.count^{vu} = 0$

Upon receiving $\{r.id, sum, count\}$ from a neighbor v If $r = \langle X \Rightarrow Y \rangle \notin C$ add it to C. If $c' = \langle \emptyset \Rightarrow X \cup Y \rangle \notin C$ add it too.

Set $r.sum^{vu} = sum, r.count^{vu} = count$

On edge vu recovery: Add vu to E^u. For all $r \in C$ set $r.sum^{uv} = r.count^{uv} = r.sum^{vu} = r.count^{vu} = 0$

On failure of edge $vu \in E^u$: Remove vu from E^u.

Main: Repeat the following for ever

Read the next transaction – T. If it is the last one in DB^u iterate back to the first one.

For every $r = \langle X \Rightarrow Y \rangle \in C$ which was generated after this transaction was last read

  If $X \subseteq T$ increase $r.count$

  If $X \cup Y \subseteq T$ increase $r.sum$

Once every M transactions

  Set $\tilde{R}[u]_t = $ the set of rules $r = \langle X \Rightarrow Y \rangle \in C$ such that $\Delta^u(r) \geq 0$ and for $r' = \langle \emptyset \Rightarrow X \cup Y \rangle$ $\Delta^u(r') \geq 0$

  For every $r = \langle X \Rightarrow Y \rangle \in \tilde{R}[u]_t$, such that $X = \emptyset$ and $i \in X$ if $r' = \langle X \setminus \{i\} \Rightarrow \{i\} \rangle \notin C$ insert r' into C with $r'.sum = r'.count = 0$, $r'.\lambda = MinConf$ and $r'.id = $ unique rule id

    For each $c_1 = \langle X \Rightarrow Y \cup \{i_1\} \rangle, c_2 = \langle X \Rightarrow Y \cup \{i_2\} \rangle \in \tilde{R}[u]_t$ such that $i_1 < i_2$, if $c_3 = \langle X \Rightarrow Y \cup \{i_1, i_2\} \rangle \notin C$ and $\forall i_3 \in Y : r_3 = \langle X \Rightarrow Y \cup \{i_1, i_2\} \setminus \{i_3\} \rangle \in \tilde{R}[u]_t$, add r_3 to C with $r_3.sum = r_3.count = 0$, $r_3.\lambda = r_1.\lambda$, and $r_3.id = $ unique rule id

  For each $r = \langle X \Rightarrow Y \rangle \in C$ and for every $vu \in E^u$

  If $r.count^{uv} + r.count^{vu} = 0$ and $\Delta^u(r) \geq 0$

  or $r.count^{uv} + r.count^{vu} > 0$ and either $\Delta^{uv}(r) < 0$ and $\Delta^u(r) > \Delta^{uv}(r)$

    or $\Delta^{uv} \geq 0$ and $\Delta^u(r) < \Delta^{uv}(r)$

    Set $r.sum^{uv} = r.sum + \sum_{wu \neq vu \in E^u} r.sum^{wu}$ and

$r.count^{uv} = r.count + \sum_{wu \neq vu \in E^u} r.count^{wu}$

    Send $\{r.id, r.sum^{uv}, r.count^{uv}\}$ over vu to v

367

system means that it is never certain whether an itemset is frequent or a rule is correct. Thus, it is impossible to guarantee that no superfluous candidates are generated. Nevertheless, at any point during execution t, it is worthwhile to use the ad hoc set of rules, $\tilde{R}[u]_t$, to try and limit the number of candidate rules. Our candidate generation criterion is thus a generalization of Apriori's criterion. Each node generates initial candidate rules of the form $\emptyset \Rightarrow \{i\}$ for each $i \in I$. Then, for each rule $\emptyset \Rightarrow X \in \tilde{R}[u]_t$, it generates $X \setminus \{i\} \Rightarrow \{i\}$ candidate rules for all $i \in X$. In addition to these initial candidate rules, the node will look for pairs of rules in $R[u]_t$ which have the same left-hand side, and right-hand sides that differ only in the last item – $X \Rightarrow Y \cup \{i_1\}$ and $X \Rightarrow Y \cup \{i_2\}$. The node will verify that the rules $X \Rightarrow Y \cup \{i_1, i_2\} \setminus \{i_3\}$, for every $i_3 \in Y$, are also correct, and then generate the candidate $X \Rightarrow Y \cup \{i_1, i_2\}$. It can be inductively proved that if $\tilde{R}[u]_t$ contains only correct rules, then no superfluous candidate rules are ever generated using this method.

The rest of Majority-Rule is straightforward. Whenever a candidate is generated, the node will begin to count its support and confidence in the local database. At the same time, the node will also begin two instances of LSD-Majority, one for the candidate's frequency and one for its confidence, and these will determine whether this rule is globally correct. Since each node runs multiple instances of LSD-Majority concurrently, messages must carry, in addition to *sum* and *count*, the identification of the rule it refers to, $r.id$. We will denote $\Delta^u(r)$ and $\Delta^{uv}(r)$ the result of the previously defined functions when they refer to the counters and λ of candidate r. Finally, $r.\lambda$ is the majority threshold that applies to r. We set $r.\lambda$ to $MinFreq$ for rules with an empty left-hand side and to $MinConf$ for all other rules.

The pseudocode of Majority-Rule is detailed in Algorithm 2.

4   Experimental Results

To evaluate Majority-Rule's performance, we implemented a simulator capable of running thousands of simulated computers. We simulated 1600 such computers, connected in a random tree overlaid on a 40×40 grid. We also implemented a simulator for a stand-alone instance of the LSD-Majority protocol and ran simulations of up to 10,000 nodes on a 100×100 grid. The simulations were run in lock-step, not because the algorithm requires that the computers work in locked-step – the algorithm poses no such limitations – but rather because properties such as convergence and locality are best demonstrated when all processors have the same speed and all messages are delivered in unit time.

We used synthetic databases generated by the standard

tool from the IBM-quest data mining group [3]. We generated three synthetic databases – T5.I2, T10.I4 and T20.I6 – where the number after T is the average transaction length and the number after I is the average pattern length. The combined size of each of the three databases is 10,000,000 transactions. Other than the number of transactions the change we made from the defaults was reducing the number of patterns. This was reduced so as to increase the proportion of correct rules from one in ten-thousands to one in a hundred candidates. Because our algorithm performs better for false rules than for correct ones this change does not impair out the validity of the results.

4.1   Locality of LSD-Majority and Majority-Rule

The LSD-Majority protocol, and consequently the Majority-Rule algorithm, are local algorithms in the sense that a correct decision will usually only require that a small subset of the data is gathered. We measure the locality of an algorithm by the average and maximum size of the environment of nodes. The environment is defined in LSD-Majority as the number of input bits received by the node and in Majority-Rule as the percent of the global database reported to the node, until system stabilization. Our experiments with LSD-Majority show that its locality strongly depends on the significance of the input: $\frac{\sum_{v \in [u]_t} s^v}{\lambda \cdot \sum_{v \in [u]_t} c^v} - 1$.

Figure 1(a) describes the results of a simulation of 10,000 nodes in a random tree over a grid, with various percentages of set input bits at the nodes. It shows that when the significance is ± 0.1 (i.e., 45% or 55% of the nodes have set input bits), the protocol already has good locality: the maximal environment is about 1200 nodes and the average size a little over 300. If the percentage of set input bits is closer to the threshold, a large portion of the data would have to be collected in order to find the majority. In the worst possible case, when the number of set input bits is equal to the number of unset input bits plus one, at least one node would have to collect all of the input bits before the solution could be reached. On the other hand, if the percentage of set input bits is further from the threshold, then the average environment size becomes negligible. In many cases different regions of the grid may not exchange any messages at all. In Figure 1(c) these results repeat themselves for Majority-Rule.

Further analysis – Figure 1(c) – show that the size of a node's environment depends on the significance in a small region around the nodes. I.e., if the inputs of nodes are independent of one another then the environment size will be random. This makes our algorithms fair: nodes' performance is not determined by its connectivity or location but rather by the data.

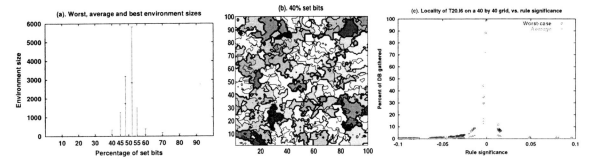

Figure 1. The locality of LSD-Majority (a) and of Majority-Rule (c) depends of the significance. The distribution of environment sizes (b) depends on the local significance and is hence random.

4.2 Convergence and Cost of Majority-Rule

In addition to locality, the other two important characteristics of Majority-Rule are its convergence rate and communication cost. We measure convergence by calculating the recall – the percentage of rules uncovered – and precision – the percentage of correct rules among all rules assumed correct – vis-a-vis the number of transactions scanned. Figure 2 describes the convergence of the recall (a) and of the precision (b). In (c) the convergence of stand-alone LSD-Majority is given, for various percentages of set input bits.

To understand the convergence of Majority-Rule, one must look at how the candidate generation and the majority voting interact. Rules which are very significant are expected to be generated early and agreed upon fast. The same holds for false candidates with extremely low significance. They too are generated early, because they are usually generated due to noise, which subsides rapidly as a greater portion of the local database is scanned; the convergence of LSD-Majority will be as quick for them as for rules with high significance. This leaves us with the group of marginal candidates, those that are very near to the threshold; these marginal candidates are hard to agree upon, and in some cases, if one of their subsets is also marginal, they may only be generated after the algorithm has been working for a long time. We remark that marginal candidates are as difficult for other algorithms as they are for Majority-Rule. For instance, DIC may suffer from the same problem: if all rules were marginal, then the number of database scans would be as large as that of Apriori.

An interesting feature of LSD-Majority convergence is that the number of nodes that assume a majority of set bits always increases in the first few rounds. This would result in a sharp reduction in accuracy in the case of a majority of unset bits, and an overshot, above the otherwise exponential convergence, in the case of a majority of set bits.

This occurs because our protocol operates in expanding wavefronts, convincing more and more nodes that there is a certain majority, and then retreating with many nodes being convinced that the majority is the opposite. Since we assume by default a majority of zeros, the first wavefront that expands would always be about a majority of ones. Interestingly enough, the same pattern can be seen in the convergence of Majority-Rule (more clearly for the precision than for the recall).

Figure 3 presents the the communication cost of LSD-Majority vis-a-vis the percentage of set input bits and of Majority-Rule vis-a-vis rule significance. For rules that are very near the threshold, a lot of communication is required, on the scale of the grid diameter. For significant rules the communication load is about ten messages per rule per node. However, for false candidates the communication load drops very fast to nearly no messages at all. It is important to keep in mind that we denote every pair of integers we send a message. In a realistic scenario, a message will contain up to 1500 bytes, or about 180 integer pairs.

5 Conclusions

We have described a new distributed majority vote protocol – LSD-Majority– which we incorporated as part of an algorithm – Majority-Rule – that mines association rules on distributed systems of unlimited size. We have shown that the key quality of our algorithm is its locality – the fact that information need not travel far on the network for the correct solution to be reached. We have also shown that the locality of Majority-Rule translates into fast convergence of the result and low communication demands. Communication is also very efficient, at least for candidate rules which turn out not to be correct. Since the overwhelming majority of the candidates usually turn out this way, the communication load of Majority-Rule depends mainly

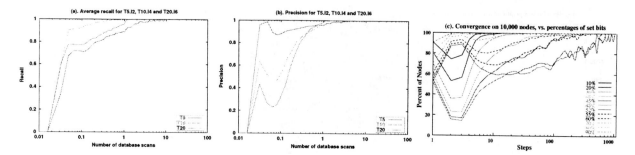

Figure 2. Convergence of the recall and precision of Majority-Rule, and of LSD-Majority.

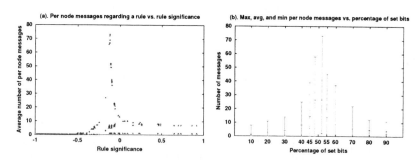

Figure 3. Communication characteristics of Majority-Rule (a), and of LSD-Majority (b). Each message here is a pair of integers.

on the size of the output – the number of correct rules. That number is controllable via user supplied parameters, namely $MinFreq$ and $MinConf$.

References

[1] R. Agrawal, T. Imielinski, and A. N. Swami. Mining association rules between sets of items in large databases. In *Proc. of the 1993 ACM SIGMOD Int'l. Conference on Management of Data*, pages 207–216, Washington, D.C., June 1993.

[2] R. Agrawal and J. Shafer. Parallel mining of association rules. *IEEE Transactions on Knowledge and Data Engineering*, 8(6):962 – 969, 1996.

[3] R. Agrawal and R. Srikant. Fast algorithms for mining association rules. In *Proc. of the 20th Int'l. Conference on Very Large Databases (VLDB'94)*, pages 487 – 499, Santiago, Chile, September 1994.

[4] S. Brin, R. Motwani, J. Ullman, and S. Tsur. Dynamic itemset counting and implication rules for market basket data. *SIGMOD Record*, 6(2):255–264, June 1997.

[5] D. Cheung, J. Han, V. Ng, A. Fu, and Y. Fu. A fast distributed algorithm for mining association rules. In *Proc. of 1996 Int'l. Conf. on Parallel and Distributed Information Systems*, pages 31 – 44, Miami Beach, Florida, December 1996.

[6] Entropia. http://www.entropia.com.

[7] E.-H. S. Han, G. Karypis, and V. Kumar. Scalable parallel data mining for association rules. *IEEE Transactions on Knowledge and Data Engineering*, 12(3):352 – 377, 2000.

[8] J.-L. Lin and M. H. Dunham. Mining association rules: Anti-skew algorithms. In *Proceedings of the 14th Int'l. Conference on Data Engineering (ICDE'98)*, pages 486–493, 1998.

[9] G. S. Manku and R. Motwani. Approximate frequency counts over data streams. In *Proceedings of the 28th International Conference on Very Large Data Bases (VLDB'02)*, Hong Kong, China, August 2002.

[10] T. C. Project. http://www.cs.wisc.edu/condor/.

[11] A. Schuster and R. Wolff. Communication-efficient distributed mining of association rules. In *Proc. of the 2001 ACM SIGMOD Int'l. Conference on Management of Data*, pages 473 – 484, Santa Barbara, California, May 2001.

[12] Seti@home. http://setiathome.ssl.berkeley.edu/.

[13] S. Thomas and S. Chakravarthy. Incremental mining of constrained associations. In *HiPC*, pages 547–558, 2000.

[14] United devices inc. http://www.ud.com/home.htm.

[15] M. J. Zaki, S. Parthasarathy, M. Ogihara, and W. Li. Parallel algorithms for discovery of association rules. *Data Mining and Knowledge Discovery*, 1(4):343–373, 1997.

MPIS: Maximal-Profit Item Selection with Cross-Selling Considerations

Raymond Chi-Wing Wong, Ada Wai-Chee Fu
Department of Computer Science and Engineering
The Chinese University of Hong Kong
cwwong,adafu@cse.cuhk.edu.hk

Ke Wang
Department of Computer Science
Simon Fraser University, Canada
wangk@cs.sfu.ca

Abstract

In the literature of data mining, many different algorithms for association rule mining have been proposed. However, there is relatively little study on how association rules can aid in more specific targets. In this paper, one of the applications for association rules - maximal-profit item selection with cross-selling effect (MPIS) problem - is investigated. The problem is about selecting a subset of items which can give the maximal profit with the consideration of cross-selling. We prove that a simple version of this problem is NP-hard. We propose a new approach to the problem with the consideration of the loss rule - a kind of association rule to model the cross-selling effect. We show that the problem can be transformed to a quadratic programming problem. In case quadratic programming is not applicable, we also propose a heuristic approach. Experiments are conducted to show that both of the proposed methods are highly effective and efficient.

1 Introduction

Recent studies in the retailing market have shown a winning edge for customer-oriented business, which is based on decision making from better knowledge about the customer behaviour. Furthermore, the behaviour in terms of sales transactions is considered significant [6]. This is also called market basket analysis. We consider the scenario of a supermarket or a large store, typically there are a lot of different items offered, and the amount of transactions can be very large. For example [11] quoted the example of American supermarket chain Wal-Mart, which keeps about 20 million sales transactions per day. This growth of data requires sophisticated method in the analysis.

At about the same time, association rule mining [3] has been proposed by computer scientists, which aims at understanding the relationships among items in transactions or market baskets. However, it is generally true that the association rules in themselves do not serve the end purpose of the business people. We believe that association rules can aid in more specific targets. Here we investigate the application of association rule mining on the problem of market basket analysis. As pointed out in [6], a major task of talented merchants is to pick the profit generating items and discard the losing items. It may be simple enough to sort items by their profit and do the selection. However, by doing that we would have ignored a very important aspect in market analysis, and that is the cross-selling effect. The cross-selling effect arises because there can

be items that do not generate much profit by themselves but they are the catalysts for the sales of other profitable items. Recently, some researchers [17] suggest that association rules can be used in the item selection problem with the consideration of relationships among items. Here we follow this line of work in what we consider as investigations of the application of data mining in the decision-making process of an enterprise.

In this paper, the problem of Maximal-Profit Item Selection with Cross-Selling Considerations (MPIS) is studied. With the consideration of the cross-selling effect, MPIS is the problem of finding a set of J items such that the total profit from the item selection is maximized, where J is an input parameter. This problem arises naturally since a store or a company typically changes the products they carry once in a while. The products that can generate the best profits should be retained and poor-profit items can be removed, then new items can be introduced into the stock. In this way the business can follow the market needs and generate the best possible results for both the business and the customers. In order to determine the profit value of an item, one can rely on expert knowledge. However, since this can be a highly complex issue especially for a large store with thousands of products for sale, we can try to apply data mining techniques, based on a history of customer purchase records.

Hence the problem is how to determine a subset of a given set of items based on a history of transaction records, so that the subset should give the best profits, with considerations of the cross-selling effects. We show that a simple version of this problem is NP-hard. We model the cross-selling factor with a special kind of association rule called *loss rule*. The rule is of the form $I_a \rightarrow \diamond d$, where I_a is an item and d is a set of items, and $\diamond d$ means any items in d. This loss rule helps to estimates the loss in profit for item I_a if the items in d are missing after the selection. The rule corresponds to the cross-selling effect between I_a and d.

To handle this problem, we propose a quadratic programming method (QP) and a heuristics method called MPIS_Alg. In QP, we express the total profit of the item selection in quadratic form and solve a quadratic optimization problem. Algorithm MPIS_Alg is a greedy approach which uses an estimate of the *benefits* of the items to prune items iteratively for maximal-profit. From our experiment, the profitabilities of our two proposed algorithms are greater than that of naive approach for all data sets. On average, the profitability of both QP and MPIS_Alg is 1.33 times higher than the naive approach for the synthetic data set. In a real drugstore data set, the best previous method HAP [26] gives a profitability that is about 2.9 times smaller than MPIS_Alg. When the number of items is large (as in the drugstore data set), the execution time of HAP is 6.5 times slower than MPIS_Alg. These shows that the MPIS_Alg is highly effective and efficient.

2 Problem Definition

Maximal-profit item selection (MPIS) is a problem of selecting a subset from a given set of items so that the estimated profit of the resulting selection is maximal among all choices. Our definition of the problem is close to [26]. Given a data set with m transactions, $t_1, t_2, ..., t_m$, and n items, $I_1, I_2, ..., I_n$. Let $I = \{I_1, I_2, ..., I_n\}$. The profit of item I_a in transaction t_i is given by $prof(I_a, t_i)$. [1] Let $S \subset I$ be a set of J selected items. In each transaction t_i, we define two symbols, t'_i and d_i, for the calculation of the total profit.

$t'_i = t_i \cap S,$	$d_i = t_i - t'_i$
t'_i	set of items selected in S in transaction t_i
d_i	set of items not selected in S in transaction t_i

Suppose we select a subset S of items, it means that some items in $I_1, ..., I_n$ will be eliminated. The transactions $t_1, ..., t_m$ might not occur in exactly the same way if some items have been removed beforehand, since customers may not make some purchase if they know they cannot get some of the items. Therefore, the profit $prof(I_a, t_i)$ can be affected if some items are removed from the stock. This is caused by the cross-selling factor. The cross-selling factor is modeled by $csfactor(D, I_a)$, where D is a set of items, and $0 \leq csfactor(D, I_a) \leq 1$. $csfactor(D, I_a)$, is the fraction of the profit of I_a that will be lost in a transaction if the items in D are not available. Note that the cross-selling factor can be determined in different ways. One way is by the domain experts. We may also have a way to derive this factor from the given history of transactions.

Definition 1 Total Profit of Item Selection: *The total profit of an item selection S is given by*
$$P = \sum_{i=1}^{m} \sum_{I_a \in t'_i} prof(I_a, t_i)(1 - csfactor(d_i, I_a))$$

We are interested in selecting a set of J items so that the total profit is the maximal among all such sets.

MPIS: *Given a set of transactions with profits assigned to each item in each transaction, and the cross-selling factors, $csfactor()$, pick a set S of J items from all given items which gives a maximum profit.*

This problem is at least as difficult as the following decision problem, which we call the decision problem for MPIS:

MPIS Decision Problem: Given a set of items and a set of transactions with profits assigned to each item in each transaction, a minimum benefit B, and cross-selling factors,

---

[1] This definition generalizes the case where profit of an item is fixed for all transactions. We note that the same item in different transactions can differ because the amount of the item purchased are different, or the item can be on discount for some transactions and the profit will be reduced. If the profit of an item is uniform over all transactions, we can set $prof(I_a, t_i)$ to be a constant over all i.

$csfactor()$, can we pick a set S of J items such that $P \geq B$?

In our proof in the following, we consider the very simple version where $csfactor(d_i, I_a) = 1$ for any non-empty set of d_i. That is, any missing item in the transaction will eliminate the profit of the other items. This may be a much simplified version of the problem, but it is still very difficult.

2.1 NP-hardness

Theorem 1 *The maximal-profit item selection (MPIS) decision problem where $csfactor(d_i, I_a) = 1$ for $d_i \neq \phi$ and $csfactor(d_i, I_a) = 0$ for $d_i = \phi$ is NP-hard.*

Proof sketch: We shall transform the problem of CLIQUE to the MPIS problem. CLIQUE [9] is an NP-complete problem defined as followd:

CLIQUE: Given a graph $G = (V, E)$ and a positive integer $K \leq |V|$, is there a subset $V' \subseteq V$ such that $|V'| \geq K$ and every two vertices in V' are joined by an edge in E ?

The transformation from CLIQUE to MPIS problem is described as follows: Set $J = K$, $B = K(K-1)$. For each vertex $v \in V$, construct an item. For each edge $e \in E$, where $e = (v_1, v_2)$, create a transaction with 2 items $\{v_1, v_2\}$. Set $prof(I_j, t_i) = 1$, where t_i is a transaction created in the above, $i = 1, 2, ..., |E|$, and I_j is an item in t_i.

It is easy to see that this transformation can be constructed in polynomial time. It is also easy to verify that when the problem is solved in the transformed MPIS, the original clique problem is also solved. Since CLIQUE is an NP-complete problem, the MPIS problem is NP-hard. □

3 Related Work

In recent years the problem of association rule mining has received much attention. We are given a set I of items, and a set of transactions. Each transaction is a subset of I. An *association rule* has the form $X \rightarrow I_j$, where $X \subseteq I$ and $I_j \in I$; the *support* of such a rule is the fraction of transactions containing all items in X and item I_j; the confidence for the rule is the fraction of the transactions containing all items in set X that also contain item I_j. The problem is to find all rules with sufficient support and confidence. Some of the earlier work include [22, 4, 21].

3.1 Item Selection Related Work

There are some recent works on the maximal-profit item selection problem. PROFSET [8, 7] models the cross-selling effects by *frequent itemsets*, which are sets of items co-occurring frequently. A *maximal frequent itemset* is a frequent itemset which does not have a frequent item superset. The profit margins of maximal itemsets are counted in the total profit. The problem is formulated as 0-1 linear programming that aims to maximize the total profit.

However, PROFSET has several drawbacks as pointed out in [26]. More details can be found in [26].

HAP [26] is a solution of a similar problem. It applies the "hub-authority" profit ranking approach [23] to solve the maximal profit item-selection problem. Items are considered as vertices in a graph. A link from I_i to I_j represents the cross-selling effect from I_i to I_j. A node I_j is a good *authority* if there are many links of the form $I_i \rightarrow I_j$ with a strong

strength of the link. The HITS algorithm [18] is applied and the items with the highest resulting authorities will be the chosen items. It is shown that the result converges to the principal eigenvectors of a matrix defined in terms of the links, confidence values, and profit values.

However, HAP also has some weaknesses. (1) Problems of dead ends or spider traps as illustrated in [25] can arise. For example, if there is an isolated subgraph with a cycle while other items are not connected, then the authority weight and hub weight of all items in the cycle are accumulated and is increased to an extremely high value, giving an over-estimating ranking for these items. (2) In HAP, the authority weight of an item I_j depends on the profit of any other item I_i with the association rule $I_i \rightarrow I_j$. It is possible that some items with low/zero profit gain very high authority weights, and are selected by HAP. In fact the real data set we shall use in the experiments exhibits this phenomenon, and HAP cannot give a competitive solution.

4 Cross selling effect by Association Rules

In Section 2, we did not specify how to determine the cross-selling effect $csfactor$ of some items for other items. In previous work [26], the concept of association rules is applied to this task. Here we also apply the ideas of association rules for the determination of $csfactor$.

Let us estimate the possible profit from a given set of transaction. If all items are selected, the profit is the same as the given profit. Suppose we have made a selection S of J items from the set of items. Now some transactions may lose profits if some items are missing. Consider a transaction t_i in our transaction history, suppose some items, says I_a, are selected in S but some items are not selected (i.e. d_i). Then if we have a rule that purchasing I_a always "implies" at least one element in d_i then it would be impossible for transaction t_i to exist after the selection of S, since t_i contains I_a and no element in d_i after the selection. The profit generated by t_i from I_a should be removed from our estimated profit.

We can model the above rule by an association rule. In fact, we can model the cross-selling factor in the total profit of item selection $csfactor(d_i, I_a)$ by $conf(I_a \rightarrow \diamond d_i)$, where $\diamond d_i$ is given by the following:

Definition 2 *Let $d_i = \{Y_1, Y_2, Y_3, ..., Y_q\}$ where Y_i refers to a single item for $i = 1, 2, .., q$, then $\diamond d_i = Y_1 \vee Y_2 \vee Y_3 \vee .... \vee Y_q$.*

The rule $I_a \rightarrow \diamond d_i$ is called a *loss rule*. The rule $I_a \rightarrow \diamond d_i$ indicates that a customer who buys the item I_a must also buy at least one of the items in d_i. If none of the items in d_i are available then the customer also will not purchase I_a. Therefore, the higher the confidence of "$I_a \rightarrow \diamond d_i$", the more likely the profit of I_a in t_i should not be counted. This is the reasoning behind the above definition.

The total profit is to estimate the amount of profit we would get from the set of transaction $t_1, ...t_m$, if the set of items is reduced to the selected set S. From Definition 1, we have

Definition 3 Total Profit of Item Selection (association rule based): *The association rule based total profit of item selection S is given by*
$$P = \sum_{i=1}^{m} \sum_{I_a \in t'_i} prof(I_a, t_i)(1 - conf(I_a \rightarrow \diamond d_i))$$

For the special cases, if all items in transaction t_i are selected in the set S, then d_i is empty, t_i will not be affected and so the profit of transaction t_i would remain unchanged. If no item in transaction t_i is selected, then the customer could not have executed the transaction t_i, then t'_i is an empty set, and the profit of transaction t_i becomes zero after we have made the selection.

The loss rule $I_a \rightarrow \diamond d_i$ is treated as an association rule. The confidence of this rule is defined in a similar manner as for the association rule:

Definition 4 $conf(I_a \rightarrow \diamond d_i)$ *is computed as*
$$\frac{no.\ of\ transactions\ containing\ I_a\ and\ any\ element\ in\ d_i}{no.\ of\ transactions\ containing\ I_a}$$

5 Quadratic Programming

Linear programming or non-linear programming has been applied for optimization problems in many companies or businesses and has saved millions of dollars in their running [12]. The problem involves a number of decision variables, an objective function in terms of these variables to be maximized or minimized, and a set of constraints stated as inequalities in terms of the variables. In linear programming, the objective function is a linear function of the variables. In quadratic programming, the objective function must be quadratic. That means the terms in the objective function involve the *square* of a variable or the *product* of two variables. If s is the vector of all variables, a general form of such a function is $P = f^T s + \frac{1}{2} s^T Q s$ where f is a vector and Q is a symmetric matrix. If the variables take binary values of 0 and 1, the problem is called zero-one quadratic programming.

In this section, we propose to tackle the problem of MPIS by means of zero-one quadratic programming. We shall show that the problem can be approximated by a quadratic programming problem. Let $s = (s_1 s_2 ... s_n)^T$ be a binary vector representing which items are selected in the set S. $s_i = 1$ if item I_i is selected in the output. Otherwise, $s_i = 0$. The total profit of item selection P can be approximated by the quadratic form $f^T s + \frac{1}{2} s^T Q s$ where f is a vector of length n and Q is an n by n matrix in which the entries are derived from the given transactions. The objective is to maximize $f^T s + \frac{1}{2} s^T Q s$, subject to $\sum_{i=1}^{n} s_i = J$. The term $\sum_{i=1}^{n} s_i = J$ means that there are J items to be selected.

With a little overloading of the term t_i, we say that $t_i = (t_{i1} t_{i2} ... t_{in})^T$ is a binary vector representing which items are in the transaction t_i. $t_{ij} = 1$ if item I_j is in the transaction t_i. Otherwise, $t_{ij} = 0$. Similarly, t'_i is a binary vector representing which items are selected in S in the transaction t_i. d_i is a binary vector representing which items are not selected in S in the transaction t_i.

Then, we have the following. For $i = 1, 2, ..., m$ and $j = 1, 2, ..., n$, $t'_{ij} = t_{ij} \times s_j$ and $d_{ij} = t_{ij} - t'_{ij}$.

n_i	number of transactions containing item I_i
n_{ij}	number of transactions containing I_i and I_j
$\|I_{i1},...I_{ij}\|$	number of transactions containing $\{I_{i1},...,I_{ij}\}$

Observation 1 *The confidence* $conf(I_j \to \diamond d_i)$ *can be approximated by* $\frac{1}{n_j}\sum_{k=1}^{n} d_{ik}n_{jk}$.

The above observation is based on the principle of inclusion-exclusion in set theory. To see this, let us consider the numerator in Definition 4 and let it equal to $g(I_a, d_i)$.

Definition 5 *Let* $D \subset I$, $D = \{Y_1, Y_2, ..., Y_q\}$ *and* $I_x \notin D$, *where* Y_i *refers to a single item for* $i = 1, 2, .., q$.

$$g(I_x, D) = \sum_{1\le i\le q}|I_x Y_i| - \sum_{1\le i<j\le q}|I_x Y_i Y_j|$$
$$+ \sum_{1\le i<j<k\le q}|I_x Y_i Y_j Y_k| - ... + (-1)^{n+1}|I_x Y_1 Y_2...Y_q|$$

where $|I_x Y_i Y_j...|$ *is the number of transactions containing the items* $I_x, Y_i, Y_j, ...$

$\square$

We have
$$conf(I_j \to \diamond d_i) = \frac{g(I_j, d_i)}{\text{no. of transactions containing item } I_j}$$
$$\approx \min\left(\frac{\sum_{1\le k<n}|I_j I_k|\times d_{ik}}{\text{no. of transactions containing item } I_j}, 1\right)$$
$$= \min\left(\frac{1}{n_j}\sum_{k=1}^{n}d_{ik}n_{jk}, 1\right)$$

The reason why the above approximation is acceptable is that the number of transactions containing a set of items $\mathcal{J}$ is typically smaller than the number of transactions containing a subset of $\mathcal{J}$. Hence $|I_j I_k I_l|$ is typically much smaller than $|I_j I_k|$, etc. From this approximation we can deduce the following theorem.

Theorem 2 *The total profit of item selection can be approximated by the quadratic form* $P = f^T s + \frac{1}{2}s^T H s$ *where* f *is a vector of size* n *and* H *is an* n *by* n *matrix.*

Proof sketch:

$$P \approx \sum_{i=1}^{m}\sum_{j=1}^{n}t'_{ij}prof(I_j, t_i)\left(1 - \frac{1}{n_j}\sum_{k=1}^{n}d_{ik}n_{jk}\right)$$
$$= \sum_{i=1}^{m}\sum_{j=1}^{n}t_{ij}s_j prof(I_j, t_i)\left(1 - \frac{\sum_{k=1}^{n}(t_{ik}-t'_{ik})n_{jk}}{n_j}\right)$$
$$= f^T s + \frac{1}{2}s^T H s$$
where
$$f = (f_j | f_j = \sum_{i=1}^{m}t_{ij}prof(I_j, t_i)(1 - \frac{1}{n_j}\sum_{k=1}^{n}t_{ik}n_{jk})$$
$$\text{for } j = 1, 2, ..., n)^T$$
$$H = (h_{jk} | h_{jk} = \frac{2n_{jk}}{n_j}\sum_{i=1}^{m}t_{ij}prof(I_j, t_i)t_{ik}$$
$$\text{for } j, k = 1, 2, ..., n) \qquad \square$$

Corollary 1 *P can be approximated by* $P' = f^T s + \frac{1}{2}s^T Q s$ *where* Q *is a symmetric* n *by* n *matrix.*

The corollary follows because
$$P = f^T s + \frac{1}{2}s^T H s = f^T s + \frac{1}{2}s^T Q s$$
where
$Q = (q_{ij})$ and $q_{ij} = \frac{1}{2}(h_{ij} + h_{ji})$ for all $i, j = 1, 2, ..., n$

Since the value of s_i is either 0 or 1, from the above corollary, we have approximated the problem of MPIS by that of 0-1 quadratic programming with the maximization of P' and an equality constraint of $\sum_i s_i = J$:

$\quad$ Maximize $P' = f^T s + \frac{1}{2}s^T Q s$

$\quad$ such that $\sum_{i=1}^{n} s_i = J$, and

$\qquad\quad s_i = 0$ or $s_i = 1$ for $i = 1, 2, .., n$

Any 0-1 quadratic programming problem is polynomially reducible to an unconstrained binary quadratic programming problem [16]. An unconstrained binary quadratic programming problem can be transformed to a binary linear programming problem (zero-one linear programming) [5]. More related properties can be found in [20] and [14]. Zero-one linear programming and quadratic programming are known to be NP-complete [24]. However, there exist programming tools which can typically return good results within a reasonable time for moderate problem sizes. We shall apply such a tool in our experiments which will be presented in Section 7.

6 Algorithm MPIS_Alg

Since quadratic programming is a difficult problem, and existing algorithms may not scale up to large data sizes, we propose also a heuristical algorithm called Maximal-Profit Item Selection (MPIS_Alg). This is an iterative algorithm. In each iteration, we estimate a selected item set with respect to each item based on its "neighborhood" in terms of cross-selling effects, and hence try to estimate a profit for each item that would include the cross-selling effect. With the estimated profit we can give a ranking for the items so that some pruning can be achieved in each iteration. The possible items for selections will become more and more refined with the iterations and when the possible set reaches the selection size, we return it as the result.

There are some factors that make this algorithm desirable: (1) We utilize the exact formula of the profitability in the iterations. This will steer the result better toward the goal of maximal profits compared to other approaches [26] that do not directly use the formula. (2) With the "neighborhood" consideration, the item pruning at each iteration usually affect only a minor portion of the set of items and hence introduce only a small amount of computation for an iteration. Compared to the HAP approach where the entire cross-selling matrix is involved in each iteration, our approach can be much more efficient when the number of items is large.

Before describing the algorithm, we define a few terms that we use. If a transaction contains I_k only, the transaction is an *individual transaction* for I_k. The **individual count** c_k, of an item I_k is the total number of individual transactions for I_k. The individual count reflects the frequency of an item appearing without association with other items.

Let Z_k be the set of transactions that contain I_k, the **average profit** is given by $p_k = (\sum_{t_i \in Z_k}prof(I_k, t_i))/|Z_k|$.

Definition 6 *We define* $\widehat{P}(A)$ *to be the estimated profit assuming that the items in set* A *are selected:*
$$\widehat{P}(A) = \sum_{i=1}^{m}\sum_{I_a \in t'_i}prof(I_a, t_i)(1 - conf(I_a \to \diamond d_i))$$

The formula $\widehat{P}(A)$ is equal to that used in Definition 3. If $A = S$, where S is the output selection set, $\widehat{P}(A)$ is equal to the final output estimated profit.

c_i	individual count of item I_i
p_i	average profits of item I_i
b_i	Benefit of item I_i
S_i	estimation set for item I_i
$e_{i,j}$	Estimated value of item I_j from item I_i; $e_{i,j} = p_j \times c_j + (p_j + p_i) \times support(I_i, I_j)$

6.1 Overall Framework

In the algorithm MPIS_Alg, there are two phases - (1) *Preparation Phase* and (2) *Main Phase*. In the Preparation Phase, the frequency and the individual count of each item and the size 2 itemsets are returned. In the Main Phase, the *benefit* of each item is evaluated. Initially the result set contains all items, a number of iterative steps of removing items with minimum estimated benefit proceeds until J items remains.

Preparation Phase

1. count the number of occurrences of each item, $n_1, n_2, ..., n_n$.
   obtain the individual count for each item, $c_1, c_2, ..., c_n$

2. generate all size 2 itemsets, with their counts.

Main Phase

1. **Estimation Set Creation -**

   In this step, the estimation sets for all items, $S_1, S_2, ..., S_n$ are computed.
   For each item I_i, calculate the **estimated value** of item I_j from item I_i: $e_{i,j} = p_j \times c_j + (p_j + p_i) \times support(I_i, I_j)$, where $support(I_i, I_j)$ is the support of the itemset $\{I_i, I_j\}$. Among these I_j items, choose $J - 1$ items with the highest estimated values. Put these items into the estimation set S_i for I_i.

2. **Item Benefit Calculation -** determine the estimated benefit b_i of each item I_i, $b_i \leftarrow \widehat{P}(S_i \cup \{I_i\})$

3. **Item Selection and Item Benefit Update**

   Let $\mathcal{I}'$ be the set of items that has not been pruned.
   (a) prune an item I_x with a smallest benefit b_x value among the items in $\mathcal{I}'$
   (b) for each remaining item I_i in $\mathcal{I}'$,
      If I_x is in S_i,
      i. remove I_x in the set S_i. Choose the item I_k which has not been selected yet in S_i with the greatest value of $e_{i,k}$. Insert I_k into the set S_i.
      ii. Calculate $b_i \leftarrow \widehat{P}(S_i \cup \{I_i\})$

4. **Iteration -** Repeat Step 3 until J items remain.

6.2 Enhancement Step

We can add a pruning step in between Step 1 and Step 2 in the above to enhance the performance. We call this the **Item Pruning** step and it prunes items with apparently small benefit. The basic idea is to compute both a lowest value and an upper value for the profit of each item. These values are generated by varying the estimated selection set for an item.

1. For each item I_i, calculate L_i and H_i, where
   $L_i = \widehat{P}(\{I_i\})$ and $H_i = \widehat{P}(S_i \cup \{I_i\}) - \widehat{P}(S_i)$

2. Find the J-th largest value (L^J) among all L_j

3. For each I_i, remove item I_i if $H_i < L^J$

L_i is an estimate of the lowest possible profit contributed by I_i; we assume that the selected set contains only I_i. In this case, the cross-selling effect may greatly reduce the profit generated from I_i. H_i is the opposite of L_i; we assume that as many as possible of the items related to I_i are selected in S_i. H_i is equal to the profit gain from adding item I_i to set S_i. Hence the cross-selling effect will diminish the profit to a much lesser extent.

For I_i, the initial profit is zero in $\widehat{P}(S_i)$, since it is not in S_i. After I_i is included in S_i, the profit from I_i should be greater than or equal to the profit that I_i generates when it is the only item selected, because of less cross-selling profit loss factors. Hence H_i and L_i satisfy the following property:

Lemma 1 $H_i \geq L_i$.

Item I_i is pruned if H_i is smaller than the values of L_j of the first J items which have the highest values of L_j. The rationale is that I_i has little chance of contributing more profit than other items.

When this pruning step is inserted, Step 2 in the Main Phase above will not need to compute the estimated benefit for all items, only the items that remain (are not pruned) will be considered when computing the estimated benefits. However, the set S_i would be updated if it initially contains items that are pruned.

Our experiments show that this step is very effective. In the IBM synthetic data set, there are 1000 items. If the number of items to be selected, J, is 500, there are only 881 remaining items after the pruning step. Note that if J is large, this enhancement step can be skipped.

6.3 Implementation Details

Here we describe how some of the steps are implemented. Some sophisticated mechanisms such as the FP-tree techniques are employed to make the computation efficient even with a vast amount of items and transactions.

6.3.1 Reading transactions from an FP-tree

In a number of cases, the transactions in the database are examined for computation; for example, in the preparation step, when we generate all size 2 itemsets; in the item benefit calculation, to determine the profit of a selection. If we actually scan the given database, which typically contains one record for each transaction, the computation will be very costly. Here we make use of the FP-tree structure [10]. We construct an FP-tree $\mathcal{FPT}$ once for all transactions, setting the support threshold to zero, and recording the occurrence count of itemsets at each tree node. With the zero threshold, $\mathcal{FPT}$ retains all information in the given set of transactions. Then we can traverse $\mathcal{FPT}$ instead of scanning the original database. The advantage of $\mathcal{FPT}$ is that it forms a single path for transactions with repeated patterns. In many applications, there exist many transactions with the same pattern, especially when the

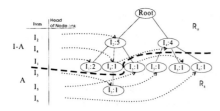

Figure 1. An example of an FP-MPIS-tree

number of transactions is large. These repeated patterns are processed only once with $\mathcal{FPT}$. From our experiments this mechanism can greatly reduce the overall running time.

6.3.2 Calculating Profit with the FP-MPIS-tree

In the definition of the profit of an item selection $\widehat{P}(A)$ (see Definition 6), we need to compute the number of transactions containing some selected items I_a and any item in set d_i (the value of $g(I_a, d_i)$), where $I_a \in A$ and $d_i \subseteq I - A$. This is computed for many selections for each iteration, hence the efficiency is important. For this task, we use the FP-MPIS-tree data structure.

In the FP-MPIS-tree, we divide the items into two sets, $I - A$ and A. Set A corresponds to items selected while $I - A$ contains those not selected. The items in set $I - A$ are inserted into FP-MPIS-tree near to the root. Similar to the FP-tree, the ordering of items in each set in the FP-MPIS-tree is based on the frequencies of items. An example is shown in Figure 1. In the figure, the set of selected items is $A = \{I_3, I_5, I_6\}$ and the set of unselected items is $I - A = \{I_1, I_2, I_4\}$.

To compute $g(I_a, d)$, we first look up the horizontal linked list (dotted links in Figure 1) of item I_a in the FP-MPIS-tree. For each node Q in the linked list, we call the function parseFPTree(Q, d). The function returns a count, we add up all the counts returned from the nodes Q and it is the value of $g(I_a, d)$.

Function parseFPTree(N, d) computes the number of transactions containing item I_a and at least one item in d in the path from root of FP-tree to N. Starting from the node N, we traverse the tree upwards towards the root of the FP-tree until we find a node M containing one element in set d or we hit the root node. If M exists, the count stored in node N is returned. The call of function parseFPTree(N, d) is quite efficient as we do not need to traverse downwards from node N. This is because all nodes below node N are selected items, no item in d will be found below N.

A further refinement for the FP-MPIS-tree is to insert only transactions that contain both selected and non-selected items. For transactions with only selected items, the profit for each selected item is simply given. For transactions with only non-selected item, the profit contribution will be zero. This refinement can greatly reduce the size of the FP-MPIS-tree. Note also that the FP-MPIS-tree is built from the FP-tree $\mathcal{FPT}$ and not from the original database.

6.3.3 Item Benefit Update

In each iteration, after we remove item I_x, we need to check the selection S_i for each item I_i in $\mathcal{I}'$. If S_i contains item I_x, it should be updated because item I_x has been removed, also a new item I_k will be selected to be included into S_i. As S_i is changed, the benefits b_i also have to be updated.

Let $S'_i \cup \{I_x\}$ be the selection before we remove item I_x while $S'_i \cup \{I_k\}$ be the selection after we have removed item I_x and added item I_k in the selection S_i. We can do the item benefit update by scanning only those transactions $\mathcal{T}$ containing at least one of item I_x and item I_k. Let $\widehat{P}'(A, \mathcal{T})$ be the profit of the item selection A generated by transactions in $\mathcal{T}$. The item benefit is updated: $b_i \leftarrow b_i + \widehat{P}'(S'_i \cup \{I_k\}, \mathcal{T}) - \widehat{P}'(S'_i \cup \{I_x\}, \mathcal{T})$. The computation of $\widehat{P}'(A, \mathcal{T})$ can be done in a similar manner as $\widehat{P}(A)$ but $\widehat{P}'(A, \mathcal{T})$ considers only transactions $\mathcal{T}$, instead of all transactions. As there are fewer transactions in $\mathcal{T}$ compared to the whole database, the update can be done very efficiently.

7 Empirical Study

We use the Pentium IV 1.5 GHz PC to conduct our experiment. Frontline System Solver is used to solve the QP problem. All algorithms other than QP are implemented in C/C++. The **profitability** is in terms of the percentage of the total profit in the data set. We compare our methods with HAP and the naive approach. The naive approach simply calculates the profits generated by each item for all transactions and select the J items with the greatest profits. Several synthetic data sets and a real data set are to be tested in our experiments.

We have tried a number of quadratic programming tools, including LINDO, TOMLAB, GAMS, BARON, OPTRIS, WSAT, Frontline System Solver, MOSEK and OPBDP. We choose Frontline System Solver (Premium Solver - Premium Solver Platform) [1] because it performs the best out of these solvers.

7.1 Synthetic Data Set

In our experiment, we use the IBM synthetic data generator in [2] to generate the data set with the following parameters (same as the parameters of [26]): 1,000 items, 10,000 transactions, 10 items per transaction on average, and 4 items per frequent itemset on average. The price distribution can be approximated by a lognormal distribution, as pointed out in [15]. We use the same settings as [26]. That is, 10% of items have the low profit range between $0.1 and $1, 80% of items have the medium profit range between $1 and $5, and 10% of items have the high profit range between $5 and $10.

7.2 Real Data Set

The real data set is obtained from a large drug store in Canada over a period of 3 month. In this data set, there are 26,128 items and 193,995 transactions. On average, each transaction contains 2.86 items. About 40% of the transactions contain a single item, 22% contain 2 items, 13% contain 3 items, the percentages for increasing sizes decrease smoothly, and there are about 3% of the transactions with more than 10 items. The greatest transaction size is 88 items. In this data set, the profit distribution of items is shown in the following table.

Profit Range	Proportion	Profit Range	Proportion
$0-$0.1	2.03%	$5-$10	10.43%
$0.1-$1	25.05%	$10-$100	7.75%
$1-$5	54.59%	$100-$400	0.15%

7.3 Results for Synthetic Data

In the first experiment, we have the same setup as in [26] but the profit follows lognormal distribution. The result is shown in Figure 2. In the figure, it is noted that the profitability lines for MPIS_Alg, QP and HAP are overlapping and the execution-time line for HAP is slightly greater than that for naive.

For profitability, we observe that, for the data set, the naive approach gives the lowest profitability among all algorithms. This is because the naive approach does not consider any cross-selling effect. Naturally the profitabilities of all algorithms increase when the number of items selected increases.

From the graph of the execution time against the selection size, the execution time of MPIS_Alg increases from 0% selection, reaching a maximum when about half the items are selected, and then decreases afterwards. Here the execution time depends on two factors. The first factor is related to the complexity of each iteration. If there are more items to be selected, the benefit calculation is more complex and updates to the benefit are more likely. The initial increase is related to the first factor. The second factor is related to the number of iterations in the algorithm. When J, the number of items selected, increases, the number of items to be removed in the iteration step decreases. Thus, the number of iterations decreases if J is large compared with n. The first factor is dominant when the selection is below 50% but the second factor becomes dominant when the selection is larger than 50%.

The quadratic programming approach (QP) used in the chosen Solver uses a variant of the Simplex method to determine a feasible region and then uses the methods described in [13] to find the solution. As the approach uses an iterative step based on the current state to determine the next step, the execution time is quite fluctuating as the execution time is mainly dependent on the problem (or which state the algorithm is in).

HAP is an iterative approach to find the authority weight of each item. The formula for the update of the authority weight is in the form $a = Ma$, where a is a vector of dimension n representing the authority weight of n items and M is an $n \times n$ matrix used in HAP to update the authority weight. In our experiment, we observed that the authority weights converge rapidly.

QP takes the longest execution time compared with other algorithms. Naive gives the shortest execution time as there are only simple operations. HAP gives the second shortest execution time for this small synthetic data set. We note that the number of iterations involved are quite small. MPIS_Alg has the second greatest execution time, but it scales much better with increasing number of items, where it can outform HAP many folds (see the next subsection).

7.4 Results for Real Data Set

With the drug store data set, we have conducted similar experiments as with the synthetic data. However, the Quadratic Programming (QP) Solver [1] does not handle more than 2000 variables. In the real data set, there are 26,128 variables (i.e. items), hence it is not possible to experiment with our QP tool.

The results of the experiments are shown in Figure 3. In the results, HAP gives the lowest profitability. The reason is as follows. In the dataset, there are some items with zero-profit and high authority weight (described in Section 3), yielding a low estimated total profit of the item selection. Suppose item I_i has zero profit, it is likely a good buy and hence can lead to high support. If there are sufficient number of purchases of other item, says item I_j, with item I_i and if item I_i usually occur in the transactions containing item I_j, the confidence of the rule $I_j \rightarrow I_i$ is quite high. This creates a high authority weight for item I_i. Items like I_i would lead to smaller profitability for HAP.

MPIS_Alg gives a greater profitability than naive approach in the real data set. For instance, if $J = 20,902$, the difference in profitabilities between these two approaches is 2%. In the real data set, the total profit is equal to $1,006,970. The difference in 2% profitability corresponds to $20,139.4, which is a significant value. If J=8709, the difference in profitabilities between the two approaches is about 8%, which corresponds to $80,557.6.

On average, the execution time of HAP is 6.5 times slower than MPIS_Alg when the problem size is large. HAP requires 6 days to find the item selection while MPIS_Alg requires about 1 day to find the solution. Since item selection is typically performed once in a while, only when a store should update the types of products it carries, the execution time is acceptable. Though the naive method is much faster, the profit gain consideration from MPIS_Alg would make it the better choice for an application.

The execution time of HAP increases significantly when the number of items increases compared with MPIS_Alg. In HAP, a *cross-selling matrix B* is updated iteratively. The matrix is of the order $n \times n$. For the real data set $n = 26,128$, and n^2 will be very large. Let a be the $n \times 1$ vector representing the authority weight of each item. In HAP, there is a process to update Ma iteratively, where $M = B^T B$. This matrix multiplication of matrix M with vector a is highly costly. Let us consider the memory required for matrix M. If double data type (8 bytes) is used for storage of each entry, then the matrix requires a memory size of about 5.08GB. If float data type (4 bytes) is required, then about 2.5GB memory is required. This large matrix cannot fit into the physical memory, causing a lot of disk accesses for virtual memory. Since the matrix M is sparse, a hash data structure can be used, so that only non-zero entries are stored. We have adopted the hash structure for the real data set, and fouud that less than 5MB memory is needed. Our results in Figure 3 are based on this enhanced hashing approach. However, the computation with this reduced size is still very massive.

We have also tried other sets of experiments where not all

377

the items are considered but only those above a minimum support threshold of 0.05% or 0.1% are considered. However, the resulting profitabilities are much lower than those shown in Figure 3. For instance, if J = 500 and min-support = 0.05%, the profitability of naive and MPIS_Alg is about 1.3%. But, if all items are considered, the profitability of those approaches is about 25%. This is explained by the existence of items that generate high profits but which are not purchased frequently enough to be counted given the support thresholds.

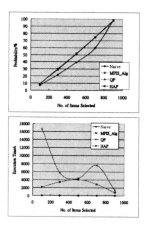

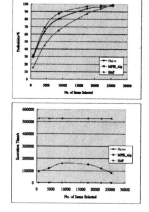

Figure 2. The Synthetic Data Set

Figure 3. The drug store data set

8 Conclusion

One of the applications of association rule - the maximal-profit item selection problem with cross-selling effect (MPIS) is discussed in this paper. We propose a modeling by the loss rule, which is used in the formulation of the total profit of the item selection. We propose both a quadratic programming approach and a heuristical approach to solve the MPIS problem. We show by experiments that these methods are efficient and highly effective. We believe that much future work can be done. The heuristical method can be enhanced with known methodologies such as hill climbing. Expert knowledge can be included in the methods, and the definition of the problem can be changed in different ways to reflect different user environments.

Acknowledgements We would like to thank M.Y. Su for his generous help in providing the source codes for the HAP solution and his other advices. We also thank Ping Quin of DBMiner Technology for providing the real dataset. This research is supported by the Hong Kong RGC Earmarked Grant UGC REF.CUHK 4179/01E.

References

[1] Frontline systems solver, http://www.solver.com/.

[2] R. Agrawal. Ibm synthetic data generator, http://www.almaden.ibm.com/cs/quest/syndata.html.

[3] R. Agrawal, T. Imilienski, and Swami. Mining association rules between sets of items in large databases. In *SIGMOD*, 1993.

[4] R. Agrawal and R. Srikant. Fast algorithms for mining association rules. In *VLDB*, 1994.

[5] J.E. Beasley. Heuristic algorithms for the unconstrained binary quadratic programming problem. In *Technical report, the Management School, Imperial College, London*, Dec 1998.

[6] T. Blischok. Every transaction tells a story. In *Chain Store Age Executive with Shopping Center Age 71 (3)*, pages 50–57, 1995.

[7] T. Brijs, B. Goethals, G. Swinnen, K. Vanhoof, and G. Wets. A data mining framework for optimal product selection in retail supermarket data: The generalized profset model. In *SIGKDD*, 2000.

[8] T. Brijs, G. Swinnen, K. Vanhoof, and G. Wets. Using association rules for product assortment decisions: A case study. In *SIGKDD*, 1999.

[9] M.R. Garey and D.S. Johnson. Computers and intractability: A guide to the theory of np-completeness. In *Freeman*, 1979.

[10] J. Han, J. Pei, and Y. Yin. Mining frequent patterns without candidate generation. In *SIGMOD*, 2000.

[11] S. Hedberg. The data gold rush. In *BYTE, October*, pages 83–99, 1995.

[12] Hiller and Lieberman. Introduction to operations research. In *McGraw Hill, Seventh Edition*, 2001.

[13] B. V. Hohenbalken. A finite algorithm to maximize certain pseudoconcave functions on polytopes. In *Mathematical Programming 8*, 1975.

[14] R. Horst, P. M. Pardalos, and N. V. Thoai. Introduction to global optimization. In *Kluwer Academic Publishers, Second Edition*, 2000.

[15] J. C. Hull. Options, futures, and other derivatives. In *Prentice Hall International, Inc. (3rd Edition)*, 1997.

[16] L.D. Iasemidis, P. Pardalos, J.C. Sackellares, and D.S. Shiau. Quadratic binary programming and dynamical system approach to determine the predictability of epileptic seizures. In *Journal of Combinatorial Optimization, Kluwer Academic*, pages 9–26, 2001.

[17] J. Kleinberg, C. Papadimitriou, and P. Raghavan. A microeconomic view of data mining. In *Knowledge Discovery Journal*, 1998.

[18] J. M. Kleinberg. Authoritative sources in a hyperlinked environment. In *Proc. ACM-SIAM Symp. on Discrete Algorithms*, 1998, Also in JACM 46:5, 1999.

[19] S. J. Leon. Linear algebra with applications. In *Prentice Hall, Fifth Edition*, 1998.

[20] J. Luo, K. R. Pattipati, and P.K. Willett. A sub-optimal soft decision pda method for binary quadratic programming. In *Proc. of the IEEE Systems, Man, and Cybernetics Conference*, 2001.

[21] H. Mannila. Methods and problems in data mining. In *Proc. of Int. Conf. on Database Theory*, 1997.

[22] H. Mannila, H. Toivonen, and A. I. Verkamo. Efficient algorithms for discovering association rules. In *KDD*, 1994.

[23] V. Safronov and M. Parashar. Optimizing web servers using page rank prefetching for clustered accesses. In *World Wide Web: Internet and Web Information Systems Volume 5, Number 1*, 2002.

[24] S. Sahni. Computationally related problems. In *SIAM J. Comput. 3*, pages 262–279, 1974.

[25] J. Ullman. Lecture notes on searching the web, http://www-db.stanford.edu/ ullman/mining/mining.html.

[26] K. Wang and M.Y. Su. Item selection by "hub-authority" profit ranking. In *SIGKDD*, 2002.

Efficient Data Mining for Maximal Frequent Subtrees

Yongqiao Xiao, Jenq-Foung Yao
Dept. of Math & Computer Science
Georgia College and State University
Milledgeville, GA 31061
{yongqiao.xiao, jf.yao}@gcsu.edu

Zhigang Li, Margaret H. Dunham *
Dept. of Computer Science & Engineering
Southern Methodist University
Dallas, TX 75275
{zgli,mhd}@engr.smu.edu

Abstract

A new type of tree mining is defined in this paper, which uncovers maximal frequent induced subtrees from a database of unordered labeled trees. A novel algorithm, PathJoin, is proposed. The algorithm uses a compact data structure, FST-Forest, which compresses the trees and still keeps the original tree structure. PathJoin generates candidate subtrees by joining the frequent paths in FST-Forest. Such candidate subtree generation is localized and thus substantially reduces the number of candidate subtrees. Experiments with synthetic data sets show that the algorithm is effective and efficient.

1 Introduction

Data mining has evolved from association rule mining [1], sequence mining [2, 4, 10], to tree mining [12, 5] and graph mining [11, 8, 7, 9]. Association rule mining and sequence mining are one-dimensional structure mining, and tree mining and graph mining are two-dimensional or higher structure mining. The applications of tree mining arise from Web usage mining, mining semi-structured data, and bioinformatics, etc.

The focus of this paper is on a new type of tree mining. As a motivating example for this new type of tree mining, consider mining the Web logs at a particular Web site. Several types of traversal patterns have been proposed to analyze the browsing behavior of the user[4, 10]. One drawback of such one-dimensional traversal patterns for the Web logs is that the document structure of the Web site, which is essentially hierarchical (a tree) or a graph, is not well captured.

In this paper, we uncover the maximal frequent subtree structures from the access sessions. The access sessions

are regarded as trees instead of sequences. The trees are unordered, and the frequent subtrees are induced subtrees and maximal. Other contributions of the paper include: a compact data structure is used to compress the trees in the database, and at the same time the original tree structure is kept; and the proposed algorithm, PathJoin, uses a new candidate subtree generation method, which is localized to the children of a node in a tree and thus substantially reduces the number of candidate subtrees.

The rest of the paper is organized as follows. In Section 2 the tree mining problem is formally defined, and then the related work is described and compared to our work. Section 3 describes the compact data structure, and the PathJoin algorithm. Section 4 reports the experimental results. The last Section concludes the paper and points out the future work.

2 Problem Statement and Related Work

2.1 Problem Statement

A *tree* is an acyclic connected directed graph. Formally, we denote a tree as $T = <N, B, r, L>$, where N is the set of nodes, B is the set of branches (directed edges), $r \in N$ is the root of the tree, and L is the set of labels on the nodes. For each branch $b = <n_1, n_2> \in B$, where $n_1, n_2 \in N$, we call n_1 the parent of n_2, and n_2 a child of n_1. If the children of each node are orderd, the tree is called an *ordered tree*, otherwise, it is an *unordered tree*. On each node $n_i \in N$, there is a label $l_i \in L$. The labels in a tree could be unique, or duplicate labels are allowed for different nodes. Without loss of generality, the labels are represented by positive integers.

Paths and Root Paths A *path* is a sequence of connected branches, i.e., $p = << n_1, n_2 >, < n_2, n_3 >, \cdots, < n_{k-1}, n_k >>$, where $n_i \in N (1 \leq i \leq k)$, and k is the number of nodes on the path. For short, we represent the path just by the nodes on the path $< n_1, n_2, \cdots, n_k >$. A node x is called an ancestor of another node y if there exists

---

*This material is based upon work supported by the National Science Foundation under Grant No. IIS-9820841 and IIS-02808741.

a path starting from x to y, and accordingly y is called a descendent of x. A path starting from the root node is called a *root path*. Since there is only one root path to any node in the tree, each root path in a tree can be uniquely identified by the last node on the path. In Figure 1, node $n3$ represents the root path $< n1, n2, n3 >$, and the labels on the path are $< 1, 2, 3 >$.

Subtrees and Root Subtrees A tree $T' = < N', B', r', L' >$ is said to be a *subtree* of another tree $T = < N, B, r, L >$, if and only if there exists a mapping $\theta : N' \rightarrow N$ such that (1) for each node $x \in N'$, $l(x) = l(\theta(x))$, where l is the labeling function $l : N \rightarrow L$, and (2) for each branch $b = < x, y > \in B'$, $< \theta(x), \theta(y) > \in B$. Such subtrees are called *induced subtrees* in [12]. The embedded subtrees defined in [12] allow the two nodes after mapping to be on the same path (ancestor/descendent relationship), that is, $< \theta(x), \cdots, \theta(y) >$ is a path in T. In this paper, a subtree is referred to as an induced subtree, unless otherwise indicated explicitly. If a tree T' is a subtree of another tree T, we also say that tree T contains T' or T' occurs in T. If a subtree has the same root as the tree, i.e., $r' = r$, the subtree is called a *root subtree*. Figure 1 shows a root subtree S of tree T.

Itemset Representation for Root Subtrees A root subtree T' of tree T can be uniquely identified by the corresponding nodes in T of the leaf nodes in T', i.e., a root subtree T' with k leaf nodes $\{y_1, y_2, \cdots, y_k\}$ can be represented by the set of nodes $\{x_1, x_2, \cdots, x_k\}$ in T, where $x_i = \theta(y_i)(1 \leq i \leq k)$. Such representation for root subtrees is called *itemset representation*, since the set of representative nodes for the subtree is similar to a k-itemset, where a k-itemset consists of k items as for association rules [1], and an item here corresponds to a representative node in the tree (i.e., the root path ending at the node). For the root subtree S of tree T in Figure 1, the itemset representation is $\{n3, n5, n7\}$.

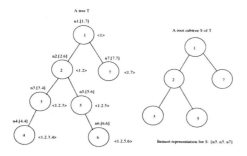

Figure 1. A Tree Example

Support and Maximal Frequent Subtrees Given a database of trees D, and a subtree S, the frequency of S

in D, $freq_D(S)$, is the total number of occurrences of S in D, i.e., $freq_D(S) = \sum_{T \in D} freq_T(S)$, where $freq_T(S)$ is 1 if S occurs in T, otherwise 0. The *support* of S in D, $sup_D(S)$, is the percentage of trees in D that contain S, i.e., $sup_D(S) = \frac{freq_D(S)}{|D|}$, where $|D|$ is the number of trees in D. Such definition excludes multiple occurrences of the subtree in a tree, thus it is called *unweighted support*. If the frequency of S includes every occurrence of S in every tree T in D, i.e., $FREQ_T(S)$ is n if S occurs n times in T, otherwise 0, the support can be defined as the ratio of the total frequency to the total size of the database (total number of nodes in all trees), i.e., $SUP(S) = \frac{\sum_{T \in D} FREQ_T(S)}{\sum_{T \in D} |T|}$, where $|T|$ is the number of nodes in $T(i.e., |N|)$. Such support is called *weighted support*, and it is similar to that in [10]. Weighted support and frequency are shown in upper case letters to distinguish from unweighted support and frequency. Given some support threshold s_{min} for unweighted or S_{min} for weighted, a subtree is said to be frequent, if the support for the subtree is not less than the threshold, i.e., $sup(X) \geq s_{min}$ for unweighted support or $SUP(X) \geq S_{min}$ for weighted support. A frequent subtree is maximal if it is not a subtree of another frequent subtree.

The Frequent Subtree Mining Problem Given a database of trees D, and some support threshold s_{min} or S_{min}, the objective is to find all maximal frequent subtrees in the database. The trees in D are assumed to be unordered trees, and the nodes in a tree could have duplicate labels, however, the labels for the children of every node are assumed to be unique. The support could be weighted or unweighted.

2.2 Related Work

In [12], Zaki presented two algorithms, TreeMiner and PatternMatcher, for mining embedded subtrees from ordered labeled trees. PatternMatcher is a level-wise algorithm similar to Apriori [1] for mining association rules. TreeMiner performs a depth-first search for frequent subtrees, and uses the novel scope-list (a vertical representation for the trees in the database) for fast support counting. FREQT was proposed in [3] for mining labeled ordered trees. FREQT uses the notion of *rightmost expansion* to generate candidate trees by attaching new nodes only to the rightmost branch of a frequent subtree. The problem of discovering frequent substructures from hierarchical semi-structured data was proposed in [5]. It assumes that the hierarchical semi-structured objects are of the same type, e.g., XML documents of the same DTD schema. Thus it is not a general-purpose subtree mining problem.

Other recent work related to frequent subtree mining include mining frequent graph patterns [7, 8, 11, 9]. Such graph mining algorithms are likely to be too general for tree mining as pointed out in [12]. The one-dimensional traversal patterns for Web usage mining include [4, 10], etc. These one-dimensional traversal patterns do not capture well the document structure of the Web site.

The maximal frequent subtree mining problem proposed by us is different from others in that: (1) the uncovered subtrees are induced subtrees of the unordered labeled trees in the database; (2) the subtrees are maximal. The trees are assumed to be unordered, because we think when analyzing the user's browsing from a Web page (e.g., home page) on a Web server, it would be more interesting to know which pages the user follows from the starting page, regardless of the order of the access; The subtrees are induced subtrees, as argued in [4, 10] that such contiguity can help analyze the user's browsing behavior for Web usage mining. The maximality of subtrees can reduce the number of meaningful patterns. Notice that we do not intend to imply that other types of frequent subtrees are not or less important.

3   Algorithm PathJoin

3.1   Outline

We propose an efficient algorithm, PathJoin, for mining the maximal frequent subtrees. For easier presentation, it is initially assumed that there are no duplicate labels in the tree. Some extensions for handling duplicate labels are described in the last subsection.

The main idea of algorithm PathJoin is as follows: first all maximal frequent paths are found, then the frequent subtrees are mined by joining the frequent paths. These maximal frequent paths are special frequent subtrees (or 1-itemsets), and joining k maximal frequent paths results in subtrees with k leaf nodes (or k-itemsets). After all frequent subtrees are found by joining the maximal frequent paths, the frequent subtrees that are not maximal are pruned, so that we have the set of all maximal frequent subtrees.

One of the features of the PathJoin algorithm is the use of a new compact data structure, *FST-Forest (Frequent SubTree-Forest)*, to find the maximal frequent paths. FST-Forest consists of compressed trees, representing the trees in the database (with infrequent 1-itemsets pruned). The idea of compressing the database was inspired by the earlier work [6] in mining association rules. In this paper, the compact structure is used to facilitate finding the maximal frequent paths, and with additional features it is also used in algorithm PathJoin for mining frequent subtrees. FST-Forest reduces the overall space requirements significantly (in most cases) due to the overlap among trees.

The PathJoin algorithm is outlined in Algorithm 1. There are only two database scans. In the first scan, the frequent size 1 subtrees (with one node) are found. In

the second scan, the trees in the database are trimmed with only frequent nodes left, and then merged into the compact structure, FST-Forest, which is done by function $constructCompressedForest$. After compressing all trees in the database to FST-Forest, the maximal frequent (root) paths are mined in each tree in FST-Forest, and then the frequent (root) subtrees are mined by joining the frequent paths. Finally, the subtrees that not maximal are pruned.

Algorithm 1 *PathJoin*

Input:

  D: database of trees.
  s_{min} *or* S_{min}: *unweighted/weighted support threshold.*
Output:
  MFST: all maximal frequent subtrees
Method:
// First database scan to find frequent 1-itemsets
*(1)   minsup = |D| * s_{min}*
           *or minsup = ($\sum_{T \in D} |T|$) * S_{min}*
(2) F_1 = { frequent size 1 subtrees};
// Second database scan to trim trees and create FST-Forest
(3)   Forest = constructCompressedForest(D, F_1);
(4)   FST = ∅;
(5)   for each tree T ∈ Forest.trees do begin
// Find the maximal frequent root paths in T
(6)   computeMFP(T, Forest, minsup);
// Find the frequent root subtrees in T
(7)   computeFST({T.root}, ∅, minsup, FST);
(8)   endfor
// Find the maximal frequent subtrees
(9)   MFST = maximize(Forest, FST);
(10)   return MFST;

3.2   Compressed Tree Construction

The compact structure, FST-Forest(or $Forest$ for short), consists of compressed trees. The construction of Forest is a three step process: identify frequent subtrees with only one node, trim the original trees in the database by removing the infrequent nodes, create Forest by appropriately merging these trimmed trees. Prior to explaining Forest creation process, we examine the Forest data structure in more detail.

The compressed trees in Forest are indexed by the root label of each tree. For each compressed tree, there is a nodelist for each label, which links together all nodes in the tree with the same label. Notice that nodelist is called header table in [6], and header table links all nodes in the entire forest, while in our structure, the nodelist is distributed to each tree in Forest to reduce overall main memory requirement during subtree mining. Figure 2 shows the FST-Forest structure. Each node in the forest is stored using the basic Node structure shown.

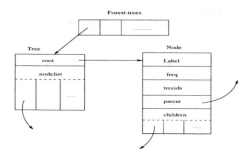

Figure 2. FST-Forest Data Structure

The treeids field in the node structure is new, and is required to reconstruct the original tree structure after compression. For a node in Forest, the treeids keeps the ids of all original trees (before being compressed to Forest) which have a root path ending at the node. To reduce the main memory requirement, the tree ids only need be saved on the leaf nodes of the original trimmed tree, since the tree ids can be merged upward(i.e., to ancestors) later in mining frequent subtrees.

To construct the Forest, each tree string (i.e., the labels by an depth-first traversal over the tree with -1 for each backward traversal as in [12]) in the database is scanned to create a tree in main memory. Then the infrequent nodes (those not in F_1) are removed from the tree yielding the trimmed trees. When creating the trimmed database, a tree in the original database may become disconnected (like a forest). If so, each connected subtree is treated as an independent tree (trimmed tree) but with the same tree id as the original tree. For the example database and an unweighted support of 50% there are only two subtrees of size one which are small: 8 and 9. When these are removed from the database we obtain the trimmed database. Figure 3 shows the original trees (upper part) and the trimmed trees (lower part). There are five trimmed trees. Two of them are the same as original trees: $T1$ and $T4$ (not shown). Three are modified from the original ones: $T2a$, $T2b$, and $T3a$.

The creation of the Forest is performed by either inserting (if no such tree with the same root label exists in Forest) or merging (a tree with the same root label already exists in Forest) these trimmed trees into Forest. In the first case, the new nodes from the trimmed tree are inserted directly to

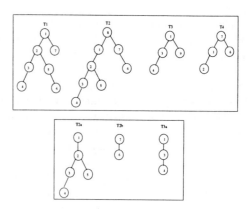

Figure 3. Original Trees vs. Trimmed Trees

Forest with the tree structure kept the same, and the nodelist updated to include the new nodes. In the second case, when a trimmed tree has common nodes with an existing tree in Forest, the frequency for the common nodes is incremented, and the new tree id is appended to the treeids if the node in the subtree is a leaf. After merging all the trimmed trees, the resulting Forest is shown in Figure 4 (frequency is shown $f = n$).

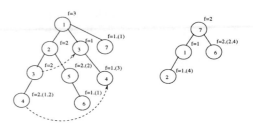

Figure 4. Compressed FST-Forest

Since the ids of the trees in the database are numbered sequentially, the treeids field on each node will be ordered after Forest is constructed. This automatic ordering is very useful in subtree expanding described in the following subsection. The treeids on the nodes are shown in the parentheses in Figure 4.

For each tree string in the database, the time for constructing the corresponding tree in main memory is linear to the string length. Determining connected subtrees with only frequent nodes can be accomplished by a breath-first traversal of the tree, which requires $O(n)$ time. Merging a subtree into Forest is like a depth-first traversal, which also requires $O(n)$ time. Overall, constructing Forest with all trees in the database needs time linear to the total number of nodes in all trees.

The space requirement for the compact structure depends on the structures of the trees in the database. In the worst case when there are no common nodes among the trees, i.e., each node is unique, there is no compression in Forest and the required memory is as large as the database. Fortunately, there are usually a lot of common nodes among the trees (the common structures of the trees are what we are trying to discover!), and thus it results in a compact Forest as shown by the experiments. Since the tree ids are stored only in the leaf nodes of the original tree (may not be leaf nodes in Forest due to merging), the memory for storing the tree ids is reduced, especially for deep trees.

3.3 Maximal Frequent Path Mining

The constructed Forest contains all paths found in the database which could possibly be frequent. However, not every path exists as a root path in Forest. For example, the path $< 2, 3 >$ is found in Figure 4, but it is not a root path. To facilitate the counting of all paths, we expand Forest to ensure that all paths from the original database are now root paths.

For those non-root paths with the same starting label X as the root label of a tree in Forest, we need to expand them to the tree. Actually all such non-root paths are linked by $nodelist[X]$ in each tree. Each node in the nodelist can be viewed as a subtree rooted at the node, and the paths starting from the node (non-root) in the subtree should be merged with the root paths of the tree with root label X. The treeids and frequency of these subtrees can be directly merged to the tree, because (1) the subtrees are disjoint (i.e., they occur in different original trees in the database); (2) for a tree rooted at X in Forest, a subtree of X rooted at node Y, and a non-root path starting from Y to node Z, the frequency of the path $< Y, \cdots, Z >$ in the tree rooted at X is the same as that of the root path $< X, \cdots, Y, \cdots, Z >$. Since tree ids are automatically ordered during Forest construction, the merging of two sets of tree ids can be done in time linear to the sum of the length of the two sets.

After expanding the subtree with root label 1 in the second tree, the first tree with root label 1 is shown in Figure 5a). Other trees in the Forest are not shown since they are not relevant while mining the tree.

As a result of expanding non-root paths (subtrees) from other trees, the tree that is being mined in Forest has all paths in the original database which start with the root node. Then the maximal frequent root paths can be found by a depth-first traversal of the tree. During the traversal for mining the maximal frequent paths, the infrequent nodes and their descendents are all removed from the tree after their treeids are merged to the closest ancestor nodes that are frequent. Such removal of infrequent nodes is valid because of the downward closure property of subtrees. That is, all subtrees of frequent trees are frequent, or equivalently, all supertrees of an infrequent tree are infrequent.

At the end of such depth-first traversal of the tree, each leaf node left in the tree corresponds to a maximal frequent path. To facilitate the subsequent frequent subtree mining, the treeids are merged upward (from descendents to ancestors) by a post-order traversal of the tree. The resulting tree after computing the maximal frequent paths in the tree with root label 1 is shown in Figure 5b. The root paths in the tree with root label 1 are all frequent. The paths terminating at the leaf nodes are maximal.

The time complexity for computing the maximal frequent paths in a tree is $O(mn + ln)$, where m and l are the total number of nodes in the subtrees that are expanded, and the number of nodes in the tree that is being mined, respectively, and n is the maximum number of tree ids on the nodes in the tree after expanding.

3.4 Frequent SubTree Mining

After expanding all subtrees with the same root label, all frequent root subtrees can be mined from the tree as shown by Theorem 1.

Theorem 1 *Given a tree T with all frequent root paths, let the label of the root node be R. All frequent subtrees with root label R are root subtrees of T.*

Proof. Straightforward using the downward closure property of frequent subtrees.

The itemset representation for root subtrees is used in the following description, i.e., each root subtree S of tree T is represented by the representative nodes in T of the leaf nodes of S. A root subtree with k leaf nodes(or k root paths) is a k-itemset, and each root path is a 1-itemset.

The main idea is to construct candidate k-itemsets by joining k 1-itemsets. For example, in Figure 5b), by joining two 1-itemsets, $n3$ and $n5$, we have a candidate 2-itemset $\{n3, n5\}$. The frequency of a candidate k-itemset is the number of common tree ids on the k 1-itemsets. The set of common tree ids of k 1-itemsets is the intersection of the tree ids of the k 1-itemset. Such k-way intersection of the tree ids can be done in linear time, since the treeids are ordered on each node.

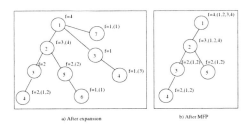

a) After expansion   b) After MFP

Figure 5. Subtree Expansion and MFP

To reduce the number of candidate itemsets, the downward closure property is used to generate candidate k-itemsets from frequent $(k-1)$-itemsets, that is, a candidate k-itemset is generated only if all its subsets $((k-1)$-itemsets) are frequent. The candidate generation is done by function $FST\_PathJoin$. Function $FST\_PathJoin$ is similar to function $apriori\_gen$ in [1]. For two itemsets $\{r_1, r_2, \cdots, r_{k-1}\}$ and $\{s_1, s_2, \cdots, s_{k-1}\}$, a candidate k-itemset $\{r_1, r_2, \cdots, r_{k-2}, r_{k-1}, s_{k-1}\}$ is generated from them if $r_i = s_i (1 \leq i \leq k-2)$ and all subsets of it are frequent. Notice that function $FST\_PathJoin$ is applied to the child nodes of a node in the tree recursively, thus it is localized, while $apriori\_gen$ is applied to all frequent itemsets.

Function 1 *computeFST(isetRecur, isetFixed, s, FST)*

> *isetRecur: itemset called recursively on its child nodes,*
> *isetFixed: itemset fixed during recursion,*
> *s: minimum support count,*
> *FST: the resulting set of frequent subtrees,*
> *output: the set of frequent child nodes of isetRecur.*

(1)   itemset = isetRecur ∪ isetFixed;
// Frequency of an itemset is the number of common tree ids
(2)   itemset.treeids = ∩_{X∈itemset} X.treeids;
(3)   if |itemset.treeids| < s then
(4)   return ∅;
(5)   FST = FST ∪ {itemset};
// Find the frequent child nodes in isetRecur
(6)   FST_1 = ∅;
(7)   for each child C of X ∈ isetRecur do begin
(8)   fx = itemset − {X};
(9)   re = {C};
(10)   RES = computeFST(re, fx, s, FST);
(11)   if RES ≠ ∅ then;
(12)   FST_1 = FST_1 ∪ {C};
(13)   endfor
// Generate candidates with two frequent child nodes
(14)   CFT_2 = FST_PathJoin(FST_1);
(15)   for (k = 2; CFT_k ≠ ∅; k++) do begin
(16)   FST_k = ∅;
(17)   for each X ∈ CFT_k do begin
(18)   fx = itemset − {Y.parent|Y ∈ X};
(19)   RES = computeFST(X, fx, s, FST);
(20)   if RES ≠ ∅ then;
(21)   FST_k = FST_k ∪ {X};
(22)   endfor
// Generate candidates with k + 1 frequent child nodes
(23)   CFT_{k+1} = FST_PathJoin(FST_k);
(24)   endfor
(25)   return FST_1;

The time complexity of the function depends on the number of frequent subtrees. For each candidate k-itemset, its frequency checking is done in time $O(kn)$, where n is the maximum number of tree ids on the nodes. The cost of function $FST\_PathJoin$ is kept minimal, since it is applied to the child nodes of a node in the tree only, that is, it is localized to a node. Such localization reduces the number of candidate subtrees substantially as shown in the experiments. There is no extra memory requirement for the frequency checking of a candidate itemset besides $1n$ for the k-way intersection.

3.5 Maximizing

There are two steps in finding the maximal frequent subtrees from the set of frequent subtrees: (1) local maximization in the tree and (2) global maximization in Forest. The local maximization is done on each tree for the frequent subtrees with the same root label. Global maximization filters those that are subtrees (non-root) of another frequent subtree. The two types of maximizations are relatively straightforward, thus the details are omitted.

After local maximization, we have maximal frequent subtrees with the same root label. Such maximal frequent subtrees within a tree in Forest could be interesting themselves. After global maximization, we have the set of all maximal frequent subtrees. For Web usage mining, these maximal frequent subtrees provide a global view of the entire Web site.

3.6 Handling Duplicate Labels

So far we have assumed that there are no duplicate labels in the trees of the database. The PathJoin algorithm can be modified a little bit to support duplicate labels.

Recall that when compressing a tree in the database into Forest, we first get the connected subtrees of the tree with only frequent nodes and each connected subtree has the same tree id as the original tree. With duplicate labels, each connected subtree with the same root label is assigned a pair of tree ids: one is the original tree id and the other is a new tree id. The pair of tree ids are added to all nodes of each connected subtree with the same root label. Notice that for these connected subtrees with unique root labels, only the original tree id is necessary (or the new tree id is the same as the original tree id). When merging a connected subtree into Forest, the pair of tree ids are also merged. For the non-root nodes with duplicate labels in a connected subtree, a pair of tree ids (original plus new) are also added the nodes and all their descendents. These pairs of tree ids are merged when expanding subtrees in function $computeMFP$.

The new tree ids are needed to prevent invalid subtree generation. For the trees in Figure 3, if $T2$ is replaced by

$T2'$ in Figure 6, the two connected subtrees have the same root label 2. In Figure 6, the pair of tree ids are shown as $x : y$ in parentheses on each node, where x and y are the original and new tree ids respectively. After merging, the root node has 3 children. Without the new tree ids, it could generate an invalid subtree, e.g., 2 1 -1 3 -1, since children with labels 1 and 3 do not appear to be the children of the node with label 2 at the same time. By checking the new tree ids, such invalid subtrees are avoided, since the two children have different new tree ids.

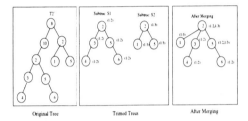

Figure 6. Handling Duplicate Labels

The frequency counting is changed as follows: for weighted support, the frequency at each node is the number of new tree ids, and for unweighted support, the frequency is the number of original tree ids.

4 Experimental Results

The performance of PathJoin was examined through a series of simulation experiments. All experiments were conducted on a Sun Blade 1000 with 1GB main memory and running Sun OS 5.8. The algorithm was implemented in C++ using Standard Template Library.

Three synthetic data sets, D10, F5 and T1M, were tested. These data sets were generated using the method in [12]. The synthetic data generation mimicks the Web site browsing behavior of the user. The parameters used in the data generation include the number of labels $N = 100$, the number of nodes in the master tree $M = 10000$, the maximum fanout of a node in the master tree $F = 10(F = 5$ for data set F5), and the maximum depth of the master tree $D = 10$, and the total number of trees in the data set $T = 100000(T = 1000000$ for T1M).

Two variations of the PathJoin algorithm were compared to examine the effect of pruning in candidate subtree generation: one uses pruning in candidate subtree generation (i.e., function $FST\_PathJoin$ checks whether the subsets of a candidate itemset are frequent) and the other does not. We did not compare our algorithm to others because of the difference of the problem defined by us from others.

4.1 Execution Time and Number of Candidate Subtrees

The execution time for the three data sets with varying minimum support is shown in Figures 7 and 8a). The execution time increases as the minimum support decreases, since there are more frequent subtrees with smaller minimum support. It can be also seen that the two variations of the algorithm (with or without pruning in candidate subtree generation) have no big difference in execution time. This is because the pruning does not prune away many candidate subtrees (less than 5%) as shown in Figure 8b). Thus the overhead for checking the subsets of the candidate subtrees offsets the saved time for frequency counting of the pruned candidate subtrees. Similar results were obtained for the other two data sets, which are not shown due to space limit. The reason that the pruning is not very effective is that the candidate subtree generation in function $computeFST$ is limited to the children of a node in a tree in Forest, i.e., it is localized. Such localization reduces the number of candidate subtrees compared to apriori_gen in [1], which is applied to all the frequent itemsets found in a pass.

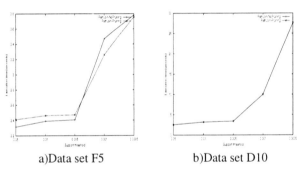

a)Data set F5 b)Data set D10

Figure 7. Execution Time

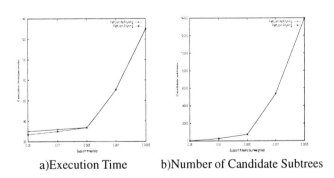

a)Execution Time b)Number of Candidate Subtrees

Figure 8. Data set T1M

4.2 Memory Usage and Scaleup

The memory usage for the compact data structure, FST-Forest, has two parts: one for the compressed tree structure, the other for the tree ids. The memory for the compressed tree structure is fixed for a data set given some minimum support threshold, while the memory for the tree ids will grow as the number of trees in the data set increases. In the experiments, the data sets with different number of trees were generated with the same parameters as for data set T1M. The minimum support was fixed to 0.5%. Figure 9a) shows the memory usage at two stages of the algorithm: the lower curve shows the the memory before expanding all subtrees with the same label, and the upper curve after computing the maximal frequent paths and merging the treeids upward. It can be seen that the memory usage is about doubled after expansion and merging. Figure 9 also shows that both the memory usage and the execution time scales linearly with respect to the change of the number of trees in the data set.

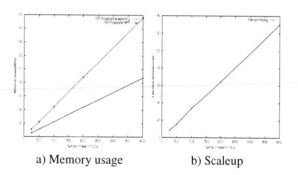

a) Memory usage   b) Scaleup

Figure 9. Memory Usage and Scaleup

5 Conclusion

A new type of tree mining (maximal induced subtrees in unordered trees) is defined in the paper. A novel algorithm, PathJoin, is proposed to discover all maximal frequent subtrees given some minimum support threshold. The algorithm uses a compact data structure, FST-Forest, to compress the trees in the database and at the same time still keeps the original tree structure. A localized candidate subtree generation method is used in the algorithm, which reduces the number of candidate subtrees substantially. The algorithm is evaluated with synthetic data sets.

The future work includes: (1) earlier identification of maximal frequent subtrees, which could potentially save a lot of time for computing the non-maximal frequent subtrees. (2) extension of FST-Forest for mining maximal frequent embedded subtrees, which allow ancestor/descendent relationship.

Acknowledgement

We would like to thank Prof. Mohammed J. Zaki for sending us the source code for the tree generation program.

References

[1] R. Agrawal and R. Srikant. Fast algorithms for mining association rules in large databases. In *Proceedings of the Twentieth International Conference on Very Large Databases*, pages 487–499, Santiago, Chile, 1994.

[2] R. Agrawal and R. Srikant. Mining sequential patterns. In *Proceedings of the 11th International Conference on Data Engineering*, Taipei, Taiwan, Mar. 1995. IEEE Computer Society Press.

[3] T. Asai, K. Abe, S. Kawasoe, H. Arimura, H. Satamoto, and S. Arikawa. Efficiently substructure discovery from large semi-structured data. In *Proceedings of the 2nd SIAM Int'l Conference on Data Mining*, april 2002.

[4] M.-S. Chen, J. S. Park, and P. S. Yu. Efficient data mining for path traversal patterns. *IEEE Transactions on Knowledge and Data Engineering*, 10(2):209–221, 1998.

[5] G. Cong, L. Yi, B. Liu, and K. Wang. Discovering frequent substructures from hierarchical semi-structured data. In *Proceedings of the 2nd SIAM Int'l Conference on Data Mining*, Arlington, VA, april 2002.

[6] J. Han, J. Pei, and Y. Yin. Mining frequent patterns without candidate generation. In *Proceedings of the ACM SIGMOD Conference*, 2000.

[7] A. Inokuchi, T. Washio, and H. Motoda. An apriori-based algorithm for mining frequent substructures from graph data. In *Proceedings of the 4th European Conference on Principles of Knowledge Discovery and Data Mining*, sep 2000.

[8] M. Kuramochi and G. Karypis. Frequent subgraph discovery. In *Proceedings of the 1st IEEE Int'l Conference on Data Mining*, nov 2001.

[9] D. Shasha, J. Wang, and R. Giugno. Algorithms and applications of tree and graph searching. In *Proceedings of the 21st ACM SIGMOD-SIGACT-SIGART Symposium on Principles of Database Systems*, pages 39–52, Madison, Wisconsin, june 2002.

[10] Y. Xiao and M. H. Dunham. Efficient mining of traversal patterns. *Data and Knowledge Engineering*, 39:191–214, 2001.

[11] X. Yan and J. Han. gspan: Graph-based substructure pattern mining. In *Proceedings of the 2002 IEEE International Conference on Data Mining (ICDM 2002), 9-12 December 2002, Maebashi City, Japan*, pages 721–724. IEEE Computer Society, 2002.

[12] M. J. Zaki. Efficiently mining frequent trees in a forest. In *Proceedings of the 8th ACM SIGKDD Int'l Conference on Knowledge Discovery and Data Mining*, Edmonton, Canada, jul 2002.

Mining Strong Affinity Association Patterns in Data Sets with Skewed Support Distribution

Hui Xiong *
Computer Science and Engineering
Univ. of Minnesota - Twin Cities
huix@cs.umn.edu

Pang-Ning Tan
Computer Science and Engineering
Michigan State University
ptan@cse.msu.edu

Vipin Kumar
Computer Science and Engineering
Univ. of Minnesota - Twin Cities
kumar@cs.umn.edu

Abstract

Existing association-rule mining algorithms often rely on the support-based pruning strategy to prune its combinatorial search space. This strategy is not quite effective for data sets with skewed support distributions because they tend to generate many spurious patterns involving items from different support levels or miss potentially interesting low-support patterns. To overcome these problems, we propose the concept of hyperclique pattern, which uses an objective measure called h-confidence to identify strong affinity patterns. We also introduce the novel concept of cross-support property for eliminating patterns involving items with substantially different support levels. Our experimental results demonstrate the effectiveness of this method for finding patterns in dense data sets even at very low support thresholds, where most of the existing algorithms would break down. Finally, hyperclique patterns also show great promise for clustering items in high dimensional space.

1 Introduction

Many data sets have inherently skewed support distributions. For example, the frequency distribution of English words appearing in text documents is highly skewed — while a few of the words appear many times, most of the words appear only a few times. Such a distribution has been observed in other application domains, including retail data, Web click-streams, and telecommunication data.

This paper examines the problem of applying association analysis [1, 2] to data sets with skewed support distributions. Existing algorithms often use a minimum support threshold to prune its combinatorial search space [2]. Two major problems arise when applying such strategy to skewed data sets.

- If the minimum support threshold is too low, many *uninteresting patterns involving items with substantially different support levels* are extracted. (We call such patterns as `cross-support` patterns.) An example of a cross-support pattern is {`Caviar, Milk`}, where `Caviar` is a low support item and `Milk` is a high support item. It is not surprising to find `Milk` in transactions that contain `Caviar` since `Milk` is present in many transactions. Cross-support patterns also tend to have very low pairwise correlations [4].

- If the minimum support threshold is too high, many *strong affinity patterns involving items with low support levels* are missed [8]. Such patterns are useful for capturing associations among rare but expensive items such as caviar and vodka or necklaces and earrings.

To illustrate these problems, consider the support distribution for the `pumsb` census data set shown in Figure 1. `Pumsb` is often used as benchmark for evaluating the performance of association rule algorithms on dense data sets. Observe the skewed nature of the support distribution, with 81.5% of the items having support less than 1% while 0.95% of them having support greater than 90%.

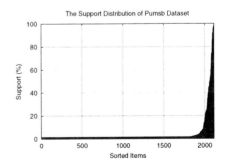

Figure 1. The support distribution of Pumsb.

We can partition the items into five disjoint groups based on their support levels, as shown in Table 1. The group

---

*Contact Author.

Table 1. Groups of items for pumsb data set.

Group	S1	S2	S3	S4	S5
Support	0-1%	1%-5%	5%-40%	40%-90%	>90%
# Items	1735	206	101	51	20

$S1$ has the lowest support level (less than or equal to 1%) but contains the most number of items, i.e., 1735 items. To detect patterns involving items from $S1$, the minimum support threshold must be less than 1%, but such a low threshold will degrade the performance of existing algorithms considerably. Our experiments showed that state-of-the-art algorithms such as Apriori [2], Charm [16], and MAFIA [5] break down when applied to pumsb at support threshold less than 40% [1]. Furthermore, if the support threshold is low, e.g., 0.05%, many cross-support patterns involving items from both $S1$ (rare items) and $S5$ (very frequent items) are generated. Just to give an indication of the scale, out of the 18847 frequent pairs involving items from $S1$ and $S5$, about 93% of them are cross-support patterns. These cross-support patterns have extremely poor correlation because the presence of the item from $S5$ does not necessarily imply the presence of the item from $S1$. It would be advantageous to develop techniques that can automatically eliminate such patterns during the mining process.

Omiecinski recently proposed an alternative to the support measure called *all-confidence* [10], which represents the minimum confidence of all association rules extracted from an itemset. Omiecinski proved that all-confidence has the desirable anti-monotone property that allows us to incorporate the measure directly into the mining process. We call the patterns derived from this measure as *hyperclique patterns*. (Note that we had independently proposed a measure called h-confidence [15] to capture the degree of affinity in a hyperclique pattern. The equivalence between h-confidence and all-confidence measures is shown in Section 2. For brevity, we will use the term h-confidence when referring to the affinity measure of hyperclique patterns.)

In this paper, we introduce a novel concept called the *cross-support property*, which is useful for eliminating candidate patterns having items with widely differing support levels. We show that h-confidence possesses such a property and develop an efficient algorithm called *hyperclique miner* that utilizes both the cross-support and anti-monotone properties of the h-confidence measure. Our experimental results suggest that hyperclique miner can efficiently discover strong affinity patterns even when the support threshold is set to zero.

Hyperclique patterns are also valuable patterns in their own right because they correspond to itemsets involving only tightly-coupled items. Discovering such patterns can

be potentially useful for a variety of applications such as item clustering, copy detection, and collaborative filtering. We demonstrate one potential application of hyperclique patterns in the area of item clustering, where such patterns can be used to provide high-quality hyperedges to seed the hypergraph-based clustering algorithms [7].

Related Work: Support-based pruning does not work well with dense data sets, nor is it effective at finding low support patterns. The concepts of maximal [3, 5] and closed itemsets [11, 16] were proposed to address these limitations. Although these concepts can identify a smaller set of representative patterns, their algorithms may still break down at low support thresholds, especially for data sets with skewed support distribution. Both closed and maximal itemsets are also not designed to explicitly remove the cross-support patterns. There has also been growing interest in developing techniques for mining association patterns without support constraints [6, 14]. However, such techniques are either limited to analyzing pairs of items [6] or does not address the cross-support problem [14].

2 Hyperclique Pattern

In this section, we describe the concept of a hyperclique pattern and introduce some important properties of the h-confidence measure.

2.1 Hyperclique Pattern Concepts

Definition 1 *The* **h-confidence** *of an itemset $P = \{i_1, i_2, \cdots, i_m\}$, denoted as $hconf(P)$, is a measure that reflects the overall affinity among items within the itemset. This measure is defined as $min\{conf\{i_1 \rightarrow i_2, \ldots, i_m\}, conf\{i_2 \rightarrow i_1, i_3, \ldots, i_m\}, \ldots, conf\{i_m \rightarrow i_1, \ldots, i_{m-1}\}\}$, where $conf$ follows from the definition of association rule confidence [1].*

Example 1 *Consider an itemset $P = \{A, B, C\}$. Assume that $supp(\{A\}) = 0.1$, $supp(\{B\}) = 0.1$, $supp(\{C\}) = 0.06$, and $supp(\{A, B, C\}) = 0.06$, where supp is the support [1] of an itemset. Then $conf\{A \rightarrow B, C\} = supp(\{A, B, C\})/supp(\{A\}) = 0.6$, $conf\{B \rightarrow A, C\} = 0.6$, and $conf\{C \rightarrow A, B\} = 1$. Hence, $hconf(P) = min\{conf\{B \rightarrow A, C\}, conf\{A \rightarrow B, C\}, conf\{C \rightarrow A, B\}\} = 0.6$.*

Definition 2 *Given a transaction database and the set of all items $I = \{I_1, I_2, \ldots, I_n\}$, an itemset P is a* **hyperclique pattern** *if and only if: 1) $P \subseteq I$ and $|P| > 0$. 2) $hconf(P) \geq h_c$, where h_c is the h-confidence threshold.*

A hyperclique pattern P is a strong-affinity association pattern because the presence of any item $x \in P$ in a transaction strongly implies the presence of $P - \{x\}$ in the same

[1]This is observed on a Sun Ultra 10 workstation with a 440MHz CPU and 128 Mbytes of memory

transaction. To that end, the h-confidence measure is designed specifically for capturing such strong affinity relationships. Nevertheless, hyperclique patterns can also miss some interesting patterns; e.g., an itemset {A, B, C} that produces low confidence rules $A \rightarrow BC$, $B \rightarrow AC$, and $C \rightarrow AB$ but a high confidence rule $AB \rightarrow C$. Such type of patterns are not the focus of this paper.

2.2 Properties of h-confidence

We illustrate three important properties of the h-confidence measure in this subsection.

2.2.1 Anti-monotone Property

As previously noted, the h-confidence measure is mathematically equivalent to the all-confidence measure proposed by Omiecinski [10], even though both measures are developed from different perspectives.

Definition 3 *The all-confidence measure [10] for an itemset $P = \{i_1, i_2, \cdots, i_m\}$ is defined as* $\min(\{conf(A \rightarrow B | \forall A, B \subset P, A \cup B = P, A \cap B = \emptyset\})$.

Lemma 1 *If $P = \{i_1, i_2, \cdots, i_m\}$ is an itemset, then $hconf(P)$ is mathematically equivalent to all-confidence(P) and is equal to*

$$\frac{supp(\{i_1, i_2, \ldots, i_m\})}{max_{1 \leq k \leq m}\{supp(\{i_k\})\}}. \quad (1)$$

Omiecinski proved that all-confidence is an anti-monotone measure [10], i.e., if an itemset $\{i_1, \ldots, i_m\}$ is above the all-confidence threshold, so is every subset of size m-1. Since h-confidence is mathematically identical to all-confidence, it is also monotonically non-increasing as the size of the hyperclique pattern increases. This anti-monotone property allows us to push the h-confidence constraint into the search algorithm. Thus, when searching for hyperclique patterns, the support of a candidate pattern $\{i_1, \ldots, i_m\}$ is counted only if all its subsets of size m-1 are hyperclique patterns.

2.2.2 Cross-Support Property

In this section, we introduce the concept of *cross-support* property. This property is useful to *avoid generating cross-support patterns*, which are patterns containing items from substantially different support levels. We also show that the h-confidence measure possesses such a property.

Before presenting the concept of *cross-support* property, we first introduce the idea of an upper bound function for a measure of association.

Definition 4 *Let f be a measure of association and $f_{\max}$ be its maximum possible value. We define upper(f) as an upper bound function for f if $\forall P : f(P) \leq upper(f(P))$, where P is an association pattern. An upper bound function is trivial if upper(f) = $f_{\max}$.*

For example $upper(supp(P)) = 1$ is a trivial upper bound function for the support measure. An example of a non-trivial upper bound function for the h-confidence measure is presented below.

Lemma 2 *Given an itemset $P = \{i_1, \ldots, i_m\}$, the h-confidence for P has the following upper bound:*

$$upper(hconf(P)) = \frac{min_{1 \leq l \leq m}\{supp(\{i_l\})\}}{max_{1 \leq k \leq m}\{supp(\{i_k\})\}}. \quad (2)$$

We will use the notion of upper bound function to describe cross-support property. In a nutshell, given a specified threshold t, if a function f has the cross-support property, we can find two itemsets from different support levels such that, for any *cross-support* pattern P, we are guaranteed to have $f(P) < t$. The formal definition of the *cross-support* property of a function f is given below.

Definition 5 *Let $I = \{i_1, i_2, \cdots, i_n\}$ be an ordered set of items, sorted according to their support values, i.e., $\forall k : supp(i_k) \leq supp(i_{k+1})$. In addition, for each item $x \in I$, let $L(x) = \{x' | supp(x') \leq supp(x)\}$ and $U(x) = \{x' | supp(x') \geq supp(x)\}$.*

A function f satisfies the cross-support property if $\exists x, y \in I$ such that $supp(x) < supp(y)$ and upper $(f(x, y)) < t$ implies $\forall P : f(P) < t$, where P is an itemset containing at least one item from $L(x)$ and at least one item from $U(y)$ and t is the specified threshold.

In the following, we provide a sufficient condition for f to satisfy the cross-support property.

Theorem 1 *Given: 1) A measure of association, f; 2) A pair of items x and y with $supp(x) < supp(y)$; 3) A pair of itemsets $L(x) = \{x' | supp(x') \leq supp(x)\}$ and $U(y) = \{y' | supp(y') \geq supp(y)\}$;*

If the following conditions hold,

1) A non-trivial upper bound function for f exists;

2) $upper(f(\{x, y\}))$ is computed using only $supp(x)$ and $supp(y)$;

3) $upper(f(\{x, y\}))$ decreases monotonically with increasing $supp(y)$ if x is fixed;

4) $upper(f(\{x, y\}))$ decreases monotonically with decreasing $supp(x)$ if y is fixed;

5) f is an anti-monotone measure when applied to patterns of size two or more;

389

Then $f(p) \leq upper(f(\{x, y\}))$, where p is a cross-support pattern that contains at least one item from $L(x)$ and at least one item from $U(y)$.

The proof of this theorem is given in [15]. As a consequence, $upper(f(\{x, y\})) < t$ implies $f(p) < t$, which means that f must satisfy the cross-support property.

Lemma 3 *The h-confidence measure satisfies the cross-support property. Furthermore, the h-confidence value for any cross-support pattern* $P = \{x_{i_1}, x_{i_2}, \ldots, x_{i_k}, y_{j_1}, y_{j_2}, \ldots, y_{j_l}\}$ *has an upper bound as* $\frac{max_{1 \leq p \leq m}\{supp(\{x_p\})\}}{min_{1 \leq q \leq n}\{supp(\{y_q\})\}}$

Lemma 3 provides an upper bound of the h-confidence values for all possible cross-support patterns from two itemsets with different support levels. Thus, if the h-confidence threshold is set higher than this upper bound, we will not generate any cross-support pattern as candidate hyperclique pattern during the mining process.

h-confidence is not the only measure that satisfies the cross-support property. Table 2 provides a list of other measures of association that possess such a property. Among the measures that do not have the *cross-support* property include support and odds ratio [13].

Table 2. Measures with the *cross-support* **property (Assume that** $supp(x) < supp(y)$**).**

Measure	Computation Formula	Upper Bound
Cosine	$\frac{supp(x,y)}{\sqrt{supp(x)supp(y)}}$	$\sqrt{\frac{supp(x)}{supp(y)}}$
Jaccard	$\frac{supp(x,y)}{supp(x)+supp(y)-supp(x,y)}$	$\frac{supp(x)}{supp(y)}$
PS	$supp(x,y)-supp(x)supp(y)$	$supp(x)(1-supp(y))$

2.2.3 Strong Affinity Property

In this subsection, we investigate the relationships between h-confidence and other similarity measures such as cosine (Lemma 4) and Jaccard (Lemma 5) measures. Our goal is to derive the lower bounds for these similarity measures in terms of the h-confidence threshold, h_c.

Definition 6 *Given a pair of items* $P = \{i_1, i_2\}$, *the cosine measure [12] for* P *can be computed as* $\frac{supp(\{i_1, i_2\})}{\sqrt{supp(i_1) \times supp(i_2)}}$, *while the Jaccard measure [12] for* P *is* $\frac{supp(\{i_1, i_2\})}{supp(\{i_1\}) + supp(\{i_2\}) - supp(\{i_1, i_2\})}$.

Lemma 4 *If* $P = \{i_1, i_2\}$ *is a size-2 hyperclique pattern, then* $cosine(P) \geq h_c$.

Lemma 5 *If* $P = \{i_1, i_2\}$ *is a size-2 hyperclique pattern, then* $Jaccard(P) \geq h_c/2$.

The above lemmas suggest that if h_c is sufficiently high, then all size-2 hyperclique patterns contain items that are strongly affiliated with each other in terms of their cosine and Jaccard values. For a hyperclique pattern that contains more than two items, we can compute the average Jaccard and cosine measure for all pairs of items within this pattern. Due to the antimonotone property of the h-confidence measure, every pair of items within a hyperclique pattern must have an h-confidence value greater than or equal to h_c. As a result, the average Jaccard or cosine measure of a hyperclique pattern must also satisfy the above lemmas.

3 Hyperclique Miner Algorithm

In this section, we design a level-wise algorithm, called hyperclique miner, for discovering hyperclique patterns.

Example 2 *We illustrate how hyperclique miner works using the running example shown in Figure 2. As can be seen, the process of searching hyperclique patterns is illustrated by the generation of branches of a set-enumeration tree. For this running example, suppose the minimum support threshold is zero and the minimum h-confidence threshold is 55%. There are two major pruning techniques incorporated into our algorithm.*

1. *We can prune itemsets by the anti-monotone property of the h-confidence measure. For instance, applying Equation 1, the h-confidence of the candidate pattern* $\{4, 5\}$ *is supp($\{4, 5\}$)/max$\{$supp($\{4\}$), supp($\{5\}$)$\}$= 0.1/0.2 = 0.5, which is less than 55%. Hence, the itemset* $\{4, 5\}$ *is not a hyperclique pattern and is immediately pruned. In turn, we can prune the candidate pattern* $\{3, 4, 5\}$ *by the anti-monotone property of the h-confidence measure since one of its subset,* $\{4, 5\}$, *is not a hyperclique pattern.*

2. *We can do pruning by the cross-support property of h-confidence. For instance, given a sorted list of items,* $\{1, 2, 3, 4, 5\}$, *suppose we split the list into two sets* $S_1 = \{1, 2\}$ *and* $S_2 = \{3, 4, 5\}$. *We can compute the upper bound of h-confidence for any cross-support pattern between these two item sets by Lemma 3. In this example, the upper bound is equal to max$\{$supp($\{3\}$), supp($\{4\}$), supp($\{5\}$)$\}$/min$\{$supp($\{1\}$), supp($\{2\}$)$\}$ = 3/9= 0.33. Therefore, the h-confidence for every cross-support pattern involving these items must be less than 33%. If the h-confidence threshold is 55%, we may prune all these cross-support patterns even before they are generated as candidate patterns. Without applying cross-support pruning, we have to generate six additional patterns, including* $\{1, 3\}$, $\{1, 4\}$, $\{1, 5\}$, $\{2, 3\}$, $\{2, 4\}$, *and* $\{2, 5\}$, *as candidate hyperclique patterns and prune them later upon computing their actual h-confidence values. Note that the anti-monotone*

property does not help us to pre-prune the six candidate patterns, since every subset of these patterns are hyperclique patterns (according to Equation 1, the h-confidence values of size-1 itemsets are 1).

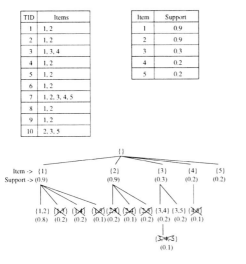

Figure 2. A running example.

Hyperclique Miner

Input:

1) a set F of K Boolean feature types F=$\{f_1, f_2, \ldots, f_K\}$

2) a set T of N transactions T=$\{t_1 \ldots t_N\}$, each $t_i \in T$ is a record with K attributes $\{i_1, i_2, \ldots, i_K\}$ taking values in $\{0, 1\}$, where the i_p is the Boolean value for the feature type f_p, for $1 \le p \le K$.

3) A user specified h-confidence threshold (*min_conf*)

4) A user specified support threshold (*min_supp*)

Output:

hyperclique patterns with h-confidence $> min\_conf$ and support $> min\_supp$

Method:

1) Get size-1 prevalent items

2) Construct item sets at different levels of support

3) **for** size of itemsets in (2, 3, ... , $K - 1$) **do**

4)   Generate candidate hyperclique patterns

5)   Prune based on the support measure

6)   Prune based on the h-confidence measure

7)   Generate hyperclique patterns

Algorithm Description: The Hyperclique Miner prunes the exponential search space based on the following three conditions: 1) Pruning based on anti-monotone property of h-confidence and support. 2) Pruning based on the upper bound of h-confidence. By Lemma 2, if the upper bound for $hconf(c)$ is less than h_c, then $hconf(c)$ must also be less than h_c. We can easily compute the upper bound of the

h-confidence for any candidate itemset since the support for every individual item is stored in memory, 3) Pruning by the *cross-support* property of h-confidence.

4   Hyperclique-based Item Clustering

This section describes how to use hyperclique patterns for clustering items in high dimensional space. For high dimensional data, traditional clustering schemes such as K-means [9] tend to produce poor results when directly applied to large, high-dimensional data sets. One promising approach proposed by Han et al. [7] is to cluster the data using a hypergraph partitioning algorithm. More specifically, a hypergraph is constructed with individual items as vertices and frequent itemsets as hyperedges connecting between these vertices. For example, if $\{A, B, C\}$ is a frequent itemset, then a hyperedge connecting the vertices for A, B, and C will be added. The weight of the hyperedge is given by the average confidence of all association rules generated from the corresponding itemset. The resulting hypergraph is then partitioned using a hypergraph partitioning algorithm such as HMETIS (http://www.cs.umn.edu/~karypis/metis/hmetis/index.html) to obtain clusters.

Although the hypergraph-based clustering algorithm has produced promising results [7], it can be further improved if the initial hypergraph contains a good representative set of high-quality hyperedges. Frequent itemsets may not provide such a good representation because they include cross-support patterns, which may have low affinity but relatively high average confidence. In addition, many low support items cannot be covered by frequent itemsets unless the minimum support threshold is sufficiently low. However, if the threshold is indeed low enough, a large number of frequent itemsets will be extracted, thus resulting in a very dense hypergraph. It will be difficult for a hypergraph partitioning algorithm to partition such a dense hypergraph, which often leads to poor clustering results.

In this paper, we use hyperclique patterns as an alternative to frequent itemsets. In the hypergraph model, each hyperclique pattern is represented by a hyperedge whose weight is equal to the h-confidence of the hyperclique pattern. For example, if $\{A, B, C\}$ is a hyperclique pattern with the h-confidence equals to 0.8, then the hypergraph contains a hyperedge that connects the vertices A, B, and C. The weight for this hyperedge is 0.8.

There are several advantages of using the hyperclique-based clustering algorithm. First, since hyperclique patterns are strong affinity patterns, they can provide a good representative set of hyperedges to seed a hypergraph-based clustering algorithm. Second, hyperclique patterns can be extracted for very low support items without making the hypergraph becomes too dense. Finally, hyperclique-based clustering algorithm is also more tolerant to noise compared to traditional clustering algorithms such as k-means because it can explicitly remove the weakly related items.

5 Experimental Evaluation

For evaluation purposes, we have performed our experiments on real data sets obtained from several application domains. The characteristics of these data sets are summarized in Table 3.

Table 3. Real Data set Characteristics.

Data set	#Item	#Record	Avg. Length	Source
Pumsb	2113	49046	74	IBM Almaden
S&P 500	932	716	75	Stock Market
Retail	14462	57671	8	Retail Store

The `pumsb` data set corresponds to a binary version of a census data set. `Retail` is a masked data set obtained from a large mail-order company. In addition, the stock market data set contains events representing the price movement of various stocks that belong to the S&P 500 index from January 1994 to October 1996.

All experiments were performed on a Sun Ultra 10 workstation with a 440 MHz CPU and 128 Mbytes of memory running the SunOS 5.7 operating system. Note that we have implemented hyperclique miner as an extension to the publicly available implementation of the Apriori algorithm by Borgelt (http://fuzzy.cs.uni-magdeburg.de/~borgelt). As a result, the performance of hyperclique miner is almost equivalent to Apriori when the h-confidence threshold is set to zero.

5.1 The Pruning Effect of Hyperclique Miner

The purpose of this experiment is to demonstrate the effectiveness of the h-confidence pruning on hyperclique pattern generation. Recently, the CHARM algorithm was proposed by Zaki et al.[16] to efficiently discover frequent closed itemsets. As shown in their paper, for a dense data set with skewed support distribution such as *Pumsb*, CHARM can achieve relatively better performance than other state-of-the-art pattern mining algorithms such as CLOSET [11], and MAFIA [5] when the support threshold is low. Hence, we chose CHARM as the baseline to compare against the performance of hyperclique miner on dense data sets (even though hyperclique miner and CHARM are actually targeted towards different kinds of patterns).

Figure 3 shows the number of patterns generated by hyperclique miner and CHARM on the `pumsb` data set. As can be seen, the number of patterns discovered by our algorithm is several orders of magnitude smaller than the number of patterns found by CHARM provided that the

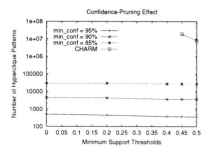

Figure 3. The effect of h-confidence pruning in terms of the number of patterns generated.

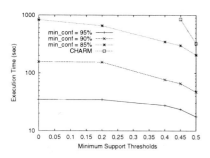

Figure 4. The effect of h-confidence pruning in terms of execution time.

h-confidence threshold is sufficiently high. In addition, CHARM has difficulties in identifying patterns when the support threshold is less than or equals to 0.4. However, our technique identifies many strong affinity patterns with very low support. For instance, we obtain a long pattern containing 9 items with the support 0.23 and h-confidence 94.2%. Recall from Table 1 that nearly 96.6% of the items have support less than 0.4. With a support threshold greater than 0.4, CHARM can only identify associations among a very small fraction of the items. Figure 4 shows the relatively performance of hyperclique miner and CHARM on `pumsb` data set. With h-confidence pruning, we can use hyperclique miner to identify hyperclique patterns even at support threshold equal to zero.

5.2 Quality of Hyperclique Patterns

Table 4 shows some of the interesting hyperclique patterns extracted from the `retail` data set. For example, we identified a hyperclique pattern involving closely related items such as Nokia battery, Nokia adapter, and Nokia cell phone. We also discovered several interesting patterns containing very low support items such as {earrings, gold ring, bracelet}. These items are expensive, rarely bought by customers, and belong to the same product category.

Table 4. Hyperclique Patterns from Retail.

Hyperclique patterns	support	h-conf
{earrings, gold ring, bracelet}	0.019%	45.8%
{nokia battery, nokia adapter, nokia cell phone}	0.049%	52.8%
{coffee maker, can opener, toaster}	0.014%	61.5%
{baby bumper pad, diaper stacker, baby crib sheet}	0.028%	72.7%
{skirt tub, 3pc bath set, shower curtain}	0.26%	74.4%

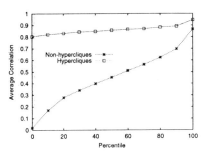

Figure 5. Average Correlation.

We also evaluated the affinity of hyperclique patterns by the correlation measure. Specifically, for each hyperclique pattern $X = \{x_1, x_2, \cdots x_k\}$, we calculate the correlation for each pair of items (x_i, x_j) within the pattern. The overall correlation of a hyperclique pattern is then defined as the average pair wise correlation. Note that this experiment was conducted on Retail data set with the h-confidence threshold 0.8 and the support threshold 0.0005.

Figure 5 compares the average correlation for hyperclique patterns versus non-hyperclique patterns. We sorted the average correlation and displayed them in increasing order. Notice that the hyperclique patterns have extremely high average pair wise correlation compared to the non-hyperclique patterns. This result supports our previous assertion that hyperclique patterns can identify itemsets that contain only tightly-coupled items.

5.3 Hyperclique-based Item Clustering

In this section, we illustrate the application of hyperclique patterns as an alternative to frequent patterns in hypergraph-based clustering approach [7]. We use the S&P 500 index data set for our clustering experiments.

Table 5 shows the dramatic increase in the number of frequent patterns as the minimum support threshold is decreased. As can be seen, the number of frequent patterns increases up to 11,486,914 when we reduce the support threshold to 1%. If all these frequent itemsets are used for hypergraph clustering, this will create an extremely dense hypergraph and makes the hypergraph-based clustering algorithm becomes computationally intractable. In [7], the authors have used a higher minimum support threshold, i.e., 3%, for their experiments and obtained 19,602 frequent

itemsets covering 440 items. A hypergraph consisting of 440 vertices and 19,602 hyperedges was then constructed and 40 partitions were generated. Out of 40 partitions, 16 of them are clean clusters as they contain stocks primarily from the same or closely related industry groups.

Table 5. Number of frequent patterns.

Support	No. of frequent patterns	items covered
3%	19602	440
2%	149215	734
1%	11486914	915

With hyperclique patterns, we can construct hypergraphs at any support threshold, and thus covering more items. For instance, with a minimum h-confidence threshold 20% and a support threshold 0%, we obtain 11,207 hyperclique patterns covering 861 items. A hypergraph consisting of 861 vertices and 11,207 hyperedges is then constructed and partitioned into smaller clusters. For comparison purposes, we partitioned the hypergraph into 80 partitions to ensure that the average size of clusters is almost the same as the average size of the 40 clusters obtained using frequent patterns. Note that for both approaches, we only use patterns containing two or more items as hyperedges.

Our experimental results suggest that the hyperclique pattern approach can systematically produce better clustering results than the frequent pattern approach. First, many items with low levels of support are not included in the frequent pattern approach. Specifically, there are 421 items covered by hyperclique pattern based clusters that are not covered by frequent pattern based clusters. Second, the hypergraph clustering algorithm can produce a larger fraction of clean clusters using hyperclique patterns than frequent patterns — 41 out of 80 partitions versus 16 out of 40 partitions. Third, all the clean clusters identified by the frequent pattern approach were also present in the results by the hyperclique pattern approach. Finally, for the same clean cluster identified by both approaches, there are more same category items included by the hyperclique based approach.

Table 6 shows some of the clean hyperclique pattern based clusters that appear at low levels of support (around 1% support). Such clusters could not be identified by the frequent pattern approach. As the table shows, our hyperclique pattern approach was able to discover retail, chemical, , health-product, power, and communication clusters. A complete list of clusters is given in Technical Report [15].

We have also applied the graph-partitioning scheme in CLUTO [2]. This algorithm takes the adjacency matrix of the similarity graph between the n objects to be clustered as input. The experiment results indicate that this approach can produce much worse clustering results than the hyperclique-based approach. For instance, out of the 80 clusters derived

---

[2]http://www.cs.umn.edu/~karypis/cluto/index.html.

Table 6. Some clean clusters

No	Discovered Clusters	Industry Group
1	Becton Dickinso↓, Emerson Electric↓, Amer Home Product↓, Johnson & Johnson↓, Merck↓, Pfizer↓, Schering-Plough↓, Warner-Lambert↓	health product
2	duPont (EI) deNemo↑, Goodrich (B.F.)↑, Nalco Chemical↑, Rohm & Haas↑, Avon Products↑	chemical
3	Federated Dept↑, Gap Inc↑, Nordstrom Inc↑, Pep Boys-Man↑, Sears↑, TJX↑, Walmart↑	Retail
4	Bell Atlantic Co↑, BellSouth Corp↑, CPC Intl↑, GTE Corp↑, Ameritech Corp↑, NYNEX Corp↑, Pacific Telesis↑, SBC Communication↑, US West Communication↑	Comm.
5	Baltimore Gas↓, CINergy Corp↓, Amer Electric Power↓, Duke Power↓, Consolidated Edi↓, Entergy Corp↓, Genl Public Util↓, Houston Indus↓, PECO Energy↓, Texas Utilities↓	Power

by CLUTO, less than 30 of them are clean clusters. This result is not surprising since the graph-partitioning scheme considers only information about pairs of items but not higher order interactions.

In addition, we also applied the improved version of the k-means clustering algorithm in CLUTO. When using cosine as the similarity measure, we were able to identify 36 clean clusters out of 80 clusters, which is worse than the hyperclique pattern approach.

Finally, we observed the following effects of the hyperclique-based clustering approach. If we set the minimum support threshold to 0% and h-confidence threshold to 20%, the discovered hyperclique patterns cover 861 items. Since there are 932 items in total, the hyperclique pattern mining algorithm must have eliminated 71 items. We examine the distribution of these 71 items in the CLUTO k-means clustering results. We observe that 68 of the items are assigned to the wrong clusters by CLUTO. As a result, we believe that the items not covered by these hyperclique patterns are potentially noise items.

6 Conclusions

In this paper, we formalized the problem of mining hyperclique patterns in data sets with skewed support distribution. We also introduced the concept of cross-support property and showed how this property can be used to avoid generating spurious patterns involving items from different support levels. Furthermore, a new algorithm called hyperclique miner was developed. This algorithm utilizes cross-support and anti-monotone properties of h-confidence for the efficient discovery of hyperclique patterns. Finally, we demonstrated applications of hyperclique patterns for discovering strong affinity patterns among low-support items and for hyperclique-based item clustering.

For future work, there is a potential for using the hyperclique concept in a variety of applications such as dimensionality reduction, copy detection, and collaborative

filtering. Also, it is valuable to exploit the *cross-support* property on some other interestingness measures.

Acknowledgments This work was partially supported by NASA grant # NCC 2 1231, NSF grant # ACI-9982274, DOE contract # DOE/LLNL W-7045-ENG-48 and by Army High Performance Computing Research Center contract number DAAD19-01-2-0014. Also, we would like to thank Dr Mohammed J. Zaki for providing us the CHARM code and Dr. Johannes Gehrke for providing us the MAFIA code. Finally, we would like to thank Dr Shashi Shekhar, Dr Ke Wang, and Mr. Michael Steinbach for valuable comments.

References

[1] R. Agrawal, T. Imielinski, and A. Swami. Mining association rules between sets of items in large databases. In *Proc. of the ACM SIGMOD*, pages 207–216, May 1993.

[2] R. Agrawal and R. Srikant. Fast algorithms for mining association rules. In *Proc. of the 20th VLDB*, 1994.

[3] R. J. Bayardo. Efficiently mining long patterns from databases. In *Proc. of the ACM SIGMOD*, 1998.

[4] S. Brin, R. Motwani, and C. Silverstein. Beyond market baskets: Generalizing association rules to correlations. In *Proc. of the ACM SIGMOD*, pages 265–276, 1997.

[5] D. Burdick, M. Calimlim, and J. Gehrke. Mafia: A maximal frequent itemset algorithm for transactional databases. In *Proc. of the ICDE*, 2001.

[6] E. Cohen, M. Datar, S. Fujiwara, A. Gionis, P. Indyk, R. Motwani, J. Ullman, and C. Yang. Finding interesting associations without support pruning. In *ICDE*, 2000.

[7] E. Han, G. Karypis, and V. Kumar. Hypergraph based clustering in high-dimensional data sets: A summary of results. *Bulletin of the Technical Committee on Data Engineering*, 21(1), March 1998.

[8] T. Hastie, R. Tibshirani, and J. Friedman. *The Elements of Statistical Learning: Data Mining, Inference, and Prediction*. Springer, 2001.

[9] A. Jain and R. Dubes. *Algorithms for Clustering Data*. Prentice Hall, 1998.

[10] E. Omiecinski. Alternative interest measures for mining associations. In *IEEE TKDE*, Jan/Feb 2003.

[11] J. Pei, J. Han, and R. Mao. Closet: An efficient algorithm for mining frequent closed itemsets. In *DMKD*, May 2000.

[12] C. J. V. Rijsbergen. *Information Retrieval (2nd Edition)*. Butterworths, London, 1979.

[13] P. Tan, V. Kumar, and J. Srivastava. Selecting the right interestingness measure for association patterns. In *Proc of the Eighth ACM SIGKDD*, 2002.

[14] K. Wang, Y. He, D. Cheung, and Y. Chin. Mining confident rules without support requirement. In *ACM CIKM*, 2001.

[15] H. Xiong, P. Tan, and V. Kumar. Mining hyperclique patterns with confidence pruning. In *Technical Report 03-006, Computer Science, Univ. of Minnesota.*, Jan 2003.

[16] M. Zaki and C.-J. Hsiao. Charm: An efficient algorithm for closed itemset mining. In *Proc. of the 2nd SDM*, 2002.

On Precision and Recall of Multi-Attribute Data Extraction from Semistructured Sources

Guizhen Yang
Department of Computer Science and Engineering
University at Buffalo
Buffalo, NY 14260-2000, USA
gzyang@cse.buffalo.edu

Saikat Mukherjee   I. V. Ramakrishnan
Department of Computer Science
Stony Brook University
Stony Brook, NY 11794-4400, USA
{saikat,ram}@cs.stonybrook.edu

Abstract

Machine learning techniques for data extraction from semistructured sources exhibit different precision and recall characteristics. However to date the formal *relationship between learning algorithms and their impact on these two metrics remains unexplored. This paper proposes a formalization of precision and recall of extraction and investigates the complexity-theoretic aspects of learning algorithms for multi-attribute data extraction based on this formalism. We show that there is a tradeoff between precision/recall of extraction and computational efficiency and present experimental results to demonstrate the practical utility of these concepts in designing scalable data extraction algorithms for improving recall without compromising on precision.*

1 Introduction

Numerous Web data sources, as illustrated in Figure 1, present organized information about entities and their attributes. For instance, each veterinarian service provider in Figure 1 corresponds to an entity whose attributes include the name of the service provider (*e.g.*, "ABC Animal Hospital"), the resident veterinarian who provides the service (*e.g.*, "John, DVM"), the address and phone number of the service provider. Usually Web pages containing this kind of information exhibit a *consistent* presentation style.

A common approach for extracting data from Web sources is to build wrappers [1, 10, 20, 17, 13, 4]. Among these assorted approaches learning-based extraction techniques [13, 16, 4, 5] are becoming important since they exhibit a high degree of automation and scalability. Extraction based on learning techniques is a two step process. In the first step, called *labeling*, examples of relevant data to be extracted from the source are supplied. This labeling step can be either manual or completely automated. In the latter case

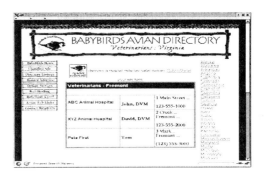

Figure 1. A List of Services Web Page

an *ontology*, encoding knowledge of the data domain, applies an attribute *identifier function* (*e.g.*, pattern matching, keyword-based search) to locate an attribute's occurrences in the data source. In the second step the labeled examples are used to automatically learn an extraction expression for pulling out all the relevant data in the source.

1.1 Precision and Recall in Learning-Based Data Extraction

Learning methods synthesize extraction expressions by a process of generalization from the labeled examples and so the set of attribute occurrences that they pull out will be a superset of the labeled examples. Hence these methods are said to increase *recall*[1]. But a problem here is that the extraction expression may be too general and pull out incorrect attribute occurrences also, thereby losing *precision*[2].

For illustration let us consider the following example: Suppose "ABC Animal Hospital" and "XYZ Animal Hospital" are supplied as two examples of the *HospitalName*

---

[1]Recall = $\frac{ce}{ce+te} \times 100\%$, where ce is the number of entities extracted correctly and te is the number of true entities not extracted.

[2]Precision = $\frac{ce}{ce+fe} \times 100\%$, where ce is the number of entities extracted correctly and fe is the number of false entities extracted.

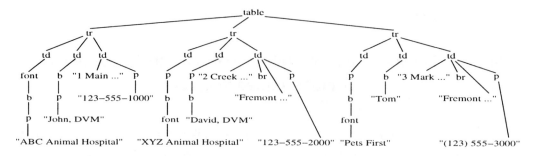

Figure 2. DOM Fragment of Figure 1

attribute. In the DOM tree (see Figure 2) corresponding to the Web page in Figure 1, the paths leading to the leaf nodes containing these text strings are $\alpha \cdot table \cdot tr \cdot td \cdot font \cdot b \cdot p$ and $\alpha \cdot table \cdot tr \cdot td \cdot p \cdot b \cdot font$, respectively, where α represents the path string from the root of the DOM tree to the $table$ tag. We can learn an extraction expression, specifically the regular expression $E_1 = \alpha \cdot table \cdot tr \cdot td \cdot font^* \cdot p^* \cdot b \cdot p^* \cdot font^*$, from these two paths. If we execute E_1 as a path query on the DOM tree, it will return the text string "Pets First". However, notice that the language[3] of E_1 also includes the path string, $\alpha \cdot table \cdot tr \cdot td \cdot p \cdot b$, which terminates on the leaf node "David, DVM". But this is an occurrence of a different attribute, *DoctorName*, in the schema. By extracting such false positives an extraction expression's increase in recall can be compromised by a reduction in precision.

Observe that different extraction expressions can be learned from the same set of examples. For instance, we can learn another expression, $E_2 = \alpha \cdot table \cdot tr \cdot td \cdot p^* \cdot b^* \cdot font \cdot b^* \cdot p^*$, from $\alpha \cdot table \cdot tr \cdot td \cdot font \cdot b \cdot p$ and $\alpha \cdot table \cdot tr \cdot td \cdot p \cdot b \cdot font$. The path string $\alpha \cdot table \cdot tr \cdot td \cdot p \cdot b$ is excluded from E_2's language. In fact none of the path strings leading to the *DoctorName* attribute data will be recognized by E_2. So E_2 retains more precision than E_1.

The above examples raises several interesting algorithmic questions: *Can we design learning algorithms without losing precision? What is the computational difficulty of such algorithms? Are there tradeoffs between precision/recall and computational efficiency?*

1.2 Our Approach

To the best of our knowledge a study of the complexity-theoretic aspects of precision and recall of extraction and their impact on the efficiency of learning extraction expressions has not been explored in the literature. In this paper we undertake such a study within the context of multi-attribute data extraction. We introduce a novel formalization of precision and recall of extraction that will serve

as the formal model for analyzing an algorithm's precision/recall characteristics.

In our model, extraction expressions are regular expressions built using the concatenation ("·") and the Kleene closure ("*") operators only. We call them *Path Abstraction Expressions* (PAEs). To handle multi-attribute entities, we associate one PAE with each attribute. When a PAE is evaluated on the DOM tree of a Web page, the leaf nodes whose path strings match this PAE will be extracted.

To learn a PAE for an attribute we generalize from both its positive and negative examples. The labeling step provides positive examples for each attribute. The set of negative examples for an attribute comprises the positive examples of all the other attributes. Based on the extent to which false positives can be excluded from a PAE's language, we ascribe different *quality* measures to the PAEs learned (see Section 2). Better quality PAEs eliminate more false positives and will therefore possess higher precision.

Our theoretical analysis shows, however, that learning good quality PAEs can be computationally intractable. Consequently, PAEs learned by practical heuristics often give rise to ambiguity when they are used to extract multi-attribute data. To this end, we model ambiguity resolution as an algorithmic problem over bipartite graphs and develop efficient algorithms for learning PAEs and resolving ambiguity. By combining domain knowledge (possibly encoded in an ontology) with these algorithms we can improve recall without much loss in precision. The experimental results, obtained from running our algorithms over 194 different Web pages listing veterinarian service providers and product descriptions, show that the overall recall achieved ranges from 58% to 100% with almost no loss in precision.

The rest of the paper is organized as follows. Section 2 formalizes different notions of PAEs with different quality measures. Complexity results on learning these classes of PAEs are presented in Section 3. Heuristics for learning PAEs and the algorithm for resolving ambiguity are also presented in Section 3. Experimental results appears in Section 4 and related work in Section 5. Finally, Section 6 concludes this paper with future work.

---

[3]The language of a regular expression is the set of strings recognized by this expression.

2 Problem Formalization

A *path abstraction expression* (*abbr.* PAE) is like a regular expression but with two restrictions: (1) it is free of the union operator ("|"); and (2) the Kleene closure operator ("*") can only apply to single symbols. The set of strings recognized by a PAE, E, is denoted as $\mathcal{L}(E)$.

By disallowing the union operator ("|") in the syntax of PAEs, we can force *generalization* in the learning algorithms. Otherwise, one can just compose a regular expression by concatenating all the input strings using the union operator. Such techniques do not really capture any regularity in the paths within a DOM tree.

Although we require that the Kleene closure operator ("*") be applied to single symbols only, this does not really impose any extra technical difficulty. We make this simplification just for the Web domain, since in reality it is very rare that a consecutive sequence of tags would repeat itself in the root-to-leaf paths of a DOM tree.

Definition 1 (Nonredundancy) *Let S be a set of strings and E a PAE such that $\mathcal{L}(E) \supseteq S$. We say that E is nonredundant w.r.t. S, iff we cannot perform either of the following operations on E to obtain a new PAE E' such that $\mathcal{L}(E') \supseteq S$: (1) Remove a symbol together with its Kleene closure operator; (2) Remove from a symbol the Kleene closure operator.*

When $\mathcal{L}(E) \supseteq S$, we will normally say that E *covers* or *generalizes* S. However, if E overgeneralizes then it will produce more false positives. Note that if we can perform either of the two operations in Definition 1 on E and obtain a new E', then $\mathcal{L}(E') \subset \mathcal{L}(E)$. Thus E' should produce less false positives in general. Therefore we require that one should learn a nonredundant PAE from examples.

Notice that nonredundant PAEs do not say anything about negative examples. To deal with negative examples we introduce the following definition.

Definition 2 (Consistency) *Let E be a PAE, POS and NEG two sets of strings. We say that E is consistent w.r.t. $\langle POS, NEG \rangle$, iff $\mathcal{L}(E) \supseteq POS$ and $\mathcal{L}(E) \cap NEG = \emptyset$.*

In the above Definition 2, the strings in POS serve as positive examples while those in NEG serve as negative examples. Intuitively, a consistent PAE generalizes all positive examples but excludes all negative examples. Therefore, extraction using consistent PAEs will have higher precision than nonredundant PAEs.

In practice we often need to extract multiple attributes of an entity. Our goal is to learn a list of PAEs, one for *each* attribute. Note that for any given attribute, the positive examples from other attributes will serve as negative examples for this attribute. If for *each* attribute, we can

learn a consistent PAE that covers the positive examples of this attribute but excludes all the positive examples of other attributes combined, then we say that this list of PAEs is unambiguous w.r.t. the given list of sets of examples.

Definition 3 (Unambiguity) *Given a list of sets of strings, $(S_1, \ldots, S_n)$, and a list of PAEs, $(E_1, \ldots, E_n)$, we say that $(E_1, \ldots, E_n)$ is unambiguous w.r.t. $(S_1, \ldots, S_n)$, iff E_i is consistent w.r.t. $\langle S_i, \bigcup_{j \neq i} S_j \rangle$ for $1 \leq i \leq n$.*

However, even when a list of PAEs is unambiguous w.r.t. examples, the languages recognized by these PAEs may still overlap. Therefore, a more desirable, better quality is that these languages are pairwise disjoint. If so, then we say the list of PAEs is *inherently* unambiguous. Clearly, inherently unambiguous PAEs are able to retain more precision than those that are only unambiguous w.r.t. the given examples.

Definition 4 (Inherent Unambiguity) *Let $(S_1, \ldots, S_n)$ be a list of sets of strings and $(E_1, \ldots, E_n)$ a list of PAEs. We say that $(E_1, \ldots, E_n)$ is inherently unambiguous w.r.t. $(S_1, \ldots, S_n)$, iff $\mathcal{L}(E_i) \supseteq S_i$ for $1 \leq i \leq n$ and $\mathcal{L}(E_i) \cap \mathcal{L}(E_j) = \emptyset$ for $1 \leq i \leq n$, $1 \leq j \leq n$, and $i \neq j$.*

We formally state our learning problems as follows.

Problem 1 (Consistent PAE) *Given two sets of strings POS and NEG, is there a PAE that is consistent w.r.t. $\langle POS, NEG \rangle$?*

Problem 2 (Unambiguous PAEs) *Given a list of sets of strings, $(S_1, \ldots, S_n)$, is there a list of PAEs, $(E_1, \ldots, E_n)$, that is unambiguous w.r.t. $(S_1, \ldots, S_n)$?*

Problem 3 (Inherently Unambiguous PAEs) *Given a list of sets of strings, $(S_1, \ldots, S_n)$, is there a list of PAEs, $(E_1, \ldots, E_n)$, that is inherently unambiguous w.r.t. $(S_1, \ldots, S_n)$?*

3 Computational Aspects of Learning PAEs

3.1 Learning Nonredundant PAEs

Algorithm *LearnPAE* takes as input a set of strings (S^+) and returns as output a nonredundant PAE (E) which generalizes this set. In Line 2, variable E is initialized with the first positive example. In Line 3, the shortest common supersequence (SCS)[4] of the string stored in E and the next positive example is computed and then assigned to E. When the loop in Line 3 terminates, E stores a common supersequence for all the strings in S^+. In Line 4, the string stored in E is generalized to a PAE that covers S^+ by adding $*$ on all the symbols in E.

---

[4]Supersequences of a string can be obtained by inserting zero or more symbols into this string.

```
Algorithm LearnPAE($S^+$)
input
    $S^+$ : a nonempty set of strings
output
    $E$ : a nonredundant PAE which covers $S^+$
begin
1.  Let $\alpha_i$ ($1 \leq i \leq n$) be a string in $S^+$.
2.  $E = \alpha_1$
3.  for $2 \leq i \leq n$ do $E = SCS(E, \alpha_i)$ endfor
4.  Put a $*$ on all the symbols of $E$.
5.  $E = $ MakeNonredundant($E, S^+$)
6.  return $E$
end
```

Algorithm *MakeNonredundant* takes as input a PAE, E, and a set, S^+, of positive examples that E covers. Upon termination it makes E nonredundant w.r.t. S^+. First, for every symbol with a $*$ in E, it is checked whether dropping the symbol together with $*$ results in a new PAE that still covers S^+. If so, then the symbol together with $*$ is dropped from E (Lines 4–7). If not, then it is checked whether dropping only $*$ from this symbol produces a new PAE that covers S^+. If it does, then the $*$ is dropped from the symbol (Lines 9–10).

```
Algorithm MakeNonredundant($E, S^+$)
input
    $E$ : a PAE which covers $S^+$
    $S^+$ : a nonempty set of strings
output
    $Q$ : a nonredundant PAE which covers $S^+$
begin
1.   $n = $ the number of symbols in $E$ excluding $*$
2.   Let $x_i$ ($1 \leq i \leq n$) be the $i$-th symbol in $E$.
3.   for $1 \leq i \leq n$ do
4.      if a $*$ is attached to $x_i$ then
5.         $R = $ drop $x_i$ together with $*$ from $E$
6.         if $R$ covers $S^+$ then
7.            $E = R$
8.         else
9.            $R = $ drop $*$ that is attached to $x_i$ from $E$
10.           if $R$ covers $S^+$ then $E = R$ endif
11.        endif
12.     endif
13.  endfor
14.  $Q = E$
15.  return $Q$
end
```

We can show that the PAE, Q, returned by algorithm *MakeNonredundant* is nonredundant w.r.t. S^+. Moreover, the complexity of algorithm *LearnPAE* is polynomial time.

3.2 Learning Consistent and Unambiguous PAEs

Recall that a consistent PAE covers all positive examples but excludes all negative examples. Since algorithm *LearnPAE* learns from positive examples only, the PAE that it produces may not be consistent. It turns out that the complexity of learning PAEs runs up very quickly once negative examples must be taken into account.

Theorem 1 *The consistent PAE problem is NP-complete.*

Therefore, one has to resort to heuristics for learning consistent PAEs. A simple heuristic is to first find a *distinguishing subsequence*[5] of symbols which is present in all positive examples but not in any negative example. If such a distinguishing subsequence exists, then a consistent PAE can be easily constructed. Here we omit details of this heuristic due to want of space.

Our goal is to extract data values for multiple attributes associated with a concept. This requires learning a list of PAEs, one per attribute. The positive and negative examples used for learning a list of PAEs are obtained in the same way as for learning consistent PAEs. To extract data values from a source with high precision and recall, it is desirable that this list of PAEs be unambiguous w.r.t. examples. However, this different learning problem also turns out to be intractable in general.

Theorem 2 *The unambiguous PAEs problem is NP-complete.*

From a computational viewpoint learning a list of PAEs that is unambiguous w.r.t. examples amounts to requiring that each PAE in this list be consistent. Therefore in practice we can repeatedly applying heuristics for learning consistent PAEs to learn an unambiguous list of PAEs.

Finally, for an inherently unambiguous list of PAEs we require that their languages be pair-wise disjoint. Such a list of PAEs has the best precision and recall properties. Although the computational complexity of this problem remains open at this time, it can be shown that it is decidable.

Theorem 3 *The inherently unambiguous PAEs problem is decidable.*

3.3 Resolving Ambiguity

Because learning an unambiguous list of PAEs is computationally difficult, one has to resort to heuristics. Since heuristics may not guarantee that all the PAEs learned are consistent, ambiguity can occur when these PAEs are used for extracting multi-attribute data. We now describe an algorithm based on bipartite graphs that uses domain knowledge to resolve ambiguity as much as possible thereby improving recall while retaining high precision.

For simplicity we assume that record boundaries are already identified and so PAEs are applied to each entity block in a DOM tree (see Section 4.1 for more details). In addition, for expositional convenience we also assume that the attributes are single-valued. Extending the techniques in this section to multivalued attributes is straightforward.

We say that a PAE *matches* an attribute value whenever it accepts the path string terminating on the leaf node in a

---

[5]Subsequences of a string can be obtained by deleting zero or more symbols from this string.

DOM tree which is labeled with this value. The ambiguity resolution algorithm takes as input a list of PAEs (E) and a set of data values (D) in an entity block and returns a set of 1–1 associations between attributes and data values. Each data value consists of a text string and the path string in the DOM tree that leads to this text string.

Our ambiguity resolution algorithm works in two steps. First domain knowledge is used to resolve ambiguity. If a data value D_j has been identified by the ontology as the value for an attribute A_i, then the pair (A_i, D_j) is added to the set of associations for that record. The data value and the corresponding PAE are deleted from D and E (note that we assume all attributes are single-valued), respectively.

Algorithm BipartiteResolution(E, D)
input
    E : a list of PAEs representing attributes
    D : a set of strings representing data values in an entity block
output
    A : a set of pairs in the form of (attribute.value)
begin
1. $A = \emptyset$
2.   Let $E_i \in E$ ($1 \leq i \leq n$) be the PAE for attribute A_i.
3.   Let $\alpha_j \in D$ ($1 \leq j \leq m$) represent the data value D_j.
4.   Create a bipartite graph G between E_i's and α_j's.
5.   **do**
6. $M = \emptyset$
7.   **for** $1 \leq i \leq n$ **do**
8.   **if** $degree(E_i) = 1$ ($edge(E_i, \alpha_k) \in G$ for some α_k) **then**
9. $X = \{E_j \mid j \neq i, edge(E_j, \alpha_k) \in G, degree(E_j) = 1\}$
10.   **if** $X = \emptyset$ **then** $M = M \cup \{E_i\}$ **endif**
11.   **endif**
12.   **endfor**
13.   **for** each $E_i \in M$ (there is only one $edge(E_i, \alpha_k) \in G$) **do**
14. $A = A \cup (A_i, D_k)$
15.   Remove all edges in G that are incident on α_k.
16.   **endfor**
17. **while** $M \neq \emptyset$
18. **return** A
end

In the second step we derive more 1–1 associations between the remaining unresolved data values and PAEs using the algorithm *BipartiteResolution*. This algorithm first constructs a bipartite graph in which the two disjoint sets of vertices are E and D, respectively, and there is an edge between $E_i \in E$ and $\alpha_j \in D$ if E_i matches α_j (Line 4).

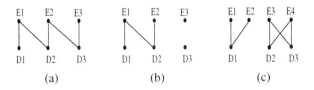

Figure 3. Bipartite Resolution

For instance, given the three records of the DOM tree in Figure 2 with the first two records as examples, suppose for *HospitalName*, *DoctorName*, and *PhoneNumber* the PAEs learned are $E_1 = table \cdot tr \cdot td \cdot p^* \cdot font^* \cdot b \cdot font^* \cdot p^*$,

$E_2 = table \cdot tr \cdot td \cdot b^* \cdot p \cdot b^*$, and $E_3 = table \cdot tr \cdot td \cdot p$, respectively. Let D_1, D_2, and D_3 represent the data values (including their path strings) "Pets First", "Tom", and "(123)555-3000" in the third record of the DOM tree, respectively. Then E_1 matches D_1 and D_2, E_2 matches D_2 and D_3, and E_3 matches D_3 only. The bipartite graph corresponding to these matchings is illustrated in Figure 3(a).

If a PAE E_i uniquely matches a data value α_k and no other PAE uniquely matches α_k, then we place a high confidence on this matching and make a 1–1 association between E_i and α_k (Lines 7–12). We also remove all edges that point to α_k (Line 15). For example, in Figure 3(a), since E_3 uniquely matches D_3 the attribute *PhoneNumber* is associated with D_3 and all edges leading into D_3 are deleted. The residual bipartite graph is shown in Figure 3(b).

The computation is repeated until it cannot derive more 1–1 associations. Continuing with the above example in Figure 3(b), E_2 now uniquely matches D_2. Therefore, the attribute *DoctorName* can be associated with D_2 and all edges leading into D_2 removed. In the final residual graph there is only one edge between E_1 and D_1. Hence the attribute *HospitalName* can be associated with D_1.

However, algorithm *BipartiteResolution* may not always derive new associations. For example, given Figure 3(c), the algorithm terminates without any new association.

4 Experimental Results

Here we describe our experimental evaluation of our theories and techniques for extracting multi-attribute data. For simplicity we assume that all records are flat (*i.e.*, without nested structures) and an attribute occurrence does not span multiple leaf nodes in a DOM tree. In Section 6 we discuss relaxing these two assumptions.

4.1 Experimental Setup

The following sequence of steps were carried out in our experiments: (1) generating data sets; (2) labeling examples; (3) learning PAEs from examples and using PAEs to extract data from Web pages; (4) manually verifying precision and recall metrics on extracted data.

Domains and Data Sets. We chose two different domains: veterinarian service providers and lighting products. For the former we focused on *referral* pages such as the one shown in Figure 1. We used a keyword-based Web search engine to retrieve a large collection of veterinarian service provider Web pages. From this collection we randomly selected 170 referral pages from different service provider Web sites. For the product domain we randomly collected 24 Web pages pertaining to lighting products. Each such page lists several product descriptions. These pages were downloaded from

Attribute Name	Actual Present	Ontology Identified	Nonredundant PAEs	Ambiguity Resolution
Hospital Name	2060	1667	420	1903
Phone Number	1841	963	101	1256
Doctor Name	1705	453	34	1000

(a)

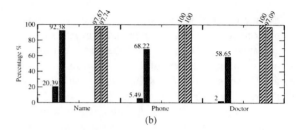

(b)

Figure 4. Aggregated Extraction Results for Veterinarian Sites

Attribute Name	PAE #	Actual Present	Ontology Identified	Consistent PAEs	Recall %	Precision %
Hospital Name	47	338	287	294	86.98	97.35
Phone Number	18	111	47	100	90.09	100
Doctor Name	7	39	26	32	82.05	100

(a)

Attribute Name	Consistent PAEs #	Recall %	Precision %
Hospital Name	47	92.38	97.74
Phone Number	18	68.22	100
Doctor Name	7	58.65	100

(b)

Figure 5. Extraction Results for Consistent PAEs in the Veterinarian Domain

4 different Web sites: 2 from Kmart, 3 from OfficeMax, 13 from Staples, and 6 from Target.

The task of data extraction is considerably simplified by identifying the boundaries of individual entities in a Web page. For instance, in Figure 2, every subtree rooted at *tr* encapsulates a service provider entity. The problem of locating such entity blocks, referred to as *record-boundary discovery* in the literature, has been addressed in a number of previous works [1, 17, 20, 13, 4, 8]. Prior to applying our data extraction algorithms we identified the boundaries of entities in a Web page.

Labeling. We used two ontologies (using ontologies for data extraction is a known idea [7]) for labeling examples: one for veterinarian services and the other for lighting products. The attributes for veterinarian services comprised *HospitalName*, *PhoneNumber*, and *DoctorName*, while *Name* and *Price* were used for lighting products.

Two keywords, *hospital* and *clinic*, were used to identify examples of the *HospitalName* attribute while one keyword, *DVM*, was used for the *DoctorName* attribute . For the *PhoneNumber* attribute we used the regular expression (in Perl syntax), [0-9]{3}-[0-9]{3}-[0-9]{4}, as the identifier function. We used the keywords, *lamp*, *bulb*, and *tube*, for the *Name* attribute of lighting products and searched the symbol $ to label examples of the *Price* attribute.

Extraction Process. Our experiments were conducted on 1GHz Pentium 4 machines each with 256MB memory. All algorithms were programmed in Java. All Web pages were parsed into DOM trees and the entity blocks identified. Note that using DOM trees for data extraction is a known idea (*e.g.*, [19]). Next the identifier functions associated with the attributes in the ontology were used to generate training examples. Based on these examples nonredundant

PAEs were learned and then used to extract attribute data from each entity block. The two-step ambiguity resolution procedure described in Section 3 was applied to make 1–1 associations. This amounts to a strong bias towards high-precision rules [5]. Finally, precision and recall metrics were manually calculated from the extracted data.

4.2 Analysis of Experimental Results

Nonredundant PAEs and Ambiguity Resolution. Figure 4 summarizes the recall and precision performance of extraction using nonredundant PAEs and the effect of ambiguity resolution. These results were aggregated over 170 veterinarian Web pages. In Figure 4(a), Column 2 lists the number of *actual* occurrences of each attribute in these pages. Column 3 shows the number of attribute values that were identified by the ontology. For example, search on the keywords, *hospital* and *clinic*, identified 1667 occurrences of the *HospitalName* attribute. Column 4 is the number of 1–1 associations between a nonredundant PAE and an attribute data value. For example, there were 420 such associations for the *HospitalName* attribute. Column 5 is the number of 1–1 associations that were made by the ambiguity resolution procedure. For instance, it resolved 1903 hospital names uniquely. Correctness of an association was manually verified over all the pages.

Figure 4(b) summarizes as bar charts the recall (shaded bars) and precision (checkered bars) performance of nonredundant PAEs, both before (illustrated by the bar on the left) and after (illustrated by the bar on the right) ambiguity resolution. Observe that there is a significant increase in recall with no loss in precision for all the three attributes after ambiguity resolution. This illustrates the effectiveness of our ambiguity resolution procedure.

Site	Attribute Name	Actual Present	Ontology Identified	Consistent PAEs
KMart	Name	18	5	18
	Price	18	18	18
OfficeMax	Name	25	7	25
	Price	25	25	25
Staples	Name	112	31	99
	Price	112	112	99
Target	Name	63	19	63
	Price	63	63	63

(a)

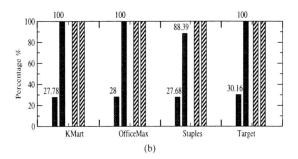

(b)

Figure 6. Extraction Results for Individual Product Sites

Consistent PAEs. Sometimes the PAEs generated by algorithm *LearnPAE* turned out to be consistent. We counted the number of consistent PAEs generated by algorithm *LearnPAE* and collected the recall and precision numbers only for those Web pages that generated such PAEs. In the table of Figure 5(a), Column 2 is the total number of Web pages where the nonredundant PAE for an attribute was consistent w.r.t. positive and negative examples. Columns 3 and 4 show the actual number of instances of that attribute in these pages and the number of instances identified by the ontology, respectively. Column 5 is the count of correct (manually ascertained) attribute data values extracted by these consistent PAEs. Columns 6 and 7 are the recall and precision numbers based on the 1–1 associations made *prior to* ambiguity resolution. In contrast observe the relatively low recall of nonredundant PAEs prior to ambiguity resolution (see the bars on the left in Figure 4(b)). This experimentally validates that consistent PAEs have superior recall and precision than nonredundant PAEs.

For yet another evidence of the superiority of consistent PAEs, observe in Figure 4(b) that after ambiguity resolution the *overall* recall of the *HospitalName* attribute is better than the *PhoneNumber* attribute which in turn is better than that of the *DoctorName* attribute. The reason can be readily explained by the number of consistent PAEs generated for the corresponding attributes, which have a high impact on the effectiveness of the bipartite graph resolution procedure. Observe in Figure 5(b) that this number is the highest for the *HospitalName* attribute and is the lowest for the *DoctorName* attribute.

Unambiguous PAEs. We ran algorithm *LearnPAE* to generate a *pair* of PAEs for extracting the *Name* and *Price* attributes from the lighting products pages of four different Web sites. These pages were all "well-structured" in the sense that the pair of PAEs produced by *LearnPAE* for each page turned out to be almost always unambiguous w.r.t. the examples identified by the ontology. The statistics for both attributes are shown in Figure 6(a), which can be interpreted the same way as those in the table of Figure 4(a). In Figure 6(b), we compare the recall (shaded) and preci-

sion (checkered) numbers of the identifier functions in the ontology (the left bar) and the unambiguous PAEs (the right bar). The statistics in Figure 6(b) are collected on the *Name* attribute only. Observe that precision is 100% while recall is almost close to 100% which experimentally demonstrates the superior quality of unambiguous PAEs.

5 Related Work

We model the notion of precision and recall that arises in wrapper building as a grammar inference problem. Therefore, to put our work in perspective we now review research in related areas, namely, grammar inference, sequence learning, and wrapper construction.

Grammar Inference. This well-known problem was first addressed in the seminal works of Gold and Angluin. Gold [9] showed that the problem of inferring a DFA of *minimum* size from positive examples is NP-complete. In [2] Angluin showed that the problem of learning a regular expression of *minimum* size from positive and negative examples is NP-complete. In our problem, however, we do not impose any constraint on the size of the PAEs learned. Our problems of learning consistent PAEs and unambiguous lists of PAEs (the problems considered in this paper) do not have equivalent counterparts in the classical works on grammar inference. Hence none of the known results is applicable.

Sequence Learning. There is a large body of work on learning subsequences and supersequences from a set of strings. The following problems are all NP-complete: (1) finding the shortest common supersequence (SCS) or the longest common subsequence (LCS) of an arbitrary number of strings over a binary alphabet [14, 18]; (2) finding a sequence which is a common subsequence/supersequence of a set of positive examples but not a subsequence/supersequence of any string in a set of negative examples [12, 15]. The semantics of PAEs differs substantially from string matching and hence their results are not applicable. Besides our problem of learning an unambiguous *list* of PAEs has no counterpart in these works.

Wrapper Construction. Research on wrapper construction for Web sources has made a transition from its early focus on manual [10, 19] and semi-automatic [1, 17] approaches to fully automated techniques based on machine learning [13, 16, 4, 5, 11, 6]. But the notion of ascribing a precision/recall metric to the learning of extraction expressions and its impact on algorithmic efficiency has not been explored in these works.

The issue of ambiguity resolution can also commonly arise in learning-based approaches to schema inference and data extraction from Web documents [6, 3] but has not been explored in the literature. Exponential-time and polynomial-time heuristics were proposed in [6, 3], respectively, to infer schemas from *unlabeled* Web documents for the purpose of automated data extraction. Recently we extended the results in this paper and showed that the problem of inferring good quality schemas from Web pages is NP-complete [21], even when the examples are labeled. Moreover, a collection of pages, generated from the *same* template, is required to learn a schema in [6, 3], but our learning techniques can apply to *individual* documents.

6 Conclusion and Future Work

Although we assumed that an attribute value resides in a single leaf node of a DOM tree, our results can be readily extended to those cases where an attribute value spans multiple leaf nodes — we will learn a list of PAEs per attribute. However, to deal with nested data types we will need to learn more expressive tree patterns. This will be an important and useful extension to our current work.

In our experimental setup, we made the simplifying assumption that record-boundary detection is able to eliminate "bad" examples. In practice the problem of "noise" in training examples cannot be ignored. We plan to address this issue and test our techniques on larger benchmark data in our future work.

Acknowledgments. This work was supported in part by NSF grants IIS-0072927, CCR-0205376, and CCR-0311512. The authors would like to thank the anonymous referees for their helpful comments and suggestions.

References

[1] B. Adelberg. NoDoSe: A tool for semi-automatically extracting structured and semi-structured data from text documents. In *ACM International Conference on Management of Data (SIGMOD)*, 1998.

[2] D. Angluin. On the complexity of minimum inference of regular sets. *Information and Control*, 39(3):337–350, 1978.

[3] A. Arasu and H. Garcia-Molina. Extracting structured data from Web pages. In *ACM International Conference on Management of Data (SIGMOD)*, 2003.

[4] N. Ashish and C. Knoblock. Wrapper generation for semi-structured Internet sources. *SIGMOD Record*, 26(4):8–15, 1997.

[5] W. Cohen, M. Hurst, and L. Jensen. A flexible learning system for wrapping tables and lists in HTML documents. In *International World Wide Web Conference (WWW)*, 2002.

[6] V. Crescenzi, G. Mecca, and P. Merialdo. RoadRunner: Towards automatic data extraction from large Web sites. In *International Conference on Very Large Data Bases (VLDB)*, 2001.

[7] D. W. Embley, D. M. Campbell, R. D. Smith, and S. W. Liddle. Ontology-based extraction and structuring of information from data-rich unstructured documents. In *ACM International Conference on Information and Knowledge Management (CIKM)*, 1998.

[8] D. W. Embley, Y. Jiang, and Y.-K. Ng. Record-boundary discovery in Web documents. In *ACM International Conference on Management of Data (SIGMOD)*, 1999.

[9] E. M. Gold. Complexity of automaton identification from given data. *Information and Control*, 37(3):302–320, 1978.

[10] J. Hammer, H. Garcia-Molina, S. Nestorov, R. Yerneni, M. M. Breunig, and V. Vassalos. Template-based wrappers in the TSIMMIS system. In *ACM International Conference on Management of Data (SIGMOD)*, 1997.

[11] C.-N. Hsu and M.-T. Dung. Generating finite-state transducers for semi-structured data extraction from the Web. *Information Systems*, 23(8):521–538, 1998.

[12] T. Jiang and M. Li. On the complexity of learning strings and sequences. *Theoretical Computer Science*, 119(2):363–371, 1993.

[13] N. Kushmerick, D. S. Weld, and R. B. Doorenbos. Wrapper induction for information extraction. In *International Joint Conference on Artificial Intelligence (IJCAI)*, 1997.

[14] D. Maier. The complexity of some problems on subsequences and supersequences. *Journal of ACM*, 25(2):322–336, 1978.

[15] M. Middendrof. On finding various minimal, maximal, and consistent sequences over a binary alphabet. *Theoretical Computer Science*, 145(1-2):317–327, 1995.

[16] I. Muslea, S. Minton, and C. Knoblock. A hierarchical approach to wrapper induction. In *Third International Conference on Autonomous Agents (Agents'99)*, 1999.

[17] M. Perkowitz, R. B. Doorenbos, O. Etzioni, and D. S. Weld. Learning to understand information on the Internet: An example-based approach. *Journal of Intelligent Information Systems*, 8(2):133–153, 1997.

[18] K.-J. Räihä and E. Ukkonen. The shortest common supersequence problem over binary alphabet is NP-complete. *Theoretical Computer Science*, 16:187–198, 1981.

[19] A. Sahuguet and F. Azavant. Web Ecology: Recycling HTML pages as XML documents using W4F. In *ACM SIGMOD Workshop on the Web and Databases (WebDB)*, 1999.

[20] S. Soderland. Learning information extraction rules for semi-structured and free text. *Machine Learning*, 34(1-3), 1999.

[21] G. Yang, I. V. Ramakrishnan, and M. Kifer. On the complexity of schema inference from Web pages in the presence of nullalbe data attributes. In *ACM Internation Conference on Information and Knowledge Management (CIKM)*, 2003.

Mining Plans for Customer-Class Transformation

Qiang Yang
Department of Computer Science
Hong Kong University of Science and Technology
Clearwater Bay, Kowloon, Hong Kong
qyang@cs.ust.hk

Hong Cheng
Department of Computer Science
University of Illinois, Urbana-Champaign
Illinois 61801 USA
hcheng3@uiuc.edu

Abstract

We consider the problem of mining high-utility plans from historical plan databases that can be used to transform customers from one class to other, more desirable classes. Traditional data mining algorithms are focused on finding frequent sequences. But high frequency may not imply low costs and high benefits. Traditional Markov Decision Process (MDP) algorithms are designed to address this issue by bringing in the concept of utility, but these algorithms are also known to be expensive to execute. In this paper, we present a novel algorithm AUPlan which automatically generates sequential plans with high utility by combining data mining and AI planning. These high-utility plans could be used to convert groups of customers from less desirable states to more desirable ones. Our algorithm adapts the Apriori algorithm by considering the concepts of plans and utilities. We show through empirical studies that planning using our integrated algorithm produces high-utility plans efficiently.

1. Introduction

In business marketing, corporations and institutions are interested in executing a sequence of marketing actions to change the class of a group of customers from an undesirable class to a more desirable one. Effective class-transformation requires careful planning. For example, a financial institution may derive marketing strategies for turning their reluctant customers into active ones and a telecommunications company may plan actions to stop their valuable customers from leaving. These marketing plans are aimed at converting groups of customers from an undesirable class to a desirable one. In universities, web-based distance-learning systems may provide students with future study plans. For example, an online learning system may devise a study plan for a student with an aim to transform the student from knowledge poor to knowledge rich.

In the past, most planning activities for such class-transformation tasks have been done by hand. However, we observe that the historical plan-execution traces in a database provide valuable knowledge which could be utilized for automatic planning. These plan traces, called *plan databases*, form sequence databases consisting of sequences of actions and states, where an action has a cost value and a plan or state has a real-valued utility measure. High-utility plans could be discovered from the plan databases and used as guidelines for future plan design. Extremely low-utility plans could also be useful, as they could be used in plan-failure analysis for understanding and improving failed plans. In this paper, we consider how to find all high-utility plans from a plan database that are able to transform customers from an undesirable class to a more desirable one.

Consider a marketing campaign planning example. Suppose that a banking company is interested in marketing to a group of 100,000 customers in the financial market to promote a special loan signup. We start with a plan database with historical campaign information in Table 1. Suppose we are interested in building a three-step plan to market to new customers. There are many candidate plans in the table to consider in order to transform as many customers as possible from non-signup status to a signup one. The signup status corresponds to a positive class that we would like to move the customers to, and the non-signup status corresponds to the initial state of our customers. Our plan will choose not only low-cost actions, but also highly successful actions from the past experience. For example, a candidate plan might be:
Step 1: Offer to reduce interest rate;
Step 2: Send flyer;
Step 3: Follow up with a home phone call.
This plan may be considered a high-utility one if it converted 85% of the initially reluctant customers to more willing ones while incurring only a cost of no more than $10.00 per customer.

This example introduced a number of interesting as-

Table 1. An example of loan signup plan database.

Plan No.	Action No.	State before action			Action Taken
		Salary	...	Signup	
1	1	50K	...	N	Send Mail
1	2	50K	...	N	Send Gift
...	...	...	...	...	...

pects for the planning problem. First, not all people in the group of 100,000 customers should be considered as candidates for the conversion. Some people should not be considered as part of marketing campaign because they are too costly or nearly impossible to convert. Second, the group-marketing problem is to use the same plan for different customers in the intended customer group, instead of a different action plan for each different customer. This makes the group-marketing problem different from the direct-marketing problem that some authors have considered in the data mining literature [8, 6]. For group or batch marketing, we are interested in finding a plan containing no conditional branches. We must build an N-step plan ahead of time, and evaluate the plan according to cross-validation from the historical records. Third, for the customers in the group to be marketed to, there are potentially many possible actions that we can use. Each action comes with an inherent cost associated with it. Fourth, it is difficult to formulate this problem as a classical planning problem, because the preconditions and effects of actions are only implicit in the database, rather than given ahead of time by "experts" in a crisp logical formulation. Finally, applying sequence mining to this database alone will not solve the problem. Sequence mining has focused on finding sequences by frequency. While in some situations highly frequent plans are useful, they do not in general give high-utility plans.

In this paper, we formulate the above problem as a combination of probabilistic planning and classical planning, where the key issue is to look for low-cost and high-profit sequences of actions for converting customer groups. Our main contribution is a novel algorithm that combines association-rule mining and AI planning. This paper is organized as follows. Section 2 discusses related work. Section 3 gives the problem formulation. Section 4 presents the *AUPlan* algorithm. Section 5 presents the empirical results. Section 6 concludes the paper.

2. Related Work

Research on plan mining is related with both planning and data mining. This section reviews these two areas. First we present the related research work in planning using MDP models. Then we review the work of frequent sequence mining and the previous plan mining work in the data mining area.

2.1. Planning by Reinforcement Learning

Reinforcement learning refers to a class of problems and associated techniques in which the learner is to learn how to make sequential decisions based on delayed reinforcement so as to maximize cumulative rewards [4, 11, 14]. In a standard reinforcement-learning model, an agent is connected to its environment via perception and action. On each step of interaction the agent receives as input, i, some indication of the current state, s, of the environment; the agent then chooses an action, a, to generate as output. The action changes the state of the environment, and the value of this state transition is communicated to the agent through a scalar reinforcement signal, r. The agent's behavior, B, should choose actions that tend to increase the long-term sum of values of the reinforcement signal. Formally, the model consists of

- a discrete set of environment states, S;
- a discrete set of agent actions, A;
- and a set of scalar reinforcement signals.

The agent's task is to find a policy π, mapping states to actions, that maximizes a measure of utility.

A reinforcement-learning task that satisfies the Markov property is called a Markov decision process (MDP). Markov property is formally defined as: the environment's response at time $t + 1$ depends only on the state and action representations at time t.

Dynamic programming techniques serve as the foundation and inspiration for the learning algorithms to determine the optimal policy given the correct model. The optimal value of a state is the expected infinite discounted sum of reward that the agent will gain if it starts in that state and executes the optimal policy. Using π as a complete decision policy, it is written

$$V^*(s) = \max_\pi E(\sum_{t=0}^\infty \gamma^t r_t) \tag{1}$$

This optimal value function is unique and can be defined as the solution to the simultaneous equations

$$V^*(s) = \max_a (R(s, a) + \gamma \sum_{s' \in S} T(s, a, s') V^*(s')), \forall s \in S \tag{2}$$

It asserts that the value of a state s is the expected instantaneous reward plus the expected discounted value of the next state, using the best available action. Given the optimal value function, we can specify the optimal policy as

$$\pi^*(s) = arg\max_a(R(s,a) + \gamma \sum_{s' \in S} T(s,a,s')V^*(s')) \quad (3)$$

Planning by post-processing of RL. Sun and Sessions [13] proposed an algorithm that addressed planning problem using reinforcement learning. This algorithm can be applied to batch marketing planning problem, but it suffers both computational inefficiency and non-optimality problems. In contrast to existing reinforcement learning algorithms that generate only reactive plans, a two-stage bottom-up process is devised, in which first reinforcement learning/dynamic programming is applied to acquire a reactive plan and then explicit plans are extracted from the reactive plan. Plan extraction is based on a beam search that performs temporal projection in a restricted fashion, guided by the value functions resulting from reinforcement learning and dynamic programming. For convenience, we call this algorithm $QPlan$ in this paper.

Sun and Sessions' $QPlan$ algorithm post-processes the reinforcement learning result to produce a sequence of actions, but it suffers two drawbacks. First, the computational cost of learning the optimal Q values is expensive in the first stage. Thus, the first stage has become a bottleneck for the entire planner. Second, the optimal policy obtained in the first stage cannot guarantee an optimal solution as a result of applying and searching plans using this policy. In the post-processing step, whenever the planner picks up an action at a time step t, it chooses the same action that can achieve the highest expected value functions for multiple states, not different actions optimal for each individual state. However, the assumption of value functions is that the optimal value of a state could only be obtained if it takes the action in the current state and follow the optimal policy forever after. Only when this assumption is satisfied, the optimality can be achieved. Therefore, a non-conditional plan (i.e., a sequence of actions) may not correspond to the optimal policy at all.

2.2. Planning by Frequent Sequence Mining

Mining sequential patterns has been studied extensively in data mining literature. These algorithms fall into several categories, including Apriori-based algorithms [1, 12, 7], lattice-based algorithms SPADE [16] and projection-based pattern-growth methods such as FreeSpan [2] and PrefixSpan [9]. These methods are aimed at finding highly frequent sequences efficiently.

Applying sequence mining algorithms to finding characteristics on highly successful plans, Han et al [3] presented a method for generating frequent plans using a *divide-and-conquer* strategy. The method exploits multi-dimensional

generalization of sequences of actions and extracts the inherent hierarchical structure and sequential patterns of plans at different levels of abstraction. These patterns are used in turn to subsequently narrow down the search for more specific patterns.

Zaki et al.[15] developed a technique for plan mining which discovers sequence-patterns indicating high incidence of plan failure. The PLANMINE sequence-mining algorithm extracts patterns of events that predict failures in databases of plan executions. It combines several techniques for pruning out un-predictive and redundant patterns which reduce the size of the returned rule set by more than three orders of magnitude.

3. Planning Problem Formulation

We now formulate the plan mining problem. To explain concepts easier, we consider such a problem in the marketing planning domain. We first consider how to build a state space from a given set of customer records.

As in any machine learning and data mining schemes, the input customer records consist of a set of attributes for each customer, along with a class attribute that describes the customer status. A customer's attribute may be his age, income, gender, credit with the bank, and so on. The class attribute may be "applied", which is a Boolean indicating whether the customer has applied and is approved for loan. As with any real customer databases, the number of attributes may be extremely large; for the KDD CUP 98 data, there are a total of 481 attributes to describe each customer. Of the many attributes, some may be removed when constructing a state. For convenience, we refer to this database table as the *Customer* table. Table 2 shows an example of *Customer* table.

Table 2. An example of *Customer* table

Customer	Interest Rate	Flyer	Salary	Signup
John	5%	Y	110K	Y
Mary	4%	N	30K	Y
...	...	...	...	...
Steve	8%	N	80K	N

A second source of input is the historical plan database. This is a database that describes how the previous actions have changed each customer's attributes as a result of the actions' execution. For example, after a customer receives a promotional mail, the customer's response to the marketing action is obtained and recorded. As a result of the mailing, the action count for the customer in this marketing campaign is incremented by one, and the customer may have decided to respond by filling out a general information form and mailing it back to the bank. The status of the customer at any instant of time is referred to as a state, and state may change as a result of executing an action. Thus, the historical plan database consists of state-action sequences, one for each participating customer. This sequence database will serve as the training data for our planner. Table 3 is an example of plan database.

Table 3. An example of plan database

State0	Action0	State1	Action1	State2
S_0	A_0	S_1	A_1	S_5
S_0	A_0	S_1	A_2	S_5
S_0	A_0	S_1	A_2	S_6
S_0	A_0	S_1	A_2	S_7
S_0	A_0	S_2	A_1	S_6
S_0	A_0	S_2	A_1	S_8
S_0	A_1	S_3		
S_0	A_1	S_4		

Given the *Customer* table and the plan database, our first task is to formulate the problem as a planning problem. In particular, we wish to find a method to map the customer records in the customer table into states using a statistical classifier. This task in itself is not trivial because it maps a large attribute space into a more concise space. The problem is more complicated when there are missing values in the database. This involves the issues of data cleaning.

After the state space is obtained, we will use a second classifier to classify the states into either desirable or undesirable states based on the training data provided in the *Customer* table. In our implementation, we use decision tree as the classification algorithm.

Next, the state-action sequences in the plan database will be used for obtaining action definitions in a state space, such that each action is represented as a probabilistic mapping from a state to a set of states. To make the representation more realistic, we will also consider the cost of executing each action.

To summarize, from the two tables we can obtain the following information:

- $f_s(r_i) = s_j$ maps a customer record r_i to a state s_j. This function is known as the customer-state mapping function;

- $p(+|s)$ is a probability function that returns the probability that state s is in a desirable class. We call this classifier the state-classification function;

- $p(s_k|s_i, a_j)$ returns the transition probability that, after executing an action a_j in state s_i, one ends up in state s_k.

We now define the utility of a given plan. Recall that a plan is a sequence of actions, starting from an initial state s. A plan is divided into stages, where each stage consists of one action and a set of possible outcome states resulting from the action. In each stage the states can be different possible states as a result of the previous action, and the action in the stage must be a same, single action. Given a plan $P = a_1 a_2 \ldots a_n$ and an initial state s, we define the utility $U(s, P)$ of the plan as follows. Let P' be the subplan of P after taking out the first action a_1; that is, $P = a_1 P'$. Then the utility of the plan P is defined recursively

$$U(s, P) = \left(\sum_{s' \in S} p(s'|s, a_1) * U(s', P') \right) - cost(a_1) \quad (4)$$

where s' is the next state resulting from executing a_1 in state s. If s is a leaf node, then the plan from the leaf node s is empty, then

$$U(s, \{\}) = p(+|s) * REWARD \quad (5)$$

$p(+|s)$ is the probability of leaf node s being in the desired class, $REWARD$ is a predefined constant that defines the maximum possible reward for the customer to be in any state.

Using Equation 4 and 5, we can evaluate the utility of a plan in the initial state.

Given a set of initial items (records in a *Customer* table), our goal is to find a sequence of actions for each initial state that converts as many of the customers in that state from the undesirable class to the desirable one – bringing in high benefits while incurring low costs. To make the computation more efficient, we require that the plan satisfy some constraints. For example, we can impose the following constraints:

- length constraint: the length of a plan is at most N; or

- success constraint: the success probability is over a threshold σ.

4 The *AUPlan* Algorithm

Given these customer database and plan traces, the *AUPlan* algorithm, shown in Table 4, will find all high utility plans in a database using a minimum utility parameter minSU; *minSU* is a minimum threshold value on the product of utility of a plan and its support value, where support carries the same meaning as in association-rule mining [1, 12, 7]. All plans generated as output must have the product of utility and support greater than the *minSU* value. A second input parameter to our algorithm is *maxlength*, which denotes the maximum length of plans in which we wish to find the high utility ones. Like Apriori-based association-rule mining algorithms, *AUPlan* searches the space of action sequences in a level-wise manner. Unlike Apriori-based algoirthms, utility-based plan mining has to use the utility of plans to guide the search. However, the utility measure does not satisfy the anti-monotone property.

Table 4. *AUPlan* algorithm

Input: A plan database, *minSU*, *maxlength*
Output: High-utility plans.

Algorithm:
1. $C_1 = \{s_j a_i\}$, $s_j a_i$ is all possible one-step plans in the planbase.
2. $K = 1$
3. While($K <= maxlength$)
   3.1 Count support for each plan P in C_k.
        Calculate utility for each plan P in C_k.
        $L_k = \{P \in C_k | sup(P) \times U(P) \geq minSU\}$
   3.2 Generate C_{k+1} from C_k.
   3.3 $K = K + 1$.
End while
4. $L = L_1 \cup L_2 \cup ... \cup L_k$
5. Partition the frequent sequences according to their initial states.
6. For each initial state s_j
   6.1 For each plan P starting with s_j
        Calculate its utility $U(s_j, P)$.
   6.2 Select the plan with highest utility for s_j.
        $plan(s_j) = argmax_P U(s_j, P)$
7. Output plans.

Even though plan utility itself does not satisfy the anti-monotone property, we can design an upper bound of utility to guarantee the anti-monotone property and still allow significant pruning of the search space. In addition, using the utility upper bound ensures the mining result accurate and complete. For a plan P, we denote the upper bound value to be $upperUtil(P)$. We denote the support of a plan P to be $sup(P)$. Pruning plans using the upper bound amounts to pruning a plan P if $upperUtil(P) \times sup(P) < minSU$. The application of the utility upper bound pruning is shown in Table 5.

Suppose the number of sequences in the database is $|N|$, the average length of sequences in the form of $s_i a_j s_{i+1} a_{j+1}...s_n$ in the database is l, the mining process iterates m times. The complexity of one database scan is $O(|C_k| * |N| * \lfloor l/2 \rfloor)$. The overall time complexity for m iterations is $O(m * |C| * |N| * \lfloor l/2 \rfloor)$, where $|C|$ is the average size of $|C_k|$.

The calculation of the transition probability is realized by matrix multiplication. We define a n by n matrix Tr_k for each action a_k, where n is the number of states. $Tr_k[i][j]$ represents the probability that the transition from state s_i to

Table 5. Candidate generation and pruning (Step 3.2) in *AUPlan*

(In Step 3.2)
if($sup(P) \times U(P) \geq minSU$)
{
    insert(L_k, P);
    for(a in action_set)
    {
        P' = append a to P;
        insert(C_{k+1}, P');
    }
}

else if($sup(P) \times U(P) < minSU$)
{
    for(a in action_set)
    {
        P' = append a to P;
        if ($upperUtil(P') \times sup(P) < minSU$)
            prune P';
        else
            insert(C_{k+1}, P');
    }
}

state s_j occurs under the action a_k. We use a 1Xn vector V' to represent the probability distribution among the states. Initially, for a starting state s_j of a plan, $V_0[j] = 1$ and $V_0[i] = 0, \forall i \neq j$. For a plan $s_j a_{i+1} a_{i+2}...a_{i+q}$, we calculate $V' = V_0 \times Tr_{i+1} \times Tr_{i+2} \times ... \times Tr_{i+q}$. The time complexity of vector and matrix multiplication is $O(qn^2)$. This is the time complexity of calculating utility for one plan. The time complexity for utility calculation for all plans in C_k in one iteration is $O(|C_k| * qn^2)$. The overall time complexity of utility calculation for all plans in m iteration is $O(\sum_{k=1}^{m} |C_k| * qn^2)$, or $O(m * |C| * qn^2)$, where $|C|$ is the average size of $|C_k|$.

The overall time complexity for m iterations is $O(m * |C| * (|N| * \lfloor l/2 \rfloor + qn^2))$, where $|C|$ is the average size of $|C_k|$.

5. Experimental Results

In order to test the hypothesis that our approach can efficiently mine good plans as compared to the optimal solutions, we run a series of simulated tests to compare *AUPlan* with planning using MDP and planning by exhaustive search.

5.1. Data Generation

We used the IBM Synthetic Generator (http://www.almaden.ibm.com/software/quest/Resources/datasets/syndata.html) to generate a *Customer* dataset with two classes and nine attributes.

The positive class has 30,000 records representing successful customers and negative has 70,000 representing unsuccessful ones. Those 70,000 negative records are treated as starting points for plan database data generation. We carried out the state abstraction and mapping by feature selection, only keeping four attributes out of nine. Those four attributes were converted from continuous range to discrete values. The state space has 400 distinct states. A classifier is trained using the C4.5 decision tree algorithm [10] on the *Customer* dataset. The classifier will be used later to decide on the class of a state. However, since our focus here is not on training the classifier, and since the choice of the classifier is fairly independent from the subsequent planning algorithms, we will not delve into details here.

We generated the plan database using a second simulator. Each of the 70,000 negative-class records is treated as an initially failed customer. A trace is then generated for the customer, transforming the customer through intermediate states to a final state. We defined four types of actions, each of which has a cost and impacts on attribute transitions. An action's impact on attribute transitions is defined by an *Action-Impact* matrix. For example, M_{ij} is a matrix representing the impact of Action i on Attribute j. The matrix is n by n if attribute j has n different values. The matrix element $M_{ij}[k][l]$ means: of the n different values of Attribute j, if the original value of Attribute j is the kth value, after action i, there is $M_{ij}[k][l]$ probability that the value of Attribute i is changed to the lth value. The plan database generation algorithm is shown in Table 6.

Given the *Customer* table and plan database, *AUPlan* will select plans in the state space. To evaluate the quality of plans found by the algorithm, we calculate the utility of each initial state s with the plan under state s. Then add up these utilities under different states. The sum of plan utility, TU, reflects the overall quality of plans returned by the algorithm over the state space.

$$TU = \sum_{s \in S} max_i U(s, P_i) \qquad (6)$$

where Pi represents different plans starting from state s.

5.2. Experimental Result

We wish to test our algorithm *AUPlan* on plan databases of different sizes against the MDP-based algorithm *QPlan* and an exhaustive search benchmark. Our test data is set up

Table 6. Plan database Generation Algorithm

Input: *maxlength*, A set of initial failed states S_i,
    a set of actions A_i with *Action-Impact* matrices.
Output: Sequences of trace data with temporal order
    $< S_i, A_j, S_{i+1}, A_{j+1}, ..., S_n >$

Algorithm:
for each initially failed state S
    while(trace_length $<$ *maxlength*)
        randomly select an action a;
        generate next state S' according to S and
        Action-Impact matrix of a;
        trace_length ++;
        if(S' is a successful state)
            break;
    end while
end for

using the IBM Synthetic Generator in the following manner. All plan databases have a total of 70,000 plans, but different plan databases have different sequence length limits. Plans in the plan database will not exceed the length limit. This variation in sequence length allows the different plan-mining algorithms to return plans of different utility values. Table 7 shows the features of the five plan databases. In these databases, *Switching Rate* refers to the percentage of customers in the 70,000 who initially belong to the failed class but can be converted successfully by some plans in corresponding plan database. It is expected that both *QPlan* and *AUPlan* will return solution plans with increasing utility values while incurring more computation when we move from DB1 to DB5.

Table 7. Features of different plan databases

plan database	Length Limit (Max # of actions)	Switching Rate (%)
Plan DB1	5	20
Plan DB2	9	40
Plan DB3	14	60
Plan DB4	29	80
Plan DB5	100	100

We compare three algorithms. The first is a most naive algorithm, which serves both as a benchmark for quality (it returns the highest possible utility) and efficiency (it performs an exhaustive search). We call this algorithm the *OptPlan* algorithm. Given an action set A and a parameter $maxlength$ for the maximum length of plans one wishes to explore, *OptPlan* tries all possible combinations of actions in a corresponding database to find optimal plans no longer than *maxlength* in length. This method will produce optimal solutions in terms of plan quality. The drawback of this method is its computation cost. Suppose the number of actions in A is $|A|$, the *maxlength* equals L. The number of length-1 plans is $|A|$, length-2 plans $|A|^2$, ..., length-L plans $|A|^L$. The number of plans, and therefore the computational time, grows exponentially with *maxlength*.

A second algorithm we compare to is the *QPlan* algorithm in [13]. As described in the related work section, this algorithm runs in two stages. In the first stage, we apply Q-learning first to get an optimal policy. We then extract plans guided by the Q-values through a beam search. Q-learning is carried out using "batch reinforcement learning" [8]. It tries to estimate the value function $Q(s, a)$ by the value-iteration algorithm. The major computational bottleneck of *QPlan* is thus from Q-learning.

To allow *QPlan* to terminate at any intermediate state that has high enough utility, we add one special *null* action to the Q-learning part of the *QPlan* algorithm. That is, besides the Q-values of each state/action pair, we learn one more Q-value $Q(s, \phi)$ for each state s, ϕ means "no action, stop at the current state". $Q(s, \phi)$ is the reward that would be obtained if no action is taken at state s. It is defined as:

$$Q(s, \phi) = p(+|s) \times REWARD \qquad (7)$$

When the agent finds that staying at a state s will bring higher utility than taking any actions from that state, it should stop taking any actions wisely. This can be realized by comparing the Q-values of $Q(s, \phi)$ and $Q(s, a)$ for all a in the action set. If $Q(s, \phi)$ is greater than $Q(s, a)$ for all a, then the agent stops at state s. Otherwise, it picks up the action a that maximizes $Q(s, a)$.

We run all three algorithms, *QPlan*, *AUPlan* and *OptPlan*, on the different plan databases and obtained the CPU time as a function of the size of plan databases. We also compared the utility of plans returned by each algorithm. For each plan database, we converted the utilities of *QPlan* and *AUPlan* as the percentage of the utility of the *OptPlan* algorithm, which is at 100% level.

Figure 1 shows the CPU time of different algorithms versus the size of plan databases. The top line corresponds to the CPU time of *OptPlan* which is at a constant for different databases in this test, because we set the parameter *maxlength* to be a constant 6 for each plan database. As *maxlength* is fixed, the number of plans by exhaustive search in *OptPlan* is also the same for different plan databases, so is the computational cost. In this case, the only difference between different plan databases is the transition probability $p(s_k|s_i, a_j)$. Note that the Y-axis is displayed in log scale. Thus the CPU time of *OptPlan* shows that exhaustive search is simply not practical at all. *AUPlan* is shown to be much more efficient than *QPlan*. This is ex-

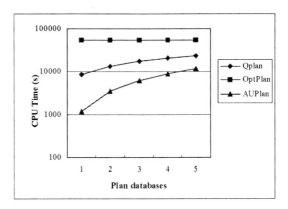

Figure 1. CPU time of Different algorithms versus different plan databases

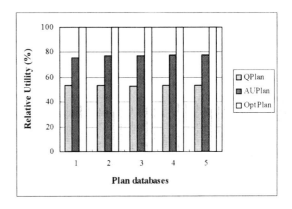

Figure 2. Relative Utility of Different algorithms vs. different plan database

pected, since *AUPlan*'s mining and pruning algorithms is able to scale up the planning problems.

We next turn to a comparison on the utility of plans found. Figure 2 shows the relative utility of different algorithms versus different plan databases. *OptPlan* has the maximal utility by exhaustive search. *AUPlan* comes next, about 80% of the optimal solution. *QPlan* have less than 60% of the optimal solution.

Figure 3 shows the relative utility of different algorithms versus *maxlength* parameter used in the *AUPlan* algorithm. *maxlength* is the maximum number of actions to be allowed in a solution plan. In this experiment, we fixed a database (DB3) and varied the *maxlength* parameter. When the *maxlength* is three, *AUPlan* has about 85% of the optimal solution. For different values of *maxlength*, *AUPlan* clearly represents a tradeoff between the optimal solution *OptPlan* and the Q-learning based solution *QPlan*.

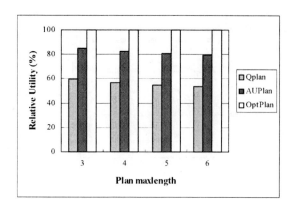

Figure 3. Relative Utility of different algorithms vs. *maxlength* **of the plans**

6 Conclusion and Future Work

We proposed a plan mining algorithm that integrates both data mining and planning to obtain high-utility plans. We add states, actions, utilities to sequence mining algorithms and returns not only the frequent sequences, but actual plans for agents to execute. In large plan databases, scalability is an important issue. Experimental results demonstrate that the integrated data mining and planning approach is more efficient and effective than planning by MDP and exhaustive search. The quality of plans by *AUPlan* is about 80% of the optimal solution in our tests.

In the future, we will consider the following directions:

- Test our algorithms on more real plan data. Our algorithms could have a broad applications, such as marketing domains, robot world, etc. If we could apply to real data, such as plans executed by robots, we could make data mining truly actionable.

- We assume the intermediate states between plan executions could be observed. If part of the data about states is not observable, our algorithms have to be modified. It is possible to formulate the problem as an approximation to POMDP [5] when the intermediate states are partially observable.

Acknowledgment The authors are supported by a Hong Kong Government RGC grant and the Hong Kong University of Science and Technology.

References

[1] R. Agrawal and R. Srikant. Mining sequential patterns. In P. Yu and A. Chen, editors, *Proceedings of 11th International Conference on Data Engineering (ICDE'95)*, pages 3–14, Taipei, Taiwan, March 1995. IEEE Computer Society Press.

[2] J. Han, J. Pei, Mortazavi-Asl, Q. Chen, U. Dayal, and M.-C. Hsu. Freespan: Frequent pattern-projected sequential pattern mining. In *Proceedings of the 2000 International Conference on Knowledge Discovery and Data Mining (KDD'00)*, pages 355–359, Boston, MA, August 2000.

[3] J. Han, Q. Yang, and E. Kim. Plan mining by divide-and-conquer. In *Proceedings of SIGMOD'99 Workshop on Research Issues on Data Mining and Knowledge Discovery (DMKD'99)*, 1999.

[4] L. Kaelbling, M. Littman, and A. Moore. Reinforcement learning: A survey. *Journal of Artificial Intelligence Research*, 4:237–285, 1996.

[5] L. P. Kaelbling, M. L. Littman, and A. R. Cassandra. Planning and acting in partially observable stochastic domains. Technical Report CS-96-08, 1996.

[6] C. Ling and C. Li. Data mining for direct marketing: Problems and solutions. In *Proceedings of the Fourth International Conference on Knowledge Discovery and Data Mining (KDD'98)*, pages 73–79, New York, 1998.

[7] F. Masseglia, F. Cathala, and P. Poncelet. The psp approach for mining sequential patterns. *Principles of Data Mining and Knowledge Discovery*, pages 176–184, 1998.

[8] E. Pednault, N. Abe, and B. Zadrozny. Sequential cost-sensitive decision making with reinforcement learning. In *Proceedings of the Eighth International Conference on Knowledge Discovery and Data Mining (KDD'02)*, pages 259–268, Edmonton, Canada, 2002.

[9] J. Pei, J. Han, B. Mortazavi-Asl, H. Pinto, Q. Chen, U. Dayal, and M.-C. Hsu. Prefixspan: Mining sequential patterns efficiently by prefix projected pattern growth. In *Proceedings of the 2001 International Conference on Data Engineering (ICDE'01)*, pages 215–226, Heidelberg, Germany, April 2001.

[10] J. R. Quinlan. *C4.5: Programming for Machine Learning*. Morgan Kaufmann Pbulishers, San Mateo, CA, 1993.

[11] S. Russell and P. Norvig. *Artificial Intelligence: A Modern Approach*. Prentice-Hall, Upper Saddle River, NJ, 1995.

[12] R. Srikant and R. Agrawal. Mining sequential patterns: Generalizations and performance improvements. In P. Apers, M. Bouzeghoub, and G. Gardarin, editors, *Proceedings of 5th International Conference on Extending Database Technology (EDBT'96)*, volume 1057, pages 3–17, SpringerVerlag, March 1996.

[13] R. Sun and C. Sessions. Learning plans without a priori knowledge. *Adaptive Behavior*, 8(3/4):225–253, 2001.

[14] R. Sutton and A. Barto. *Reinforcement Learning: An Introduction*. MIT Press, Cambridge, MA, 1998.

[15] M. Zaki, N. Lesh, and M. Ogihara. Planmine: Sequence mining for plan failures. In *Proceedings of the Fourth International Conference on Knowledge Discovery and Data Mining (KDD'98)*, 1998.

[16] M. J. Zaki. Spade: An efficient algorithm for mining frequent sequences. *Machine Learning, special issue on Unsupervised Learning*, 42(1/2):31–60, Jan/Feb 2001.

Segmenting Customer Transactions Using a Pattern-Based Clustering Approach

Yinghui Yang and Balaji Padmanabhan

Operations and Information Management Department
The Wharton School, University of Pennsylvania
{yiyang, balaji}@wharton.upenn.edu

Abstract

Grouping customer transactions into categories helps understand customers better. The marketing literature has concentrated on identifying important segmentation variables (e.g. customer loyalty) and on using clustering and mixture models for segmentation. The data mining literature has provided various clustering algorithms for segmentation. In this paper we investigate using "pattern-based" clustering approaches to grouping customer transactions. We argue that there are clusters in transaction data based on natural behavioral patterns, and present a new technique, YACA, that groups transactions such that itemsets generated from each cluster, while similar to each other, are different from ones generated from others. We present experimental results from user-centric Web usage data that demonstrates that YACA generates a highly effective clustering of transactions.

1. Introduction

Firms are increasingly realizing the importance of understanding and leveraging customer level data, and critical business decision models are being built upon analyzing such data. For example, Amazon.com offers distinct home pages and recommends new products for customers based on personalization models built from data. Most credit card and cellular phone fraud alerts are also issued from the analysis of customer level data. Consumer brand choice models and pricing models are heavily used in marketing endeavors.

While the expectation for customer level data analysis is high, there are still problems with existing analysis methods. Consumers still receive significant amount of mail advertising products that they are not interested in, and online recommendations are still far from perfect. In order to create more successful personalized systems and build more accurate consumer behavior models for customers, firms need to understand their customers better. This includes understanding customers'

preferences through facts and customers' behavior through analyzing their transaction data. There has been much research done in this direction, and clustering transactions to learn segments has been one research stream that has generated a variety of useful approaches.

In the marketing literature, market segmentation approaches have often been used to divide customers into groups in order to implement different strategies. It has been long established that customers demonstrate heterogeneity in their product preferences and buying behaviors [2], and that the model built on the market in aggregate is less efficient than models built for individual segments. Much of this research focuses on examining how variables like demographics, socioeconomic status, personality and attitudes can be used in predicting differences in consumption and brand loyalty. Distance-based clustering techniques, such as *k*-means, and parametric mixture models, such as gaussian mixture models, are two main approaches used in segmentation. While both these approaches have produced good results in various applications, there are well known drawbacks to these methods. For clustering approaches to segmentation, the actual technique used has often been ad-hoc. It is generally not clear why a distance-based clustering in an *n* dimensional space, while convenient, is the appropriate manner to group customers. For mixture models, using changing model parameters to represent the difference between segments can often oversimplify the difference between segments and can ignore variables and patterns that are not captured by the parametric models.

In our research we study a new approach to segmenting customer transactions, one that is based on the idea that there may exist natural behavioral patterns in different groups of transactions. For example, a set of behavioral patterns that distinguish a group of wireless subscribers may be:

• Their call duration during weekday mornings is short and these calls are within the same geographical area.
• They call from outside the home area on weekdays and from the home area on weekends.
• They have several "data" calls on weekdays.

The above set of three patterns may be representative of a group of 'consultants' who travel frequently and exhibit a set of common behavioral patterns. This example suggests that there may be natural clusters in data, characterized by a set of typical behavioral patterns. In such cases, appropriate "pattern-based clustering" approaches can be an intuitive method for grouping customer transactions.

At the highest level, the idea here is to cluster customer transactions such that patterns generated from each cluster, while similar to each other, are very different from the patterns generated from other clusters. We suggest that different domains may have different representations for what "patterns" are, and on how to define differences between sets of patterns. In the above example, rules are an effective representation for patterns generated from the wireless data, but in a different domain, such as time series data on stock prices, representations for patterns may be based on "shapes" in the time series. It is easy to see that traditional distance-based clustering techniques and mixture models are not well suited to learning clusters where the fundamental characterization is a set of patterns such as the ones above.

A reason why pattern-based clustering techniques can generate natural clusters from customer transactions is that such transactions often have natural categories *that are not directly observable from the data*. For example, Web transactions may be for work, for entertainment, shopping for self, shopping as gifts, transactions made while in a happy mood etc. However, customers do not indicate whether they are happy or sad, for example, before starting each transaction. However, the set of patterns corresponding to transactions in each category will be different. Transactions at work may be quicker and more focused while transactions for entertainment may be long and across a broader set of sites. Hence grouping transactions such that the patterns generated from each cluster are 'very different' from those generated from another cluster may be an effective method for learning the natural categorizations. This argument suggests a natural evaluation technique that is used in this paper. We combine transactions with a known natural category – Web transactions from different users (without maintaining the user ID) - and examine how well pattern-based clustering does in separating transactions that belong to the individual users as compared to traditional clustering techniques.

Motivated by the above argument, in this paper we investigate the utility of pattern-based clustering for grouping Web transactions. In particular, we argue that itemsets are a natural representation for patterns in Web transactions and present YACA, a pattern-based clustering algorithm for domains where itemsets are the natural representation.

In general the idea of using patterns to group data has been applied for other specific examples in the literature [11] and in particular, there has been prior work that clustered based on items [3, 8, 12, 13]. We describe these in the related work in Section 5. The rest of this paper is structured as follows. In Section 2 we describe the domain and develop an objective function that will be used to generate the pattern-based clusters. This is followed by a description of YACA, the algorithm used to generate the clusters. We present experimental results in Section 4 followed by related work and conclusions.

2. Pattern-Based Clustering of Web Transactions

In this paper we assume that users' Web transactions are data records containing categorical and numeric attributes created from the raw data consisting of a series of URLs visited. In our experiments, we start with real session-level Web browsing data for users (provided by a market data vendor [10]) and create 46 features describing the session. The specific features are listed in Table 1.

Note that the features include those about time (e.g. average time spent per page), quantity (e.g. number of sites visited) and the order of pages visited (e.g. first site) and that the features include both categorical and numeric types. A conjunction of atomic conditions on these attributes is a good representation for common behavioral patterns in the transaction data. For example {*starting_time = morning, average_time_page < 2 minutes, num_categories = 3, total_time < 10 minutes*} is a behavioral pattern that may capture a user's specific 'morning' pattern of Web usage that involves looking at multiple sites (e.g. work email, news, finance etc) in a focused manner such that the total time spent is low. Another common pattern for this (same) user may be {*starting_time = night, most_visted_category = games*} reflecting her typical behavior at the end of days. Hence, in order to capture the typical behavioral patterns in Web transactions, we use itemsets as the representation for patterns. Note that in general we assume that the items in the itemsets can involve both categorical and numeric attributes as described in the examples above, and the functions defined below for the clusters are for the general case. However in the implementation described in Section 4, we bin the numeric attributes into categories to enable the application of Apriori-type methods for learning the frequent itemsets from the data. Below we describe the objective function of the pattern-based clustering method.

Table 1. Features of a session

Categories	Metric	Definition
Time-related	Total time	
	Average time per page	Total time/ # of pages
	Average time per site	Total time/ # of sites
	Average time per category	Total time/ # of categories
	Starting time	
	Starting day	
	Most visited site	
	Most visited category	
Quantity-related	number of pages	
	number of sites	
	number of categories	
	average # of pages per site	# of pages / # of sites
	average # of sites per categories	# of sites / # of categories
	# of sites for each category (total 27 categories)	
Order-related	first site	
	second site	
	last site	
	first category	
	second category	
	last category	

Page: individual Web page, each hit is a page;
Site: domain name, such as www.yahoo.com ;
Category: Such as "travel site", "news site" etc.

Consider a collection of transactions to be clustered $\{ T_1, T_2, \ldots, T_n \}$. Each transaction T_i contains a subset of a list of candidate items $\{ i_1, i_2, \ldots, i_m \}$. A clustering C is a partition $\{ C_1, C_2, \ldots, C_k \}$ of $\{ T_1, T_2, \ldots, T_n \}$ and each C_i is a cluster. The goal of our method is to maximize the difference between clusters and the similarity of transactions within clusters. In another word, we cluster to maximize a quantity M, where M is defined as follows:

$$M(C_1, C_2, \ldots, C_k) = Difference\,(C_1, C_2, \ldots, C_k) + \sum_{i=1}^{k} Similarity\,(C_i)$$

More specifically, the difference is defined based on the idea that frequent itemsets generated from each cluster C_i are "very different" from the frequent itemsets generated from other clusters. "Very different" is defined based on the difference in support values of the itemsets generated in each cluster.

Note that this suggests that itemsets are generated for each cluster separately (i.e. based on the transactions within that cluster only). However, to avoid repeated executions of the itemset discovery routine, in practice we can generate the set of all itemsets once (from the entire transaction data), and re-calibrate the support values for the itemsets in any cluster as needed. For example, assume that the total data size is 100,000

transactions and the minimum number of transactions in a cluster is set to 1000. For a minimum support of 5%, the smallest frequent itemset in any cluster has a support of 50 transactions. Hence we set the minimum support to (50/100,000) for the entire database to learn the set of all itemsets that could be frequent in any cluster. Subsequently for any group of transactions we update the set of frequent itemsets by determining the actual support values for all the itemsets within this set of transactions.

Let FIS be the set of all the frequent itemsets (we call it the candidate itemsets) based on the entire transaction data (before any clustering). After clustering, we calculate the support for each itemset in FIS for each cluster. Note that a candidate itemset is frequent in the entire set of transactions before clustering, but not necessarily frequent for each cluster. Specifically, FIS = $\{is_1, is_2, \ldots, is_p\}$ where is_i is an itemset in FIS and s_{ij} is the support of itemset i in cluster j (see Table 2).

Table 2. Matrix of itemsets' supports

	C_1	C_2	$\ldots$	C_k
is_1	s_{11}	s_{12}	$\ldots$	s_{1k}
is_2	s_{21}	s_{22}	$\ldots$	s_{2k}
$\ldots$	$\ldots$	$\ldots$	$\ldots$	$\ldots$
is_p	s_{p1}	s_{p2}	$\ldots$	s_{pk}

Next, we define the difference between two clusters and the similarity of the transactions within a cluster using the support of the itemsets.

Definition 1 (Difference of two clusters)

$$Difference \ (C_i, C_j) = \sum_{a=1}^{p} \frac{\left| \dfrac{S_{ai}}{|C_i|} - \dfrac{S_{aj}}{|C_j|} \right|}{\dfrac{1}{2} \left(\dfrac{S_{ai}}{|C_i|} + \dfrac{S_{aj}}{|C_j|} \right)}$$

$|C_i|$ is the number of transactions in cluster C_i and p is the number of itemsets in *FIS*. This is a good measure since for every itemset, it calculates the difference between the pattern in each cluster by computing the difference between the support values (adjusted by the actual support values). For example, if the itemset {*starting_time=afternoon, most_visited_category=sports*} occurs in 3% of the transactions in cluster-1 while it occurs 9% of time in cluster-2, the difference is 1, while if it occurs 50% and 75% of time respectively the difference is 0.4.

Note that we have defined the difference between two clusters only. This is sufficient since hierarchical clustering techniques can be used to repeatedly cluster the transactions into two groups in such a way that the process results in clustering the transactions into an arbitrary number of clusters (which is generally desirable since the number of clusters do not have to be specified upfront). Clearly, alternative definitions of difference are possible and the above function, though intuitive, is one among possibly several reasonable difference definitions between sets of itemsets.

Definition 2 (Intra-cluster similarity):
Here, our goal is to define a metric that captures what it means for patterns in one cluster to be "similar" to each other. An itemset is considered "good" if it is frequent and hence we define similarity based on the number of frequent itemsets within a cluster.
Similarity $S(C_i)$ = the number of frequent itemsets in cluster C_i

In this section we described the use of itemsets for clustering Web transactions and presented an objective function to maximize in order to generate the pattern-based clusters. In the next section we describe YACA, an algorithm for pattern-based clustering.

3. The Clustering Algorithm

The ideal algorithm will be one which maximizes M (defined in previous section). However, for the objective function defined above, if there are n transactions and two clusters that we are interested in learning, the number of possible clustering schemes to examine is 2^n. Hence we need a heuristic approach.

After we get *FIS*, as described in Section 2, we convert the initial transactions into the format in Table 3, where the rows represent transactions to be clustered and the columns represents itemsets. A "1" in a cell indicates that a certain transaction contains a certain itemset.

Table 3. Transaction represented in itemsets

	is_1	is_2	...	is_p
T_1	1	0	...	0
T_2	1	0	...	1
...	...	...	...	...
T_n	0	1	...	0

We use $T'=\{ T'_1, T'_2, \ldots, T'_n \}$ to represent this new transaction set. Instead of clustering the original transactions, we convert the problem into clustering these binary vectors and present a divisive hierarchical algorithm. The entire transaction set is first divided into two clusters. Each cluster is further divided into two clusters if it has more than a predefined number of transactions. This process is repeated until no cluster is big enough to be divided further. In addition to cluster size, we assume the stopping conditions are user-specified and can contain additional criteria such that if a cluster's size is bigger than the threshold but its quality is very good (contains very similar transactions), we can stop dividing that cluster.

In order to generate balanced clusters, we introduce another component to M. Also because each division creates two clusters, the revised M is specified as follows:

$$M(C_1, C_2) = K_1 \cdot D(C_1, C_2) + K_2 \cdot S(C_1) + K_3 \cdot S(C_2) - K_4 \cdot |N_1 - N_2|$$

K_1, K_2, K_3, K_4 are user-specified weights (can be decided based on different applications),
$D(C_1, C_2)$ represents the inter-cluster difference,
$S(C_1)$ and $S(C_2)$ are the intra-cluster similarity for cluster-1 and cluster-2 respectively, and
N_1 and N_2 are the number of transactions in cluster-1 and cluster-2 respectively.

The candidate itemsets are generated from association rule discovery algorithms such as Apriori [1]. Figure 1 describes the algorithm YACA.

For each division, a randomly chosen first transaction and the 'most different' transaction (in terms of Euclidean distance) from the first transaction are chosen to form two initial clusters, C_1 and C_2. Then, every other transaction is either assigned to C_1 or C_2 whichever maximizes M.

Input: $C = \{ C_0 \}$
$\qquad C_0 = \{ T'_1, T'_2, \ldots, T'_n \}$ – the converted transactions to be clustered (see Table 3)
Output: Clusters $C = \{ C_1, C_2, \ldots, C_f \}$

Repeat {
Choose any cluster $X = \{ T_1, T_2, \ldots Ts \}$ from C such that the stopping condition is not satisfied for X;
$C_1 = \{\}, C_2 = \{\}$;
Assign T_1 in X to C_1;
Assign T_m to $C_2 \mid T_m$ is 'most different' from T_1;
for i=1 to s {
$\qquad$ Allocate T_i to C_1 or C_2 to maximize M;
$\qquad$ }
$C = (C - X) \cup C_1 \cup C_2$;
} While the stopping condition is not satisfied for every X in C

Figure 1 *Algorithm YACA*

4. Experiments: Clustering user-centric Web transactions

Evaluating whether our grouping of transactions using patterns is "good" is a hard problem since it, like any other clustering technique, is an unsupervised learning technique. However, as mentioned in the introduction, in order to test the efficacy of pattern-based clustering it is natural to combine transactions with a known category – Web transactions from different users (without maintaining the user ID) - and examine how the method does in separating transactions that belong to the individual users as compared to traditional clustering techniques. This is the approach used in our experiments. We pick out the sessions belonging to a certain number of users to form a sub-dataset which is used as the input to YACA. The users we picked out are those who have the most sessions. The most active users have approximately 2500 sessions over that year. In order to demonstrate the robustness of our approach, we constructed 30 such sub-datasets. Among these 30 datasets, 10 datasets contain sessions from 2 users, 10 contain sessions from 3 users, and 10 contain sessions from 4 users. There are approximately 5000 sessions in each of the 2-user datasets, 7500 sessions in each 3-user set, and 10000 in each 4-user set. The transactions of each user capture his/her online activity over a period of a year.

To construct the data, we start with user-centric data provided by a market data vendor. User-centric Web transaction data is data collected at the user level, and thus captures the entire Web surfing behavior for each user. First, we group individual hits into sessions using a common rule of thumb that groups consecutive hits within 30 minutes of each other into a session. As

described in Section 2 (see Table 1), we create features to describe the user's behavior for each session and construct 46 features for each session. We create an item for each value of the categorical features and categorize the continuous variables according to their value distribution (uniformly binned), and create an item for each bin. After itemizing, we create a session (transaction) by item matrix (Table 4) with binary values for each sub-dataset. A "1" in a cell indicates that a certain transaction contains a certain item. $T_1.T_2,\ldots,T_n$ correspond to the sessions in a sub-dataset. Depending on the sub-dataset, there are approximately 2000 to 5000 items for each sub-dataset.

Table 4. Transactions represented in items

	i_1	i_2	...	i_p
T_1	1	0	...	1
T_2	1	1	...	0
...	...	...	...	...
T_n	0	1	...	1

From this matrix, we use Apriori to discovery the candidate itemsets and create a matrix like the one in Table 3 used as the input to YACA. In the experiment, the minimum support we set for Apriori to discover frequent itemsets is 3%. There are 2000 to 6500 itemsets (we restricted these to have a maximum of 4 items) for different sub-datasets.

In order to compare the performance of YACA, we implemented three different methods: (i) Hierarchical k-means on data represented in items as in Table 4 (the "$k$means-items" approach) (ii) Hierarchical k-means on data represented in itemsets as in Table 3 (the "$k$means-itemsets" approach) and (iii) YACA on data represented in itemsets as in Table 3 (the "YACA-itemsets" approach). Hierarchical k-means is described in Figure 2.

Input: $C = \{ C_0 \}$
$\qquad C_0 = \{ T'_1, T'_2, \ldots, T'_n \}$ - the converted transaction set to be clustered (the transactions can take the forms both as that in Table 4 ("k-means-items" approach) and that in Table 3 ("$k$means-itemsets" approach).
Output: Clusters $C = \{ C_1, C_2, \ldots, C_f \}$

Repeat {
Choose any cluster $X = \{ T_1, T_2, \ldots Ts \}$ from C such that the stopping condition is not satisfied for X;
Use k-means to cluster X into 2 clusters C_1 and C_2;
$C = (C - X) \cup C_1 \cup C_2$;
} While the stopping condition is not satisfied for every X in C

Figure 2. Hierarchical k-means

The reason we use hierarchical k-means is because the number of natural clusters are not known in advance. This is particularly useful since even for a sub-dataset containing transactions from 2 users, we expect more than 2 clusters, since each user may have more than one behavior pattern. Note that if we use just k-means instead of hierarchical k-means, we get inferior results. For example, when we applied k-means on a 2-user dataset, each resulting cluster contains approximately 50% of the transactions from each user. By using hierarchical clustering, around 70% of the clusters we get are more than 95% pure (a cluster is considered "95% pure" if at least 95% of transactions in the cluster belong entirely to a single user). When we cluster using YACA, we set the value of K_1 to be 1, K_2 and K_3 to be 1.1, K_4 to be 100, and the support threshold that we used to define large itemsets to be 2%, and have the same value for these parameters through out the entire experiment. These values are chosen to bring the four components of M to relatively compatible scales. We only consider itemsets which contain less than 4 items and the stopping criterion is that the size of the cluster is smaller than 5% of the size of the dataset to be clustered.

Figures 3~5 present the results on the 30 datasets. The number of clusters generated for each sub-dataset is between 20 and 100 and the three methods generate relatively balanced clusters. Hence we use the percentage of 95% pure clusters generated to measure the goodness of the clustering algorithms. This is a strong measure given that all the datasets contain approximately equal number of transactions from each user.

Overall the results are striking and all three figures demonstrate the same pattern. YACA significantly outperforms k-means-itemsets which in turn outperforms $k$means-items. On average, for the two-user datasets, YACA outperforms $k$means-itemsets by 25% and $k$means-items by 81%. For the three-user datasets, YACA outperforms $k$means-itemsets by 40% and $k$means-items by 125% and for the four-user datasets, , YACA outperforms $k$means-itemsets by 133% and $k$means-items by 274%. These numbers are highly significant and suggest that pattern-based clustering techniques may be a natural approach to cluster consumer transactions such as Web transactions considered in this paper. We also ran experiments for alternate definitions of "pure" clusters (e.g. "80% pure"), and the results are similar. For lack of space, we do not report all the results here.

In addition to the quantitative results, there are several examples of interesting clusters discovered in the data. For example:

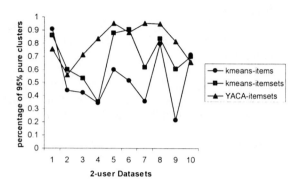

Figure 3. Results for 10 two-user datasets

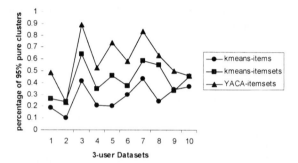

Figure 4. Results for 10 three-user datasets

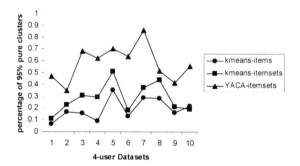

Figure 5. Results for 10 four-user datasets

- Two significant itemsets in a cluster were {*starting_day = Saturday, most_visited_category = sports*} and {*starting_day = Sunday, most_visited_category = services such as chat rooms*} – reflecting a weekend behavior pattern of one of the users in the data.
- A highly significant itemset in a cluster was {*start category = search, most visited category = retail*} indicating shopping patterns driven by Web searches rather than going to favorite sites to make purchases.

- Two most significant itemsets in one of the clusters were: (1) *{first_category = ISP, news_category = 1}* with support 71.3% - in contrast, the support for this itemset over the entire dataset was just 3.18%; (2) *{average # of sites per category = 1, first_site = site187, retail category = 1}* with support 51.7% - again, in contrast the support over the entire dataset was just 5%. Both these itemsets are reflective of a behavior that is more complex - indicating a more focused browsing behavior perhaps - than the first two examples above.

In general, the itemsets in some of the clusters suggest highly explainable behavior patterns (as in the first two examples above), while in other cases it is more difficult to place a single behavior type (third example) based on the itemsets in the cluster. This may be in part due to the fact that consumer behavior in the real-world is highly complex. In such cases, the clusters generated can still be useful by providing a starting point for a deeper understanding of consumer behavior.

5. Related Work

Traditional clustering algorithms usually employ a distance metric based (e.g., euclidean) similarity measure in order to partition the data. As pointed out in [7], while the traditional distance-based clustering approaches can yield satisfactory results for numeric attributes, it is not appropriate for data sets with categorical attributes. In the recent past, there has been much work done on clustering large categorical databases (ROCK[7], [8], STIRR[6], LargeItem[12], CLOPE[13]). [7] presents a concept of clustering based on links between data points. They consider a pair of points to be neighbors if their similarity exceeds a certain threshold. The similarity value for pairs of points can be based on any non-metric similarity function. The number of links between a pair of points is then the number of common neighbors for the points. During clustering, they merge clusters/points with the most number of links. The drawback of this method is the heavy computational cost, and sampling has to be used when scaling to large datasets. Also, there may exist undesirable mergers because of the large number of pairs whose similarities barely exceed the threshold.

The idea of pattern-based clustering is not new. [11] considers two objects similar if they exhibit a coherent pattern on a subset of dimensions. The definition of a pattern is based on the correlation between attributes of objects to be clustered. The specific definition of a pattern used in [11] makes it more suitable for numerical data. This paper uses a set of itemsets as the representation of patterns in each cluster. Hence within the clustering methods dealing with categorical data,

those using the concept of large items/itemsets and association rules are particularly relevant to this paper. [8] addresses the problem of clustering related customer transactions in a market basket database. Frequent itemsets used to generate association rules are used to construct a weighted hypergraph. Each frequent itemset is a hyperedge in the weighted hypergraph and the weight of the hyperedge is computed as the average of the confidences for all possible association rules that can be generated from the itemset. Then, a hypergraph partitioning algorithm from [9] is used to partition the items such that the sum of the weights of hyperedges that are cut due to the partitioning is minimized. The result is a clustering of items (not transactions) that occur together in the transactions. Finally, the item clusters are used as the description of the cluster and a scoring metric is used to assign customer transactions to the best item cluster. The approach in [8] makes the assumption that itemsets that define clusters are disjoint and have no overlap among them. This may not be true in practice since transactions in different clusters may have a few common items.

[12] introduces a clustering criterion suggesting that there should be many large items within a cluster and little overlapping of such items across clusters. They then use this criterion to search for a good clustering solution. [12] also points out that, for transaction data, methods using pairwise similarity, such as k-means, have problems in forming a meaningful cluster. For transactions that come naturally in collection of items, it is more meaningful to use item/rule based methods. [13] addresses a similar problem and our work is most similar to LargeItem[12] and CLOPE[13] in that we do not use any pairwise distance function. We define a global goal and use this goal to guide the clustering process. Compared to LargeItem[12] and CLOPE[13], our method takes a new perspective of associating itemsets with behavior patterns, and using that concept to guide the clustering process. Using this approach, we are able to identify the distinguishing itemsets representing a cluster of transactions. As noted previously, in this paper behavioral patterns describing a cluster are represented by a *set* of itemsets (for example, a set of two itemsets *{weekend, second site = eonline.com}* and *{weekday, second site = cnbc.com}*). We allow the possibility to find a *set of itemsets* to describe a cluster instead of just a set of items which is the focus of other item/itemsets related work. This is important for clustering Web transaction data. We also illustrate in the paper how we cluster Web transaction data with both numeric data and categorical data. On a different note, document clustering methods also use the concept of *terms* (similar to items) for clustering. However, document clustering tends to have their special treatment for documents and we do not discuss them here. See [14] for some common

approaches in document clustering, and see [3] for a recent approach utilizing the concept of term set.

Finally, another important category of clustering algorithms is model-based clustering [4, 5]. The data is viewed as coming from a mixture of probability distributions, each representing a different cluster. If we view the patterns representing a cluster as a type of model, the spirit of our approach is similar to that of model-based clustering. Model-based methods can provide good cluster results if the data does approximate the assumed distribution, but it can simplify the differences between clusters and ignore other attributes not in the hypothesized distribution and also ignores patterns across attributes.

6. Discussion

As mentioned in the introduction, the existence of natural categories of customer behavior is intuitive, and these categories influence the transactions observed. We suggest that pattern-based clustering techniques, such as the one described in this paper, may be effective in learning such natural categories and can, hence, enable firms to understand their customers better and build more accurate customer models. In this paper we presented a new approach, YACA, for pattern-based clustering of Web transactions and demonstrated that the technique performs highly effectively as compared to traditional techniques.

There are limitations of this work, which suggest opportunities for future work. First, the choice of pattern representation for a domain and the subsequent difference and similarity definitions that need to be derived, continue to be subjective. While we argued that itemsets are good for Web transactions, it is harder to claim that they are the "best" representation technique. Similarly the difference and similarity definitions are intuitive but there may be alternatives. The algorithm proposed, YACA, is a heuristic approach that incrementally and hierarchically clusters the transactions and in future work we will investigate means to improve the efficiency. Overall, the results in our experiments suggest that pattern-based clustering can be highly effective, and we hope to investigate approaches to extend the solutions along the lines described above in future work.

References

[1] Agrawal, R., Mannila, H., Srikant, R., Toivonen, H. and Verkamo, A. I., "Fast Discovery of Association Rules", Advances in Know. Discovery and Data Mining, Chapter 12, AAAI/MIT Press, 1995.

[2] Allenby, G. M. and Rossi, P. E., "Marketing Models of Consumer Heterogeneity", Journal of Econometrics 89(1999) 57-78.

[3] Beil, F., Eater, M. and Xu, X., "Frequent Term-Based Text Clustering", Proc. 8th Int. Conf. on Knowledge Discovery and Data Mining (KDD '2002), Edmonton, Alberta, Canada, 2002.

[4] Fraley, C. and Raftery, A. E., "How many clusters? Which clustering method? - Answers via Model-Based Cluster Analysis". Technical Report no. 329, Department of Statistics, University of Washington, Computer Journal 41:578-588 (1998).

[5] Fraley, C. and Raftery, A. E., "Model-Based Clustering, Discriminant Analysis, and Density Estimation", Tech. Rep. 380, Department of Statistics, University of Washington, Seattle, WA, Oct. 2000. Journal of the American Statistical Association 97:611-631 (2002).

[6] Gibson, D. , Kleinberg, J. , Raghavan, P. , "Clustering Categorical Data: An Approach Based on Dynamical Systems", the VLDB Conference, New York City, New York, August 1998.

[7] Guha, S. , Rastogi, R., Shim K. , "ROCK: A Clustering Algorithm for Categorical Attributes", the 15th International Conference on IEEE Data Engineering, Sydney, Australia, 1999.

[8] Han, E., Karypis, G., Kumar, V. and Mobasher, B., "Clustering based on association rule hypergraphs", in Proceedings of the SIGMOD'97 Workshop on Research Issues in Data Mining and Knowledge Discovery. 1997, ACM.

[9] Karypis, G., Aggarwal, R., Kumar, V. and Shekhar, S., "Multilevel hypergraph partitioning: application in VLSI domain". In Proceedings of the ACM/IEEE Design Automation Conference, Canada (1997).

[10] Kimbrough, S., Padmanabhan, B. and Zheng, Z., "On Usage Metric for Determining Authoritative Sites", Procs. Workshop on Information Technology and Systems WITS 2000, December 2000.

[11] Wang, H., Yang, J., Wang, W., and Yu, P.S., "Clustering by Pattern Similarity in Large Data Sets", Proc. ACM SIGMOD Conference, Madison, WI, June 2002.

[12] Wang, K., Xu, C. and Liu, B. "Clustering Transactions Using Large Items", Proc. 8th Int. Conf. on Information and Knowledge Management (ACM CIKM'99), Kansas City, November, 1999.

[13] Yang, Y., Guan, X., You, J., "CLOPE: A Fast and Effective Clustering Algorithm for Transactional Data", SIGKDD '02, July 23-26, 2002, Edmonton, Alberta, Canada.

[14] Zhao, Y. and Karypis, G., "Criterion functions for document clustering: experiments and analysis", Tech. Report #01-40, Department of Comp. Sci. & Eng., U. Minnesota, 2002.

A new optimization criterion for generalized discriminant analysis on undersampled problems

Jieping Ye[*]   Ravi Janardan[*]   Cheong Hee Park[*]   Haesun Park[*]

Abstract

A new optimization criterion for discriminant analysis is presented. The new criterion extends the optimization criteria of the classical linear discriminant analysis (LDA) by introducing the pseudo-inverse when the scatter matrices are singular. It is applicable regardless of the relative sizes of the data dimension and sample size, overcoming a limitation of the classical LDA. Recently, a new algorithm called LDA/GSVD for structure-preserving dimension reduction has been introduced, which extends the classical LDA to very high-dimensional undersampled problems by using the generalized singular value decomposition (GSVD). The solution from the LDA/GSVD algorithm is a special case of the solution for our generalized criterion in this paper, which is also based on GSVD.

We also present an approximate solution for our GSVD-based solution, which reduces computational complexity by finding sub-clusters of each cluster, and using their centroids to capture the structure of each cluster. This reduced problem yields much smaller matrices of which the GSVD can be applied efficiently. Experiments on text data, with up to 7000 dimensions, show that the approximation algorithm produces results that are close to those produced by the exact algorithm.

1 Introduction

Many interesting data mining problems involve data sets represented in very high dimensional spaces. We consider dimension reduction of high-dimensional, undersampled data, where the dimension of the data points is higher than the number of data points.

One application area of interest in this paper is vector space based information retrieval. The dimension of the document vectors is typically very high, due to a large number of terms that appear in the collection of the documents. In the vector space based-model, documents are represented as column vectors in a term-document matrix. For an $m \times n$ term-document matrix $A = (a_{ij})$, its (i, j)-th term a_{ij} represents the weighted frequency of term i in document j.

When the documents are already clustered, we would like to find a dimension-reducing transformation that preserves the cluster structure of the original full space even after the dimension reduction. Throughout the paper, the input documents are assumed to have been already clustered before the dimension reduction step. When the documents are not clustered, then efficient clustering algorithms such as K-Means [3, 8] can be applied before the dimension reduction step. We seek a reduced representation of the document vectors, which best preserves the structure of the original document vectors.

Latent Semantic Indexing has been widely used for dimension reduction of text data [1, 2]. It is based on lower rank approximation of the term-document matrix from the singular value decomposition (SVD) [6]. Although the SVD provides the optimal reduced rank approximation of the matrix when the difference is measured in the L_2 or Frobenius norm, it has limitations in that it does not consider cluster structure in the data and is expensive to compute. Moreover, the choice of the optimal reduced dimension is difficult to determine theoretically.

The Orthogonal Centroid Method has been introduced [10], as a dimension reduction method that maximizes the separation between clusters. The main advantage of this method is its computational efficiency since a dimension-reducing transformation based on the symmetric eigenvalue

---

[*]Department of Computer Science & Engineering, University of Minnesota, Minneapolis, MN 55455, U.S.A. {jieping,janardan,chpark,hpark}@cs.umn.edu. Research of J. Ye and R. Janardan is sponsored, in part, by the Army High Performance Computing Research Center under the auspices of the Department of the Army, Army Research Laboratory cooperative agreement number DAAD19-01-2-0014, the content of which does not necessarily reflect the position or the policy of the government, and no official endorsement should be inferred. Research of C. Park and H. Park has been supported in part by the National Science Foundation Grant No. CCR-0204109 and ACI-0305543. Any opinions, findings and conclusions or recommendations expressed in this material are those of the authors and do not necessarily reflect the views of the National Science Foundation.

decomposition can be computed by a simple orthogonal decomposition of the matrix that involves only the centroids of the clusters. A disadvantage of the Orthogonal Centroid method is that it does not take into account the within-cluster relationship.

The linear discriminant analysis (LDA) method has been applied for decades for dimension reduction (feature extraction) of clustered data in pattern recognition [5]. It is classically formulated as an optimization problem on covariance matrices. A serious disadvantage of the LDA is that its objective function requires that at least one of the covariance matrices be nonsingular. In many modern data mining problems such as information retrieval, facial recognition, and microarray data analysis, all of the covariance matrices in question can be singular since the data items are from a very high-dimensional space and in general the number of sample data points does not exceed this dimension. Recently, a generalization of LDA based on the generalized singular value decomposition (GSVD) has been developed [7], which is applicable regardless of the data dimension, and, therefore can be used for undersampled problems. The classical LDA solution becomes a special case of this LDA/GSVD method. In [7], the solution from LDA/GSVD is justified to preserve the cluster structure in the original full space after dimension reduction. However, no explicit global objective function has been presented.

In this paper, we present a new generalized optimization criterion for discriminant analysis. Our class-preserving projections are tailored for extracting the class structure of high dimensional data, and are closely related to the classical linear discriminant analysis. The main advantage of the new criterion is that it is applicable to undersampled problems. A detailed mathematical derivation of the proposed new optimization problem is presented. The GSVD technique is the key component for the derivation. The solution from the LDA/GSVD algorithm is a special case of the solution for this new criterion. Since there is no approximation involved in the proposed algorithm, we call it the *exact algorithm*, to distinguish it from the approximation algorithm introduced below.

One limitation of the GSVD-based method is its high computational complexity in handling large matrices. We propose an approximation algorithm based on sub-clustering of clusters to reduce the cost of computing the SVD involved in the computation of GSVD. Each cluster is further sub-clustered so that the overall structure of each cluster can be represented by the set of centroids corresponding to each sub-clusters. As a result, only a few vectors are needed to define the scatter matrices, thus reducing the computational complexity. Experimental results show that the approximation algorithm produces results close to those produced by the exact one.

Due to space constraints we omit numerous proofs and details here; these can be found in the full paper [12].

2 Classical discriminant analysis

Given a term-document matrix $A \in R^{m \times n}$, we consider finding a linear transformation $G^T \in R^{\ell \times m}$ that maps each column a_i, for $1 \leq i \leq n$, of A in the m-dimensional space to a column y_i in the ℓ-dimensional space:

$$G^T : a_i \in R^{m \times 1} \to y_i \in R^{\ell \times 1}. \tag{1}$$

Assume the original data is already clustered. The goal here is to find the transformation G^T such that cluster structure of the original full high-dimensional space is preserved in the reduced dimensional space. Let the document matrix A be partitioned into k clusters as $A = [A_1, \ A_2, \ \cdots, \ A_k]$, where $A_i \in R^{m \times n_i}$, and $\sum_{i=1}^{k} n_i = n$.

Let N_i be the set of column indices that belong to the ith cluster, i.e., a_j, for $j \in N_i$, belongs to the ith cluster.

In general, if each cluster is tightly grouped, but well separated from the other clusters, the quality of the cluster is considered to be high. In discriminant analysis [5], two scatter matrices, within-cluster and between-cluster scatter matrices are defined to quantify the quality of the cluster, as follows:

$$S_w = \sum_{i=1}^{k} \sum_{j \in N_i} (a_j - c^{(i)})(a_j - c^{(i)})^T,$$

$$S_b = \sum_{i=1}^{k} n_i (c^{(i)} - c)(c^{(i)} - c)^T, \tag{2}$$

where the centroid $c^{(i)}$ of the ith cluster is defined as $c^{(i)} = \frac{1}{n_i} A_i e^{(i)}$, where $e^{(i)} = (1, \cdots, 1)^T \in R^{n_i \times 1}$, and the global centroid c is defined as $c = \frac{1}{n} A e$, where $e = (1, \cdots, 1)^T \in R^{n \times 1}$.

Define the matrices

$$H_w = [A_1 - c^{(1)}(e^{(1)})^T, \cdots, A_k - c^{(k)}(e^{(k)})^T] \in R^{m \times n},$$

$$H_b = [\sqrt{n_1}(c^{(1)} - c), \cdots, \sqrt{n_k}(c^{(k)} - c)] \in R^{m \times k}. \tag{3}$$

Then the scatter matrices S_w and S_b can be expressed as

$$S_w = H_w H_w^T, \quad S_b = H_b H_b^T. \tag{4}$$

The traces of the two scatter matrices can be computed as follows,

$$\text{trace}(S_w) = \sum_{i=1}^{k} \sum_{j \in N_i} (a_j - c^{(i)})^T (a_j - c^{(i)}) = \sum_{i=1}^{k} \sum_{j \in N_i} ||a_j - c^{(i)}||^2$$

$$\text{trace}(S_b) = \sum_{i=1}^{k} n_i (c^{(i)} - c)^T (c^{(i)} - c) = \sum_{i=1}^{k} n_i ||c^{(i)} - c||^2.$$

Hence, trace (S_w) measures the closeness of the vectors within the clusters, while trace (S_b) measures the separation between clusters.

In the lower-dimensional space resulting from the linear transformation G^T, the within-cluster and between-cluster matrices become

$$
\begin{aligned}
S_w^L &= (G^T H_w)(G^T H_w)^T = G^T H_w H_w^T G = G^T S_w G, \\
S_b^L &= (G^T H_b)(G^T H_b)^T = G^T H_b H_b^T G = G^T S_b G.
\end{aligned} \tag{5}
$$

An optimal transformation G^T would maximize $\mathrm{trace}\,(S_b^L)$ and minimize $\mathrm{trace}\,(S_w^L)$. Common optimizations in classical discriminant analysis include

$$
\max_{G^T}\left\{\mathrm{trace}((S_w^L)^{-1}S_b^L)\right\} \text{ and } \min_{G^T}\left\{\mathrm{trace}((S_b^L)^{-1}S_w^L)\right\}. \tag{6}
$$

If we focus on the criterion of maximizing

$$
F_0(G) = \mathrm{trace}\left(\left(G^T S_w G\right)^{-1}\left(G^T S_b G\right)\right), \tag{7}
$$

the solution can be obtained by solving the following eigen problem [5]: $S_w^{-1}S_b x = \lambda x$, for $\lambda \neq 0$.

If we switch between S_w and S_b in (7), the problem becomes a minimization problem. One limitation of classical discriminant analysis is that the within-class scatter matrix S_w is assumed to be nonsingular.

3 Generalization of discriminant analysis

Classical discriminant analysis expresses its solution by solving a generalized eigenvalue problem when S_b or S_w is nonsingular. However, for a general document matrix A, the number of document n may be smaller than its dimension m, then matrix H_w and H_b are not of full column rank, hence matrix S_w and S_b are both singular. In this paper, we define a new criterion F_1 below, where the non-singularity of the matrix S_w or S_b is not required. The new criterion aims to minimize the within-class distance, $\mathrm{trace}\,(S_w^L)$, and maximize the between-class distance, $\mathrm{trace}\,(S_b^L)$. It is defined as

$$
F_1(G) = \mathrm{trace}\left((S_b^L)^+ S_w^L\right). \tag{8}
$$

The new criterion is a natural extension of the classical one in Equation (6), where the inverse of a matrix is replaced by the pseudo-inverse [6]. While the inverse of a matrix may not exist, the pseudo-inverse of any matrix is well defined. Moreover, when the matrix is invertible, its pseudo-inverse is the same as its inverse.

Here the trace optimization is to find an optimal transformation matrix G^T such that $F_1(G)$ is minimum, under certain constraint defined in more detail in Section 3.3. We switch the roles of S_b^T and S_w^T in the F_1 criterion, compared with the F_0 criterion in classical discriminant analysis defined in Equation (7), since the value of $\mathrm{trace}\left((S_w^L)^+ S_b^L\right)$ can be infinity.

We show how to solve the above optimization problem in Section 3.3. The main technique applied here is the GSVD, briefly introduced in Section 3.1. The constraint on the optimization problem is based on the observations in Section 3.2.

3.1 Generalized singular value decomposition

The Generalized Singular Value Decomposition (GSVD) was first introduced in [11]. A simple algorithm to compute GSVD can be found in [7], derived from [9].

The GSVD on the matrix pair (H_b^T, H_w^T), will give orthogonal matrices $U \in R^{k \times k}, V \in R^{n \times n}$, and a nonsingular matrix $X \in R^{m \times m}$, such that

$$
\left[\begin{array}{cc} U & 0 \\ 0 & V \end{array}\right]^T K X = \left[\begin{array}{cc} \Sigma_1 & 0 \\ \Sigma_2 & 0 \end{array}\right], \tag{9}
$$

where $\Sigma_1 = \left[\begin{array}{ccc} I_b & 0 & 0 \\ 0 & D_b & 0 \\ 0 & 0 & 0_b \end{array}\right]$, $\Sigma_2 = \left[\begin{array}{ccc} 0_w & 0 & 0 \\ 0 & D_w & 0 \\ 0 & 0 & I_w \end{array}\right]$.

Here $I_b \in R^{r \times r}$ is an identity matrix with $r = \mathrm{rank}(K) - \mathrm{rank}(H_w^T)$, $D_b = \mathrm{diag}(\alpha_{r+1}, \cdots, \alpha_{r+s})$, and $D_w = \mathrm{diag}(\beta_{r+1}, \cdots, \beta_{r+s}) \in R^{s \times s}$ are diagonal matrices with $s = \mathrm{rank}(H_b) + \mathrm{rank}(H_w) - \mathrm{rank}(K)$, satisfying $1 > \alpha_{r+1} \geq, \cdots, \geq \alpha_{r+s} > 0, 0 < \beta_{r+1} \leq, \cdots, \leq \beta_{r+s} < 1$, and $\alpha_i^2 + \beta_i^2 = 1$ for $i = r+1, \cdots, r+s$.

It follows from (9) that,

$$
\begin{aligned}
X^T H_b H_b^T X &= \left[\begin{array}{cc} \Sigma_1^T \Sigma_1 & 0 \\ 0 & 0 \end{array}\right] \equiv D_1, \\
X^T H_w H_w^T X &= \left[\begin{array}{cc} \Sigma_2^T \Sigma_2 & 0 \\ 0 & 0 \end{array}\right] \equiv D_2.
\end{aligned}
$$

It is easy to check that

$$
S_b^L = \tilde{G} D_1 \tilde{G}^T, \quad S_w^L = \tilde{G} D_2 \tilde{G}^T, \tag{10}
$$

where the matrix

$$
\tilde{G} = (X^{-1}G)^T. \tag{11}
$$

We will use the above representations for S_b^L and S_w^L in Section 3.3 for the minimization of F_1.

3.2 Linear subspace spanned by the centroids

Let $c = \mathrm{span}\{c^{(1)}, \cdots, c^{(k)}\}$ be a subspace in R^m spanned by the k centroids of the document vectors. In the lower dimensional space transformed by G^T, the linear subspace spanned by the k centroids in the reduced space is $c_L = \mathrm{span}\{c_L^{(1)}, \cdots, c_L^{(k)}\}$, where $c_L^{(i)} = G^T c^{(i)}$, for $i = 1, \cdots, k$.

In this section, we study the relation between the dimension of the subspace c and the rank of the matrix H_b, as well as the corresponding ones in the reduced space.

The main result is as follows:

Lemma 3.1 *Let c and c_L be defined as above and H_b be defined as in (3). Let $dim(c)$ and $dim(c_L)$ denote the dimensions of the subspaces c, c_L respectively. Then*

1 *$dim(c) = \mathrm{rank}(H_b) + 1$, or $\mathrm{rank}(H_b)$, and $dim(c_L) = \mathrm{rank}(G^T H_b) + 1$, or $\mathrm{rank}(G^T H_b)$;*

2 *If $dim(c) = \mathrm{rank}(H_b)$, then $dim(c_L) = \mathrm{rank}(G^T H_b)$. If $dim(c_L) = \mathrm{rank}(G^T H_b) + 1$, then $dim(c) = \mathrm{rank}(H_b) + 1$.*

The proof of this Lemma appears in the full paper [12].

3.3 Generalized discriminant analysis using F_1 measure

We start with a more general optimization problem as follows,

$$\min_G F_1(G) \text{ subject to } \text{rank}(G^T H_b) = \delta, \qquad (12)$$

for some $\delta > 0$. The optimization in Equation (12) depends on the value of δ. The optimal transformation G we are looking for in this section is a special case of the above formulation, where we set $\delta = \text{rank}(H_b)$. This choice of δ guarantees that the dimension of the linear space c spanned by the centroids in the original high dimension space and the corresponding one c_L in the transformed lower dimensional space are close to each other, as shown in the following Proposition 3.1.

To solve the optimization problem in (12), we need the following three lemmas, where the proof of the first two lemmas are straightforward from the definition of the pseudo-inverse [6].

Lemma 3.2 *For any matrix* $A \in R^{m \times n}$, *we have* $\text{trace}(AA^+) = \text{rank}(A)$.

Lemma 3.3 *For any matrix* $A \in R^{m \times n}$, *we have* $(AA^T)^+ = (A^+)^T A^+$.

The following Lemma is critical for our main result:

Lemma 3.4 *Let* $\Sigma = \text{diag}(\sigma_1, \cdots, \sigma_u)$ *be any diagonal matrix with* $\sigma_1 \geq \cdots \geq \sigma_u > 0$. *Then for any matrix* $M \in R^{v \times u}$ *with* $\text{rank}(M) = \delta$, *the following inequality holds:* $\text{trace}\left(\left(M\Sigma M^T\right)^+ MM^T\right) \geq \sum_{i=1}^{\delta} \frac{1}{\sigma_i}$. *Furthermore, the equality holds if and only if* $M = U \begin{pmatrix} D & 0 \\ 0 & 0 \end{pmatrix}$, *for some orthogonal matrix* $U \in R^{v \times v}$ *and matrix* $D = \Sigma^1 Q \Sigma^2 \in R^{\delta \times \delta}$, *where* $Q \in R^{\delta \times \delta}$ *is orthogonal and* $\Sigma^1, \Sigma^2 \in R^{\delta \times \delta}$ *are diagonal matrices with positive diagonal entries.*

The proof of this Lemma appears in the full paper [12].

We are now ready to present our main result for this section. To solve the minimization problem in (12), we first give a lower bound on the objective function F_1 in Theorem 3.1. A sufficient condition on G^T, under which the lower bound computed in Theorem 3.1 is obtained, is presented in Corollary 3.1. A simple solution is then presented in Corollary 3.2.

The optimal solution for our generalized discriminant analysis presented in this paper is a special case of the solution in Corollary 3.2, where we set $\delta = \text{rank}(H_b)$, which is justified in Proposition 3.1.

Theorem 3.1 *Assume the transformation matrix* $G^T \in R^{\ell \times m}$ *satisfies* $\text{rank}(G^T H_b) = \delta$, *for some integer* $\delta > 0$, *then the following inequality holds,*

$$
\begin{aligned}
F_1 &= \text{trace}\left((S_b^L)^+(S_w^L)\right) \\
&\geq \begin{cases} \sum_{i=r+1}^{\delta} \left(\frac{\beta_i}{\alpha_i}\right)^2 & \text{if } \delta \geq r+1 \\ 0 & \text{if } \delta < r+1, \end{cases}
\end{aligned}
\qquad (13)
$$

where $S_b^L = G^t S_b G$ *and* $S_w^L = G^T S_w G$ *are defined in (5).*

Proof First consider the easy case when $\delta < r + 1$. Since both $(S_b^L)^+$ and S_w^L are semi-positive definite, $\text{trace}\left((S_b^L)^+(S_w^L)\right) \geq 0$. Next consider the case when $\delta \geq r+1$.

Recall from Equation (10) that by the GSVD,

$$S_b^L = \tilde{G} D_1 \tilde{G}^T, \quad S_w^L = \tilde{G} D_2 \tilde{G}^T,$$

where $\tilde{G}$ is defined in (11). Partition $\tilde{G}$ into

$$\tilde{G} = \begin{pmatrix} G_1 & G_2 & G_3 & G_4 \end{pmatrix},$$

such that $G_1 \in R^{\ell \times r}, G_2 \in R^{\ell \times s}, G_3 \in R^{\ell \times (t-r-s)}$, and $G_4 \in R^{\ell \times (m-t)}$.

Let $G_{123} = \begin{pmatrix} G_1 & G_2 & G_3 \end{pmatrix}$. Since D_1 and D_2 are diagonal matrices and the last $m - t$ diagonal entries are zero, it follows that

$$
\begin{aligned}
S_b^L &= G_{123} \Sigma_1^T \Sigma_1 G_{123}^T, \\
S_w^L &= G_{123} \Sigma_2^T \Sigma_2 G_{123}^T
\end{aligned}
\qquad (14)
$$

Since $\alpha_i^2 + \beta_i^2 = 1$, for $i = 1, 2, \cdots, t$, we have $\Sigma_1^T \Sigma_1 + \Sigma_2^T \Sigma_2 = I_t$, here $I_t \in R^{t \times t}$ is an identity matrix. Therefore,

$$S_w^L + S_b^L = G_{123} G_{123}^T = G_{12} G_{12}^T + G_3 G_3^T. \qquad (15)$$

Define $G_{12} = \begin{pmatrix} G_1 & G_2 \end{pmatrix}$. It follows from Equation (14) and Equation (15) that

$$
\begin{aligned}
\text{trace}((S_b^L)^+(S_w^L + S_b^L)) &= \text{trace}((S_b^L)^+(G_{123} G_{123}^T)) \\
&= \text{trace}((G_{123}\Sigma_1 \Sigma_1^T G_{123}^T)^+ G_{123} G_{123}^T) \\
&\geq \text{trace}\left(\left(G_{12}\Sigma G_{12}^T\right)^+ G_{12} G_{12}^T\right) \\
&\geq \sum_{i=1}^{r} 1 + \sum_{i=r+1}^{\delta} \frac{1}{\alpha_i^2},
\end{aligned}
\qquad (16)
$$

where $\Sigma = \begin{pmatrix} I_b & 0 \\ 0 & D_b^2 \end{pmatrix}$. The first inequality follows, since $G_3 G_3^T$ is positive semi-definite, and the equality holds if $G_3 = 0$. The second inequality follows from Lemma 3.4 and the equality holds if and only if $G_{12} = U \begin{pmatrix} D & 0 \\ 0 & 0 \end{pmatrix} \in R^{\ell \times r+s}$, for some orthogonal matrix $U \in R^{\ell \times \ell}$ and some matrix $D = \Sigma^1 Q \Sigma^2 \in R^{\delta \times \delta}$, as stated in Lemma 3.4.

By the property of the pseudo-inverse in Lemma 3.2, $\text{trace}((S_b^L)^+ S_b^L) = \text{rank}(S_b^L) = \delta$. Therefore,

$$
\begin{aligned}
F_1 &= \text{trace}((S_b^L)^+ S_w^L) \\
&= \text{trace}((S_b^L)^+(S_w^L + S_b^L)) - \text{trace}((S_b^L)^+ S_b^L) \\
&\geq \sum_{i=1}^{r} 1 + \sum_{i=r+1}^{\delta} \frac{1}{\alpha_i^2} - \delta \\
&= \sum_{i=r+1}^{\delta} \left(\frac{\beta_i}{\alpha_i}\right)^2,
\end{aligned}
\qquad (17)
$$

where the inequality follows from (16). ∎

Theorem 3.1 gives a lower bound on F_1, when δ is fixed. From the arguments above, all the inequalities become equality if $G_{12} = U \begin{pmatrix} D & 0 \\ 0 & 0 \end{pmatrix} \in R^{\ell \times r+s}$, and $G_3 = 0$. A simple case is when U and D are both set to be identity matrices, which is summarized in the following Corollary.

Corollary 3.1 *Let* G^T, $\bar{G}$ *be defined as in Theorem 3.1 and* $\delta > r + 1$, *then the equality* $F_1 = trace((S_b^L)^+ S_w^L) = \sum_{i=r+1}^{\delta} \left(\frac{\beta_i}{\alpha_i}\right)^2$ *holds, under the condition that the partition of* $\bar{G} = \begin{pmatrix} G_1, & G_2, & G_3, & G_4 \end{pmatrix}$ *satisfies* $G_{12} = \begin{pmatrix} I_\delta & 0 \\ 0 & 0 \end{pmatrix}$ *and* $G_3 = 0$, *where* $G_{12} = \begin{pmatrix} G_1, & G_2 \end{pmatrix}$.

Theorem 3.1 does not mention the connection between ℓ, the row dimension of the transformation matrix G^T and δ. We can choose the transformation matrix G^T with large row dimension ℓ and still satisfies the condition stated in Corollary 3.1. However we are more interested in a lower dimensional representation of the original, while keeping the same information from the original data.

The following Corollary says the smallest possible value for ℓ is δ, and more importantly we can find a transformation G^T with its row dimension equal δ, which also satisfies the condition stated in Corollary 3.1.

Corollary 3.2 *For every* $\delta \leq r + s$, *there exists a transformation* $G^T \in R^{\delta \times m}$, *such that the equality in (13) holds, i.e. the minimum value for* F_1 *is obtained. Furthermore for any transformation* $(G')^T \in R^{\ell \times m}$, *such that the assumption in Theorem 3.1 holds, we have* $\ell \geq \delta$.

Proof Construct a transformation $G^T \in R^{\delta \times m}$, such that

$$\bar{G} = (X^{-1}G)^T = \begin{pmatrix} G_{12}, & G_3, & G_4 \end{pmatrix}$$

satisfies $G_{12} = \begin{pmatrix} I_\delta & 0 \end{pmatrix}$, $G_3 = 0$, and $G_4 = 0$, where $I_\delta \in R^{\delta \times \delta}$ is an identity matrix. Hence $G^T = X_\delta^T$, where $X_\delta \in R^{\delta \times m}$ contains the first δ columns of the matrix X. By Corollary 3.1, the equality in (13) holds under the above transformation G^T. This completes the proof for the first part.

For any $(G')^T \in R^{\ell \times m}$, such that $rank((G')^T H_b) = \delta$, it is clear $\delta \leq rank((G')^T) \leq \ell$. Hence $\ell \geq \delta$. ∎

Remark 3.1 Theorem 3.1 shows the minimum value of the objective function F_1 is dependent on the rank of the matrix $G^T H_b$. Corollary 3.2 constructs a simple solution for the optimization problem. In our implementation, we chose $\delta = rank(H_b)$, its maximum possibility. One nice property of this choice is stated in the following Proposition:

Proposition 3.1 *If* $\delta \equiv rank(G^T H_b)$ *equals to* $rank(H_b)$, *then* $|\mathcal{C}| - 1 \leq |\mathcal{C}_L| \leq |\mathcal{C}|$.

Algorithm 1: Exact algorithm
1. Form the matrices H_b and H_w as in Eq. (3).
2. Compute GSVD on the matrix pair (H_b^T, H_w^T) to obtain the matrix X as in Eq. (9),
3. $\delta^\star \leftarrow rank(H_b)$.
4. $G^T \leftarrow X_{\delta^\star}^T$, where $X_{\delta^\star}$ contains the first $\delta^\star$ columns of the matrix X.

Proof The proof follows directly from Lemma 3.1. ∎

Proposition 3.1 implies choosing $\delta = rank(H_b)$ keeps the same or one less degree of linear independence of the centroids in the reduced space as the one in the original space. With the above choice, the reduced dimension under the transformation G^T is $rank(H_b)$. We use $\delta^\star = rank(H_b)$ to denote the optimal reduced dimension for our generalized discriminant analysis (also called exact algorithm) throughout the rest of the paper. In this case, we can choose $G^T = X_{\delta^\star}^T$, where $X_{\delta^\star}$ contains the first $\delta^\star$ columns of the matrix X as in Corollary 3.2. The pseudo-code for our main algorithm is shown in **Algorithm 1**.

4 Approximation algorithm

One of the limitations of the above exact algorithm is the expensive computation of the generalized singular value decomposition of the matrix $K \in R^{n+k \times m}$. For large text document data, both n and m can be large, hence the exact algorithm may not be applicable. In this section, an efficient approximation algorithm is presented to overcome this limitation.

The K-Means algorithm [3, 8] is widely used to capture the structure of the scattered data, by decomposing the whole data set as a disjoint union of small sets, called clusters. The K-Means algorithm aims to minimize the the distance within each cluster, hence the centroid of the each cluster represents well the data points in the same cluster, while the centroids of the resulting clusters give a good approximation of the original data set.

In Section 2, we use the matrix H_w to capture the closeness of the vectors within each cluster. However, the dimension of $H_w \in R^{m \times n}$ is very high, since we use every point in the document data. To simplify the model, we attempt to use the centroids only to approximate the structure of each cluster, by apply K-Means algorithm to each cluster.

More specifically, if $(\pi_1, \pi_2, \cdots, \pi_k)$ are the k clusters in the text document data, with the size of each cluster $|\pi_i| = n_i$, and $\sum_{i=1}^k n_i = n$. K-Means algorithm is applied to each cluster π_i to produce s_i sub-clusters $\{\pi_i^{(j)}\}_{j=1}^{s_i}$, with $\pi_i = \cup_{j=1}^{n_i} \pi_i^{(j)}$ and the size of each sub-cluster $|\pi_i^{(j)}| = n_i^j$. Let $c_i^{(j)}$ be the centroid for each sub-cluster $\pi_i^{(j)}$. The within cluster distance in the ith cluster $\sum_{j \in \pi_i} ||a_j - c^{(i)}||^2$ can be approxi-

Algorithm 2: Approximation algorithm
1. Form the matrix H_b as defined in Eq. (3).
2. Run K-Means algorithm on each π_i with $s_i = s'$.
3. Form the matrix $\tilde{H}_w$ as defined in Eq. (18)
4. Compute GSVD on the matrix pair $(H_b^T, \tilde{H}_w^T)$ to obtain the matrix X as in Eq. (9).
3. $\delta^\star \leftarrow \text{rank}(H_b)$.
4. $G^T \leftarrow X_{\delta^\star}^T$, where $X_{\delta^\star}$ contains the first $\delta^\star$ columns of the matrix X.

mated as $\sum_{u=1}^{s_i} \sum_{a_j \in \pi_i^{(u)}} ||a_j - c^{(i)}||^2 \sim \sum_{u=1}^{s_i} n_i^u ||c_i^{(u)} - c^{(i)}||^2$, by approximating every point a_j in the sub-cluster $\pi_i^{(u)}$ by its centroid $c_i^{(u)}$.

Hence the matrix H_w can be approximated as

$$[\sqrt{n_1^1}(c_1^{(1)} - c^{(1)}), \quad \cdots \quad , \sqrt{n_1^{s_1}}(c_1^{(s_1)} - c^{(1)}), \cdots,$$
$$\sqrt{n_k^1}(c_k^{(1)} - c^{(k)}), \quad \cdots \quad , \sqrt{n_k^{s_k}}(c_k^{(s_k)} - c^{(k)})] \in R^{m \times M}, \quad (18)$$

where $M = \sum_{i=1}^{k} s_i$ is the total number of centroids, which is typically much smaller than n, the total number of data points in the original text document data, thus reducing the complexity of the GSVD computation dramatically. The main steps for our approximation algorithm are summarized in **Algorithm 2**. For simplicity, in our implementation we chose all the s_i's to have the same value s'. We discuss below the choice for s'.

To test the efficacy of the approximation algorithm, we have applied it to numerous data sets. Experiments show the approximation algorithm produces similar results to the exact ones.

4.1 The value for s'

The number of sub-clusters s' within each cluster π_i will determine the complexity of the approximation algorithm. If s' is too large, the approximation algorithm will produce results close to the one using all the points, while the computation of the GSVD will still be expensive. For our problem, we only apply the K-Means algorithm to the data points belonging to the same cluster of the original document set, which are already close to each other. Indeed, in our experiments, we found that small values of s' worked well; in particular, choosing s' around 6 to 10 gave good results.

5 Experimental results

5.1 Datasets

In the following experiments, we used three different datasets, summarized in Table 5.1. More details on these datasets can be found in [12].

Data Set	1	2	3
Source	TREC	Reuters-21578	
# of documents	210	320	490
# of terms	7454	2887	3759
# of classes	7	4	5

Table 1. Summary of datasets used for evaluation

5.2 Experimental methodology

To evaluate the proposed methods in this paper, we compared them with several other well known dimension reduction methods on the three datasets. The K-Nearest Neighbor algorithm (for $K = 1, 7, 15$) [4] was applied to evaluate the quality of different dimension-reduction algorithms as in [10, 7]. For each method, we applied 10-fold cross validation to compute misclassification rate.

The clustering using the K-Means in the approximation algorithm is sensitive to the choices of the initial centroids. To mitigate this, we ran the algorithm 10 times, and the initial centroids for each run were generated randomly. The final result is the average over the 10 different runs.

5.3 Results

5.3.1 Effect of s' on the approximation algorithm

As mentioned in Section 4, our approximation algorithm worked well for small values of s'. We tested our approximation algorithm on Datasets 1–3 for different values of s', ranging from 2 to 30, and computed the misclassification rates. $K = 7$ nearest neighbors have been used for classification. As seen from Figure 1, the rates did not fluctuate very much within the range. In our experiments, we chose $s' = 8$.

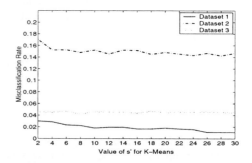

Figure 1. Effect of s' on the approximation algorithm using Datasets 1–3

5.3.2 Comparison of misclassification rates

We made a comparison of our exact and approximation algorithms with other competing algorithms based on the misclassification rates, using the three datasets in Table 5.1.

The results for Datasets 1–3 are summarized in Figure 2, where the x-axis is three different choices of K ($K = 1, 7, 15$) used in KNN for classification, and the y-axis is the misclassification rate. For each K, the misclassification rates for different methods ("FULL", "LSI-1","LSI-2", "OCM", "EXACT", and "APPR") are ordered from left to right. Here "FULL" is the method without any dimension algorithm, "LSI-1" is the Latent Semantic Indexing algorithm with reduced dimension $N = \delta^\star$, where $\delta^\star$ is the optimal reduced dimension in our exact algorithm, and "LSI-2" is the Latent Semantic Indexing algorithm with the reduced dimension $N = 100$. "OCM" is the Orthogonal Centroid Method. "EXACT" and "APPR" are the exact and approximation algorithms proposed in this paper.

In Dataset 1, since the number of terms (7454) in the term document matrix is larger than the number of documents (210), both S_w and S_b are singular and classical discriminant analysis breaks down. However our proposed generalized discriminant analysis circumvents this problem. Our exact and approximation algorithm reduce the dimension $m = 7454$ to $\delta^\star = 6$, while the orthogonal centroid method (OCM) reduces the dimension to seven. We applied LSI with the reduced dimension $N = 6$ and $N = 100$. As shown in Figure 2 (Left graph), our exact and approximation algorithms work better than the other methods, while the results produced by the approximation algorithm are fairly close to those of the exact one. It also shows better performance of OCM over LSI and Full.

For Datasets 2 and 3, the number of documents is smaller than the document dimension, hence classical discriminant analysis again breaks down. Again, the results from Figure 2 show that our exact and approximation algorithms perform better than the other methods. More interestingly, the approximation algorithm works almost as well as the exact one.

5.3.3 Effect of the reduced dimension on the exact and approximation algorithms and on LSI

As is well known, the choice of the reduced dimension is a serious problem for LSI. In Section 3, we show our exact algorithm using generalized discriminant analysis has optimal reduced dimension $\delta^\star$, which equals the rank of the matrix H_b and is typically very small. We also mentioned in Section 3, that our exact algorithm may not work very well if the reduced dimension is chosen to be much smaller than the optimal one.

Figure 3 illustrates the effect of different choices for the reduced dimension on our exact and approximation algo-

rithms and on LSI. $K = 7$ nearest neighbors have been used for classification. The x-axis is the value for the reduced dimension, and the y-axis is the misclassification rate. For each reduced dimension, the results for our exact and approximation algorithms and LSI are ordered from left to right. Our exact and approximation algorithms outperform LSI in almost all cases, especially for reduced dimension around $\delta^\star$. The results also show and further confirm our theoretical results on the optimal choice of the reduced dimension for our exact algorithm as discussed in Section 3.

5.4 Analysis

The results from the previous section show several interesting points: 1) In general, the dimension reduction algorithms, like OCM and our exact and approximation algorithms do improve the performance for classification, even for very high dimensional data sets, like those derived from text documents. The dimensional reduction step may be time-consuming, but it dramatically reduces the query time; 2) Algorithms using the label information like our proposed exact and approximation algorithms, and the Orthogonal Centroid Method have better performance than those without using the label information, like LSI. The results also show better performance of our proposed exact and approximation algorithms over the Orthogonal Centroid Method; 3) Our approximation algorithm deals with a much smaller size problem, compared with the one in the exact algorithm. However, the results from all the experiments show they have similar misclassification rates, while the approximation algorithm has much lower running time complexity.

6 Conclusions

A new criterion for generalized linear discriminant analysis is presented. The new criterion is applicable to the undersampled problems, thus overcoming the limitation of the classical linear discriminant analysis. A new formulation for the proposed generalized linear discriminant analysis based on the trace optimization is discussed. Generalized singular value decomposition is applied to solve the optimization problem. The solution from LDA/GSVD is a special case of the solution for this new optimization problem.

The exact algorithms involve $H_w \in R^{m \times n}$ with high column dimension n. To reduce the decomposition time for the exact algorithm, an approximation algorithm is presented, which applies K-Means algorithm to each cluster and replace the cluster by the centroids of the resulting subclusters. The column dimension of the matrix H_w is reduced dramatically, therefore reducing the complexity for the computation of GSVD. Experiments on various real data sets show that the approximation algorithm produces results close to those produced by the exact algorithm.

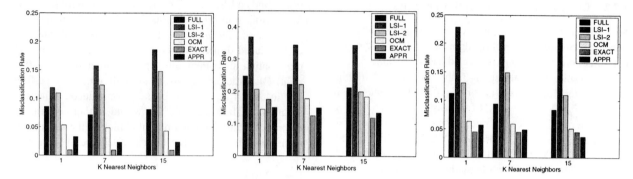

Figure 2. Performance of different dimension reduction methods using Dataset 1 (Left), Dataset 2 (Middle), and Dataset 3 (Right). Algorithms FULL, LSI-1, LSI-2, OCM, EXACT, and APPR are ordered from left to right.

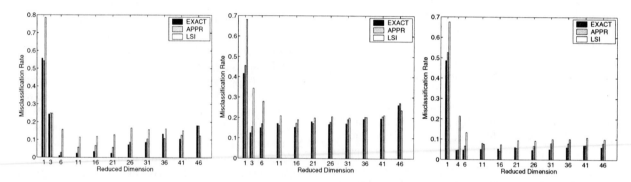

Figure 3. Comparison between our exact algorithm, approximation algorithm and LSI on different values of reduced dimension using Dataset 1 (Left, optimal reduced dimension $\delta^\star = 6$), Dataset 2 (Middle, optimal reduced dimension $\delta^\star = 3$), and Dataset 3 (Right, optimal reduced dimension $\delta^\star = 4$). The results for our exact, approximation algorithms and for LSI are ordered from left to right.

References

[1] M.W. Berry, S.T. Dumais, and G.W. O'Brien. Using linear algebra for intelligent information retrieval. *SIAM Review*, 37:573-595, 1995.

[2] S. Deerwester, S.T. Dumais, G.W. Furnas, T.K. Landauer, and R. Harshman. Indexing by latent semantic analysis. *J. of the Society for Information Science*, 41, pp. 391–407, 1990.

[3] I.S. Dhillon and D.S. Modha. Concept Decompositions for Large Sparse Text Data using Clustering. *Machine Learning*. 42, pp. 143–175, 2001.

[4] R.O. Duda and P.E. Hart, and D. Stork. Pattern Classification. Wiley, 2000.

[5] K. Fukunaga. *Introduction to Statistical Pattern Recognition*, 2nd edition. Academic Press, Inc., 1990.

[6] G.H. Golub, and C.F. Van Loan. Matrix Computations, John Hopkins Univ. Press, 3rd edition, 1996.

[7] P. Howland, M. Jeon, and H. Park. Cluster structure preserving dimension reduction based on the generalized singular value decomposition. *SIMAX*, 25(1), pp. 165–179, 2003.

[8] A.K. Jain, and R.C. Dubes. Algorithms for Clustering Data. *Prentice Hall*, 1988.

[9] C.C. Paige, and M.A.Saunders. Towards a generalized singular value decomposition, *SIAM Journal on Numerical Analysis*. 18, pp. 398–405, 1981.

[10] H. Park, M. Jeon and J.B. Rosen. Lower dimensional representation of text data based on centroids and least squares. *BIT*, 43(2), pp. 1–22, 2003.

[11] C. F. Van Loan. Generalizing the singular value decomposition. *SIAM Journal on Numerical Analysis*, 13(1), pp. 76–83, 1976.

[12] J. Ye, R. Janardan, C.H. Park, and H. park. A new optimization criterion for generalized discriminant analysis on undersampled problems. Technical Report TR03-026. University of Minnesota, 2003.

Sentiment Analyzer: Extracting Sentiments about a Given Topic using Natural Language Processing Techniques

Jeonghee Yi[†]   Tetsuya Nasukawa[‡]   Razvan Bunescu* *   Wayne Niblack[†]

[†] IBM Almaden Research Center, 650 Harry Rd, San Jose, CA 95120, USA
`{jeonghee, niblack}@almaden.ibm.com`
[‡] IBM Tokyo Research Lab, 1623-14 Shimotsuruma, Yamato-shi, Kanagawa-ken 242-8502, Japan
`nasukawa@jp.ibm.com`
* Dept. of Computer Science, University of Texas, Austin, TX 78712, USA
`razvan@cs.utexas.edu`

Abstract

We present Sentiment Analyzer (SA) that extracts sentiment (or opinion) about a subject from online text documents. Instead of classifying the sentiment of an entire document about a subject, SA detects all references to the given subject, and determines sentiment in each of the references using natural language processing (NLP) techniques. Our sentiment analysis consists of 1) a topic specific feature term extraction, 2) sentiment extraction, and 3) (subject, sentiment) association by relationship analysis. SA utilizes two linguistic resources for the analysis: the sentiment lexicon and the sentiment pattern database. The performance of the algorithms was verified on online product review articles ("digital camera" and "music" reviews), and more general documents including general webpages and news articles.

1. Introduction

Today, a huge amount of information is available in on-line documents such as web pages, newsgroup postings, and on-line news databases. Among the myriad types of information available, one useful type is the *sentiment*, or *opinions* people express towards a *subject*. (A *subject* is either a topic of interest or a feature of the topic.) For example, knowing the reputation of their own or their competitors' products or brands is valuable for product development, marketing and consumer relationship management. Traditionally, companies conduct consumer surveys for this purpose. Though well-designed surveys can provide quality es-

timations, they can be costly especially if a large volume of survey data is gathered.

There has been extensive research on automatic text analysis for sentiment, such as sentiment classifiers[13, 6, 16, 2, 19], affect analysis[17, 21], automatic survey analysis[8, 16], opinion extraction[12], or recommender systems [18]. These methods typically try to extract the overall sentiment revealed in a document, either positive or negative, or somewhere in between.

Two challenging aspects of sentiment analysis are: First, although the overall opinion about a topic is useful, it is only a part of the information of interest. Document level sentiment classification fails to detect sentiment about individual aspects of the topic. In reality, for example, though one could be generally happy about his car, he might be dissatisfied by the engine noise. To the manufacturers, these individual weaknesses and strengths are equally important to know, or even more valuable than the overall satisfaction level of customers.

Second, the association of the extracted sentiment to a specific topic is difficult. Most statistical opinion extraction algorithms perform poorly in this respect as evidenced in [3]. They either i) assume the topic of the document is known *a priori*, or ii) simply associate the opinion to a topic term co-existing in the same context. The first approach requires a reliable *topic* or *genre classifier* that is a difficult problem in itself. A document (or even a portion of a document as small as a sentence) may discuss multiple topics and contain sentiment about multiple topics.

For example, consider the following sentences from which *ReviewSeer*[3] found positive opinions about the NR70 PDA:

1. As with every Sony PDA before it, the NR70 series is equipped with Sony's own Memory Stick expansion.

---

* The author's work on a portion of the feature term selection algorithm development was performed while the author was on summer internship at IBM Almaden Research Center.

2. Unlike the more recent T series CLIEs,
   the NR70 does not require an add-on
   adapter for MP3 playback, which is
   certainly a welcome change.
3. The Memory Stick support in the NR70
   series is well implemented and functional,
   although there is still a lack of non-
   memory Memory Sticks for consumer
   consumption.

Based on our understanding of the *ReviewSeer* algorithm, we suppose their statistical method (and most other statistical opinion extraction methods) would assign the same polarity to Sony PDA and T series CLIEs as that of NR70 for the first two sentences. That is wrong for T series CLIEs, although right for Sony PDA. We notice that the third sentence reveals a negative aspect of the NR70 (i.e., the lack of non-memory Memory Sticks) as well as a positive sentiment in the primary phrase.

We anticipated the shortcomings of the purely statistical approaches, and in this paper we show that the analysis of grammatical sentence structures and phrases based on NLP techniques mitigates some of the shortcomings. We designed and developed *Sentiment Analyzer (SA)* that

- extracts topic-specific features

- extracts sentiment of each sentiment-bearing phrase

- makes (topic|feature, sentiment) association

SA detects, for each occurrence of a topic spot, the sentiment specifically about the topic. It produces the following output for the above sample sentences provided that Sony PDA, NR70, and T series CLIEs are specified topics:

1. Sony PDA - positive
   NR70 - positive
2. T series CLIEs - negative
   NR70 - positive
3. NR70 - positive
   NR70 - negative

The rest of this paper is organized as follows: Section 2 describes the feature term extraction algorithm and reports the experimental results for feature term selection. Section 3 describes the core sentiment detection algorithms and experimental results. Section 4 summarizes related work and compares them with our algorithms. Finally, we conclude with a discussion in Section 5.

2. Feature Term Extraction

A *feature term* of a topic is a term that satisfies one of the following relationships:

- a *part-of* relationship with the given topic.

- an *attribute-of* relationship with the given topic.

This **camera** has everything that you need. It takes great **pictures** and is very easy to use. It has very good **documentation**. Bought 256 MB **memory card** and can take a huge number of **pictures** at the highest **resolution**. Everyone is amazed at the **resolution** and clarity of the **pictures**. The results have been excellent from **macro shots** to **telephoto nature shots**. **Manuals** and **software** are not easy to follow. Good **Battery Life** 200 on 1GB **drive** Best **Remote** I have seen on any **camera**. The **battery** seems to last forever but you will want a spare anyway. The best **built in flash** I have seen on any **camera**. The G2 has enough **features** to keep the consumer and pro creative for some time to come!

Figure 1. Sample digital camera review

- an *attribute-of* relationship with a known feature of the given topic.

For the digital camera domain, a feature can be a *part of* the camera, such as lenses, battery or memory card; an *attribute*, such as price or size; or an *attribute of a feature*, such as battery life (an attribute of feature battery). Figure 1 is a portion of an actual review article from www.cnet.com. The phrases in bold are the features we intend to extract. We apply the feature term extraction algorithm described in the rest of this section to a set of documents having the same topic.

2.1. The Candidate Feature Term Selection

Based on the observation that feature terms are nouns, we extract only noun phrases from documents and apply feature selection algorithms described in Section 2.2. Specifically, we implemented and tested the following three candidate term selection heuristics.

2.1.1. Base Noun Phrases (BNP). BNP restricts the candidate feature terms to one of the following base noun phrase (BNP) patterns: *NN, NN NN, JJ NN, NN NN NN, JJ NN NN, JJ JJ NN*, where *NN* and *JJ* are the part-of-speech(POS) tags for nouns and adjectives respectively defined by Penn Treebank[10].

2.1.2. Definite Base Noun Phrases (dBNP). dBNP further restricts candidate feature terms to definite base noun phrases, which are noun phrases of the form defined in Section 2.1.1 that are preceded by the definite article "the." Given that a document is focused on a certain topic, the definite noun phrases referring to topic features do not need any additional constructs such as attached prepositional phrases or relative clauses, in order for the reader to establish their referent. Thus, the phrase "the battery," instead of "the battery of the digital camera," is sufficient to infer its referent.

2.1.3. Beginning Definite Base Noun Phrases (bBNP). bBNP refers to *dBNP* at the beginning of sentences followed by a verb phrase. This heuristic is based on the observation that, when the focus shifts from one feature to another, the new feature is often expressed using a definite noun phrase at the beginning of the next sentence.

2.2. Feature Selection Algorithms

We developed and tested two feature term selection algorithms based on a mixture language model and likelihood ratio. They are evaluated in Section 2.3.

2.2.1. Mixture Model. This method is based on the mixture language model by Zhai and Laffertry[23]: they assume that an observed documents d is generated by a mixture of the query model and the corpus language model. In our case, we may consider our language model as the mixture (or a linear combination) of the general web language model θ_W (similar to the corpus language model) and a topic-specific language model θ_T (similar to the query model):

$$\theta = \alpha\theta_W + \beta\theta_T$$

where α, β are given and sum to 1. α indicates the amount of background noise when generating a document from the topic-specific model. θ, θ_W and θ_T have multinomial distributions, $\theta_W = (\theta_{W_1}, \theta_{W_2}, ...\theta_{W_k})$, $\theta_T = (\theta_{T_1}, \theta_{T_2}, ...\theta_{T_k})$, and $\theta = (\theta_1, \theta_2, ...\theta_k)$, where k is the number of words in the corpus. Intuitively, by calculating the topic-specific model, θ_T, noise words can be deleted, since the topic-specific model will concentrate on words occurring frequently in topic-related documents, but less frequently in the whole corpus. The maximum likelihood estimator of θ_W can be calculated directly as:

$$\hat{\theta_{W_i}} = \frac{df_i}{\sum_j df_j}$$

where df_i is the number of times word i occurs in the whole corpus. The problem of finding θ_T can be generalized as finding the maximum likelihood estimation of multinomial distribution θ_T.

Zhang et al.[24] developed an $O(k\log(k))$ algorithm that computes the exact maximum likelihood estimation of the multinomial distribution of q in the following mixture model of multinomial distributions, $p = (p_1, p_2, ...p_k)$, $q = (q_1, q_2, ...q_k)$, and $r = (r_1, r_2, ...r_k)$:

$$r = \alpha p + \beta q$$

Let f_i be the observed frequency of word i in the documents that are generated by r. Sort $\frac{p_i}{f_i}$ so that $\frac{f_1}{p_1} > \frac{f_2}{p_2} > ... > \frac{f_k}{p_k}$. Then, find t that satisfies:

$$\frac{\frac{\beta}{\alpha} + \sum_{j=1}^{t} p_j}{\sum_{j=1}^{t} f_j} - \frac{p_t}{f_t} > 0$$

$$\frac{\frac{\beta}{\alpha} + \sum_{j=1}^{t+1} p_j}{\sum_{j=1}^{t+1} f_j} - \frac{p_{t+1}}{f_{t+1}} \leq 0$$

	D_+	D_-
bnp	C_{11}	C_{12}
$\overline{bnp}$	C_{21}	C_{22}

Table 1. Counts for a bnp [9]

Then, the q_i's are given by:

$$q_i = \begin{cases} \frac{f_i}{\lambda} - \frac{\alpha}{\beta}p_i & \text{if } 1 \leq i \leq t \\ 0 & \text{otherwise} \end{cases} \quad (1)$$

$$\lambda = \frac{\sum_{i=1}^{t} f_i}{1 + \frac{\alpha}{\beta}\sum_{i=1}^{t} p_i}$$

The following feature selection algorithm is the direct result of Equation 1.

Algorithm: For feature term selection, compute θ_{T_i} as follows:

$$\theta_{T_i} = \begin{cases} \frac{f_i}{\lambda} - \frac{\alpha}{\beta}\theta_{W_i} & \text{if } 1 \leq i \leq t \\ 0 & \text{otherwise} \end{cases} \quad (2)$$

$$\lambda = \frac{\sum_{i=1}^{t} f_i}{1 + \frac{\alpha}{\beta}\sum_{i=1}^{t} \theta_{W_i}}$$

Then sort candidate feature terms in decreasing order of θ_{T_i}. Feature terms are those whose θ_{T_i} score satisfy a predefined confidence level. Alternatively we can simply select only the top N terms.

2.2.2. Likelihood Test. This method is based on the likelihood-ratio test by Dunning [4]. Let D_+ be a collection of documents focused on a topic T, D_- those not focused on T, and bnp a candidate feature term extracted from D_+ as defined in Section 2.1. Then, the likelihood ratio $-2log\lambda$ is defined as follows:

$$-2log\lambda = -2log\frac{\max_{p_1 \leq p_2} L(p_1, p_2)}{\max_{p_1, p_2} L(p_1, p_2)}$$

$$p_1 = p(d \in D_+ | bnp \in d)$$

$$p_2 = p(d \in D_+ | \overline{bnp} \in d)$$

where $L(p_1, p_2)$ is the likelihood of seeing bnp in both D_+ and D_-.

Assuming that each bnp is a Bernoulli event, the counts from Table 1 follow a binomial distribution, and the following likelihood ratio is asymptotically χ^2 distributed.

$$-2log\lambda = -2log\frac{\max_{p_1 \leq p_2} b(p_1, C_{11}, C_{11} + C_{12}) * b(p_2, C_{21}, C_{21} + C_{22})}{\max_{p_1, p_2} b(p_1, C_{11}, C_{11} + C_{12}) * b(p_2, C_{21}, C_{21} + C_{22})}$$
$$\text{where } b(p, k, n) = p^k \cdot (1 - p)^{n-k}$$

$$-2log\lambda = \begin{cases} -2 * lr & \text{if } r_2 < r_1 \\ 0 & \text{if } r_2 \geq r_1 \end{cases} \quad (3)$$

$$r_1 = \frac{C_{11}}{C_{11}+C_{12}}, \quad r_2 = \frac{C_{21}}{C_{21}+C_{22}}$$
$$r = \frac{C_{11}+C_{21}}{C_{11}+C_{12}+C_{21}+C_{22}}$$
$$lr = (C_{11}+C_{21})log(r) + (C_{12}+C_{22})log(1-r) - C_{11}log(r_1)$$
$$-C_{12}log(1-r_1) - C_{21}log(r_2) - C_{22}log(1-r_2)$$

The higher the value of $-2log\lambda$, the more likely the bnp is relevant to the topic T.

429

	$|D_+|$	$|D_-|$	source
digital camera	485	1838	www.cnet.com www.dpreview.com www.epinions.com, www.steves-digicams.com
music	250	2389	www.epinions.com

Table 2. The product review datasets

	digital camera (38)	music (31)
BNP-M	63%	61%
dBNP-M	68%	32%
bBNP-M	32%	29%
BNP-L	68%	92%
dBNP-L	81%	96%
bBNP-L	97%	100%

Table 3. Precision of feature term extraction algorithms

Algorithm: For each bnp, compute the likelihood score, $-2log\lambda$, as defined in equation 3. Then, sort bnp in decreasing order of their likelihood score. Feature terms are all bnp's whose likelihood ratio satisfy a pre-defined confidence level. Alternatively simply only the top N bnp's can be selected.

2.3. Evaluation

2.3.1. The Dataset. We carried out experiments on two domains: digital camera and music review articles. Each dataset is a mix of manually labeled topic domain documents (D_+) and non-topic domain documents (D_-) that are randomly selected from the web pages collected by our web-crawl. The datasets are summarized in Table 2.

2.3.2. Experimental Results. We ran the two feature extraction algorithms in six different settings on the product review datasets:

- *BNP-M*: Mixture Model with *BNP*
- *dBNP-M*: Mixture Model with *dBNP*
- *bBNP-M*: Mixture Model with *bBNP*
- *BNP-L*: Likelihood Test with *BNP*
- *dBNP-L*: Likelihood Test with *dBNP*
- *bBNP-L*: Likelihood Test with *bBNP*

First, *BNP*, *dBNP* and *bBNP* were extracted from the review pages and the Mixture Model and Likelihood Test were applied on the respective bnp's. Terms with likelihood ratio above 0 were extracted for *bBNP-L*: 38 and 31 feature terms for digital camera and music datasets respectively. For the rest of the settings, the thresholding scheme was applied giving the same number of terms (i.e., 38 and 31 respectively for digital camera and music datasets) at the top of the lists. This thresholding gives the best possible precision scores for the other settings, since terms on the top of the

Digital Camera	camera, picture, flash, lens, picture quality, battery, software, price, battery life, viewfinder, color, feature, image, menu, manual, photo, movie, resolution, quality, zoom
Music Albums	song, album, track, music, piece, band, lyrics, first movement, second movement, orchestra guitar, final movement, beat, production, chorus first track, mix, third movement, piano, work

Table 4. Top 20 feature terms extracted by *bBNP-L* in the order of their rank

list are more likely to be feature terms. We used the Ratnaparkhi POS tagger[14] to extract bnp's. $\alpha = 0.3$ was used for the computation of the Mixture Model. (Other values of α were used, which did not produce any better results than what are reported here.) The extracted feature terms were manually examined by two human subjects and only the terms that both subjects labeled as feature terms were counted for the computation of the precision.

The precision scores are summarized in Table 3. *bBNP-L* performed impressively well. The Likelihood Test method consistently performed better than the Mixture Model algorithm. Its performance continued improving with increasing level of restrictions in the candidate feature terms, perhaps because, with further restriction, the selected candidate terms are more probable feature terms. On the contrary, interestingly, the increasing level of restrictions had the reverse effect with the Mixture Model algorithm. This might be because the restrictions caused too much perturbation on term distributions for the algorithm to reliably estimate the multinomial distribution of the topic-specific model. We need further investigation to explain the behavior.

The top 20 feature terms extracted by *bBNP-L* from the digital camera and music datasets are listed in Table 4.

3. Sentiment Analysis

In this section, we describe the linguistic resources used by sentiment analysis (3.1), define the scope of sentence structures that *SA* is dealing (3.2), sentiment phrase identification and sentiment assignment (3.3), and relationship analysis (3.4).

3.1. Linguistic Resources

Sentiment about a subject is the orientation (or polarity) of the opinion on the subject that deviates from the neutral state. Sentiment that expresses a desirable state (e.g., The picture is flawless.) has *positive* (or "+") polarity, while one representing an undesirable state (e.g., The product fails to meet our quality expectations.) has *negative* (or "-") polarity. The *target* of sentiment is the subject that the sentiment is directed to: the picture and the product for the examples above. *SA* uses sentiment terms defined in the *sentiment lexicon* and sentiment patterns in the *sentiment pattern database*.

3.1.1. Sentiment Lexicon.

The *sentiment lexicon* contains the sentiment definition of individual words in the following form:

```
<lexical_entry> <POS> <sent_category>
```

- lexical_entry is a (possibly multi-word) term that has sentimental connotation.
- POS is the required POS tag of lexical entry.
- sentiment_category: +|-

The following is an example of the lexicon entry:

```
"excellent" JJ +
```

We have collected sentiment words from several sources: General Inquirer (GI)[1], Dictionary of Affect of Language (DAL)[2][21], and WordNet[11]. From GI, we extracted all words in Positive, Negative, and Hostile categories. From DAL, we extracted words whose affect scores are one standard deviation higher (*positive*) or lower (*negative*) than the mean. From WordNet, we extracted synonyms of known sentiment words. At present, we have about 3000 sentiment term entries including about 2500 adjectives and less than 500 nouns.

3.1.2. Sentiment Pattern Database.

Our sentiment pattern database contains sentiment extraction patterns for sentence predicates. The database entry is defined in the following form:

```
<predicate> <sent_category> <target>
```

- predicate: typically a verb
- sent_category: +|-| [~]source
  source is a sentence component (SP|OP|CP|PP) whose sentiment is transferred to the target. SP, OP, CP, and PP represent subject, object, complement (or adjective), and prepositional phrases, respectively. The opposite sentiment polarity of source is assigned to the target, if ~ is specified in front of source.
- target is a sentence component (SP|OP|PP) the sentiment is directed to.

Some verbs have positive or negative sentiment by themselves, but some verbs (we call them *trans* verb), such as "be" or "offer", do not. The sentiment of a subject in a sentence with a *trans* verb is determined by another component of the sentence. Some example sentiment patterns and sentences matching with them are:

```
impress +  PP(by;with)
        I am impressed by the picture quality.
be CP SP
        The colors are vibrant.
offer OP SP
        IBM offers high quality products.
        IBM offers mediocre services.
```

Initially, we collected sentiment verbs from GI, DAL, and WordNet. For GI and DAL, the sentiment verb extraction is the same as the sentiment term extraction as described in Section 3.1.1. From WordNet we extracted verbs from the *emotion cluster*. From the training datasets described in Section 2.3.1, we manually refined some of the patterns. The refinements typically involve the specification of sentiment source and target, as the typical error *SA* initially introduced was the association of the discovered sentiment to a wrong target. Currently, we have about 120 sentiment predicate patterns in the database.

3.2. Scope of Sentiment Analysis

As a preprocessing step to our sentiment analysis, we extract sentences from input documents containing mentions of subject terms of interest. Then, *SA* applies sentiment analysis to *kernel sentences* [7] and some text fragments. Kernel sentences usually contain only one verb. For kernel sentences, *SA* extracts the following types of *ternary expressions (T-expressions)*[7]:

- positive or negative sentiment verbs:
  ```
  <target, verb, "">
  ```
- trans verbs:
  ```
  <target, verb, source>
  ```

The following illustrates *T-expressions* of given sentences:
```
<the camera, like, "">
    ex. I like the camera.
<the digital zoom, be, too grainy>
    ex. The digital zoom is too grainy.
```

For text fragments, *SA* extracts *binary expressions (B-expressions)*,

```
<adjective, target>
ex. good quality photo : <good quality, photo>
```

3.3. Sentiment Phrases and Sentiment Assignment

After parsing each input sentence by a syntactic parser, *SA* identifies sentiment phrases from subject, object, adjective, and prepositional phrases of the sentence.

Adjective phrases: Within the phrase, we identify all sentiment adjectives defined in the sentiment lexicon. For example, vibrant is positive sentiment phrase for the sentence "The colors are vibrant."

Subject, object and prepositional phrases: We extract all base noun phrases of the forms defined in Section 2.1.1 that consist of at least one sentiment word. The sentiment of the phrase is determined by the sentiment words in the phrase. For example, excellent pictures (JJ NN) is a positive sentiment phrase because excellent (JJ) is a positive sentiment word. For a sentiment phrase with a word with negative meaning, such as not,no, never, hardly, seldom, or little, the polarity of the sentiment is reversed.

---

1   http://www.wjh.harvard.edu/~inquirer/
2   http://www.hdcus.com

3.4. Semantic Relationship Analysis

SA extracts *T-* and *B-expressions* in order to make (subject, sentiment) association. From a *T-expression*, sentiment of the *verb* (for sentiment verbs) or *source* (for *trans* verb), and from a *B-expression*, sentiment of the *adjective*, is assigned to the *target*.

3.4.1. Sentiment Pattern based Analysis. For each sentiment phrase detected (Section 3.3), *SA* determines its *target* and final polarity based on the sentiment pattern database (Section 3.1.2). *SA* first identifies the *T-expression*, and tries to find matching sentiment patterns. Once a matching sentiment pattern is found, the *target* and sentiment assignment are determined as defined in the sentiment pattern.

Some sentiment patterns define the *target* and its sentiment explicitly. Suppose the following sentence, sentiment pattern, and subject is given:

```
I am impressed by the flash capabilities.
pattern : "impress" + PP(by;with)
subject : flash
```

SA first identifies the *T-expression* of the sentence:
```
<flash capability, impress, "">
```
and directly infers that the *target* (PP lead by "by" or "with"), the `flash capabilities`, has positive sentiment: (`flash capability, +`).

For sentences with a *trans* verb, *SA* first determines the sentiment of *source*, and assigns the sentiment to the *target*. For example, for the following sentence and the given subject term `camera`:

```
This camera takes excellent pictures.
```

SA first parses the sentence and identifies:
- matching sentiment pattern: `<"take" OP SP>`
- subject phrase (SP): `this camera`
- object phrase (OP): `excellent pictures`
- sentiment of the OP: `positive`
- *T-expression*: `<camera, take, excellent picture>`

From this information, *SA* infers that the sentiment of *source* (OP) is positive, and associates positive sentiment to the *target* (SP): (`camera, +`).

During the semantic relationship analysis, *SA* takes *negation* into account at the sentence level: if an adverb with negative meaning (such as `not`, `never`, `hardly`, `seldom`, or `little`) appears in a verb phrase, *SA* reverses the sentiment of the sentence assigned by the corresponding sentiment pattern. For example, *SA* detects negative polarity from the following sentence:

```
This camera is not good for novice users.
```

3.4.2. Analysis without Sentiment Pattern. There are many cases where sentiment pattern based analysis is not possible. Common cases include:
- No corresponding sentiment pattern is available.
- The sentence is not complete.
- Parser failure, possibly due to missing punctuation,

	Precision	Recall	Accuracy
SA	87%	56%	85.6%
Collocation	18%	70%	N/A
ReviewSeer	N/A	N/A	88.4%

Table 5. Performance comparison of sentiment extraction alorithms on the product review datasets.

wrong spelling, etc.

Examples of fragments containing sentiment are:
```
Poor performance in a dark room. (1)
Many functionalities for the price. (2)
```
SA creates *B-expressions* and makes the sentiment assignment on the basis of the phrase sentiment. The *B-expressions* and sentiment associations of sentences (1) and (2) are:
```
(1ᴮ) <poor, performance>   : (performance, -)
(2ᴮ) <many, functionality> : (functionaliry, +)
```

3.5. Evaluation

For experiments, we used the Talent[3] shallow parser for sentence parsing, and *bBNP-L* for feature extraction.

3.5.1. Product Review Dataset. We ran *SA* on the review article datasets (Section 2.3.1). The review articles are a special class of web documents that typically have a high percentage of sentiment-bearing sentences. For each subject term, we manually assigned the sentiment. Then, we ran *SA* for each sentence with a subject term and compared the computed sentiment label with the manual label to compute the accuracy. The result is compared with the collocation algorithm and the best performing algorithm of *ReviewSeer*[3]. To our knowledge, *ReviewSeer* is by far the latest and the best opinion classifier. The collocation algorithm assigns the polarity of a sentiment term to a subject term, if the sentiment term and the subject term exist in the same sentence. If positive and negative sentiment terms co-exist, the polarity with more counts is selected.

The overall precision and recall of *SA* are 87% and 56%, respectively (Table 5). The accuracy of the best performing algorithm of *ReviewSeer* is 88.4% (vs. 85.6% of *SA*). The precision of the Collocation algorithm is significantly lower, only 18%, as expected, with high recall of 70%.

Although the results provide a rough comparison, they are not directly comparable. First, the test datasets are not the same. Although both *SA* and *ReviewSeer* use product review articles, the actual datasets are not identical. (We are not aware of any benchmark dataset for sentiment classification for evaluation purposes.) They have combined more categories (7 categories vs. 2 categories for *SA*). Secondly,

---

3   http://flahdo.watson.ibm.com/Talent/talent_project.htm

	Precision	Accuracy	Acc. w/o *I class*
SA(Petroleum, Web)	86%	90%	N/A
SA(Pharmaceutical, Web)	91%	93%	N/A
SA(Petroleum, News)	88%	91%	N/A
ReviewSeer (Web)	N/A	38%	68%

Table 6. The performance of *SA* and *ReviewSeer* on general web documents and news articles.

ReviewSeer is a document level sentiment classifier, while *SA* is per subject-spot level. Third, *ReviewSeer* does not try to do subject association.

ReviewSeer might have produced better accuracy with fewer categories. On the other hand, since they do not try (subject, sentiment) association, their accuracy is not affected by the potential association error, while *SA*'s is. That is, even though *SA* extracts sentiment polarity accurately, we consider it a failure if the (subject, sentiment) association is made wrong. It is not clear how much the subject association would impact *ReviewSeer*'s accuracy. However, the experimental results on general web documents (Section 3.5.2) reveal how much subject association error degrades, at least partially, the accuracy of *ReviewSeer*.

3.5.2. General Web Documents. Sentiment expressions in general Web documents are typically very sparse in comparison to the review articles. This characteristic of general web documents may work against a document level classifier as there might not be enough sentiment-bearing expressions in a document to classify the entire document as sentiment-bearing.

In order to mitigate the problem, *ReviewSeer* applied the algorithm on the individual sentences with a subject word. This makes the comparison with *SA* on more equal ground. Table 6 lists the results.

SA achieves high precision (86% ∼ 91%) and even higher accuracy (90% ∼ 93%) on general Web documents and news articles. The precision of *SA* was computed only on the test cases that *SA* extracted as either *positive* or *negative*, but did not include *neutral* cases. The accuracy of *SA* included the *neutral* cases as well, as did *ReviewSeer*'s. The accuracy of *SA* is higher than the precision, because the majority of the test cases do not have any sentiment expression, and *SA* correctly classifies most of them as neutral.

On the contrary, *ReviewSeer* suffered with sentences from general web documents: the accuracy is only 38% (down from 88.4%). (The accuracy is computed based on the figures from Table 14 of [3]: we have averaged the accuracies of the three equal-size groups of a test set, 21%, 42% & 50%, respectively.) The accuracy was improved to 68% after removing difficult cases and using only clearly positive or negative sentences about the given subject. The set of difficult testing cases eliminated (called *I class*) include sentences that were ambiguous when taken out of context (*case i*), were not describing the product (*case ii*), or did not express any sentiment at all (*case iii*).

The challenge here is that these difficult cases are the majority of the sentences that any sentiment classifier has to deal with: 60% (356 out of 600) of the test cases for the *ReviewSeer* experiment and even more (as high as over 90% on some domain) in our experiments. *Case i* is difficult for any sentiment classifier. We believe *case ii* is where the purely statistical methods do not perform well and sophisticated NLP can help. *SA* tries to solve the (subject, sentiment) association problem *case ii* by the relationship analysis. *SA* handles the neutral cases *iii* already very well as discussed earlier.

4. Previous Work

[1] describes a procedure that aims at extracting *part-of* features, using possessive constructions and prepositional phrases, from news corpus. By contrast, we extract both *part-of* and *attribute-of* relations.

Some of the previous works on sentiment-based classification focused on classifying the semantic orientation of individual words or phrases, using linguistic heuristics, a preselected set of seed words, or by human labeling [5, 21]. [5] developed an algorithm for automatically recognizing the semantic orientation of adjectives. [22] identifies *subjective* adjectives (or sentiment adjectives) from corpora.

Past work on sentiment-based categorization of entire documents has often involved either the use of models inspired by cognitive linguistics [6, 16] or the manual or semi-manual construction of discriminant-word lexicons [2, 19]. [6] proposed a sentence interpretation model that attempts to answer directional queries based on the deep argumentative structure of the document, but with no implementation detail or any experimental results. [13] compares three machine learning methods (Naive Bayes, maximum entropy classification, and SVM) for sentiment classification task. [20] used the average "semantic orientation" of the phrases in the review. [15] analysed emotional affect of various corpora computed as average of affect scores of individual affect terms in the articles. The sentiment classifiers often assumes 1) each document has only one subject, and 2) the subject of each document is known. However, these assumptions are often not true, especially for web documents. Moreover, even if the assumptions are met, sentiment classifiers are unable to reveal the sentiment about individual features, unlike *SA*.

Product Reputation Miner [12] extracts positive or negative opinions based on a dictionary. Then it extracts characteristic words, co-occurrence words, and typical sentences for individual target categories. For each characteristic word or phrase they compute frequently co-occurring terms. However, their association of characteristic terms and co-occurring terms does not necessarily mean relevant opinion as was seen in collocation experiments. In contrast, our NLP based relationship analysis associates subjects to the corresponding sentiments.

ReviewSeer [3] is a document level opinion classifier that uses mainly statistical techniques and some POS tagging information for some of their text term selection algorithms. It achieved high accuracy on review articles. However, the performance sharply degrades when applied to sentences with subject terms from the general web documents. In contrast, *SA* continued to perform with high accuracy. Unlike *ReviewSeer*, *SA* handles the neutral cases and subject association very well. In fact, the relationship analysis of *SA* was designed for these kinds of difficult cases.

5. Discussion and Future Work

We applied NLP techniques to sentiment analysis. The feature extraction algorithm successfully identified topic related feature terms from online review articles, enabling sentiment analysis at finer granularity. *SA* consistently demonstrated high quality results of 87% for review articles, $86 \sim 91\%$ (precision) and $91 \sim 93\%$ (accuracy) for the general web pages and news articles. The results on review articles are comparable with the state of the art sentiment classifiers, and the results on general web pages are better than those of the state of the art algorithms by a wide margin (38% vs. $91 \sim 93\%$).

However, from our initial experience with sentiment detection, we have identified a few areas of potentially substantial improvements. We expect full parsing will provide better sentence structure analysis, thus better relationship analysis. Second, more advanced sentiment patterns currently require a fair amount of manual validation. Although some amount of human expert involvement may be inevitable in the validation to handle the semantics accurately, we plan on more research on increasing the level of automation.

References

[1] M. Berland and E. Charniak. Finding parts in very large corpora. In *Proc. of the 37th ACL Conf.*, pages 57–64, 1999.

[2] S. Das and M. Chen. Yahoo! for anazon: Extracting market sentiment from stock message boards. In *Proc. of the 8th APFA*, 2001.

[3] K. Dave, S. Lawrence, and D. M. Pennock. Mining the peanut gallery: Opinion extraction and semantic classification of product reviews. In *Proc. of the 12th Int. WWW Conf.*, 2003.

[4] T. E. Dunning. Accurate methods for the statistics of surprise and coincidence. *Computational Linguistics*, 19(1), 1993.

[5] V. Hatzivassiloglou and K. R. McKeown. Predicting the semantic orientation of adjectives. In *Proc. of the 35th ACL Conf.*, pages 174–181, 1997.

[6] M. Hearst. Direction-based text interpretation as an information access refinement. *Text-Based Intelligent Systems*, 1992.

[7] B. Katz. From sentence processing to information access on the world wide web. In *Proc. of AAAI Spring Symp. on NLP*, 1997.

[8] H. Li and K. Yamanishi. Mining from open answers in questionnaire data. In *Proc. of the 7th ACM SIGKDD Conf.*, 2001.

[9] C. Manning and H. Schutze. *Foundations of Statistical Natural Language Processing*. MIT Press, 1999.

[10] M. P. Marcus, B. Santorini, and M. A. Marcinkiewicz. Building a large annotated corpus of english: the penn treebank. *Computational Linguistics*, 19, 1993.

[11] G. A. Miller. Nouns in WordNet : A lexical inheritance system. *Int. J. of Lexicography*, 2(4):245–264, 1990. Also available from ftp://ftp.cogsci.princeton.edu/pub/wordnet/5papers.ps.

[12] S. Morinaga, K. Yamanishi, K. Teteishi, and T. Fukushima. Mining product reputations on the web. In *Proc. of the 8th ACM SIGKDD Conf.*, 2002.

[13] B. Pang, L. Lee, and S. Vaithyanathan. Thumbs up? sentiment classification using machine learning techniques. In *Proc. of the 2002 ACL EMNLP Conf.*, pages 79–86, 2002.

[14] A. Ratnaparkhi. A maximum entropy model for part-of-speech tagging. In *Proc. of the EMNLP Conf.*, pages 133–142, 1996.

[15] L. Rovinelli and C. Whissell. Emotion and style in 30-second television advertisements targeted at men, women, boys, and girls. *Perceptual and Motor Skills*, 86:1048–1050, 1998.

[16] W. Sack. On the computation of point of view. In *Proc. of the 12th AAAI Conf.*, 1994.

[17] P. Subasic and A. Huettner. Affect analysis of text using fuzzy semantic typing. *IEEE Trans. on Fuzzy Systems, Special Issue*, Aug., 2001.

[18] L. Terveen, W. Hill, B. Amento, D. McDonald, and J. Creter. PHOAKS: A system for sharing recommendations. *CACM*, 40(3):59–62, 1997.

[19] R. M. Tong. An operational system for detecting and tracking opinions in on-line discussion. In *SIGIR Workshop on Operational Text Classification*, 2001.

[20] P. D. Turney. Thumbs up or thumbs down? semantic orientation applied to unsupervised classification of reviews. In *Proc. of the 40th ACL Conf.*, pages 417–424, 2002.

[21] C. Whissell. The dictionary of affect in language. *Emotion: Theory, Research, and Experience*, pages 113–131.

[22] J. M. Wiebe. Learning subjective adjectives from corpora. In *Proc. of the 17th AAAI Conf.*, 2000.

[23] C. Zhai and J. Lafferty. Model-based feedback in the language modeling approach to information retrieval. In *Proc. of the 10th Information and Knowledge Management Conf.*, 2001.

[24] Y. Zhang, W. Xu, and J. Callan. Exact maximum likelihood estimation for word mixtures. In *ICML Workshop on Text Learning*, 2002.

Cost-Sensitive Learning by Cost-Proportionate Example Weighting

Bianca Zadrozny, John Langford*, Naoki Abe
Mathematical Sciences Department
IBM T. J. Watson Research Center
Yorktown Heights, NY 10598

Abstract

We propose and evaluate a family of methods for converting classifier learning algorithms and classification theory into cost-sensitive algorithms and theory. The proposed conversion is based on cost-proportionate weighting of the training examples, which can be realized either by feeding the weights to the classification algorithm (as often done in boosting), or by careful subsampling. We give some theoretical performance guarantees on the proposed methods, as well as empirical evidence that they are practical alternatives to existing approaches. In particular, we propose costing, *a method based on cost-proportionate rejection sampling and ensemble aggregation, which achieves excellent predictive performance on two publicly available datasets, while drastically reducing the computation required by other methods.*

1 Introduction

Highly non-uniform misclassification costs are very common in a variety of challenging real-world data mining problems, such as fraud detection, medical diagnosis and various problems in business decision-making. In many cases, one class is rare but the cost of not recognizing some of the examples belonging to this class is high. In these domains, classifier learning methods that do not take misclassification costs into account do not perform well. In extreme cases, ignoring costs may produce a model that is useless because it classifies every example as belonging to the most frequent class even though misclassifications of the least frequent class result in a very large cost.

Recently a body of work has attempted to address this issue, with techniques known as cost-sensitive learning in the machine learning and data mining communities. Current cost-sensitive learning research falls into three categories. The first is concerned with making particular classifier learners cost-sensitive [3, 7]. The second uses Bayes risk theory to assign each example to its lowest risk

class [2, 19, 14]. This requires estimating class membership probabilities and, in the case where costs are non-deterministic, also requires estimating expected costs [19]. The third category concerns methods for converting arbitrary classification learning algorithms into cost-sensitive ones [2]. The work described here belongs to the last category.

In particular, the approach here is akin to the pioneering work of Domingos on MetaCost [2], which also is a general method for converting cost-sensitive learning problems to cost-insensitive learning problems. However, the method here is distinguished by the following properties: (1) it is even simpler; (2) it has some theoretical performance guarantees; and (3) it does not involve any probability density estimation in its process: MetaCost estimates conditional probability distributions via bagging with a classifier in its procedure, and as such it also belongs to the second category (Bayes risk minimization) mentioned above.

The family of proposed methods is motivated by a folk theorem that is formalized and proved in section 2.1. This theorem states that altering the original example distribution D to another $\hat{D}$, by multiplying it by a factor proportional to the relative cost of each example, makes any error-minimizing classifier learner accomplish expected cost minimization on the original distribution. Representing samples drawn from $\hat{D}$, however, is more challenging than it may seem. There are two basic methods for doing this: (i) Transparent Box: Supply the costs of the training data as example weights to the classifier learning algorithm. (ii) Black Box: resample according to these same weights.

While the transparent box approach cannot be applied to arbitrary classifier learners, it can be applied to many, including any classifier which only uses the data to calculate expectations. We show empirically that this method gives good results. The black box approach has the advantage that it can be applied to any classifier learner. It turns out, however, that straightforward sampling-with-replacement can result in severe overfitting related to duplicate examples.

We propose, instead, to employ *cost-proportionate rejection sampling* to realize the latter approach, which allows us to independently draw examples according to $\hat{D}$. This method comes with a theoretical guarantee: In the worst case it produces a classifier that achieves at least as good

---

*This author's present address: Toyota Technological Institute at Chicago, 427 East 60th Street, Second Floor - Press Building, Chicago, IL 60637.

435

approximate cost minimization as applying the base classifier learning algorithm on the entire sample. This is a remarkable property for a subsampling scheme: in general, we expect any technique using only a subset of the examples to compromise predictive performance.

The runtime savings made possible by this sampling technique enable us to run the classification algorithm on multiple draws of subsamples and average over the resulting classifiers. This last method is what we call *costing* (cost-proportionate rejection sampling with aggregation). Costing allows us to use an arbitrary cost-insensitive learning algorithm as a black box in order to accomplish cost-sensitive learning, achieves excellent predictive performance and can achieve drastic savings of computational resources.

2 Motivating Theory and Methods

2.1 A Folk Theorem

We assume that examples are drawn independently from a distribution D with domain $X \times Y \times C$ where X is the input space to a classifier, Y is a (binary) output space and $C \subset [0, \infty)$ is the importance (extra cost) associated with mislabeling that example. The goal is to learn a classifier $h : X \to Y$ which minimizes the expected cost,

$$E_{x,y,c \sim D}[c\,I(h(x) \neq y)]$$

given training data of the form: (x, y, c), where $I(\cdot)$ is the indicator function that has value 1 in case its argument is true and 0 otherwise. This model does not explicitly allow using cost information at prediction time although X might include a cost feature if that is available.

This formulation of cost-sensitive learning in terms of one number per example is more general than "cost matrix" formulations which are more typical in cost-sensitive learning [6, 2], when the output space is binary.[1] In the cost matrix formulation, costs are associated with false negative, false positive, true negative, and true positive predictions. Given the cost matrix and an example, only two entries (false positive, true negative) or (false negative, true positive) are relevant for that example. These two numbers can be further reduced to one: (false positive - true negative) or (false negative - true positive), because it is the difference in cost between classifying an example correctly or incorrectly which controls the importance of correct classification. This difference is the importance c we use here. This setting is more general in the sense that the importance may vary on a example-by-example basis.

A basic folk theorem [2] states that if we have examples drawn from the distribution:

$$\hat{D}(x,y,c) \equiv \frac{c}{E_{x,y,c \sim D}[c]} D(x,y,c)$$

---

[1] How to formulate the problem in this way when the output space is not binary is nontrivial and is beyond the scope of this paper.

[2] We say "folk theorem" here because the result appears to be known by some and it is straightforward to derive it from results in decision theory, although we have not found it published.

then optimal error rate classifiers for $\hat{D}$ are optimal cost minimizers for data drawn from D.

Theorem 2.1. *(Translation Theorem) For all distributions, D, there exists a constant $N = E_{x,y,c \sim D}[c]$ such that for all classifiers, h:*

$$E_{x,y,c \sim \hat{D}}[I(h(x) \neq y)] = \frac{1}{N} E_{x,y,c \sim D}[c\,I(h(x) \neq y)]$$

Proof.

$$
\begin{aligned}
E_{x,y,c \sim D}[c\,I(h(x) \neq y)] &= \sum_{x,y,c} D(x,y,c)c\,I(h(x) \neq y) \\
&= N \sum_{x,y,c} \hat{D}(x,y,c) I(h(x) \neq y) \\
&= N E_{x,y,c \sim \hat{D}}[I(h(x) \neq y)]
\end{aligned}
$$

$$\text{where} \qquad \hat{D}(x,y,c) = \frac{c}{N} D(x,y,c).$$

$\square$

Despite its simplicity, this theorem is useful to us because the right-hand side expresses the expectation we want to control (via the choice of h) and the left-hand side is the probability that h errs under another distribution. Choosing h to minimize the rate of errors under $\hat{D}$ is equivalent to choosing h to minimize the expected cost under D. Similarly, ε-approximate error minimization under $\hat{D}$ is equivalent to $N\varepsilon$-approximate cost minimization under D.

The prescription for coping with cost-sensitive problems is straightforward: re-weight the distribution in your training set according to the importances so that the training set is effectively drawn from $\hat{D}$. Doing this in a correct and general manner is more challenging than it may seem and is the topic of the rest of the paper.

2.2 Transparent Box: Using Weights Directly

2.2.1 General conversion

Here we examine how importance weights can be used within different learning algorithms to accomplish cost-sensitive classification. We call this the transparent box approach because it requires knowledge of the particular learning algorithm (as opposed to the black box approach that we develop later).

The mechanisms for realizing the transparent box approach have been described elsewhere for a number of weak learners used in boosting, but we will describe them here for completeness. The classifier learning algorithm must use the weights so that it effectively learns from data drawn according to $\hat{D}$. This requirement is easy to apply for all learning algorithms which fit the statistical query model [13].

As shown in figure 1, many learning algorithms can be divided into two components: a portion which calculates the (approximate) expected value of some function (or query) f and a portion which forms these queries and uses their output to construct a classifier. For example, neural networks, decision trees, and Naive Bayes classifiers can be

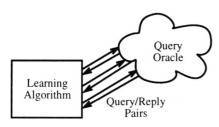

Figure 1. The statistical query model.

constructed in this manner. Support vector machines are not easily constructible in this way, because the individual classifier is explicitly dependent upon individual examples rather than on statistics derived from the entire sample.

With finite data we cannot precisely calculate the expectation $E_{x,y \sim D}[f(x,y)]$. With high probability, however, we can approximate the expectation given a set of examples drawn independently from the underlying distribution D.

Whenever we have a learning algorithm that can be decomposed as in figure 1, there is a simple recipe for using the weights directly. Instead of simulating the expectation with $\frac{1}{|S|} \sum_{(x,y) \in S} f(x,y)$, we use $\frac{1}{\sum_{(x,y,c) \in S} c} \sum_{(x,y,c) \in S} cf(x,y)$. This method is equivalent to importance sampling for $\hat{D}$ using the distribution D, and so the modified expectation is an unbiased Monte Carlo estimate of the expectation w.r.t. $\hat{D}$.

Even when a learning algorithm does not fit this model, it may be possible to incorporate importance weights directly. We now discuss how to incorporate importance weights into some specific learning algorithms.

2.2.2 Naive Bayes and boosting

Naive Bayes learns by calculating empirical probabilities for each output y using Bayes' rule and assuming that each feature is independent given the output:

$$P(y|x) = \frac{P(x|y)P(y)}{P(x)} = \frac{\prod_i P(x_i|y)P(y)}{\prod_i P(x_i)}$$

Each probability estimate in the above expression can be thought of as a function of empirical expectations according to D, and thus it can be formulated in the statistical query model. For example, $P(x_i|y)$ is just the expectation of $I(\mathbf{x_i} = x_i) \wedge I(\mathbf{y} = y)$ divided by the expectation of $I(\mathbf{y} = y)$. More specifically, to compute the empirical estimate of $P(x_i|y)$ with respect to D, we need to count the number of training examples that have y as output, and those having x_i as the i-th input dimension among those. When we compute these empirical estimates with respect to $\hat{D}$, we simply have to sum the weight of each example, instead of counting the examples. (This property is used in the implementation of boosted Naive Bayes [5].)

To incorporate importance weights into AdaBoost [8], we give the importance weights to the weak learner in the first iteration, thus effectively drawing examples from $\hat{D}$. In the subsequent iterations, we use the standard AdaBoost

rule to update the weights. Therefore, the weights are adjusted according to the accuracy on $\hat{D}$, which corresponds to the expected cost on D.

2.2.3 C4.5

C4.5 [16] is a widely used decision tree learner. There is a standard way of incorporating example weights to it, which in the original algorithm was intended to handle missing attributes (examples with missing attributes were divided into fractional examples, each with a smaller weight, during the growth of the tree). This same facility was later used by Quinlan in the implementation of boosted C4.5 [15].

2.2.4 Support Vector Machine

The SVM algorithm [11] learns the parameters a and b describing a linear decision rule $h(x) = \text{sign}(a \cdot x + b)$, so that the smallest distance between each training example and the decision boundary (the margin) is maximized. It works by solving the following optimization problem:

$$\text{minimize: } V(a,b,\xi) = \tfrac{1}{2}a \cdot a + C \sum_{i=1}^n \xi_i$$
$$\text{subject to: } \forall i: \quad y_i[a \cdot x_i + b] \geq 1 - \xi_i, \ \xi_i > 0$$

The constraints require that all examples in the training set are classified correctly up to some slack ξ_i. If a training example lies on the wrong side of the decision boundary, the corresponding ξ_i is greater than 1. Therefore, $\sum_{i=1}^n \xi_i$ is an upper bound on the number of training errors. The factor C is a parameter that allows one to trade off training error and model complexity. The algorithm can be generalized to non-linear decision rules by replacing inner products with a kernel function in the formulas above.

The SVM algorithm does not fit the statistical query model. Despite this, it is possible to incorporate importance weights in a natural way. First, we note that $\sum_{i=1}^n c_i \xi_i$, where c_i is the importance of example i, is an upper bound on the total cost. Therefore, we can modify $V(a,b,\xi)$ to

$$V(a,b,\xi) = \tfrac{1}{2}a \cdot a + C \sum_{i=1}^n c_i \xi_i.$$

Now C controls model complexity versus total cost.

The SVMLight package [10] allows users to input weights c_i and works with the modified $V(a,b,\xi)$ as above, although this feature has not yet been documented.

2.3 Black Box: Sampling methods

Suppose we do not have transparent box access to the learner. In this case, sampling is the obvious method to convert from one distribution of examples to another to obtain a cost-sensitive learner using the translation theorem (Theorem 2.1). As it turns out, straightforward sampling does not work well in this case, motivating us to propose an alternative method based on rejection sampling.

2.3.1 Sampling-with-replacement

Sampling-with-replacement is a sampling scheme where each example (x, y, c) is drawn according to the distribution $p(x, y, c) = \frac{c}{\sum_{(x,y,c) \in S} c}$. Many examples are drawn to create a new dataset S'. This method, at first pass, appears useful because every example is effectively drawn from the distribution $\hat{D}$. In fact, very poor performance can result when using this technique, which is essentially due to overfitting because of the fact that the examples in S' are not drawn *independently* from $\hat{D}$, as we will elaborate in the section on experimental results (Section 3).

Sampling-without-replacement is also not a solution to this problem. In sampling-without-replacement, an example (x, y, c) is drawn from the distribution $p(x, y, c) = \frac{c}{\sum_{(x,y,c) \in S} c}$ and the next example is drawn from the set $S - \{x, y, c\}$. This process is repeated, drawing from a smaller and smaller set according to the weights of the examples remaining in the set.

To see how this method fails, note that sampling-without-replacement m times from a set of size m results in the original set, which (by assumption) is drawn from the distribution D, and not $\hat{D}$ as desired.

2.3.2 Cost-proportionate rejection sampling

There is another sampling scheme called rejection sampling [18] which allows us to draw examples independently from the distribution $\hat{D}$, given examples drawn independently from D. In rejection sampling, examples from $\hat{D}$ are obtained by first drawing examples from D, and then keeping (or accepting) the sample with probability proportional to $\hat{D}/D$. Here, we have $\hat{D}/D \propto c$, so we accept an example with probability c/Z, where Z is some constant chosen so that $\max_{(x,y,c) \in S} c \leq Z$,[3] leading to the name *cost-proportionate rejection sampling*. Rejection sampling results in a set S' which is generally smaller than S. Furthermore, because inclusion of an example in S' is independent of other examples, and the examples in S are drawn independently, we know that the examples in S' are distributed independently according to $\hat{D}$.

Using cost-proportionate rejection sampling to create a set S' and then using a learning algorithm $A(S')$ is guaranteed to produce an approximately cost-minimizing classifier, as long as the learning algorithm A achieves approximate minimization of classification error.

Theorem 2.2. *(Correctness) For all cost-sensitive sample sets S, if cost-proportionate rejection sampling produces a sample set S' and $A(S')$ achieves ε classification error:*

$$E_{x,y,c \sim \hat{D}}[I(h(x) \neq y)] \leq \varepsilon$$

---

[3] In practice, we choose $Z = \max_{(x,y,w) \in S} c$ so as to maximize the size of the set S'. A data-dependent choice of Z is *not* formally allowed for rejection sampling. However, the introduced bias appears small when $|S| \gg 1$. A precise measurement of "small" is an interesting theoretical problem.

then $h = A(S')$ approximately minimizes cost:

$$E_{x,y,c \sim D}[c\, I(h(x) \neq y)] \leq \varepsilon N$$

where $N = E_{x,y,c \sim D}[c]$.

Proof. Rejection sampling produces a sample set S' drawn independently from $\hat{D}$. By assumption $A(S')$ outputs a classifier h such that

$$E_{x,y,c \sim \hat{D}}[I(h(x) \neq y)] \leq \varepsilon$$

By the translation theorem (Theorem 2.1), we know that

$$E_{x,y,c \sim \hat{D}}[I(h(x) \neq y)] = \frac{1}{N} E_{x,y,c \sim D}[c\, I(h(x) \neq y)]$$

Thus,

$$E_{x,y,c \sim D}[c\, I(h(x) \neq y)] \leq \varepsilon N.$$

$\square$

2.3.3 Sample complexity of cost-proportionate rejection sampling

The accuracy of a learned classifier generally improves monotonically with the number of examples in the training set. Since cost-proportionate rejection sampling produces a smaller training set (by a factor of about N/Z), one would expect worse performance than using the entire training set.

This turns out to not be the case, in the *agnostic PAC-learning model* [17, 12], which formalizes the notion of probably approximately optimal learning from arbitrary distributions D.

Definition 2.1. *A learning algorithm A is said to be an agnostic PAC-learner for hypothesis class H, with sample complexity $m(1/\varepsilon, 1/\delta)$ if for all $\varepsilon > 0$ and $\delta > 0$, $m = m(1/\varepsilon, 1/\delta)$ is the least sample size such that for all distributions D (over $X \times Y$), the classification error rate of its output h is at most ε more than the best achievable by any member of H with probability at least $1 - \delta$, whenever the sample size exceeds m.*

By analogy, we can formalize the notion of *cost-sensitive* agnostic PAC-learning.

Definition 2.2. *A learning algorithm A is said to be a cost-sensitive agnostic PAC-learner for hypothesis class H, with cost-sensitive sample complexity $m(1/\varepsilon, 1/\delta)$, if for all $\varepsilon > 0$ and $\delta > 0$, $m = m(1/\varepsilon, 1/\delta)$ is the least sample size such that for all distributions D (over $X \times Y \times C$), the expected cost of its output h is at most ε more than the best achievable by any member of H with probability at least $1 - \delta$, whenever the sample size exceeds m.*

We will now use this formalization to compare the cost-sensitive PAC-learning sample complexity of two methods: applying a given base classifier learning algorithm to a sample obtained through cost-proportionate rejection sampling, and applying the same algorithm on the original training set. We show that the cost-sensitive sample complexity of the latter method is lower-bounded by that of the former.

Theorem 2.3. *(Sample Complexity Comparison) Fix an arbitrary base classifier learning algorithm A, and suppose that $m_{orig}(1/\varepsilon, 1/\delta)$ and $m_{rej}(1/\varepsilon, 1/\delta)$, respectively, are cost-sensitive sample complexity of applying A on the original training set, and that of applying A with cost-proportionate rejection sampling. Then, we have*

$$m_{orig}(1/\varepsilon, 1/\delta) = \Omega(m_{rej}(1/\varepsilon, 1/\delta)).$$

Proof. Let $m(1/\varepsilon, 1/\delta)$ be the (cost-insensitive) sample complexity of the base classifier learning algorithm A. (If no such function exists, then neither $m_{\mathrm{orig}}(1/\varepsilon, 1/\delta)$ nor $m_{\mathrm{rej}}(1/\varepsilon, 1/\delta)$ exists, and the theorem holds vacuously.) Since Z is an upper bound on the cost of misclassifying an example, we have that the cost-sensitive sample complexity of using the original training set satisfies

$$m_{\mathrm{orig}}(1/\varepsilon, 1/\delta) = \Theta(m(Z/\varepsilon, 1/\delta))$$

This is because given a distribution that forces ε more classification error than optimal, another distribution can be constructed, that forces εZ more cost than optimal, by assigning cost Z to all examples on which A errs.

Now from Theorem 2.2 and noting that the central limit theorem implies that cost-proportionate rejection sampling reduces the sample size by a factor of $\Theta(N/Z)$, the cost-sensitive sample complexity for rejection sampling is:

$$m_{\mathrm{rej}}(1/\varepsilon, 1/\delta) = \Theta\left(\frac{Z}{N} m(N/\varepsilon, 1/\delta)\right). \tag{1}$$

A fundamental theorem from PAC-learning theory states that $m(1/\varepsilon, 1/\delta) = \Omega((1/\varepsilon)\ln(1/\delta))$ [4]. When $m(1/\varepsilon, 1/\delta) = \Theta((1/\varepsilon)\ln(1/\delta))$, Equation (1) implies:

$$m_{\mathrm{rej}}(1/\varepsilon, 1/\delta) = \Theta\left(\frac{Z}{N}\frac{N}{\varepsilon}\ln(1/\delta)\right) = \Theta\left(m_{\mathrm{orig}}(1/\varepsilon, 1/\delta)\right)$$

Finally, note that when $m(1/\varepsilon, 1/\delta)$ grows faster than linear in $1/\varepsilon$, we have $m_{\mathrm{rej}}(1/\varepsilon, 1/\delta) = o(m_{\mathrm{orig}}(1/\varepsilon, 1/\delta))$, which finishes the proof. ☐

Note that the linear dependence of sample size on $1/\varepsilon$ is only achievable by an ideal learning algorithm, and in practice super-linear dependence is expected, especially in the presence of noise. Thus, the above theorem implies that *cost-proportionate rejection sampling* minimizes cost better than no sampling for worst case distributions.

This is a remarkable property about any sampling scheme, since one generally expects that predictive performance is compromised by using a smaller sample. Cost-proportionate rejection sampling seems to *distill* the original sample and obtains a sample of smaller size, which is at least as informative as the original.

2.3.4 Cost-proportionate rejection sampling with aggregation (costing)

From the same original training sample, different runs of cost-proportionate rejection sampling will produce different training samples. Furthermore, the fact that rejection sampling produces very small samples means that the time required for learning a classifier is generally much smaller.

We can take advantage of these properties to devise an ensemble learning algorithm based on repeatedly performing rejection sampling from S to produce multiple sample sets $S'_1, ..., S'_m$, and then learning a classifier for each set. The output classifier is the average over all learned classifiers. We call this technique *costing*:

Costing(Learner A, Sample Set S, count t)

1. **For** $i = 1$ **to** t **do**

   (a) S' = **rejection sample from S with acceptance probability** c/Z.

   (b) **Let** $h_i \equiv A(S')$

2. **Output** $h(x) = \mathrm{sign}\left(\sum_{i=1}^{t} h_i(x)\right)$

The goal in averaging is to improve performance. There is both empirical and theoretical evidence suggesting that averaging can be useful. On the empirical side, many people have observed good performance from bagging despite throwing away a $1/e$ fraction of the samples. On the theoretical side, there has been considerable work which proves that the ability to overfit of an average of classifiers might be smaller than naively expected when a large margin exists. The preponderance of learning algorithms producing averaging classifiers provides significant evidence that averaging is useful.

Note that despite the extra computational cost of averaging, the overall computational time of costing is generally much smaller than that of a learning algorithm using sample set S (with or without weights). This is the case because most learning algorithms have running times that are super-linear in the number of examples.

3 Empirical evaluation

We show empirical results using two real-world datasets. We selected datasets that are publicly available and for which cost information is available on a per example basis. Both datasets are from the direct marketing domain. Although there are many other data mining domains that are cost-sensitive, such as credit card fraud detection and medical diagnosis, publicly available data are lacking.

3.1 The datasets used

3.1.1 KDD-98 dataset

This is the well-known and challenging dataset from the KDD-98 competition, now available at the UCI KDD repository [9]. The dataset contains information about persons who have made donations in the past to a particular charity. The decision-making task is to choose which donors to mail a request for a new donation. The measure of success is the total profit obtained in the mailing campaign.

The dataset is divided in a fixed way into a training set and a test set. Each set consists of approximately 96000 records for which it is known whether or not the person made a donation and how much the person donated, if a donation was made. The overall percentage of donors is about 5%. Mailing a solicitation to an individual costs the charity $0.68. The donation amount for persons who respond varies from $1 to $200. The profit obtained by soliciting every individual in the test set is $10560, while the profit attained by the winner of the KDD-98 competition was $14712.

The importance of each example is the absolute difference in profit between mailing and not mailing an individual. Mailing results in the donation amount minus the cost of mailing. Not mailing results in zero profit. Thus, for positive examples (respondents), the importance varies from $0.32 to $199.32. For negative examples (non-respondents), it is fixed at $0.68.

3.1.2 DMEF-2 dataset

This dataset can be obtained from the DMEF dataset library [1] for a nominal fee. It contains customer buying history for 96551 customers of a nationally known catalog. The decision-making task is to choose which customers should receive a new catalog so as to maximize the total profit on the catalog mailing campaign. Information on the cost of mailing a catalog is not available, so we fixed it at $2.

The overall percentage of respondents is about 2.5%. The purchase amount for customers who respond varies from $3 to $6247. As is the case for the KDD-98 dataset, the importance of each example is the absolute difference in profit between mailing and not mailing a customer. Therefore, for positive examples (respondents), the importance varies from $1 to $6245. For negative examples (non-respondents), it is fixed at $2.

We divided the dataset in half to create a training set and a test set. As a baseline for comparison, the profit obtained by mailing a catalog to every individual on the training set is $26474 and on the test set is $27584.

3.2 Experimental results

3.2.1 Transparent box results

Table 1 (top) shows the results for Naive Bayes, boosted Naive Bayes (100 iterations) C4.5 and SVMLight on the KDD-98 and DMEF-2 datasets, with and without the importance weights. Without the importance weights, the classifiers label very few of the examples positive, resulting in small (and even negative) profits. With the costs given as weights to the learners, the results improve significantly for all learners, except C4.5. Cost-sensitive boosted Naive Bayes gives results comparable to the best so far with this dataset [19] using more complicated methods.

We optimized the parameters of the SVM by cross-validation on the training set. Without weights, no setting of the parameters prevented the algorithm of labeling all examples as negatives. With weights, the best parameters were

KDD-98:

Method	Without Weights	With Weights
Naive Bayes	0.24	12367
Boosted NB	-1.36	14489
C4.5	0	118
SVMLight	0	13683

DMEF-2:

Method	Without Weights	With Weights
Naive Bayes	16462	32608
Boosted NB	121	36381
C4.5	0	478
SVMLight	0	36443

Table 1. Test set profits with transparent box.

a polynomial kernel with degree 3 and $C = 5 \times 10^{-5}$ for KDD-98 and a linear kernel with $C = 0.0005$ for DMEF-2. However, even with this parameter setting, the results are not so impressive. This may be a hard problem for margin-based classifiers because the data is very noisy. Note also that running SVMLight on this dataset takes about 3 orders of magnitude longer than AdaBoost with 100 iterations.

The failure of C4.5 to achieve good profits with importance weights is probably related to the fact that the facility for incorporating weights provided in the algorithm is heuristic. So far, it has been used only in situations where the weights are fairly uniform (such as is the case for fractional instances due to missing data). These results indicate that it might not be suitable for situations with highly non-uniform costs. The fact that it is non-trivial to incorporate costs directly into existing learning algorithms is the motivation for the black box approaches that we present here.

3.2.2 Black box results

Table 2 shows the results of applying the same learning algorithms to the KDD-98 and DMEF-2 data using training sets of different sizes obtained by sampling-with-replacement. For each size, we repeat the experiments 10 times with different sampled sets to get mean and standard error (in parentheses). The training set profits are on the original training set from which we draw the sampled sets.

The results confirm that application of sampling-with-replacement to implement the black box approach can result in very poor performance due to overfitting. When there are large differences in the magnitude of importance weights, it is typical for an example to be picked twice (or more). In table 2, we see that as we increase the sampled training set size and, as a consequence, the number of duplicate examples in the training set, the training profit becomes larger while the test profit becomes smaller for C4.5.

Examples which appear multiple times in the training set of a learning algorithm can defeat complexity control mechanisms built into learning algorithms For example, suppose that we have a decision tree algorithm which divides the training data into a "growing set" (used to construct a tree)

KDD-98:

	1000		10000		100000	
	Training	Test	Training	Test	Training	Test
NB	11251 (330)	10850 (325)	12811 (155)	11993 (185)	12531 (242)	12026 (256)
BNB	11658 (311)	11276 (383)	13838 (65)	12886 (212)	14107 (152)	13135 (159)
C4.5	11124 (255)	9548 (331)	22083 (271)	7599 (310)	40704 (152)	2259 (107)
SVM	10320 (372)	10131 (281)	11228 (182)	11015 (161)	13565 (129)	12808 (220)

DMEF-2:

	1000		10000		100000	
	Training	Test	Training	Test	Training	Test
NB	33298 (495)	34264 (419)	32742 (793)	33956 (798)	33511 (475)	34506 (405)
BNB	33902 (558)	30304 (660)	34802 (806)	31342 (772)	34505 (822)	31889 (733)
C4.5	37905 (1467)	24011 (1931)	67960 (763)	9188 (458)	72574 (1205)	3149 (519)
SVM	28837 (1029)	30177 (1196)	31263 (1121)	32585 (891)	34309 (719)	33674 (600)

Table 2. Profits using sampling-with-replacement.

and a "pruning set" (used to prune the tree for complexity control purposes). If the pruning set contains examples which appear in the growing set, the complexity control mechanism is defeated.

Although not as markedly as for C4.5, we see the same phenomenon for the other learning algorithms. In general, as the size of the resampled size grows, the larger is the difference between training set profit and test set profit. And, even with 100000 examples, we do not obtain the same test set results as giving the weights directly to Boosted Naive Bayes and SVM.

The fundamental difficulty here is that the samples in S' are not drawn *independently* from $\hat{D}$. In particular, if $\hat{D}$ is a density, the probability of observing the same example twice given independent draws is 0, while the probability using sampling-with-replacement is greater than 0. Thus sampling-with-replacement fails because the sampled set S' is not constructed independently.

Figure 2 shows the results of costing on the KDD-98 and DMEF-2 datasets, with the base learners and $Z = 200$ or $Z = 6247$, respectively. We repeated the experiment 10 times for each t and calculated the mean and standard error of the profit. The results for $t = 1$, $t = 100$ and $t = 200$ are also given in table 3.

In the KDD-98 case, each resampled set has only about 600 examples, because the importance of the examples varies from 0.68 to 199.32 and there are few "important" examples. About 55% of the examples in each set are positive, even though on the original dataset the percentage of positives is only 5%. With $t = 200$, the C4.5 version yields profits around $15000, which is exceptional performance for this dataset.

In the DMEF-2 case, each set has only about 35 examples, because the importances vary even more widely (from 2 to 6246) and there are even fewer examples with a large importance than in the KDD-98 case. The percentage of positive examples in each set is about 50%, even though on the original dataset it was only 2.5%.

For learning the SVMs, we used the same kernels as we did in section 2.2 and the default setting for C. In that

KDD-98:

	1	100	200
NB	11667 (192)	13111 (102)	13163 (68)
BNB	11377 (263)	14829 (92)	14714 (62)
C4.5	9628 (511)	14935 (102)	15016 (61)
SVM	10041 (393)	13075 (41)	13152 (56)

DMEF-2:

	1	100	200
NB	26287 (3444)	37627 (335)	37629 (139)
BNB	24402 (2839)	37376 (393)	37891 (364)
C4.5	27089 (3425)	36992 (374)	37500 (307)
SVM	21712 (3487)	33584 (1215)	35290 (849)

Table 3. Test set profits using costing.

section, we saw that by feeding the weights directly to the SVM, we obtain a profit of $13683 on the KDD-98 dataset and of $36443 on the DMEF-2 dataset. Here, we obtain profits around $13100 and $35000, respectively. However, this did not require parameter optimization and, even with $t = 200$, was much faster to train. The reason for the speedup is that the time complexity of SVM learning is generally superlinear in the number of training examples.

4 Discussion

Costing is a technique which produces a cost-sensitive classification from a cost-insensitive classifier using only black box access. This simple method is fast, results in excellent performance and often achieves drastic savings in computational resources, particularly with respect to space requirements. This last property is especially desirable in applications of cost-sensitive learning to domains that involve massive amount of data, such as fraud detection, targeted marketing, and intrusion detection.

Another desirable property of any reduction is that it applies to the theory as well as to concrete algorithms. Thus, the reduction presented in the present paper allows us to automatically apply any future results in cost-insensitive classification to cost-sensitive classification. For example, a

441

KDD-98:

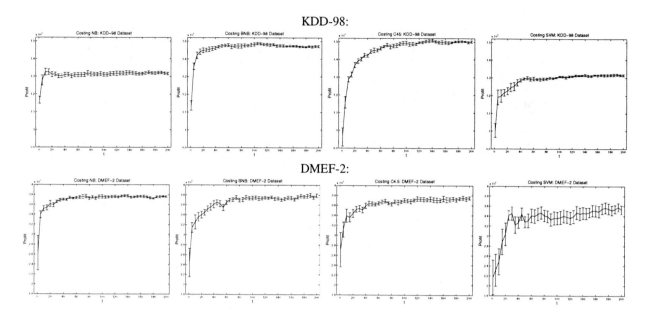

DMEF-2:

Figure 2. Costing: test set profit vs. number of sampled sets.

bound on the future error rate of $A(S')$ implies a bound on the expected cost with respect to the distribution D. This additional property of a reduction is especially important because cost-sensitive learning theory is still young and relatively unexplored.

One direction for future work is multiclass cost-sensitive learning. If there are K classes, the minimal representation of costs is $K - 1$ weights. A reduction to cost-insensitive classification using these weights is an open problem.

References

[1] Anifantis, S. The DMEF Data Set Library. The Direct Marketing Association, New York, NY, 2002. [http://www.the-dma.org/dmef/dmefdset.shtml]

[2] Domingos, P. MetaCost: A general method for making classifiers cost sensitive. *Proceedings of the 5th International Conference on Knowledge Discovery and Data Mining*, 155-164, 1999.

[3] Drummond, C. & Holte, R. Exploiting the cost (in)sensitivity of decision tree splitting criteria. *Proceedings of the 17th International Conference on Machine Learning*, 239-246, 2000.

[4] Ehrenfeucht, A., Haussler, D., Kearns, M. & Valiant. A general lower bound on the number of examples needed for learning. *Information and Computation*, *82:3*, 247-261, 1989.

[5] Elkan, C. *Boosting and naive bayesian learning* (Technical Report). University of California, San Diego, 1997.

[6] Elkan, C. The foundations of cost-sensitive learning. *Proceedings of the 17th International Joint Conference on Artificial Intelligence*, 973-978, 2001.

[7] Fan, W., Stolfo, S., Zhang, J. & Chan, P. AdaCost: Misclassification cost-sensitive boosting. *Proceedings of the 16th International Conference on Machine Learning*, 97-105, 1999.

[8] Freund, Y. & Schapire, R. E. A decision-theoretic generalization of on-line learning and an application to boosting. *Journal of Computer and System Sciences*, *55:1*, 119-139, 1997.

[9] Hettich, S. & Bay, S. D. The UCI KDD Archive. University of California, Irvine. [http://kdd.ics.uci.edu/].

[10] Joachims, T. Making large-scale SVM learning practical. In *Advances in Kernel Methods - Support Vector Learning*. MIT Press, 1999.

[11] Joachims, T. Estimating the generalization performance of a SVM efficiently. *Proceedings of the 17th International Conference on Machine Learning*, 431-438, 2000.

[12] Kearns, M., Schapire, R., & Sellie, L. Toward Efficient Agnostic Learning. *Machine Learning*, *17*, 115-141, 1998.

[13] Kearns, M. Efficient noise-tolerant learning from statistical queries. *Journal of the ACM*, *45:6*, 983-1006, 1998.

[14] Margineantu, D. Class probability estimation and cost-sensitive classification decisions. *Proceedings of the 13th European Conference on Machine Learning*, 270-281, 2002.

[15] Quinlan, J. R. Boosting, Bagging, and C4.5. *Proceedings of the Thirteenth National Conference on Artificial Intelligence*, 725-730, 1996.

[16] Quinlan, J. R. *C4.5: Programs for Machine Learning*. San Mateo, CA: Morgan Kaufmann, 1993.

[17] Valiant, L. A theory of the learnable. *Communications of the ACM*, *27:11*, 1134-1142, 1984.

[18] von Neumann, J. Various techniques used in connection with random digits, *National Bureau of Standards*, *Applied Mathematics Series*, *12*, 36-38, 1951.

[19] Zadrozny, B. and Elkan, C. Learning and making decisions when costs and probabilities are both unknown. *Proceedings of the 7th International Conference on Knowledge Discovery and Data Mining*, 203-213, 2001.

CBC: Clustering Based Text Classification Requiring Minimal Labeled Data

Hua-Jun Zeng[1] Xuan-Hui Wang[2] Zheng Chen[1] Hongjun Lu[3] Wei-Ying Ma[1]

[1]*Microsoft Research Asia*
Beijing, P. R. China
{i-hjzeng, zhengc,
wyma}@microsoft.com

[2]*University of Science and*
Technology of China,
Anhui Hefei, P. R. China
xhwang6@mail.ustc.edu.cn

[3]*Department of Computer*
Science, HKUST, Clear Water
Bay, Kowloon, Hong Kong
luhj@cs.ust.hk

Abstract

Semi-supervised learning methods construct classifiers using both labeled and unlabeled training data samples. While unlabeled data samples can help to improve the accuracy of trained models to certain extent, existing methods still face difficulties when labeled data is not sufficient and biased against the underlying data distribution. In this paper, we present a clustering based classification (CBC) approach. Using this approach, training data, including both the labeled and unlabeled data, is first clustered with the guidance of the labeled data. Some of unlabeled data samples are then labeled based on the clusters obtained. Discriminative classifiers can subsequently be trained with the expanded labeled dataset. The effectiveness of the proposed method is justified analytically. Our experimental results demonstrated that CBC outperforms existing algorithms when the size of labeled dataset is very small.

1. Introduction

Text classification is a supervised learning task of assigning natural language text documents to one or more predefined categories or classes according to their contents. While it is a classical problem in the field of information retrieval for a half century, it has recently attracted an increasing amount of attention due to the ever-expanding amount of text documents available in digital form. Its applications span a number of areas including auto-processing of emails, filtering junk emails, cataloguing Web pages and news articles, etc. A large number of techniques have been developed for text classification, including Naive Bayes (Lewis 1998), Nearest Neighbor (Masand 1992), neural networks (Ng 1997), regression (Yang 1994), rule induction (Apte 1994), and Support Vector Machines (SVM) (Vapnik 1995, Joachims 1998). Among them SVM has been recognized as one of the most effective text classification methods. Yang & Liu gave a comparative study of many algorithms (Yang 1999).

As supervised learning methods, most existing text classification algorithms require sufficient training data so that the obtained classification model can generalize well.

When the number of training data in each class decreases, the classification accuracy of traditional text classification algorithms degrade dramatically. However, in practical applications, labeled documents are often very sparse because manually labeling data is tedious and costly, while there are often abundant unlabeled documents. As a result, exploiting these unlabeled data in text classification has become an active research problem in text classification recently. The general problem of exploiting unlabeled data in supervised learning leads to a semi-supervised learning or labeled-unlabeled problem in different context.

The problem, in the context of text classification, could be formalized as follows. Each sample text document is represented by a vector $x \in \Re^d$. We are given two datasets D_l and D_u. Dataset D_l is a labeled dataset, consisting of data samples (x_i, t_i), where $1 \leq i \leq n$, and t_i is the class label with $1 \leq t_i \leq c$. Dataset D_u is an unlabeled dataset, consisting of unlabeled sample data x_i, $n+1 \leq i \leq n+m$. The semi-supervised learning task is to construct a classifier with small generalization error on unseen data[1] based on both D_l and D_u. There have been a number of work reported in developing semi-supervised text classification recently, including Co-Training (Blum & Mitchell, 1998), Transductive SVM (TSVM) (Joachims, 1999), and EM (Nigram et al., 2000); and a comprehensive review could be found in Seeger (2001).

While it has been reported that those methods obtain considerable improvement over traditional supervised methods when the size of training dataset is relatively small, our experiments indicated that they still face difficulties when the labeled dataset is *extremely* small, e.g. containing less than 10 labeled examples in each class. This is somehow expected as most of those methods adopt the same iterative approach which train an initial classifier heavily based on the distribution presented in the labeled data. When containing very small number of samples, and the samples are far apart from corresponding class centers due to the high dimensionality, those

---

[1] A transductive setting of this problem just uses seen unlabeled data as testing data.

443

methods will often have a poor starting point and cumulate more errors in iterations. On the other hand, although there are much more unlabeled data sample available which should be more representative, they are not made full use of in the classification process.

The above observation motivated our work reported in this paper. We present CBC, a clustering based approach for text documents classification with both labeled and unlabeled data. The philosophical difference between our approach and existing ones is that, we treat semi-supervised learning as *clustering* aided by the *labeled* data, while the existing algorithms treated it as *classification* aided by the *unlabeled* data. Traditional clustering is unsupervised and requires no training examples. However, the labeled data can provide important hint for the latent class variables. The labeled data also help determine parameters associated with clustering methods, thus impacting on the final clustering result. Furthermore, the label information could be propagated to unlabeled data according to clustering results. The expanded labeled set could be used in subsequent discriminative classifiers to obtain low generalization error on unseen data. Experimental results indicated that our approach outperforms existing approaches, especially when the original labeled dataset is very small.

Our contributions can be summarized as follows. (1) We proposed a novel clustering based classification approach that requires minimal labeled data in the training dataset to achieve high classification accuracy; (2) We provided analysis that gives some insight to the problem and proposed various implementation strategies; (3) We conducted comprehensive experiments to validate our approach and study related issues. The remainder of the paper is organized as follows. Section 2 reviews several existing methods. Our approach is outlined in Section 3 with some analysis. The detailed algorithm is then presented in Section 4. A performance study using several standard text datasets is presented in Section 5. Finally, Section 6 concludes the paper.

2. Semi-Supervised Learning: Motivations

As defined in the previous section, semi-supervised learning uses both the labeled dataset D_l and the unlabeled dataset D_u to construct a classification model. However, how the unlabeled data could help in classification is not a trivial problem. Different methods were proposed according to different view of unlabeled data.

Expectation-Maximization (EM) (Dempster et al, 1977) has a long history in semi-supervised learning. The motivation of EM is as follows. Essentially, any classification method is to learn a conditional probability model $P(t|x,\theta)$, from a certain model family to fit the real joint distribution $P(x, t)$. With unlabeled data, a standard statistical approach to assessing the fitness of learned models $P(t|x,\theta)$ is

$$\sum_{x \in D_l} \log P(x|t_i,\theta)P(t_i) + \sum_{x \in D_u} \log \sum_t P(x|t,\theta)P(t) \quad (1)$$

where the latent labels of unlabeled data are treated as missing variables. Given Eq. 1, a Maximum Likelihood Estimation (MLE) process can be conducted to find an optimal θ. Because the form of likelihood often makes it difficult to maximize by partial derivatives, Expectation-Maximization (EM) algorithm is generally used to find a local optimal θ. For example, Nigram et al. (2000) combined EM with Naive Bayes and got improved performance over supervised classifiers. Theoretically if a θ close to the global optima could be found, the result will also be optimal under the given model family. However, the selection of a plausible model family is difficult, and the local optima problem is serious especially when given a poor starting point. For example, in Nigram's approach, EM is initialized by Naive Bayes classifiers on labeled data, which may be heavily biased when there is no sufficient labeled data.

Co-Training and TSVM methods were proposed more recently and have shown superior performance over EM in many experiments. Co-Training method (Blum & Mitchell, 1998) splits the feature set by $x=(x_1, x_2)$ and trains two classifiers θ_1 and θ_2 each of which is sufficient for classification. With the assumption of compatibility, i.e. $P(t|x_1,\theta_1)= P(t|x_2,\theta_2)$, Co-Training uses unlabeled data to place an additional restriction on the model parameter distribution $P(\theta)$, thus improving the estimation of real θ. The algorithm initially constructs two classifiers based on labeled data, and mutually selects several confident examples to expand the training set. This is based on the assumptions that an initial "weak predictor" could be found and the two feature sets are conditional independent. However, when labeled dataset is small, it is often heavily biased against the real data distribution. The above assumptions will be seriously violated.

TSVM (Joachims, 1999) adopts a totally different way of exploiting the unlabeled data. It maximizes margin over both the labeled data and the unlabeled data. TSVM works by finding a labeling $t_{n+1}, t_{n+2}, ..., t_{n+m}$ of the unlabeled data D_u and a hyperplane $<w, b>$ which separates both D_l and D_u with maximum margin. TSVM expects to find a low-density area of data and constructs a linear separator in this area. Although empirical results indicate the success of the method, there is a concern that the large margin hyperplane over the unlabeled data is not necessary to be the real classification hyperplane (Zhang, 2000). In text classification, because of the high dimensionality and data sparseness, there are often many low-density areas between positive and negative labeled examples.

Instead of using two conditional independent features in the co-training setting, Raskutti (2002) co-trained two SVM classifiers using two feature spaces from different views. One is the original feature space and the other is derived from clustering the labeled and unlabeled data. Nigam K. & Ghani R. (2002) proposed two hybrid algorithms, co-EM and self-training, using two randomly split features in co-training setting. After exhaustive experiments, they found that co-training is better than non-co-training algorithms such as self-training.

As a summary, all existing semi-supervised methods still work in the supervised fashion, that is, they pay more attention to the labeled dataset, and rely on the distribution presented in the labeled dataset heavily. With the help of the unlabeled data, extra information on data distribution can help to improve the generalization performance. However, if the number of samples contained in the labeled data is extremely small, such algorithms may not work well as the labeled data can hardly represent the distribution in unseen data from the beginning. This is often the case for text classification where the dimensionality is very high and a labeled dataset of small size just represents a few isolated points in a huge space. In Figure 1, we depict the results of applying two algorithms to a text classification problem. The X-axis is the number of samples in each class, and the Y-axis is their performance in terms of F_{Micro} that will be defined in Section 5. We can see that the performance of both algorithms degrades dramatically when the number of samples in each class dropped to less than 16.

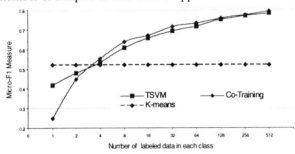

Figure 1. Performance of two existing algorithms with different size of labeled data (No. classes = 5, total number of training data samples = 4000)

In Figure 1, we depict another line, the dotted line, to indicate the performance of using a clustering method, k-means, to cluster the same set of training data. In the experiments, we ignore the labels; hence it represents the performance of unsupervised learning. It is interesting to see that when the number of labeled data in each class is less than 4, unsupervised learning in fact gives better performance than both semi-supervised learning algorithms. This motivated us to develop a clustering based approach to the problem of semi-supervised learning.

3. Clustering Based Classification

Our approach clusters the unlabeled data with the guidance of labeled data first. With those clusters, some originally unlabeled data can be viewed as labeled data with high confidence. Such an expanded labeled dataset can be subsequently used in classification algorithms to construct the final classification model.

3.1. The Basic Approach

CBC consists of the following two steps:
1. **Clustering step**: to cluster the training dataset including both the labeled and unlabeled data and expand the labeled set according to the clustering result;
2. **Classification step**: to train classifiers with the expanded labeled data and remaining unlabeled data.

Figure 2 gives an example to illustrate the traditional approach and our clustering based approach, respectively. The black points and grey points in the Figure represent data samples of two different classes. We have very small number of labeled data, e.g. one for each class, represented by the points with "+" and "−" signs. Apparently, a classification algorithm trained with these two points will most likely find line A as shown in Figure 2(a) as the class boundary; and it's also rather difficult to

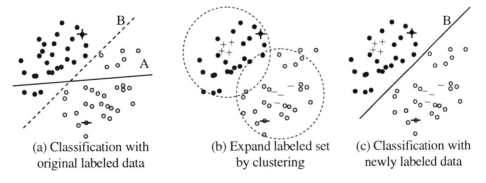

| (a) Classification with | (b) Expand labeled set | (c) Classification with |
| original labeled data | by clustering | newly labeled data |

Figure 2. An illustrative example of clustering based classification. The black and gray data points are unlabeled examples. The big "+" and "−" are two initially labeled example, and small "+" and "−" are examples expanded by clustering.

discover the real boundary B even with the help of those unlabeled data points. Firstly, because the initial labeled samples are highly biased, they will cause poor starting points for iterative reinforcement algorithms such as Co-Training and EM. Moreover, TSVM algorithm may also take line A as the result because it happens to lie in a low density area.

Our clustering based approach is shown in Figure 2(b) and (c). During the first step, a clustering algorithm is applied to the training samples. In the example, it results in two clusters. Then we propagate the labels of the labeled data samples to the unlabeled samples which are closest to cluster centroids. As a result, we have more labeled data samples, as shown in Figure 2(b). The second step of the approach is to use the expanded labeled data and remaining unlabeled data to train a classifier. As the result, we can obtain the better class boundary, as shown in Figure 2(c).

From the above description, we can see that, our approach aims to combining the merits of both clustering and classification methods. That is, we use clustering method to reduce the impact of the bias caused by the initial sparse labeled data. At the same time, with sufficient expanded labeled data, we can use discriminative classifiers to achieve better generalization performance than pure clustering methods.

3.2. Benefits of the Clustering Based Approach

In this subsection, we further analyze the benefit of integrating clustering into the classification process.

First, clustering methods are more robust to the bias caused by the initial sparse labeled data. Let us take k-means, the most popular clustering algorithm as an example. In essence, k-means is a simplified version of EM working on spherical Gaussian distribution models. They can be approximately described by MLE of k spherical Gaussian distributions, where the means μ_1, …, μ_k and the identical covariances Σ are latent variables. Thus with the aid of labeled data, the objective is to find an optimal $\theta = <\mu_1, …, \mu_k, \Sigma>$ to maximize the log-likelihood of Eq. 1, where the $P(x|t_i, \theta)$ equals to

$$\frac{1}{(2\pi)^{d/2} \cdot |\Sigma|^{1/2}} \cdot \exp(-\frac{1}{2}(x - \mu_i)^T \Sigma^{-1}(x - \mu_i)) \quad (2)$$

When the number of labeled examples is small, the bias of labeled example will not affect much the likelihood estimation and the finding of the optimal θ.

Second, our clustering method is in fact a generative classifier, i.e., it constructs a classifier derived from the generative model of its data $P(x|t, \theta)$. Ng & Jordan theoretically and empirically analyzed the asymptotic performance of generative classifier and discriminative classifier (such as logistic regression, which is a general form of SVM). They showed that generative classifiers

reach their asymptotic performance faster than discriminative classifiers (Ng & Jordan 2002). Thus our clustering method is more effective with small training data; and easier to achieve high performance when the labeled data is sparse. To address the problem that generative classifiers usually lead to higher asymptotic error than discriminative classifiers, discriminative classification method such as TSVM can be used in the second step of our approach, i.e., after clustering unlabeled data and expanding the labeled data set.

Our clustering is guided by labeled data. Generally, clustering methods address the issue of finding a partition of available data which maximizes a certain criterion, e.g. intra-cluster similarity and inter-cluster dissimilarity. The labeled data could be used to modify the criterion. There are also some parameters associated with each clustering algorithm, e.g. the number k in k-means, or split strategy of dendrogram in hierarchical clustering. The labeled data can also be used to guide the selection of these parameters. In our current implementation, we use the *soft-constraint* version of k-means algorithm for clustering, where k is equal to the number of classes in the given labeled data set. The detailed algorithm is described in Section 4.

3.3. Combining Clustering with Classification

After the clustering step, we select from unlabeled data examples that are confidently clustered (i.e. examples with high likelihood) and combine them with original labeled data to train the classifier. Because more labeled data are used, the obtained classifier is expected to be more accurate.

One key issue here is how to expand the labeled dataset. In principle, we can just assign the label to the most confident $p\%$ of examples from each of the resulting clusters. If we choose $p=100\%$ after first clustering process, all data are used as labeled data to train a classifier.

First, we need to determine the value of p. The selection of p is a tradeoff between the number of labeled samples and possible noise introduced by the labeling error. Obviously, with higher p, a large labeled dataset will be obtained. In general, a classifier with higher accuracy can be obtained with more training samples. On the other hand, when we expand more samples, we might introduce incorrectly labeled samples into the labeled dataset, which become noise and will degrade the performance of a classification algorithm. The selection of p will be described in the experiment.

Second, we need to choose "confident examples". Note that any learned model is an estimation of the real data model $P(x,t)$. We can find examples that are confidently classified by a given model if a slightly change of θ has no impact on them. When more examples are given, the model estimation will become more accurate, and the number of confident examples will grow.

As illustrated in Figure 2 (a) and (b), even when some of the data points are wrongly classified, the most confident data points, i.e. the ones nearest to the centroid under clustering model, are confidently classified. That is, a slightly change the centroid will not affect the label of these data.

We assume that class labels t are uniformly distributed. Since the Gaussian is spherical, the log-likelihood of a given data point and the estimated label is

$$\log(P(x^*, t^* | \theta)) = \log(P(x^* | t^*, \theta) P(t^* | \theta) = -c_1 \|x - \mu^*\|^2 + c_2 \quad (3)$$

where c_1 and c_2 are positive constants. Thus the most confident examples are the ones which minimize $\|x - \mu^*\|^2$, i.e. the ones which are nearest to the centroid.

4. The Algorithm

In this section, we present the detailed algorithm when CBC is applied to text data, which is generally represented by sparse term vectors in a high dimensional space. Following the traditional IR approach, we tokenize all documents into terms and construct one component for each distinct term. Thus each document is represented by a vector $(w_{i1}, w_{i2}, ..., w_{id})$ where w_{ij} is weighted by TFIDF (Salton, 1991), i.e. $w_{ij} = TF_{ij} \times \log(N / DF_j)$, where N is total number of documents.

Assuming the term vectors are normalized, cosine function is a commonly used similarity measure for two documents: $sim(doc_j, doc_k) = \sum_{t=1}^{d} w_{ij} \cdot w_{ik}$. This measure is also used in the clustering algorithm to calculate the distance from an example to a centroid (which is also normalized).

This simple representation proves to be efficient for supervised learning (Joachims, 1998), e.g. in most tasks they are linear separable. For the classification step, we use a TSVM classifier with a linear kernel. The detailed algorithm is presented as following table.

During the clustering step, a *soft-constrained* version of k-means is used. We compute the centroids of the labeled data for each class (which is called "labeled centroids") and use them as the initial centroids for k-means. The k value is set to the number of classes in the labeled data. Then we run k-means on both labeled and unlabeled data. The loop is terminated when clustering result doesn't change anymore, or just before a labeled centroid being assigned to a wrong cluster. This sets "soft constraints" on clustering because the constraints are not based on exact examples but on their centroid. The constraints will reduce bias in the labeled examples. Finally, unlabeled data are assigned the same labels as labeled centroid in the same cluster.

Algorithm CBC

Input:
- Labeled data set D_l
- Unlabeled data set D_u.

Output:
- The full labeled set $D_l' = D_l + (D_u, T_u^*)$
- A classifier L

1. Initialize current labeled and unlabeled set $D_l' = D_l$, $D_u' = D_u$
2. Clustering Step
   - Calculate initial centroids $o_i = \sum_{\forall j, t_j = i} x_j$, $i=1...c$, $x_j \in D_l$, and set current centroids $o_i^* = o_i$.
   - The label of the centroids $t(o_i) = t(o_i^*)$ are equal to labels of the corresponding examples.
   - Repeat until cluster result doesn't change any more
     - Calculate the nearest centroids o_j^* for each o_i. If $t(o_i) \neq t(o_j^*)$, exit the loop.
     - Assign $t(o_i^*)$ to each $x_i \in D_l + D_u$ that are nearer to o_i^* than to other centroids.
     - Update current centroids $o_i^* = \sum_{\forall j, t_j = i} x_j$, $i=1...c$, $x_j \in D_l + D_u$.
   - From each cluster, select $p\%$ examples $x_i \in D_u'$ which is nearest to o_i^*, and add them to D_l'.
3. Classification Step
   - Train a TSVM classifier based on D_l' and D_u'.
   - Classify all unlabeled examples $x_i \in D_u'$ and add them to D_l'.

After clustering, we select the most confident examples (i.e. examples nearest to cluster centroids) to form a new labeled set, together with the remaining unlabeled data, to train a TSVM classifier. It should be noted that the time complexity of a TSVM classifier is much higher than that of a SVM classifier. When there is no unlabeled data, TSVM becomes a pure SVM and runs much faster. In our algorithm, if $p=100\%$ the classification is done by a standard SVM classifier.

5. A Performance Study

To evaluate the effectiveness of our approach, comprehensive performance study has been conducted using several standard text dataset.

5.1. Datasets

Three commonly used datasets, 20-Newsgroups, Reuters-21578, and Open Directory Project (ODP) webpages were used in our experiments. For each document, we extract features from its title and body separately for Co-Training algorithm, and extract a single feature vector from both title and body for all other algorithms. Stop-words are eliminated and stemming is performed for all features. TFIDF is then used to index both titles and bodies, where IDF is calculated only based on the training dataset. The words that appear only in the test dataset but not in the train dataset are discarded.

From the 20-Newsgroups dataset[2], we only select the five comp.* discussion groups, which forms a very confusing but evenly distributed dataset for classification, i.e. there are almost 1000 articles in each group. We choose 80% of each group as training set and the remaining 20% as test set, which give us 4000 train examples and 1000 test examples. Such a split is similar to what used in Nigam K. & Ghani R. (2002). After preprocessing, there are 14,171 distinct terms, with 14,059 in body feature, and 2,307 in title feature.

The dataset Reuters-21578 is downloaded from Yiming Yang's homepage[3]. We use the ModApte split to form the training set and test set, where there are 7,769 training examples and 3,019 test examples. From the whole dataset, we select the biggest ten classes: *earn, acq, money-fx, grain, crude, trade, interest, ship, wheat,* and *corn*. After selecting the biggest ten classes, there are 6,649 training examples and 2,545 test examples. After preprocessing, there are only 7,771 distinct terms, with 7,065 in body feature and 6,947 in title feature respectively.

The ODP webpages dataset used in our experiments is composed of the biggest six classes in the second level of ODP directory[4]: *Business/Management* (858 documents), *Computers/Software* (2,411), *Shopping/Crafts* (877) *Shopping/Home&Garden* (1,170), *Society/Religion &Spirituality* (886), and *Society/ Holidays* (881). We select 50% of each category as the training data and the remainder as the test data. From the experiment result below, we can see that there is only a small difference between 90% and 50%. The webpages are preprocessed by a HTML parser and pure text is extracted. After preprocessing, there are 16,818 distinct terms on body, 3,729 on title and 17,050 on title+body.

The Jochims's SVM-light package[5] is used for SVM and TSVM classification. We use a linear kernel and set the weight *C* of the slack variables to default. The basic classifiers for the two feature sets in the Co-Training method are Naive Bayes. During each iteration, we add 1% of examples with the maximal classification confidence, i.e. examples with largest margin, into the labeled set. And the performance is evaluated on the combined features.

[2] Available at http://www.ai.mit.edu/people/jrennie/20Newsgroups/.
[3] http://www-2.cs.cmu.edu/~yiming/
[4] http://dmoz.org/
[5] Available at http://svmlight.joachims.org/.

5.2. Evaluation Metrics

We use micro-averaging of F1 measure among all classes to evaluate the classification result.

Since it is a multi-classification problem, the TSVM or SVM in our algorithm construct several one-to-many binary classifiers. For each class $i \in [1,c]$, let A_i be the number of documents whose real label is i, and B_i the number of documents whose label is predicted to be i, and C_i the number of correctly predicted examples in this class. The precision and recall of the class i are defined as $P_i = C_i/B_i$ and $R_i = C_i/A_i$ respectively.

F1 Measure could be used to combine precision and recall into a unified measure. Because of the difference of F1 for different classes, two averaging functions could be used to judge the combined performance. The first is *macro-averaging*:

$$FI_{macro} = \frac{1}{c} \cdot \sum_{i=1}^{c} \frac{2 \times P_i \times R_i}{P_i + R_i} \qquad (4)$$

The second averaging function is *micro-averaging*, which first calculates the total precision and recall on all classes $P = \Sigma C_i/\Sigma B_i$ and $R = \Sigma C_i/\Sigma A_i$, and the F1 measure is:

$$FI_{micro} = \frac{2 \times P \times R}{P + R} \qquad (5)$$

Because the micro-averaging of F1 is in fact a weighted average over all classes, which is more plausible for highly unevenly distributed classes, we use this measure in the following experiments.

5.3. Results

We first evaluate our algorithms and compare them with TSVM and Co-Training on 5 comp.* newsgroups data set (See Figure 3). In our algorithm, we set the parameter *p* to 100%, which means to propagate label information to all the examples. This is because in most of our experiment the classification performance of *p*=100% is higher than that of any other *p*<100%.

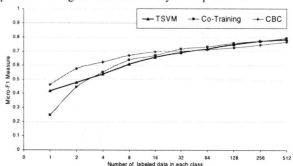

Figure 3. Comparative study of TSVM, Co-Training, and our algorithm CBC when given small training data on 5 comp. newsgroups data set.*

The algorithms run several rounds with the number of labeled examples ranging from 1, 2, 4, 8, ..., 512 per class. For each number of labeled data, we randomly choose 10 sets to test the three methods, and draw the average of them on Figure 3.

From Figure 3, we can see that when the number of the labeled data is very small, CBC performs significantly better than the other algorithms. For example, when the number of the labeled data in each class is 1, our method outperforms TSVM by 5% and Co-Training by 22%; when the number is 2, our method outperforms TSVM by 9% and Co-Training by 12%. Only when the number of the labeled samples exceeds 64, the performances of TSVM and Co-Training achieves a slightly better performance than our method.

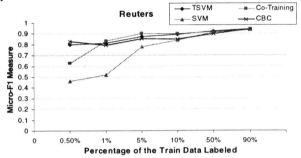

Figure 4. Micro-F1 of four algorithms on the Reuters data set

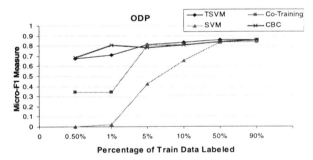

Figure 5. Micro-F1 of four algorithms on the ODP data set

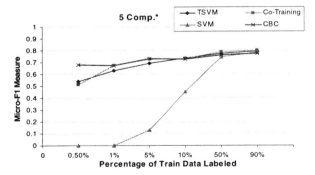

Figure 6. Micro-F1 of four algorithms on the 5 comp.* newsgroups data set

To evaluate the performance of CBC with a large range of labeled data, we run the same algorithm together with TSVM, Co-Training and SVM on different percentage of the labeled data on the above 3 datasets. Figure 4, 5, and 6 illustrate the results. The horizontal axis indicates the percentage of the labeled data in all training data, and the vertical axis is the value of Micro-F1 measure. We vary the percentage from 0.50% to 90%. The performance of a basic SVM which do not exploit unlabeled data is always the worst because the labeled data is too sparse for SVM to effectively generalize.

In all datasets, CBC performs best when labeled data percentage is less than 1%. When the number of labeled documents increases, the performance of our algorithm is still comparative to other methods. The Co-Training algorithm has low performance when training data is small because it is based on the assumptions that an initial "weak predictor" could be found. When training data is rather small, it is often largely biased against the real data distribution. However, Co-Training sometimes got superior result than others, especially in Figure 4 which uses Reuters dataset, because it exploits the feature split to form two views of the training data. In Figure 4, 5, and 6, TSVM always has an intermediate performance between Co-Training and our algorithm.

One limitation of our algorithm is that with the increase of labeled data, the performance grows slowly, and sometimes will drop (as in Figure 4 based on Reuters set). This could be explained by the simple method of integration of labeled examples in the clustering step. In fact, labeled examples can not only provide constraints of the clustering, but are also used to modify the similarity measure. We hope this can be further evaluated in future works.

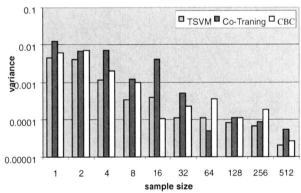

Figure 7. Variance of different algorithms given different labeled data size (each calculated over 10 randomly selected samples).

Finally we evaluate the stability of the algorithms by the variance of the three algorithms calculated over 10 randomly selected examples under different sample size (see Figure 7). This experiment is also conducted on 5 comp.* newsgroups. As can be seen from Figure 7, generally the TSVM algorithm has smallest variance and Co-Training has largest variance. It is natural to understand the large variance of Co-Training, as the reason mentioned before that the initial labeled data has large impact on the initial weak predictor. The variance of our algorithm is lower than Co-Training but higher than TSVM. It is mainly because our simple version of constrained k-means algorithm may also fall into a local minimal given a poor starting point.

6. Conclusion and Future Work

This paper presented a clustering based approach for semi-supervised text classification. The experiments showed the superior performance of our method over existing methods such as TSVM and Co-Training, when labeled data size is very small. When there is sufficient labeled data, our method is comparable to TSVM and Co-Training.

To the best of our knowledge, no work has been focused on clustering examples aided by labeled data has been reported. Some works on constraint clustering (Wagstaff et al., 2001; Klein et al., 2002) could be considered most relevant ones. They use prior knowledge in the form of cannot-link and must-link constraints to guide clustering algorithms. While in our case, the labeled data provide not only these constraints but also label information which could be exploited to assign labels for unlabeled data.

The constrained clustering method in this paper may not be sophisticated enough to capturer all information carried in labeled data. We plan to evaluate other clustering methods and further adjust the similarity measure with the aid of labeled examples.

7. References

[1] Apte, C., Damerau, F., & Weiss, S.M. (1994) Automated learning of decision rules for text categorization. ACM TOIS, Vol 12, No. 3. 223-251

[2] Bhavani Raskutti, Herman Ferra, & Adam Kowalczyk. (2002). Combining Clustering and Co-Training to enhance text classification using unlabeled data. In Proceedings of the SIGKDD Conference.

[3] Blum, A. & Mitchell, T. (1998). Combining labeled and unlabeled data with Co-Training. In Proceedings of the 11th COLT Conference (pp. 92-100).

[4] Dempster, A. P., Laird, N.M., & Rubin, D. B. (1977). Maximum likelihood from incomplete data via the EM algorithm. Journal of the Royal Statistical Society, Series B, 39(1), 1-38.

[5] Joachims, T. (1998). Text categorization with support vector machines: Learning with Many Relevant Features. In Proceedings of the ECML'98 (pp. 137--142).

[6] Joachims, T. (1998). Text categorization with support vector machines: Learning with many relevant features. In Proceedings of ECML'98.

[7] Joachims, T. (1999). Transductive inference for text classification using support vector machines. In Proceedings of 16th ICML Conference (pp. 200-209).

[8] Klein, D., Kamvar, S. D., & Maning, C. D. (2002). From instance-level constraints to space-level constraints: making the most of prior kowldege in data clustering. In Proceedings of the 19th ICML Conference.

[9] Lewis, D.D (1998). Naive Bayes at forty: The independence assumption in information retrieval. In Proceedings of ECML'98.

[10] Masand, B., Linoff, G., & Waltz, D. (1992). Classifying news stories using memory based reasoning. In Proceedings of the 15th ACM SIGIR Conference, 59-64.

[11] Ng, A. Y., & Jordan, M. I. (2002). On discriminative vs. generative classifiers: A comparison of logistic regression and naive Bayes. Advances in Neural Information Processing Systems 14.

[12] Ng, T.H., Goh, W.B., & Low, K.L. (1997). Feature selection, perception learning and a usability case study for text categorization. In Proceedings of the 20th SIGIR Conference.

[13] Nigam K. & Ghani R. (2002). Analyzing the effectiveness and applicability of co-training. In Proceedings of 9th CIKM Conference.

[14] Nigam, K., McCallurn, A. K., Thrun, S. & Mitchell, T. (2000). Text classification from labeled and unlabeled documents using EM. Machine Learning, 39(2/3):103-134.

[15] Salton, G. (1991). Developments in automatic text retrieval. Science, 253:974-979.

[16] Seeger, M. (2001). Learning with labeled and unlabeled data. Technical report, Edinburgh University.

[17] Vapnik, V. N. (1995). The nature of statistical learning theory. New York: Springer-Verlag.

[18] Wagstaff, K., Cardie, C., Rogers, S., & Caruana, R. (2001). Constrained k-means clustering with background knowledge. In Proceedings of the 18th ICML Conference.

[19] Yang, Y. & Chute, C.G. (1994). An example-based mapping method for text categorization and retrieval. ACM TOIS, Vol 12, No. 3, 252-277.

[20] Yang, Y. & Liu, X. (1999). An re-examination of text categorization. In Proceedings of the 22th ACM SIGIR Conference.

[21] Zhang, T. & Oles, F. (2000). A probability analysis on the value of unlabeled data for classification problems. In Proceedings of the 17th ICML Conference.

Regression Clustering

Bin Zhang

Hewlett-Packard Research Laboratories, Palo Alto, CA 94304

bzhang@hpl.hp.com

Abstract

Complex distribution in real-world data is often modeled by a mixture of simpler distributions. Clustering is one of the tools to reveal the structure of this mixture. The same is true to the datasets with chosen response variables that people run regression on. Without separating the clusters with very different response properties, the residue error of the regression is large. Input variable selection could also be misguided to a higher complexity by the mixture. In Regression Clustering (RC), K (>1) regression functions are applied to the dataset simultaneously which guide the clustering of the dataset into K subsets each with a simpler distribution matching its guiding function. Each function is regressed on its own subset of data with a much smaller residue error. Both the regressions and the clustering optimize a common objective function. We present a RC algorithm based on K-Harmonic Means clustering algorithm and compare it with other existing RC algorithms based on K-Means and EM.

1. Introduction

Two important data mining techniques are regression on the datasets with chosen response variables, and clustering on the datasets that do not have response information. The RC algorithm handles the case in between: the datasets that have response variables but they do not contain enough information to guarantee high quality learning, the missing part of the response is essential. Missing information is generally caused by insufficiently controlled data collection, due to a lack of means, a lack of understanding or other reasons. For example, sales or marketing data collected on all customers may not have the label on a proper segmentation of the customers.

Clustering algorithms partition (hard or soft) a dataset into a finite number of subsets each containing similar data points. Dissimilarity labeled by the index of the partitions provides additional supervision to the K regressions running in parallel so that each regression works on a subset of similar data. The K regressions in turn provide the model of dissimilarity for clustering to partition the data. The linkage is a common objective function minimized by both the regressions and the clustering. Neither can be properly performed alone.

The concept of regression clustering is not new. A number of earlier papers are reviewed in the next section. This paper adds a new member, Regression-K-Harmonic Means clustering, to the family of RC algorithms and compares its performance with others.

1.1. Related Previous Work

Regression clustering has been studied under a number of different names: *Clusterwise Linear Regression* in Spath [14-17], DeSarbo and Cron [2], Hennig [6-8] and others; *Trajectory clustering using mixtures of regression models* by Gaffney and Smith [4]; *Fitting Regression Model to Finite Mixtures* by Williams [20]; *Clustered Partial Linear Regression* by Torgo [19]. We choose the name Regression-Clustering because a) RC is not limited to linear regressions; b) Comparing RC with center-based clustering algorithms, KM, KHM, and EM, the centers are replaced by regression functions -- RCs are just regression-function-centered clustering algorithms; c) By examining the computational structure, the clustering algorithm represents the main (outer) loop or the overall program structure, and the regression is called only as a subroutine to update the "centers".

Clusterwise Linear Regression by Spath [14-17] used linear regression and partition of the dataset in his algorithm that locally minimize the total mean square error over all K-regression (Eq. (2)). He also developed an incremental version to allow adding new observations into the dataset. Spath's algorithm is based on *K-means* clustering algorithm. DeSarbo [2] used maximum likelyhood methodology for performing clusterwise linear regression, locally minimizing the objective function (Eq. (16)). A marketing application is presented in his paper. We will briefly introduce the details of his work in section 6 for comparison. Hennig continued the research of Clustered Linear Regression using the same linear mixing of Gaussian density functions. The number of clusters in his work is treated as unknown. Gaffney and

Smyth's work [4] is also based on EM clustering algorithm.

1.2. Contributions of This Paper

Previous work on RC used K-Means and EM in their algorithms, these RC algorithms will have the same well-known problem of being sensitive to the initialization of the regression functions as the K-Means and EM being sensitive to the initialization of the centers.

The author developed a center-based clustering algorithm, K-Harmonic Means, which is much less sensitive to initialization of centers. It is demonstrated through a large number of experiments on randomly generated datasets that KHM converges to better local optimum than K-Means and EM, measured by a common objective function of K-Means (Zhang [23][24]).

In this paper, we add a new algorithm RC-KHM to the family of RC algorithms (Section 4 and 5), provide performance comparisons of the three RC algorithms based on extensive experimental results (Section 11 and **Fig. 5.**), and give an interpretation of the K-regression functions as a predictor and its combination with a K-way classifier (Section 10).

The rest of the paper is organized in sections as: Section 2, defining the problem; Section 3 and 4, the RC-KM and its special case LinReg-KM. Section 5 and 6, the new RC-K-Harmonic Means and its special case LinReg-KHM; Section 7 and 8, the RC-Expectation Maximiza-tion algorithm and LinReg-EM; Section 9, computational costs; Section 10, probability interpretation of the K re-gression functions as predictors; Section 11, experimental results and comparisons; Section 12, Conclusions.

2. The Problem

Given a dataset with supervising responses, $Z = (X, Y) = \{(x_i, y_i) \mid i = 1, ..., N\}$, a (constrained) family of functions $\Phi = \{f\}$ and an loss function $e() \geq 0$, regression solves the following minimization problem,

$$f^{opt} = \arg\min_{f \in \Phi} \sum_{i=1}^{N} e(f(x_i), y_i) \qquad (1)$$

Usually, $\Phi = \{\sum_{l=1}^{m} \beta_l h(x, a_l) \mid \beta_l \in R, a_l \in R^n\}$, linear expansions of simple parametric functions such as polynomials of degree up to m, Fourier series of bounded frequency, neural networks, RBF, ... Usually, $e(f(x), y) = \| f(x) - y \|^p$, with $p=1,2$ most widely used. (1) is not effective when the data set contains a mixture of very different response characteristics as

shown in **Fig. 1a**. It is much better to find the partitions in the data and learn a separate function on each partition as shown in **Fig. 1b**.

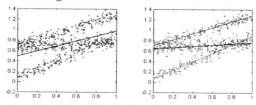

Fig. 1: a) Left: a single function is regressed on all training data which is a mixture of three different distributions.   b) Right: three regression functions, each regressed on a subset found by RC.   The residue errors are much smaller.

We assume that there are K partitions in the data. Determining the right K has been discussed in the clustering context [5][18], which still applies under our new setting. K can also be determined (or bounded) by other aspects of the original problem.

In RC algorithms, K regression functions $M = \{f_1, ..., f_K\} \subset \Phi$ are applied to the data, each of which finds a partition Z_k and regress on it. Both parts of the process -- the K regressions and the partitioning of the dataset – optimize a common objective function. The partition of the dataset can be a "soft" partition given by K density functions defined on the dataset.

3. The RC-KM Algorithm

Clusterwise Linear Regression [14] is the simplest RC algorithm. We review it as an introduction to RC. The K regressions do not have to be linear.

RC-KM solves the following optimization problem,

$$\min_{\{f_k\} \subset \Phi; \{Z_k\}} Perf_{RC-KM} = \sum_{k=1}^{K} \sum_{(x_i, y_i) \in Z_k} e(f_k(x_i), y_i), \ (2)$$

where $Z = \bigcup_{k=1}^{K} Z_k$ $(Z_k \cap Z_{k'} = \varnothing, k \neq k')$. The optimization is over both the K regression functions and the partition. The optimal partition will satisfy

$$Z_k = \{(x, y) \in Z \mid e(f_k^{opt}(x), y) \leq e(f_{k'}^{opt}(x), y) \quad \forall k' \neq k\}, (3)$$

which allows us to replace the function in (2) by

$$Perf_{RC-KM}(Z, \{f_k\}_{k=1}^{K}) = \sum_{i=1}^{N} MIN\{e(f_k(x_i), y_i) \mid k=1, ..., K\} (4)$$

RC-KM Algorithm, a monotone-convergent algorithm to find a local optimum of (2):

Step1: Pick K functions $f_1^{(0)}, ..., f_K^{(0)} \in \Phi$ randomly, or by any heuristics that are believed to give a good start.

452

Step2: Clustering Phase: In the *r*-th iteration, *r=1, 2, …,* repartition the dataset as

$$Z_k^{(r)} = \{(x,y) \in Z \mid e(f_k^{(r-1)}(x), y) \le e(f_{k'}^{(r-1)}(x), y) \quad \forall k' \ne k\}. \quad (5)$$

(A tie can be resolved randomly among the winners.) Intuitively, each data point is associated with the regression function that gives the smallest approximation error on it. Algorithmically, a data point in $Z_k^{(r-1)}$ is moved to $Z_{k'}^{(r)}$ iff $e(f_{k'}^{(r-1)}(x), y) < e(f_k^{(r-1)}(x), y)$ and $e(f_{k'}^{(r-1)}(x), y) \le e(f_{k''}^{(r-1)}(x), y)$ for all $k'' \ne k, k'$. $Z_k^{(r)}$ gets all the data points in $Z_k^{(r-1)}$ that are not moved.

Step3: Regression Phase: Run any regression optimization algorithm that gives the following

$$f_k^{(r)} = \arg\min_{f \in \Phi} \sum_{(x_i, y_i) \in Z_k} e(f(x_i), y_i) \text{ for } k = 1, …, K. \quad (6)$$

(The regression algorithm is selected by the nature of the original problem or other criteria. RC adds no additional constraint on its selection.)

Step4: Stopping Rule: Run Step 2 and Step 3 repeatedly until there is no more data points changing its membership.

Step 2 and Step 3 never increase the value of the objective function in (2). If any data changes its member-ship in Step 2, the objective function is strictly decreased. Therefore, the algorithm stops in finite number of iterations.

4. MSE Linear Regression with K-Means Clustering -- LinReg-KM

With $\bar{D}$ functions $h_1(x), …, h_{\bar{D}}(x)$ chosen as the basis, we consider the function class $\Phi = \{\sum_{l=1}^{\bar{D}} c_l h_l(x) \mid c_l \in R\}$. To simplify the notations, let $\bar{x} = (h_1(x), … , h_{\bar{D}}(x))$ and $\bar{X} = [\bar{x}_i]_{N \times \bar{D}}$. As an example, for the set of two-variable (*D=2*) polynomials up to degree 2, the basis functions are $h_1(x) = 1$, $h_2(x) = x_1$, $h_3(x) = x_2$, $h_4(x) = x_1^2$, $h_5(x) = x_1 x_2$, $h_6(x) = x_2^2$. We have

$$\bar{X} = \begin{bmatrix} 1 & x_{1,1} & x_{1,2} & x_{1,1}^2 & x_{1,1}x_{1,2} & x_{1,2}^2 \\ … & … & … & … & … & … \\ 1 & x_{N,1} & x_{N,2} & x_{N,1}^2 & x_{N,1}x_{N,2} & x_{N,2}^2 \end{bmatrix}.$$

With the MSE $e(f(x), y) = |f(x) - y|^2$, LinReg-KM minimizes the objective function

$$Perf_{LinReg-KM}(Z, \{f_k\}_{k=1}^K) = \sum_{i=1}^N \min_{1 \le k \le K} \{\| \bar{x}_i * c_k - y_i \|^2\}.$$

With row-partition of Z into K subsets $Z_1, …, Z_K$, matrices $\bar{X}$ and Y are row-partitioned accordingly, $\bar{X} \to \bar{X}_1, …, \bar{X}_K$ and $Y \to Y_1, …, Y_K$, the coefficients of the optimal function on the *k*-th subset is (Step 3 of the RC-KM)

$$c_k = (\bar{X}_k^T * \bar{X}_k)^{-1} \bar{X}_k^T * Y_k. \quad (7)$$

The matrix of losses used for the comparisons in Step 2 of RC-KM is

$$E = [e(f_k(x_i), y_i)]_{N \times K} = abs(\bar{X} * [c_1, …, c_K] - [Y, …, Y]). \quad (8)$$

(squaring is monotone and not necessary.)

5. RC-K-Harmonic Means Algorithm (RC-KHM)

K-Means clustering algorithm is known to be sensitive to the initialization of its centers. The same is true for RC-KM. Convergence to a poor local optimum has been observed quite frequently (See **Fig 5**).

K-Harmonic Means clustering algorithm showed very strong insensitivity to initialization due to its dynamic weighting of the data points (Zhang 2001, 2003). The regression clustering algorithm RC-KHM$_p$ is presented in this section. It is shown experimentally that it out-performs RC-KM and RC-EM.

RC-KHM$_p$'s objective function is defined by replacing the *MIN()* function in (4) by the harmonic average *HA()*. The error function is $e(f_k(x_i), y_i) = \| f_k(x_i) - y_i \|^p$, $p \ge 2$,

$$Perf_{RC-KHM_p}(Z, M) = \sum_{i=1}^N HA_{1 \le k \le K} \{\| f_k(x_i) - y_i \|^p\} = \sum_{i=1}^N \frac{K}{\sum_{k=1}^K \frac{1}{\| f_k(x_i) - y_i \|^p}} \quad (9)$$

An iterative algorithm (see Zhang 2001) is available for finding a local optimum of (9).

RC-KHM Algorithm:

Step 1: Pick K functions $f_1^{(0)}, …, f_K^{(0)} \in \Phi$ randomly.

Step 2: Clustering Phase: In the *r*-th iteration, let

$$d_{i,k} = \| f_k^{(r-1)}(x_i) - y_i \|. \quad (10)$$

a) The hard partition $Z = \bigcup_{k=1}^K Z_k$, in RC-KM, is replaced by a "soft" membership function – the *i*-th data point is associated with the *k*-th regression function with probability

$$p(Z_k \mid z_i) = d_{i,k}^{p+q} / \sum_{l=1}^K d_{i,l}^{p+q}. \quad (11)$$

The choice of q (>=*1*) will put the regression's error function in L^q-space. See (13). (This is more general than the *K*-Harmonic Means clustering algorithm presented before, which had $q = 2$.) For simpler notations, we do not index $p(Z_k | z_i)$ and $a_p(z_i)$ in (12) by q. Quantities $d_{i,k}$, $p(Z_k | z_i)$, and $a_p(z_i)$ should be indexed by the iteration r, which is also dropped.

b) In RC-KHM, not all data points fully participate in all iterations like in RC-KM. Each data point's participation is weighted by

$$a_p(z_i) = \sum_{l=1}^{K} d_{i,l}^{p+q} \Big/ \sum_{l=1}^{K} d_{i,l}^{p} . \qquad (12)$$

$a_p(z_i)$ is small if and only if z_i is close to one of the functions (i.e. done for it). Weighting function $a_p(z_i)$ changes in each iteration as the regression functions are updated. If all functions drifted away from a point z_i in the last iteration, $a_p(z_i)$ goes up. More details on this weighting function are in (Zhang 2001).

Step 3: Regression Phase: Run any regression optimization algorithm that gives the following

$$f_k^{(r)} = \arg\min_{f \in \Phi} \sum_{i=1}^{N} a_p(z_i) p(Z_k | z_i) \| f(x_i) - y_i \|^q$$

for $k = 1, ..., K$. $\qquad (13)$

Step 4: Since there is no discrete membership change in RC-KHM, the stopping rule is replaced by measuring the changes to its objective function (9), when the change is smaller than a threshold, the iteration is stopped.

6. Linear Regression with K-Harmonic Means Clustering -- LinReg-KHM

For linear regression, we choose $q=2$. Writing (13) in matrix form, we have

$$c_k^{(r)} = \arg\min_{c} \left(\bar{X} * c - Y \right)^T * diag_{1 \le i \le N} \left(a_p(z_i) p(Z_k | z_i) \right) * \left(\bar{X} * c - Y \right) \qquad (14)$$

and its solution is

$$c_k^{(r)} = \left(\bar{X}^T * \left[\bar{x}_i \Big/ d_{i,k}^{p+2} \left(\sum_{l=1}^{K} \frac{1}{d_{i,l}^p} \right)^2 \right]_{N \times \bar{D}} \right)^{-1} * \bar{X}^T * \left[y_i \Big/ d_{i,k}^{p+2} \left(\sum_{l=1}^{K} \frac{1}{d_{i,l}^p} \right)^2 \right]_{N \times \bar{D}} \qquad (15)$$

where $d_{i,k} = \| \bar{x}_i * c_k^{(r-1)} - y_i \|$. $([\alpha]_{N \times \bar{D}}$ is a matrix of size $N \times \bar{D}$ with entries α being one of three possibilities: row vectors, column vectors or scalars.) The inversion in (15) is on a $\bar{D} \times \bar{D}$ matrix.

7. The RC-EM Algorithm

One of the applications of the general EM algorithm (McLachlan and Krishnan [11]) is on probability density estimation or clustering. The best of the linear mixing of

Gaussian EM clustering algorithm is the natural probability interpretation of its linear mixing (superposition). We include a brief presentation of RC-EM for comparing the performance of all three algorithms in Section 11. The objective function for RC-EM is defined as

$$Perf_{RC-EM}(Z,M) =$$
$$-\log \left\{ \prod_{i=1}^{N} \sum_{k=1}^{K} \frac{p_k}{\sqrt{(2\pi)^d |\Sigma_k|}} EXP \left(-\frac{1}{2} (f_k(x_i) - y_i) \Sigma_k^{-1} (f_k(x_i) - y_i)^T \right) \right\} \qquad (16)$$

where $d = dim(Y)$. In case $d=1$, $(f_k(x_i) - y_i)$ is just a real number and $\Sigma_k^{-1} = 1/\sigma_k^2$. In higher dimensions, restriction to the covariance matrix Σ_k is necessary for EM to work properly. Σ_k = diagonal matrix is often used.

The RC-EM recursion is given by

E-Step:

$$p(Z_k^{(r)} | z_i) = \frac{\frac{p_k^{(r-1)}}{\sqrt{|\Sigma_k|}} EXP(-\frac{1}{2}(f_k^{(r-1)}(x_i) - y_i) \Sigma_{r-1,k}^{-1} (f_k^{(r-1)}(x_i) - y_i)^T)}{\sum_{k=1}^{K} \frac{p_k^{(r-1)}}{\sqrt{|\Sigma_k|}} EXP(-\frac{1}{2}(f_k^{(r-1)}(x_i) - y_i) \Sigma_{r-1,k}^{-1} (f_k^{(r-1)}(x_i) - y_i)^T)} \qquad (17)$$

M-Step: $p_k^{(r)} = \frac{1}{N} \sum_{i=1}^{N} p(Z_k^{(r)} | z_i) \qquad (18)$

$$f_k^{(r)} = \arg\min_{f \in \Phi} \sum_{i=1}^{N} p(Z_k^{(r)}, z_i) \| f(x_i) - y_i \|^2 \qquad (19)$$

$$\Sigma_{r,k} = \frac{\sum_{i=1}^{N} p(Z_k^{(r)} | z_i)(f_k^{(r)}(x_i) - y_i)^T (f_k^{(r)}(x_i) - y_i)}{N * p_k^{(r)}} \qquad (20)$$

8. MSE Linear Regression with EM Clustering -- LinReg-EM

When MSE linear regression is used, (19) can be solved and takes the following special form, while all other formulas (16)-(18) and (20) remain the same.

$$c_k^{(r)} = \left(\bar{X}^T * [p(Z_k^{(r)}, z_i) \bar{x}_i]_{N \times \bar{D}} \right)^{-1} * \bar{X}^T * [p(Z_k^{(r)}, z_i) y_i]_{N \times 1} \qquad (21)$$

Very strong similarity between (21) and LinReg-KHM's (15), or between (21) and LinReg-KM' (7) can be observed.

9. Computational Costs for RCs with MSE Linear Regression

We compare the cost of one iteration of RC with the cost of single function linear regression on the whole dataset without clustering for all three examples LinReg-KM, LinReg-KHM and LinReg-EM. This comparison shows the cost ratio of switching from single function regression to RC.

The cost of forming $\overline{X}$ is common to both RC and single linear regression. In single linear regression, the cost of calculating $c = (\overline{X}^T * \overline{X})^{-1} \overline{X}^T * Y$ is the sum of (an unit of calculation here is multiplying two numbers and adding the result to another number): $\overline{D}^2 * N$ units for forming $\overline{X}^T * \overline{X}$, $\overline{D}^2 + \overline{D} * N$ units for forming $\overline{X}^T * Y$ and $\beta \overline{D}^3$ for solving $(\overline{X}^T * \overline{X}) * c = \overline{X}^T * Y$, β is a small constant, where $\overline{D} = m+1$ if $D=1$, or $\overline{D} = \dfrac{D^{m+1}-1}{D-1}$ for $D >1$. $D=dim(X)$. $N \geq \overline{D}$, otherwise the regression has infinite solutions. We assume that $N \gg \overline{D}$, otherwise the potential of over fitting (and/or over shooting) is high. In any case the dominate term is $O(\overline{D}^2 * N)$. Let N_k be the size of the kth cluster, the costs of K regressions are $\sum_{k=1}^{K} \overline{D}^2 * N_k = \overline{D}^2 * N$ units for all $\overline{X}_k^T * \overline{X}_k$, $k=1,\dots,K$, $K\overline{D}^2 + \overline{D} * N$ units for all $\overline{X}_k^T * Y_k$ and $K\beta \overline{D}^3$ for solving K linear equations, $(\overline{X}_k^T * \overline{X}_k) * c_k = \overline{X}_k^T * Y_k$. K is very small and we do not expect it ever to be large (say > 50). The repartition cost for LinReg-KM is $O(\overline{D} * N * K)$ due to the number of error function evaluations and comparisons. Therefore, the cost of each iteration of LinReg-KM is at the same order of complexity as the simple single function regression.

We observed a quick convergence at start in all experiments but some of them had a long tail. (See Section 11.2)

The cost of calculating the repartition probabilities in LinReg-KHM and LinReg-EM are in the same order as the repartition cost in LinReg-KM.

With input variable selection, not all the variables selected for the single function regression need to appear in the selected variables for each subset. Therefore, the dimensionality of the regression problem on each subset may become lower.

10. Probability Interpretation of RC's K Regression Functions

Regression results are most often used for predictions, $y = f(x)$ is taken as a prediction of the response at a new $x \notin X$. With K regression functions

returned by RC, we get K predictions $\{f_k(x)\}_{k=1}^{K}$ on the same input x, which is interpreted in this section.

Assuming that dataset X is iid sampled from a hidden density distribution $P()$. Kernel density estimation on the K X-projections of $Z_k = \{p(Z_k | z) \mid z = (x,y) \in Z\}$ (for KHM and EM see (11) & (17), for KM they are the real subsets) gives

$$\hat{P}(x | X_k) = \frac{\dfrac{1}{N} \sum_{i=1}^{N} p(Z_k | z_i) H\left(\dfrac{x_i - x}{h}\right)}{\hat{P}(X_k)} \tag{22}$$

with

$$\hat{P}(X_k) = \frac{1}{N} \sum_{i=1}^{N} p(Z_k | z_i). \tag{23}$$

$H()$ in (22) is a symmetric kernel and h the bandwidth (See [13]). If we add the density estimation of each subset, we get the kernel density estimation on the whole dataset,

$$\hat{P}(x) = \sum_{k=1}^{K} \hat{P}(x | X_k)\hat{P}(X_k) = \frac{1}{N} \sum_{i=1}^{N} H\left(\frac{x_i - x}{h}\right). \tag{24}$$

Bayes' inversion gives the probability of x belongs to each subset,

$$\hat{P}(X_k | x) = \frac{\hat{P}(x | X_k)\hat{P}(X_k)}{\hat{P}(x)} = \frac{\sum_{i=1}^{N} p(Z_k | z_i) H\left(\dfrac{x_i - x}{h}\right)}{\sum_{i=1}^{N} H\left(\dfrac{x_i - x}{h}\right)} \tag{25}$$

Let $\tilde{f}(x)$ be the random variable prediction which equals $f_k(x)$ with probability $P(X_k | x)$, and the expected value of this prediction is estimated by

$$E(\tilde{f}(x) | x) \approx \sum_{k=1}^{K} f_k(x)\hat{P}(X_k | x) = \frac{\sum_{i=1}^{N}\left[\sum_{k=1}^{K} f_k(x)p(Z_k | z_i)\right] H\left(\dfrac{x_i - x}{h}\right)}{\sum_{i=1}^{N} H\left(\dfrac{x_i - x}{h}\right)} \tag{26}$$

A random variable contains more information than its expectation; therefore, RC's prediction $\tilde{f}(x) | x$, a random variable, gives more information than its expectation $E(\tilde{f}(x) | x)$. Instead of giving a single valued prediction with a large uncertainty, $\tilde{f}(x) | x$ gives K possible values each with a much smaller uncertainty. The significant part of the uncertainty is described by the probability distribution $\{P(X_k | x)$, $k=1,\dots,K\}$.

A classifier, $k=C(x)$, can be trained using the labels provided by the clustering phase of the RC algorithm. In case the false classification rate of C is low, which may not be true for some datasets, a prediction on x can be $f_{C(x)}(x)$.

11. Experimental Results

We conducted three sets of experiments: Set 1 for visualization of RC, and Set 2 for statistical comparisons of LinReg-KM, LinReg-KHM and LinReg-EM.

11.1. Visualization Experiments

This section visually demonstrates RC. Statistical performance analysis and comparison of different variations of RCs are in the next section.

Dimensionality of X is 1, so that 2-dimensional visualization can be presented. Linear regression RC is already demonstrated in **Fig.1b**. We do both quadratic (**Fig. 2**) and trigonometric (**Fig. 3**) regressions in this section.

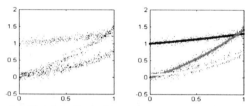

Fig. 2. _N=600, D=1, K=3_. On the left is the result of simple quadratic regression on the whole dataset. On the right is LinReg-KHM.

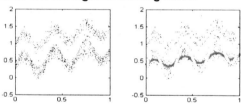

Fig. 3. _N=1200, D=1, K=3_. $\Phi = \{a_1 \sin(6\pi x) + a_2 x + a_3 \mid a_i \in R\}$ **and the data set is a mixture of three subsets generated by three functions in Φ with added Gaussian noise. Left: one regression function is applied to the whole dataset. Right: three regression functions are used. Each of them found a very good approximation of the original functions used to generate the dataset.**

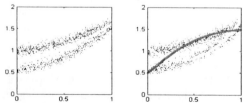

Fig. 4. A local optimum. It happens to all three RC algorithms, RC-KM, RC-KHM, and RC-EM.

Ploy-KHM, with the version KHM presented in Zhang at. el [22] which is better for one and two dimensional spaces, is used in this section.

A local optimum is shown in **Fig. 4**. This tells us how the algorithms may fail to reach the global optimum. Knowing this helps to manually correct it, by providing a special initialization after seeing a suspected result.

11.2 Statistical Comparisons of LinReg-KM, LinReg-KHM and LinReg-EM

Twelve sets of experiments, with $D = 2, 4, 6, 8$ and $K = 3, 6, 9$, are conducted. In each set, 60 datasets with $N = 50*D*K$ are generated by randomly picking N points on K randomly generated hyperplanes and then adding Gaussian noise to the y-components. The regression functions are linear (hyperplanes). For each dataset, a common initialization of the regression functions is used for all three different algorithms.

To make direct comparisons of three algorithms possible, we have to measure them by a common performance measure, which is chosen to be the LinReg-KM's objective function in (2). After LinReg-KHM and LinReg-EM converged, we discard its own performance measure, and re-measure its result by the LinReg-KM's. Doing so is slightly in favor of LinReg-KM. We use the notations $Perf_{KHM/KM}$ and $Perf_{EM/KM}$ for these re-measurements.

Taking advantage of the known partitions of the synthetic datasets, we calculated a $Perf_{baseline}$, by running regression on each of the K subsets and add them up, for comparing against the performance of LinReg-KM and LinReg-KHM. $Perf_{baseline}$ is close to the global optimum.

The results are in **Fig 5**. Each curve has 60 points from the 60 runs of RC, without interpolation. Four curves in each plot, which are frequency-estimations of the accumulative distributions in (22)-(25), with *v-axis* horizontal and *prob-axis* vertical,

$$\Pr\left(\frac{Perf_{KHM/KM}}{Perf_{EM/KM}} < v\right), \quad \Pr\left(\frac{Perf_{KHM/KM}}{Perf_{baseline}} < v\right),$$

$$\Pr\left(\frac{Perf_{RC-KM}}{Perf_{baseline}} < v\right), \quad \Pr\left(\frac{Perf_{EM/KM}}{Perf_{baseline}} < v\right)$$

$$(22\text{-}25)$$

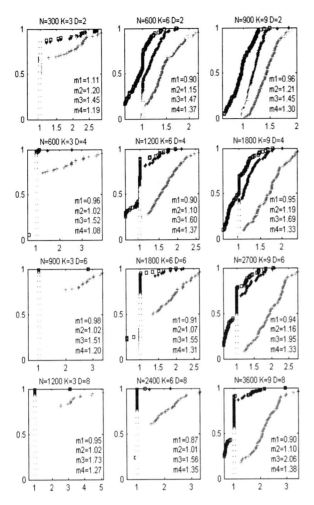

Fig 5. The accumulative distribution of the performance ratios. Icons and the text in each plot: black squares: LinReg-KHM over LinReg-EM; blue (*)'s: LinReg-KHM over the baseline; red (+)'s: LinReg-KM over the baseline and green triangles: LinReg-EM over the baseline. m1 = mean of the ratios of LinReg-KHM over LinReg-EM, m2 = mean of the ratios of LinReg-KHM over the baseline, m3 = mean of the ratios of LinReg-KM over the baseline, and m4 = mean of the ratios of LinReg-EM over the baseline.

The plot of (22), in black squares, shows how often LinReg-KHM performed better then LinReg-EM, with equal performance when the ratio is 1.

The plot of (23), in blue (*)'s, shows how well LinReg-KHM performed against the $Perf_{baseline}$, which should be very close to the true optimum. When the value is close to 1, a very good approximation of the global optimum was found.

The plot of (24) in red (+)'s and (25) in green triangles shows how well LinReg-KM and LinReg-EM performed against the $Perf_{baseline}$.

We truncated the x-axis to make the interesting part of the plot (near 1) more readable.

In addition to the plotted distributions in (22)-(25), the expectation is also given on each plot,

$$m1 \approx E\left(\frac{Perf_{KHM/KM}}{Perf_{EM/KM}}\right), m2 \approx E\left(\frac{Perf_{KHM/KM}}{Perf_{baseline}}\right), \quad (26)$$

$$m3 \approx E\left(\frac{Perf_{KM}}{Perf_{baseline}}\right), m4 \approx E\left(\frac{Perf_{EM/KM}}{Perf_{baseline}}\right).$$

Observations: A) Except for *K=3 and D=2,* LinReg-KHM performed the best among the three. As *K* and *D* increase, the performance gaps become larger; *B)* LinReg-EM performed better than LinReg-KM on average for all *K* and *D*. This is due to the low dimensionality of the *Y*-space *(dim(Y)=1)*, where the clustering algorithms are applied; *C)* In my previous comparisons on the performance of center-based clustering algorithms (Zhang 2003), *K*-means performed better than EM on average on datasets with dimensionality > 1. The higher the dimensionality of the data, the more K-Means outperform EM.

12. Conclusions

Clustering recovers a discrete estimation of the missing part of the responses and provides each regression function with the right subset of data. A new regression clustering algorithm RC-KHM is presented. LinReg-KHM outperforms both LinReg-EM and LinReg-KM.

In the general form of RCs, the regression part of the algorithm is completely general, no requirements is added to it by the RC algorithm. This implies that a) RC algorithms work with any type of regression; b) RC can be built on top of existing regression libraries and call the existing regression program as a subroutine.

We give two other advantages of using RC. Regression helps with understanding the data by replacing it with an analytical function plus a residue noise. When the noise is small, the function describes the data well. RC does a much better job requirements is added to it by the RC algorithm. This implies that a) RC algorithms work with any type of regression; b) RC can be built on top of existing regression libraries and call the existing regression program as a subroutine.

We give two other advantages of using RC. Regression helps with understanding the data by replacing it with an analytical function plus a residue noise. When the noise is small, the function describes the data well. RC does a much better job on this. The compact representation of data by a regression function can also be considered as (or part of) data compression. With a significantly smaller mean residue noise, RC does a much better job on this too.

EM's linear mixing of simple distributions has the most natural probability interpretation. To benefit from both the EM's probability model and the KHM algorithm's robust convergence, we recommend running RC-KHM first and use its converged results to initialize RC-EM. RC-KHM does not supply the initial values for $p_k^{(r)}$ and $\Sigma_{r,k}$. To solve this problem, keep the initial function-centers fixed at the RC-KHM's output for a number of iterations to let the probabilities $p_k^{(r)}$ and $\Sigma_{r,k}$ to converge under RC-EM before setting the function-centers free.

References

[1] Dempster, A. P., Laird, N.M., and Rubin, D.B. (1977), "Miximum Likelyhood from Incomplete Data via the EM Algorithm", Journal of the Royal Statistical Society, Series B, 39(1):1-38

[2] DeSarbo, W. S., Corn, L. W. (1988), "A Maximum Likelihood Methodology for Cluterwise Linear Regression," J. of Classification, 5:249-282

[3] Duda, R., Hart, P. (1972), "Pattern Classification and Scene Analysis", John Wiley & Sons

[4] Gaffney, S., and P. Smyth, `Trajectory clustering using mixtures of regression models,' in Proceedings of the ACM 1999 Conference on Knowledge Disovery and Data Mining, S. Chaudhuri and D. Madigan (eds.), New York, NY: ACM, 63--72, August 1999.

[5] Hamerly, G. and Elkan C., **Learning the k in k-means**. To appear in the Seventeenth Annaul Conference on Neural Information Processing Systems (NIPS 2003)

[6] Hennig, C. (1997), "Datenanalyse mit Modellen Fur Cluster Linear Regression." Dissertation, Institut Fur Mathmatsche Stochastik, Universitat Hamburg

[7] Hennig, C. (1999): Models and Methods for Clusterwise Linear Regression in Gaul, W. and Locarek-Junge, H. (Eds.): Classification in the Information Age, Springer, Berlin, p. 179-187.

[8] Hennig, C. (2002): Fixed point clusters for linear regression: computation and comparison (Part of Preprint 2000-02) Journal of Classification 19, 249-276.

[9] Lazarevic A. Xu X., Fietz T. and Obradovic Z. (1999): "Clustering-Regression-Ordering Steps for Knowledge Discovery in Spatial Databases", International Joint Conference on Neural Networks (IJCNN'99), July 10-16, Washington, DC. Paper (pdf 221k)

[10] MacQueen, J. (1967), "Some Methods for Classification and Analysis of Multivariate Obser-vations". Pp. 281-297 in: L. M. Le Cam & J. Neyman [eds.] Proceedings of the fifth Berkeley symposium on mathematical statistics and probability, Vol. 1. University of California Press, Berkeley. xvii + 666 p

[11] McLachlan, G. J. and Krishnan, T. (1997), "The EM Algorithm and Extensions.", John Wiley & Sons

[12] Montgomery, D. C., Peck, E. A., Vining, G. G. (2001), "Introduction to Linear Regression Analy-sis", John Wiley & Sons; 3rd edition, April

[13] Silverman, B. W. (1998), "Density Estimation for Statistics and Data Analysis," Chapman & Hall/CRC.

[14] Spath, H. (1979), Algorithm 39: Clusterwise Linear Regression, Computing, 22, 367-73.

[15] Spath, H. (1981), "Correction to Algorithm 39: Clusterwise Linear Regression," Computing, 26, 275.

[16] Spath, H. (1982), "Algorithm 48: A Fast Algorithm for Clusterwise Linear Regression," Computing, 29, 175-181.

[17] Spath, H. (1985), "Cluster Dissection and Analysis," New York: Wiley.

[18] Tibshirani, R., Walther, G., and Hastie, T. (2000), "Estimating the Number of Clusters in a Dataset via the Gap Statistic", Available at http://www-stat.stanford.edu/~tibs/research.html.

[19] Torgo,L., and Pinto da Costa,J. (2000): "Clustered Partial Linear Regression," Machine Learning, 50 (3), pp. 303-319. Kluwer Academic Publishers.

[20] Williams, J. (2000), "Fitting Regression Models to Finite Mixtures," ANZMAC Visionary Marketing for the 21th Century: Facing the Challenge, 1409-1414.

[21] Wedel, M. and Steenkamp, J. B. (1991) `A clusterwise regression method for simultaneous fuzzy market structuring and benefit segmentation,' Journal of Marketing Research, 28, pp.385--96.

[22] Zhang, B., Hsu, M., Dayal, U. (2000), "K-Harmonic Means", Intl. Workshop on Temporal, Spatial and Spatio-Temporal Data Mining, Lyon, France Sept. 12.

[23] Zhang, B. (2001), "Generalized K-Harmonic Means–Dynamic Weighting of Data in Unsupervised Learn-ing,", the First SIAM International Conference on Data Mining (SDM'2001), Chicago, USA, April 5-7.

[24] Zhang, B. (2003), "Comparison of the Performance of Center-based Clustering Algorithms", the proceedings of PAKDD-03, Seoul, South Korea, April.

Model-based Clustering with Soft Balancing

Shi Zhong
Dept. of Computer Science and Engineering
Florida Atlantic University
777 Glades Road, Boca Raton, FL 33431
zhong@cse.fau.edu

Joydeep Ghosh
Dept. of Electrical and Computer Engineering
The University of Texas at Austin
1 University Station, Austin, TX 78712-1084
ghosh@ece.utexas.edu

Abstract

Balanced clustering algorithms can be useful in a variety of applications and have recently attracted increasing research interest. Most recent work, however, addressed only hard balancing by constraining each cluster to have equal or a certain minimum number of data objects. This paper provides a soft balancing strategy built upon a soft mixture-of-models clustering framework. This strategy constrains the sum of posterior probabilities of object membership for each cluster to be equal and thus balances the expected number of data objects in each cluster. We first derive soft model-based clustering from an information-theoretic viewpoint and then show that the proposed balanced clustering can be parameterized by a temperature parameter that controls the softness of clustering as well as that of balancing. As the temperature decreases, the resulting partitioning becomes more and more balanced. In the limit, when temperature becomes zero, the balancing becomes hard and the actual partitioning becomes perfectly balanced. The effectiveness of the proposed soft balanced clustering algorithm is demonstrated on both synthetic and real text data.

1 Introduction

Clustering algorithms have been widely studied across multiple disciplines for several decades [13, 15, 16]. A central goal of clustering is to group similar data objects together and to extract a compact representation for each group. Current clustering methods can be divided into discriminative (similarity-based) approaches [29, 14, 19] and generative (model-based) approaches [22, 4, 7]. Similarity-based approaches focus on partitioning data objects according to a data-pairwise (dis)similarity measure, whereas model-based approaches aim at estimating a set of generative models for each cluster, usually through a maximum likelihood approach. This paper is based on model-based clustering.

In many data mining applications, it is often desirable to have (approximately) balanced clusters. For example, pre-clustering is sometimes used to build an indexing structure to facilitate search in very large databases. When a query comes in, the search engine can first check the cluster representatives and then only search the individual records in those closely matched clusters. If the clusters are very skewed in size, the worst case search time can be close to the time needed to search over all data records. Therefore, balanced clusters can significantly reduce search time. Similarly, in a clustering of a large corpus of documents to generate topic hierarchies, balancing can greatly improve navigation by avoiding the generation of highly skewed hierarchies.

In addition to application requirements, balanced clustering is sometimes also helpful because it tends to decrease sensitivity to initialization and to avoid outlier clusters (highly under-utilized representatives) from forming, and thus has a beneficial regularizing effect. This is especially useful for k-means type algorithms, including the soft EM variant [5], which are increasingly prone to yielding unbalanced solutions as the input dimensionality increases. This problem is exacerbated when a large (tens or more) number of clusters are needed, and it is well known that both hard and soft k-means invariably result in some near-empty clusters in such scenarios [6, 3].

Many clustering algorithms produce somewhat balanced clusters even though there are no explicit balancing constraints in their objective functions. For example, in divisive hierarchical clustering, one can pick the largest cluster to split at each iteration, resulting in a set of relatively balanced clusters. Frequency sensitive competitive learning [1, 11] penalizes the distance to large clusters thus eliminates empty clusters. Spectral graph partitioning algorithms [9, 17, 23] use a modified minimum cut objective that favors balanced partitioning since exact minimum cut solution often leads to completely useless results (e.g., one point in one cluster and all other points in the other in a bipartitioning). These algorithms, however, do not guarantee the level of balancing and have no principled way of adjusting it in the final clustering results.

The problem of clustering large scale data under constraints such as balancing has recently received attention in the data mining literature [6, 28, 25, 2, 32]. Since balancing is a global property, it is difficult to obtain near-linear time algorithms to achieve this goal while retaining high cluster quality [12]. Banerjee and Ghosh [3] proposed a three-step framework for balanced clustering: sampling, balanced clustering of the sampled data, and populating the clusters with the remaining data points in a balanced fashion. This algorithm has relatively low complexity of $O(N\log(N))$ but relies on the assumption that the data itself is very balanced (for the sampling step to work). Here N is the number of data objects. Bradley et al. [6] developed a constrained version of the k-means algorithm. They constrained each cluster to be assigned at least a minimum number of data points at each iteration. The data assignment subproblem was formulated as a minimum cost flow problem, which has a high ($O(N^3)$) complexity. In a previous work [32], we presented a general framework for adapting any hard model-based clustering to provide balanced solutions. An efficient heuristic was developed to solve the completely balanced data assignment subproblem in $O(K^2N + KN\log N)$ time, where K is the number of clusters.

These existing balanced clustering algorithms, however, mostly concentrated on hard balancing that constrains each cluster to have equal or certain minimum number of data objects. In many situations, strict balance is not required or desired. The contribution of this paper is a soft balancing strategy built on a general soft model-based clustering framework. Instead of constraining the actual number of data objects in each cluster to be equal, we constrain the expected number of data objects in each cluster to be equal. This is realized by setting the sum of posterior probabilities to be equal to N/K for each cluster. The resulting algorithm is parameterized by a temperature parameter, which controls the softness of clustering as well as that of balancing. Therefore, it provides a knob for users to adjust the level of balancing for different applications. Also, it turns out that this soft balancing strategy is computationally more efficient compared to hard balancing and has a time complexity of $O(KN)$. Finally, the proposed soft balancing is a general method that can be applied to any situation for which good generative models exist.

The organization of this paper is as follows. Section 2 gives an information-theoretic derivation of soft model-based clustering. Section 3 details the soft balancing strategy built upon the general model-based clustering framework. Section 4 demonstrates the effectiveness of the proposed soft balanced clustering algorithms through experimental results on both synthetic and real text data. Finally,

Section 5 summarizes this paper with some concluding remarks.

2 Soft Model-based Clustering

In this section, we present a principled, information-theoretic derivation of model-based clustering. The derivation process is similar to that of deterministic annealing [24] and provides a useful generalization of the standard mixture-of-models clustering [22, 4, 7]. The resulting algorithm is parameterized by a temperature parameter T, which governs the randomness of posterior data assignments. As we will see, the standard mixture-of-models clustering corresponds to the special case $T = 1$ whereas k-means clustering corresponds to the special case $T = 0$.

In model-based clustering, one estimates K models from N data objects, with each model representing a cluster. Let X be the set of all data objects and Y the set of all cluster indices. Let the likelihood of a data object x given a cluster y be $P(x|\lambda_y)$ and the joint probability for X and Y be $P(x,y)$. We aim to maximize the expected log-likelihood

$$
\begin{aligned}
L &= \sum_{x,y} P(x,y)\log p(x|\lambda_y) \\
&= \sum_x P(x)\sum_y P(y|x)\log p(x|\lambda_y) .
\end{aligned}
\tag{1}
$$

Note that in practice it is unavoidable to use a sample average to calculate (1), i.e., to set the prior $P(x)$ to be constant ($1/N$). As N goes to infinity, the sample average approaches the expected log-likelihood asymptotically.

Directly maximizing (1) over $P(y|x)$ and λ_y leads to a generic model-based k-means algorithm [32], which iterates between the following two steps:

$$
P(y|x) = \begin{cases} 1, & y = \arg\max_{y'}\log p(x|\lambda_{y'}); \\ 0, & \text{otherwise}, \end{cases}
\tag{2}
$$

and

$$
\lambda_y = \arg\max_\lambda \sum_x P(y|x)\log p(x|\lambda) .
\tag{3}
$$

The posterior probability $P(y|x)$ in (2) is actually conditioned on current parameters $\Lambda = \{\lambda_1, ..., \lambda_K\}$, but for simplicity we use $P(y|x)$ instead of $P(y|x, \Lambda)$ where there is no confusion. Equation (2) represents a hard data assignment strategy—each data object x is assigned, with probability 1, to the cluster y that gives the maximum $\log p(x|\lambda_y)$. When equi-variance spherical Gaussian models are used, this model-based k-means algorithm reduces to the standard k-means algorithm [21, 20]. It is well known that the k-means algorithm tends to quickly get stuck in a local solution. One way of alleviating this problem is to use soft assignments.

To introduce some randomness/softness to the data assignment step, we add entropy terms to (1) to get an entropy-constrained objective function. The new objective function is

$$L_1 = L + T \cdot H(Y|X) - T \cdot H(Y) = L - T \cdot I(X;Y), \quad (4)$$

where $H(Y) = -\sum_y P(y) \log P(y)$ is the cluster prior entropy, $H(Y|X) = -\sum_x P(x) \sum_y P(y|x) \log P(y|x)$ the average posterior entropy, and $I(X;Y)$ the mutual information between X and Y. The parameter T is a Lagrange multiplier used to tradeoff between maximizing the average log-likelihood L and minimizing the mutual information between X and Y (i.e., compressing data X into clusters Y). If we fix $H(y)$, minimizing $I(X;Y)$ is equivalent to maximizing the average posterior entropy $H(Y|X)$, or maximizing the randomness of posterior data assignments.

Note the added entropy terms do not change the model re-estimation formula (3) since the model parameters that maximize L also maximize L_1. To solve for $P(y|x)$ under constraint $\sum_y P(y|x) = 1$, we first construct the Lagrangian $\mathcal{L} = L_1 + \sum_x \xi_x (\sum_y P(y|x) - 1)$ and then let the partial derivative $\frac{\partial \mathcal{L}}{\partial P(y|x)} = 0$. The resulting $P(y|x)$ is given by

$$P(y|x) = \frac{P(y)p(x|\lambda_y)^{\frac{1}{T}}}{\sum_{y'} P(y')p(x|\lambda_{y'})^{\frac{1}{T}}}. \quad (5)$$

If necessary, $P(y)$ can be estimated from the data as $P(y) = \sum_x P(x)P(y|x)$. Now we get a model-based clustering algorithm parameterized by the parameter T, which has a temperature interpretation in deterministic annealing [24]. A standard deterministic annealing algorithm for model-based clustering is shown in Fig. 1. Note that at each temperature, the EM algorithm [8] is used to maximize (4), with cluster labels Y being the hidden variable and (5) and (3) corresponding to E-step and M-step, respectively.

It can be shown that plugging (5) into (4) and setting $T = 1$ reduce the objective function to

$$L_1^* = \sum_x P(x) \log \left(\sum_y P(y)p(x|\lambda_y) \right), \quad (6)$$

which is exactly the (incomplete data log-likelihood) objective function that the standard mixture-of-models clustering algorithm maximizes. It is a common practice to refer to the mixture-of-models clustering that maximizes (6) as EM clustering. As T goes to 0, (5) reduces to (2) and the algorithm reduces to model-based k-means, independent of the actual $P(y)$'s (unless they are 1 and 0's). For any $T > 0$, iterating between (5) and (3) gives a soft model-based clustering algorithm that maximizes (4) for a given T.

This analysis makes it clear that model-based k-means and EM clustering can be viewed as two special stages of

---

Algorithm: model-based clustering via deterministic annealing

Input: A set of N data objects $X = \{x_1, ..., x_N\}$, model structure $\Lambda = \{\lambda_1, ..., \lambda_K\}$, temperature decreasing rate $\alpha, 0 < \alpha < 1$, and final temperature T_f (usually a small positive value close to 0).

Output: Trained models Λ and a partition of the data objects given by the cluster identity vector $Y = \{y_1, ..., y_N\}, y_n \in \{1, ..., K\}$.

Steps:

1. Initialization: initialize the model parameters Λ and set T to be high (a large number);

2. Optimization: optimize (4) by iterating between (5) and (3) until convergence;

3. Annealing: lower the temperature parameter $T^{(new)} = \alpha T^{(old)}$, go to step 4 if $T < T_f$, otherwise go back to step 2.

4. For each data object x_n, set $y_n = \arg\max_y P(y|x_n)$.

Figure 1. Deterministic annealing algorithm for model-based clustering.

---

a deterministic annealing process, with $T = 0$ and $T = 1$, respectively, and they optimize two different objective functions (L vs. $L - I(X;Y)$). Since larger T indicates smoother objective function and a smaller number of local solutions, theoretically the EM clustering ($T = 1$) should have a better chance of finding good local solutions than the model-based k-means algorithm ($T = 0$). So it makes sense to use the EM clustering results to initialize the model-based k-means, which has been heuristically used in practice (e.g., using mixture-of-Gaussians to initialize standard k-means). It can be viewed as a one-step deterministic annealing algorithm (temperature decreases one time from $T = 1$ to $T = 0$). Of course, a better approach is always to start at a high $T \gg 1$ and gradually reduce T toward 0.

The computational complexity for all the algorithms described above is linear in the number of data objects N, provided that we use a constant (maximum) number of iterations and a model training algorithm that has linear complexity.

3 Model-based clustering with soft balancing

In previous work [32], we have built a generic balanced hard clustering algorithm, based upon model-based k-means. In this section we shall show how we can build soft balancing based on the soft model-based clustering framework presented in the previous section.

Instead of enforcing the exact number of data objects

grouped into each cluster to be equal, we constrain the sum of posterior probabilities for each cluster to be equal to N/K, which equalizes the expected number of objects assigned to each cluster. This is a soft balancing constraint in that the actual partitioning can be unbalanced. Our experimental results show that the softness of balancing can be characterized by T, the same parameter that parameterizes the softness of clustering.

After taking into account the soft balancing constraints

$$\sum_x P(y|x) = \frac{N}{K}, \; \forall y \; , \tag{7}$$

we construct the Lagrangian w.r.t. $P(y|x)$ as

$$\begin{aligned} \mathcal{L} &= L_1 + \sum_x \xi_x \left(\sum_y P(y|x) - 1 \right) \\ &+ \sum_y \eta_y \left(\sum_x P(y|x) - \frac{N}{K} \right), \end{aligned}$$

where ξ_x and η_y are Lagrange multipliers. Taking the derivative $\frac{\partial \mathcal{L}}{\partial P(y|x)} = 0$, and after some algebra, we get

$$P(y|x) = \frac{P(y) \left[e^{\eta_y} p(x|\lambda_y) \right]^{\frac{1}{T}}}{\sum_{y'} P(y') \left[e^{\eta_{y'}} p(x|\lambda_{y'}) \right]^{\frac{1}{T}}}. \tag{8}$$

For balance clustering, it makes sense to set $P(y)$ to be $1/K$, which eliminates $P(y)$ from (8). For simplicity, let $\beta_y = e^{\eta_y}$. Plugging (8) into (7), we get

$$\sum_x \frac{[\beta_y p(x|\lambda_y)]^{\frac{1}{T}}}{\sum_{y'} [\beta_{y'} p(x|\lambda_{y'})]^{\frac{1}{T}}} = \frac{N}{K}. \tag{9}$$

To solve for β_y's in (9), we take an iterative optimization approach since a closed form solution is not available in general. The iterative formula for β_y can be derived from (9) as

$$\beta_y^{(t+1)} = \left(\frac{N/K}{\sum_x \frac{p(x|\lambda_y)^{\frac{1}{T}}}{\sum_{y'} \left(\beta_{y'}^{(t)} p(x|\lambda_{y'}) \right)^{\frac{1}{T}}}} \right)^T, \tag{10}$$

where t is the iteration number. We use $\beta_y^{(0)} = 1, \forall y$. To avoid possible underflow problem with very small likelihood $p(x|\lambda_y)$, we operate on log-likelihood $\log p(x|\lambda_y)$ and $\log \beta_y$ using the following implementation:

$$\log \beta_y^{(t+1)} = T \cdot \log \left(\frac{N}{K} \right) -$$

$$T \cdot \log \left(\sum_x \frac{e^{\frac{1}{T} \log p(x|\lambda_y)}}{\sum_{y'} e^{\frac{1}{T} \left(\log \beta_{y'}^{(t)} + \log p(x|\lambda_{y'}) \right)}} \right). \tag{11}$$

Now we have a soft balancing strategy parameterized by the temperature, T. Experimental results show that the iterative estimation of $\log \beta_y$ converges fast for a high T but can be very slow for a low T. For example, in an experiment on estimating nine cluster models from the *tr11* dataset (see Section 4.3), we need about 60 iterations for $T = 0.1$, 120 iterations for $T = 0.04$, and 400 iterations for $T = 0.01$. To avoid long estimation time for a low temperature (e.g., $T = 0.01$), we take an annealing approach for computing $\log \beta_y$. That is, starting from a high temperature (e.g., $T = 0.1$) and quickly lower the temperature toward $T = 0.01$. At every temperature we run a small number of iterations and initialize $\log \beta_y$'s using the values computed from previous temperature. Due to space limit, training curves are omitted in this paper. But we observe that by just iterating 30 times at $T = 0.1$, then 30 times at $T = 0.04$, and then 40 times at $T = 0.01$, we get converged results for $T = 0.01$ in 100 iterations.

Compared to hard balancing, soft balancing for model-based clustering can be solved exactly and efficiently using the iterative strategy described above. If we use a fixed number of maximum iterations, the time complexity for computing $\log \beta$'s will be $O(KN)$. In hard balancing [6, 32], a linear programming problem has to be solved and the time complexity is $O(K^3 N^3)$ for an exact solution and $O(K^2 N + KN \log N)$ even for an approximate solution. This is not surprising since for hard clustering, the posterior probabilities $P(y|x)$ are either 0's or 1's, creating a much harder integer programming problem.[1] For this reason, we recommend using a temperature T away from 0 (e.g., let $T > \delta$, where $\delta > 0$ is a small positive number) for our soft balancing strategy.

4 Experimental results and discussions

In this section, we first introduce several criteria used to evaluate balanced clustering results, followed by results and discussions on both synthetic datasets and real text document datasets.

4.1 Clustering evaluation

To evaluate the performance of our balanced clustering algorithms, we use three criteria—balance, objective function value, and mutual information between cluster labels and class labels (if they exist).

We measure the balance of a clustering by normalized entropy (of the distribution of cluster sizes) that is defined

---

[1]Fortunately, the resulting integer programming problem can be reduced to a linear programming problem [6]. Even so, the complexity is still high.

as

$$N_{entro} = -\frac{1}{\log K} \sum_{j=1}^{K} \frac{N_j}{N} \log \left(\frac{N_j}{N} \right), \quad (12)$$

where N_j is the number of data objects in cluster j. A normalized entropy of 1 means perfectly balanced clustering and 0 extremely unbalanced clustering.

The expected log-likelihood objective (1) is used as an internal measure of clustering quality. For the text datasets, where class labels are available, we calculate a normalized mutual information (NMI) criterion as an external measure of how well the clustering results conform to existing class labels. There are several choices for normalization; we shall follow the definition given in [26]:

$$NMI = \frac{\sum_{h,l} n_{h,l} \log \left(\frac{N \cdot n_{h,l}}{n_h n_l} \right)}{\sqrt{\left(\sum_h n_h \log \frac{n_h}{N} \right) \left(\sum_l n_l \log \frac{n_l}{N} \right)}}, \quad (13)$$

where n_h is the number of data objects in class h, n_l the number of objects in cluster l and $n_{h,l}$ the number of objects in class h as well as in cluster l. The NMI value is 1 when clustering results perfectly match the external category labels and close to 0 for a random partitioning. This is a better measure than purity or entropy which are both biased towards high K solutions [27, 26].

4.2 Results on synthetic datasets

We first tested the soft balanced clustering algorithms on a synthetic dataset—the t4 dataset (Fig. 2(a)) included in the CLUTO toolkit [18]. There are no ground truth labels for this dataset but there are six natural clusters plus a lot of noise according to human judgment. The best algorithm that can identify all the six natural clusters uses a hybrid partitional-hierarchical approach [19, 18]. It partitions the data into a large number (e.g., 30) of clusters and then merges them back to a proper granularity level.

We intend to use our balanced clustering algorithm to get a partition of 30 clusters. These fine granularity clusters can be merged using a hierarchical clustering algorithm to form a cluster hierarchy, for further interactive analysis. But here we are only concerned with the partitional step. Spherical Gaussian distributions are used to model the clusters.

The balanced clustering results are shown in Fig. 2. As can be seen from the histogram distribution of cluster sizes in Fig. 2(d), model-based clustering with soft balancing can generate more balanced results (higher normalized entropy) than model-based clustering without balancing. Furthermore, low temperature (Fig. 2(d)) leads to more balanced actual partitioning, as well as better clustering quality in terms of the average log-likelihood measure for this dataset. This phenomenon was also observed in [2]. Fig. 2(c) indicates that our algorithm generates unbalanced solutions when the temperature is high.

4.3 Results on text datasets

We used two datasets from the CLUTO toolkit[2] [18]. A summary of the datasets is shown in Table 1. The traditional vector space representation is used for text documents, i.e., each document is represented as a high dimensional vector of "word"[3] counts in the document. The dimensionality equals the number of words in the vocabulary used. All the datasets have already been preprocessed [30]. We further removed those words that appear in two or fewer documents.

Table 1. Summary of text datasets. (For each dataset, n_d is the total number of documents, n_w the total number of words, and K the number of classes.)

Data	Source	n_d	n_w	K
classic	CACM/CRANFIELD/ CISI/MEDLINE	7094	41681	4
tr11	TREC	414	6429	9

Further, we used standard multinomial models with Laplacian smoothing for model-based clustering of text documents [31].

The soft balanced clustering results for *tr11* and *classic* datasets are shown in Fig. 3, with results for *tr11* on the left column and results for *classic* on the right. The first row shows balance measures, the second row average log-likelihood measures, and the last row normalized mutual information measures across seven different temperatures. The x-axis is on a $\log T$ scale, which provides a better visualization than using the T scale. The vertical bar at each temperature shows ± 1 *standard deviation* over 10 runs of each experiment (with random initialization for each run). The balance of clusterings has a general trend of going down with increasing temperature. But the clustering quality, in terms of both average log-likelihood and normalized mutual information, seems to peak somewhere in the middle. This is intuitive in that toward very low temperature settings, a highly balanced clustering starts grouping distant data objects together, whereas toward the other end, highly fuzzy posterior assignments fail to discriminate between different clusters and thus fail to generate a good partitioning.

---

[2]http://www.cs.umn.edu/~karypis/CLUTO/files/datasets.tar.gz.
[3]Used in a broad sense since it may represent individual words, stemmed words, tokenized words, short phrases, etc.

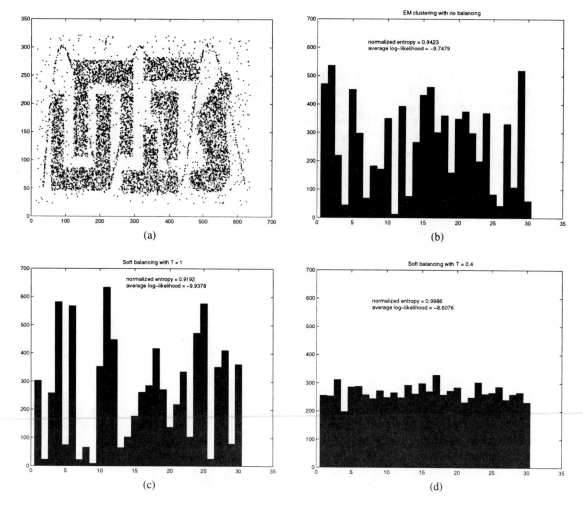

Figure 2. Balanced clustering results on *t4* dataset: (a) *t4* dataset; histogram distribution of cluster sizes when clustering *t4* into 30 groups using (b) EM clustering with spherical Gaussian models and no balancing; (c) mixture-of-spherical Gaussians clustering with soft balancing (T=1); (d) mixture-of-spherical Gaussians clustering with soft balancing (T=0.4).

5 Concluding remarks

The soft balancing strategy presented in this paper offers a continuous spectrum of solutions depending on where the temperature knob is set. One end of the spectrum (zero temperature) provides hard balancing where all posterior probabilities are either 0 or 1. Toward the other end (high temperature), we can get very unbalanced clusterings even when the expected number of data objects in each cluster is constrained to be equal. Experimental results show that clusterings of the highest quality often occur in the middle of the spectrum.

The proposed soft balancing also has a computational advantage compared to hard balanced clustering algorithms.

With a complexity linear in the number of data objects, it is better positioned for large scale data mining applications.

Since the proposed algorithm is built on a general model-based clustering framework, it can be readily applicable to a wide range of data types. For example, balanced time series clustering can be constructed with appropriate models (e.g., Markov chains or hidden Markov models), and can be useful in financial world for building balanced portfolios.

There are several model selection methods [10] for estimating number of clusters in a general model-based clustering framework. Future work should study the interaction between model selection and balancing.

Acknowledgments

This research was supported in part by NSF grants IDM-0307792 and ITR-0312471.

References

[1] S. C. Ahalt, A. K. Krishnamurthy, P. Chen, and D. E. Melton. Competitive learning algorithms for vector quantization. *Neural Networks*, 3(3):277–290, 1990.

[2] A. Banerjee and J. Ghosh. Frequency sensitive competitive learning for clustering on high-dimensional hyperspheres. In *Proc. IEEE Int. Joint Conf. Neural Networks*, pages 1590–1595, May 2002.

[3] A. Banerjee and J. Ghosh. On scaling up balanced clustering algorithms. In *Proc. 2nd SIAM Int. Conf. Data Mining*, pages 333–349, April 2002.

[4] J. D. Banfield and A. E. Raftery. Model-based Gaussian and non-Gaussian clustering. *Biometrics*, 49(3):803–821, September 1993.

[5] J. A. Blimes. A gentle tutorial of the EM algorithm and its application to parameter estimation for Gaussian mixture and hidden Markov models. Technical report, University of California at Berkeley, April 1998.

[6] P. S. Bradley, K. P. Bennett, and A. Demiriz. Constrained k-means clustering. Technical Report MSR-TR-2000-65, Microsoft Research, Redmond, WA, 2000.

[7] I. V. Cadez, S. Gaffney, and P. Smyth. A general probabilistic framework for clustering individuals and objects. In *Proc. 6th ACM SIGKDD Int. Conf. Knowledge Discovery and Data Mining*, pages 140–149, 2000.

[8] A. P. Dempster, N. M. Laird, and D. B. Rubin. Maximum-likelihood from incomplete data via the EM algorithm. *Journal of the Royal Statistical Society B*, 39(1):1–38, 1977.

[9] I. S. Dhillon. Co-clustering documents and words using bipartite spectral graph partitioning. In *Proc. 7th ACM SIGKDD Int. Conf. Knowledge Discovery and Data Mining*, pages 269–274, 2001.

[10] C. Fraley and A. E. Raftery. How many clusters? Which clustering method? Answers via model-based analysis. *The Computer Journal*, 41(8):578–588, 1998.

[11] A. S. Galanopoulos, R. L. Moses, and S. C. Ahalt. Diffusion approximation of frequency sensitive competitive learning. *IEEE Trans. Neural Networks*, 8(5):1026–1030, September 1997.

[12] J. Ghosh. Scalable clustering. In N. Ye, editor, *Handbook of Data Mining*, pages 341–364. Lawrence Erlbaum Assoc., 2003.

[13] J. A. Hartigan. *Clustering Algorithms*. John Wiley & Sons, 1975.

[14] P. Indyk. A sublinear-time approximation scheme for clustering in metric spaces. In *40th Annual IEEE Symp. Foundations of Computer Science*, pages 154–159, 1999.

[15] A. K. Jain and R. C. Dubes. *Algorithms for Clustering Data*. Prentice Hall, New Jersey, 1988.

[16] A. K. Jain, M. N. Murty, and P. J. Flynn. Data clustering: A review. *ACM Computing Surveys*, 31(3):264–323, 1999.

[17] R. Kannan, S. Vempala, and A. Vetta. On clusterings — good, bad and spectral. In *41st Annual IEEE Symp. Foundations of Computer Science*, pages 367–377, 2000.

[18] G. Karypis. *CLUTO - A Clustering Toolkit*. Dept. of Computer Science, University of Minnesota, May 2002.

[19] G. Karypis, E.-H. Han, and V. Kumar. Chameleon: Hierarchical clustering using dynamic modeling. *Computer*, 32(8):68–75, 1999.

[20] S. P. Lloyd. Least squares quantization in PCM. *IEEE Trans. Information Theory*, IT-28:129–137, March 1982.

[21] J. MacQueen. Some methods for classification and analysis of multivariate observations. In *Proc. 5th Berkeley Symp. Math. Statistics and Probability*, pages 281–297, 1967.

[22] G. McLachlan and K. Basford. *Mixture Models: Inference and Applications to Clustering*. Marcel Dekker, New York, 1988.

[23] A. Y. Ng, M. I. Jordan, and Y. Weiss. On spectral clustering: analysis and an algorithm. In T. G. Dietterich, S. Becker, and Z. Ghahramani, editors, *Advances in Neural Information Processing Systems*, volume 14, pages 849–856. MIT Press, 2002.

[24] K. Rose. Deterministic annealing for clustering, compression, classification, regression, and related optimization problems. *Proceedings of IEEE*, 86(11):2210–2239, 1998.

[25] A. Strehl and J. Ghosh. Cluster ensembles — a knowledge reuse framework for combining partitions. *Journal of Machine Learning Research*, 3:583–617, 2002.

[26] A. Strehl and J. Ghosh. Relationship-based clustering and visualization for high-dimensional data mining. *INFORMS Journal on Computing: Special Issue on Web Mining*, 15(2):208–230, 2003.

[27] A. Strehl, J. Ghosh, and R. J. Mooney. Impact of similarity measures on web-page clustering. In *AAAI Workshop on AI for Web Search*, pages 58–64, July 2000.

[28] A. K. H. Tung, R. T. Ng, L. V. D. Lakshmanan, and J. Han. Constraint-based clustering in large databases. In *Proc. 8th Int. Conf. Database Theory*, pages 405–419, 2001.

[29] V. Vapnik. *Statistical Learning Theory*. John Wiley, New York, 1998.

[30] Y. Zhao and G. Karypis. Criterion functions for document clustering: experiments and analysis. Technical Report #01-40, Department of Computer Science, University of Minnesota, November 2001.

[31] S. Zhong and J. Ghosh. A comparative study of generative models for document clustering. In *SIAM Int. Conf. Data Mining Workshop on Clustering High Dimensional Data and Its Applications*, San Francisco, CA, May 2003.

[32] S. Zhong and J. Ghosh. Scalable, balanced model-based clustering. In *Proc. 3rd SIAM Int. Conf. Data Mining*, pages 71–82, San Francisco, CA, May 2003.

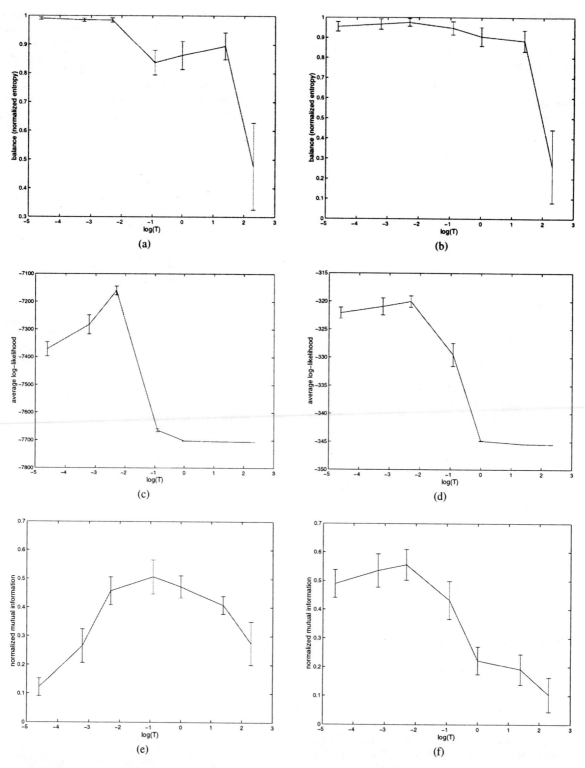

Figure 3. Soft balanced clustering results for *tr11* **and** *classic* **datasets: balance (normalized entropy) results for (a)** *tr11* **and (b)** *classic*; **average log-likelihood results for (c)** *tr11* **and (d)** *classic*; **normalized mutual information results for (e)** *tr11* **and (f)** *classic*.

Research-Track Short Papers

Integrating Fuzziness into OLAP for Multidimensional Fuzzy Association Rules Mining

Reda ALHAJJ
ADSA Lab & Department of Computer Science
University of Calgary
Calgary, Alberta, Canada
alhajj@cpsc.ucalgary.ca

Mehmet KAYA
Department of Computer Engineering,
Fırat University
23119, Elazığ, Turkey
kaya@firat.edu.tr

Abstract

This paper contributes to the ongoing research on multidimensional online association rules mining by proposing a general architecture that utilizes a fuzzy data cube for knowledge discovery. Three different methods are introduced to mine fuzzy association rules in the constructed fuzzy data cube, namely single dimension, multidimensional and hybrid association rules mining. Experimental results obtained for each of the three methods on the adult data of the United States census in 2000 show their effectiveness and applicability.

1. Introduction

Earlier approaches for quantitative association rules mining require discretizing the domains of quantitative attributes into intervals in order to discover quantitative association rules. But, these intervals may not be concise and meaningful enough for humans to obtain nontrivial knowledge from the discovered rules. Also, existing quantitative mining algorithms either ignore or over-emphasize elements near the boundary of an interval.

Instead of using sharp intervals, some work has recently been done on the use of fuzzy sets in discovering association rules among quantitative attributes in flat tables, e.g., [3, 9]. These approaches assume a flat relational table structure.

In this paper, we apply the same fuzziness concepts to OLAP data mining, where the basic structure is a *data cube*. A cube is a set of data organized similar to a multidimensional array of values representing measures over several dimensions. Explicitly, OLAP mining integrates online analytical processing with data mining; this substantially enhances the power and flexibility of data mining and makes mining an interesting exploratory process, e.g., [7, 8]. So, generating online association rules is considered an important research area of data mining, e.g., [1, 4, 5, 6]. Although these algorithms improved the online generation of association rules, it is still an open problem. They use data cubes with binary attributes, whereas most real life databases include quantitative attributes. Motivated by this, we developed a novel approach for online association rules mining.

We contribute to the ongoing research on multidimensional online data mining by proposing a general architecture that constructs and uses a fuzzy data cube for knowledge discovery. This allows users to query a given database for fuzzy association rules for different values of support and confidence. We present three different methods to mine fuzzy association rules in the constructed fuzzy data cube, namely one-dimensional, multi-dimensional and hybrid (integrates the two other methods) fuzzy association rules mining. To the best of our knowledge, this is the first attempt to utilize fuzziness in OLAP mining. Experimental results obtained on the adult data of United States census in 2000 show the effectiveness and applicability of the proposed three methods.

The rest of this paper is organized as follows. Section 2 introduces the basic terminology used in the rest of the paper. Section 3 presents the three proposed fuzzy data cube based mining methods. Experimental results for the adult data of the United States census in 2000 are reported and discussed in Section 4. Section 5 includes a summary and the conclusions.

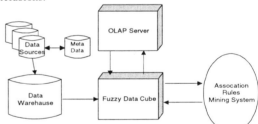

Figure 1 Architecture of the OLAP-based fuzzy association rules mining system

2. Fuzzy Data Cube Construction

Our target is to integrate fuzziness with OLAP association rules mining. To achieve this, we constructed a model that builds a fuzzy data cube first, and then utilizes the fuzzy data cube in mining fuzzy association rules. The proposed architecture, shown in Figure 1, consists of three main parts: 1) data warehouse, 2) fuzzy data cube and OLAP server, and 3) fuzzy association rules mining system. The major task of an OLAP server is to compute user's OLAP instructions, such as creating data cube, drilling, dicing, etc. The fuzzy association rules mining system is responsible for the extraction of fuzzy association rules from the constructed fuzzy data cube.

So, consider a quantitative attribute, say x. It is possible to define some fuzzy sets for x, with a membership function per fuzzy set, such that each value of x qualifies to be in one or more of these fuzzy sets. Let $F_x=\{f_x^1, f_x^2,..., f_x^l\}$ be a set of l fuzzy sets associated with x. Membership function of the j-th fuzzy set in F_x, denoted $\mu_{f_x^j}$, represents a mapping from the domain of x into the interval [0,1]. If $\mu_{f_x^j}(v)=1$ then value v of x totally belongs to fuzzy set f_x^j. On the other hand, $\mu_{f_x^j}(v)=0$ means that v is not a member of f_x^j. All other values between 0 and 1, exclusive, specify "partial membership". This concept is used next in building a fuzzy data cube.

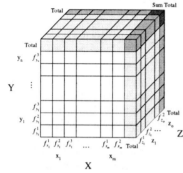

Figure 2 An example 3-dimensional fuzzy data cube

Figure 3 An example 2-dimensional fuzzy data cube

Consider a data cube with n dimensions, and given an association rules mining task involved with dimensions d_1, d_2, ..., d_n of the data cube. Each dimension of the cube contains $\sum_{i=1}^{k} l_i + 1$ values, where l_i is the number of membership functions of attribute x_i, k is the number of attributes, both in dimension X, and "+1" represents a special "Total" value in which each cell stores the aggregation value of the previous rows. Finally, a three-dimensional fuzzy data cube is shown in Figure 2, where each dimension has two attributes and the number of membership functions of each attribute varies between 2 and 3.

As the target is to find out some interesting and potentially useful fuzzy association rules with enough support and high confidence, we end this section with the definition of fuzzy association rule.

Consider a database of transactions T, its set of attributes I, and the fuzzy sets associated with quantitative attributes in I. Each transaction t_i contains values of some attributes from I and each quantitative attribute in I is associated with at least two corresponding fuzzy sets. A fuzzy association rule is defined as follows.

If $X=\{x_1, x_2, ..., x_p\}$ is $A=\{f_1, f_2, ..., f_p\}$ then
$Y=\{y_1, y_2, ..., y_q\}$ is $B=\{g_1, g_2, ..., g_q\}$,

where X, Y are itemsets, i.e., disjoint subsets of I, and A and B contain the fuzzy sets associated with corresponding attributes in X and Y, respectively, i.e., f_i is a fuzzy set related to attribute x_i and g_j is a fuzzy set related to attribute y_j.

3. OLAP Mining of Fuzzy Association Rules

3.1. Single Dimension Method

Single dimension association rules mining concentrates on the correlation within one dimension by grouping the other dimension. Shown in Figure 3 is an example of such a cube with two dimensions involved in the single dimension association rules mining process. One of the dimensions is referred to as transaction dimension and the set of attributes associated with it constitute the other dimension.

By grouping attributes in the transaction dimension, a transaction table can be transformed into a set-based table in which items sharing the same transactional attribute are merged into one tuple. Note that there is no point in partitioning attributes in the transactional dimension into fuzzy sets because the mining process is performed in the non-transactional dimension.

After constructing the fuzzy data cube, the process of association rules mining starts by identifying large itemsets. An itemset is large if it is a combination of items that have a support over a predefined minimum support. The mining process and hence identifying large itemsets is performed based on the sum of sharing rates, denoted SR, and defined in terms of the degree of membership in the fuzzy sets. If more than one membership function intersect with the real values of an attribute, then all the cells related to these functions are updated. So, each cell in Figure 3 stores an SR value.

To generate fuzzy association rules, all sets of items that have a support above a user specified threshold should be determined first. Itemsets with at least a minimum support value are called large itemsets. The fuzzy support value of itemset Y and its corresponding set of fuzzy sets F, denoted $FSupport(Y, F)$ is computed as:

$$FSupport(Y,F)=\frac{\sum_{for\,all\,x_i\,in\,X} \prod_{y_j \in Y} SR_{(y_j, f_j^*)} (f_j^n \in F, x_i . f_j^n)}{sumTotal}$$

3.2. Multidimensional Method

In this method, the correlation is among a set of dimensions, i.e., the items forming a rule come from different dimensions. Therefore, each dimension should be partitioned at the fuzzy set level.

The table in Figure 3:

		x_1	x_2	Sum Total
	Total	32.98	29.38	62.36
	f_2^3	3.10		3.10
y_2	f_2^2	6.48	11.08	17.56
	f_2^1	8.04	5.18	13.22
y_1	f_1^2	5.12	7.46	12.58
	f_1^1	10.24	5.66	15.9
		x_1	x_2	Total

Dimension Y (left axis) / Dimension X (Transaction Dimension)

Here, consider a fuzzy data cube with 3 dimensions, if values of attributes x_i, y_j and z_k have membership degrees $\mu^m(x_i)$, $\mu^n(y_j)$ and $\mu^o(z_k)$ in fuzzy sets f_i^m, f_j^n and f_k^o, respectively, then sr of the fuzzy sets of the corresponding cell is computed as $\mu^m(x_i) \cdot \mu^n(y_j) \cdot \mu^o(z_k)$. This may be generalized for n-dimensions. So, the frequency for each itemset can be directly obtained from one cell of the fuzzy cube. In a way similar to the single dimension case, each cell stores the product of the membership grades of different items, one item per dimension. As the example data cube shown in Figure 2 has three dimensions, each cell stores the product of the membership grades of three items, one from each of the three dimensions. Finally, the fuzzy support value of each cell is calculated as follows:

$$FSupport = \frac{SR}{sumTotal}.$$

3.3. Hybrid Method

This method is based on a hybrid structure, which combines single and multidimensional rules without repetitive items within one dimension. In this case, each candidate itemset can be written as $L_{h\backslash brid} = L_{single} \bigcup L_{multi}$, where L_{single} and L_{multi} are the items from one dimension and multi-dimensions, respectively.

The reason for using this new method is to provide the opportunity for one dimension to dominate over others. This dominating dimension corresponds to the one referred to as non-transactional dimension in the single dimension method. The motivation is to overcome the database size problem as follows; instead of looking for all possible associations, we look for rules containing specific items in a fuzzy data cube. The problem is reduced into how to efficiently identify itemsets which are relevant to our data requirements, and then construct association rules that satisfy our needs. This way, we avoid considering data and rules that do not meet the current data requirements.

To illustrate this, consider the 3-dimensional fuzzy data cube shown in Figure 2. If the three dimensions X, Y and Z are assumed to represent the transaction, the dominating (non-transaction) and the other dimension, respectively, then we can obtain a rule including the triplet (y_1, y_2, z_1), with its fuzzy support calculated as:

$$FSupport = \frac{\sum_{forall\ x_i\ only\ in\ z_i \in Z} \prod_{y_j \in Y} SR_{(x_j,f_j^n)}[f_j^n \in F, (x_i.f_i^m).(y_j.f_j^n)]}{sumTotal}$$

4. Experimental Results

We performed some empirical tests in order to evaluate the performance of the proposed approach. All of the experiments were conducted on a Pentium III, 1.4GHz CPU with 512 MB of memory and running Windows 2000. As experimental data, we constructed the fuzzy data cube using 10 attributes and 100K transactional records from the adult data of the United States census in 2000.

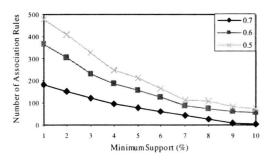

Figure 4 Effect of different minimum confidence values on mining 2-dimensional fuzzy data cube

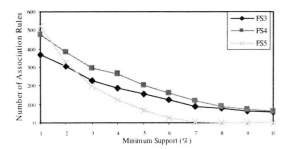

Figure 5 Effect of different numbers of fuzzy sets on mining 2-dimensional fuzzy data cube

Three sequences of tests were carried out, one for each of the three methods presented in Section 3. Each set of tests necessitates the construction of a fuzzy data cube which complies with the requirements of the method under investigation; for each dimension of the cube, a set of attributes was picked up from the experimental database. Finally, each set consists of two experiments to evaluate our approach with respect to the following dimensions: 1) number of association rules generated for different values of minimum support and different minimum confidence values, namely, 0.5, 0.6 and 0.7; and 2) number of association rules generated for different values of minimum support and different numbers of fuzzy sets, namely 3, 4 and 5 fuzzy sets, denoted FS3, FS4 and FS5, respectively. Note that in the experiments, unless otherwise specified, the minimum confidence and the number of fuzzy sets have been set to 0.6 and 4, respectively.

The first set of experiments was carried out to test the first method on a 2-dimensional fuzzy data cube with 6 attributes used to construct the non-transaction dimension; the results are shown in Figures 4 and 5. According to Figure 4, the number of the rules mined decreases as the minimum support value increases. This is quite consistent with our intuition. Also, the curve is smoother as the minimum confidence value increases. This means that the minimum support value has large effect on the number of mined rules for smaller minimum confidence values. As Figure 5 is concerned, larger number of fuzzy sets generates more rules for FS3 and FS4. However, as the minimum support value increase, the curve of FS5 drops quickly and after a particular minimum support value, it generates fewer rules than the others. This is reasonable since a large number of fuzzy sets will easily scatter quantities of an item from different transactions in different sets.

In the second set of experiments, we applied the second method on a 3-dimensional fuzzy data cube; each dimension has 3 quantitative attributes. The results are shown in Figures 6 and 7. The curves plotted in Figure 6 show the relationships between number of rules mined and minimum support values for different values of minimum confidence.

The numbers of association rules produced for different number of fuzzy sets are given in Figure 7. In this case, each itemset of a given rule is coming from different dimensions. It is worth mentioning that the same interpretation about Figures 4 and 5 is valid for Figures 6 and 7, respectively.

The last set of experiments is dedicated to testing the hybrid method on the same 3-dimentional fuzzy data cube used in the previous set of experiments. The results are shown in Figures 8 and 9. The same interpretation for Figures 4 and 5 are also valid for Figures 8 and 9, respectively. As the results obtained from all the three methods are consistent, it is anticipated that our approach presented in this paper is equally effective regardless of the number of fuzzy sets utilized in the process.

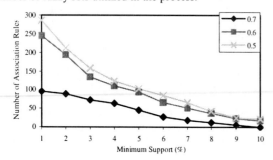

Figure 6 Effect of different minimum confidence values on mining 3-dimensional fuzzy data cube

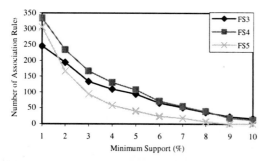

Figure 7 Effect of different numbers of fuzzy sets on mining 3-dimensional fuzzy data cube

5. Summary and Conclusions

In this paper, we proposed a general architecture that utilizes a fuzzy data cube for knowledge discovery in quantitative attributes. Also, we presented three different methods for the online mining of fuzzy association rules from the proposed architecture. One method deals with the

mining of fuzzy association rules in 2-dimensional fuzzy data cube. The other two methods handle the mining process in multidimensional fuzzy data cube. We have already tested the last two methods on a 3-dimensional fuzzy data cube. The experiments conducted on adult data of the United States census in 2000 showed that the proposed approach produces meaningful results and has reasonable efficiency.

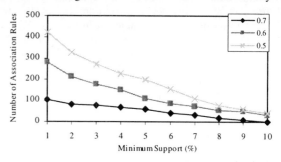

Figure 8 Effect of different minimum confidence values on mining 3-dimensional fuzzy data cube for the hybrid case

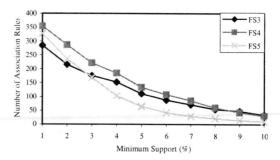

Figure 9 Effect of different numbers of fuzzy sets on mining 3-dimensional fuzzy data cube for the hybrid case

References

[1] C.C. Agarwal and P.S. Yu, "A new approach to online generation of association rules," *IEEE TKDE*, Vol.13, No.4, pp.527-540, 2001.

[2] R. Agrawal, A. Gupta, S. Sarawagi, "Modeling Multidimensional Databases," *Proc. of IEEE ICDE*, 1997.

[3] K.C.C. Chan and W.H. Au, "Mining Fuzzy Association Rules," *Proc. of ACM CIKM*, pp.209-215, 1997.

[4] J. Han and Y. Fu, "Mining multiple-level association rules in large databases," *IEEE TKDE*, Vol.11, pp.798-804, 1999.

[5] C. Hidber, "Online Association Rule Mining," *Proc. of ACM SIGMOD*, pp. 145-156, 1999.

[6] M. Kamber, J. Han and J.Y. Chiang, "Meta-rule guided mining of multidimensional association rules using data cubes," *Proc. of ACM KDD*, pp.207-210, 1997.

[7] M. Kaya, R. Alhajj, F. Polat and A. Arslan, "Efficient Automated Mining of Fuzzy Association Rules," *Proc. of DEXA*, 2002.

[8] D. Margaritis, C. Faloutsos and S. Thrun, "NetCube: A Scalable Tool for Fast Data Mining and Compression," *Proc. of VLDB*, 2001.

[9] W. Zhang, "Mining Fuzzy Quantitative Association Rules," *Proc. of IEEE ICTAI*, pp.99-102, 1999.

Analyzing High-Dimensional Data by Subspace Validity*

Amihood Amir,[†] Reuven Kashi, Nathan S. Netanyahu[‡]
Bar-Ilan University
Department of Computer Science
52900 Ramat-Gan, Israel
{amir,kashi,nathan}@cs.biu.ac.il

Daniel Keim, Markus Wawryniuk
University of Konstanz
Computer & Information Scienc
78457 Konstanz, Germany
{keim,wawryniu}@informatik.uni-konstanz.de

Abstract

We are proposing a novel method that makes it possible to analyze high dimensional data with arbitrary shaped projected clusters and high noise levels. At the core of our method lies the idea of subspace validity. We map the data in a way that allows us to test the quality of subspaces using statistical tests. Experimental results, both on synthetic and real data sets, demonstrate the potential of our method.

1. Introduction

The concept of "cluster" is somewhat elusive. From an intuitive sense, it means points in a cluster are "close" to each other while they are "far" from other points. The meaning of "closeness" corresponds to the meaning of "similarity". This definition raises some questions:

Projected Clusters: Typically, a relation may exist between some, but not all, variables. Consequently, the clusters are not defined over all attributes, i.e. values in some attributes are similar, but in other attributes not. It is possible that projecting the space into a smaller dimensional space will yield interesting clusters that do not exist in the original data space.

Topology: Clusters may have different shapes and linear dependencies. We may be interested in identifying a plane in a multidimensional space as a cluster.

Dimensions: A Cluster spreads over a subset of dimensions, implying a relationship between these dimensions. Different clusters may also share some dimensions, meaning that different values of a variable v relate to some subset of variables, while other values of v relate to a different set of variables.

Overlaps: It is possible that under a certain projection, two clusters overlap and can not be distinguished, whereas in another projection they are separated. In an even more drastic situation, a cluster may not be identified under *any* projection!

For clustering visual methods have proven to be quite successful. Such methods use the perceptual capabilities of the human. Knowledge about the domain/task flows into the process step by step and is exploited both for a successful understanding of dependencies in the particular domain and for ferring out and separating clusters [6, 7].

Albeit the success of such visualization methods, it is necessary to develop automated clustering algorithms. The reason for this need is the existence of very large high dimensional data sets that need to be analyzed. Considering all different 2- or 3-dimensional projections is clearly not a feasible number for interactive human analysis.

Automated methods have the advantage of speed but the disadvantage of lacking domain knowledge. Harnessing such knowledge through preprocessing work or by machine learning methods is a laborious process and the state-of-the-art is far from satisfactory. The above mentioned challenges of cluster finding do not have good solutions by current methods of automatic data exploration.

---

*This work was partially funded by the Information Society Technologies programme of the European Commission, Future and Emerging Technologies under the IST-2001-33058 PANDA project (2001-2004).

[†]Partially supported by NSF grant CCR-01-04494, and ISF grant 282/01.

[‡]And: Univiversity of Maryland, Center for Automation Research, College Park, MD 20742

Current methods for cluster finding differ in their requirements of domain knowledge and they require parameters (such as the requested number of clusters) as input for the algorithm. In addition, they depend on the amount of noise in the data and that affects the quality of the results.

2. Our Contribution

We are proposing a novel method that makes it possible to analyze high dimensional data with high noise levels. Our method requires no domain knowledge in advance, yet it discovers projected clusters and allows separating overlapping clusters with different topologies.

At the core of our method lies the idea of *subspace validity*. We map the data in a way that allows us to test the parameters of a one-dimensional subspace. It is possible to perform various statistical tests efficiently in one dimension. In these projections, one of the variables is designated as the subspace whose validity is checked by various statistical means. The result of these tests allows us to reach a conclusion about clustering in the low-dimensional subspace.

Our goal is analyzing high-dimensional data sets in order to find structures and patterns that can be considered as interesting to the end user. It is accepted that if the human eye would perceptually capture a pattern in a subset of data points, then it is considered as valuable information which should be noticed and investigated further. The traditional way to capture such "similar" data objects is by the various definitions of clustering in the literature. Therefore, to demonstrate the efficiency and effectiveness of our proposed method, we compare it against clustering algorithms in the databases literature. However, it should be stressed that we are not defining "clusters" in any traditional formal sense. We are seeking a more general method that can automatically detect "interesting" structures in high dimensional data sets. Therefore, our use of the word "clusters" to define such structures is intentionally quite loose.

3. The Subspace Validity Algorithm

Given a m-dimensional database DB, we first project the data set onto every subset of 3 dimensions. For each 3-dimensional projection, we designate one dimension (i.e., attribute) as the *vertical dimension*, i.e., the one-dimensional subspace whose subspace validity is tested. The proposed approach has four major stages.

Constructing compact images from the data. The first stage consists of building compact 2-dimensional images for every triple of dimensions $\langle X, Y, Z \rangle$. Let M_{XY} denote the image matrix. In every M_{XY} entry or pixel (x, y) we store information about the conditional distribution $P(Z|(x, y))$ of the Z variable associated with that entry.

Feature extraction from the image. Recall that for the same (x, y) location in the image M_{XY}, there can be many z values in the Z dimension. A feature function returns for each pixel an extracted feature vector associated with that pixel. These values are assigned to $M_{XY}^{Z}(x, y)$. In our implementation we used the Haar wavelet transformation for our feature function.

Let us illustrate this idea with a simple case. In [4], a single representative value was chosen for each entry of M_{XY}, the *median* of all Z values at location (x, y), assuming a unimodal distribution at that location.

Image segmentation. Since M_{XY}^{Z} represents an image, we can segment the image by applying standard *image segmentation* techniques. The segmentation of M_{XY}^{Z} yields regions, such that the pixels of a region have similar features. The strategy we have used for segmentation is based on region growing.

Region analysis. At this stage we have possibly a large number of different regions of the various X and Y attributes, such that the values of the associated vertical Z dimensions in each such region are distributed in a similar manner. Using this information about the regions, we can analyze the data points in order to further discover prospective clusters either in the same attribute subspace or in some augmented subspace projections.

The clustering scheme we have used consists of the following characteristics:

1. Consider the two-dimensional projection on X and Y. A pixel stores information about the distribution of the Z values of the points which are mapped to the corresponding cell.

2. We find regions (dense and compact) with similar distribution of Z.

3. A region corresponds to a low-dimensional cluster. In order to augment the set of dimensions which define the cluster, we partition all points into two sets; points which belong to the region and points which do not. The two subsets are processed recursively. We use the *partition tree* concept which is a generalization of the separator tree concept used in HD-Eye [6].

4. Searching for projected clusters is motivated by the fact that it might not be possible to augment a certain dimension set, i.e., the cluster is not defined in all dimensions; it is a projected cluster.

5. Clusters correspond to the leafs of the partition tree.

4. Evaluation and Comparison

In the experiments, we use a number of data sets with controlled characteristics, such as the number of dimensions or noise level, as well as real data sets. In the exper-

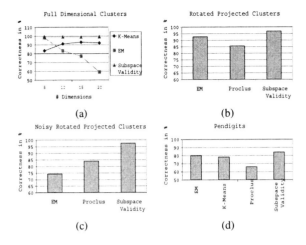

Full Dimensional Clusters	Rotated Projected Clusters
(a)	(b)

Noisy Rotated Projected Clusters	Pendigits
(c)	(d)

Figure 1. Experimental results

iments, we compare our new approach to existing methods including Expectation Maximization (EM) [5], K-Means and PROCLUS [1].

In the first experiment, we present the effectiveness of our approach on clusters which are defined in all dimensions, which we will refer to as full-dimensional clusters. The type of data we generated is similar to the data created in [1], taking into account that all dimensions are selected. The results are shown in Figure 1(a). The performance of K-Means remains constant and EM is degenerating with increasing dimensionality, whereas our solution provides the best overall effectiveness.

Full-dimensional clusters are unlikely to occur in high-dimensional data sets. Real clusters often describe linear dependencies between the dimensions which define the cluster. Therefore we analyze the ability of the algorithms to find rotated projected clusters. The type of data we generated is similar to the data created in [1] and [2]. The results are shown in Figure 1(b). The results represent the average correctness over a number of data sets of this type. Subspace Validity has the best overall correctness. EM performs surprisingly well and provides a better performance than PROCLUS.

In the next experiment, we examined the effect of noise in the data. For this series of experiments, we added random noise to the data sets from our second experiments and repeated the tests. The new results (see Figure 1(c)) show that the effectiveness of our method remains unchanged, but the performance of EM and PROCLUS degenerates. Interestingly, the performance of EM degenerates much faster than the performance of PROCLUS.

We performed experiments with two real data sets. The first one is the *pendigits* data set from the University of California at Irvine's Machine Learning Reposi-

tory (www.ics.uci.edu/~mlearn/MLRepository.html). The pendigits data set contains 7,494 tuples and 16 dimensions that describe handwritten digits. The results of this experiment is shown in Figure 1(d). With our method we get the best correctness of 84%, followed by EM with 80% and K-Means with 78%. From the extremely low classification rate of PROCLUS (only 66%, we tested all kinds of values for the number of bounded dimensions), we may conclude that clusters are spread over all dimensions.

Our second real data set is the census data set *nhis93ac* (NHIS – National Health Interview Survey 1993). The data set is available from (http://ferret.bls.census.gov/). It has several hundred numeric and nominal attributes and consists of 45951 records. The numerical attributes *AGE, BDAY12, DV12, EDUC, INCFAMR, NCOND, WEIGHT* were selected. Since the data does not come with a known classification, we have to judge the accuracy of the clusters by looking at the results. For this purpose, we use the Subspace Validity plots.

An example can be seen in Figure 2. The clusters are defined in three dimensions, namely AGE, WEIGHT and NCOND. The AGE attribute is on the horizontal axis, WEIGHT is the vertical axis, and NCOND is the vertical dimension and is represented by a symbol.[1] Recall that a region in the X, Y projection with the same symbol means that the pixels belonging to the region have a similar data distribution in the vertical dimension Z. Therefore, same symbol means a cluster with similar data points in the third attribute. The clusters can be easily understood with the histogram of Z. Those histograms are shown in Figure 2(b),(c) and (d). The histogram is shown with gray bars, and the black line indicates the histogram of the full data set. One can see that the data points falling in the region marked with squares have lower values compared to the full data set, because the leftmost bin of the histogram for the region in Figure 2(b) is more than 10% higher than the histogram corresponding to the full dataset. Analogously, one can see that points falling in the region with solid circles have a similar distribution in the Z attribute as the full data set. But points falling in the region with the triangle point-up have higher values compared to the full data set. The pixels labeled with the plus sign are outliers. They belong to regions with very low support. The number of points falling in a particular region is 22946, 17509 and 5182, respectively. The clusters found by our method tell a very interesting story. The diagonal in the projected cluster from top left to bottom right indicates something that insurance companies love to find. The number of medical conditions increases at a younger age when the weight is greater. In fact, the diagonal can even predict at what weight and at what age one can expect the problems to accumulate.

---

[1]In reality we use colors, which will increase considerably the ability to recognize the regions.

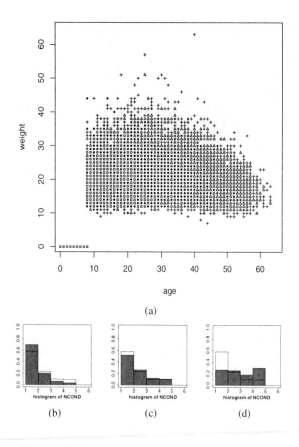

(a)

(b)   (c)   (d)

Figure 2. An example from a census data set

5. Related Work

Cluster finding has been an extensively studied problem for many years by the statistics, machine learning and database communities. For the *full-dimensional* case many clustering algorithms have been proposed [8].

The idea of *projected clustering* has attracted a lot of attention during the last few years. One of the first algorithms dealing with projected clustering is CLIQUE [3]. The algorithm mines the projection space bottom up by searching frequent combinations of histogram bins which are assembled to clusters on a single linkage basis.

The algorithms PROCLUS [1] and ORCLUS [2] are k-means like algorithms. Each cluster found is described by a centroid and a set of vectors, spanning the subspace of the projected cluster. PROCLUS reduces the full-dimensional data space to the subspace spanned by the dimensions with the smallest variance (which are treated independently) with the result that only axes-parallel projected clusters can be found. In contrast, ORCLUS determines for each cluster the eigenvectors of the covariance matrix with the smallest eigenvalues and therefore allows arbitrary orientations.

The most recent method DOC [9] defines a projected

cluster as a hyperbox, with a boundary size of w in the bounded dimensions and an unbounded size in the other dimensions. DOC uses sampling to center the boxes, and an optimal projected cluster maximizes a quality function.

6. Conclusions and Future Work

We have shown a methodology for finding projected clusters in high dimensional data sets. Our idea resulted in an effective way of automatically considering low dimensional projections of the data set and analyze them appropriately to obtain meaningful projected clusters. Our method constructs higher dimensional clusters from data on small dimensional projections of those clusters. In future research we plan to pursue faster implementation for our approach as well as extending it into a visual data mining system.

References

[1] C. C. Aggarwal, C. M. Procopiuc, J. L. Wolf, P. S. Yu, and J. S. Park. Fast algorithms for projected clustering. In *Proc. ACM SIGMOD International Conference on Management of Data, June 1-3, 1999, Philadephia, Pennsylvania, USA*, pages 61–72. ACM Press, 1999.

[2] C. C. Aggarwal and P. S. Yu. Finding generalized projected clusters in high dimensional spaces. In *Proc. of the 2000 ACM SIGMOD International Conference on Management of Data, May 16-18, 2000, Dallas, Texas, USA*, pages 70–81. ACM, 2000.

[3] R. Aggrawal, J. Gehrke, D. Gunopulos, and P. Raghavan. Automatic subspace clustering of high dimensional data for data mining applications. In *Proc. ACM SIGMOD International Conference on Management of Data, June 2-4, 1998, Seattle, Washington, USA*, pages 94–105. ACM Press, 1998.

[4] A. Amir, R. Kashi, and N. S. Netanyahu. Analyzing quantitative databases: Image is everything. In *VLDB 2001, Proc. of 27th International Conference on Very Large Data Bases*, pages 89–98, Roma, Italy, September 11-14 2001.

[5] A. P. Dempster, N. Laird, and D. Rubin. Maximum likelihood for incomplete data via the EM algorithm. *J. of the Royal Statistical Society, ser. B*, 39:1–38, 1977.

[6] A. Hinneburg, M. Wawryniuk, and D. A. Keim. Hd-eye: Visual mining of high-dimensional data. *IEEE Computer Graphics & Applications Journal*, 19(5):22–31, September 1999.

[7] D. A. Keim. Information visualization and visual data mining. *IEEE Transactions on Visualization and Computer Graphics (TVCG)*, 8(1):1–8, January–March 2002.

[8] D. A. Keim and A. Hinneburg. Clustering techniques for large data sets - from the past to the future. In *Tutorial Notes for ACM SIGKDD 1999 International Conference on Knowledge Discovery and Data Mining*, pages 141–181, San Diego, CA, 1999. ACM Press.

[9] C. M. Procopiuc, M. Jones, P. K. Agarwal, and T. M. Murali. A monte carlo algorithm for fast projective clustering. In *Proc. of the ACM SIGMOD international conference on Management of data*, pages 418–427. ACM Press, 2002.

Objective and Subjective Algorithms for Grouping Association Rules

Aijun An,   Shakil Khan
Department of Computer Science
York University
Toronto, Ontario M3J 1P3 Canada
aan,skhan@cs.yorku.ca

Xiangji Huang
School of Analytic Studies and
Information Technology, York University
Toronto, Ontario M3J 1P3 Canada
jhuang@cs.yorku.ca

Abstract

We propose two algorithms for grouping and summarizing association rules. The first algorithm recursively groups rules according to the structure of the rules and generates a tree of clusters as a result. The second algorithm groups the rules according to the semantic distance between the rules by making use of an automatically tagged semantic tree-structured network of items. We provide a case study in which the proposed algorithms are evaluated. The results show that our grouping methods are effective and produce good grouping results.

1   Introduction

A common problem in association rule mining is that a large number of rules are often generated from the database, which makes it difficult for human users to analyze and make use of the rules. Solutions have been proposed to overcome this problem, which include constraint-based data mining, post-pruning rules, and grouping rules. In this paper, we focus on grouping association rules. Several studies have been conducted to group association rules. One of approaches, presented in [3], uses heuristic methods based on geometric properties of two-dimensional grids to cluster discovered rules in the two-dimensional space. The problem of the approach is that it is limited to only the rules with two fixed attributes in their antecedents. Another approach presented in [6] lifts the two-dimensional restriction, but grouping is only based on numeric attributes. A third approach was proposed in [5], in which rules are grouped into clusters according to a distance measure between two association rules. The distance measure is defined as the number of transactions on which the two rules differ. A limitation of this approach is that rules that belong to the same cluster may have substantially different structures and thus it is difficult to describe the rule cluster to the user. Another similarity-based approach was described in [1], in which the similarity measure is based on attribute hierar-

chies. The attribute hierarchy is a tree structure provided by the human expert. By specifying a rule aggregation level, the rules are generalized using the non-leaf nodes at the aggregation level, and the rules with the same aggregated rule are grouped together. The benefit of this approach is that each group can be described by the aggregated rule. However, this approach requires the intensive user interaction during the grouping process. The user must specify the aggregation level. When the attribute hierarchy is huge, the user may not have a clear idea about what would be the appropriate aggregation level.

We propose two algorithms for grouping association rules. The first algorithm, called the Objective Grouping algorithm (the *OG* algorithm), groups the rules according to the syntactic structure of the rules without using any domain knowledge. The second algorithm, referred to as the Subjective Grouping algorithm (the *SG* algorithm), incorporates domain knowledge and groups the rules according to the semantic information of the objects in the rules. Both algorithms group similar rules together and provide users with a high-level overview of the rules. In addition, the two algorithms require little intervention from the user during the rule grouping process and can be applied to association rules that are derived from a database containing a large number of different items or attributes.

2   The Objective Grouping Algorithm

Let I be a set of all items in a domain and D be a set of transactions over I. A transaction is a subset of I. The association rule is an implication of the form $A \rightarrow B$, where $A \subseteq I$, $B \subseteq I$, and $A \cap B = \emptyset$. A is called the antecedent of the rule and B is called the consequent of the rule. Let R be a set of association rules over I. Let $a, b \in I$ and $\rho = \{a\} \rightarrow \{b\}$. Note that ρ may or may not be in R. The *cover* of ρ in R, $cover_R(\rho)$, is defined as[1] $cover_R(\rho) = \{r \in R | r = A \rightarrow B, a \in A, b \in B\}$. Intuitively, $cover_R(\rho)$

---

[1] Our definitions of *cover* and *seed rule* are recast from the definitions of *coverage list* and *ancestor rule* in [4].

contains all the rules in R that have a in their antecedent and b in their consequent. Again, note that $\rho \notin cover_R(\rho)$ when $\rho \notin R$. The *seed rule* of the cover of ρ in R is defined to be ρ. The *size* of the cover of ρ in R, $size_R(\rho)$, is the number of rules in $cover_R(\rho)$.

The basic idea of the OG algorithm is to recursively group rules with common items in their antecedents and consequents until some criteria are satisfied. The result of the algorithm is a tree of clusters, in which each leaf node is a rule and each non-leaf node is a cluster that contains all the rules in its children. In addition, each cluster has a unique label or group name, which is the ancestor rule of the cluster. For example, given a set of association rules $\{ab \rightarrow cd, bcd \rightarrow ae, abe \rightarrow d, ac \rightarrow d, b \rightarrow a, d \rightarrow c\}$, the OG algorithm can generate a tree of clusters shown in Figure 1, where non-leaf nodes denote clusters.

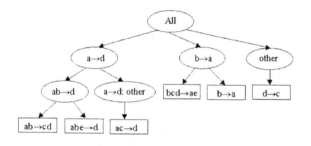

Figure 1. Sample Output of the OG Algorithm

The OG algorithm is presented in Figure 2. It takes four inputs: I, R, $threshold$ and $depth$, which are explained in the figure. The $depth$ parameter should be 1 when the algorithm is first called. The algorithm works as follows. As long as the number of ungrouped rules is greater than a certain predefined limit[2], it tries to group the rules in the following manner. First, it searches for a seed rule ρ (with single item antecedent and single item consequent) that has the $depth$'th largest size of cover in R by enumerating over all possible combinations. Here, rather than considering the largest cover, we search for the $depth$'th largest cover to avoid grouping items using the same seed rule over and over again, in a recursive call. The reason behind this is that we have already classified the largest cover into one group in one of the upper levels of recursion. After a seed rule ρ is selected, the cover of ρ in R is computed and all the rules in the cover is grouped into a single cluster, labeled as group ρ. Next, if $cover_R(\rho)$ has more than $threshold$ elements, we recursively group them. To reduce the complexity of the process, when we recursively call the OG algorithm, we reduce the size of the itemset I by keeping only the items that appear in $cover_R(\rho)$. For the rest of the rules in R, i.e., for $R - cover_R(\rho)$, we repeat this procedure until the

---

[2]In the algorithm, we reuse the $threshold$ to define this limit. Another threshold can be used for this purpose.

Algorithm: Objective_Grouping
Input: I = a set of items;
  R = a set of association rules over I;
  $threshold$ = the maximum number of rules in a group;
  $depth$ = the depth of recursive call.
Output: $Output$=the grouped version of R.
Begin

1. $Output \leftarrow \emptyset$;

2. **While** $|R| > threshold$ **Begin**

3.   **For** $i = 1$ to $|I|$

4.   **For** $j = 1$ to $|I|$

5. $count_{i,j} = 0$;

6.   **For** $i = 1$ to $|R|$

7.   **For** each item a in the antecedent

8.   **For** each item b in the consequent

9. $count_{a,b} \leftarrow count_{a,b} + 1$;

10.   **If** the $depth$'th largest $count_{a,b} = 0$, **Return** R;

11. $(x, y) \leftarrow$ the index of the $depth$'th largest $count_{a,b}$

12. $\rho \leftarrow$ rule $\{x\} \rightarrow \{y\}$;

13.   Compute $cover_R(\rho)$;

14.   Group all the rules in $cover_R(\rho)$ with label "ρ"

15.   **If** $|cover_R(\rho)| > threshold$ **Begin**

16. $I_\rho \leftarrow$ all the items appearing in $cover_R(\rho)$;

17. $cover_R(\rho) \leftarrow$ **Objective_Grouping**$(I_\rho, cover_\rho, threshold, depth + 1)$;

18.   **End**

19. $Output \leftarrow Output \cup cover_R(\rho)$;

20. $R \leftarrow R - cover_R(\rho)$;

21. **End**

22. Group R with label "other";

23. $Output \leftarrow Output \cup other$;

24. **Return** $Output$;

End

Figure 2. The Objective Grouping Algorithm

number of leftover rules is less than $threshold$. Finally, we group and label these leftovers as the "other" group and terminate the procedure.

3 The Subjective Grouping Algorithm

The SG algorithm makes use of domain knowledge. The domain knowledge it uses is a tagged semantic network, which is a special type of taxonomy or *is-a*-hierarchy. The semantic network is provided by domain experts and has the following properties. (1) The taxonomy contains one or more trees. Each node in a tree represents an object or item. The upper level nodes represent generalization of their children. (2) Both leaf and non-leaf nodes of the taxonomy can be present in the antecedent and consequent of a rule. (3) Each node of the taxonomy is associated with a pair of numbers, which represents the relative position of the node

478

in the taxonomy. We call this pair of numbers the *Relative Semantic Position* (RSP) of the node. Generally, if two objects are closer to each other in terms of their semantic distance, their RSPs are also closer and vice versa. RSPs can be specified by domain experts. But to reduce the degree of user intervention, we assign a RSP to each node automatically as follows. We define the RSP of a node to consist of two numbers, denoted as $(hpos, vpos)$, where $hpos$ represents the horizontal position of the node in the tree and $vpos$ represents the vertical position of the node in the tree. We use the level of the node in the tree to represent the vertical position of the node. To assign a $hpos$ to each node, we first create a completely balanced tree by adding artificial nodes to the tree, do an in-order traversal of the balanced tree, and then remove the artificial nodes. While performing in-order traversal of the tree, we assign gradually monotonically increasing integers to the nodes of the tree as their $hpos$ values. Therefore, the $hpos$ value of a node is the position of the node in the balanced tree's in-order traversal sequence. Figure 3 illustrates a tagged unbalanced tree with its RSPs assigned by this method. The benefit of this method for assigning RSPs is that the tree can be easily visualized using the RSP values in a two dimensional space. If the semantic network contains multiple trees, we can either make it a single tree by adding a root node on top of all the trees, or assign RSPs for each tree individually but with different value ranges.

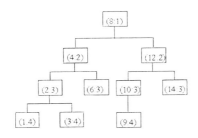

Figure 3. A Tagged Tree with RSP Values

Having assigned a RSP to each node of the taxonomy, we use RSPs to represent the objects or items in each association rule. We then calculate the average RSP of all the elements in a rule's antecedent and the average RSP of all the elements in the rule's consequent. The rule is then represented by two mean RSPs. Since each of the two mean RSPs corresponds to a point in a two-dimensional space, the rule can be further represented by a directed line segment (pointing from the antecedent mean to the consequent mean) in the two dimensional space. For example, consider the following rule described by the RSPs of its objects: $\{(2,3), (4,2)\} \rightarrow \{(9,4), (10,3)\}$. We can represent the rule using the mean RSPs of its antecedent and consequent as $\{3, 2.5\} \rightarrow \{(9.5, 3.5)\}$ and further depict the rule using a directed line segment, as shown in Figure 4.

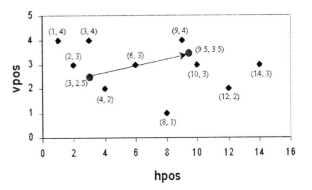

Figure 4. A Rule Represented by a Line Segment in the Object Taxonomy Space

Once the rules are represented using line segments, the problem of grouping association rules is converted to the problem of clustering line segments. We can use a standard clustering algorithm to cluster the line segments, and modify the distance function used in the clustering algorithm to measure the distance between two line segments. Our distance function is defined as $Distance(s_1, s_2) = 1 - cos(s_1, s_2) + NDist(c_1, c_2) + NDiff(length(s_1), length(s_2))$, where s_1 and s_2 are two line segments, $cos(s_1, s_2)$ takes the cosine of the angle between s_1 and s_2, c_1 and c_2 are the center points of s_1 and s_2 respectively, $NDist$ represents normalized distance and $NDiff$ denotes the normalized difference, and $length(x)$ computes the length of segment x.

The SG algorithm is presented in Figure 5. It groups together rules with similar antecedents and similar consequents, and labels each group by the mean RSPs of the rules in the group, which indicate the position of the group in the semantic network. The algorithm can generate a hierarchy of clusters if a hierarchical clustering method is used for grouping line segments.

4 A Case Study

We have applied the OG and SG algorithms to group association rules discovered in a Web mining application. The data set used in the application is the Web log data produced by Livelink[3], which provides automatic management and retrieval of a wide variety of information objects. From the data set, a large number of rules were generated. We first ranked the rules according to an interestingness measure [2] and then selected the top 100 rules for use in our evaluation. In the evaluation, we asked our domain expert to group the 100 rules and then compared the results from the OG and SG algorithms with the expert grouping. Our domain expert

---

[3]Livelink is a commercial product of Open Text Corporation (http://www.opentext.com).

Algorithm: Subjective_Grouping
Input: a tagged tree or forest;
      a set of mined association rules R;
Output: a set of grouped association rules
Begin

1. **For** each rule in R **Begin**

2.   Replace each item in the rule with its RSP;

3.   Compute the mean of RSPs of all the items in the antecedent of the rule and the mean of RSPs of all the items in the consequent;

4.   Add the two means and the rule id as a record in table T

5. **End**

6. Call a clustering algorithm to group the line segments (represented by the two means) in T, using our distance function;

7. Label each group with the mean of RSPs in the antecedents and the mean of RSPs in the consequents of the rules in the group;

8. **Return** the grouped association rules;

End

Figure 5. The Subjective Grouping Algorithm

Group size	1	2	3	4	5	20	25	26
Num. of groups	4	4	1	1	2	1	1	1

Table 1. Group Size Distribution from Experts

groups the 100 rules into 15 groups. The distribution of the group size is shown in Table 1. The results of OG and SG are shown in Table 2. There are two runs of the OG algorithm (OG-1 and OG-2), using two different thresholds (i.e., the maximum numbers of the rules in a cluster). Each run of OG produces a tree of clusters. The table shows the number of levels of the cluster tree, the number of clusters at the lowest non-leaf level (shown in the table as No. of clusters), the number of lowest non-leaf level clusters that are completely the same as a cluster from the expert (No. of compl. cor. clusters) and the grouping accuracy. The grouping accuracy is calculated as follows. For each pair of rules, we know whether they should belong to the same group based on the grouping result from the domain expert. If two rules that should belong to the same group are clustered into the same group or if two rules that should not belong to the same group are clustered into different groups, we call it a "match"; otherwise, it is a mis-match. The grouping accuracy is defined as $accuracy = \frac{Number\ of\ matches}{Total\ number\ of\ rule\ pairs}$.

The information objects in the Livelink environment are organized into a structure that contains over 2000 trees. To run the SG algorithm, we first tagged the trees with our automatic tagging method. We then used a hierarchical agglomerative clustering algorithm to cluster the line segments within the SG program. The program generates a dendrogram that shows the levels of nested merging. When we evaluate the performance, we cut the dendrogram at the level where there are 15 clusters, and based on these clusters we calculate the grouping accuracy. Due to the use of hierarchical clustering, the result of grouping is also a tree of clusters. The number of levels shown in Table 2 for the SG run is the level of the tree produced on top of the 15 clusters. In general, the program can do k-way clustering. Here we set k to be 15, which is the actual number of groups produced by the expert. From Table 2 we can see that the SG algorithm produces more accurate results than the OG algorithm.

5 Conclusions

We have presented two new algorithms for grouping a large number of (interesting) association rules. We also presented a case study in which we applied the two algorithms to group a set of interesting association rules discovered from the Livelink log data. Our experiment shows that both methods are effective and produce good grouping result with respect to the expert grouping result.

Acknowledgment

We would like to thank Open Text Corporation and CITO for supporting this research, and Mr. Miao Wen for his help in implementing the algorithms presented in the paper.

References

[1] Adomavicius, G. and Tuzhilin, A. "Expert-driven validation of rule-based user models in personalization applications", *Data Mining and Knowledge Discovery*, vol.5, nos.1/2, January/April 2001.

[2] Huang, X., An, A., Cercone, N and Promhouse, G. "Discovery of Interesting Association Rules from Livelink Web Log data", *Proc. of the IEEE Int. Conf. on Data Mining (ICDM'02)*, Maebashi City, Japan, 2002.

[3] Lent, B., Swami, A.N., and Widom, J. "Clustering Association Rules", *Proc. of ICDE*, 1997.

[4] Sahar, S., "Interestingness via What is not Interesting", *Proceedings of KDD'99*, 1999, pp.332-336.

[5] Toivonen, H., Klemettinen, M., Ronkainen, P., Hatonen, K. and Mannila, H. "Pruning and grouping discovered association rules", *Proc. of KDD'95*.

[6] Wang, K., Tay, S.H.W. and Liu, B. "Interestingness-based interval merger for numeric association rules", *Proc. of KDD'98*.

Run	Threshold	No. of levels	No. of clusters	No. of compl. cor. clusters	Accuracy
OG-1	26	3	11	6	81.2%
OG-2	20	4	13	4	71.5%
SG	15	9	15	12	93.7%

Table 2. Results of the OG and SG Algorithm

Efficient Subsequence Matching in Time Series Databases Under Time and Amplitude Transformations

Tassos Argyros
School of Electrical and Computer Engineering
National Technical University of Athens
Athens, Greece
targyros@cs.ntua.gr

Charis Ermopoulos
School of Electrical and Computer Engineering
National Technical University of Athens
Athens, Greece
ermop@cs.ntua.gr

Abstract

Subsequence matching in large time series databases has attracted a lot of interest and many methods have been proposed that cope with this problem in an adequate extend. However, locating subsequence matches of arbitrary length, under time and amplitude transformations, has received far less attention and is still an open problem. In this paper we present an efficient algorithm for variable-length subsequence matching under transformations that guarantees no false dismissals. Further, this algorithm uses a novel similarity criterion for determining similarity under amplitude transformations in a most efficient way. Finally, our algorithm has been tested in various experiments on real data, resulting in a running time improvement of one order of magnitude compared to the naive approach.

1. Introduction

The problem of efficiently locating matches of a given time sequence in a large temporal database has recently attracted a lot of interest in the research community and many methods have been proposed that cope with this problem in an adequate extend [1, 12, 9, 5]. However, most of the proposed methods locate matches of the same length. Finding matches under *time scaling* of a given time sequence within a large database, efficiently and with no false dismissals, is still an open problem.

The specific problem is very important, since it is profoundly related with self-similarity in time series. In a nutshell, self-similarity simply means reproducing oneself on different time scales. It is now known that a widely extended range of man-made and natural phenomena exhibit self-similarity and power-law behavior. Some examples include financial time series [14] and human speech signals [15]. The proposed algorithm is ideal for analyzing large self-similar time sequences as the ones mentioned, while most of the relevant existing methods are either computationally inefficient or use approximation methods that allow false dismissals.

In this paper we present a method that can locate any scaled occurrence (under scaling in both time and amplitude axes) of a query sequence in a large time series database; in fact, the method guarantees no false dismissals. The proposed method is efficient (outperforms the naive approach for over an order of magnitude), reliable (a proof that it has no false dismissals is presented in [2]) and its applications extend in a broad range of scientific and financial areas.

2. Similarity under V-axis transformations—the CD-criterion

In order to decide on the similarity of time series that appear under different scale and offset in V-axis, we need to define time series similarity in a more flexible manner. Such flexibility can be achieved by using the following similarity measure.

Definition 2.1 *Given two time series, $T[1 \ldots n]$ and $Q[1 \ldots n]$ and a positive real constant ϵ, we define T to be ϵ-similar to Q if there exist real constants c and d such that*

$$\sum_{i=1}^{n} (c \cdot T[i] + d - Q[i])^2 < \epsilon.$$

We now propose the *CD-criterion* which enables us to decide (without error) whether a time series is ϵ-similar to another—that is, similar under amplitude scale and shift transformations.

Theorem 2.1 *Given two time series, $T[1 \ldots n]$ and*

481

$Q[1 \ldots n]$, T is ϵ-similar to Q if and only if

$$\left(\Sigma(T) \cdot (T \cdot Q) - \|T\|^2 \cdot \Sigma(Q) \right)^2 -$$

$$- \Big(\left(\Sigma(T)^2 - n \cdot \|T\|^2 \right) \cdot$$

$$\cdot \left(\epsilon \cdot \|T\|^2 + (T \cdot Q)^2 - \|T\|^2 \cdot \|Q\|^2 \right) \Big) > 0, \ (1)$$

where $\Sigma(T) = \sum_{i=1}^{n} T[i]$, $\|T\| = \sqrt{\sum_{i=1}^{n} T[i]^2}$ (respectively for Q) and $T \cdot Q = \sum_{i=1}^{n} (T[i] \cdot Q[i])$.

Notice that inequality (1) includes only the arguments $\Sigma(T)$, $\|T\|$, $\Sigma(Q)$, $\|Q\|$, $T \cdot Q$ and ϵ. Thus, in case we are interested in comparing two time series T, Q in a "growing window" or "sliding window" scan, the evaluation of the sums $(\Sigma(T), \|T\|, T \cdot Q$ etc.) involved in (1) can be done recursively by adding to the previously calculated sums the remaining terms and thus reducing the amount of computations needed. Moreover, the above theorem can be extended as to apply for other transformations such as skew [2].

3. Efficient subsequence matching

In this section we present an algorithm that locates all scaled occurrences of a query time series Q in a much larger time series (database) D. Before describing the method, we need to define time scaling.

3.1. Time scaling

Here we give the basic definitions on time scaling. We will only consider compressing a time series, since this should be adequate for our algorithm in the next section. Let $T[1 \ldots n]$ be a time series and m an integer with $0 < m < n$. There are many ways to define the scaling of T from n to m points. Our approach scales a large time sequence T into a smaller length by grouping sequential points of T and taking their averages in order to to form the smaller sequence. Taking averages has been used successfully as an approximation and dimensionality reduction technique in time series [12]; the main advantage of this type of scaling is its robustness to noise.

Definition 3.1 Let $T[1 \ldots n]$ be a time series, m be an integer such that $1 \leq m < n$ and $l = n \mod m$. We define the scaling of T to size m, and denote by $\mathcal{S}_m(T)$, a time sequence $T_S[1 \ldots m]$ where

$$T_S[i] = \begin{cases} \dfrac{1}{\lceil \frac{n}{m} \rceil} \displaystyle\sum_{j=(i-1) \cdot \lceil \frac{n}{m} \rceil + 1}^{i \cdot \lceil \frac{n}{m} \rceil} T[j], & \text{if } 1 \leq i \leq l, \\[2em] \dfrac{1}{\lfloor \frac{n}{m} \rfloor} \displaystyle\sum_{j=l+(i-1) \cdot \lfloor \frac{n}{m} \rfloor + 1}^{l+i \cdot \lfloor \frac{n}{m} \rfloor} T[j], & \text{if } l < i \leq m. \end{cases}$$

Let us now focus on the scaled matching of sequences. We consider a subsequence of D a scaled match if, scaled to $|Q|$ points and under some transformations (as described in the previous section), the scaled subsequence can become "similar" to Q (in the way that ϵ-similarity defines). Note that for brevity and clarity of presentation we are interested only in matches of length larger that $|Q|$ (actually, for most practical applications this is adequate).

Note that we would probably want to set a lower and upper bound on the size of a match for a given Q. The need for an upper bound comes from the fact that if we scale very large sequences into small sizes we lose so much information from scaling that virtually any use of the scaled sequence becomes meaningless. In a similar manner, we would probably not be interested in the scaling (expansion) of, e.g. two points to thirty. Therefore a lower bound should also exist. Our algorithm uses both lower and upper scaling bounds as input parameters.

3.2. The algorithm

In this section we first present the naive approach and then give a detailed description of our algorithm.

3.2.1 The naive approach

Let us again consider a large time sequence $D[1 \ldots n]$ and a much smaller $Q[1 \ldots m]$. The task that we want to perform is "find all scaled matches—within some given scale bounds—of Q in D". Obviously, the problem itself is rather complex. The naive approach is to begin at position 1 of D, get a window of minimum size w_{min} (where w_{min} is the lower scaling bound as described in the previous section), scale $D[1 \ldots w_{min}]$ to m points and see whether it matches Q under some similarity measure. With the left side of the window anchored in $D[1]$, check in a similar manner if $D[1 \ldots i]$ (scaled to m points) matches Q, for all i, $w_{min} < i \leq w_{max}$ (where w_{max} is the upper scaling bound). After this step, repeat the same procedure with the window anchored at position $D[2]$, then $D[3]$ etc.

3.2.2 Description of the algorithm

For the description that follows, let again $Q[1 \ldots m]$ the query sequence, with $m \geq 3$, and $D[1 \ldots n]$ the database sequence. Let w_{min} and w_{max}, $w_{min} < w_{max}$, be the lower and upper window lengths, meaning that we are interested in finding scaled matches of Q in D with length ranging from w_{min} to w_{max}. In order to enhance the clarity of presentation, we will consider w_{min} and w_{max} to be multiples of $|Q| = m$. The implementation of the more general case is straightforward. Let thus, $w_{min} = k_{min} \cdot m$ and $w_{max} = k_{max} \cdot m$ for appropriate k_{min} and k_{max}.

The algorithm is an iterative procedure. In each iteration, the algorithm decides whether or not there exist any scaled matches of windows whose left side is anchored at a specific point of D. In more detail, let us consider the iteration that anchors the windows on $D[i]$. As mentioned before, the naive approach consists of checking all possible windows from $D[i \ldots i + w_{min} - 1]$ to $D[i \ldots i + w_{max} - 1]$ (candidate windows). However, the algorithm starts (*initialization step*) by checking only whether the windows $D[i \ldots i + 3 \cdot k_{min} - 1], D[i \ldots i + 3 \cdot (k_{min} + 1) - 1], \ldots, D[i \ldots i + 3 \cdot k_{max} - 1]$, are scaled matches of $Q[1 \ldots 3]$. By performing this check, we have actually checked all the three-point-scaled prefix subsequences of all candidate windows at the specific anchoring. This is because, if we scale a window of size l to m points, then due to the fact that $k_{min} \leq \frac{l}{m} \leq k_{max}$, each scaled point of the window will be an average of at least k_{min} and at most k_{max} points. In other words, if we consider a candidate window W, and scale it to m points, $W_S[1 \ldots m]$ (remember that $m = |Q|$) then $W_S[1 \ldots 3]$ will have been checked whether or not it matches $Q[1 \ldots 3]$ in the initialization step. Therefore if we have no matches after performing this step, we can be sure that there are no scaled matches of Q that start in $D[i]$ and thus the iteration ends.

However, if there are some matches in the initialization step then we take the set $\mathcal{M}_3$ that contains all of the above windows (scaled to three points) that are scaled matches of $Q[1 \ldots 3]$. We would like now to check whether or not there exist scale matches of size four. The key observation is that in order for a window M (scaled to $M_S[1 \ldots 4]$) to be a scale match of $Q[1 \ldots 4]$, then the prefix subsequence of M_S, i.e. $M_S[1 \ldots 3]$, should belong to the set $\mathcal{M}_3$. Therefore, we only need to examine the windows that are "*extensions*" of the windows in the set $\mathcal{M}_3$. More formally, we define extensions as following.

Definition 3.2 *Let a time sequence $D[1 \ldots d]$ and a window (subsequence) $W[1 \ldots n]$ of D anchored at $D[i]$. Let further its scaling to m points, $W_S[1 \ldots m]$. As an extension of the window W we define a window of greater size W', anchored (as well) in $D[i]$, that, when scaled to $m + 1$ points, $W'_S[1 \ldots m + 1]$, W_S is a prefix subsequence of W'_S, i.e. $W_S[1 \ldots m] \equiv W'_S[1 \ldots m]$.*

It can be easily proved that if m does not divide n, the extension of a window $W[1 \ldots n]$ scaled to $W_S[1 \ldots m]$ points is $W[1 \ldots n + \lfloor \frac{n}{m} \rfloor]$; and if m divides n we have two extensions, $W[1 \ldots n + \frac{n}{m}]$ and $W[1 \ldots n + \frac{n}{m} - 1]$.

Returning to our algorithm, the extensions of the set $\mathcal{M}_3$ consists of the set of *candidate windows* (of size four) $\mathcal{C}_4$. The windows that, scaled to four points, actually match (under the CD-criterion) $Q[1 \ldots 4]$ compose the set $\mathcal{M}_4$. Obviously, it holds $\mathcal{M}_4 \subseteq \mathcal{C}_4$. In the same manner, we continue by constructing $\mathcal{C}_5$, $\mathcal{M}_5$, etc. until, for a number t, the set

$\mathcal{M}_t$ is empty. It is obvious that the scaled matches that we are interested in are the elements of the set $\mathcal{M}_m$. Therefore, if $t < m$ we have no matches at that offset and thus the algorithm continues at the next offset without returning any matches. Since most times the case is that t is much smaller than m, the above algorithm performs an extensive pruning on the number of candidate windows that have to be checked.

As mentioned before, our algorithm has no false dismissals. A proof of this is presented in [2].

3.2.3 Implementation of the sets $\mathcal{M}$ and $\mathcal{C}$

As mentioned in Section 2, the CD-criterion gives us the ability to perform very efficient "growing window" matches. In order to implement this feature in this algorithm, when we insert a sequence $D[1 \ldots m]$ into a set, e.g. $\mathcal{C}_{k+1}$, we actually store the attributes needed to compute the CD-criterion ($\|D\|$, $\Sigma(D)$ etc.). In fact, these attributes can be computed recursively; e.g. the attributes of the set $\mathcal{C}_{k+1}$ can be computed efficiently using (recursively) the respective attributes of the set $\mathcal{M}_k$. The reason why we are able to do this is that for all new window "extensions" that we insert in the set $\mathcal{C}_{k+1}$ we have the attributes of their prefixes stored in the set $\mathcal{M}_k$. For example, if we insert a scaled window $W_S[1 \ldots k+1]$ in $\mathcal{C}_{k+1}$, we would already have the attributes of $W_S[1 \ldots k]$ stored in $\mathcal{M}_k$. Therefore, we only need to compute the value of $W_S[k + 1]$ and then compute recursively the new attribute values, instead of recalculating the attributes from the beginning.

4. Experiments

For our experiments we used the following time series: Dow Jones Industrial Average Index (daily, 1915–1990, 18,840 points), NYSE Finance Index (daily, 1966–1998, 8,310 points) and network traffic data (approximately one million points—source: http://ita.ee.lbl.gov/html/contrib/BC.html).

Time Series	Running time of the proposed algorithm / Running time of the naive algorithm
Stock Data	0.143
Network Traffic Data	0.091

Table 1. Comparison of the proposed algorithm versus the naive.

In Table 1 we present the relative average running times of the experiments conducted. It is obvious that the pruning performed by our algorithm, together with the efficient implementation that was described in section 3.2.3, speeds up the process of extracting matching subsequences up to over an order of magnitude.

5. Related work

The problem of efficiently discovering matches of a small query sequence in a large database has attracted a lot of attention and a number of approaches have been proposed. A large fraction of them is based on indexing. Pioneer work on this approach was done by Agrawal et al. in [1] and subsequent research has produced significant results in diverse variations of the initial idea [5, 3, 10, 9]. Although indexing is used very extensively, creating an index that can handle queries of arbitrary length along with time and amplitude scaling is non-trivial, mostly due to the vast number of candidate subsequences.

Concerning the problem of finding scaled matches of different lengths, there have been proposed a number of techniques that solve the problem approximately, including [13, 7, 16]. However, since all these approaches approximate time series, it follows that they cannot be applied to our problem without false dismissals. Moreover, much recent research has concentrated on Dynamic Time Warping (DTW) with interesting results [17, 11, 8]. However, DTW is inappropriate for our problem both due to its different definition of scaling and to its high complexity.

Regarding amplitude shift and scaling, Chu and Wong [3] have proposed a transformation of time sequences that is shift invariant. However, this approach requires more computations than the CD-criterion we propose. Furthermore, it seems hard to extend the shift invariant transformation so as to include more operations (other than shifting and scaling) like skew [2]. A variation of the above idea is also presented in [6]. In [4] a method is proposed for identifying similar time series under some linear (amplitude only) transformations. However, in order to find whether two time series are similar or not, they propose an approximation algorithm that (due to approximation) may yield false results.

6. Acknowledgments

We would like to thank Foto Afrati for invaluable comments on a draft of this paper. Also, Alexander Dimakis for insightful discussions on some aspects of this paper.

References

[1] R. Agrawal, C. Faloutsos, and A. Swami. Efficient similarity search in sequence databases. In *Proceedings of the 4th Int'l Conf. on Foundations of Data Organization and Algorithms*, pages 69–84, Chicago, IL, 1993.

[2] T. Argyros and C. Ermopoulos. Efficient subsequence matching in time series databases under time and amplitude transformations (extended version). In http://ieee.ntua.gr/~targyros/transform03.pdf.

[3] K. Chu and M. Wong. Fast time-series searching with scaling and shifting. In *Proceedings of ACM Principles on Database Systems*, pages 237–248, Philadelphia, PA, 1999.

[4] G. Das, D. Gunopulos, and H. Mannila. Finding similar time series. In *1st European Symposium on Principles of Data Mining and Knowledge Discovery*, pages 88–100, Trondheim, Norway, 1997.

[5] C. Faloutsos, M. Ranganathan, and Y. Manolopoulos. Fast subsequence matching in time-series databases. In *Proceedings of ACM SIGMOD Int'l Conf. on Managment of Data*, pages 419–429, Minneapolis, MN, 1994.

[6] T. Kahveci, A. Singh, and A. Gurel. Similarity searching for multi-attribute sequences. In *Proceedings of 14th Int'l Conf. on Scientific and Statistical Database Management*, pages 175–186, Edinburgh, Scotland.

[7] E. Keogh. A fast and robust method for pattern matching in time series databases. In *Proceedings of Ninth Int'l Conf. on Tools with Artificial Intelligence*, pages 578–584, Newport Beach, CA, 1997.

[8] E. Keogh. Exact indexing of dynamic time warping. In *Proceedings of the 28th Int'l Conf. on Very Large Data Bases*, pages 406–417, Hong Kong, China, 2002.

[9] E. Keogh, K. Chakrabarti, S. Mehrotra, and M. Pazzani. Locally adaptive dimensionality reduction for indexing large time series databases. In *Proceedings of ACM SIGMOD Conf. on Managment of Data*, pages 151–162, Santa Barbara, CA, 2001.

[10] E. Keogh, K. Chakrabarti, M. Pazzani, and S. Mehrotra. Dimensionality reduction for fast similarity search in large time series databases. *Journal of Knowledge and Information Systems*, 3(3):263–286, 2000.

[11] E. Keogh and M. Pazzani. Scaling up dynamic time warping to massive datasets. In *Proceedings of the 3rd European Conf. on Principles and Practice of Knowledge Discovery in Databases*, pages 1–11, Prague, Czech Republic, 1999.

[12] E. Keogh and M. Pazzani. A simple dimensionality reduction technique for fast similarity search in large time series databases. In *Proceedings of 4th Pacific- Asia Conf. on Knowledge Discovery and Data Mining*, pages 122–133, Kyoto, Japan, 2000.

[13] E. Keogh and P. Smyth. A probabilistic approach to fast pattern matching in time series databases. In *Proceedings of 3rd Int'l Conf. on Knowledge Discovery and Data Mining*, pages 24–30, Menlo Park, CA, 1997.

[14] B. Mandelbrot. *Fractals and Scaling in Finance: Discontinuity, Concentration, Risk*. Springer-Verlag, NY, 2000.

[15] P. Maragos, A. Dimakis, and I. Kokkinos. Some advances in nonlinear speech modeling using modulations, fractals and chaos. In *Proceedings of IEEE Int'l Conf. on Digital Signal Processing*, pages 325–332, Santorini, Greece, 2002.

[16] C. Perng, H. Wang, S. Zhang, and S. Parker. Landmarks: a new model for similarity-based pattern querying in time series databases. In *Proceedings of 16th Int'l Conf. on Data Engineering*, pages 33–42, San Diego, CA, 2000.

[17] B. Yi, V. Jagadish, and C. Faloutsos. Efficient retrieval of similar time sequences under time warping. In *Proceedings of the 14th Int'l Conf. on Data Engineering*, pages 201–208, Orlando, FL, 1998.

A Fast Algorithm for Computing Hypergraph Transversals and its Application in Mining Emerging Patterns

James Bailey, Thomas Manoukian and Kotagiri Ramamohanarao
Department of Computer Science & Software Engineering
The University of Melbourne, Australia
{jbailey,tcm,rao}@cs.mu.oz.au

Abstract

Computing the minimal transversals of a hypergraph is an important problem in computer science that has significant applications in data mining. In this paper, we present a new algorithm for computing hypergraph transversals and highlight their close connection to an important class of patterns known as emerging patterns. We evaluate our technique on a number of large datasets and show that it outperforms previous approaches by a factor of 9-29 times.

Introduction Analysis of hypergraphs is an important problem in discrete mathematics which has many applications in computer science. Example areas range from minimal diagnosis and propositional circumscription [10], to learning boolean formulae [2], and boolean switching theory [4].

The hypergraph minimal transversal problem is particularly significant from a data mining perspective. Indeed, the algorithmic complexity of mining maximal frequent itemsets and minimal infrequent itemsets is closely linked to the complexity of computing minimal hypergraph transversals [6].

Minimal infrequent itemsets are minimal itemsets such that their frequency is less than α in the dataset being mined (where α is some threshold ≥ 1). They are interesting because of their connection to *contrast* or *emerging patterns*. Consider the transactions for class A: $\{\{b, d, g, j\}, \{c, e, g, j\}, \{c, f, h, j\}, \{a, f, h, j\}\}$ and class B: $\{\{a, d, g, j\}, \{a, d, g, i\}, \{c, f, h, i\}, \{a, e, g, j\}\}$. Suppose we are interested in finding minimal contrasts between them. The transactions in Class A contain the following contrast patterns: Transaction 1 $\{b\}$, Transaction 2 $\{ce, cg, cj\}$, Transaction 3 $\{cj, fj, hj\}$, Transaction 4 $\{af, ah, fj, hj\}$.

The relationship to hypergraphs is natural. These are defined by a set of vertices $V = \{v_1, v_2, ..., v_n\}$ and a set of edges E, where each edge is some subset of V. A *transversal* of a hypergraph is any set of vertices that contains at least one element of every edge. A *minimal transversal* is a transversal such that no proper subset is also a transversal.

Each transaction t in Class A can be thought of as inducing a hypergraph with respect to all the transactions in Class B. The vertex set corresponds to the elements of t. Hypergraph edges are individually defined by subtracting a transaction in the negative dataset from the vertex set. So, for $t = 3 = \{c, f, h, j\}$ in class A, we have a hypergraph with vertex set $\{c, f, h, j\}$ and edges: Hyperedge 1 $\{c, f, h\}$, Hyperedge 2 $\{c, f, h, j\}$, Hyperedge 3 $\{j\}$, Hyperedge 4 $\{c, f, h\}$. The three minimal transversals of this hypergraph are $\{cj, fj, hj\}$, these correspond precisely to the contrast patterns listed above for transaction 3 in class A.

Efficiently finding minimal hypergraph transversals (and thus mining minimal infrequent itemsets and emerging patterns) is a computationally difficult task. Hypergraphs with many vertices (high dataset dimensionality) and many edges (high dataset volume) can contain huge numbers of patterns - an exponential number in the worst case.

In this paper, we investigate the problem of efficiently finding minimal hypergraph transversals in the data mining context. Our main contributions are threefold:

- We identify the correspondence between computing minimal hypergraph transversals and data mining of emerging patterns. This connection has not, to our knowledge, been made elsewhere.

- We present a new algorithm for efficiently computing minimal transversals based on a guided partitioning heuristic.

- We discuss experiments performed on several large datasets that demonstrate our algorithm significantly outperforms previous approaches.

Hypergraphs The study of hypergraphs [1] and their related problems is a well established field of discrete mathematics. In this section we overview three known algorithms for computing minimal transversals. See [4, 5] for a formal presentation.

Work by Berge [1] proposed a cross-product based algorithm for solving the problem. The method involves iteratively finding partial minimal transversals of the input hypergraph until the entire minimal transversal set is computed. For each edge, e_i, we calculate the cross-product between e_i and the minimal transversal set calculated so far. The result of this cross product operation is then minimised.

The precise complexity of hypergraph transversal is an open problem. Work in [5] presented an algorithm that solves an equivalent problem, monotone Boolean duality and has the best known complexity. *Algorithm B* was presented to solve this problem in $\mathcal{O}(nm) + m^{\log m}$ time where n is the number of variables and m is the combined size of the input and output.

Work in [7] identified two primary drawbacks in the method of Berge; a large amount of memory is required to store partial transversals, no transversal is available for output until all have been found. The basis of their algorithm is to traverse, depth first, a tree of transversals. This feature means both issues are addressed.

Emerging Patterns *Emerging Patterns*, or EPs, were introduced in [3] as a means of contrasting disjoint sets of relational data. EPs are simply defined as itemsets whose frequency of occurrence, or support, differs substantially between two sets of data. They have been shown to be a powerful tool in the field of classification [8]. An important particular case of EPs, *Jumping Emerging Patterns*, or JEPs, refer to those itemsets that exist in one dataset and are totally absent from the other.

In the work that introduced them, the process of finding all EPs satisfying some support constraints relied on a function *Border-Diff*, which discovers unique minimal subsets that exist within one set when contrasted against a group of other sets.

The *Border-Diff* operator [3] is reminiscent of the algorithm of Berge, also using the strategy of generating partial results, in this case, partial EPs. No connection to hypergraphs was made in [3] though.

This operator has two input parameters: a reference set of itemsets, or negative instances (transactions), N and a single positive instance (transaction), p. The process initially involves finding all subsets of p that do not exist in at least one element of N. This is simply the set of differences $Diffs = \{p - n_i, \forall\, n_i \in N\}$. Taking these differences, the generation based on partial expansions of the cross-product follows in a similar manner as the Berge algorithm, with the set of differences taking the place of the set of edges found in a hypergraph.

The principal difference is a mechanism to avoid the generation of non-minimal itemsets. One observation lies in the fact that given a set of itemsets comprising the partial expansion up to some iteration j, PE_j, on processing the difference in iteration $j + 1$, d_{j+1}, we need not consider those elements $pe \in PE_j$ for which $pe \cap d_{j+1} \neq \emptyset$.

An additional optimisation, further to the scheme of [1], centers on the initial set of differences. Due to the incremental nature of the process, The order in which one iterates through the differences can be significant. By processing them in increasing order of cardinality, the search space can be reduced.

It is also possible to compute minimal hypergraph transversals in a bottom-up, levelwise manner. This connection has been pointed out in [6, 9]. Work in [11] presents algorithms which are based on this idea. Here, itemsets are grown, one item at a time, until a transversal is found. A set enumeration tree can be used to guide the growth process. The major problem with this strategy is that minimal transversals do not possess the monotonic property that could allow the well-known a-priori optimisation to be used (cease growing an itemset once it isn't a transversal). Instead, they possess an anti-monotonic property (all supersets of a minimal transversal are themselves transversals). The amount of pruning that can be done when growing bottom-up is thus vastly reduced and consequently the method is not competitive with respect to the other schemes when the dimensionality becomes large.

A New Partitioning Algorithm While the methods of [3] and [7] both improve on the algorithm of Berge, all three are susceptible to the fact that when the number of items or vertices is large, potential worst-case exponential behaviour becomes a practical problem, the size of partial expansions grows very quickly and thus the task of keeping intermediate transversals minimal becomes a bottleneck.

Our system, is fundamentally designed to prevent situations in which prohibitively large (with respect cardinality) edges have their cross-product computed. We achieve this by a divide and conquer approach, which iterates through specific subsets of edges. The key is the manner in which we identify candidate subsets of edges such that cross-product expansion/minimisation is more tightly controlled. The process of partitioning is recursive.

Partitioning any edge set is based on the frequency of the vertices that comprise them. All partitions are induced by a particular vertex. Given some vertex, v a partition of edges is simply those which do not contain v. This first step ensures that the number of edges in any induced partition is smaller or equal to the set of edges from which it was projected. So by iterating through each vertex, we induce some partition. Our method of avoiding an expensive round of expansion/minimisation is to manufacture one of two kinds of partitions: i) those having many edges, where each has relatively low cardinality, or ii) those having few edges, when the cardinality of individual edges is high. This objective requires that edges in any partition must have their cardinality reduced. This is done by modifying each edge in any partition by projecting out only those vertices previously considered in prior iterations. The choice of a total vertex ordering is crucial, due to its effect on cardinality reduction of the edges.

Clearly, by selecting the least frequent vertex in the edges, we project a significant number of them (those not containing this vertex). By masking out those vertices that succeed the least frequent vertex from the partition, we generate the emptyset, a base example of our preferred partition i). Conversely when the last vertex is considered, no vertices remain to be masked out, however, the least number of edges are projected, a case of scenario ii). By forming such partitions, we have control over what we choose to input to a subroutine which generates minimal transversals. Here, we utilise a version of Berge with optimisations attributable to Dong and Li [3] as the subroutine in our algorithm. Our Partition algorithm utilises a global variable (Min_Tvs) to store the final set of minimal transversals. Determining whether to apply the algorithm recursively is based on whether the partition is still 'too large'. To measure this, we use a simple metric based on i) the number of edges in a partition (par_num_edges) and ii) the average edge cardinality multiplied by the number of edges (par_volume). The function Add_Min_Can combines candidates (Can_Tvs) which are minimal for the partition (but possibly not globally), with the global set of transversals so far Min_Tvs. As all transversals are computed with respect some partition, the relevant vertices (Par_Ver) must be appended to each output of the $Optimised\_Berge$ subroutine. The algorithm is invoked by the top-level call Partition(edges,$\emptyset$) and Min_Tvs is initially $\emptyset$.

Experimental Results

We now experimentally study the algorithms discussed in the previous section. We examine three large datasets from the UCI Machine Learning Repository [1] - Waveform, Satimage and Splice. Statistics for these are shown in table 1. All experiments were carried out on a 500MHz Pentium III PC, with 512MB of memory, running Linux(Mandrake 8.2). All times are measured in seconds.

The overall outline of each experiment is as follows: A single (positive) transaction p is chosen from the first class within a dataset. The entire set of negative transactions corresponds to all the transactions in the other classes. m of these transactions are then randomly chosen to yield a smaller negative set N. Together, p and N induce a set of vertices and hypergraph edges, as explained earlier. The time taken to calculate the minimal transversals of this hy-

---

[1] www.ics.uci.edu/~mlearn/MLRepository.html

Algorithm 1 Partition(E, Par_Ver)

1: **Input**: A set of hypergraph edges, E
    A set of partitioned on vertices, Par_Ver
2: $ver\_universe$ = set of all vertices in hypergraph
3: Generate frequency table for all vertices
4: Order vertices in increasing frequency $\Rightarrow [v_1, \ldots, v_k]$
5: **for** $v = v_1$ to v_k **do**
6:   $Partition = \emptyset$
7:   $ver\_universe = ver\_universe - v$
8:   **for all** $edge \in E$ **do**
9:     **if** $v \notin edge$ **then**
10:       $Partition = Partition \cup (edge - ver\_universe)$
11:     **end if**
12:   **end for**
13:   $Par\_Ver = Par\_ver \cup v$
14:   **if** $par\_num\_edges \geq 2$ AND $par\_volume \geq 50$ **then**
15:     Partition($Partition$, Par_Ver)
16:   **else**
17:     Can_Tvs = Optimised_Berge($Partition$)
18:     Add_Min_Can(Can_Tvs, Min_Tvs, Par_Ver)
19:   **end if**
20:   $Par\_Ver = Par\_ver - v$
21: **end for**

---

pergraph is measured. This time is then averaged over k different choices for p, where k is 100. The procedure is then repeated for different choices of m. The results for all classes were very similar.

The second column of each table shows the average number of transactions (from classes other than the one being considered) from which hypergraph edges were generated. We ensured we were dealing with simple hypergraphs (ones with no non-minimal edges) by performing an initial minimisation step and thus the the value in parentheses is the actual number of edges used as input. The third column shows the average number of transversals generated per problem instance.

We considered the collection of algorithms previously mentioned. Aside from our algorithm (Partition), we chose *Border-Diff* [3] and two hypergraph transversal algorithms, *Algorithm B* of Fredman-Khachiyan [5] and Kavvadias-Stavropoulos [7]. We implemented *Border-Diff*, the Fredman-Khachiyan algorithm and a Level-Wise system. We were able to obtain an executable of the Kavvadias-Stavropoulos algorithm. Preliminary work (results excluded due to lack of space) showed that both the Fredman-Khachiyan algorithm and the Level-Wise approach were uncompetitive. For Fredman-Khachiyan this is due to the conservative manner in which it decomposes prime implicants, splitting on a single variable per recursive call. Its complexity (in terms of the number of recursive calls made) is a function of the size of the input and output and its cost on the modest Waveform dataset was prohibitive (~1600 times slower than Partition and ~92 times slower than

Dataset	#classes	#attrs	#vertices	#transactions
Waveform	3	21	105	5000
Satimage	6	36	180	6435
Splice	3	60	287	3175

Table 1. DATASET CHARACTERISTICS

WAVEFORM DATASET					
CLASS	N (EDGES)	TVS/CALL	AVE TIME/CALL		RATIO
			PART	B-DIFF	
0	3343(562)	4988	0.44	5.35	12.16
SATIMAGE DATASET					
CLASS	N (EDGES)	TVS/CALL	AVE TIME/CALL		RATIO
			PART	B-DIFF	
1	1000(163)	5128	0.40	10.31	25.78
	1250(186)	6021	0.49	14.12	28.82
SPLICE DATASET					
CLASS	N (EDGES)	TVS/CALL	AVE TIME/CALL		RATIO
			PART	B-DIFF	
EI	75(75)	56393	5.59	50.82	9.09
	100(99)	88560	8.95	108.41	12.11

Table 2. PARTITION AND BORDER-DIFF

WAVEFORM DATASET					
CLASS	N (EDGES)	TVS/CALL	AVE TIME/CALL		RATIO
			PART	KAV-STA	
0	3343(562)	4988	0.96	25.92	27.00
SATIMAGE DATASET					
CLASS	N (EDGES)	TVS/CALL	AVE TIME/CALL		RATIO
			PART	KAV-STA	
1	1000(163)	5128	0.48	11.44	23.83
	1250(186)	6021	0.58	15.98	27.55
SPLICE DATASET					
CLASS	N (EDGES)	TVS/CALL	AVE TIME/CALL		RATIO
			PART	KAV-STA	
EI	100(99)	88560	9.07	80.56	8.88
	125(124)	124739	13.08	180.13	13.77

Table 3. PARTITION AND KAVVADIAS-STAVROPOULOS

Kavvadias-Stavropoulos and *Border-Diff* on half the number of instances shown here). The SE-Tree, while competitive for Waveform, suffered from a performance blowout on Satimage (~241 times slower than Partition). With this approach, the dimensionality of the initial positive instance determines the potential search space. When this increases, the search space that must be examined (without the assistance of the a-priori property) becomes prohibitive and the algorithm becomes impractical.

Table 2 shows the results of a single *Border-Diff* call averaged over 100 calls. The results in this table clearly indicate the strength of our partitioning mechanism for handling these challenging datasets. There are many instances in which the improvement is more than an order of magnitude. Next, evaluation of our partitioning algorithm against the Kavvadias-Stavropoulos algorithm is presented in table 3. The results are also very impressive. Our system is considerably faster in all the cases. The improvements against *Border-Diff* and the Kavvadias-Stavropoulos algorithm are proportional to the number of edges, an expected, yet important result. Clearly, our partitioning algorithm is uniformly superior on all problem instances considered.

Acknowledgements: This work was supported in part by an Expertise Grant from the Victorian Partnership for Advanced Computing. Thanks to Elias Stavropoulos for providing an executable for the algorithm in [7].

References

[1] C. Berge. *Hypergraphs, North Holland Mathematical Library*, volume 45. Elsevier, 1989.

[2] E. Boros, V. Gurvich, L. Khachiyan, and K. Makino. On the Complexity of Generating Maximal Frequent and Minimal Infrequent Sets. In *Proceedings of STACS 2002*, pages 133–141, 2002.

[3] G. Dong and J. Li. Efficient Mining of Emerging Patterns: Discovering Trends and Differnces. In *Proceedings of KDD'99*, pages 43–52, 1999.

[4] T. Eiter and G. Gottlob. Identifying the Minimal Transversals of a Hypergraph and Related Problems. *SIAM Journal on Computing*, 24(6):1278–1304, 1995.

[5] M. L. Fredman and L. Khachiyan. On the Complexity of Dualization of Monotone Disjunctive Normal Forms. *Journal of Algorithms*, 21(3):618–628, 1996.

[6] D. Gunopulos, R. Khardon, H. Mannila, and H. Toivonen. Data Mining, Hypergraph Transversals, and Machine Learning. In *Proceedings of PODS'97*, pages 209–216, 1997.

[7] D. Kavvadias and E. C. Stavropoulos. Evaluation of an Algorithm for the Transversal Hypergraph Problem. In *Proceedings of WAE'99*, pages 72–84, 1999.

[8] J. Li, G. Dong, and K. Ramamohanarao. Making use of the most Expressive Jumping Emerging Patterns for Classification. In *Proceedings of PAKDD'00*, pages 220–232, 2000.

[9] H. Mannila and H. Toivonen. Levelwise Search and Borders of Theories in Knowledge Discovery. *Data Mining and Knowledge Discovery*, 3(1):241–258, 1997.

[10] R. Reiter. A Theory of Diagnosis from First Principles. *Artificial Intelligence*, 32(1):57–95, 1987.

[11] R. Rymon. An SE-Tree-Based Prime Implicant Generation Algorithm. *Annals of Mathematics and Artificial Intelligence*, 11(1-4):351–366, 1994.

Mining Relevant Text from Unlabelled Documents

Daniel Barbará   Carlotta Domeniconi   Ning Kang

Information and Software Engineering Department

George Mason University

Fairfax, VA 22030

{dbarbara,cdomenic,nkang}@gmu.edu

Abstract

Automatic classification of documents is an important area of research with many applications in the fields of document searching, forensics and others. Methods to perform classification of text rely on the existence of a sample of documents whose class labels are known. However, in many situations, obtaining this sample may not be an easy (or even possible) task. In this paper we focus on the classification of unlabelled documents into two classes: relevant and irrelevant, given a topic of interest. By dividing the set of documents into buckets (for instance, answers returned by different search engines), and using association rule mining to find common sets of words among the buckets, we can efficiently obtain a sample of documents that has a large percentage of relevant ones. This sample can be used to train models to classify the entire set of documents. We prove, via experimentation, that our method is capable of filtering relevant documents even in adverse conditions where the percentage of irrelevant documents in the buckets is relatively high.

1. Introduction

In information retrieval, such as content based image retrieval or web page classification, we face an asymmetry between positive and negative examples [10, 2]. Suppose, for example, we submit a query to multiple search engines. Each engine retrieves a collection of documents in response to our query. Such collections include, in general, both relevant and irrelevant documents. Suppose we want to discriminate the relevant documents from the irrelevant ones. The set of all relevant documents in all retrieved collections represent a sample of the positive class, drawn from an underlying unknown distribution. On the other hand, the irrelevant documents may come from an unknown number of different "negative" classes. In general, we cannot approximate the distributions of the negative classes, as we may

have too few representatives for each of them. Hence, we are facing a problem with an unknown number of classes, with the user interested in only one of them.

Modelling the above scenario as a two-class problem, may impose misleading requirements, that can yield poor results. We are definitely better off focusing on the class of interest, as positive examples in this scenario have a more compact support, that reflects the correlations among their feature values.

Moreover, more often than not, the class labels of the data are unknown, either because the data is too large for an expert to label it, or because no such expert exists. In this work we eliminate the assumption of having even partially labelled data. We focus on document retrieval, and develop a technique to mining relevant text from unlabelled documents. Specifically, our objective is to identify a sample of positive documents, representative of the underlying class distribution. The scenario of a query submitted to multiple search engines will serve as running example throughout the paper, although the technique can be applied to a variety of scenarios and data. Our approach reflects the asymmetry between positive and negative data, and does not make any particular and unnecessary assumption on the negative examples.

2 Related Work

In [4] the authors discuss a hierarchical document clustering approach using frequent set of words. Their objective is to construct a hierarchy of documents for browsing at increasing levels of specificity of topics.

In [1] the authors consider the problem of enhancing the performance of a learning algorithm allowing a set of unlabelled data augment a small set of labelled examples. The driving application is the classification of Web pages. Although similar to our scenario, the technique depends on the existence of labelled data to begin with.

The authors in [6] exploit semantic similarity between terms and documents in an unsupervised fashion. Documents that share terms that are different, but semantically related, will be considered as unrelated when text documents are represented as a *bag of words*. The purpose of the work in [6] is to overcome this limitation by learning a *semantic proximity matrix* from a given corpus of documents by taking into consideration high order correlations. Two methods (both yielding to the definition of a kernel function) are discussed. In particular, in one model, documents with highly correlated words are considered as having similar content. Similarly, words contained in correlated documents are viewed as semantically related.

3   The DocMine Algorithm

Given a document, it is possible to associate with it a *bag of words* [5, 3, 7]. Specifically, we represent a document as a binary vector $\mathbf{d} \in \Re^n$, in which each entry records if a particular word stem occurs in the text. The dimensionality n of $\mathbf{d}$ is determined by the number of different terms in the corpus of documents (size of the *dictionary*), and each entry is indexed by a specific term.

Going back to our example, suppose we submit a query to s different search engines. We obtain s collections, or *buckets*, of documents $B_j = \{\mathbf{d}_i\}_j, \quad j = 1, \ldots, s$.

While many documents retrieved by a specific search engine (a bad one) might be irrelevant, the relevant ones are expected to be more frequent in the majority of buckets. In addition, since we can assume that positive documents are drawn from a single underlying distribution, a compact support unifies them across all buckets. On the other hand, the negatives manifest a large variation. We make use of these characteristics to develop a technique that discriminates relevant documents from the irrelevant ones. In details, we proceed as follows.

We mine each bucket B_j to find the frequent itemsets that satisfy a given support level. Each resulting itemset is a set of words. The result of this process is a collection of sets of itemsets, one set for each bucket: $F_j = \{W_i | W_i \text{ is a frequent itemset in bucket } j\ \}$ for $j = 1, \ldots, s$, where it is possible that $F_j = \emptyset$, for some j. Now we compute all itemsets that are frequent in m buckets: $I_m = \{W_i | W_i \in F_{j_1} \cap F_{j_2} \cap \ldots \cap F_{j_m}\}$, for distinct $j_1, \ldots, j_m$. In general $m = \lfloor s/2 \rfloor + 1$. In our experiments we set $m = s$ since we consider a limited number of buckets ($s = 5$), driven by the number of available documents per topic. We wish now to retrieve the documents that *support* the itemsets that are frequent in m buckets. Then, for each $W_i \in I_m$, we select, in each of the m buckets that contain W_i as frequent itemset, the documents that has W_i expressed within. The resulting collection of documents P represent the presumed positive documents, relevant to our query.

The algorithm, which we call DocMine (**Doc**ument **Min**ing), is summarized in the following. The algorithm

takes as input the s buckets of documents, and the minimum support (Sup_{min}) for the computation of frequent itemsets.

1. **Input**: s buckets of documents $B_j = \{\mathbf{d}_i\}_j, j = 1, \ldots, s$, Sup_{min}, m.

2. Compute frequent itemsets in each bucket B_j:

    $$F_j = \{W_i | W_i \text{ is a frequent itemset in bucket } j\},$$
    $$j = 1 \ldots, s$$

3. Compute all itemsets that are frequent in m buckets:

    $$I_m = \{W_i | W_i \in F_{j_1} \cap F_{j_2} \cap \ldots \cap F_{j_m}\}$$

4. Set $P = \emptyset$.

5. for each $W_i \in I_m$

    - for each $l = 1, \ldots, m$ such that $W_i \in \cap_{l=1}^m F_{j_l}$

        - for each $\mathbf{d} \in B_{j_l}$

            * if $\mathbf{d}$ contains W_i

                · $P = P \cup \{\mathbf{d}\}$

6. **Output**: the set P (presumed positive documents)

It is important to remark that the DocMine algorithm can be tuned to ignore itemsets of small size. Some words, in fact, may be common to documents of different topics (they would not discriminate). Our experience tells us that, for instance, combinations of two frequent words are not sufficient to discriminate among different topics.

4   Experimental Results

To test the feasibility of our approach we use the Reuters-21578 text categorization collection [8], omitting empty documents and those without labels. Common and rare words are removed, and the vocabulary is stemmed with the Porter Stemmer [9]. After stemming, the vocabulary size is 12113.

In our experiments, we consider five buckets of documents ($s = 5$), and vary the percentage R of relevant documents (i.e., concerning the topic of interest) in each bucket from 50% to 80%. As topics of interest, we select the topics with the largest number of documents available in the data set. Once we have identified a topic, the non relevant documents are randomly selected from the remaining topics. We observe that some documents in the Reuters data have multiple topics associated (e.g., *grain* and *crops*). In our experiments, a document is considered positive if it has the topic of interest among its associated topics. For each topic examined, we test three different values of the minimum support (10%, 5%, 3%).

We have also investigated different threshold values (from 2 to 5) for the cardinality of the frequent itemsets ($|W_i|$). Only frequent itemsets of size above (or equal to) the threshold are considered for the retrieval of relevant documents. The rationale beyond this test is that if an item is too common across different documents, then it would have little discriminating power. The setting of a proper threshold for $|W_i|$ allows to discard frequently used words (not removed during preprocessing) that are not discriminating. Our experiments show that threshold values of 4 or 5 (depending on the value of the minimum support) give good results.

In the following tables we report, for each value of R, the number of (retrieved) documents in P ($|P|$), the number of positive (relevant) documents in P ($|P^+|$), the percentage of positive documents in P ($\%|P^+|$) –precision –, and the percentage of positive documents retrieved by P (r) – recall–. Each caption has (in parenthesis) the total number of positive documents versus the total number of documents in the five buckets.

We have considered different topics in our experiments. For lack of space, we report only the results for the topic *earn* (3776 documents). Similar results were obtained for the other topics. We distribute all the available positives among the buckets, and adjust the number of negatives accordingly to the R value considered.

Tables 1-4 show the results. Figures 1-3 plot the precision values for the topic *earn*, for increasing threshold t on the itemset size $|W_i|$. Each line corresponds to a value of R (percentage of positive documents in each bucket). The plots show that, in each case, the setting of $t = 5$ allows the achievement of a precision value very close to 1. For larger support values (5% and 10%), $t = 4$ suffices for the selection of an almost "pure" sample of documents. Even in the adverse condition of 50% of irrelevent documents in the buckets, the DocMine algorithm is able to achieve a very high precision.

These results are very promising for the purpose of constructing a classifier that uses the selected collection of documents P as a positive sample.

5   Conclusions

We have introduced a new algorithm, based on association rule mining, to select a representative sample of positive examples from a given set of unlabelled documents. Our experiments show that our method is capable of selecting sets of documents with precision above 90% in most cases, when frequent itemsets of cardinality 4 or 5 are considered. We emphasize that, in all cases, the precision tends to reach high levels, as the cardinality of the common itemsets grows, regardless of the value of the support, or the percentage of relevant documents in the original buckets.

Table 1. Topic *earn*: $R = 50\%$ (3776/7552).

Sup_{min}	$|W_i|$	$|P|$	$|P^+|$	$\%|P^+|$	r
	≥ 2	5323	2824	0.53	0.74
10%	≥ 3	2538	2204	0.87	0.58
	≥ 4	1848	1848	1.00	0.49
	≥ 5	1103	1103	1.00	0.29
	≥ 2	6441	3012	0.47	0.80
5%	≥ 3	4653	2597	0.56	0.69
	≥ 4	1972	1913	0.97	0.51
	≥ 5	1284	1284	1.00	0.34
	≥ 2	7246	3597	0.50	0.95
3%	≥ 3	5789	2943	0.51	0.78
	≥ 4	3671	2408	0.66	0.64
	≥ 5	1642	1628	0.99	0.43

Table 2. Topic *earn*: $R = 60\%$ (3776/6294).

Sup_{min}	$|W_i|$	$|P|$	$|P^+|$	$\%|P^+|$	r
	≥ 2	4453	2932	0.66	0.78
10%	≥ 3	2725	2250	0.83	0.60
	≥ 4	1842	1841	0.99	0.49
	≥ 5	1403	1403	1.00	0.37
	≥ 2	5684	3507	0.62	0.93
5%	≥ 3	3985	2668	0.67	0.71
	≥ 4	2045	1999	0.98	0.53
	≥ 5	1381	1376	0.99	0.36
	≥ 2	5859	3561	0.61	0.94
3%	≥ 3	4636	2928	0.63	0.78
	≥ 4	3311	2490	0.75	0.66
	≥ 5	1879	1875	0.99	0.50

Table 3. Topic *earn*. $R = 70\%$ (3776/5394).

Sup_{min}	$|W_i|$	$|P|$	$|P^+|$	$\%|P^+|$	r
	≥ 2	3592	2940	0.82	0.78
10%	≥ 3	2515	2274	0.90	0.60
	≥ 4	1849	1842	0.99	0.49
	≥ 5	1674	1674	1.00	0.44
	≥ 2	4784	3467	0.72	0.92
5%	≥ 3	3253	2747	0.84	0.73
	≥ 4	2027	1989	0.98	0.53
	≥ 5	1644	1642	0.99	0.43
	≥ 2	4982	3555	0.71	0.94
3%	≥ 3	4422	3447	0.78	0.91
	≥ 4	3550	3079	0.87	0.81
	≥ 5	1807	1803	0.99	0.48

References

[1] Blum, A., Mitchell T. (1998). Combining Labelled and Unlabelled Data with Co-Training. *Proceedings of the 1998 Conference on Computational Learning Theory.*

[2] Chen, Y., Zhou, X. S., Huang, T. S. (2001). One-class SVM for learning in image retrieval. *Proceedings of the International Conference on Image Processing.*

[3] Dumais, S. T., Letsche, T. A., Littman, M. L., & Landauer, T. K. (1997). Automatic cross-language retrieval using latent semantic indexing. *AAAI Spring Symposium on Cross-Language Text and Speech Retrieval.*

[4] Fung, B. C. M., Wang, K., & Ester M. (2003). Hierarchical Document Clustering Using Frequent Itemsets. *Proceedings of the SIAM International Conference on Data Mining.*

[5] Joachims, T. (1998). Text categorization with support vector machines. *Proceedings of the European Conference on Machine Learning.*

[6] Kandola, J., Shawe-Taylor, J., & Cristianini, N. (2002). Learning Semantic Similarity. *Neural Information Processing Systems (NIPS).*

[7] Leopold, E., & Kindermann, J. (2002). Text categorization with support vector machines, how to represent texts in input space? *Machine Learning,* **46**:423-444.

[8] Lewis, D., Reuters-21578 Text Categorization Test Collection Distribution 1.0. http://kdd.ics.uci.edu/databases/reuters21578/reuters21578.html

[9] Porter, M. (1980). An algorithm for suffix stripping, Program, **14**(3):130-137 http://www.tartarus.org/~martin/PorterStemmer

[10] Zhou, X. S., & Huang, T. S. (2001). Small sample learning during multimedia retrieval using BiasMap. *Proceedings of the IEEE Conference on Computer Vision and Pattern Recognition.*

Table 4. Topic *earn*: $R = 80\%$ **(3776/4720).**

Sup_{min}	$|W_i|$	$|P|$	$|P^+|$	$\%|P^+|$	r
10%	≥ 2	3192	2810	0.88	0.74
	≥ 3	2398	2279	0.95	0.60
	≥ 4	1394	1393	0.99	0.37
	≥ 5	1205	1205	1.00	0.32
5%	≥ 2	4151	3483	0.84	0.92
	≥ 3	3003	2763	0.92	0.73
	≥ 4	2126	2111	0.99	0.56
	≥ 5	1589	1587	0.99	0.42
3%	≥ 2	4294	3493	0.81	0.93
	≥ 3	3854	3275	0.85	0.87
	≥ 4	3059	2780	0.91	0.74
	≥ 5	2447	2377	0.97	0.63

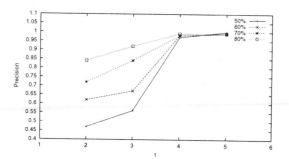

Figure 2. Precision values for topic *earn* **and** $Sup_{min} = 5\%$**. The x-axis is the minimum cardinality of common itemsets (**t**).**

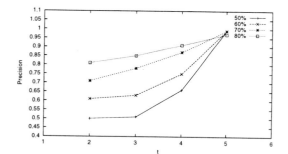

Figure 1. Precision values for topic *earn* **and** $Sup_{min} = 3\%$**. The x-axis is the minimum cardinality of common itemsets (**t**).**

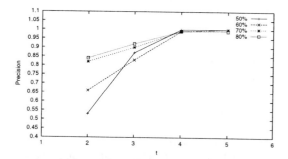

Figure 3. Precision values for topic *earn* **and** $Sup_{min} = 10\%$**. The x-axis is the minimum cardinality of common itemsets (**t**).**

A User-driven and Quality-oriented Visualization for Mining Association Rules

Julien Blanchard, Fabrice Guillet, Henri Briand
IRIN – Polytech'Nantes – University of Nantes
La Chantrerie – BP50609
44306   Nantes cedex 3   France
{julien.blanchard, fabrice.guillet, henri.briand}@polytech.univ-nantes.fr

Abstract

On account of the enormous amounts of rules that can be produced by data mining algorithms, knowledge validation is one of the most problematic steps in an association rule discovery process. In order to find relevant knowledge for decision-making, the user needs to really rummage through the rules. Visualization can be very beneficial to support him/her in this task by improving the intelligibility of the large rule sets and enabling the user to navigate inside them. In this article, we propose to answer the association rule validation problem by designing a human-centered visualization method for the rule rummaging task. This new approach based on a specific rummaging model relies on rule interestingness measures and on interactive rule subset focusing and mining. We have implemented our representation by developing a first experimental prototype called ARVis.

1. Introduction

Among the knowledge models used in Knowledge Discovery in Databases (KDD), association rules [1] have become a major concept and received significant research attention. These rules are implicative tendencies of the form $X \rightarrow Y$ where X and Y are conjunctions of database items (boolean variables). One of most problematic steps in an association rule discovery process is the post-processing of the rules, i.e. the interpretation, evaluation and validation of the rules after their extraction. Indeed the data mining algorithms can produce enormous amounts of rules. In practice, it is very tedious for the user (a decision-maker specialized in the data studied) to find interesting knowledge for decision-making in a corpus that can hold hundreds of thousands of rules or even millions of rules with large business databases. This problem is due to the unsupervised nature of association rule discovery: the user does not make his/her goals explicit and does not specify any endogenous variable.

Three kinds of approaches aim at helping the user appropriate the bulks of association rules: reducing the number of rules with interestingness measures [13] or summary techniques [11], exploring the rules with interactive tools like rule browsers [9] or query languages [8], and visualizing the rule sets with visual representations like matrices or graphs [6, 14]. In this article, to apprehend the problem of rule validation, we have opted for defining the user's task as a prerequisite. Indeed in order to efficiently assist the user in his/her search for the interesting knowledge, the KDD process should be considered not from the point of view of the discovery algorithms but from that of the user's, as a user-centered and task-oriented decision support system [4]. From the definition of the user's task and the cognitive constraints which ensue, we propose an appropriate model of rule rummaging which follows from our previous works on the exploration of rule sets using graphs [10]. Then we present an interactive visualization method for the human-centered process of association rule rummaging. This method combines the three approaches described before with a tight association of interestingness measures, a strong interactivity with the user, and a visual representation. We have implemented our new visualization method in a first rule mining prototype called ARVis. Including an online algorithm of rule extraction, ARVis allows the user to mine the rules interactively *via* the visual representation all along the rummaging process.

In the next part we define the user's task and our model for the human-centered rummaging of association rules. Then we present our interactive visualization method and the choices we made for ARVis regarding the rule set structure, the visual metaphor, and the interactions.

2. Human-centered rummaging of association rules

2.1. User's task

During the knowledge validation step in the post-processing of the rules, the user is faced with the rules extracted by data mining algorithms and described by interestingness measures. The user's task is then to find interesting rules for decision-making in these long lists. Inspired by research works on the user's behavior in a knowledge discovery process [2] on the one hand, and

493

also by cognitive principles of information processing in the context of decision models [12] on the other hand, we consider that the user applies a focusing strategy to apprehend the bulk of rules: faced with a large amount of information, the user focuses his/her attention on a limited and therefore more intelligible subset of potentially useful information. To facilitate the user's post-processing task, we have developed a model of human-centered rummaging which supports his/her focusing strategy by allowing to isolate a rule subset, to explore it, and to change it in an iterative way until he/she is able to reach a decision.

2.2. Rule rummaging model

Our rule rummaging model consists in letting the user navigate as he/she wishes through the voluminous rule set by focusing on the successive limited subsets to explore. The user drives a series of local explorations by trial and error through the whole rule set from which only the selected portion is gradually visited. Implementing such a rule rummaging process implies structuring the rule set to allow the user to focus on rule subsets and navigate from one to another. More precisely, we need to group the rules together into subsets and combine these subsets among themselves by neighborhood relations (figure 1). At each navigation step, to access a new rule subset after exploring the current one, the user has the choice among all the neighboring subsets, i.e. those reachable by the neighborhood relation. This relation can be implemented by a retrieval procedure if the rule set is already extracted (post-analysis of rules), or by a local algorithm for constraint-based rule extraction (inductive database approach [7]) so that the user drives the data mining interactively from the rummaging process.

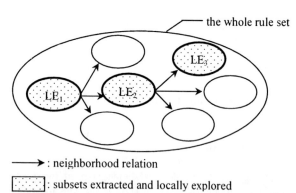

the whole rule set

$\longrightarrow$: neighborhood relation

[:::::]: subsets extracted and locally explored

Figure 1. The neighborhood relation allows to mine the rule subsets according to the user's navigation

3. Visualization for rule rummaging in the ARVis tool

In this part, we describe the choices we made to implement the human-centered rummaging process in ARVis. The rules are here described by three interestingness measures: support, confidence [1], and implication intensity (respectively noted *sp*, *cf* and *ii*). Support evaluates the generality of the rules and confidence its validity (success rate), while implication intensity evaluates the rule statistical surprisingness by quantifying the unlikelihood of the number of counter-examples compared to a probabilistic model [3, 5]. Each measure is associated to a minimal threshold set by the user and exploited to filter the rules: s_{sp}, s_{cf}, s_{ii}.

3.1. Relation of specialization/generalization

Given the set I of items relative to the studied domain, the rules are of the form $X \rightarrow y$ where X is an itemset $X \subseteq I$ and y is an item $y \in I \setminus X$. We have chosen to structure the rule set by creating rule subsets $RULES(X)$, each corresponding to an itemset $X \subseteq I$. Each subset $RULES(X)$ contains two kinds of rules, the specific ones $RULESspe(X)$ and the general ones $RULESgen(X)$:

$$RULES(X) = RULESspe(X) \cup RULESgen(X).$$

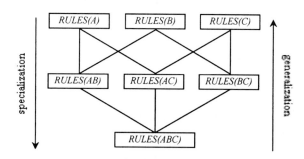

Figure 2. The relations of specialization and generalization among the rule subsets (with a set of items $I = \{A, B, C\}$)

The specific and general rules are defined as:
$RULESspe(X) = \{ X \rightarrow y$ such as:
$y \in I \setminus X, sp(X \rightarrow y) \geq s_{sp}, cf(X \rightarrow y) \geq s_{cf}, ii(X \rightarrow y) \geq s_{ii} \}$
$RULESgen(X) = \{ X \setminus \{y\} \rightarrow y$ such as: $y \in X,$
$sp(X \setminus \{y\} \rightarrow y) \geq s_{sp}, cf(X \setminus \{y\} \rightarrow y) \geq s_{cf}, ii(X \setminus \{y\} \rightarrow y) \geq s_{ii} \}$

The specific rules have all the same left-hand side and only their right-hand sides differ, while the general rules are all built from the same items. We use as neighborhood relation a relation of specialization among the subsets and its symmetrical relation of generalization (see the graph figure 2). Specializing a subset $RULES(X)$ amounts to adding an item to the itemset X, whereas an item is removed by generalizing.

3.2. Quality-oriented visual metaphor

To generate a visual representation of the rules, we take advantage of the user's focusing strategy by only representing the current subset at each navigation step. Each rule subset is visualized using a 3D "information landscape" representation. With the use of 3D instead of 2D, the most important information can be displayed in the foreground, letting the less important information in the background. For each rule subset, the landscape is shared into two areas: one is dedicated to the specific rules, and the other one to the general rules.

Figure 3. Two arenas in a landscape

We symbolize each rule by the following object: a sphere perched on top of a cone in the landscape. In the specific rule and the general rule areas, the objects are laid-out in the landscape on an arena (a "glass" half-bowl) to reduce occultation (figure 3). We have opted for the following visual metaphor to represent the rule subsets (figure 4):
- the object position represents the implication intensity,
- the sphere visible area represents the support,
- the cone height represents the confidence,
- the object color is used redundantly to represent a weighted average of the three measures.

This visual metaphor stresses the good rules whose visualization and access are made easier compared to the worse rules. Furthermore, some complementary text labels appear above each object to give the name of the corresponding rule and provide the numerical values for support, confidence and implication intensity.

3.3. Interactions

The user interacts in three different ways with the visual representation: by visiting the rule subsets, by filtering the rules on the interestingness measures, and by navigating among the subsets.

The user can wander freely over the 3D landscape to browse the rules and examine them more closely. To

facilitate the user's exploration, there exist predefined viewpoints for the overall vision of each arena and for the close vision of each object.

During the subset local explorations, the user can filter the rules in the landscape by dynamic queries on the interestingness measures *via* sliders. These queries alter the thresholds s_{sp}, s_{cf}, s_{ii} on the measures to make only the rules with sufficient quality appear.

Finally, to drive his/her rummaging process, the user can navigate from one rule subset to another by clicking on the objects in the landscape. By clicking on a specific (respectively general) rule $X \rightarrow x$, he/she triggers the relation of specialization (resp. generalization), the current subset is thus replaced by the new more specific subset $RULES(X \cup \{x\})$ (resp. the new more general subset $RULES(X)$) and the representation is updated. Besides, the more specific or more general subsets the user can reach are represented in a shrunk version inside the spheres of the current landscape. This allows to anticipate whether a subset is worth exploring or not.

The relations of specialization/generalization are implemented using the hybrid mining algorithm presented in [10]. The first step of this algorithm is the "frequent itemset" mining procedure of the well-known *A Priori* algorithm [1]. The second step is an online local procedure polynomial in number of items which dynamically computes the rule subsets $RULES(X)$. Therefore, only the rules required by the user along his/her rummaging process are extracted.

4. Conclusion

In this paper, we have presented an interactive visualization method specially designed to support association rule mining and post-processing in a KDD process. This new approach is based on our human-centered model of rule rummaging appropriate to the user's task. It enables him/her to navigate through the voluminous rule set by carrying out a series of local explorations of limited subsets he/she focuses on. The user can thus comprehend the bulk of rules more easily to find relevant knowledge for decision-making. Coupled with an online algorithm of rule extraction, the visualization allows to interactively drive the data mining by producing only the rules required by the user. The subjectivity present in the rule validation step can thus be exploited in the KDD process to reduce the rule profusion. Moreover, our visualization takes advantage of the rules' names, used in the interactions to navigate among the subsets, but also of the interestingness measures, highlighted in the representation, which is original compared to the other rule set visualization methods.

We have developed ARVis, a first rule mining prototype implementing our visualization method. ARVis is built on a client/server architecture. On the server side, a CGI program takes charge of the local extraction of the rules and of the visual representation construction in VRML. The rules and the 3D landscapes are therefore generated dynamically. On the client side, the user visualizes the landscapes with a web browser equipped with a relevant VRML plug-in. The tool can be used with shutterglasses to provide stereoscopic display in order to improve the perception of depth. Our future works will mainly concern:

- developing the tool for rule rummaging in Java3D,
- implementing additional neighborhood relations with appropriate local mining algorithms.

Mining and Knowledge Discovery, Springer, L.N.A.I. 1510, 1998, 318-327.

[6] Han, J., Chiang, J., Chee, S., Chen, J., Cheng, S., Gong, W., Kamber, M., Koperski, K., Liu, G., Lu, Y., Stefanovic, N., Winstone, L., Xia, B., Zaiane, O.R., Zhang, S., and Zhu, H., "DBMiner: a system for data mining in relational databases and data warehouses", *Proc. of CASCON'97*, 1997, 249-260.

[7] Imielinski, T., and Mannila, H., "A database perspective on knowledge discovery", *Communications of the ACM 39(11)*, 1996, 58-64.

[8] Imielinski, T., and Virmani, A., "MSQL: a query language for database mining", *Journal of data mining and knowledge discovery 3(4)*, 1999, 373-408.

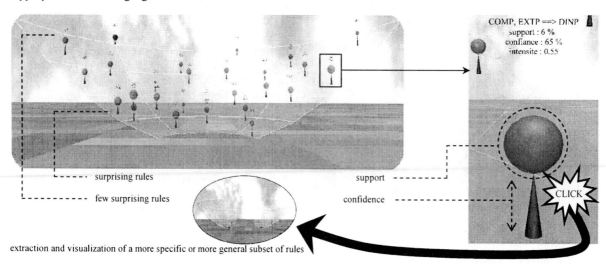

surprising rules

few surprising rules

support

confidence

extraction and visualization of a more specific or more general subset of rules

Figure 4. The visual metaphor and the interactions in ARVis

5. References

[1] Agrawal, R., Mannila, H., Srikant, R., Toivonen, H., and Verkamo, A.I., "Fast discovery of association rules", *Advances in Knowledge Discovery and Data Mining*, AAAI/MIT Press, U.M. Fayyad, G. Piatetsky-Shapiro, and P. Smyth (Eds.), 1996, 307-328.

[2] Bandhari, I., "Attribute focusing: machine-assisted knowledge discovery applied to software production process control", *Knowledge acquisition 6*, 1994, 271-294.

[3] Blanchard, J., Kuntz, P., Guillet, F., and Gras, R., "Implication intensity: from the basic statistical definition to the entropic version", *Statistical Data Mining and Knowledge Discovery*, CRC Press, H. Bozdogan (Ed.), 2003, 473-485.

[4] Brachman, J.R., and Anand, T., "The process of knowledge discovery in databases: a human-centered approach", *Advances in Knowledge Discovery and Data Mining*, AAAI/MIT Press, U.M. Fayyad, G. Piatetsky-Shapiro, and P. Smyth (Eds.), 1996, 37-58.

[5] Guillaume, S., Guillet, F., and Philippe, J., "Improving the discovery of association rules with intensity of implication", *Proc. of the 2nd European Conference of Principles of Data*

[9] Klemettinen, M., Mannila, H., and Toivonen, H., *Interactive exploration of discovered knowledge: a methodology for interaction, and usability studies*, Technical report C-1996-3, University of Helsinki, 1996.

[10] Kuntz, P., Guillet, F., Lehn, R., and Briand, H., "A user-driven process for mining association rules", *Proc. of the 4th European Conference of Principles of Data Mining and Knowledge Discovery*, Springer, L.N.A.I. 1910, 2000, 160-168.

[11] Liu, B., Hu, M., and Hsu, W., "Multi-level organization and summarization of the discovered rules", *Proc. of the 6th ACM SIGKDD International Conference on Knowledge Discovery and Data Mining*, 2000, 208-217.

[12] Montgomery, H., "Decision rules and the search for dominance structure: toward a process model of decision-making", *Analyzing and Aiding Decision Processes*, P.C. Humphreys, O. Svenson, and A. Vari (Eds.), 1983, 471-483.

[13] Tan, P., Kumar, V., and Srivastava, J., "Selecting the right interestingness measure for association patterns", *Proc. of the 8th ACM SIGKDD International Conference on Knowledge Discovery and Data Mining*, 2000, 32-41.

[14] Wong, P.C., Whitney, P., and Thomas, J., "Visualizing association rules for text mining", *Proc. of the IEEE Symposium on Information Visualization InfoVis'99*, 1999, 120-123.

Towards Simple, Easy-to-Understand, yet Accurate Classifiers

Doina Caragea
Artificial Intelligence Research Laboratory
Department of Computer Science
Iowa State University
226 Atanasoff Hall, Ames, IA 50011, USA
dcaragea@cs.iastate.edu

Dianne Cook
Virtual Reality Applications Center
Department of Statistics
Iowa State University
325 Snedecor Hall, Ames, IA 50011, USA
dicook@iastate.edu

Vasant Honavar
Artificial Intelligence Research Laboratory
Department of Computer Science
Iowa State University
226 Atanasoff Hall, Ames, IA 50011, USA
honavar@cs.iastate.edu

Abstract

We design a method for weighting linear support vector machine classifiers or random hyperplanes, to obtain classifiers whose accuracy is comparable to the accuracy of a non-linear support vector machine classifier, and whose results can be readily visualized. We conduct a simulation study to examine how our weighted linear classifiers behave in the presence of known structure. The results show that the weighted linear classifiers might perform well compared to the non-linear support vector machine classifiers, while they are more readily interpretable than the non-linear classifiers.

1 Introduction

Support vector machines (SVMs) [9] have been shown to build accurate rules in complex classification problems, but the results often provide little insight into the class structure in the data.

When the data is linearly separable, we can understand the nature of the boundaries between classes by looking at the separating hyperplane or the normal to this hyperplane. In high-dimensional spaces the normal to the separating hyperplane is visualized using tour methods [4, 5]. When data is non-linearly separable, the visualization is more difficult because the boundaries between classes are non-linear.

We have designed a classifier based on weighting linear support vector machines or random hyperplanes, whose accuracy is comparable to the accuracy of a support vector machine classifier with non-linear kernel, and whose results can be readily visualized. We have shown this by conducting a simulation study on artificially generated data sets. We expect that this approach will be useful for data with a relatively low number of variables (features), less than 20, where it is possible to visually explore the space.

2 SVM and Visualization

The output of the SVM classifier, using linear kernels, is the normal to the separating hyperplane, which is itself a linear combination of the data. Thus the natural way to examine the result is to look at the data projected into this direction. It may also be interesting to explore the neighborhood of this projection by changing the coefficients to the projection. This is available in a visualization technique called a manually-controlled tour.

Generally, tours display projections of variables, $\mathbf{x}'\mathbf{A}$ where $\mathbf{A}$ is a $p \times d(< p)$-dimensional projection matrix. The columns of A are orthonormal. Often $d = 2$ because the display space on a computer screen is 2-dimensional, but it can be 1 or 3, or any value between 1 and p. The earliest form of the tour presented the data in a continuous movie-like manner [1], but recent developments have provided guided tours [5] and manually controlled tours [4]. Here we are going to use a $d = 2$-dimensional manually-controlled tour to recreate the separating boundary between two groups in the data space. Figure 1 illustrates the tour approach.

497

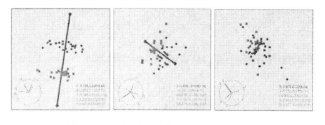

Figure 1. Three tour projections of a 5-dimensional data set where the two groups are readily separated. The normal to the separating hyperplane is shown as a vector in the space, and the axes at bottom left and right represent the projection coordinates. The left plot shows a projection where the groups are well-separated, and the plot at right shows a projection where they are less separated. The magnitude of the projection coefficients indicate variable importance, the larger the coefficient - in the direction of separation - the more important the variable. For example, the left plot shows $\frac{-0.169}{5.34}V_1 - \frac{0.803}{4.71}V_2 - \frac{0.366}{20}V_3 + \frac{0.269}{20}V_4 + \frac{0.346}{20}V_5$ horizontally, and $\frac{0.006}{5.34}V_1 + \frac{0.120}{4.71}V_2 + \frac{0.618}{20}V_3 + \frac{0.642}{20}V_4 + \frac{0.438}{20}V_5$ vertically. The separation between groups is in the vertical direction which is primarily variables 4,5,6.

3 Weighted Linear SVMs

We design a method for combining linear classifiers generated either using the SVM algorithm or randomly on subsamples of data, and we use this method to classify new non-linearly separable data.

We assume that a training set E of size l is given and N hyperplanes $h_1, h_2, \cdots, h_N$ are generated using the SVM algorithm. To generate a hyperplane h_i, we randomly divide the training set into two subsets. One subset is used for generating the linear classifier and the other is used for estimating its error, $error(h_i)$.

If x is a new data example that needs to be classified, we estimate the "probability" $P(+1|x)$ that x belongs to the positive class, and the "probability" $P(-1|x)$ that x belongs to the negative class, as follows, and then we assign to x the class with larger "probability": $P(+1|x) = \sum_{i=1}^{N} P(+1|x, h_i) * 2^{error(h_i)}$, $P(-1|x) = \sum_{i=1}^{N} P(-1|x, h_i) * 2^{error(h_i)}$. In order to estimate the "probabilities" $P(+1|x, h_i)$ and $P(-1|x, h_i)$, we use the method described in [6], which is based on binning the training examples according to their scores computed by SVM (i.e., the distances from the points to the separating hyperplane). More exactly, the training examples are

ranked according to their scores with respect to a hypothesis h_i and then they are grouped in b subsets of equal size. A new test example x is placed in the corresponding subset j according to the score that h_i assigns to it. The "probability" that x belongs to the positive class is estimated as the fraction of positive training examples that fall into the subset j, while the "probability" that x belongs to the negative class is given by the fraction of negative training examples that fall into j.

One may ask why use hyperplanes generated with SVM algorithm instead of randomly generated hyperplanes. The advantage of using the hyperplanes generated by SVM is that they are guided toward a reasonable solution for the given data, while the random hyperplanes can be arbitrarily good or bad. So, in general, we expect that a larger number of random hyperplanes is needed, especially for higher dimensional data. For comparison, we designed a similar method to the one described above for randomly generated hyperplanes. We generated N random hyperplanes and assigned scores to the test examples based on the distances from those examples to the random hyperplanes.

4 Examining SVM Through Simulation

For the experiments in this paper, we used SVM^{light}3.50 [8] implementation (svmlight.joachims.org) of SVM algorithm. The parameters used were chosen by trying various values and choosing the ones that gave the best results in terms of accuracy. We also used the tour methods available in the data visualization package GGobi (www.ggobi.org).

The data sets used were generated by varying the shape of clusters and the number of variables. The first three data sets (plotted in Figure 2) contain 2 classes, and 2 variables, and the fourth data set contains 2 classes and 5 variables. There are 500 instances in each data set. Data set 1 contains

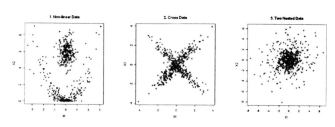

Figure 2. Simulated Data Sets: 2-Dimensional data sets used to examine the SVM behavior under different distributions

two non-linearly separable clusters. It is motivated by previous observations [3]. Data sets 2 and 3 exhibit classes that are highly non linearly separable. One data set contains two ellipses that intersect in their centers (normals with the same mean). The other contains one cluster nested inside the other (generated from normal distributions with the same mean, but different variance). Data set 4 is similar to the third data set, but in 5 dimensions, a very difficult data set to classify using linear boundaries.

We perform two sets of experiments for all three methods we want to compare (i.e., non-linear SVM, weighted linear SVM and weighted random hyperplanes). The first set of experiments is meant to compare the performance of the three methods, while the second set is meant to show how we can visualize the results of the methods used.

For each run of the three methods we compare, we randomly divide the data set into a training set containing 400 example and a test set containing 100 examples. The non-linear SVM (Non-Lin SVM) uses these sets as training and test sets. For the weighted linear SVM (Lin SVM) and the random hyperplanes (Rnd Hyp) methods, we split the training set further into a set containing 300 examples, (used to train the individual linear SVMs) and a set containing 100 examples (used to estimate the probabilities corresponding to the test examples, and also the error of each linear classifier generated). The number of bins is 5, so the size of each bin is 20. The same test set as in the case of non-linear SVM is used for the weighted linear SVM and weighted random hyperplanes methods.

4.1 Visual Results

Simulation Set 1: To show how the three methods used in the paper perform compared to each other, we ran them 100 times and recorded the accuracy on the test set. The average test accuracy over 100 runs for the four simulated data sets is shown in the Table 1. It appears that in general the non-linear kernel SVM performs better than the other two methods, but the difference is not always significant. The use of the kernel brings a gain over the other two linear methods in terms of accuracy, however it pays off in terms of the understanding of the separation between classes.

The performance of the Lin SVM and Rnd Hyp is comparable for Cross and Two Nested data sets, but the Rnd Hyp performs better in the case of the Non-Linear and 5d Nested data sets. This can be explained by the better chance that the Rnd Hyp has to find hyperplanes that are not very accurate by themselves, but they contribute to the global accuracy when they are used in combination with others (if the number of hyperplanes is large enough). This is not the case for the hyperplanes obtained with SVM that are biased toward the best hyperplane given the data.

Simulation Set 2: The goal of the second set of experiments is to show how we can visualize the results of the methods designed. We performed 8 runs for each 2-dimensional data set, using h=2, 5, 10, 20, 25, 50, 75, 100

Table 1. The average test accuracy over 100 runs for the four simulated data sets

Data Set	Non-Lin SVM	Lin-SVM	Rnd Hyp
Non-Linear	0.9989	0.8915	0.9215
Cross	0.8509	0.8281	0.8201
Two Nested	0.7654	0.7044	0.7192
5d Nested	0.8108	0.7150	0.8126

hyperplanes for each run, respectively. The graphical results for h=5, 50 and 100 are shown in Figure 3 for Non-Linear data, Cross data and Two-Nested data, in the case of Lin SVM and Rnd Hyp methods. Separation boundaries appeared comparable for the two methods. In addition, separation boundaries, especially in the case with random hyperplanes, improve with the number of hyperplanes, covering towards the true boundaries.

The Figure 4 shows the graphical results for the 5-dimensional data. Here we performed only one run using 5 hyperplanes.

5 Discussion

The proposed method for combining linear classifiers outperforms SVM using non-linear kernels in some cases. Even in cases where SVM with non-linear kernel outperforms the weighted combination of linear classifiers, the loss in accuracy is compensated by the ease of understanding of the results through visualization.

Various weighting schemes for combining classifiers exist in literature [2, 7]. Our purpose was to show how one particular scheme can be easily visualized. Similar visualization methods can be applied for any other weighting scheme based on linear classifier.

More experiments with higher dimensional data sets are underway. Different ways to visualize the normal to the separating hyperplane in higher dimensional spaces are explored.

Acknowledgements

This work has been supported in part by grants from the National Science Foundation (#9982341, #9972653), the Carver Foundation, Pioneer Hi-Bred, Inc., John Deere Foundation, the ISU Graduate College, and the IBM.

References

[1] D. Asimov. The Grand Tour: A Tool for Viewing Multidimensional Data. *SIAM Journal of Scientific and Statistical Computing*, 6(1):128–143, 1985.

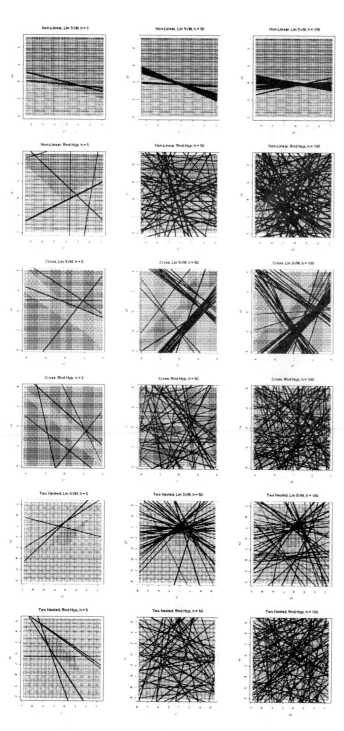

Figure 4. (Top row) This plot shows 4 projections of the 5-dimensional nested data, with the normals to 5 hyperplanes drawn as vectors over the data. We would expect that the best solution using hyperplanes will bound the groups with the smaller variance using planes tangent to the surface of a sphere. That is, the normals to the boundary hyperplanes will be uniformly distributed in all directions, which is what we see in the 5 normals here. **(Bottom row)** This plot is similar to the above, 4 projections of the 5-dimensional nested data with the 5 randomly generated normals overlaid.

[2] L. Breiman. Bagging Predictors, In *Machine Learning*, Vol. 24, No. 2, 1996.

[3] D. Caragea, D. Cook and V. Honavar. Gaining Insights into Support Vector Machine Pattern Classifiers Using Projection-Based Tour Methods, In Proceedings of the KDD Conference, San Francisco, CA, 2001.

[4] D. Cook and A. Buja. Manual Controls For High-Dimensional Data Projections. *Journal of Computational and Graphical Statistics*, 6(4):464–480, 1997.

[5] D. Cook, A. Buja, J. Cabrera, and C. Hurley. Grand Tour and Projection Pursuit. *Journal of Comp. and Graphical Statistics*, 4(3):155–172, 1995.

[6] J. Drish. Obtaining Calibrated Probability Estimates from Support Vector Machines. San Diego, 2001.

[7] T. Dietterich. Ensemble Methods in Machine Learning. In: *Lecture Notes in Computer Science*, Vol. 1857, 2000.

[8] T. Joachims. *Making Large-Scale SVM Learning Practical*. MIT Press, 1999.

[9] V. Vapnik. *The Nature of Statistical Learning Theory*. Springer-Verlag, New York, NY, 1999.

Figure 3. Visual Results for Lin-SVM and Rnd Hyp: three runs for h=5,50 and 100 are shown. A grid over data is generated and the classifiers constructed are used to classify the points in the grid. The two classes are identify by different colors. For each data set, the first raw shows the performance of the Lin-SVM on the grid, while the second raw shows the performance of the Rnd Hyp on the grid.

Validating and Refining Clusters via Visual Rendering

Keke Chen   Ling Liu

College of Computing, Georgia Institute of Technology
{kekechen, lingliu}@cc.gatech.edu

Abstract

The automatic clustering algorithms are known to work well in dealing with clusters of regular shapes, e.g. compact spherical/elongated shapes, but may incur higher error rates when dealing with arbitrarily shaped clusters. Although some efforts have been devoted to addressing the problem of skewed datasets, the problem of handling clusters with irregular shapes is still in its infancy, especially in terms of dimensionality of the datasets and the precision of the clustering results considered. Not surprisingly, the statistical indices works ineffective in validating clusters of irregular shapes, too. In this paper, we address the problem of clustering and validating arbitrarily shaped clusters with a visual framework (VISTA). The main idea of the VISTA approach is to capitalize on the power of visualization and interactive feedbacks to encourage domain experts to participate in the clustering revision and clustering validation process.

1. Introduction

Over the past decades most of the clustering research has been focused on automatic clustering algorithms and statistical validity indices. The automatic methods are known to work well in dealing with clusters of regular shapes, e.g. compact spherical or elongated shapes, but incur high error when dealing with arbitrarily shaped clusters. Some new algorithms like CURE [2], WaveCluster [12], DBSCAN [9], and OPTICS [15] have addressed this problem and try to solve it in restricted situations (low dimensional datasets or the cluster shapes are elongated/enlarged). Yet it is still considered as an unsolved hard problem due to the complexity in multi-dimensional space and the unpredictable skewed cluster distributions.

Since clustering is an unsupervised process, cluster validity indices are used to evaluate the quality of clusters, (the compactness or density of clusters, and the dissimilarity between clusters, etc.[11]) and particularly, cluster validity indices are used to decide the optimal number of clusters. The arbitrarily shaped clusters also make the traditional statistical cluster validity indices ineffective [11], which leaves it difficult to determine the optimal cluster structure.

It is possible to invent some complicated automatic clustering algorithms or statistical methods to adapt various specific irregular situations. However, the irregularity cannot be anticipated in applications. Some irregularly shaped clusters may be formed by combining two regular clusters or by splitting one large cluster with the incorporation of domain knowledge. There are no general rules to describe the irregularity. Therefore, the automatic algorithms or statistical methods are not flexible enough to adapt all application-specific requirements.

One feature of the automatic clustering algorithms is that it almost excludes human from the clustering process. What the user can do is usually setting the parameters before the clustering algorithm running, waiting for the algorithm producing the results, validating the results and repeating the entire process if the results are not satisfactory. Once the clustering algorithm starts running, the user cannot monitor or steer the cluster process, which also makes it hard to incorporate domain knowledge into the clustering process and especially inconvenient for large-scale clustering since the iterative cycle is long.

Since the geometry and density features of clusters derived from the distance (similarity) relationship, determines the validity of clustering results, no wonder that visualization is the most intuitive method for validating clusters, especially the clusters in irregular shape. However, cluster visualization is also highly challenging because of the difficulty in visualizing multi-dimensional (>3D) datasets.

Generally speaking, clustering algorithms and validity indices have to answer the two questions: "how to recognize the special structure of each particular dataset?" and "how to refine a given imprecise cluster definition?" In this paper, we propose a visual framework that allows the user to be involved into the clustering/validating process via interactive visualization. The core of the visual framework is the visual cluster rendering system VISTA. VISTA can work with any algorithmic results – at the beginning, VISTA imports the algorithmic clustering result into the visual cluster rendering system, and then lets the user participate in the following "clustering-evaluation" iterations interactively. With the reliable mapping mechanism employed by VISTA system, the user can visually validate the defined clusters via interactive operations. The interactive operations also allow the user to refine the clusters or incorporate domain knowledge to define better cluster structure.

We organize the paper as following. The visual framework and VISTA system are introduced in section 2; in section 3, two empirical examples are demonstrated in details to show the power of VISTA in validating and refining clusters for real datasets. The related work is discussed in section 4. Finally, we conclude our work.

2. VISTA visual framework

Most frequently, the clustering is not finished when the computer/algorithm finishes unless the user has evaluated, understood and accepted the patterns or results, therefore, the user has to be involved in the "clustering – analysis/evaluation" iteration. Concrete discussion about the framework can be found in [8]. We observed that with automatic approaches clustering phase and validating phase should only be done in sequence. In order to interweave these two phases to improve the efficiency, we develop an interactive cluster visual rendering system to get human involved in. With this framework, the user can participate in the clustering process, validating the clusters, monitoring and steering the clustering process.

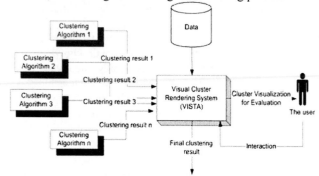

Figure 1. VISTA validating and refining clusters

There are some challenges for interactive cluster visualization techniques, among which the most challenging one is cluster preserving – the clusters appearing in the 2D/3D visualization should be the real clusters in k-D (k>=3) space. Since a k-D to 2D/3D mapping inevitably introduces visual bias, such as broken clusters, overlapping clusters or fake clusters formed by outliers, additional interactive rendering techniques are needed to improve the visual quality.

In VISTA cluster rendering system, we use a linear (or affine) mapping [13] – α-mapping to avoid the breaking of clusters after mapping, but the overlapping and fake clusters may still exist. The compensative techniques are interactive operations to produce dynamic visualization. The interactive operations are used to change the projection plane, which allows the user to observe the datasets from different perspectives. While the visual cluster rendering system is combined with the algorithmic result, the two can improve each other.

To illustrate how the VISTA works, we will briefly introduce the α-mapping and some interactive operations. The initial version of VISTA is used to render Euclidean datasets, where the similarity is defined by Euclidean distance, since the Euclidean distance is widely used in applications.

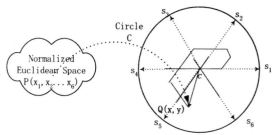

Figure 2. Illustration of α-mapping with $k=6$

We invent a linear mapping α-mapping that partially preserves k-dimensional (k-D) information in 2D space and is used to build a k-parameter-adjustable interactive visualization system. A k-axis 2D star coordinates is defined by an origin $\vec{o}\,(x_0,\ y_0)$ and k coordinates $S_1, S_2, ..., S_k$, which represent the k dimensions in 2D spaces. The k coordinates are equidistantly distributed on the circumference of the circle C, as in Figure 2, where the unit vectors are $\vec{S}_i = (\hat{u}_{xi}, \hat{u}_{yi})$, $i= 1..k$, $\hat{u}_{xi} = \cos(2\pi/i), \hat{u}_{yi} = \sin(2\pi/i)$. The radius c of the circle C is the scaling factor, which determines the size and the detail level of the visualization. Let a 2D point $Q\,(x, y)$ represent the mapping of a k-dimensional max-min normalized (with normalization bounds [-1, 1]) data point $P(x_0, x_1,...x_i...,x_k)$ on the 2D star coordinates.

α-mapping:

$$A(x_1,..., x_k, \alpha_1,..., \alpha_k) = (c/k)\sum_{i=1}^{k}\alpha_i x_i \vec{s}_i - \vec{o} \quad (1)$$

i.e. the position of $Q\,(x, y)$ is determined by,

$$\left\{(c/k)\sum_{i=1}^{k}\alpha_i x_i \cos(2\pi/i) - x_0, \quad (c/k)\sum_{i=1}^{k}\alpha_i x_i \sin(2\pi/i) - y_0\right\}$$

The α_i ($i = 1,2,...k$, $-1\leq\alpha_i \leq 1$) in the definition are dimensional adjustment parameters, one for each of the k dimensions. α_i is set to 0.5 initially.

The α-mapping has two important properties: (1) the mapping is linear, and thus it does not break clusters and the gaps in visualization are the real gaps in the original space. (2) The mapping is dimension-by-dimension adjustable by α_i, which enables the dynamic rendering operations to find the cluster overlapping.

Since α-parameter adjustment is the most frequently used one, some operations, such as random rendering and automatic rendering, are used to increase the efficiency of α-parameter adjustment [1]. Another set of set-oriented operations are used to refine visual cluster definition after we get initial cluster visualization with α-parameter

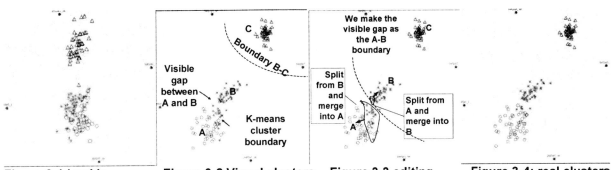

Figure 3-1 load in   **Figure 3-2 Visual clusters**   **Figure 3-3 editing**   **Figure 3-4: real clusters**

* k-means result, RMSSTD =0.4108, RS = 0.8002, S_Dbw = 1.4158.   After editing, EMSSTD = 0.4396, RS=0.7712, S_Dbw =1.5115

adjustment. These operations include subset selection, cluster marking, cluster splitting, cluster merging, and hierarchical structure defining. Domain knowledge in form of labelled items can be incorporated into visualization conveniently. Due to the space limitation, we will not introduce them concretely.

3. Empirical study

In this section, we will introduce two examples of visual rendering. The first one demonstrates the ability of VISTA visual validating and interactive refining. The second one shows how to incorporate domain knowledge into VISTA visual cluster rendering. The datasets used in the examples can be found at UCI Machine Learning database (http://www.ics.uci.edu/~mlearn/).

3.1 Analyzing the "Iris" dataset

In this example, we will use the most popular clustering algorithm – k-means [6] to produce the clustering result on the dataset "iris", and then import the result into VISTA system. With VISTA system, we will validate the k-means result visually and then try to refine the clusters to improve the quality of the k-means clusters. The quality of clusters is also evaluated by statistical indices RMSSTD, RS, and S_Dbw [11] to see if the statistical indices are consistent with the visual improvement.

"Iris" dataset is a famous dataset widely used in pattern recognition and clustering. It is a 4-D dataset containing 150 instances, and there are three clusters, each has 50 instances. One cluster is linearly separable from the other two; the latter two are not exactly linearly separable from each other according to the literature.

In initial visualization Figure 3-1, we can find one cluster has been separated from the other two. After interactive cluster rendering, mainly the α-parameter adjustment, the visual boundaries become clearer (Figure 3-2). The boundary B-C clearly separates cluster C from the other two clusters. The gap between cluster A and B can be visually perceived. The α-mapping model confirms that this gap does exist in the 4-D space. We make this gap as the visual boundary A-B. This visually

perceived boundary A-B is not consistent with the k-means boundary, but we have more confidence with it since it has been intuitively confirmed. As the literature of the "iris" dataset mentioned, the two clusters are not linearly separable. To further refine the cluster definition, we can also informally define a small "ambiguous area" around the gap between A and B, the points in which have equal probability of belonging to A or B.

With this visual boundary, we can edit the k-means result as Figure 3-3 shows. After editing, the points are shown more homogeneously distributed in the clusters. The visual partition is also highly consistent with the real cluster distribution (comparing Figure 3-3 and 3-4). However, the statistical validity indices do not agree with the visual improvement. All of the three indices show the visual re-partitioning reduces the cluster quality. (Smaller RMSSTD, larger RS and the smaller S_Dbw imply the better quality. [11]).

Extended experiments with trained users show all users can find the visualization like Figure 3-2 in less than 2 minutes, which means visual validity could be very practical in exploring datasets. Experimental results on various datasets, showing the effectiveness and efficiency of visual validating and rendering, are not listed here, due to the space limitation.

3.2 Incorporating domain knowledge

Domain knowledge plays a critical role in the clustering process [8]. It is the semantic explanation to the data, which is different from the structural clustering criteria, such as distance between points and usually leads to a high-level cluster definition, for example, splitting or combining the parts of the basic clusters.

Domain knowledge can be represented in various forms [8]. In VISTA system, we define the domain knowledge as additional labeled items to the original dataset. The labels indicate the domain criterion about the clustering. We name the labeled items "landmarks". The number of landmarks is usually so small that they cannot work effectively as a training dataset to classify the entire datasets with classification algorithms.

When visualizing a dataset, the landmark points are loaded and visualized in different colors according to their labels. This guiding information can direct the user to define the high-level cluster structure, or repartition the algorithmic clustering results. The alternative method is to visualize the dataset first and then sample some points from the "critical areas" on the visualization such as the connection/boundary area. The sample points then work as the "landmarks". It is very inefficient or clumsy to incorporate such functionality into automatic algorithms.

We use the "shuttle" dataset and the alternative method to demonstrate how the VISTA system incorporates the domain knowledge into the clustering process. "Shuttle" dataset is a 9-D dataset. It has three large clusters and some tiny clusters in irregular shapes. We use the testing dataset, which has 14500 items for visualization.

Several points are interactively picked from the critical areas in the initial visualization (Figure 4-1) working as the landmarks. Using the labels from the original datasets to mimic the domain expert, the "landmarks" show we could partition the dataset in the way of Figure 4-2.

4. Related work

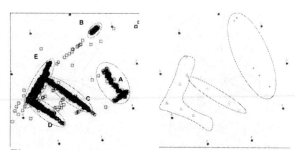

Figure 4-1: Initial   **Figure 4-2: landmarks**

The common framework of cluster analysis is described in the clustering review paper [14]. Recently, some algorithms [2][7][9][10][12][15]have been developed aiming at the arbitrarily shaped clusters. Some typical statistical validity indices are introduced in [11].

The early research on general plot-based data visualization is Grand Tour and Projection Pursuit [3]. L.Yang [4] utilizes the Grand Tour technique to show projections of datasets in an animation. Star Coordinates [5] is a visualization system designed to visualize and analyze the clusters interactively. We utilize the form of Star Coordinates and build the normalized α-mapping model in our system. HD-Eye [14] is another interactive visual clustering system based on density-plots of any two interesting dimensions. The 1D visualization based OPTICS [15] works well in finding the basic arbitrarily shaped clusters but lacks the ability in helping understand the inter-cluster relation. In the KDD 2002 tutorial [7], more visualization methods were also discussed.

5. Conclusion

Most of researchers have focused on automatic clustering algorithms, but very few have addressed the human factor in the clustering process, especially in dealing with arbitrarily shaped clusters. The VISTA system demonstrates some possible ways to introduce the users into the clustering process, and helps them validating and refining the clustering results visually.

Reference

[1] Keke Chen and Ling Liu: "Cluster Rendering of Skewed Datasets via Visualization". ACM Symposium on Applied Computing 2003, Melborne, FL.

[2] G.Guha, R.Rastogi, and K.Shim. "CURE: An efficient clustering algorithm for large databases", in Proc. of the 1998 ACM SIGMOD

[3] Cook, D.R, Buja, A., Cabrea, J., and Hurley, H. "Grand tour and projection pursuit", Journal of Computational and Graphical Statistics, V23, pp. 225-250

[4] Li Yang. "Interactive Exploration of Very Large Relational Datasets through 3D Dynamic Projections", in Proc. of SIGKDD2000

[5] E. Kandogan. "Visualizing Multi-dimensional Clusters, Trends, and Outliers using Star Coordinates", in Proc. of SIGKDD2001.

[6] A. Jain and R.Dubes. "Algorithms for Clustering Data", Prentice hall, Englewood Cliffs, NJ, 1988

[7] Grinstein G., Ankerst M., Keim D.A.: Visual Data Mining: Background, Applications, and Drug Discovery Applications", Tutorial at ACM SIGKDD2002.

[8] Jain, A.K., Murty, M.N. and Flynn, P.J.: Data Clustering: A Review. ACM Computing Surveys, 31(3), P264-323

[9] Ester, M., Kriegel, H., Sander, J. and Xu, X. "A Density-based Algorithm for Discovering Clusters in Large Spatial Databases with Noise"

[10] Hinneburg, A. and Keim, D. " An Efficient Approach to Clustering in Large Multimedia Databases with Noise", in Proc. of KDD-98, pp. 58-65

[11] Maria Halkidi, Yannis Batistakis, Michalis Vazirgiannis: "Cluster Validity Methods: Part I&II", SIGMOD Record, Vol31, No.2&3, 2002

[12]G.Sheikholeslami, S.Chatterjee, and A.Zhang. "Wavecluster: A multi-resolution clustering approach for very large spatial databases", In Proc. VLDB98', 1998

[13] Jean Gallier: "Geometric methods and applications: for computer science and engineering", Springer-Verlag, NY, c2001

[14] A. Hinneburg, D. Keim, and M. Wawryniuk: "Visual Mining of High-dimensional data", IEEE Computer Graphics and Applications. V19, No 5, 1999

[15] M. Ankerst, M. Breunig, H. Kriegel and J. Sander: "OPTICS: Ordering Points To Identify the Clustering Structure", in proc. of SIGMOD1999

Icon-based Visualization of Large High-Dimensional Datasets

Ping Chen*   Chenyi Hu†   Wei Ding‡   Heloise Lynn, Yves Simon§

Abstract

High dimensional data visualization is critical to data analysts since it gives a direct view of original data. We present a method to visualize large amount of high dimensional data. We divide dimensions of data into several groups. Then, we use one icon to represent each group, and associate visual properties of each icon with dimensions in each group. A high dimensional data record will be represented by multiple different types of icons located in the same position. Furthermore, we use summary icons to display local details of viewer's interests and the whole data set at meantime. We show its effectiveness and efficiency through a case study on a real large data set.

1 Introduction

Data visualization plays an important role in discovering knowledge since the human eye-brain system is still the best existing pattern recognition device. Data visualization is a rapidly expanding research area due to the huge increase of number and size of datasets that need to be visualized and interpreted. Data visualization techniques may range from simple scatter plots and histogram plots over parallel coordinates to 3D visual reality systems.

Visualization techniques, such as EXVIS [8], Chernoff Faces [1] [3], icons [5] and m-Arm Glyph [7], are often called glyph-based methods. Glyphs are graphical entities whose visual features such as shape, orientation, color and size are controlled by attributes in an underlying dataset, and glyphs are often used for interactive exploration of data sets [9]. Glyph-based techniques range from representation via individual icons to

*Department of Computer and Mathematical Sciences,Univ. of Houston-Downtown, 1 Main St. Houston, TX 77002

†Computer Science Department,Univ. of Central Arkansas,201 Donaghey Ave. Conway, AR 72035

‡Division of Computing and Mathematics,Univ. of Houston-Clear Lake,2700 Bay Area Blvd. Houston, TX 77058

§Lynn Inc.,14732 F Perthshire Rd.,Houston, TX 77079

the formation of texture and color patterns through the overlay of many thousands of glyphs [2]. Chernoff used facial characteristics to represent information in a multivariate dataset [1] [3]. Each dimension of the data set controls one facial feature such as nose, eyes, eyebrows, mouth, and jowls. Glyphmaker proposed by Foley and Ribarsky can visualize multivariate datasets in an effective, interactive fashion [4]. Levkowitz described a prototype system for combining colored squares to produce patterns to represent an underlying multivariate dataset [6]. In [5] an icon encodes six dimensions by color coding six different lines within a square icon. In [2] Levkowitz describes the combination of textures and colors in a visualization system. The m-Arm Glyph by Pickett and Grinstein [7] consists of a main axis and m arms, and the length and thickness of each arm and the angles between each arm and main axis are used to encode different dimensions of a data set.

2 Visualizing high dimensional data

Data visualization is the graphic presentation of a data set, with the goal of helping and providing the viewer with a qualitative understanding of the embedded information in a natural and direct way. And a visualization process includes Rendering data(forward transformation) stage, Reverse transformation stage, Knowledge extraction stage.

The basic requirement for rendering data is that different values should be displayed differently, the more the original values are, the more different they should look. Rendering data takes two steps:

1. *Association step*

   Associate data dimensions/columns with visual elements. The association is as the following:

   $$D = \{d_1, d_2, \cdots, d_n\}$$
   $$V = \{v_1, v_2, \cdots, v_m\}$$
   $$F_a : D \rightarrow V \quad (1)$$

   where D is the set of n dimensions in a data set, and d_i is the ith dimension in D; V is the space of m visual elements which include visual objects and their features, and v_j is the jth element in V.

2. *Transformation step*

Choose a transformation function for each dimension-visual element pair which maps each value in that dimension to a member in that visual element domain. The function is:

$$F_i : d_i \rightarrow v_i (i = 1, 2, \cdots, n) \qquad (2)$$

where d_i is the set of values of ith dimension, and v_i is the set of members of ith visual element.

During the association step of rendering data a visualization system associates visual elements with dimensions from a data set. One visual element is one visual feature of a visual object. The visual objects (these objects are differentiated by their shapes and styles) could be point, line, polyline, glyph, 2-D or 3-D surface, 3-D solid, image, text, etc. And for each visual object, we may choose from the following visual features, color, location, shape/style, texture, size/length/width/depth, orientation, relative position/motion, etc.

Existing methods use only one icon's visual features to represent a data record, as the dimensions of the data record become higher, more features from the icon has to used if no dimension reduction techniques adopted, which results in a complex icon. A complex icon is hard to understand and computationally expensive, which will hurt visualization quality and make large data set visualization impractical.

In our technique, we use a group of icons' visual features to represent one data record. This group of icons are located in the same position to tell a viewer that this whole group represent the same data record. Icons in one group should be of different types(shapes). And for each icon of this group, we associate one of its selected visual features with one dimension in a data set. In three-dimensional space the position of one icon can represent three dimensions, but since all icons in the group will share the same position, only three dimensions can be represented by the position of a icon group. If there are some identical triples in the three dimensions of a data set selected to be displayed by position, we can not use position to encode any dimensions any more. Instead we only associate dimensions with icon visual features and display groups of icons uniformly (or any way specified by a viewer) in the space, in this case, icon positions do not represent any information except icons in the same position are for the same data record. Suppose the number of selected icon types is N, and the number of selected features from each icon is M, and we are able to choose three dimensions which

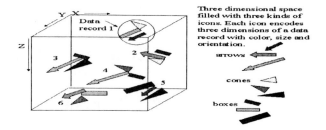

Figure 1. A sample figure to visualize a twelve-dimensional data set with six records.

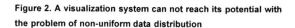

Figure 2. A visualization system can not reach its potential with the problem of non-uniform data distribution

do not have identical triples, the number of dimensions which can be displayed is: $3 + M \times N$. If we want the user to be able to associate the features of icons with original data dimensions easily, M and N can not be too large. Our estimation of M and N could be up to around 10, , and our technique could handle up to around 50 dimensions.

If we choose color, size and orientation as the visual features for icon "box", "arrow" and "cone", we will have a sample figure as Figure 1. By using multiple icons located in the same position our method can effectively visualize a data set with higher dimensions than existing methods. Within the data set, it is common that the data values are clustered, and the data distribution is not uniform. Non-uniform data distribution can hurt our visualization efforts, which is shown by the following example. Suppose we have a one-dimensional dataset as $\{1, 1, 1, 1, 1, 5, 10, 10, 100\}$, and we choose the color of icon "bar" to represent it, and our transformation function is:

$\{value | 1 \leq value \leq 10\} \longrightarrow red$

$\cdots$

$\{value | 91 \leq value \leq 100\} \longrightarrow blue$

And the dataset will be visualized as Figure 2, although the visualization system can use ten different colors, most icons are blue because most data values fall into the interval $[1, 10]$ represented by blue. We can not tell the difference of these data values any more, and visualization is less effective. Instead, we find the data clusters first for each dimension i with data clustering techniques.For one-dimensional data set clustering we have lots of clustering algorithms to choose from.

Let k_i be the number of clusters for the ith dimension. Then, we divide v_i (set of members of ith visual

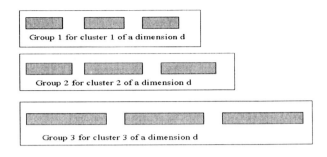

Figure 3. We divide members of "bar's size" into three groups, each group has three members.

Figure 4. Failure to reveal critical information from a data set with non-uniform knowledge distribution problem

element) into k_i groups, i.e.

$v_i = \{v_{ij} | 1 \leq j \leq k_i\}$.

The transformation between the ith data dimension and its visual element will be determined according to the cluster which the data value belongs to. Let us use c_{ij} to denote the jth cluster of data in the ith dimension, then we have:

$$C_i = \{c_{ij}\}(1 \leq i \leq n, 1 \leq j \leq k_i) \qquad (3)$$

where C_i is the set of clusters in dimension i, n is the number of dimensions in a data set, k_i is the number of clusters in dimension i. We divide members in visual element V_i into k_i groups:

$$V_i = \{v_{ij}\}(1 \leq i \leq n, 1 \leq j \leq k_i) \qquad (4)$$

where v_{ij} is a group of members in visual element i. For example, if we choose visual element "bar's size", as shown in Figure 3, we could divide different sized bars into three groups, and each group has three members of visual element "bar's size".

Then the transformation between data dimensions and visual elements will be:

$$F_{ij} : C_{ij} \rightarrow V_{ij}(1 \leq i \leq n, 1 \leq j \leq k_i) \qquad (5)$$

In "Rendering data" stage we perform association and transformation on the original data and then perform rendering. Viewers have to be aware of and understand the association and transformation during the visualization process, and be able to reverse the transformed display and restore the original picture in their mind.

This requirement makes a complex transformation in the first stage infeasible.

Rendering millions of icons is computationally expensive, and interpretion and analysis done by the user is even harder. A visualization system has to provide not only a "loyal" picture of the original dataset, but also a "better" picture for easier interpretion and knowledge extraction. Previously we specified the basic requirement for a visualization system as:

"Different data values should be visualized differently, and the more different the data values are, the more different they should look".

But what a viewer really want is the information or knowledge represented by the data values, so the above requirement can be better stated as:

"Different information should be visualized differently, and the more different the information is, the more different it should look".

To help a viewer on knowledge extraction a visualization system has to deal with the problem of non-uniform knowledge/information distribution. It is common in some data sets or fields that a small difference of a value could mean a big difference, which means the knowledge and information is not distributed uniformly within data values. Of course, a user would like a visualization system to be able to show these meaningful differences clearly. To be specific, two differences of same amount in data values may not necessarily be rendered by the identical difference in visual elements on the screen. Instead the difference representing more information should be displayed more significantly to get attention from a viewer. Suppose we have a one dimensional data set which saves human body temperatures, $\{36.5, 37.0, 37.5, 38.0, 38.5, 39.0, 39.5, 40.0, 40.5, 41.0, 41.5, 42.0\}$, and this data set is uniformly distributed. We still use a bar's color to visualize the data set, and our transformation function will map the values uniformly since the dataset has a uniform distribution:

$\{value | 36.0 \leq value < 38.0\} \longrightarrow red$
$\{value | 38.0 \leq value < 40.0\} \longrightarrow orange$
$\{value | 40.0 \leq value \leq 42.0\} \longrightarrow blue$

And the dataset will be visualized as the above figure. The visualization system visualizes the data loyally. Both 40.0 and 42.0 are represented by blue, but as human body temperatures 40.0 and 42.0 could mean a difference of life and death. From the above example, it is clear that integration of domain knowledge into a visualization system is very important due to non-uniform knowledge distribution. To a visualization system integration of domain knowledge can be achieved by choosing proper association function and transformation functions during visualization process.

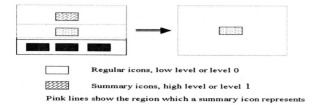

Regular icons, low level or level 0

Summary icons, high level or level 1

Pink lines show the region which a summary icon represents

Figure 5. Figures with summary icons

3 Summary icons and a case study

To display the local details and overall context of a data set at the same time, we use summarization. We use "summary" icons to display summarized data for "uninteresting" parts of a dataset, and regular icons to display the "interesting" parts of a data set which will show all details. One feature of a summary icon do not represent one field in a data record, instead it represents a statistical parameter (summary) of the fields from multiple underlying data records, such as sum, mean, median. By this way, we can build a hierarchical structure of icons as in Figure 5. The icons in low level represent only one record, the icons in high level will be a summary of icons/records below it. The icons on the high level are more general, they summarize information from a lot of records, and the icons on the low level are more specialized or local, and they represent and visualize only one record.

Using temperature set Figure 4, we use some summary icons to summarize some data values shown in Figure 5. The left figure in 5 shows two level-one summary icons, the top bar represents the average of first three values and middle bar represents the average of value 4 ,5 and 6. The right figure in 5 use one summary icon to represent the average of all values in this set.

In case study we use a large dataset that encodes multiple data fields at a single spatial location. This set of 12-dimensional geophysical data was obtained with man-made earthquakes to discover oil underground. These data were recorded as nine SGY files. Each file includes some headers and 6,172,871 one-dimensional records. These records are data samples from 111 × 111 locations within 2 seconds after an explosion. Data represents three different properties in geophysical science, which are interval velocity, amplitude of the 5-45 degree angles of incidence, and amplitude of the 35-55 degree angles of incidence. Each property has three dimensions. We used three different icons: parallelogram, box, and pyramid. The experiment is run on a PC with Pentium III 1GHz CPU, 256 MB RAM, and a 16 MB video card. View rendering (move, rotate, zoom) can be done in real time.

4 Conclusion

Using multiple icons located in one position is an effective and efficient method for large high dimensional data set visualization. Summary icons can help display local data details and overall context at the same time.

References

[1] Bruckner, L.A., On chernoff faces. In Graphical Representation of Multivariate Data, P.C.C. Wang, Ed. Academic Press, New York, New York, pages 93-121, 1978.

[2] Christopher, G. Healey, James T. Enns, Large Datasets at a Glance: Combining Textures and Colors in Scientific Visualization. IEEE Transactions on Visualization and Computer Graphics, Volume 5, Issue 2, 1999.

[3] Chernoff, H. The use of facesto represent points in k-dimensional space graphically. Journal of the American Statistical Association 68, 342, pages 361-367, 1973.

[4] Foley, J., and Ribarsky, W. Next-generation data visualization tools. Scientific Visualization: Advances and Challenges, L. Rosenblum, Ed. Academic Press, San Diego, California, pages 103-127, 1994.

[5] Levkowitz, H. Color Icons: Merging Color and Texture Perception for Integrated Visualization of Multiple Parameter, Proceedings of IEEE Visualization'91 Conference, San Diego, CA, Oct. 1996

[6] Laidlaw, D. H., Ahrens, E.T., Kremers, D., Avalos, M.J., Jacobs, R.E., and Readhead, C. Visualizing diffusion tensor images of the mouse spinal cord. Proceedings of Visualization '98, pages 127-134, 1998

[7] Pickett, R. M. and Grinstein, G. G., Iconographics Displays for Visualizing Multidimensional Data. Proceedings of the 1988 IEEE Conference on Systems, Man and Cybernetics. Beijing and Shenyang, People's Republic of China, 1988.

[8] Grinstein, G. G., Pickett, R. M. and Williams, M., EXVIS: An Exploratory Data Visualization Environment. Proceedings of Graphics Interface '89 pages 254-261, London, Canada, 1989.

[9] Wegenkittl, R., Lffelmann, H., Grller, E., Visualizing the behavior of higher dimensional dynamical systems. Proceedings of the conference on Visualization '97, 1997 , Phoenix, Arizona, United States

Indexing and Mining Free Trees

Yun Chi, Yirong Yang, Richard R. Muntz
Department of Computer Science
University of California, Los Angeles, CA 90095
{ychi,yyr,muntz}@cs.ucla.edu

Abstract

Tree structures are used extensively in domains such as computational biology, pattern recognition, computer networks, and so on. In this paper, we present an indexing technique for free trees and apply this indexing technique to the problem of mining frequent subtrees. We first define a novel representation, the canonical form, for rooted trees and extend the definition to free trees. We also introduce another concept, the canonical string, as a simpler representation for free trees in their canonical forms. We then apply our tree indexing technique to the frequent subtree mining problem and present FreeTreeMiner, a computationally efficient algorithm that discovers all frequently occurring subtrees in a database of free trees. We study the performance and the scalability of our algorithms through extensive experiments based on both synthetic data and datasets from two real applications: a dataset of chemical compounds and a dataset of Internet multicast trees.

1 Introduction

Graphs are used extensively in various areas such as computational biology, chemistry, pattern recognition, computer networks, etc. Among all graphs, a particularly useful family is the family of *free trees*–the connected, acyclic and undirected graphs. Some real applications using free trees include the evolutionary tree (or phylogeny) for analysis of molecular evolution, the *shape axis tree* for representing shapes in pattern recognition, and the multicast trees in computer networking. In addition to being unrooted, trees in these applications are often *labeled*, with labels attached to vertices and edges where these labels are not necessarily unique. In this paper, we study some issues in databases of labeled free trees.

In the above applications, two problems are important from the database point of view. The first one is how to index trees. The second is how to efficiently discover *interesting* patterns. One type of interesting patterns consists of those patterns that are embedded in a lot of transactions in a database. In this paper, we present our approaches to solving these two important problems. Some of the main contributions of our work are: (1) We introduce a unique representation, the canonical form, for a free tree and give an efficient algorithm to convert a free tree to its canonical form. An equivalent representation, the canonical string, is also introduced to simplify certain operations such as comparing or searching free trees. (2) We apply the canonical form of free trees to the frequent subtree mining problem. In mining procedures, canonical forms are used to index frequent trees and candidate trees; they are also used to speed up the join step. (3) We have implemented all of our algorithms and have extensive experimental analysis. We use both synthetic data and real application data to evaluate the performance of our algorithm.

2 Canonical Form for Labeled Free Trees

In this section, we give a unique representation for labeled free trees, i.e. a canonical form that represents labeled free trees in the same equivalence class where the relation defining the equivalence classes is an isomorphism. Two labeled trees T_1 and T_2 are *isomorphic* to each other if there is a one-to-one mapping from the vertices of T_1 to the vertices of T_2 that preserves vertex labels, edges labels, and adjacency.

2.1 Labeled, Rooted, Ordered Trees

A *rooted tree* is a tree in which one vertex is singled out as the root. We say that a rooted tree is *ordered* if the set of children of each vertex in the tree is ordered. If a labeled rooted tree is ordered, then there are ways to represent the tree in a unique form. [5] is one example in which a depth-first traversal is used to obtain unique string representations for rooted ordered trees. Notice that when a rooted tree is ordered, the isomorphism does not really apply–two rooted ordered trees are either the same or not.

509

2.2 Labeled, Rooted, Unordered Trees

We assume that for the trees in our databases, both vertices and edges are labeled and there exist total orders among vertex labels and edge labels. We define the total order among trees based on the ordering for labels.

Let's first assume that the trees are rooted. (Later, we will extend our definition to free trees.) If a tree is rooted, without loss of generality we can assume that all edge labels are identical, because each edge connects a vertex with its parent and we can consider an edge, together with its label, as a part of the child vertex. (For the root, we can assume that there is a *null* edge connecting to it from above.)

There are two concepts we want to define: the *canonical form* for a rooted tree and the *order* among rooted trees. These two concepts are defined mutually recursively (notice that in the definition below we assume that all edge labels are identical):

Definition 1 (Canonical Form and Order for Labeled, Rooted, Unordered Trees). *For labeled rooted trees with height 0 (i.e., trees consisting of a single vertex), the canonical forms are the vertices themselves and the order among such trees is defined by the order of the vertex labels.*

For a labeled rooted tree with height h where $h > 0$, the canonical form is obtained by first normalizing all subtrees of the root then rearranging the subtrees in increasing order (from the left to right in illustrating examples).

For a pair of labeled rooted trees (in their canonical forms) with heights less than or equal to h where $h > 0$, their order is defined by first comparing the labels of their roots then comparing their corresponding subtrees from the left to the right until their relative order is resolved.

Essentially, after normalizing rooted trees into their canonical forms, we can compare two trees; the normalization of a tree with height $h > 0$ depends on the order among the subtrees (whose heights are less than h) of the root. It is easy to see that the above definition introduces a total order among all rooted trees. Figure 1 gives a rooted tree and its canonical form. Notice two things in the example: first, an edge connects a child vertex to its parent and the edge label is considered as a part of the vertex label of the child– this is why the branch "2,*D*" is *less* than branch "3,*C*" at the leaf level; second, in comparing two (sub)trees, if root nodes have different number of subtrees, then we need to conceptually pad the smaller set of subtrees with subtrees having the largest possible label–this is why we switch the two subtrees of the root to get the canonical form in our example.

2.3 Labeled Free Trees

Free trees do not have roots, but we can uniquely create roots for them for the purpose of constructing a unique

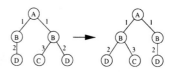

Figure 1. A Labeled, Rooted, Unordered Tree (left) and Its Canonical Form (right)

canonical form for each free tree. Starting from a free tree in each step we remove all leaf vertices (together with their incident edges), and we repeat the step until a single vertex or two adjacent vertices are left. For the first case, the tree is called a *central tree* and the remaining vertex is called the *centre*; for the second case, the tree is called a *bicentral tree* and the pair of remaining vertices are called the *bicentre*. The procedure takes $O(k)$ time where k is the number of vertices in the free tree. Figure 2 shows a central tree and a bicentral tree as well as the procedure to obtain the corresponding centre and bicentre.

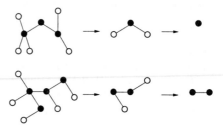

Figure 2. A Central Tree (above) and A Bicentral Tree (below)

If we relax the definition of rooted trees to allow a pair of roots (together with an edge connecting them) then from an arbitrary free tree we can obtain a rooted tree. After obtaining such a rooted tree with a root or a pair of roots, we can extend the definition of canonical form to an arbitrary labeled free tree. Notice that for a bicentral tree, the order of the pair of roots is fixed in its canonical form.

2.4 Normalizing Rooted Trees

We now show a bottom-up procedure to normalize labeled rooted trees. The procedure is based on a tree isomorphism algorithm given in [2]. Figure 3 gives a running example on how to obtain the canonical form for a labeled rooted tree. In the figure, we start from the original tree, normalize level by level bottom-up using the orders among subtrees at each level, until finally we obtain the canonical form. Notice that we have used (acyclic, directed) multigraph to represent trees in intermediate steps in order to combine subtrees that are *equal*. It is straightforward to extend this procedure to rooted trees obtained from bicentral free trees.

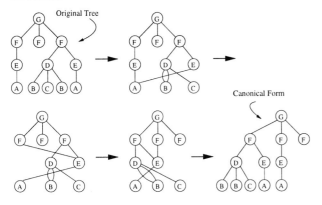

Figure 3. To Obtain the Canonical Form of A Rooted Tree

The key step in each level of the procedure is sorting. With appropriate data structures, the running time for the normalization is $O(c \cdot k \log k)$, where c is the maximal fanout of the tree and k is the number of vertices in the tree: assuming there are k_h vertices in each level of the tree for $h = 0, 1, 2, \ldots$, to sort vertices at level h, it takes $O(k_h \log k_h)$ comparisons; the total number of comparison for normalizing the whole tree is $\sum_h O(k_h \log k_h)$ which is $O(k \log k)$ (notice that $\sum_h (k_h \log k_h) \leq \sum_h (k_h \log k) = k \log k$); the time for each comparison is bounded by the maximal fan-out c of the tree because we can consider c as the length of the "keys" to be compared.

2.5 Converting to Canonical Strings

A canonical string representation for labeled trees is equivalent to, but simpler than, canonical forms. There are two ways to define a canonical string–one based on depth-first tree traversal and the other based on breadth-first tree traversal. Assume two special symbols, "#" and "$", are not in the alphabet of edge labels and vertex labels. To get the first canonical string, we traverse a tree in canonical form in depth-first fashion, using "$" to represent a backtrack and "#" to represent the end of the string. The depth-first canonical string for the example in Figure 3 is $G1F1D1B\$1B\$1C\$\$1E1A\$\$\$1F1E1A\$\$\$1F\#$, assuming all edges have label "1". If we assume "#" is greater than "$" and both are greater than any other symbols in the alphabet of vertex labels and edge labels, then the lexicographical order among depth-first canonical strings turns out to be the same as the order among trees in canonical forms. In other words, we could have defined the canonical form for a rooted unordered tree as the ordered tree derived

from the unordered tree that gives the minimum depth-first string encoding.

We obtain the second type of canonical string by scanning a tree in canonical form top-down level by level in a breadth-first fashion: we use "$" to partition the families of siblings and use "#" to indicate the end of the canonical string. The canonical string for the example in Figure 3 is $G\$1F1F1F\$1D1E\$1E\$\$1B1B1C\$1A\$1A\#$, assuming all edges have label "1". The order among breadth-first canonical strings is a total order, although it is not the same total order as the order among trees in canonical form. Because we use canonical form for indexing and any total order will work for this purpose, we can use either the depth-first canonical string or the breadth-first canonical string.

It is easy to see that the procedures for obtaining both types of canonical strings take $O(k)$ time where k is the number of vertices in the original tree. In addition, it is easy to prove that the length of the two types of canonical strings are both bounded by $3k$. In the actual implementation we have chosen the breadth-first canonical string and put some additional information, such as the number of roots and the number of vertices of a tree, in the canonical strings to expedite other operations on them.

2.6 Indexing Labeled Free Trees

With canonical forms (or canonical strings), we introduce a unique representation for labeled free trees. With such a unique representation, a traditional indexing method such as hashing can be used on databases of free trees. In addition, we also introduce a total order among labeled free trees. Hence we can apply traditional database indexing methods that depend on such a total order, such as B-trees, on databases of free trees. Notice that our canonical form applies to rooted, unordered trees as well. Therefore, it can be used in many applications related to rooted trees such as indexing XML documents.

3 Mining Frequent Subtrees

In this section, we apply our tree indexing technique to the frequent subtree mining problem. First, let's define the problem.

Frequent Subtree Mining Problem Let D denote a database where each transaction $t \in D$ is a labeled free tree. For a given pattern s (which is a free tree) we say s occurs in a transaction t (or t *supports* s) if there exists a subtree of t that is isomorphic to s. The *support* of a pattern s is the fraction of transactions in database D that supports s. A pattern s is called *frequent* if its support is greater than or equal to a *minimum support* (*minsup*) specified by a user. The frequent subtree mining problem is to find all frequent patterns in a given database.

Figure 4 gives *FreeTreeMiner*, our algorithm for solving the frequent subtree mining problem. Our algorithm, like many other studies on the frequent itemsets mining problem, is based on the *Apriori* method [1]. The two main steps in the above algorithm are (1) candidate generation and (2) frequency counting. We now describe each in detail.

Algorithm **FreeTreeMiner**(D, *minsup*)
1:    $F_2, F_3, F_4 \leftarrow$ {frequent 2, 3, and 4-trees};
2:    **for** ($k \leftarrow 5$; $F_{k-1} \neq \emptyset$; $k++$) **do**
3:        $C_k \leftarrow$ candidate-generate(F_{k-1});
4:        **for each** transaction $t \in D$ **do**
5:            **for each** candidate $c \in C_k$ **do**
6:                **if** (t supports c) **then** $c.count++$;
7:        $F_k \leftarrow \{c \in C_k | c.count \geq minsup\}$;
8:    *Answer* $\leftarrow$ Union all F_k's;

Figure 4. The FreeTreeMiner Algorithm

For candidate generation, if we have discovered all the frequent k-trees, we can combine a pair of frequent k-trees to get a candidate for frequent $(k+1)$-trees, as long as this pair of k-trees share all structure but one leaf vertex. Therefore, a self-join on the list of all the frequent k-trees is needed. In our algorithm, we use the indexing technique that we introduced previously to expedite the self-join step. For a frequent k-tree, we remove one of its leaves. The remaining graph is a tree with $k - 1$ vertices. We call this $(k-1)$-tree a *core* of the k-tree and the removed vertex (together with the removed edge) the corresponding limb. The number of cores for a frequent k-tree is equal to the number of its leaves because each leaf can be a limb. A pair of frequent k-trees can be joined to obtain a candidate $(k+1)$-tree if and only if they share a core with $k - 1$ vertices. For each frequent k-tree, we can remove one leaf at a time to obtain all its possible cores, then register the k-tree to all its cores where the cores are indexed using our free tree indexing technique. Two frequent k-trees registered at the same core can be joined together to create candidate $(k+1)$-trees.

In the frequency counting step, we verify if a candidate tree is frequent or not by checking its support in the database. The key work is for each transaction t in the database and each candidate c, we want to check if t supports c. That is, we want to detect if c is embedded in t. This is a subtree isomorphism problem. We have implemented, with some variations, the $O(k^{1.5}n)$ algorithm described in [4] (where n is the number of vertices in t and k is the number of vertices in c). The main idea of the algorithm is to first fix a root r for t (we call the resulting rooted tree t^r) then test for each vertex v of c if the rooted tree c^v with v as the root is isomorphic to some subtree of t^r. The test is done on each subtree of t^r in a postorder and is reduced to maximum bipartite matching problems.

4   Experimental Results

We performed three sets of experiments to evaluate the performance of the *FreeTreeMiner* algorithm: a group of synthetic datasets, a chemical compounds dataset, and a multicast trees dataset. The main results are (1) The running time of our *FreeTreeMiner* algorithm scales linearly with the number of transactions in a database. (2) The running time scales with the size of the frequent trees in a nonlinear fashion because of the subtree isomorphism checking algorithm. (3) The number of intermediate frequent subtrees increases exponentially with the size of the maximal frequent subtree.

5   Conclusions

In this paper we introduced a novel indexing technique for databases of labeled free trees, which is based on a unique representation, the canonical form, for free trees that represents a free tree by its isomorphism family. With the canonical form and its equivalent representation the canonical string, we assigned a total order among all labeled free trees and therefore we can apply traditional indexing techniques to databases of free trees. We also defined the frequent subtree mining problem and presented an efficient algorithm, which is based on our indexing technique, to discover all frequent subtrees in a database. We used both synthetic and real application datasets to study the performance of our algorithm.

We refer interested readers to the full version of this paper [3] for a more detailed description.

This material is based upon work supported by the National Science Foundation under Grant Nos. 0086116 and 0085773. Any opinions, findings, and conclusions or recommendations expressed in this material are those of the authors and do not necessarily reflect the views of the National Science Foundation.

References

[1] R. Agrawal and R. Srikant. Fast algorithms for mining association rules. In *VLDB 94*, September 1994.

[2] A. V. Aho, J. E. Hopcroft, and J. E. Ullman. *The Design and Analysis of Computer Algorithms*. Addison-Wesley, 1974.

[3] Y. Chi, Y. Yang, and R. R. Muntz. Indexing and mining free trees. In *ICDM 2003*, November 2003. Full version available as Technical Report CSD-TR No. 030041 at ftp://ftp.cs.ucla.edu/tech-report/2003-reports/030041.pdf.

[4] M. J. Chung. $O(n^{2.5})$ time algorithm for subgraph homeomorphism problem on trees. *Journal of Algorithms*, 8:106–112, 1987.

[5] M. J. Zaki. Efficiently mining frequent trees in a forest. In *8th ACM SIGKDD*, July 2002.

T-Trees, Vertical Partitioning and Distributed Association Rule Mining

Frans Coenen, Paul Leng and Shakil Ahmed
Department of Computer Science, The University of Liverpool
Liverpool, L69 3BX, UK
{frans,phl,shakil}@csc.liv.ac.uk

Abstract

In this paper we consider a technique (DATA-VP) for distributed (and parallel) Association Rule Mining that makes use of a vertical partitioning technique to distribute the input data amongst processors. The proposed vertical partitioning is facilitated by a novel compressed set enumeration tree data structure (the T-tree), and an associated mining algorithm (Apriori-T), that allows for computationally effective distributed/parallel ARM when compared with existing approaches.

1 Introduction

An approach to distributed/parallel Association Rule Mining (ARM), DATA-VP, that makes use of a vertical partitioning approach to distributing the input data is described. Using this approach each partition can be mined in isolation while at the same time taking into account the possibility of the existence of large itemsets dispersed across two or more partitions. To facilitate the partitioning a compressed set enumeration tree data structure (the T-tree), developed by the authors, is used together with an associated ARM algorithm — Apriori-T. The approach described offers significant advantages with respect to computational efficiency when compared to alternative mechanisms for (a) dividing the input data between processors and/or (b) achieving distributed/parallel ARM.

2 The T-tree and the Apriori-T algorithm

A significant consideration, with respect to ARM, is the nature of the data structures used to store itemsets as the algorithm progresses. The authors have developed a number of compressed set enumeration tree structures to support ARM including the T-tree (Total Support Tree) [7, 6], and a number of serial ARM algorithms to be used in association with these structures. Of particular relevance, with respect to this paper, is the Apriori-T algorithm.

The T-tree differs from more standard set enumeration trees in that the nodes at the same level in any sub-branch are organised into 1-D arrays so that array indexes represent column numbers. For this purpose it is more convenient to build a "reverse" version of the tree (see Figure 1(a)), which permits direct indexing with attribute/column numbers. The T-tree offers two initial advantages over standard set enumeration trees: (1) fast traversal of the tree using indexing mechanisms, and (2) reduced storage, in that itemset labels are not required to be explicitly stored, and thus no sibling references (pointers) are required. The implementation of this structure is illustrated in Figure 1(b) where nodes in the T-tree are objects comprising a support value and a reference to an array of child T-tree nodes.

The Apriori-T algorithm combines the classic Apriori ARM algorithm [2] with the T-tree data structure[1]. As each level is processed, candidates are added as a new level of the T-tree, their support is counted, and those that do not reach the required support threshold pruned. When the algorithm terminates, the T-tree contains only large itemsets. At each level, new candidate itemsets of size K are generated from identified large K-1 itemsets, using the *downward closure property of itemsets*, which in turn may necessitate the inspection of neighbouring branches in the T-tree to determine if a particular K-1 subset is supported. We refer to this process as *X-checking*. Note that X-checking adds a computational overhead; offset against the additional effort required to establish whether a candidate K itemset, all of whose K-1 itemsets may not necessarily be supported, is or is not a large itemset.

The number of candidate nodes generated during the construction of a T-tree, and consequently the computational effort required, is very much dependent on the distribution of columns within the input data. Best results are produced by reordering the dataset, according to the support counts for the 1-itemsets, so that the most frequent 1-itemsets occur first ([5]).

---

[1] Elsewhere [5] the authors have described an algorithm, Apriori-TFP, which uses both the T-tree structure and another set-enumeration tree, the P-tree. In this paper we examine methods using only the T-tree structure.

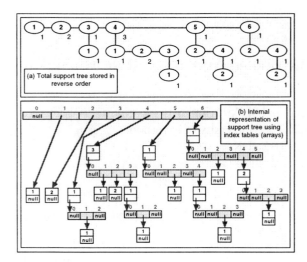

Figure 1. The T-tree for the data set $\{\{1,3,4\},\{2,4,5\},\{2,4,6\}\}$. **Note that, for ease of processing, items/attributes are enumerated commencing with** 1

3 The distributed Apriori-T Algorithm with Vertical Partitioning (DATA-VP)

The DATA-VP algorithm commences by distributing the input dataset over the available number of processes using a vertical partitioning strategy. Initially the set of single attributes (columns) is split equally between the available processes so that an *allocationItemSet* (a sequence of single attributes) is defined for each process in terms of a *startColNum* and *endColNum*:

$$allocationItemSet = \{n|startColNum < n \leq endColNum\}$$

Each process will have its own *allocationItemSet* which is then used to determine the subset of the input dataset to be considered by the process. Using its *allocationItemSet* each process will proceed as follows:

1. Remove all records in the input dataset that do not intersect with the *allocationItemSet*.

2. From the remaining records remove those attributes whose column number is greater than *endColNum*. We cannot remove those attributes whose identifiers are less than *startColNum* because these may represent the "leading sub-string" of large itemset to be included in the sub T-tree counted by the process.

The input dataset distribution procedure, given an *allocationItemSet*, can be summarised as follows:

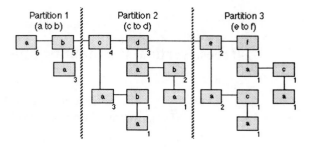

Figure 2. Distributed T-tree representing the vertical partitioning presented in the example

$$\forall records \in input\ data$$
$$if\ (record \cap allocationItemSet \equiv true)$$
$$record = \{n|n \in record\ n \leq endColNum\}$$
$$else\ delete\ record$$

For example — given the data set $\{\{a,c,f\},\{b\},\{a,c,e\},\{b,d\},\{a,e\},\{a,b,c\},\{d\},\{a,b\},\{c\},\{a,b,d\}\}$, and assuming three processes, the above partitioning process will result in three dataset partitions:

Process 1 (a to b): $\{\{a\},\{b\},\{a\},\{b\},\{a\},\{a,b\},\{\},\{a,b\},\{\},\{a,b\}\}$
Process 2 (c to d): $\{\{a,c\},\{\},\{a,c\},\{b,d\},\{\},\{a,b,c\},\{d\},\{\},\{c\},\{a,b,d\}\}$
Process 3 (e to f): $\{\{a,c,f\},\{\},\{a,c,e\},\{\},\{a,e\},\{\},\{\},\{\},\{\},\{\}\}$

Figure 2 shows the resulting sub T-trees assuming all combinations represented by each partition are supported.

Note that because the input dataset is ordered according to the frequency of 1-itemsets the size of the individual partitioned sets does not necessarily increase as the *endColNum* approaches N (the number of columns in the input dataset); in the later partitions, the lower frequency leads to more records being eliminated. Thus the overall result of the vertical partitioning is that the overall size of the dataset (applicable to the process in question) is reduced. Once partitioning is complete each partition can be mined, using the Apriori-T algorithm, in isolation.

The DATA-VP algorithm can thus be summarised as follows:

1. Start all processes, Master plus a number of Workers.

2. Master determines the division of *allocationItemSet* according to the total number of available processes and transmits this information to the Workers.

3. Each process then generates a T-tree for its allocated partition (a sub tree of the final T-tree).

4. On completion each process transmits its partition of the T-tree to all other processes which are then merged

into a single T-tree (so that each process has a copy of the final T-tree ready for the next stage in the ARM process — rule generation).

The process begins with a top-level "tree" comprising only those 1-itemsets included in its *allocationItemSet*. The process will then generate the candidate 2-itemsets that belong in its sub T-tree. These will comprise all the possible pairings between each element in the *allocationItemSet* and the lexicographically preceding attribute; of those elements (see Figure 2). The support values for the candidate 2-itemsets are then determined and the sets pruned to leave only large 2-itemsets. Candidate sets for the third level are then generated. Again, no attributes from succeeding *allocationItemSet* are considered, but the possible candidates will, in general, have subsets which are contained in preceding *allocationItemSet* and which, therefore, are being counted by some other process. To avoid the overhead involved in X-checking, which in this case would require message-passing between the processes concerned, X-checking does not take place. Instead, the process will generate its candidates assuming, where necessary, that any subsets outside its local T-tree are large.

4 Related Work

Generally speaking two types of parallel/distributed ARM algorithms can be identified [4]:

Data Distribution (e.g. Agrawal and Schafer's "count distribution algorithm" [1]): The data is apportioned amongst the processes, typically by "horizontally" segmenting the dataset into sets of records. Each process then mines its allocated segment (exchanging information on-route as necessary).

Task Distribution (e.g. Agrawal is Schafer's "data distribution algorithm" [1]): Each process has access to the entire dataset but is responsible for some subset of the set of candidate itemsets generated at each level.

To evaluate the DATA-VP algorithm (see below) we will compare its performance with a data parallel Apriori-T algorithm (DATA-DD), and an Apriori-T version of the task parallel approach (DATA-TD).

5 Evaluation

The implmentation of the algorithms was carried oput using Java Spaces [3]. The evaluation presented here uses five processes and the data set `T20.I10.D500K.N500` (generated using the IBM Quest generator used in Agrawal and Srikant [2]), although the research team have obtained similar results using other data sets. In all case the dataset has been preprocessed so that it is ordered.

	Support %			
	2.0	1.5	1.0	0.5
DATA-DD	3472	4621	8855	36119
DATA-TD	695	924	1771	7225
DATA-VP	11	21	60	228

Table 1. Average Total size (Kbytes) of messages sent and read/taken per process

5.1 Number of T-tree Messages

The most significant overhead of any distributed/parallel ARM algorithm is the number of messages sent and received between processes. For DATA-DD and DATA-TD processes are required to exchange information as each level of the T-tree is constructed; the number of levels will equal the size of the largest supported set. For DATA-VP the number of messages sent is independent of the number of levels in the T-tree; communication takes place only at the end of the tree construction. DATA-VP therefore has a clear advantage in terms of the number of messages sent.

5.2 Amount of Data Sent and Received

Table 1 shows the average amount of data sent and received by each process for each of the Apriori-T algorithms under consideration assuming five processes. Note that:

- With respect to DATA-DD, for each generated T-tree level, un-pruned levels of the T-tree are passed from one process to another (and then pruned).

- In the case of DATA-TD pruned sections of levels in the T-tree are passed from one process to another.

- DATA-VP passes entire pruned sub T-trees (pruned T-tree branches, not entire levels). Consequently the amount of data passed between processes when using DATA-VP is significantly less than that associated with the other approaches.

- In the case of DATA-DD adding more processes increases the amount of communication, because all processes send data to all others. In the case of DATA-TD and DATA-VP, however, each process sends only the set of candidates it is counting or has counted, which becomes proportionately smaller as the number of processes is increased; i.e. for these methods the messaging overhead remains approximately constant.

5.3 Number of Updates

The number of support value updates/incrementations per process is a good indication of the amount of work done by each process. Table 2 gives the number of updates for

	Support %			
	2.0	1.5	1.0	0.5
DATA-VP, -DD, -TD	20	22	30	57
Apriori-T (with X-check)	99	111	148	285
Apriori-T (No X-check)	99	111	148	286

Table 2. Average number of updates ($\times 10^6$) to generate a final T-tree per process

	Support %			
	2.0	1.5	1.0	0.5
DATA-DD	13	16	25	99
Apriori-T (No X-check)	15	19	31	95
DATA-TD	9	9	16	66
DATA-VP	3	4	10	31

Table 3. Average execution time (seconds) per process

each of the algorithms under consideration for a range of support thresholds and using five processes. Note that:

- Table 2 includes, for comparison, values for the serial form of the Apriori-T algorithm with and without X-checking.

- DATA-DD, DATA-TD and DATA-VP all have the same average number of updates (as would be expected).

5.4 Execution Time

The overall execution time for each algorithm is arguably the most significant performance parameter. A set of times (seconds) is presented in Table 3. The table includes execution times using the Apriori-T serial algorithm (without X-checking as this provides a slightly better result for this data set).

In terms of execution time the Task Distribution algorithms, DATA-TD, and (especially) the vertical partitioning algorithm DATA-VP, perform much better than the data distribution algorithm (DATA-DD) because of the messaging overhead. Note also that, for DATA-DD, as further processes are added, the increasing overhead of messaging more than outweighs any gain from using additional processes, so that distribution/parallelisation becomes counter productive. DATA-TD shows some gain from the addition of further processes, however DATA-VP gives the best results and the best scaling.

6 Summary and Conclusions

We have described the DATA-VP approach to distributed/parallel ARM founded on the T-tree data structure and the associated Apriori-T algorithm. We have evaluated DATA-VP against established data and task distribution approaches. The principal advantages offered by DATA-VP are: (1) minimal amount of message passing compared to DATA-DD and DATA-TD, (2) minimal message size, especially with respect to DATA-DD but also when compared to DATA-TD, and (3) enhanced efficiency as the number of processes increases, unlike DATA-DD.

Our experimental evaluation of DATA-VP clearly demonstrates that the approach performs much better than those methods that use data and task distributed approaches. This is largely due to the T-tree data structure which: (a) facilitates vertical distribution of the input dataset, and (b) readily lends itself to distribution/parallelisation.

More generally we have demonstrated that both the T-tree data structure and the Apriori-T algorithm are good generic mechanisms that can be used effectively to implement many approaches to distributed/parallel ARM.

References

[1] Agrawal, R, and Shafer, J.C. (1996). Parallel Mining of Association Rules. IEEE Transactions on Knowledge and Data Engineering, Vol 8, No 6, pp962-969.

[2] Agrawal, R. and Srikant, R. (1994). *Fast algorithms for mining association rules*. Proc. 20th VLDB Conference, Morgan Kaufman, pp487-499.

[3] Arnold, K., Freeman, E. and Hupfer, S. (1999). *JavaSpaces: Principles, Patterns and Practice*. Addison Wesley.

[4] Chattratichat, J., Darlington, J., Ghanem, M., Guo, Y., Hning, H., Khler, M., Sutiwaraphun, J., To H. W., Yang, D. (1997). *Large Scale Data Mining: Challenges and Responses*. Proc. 3rd Int.Conf. on Knowledge Discovery and Data mining (KDD'97), pp143-146.

[5] Coenen, F. and Leng, P. (2001). *Optimising Association Rule Algorithms Using Itemset Ordering*. Research and Development in Intelligent Systems XVIII: Proc ES2001 Conference, eds M Bramer, F Coenen and A Preece, Springer, pp53-66.

[6] Coenen, F., Goulbourne, G. and Leng, P., (2003). *Tree Structures for Mining association Rules*. To appear in the journal of Data Mining and Knowledge Discovery.

[7] Goulbourne, G., Coenen, F. and Leng, P. (2000). *Algorithms for Computing Association Rules Using a Partial-Support Tree*. Journal of Knowledge-Based Systems, Vol (13), pp141-149.

Information Theoretic Clustering of Sparse Co-Occurrence Data

Inderjit S. Dhillon and Yuqiang Guan
Department of Computer Sciences
University of Texas
Austin, TX 78712-1188, USA
inderjit, yguan@cs.utexas.edu

Abstract

A novel approach to clustering co-occurrence data poses it as an optimization problem in information theory which minimizes the resulting loss in mutual information. A divisive clustering algorithm that monotonically reduces this loss function was recently proposed. In this paper we show that sparse high-dimensional data presents special challenges which can result in the algorithm getting stuck at poor local minima. We propose two solutions to this problem: (a) a "prior" to overcome infinite relative entropy values as in the supervised Naive Bayes algorithm, and (b) local search to escape local minima. Finally, we combine these solutions to get a robust algorithm that is computationally efficient. We present experimental results to show that the proposed method is effective in clustering document collections and outperforms previous information-theoretic clustering approaches.

1 Introduction

Clustering is a central problem in unsupervised learning [5]. Presented with a set of data points, clustering algorithms group the data into clusters according to some notion of similarity between data points. However, the choice of similarity measure is a challenge and often an *ad hoc* measure is chosen. Information Theory comes to the rescue in the important situations where non-negative co-occurrence data is available. A novel formulation poses the clustering problem as one in information theory: find the clustering that minimizes the loss in (mutual) information [8, 4]. This information-theoretic formulation leads to a "natural" divisive clustering algorithm that uses relative entropy as the measure of similarity and monotonically reduces the loss in mutual information [4].

However, sparse and high-dimensional data presents special challenges and can lead to qualitatively poor local minima. In this paper, we demonstrate these failures and

then propose two solutions to overcome these problems. First, we use a prior as in the supervised Naive Bayes algorithm to overcome infinite relative entropy values caused by sparsity. Second, we propose a local search strategy that is highly effective for high-dimensional data. We combine these solutions to get an effective, computationally efficient algorithm. A prime example of high-dimensional co-occurrence data is word-document data; we show that our algorithm returns clusterings that are better than those returned by previous information-theoretic approaches.

The following is a brief outline of the paper. Section 2 presents the information-theoretic framework and divisive clustering algorithm of [4]. The problems due to sparsity and high-dimensionality are illustrated in Section 3. We present our two-pronged solution to the problem in Section 4. Detailed experimental results are given in Section 5.

A word about notation. Upper-case letters such as X, Y will denote random variables, while lower-case letters such as x, y denote individual set elements. $\hat{Y}$ denotes a random variable obtained from a clustering of Y while $\hat{y}$ denotes an individual cluster. Probability distributions will be denoted by $p(X)$, $p(X|y)$. Boldfaced letters, such as $\mathbf{y}$, $\hat{\mathbf{y}}$, will denote $p(X|y), p(X|\hat{y})$ for brevity. The logarithmic base 2 is used throughout this paper.

2 Divisive Information-Theoretic Clustering

Let X and Y be two discrete random variables that take values in the sets $\{x_1, x_2, \ldots, x_m\}$ and $\{y_1, y_2, \ldots, y_n\}$ respectively. Suppose that we know their joint probability distribution $p(X, Y)$; often this can be estimated using co-occurrence data. Consider the case where we want to cluster Y. Let $\hat{Y}$ denote the "clustered" random variable that ranges over the disjoint clusters $\hat{y}_1, \ldots, \hat{y}_k$, i.e.,

$$\cup_{i=1}^k \hat{y}_i = \{y_1, \ldots, y_n\}, \text{ and } \hat{y}_i \cap \hat{y}_j = \phi, \quad i \neq j.$$

A novel information-theoretic approach to clustering is to seek the clustering which gives the smallest loss in mutual information [8, 4], i.e. to minimize

$$I(X;Y) - I(X;\hat{Y}) = \sum_{\hat{y}} \sum_{y \in \hat{y}} p(y) KL(p(X|y), p(X|\hat{y})), \tag{1}$$

where $I(X;Y)$ is mutual information between random variable X and Y and KL stands for Kullback-Leibler divergence [1]. The above expression for the loss in mutual information suggests a "natural" divisive clustering algorithm (DITC), which iteratively (i) re-partitions the distributions $p(X|y)$ by their closeness in KL-divergence to the cluster distributions $p(X|\hat{y})$, and (ii) subsequently, given the new clusters, re-computes the new cluster distributions. This procedure is iterated until change in objective function value as given in (1) is less than, say, 10^{-3}. See [4] for details.

3 Challenges due to Sparsity and High-Dimensionality

Unfortunately, Algorithm DITC can falter in the presence of sparsity and high-dimensionality.

Example 1 *(Sparsity) Consider the three conditional distributions:*

	$\mathbf{y}_1$	$\mathbf{y}_2$	$\mathbf{y}_3$
	.1	0	0
	.9	.9	.1
	0	.1	.9

Suppose we want to cluster $\mathbf{y}_1, \mathbf{y}_2$ and $\mathbf{y}_3$ into two clusters; clearly the optimal clustering puts $\{\mathbf{y}_1, \mathbf{y}_2\}$ in one cluster and $\{\mathbf{y}_3\}$ in the other. However suppose the initial clusters are $\hat{\mathbf{y}}_1 = \{\mathbf{y}_1\}$ and $\hat{\mathbf{y}}_2 = \{\mathbf{y}_2, \mathbf{y}_3\}$. Then the cluster distributions will be $\hat{\mathbf{y}}_1 = (.1, .9, 0)$ and $\hat{\mathbf{y}}_2 = (0, .5, .5)$, respectively. The Kullback-Leibler divergences $KL(\mathbf{y}_1, \hat{\mathbf{y}}_2)$, $KL(\mathbf{y}_2, \hat{\mathbf{y}}_1)$ and $KL(\mathbf{y}_3, \hat{\mathbf{y}}_1)$ are infinite. Therefore Algorithm DITC gets stuck in this initial clustering and misses the optimal partition due to the presence of zeros in the cluster distributions $\hat{\mathbf{y}}_1$ and $\hat{\mathbf{y}}_2$ that result in infinite KL-divergences.

Example 2 *(High dimensionality) For the second example, we took a collection of 30 documents consisting of 10 documents each from the three distinct classes MEDLINE, CISI and CRAN (see Section 5 for details). These 30 documents contain a total of 1073 words and so the data is very high-dimensional. However, when we run DITC using the word-document co-occurrence data, there is hardly any movement of documents between clusters irrespective of the starting partition.*

4 Proposed Algorithm

In this section, we propose a computationally efficient algorithm that avoids the above problems due to sparsity

and high-dimensionality. As in the supervised Naive Bayes method, we wish to perturb $p(X|\hat{y})$ to avoid zero probabilities. Recall that in our unsupervised case $p(X|\hat{y})$ refers to a cluster distribution. The important question is: what should be the perturbation? For reasons outlined below, we perturb the cluster distribution to:

$$p'(X|\hat{y}) = \frac{1}{1+\alpha} \left(p(X|\hat{y}) + \alpha \cdot u(X) \right), \tag{2}$$

where α is a constant and $u(X)$ is the uniform distribution $(\frac{1}{m}, ..., \frac{1}{m})$. The value of this prior has a pleasing property: the perturbed cluster distribution $p'(X|\hat{y})$ can be interpreted as the mean distribution for $\hat{y}$ obtained after perturbing each element of the input joint distribution $p(x, y)$ to

$$p'(x, y) = \frac{1}{1+\alpha} \left(p(x, y) + \frac{\alpha}{m} p(y) \right).$$

Note that if $\alpha = \frac{m}{\sum_x N(x, \hat{y})}$ in (2), where $N(x, \hat{y})$ is the frequence of x in cluster $\hat{y}$, we get Laplace's rule of succession used in supervised Naive Bayes, i.e., $p'(x|\hat{y}) = \frac{1 + N(x, \hat{y})}{m + \sum_x N(x, \hat{y})}$. What should be the value of α in our clustering algorithm? Experimental results reveal that an "annealing" approach helps, i.e., start the algorithm with a large value of α and decrease α progressively as the number of iterations increase. Algorithm DITC_prior is same as DITC except that the cluster distributions are computed as in (2) and α is halved at every iteration. Our prior has the same influence as the temperature in deterministic annealing [7] through a slightly different mechanism: when the prior is big all the $p(X|\hat{y})$'s are uniform, i.e., the joint entropy $H(X, \hat{Y})$ is large, thus $KL(p(X|y), p(X|\hat{y}))$ is almost the same for all y and $\hat{y}$. As the prior decreases $H(X, \hat{Y})$ is decreased.

To further improve our algorithm, we turn to a local search strategy, called *first variation* in [3], that allows us to escape undesirable local minimum, especially in the case of high-dimensionality. Precisely, a first variation of a partition $\{\hat{y}_j\}_{j=1}^k$ is a partition $\{\hat{y}'_j\}_{j=1}^k$ obtained by removing a distribution y from a cluster $\hat{y}_j$ and assigning it to an existing cluster $\hat{y}_l$. Among all the kn possible first variations, corresponding to each combination of y and $\hat{y}_l$, we choose the one that gives the smallest loss in mutual information. As in [3], a chain of first variations are implemented for our DITC_LocalSearch algorithm, which iterates over DITC followed by a chain first variations. Finally, our algorithm DITC_PLS incorporates both the ideas of priors and local search, i.e., it iteratively runs DITC_prior and a chain of first variations till it converges. Lack of space prevents us from giving a more detailed description of the algorithm which may be found in [2].

	MED	CRAN	CISI		MED	CRAN	CISI
$\hat{y}_1$	**847**	41	275	$\hat{y}_1$	**1016**	1	2
$\hat{y}_2$	142	**954**	86	$\hat{y}_2$	1	**1389**	1
$\hat{y}_3$	44	405	**1099**	$\hat{y}_3$	16	9	**1457**

DITC results   DITC_prior results

Table 1. Confusion matrices for 3893 **documents,** 4303 **words (**CLASSIC3**)**

5 Experimental Results

We now present experimental results for our information-theoretic algorithm applied to the task of clustering document collections using word-document co-occurrence data.

For our test data, we use various subsets of the 20-newsgroup data (NG20) [6] and the SMART collection (ftp://ftp.cs.cornell.edu/pub/smart). NG20 consists of approximately 20,000 newsgroup postings collected from 20 different usenet newsgroups. We report results on NG20 and various subsets of this data set of size 500 each: Binary, Multi5, Multi10 and NG10 (see [2] for details). In order for our results to be comparable, we applied the same preprocessing as in [8] to all the news group data sets, i.e. we removed stopwords and selected the 2000 words with the highest contribution to the mutual information, removed documents with less than 10 word occurrences and removed all the headers except the subject line.

From SMART, we used MEDLINE, CISI, and CRANFIELD subcollections, which consist of 1033, 1460 and 1400 abstracts respectively. We also created 3 subsets of 30, 150, and 300 documents respectively; each data set was created by equal sampling of the three collections. After removing stopwords, the number of words for the 30, 150 and 300 document data sets is 1073, 3658 and 5577 respectively. We refer to the entire data set as CLASSIC3 and the subsets as C30, C150 and C300 respectively.

Since we know the underlying class labels for our data sets, we can evaluate clustering results by forming a confusion matrix where entry(i, j) gives the number of documents in cluster i that belong to the true class j. For an objective evaluation measure, we use micro-averaged precision which was also used in [8].

We first demonstrate that Algorithm DITC_PLS (with prior and local search) is superior to Algorithms DITC_prior and DITC_LocalSearch.

Algorithm DITC_prior cures the problem of sparsity to some extent and its results are superior to DITC, for example, Table 1 shows the confusion matrices resulting from the two algorithms. An interesting option in DITC_prior is the starting value of α. Indeed, as Figures 1 show, the starting values of α can result in quite different values of

	MED	CRAN	CISI		MED	CRAN	CISI
$\hat{y}_1$	1	15	29	$\hat{y}_1$	**50**	0	1
$\hat{y}_2$	**13**	11	8	$\hat{y}_2$	0	**50**	0
$\hat{y}_3$	**36**	24	13	$\hat{y}_3$	0	0	**49**

DITC_prior results   DITC_LocalSearch results

Table 2. Algorithm DITC_LocalSearch yields better confusion matrix than DITC_prior (150 **documents,** 3652 **words)**

	MED	CRAN	CISI		MED	CRAN	CISI
$\hat{y}_1$	**45**	38	35	$\hat{y}_1$	**97**	0	0
$\hat{y}_2$	31	26	**33**	$\hat{y}_2$	1	**100**	0
$\hat{y}_3$	24	**36**	32	$\hat{y}_3$	2	0	**100**

DITC_prior results   DITC_LocalSearch results

Table 3. Algorithm DITC_LocalSearch yields better confusion matrix than DITC_prior (300 **documents,** 5577 **words)**

mutual information preserved, $\frac{I(X;\hat{Y})}{I(X;Y)}$, and micro-averaged precision. The trend for DITC_prior in Figures 1 appears to be that larger starting values of α lead to better results (we observe this trend over other data sets too). This behavior is interesting and needs further study. Note that larger α values correspond to starting with "smeared" cluster distributions, or in other words, with high joint entropy values $H(X, \hat{Y})$.

However, the starting values of α cease to be an issue when we use DITC_PLS, which is seen to be "immune" to different starting values in Figure 1. Note that these figures validate our optimization criterion: there is a definite correlation between the mutual information preserved and micro-averaged precision, which was also observed in [8]. DITC_PLS is seen to be more stable than DITC_prior in addition to yielding higher quality results. Tables 2 and 3 further show that DITC_LocalSearch also yields better clustering than DITC_prior. However, DITC_PLS is computationally more efficient than DITC_LocalSearch since it has better starting partitions before invoking the slower local search procedure; hence DITC_PLS is our method of choice.

We now compare our Algorithm DITC_PLS with previously proposed information-theoretic algorithms. [9] proposed the use of an agglomerative algorithm that first clusters words, and then uses this clustered feature space to cluster documents using the same agglomerative information bottleneck method. More recently [8] improved the clustering results in [9] by using sequential information bottleneck (sIB). We implemented the sIB algorithm for purpose of comparison; since the sIB method starts with a random partition we ran 10 trials and report the average per-

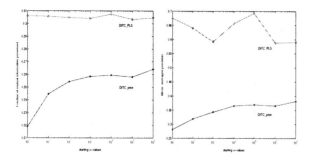

Figure 1. Mutual information preserved and Micro-averaged precision for DITC_prior with various starting α-values on Multi10

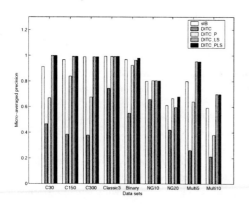

Figure 2. Micro-averaged precision results.

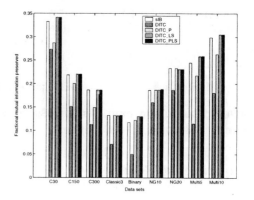

Figure 3. Fraction of mutual information preserved

Data set	sIB	DITC	DITC_prior
Classic3 (3893 documents)	95	1.35	1.67
NG10 (20000 documents)	2459	16.71	14.75
NG20 (20000 documents)	6244	35.87	29.92

Table 4. Computation time (in seconds) on large data sets (≥ 3000 documents)

NSF CAREER Award No. ACI-0093404 and Texas Advanced Research Program grant 003658-0431-2001.

formance numbers in Figures 2 and 3, which also contain performance results for our algorithms (recall that our algorithm is deterministic due to the deterministic initialization shceme we use). Figures 2 and 3 again reveal the correlation between the preserved mutual information and micro-averaged precision. DITC_PLS is seen to be the best algorithm, and beats sIB on at least 3 of the data sets; for example, the average micro-averaged precision of sIB on Multi5 is .8 while DITC_PLS yields .95. Note that numbers for our sIB implementation are averages of 10 runs while the published numbers in [8] are the best among 15 restarts. Also, the Binary, Multi10 and Multi5 datasets in our work and in [8] are formed by a random sampling of the newsgroups, so the data sets are a bit different. However, the NG10 and NG20 data sets used by us and [8] are identical, and so are the micro-averaged precision values (see [8, Table 2]).

For the large data sets, CLASSIC3, NG10, NG20, DITC_prior gives results that are comparable to those with prior and local search, see Figures 2 and 3. This leads to considerable savings in time since DITC_prior is much faster than sIB as shown in Table 5.

Acknowledgments. This research was supported by

References

[1] T. Cover and J. Thomas. *Elements of Information Theory*. John Wiley & Sons, New York, USA, 1991.

[2] I. S. Dhillon and Y. Guan. Information theoretic clustering of sparse co-occurrence data. Technical Report TR-03-39, Dept. of Computer Sciences, University of Texas, Sept 2003.

[3] I. S. Dhillon, Y. Guan, and J. Kogan. Iterative clustering of high dimensional text data augmented by local search. In *Proc. of IEEE International Conf. on Data Mining*, 2002.

[4] I. S. Dhillon, S. Mallela, and R. Kumar. A divisive information-theoretic feature clustering algorithm for text classification. *J. of Mach. Learning Res.*, 3:1265–1287, 2003.

[5] R. O. Duda, P. E. Hart, and D. G. Stork. *Pattern Classification*. John Wiley & Sons, 2nd edition, 2000.

[6] K. Lang. News Weeder: Learning to filter netnews. In *Proc. 12th Int'l Conf. Machine Learning*, pages 331–339, 1995.

[7] K. Rose. Deterministic annealing for clustering, compression, classification, regression, and related optimization problems. *Proc. IEEE*, 86(11):2210–2239, 1998.

[8] N. Slonim, N. Friedman, and N. Tishby. Unsupervised document classification using sequential information maximization. In *ACM SIGIR*, 2002.

[9] N. Slonim and N. Tishby. Document clustering using word clusters via the information bottleneck method. In *ACM SIGIR*, pages 208–215, 2000.

Links Between Kleinberg's Hubs and Authorities, Correspondence Analysis, and Markov Chains

Francois Fouss & Marco Saerens
Université Catholique de Louvain
Place des Doyens 1
B-1348 Louvain-la-Neuve, Belgium
{fouss, saerens}@isys.ucl.ac.be

Jean-Michel Renders
Xerox Research Center Europe
Chemin de Maupertuis 6
F-38240 Meylan (Grenoble), France
jean-michel.renders@xrce.xerox.com

Abstract

*In this work, we show that Kleinberg's hubs and authorities model is closely related to both correspondence analysis, a well-known multivariate statistical technique, and a particular Markov chain model of navigation through the web. The only difference between correspondence analysis and Kleinberg's method is the use of the **average** value of the hubs (authorities) scores for computing the authorities (hubs) scores, instead of the **sum** for Kleinberg's method. We also show that correspondence analysis and our Markov model are related to SALSA, a variant of Kleinberg's model.*

1. Introduction

Exploiting the graph structure of large document repositories, such as the web environment, is one of the main challenges of computer science and data mining today. In this respect, Kleinberg's proposition to distinguish web pages that are hubs and authorities (see [4]; the HITS algorithm) has been well-received in the community.

In this paper, we show that Kleinberg's hubs and authorities procedure [4] is closely related to both correspondence analysis (see for instance [3]), a well-known multivariate statistical analysis technique, and a particular Markov chain model of navigation through the web that provides the same results as correspondence analysis. We further show that correspondence analysis and the Markov model are related to SALSA [5], a variant of Kleinberg's model. This puts new lights on the interpretation of Kleinberg's procedure since correspondence analysis has a number of interesting properties that makes it well suited for the analysis of frequency tables. On the other hand, the proposed Markov model could easily be extended to more general structures, such as relational databases.

2. Kleinberg's procedure

In [4], Kleinberg introduced a procedure for identifying web pages that are good hubs or good authorities, in response to a given query. The following example is often mentioned. When considering the query "automobile makers", the home pages of Ford, Toyota and other car makers are considered as good authorities, while web pages that list these home pages are good hubs.

To identify good hubs and authorities, Kleinberg's procedure exploits the graph structure of the web. Each web page is a node and a link from page a to page b is represented by a directed edge from node a to node b. When introducing a query, the procedure first constructs a focused subgraph G, and then computes hubs and authorities scores for each node of G. Let n be the number of nodes of G. We now briefly describe how these scores are computed. Let $\mathbf{W}$ be the adjacency matrix of the subgraph G; that is, element w_{ij} (row i, column j) of matrix $\mathbf{W}$ is equal to 1 if and only if node (web page) i contains a link to node (web page) j; otherwise, $w_{ij} = 0$. We respectively denote by $\mathbf{x}^h$ and $\mathbf{x}^a$ the hubs and authorities $n \times 1$ column vector scores corresponding to each node of the subgraph.

Kleinberg uses an iterative updating rule in order to compute the scores. Initial scores at $k = 0$ are all set to 1, i.e. $\mathbf{x}^h = \mathbf{x}^a = \mathbf{1}$ where $\mathbf{1} = [1, 1, \ldots, 1]^T$, a column vector made of 1 (T is the matrix transpose). Then, the following mutually reinforcing rule is used: the hub score for node i, x_i^h, is set equal to the normalized sum of the authority scores of all nodes pointed by i and, similarly, the authority score of node j, x_j^a, is set equal to the normalized sum of hub scores of all nodes pointing to j. This corresponds to the following updating rule:

$$\mathbf{x}^h(k+1) = \frac{\mathbf{W}\mathbf{x}^a(k)}{\|\mathbf{W}\mathbf{x}^a(k)\|_2} \quad (1)$$

$$\mathbf{x}^a(k+1) = \frac{\mathbf{W}^T\mathbf{x}^h(k)}{\|\mathbf{W}^T\mathbf{x}^h(k)\|_2} \quad (2)$$

where $\|\mathbf{x}\|_2$ is the Euclidian norm, $\|\mathbf{x}\|_2 = (\mathbf{x}^T\mathbf{x})^{1/2}$.

Kleinberg [4] showed that when following this update rule, $\mathbf{x}^h$ converges to the normalized principal (or dominant) right eigenvector of the symmetric matrix $\mathbf{WW}^T$, while $\mathbf{x}^a$ converges to the normalized principal eigenvector of the symmetric matrix $\mathbf{W}^T\mathbf{W}$, provided that the eigenvalues are distinct.

Indeed, the equations (1), (2) result from the application of the power method, an iterative numerical method for computing the dominant eigenvector of a symmetric matrix [2], to the following eigenvalue problem:

$$\mathbf{x}^h \propto \mathbf{W}\mathbf{x}^a \Rightarrow \mathbf{x}^h = \mu\mathbf{W}\mathbf{x}^a \qquad (3)$$
$$\mathbf{x}^a \propto \mathbf{W}^T\mathbf{x}^h \Rightarrow \mathbf{x}^a = \eta\mathbf{W}^T\mathbf{x}^h \qquad (4)$$

where $\propto$ means "proportional to". This means that each hub node, i, is given a score, x_i^h, that is proportional to the sum of the authorities nodes scores to which it links to. Symmetrically, to each authorities node, j, we allocate a score, x_j^a, which is proportional to the sum of the hubs nodes scores that point to it. By substituting (3) in (4) and vice-versa, we easily obtain

$$\mathbf{x}^h = \mu\eta\mathbf{WW}^T\mathbf{x}^h = \lambda\mathbf{WW}^T\mathbf{x}^h$$
$$\mathbf{x}^a = \mu\eta\mathbf{W}^T\mathbf{W}\mathbf{x}^a = \lambda\mathbf{W}^T\mathbf{W}\mathbf{x}^a$$

which is an eigenvalue/eigenvector problem.

Many extensions of the updating rules (1), (2) were proposed. For instance, in [5] (the SALSA algorithm), the authors propose to normalise the matrices $\mathbf{W}$ and $\mathbf{W}^T$ in (3) and (4) so that the new matrices verify $\mathbf{W}'\mathbf{1} = \mathbf{1}$ and $\mathbf{W}^{T\prime}\mathbf{1} = \mathbf{1}$ (the sum of the elements of each row of $\mathbf{W}'$ and $\mathbf{W}^{T\prime}$ is 1). In this case, (3) and (4) can be rewritten as

$$x_i^h \propto \frac{\sum_{j=1}^n w_{ij}x_j^a}{w_{i.}} \text{ with } w_{i.} = \sum_{j=1}^n w_{ij} \qquad (5)$$
$$x_j^a \propto \frac{\sum_{i=1}^n w_{ij}x_i^h}{w_{.j}} \text{ with } w_{.j} = \sum_{i=1}^n w_{ij} \qquad (6)$$

This normalization has the effect that nodes (web pages) having a large number of links are not privileged with respect to nodes having a small number of links. The relations (5) and (6) are not explicitly used in order to compute hubs and authorities scores (it would lead to the dominant right eigenvector, which is a trivial one, $\mathbf{1}$), but lead to an eigenvalue/eigenvector problem, as will become clear in next section. In the SALSA algorithm, the hubs and authorities scores are the "steady-state values" computed from the corresponding Markov model (see section 4).

3. Links with correspondence analysis

Correspondence analysis is a standard multivariate statistical analysis technique aiming to analyse frequency tables [3]. Suppose that we have a table of frequencies, $\mathbf{W}$,

for which each cell, w_{ij}, represents the number of cases having both values i for the row variable and j for the column variable (we simply use the term "value" for the discrete value taken by a categorical variable). In our case, the records are the directed edges; the row variable represents the index of the origin node of the edge (hubs) and the column variable the index of the end node of the edge (authorities).

Correspondence analysis associates a score to the values of each of these variables. These scores relate the two categorical variables by what is called a "**reciprocal averaging**" relation [3]:

$$x_i^h \propto \frac{\sum_{j=1}^n w_{ij}x_j^a}{w_{i.}} \text{ with } w_{i.} = \sum_{j=1}^n w_{ij} \qquad (7)$$
$$x_j^a \propto \frac{\sum_{i=1}^n w_{ij}x_i^h}{w_{.j}} \text{ with } w_{.j} = \sum_{i=1}^n w_{ij} \qquad (8)$$

which is exactly the same as (5) and (6). This means that each hub node, i, is given a score, x_i^h, that is proportional to the average of the authorities nodes scores to which it links to. Symmetrically, to each authorities node, j, we allocate a score, x_j^a, which is proportional to the average of the hubs nodes scores that point to it.

Now, by defining the diagonal matrix $\mathbf{D}^h = \text{diag}(1/w_{i.})$ and $\mathbf{D}^a = \text{diag}(1/w_{.j})$ containing the number of links, we can rewrite (7) and (8) in matrix form

$$\mathbf{x}^h \propto \mathbf{D}^h\mathbf{W}\mathbf{x}^a \Rightarrow \mathbf{x}^h = \mu\mathbf{D}^h\mathbf{W}\mathbf{x}^a \qquad (9)$$
$$\mathbf{x}^a \propto \mathbf{D}^a\mathbf{W}^T\mathbf{x}^h \Rightarrow \mathbf{x}^a = \eta\mathbf{D}^a\mathbf{W}^T\mathbf{x}^h \qquad (10)$$

In the language of correspondence analysis, the row vectors of $\mathbf{D}^h\mathbf{W}$ are the hub **profiles**, while the row vectors of $\mathbf{D}^a\mathbf{W}^T$ are the authorities **profiles**. These vectors sum to one. Notice that (9) and (10) differ from (3) and (4) only by the fact that we use the **average value** in order to compute the scores, instead of the sum.

Now, from (9), (10), we easily find

$$\mathbf{x}^h = \mu\eta\mathbf{D}^h\mathbf{W}\mathbf{D}^a\mathbf{W}^T\mathbf{x}^h = \lambda\mathbf{D}^h\mathbf{W}\mathbf{D}^a\mathbf{W}^T\mathbf{x}^h \quad (11)$$
$$\mathbf{x}^a = \mu\eta\mathbf{D}^a\mathbf{W}^T\mathbf{D}^h\mathbf{W}\mathbf{x}^a = \lambda\mathbf{D}^a\mathbf{W}^T\mathbf{D}^h\mathbf{W}\mathbf{x}^a \quad (12)$$

Correspondence analysis computes the **subdominant right eigenvector** of the matrices $\mathbf{D}^h\mathbf{W}\mathbf{D}^a\mathbf{W}^T$ and $\mathbf{D}^a\mathbf{W}^T\mathbf{D}^h\mathbf{W}$. Indeed the right principal eigenvector is a trivial one, $\mathbf{1} = [1, 1, \ldots, 1]^T$, with eigenvalue $\lambda = 1$ (all the other eigenvalues are real positive and smaller that 1; see [3]) since the sum of the columns of $\mathbf{D}^h\mathbf{W}\mathbf{D}^a\mathbf{W}^T$ (respectively $\mathbf{D}^a\mathbf{W}^T\mathbf{D}^h\mathbf{W}$) is one for each row.

In standard correspondence analysis, this subdominant right eigenvector has several interesting interpretations in terms of "optimal scaling", of the "best approximation" in terms of chi-square distance to the original matrix, or of the linear combinations of the two sets of values that are "maximally correlated", etc. (see for instance [3]).

The next eigenvectors can be computed as well; they are related to the proportion of chi-square computed on the original table of frequencies that can be explained by the first m eigenvectors: they measure the departure to independence of the two discrete variables. Correspondence analysis is therefore often considered as an "equivalent" of principal components analysis for frequency tables.

4. A Markov chain model of web navigation

We now introduce a Markov chain model of random web navigation that provides the same results as correspondence analysis, and is therefore closely related to Kleinberg's procedure and SALSA. Hence, it provides a new interpretation for both correspondence analysis and Kleinberg's procedure. Notice that this random walk model is quite similar to the one proposed in SALSA ([5]; for other random walk models of web navigation, see PageRank [7] or [6]).

We first define a **Markov chain** in the following way. We associate a state of the Markov chain to every hub and every authority node ($2n$ in total); we also define a random variable, $s(k)$, representing the state of the Markov model at time step k. Moreover, let S^h be the subset of states that are hubs and S^a be the subset of states that are authorities. We say that $s^h(k) = i$ (respectively $s^a(k) = i$) when the Markov chain is in the state corresponding to the ith hub (authority) at time step k. As in [5], we define a random walk on these states by the following single-step transition probabilities

$$P(s^h(k+1) = i | s^a(k) = j) = \frac{w_{ij}}{w_{.j}} \quad (13)$$

$$P(s^a(k+1) = j | s^h(k) = i) = \frac{w_{ij}}{w_{i.}} \quad (14)$$

All the other transitions being impossible: $P(s^a(k+1) = j | s^a(k) = i) = 0$ and $P(s^h(k+1) = j | s^h(k) = i) = 0$, for all i, j. In other words, to any hub page, $s^h(k) = i$, we associate a non-zero probability of jumping to an authority page, $s^a(k+1) = j$, pointed by the hub page (equation 14), which is inversely proportional to the number of directed edges leaving $s^h(k) = i$. Symmetrically, to any authority page $s^a(k) = i$, we associate a non-zero probability of jumping to a hub page $s^h(k+1) = j$ pointing to the authority page (equation 13), which is inversely proportional to the number of directed edges pointing to $s^a(k) = i$.

We suppose that the Markov chain is irreducible, that is, any state can be reached from any other state. If this is not the case, the Markov chain can be decomposed into closed sets of states which are completely independent (there is no communication between them), each closed set being irreducible. In this situation, our analysis can be performed on these closed sets instead of the full Markov chain.

Now, if we denote the probability of being in a state by $x_i^h(k) = P(s^h(k) = i)$ and $x_i^a(k) = P(s^a(k) = i)$, and we define $\mathbf{P}^h$ as the transition matrix whose elements are $p_{ij}^h = P(s^h(k+1) = j | s^a(k) = i)$ and $\mathbf{P}^a$ as the transition matrix whose elements are $p_{ij}^a = P(s^a(k+1) = j | s^h(k) = i)$, from equations (13) and (14),

$$\mathbf{P}^h = \mathbf{D}^a \mathbf{W}^T \quad (15)$$
$$\mathbf{P}^a = \mathbf{D}^h \mathbf{W} \quad (16)$$

The evolution of the Markov model is characterized by

$$\mathbf{x}^h(k+1) = (\mathbf{P}^h)^T \mathbf{x}^a(k) \quad (17)$$
$$\mathbf{x}^a(k+1) = (\mathbf{P}^a)^T \mathbf{x}^h(k) \quad (18)$$

It is easy to observe that the Markov chain is periodic with period 2: each hub (authority) state could potentially be reached in one jump from an authority (hub) state but certainly not from any other hub (authority) state. In this case, the set of hubs (authorities) corresponds to a subset which itself is an irreducible and aperiodic Markov chain whose evolution is given by

$$\mathbf{x}^h(k+2) = (\mathbf{P}^h)^T (\mathbf{P}^a)^T \mathbf{x}^h(k) = (\mathbf{Q}^h)^T \mathbf{x}^h(k)$$
$$\mathbf{x}^a(k+2) = (\mathbf{P}^a)^T (\mathbf{P}^h)^T \mathbf{x}^a(k) = (\mathbf{Q}^a)^T \mathbf{x}^a(k)$$

where $\mathbf{Q}^h$ and $\mathbf{Q}^a$ are the transition matrices of the corresponding Markov models for the hubs and authorities. These Markov chains are aperiodic since each link (corresponding to a transition) can be followed in both directions (from hub to authority and from authority to hub) so that, when starting from a state, we can always return to this state in two steps. Hence, all the diagonal elements of $\mathbf{Q}^h$ and $\mathbf{Q}^a$ are non-zero and the Markov chains are aperiodic.

Therefore, the transition matrices of the corresponding Markov chains for hubs and authorities are

$$\mathbf{Q}^h = \mathbf{P}^a \mathbf{P}^h = \mathbf{D}^h \mathbf{W} \mathbf{D}^a \mathbf{W}^T \quad (19)$$
$$\mathbf{Q}^a = \mathbf{P}^h \mathbf{P}^a = \mathbf{D}^a \mathbf{W}^T \mathbf{D}^h \mathbf{W} \quad (20)$$

The matrices appearing in these equations are equivalent to the ones appearing in (11), (12). Now, it is well-know that the subdominant (the dominant right eigenvector is trivially **1**) right eigenvector – as computed in correspondence analysis – of the transition matrix, $\mathbf{Q}$, of an irreducible, aperiodic, Markov chain measures the departure of each state from the "equilibrium position" or "steady-state" probability vector (for a precise definition, see the appendix A or [9]), $\boldsymbol{\pi}$, which is given by the first left eigenvector of the transition matrix $\mathbf{Q}$: $\mathbf{Q}^T \boldsymbol{\pi} = \boldsymbol{\pi}$, subject to $\sum_{i=1}^n \pi_i = 1$, with eigenvalue $\lambda = 1$. This principal left eigenvector, $\boldsymbol{\pi}$, is unique and positive and is called the "steady state" vector; it corresponds to the probability of finding the Markov chain in state $s = i$ in the long-run behavior, $\lim_{k \to \infty} P(s(k) = i) = \pi_i$, and is independent of the initial distribution of states at $k = 0$. The elements of the subdominant right eigenvector of $\mathbf{Q} = \mathbf{Q}^h$ or $\mathbf{Q}^a$ can thus be interpreted as a kind of "distance" from each state to its "steady-state" value. The states of the Markov chain are often classified by means of the values of this subdominant eigenvector as well as the few next eigenvectors [9].

Lempel and Moran [5], in the SALSA algorithm, propose, as hubs and authorities scores, to compute the steady-state vectors, $\boldsymbol{\pi}^h$ and $\boldsymbol{\pi}^a$, corresponding to the hubs and the authorities transition matrices, $\mathbf{Q}^h$, $\mathbf{Q}^a$. We propose instead (or maybe in addition) to use the subdominant right eigenvector, which produces the same results as correspondence analysis, and which is often used in order to characterise the states of the Markov chain, as already mentionned. Eventually, the next eigenvectors/eigenvalues could be computed as well; they correspond to higher-order corrections.

5. Conclusions

We showed that Kleinberg's method for computing hubs and authorities scores is closely related to correspondence analysis, a well-known multivariate statistical analysis method. This will allow to provide new interpretations of Kleinberg's method. We then introduce a random walk model of navigation through the web, related to SALSA, and we show that this model is equivalent to correspondence analysis. This random walk model has an important advantage: it could easily be extended to more complex structures, such as relational databases.

References

[1] P. Bremaud. *Markov Chains: Gibbs Fields, Monte Carlo Simulation, and Queues.* Springer-Verlag New York, 1999.

[2] G. H. Golub and C. F. V. Loan. *Matrix Computations, 3th Ed.* The Johns Hopkins University Press, 1996.

[3] M. J. Greenacre. *Theory and Applications of Correspondence Analysis.* Academic Press, 1984.

[4] J. M. Kleinberg. Authoritative sources in a hyperlinked environment. *Journal of the ACM*, 46(5):604–632, 1999.

[5] R. Lempel and S. Moran. Salsa: The stochastic approach for link-structure analysis. *ACM Transactions on Information Systems*, 19(2):131–160, 2001.

[6] A. Y. Ng, A. X. Zheng, and M. I. Jordan. Link analysis, eigenvectors and stability. *International Joint Conference on Artificial Intelligence (IJCAI-01)*, 2001.

[7] L. Page, S. Brin, R. Motwani, and T. Winograd. The pagerank citation ranking: Bringing order to the web. *Technical Report, Computer System Laboratory, Stanford University*, 1998.

[8] A. Papoulis and S. U. Pillai. *Probability, Random Variables and Stochastic Processes.* McGraw-Hill, 2002.

[9] W. J. Stewart. *Introduction to the Numerical Solution of Markov Chains.* Princeton University Press, 1994.

A. Appendix: Distance to steady state vector

In this appendix, we show that the entries of the subdominant right eigenvector of the transition matrix $\mathbf{Q}$ of the aperiodic, irreducible Markov chains for hubs and authorities can be interpreted as a distance to the "steady-state" vector, $\boldsymbol{\pi}$. From (19), (20), we can easily show that $\mathbf{Q}$ is positive semidefinite so that all its eigenvalues are positive real and its eigenvectors are real. Moreover, since $\mathbf{Q}$ is stochastic nonnegative, all the eigenvalues are ≤ 1, and the eigenvalue 1 has multiplicity one. The proof is adapted from [8], [9], [1].

Let $\mathbf{e}_l = [0, 0, \ldots, 1, \ldots, 0]^{\mathrm{T}}$ be the column vector with the lth component equal to 1, all others being equal to 0. $\mathbf{e}_l$ will denote that, initially, the system starts in state l. After one time step, the probability density of finding the system in one state is $\mathbf{x}(1) = \mathbf{Q}^{\mathrm{T}} \mathbf{e}_l$, and after k steps, $\mathbf{x}(k) = (\mathbf{Q}^{\mathrm{T}})^k \mathbf{e}_l$. Now, the idea is to compute the distance

$$d_l(k) = \| (\mathbf{Q}^{\mathrm{T}})^k \mathbf{e}_l - \boldsymbol{\pi} \|_2 \qquad (21)$$

in order to have an idea of the rate of convergence to the steady state when starting from a particular state $s = l$.

Let $(\lambda_i, \mathbf{u}_i)$, $i = 1, 2, \ldots n$ represent the n right eigenvalue/eigenvectors pairs of $\mathbf{Q}$ in decreasing order of λ_i. Thus $\mathbf{Q}\mathbf{U} = \mathbf{U}\boldsymbol{\Lambda}$ where $\mathbf{U}$ is the $n \times n$ matrix made of the column vectors $\mathbf{u}_i$ which form a basis of $\Re^n$, $\mathbf{U} = [\mathbf{u}_1, \mathbf{u}_2, \ldots, \mathbf{u}_n]$, and $\boldsymbol{\Lambda} = \mathrm{diag}(\lambda_i)$. Hence,

$$\mathbf{Q} = \mathbf{U}\boldsymbol{\Lambda}\mathbf{U}^{-1} = \mathbf{U}\boldsymbol{\Lambda}\mathbf{V} \qquad (22)$$

where we set $\mathbf{V} = \mathbf{U}^{-1}$. We therefore obtain $\mathbf{V}\mathbf{Q} = \boldsymbol{\Lambda}\mathbf{V}$ where $\mathbf{V} = [\mathbf{v}_1, \mathbf{v}_2, \ldots, \mathbf{v}_n]^{\mathrm{T}}$, so that the column vectors $\mathbf{v}_i$ are the left eigenvectors of $\mathbf{Q}$, $\mathbf{v}_i^{\mathrm{T}} \mathbf{Q} = \lambda_i \mathbf{v}_i^{\mathrm{T}}$: the rows of $\mathbf{V}$ are $\mathbf{v}_i^{\mathrm{T}}$. Moreover, since $\mathbf{V}\mathbf{U} = \mathbf{I}$, we have $\mathbf{v}_i^{\mathrm{T}} \mathbf{u}_j = \delta_{ij}$.

Hence, from (22),

$$
\begin{aligned}
\mathbf{Q}^k &= \mathbf{U}\boldsymbol{\Lambda}^k \mathbf{V} = \sum_{i=1}^n \lambda_i^k \mathbf{u}_i \mathbf{v}_i^{\mathrm{T}} \\
&= \mathbf{1}\boldsymbol{\pi}^{\mathrm{T}} + \sum_{i=2}^n \lambda_i^k \mathbf{u}_i \mathbf{v}_i^{\mathrm{T}} \\
&= \mathbf{1}\boldsymbol{\pi}^{\mathrm{T}} + \lambda_2^k \mathbf{u}_2 \mathbf{v}_2^{\mathrm{T}} + O((n-2)\lambda_3^k) \qquad (23)
\end{aligned}
$$

since $\lambda_i < 1$ for $i > 1$ and the eigenvalues/eigenvectors are sorted in decreasing order of eigenvalue. Let us now return to (21)

$$
\begin{aligned}
d_l(k) &= \left\| (\mathbf{Q}^{\mathrm{T}})^k \mathbf{e}_l - \boldsymbol{\pi} \right\|_2 \\
&\simeq \left\| (\boldsymbol{\pi}\mathbf{1}^{\mathrm{T}} + \lambda_2^k \mathbf{v}_2 \mathbf{u}_2^{\mathrm{T}}) \mathbf{e}_l - \boldsymbol{\pi} \right\|_2 \\
&\simeq \left\| \boldsymbol{\pi} + \lambda_2^k \mathbf{v}_2 \mathbf{u}_2^{\mathrm{T}} \mathbf{e}_l - \boldsymbol{\pi} \right\|_2 \\
&\simeq \lambda_2^k \left\| \mathbf{v}_2 \right\|_2 u_{2l}
\end{aligned}
$$

where u_{2l} is l^{th} component of $\mathbf{u}_2$. Since the only term that depends on the initial state, l, is u_{2l}, the eigenvector $\mathbf{u}_2$ can be interpreted as a distance to the steady-state vector. ∎

Fast PNN-based Clustering Using K-nearest Neighbor Graph

Pasi Fränti, Olli Virmajoki and Ville Hautamäki

Department of Computer Science, University of Joensuu, PB 111, FIN-80101 Joensuu, Finland.
franti@cs.joensuu.fi, ovirma@cs.joensuu.fi, villeh@cs.joensuu.fi

Abstract

Search for nearest neighbor is the main source of computation in most clustering algorithms. We propose the use of nearest neighbor graph for reducing the number of candidates. The number of distance calculations per search can be reduced from O(N) to O(k) where N is the number of clusters, and k is the number of neighbors in the graph. We apply the proposed scheme within agglomerative clustering algorithm known as the PNN algorithm.

1. Introduction

Agglomerative clustering is popular method for generating the clustering hierarchically by a sequence of merge operations. *Ward's method* [1] selects the cluster pair to be merged that minimizes the increase in distortion function value. In vector quantization, it is known as the *pairwise nearest neighbor* (*PNN*) method [2].

The main drawback of the PNN is its slowness. The original implementation requires $O(N^3)$ distance calculations. An order of magnitude faster algorithm has been introduced in [3] but the method is still lower bounded by $\Omega(N^2)$. The main source of computation originates from the search of the nearest neighbor cluster.

Another approach is to use graph theoretical methods. In [4], a complete undirected graph is created where the nodes correspond to the data vectors, and the edge costs to vector distances according to a given *distortion* measure. The resulting graph can be trimmed to a *minimal spanning tree*. Clustering can then be generated by iteratively dividing the cluster by removing longest edges from the graph. In the final graph, clusters are defined by the separate components in the graph. This can be seen as a variant of a split-based clustering with *single-linkage* criterion.

In this work, we introduce fast agglomerative clustering algorithm motivated by the graph-based approaches. In our approach, however, we process the data at the cluster level so that every node in the graph represents a cluster, not a single vector. The edges of the graph represent inter cluster connections between nearby clusters. The graph is used as a search structure for reducing the number of distance calculations.

The proposed approach has two specific problems to solve: (1) how to generate the graph efficiently, and (2) how to utilize it. Standard solutions for minimum spanning tree take $O(N^2)$ time, which would prevent any speed-up. We propose solution for the first problem by considering Mean-distance ordered partial search [5]. We study the second sub-problem in detail and propose double-linked list, and use heap for efficient search for the cluster pair to be merged. We will show by experiments that a relatively small neighborhood size is sufficient for preserving the good quality clustering results.

2. Pairwise nearest neighbor method

The *clustering problem* is defined here as a combinatorial optimization problem. Given a set of N data vectors $X=\{x_1, x_2, ..., x_N\}$, partition the data set into M clusters so that a given distortion function is minimized. Partition $P=\{p_1, p_2, ..., p_N\}$ defines the clustering by giving for each data vector the index of the cluster where it is assigned to. A *cluster* s_a is defined as the set of data vectors that belong to the same partition a.

The clustering is then represented as the set $S=\{s_1, s_2, ..., s_M\}$. In vector quantization, the output of the clustering is a codebook $C=\{c_1, c_2, ..., c_M\}$, which is usually the set of cluster centroids. We assume that the vectors belong to Euclidean space, and use the mean square error (*MSE*) as the distortion function.

The *pairwise nearest neighbor* (*PNN*) method [1,2] generates the clustering hierarchically by a sequence of merge operations. At each step, two nearby clusters are merged. The method uses greedy strategy by choosing the cluster pair that increases the *MSE* least. A fast variant with linear memory consumption is given in [3].

3. K-nearest neighbor graph

We define *k-nearest neighbor graph* (*kNN graph*) as a weighted directed graph, in which every node represents a single cluster, and the edges correspond to pointers to neighbor clusters. Every node has k neighbors. The distance of clusters is defined by the merge distortion function. Note that this is not the only possible definition: others have been given in [6], [7].

The graph is utilized as a search structure: every time we need to search for the nearest neighbor, we consider only the clusters that are neighbors in the graph structure. Thus, the use of the graph approximates the $O(N)$ time full search by a faster $O(k)$ time search method.

3.1. MPS for searching nearest neighbor

The graph can be constructed by brute force but at the cost of $O(N^2)$ time. We therefore propose a faster method based on the *Mean-distance ordered partial search* (MPS). It was originally proposed for K-means clustering (GLA) in [5] but generalized to the PNN in [8].

The MPS method stores the component sums of each cluster centroid (code vectors). The component sums correspond to the projections of the vectors to the diagonal axis of the vector space. In typical data sets, the code vectors are highly concentrated along the diagonal axis, and therefore, the distance of their component sums highly correlate to their real distance. Then, given the cost function value of the best candidate found so far, vectors outside the radius defined by a given pre-condition can be excluded in the calculations, see Fig. 1.

The pre-condition is utilized as follows. The vectors are sorted according to their component sums, and then proceed in the order given by the sorting. The search starts from the given cluster, and proceeds bi-directionally along the projection axis. If the pre-condition holds true, the calculation the candidate cluster can be rejected.

3.2. MPS for searching k neighbors

For finding the k nearest clusters, we relax the condition of the graph and find any k neighbors instead of the nearest ones. This is a reasonable modification because the optimality of the graph cannot be guaranteed during the process of the PNN algorithm. Thus, by relaxing the definition of the k-nearest neighbor graph, speed-up can be obtained at a slight increase in the distortion.

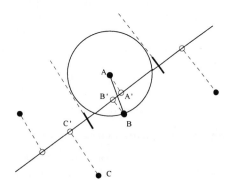

Fig. 1. Vectors (black dots) and their projections (empty dots) according to the component sums.

In particular, we use the exact MPS method for finding the nearest neighbor but stop the search immediately when it has been found. In addition to this, we maintain ordered list of the k best candidates found so far. The rest of the neighbors are then chosen simply from the list of the candidates no matter whether they are actually the k-1 nearest or not. It is expected that the rest of the candidates are nearby vectors although not necessarily the nearest ones. Even if some links were missing, vectors in the same cluster are most likely to be connected anyhow.

4. Graph-PNN

The proposed Graph-PNN is based on the exact PNN method but we utilize the graph structure in the search of nearest neighbor clusters.

4.1. Simple implementation

The main structure of the algorithm is given in Fig. 2. The algorithm starts by initializing every data vector as its own clusters, and by constructing the neighborhood graph. The algorithm iterates by removing nodes from the graph until the desired number of clusters has been reached.

At first, the edge with smallest weight is found, and the nodes (s_a and s_b) are merged. The algorithm creates a new node s_{ab} from the clusters s_a and s_b, which are removed from the graph. The corresponding edge costs are updated. The algorithm must also calculate cost values for the outgoing edges from the newly created node s_{ab}. The k nearest neighbors is found among the $2k$ neighbors of the previously merged nodes s_a and s_b. The merge procedure is illustrated in Fig. 3 for a sample 2NN graph (k=2).

```
GraphPNN(X, M) → S

    FOR i←1 to N DO
        s_i ← {x_i};
    FOR ∀(s_i; i ∈ [1, N]) DO

        Find k nearest neighbors;

    REPEAT

        (s_a, s_b) ← SearchNearestClustersInGraph(S);
        s_ab ← Merge(s_a, s_b);
        Find the k nearest neighbors for s_ab;
        Update the nodes that had s_a and s_b as neighbors;
    UNTIL |S|=M;
```

Fig. 2. Structure of the Graph-PNN.

4.2. Double linked list

The PNN iterations take $O(1)$ time to find the smallest distance if we use heap structure. The update of the data structures and recalculation of the distances for merged node takes $O(2k^2 + \log N + kN + N)$ time. The first term $(2k^2)$ originates from the update of the data structures and recalculation of the distances. The second term (log N) comes from the update of the heap structure. The third and fourth terms ($kN+N$) comes from updating edges that pointed to the obsolete nodes, and the time needed to recalculate those edge values.

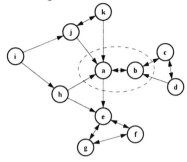

Fig. 3. Illustration of the graph where a and b are to be merged.

To sum up, one step requires O(kN) time, which sums up to O(τN^2), where τ is the number of incoming pointers. In general, this is too much and we therefore consider the double linked list (Fig. 4), in which we maintain for every node two lists: the first list points to the neighbor clusters, and the second list contains so called "back pointers" to clusters that have the node as their nearest neighbors. In this way, we can eliminate O(N) time loops, and the time complexity becomes O(τN log N), see Tables 1 and 2.

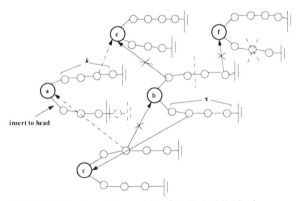

Fig. 4. Illustration of the update of the linked list in the merge procedure of the clusters a and b in the neighborhood graph.

5. Experiments

We consider three data sets from [3], [10], and number of clusters fixed to M=256. The illustrations in Fig. 5 show that the PNN iterations can be performed efficiently and that the graph creation is the bottleneck of the algorithm. The results also indicate that a very small neighborhood size, such as k=3, is sufficient for obtaining high quality clustering.

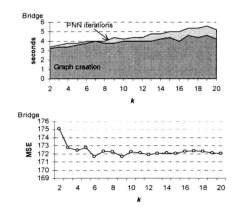

Fig. 5. Effect of the neighborhood size on running time.

The running times and the number of distance calculations are summarized in Table 3. Comparative results are given for the fast exact *PNN* [3], and the fast exact *PNN* with several speed-up methods as proposed in [8]. The results show that the *graph PNN* is significantly faster than the fast exact *PNN*. The graph creation is evidently a bottleneck in the *Graph-PNN*. We therefore consider limiting the search of MPS by a control parameter, see Fig. 6.

Comparative results are shown in Table 4 including *Fast PNN* [3], and its faster variant [8] using three practical speed-up techniques such as the *PDS*, *MPS* and *Lazy evaluation* of the distances. The *GLA* has also two variants: the original method [9], and a faster variant that uses PDS, MPS and activity detection for speed-up [10]. Results are given also for *Graph-PNN + GLA*, in which the data is first processed by the *Graph-PNN* and the result is input to the *GLA*.

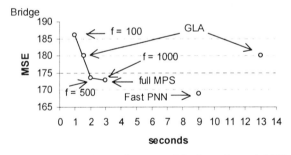

Fig. 6. Time-distortion performance of the *limited search MPS*.

6. Conclusion

Fast Graph-based PNN has been proposed. We found out that a relatively small neighborhood size ($k = 2, 3, 4$ or 5) can produce clustering results close to the exact PNN method but with a significantly smaller number of distance calculations and shorter running time.

Table 1: Estimated number of steps and distance calculations of the PNN iterations (*Bridge*).

Steps:	Fast PNN		Graph PNN (simple)		Graph PNN (double-linked)	
	Steps	Distances	Steps	Dists	Steps	Dists
SearchNearest( )	N	-	1	-	1	-
Merge(a, b)	N	-	$2 k^2 + \log N$	$2 k$	$2 k^2 + \tau k + \log N$	$2 k$
FindNeighbors(a, b)	N	-	$k N$	-	τk	-
RemoveLast( )	N	-	$k + 2 \log N$	-	$\log N$	-
UpdateDistances( )	$N (1+\tau)$	τN	$N + \tau \log N / k$	τ	$\tau (1 + \log N / k)$	τ

Table 2: Observed number of steps and distance calculations of the PNN iterations (*Bridge*).

	Fast PNN		Graph PNN (simple)		Graph PNN (double-linked)	
	Steps	Distances	Steps	Distances	Steps	Distances
SearchNearests( )	8 357 760	-	3 840	-	3 840	-
Merge(a, b)	8 357 760	-	67 362	8 210	108 410	8 217
FindNeighbors(a, b)	8 357 760	-	16 715 520	-	30 868	-
RemoveLast( )	8 349 185	-	90 979	-	45 514	-
UpdateDistances( )	48 538 136	40 166 328	8 478 587	11 285	145 722	11 261
Total	81 960 601	40 166 328	25 356 288	19 495	334 354	19 478

Table 3. Summary of the running times and the number of distance calculations.

		Bridge		House		Miss America	
		Distance calculations	Run time	Distance calculations	Run time	Distance calculations	Run time
Fast PNN		48 552 888	79	2 237 460 562	1574	128 323 740	229
Fast PNN	+MPS+PDS+lazy	6 167 439	9	37 752 863	190	83 323 889	106
Graph PNN	Graph creation	2 341 547	3	19 017 163	17	32 440 442	46
	Iterations	24 431	< 1	166 475	1	40 446	< 1
	Total	2 365 978	3	19 183 638	18	32 480 888	46

Table 4. Comparison of the Graph-PNN with other methods.

		Bridge (N=)		House		Miss America	
		Run time	MSE	Run time	MSE	Run time	MSE
Fast PNN	Full search	79	168.92	1574	6.27	229	5.36
	+PDS+MPS+Lazy	9	168.92	190	6.26	106	5.37
Graph PNN	Full MPS	3	172.96	18	6.47	46	5.49
	Limited search MPS	3	173.46	13	6.59	5	5.67
Graph PNN + GLA	Full MPS	4	166.85	19	6.14	48	5.31
	Limited search MPS	3	167.06	14	6.16	8	5.38
GLA	Full search	13	179.95	22.8	7.77	19.7	5.95
	+PDS+MPS+Activity	1.6	180.02	3	7.80	8.3	5.95

7. References

[1] J.H. Ward, "Hierarchical grouping to optimize an objective function," *J. Amer. Statist.Assoc.*, 58, 236-244, 1963.

[2] W.H. Equitz, "A new vector quantization clustering algorithm," *IEEE-ASSP*, 37(10), 1568-1575, Oct. 1989.

[3] P. Fränti, T. Kaukoranta, D.-F. Shen and K.-S. Chang, "Fast and memory efficient implementation of the exact PNN," *IEEE-IP*, 9(5), 773-777, May 2000.

[4] J.C. Cover and G.J.S. Ross, "Minimum spanning trees and simple-linkage cluster analysis," *Applied Statistics*, 18, 54-64, 1969.

[5] S.-W. Ra and J.K. Kim, "A fast mean-distance-ordered partial codebook search algorithm for image vector quantization," *IEEE-CS*, 40(9), 576-579, September 1993.

[6] S. Arya and D.M. Mount, "Algorithm for fast vector quantization," *IEEE Data Compresion Conference*, Snowbird Utah, 381-390, 1994.

[7] A.D. Constantinou, R.D. Bull and C.N. Canagarajah, "A new class of VQ codebook design algorithms using adjacency maps," *SPIE Electronics Imaging 2000*, San Jose, 3974, 625-634, 2000.

[8] O. Virmajoki, P. Fränti, T. Kaukoranta, "Practical methods for speeding-up the pairwise nearest neighbor method", *Optical Engineering*, 40(11), 2495-2504, November 2001.

[9] Y. Linde, A. Buzo and R.M. Gray, "An Algorithm for Vector Quantizer Design," *IEEE-COM*, 28(1), 84-95, Jan. 1980.

[10] T. Kaukoranta, P. Fränti and O. Nevalainen, "A fast exact GLA based on code vector activity detection", *IEEE-IP*, 9(8), 1337-1342, Aug. 2000.

The Rough Set Approach to Association Rule Mining

J. W. Guan[1][2]   D. A. Bell[2]   D. Y. Liu[1]
[1]College of Computer Science and Technology
Jilin University
130012, Changchun, P.R.CHINA
[2]School of Computer Science
The Queen's University of Belfast, Belfast
BT7 1NN, Northern Ireland, U.K.
{j.guan,da.bell}@qub.ac.uk

Abstract

In transaction processing, an association is said to exist between two sets of items when a transaction containing one set is likely to also contain the other. In information retrieval, an association between two sets of keywords occurs when they co-occur in a document. Similarly, in data mining, an association occurs when one attribute set occurs together with another. As the number of such associations may be large, maximal association rules are sought, e.g., Feldman et al (1997, 1998).

Rough set theory is a successful tool for data mining. By using this theory, rules similar to maximal associations can be found. However, we show that the rough set approach to discovering knowledge is much simpler than the maximal association method.

Keywords: Rough Set, Data Mining, Knowledge Discovery in Databases.

1   Introduction

Consider the analysis of supermarket basket data where associations like "82% of customers who buy spaghetti also buy Italian sauces" may be found. On the other hand, in information retrieval, an association between the keywords " bridle ways " and " jogging paths " means they co-occur in several documents. One method of data mining is to seek to identify association rules by which we can infer the existence of one attribute set from another. Generally, the number of such associations may be large. For example, from a (single) record " bright sunshine, water sprinkler off, external temperature drop, thermostat flips, room temperature increase " a large number of associations may be discovered: " water sprinkler off, room temperature increase " is

associated with " bright sunshine "; etc. Only some of these reflect insights into our world.

While regular association rules are based on the notion of *frequent sets of attributes* which appear in many records, maximal association rules are based on *frequent maximal sets of attributes* which appear maximally in many records. While the regular association rule $X \rightarrow Y$ for attribute sets X and Y means that if X then Y (with some *confidence*), the maximal association rule $X \rightarrow Y$ means that if X maximally then Y maximally (Feldman et al 1997, 1998). We can also apply this to documents for information retrieval.

For maximal associations, there is only one maximal association, e.g., with more records it might be possible to identify one between " *external events*: bright sunshine, water sprinkler off, external temperature drop " and " *internal events*: thermostat flips, room temperature increase ".

Rough set theory is a useful tool for data mining. By using this theory, rules that are similar to maximal associations can be found. However, we show that the rough set approach to discovering knowledge is much simpler than the maximal association method. We focus on information retrieval.

Let D be a document collection containing documents $d_1, d_2, ..., d_N$. The vocabularies of collection D and document d are denoted by V^D and V^d, respectively.

In order to illustrate the Feldman method, this paper uses the following example.

Example 1.1 (Feldman et al 1997) There are 10 articles referring to "corn" which also refer to USA and Canada, and other 20 different articles concern "fish" and the countries USA, Canada and France. We can write

{USA,Canada,corn}=V^{d_i} for $i = 1, 2, ..., 10$;

{USA,Canada,France,fish}=V^{d_j}

for $j = 11, 12, ..., 30$.

This paper is organized as follows. Section 2 discusses

the support documents of a keyword set. Sections 3-6 introduce partitioning of the indexing vocabulary of terms and the definition of maximality, and then discuss maximal associations. Finally, we introduce the rough set approach to association rule mining.

2 The Support Documents of a Keyword Set

Let $V^D = \{t_1, t_2, ..., t_n\}$, where t are keywords. Let $X \subseteq V^D$ be a subset of the collection vocabulary. Denote $X^D = \{d | X \subseteq V^d\}$, i.e. the set of documents in which elements of X occur. That is, in an information table, we say that a document d *supports* a given set of terms or keywords X if $X \subseteq V^d$. The *strength* of X in the information table, denoted by $stg(X)$, is the number of documents d supporting X:
$$stg(X) = |\{d | X \subseteq V^d\}| = |X^D|.$$
An *association* between X and Y is an expression of the form $X \rightleftharpoons Y$, where X and Y are sets of terms/keywords; the *strength* of the association $stg(X \rightleftharpoons Y)$ is the strength of $X \cup Y$, i.e., the number of documents supporting $X \cup Y$
$$stg(X \rightleftharpoons Y) = stg(X \cup Y) = |(X \cup Y)^D|,$$
and the *confidence* of the association $cfi(X \rightleftharpoons Y)$ is
$$\frac{stg(X \cup Y)}{\max(stg(X), stg(Y))} = \frac{|(X \cup Y)^D|}{\max(|X^D|, |Y^D|)}.$$
An *association rule* is a rule of the form $X \rightarrow Y$, where X and Y are sets of terms; the *strength* of the association rule $stg(X \rightarrow Y)$ is
$$stg(X \rightarrow Y) = stg(X \cup Y) = |(X \cup Y)^D|,$$
and the *confidence* of the rule $cfi(X \rightarrow Y)$ is
$$stg(X \cup Y)/stg(X) = \frac{|(X \cup Y)^D|}{|X^D|}.$$

Example 2.1 For example 1.1, it can be found that associations (with the given cardinalities) are

{USA,Canada} $\rightleftharpoons$ {fish} with confidence
$$\frac{|(\{USA, Canada\} \cup \{fish\})^D|}{\max(|\{USA, Canada\}^D|, |\{fish\}^D|)} = \frac{20}{\max(30, 20)} = 66\%,$$
{USA,Canada,France} $\rightleftharpoons$ {fish} with confidence
$$\frac{|(\{USA, Canada, France\} \cup \{fish\})^D|}{\max(|\{USA, Canada, France\}^D|, |\{\{fish\}^D|)} = \frac{20}{\max(20, 20)} = 100\%,$$
{USA,Canada} $\rightleftharpoons$ {corn} with confidence
$$\frac{|(\{USA, Canada\} \cup \{corn\})^D|}{\max(|\{USA, Canada\}^D|, |\{corn\}^D|)} = \frac{10}{\max(30, 10)} = 33\%.$$
Feldman et al argue that this confidence is too low to indicate a strong connection between USA-Canada and "corn". Of course, this is an application-dependent judgement.

Also, association rules are

{USA,Canada} $\rightarrow$ {fish} with confidence
$$\frac{|(\{USA, Canada\} \cup \{fish\})^D|}{|\{USA, Canada\}^D|} = 20/30 = 66\%,$$
{USA,Canada,France} $\rightarrow$ {fish} with confidence
$$\frac{|(\{USA, Canada, France\} \cup \{fish\})^D|}{|\{USA, Canada, France\}^D|} = 20/20 = 100\%,$$
{USA,Canada} $\rightarrow$ {corn} with confidence
$$\frac{|(\{USA, Canada\} \cup \{corn\})^D|}{|\{USA, Canada\}^D|} = 10/30 = 33\%.$$

Again, this confidence is judged to be too low to represent the strong connection between USA-Canada and "corn".

Therefore, Feldman et al introduce the definition of maximality. An example of a maximal association rule is

{USA,Canada} $\rightarrow$ {corn} and it has " confidence " 10/10=100%

since whenever USA-Canada appear *maximally* without any other country (in and only in documents d_1-d_{10}), "corn" also appears *maximally* without any other goods (also in and only in documents d_1-d_{10}).

3 Partitioning the Indexing Vocabulary

For the definition of maximality, an underlying taxonomy τ of terms is used. Then the "interesting" correlations between terms from different categories can be obtained.

Let $A = V^D$ be partitioned to classes $T_1, T_2, ..., T_K$. We denote the partition by $A/\tau : T_1, T_2, ..., T_K$; or $A/\tau = \{T_1, T_2, ..., T_K\}$, where τ is the corresponding equivalence relation of the partition such that $a\tau b$ for $a, b \in A$ if and only if a and b are in the same class, and $T_k \in 2^A; T_k \neq \emptyset; T_i \cap T_j = \emptyset$ when $i \neq j; A = \cup_{k=1}^K T_k$. The partition is called a *taxonomy*. Each class is called a *category*.

Example 3.1 For example 1.1, the vocabulary of terms A can be partitioned as follows: $A/\tau = \{T_1, T_2\}$, where $T_1 = countries = \{USA, Canada, France\}, T_2 = topics = \{corn, fish\}$. The taxonomy is {countries, topics}, and countries and topics are categories.

4 Maximally Supported Sets

From a given underlying taxonomy τ of attributes, the definition of maximality can be introduced, and "interesting" correlations between terms from different categories can be obtained.

For a given subset $X \subseteq A (X \neq \emptyset)$, we can find a unique decomposition $X = X_1 \cup X_2 \cup ... \cup X_K$ such that $X_1 \subseteq T_1, X_2 \subseteq T_2, ..., X_K \subseteq T_K$, where $T_k (k = 1, 2, ..., K)$ are categories of τ. We call T_k the *corresponding category* of X_k.

Given a category T_k, for an $X_k \subseteq T_k (X_k \neq \emptyset)$ and document d, we say that d *supports* X_k or X_k *occurs* in d if $X_k \subseteq V^d \cap T_k$. The *support/occurrence collection* of X_k in the document collection D, denoted by $(X_k)^D$, is the sub-collection of documents supporting X_k:
$$(X_k)^D = \{d | X_k \subseteq V^d \cap T_k\}.$$

This set X_k of terms can also be denoted by a *taxonomy pair* $\{X_k : T_k\}$ to indicate its category. The strength $stg(X_k)$ is equal to the number of documents supporting X_k:
$$stg(X_k) = |\{d | X_k \subseteq V^d \cap T_k\}| = |(X_k)^D|,$$

and pair $\{X_k : T_k\}$ can be denoted by $\{X_k : T_k\}(X_k)^D$ with its support collection $(X_k)^D$ added when $(X_k)^D \subset D$. We call X_k a *clause* co-occurring in $(X_k)^D$.

Now for an $X_k \subseteq T_k$ $(X_k \neq \emptyset)$ and document d, we say that d *maximally supports* X_k if $X_k = V^d \cap T_k$. The *max-support collection* of X_k in the document collection D, denoted by $(X_k)^{D,\max}$, is the sub-collection of documents maximally supporting X_k: $(X_k)^{D,\max} = \{d | X_k = V^d \cap T_k\}$. This set X_k of terms can also be denoted by a *taxonomy pair* $\{X_k : T_k\}$ to indicate its category. The max-strength $msg(X_k)$ is equal to the number of documents maximally supporting X_k:

$$msg(X_k) = |\{d | X_k = V^d \cap T_k\}| = |(X_k)^{D,\max}|,$$

and pair $\{X_k : T_k\}$ can be denoted by $\{X_k : T_k\}_{\max}(X_k)^{D,\max}$ with its max-support collection $(X_k)^{D,\max}$ added when $(X_k)^{D,\max} \subset D$. We call X_k a *sentence* co-occurring in $(X_k)^{D,\max}$.

Example 4.1 Continue example 1.1.

For $T_1 = countries$, the following 2 sentences and their co-occurrence collection can be found:

$\{\{Canada, France, USA\} : countries\}_{\max}\{d_{11}\text{-}d_{30}\}$
$\{\{Canada, USA\} : countries\}_{\max}\{d_1\text{-}d_{10}\}$

For $T_2 = topics$, the following 2 sentences and their co-occurrence collection can be found:

$\{\{corn\} : topics\}_{\max}\{d_1\text{-}d_{10}\}$
$\{\{fish\} : topics\}_{\max}\{d_{11}\text{-}d_{30}\}$.

Given a taxonomy τ, for a given $X = X_1 \cup X_2 \cup ... \cup X_K$ $(X \neq \emptyset; X_k \subseteq T_k$ for $k = 1, 2, ..., K$; and so there is at least one k such that $X_k \neq \emptyset$) and document d, we say that d *supports* X if $X_k \subseteq V^d \cap T_k$ for all k. The *support/occurrence collection* of X in the document collection D, denoted by X^D, is the sub-collection of documents supporting X; $X^D = \{d | X_k \subseteq V^d \cap T_k; k = 1, 2, ..., K\}$. This set X of terms can also be denoted by a vector of *taxonomy pairs* $\{X_k : T_k\}$ in a Cartesian product space $2^{T_1} \times 2^{T_2} \times ... \times 2^{T_K}$ to indicate the component categories. The strength $stg(X)$ is equal to the number of documents supporting X:

$$stg(X) = |\{d | X_k \subseteq V^d \cap T_k; k = 1, 2, ..., K\}| = |X^D|,$$

and the vector can be denoted as

$$(\{X_1 : T_1\}, \{X_2 : T_2\}, ..., \{X_K : T_K\})X^D$$

with its support collection added when $X^D \subset D$. We call X a *clause* co-occurring in X^D.

Now for an $X = X_1 \cup X_2 \cup ... \cup X_K$ (where $X_k \neq \emptyset$ and $X_k \subseteq T_k$ for $k = 1, 2, ..., K$) and document d, we say that d *maximally supports* X if $X_k = V^d \cap T_k$ for all k. The *max-support collection* of X in the document collection D, denoted by $X^{D,\max}$, is the sub-collection of documents maximally supporting X:

$$X^{D,\max} = \{d | X_k = V^d \cap T_k; k = 1, 2, ..., K\}.$$

This set X of terms can also be denoted by a vector of *taxonomy pairs* $\{X_k : T_k\}$ in a Cartesian product space $2^{T_1} \times 2^{T_2} \times ... \times 2^{T_K}$ to indicate the component categories. The max-strength $msg(X)$ is equal to the number of documents maximally supporting X:

$$msg(X) = |X^{D,\max}|,$$

and the vector can be denoted as

$$(\{X_1 : T_1\}, \{X_2 : T_2\}, ..., \{X_K : T_K\})_{\max}X^{D,\max}$$

with its max-support collection added when $X^{D,\max} \subset D$. We call X a *sentence* co-occurring in $X^{D,\max}$.

Example 4.2 For example 1.1, sentences for the taxonomy are

$(\{Canada, France, USA\} : countries,$
$\{fish\} : topics)_{\max}\{d_{11}\text{-}d_{30}\}$
$(\{Canada, USA\} : countries,$
$\{corn\} : topics)_{\max}\{d_1\text{-}d_{10}\}.$

5 Maximal Associations

A *maximal association* between V and W is an expression of the form $V \rightleftharpoons W$, where V and W are sentences from 2 different categories. The *strength* of the association is $msg(V \cup W)$, and confidence of the association is $msg(V \cup W)/max(msg(V), msg(W))$.

Example 5.1 For example 1.1, the following maximal associations can be found:

$\{Canada, France, USA\} : countries$
$\rightleftharpoons \{fish\} : topics$ with strength $msg = |\{d_{11}\text{-}d_{30}\}| = 20$ and confidence $20/\max(20, 20) = 1 = 100\%$

$\{Canada, USA\} : countries$
$\rightleftharpoons \{corn\} : topics$ with strength $msg = |\{d_1\text{-}d_{10}\}| = 10$ and confidence $10/\max(10, 10) = 1 = 100\%$

6 Maximal Association Rules

A *maximal association rule* is an expression of the form $V \rightarrow W$, where V and W are sentences from 2 different categories. The *strength* of the association rule is $msg(V \cup W)$, and confidence of the association is $msg(V \cup W)/msg(V)$.

Example 6.1 For example 1.1, the following maximal association rules can be found:

$\{Canada, France, USA\} : countries$
$\rightarrow \{fish\} : topics$ with strength $msg = |\{d_{11}\text{-}d_{30}\}| = 20$ and confidence $20/20 = 1 = 100\%$

$\{Canada, France, USA\} : countries$
$\leftarrow \{fish\} : topics$ with strength $msg = |\{d_{11}\text{-}d_{30}\}| = 20$ and confidence $20/20 = 1 = 100\%$

$\{Canada, USA\} : countries$

$\rightarrow \{corn\}$: $topics$ with strength $msg = |\{d_1\text{-}d_{10}\}| = 10$ and confidence $10/10 = 1 = 100\%$

$\{Canada, USA\}$: $countries$

$\leftarrow \{corn\}$: $topics$ with strength $msg = |\{d_1\text{-}d_{10}\}| = 10$ and confidence $10/10 = 1 = 100\%$

7 Rough Set Approach

Using the rough set method (Pawlak 1991, Bell Guan 1998, Guan Bell 1998), we can much more easily discover similar knowledge to maximal association rules. For a given sentence, we use the theory to recognize its support/occurrence documents. Now, an information table can be designed for sentences as follows.

$D\backslash 2^{T_1}$	T_1	T_2	...	T_K
d_1	$T_1 \cap V^{d_1}$	$T_2 \cap V^{d_1}$	...	$T_K \cap V^{d_1}$
d_2	$T_1 \cap V^{d_2}$	$T_2 \cap V^{d_2}$	...	$T_K \cap V^{d_2}$
...	...	...	...	...
d_i	$T_1 \cap V^{d_i}$	$T_2 \cap V^{d_i}$	...	$T_K \cap V^{d_i}$
...	...	...	...	...
d_N	$T_1 \cap V^{d_N}$	$T_2 \cap V^{d_N}$	...	$T_K \cap V^{d_N}$

For example, the information table for Example 1.1 can be designed as follows:

$D\backslash 2^{T_k}$	$T_1 = countries$	$T_2 = topics$
$d_1 : d_{10}$	$\{Canada, USA\}$	$\{corn\}$
$d_{11} : d_{30}$	$\{Canada, France, USA\}$	$\{fish\}$

The Information Table for Example 1.1

Then it can be found that partitions
$D/countries$ is
$\{Canada,USA\}D_{11}, \{Canada,France,USA\}D_{12}$, where
$D_{11} = \{d_1 : d_{10}\}, D_{12} = \{d_{11} : d_{30}\}$;
$D/topics$ is $\{corn\}D_{21}, \{fish\}D_{22}$, where
$D_{21} = \{d_1 : d_{10}\}, D_{22} = \{d_{11} : d_{30}\}$; and
$D/countries \cap topics$ is
$(\{Canada, USA\} : countries,$
$\{corn\} : topics)\{d_1 : d_{10}\}$
$(\{Canada, France, USA\} : countries,$
$\{fish\} : topics)\{d_{11} : d_{30}\}$
That is, we find the same associations/co-occurrences as the maximal ones discovered in Examples 5.1. However, as these examples show, the rough set approach to discover knowledge is much simpler than the maximal association method.

8 Conclusion

While regular association rules are based on the notion of *frequent sets of attributes* which appear in many documents, maximal association rules are based on *frequent*

maximal sets of attributes which appear maximally in many documents. Moreover, while the regular association rule $X \rightarrow Y$ means that if X then Y (with some *confidence*), the maximal association rule $X \rightarrow Y$ means that if X maximally then Y maximally.

Feldman et al argue that the regular concept of confidence is too low to indicate strong connections, and they introduce maximal associations to improve the quality of mined association rules.

By using rough set theory, rules that are similar to maximal associations can be found. However, we demonstrate that the rough set approach to discover knowledge is much simpler than the maximal association method.

References

[1] Bell, D.A.; Guan, J. W. 1998, Computational methods for rough classification and discovery, *Journal of the American Society for Information Science, Special Topic Issue on Data Mining*, Vol.49(1998), No.5, 403-414.

[2] Feldman, R.; Aumann, Y.; Amir, A.; Zilberstain, A.; Kloesgen, W. Ben-Yehuda, Y. 1997, Maximal association rules: a new tool for mining for keyword co-occurrences in document collection, in *Proceedings of the 3rd International Conference on Knowledge Discovery (KDD 1997)*, 167-170.

[3] Feldman, R.; Fresko, M.; Kinar, Y.; Lindell, Y.; Liphstat, O.; Rajman, M.; Schler, Y.; Zamir, O. 1998, Text mining at the term level, in *Proceedings of the 2nd European Symposium on Knowledge Discovery in Databases, PKDD'98, Nantes, France, 23-26 September 1998; Lecture Notes in Artificial Intelligence 1510: Principles of Data Mining and Knowledge Discovery*, Jan M. Zytkow Mohamed Quafafou eds.; Springer, 65-73.

[4] Guan, J. W. ; Bell, D. A. 1998, Rough computational methods for information systems, *Artificial Intelligence — An International Journal*, Vol.105(1998), 77-104.

[5] Pawlak, Z. (1991). Rough sets: theoretical aspects of reasoning about data. Kluwer.

Comparing Pure Parallel Ensemble Creation Techniques Against Bagging

Lawrence O. Hall, Kevin W. Bowyer[1], Robert E. Banfield, Divya Bhadoria
W. Philip Kegelmeyer[2] and Steven Eschrich
Computer Science & Engineering, University of South Florida, Tampa, Florida 33620-5399
{hall, rbanfiel, dbhadori}@csee.usf.edu

[1] Computer Science & Engineering, 384 Fitzpatrick Hall, Notre Dame, IN 46556
kwb@cse.nd.edu

[2] Sandia National Labs, Biosystems Research Dept, POB 969, MS 9951, Livermore, CA 94551-0969
wpk@ca.sandia.gov

Abstract

We experimentally evaluate randomization-based approaches to creating an ensemble of decision-tree classifiers. Unlike methods related to boosting, all of the eight approaches considered here create each classifier in an ensemble independently of the other classifiers. Experiments were performed on 28 publicly available datasets, using C4.5 release 8 as the base classifier. While each of the other seven approaches has some strengths, we find that none of them is consistently more accurate than standard bagging when tested for statistical significance.

1 Introduction

This paper compares eight methods of creating an ensemble without incrementally focusing on misclassified examples as in boosting [8, 14]. Bagging [4], three variations of random forests [5], three variations of randomized C4.5 [9] (which we will call by the more general name "random trees"), and random subspaces [10] are compared. Their classification accuracy is evaluated through a series of 10-fold stratified cross validation experiments on 28 data sets. The base classifier is a modification of the C4.5 release 8 [13] that we call USFC4.5. USFC4.5 produces identical output to C4.5 release 8 with default settings, but has significant added functionality. Each ensemble creation approach compared here can be distributed in a simple way across a set of processors. This makes them suitable for learning from very large data sets [11, 2, 7].

The experimental results show that the random tree approaches and random forests methods gave a statistically significant, though small, increase in accuracy over building a single decision tree. However, in head-to-head comparisons with bagging, none of the ensemble building methods was generally significantly more accurate than bagging.

2 Ensemble Creation Techniques Evaluated

Ho's random subspace method of creating a decision forest utilizes the random selection of attributes or features in creating each decision tree. Ho used a randomly chosen 50% of the attributes to create each decision tree in an ensemble. The ensemble size was 100 trees. Ho found the random subspace approach was better than bagging and boosting for a single train/test data split for four data sets taken from the stat log project [3]. Fourteen other data sets were split into two halves randomly, for train and test. This was done 10 times for each of the data sets. The maximum and minimum accuracy results were deleted and the other eight runs were averaged. There was no evaluation of statistical significance. The conclusion was that random subspaces was better for data sets with a large number of attributes. This result, and some results from other papers listed below, conflict with our conclusions. We discuss those conflicts in Section 5.

Breiman's random forest approach to creating an ensemble also utilizes a random choice of attributes in the construction of each CART decision tree [6, 5]. However, a random selection of attributes occurs at each node in the tree. Potential tests from these random attributes are evaluated and the best one is chosen. So, it is possible for each of the attributes to be utilized in the tree. The number of random attributes chosen for evaluation at each node is a variable in this approach. Additionally, bagging is used to create the training set for each of the trees that make up the random forests. In [5], random forest experiments were conducted on 20 data sets and compared with Adaboost on the same data sets. Ensembles of 100 trees were built for the random forests and 50 for Adaboost. For the zip-code data set 200 trees were used. A random 10% of the data was left out of the training set to serve as test data. This was done 100 times and the results averaged. The random forest with a single attribute randomly chosen at each node was better than Adaboost on 11 of the 20 data sets. There was no evaluation of statistical significance. It was significantly faster to build the ensembles using random forests. In the experiments in this paper, we consider random subsets of size 1, 2 and $\lfloor \log_2(n) + 1 \rfloor$ where n, is the number of attributes.

Dietterich introduced an approach which he called randomized C4.5 [9], which comes under our more general description of random trees. In this approach, at each node in the decision tree the 20 best tests are determined and the actual test used is randomly chosen from among them. With continuous attributes, it is possible that multiple tests from the same attribute will be in the top 20. All tests (in C4.5) must be kept to determine the best 20, which can make this approach memory intensive. Dietterich experimented with 33 data sets from the UC Irvine repository. For all but three, a 10-fold cross validation was done. The best result from a pruned (certainty factor of 10) or unpruned ensemble was reported. Test results were evaluated for statistical significance at the 95% confidence level. It was found that randomized C4.5 was better than C4.5 14 times and equivalent 19 times. It was better than bagging with C4.5 6 times, worse 3 times and equivalent 24 times. From this, it was concluded that the approach tends to produce an equivalent or better ensemble than bagging. It has the advantage that you do not have to create multiple instances of a training set.

3 Algorithm Modifications

We describe our implementation of random forests and a modification to Dietterich's randomized C4.5 method. In the random forest implementation, in the event that the attribute set randomly chosen provides a negative information gain, our approach is to randomly re-choose attributes until a positive information gain is obtained. This enables each test to improve the purity of the resultant leaves to at least some degree. The same approach was also used in the WEKA system [15].

We have made a modification to the randomized C4.5[1] ensemble creation method in which only the best test from

---

[1]On a code implementation note, we have added a –pure flag which allows trees to be grown to single example leaves, which we call pure trees. MINOBJS is set to one (which means a test will be attempted any time there are two or more examples at a node), tree collapsing is not allowed and dynamic changes in the minimum number of examples in a branch for a test to be used are not allowed. All unpruned trees were built with the pure flag.

each attribute is allowed to be among the best set (of a given size) from which one is randomly chosen. We will call it the random tree B (RTB) approach. A slightly more memory efficient perturbation of this approach is to keep $sqrt(n)$ best attributes to randomly choose. In the rest of the paper, we will call our ensemble creation method RTB and Dietterich's original method random trees.

4 Experimental Results

Experiments were done on 28 data sets; 26 from the UC Irvine repository [12], credit-g from NIAAD (www.liacc.up.pt/ML) and phoneme from the ELENA project. The data sets have from 4 to 69 attributes and the attributes are a mixture of continuous and nominal[2] values. The ensemble size was 200 trees for the Dietterich and RTB approaches. There were 100 trees used in the random forest approach and in the ensemble for the random subspace approach. The size of the ensembles was chosen to allow for comparison with previous work (and corresponds with those authors' recommendations).

For the RTB approach, we used a random test from the 20 attributes with maximal information gain and a random test from the square root of the number of attributes, which of course will vary with the size of the attribute space. In the random subspace approach of Ho, exactly half ($\lceil n/2 \rceil$) of the attributes were chosen each time. For the random forest approach, we used a single attribute, 2 attributes and $\lfloor log_2 n + 1 \rfloor$ attributes (which will be abbreviated as Random Forests-lg in the following).

For each data set, a 10-fold cross validation was done. For each fold, an ensemble is built by each method and tested on the held out data. We also built a single C4.5 tree, with default pruning, on each of the folds. The accuracy of each ensemble method is compared against the single default pruned decision trees. The ensembles consist solely of unpruned trees.

For these experiments, with 8 classification methods and 28 data sets, there are 224 comparisons, and so about 11 errors in the comparisons at the 95% confidence level. Hence, we look at statistical significance at the 99% level, as shown in Table 1. Compared to C4.5 a random forest ensemble created using $log_2 n + 1$ attributes is very good and RTB-20 is the best by a rather small increment. Random subspaces ties for the most times as statistically significantly more accurate than C4 .5, but is also less accurate the most times. Several ensemble algorithms are very close and hard to pick among. We can create a summary score for each ensemble algorithm by providing 1 point for a win, and 1/2 point for a tie. Using this scoring approach, the random forest approaches have a score of 16.5 for 2 and lg attributes

---

[2]As done by Dietterich, the attribute physician-fee-freeze has been left out of the voting data set to make it more difficult.

534

Table 1. Statistical significance at 99% level: + indicates more accurate, - indicates no difference, X means less accurate than C4.5.

Data Set	RTB sqrt	RTB 20	RT	RS	Bagging	RF 1	RF 2	RF lg
anneal	-	-	-	-	-	-	-	-
audiology	-	-	-	-	-	-	-	-
autos	-	-	-	-	-	-	-	-
breast-y	-	-	-	-	-	-	-	-
breast-w	-	+	+	+	-	-	-	-
glass	-	-	-	+	-	-	+	-
heart-v	-	-	-	-	-	-	-	-
heart-s	-	-	-	-	-	-	-	-
heart-h	-	-	-	-	-	-	-	-
heart-c	-	-	-	-	-	-	-	-
iris	-	-	-	-	-	-	-	-
hepatitis	-	+	-	+	-	+	+	+
hypo	-	-	-	-	-	-	-	-
horse-colic	-	-	-	-	-	-	-	-
waveform	+	+	+	+	+	+	+	+
voting	-	-	-	-	-	-	-	-
vehicle	-	-	-	-	-	-	-	-
soybean	-	-	-	-	-	-	-	-
sonar	+	+	+	+	-	+	+	+
sick	-	-	-	X	-	X	-	-
primary	-	-	-	-	-	-	-	-
phoneme	-	+	-	X	+	+	+	+
lymph	-	+	-	-	-	-	-	-
labor	-	-	-	-	-	-	-	-
krkp	-	-	-	X	-	X	-	-
credit-g	+	-	+	+	+	+	-	+
credit-a	-	-	-	-	-	-	-	-
pima	-	-	-	-	-	-	-	-
Summary								
Better	3	6	4	6	3	5	5	5
Similar	25	22	24	19	25	21	23	23
Worse	0	0	0	3	0	2	0	0
Score	15.5	17	16	15.5	15.5	15.5	16.5	16.5

RT = Random Trees, RS = Random Subspaces, RF = Random Forests.

with RTB-20 at 17. On the other hand, most of the others amassed 15.5 points.

An interesting question is how would these approaches rank if the average accuracy, regardless of significance, was the criterion. In this case random forests-lg and bagging appear the best (22.5 and 21.5 points respectively). The other random forest approaches are at 21 points with random trees and random subspaces at 20. Now, RTB-20 is the weakest approach at 18.5 points. Clearly, utilizing statistical significance tests changes the conclusions that one would make given these experimental results. It is worth noting that all

Table 2. Pairwise win-lose-tie comparisons with significance at the 99% level.

wins-loses-ties row versus col	C4.5	RTB-20	Random Forests-lg
Bagging	3-0-25	1-1-26	0-1-27
Random Forests-lg	5-0-23	3-1-24	
RTB-20	6-0-22		

scores are well above 14 which means they are each better than growing a single pruned tree on average.

At the outset of the study, it was expected that one or more of these approaches would be an unambiguous winner over bagging in terms of accuracy. This was not the case, despite the earlier observation that, for instance, RTB-20 and random forests-lg seem to be better than a single C4.5 tree more often than bagging. When the two most competitive techniques are compared *directly* to bagging and each other (using the same methods for evaluating statistical significance at 99%), the results are as in Table 2. There we see bagging proves equivalent to RTB-20 and has one loss compared to random forests-lg. It was shown to be slightly worse than random trees (randomized C4.5) in previous work.

5 Discussion

Since the random forest approach utilizes bagging to create the training sets for the trees of its ensembles, one might expect that its accuracy was less than C4.5 on some of the same data sets for which bagging was less accurate. We found that random forests with one, two or $log_2 n + 1$ random attributes to choose from was able to outperform C4.5 when bagging was worse two times for the first two approaches and three times with random forests-lg attributes. It was better than bagging was when compared with C4.5 twice when using two attributes. There were two cases in which random forests were worse than C4.5 when a bagged ensemble was better.

All the data sets used here, except Pima, were also used in the original randomized C4.5 paper [9], which found no losses to C4.5 at the 95% level. Our study finds only one loss. However, the previous study finds more wins in the (14 of 33 data sets) than we do. The difference could be due to our use of release 8 of C4.5, which is better at handling continuous valued attributes. Another big difference is that we utilized only unpruned trees. Dietterich chose the best of the pruned (certainty factor of 10) and unpruned trees.

In the random forests work, the ensembles obtained were compared with those obtained from Adaboost. On 19 data sets it was better 11 times and worse 8 times. There was no statistical test used to determine if the wins and losses were significant. Boosting is usually better than bagging unless there is noise in the data set [1]. We have nine data sets in common. It is difficult to draw direct conclusions, but this approach is one of the most competitive, which one would expect given the results in [5].

There are five data sets in common from the random subspaces paper [10]. In the experiments reported in the original paper random subspaces was better on all of these data sets. Here, at the 99% confidence level it is better once, worse once, and equivalent three times. We do not know what release of C4.5 was used. However, a twofold cross validation was done 10 times and the outliers were removed (highest accuracy and lowest accuracy) with the remaining 8 averaged. Using a twofold cross validation the training set will be significantly smaller. The "data starvation" in the training set probably hurts the accuracy of the single tree more than it hurts the accuracy of the ensemble. Other work has shown that ensembles can recover accuracy with reduced training set sizes [7].

Random subspaces was not expected to do well when there are a small number of attributes. It's performance is less than a single classifier for Phoneme which has just five attributes and this was not unexpected. Also, it is no better than a single classifier on the Iris and Pima data sets which have only 4 and 8 attributes respectively. So, it was perhaps a lower performer partly due to the data sets chosen.

There are some computational advantages to random trees and random forests. Utilizing random trees it is not necessary to re-sample the training data in creating the individual trees. Random forests use a relatively small number of attributes in determining a test at a node which makes the tree faster to build.

It is possible to use the out of bag error to decide when to stop adding classifiers to a random forest ensemble or bagged ensemble. A stopping criterion of the error leveling off suffices. This, perhaps, would boost the performance of the random forests on the data sets utilized here.

Random trees and random forests can only be directly used to create ensembles of decision trees. The random subspace approach, which is less competitive than bagging, but faster because it uses less attributes, could be utilized with other learning algorithms such as neural networks.

Given the results presented here, it is perhaps worthwhile to explicitly consider the question — what would constitute a convincing experimental demonstration that a new technique achieves a general improvement in accuracy over simple bagging? Certainly the experiments should involve a "large" number of different datasets, say, in the range of 30 or more. Also, the comparison on each individual dataset should be in terms of whether or not the new technique achieves a statistically significant increase in accuracy. For this point, a paired t test on 10-fold or 20-fold cross-validation seems appropriate. The issue then becomes, on what fraction of the datasets should the new technique achieve a statistically significant increase in accuracy in order for us to accept that it offers a general improvement over bagging?

Acknowledgments: This research was partially supported by the Department of Energy through the ASCI Views Data Discovery Program, Contract number: DE-AC04-76DO00789 and the National Science Foundation under grant EIA-0130768.

References

[1] E. Bauer and R. Kohavi. An empirical comparison of voting classification algorithms: Bagging, boosting, and variants. *Machine Learning*, 36(1,2):105–139, 1999.

[2] K. Bowyer, N. Chawla, J. T.E. Moore, L. Hall, and W. Kegelmeyer. A parallel decision tree builder for mining very large visualization datasets. In *IEEE Systems, Man, and Cybernetics Conference*, pages 1888–1893, 2000.

[3] P. Brazdil and J.Gama. The statlog project- evaluation / characterization of classification algorithms. Technical report, The STATLOG Project- Evaluation / Characterization of Classification Algorithms, http://www.ncc.up.pt/liacc/ML/statlog/, 1998.

[4] L. Breiman. Bagging predictors. *Machine Learning*, 24:123–140, 1996.

[5] L. Breiman. Random forests. *Machine Learning*, 45(1):5–32, 2001.

[6] L. Breiman, J. Friedman, R. Olshen, and P. Stone. *Classification and Regression Trees*. Wadsworth International Group, Belmont, CA., 1984.

[7] N. Chawla, T. Moore, L. Hall, K. Bowyer, W. Kegelmeyer, and C. Springer. Distributed learning with bagging-like performance. *Pattern Recognition Letters*, 24:455–471, 2003.

[8] M. Collins, R. Schapire, and Y. Singer. Logistic regression, AdaBoost and Bregman distances. In *Proceedings of the Thirteenth Annual Conference on Computational Learning Theory*, pages 158–169, 2000.

[9] T. Dietterich. An experimental comparison of three methods for constructing ensembles of decision trees: bagging, boosting, and randomization. *Machine Learning*, 40(2):139–157, 2000.

[10] T. Ho. The random subspace method for constructing decision forests. *IEEE Transactions on Pattern Analysis and Machine Intelligence*, 20(8):832–844, 1998.

[11] G. Hulten and P. Domingos. Learning from infinite data in finite time. In *Advances in Neural Information Processing Systems 14*, pages 673–680, Cambridge, MA, 2002. MIT Press.

[12] C. Merz and P. Murphy. *UCI Repository of Machine Learning Databases*. Univ. of CA., Dept. of CIS, Irvine, CA. http://www.ics.uci.edu/˜mlearn/MLRepository.html.

[13] J. Quinlan. *C4.5: Programs for Machine Learning*. Morgan Kaufmann, 1992. San Mateo, CA.

[14] R. Schapire. The strength of weak learnability. *Machine Learning*, 5(2):197–227, 1990.

[15] I. H. Witten and E. Frank. *Data Mining: Practical machine learning tools with Java implementations*. Morgan Kaufmann, San Francisco, 1999.

Improving Home Automation by Discovering Regularly Occurring Device Usage Patterns

Edwin O. Heierman, III   Diane J. Cook
Department of Computer Science and Engineering
University of Texas at Arlington
{heierman,cook}@cse.uta.edu

Abstract

The data stream captured by recording inhabitant-device interactions in an environment can be mined to discover significant patterns, which an intelligent agent could use to automate device interactions. However, this knowledge discovery problem is complicated by several challenges, such as excessive noise in the data, data that does not naturally exist as transactions, a need to operate in real time, and a domain where frequency may not be the best discriminator. In this paper, we propose a novel data mining technique that addresses these challenges and discovers regularly-occurring interactions with a smart home. We also discuss a case study that shows the data mining technique can improve the accuracy of two prediction algorithms, thus demonstrating multiple uses for a home automation system. Finally, we present an analysis of the algorithm and results obtained using inhabitant interactions.

1. Introduction

Several research efforts are focused on home automation. The Intelligent Room [2] uses an array of sensors and AI techniques to interpret inhabitant activities within the environment and provide automated assistance. The Neural Network House [6] balances the goals of anticipating inhabitant needs and energy conservation by use of a neural network. The MavHome [3] project uses an intelligent and versatile home agent that perceives the state of the home through sensors and acts on the environment through effectors.

Our research is unique in that it looks at improving home automation by discovering regular usage patterns in a data stream collected from user interactions with the home appliances and devices. These patterns, if predictable, can be automated for the user or even improved in a way that achieves the same end result in less time or energy cost. However, the numerous noisy patterns contained within the data complicate the problem. For example, it would be difficult, and undesirable, to automate appliance interactions for

random and frequent trips to the kitchen to get a drink of water. It is important to filter out this noise, because embedded within the collected data are significant patterns that can be automated, such as the appliance interactions that occur when inhabitants wake and prepare to leave for work. Our goal is to discover significant patterns worthy of automation so that an agent can reduce inhabitant interactions, without generating unnecessary device actions.

Therefore, we propose a framework based on a novel data-mining algorithm ED (**E**pisode **D**iscovery) that discovers behavior patterns within a sequential data stream. The pattern knowledge and corresponding filtered data can be provided to a prediction algorithm or decision learner to improve home automation. In addition, the framework processes the interactions incrementally and can be used in a real-time system.

Several important characteristics of the home automation problem influence our discovery technique. First, the input sequence consists of histories of device interactions (episodes) with no indicated pattern start or stop points. Second, ordering information of actions within the pattern must be discovered. Third, the discovery needs to balance episode length with frequency and periodicity or regularity. Finally, the dataset will be of moderate size, which allows for the use of techniques that might not be suitable for extremely large datasets.

With these characteristics in mind, we developed an approach that mines a device activity stream to discover subsequences, or episodes, that are closely related in time. These episodes may be totally or partially ordered, and are evaluated based on information theory principles.

The following scenario, executed by the MavHome smart home for an inhabitant named Bob, illustrates the potential uses of the ED algorithm. Bob's alarm goes off at 7:00, which signals MavHome to turn on the bedroom light as well as the coffee maker in the kitchen. When Bob steps into the bathroom, MavHome turns on the light, displays the morning news on the bathroom video screen, and turns on the shower. When Bob finishes grooming, the bathroom light turns off while the kitchen light and menu/schedule display turns on, and the news program moves to the kitchen screen. When Bob leaves for work, MavHome secures the home, and starts the lawn sprinklers. Because the refrigerator is low on milk and cheese, MavHome places a grocery order to arrive just before Bob comes home.

In order to provide such a level of automation, MavHome can use ED to mine the event history of the devices. Upon mining the data, ED discovers that some activities such as {alarm on, alarm off, bedroom light on, coffee maker on, bathroom light on, bathroom video on, shower on} occur on a daily basis, while others such as {sprinkler on, sprinkler off} occur weekly. ED identifies these collections as significant episodes because they provide compression of the event history. Once the significant episodes are identified, MavHome can use this knowledge to provide the desired device automation.

Several works address the problem of discovering sequences. Agrawal [1] mines sequential patterns from time-ordered transactions using variations of the Apriori property. Mannilla [5] discovers frequent parallel and serial episodes using a window of user-defined size to slide over an event stream. Our work uses the same definition for an episode, and employs the sliding window to identify episodes. The Apriori support measure, however, is supplanted with a Minimum Description Length (MDL) evaluation measure.

2. The Episode Discovery (ED) Algorithm

Given an input stream S of event occurrences O, ED:

1. Partitions S into Maximal Episodes, P_{max}.
2. Creates Itemsets, I, from the Maximal Episodes.
3. Creates a Candidate Significant Episode, C, for each Itemset I, and computes one or more Significance Values, V, for each candidate.
4. Identifies Significant Episodes by evaluating the Significance Values of the candidates.

First, our technique generates maximal episodes, P_i, from the input sequence, S, by incrementally processing each event occurrence, O_j. An episode window maintains the occurrences and is pruned when an occurrence is outside of the allowable window time frame due to the addition of a new event occurrence. The window contents prior to pruning are maximal for that particular window instance, and are used to generate a maximal episode.

Next, the algorithm constructs an initial collection of itemsets, one for each maximal episode. Additional itemsets are generated so that the episode subsets of the maximal episodes can be evaluated for significance. To avoid generating the power set of each maximal episode itemset, ED must prune the complete set of potential itemsets in a tractable manner, while ensuring itemsets leading to significant episodes are retained.

Because frequency is not our only discriminator of interestingness, pruning based on the Apriori measure of frequency is not sufficient. Nevertheless, we can prune

the itemset search space by selecting a subset of an episode itemset as an additional itemset based on one of the following conditions:

- The subset represents the intersection of multiple maximal episode itemsets. Because the subset represents event occurrences in multiple episodes, it may be more significant than its parents.
- The subset represents the difference between a maximal episode itemset and one of its subset itemsets. If a subset itemset is significant, then the remainder of the maximal episode itemset must be evaluated to see if it is also significant.

Our approach relies on the following principle to prune the itemset space: subset itemsets that have the same episode occurrences as their parent itemset do not need to be generated as candidates. Because these subset itemsets are shorter in length, but have the same frequency and regularity as their parent, their value cannot be greater than the parent. Our pruning method generates smaller itemsets from larger ones, which is essentially the opposite of an Apriori approach [1] where larger itemsets are generated from smaller ones.

Once the itemsets have been generated, a significant episode candidate C_n is created for each itemset I_n. Next, each maximal episode is compared with the I_n of each candidate. If the maximal episode contains all of I_n, then the maximal episode is added to the episode set of the candidate as an occurrence of the itemset.

ED evaluates the candidates by making use of the MDL principle, which targets patterns that can be used to minimize the description length of a database by replacing each instance of the pattern with a pointer to the pattern definition. Our MDL-based evaluation measure thus identifies patterns that balance frequency and length. Instances of a regular (daily, weekly) sequence can be removed without storing a pointer to the sequence definition, because the regularity of the sequence is stored with the sequence definition. Regular sequences thus further compress the description length of the data. The larger the potential amount of compression a pattern provides, the greater the impact that results from automating the pattern. Therefore, the resulting amount of compression represents the pattern's significance value. ED detects daily and weekly periodic patterns, and adjusts the description length to account for too frequent or infrequent deviations from the expected regularity.

Once the candidates have been evaluated, ED greedily identifies the significant episodes as those meeting a user-configurable minimum significance (compression) value. Because a high level of confidence is desired before automating an episode, we chose 80% as the minimum compression. After selecting a candidate, the algorithm marks the events that represent instances of the candidate's pattern, which allows ED to construct a filtered input stream. These steps are repeated until all candidates have been processed.

The knowledge that ED obtains by mining the device-interaction history can be used in a variety of ways. The filtered input stream could be provided to a prediction algorithm, improving the algorithm's accuracy by removing noise from its training data. Also, the significant episodes can be used to segment a decision learner's state space into meaningful partitions and enhance scalability of the algorithm. Finally, an episode's temporal information, such as episode start and stop times, can be used to enhance automation decisions.

3. Case Study

To validate the ED algorithm, we conducted a case study to demonstrate that regular episodes could be discovered, and also that the filtered input stream, significant episodes, and temporal knowledge of the significant episodes could be used effectively. We selected the **I**ncremental **P**robabilistic **A**ction **M**odeling (IPAM) sequential prediction algorithm [4] and a **B**ack-**P**ropagation **N**eural **N**etwork (BPNN) for this case study. IPAM is a frequency-based prediction algorithm that maintains a probability distribution for the next event given the current state. Both algorithms could be used to predict the next action that might occur in a home environment. Because these algorithms by themselves may not fare well in the home environment due to noisy data, we felt they would be ideal candidates. The goal was to show that by training each algorithm on filtered data and using the significant episode temporal knowledge when performing a prediction, ED could improve the predictive accuracy of the algorithms.

Using a synthetic data generator, we created five randomly-generated scenarios from a device usage description that covers typical device interactions over a six-month time period. The scenario generator supports generating random noisy patterns, allows the occurrences of the patterns to overlap, and allows the pattern order to be varied. Our scenario definition includes twenty-two devices with on and off states. Fourteen regularly-occurring daily and weekly patterns were defined that ED should discover, as well as sixty-eight noisy patterns. Eight devices were used as part of both the regularly-occurring patterns and the noisy patterns. Each scenario contains close to 13,000 device interactions, of which less than 5,000 are part of a regularly-occurring pattern.

We tested the algorithms in the following manner. First we trained each prediction algorithm (IPAM, BPNN) on the entire scenario dataset, using parameter values that maximized the performance based on initial testing. Next, ED mined the scenario dataset to identify

the significant episodes, and marked the device interactions that were part of the discovered significant episodes. ED was configured to use a fifteen-minute sliding window in order to partition the input stream. We then trained a version of each algorithm (IPAM+ED, BPNN+ED) on the filtered data.

Once the algorithms were trained, the synthetic data generator used the same scenario description to randomly create a test scenario that covered the same twenty-two devices over an additional one-month period. Using the test dataset, each algorithm predicted the next event occurrence based on the current event occurrence. For IPAM+ED and BPNN+ED, we used the significant episode temporal information to perform a prediction only when the following conditions were met:

- Event e of the current event occurrence O is a member of one of the significant episodes, and
- The time of O falls within the time-of-day range of the episodes the significant episode represents.

Thus, the combined approach should automate regular device interactions while ignoring unnecessary interactions, which, as we noted previously, is very important for a home environment.

ED was able to correctly discover the pre-defined significant episodes in all of the datasets, and appreciably improved the accuracy of both algorithms across all five scenarios, as can be seen in Table 1. Therefore, we conclude that the knowledge discovered by ED can be used to consistently improve the predictive accuracy of the case study algorithms. One reason for the improvement was that the algorithms were trained on significant, noise-free data. In addition, the predictions were filtered so that predictions were not performed on data that was considered noise. ED not only improved the accuracy of the algorithms, it also significantly reduced the total number of false predictions (and resulting wasteful automations) each algorithm made.

Table 1 Averaged Scenario Prediction Results

Approach:	IPAM	IPAM+ED	BPNN	BPNN+ED
Accuracy:	41.0 %	73.6 %	63.6%	85.6%

4. Algorithm Analysis

We performed additional testing that compared the algorithm against a frequency-based approach, evaluated the runtime performance of the algorithm, and tested ED using real inhabitant interactions collected from our MavHome environment.

For comparison purposes, we modified ED to discover the most frequently occurring episodes. The algorithm selected an episode as significant if it occurred a minimum number of times. We varied this support level from 50 to 200 in increments of 50, and tested the accuracy of the BPNN+ED predictor on the synthetic datasets. The results are shown in Table 2. The highest accuracy obtained was 64%, which is well below the 85.6% achieved by our MDL approach. In addition, no weekly episodes were discovered, and noisy patterns were selected as significant episodes in all of the test runs. We conclude that the ED algorithm using our MDL-based approach outperforms a frequency-based approach on the synthetic datasets.

Table 2 Frequency-based Results

Support:	50	100	150	200
Accuracy:	46%	53%	64%	54%

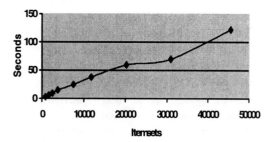

Figure 1 Itemset vs. Processing Time Plot

Our tests also show that ED is an efficient algorithm for the home automation domain. We empirically analyzed the runtime complexity of the algorithm by varying the window width, and in Figure 1 we show a plot of the number of itemsets generated versus the processing time. The results indicate that the algorithm achieves a near-linear performance on the synthetic datasets.

Finally, we collected one month of device interaction data from six participants in our MavHome environment laboratory. The dataset consists of 618 interactions contained in patterns occurring once a week, multiple times a week, and randomly. We used ED to mine the data with window widths ranging from 2 to 10 minutes and compression minimums ranging from 20% to 60%. ED was able to correctly identify the patterns of three of the inhabitants as significant episodes that occur weekly. The results of this testing highlighted the following:

- The algorithm must be improved to discover the regularity of the patterns. ED only discovered daily or weekly patterns, and was unable to discover the patterns that occurred multiple times in a week.
- The approach used to determine membership in a significant episode needs improvement. Several of the significant episodes contained anomalous episode occurrences, which incorrectly increased the time-of-

day range of the episodes to an excessively large value.

5. Conclusions and Future Work

We have demonstrated that ED provides an efficient mechanism for identifying significant episodes in sequential data. ED can be used to comprehend the nature of the activities occurring within the environment, and to improve the predictive accuracy of a home agent. We anticipate that ED will serve as a penultimate component that helps identify the activities that a smart home agent should automate.

In our future work, we intend to test ED on interaction data collected from the MavHome residence, and to incorporate additional prediction and decision learner algorithms. In addition, we are currently applying auto-correlation techniques to automatically detect regularity intervals in the observed data. We are also investigating automatically discovering the optimal window width by evaluating compression values between windows. Finally, we intend to enhance the approach used to determine membership in a significant episode by providing statistical information on the likelihood an event occurrence is part of a significant episode.

6. REFERENCES

[1] R. Agrawal and R. Srikant, "Mining sequential patterns," *Proc. 11th International Conference Data Engineering (ICDE 1995)*, Taipei, Taiwan, pp. 3-14, March 1995.

[2] M. Coen. Design principles for Intelligent Environments. *AAAI Spring Symposium*, Stanford, pp. 36-43, March 1998.

[3] S. Das, D. Cook, A. Bhattacharaya, E. Heierman, and T. Lin. The Role of Prediction Algorithms in the MavHome Smart Home Architecture. *IEEE Wireless Communications*, vol. 9, no. 6, pp. 77-84, December 2002.

[4] B. Davison and H. Hirsh. Predicting Sequences of User Actions. In *Technical Report*, Rutgers, The State University of New York, 1998.

[5] H. Mannila, H. Toivonen, and A. Verkamo, "Discovering frequent episodes in sequences," *Proc. 1st International Conference on Knowledge Discovery and Data Mining (KDD'95)*, Montreal, Canada, pp. 210-215, August 1995.

[6] M. Mozer. An intelligent environment must be adaptive. *IEEE Intelligent Systems*, vol. 14, no. 2, pp. 11-13, March/April 1999.

Ontologies Improve Text Document Clustering

Andreas Hotho, Steffen Staab, Gerd Stumme
{hotho,staab,stumme}@aifb.uni-karlsruhe.de
Institute AIFB, University of Karlsruhe,
76128 Karlsruhe, Germany

Abstract

Text document clustering plays an important role in providing intuitive navigation and browsing mechanisms by organizing large sets of documents into a small number of meaningful clusters. The bag of words representation used for these clustering methods is often unsatisfactory as it ignores relationships between important terms that do not co-occur literally. In order to deal with the problem, we integrate core ontologies as background knowledge into the process of clustering text documents. Our experimental evaluations compare clustering techniques based on pre-categorizations of texts from Reuters newsfeeds and on a smaller domain of an eLearning course about Java. In the experiments, improvements of results by background knowledge compared to a baseline without background knowledge can be shown in many interesting combinations.

1 Introduction

With the abundance of text documents available through corporate document management systems and the World Wide Web, the efficient, high-quality partitioning of texts into previously unseen categories is a major topic for applications such as information retrieval from databases, business intelligence solutions or enterprise portals. So far, however, existing text clustering solutions only relate documents that use identical terminology, while they ignore *conceptual similarity* of terms such as defined in terminological resources like WordNet [7].

In this paper we investigate which beneficial effects can be achieved for text document clustering by integrating an explicit conceptual account of terms found in thesauri and ontologies like WordNet. In order to come up with this result we have performed empirical evaluations. This short paper summarizes the main results, while a more in-depth discussion can be found in [4]. In particular, we analyse our novel clustering technique in depth in order to find explanations of when background knowledge may help.

We compare a baseline with different strategies for representing text documents that take background knowledge into account to various extent (Section 2). For instance, terms like "beef" and "pork" are found to be similar, because they both are subconcepts of "meat" in WordNet. The clustering is then performed with Bi-Section-KMeans, which has been shown to perform as good as other text clustering algorithms — and frequently better [8]. For the evaluation (cf. Section 3), we have investigated two text corpora which both come with a set of categorizing labels attached to the documents, *(i)*, the Reuters corpus on newsfeeds, and *(ii)*, a smaller domain of an eLearning course about Java (henceforth called Reuters and Java dataset, respectively). The evaluation results (cf. Section 4) compare the original classification with the partitioning produced by clustering the different representations of the text documents. Briefly, we report also the results we have achieved for the Java corpus, in conjunction with Wordnet on one hand, and with a domain specific ontology on the other hand.

2 Compiling Background Knowledge into the Text Document Representation

Based on the initial text document representation as a bag of words, we have first applied stopword removal. Then we performed stemming, pruning and tfidf weighting in all different combinations. This also holds for the document representation involving background knowledge described subsequently. When stemming and/or pruning and/or tfidf weighting was performed, we have always performed them in the order in which they have been listed here.

The background knowledge we have exploited is given through an ontology like Wordnet. Wordnet assigns words of the English language to sets of synonyms called 'synsets'. We consider the synsets as concepts, and use them to extend the bag-of-word model.

2.1 Term vs. Concepts Vector Strategies

Enriching the term vectors with concepts from the core ontology has two benefits. First it resolves synonyms; and second it introduces more general concepts which help identifying related topics. For instance, a document about beef may not be related to a document about pork by the cluster algorithm if there are only 'beef' and 'pork' in the term vector. But if the more general concept 'meat' is added to both documents, their semantical relationship is revealed. We have investigated different strategies (HYPINT) for adding or replacing terms by concepts:

Add Concepts ("add"[1]). When applying this strategy, we have extended each term vector $\vec{t_d}$ by new entries for Wordnet concepts c appearing in the document set. Thus, the vector $\vec{t_d}$ was replaced by the concatenation of $\vec{t_d}$ and $\vec{c_d}$, where $\vec{c_d} := (\text{cf}(d, c_1), \ldots, \text{cf}(d, c_l))$ is the concept vector with $l = |C|$ and $\text{cf}(d, c)$ denotes the frequency that a concept $c \in C$ appears in a document d as indicated by applying the reference function Ref_C to all terms in the document d. For a detailed definition of cf, see next subsection.

Hence, a term that also appeared in Wordnet as a synset would be accounted for at least twice in the new vector representation, i. e., once as part of the old $\vec{t_d}$ and at least once as part of $\vec{c_d}$. It could be accounted for also more often, because a term like "bank" has several corresponding concepts in Wordnet.

Replace Terms by Concepts ("repl"). This strategy works like 'Add Concepts' but it expels all terms from the vector representations $\vec{t_d}$ for which at least one corresponding concept exists. Thus, terms that appear in Wordnet are only accounted at the concept level, but terms that do not appear in Wordnet are not discarded.

Concept Vector Only ("only"). This strategy works like 'Replace Terms by Concepts' but it expels *all* terms from the vector representation. Thus, terms that do not appear in Wordnet are discarded; $\vec{c_d}$ is used to represent document d.

2.2 Strategies for Disambiguation

The assignment of terms to concepts in Wordnet is ambiguous. Therefore, adding or replacing terms by concepts may add noise to the representation and may induce a loss of information. Therefore, we have also investigated how the choice of a "most appropriate" concept from the set of alternatives may influence the clustering results.

While there is a whole field of research dedicated to word sense disambiguation (e.g., cf. [5]), it has not been our intention to determine which one could be the most appropriate, but simply whether word sense disambiguation is needed at all. For this purpose, we have considered two simple disambiguation strategies besides of the baseline:

All Concepts ("all"). The baseline strategy is not to do anything about disambiguation and consider all concepts for augmenting the text document representation. Then, the

concept frequencies are calculated as follows:
$$\text{cf}(d, c) := \text{tf}(d, \{t \in T \mid c \in Ref_C(t)\}) .$$
with $\text{tf}(d, T')$ being the sum of the frequencies[2] of all terms $t \in T$ in document d and with $Ref_C(t)$ being the set of all concepts (synsets) assigned to term t in the ontology.

First Concept ("first"). Wordnet returns an *ordered* list of concepts when applying Ref_C to a set of terms. Thereby, the ordering is supposed to reflect how common it is that a term reflects a concept in "standard" English language. More common term meanings are listed before less common ones.

For a term t appearing in S_C, this strategy counts only the concept frequency cf for the first ranked element of $Ref_C(t)$, i.e. the most common meaning of t. For the other elements of $Ref_C(t)$, frequencies of concepts are not increased by the occurrence of t. Thus the concept frequency is calculated by: $\text{cf}(d, c) := \text{tf}(d, \{t \in T \mid \text{first}(Ref_C(t)) = c\})$ where $\text{first}(Ref_C)$ gives the first concept $c \in Ref_C$ according to the order from Wordnet.

Disambiguation by Context ("context"). The sense of a term t that refers to several different concepts $Ref_C(t) := \{b, c, \ldots\}$ may be disambiguated by a simplified version of [1]'s strategy: Define the semantic vicinity of a concept c to be the set of all its direct sub- and superconcepts $V(c) := \{b \in C \mid c \prec b \text{ or } b \prec c\}$. Collect all terms that could express a concept from the conceptual vicinity of c by $U(c) := \bigcup_{b \in V(c)} Ref_C^{-1}(b)$. The function $\text{dis}: D \times T \to C$ with $\text{dis}(d, t) := \text{first}\{c \in Ref_C(t) \mid c \text{ maximizes } \text{tf}(d, U(c))\}$. disambiguates term t based on the context provided by document d. Now $\text{cf}(d, c)$ is defined by $\text{cf}(d, c) := \text{tf}(d, \{t \in T \mid \text{dis}(d, t) = c\})$.

2.3 Strategies for considering the concept hierarchy

The third set of strategies varies the amount of background knowledge. Its principal idea is that if a term like 'beef' appears, one does not only represent the document by the concept corresponding to 'beef', but also by the concepts corresponding to 'meat' and 'food' etc. up to a certain level of generality.

The following procedure realizes this idea by adding to the concept frequency of higher level concepts in a document d the frequencies that their subconcepts (at most r levels down in the hierarchy) appear, *i.e.* for $r \in \mathbb{N}_0$: The vectors we consider are of the form $\vec{t_d} := (\text{tf}(d, t_1), \ldots, \text{tf}(d, t_m), \text{cf}(d, c_1), \ldots, \text{cf}(d, c_n))$ (the concatenation of an initial term representation with a concept vector). Then the frequencies of the concept vector part are updated in the following way: For all $c \in C$, replace $\text{cf}(d, c)$ by $\text{cf}'(d, c) := \sum_{b \in H(c,r)} \text{cf}(d, b)$, where

---

[1]These abbreviations are used below in Section 4.2

[2]or tfidf's if this weighting is applied

$H(c,r) := \{c'|\exists c_1,\ldots,c_i \in C\colon c' \prec c_1 \prec \ldots \prec c_i = c, \; 0 \leq i \leq r\}$ gives for a given concept c the r next subconceps in the taxonomy. In particular $H(c,\infty)$ returns all subconcepts of c. This implies: The strategy $r = 0$ does not change the given concept frequencies, $r = n$ adds to each concept the frequency counts of all subconcepts in the n levels below it in the ontology and $r = \infty$ adds to each concept the frequency counts of all its subconcepts.

3 Experimental Setting

Our incorporation of background knowledge is rather independent of the concrete clustering method. The only requirements we had were that the baseline could achieve good clustering results in an efficient way e.g. on the Reuters corpus. In [8] it has been shown that Bi-Section-KMeans – a variant of KMeans – fulfilled these conditions, while frequently outperforming standard KMeans as well as agglomerative clustering techniques.

In the experiments we have varied the different strategies for plain term vector representation and for vector representations containing background knowledge as elaborated above. We have clustered the representations of the corpora using Bi-Section-KMeans and have compared the pre-categorization with our clustering results using standard measures for this task like purity and F-measure.

The Reuters-Corpus. We have performed most of our evaluations on the Reuters-21578 document set ([6][3]). The reason was that it comprises an *a priori* categorization of documents (which we need for evaluating our approach), its domain is broad enough to be realistic, and the content of the news were understandable for non-experts (like us) in order to be able to explain results.

To be able to perform evaluations for more different parameter settings, we derived several different subsets of the Reuters corpus. In this short paper, we focus on a corpus which does not include "outlier categories" with less than 15 documents, and restricts all categories to max. 100 documents by sampling. This corpus, called PRC-min15-max100, consists of 46 categories and 2619 documents with an average of 56.93 documents per category. Our extensive evaluation shows, however, that the results did not change significantly when choosing different subsets.

The Java-Corpus. The Java-Corpus is a small dataset containing web pages of an eLearning course about the programming language Java (cf [2]). There are 94 documents distributed among 8 classes with 2013 different word stems and 20394 words overall.

[3]http://www.daviddlewis.com/resources/testcollections/reuters21578/

In [3], Nicola Henze has described an ontology for the programming language Java. The ontology has been modeled to support an open, adaptive hypermedia system and consists of 521 concepts and twelve non-taxonomic relations. The maximal depth of the taxonomy is 12 with an average of 6.3. We used this domain specific ontology as another source of background knowledge.

4 Results

Each evaluation result described in the following denotes an average from 20 test runs performed on the given corpus for a given combination of parameter values with randomly chosen initial values for Bi-Section-KMeans. The results we report here have been achieved for $k = 60$ clusters for the Reuters and $k = 10$ clusters for the java corpus. Varying the number k of clusters for the parameter combinations described below has not altered the overall picture.

On the results we report in the text, we have applied t-tests to check for significance with a confidence of 99.5%. All differences that are mentioned below are significant within a confidence of $\alpha = 0.5\%$.

4.1 Clustering without Background Knowledge on Reuters Dataset

Without background knowledge, averaged purity values for PRC-min15-max100 ranged from 46.1% to 57%. We have observed that tfidf weighting decisively increased purity values irrespective of what the combination of parameter values was. Pruning with a threshold of 5 or 30 has not always shown an effect. But it always increased purity values when it was combined with tfidf weighting.

4.2 Clustering with Background Knowledge on Reuters Dataset

For clustering using background knowledge, we have also performed pruning and tfidf weighting as described above. The thresholds and modifications have been enacted on concept frequencies (or mixed term/concept frequencies) instead of term frequencies only. We have computed the purity results for varying parameter combinations as described before.

Results on Reuters-21578 PRC-min15-max100. The baseline, i. e., the representation without background knowledge with tfidf weighting and a pruning threshold of 30 returns an average purity of 57%. The best overall value is achieved by the following combination of strategies: Background knowledge with five levels of hypernyms ($r = 5$), using "disambiguation by context"[4] and term vectors extended by concept

[4]The "first" strategy produced results that were not significantly different.

Table 1. Results on PRC-min15-max100 for $k = 60$ and $prune = 30$ (with background knowledge also HYPDIS = context, avg denotes average over 20 cluster runs and std denotes standard deviation)

Ontology	HYPDEPTH (r)	HYPINT	Purity avg ± std	InversePurity avg ± std	F-Measure avg ± std	Entropy avg ± std
false			**0,57 ± 0,019**	**0,435 ± 0,016**	**0,479 ± 0,016**	**1,329 ± 0,038**
true	0	add	0,585 ± 0,014	0,449 ± 0,018	0,492 ± 0,017	1,260 ± 0,052
		only	0,603 ± 0,019	0,460 ± 0,020	0,504 ± 0,021	1,234 ± 0,038
	5	add	**0,618 ± 0,015**	**0,473 ± 0,019**	**0,514 ± 0,019**	**1,178 ± 0,040**
		only	0,593 ± 0,01	0,459 ± 0,017	0,500 ± 0,016	1,230 ± 0,039

Table 2. Results on Java dataset for $k = 10$ and $prune = 17$ (with background knowledge also HYPDIS = first, HYPDEPTH = 1, avg denotes average over 20 cluster runs and std denotes standard deviation)

Ontology	HYPINT	Purity avg ± std	InversePurity avg ± std	F-Measure avg ± std	Entropy avg ± std
false		**0,61 ± 0,051**	**0,662 ± 0,062**	**0,602 ± 0,047**	**0,845 ± 0,102**
Wordnet	add	0,634 ± 0,070	0,665 ± 0,051	0,626 ± 0,062	0,803 ± 0,125
Java ontology	add	0,651 ± 0,076	**0,685 ± 0,064**	**0,646 ± 0,061**	**0,745 ± 0,122**
Wordnet	only	0,630 ± 0,052	0,635 ± 0,051	0,610 ± 0,051	0,825 ± 0,093
Java ontology	only	**0,669 ± 0,041**	0,646 ± 0,026	0,637 ± 0,036	0,751 ± 0,085

frequencies. Purity values then reached 61.8%, thus yielding a relative improvement of 8.4% compared to the baseline.

Inverse Purity, F-Measure, Entropy on Reuters-21578 PRC-min15-max100. We observed that purity does not discount evaluation results when splitting up large categories. Therefore, we have investigated how inverse purity, F-measure and entropy would be affected for the best baseline (in terms of purity) and a typically good strategy based on background knowledge (again measured in terms of purity). Table 1 summarizes the results. It shows, e. g., that background knowledge is favored over the baseline by 51.4% over 47.9% wrt. F-measure, and showing similar relations for inverse purity and entropy.

4.3 Results on Java dataset

In order to assure that our observations do not depend on some specific structure of the Reuters dataset, we also performed our experiments on the Java dataset. The major results are shown in Table 2. They indeed back up our observations gained from the Reuters dataset, as the results on the Java dataset with Wordnet on one hand, and the domain specific ontology on the other hand are analogous to the results on the Reuters corpus. Additionally, we could make two more observations: (1) The amount of hypernyms that should be added depends on the size of the thesaurus: The java ontology is too small to derive worth from more than one level of generalization, HYPDEPTH=1 achieves the best

values. (2) An ontology tailored to the domain improves the clustering. The purity, for instance, increases by 1.7 points for the 'add' strategy, and by 3.9 points for the 'only' strategy. The other measures improved as well when using the domain specific ontology.

In this short paper, we could only briefly present the most significant results of our extensive evaluation. More details are given in [4].

References

[1] E. Agirre and G. Rigau. Word sense disambiguation using conceptual density. In *Proc. of COLING'96*, 1996.

[2] M. Gutschke. Kategorisierung von textuellen lernobjekten mit methoden des maschinellen lernens. Studienarbeit, Universität Hannover, Hannover, 2003.

[3] N. Henze. Towards open adaptive hypermedia. In *9. ABIS-Workshop 2001, im Rahmen der Workshopwoche "Lernen - Lehren - Wissen - Adaptivität" (LLWA 01)*, Dortmund, 2001.

[4] A. Hotho, S. Staab, and G. Stumme. Text clustering based on background knowledge. Technical Report 425, University of Karlsruhe, Institute AIFB, 2003. 36 pages.

[5] N. Ide and J. Véronis. Introduction to the special issue on word sense disambiguation: The state of the art. *Computational Linguistics*, 24(1):1–40, 1998.

[6] D. Lewis. Reuters-21578 text categorization test collection, 1997.

[7] G. Miller. WordNet: A lexical database for english. *CACM*, 38(11):39–41, 1995.

[8] M. Steinbach, G. Karypis, and V. Kumar. A comparison of document clustering techniques. In *KDD Workshop on Text Mining*, 2000.

The Hybrid Poisson Aspect Model for Personalized Shopping Recommendation

Chun-Nan Hsu
Institute of Information Science
Academia Sinica
Taipei, Taiwan
chunnan@iis.sinica.edu.tw

Hao-Hsiang Chung & Han-Shen Huang
Department of Computer Sci. & Info. Eng.
National Taiwan University
Taipei, Taiwan
{r89057,d5526013}@csie.ntu.edu.tw

Abstract

Predicting an individual customer's likelihood of purchasing a specific item forms the basis of many marketing activities, such as personalized shopping recommendation. Collaborative filtering and association rule mining can be applied to this problem, but in retail supermarkets, the problem becomes particularly challenging because of the sparsity and skewness of transaction data. This paper presents HyPAM (Hybrid Poisson Aspect Model), a new probabilistic graphical model that combines a Poisson mixture with a latent aspect class model to model customers' shopping behavior. We empirically compare HyPAM with two well-known recommenders, GroupLens (a correlation-based method), and IBM SmartPad (association rules and cosine similarity). Experimental results show that HyPAM outperforms the other recommenders by a large margin for two real-world retail supermarkets, ranking most of actual purchases in the top ten percent of the most likely purchased items. We also present a new visualization method, rank plot,to evaluate the quality of recommendations.

1. Introduction

This paper addresses the problem of predicting an individual customer's likelihood of purchasing a specific item in retail supermarket applications. The predicted likelihood forms the basis of many marketing activities, such as personalized shopping recommendation. We focus on a *collaborative filtering* [6] approach, where prediction is derived from historical transaction data. Transaction data may provide valuable clues. However, a customer usually only buys a very small subset of all items, and a large portion of sales is always concentrated on a very small portion of items. As a result, the transaction data are typically extremely *sparse* and *skewed*, making the problem challenging.

This paper presents HyPAM (Hybrid Poisson Aspect Model), a probabilistic graphical model designed to overcome data sparsity and skewness. Unlike previous work in collaborative filtering, HyPAM explicitly models customers' shopping behavior by assuming that customers can be clustered into groups based on their historical transaction data and that a latent *aspect* class [7] can relate customer groups with their likelihood of purchasing a given item. The model performs well in our experiment for two real-world retail supermarkets, and outperforms two well-known collaborative filtering recommenders, GroupLens [12], based on correlation, and IBM SmartPad [8], based on association rules and cosine similarity, by a large margin.

2. Hybrid Poisson Aspect Model

The goal of HyPAM is to predict the probability that a customer will purchase an item. HyPAM contains a cluster model, which is a Poisson mixture, to cluster customers into groups; and an aspect model [7], which has a multinomial latent variable to model the relationships between customer groups and items. Figure 1 shows the Bayesian network representation of HyPAM. In the dotted box is the cluster model and in the dashed box the aspect model.

A customer u_i is represented by a set of F random variables $(X_1, \ldots, X_F)$, where X_f is the random variable for the number of purchases of the f-th item in a given period of time. The cluster model partitions the customers into L clusters. $U^c = u_l^c$ denotes the event that the customer is in the l-th cluster. The distribution $P(X_f|u_l^c)$ is modeled by the *Poisson distribution*:

$$P(X_f|u_l^c) = P(X_f|\lambda_{lf}) = e^{-\lambda_{lf}} \frac{(\lambda_{lf})^{X_f}}{X_f!}, \quad (1)$$

where λ_{lf} is the expected number that the f-th item is purchased given that the customer belongs to cluster u_l^c. Therefore, $P(u_i|u_l^c)$, the probability that customer u_i belongs to cluster u_l^c, is:

$$P(u_i|u_l^c) = \prod_{\{f|x_{if} \neq 0\}} P(X_f = x_{if}|u_l^c). \quad (2)$$

0-7695-1978-4/03 $17.00 © 2003 IEEE

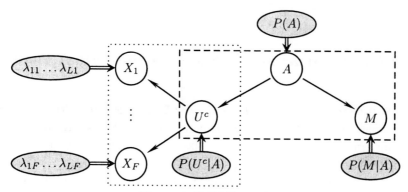

Figure 1. HyPAM and its parameters

The f-th item is treated as "unseen" instead of "uninterested" if $x_{if} = 0$ to prevent HyPAM from recommending only those items that are frequently purchased.

The aspect model partitions the co-occurrence data over $\mathcal{U}^c \times \mathcal{M}$ into K aspects, denoted by $a_1, \ldots, a_K$. The aspect model is inspired by [7] but we have customer clusters instead of individual customers to relate to items.

3. Training HyPAM

We apply the Expectation Maximization (EM) algorithm [5] to learn the parameters of HyPAM because of the hidden nodes U^c and A. Figure 1 shows all the parameters of HyPAM. Let D be the training data set, and $d^1, \ldots, d^N$ be the instances in D. Each d^n must have the form $(\mathbf{x}^n, m^n)_{1 \le n \le N}$, where N is the number of total transactions and m^n is the item. $\mathbf{x}^n = (x_1^n, \ldots, x_F^n)$ indicates the number of items that customer u_n have bought. In the E-step, we compute the distributions for a^n and u^{cn} to fill the missing values. The filled instance is of the form $\{d^n, a^n, u^{cn}\}$, for $n = 1, \ldots, N$. In the M-step, we re-estimate new parameters for HyPAM.

E-step : Let Θ be the current parameter set, and Θ' the set for the next iteration. E-step is to compute the probability $P(a^n = a_k, u^{cn} = u_l | \mathbf{x}^n, m^n; \Theta)$, that is:

$$\frac{P_\Theta(a_k) P_\Theta(u_l^c | a_k) P_\Theta(m^n | a_k) P_\Theta(\mathbf{x}^n | u_l)}{\sum_{k,l} P_\Theta(a_{k'}) P_\Theta(u_{l'}^c | a_{k'}) P_\Theta(m^n | a_{k'}) P_\Theta(\mathbf{x}^n | u_{l'})}, \quad (3)$$

where $P_\Theta(\mathbf{x}^n | u_l)$ can be estimated by Equation (2).

For the sake of conciseness, we will use p_{kl}^n to abbreviate $P(a^n = a_k, u^{cn} = u_l | \mathbf{x}^n, m^n; \Theta)$, p_k^n for $P(a^n = a_k, | \mathbf{x}^n, m^n; \Theta) = \sum_{l=1}^L p_{kl}^n$, and p_l^n for $P(u^{cn} = u_l | \mathbf{x}^n, m^n; \Theta) = \sum_{k=1}^K p_{kl}^n$.

M-step : M-step maximizes $Q(\Theta'; \Theta)$ to obtain the new parameters. $Q(\Theta'; \Theta)$ can be derived as follows:

$$Q(\Theta'; \Theta) = E[\log P(Z; \Theta') | D; \Theta]$$
$$= \sum_{n,k,l} p_{kl}^n \log P_{\Theta'}(\mathbf{x}^n | u_l^c) P_{\Theta'}(u_l^c | a_k) P_\Theta(a_k) P_\Theta(m^n | a_k).$$

Then, we compute the derivatives of every parameter to update Θ. Here are the results:

$$\lambda_{lf} = \frac{\sum\limits_{\{n | x_f^n > 0\}} p_l^n x_f^n}{\sum\limits_{\{n | x_f^n > 0\}} p_l^n}, \quad (4)$$

$$P_{\Theta'}(a_k) = \frac{1}{N} \sum_{n=1}^N \bar{q}_k^n, \quad (5)$$

$$P_{\Theta'}(u_l^c | a_k) = \frac{\sum\limits_{n=1}^N p_{kl}^n}{\sum\limits_{n=1}^N p_k^n}, \quad (6)$$

$$P_{\Theta'}(m_{j'} | a_k) = \frac{\sum\limits_{\{n | m^n = m_j\}} p_k^n}{\sum\limits_{n=1}^N p_k^n}. \quad (7)$$

4. Previous Work

Previous work in *collaborative filtering* [6] can be classified into *memory-based* and *model-based* [3]. In memory-based approaches, the whole transaction database is used in recommendation. For example, GroupLens [12] predicts customers' preference ratings by computing Pearson correlation coefficient. Model-based approaches learn an abstract model from data, and are queried subsequently for recommendations (see e.g., [2, 3, 4, 7, 11]). However, all these approaches require customers' preference ratings, rarely available in transaction data of retail supermarkets.

Another prevailing method is to "mine" association rules [1] of items and then used the rules for recommendation. Lawrence et al. [8] developed a sophisticated system based on association rule mining for IBM's SmartPad project. In this method, an item is represented by a vector, indicating the degree of association between this item and other items. Similarly, a customer is represented by a

Table 1. Experimental Results for Ta-Feng (top) and B&Q (bottom)

Algorithms	Given 2		Given 5		Given 10		All but 1	
	RS	LI	RS	LI	RS	LI	RS	LI
GroupLens	0.0285	0.836	0.0295	0.827	0.0302	0.812	0.0247	0.930
IBM	0.0639	0.709	0.0690	0.779	0.0671	0.774	0.0645	0.842
L10_K10	0.219	0.948	0.209	0.943	0.194	0.935	0.258	0.987
L10_K20	0.219	0.948	0.209	0.943	0.195	0.935	0.256	0.987
L20_K10	0.219	0.948	0.209	0.942	0.195	0.935	0.257	0.987
L20_K20	0.219	0.948	0.209	0.943	0.195	0.935	0.260	0.987

Algorithms	Given 2		Given 5		Given 10		All but 1	
	RS	LI	RS	LI	RS	LI	RS	LI
GroupLens	0.0163	0.763	0.0147	0.760	0.0150	0.753	0.0123	0.887
IBM	0.098	0.243	0.092	0.292	0.063	0.293	0.0131	0.390
L10_K10	0.243	0.978	0.251	0.979	0.262	0.975	0.179	0.979
L10_K20	0.243	0.978	0.251	0.979	0.262	0.975	0.179	0.978
L20_K10	0.243	0.978	0.251	0.979	0.262	0.975	0.179	0.978
L20_K20	0.243	0.978	0.251	0.979	0.262	0.976	0.179	0.979

RS: Rank Score   LI: Lift Index

vector, indicating this customer's preference toward those items. The vectors are prepared in advance from the mined association rules. The likelihood of purchasing an item for a customer is estimated by computing the cosine of the angle between the vector for the item and the vector for the customer. The IBM method and GroupLens will be compared with HyPAM in our experiment.

5. Experimental Evaluation

The data sets in our experiment are the courtesy of two large real-world retail supermarkets, Ta-Feng and B&Q . Ta-Feng is a membership retailer warehouse that sells a wide range of merchandise, from food and grocery to office supplies and furniture. The data set contains shopping records collected within four months, from November, 2000 to February, 2001. Unlike Ta-Feng, B&Q is a large international DIY home improvement and garden retailer chain. Our data set is provided by the largest B&Q store in Taipei. This data set contains the transaction data of the fourth quarter in 2001. Both data sets are very sparse and skewed [10].

We randomly select 15,000 customers as the training set, and another non-overlapping 1,000 customers as the test set. For the target customers in the test set, we apply *Given 2*, *Given 5*, *Given 10*, and *All but one* protocols [3] to choose given purchases. The performance is evaluated by *rank score* [3] and *lift index* [9], and visualized by *rank plot*.

Recommender systems based on HyPAM, GroupLens, and IBM method are trained with both data sets and tested with each protocol. We use four settings for U^c and A. Let L and K denote the number of states of U^c and A, respectively. For example, L20_K10 means a HyPAM model that

uses 20 clusters and 10 aspects. For GroupLens, we have to transfer the purchases to ratings. If a customer purchases r items, the rating is r for $0 < r \le 10$ and 10 if r exceeds ten. The IBM method requires association rules mined from the data sets in advance. The support and confidence thresholds [1] for Ta-Feng data set are 50 and 0.2, respectively and for B&Q data set are 25 and 0.1, respectively.

Table 1 shows the rank scores and lift index scores by the recommenders for Ta-Feng and B&Q data sets. HyPAM outperforms the other two recommenders by a large margin in all combinations of experimental setting. Both rank scores and lift index scores are not sensitive to the number of clusters and aspects of HyPAM, with almost identical results for all combinations.

These metrics, however, may yield discrepant results because the rank score favors a ranked list that predicts one or two items at the top accurately, while the lift index favors one with a better overall predictive accuracy. Hence, we use a new visualization method *rank plot* to visually compare the rank lists, as shown in Figure 2. Each actual purchase is presented by a spot at its position in the ranked list. The x-axis represents customer ID and the y-axis represents rank. The more the spots concentrate at the top, the better the ranked lists. As we can see, most of purchased items are ranked in the top ten percent of all items by HyPAM, which apparently outperforms the other two approaches.

6. Conclusion

HyPAM offers a general approach to personalized shopping recommendation by predicting the likelihood that a customer will purchase a given item. HyPAM combines the

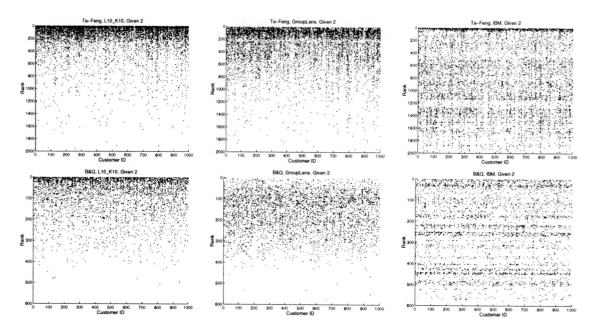

Figure 2. Rank plots for Ta-Feng (top) and B&Q (bottom) data sets by HyPAM L10_K10 (left), GroupLens (center) and IBM (right) with protocol Given 2.

cluster model and the aspect model to provide generalization for the customers and relations between customers and items. HyPAM uses the Poisson distribution to model the distribution of the purchases for an item given a customer cluster, in which the never-purchased items are regarded as "unseen" for the customers. These features are critical for handling skewed and sparse transaction data. The data sets and complete results are available for download at our website[1].

References

[1] R. Agrawal and R. Srikant. Fast algorithms for mining association rules. In *Proceedings of the 20th International Conference on Very Large Data Bases*, pages 487–499, 1994.

[2] D. Billsus and M. J. Pazzani. Learning collaborative information filters. In *Proceedings of the Fifteenth International Conference on Machine Learning*, pages 46–54, Jul 1998.

[3] J. S. Breese, D. Heckerman, and C. Kadie. Empirical analysis of predictive algorithms for collaborative filtering. In *Proceedings of the 14th Conference on Uncertainty in Artificial Intelligence*, pages 43–52, 1998.

[4] I. V. Cadez, P. Smyth, and H. Mannila. Probabilistic modeling of transaction data with applications to profiling, visualization, and prediction. In *Proceedings of the 7th ACM International Conference on Knowledge Discovery and Data Mining*, pages 37–46, 2001.

[5] A. Dempster, N. Laird, and D. Rubin. Maximum likelihood from incomplete data via the em algorithm. *Journal of the Royal statistical Society*, B39:1–37, 1977.

[6] D. Goldberg, D. Nichols, B. M. Oki, and D. Terry. Using collaborative filtering to weave an information tapestry. *Communications of the ACM*, 35(12):61–70, Dec 1992.

[7] T. Hofmann. Probabilistic latent semantic analysis. In *Proceedings of the 15th Conference on Uncertainty in Artificial Intelligence*, pages 289–296, 1999.

[8] R. D. Lawrence, G. S. Almasi, V. Kotlyar, M. S. Viveros, and S. Duri. Personalization of supermarket product recommendations. *Data Mining and Knowledge Discovery*, 5:11–32, 2001.

[9] C. Ling and C. Li. Data mining for direct marketing: Problems and solutions. In *Proceedings of the 4th International Conference on Knowledge Discovery and Data Mining*, pages 73–79, 1998.

[10] C. Hsu, H. Chung, and H. Huang. Data Mining Skewed and Sparse Transaction Data for Personalized Shopping Recommendation. Submitted for publication, 2003.

[11] A. Popescul, L. Ungar, D. Pennock, and S. Lawrence. Probabilistic models for unified collaborative and content-based recommendation in sparse-data environments. In *Proceedings of the Seventeenth Conference on Uncertainty in Artificial Intelligence*, pages 437–444, 2001.

[12] P. Resnick, N. Iacovou, M. Suchak, P. Bergstorm, and J. Riedl. GroupLens: An Open Architecture for Collaborative Filtering of Netnews. In *Proceedings of ACM Conference on Computer Supported Cooperative Work*, pages 175–186, 1994.

---

[1] http://chunnan.iis.sinica.edu.tw/hypam/HyPAM.html

Efficient Mining of Frequent Subgraphs in the Presence of Isomorphism

Jun Huan, Wei Wang, Jan Prins
Department of Computer Science
University of North Carolina, Chapel Hill
{huan, weiwang, prins}@cs.unc.edu

Abstract

Frequent subgraph mining is an active research topic in the data mining community. A graph is a general model to represent data and has been used in many domains like cheminformatics and bioinformatics. Mining patterns from graph databases is challenging since graph related operations, such as subgraph testing, generally have higher time complexity than the corresponding operations on itemsets, sequences, and trees, which have been studied extensively. In this paper, we propose a novel frequent subgraph mining algorithm: FFSM, which employs a vertical search scheme within an algebraic graph framework we have developed to reduce the number of redundant candidates proposed. Our empirical study on synthetic and real datasets demonstrates that FFSM achieves a substantial performance gain over the current start-of-the-art subgraph mining algorithm gSpan.

1. Introduction

Mining frequent patterns of semi-structured data such as trees and graphs has attracted much research interest because of its wide-range application areas such as bioinformatics and cheminformatics [1, 4], web log mining [10], video indexing [6], and efficient database indexing [2]. Given a set S of labeled graphs (referred to as a *graph database*), the *support* of an arbitrary graph g is the fraction of all graphs in S of which g is a subgraph [9, 8, 3]. Graph g is *frequent* if the support of g meets a certain support threshold (*minSupport*). The problem of *frequent subgraph mining* is to find all (connected) frequent subgraphs from a graph database.

At the core of any frequent subgraph mining algorithm are two computationally challenging problems 1) subgraph isomorphism: determining whether a given graph is a subgraph of another graph and 2) an efficient scheme to enumerate all frequent subgraphs. Generally the number of possible isomorphisms/subgraphs increases with the graph size, the graph complexity, and the number of graphs in

graph databases. To develop a solution that scales to complex graphs and large databases, it is imperative to focus on efficient frequent pattern enumeration and isomorphism test algorithms. This is the basic motivation for this work.

Several efficient subgraph mining algorithms have been proposed and a recent review is presented in [3]. The algorithms most closely related to our current effort are [9, 1].

In [9], a novel canonical form of graphs called DFS code and a novel data structure called *DFS code tree* are proposed. Involving a simple single-edge growth scheme and Ullman's subgraph matching algorithm, the preorder traversal of the DFS code tree enumerates all frequent connected subgraphs of a graph database.

In [1], a depth first scheme is proposed following the idea of the Eclat association mining algorithm [11]. Candidate graphs are proposed guided by information from sibling nodes.

Contributions We developed FFSM (**F**ast **F**requent **S**ubgraph **M**ining) targeting efficient subgraph testing and a better candidate subgraph enumeration scheme. The key features of our method are: (i) a novel graph canonical form and two efficient candidate proposing operations: FFSM-Join and FFSM-Extension, (ii) an algebraic graph framework (suboptimal CAM tree) to guarantee that all frequent subgraphs are enumerated unambiguously and (iii) completely avoiding subgraph isomorphism testing by maintaining an embedding set for each frequent subgraph.

Our experimental study shows that FFSM is competitive with gSpan on all inputs and outperforms gSpan by a factor of seven on a commonly studied chemical compound benchmark.

2. Mining Frequent Subgraphs

2.1. Canonical Adjacency Matrix

In FFSM, every graph is represented by an adjacency matrix M. Slightly different from the adjacency matrix used for an unlabeled graph, every diagonal entry of M is filled with the label of the corresponding node and every

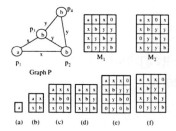

Figure 1. Top: A labeled graph P and two adjacency matrices for P. After applying the total ordering, we have $code(M_1) = $ "$axbxyb0yyb$" $\geq code(M_2) = $ "$axb0ybxyyb$". For an adjacency matrix M, each off-diagonal none-zero entry in the lower triangular part is referred to as an *edge entry*. All edge entries are ordered according to their relative positions in the code. For M_1, $m_{2,1}, m_{4,3}$, and $m_{4,2}$ are the first, last, second-to-last edge entries of M_1, respectively. $m_{4,4}$ is denoted as the last node of M_1. Bottom: examples of submatrices. Matrix (a) is the submatrix of matrix (b), which itself is the submatrix of (c) and so forth.

off-diagonal entry is filled with the label of the corresponding edge, or zero if there is no edge.

Given an $n \times n$ adjacency matrix M of a graph G with n nodes, we define the *code* of M, denoted by $code(M)$, as the sequence of lower triangular entries of M (including entries on the diagonal) in the order: $m_{1,1}m_{2,1}m_{2,2}...m_{n,1}m_{n,2}...m_{n,n-1}m_{n,n}$ where $m_{i,j}$ represents the entry at the ith row and jth column in M.

We use standard lexicographic order on sequences to define a total order of two arbitrary codes p and q. Given a graph G, its *canonical form* is the maximal code among all its possible codes. The adjacency matrix M which produces the canonical form is denoted as G's *canonical adjacency matrix* (CAM). For example, the adjacency matrix M_1 shown in Figure 1 is the CAM of the graph P in the same figure, and $code(M_1)$ is the canonical form of the graph.

Notice that we use maximal code rather than the minimal code used by [5, 4] in the above canonical form definition. This definition provides important properties for subgraph mining, as explained below.

Theorem 2.1 *Given a connected graph G and one of its subgraphs H, let G's CAM be A and H's CAM be B, then we have $code(A) \geq code(B)$.*

We define the *maximal proper submatrix* (submatrix in short) of an adjacency matrix M as the matrix obtained by removing the last edge entry e of M (also removing the symmetric entry of e in M and the resulting unconnected node, if applicable). For submatrices we have the following two corollaries:

Corollary 2.2 *Given a CAM M of a connected graph G*

and M's submatrix N, N represents a connected subgraph of G.

Corollary 2.3 *Given a connected graph G with CAM M, M's submatrix N, and a graph H which N represents, N is the CAM of H.*

Several examples of submatrices are given at the bottom of Figure 1. The formal proof of the theorem and corollaries are presented in [3] and omitted here due to space limitations.

If we let an empty matrix be the submatrix of any matrix with size 1, we can organize the CAMs of all connected subgraphs of a graph G into a rooted tree as follows: (i) The root of the tree is an empty matrix; (ii) Each node in the tree is a distinct connected subgraph of G, represented by its CAM; (iii) For a given none-root node (with CAM M), its parent is the graph represented by M's submatrix.

The tree obtained in this fashion is denoted as the *CAM tree* of the graph G.

2.2 Exploring the CAM Tree: Join, Extension and Suboptimal CAMs

The current methods for enumerating all the subgraphs might be classified into two categories: one is the join operation adopted by FSG and AGM [4, 5] and another one is the extension operation proposed by [1, 9]. The major concerns for the join operation are that a single join might produce multiple candidates and that a candidate might be redundantly proposed by many join operations [5]. The concern for the extension operation is to restrict the nodes that a newly introduced edge may attach to.

We list some of the key design challenges to achieve efficient subgraph enumeration:

(i) Can we design a join operation such that every distinct CAM is generated only once?

(ii) Can we improve the join operation such that only a few (say at most two) CAMs are generated from a single join operation?

(iii) Can we design an extension operation such that every edge might be attached to only one node in a graph represented by its CAM?

In order to tackle these challenges, we augment the CAM tree with a set of *suboptimal canonical adjacency matrices*, and introduce two new operations: FFSM-Join and FFSM-Extension.

Given two adjacency matrices M and N, we define a binary operation *join* which produces a set of matrices as the result of superimposing M and N. We define a unary operation *extension* on a matrix M to produce a set of matrices, each of which has one additional node v and one additional edge entry connecting v and the last node in M. Examples of the join and extension operations are given in Figure 2

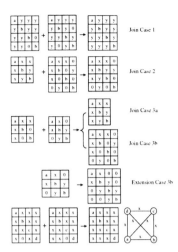

Figure 2. Examples of the join/extension operation

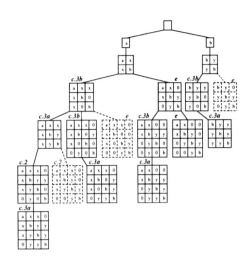

Figure 3. the Suboptimal CAM Tree for graph P in Figure 1. Matrices with solid boundary are CAMs and those with dash boundary are proper suboptimal CAMs. The label on top of each adjacency matrix M indicates the operation by which M might be proposed. A join operation is specified by a label **c.** and then the type of the operation (e.g. **c.3a** stands for join case3a). **e** specifies an extension operation.

(further details are given in [3]). At the bottom of Figure 2 we show a case in which a graph might be redundantly proposed by FSG $\binom{6}{2} = 15$ times (Joining any two distinct five-edge subgraphs G_1 and G_2 of the graph G will restore G by the join operation proposed by FSG). As shown in the graph, FFSM-Join completely removes the redundancy after "sorting" the subgraphs by their canonical forms.

Given a graph G, a *suboptimal canonical adjacency matrix (simply, suboptimal CAM)* of G is an adjacency matrix M of G such that its submatrix N is the CAM of the graph N represents. By definition, every CAM is a suboptimal CAM (by Corollary 2.3) and we denote a *proper suboptimal CAM* as a suboptimal CAM that itself is not a CAM.

Clearly, all suboptimal CAMs of a graph G could be organized as a tree in a similar way to the construction of the CAM tree. One such example for the graph in Figure 1 is shown in Figure 3. The suboptimal CAM tree is "complete" in the sense that all nodes could be enumerated by either a join operation or an extension operation. This is formally stated in the following theorem.

Theorem 2.4 *For a graph G, let $C_{k-1}(C_k)$ be the set of the suboptimal CAMs of all $(k-1)$-edge (k-edge) subgraphs of G ($k \geq 2$). Every member of C_k can be enumerated unambiguously either by joining two members of C_{k-1} or by extending a member in C_{k-1}.*

2.3. Embeddings of a Frequent Subgraph

Given a graph $G = (V, E, \Sigma, l)$ where Σ is a set of available labels and $l : V \cup E \to \Sigma$ is a function assign labels to vertices and edges [3], a node list $L = u_1, u_2, \ldots, u_n \subset V$ is *compatible* with an $n \times n$ adjacency matrix M iff: (i)$\forall$ $i, (m_{i,i} = l(u_i))$ and (ii)$\forall$ $i, j(i \neq j), (m_{i,j} \neq 0 \Rightarrow (m_{i,j} = l(u_i, u_j))$, where $0 < i, j \leq n$.

Given a suboptimal CAM M with size n, a graph G in a graph database GD, and a node list L of G compatible with M, an *embedding* o_M of M is a two-element tuple $o_M = (g_i, L)$ where g_i is the graph G's transaction id. The set of all possible embeddings of a suboptimal CAM is defined as its *embedding set*.

Given two suboptimal CAMs P and Q, and a suboptimal CAM $A \in join(P, Q)$, the relation between A's embedding set and those of P and Q can easily be established. For example, for join case 1, we have $O_A = O_P \cap O_Q$, where O_A, O_P, and O_Q are the embedding sets of suboptimal CAM A, P, and Q, respectively. For other join types/extensions, similar relations can be obtained with details given in [3].

FFSM

1: $S \leftarrow$ { the CAMs of the frequent nodes }
2: $P \leftarrow$ { the CAMs of the frequent edges }
3: FFSM-Explore(P, S);

FFSM-Explore (P, S)

1: **for** $X \in P$ **do**
2:     **if** ($X.isCAM$) **then**
3:         $S \leftarrow S \cup \{X\}, C \leftarrow \Phi$
4:         **for** $Y \in P$ **do**
5:             $C \leftarrow C \cup$ FFSM-Join(X, Y)
6:         **end for**
7:         $C \leftarrow C \cup$ FFSM-Extension(X)

```
8:      remove CAM(s) from $C$ that is either infrequent
        or not suboptimial
9:      FFSM-Explore($C$, $S$)
10: **end if**
11: **end for**
```

3. Experimental Study

We performed our experimental study using a single processor of a 2GHz Pentium Xeon with 512KB L2 cache and 2GB main memory, running RedHat Linux 7.3. The FFSM algorithm is implemented using the C++ programming language and compiled using g++ with O3 optimization. For gSpan, we used an executable kindly provided by Xifeng Yan and Jiawei Han for performance comparison purpose.

Chemical Compound Datasets We used a set of benchmark chemical compound datasets to evaluate the performance of the FFSM algorithm. The first two we used are from the DTP AIDS Antiviral Screen dataset from National Cancer Institute. In this dataset, chemicals are classified into three classes: confirmed active (**CA**), confirmed moderately active (**CM**) and confirmed inactive (**CI**) according to experimentally determined activities against AIDS virus. There are total 423, 1083, and 42115 chemicals in the three classes, respectively. For our own purposes, we formed two datasets consisting of all CA compounds and of all CM compounds and refer to them as DTP CA/DTP CM thereafter. The DTP datasets can be downloaded from *http://dtp.nci.nih.gov/docs/aids/aids_data.html*.

The third dataset we used is the Predicative Toxicology Evaluation Challenge (PTE) [7], which can be downloaded from *http://web.comlab.ox.ac.uk/oucl/research/areas/ machlearn/PTE/*. We follow exactly the same procedure described in [1, 9] for building graphs from all the above datasets.

Figure 4 shows the performance comparison between FFSM and gSpan, using various support thresholds for the DTP CM dataset. From the curve, we find that FFSM always outperforms gSpan by a factor up to seven. We observe a similar trend using DTP CA and PTE dataset and find a speedup of two fold and three fold, respectively [3].

Synthetic Datasets We also tested FFSM and gSpan on various synthetic graph datasets and found FFSM is always competitive with gSpan. Details are provided in [3].

4 Conclusions

We presented a new algorithm FFSM for the frequent subgraph mining problem. Comparing to existing algorithms, FFSM achieves substantial performance gain by efficiently handling the underlying subgraph isomorphism problem, which is a time-consuming step and by introducing two efficient subgraph enumeration operations, together with an algebraic graph framework developed for reduce the number of redundant candidates proposed. Performance

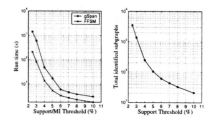

Figure 4. Left: FFSM and gSpan performance comparison under different support values for DTP CM dataset. Right: Total frequent pattern identified by the algorithms.

evaluation using various real datasets demonstrated a wide margin performance gain of FFSM over gSpan. The efficiency of FFSM is further confirmed using the synthetic datasets.

Acknowledgement We thank Mr. Michihiro Kuramochi and Dr. George Karypis in University of Minnesota for providing the synthetic data generator. We thank Mr. Xifeng Yan and Dr. Jiawei Han in University of Illinois at Urbana Champaign for providing the gSpan executable.

References

[1] C. Borgelt and M. R. Berhold. Mining molecular fragments: Finding relevant substructures of molecules. *In ICDM'02*.

[2] R. Goldman and J. Widom. Dataguides: Enabling query formulation and optimization in semistructured databases. *In VLDB'97*.

[3] J. Huan, W. Wang, and J. Prins. Efficient mining of frequent subgraph in the presence of isomorphism. *UNC computer science technique report TR03-021*, 2003.

[4] A. Inokuchi, T. Washio, and H. Motoda. An apriori-based algorithm for mining frequent substructures from graph data. *In PKDD'00*.

[5] M. Kuramochi and G. Karypis. Frequent subgraph discovery. *In ICDM'01*.

[6] K. Shearer, H. Bunks, and S. Venkatesh. Video indexing and similarity retrieval by largest common subgraph detection using decision trees. *Pattern Recognition*, 34(5):1075–91, 2001.

[7] A. Srinivasan, R. D. King, S. H. Muggleton, and M. Sternberg. The predictive toxicology evaluation challenge. *In Proc. of the 15th International Joint Conference on Artificial Intelligence (IJCAI)*, pages 1–6, 1997.

[8] N. Vanetik, E. Gudes, and E. Shimony. Computing frequent graph patterns from semi-structured data. *ICDM'02*, 2002.

[9] X. Yan and J. Han. gspan: Graph-based substructure pattern mining. *In ICDM'02*.

[10] M. J. Zaki. Efficiently mining frequent trees in a forest. *In SIGKDD'02*.

[11] M. J. Zaki, S. Parthasarathy, M. Ogihara, and W. Li. New algorithms for fast discovery of association rules. *In SIGKDD'97*.

Comparing Naive Bayes, Decision Trees, and SVM with AUC and Accuracy

Jin Huang   Jingjing Lu*   Charles X. Ling
Department of Computer Science
The University of Western Ontario
London, Ontario, Canada N6A 5B7
{jhuang, jlu, cling}@csd.uwo.ca

(* Research Visitor from Yan Cheng, Jiang Su Province, China)

Abstract

Predictive accuracy has often been used as the main and often only evaluation criterion for the predictive performance of classification or data mining algorithms. In recent years, the area under the ROC (Receiver Operating Characteristics) curve, or simply AUC, has been proposed as an alternative single-number measure for evaluating performance of learning algorithms. In our previous work, we proved that AUC is, in general, a better measure (defined precisely) than accuracy. Many popular data mining algorithms should then be re-evaluated in terms of AUC. For example, it is well accepted that Naive Bayes and decision trees are very similar in accuracy. How do they compare in AUC? Also, how does the recently developed SVM (Support Vector Machine) compare to traditional learning algorithms in accuracy and AUC? We will answer these questions in this paper. Our conclusions will provide important guidelines in data mining applications on real-world datasets.

1 Introduction

The predictive ability of a classification algorithm is typically measured by its predictive accuracy (or error rate, which is 1 minus the accuracy) on the testing examples. Most classifiers (including C4.5 and Naive Bayes) can also produce probability estimations or "confidence" of the class prediction. Unfortunately, this information is completely ignored in accuracy.

In recent years, the ROC (Receiver Operating Characteristics) curve [9, 5], which is plotted with the probability of the class prediction, has been introduced to evaluate performance of machine learning algorithms [19, 20]. Bradley [2] compared popular machine learning algorithms using AUC (area under the curve) of ROC, [1] and found that AUC ex-

hibits several desirable properties compared to accuracy. An additional benefit of AUC is that it is a way of measuring ranking, which is very useful in many data mining applications. However, no formal arguments or criteria were established for comparing the two measures. Recently, other researchers used AUC to construct learning algorithms [8, 15]. But it is not clear if and why AUC is a better measure than accuracy. In general, how can we compare any two evaluation measures for learning algorithms? How can we establish that one measure is "better" than another for any two measures?

In our recent work [14], we gave formal definitions on the (strict) consistency and discriminancy to compare any two measures. However, for AUC and accuracy, we found counter examples which show that AUC and accuracy are not strictly consistent, and AUC is not strictly discriminant than accuracy. We then extended the definitions to the degree of consistency and degree of discriminancy, and we defined that a measure is better than the other based on the degree of consistency and degree of discriminancy. Then we applied these definitions to AUC and accuracy, and verified empirically and proved theoretically that AUC is a better measure than accuracy. That is, AUC is indeed statistically consistent and more discriminant than accuracy. Details can be found in [14].

However, most previous work only focussed on comparing the learning algorithms in accuracy. A well-accepted conclusion in the machine learning community is that the popular decision tree learning algorithm C4.5 [21] and Naive Bayes are very similar in predictive accuracy [11, 12, 6]. How do popular learning algorithms, such as decision trees and Naive Bayes, compare in terms of the better measure AUC? How does recent Support Vector Machine (SVM) compare to traditional learning algorithms such as Naive Bayes and decision trees? In this paper, we will answer these questions experimentally.

---

[1] AUC of ROC is simply called AUC in our paper.

2 Empirical Comparison of Naive Bayes, Decision trees, and SVM

We first compare Naive Bayes and decision trees with AUC and accuracy in Section 2.1, and we then add SVM in our comparison in Section 2.2. This is because we only use binary datasets in comparisons with SVM (see Section 2.2 for details).

2.1 Comparing of Naive Bayes and Decision Trees

The popular decision tree learning algorithm C4.5 have been recently observed to produce poor probability estimations on AUC [22, 20, 18]. Several improvements have been proposed, and we want to include a recent improvement, C4.4 [18], in our comparison.

We conduct our experiments to compare Naive Bayes, C4.5, and its recent improvement C4.4, using both accuracy and AUC as the evaluation criterion. We use 18 datasets with a relatively large number of examples from the UCI repository [1].

Our experiments follow the procedure below:

1. The continuous attributes in all datasets are discretized by the entropy-based method described in [7].

2. For each dataset, create 10 pairs of training and testing sets with 10-fold cross-validation, and run Naive Bayes, C4.5, and C4.4 on the *same* training sets and test them on the *same* testing sets to obtain the testing accuracy and AUC scores.

The averaged results on accuracy are shown in Table 2.1, and on AUC in Table 2.1. As we can see from Table 2.1, the three algorithms have very similar predictive accuracy. The two tailed, paired t-test with 95% confidence level (same for other t-tests in the rest of the paper) shows that there is no statistical difference in accuracy between Naive Bayes and C4.4, Naive Bayes and C4.5, and C4.4 and C4.5. This verifies results of previous publications [11, 12, 6].

When we analyze the table for AUC (see Table 2.1), we get some very interesting and surprising results. The average predictive AUC score of Naive Bayes is slightly higher than that of C4.4, and much higher than that of C4.5. The paired t-test shows that the difference between Naive Bayes and C4.4 is not significant, but the difference between Naive Bayes and C4.5 is significant. (The difference between C4.4 and C4.5 is also significant, as observed by [18]). That is, Naive Bayes outperforms C4.5 in AUC with significant difference. This verifies our second hypothesis mentioned above.

This conclusion is quite significant to the machine learning and data mining community. Previous research concluded that Naive Bayes and C4.5 are very similar in pre-

Dataset	NB	C4.4	C4.5
breast	97.5±2.9	92.9±3.0	92.8±1.2
cars	86.4±3.7	88.9±4.0	85.1±3.8
credit	85.8±3.0	88.1±2.8	88.8±3.1
dermatology	98.4±1.9	94.0±3.5	94.0±4.2
echocardio	71.9±1.8	73.6±1.8	73.6±1.8
ecoli	96.7±2.2	96.4±3.1	95.5±3.9
glass	71.8±2.4	73.3±3.9	73.3±3.0
heart	80.8±7.3	78.9±7.6	81.2±5.6
hepatitis	83.0±6.2	81.3±4.4	84.02±4.0
import	96.1±3.9	100.0±0.0	100.0±0.0
iris	95.3±4.5	95.3±4.5	95.3±4.5
liver	62.3±5.7	60.5±4.8	61.1±4.9
mushroom	97.2±0.8	100.0±0.0	100.0±0.0
pima	71.4±5.8	71.9±7.1	71.7±6.8
solar	74.0±3.2	73.0±3.1	73.9±2.1
thyroid	95.7±1.1	96.0±1.1	96.6±1.1
voting	91.4±5.6	95.7±4.6	96.6±3.9
wine	98.9±2.4	95.0±4.9	95.5±5.1
Average	**86.4**	**86.4**	**86.6**

Table 1. Predictive accuracy values of Naive Bayes, C4.4, and C4.5

diction measured by accuracy [11, 12, 6]. As we have established in this paper, AUC is a better measure than accuracy. Further, our results show that Naive Bayes and C4.4 outperform the most popular decision tree algorithm C4.5 in terms of AUC. This indicates that Naive Bayes (and C4.4) should be favoured over C4.5 in machine learning and data mining applications, especially when ranking is important.

2.2 Comparing Naive Bayes, Decision Trees, and SVM

In this section we compare accuracy and AUC of Naive Bayes, C4.4, and C4.5 to the recently developed SVM on the datasets from the UCI repository. Such an extensive comparison with a large number of benchmark datasets is still rare [17]; most previous work limited to only a few comparisons, with the exception of [17]. SVM is essentially a binary classifier, and although extensions have been made to multiclass classification [23, 10] there is no consensus which is the best. Therefore, we take the 13 binary-class datasets from the 18 datasets in the experiments involving SVM. [17] also only used binary datasets for the classification for the same reason.

For SVM we use the software package LIBSVM [4] modified to directly output the evaluation of the hyperplane target function as scores for ranking. We used the Gaussian Kernel for all the experiments. The parameters C (penalty for misclassification) and gamma (function of the deviation of the Gaussian Kernel) were determined by searching for

Dataset	NB	C4.4	C4.5
breast	97.5±0.9	96.9±0.9	95.1±2.4
cars	92.8±3.3	94.1±3.2	91.4±3.5
credit	91.9±3.0	90.4±3.2	88.0±4.1
dermatology	98.6±0.1	97.5±1.1	94.6±3.3
echocardio	63.8±2.1	69.4±2.2	68.9±2.3
ecoli	97.0±1.1	97.0±1.0	94.3±3.6
glass	76.1±2.4	73.1±2.6	71.3±3.3
heart	82.7±6.1	80.1±7.8	76.2±7.0
hepatitis	76.5±4.4	62.9±8.2	59.2±6.8
import	91.7±4.5	94.4±2.0	95.1±2.6
iris	94.2±3.4	91.8±3.8	92.4±4.6
liver	61.5±5.9	59.6±5.7	60.5±5.0
mushroom	99.7±0.1	99.9±0.0	99.9±0.0
pima	75.9±4.2	73.4±7.3	72.4±7.4
solar	88.7±1.7	87.7±1.9	85.2±2.8
thyroid	94.9±1.8	94.3±2.6	92.1±5.5
voting	91.4±3.7	95.2±2.2	93.4±3.7
wine	95.3±1.8	94.4±1.2	91.6±4.0
Average	**87.2**	**86.2**	**84.5**

Table 2. Predictive AUC values of Naive Bayes, C4.4, and C4.5

the maximum accuracy in the two-dimensional grid formed by different values of C and gamma in the 3-fold cross-validation on the training set (so the testing set in the original 10-fold cross-validation is not used in tuning SVM). C was sampled at $2^{-5}, 2^{-3}, 2^{-1}, ..., 2^{15}$, and gamma at $2^{-15}, 2^{-13}, 2^{-11}, ..., 2^{3}$. Other parameters are set default values by the software. This experiment setting is similar to the one used in [17]. The experiment procedure is the same as discussed earlier.

The predictive accuracy and AUC of SVM on the testing sets of the 13 binary datasets are listed in Table 2.2. As we can see, the average predictive accuracy of SVM on the 13 binary datasets is 87.8%, and the average predictive AUC is 86.0%. From Table 2.1 we can obtain the average predictive accuracy of Naive Bayes, C4.4, and C4.5 on the 13 binary datasets is 85.9%, 86.5%, and 86.7%, respectively. Similarly, from Table 2.1 we can obtain the average predictive AUC of Naive Bayes, C4.4, and C4.5 on the 13 binary datasets is 86.0%, 85.2%, and 83.6%, respectively.

Some interesting conclusions can be drawn. First, the average predictive accuracy of SVM is slightly higher than other algorithms in comparison. However, the paired t-test shows that the difference is *not* statistically significant. Secondly, the average predictive AUC scores showed that SVM, Naive Bayes, and C4.4 are very similar. In fact, there is no statistical difference among them. However, SVM does have significantly higher AUC than C4.5, so does Naive Bayes and C4.4 (as observed in the early comparison in Section 2.1). Our results on SVM may be incon-

sistent with some other comparisons involving SVM which showed superiority of SVM over other learning algorithms [17, 13, 3]. We think that one major difference is data pre-processing: we have discretized all numerical attributes (see Section 2.1) as Naive Bayes requires all attributes to be discrete. Discretization is also an important pre-processing step in data mining [16]. The discretized attributes are named 1, 2, 3, and so on. Decision trees and Naive Bayes then take discrete attributes directly. For SVM, those values are taken as numerical attributes after normalization. In most previous comparisons, numerical attributes are used directly in SVM. However, we think that our comparisons are fair since all algorithms use the same training and testing datasets after discretization. If there is loss of information during discretization, the decision trees, Naive Bayes, and SVM would suffer equally from it. The other difference is that we did not seek for problem-specific, best kernels for SVM. This is fair as Naive Bayes, C4.5, and C4.4, are run automatically in the default, problem-independent parameter settings.

Dataset	Accuracy	AUC
breast	96.5±2.3	97.3±1.3
cars	97.0±1.3	98.6±0.4
credit	86.4±2.9	90.4±3.0
echocardio	73.6±1.8	71.5±2.0
ecoli	96.4±3.1	95.0±2.8
heart	79.7±8.2	82.1±8.3
hepatitis	85.8±4.2	64.2±8.7
import	100.0±0.0	93.8±0.6
liver	60.5±4.8	61.6±5.6
mushroom	99.9±0.1	99.9±0.0
pima	72.2±6.3	72.2±7.5
thyroid	96.7±1.3	95.8±3.3
voting	97.0±3.5	95.3±0.7
Average	**87.8**	**86.0**

Table 3. Predictive accuracy and AUC of SVM on the 13 binary datasets

To summarize, our extensive experiments in this section allows us to draw the following conclusions:

- The average predictive accuracy of the four learning algorithms compared: Naive Bayes, C4.5, C4.4, and SVM, are very similar. There is no statistical difference between them. The recent SVM does produce slightly higher average accuracy but the difference on the 13 binary datasets is not statistically significant.

- The average predictive AUC values of Naive Bayes, C4.4, and SVM are very similar (no statistical difference), and they are all higher with significant difference than C4.5.

Our conclusions will provide important guidelines in data mining applications on real-world datasets.

3 Conclusions

In our previous work, we proved that AUC is, in general, a better measure than accuracy. Many popular data mining algorithms should then be re-evaluated in terms of AUC. We compare experimentally Naive Bayes, C4.5, C4.4, and SVM in both accuracy and AUC, and conclude that they have very a similar predictive accuracy. In addition, Naive Bayes, C4.4, and SVM produce similar AUC scores, and they all outperform C4.5 in AUC with significant difference. Our conclusions will provide important guidelines in data mining applications on real-world datasets.

Acknowledgements

We gratefully thank Foster Provost for kindly providing us with the source codes of C4.4, which is a great help to us in the comparison of C4.5 and C4.4 to other algorithms. Jianning Wang, Dansi Qian, and Huajie Zhang also helped us at various stages of the experiments.

References

[1] C. Blake and C. Merz. UCI repository of machine learning databases. http://www.ics.uci.edu/~mlearn/MLRepository.html, 1998. University of California, Irvine, Dept. of Information and Computer Sciences.

[2] A. P. Bradley. The use of the area under the ROC curve in the evaluation of machine learning algorithms. *Pattern Recognition*, 30:1145–1159, 1997.

[3] M. Brown, W. Grundy, D. Lin, and N. C. et al. Knowledge-based analysis of microarray gene expression data using support vector machines. In *Proceedings of the National Academy of Sciences*, pages 262–267, 2000.

[4] C. C. Chang and C. Lin. Libsvm: A library for support vector machines (version 2.4), 2003.

[5] C.W.Therrien. *Decision Estimation and Classification: An Introduction to Pattern Recognition and Related Topics*. Wiley, New York, 1989.

[6] P. Domingos and M. Pazzani. Beyond independence: conditions for the optimality of the simple Bayesian classifier. In *Proceedings of the Thirteenth International Conference on Machine Learning*, pages 105 – 112, 1996.

[7] U. Fayyad and K. Irani. Multi-interval discretization of continuous-valued attributes for classification learning. In *Proceedings of Thirteenth International Joint Conference on Artificial Intelligence*, pages 1022–1027. Morgan Kaufmann, 1993.

[8] C. Ferri, P. A. Flach, and J. Hernandez-Orallo. Learning decision trees using the area under the ROC curve. In *Proceedings of the Nineteenth International Conference on Machine Learning (ICML 2002)*, pages 139–146, 2002.

[9] K. Fukunaga. *Introduction to Statistical Pattern Recognition*. Academic Press, second edition, 1990.

[10] C. Hsu and C. Lin. A comparison on methods for multiclass support vector machines. Technical report, Department of Computer Science and Information Engineering, National Taiwan University, Taipei, Taiwan, 2001.

[11] I. Kononenko. Comparison of inductive and naive Bayesian learning approaches to automatic knowledge acquisition. In B. Wielinga, editor, *Current Trends in Knowledge Acquisition*. IOS Press, 1990.

[12] P. Langley, W. Iba, and K. Thomas. An analysis of Bayesian classifiers. In *Proceedings of the Tenth National Conference of Artificial Intelligence*, pages 223–228. AAAI Press, 1992.

[13] Y. Lin. Support vector machines and the bayes rule in classification. *Data Mining and Knowledge Discovery*, 6(3):259–275, 2002.

[14] C. X. Ling, J. Huang, and H. Zhang. AUC: a statistically consistent and more discriminating measure than accuracy. In *Proceedings of 18th International Conference on Artificial Intelligence (IJCAI-2003)*, pages 329–341, 2003.

[15] C. X. Ling and H. Zhang. Toward Bayesian classifiers with accurate probabilities. In *Proceedings of the Sixth Pacific-Asia Conference on KDD*, pages 123–134. Springer, 2002.

[16] H. Liu, F. Hussain, C. L. Tan, and M. Dash. Discretization: An enabling technique. *Data Mining and Knowledge Discovery*, 6(4):393–423, 2002.

[17] D. Meyer, F. Leisch, and K. Hornik. Benchmarking support vector machines. Technical report, Vienna University of Economics and Business Administration, 2002.

[18] F. Provost and P. Domingos. Tree induction for probability-based ranking. *Machine Learning*, 2003. To appear.

[19] F. Provost and T. Fawcett. Analysis and visualization of classifier performance: comparison under imprecise class and cost distribution. In *Proceedings of the Third International Conference on Knowledge Discovery and Data Mining*, pages 43–48. AAAI Press, 1997.

[20] F. Provost, T. Fawcett, and R. Kohavi. The case against accuracy estimation for comparing induction algorithms. In *Proceedings of the Fifteenth International Conference on Machine Learning*, pages 445–453. Morgan Kaufmann, 1998.

[21] J. Quinlan. *C4.5: Programs for Machine Learning*. Morgan Kaufmann: San Mateo, CA, 1993.

[22] P. Smyth, A. Gray, and U. Fayyad. Retrofitting decision tree classifiers using kernel density estimation. In *Proceedings of the 12th International Conference on machine Learning*, pages 506–514, 1995.

[23] J. A. K. Suykens and J. Vandewalle. Multiclass least squares support vector machines. In *IJCNN'99 International Joint Conference on Neural Networks*, Washington, DC, 1999.

SVM Based Models for Predicting Foreign Currency Exchange Rates

Joarder Kamruzzaman
GSCIT, Monash University
Churchill, Victoria, Australia

Ruhul A Sarker
School of Computer Science
University of NSW, Canberra, Australia

Iftekhar Ahmad
GSCIT, Monash University
Churchill, Victoria, Australia

Abstract

Support vector machine (SVM) has appeared as a powerful tool for forecasting forex market and demonstrated better performance over other methods, e.g., neural network or ARIMA based model. SVM-based forecasting model necessitates the selection of appropriate kernel function and values of free parameters: regularization parameter and ε–insensitive loss function. In this paper, we investigate the effect of different kernel functions, namely, linear, polynomial, radial basis and spline on prediction error measured by several widely used performance metrics. The effect of regularization parameter is also studied. The prediction of six different foreign currency exchange rates against Australian dollar has been performed and analyzed. Some interesting results are presented.

1. Introduction

Exchange rate prediction is one of the challenging applications of modern time series forecasting and very important for the success of many businesses and financial institutions. The rates are inherently noisy, non-stationary and deterministically chaotic [12]. One general assumption is made in such cases is that the historical data incorporate all those behaviour. As a result, the historical data is the major input to the prediction process. There are several forecasting techniques available; those are developed mainly based on different assumptions, mathematical foundations and specific model parameters. However, for better result, it is important to find the appropriate technique for a given forecasting task.

For more than two decades, Box and Jenkins' Auto-Regressive Integrated Moving Average (ARIMA) technique [1] has been widely used for time series forecasting. However, ARIMA is a general univariate model and it is developed based on the assumption that the time series being forecasted are linear and stationary [2]. In recent years, Neural Networks has found useful applications in financial time-series analysis and forecasting [9], [11-14]. In several applications, Tang and Fishwich [9], Jhee and Lee [5], Wang and Leu [11], Hill *et al.* [4], Kamruzzaman and Sarker [6] and many other researchers have shown that ANNs perform better than ARIMA models, specifically, for more irregular series and for multiple-period-ahead forecasting. Zhang and Hu [14] analysed backpropagation neural networks' ability to forecast an exchange rate. Recently, Yao *et al.* [12] evaluated the capability of a backpropagation neural-network model as forecasting tool of Singapore forex market. Medeiros [8] proposed neuro-coefficient smooth transition autoregression to model and forecast monthly exchange rate time series. Zimmermann *et al.* [13] developed a neural network modelling to analyse the decisions and interaction of multiple agents to capture the price dynamics of multiple forex market. In [6], Kamruzzaman and Sarker investigated three

ANN based forecasting models using Standard Backpropagation, Scaled Conjugate Gradient and Backpropagation with Bayesian Regularization with six moving average technical indicators to predict six major currencies against Australian dollar. However, there are several disadvantages for NN based model: (i) dependency on a large number of parameters, e.g, network size, learning parameters and initial weight chosen, (ii) possibility of being trapped into local minima resulting in a very slow convergence, and (iii) over-fitting on training data resulting in poor generalization ability.

Recent research has been directed to Support Vector Machine (SVM) which has emerged as a new and powerful technique for learning from data and in particular for solving classification and regression problems with better performance [2], [3], [10]. Study in [7] with Australian forex data showed better forecasting of exchange rate by SVM based model compared to NN based model. The main advantage of SVM is its ability to minimize structural risk as opposed to empirical risk minimization as employed by the NN system. This paper reports a further investigation of the study in [6-7]. One aim of this paper is to investigate the effect of various kernel functions on predicting forex market. Forecasting performance is evaluated in term of five commonly used metrics measuring accuracy and upward/downward trend of the market. The effect of selecting free parameters of SVMs on prediction error is also investigated.

2. Support Vector Machine Regression Model

SVMs originate from Vapnik's statistical learning theory [10], and their major advantage over NN is that they formulate the regression problem as a quadratic optimization problem. SVMs perform by nonlinearly mapping the input data into a high dimensional feature space by means of a kernel function and then do the linear regression in the transformed space. The whole process results in nonlinear regression in the low-dimensional space.

Given a data set $G = \{(x_i, y_i)\}_{i=1}^{N}$ realizing some unknown function $g(x)$, we need to determine a function f that approximates $g(x)$, based on the knowledge of G as below.

$$f(x) = \sum_i \omega_i \phi_i(x) + b$$

where $\phi_i(x)$ are the features, coefficients ω_i and b have to be estimated from data. In SVM regression, Vapnik proposed the use of ε-insensitive loss function where error below is not penalized, ε being known *a priori*. Then the unknown coefficient is estimated by minimizing the following risk function.

$$R = C \frac{1}{N} \sum_{i=1}^{N} |y_i - f(x_i)|_\varepsilon + \frac{1}{2} \|\omega\|^2$$

The first term describes the ε-insensitive loss function and the second term is a measure of function flatness. The constant C>0 is a regularized constant determining the trade-off between the training error and model flatness. Using the slack variables ζ and ζ^*, the optimization problem solved by SVM under appropriate constraints depends on the finite number of parameters and has the following form.

$$f(x_i, \alpha_i, \alpha_i^*) = \sum_{i=1}^{N} (\alpha_i - \alpha_i^*) K(x, x_i) + b$$

$K(x, x_i)$ is called kernel function. Coefficients α, α^* are obtained by maximizing the following quadratic form:

$$W(\alpha, \alpha^*) = \sum_{i=1}^{N} y_i(\alpha_i - \alpha_i^*) - \varepsilon \sum_{i=1}^{N} (\alpha_i + \alpha_i^*) + \frac{1}{2} \sum_{i,j=1}^{N} (\alpha_i - \alpha_i^*)(\alpha_j - \alpha_j^*) K(x_i, x_j)$$

The constraints $0 \le \alpha_i^*, \alpha_j \le C$, $\sum_{i=1}^{N} (\alpha_i^* - \alpha_i) = 0$ and the above equations define the optimization problem. Only a number of coefficients satisfy $\alpha_i^* - \alpha_i \ne 0$ and the associated points to those coefficients are called support vectors.

Kernel Function: The value of the kernel function $K(x_i, x_j)$ is equal to the inner product of two vectors x_i and x_j in the feature space $\phi(x_i)$ and $\phi(x_j)$ satisfying Mercer's condition [3]. The kernel functions used in this study are the followings.

Linear : $K(x_i, x_j) = \langle x_i \cdot x_j \rangle$

Polynomial : $K(x_i, x_j) = (\langle x_i \cdot x_j \rangle + 1)^d$, d=degree

Radial Basis : $K(x_i, x_j) = \exp(-\|x_i - x_j\|^2 / 2\sigma^2)$, σ=width

Spline : $K(x_i, x_j) = 1 + \langle x_i \cdot x_j \rangle + (1/2) \langle x_i \cdot x_j \rangle \min(\langle x_i \cdot x_j \rangle)$
$- (1/6) \min(\langle x_i \cdot x_j \rangle)^3$

3. Forecasting Model and Evaluation

Technical and fundamental analyses are the two major financial forecasting methodologies. In recent times, technical analysis has drawn particular academic interest due to the increasing evidence that markets are less efficient than was originally thought. In this study, we used time delay moving average as technical data. The advantage of moving average is its tendency to smooth out some of the irregularity that exits between market days [12]. We used moving average values of past weeks to build SVM model to predict following week's rate. The indicators are MA5 (moving average on 5 days), MA10, MA20, MA60, MA120 and X_i, last week's closing rate. Exchange rate for the period $i+1$ is predicted. These six indicators are used as inputs to construct support vectors.

Forecasting performance of the above model is evaluated against six widely used statistical metrics [7], namely, Normalized Mean Square Error (NMSE), Mean Absolute Error (MAE), Directional Symmetry (DS), Correct Up trend (CU) and Correct Down trend (CD). NMSE and MAE measure the deviation between actual and forecasted value. Smaller values of these metrics indicate higher accuracy in forecasting. DS measures correctness in predicted directions. CU and CD measure the correctness of predicted upward

trend and downward trend, respectively. Higher values of DS, CU and CD indicate correctness in trend prediction. A detail formulation of these metrics are presented in [6].

4. Experimental Results and Analysis

In this study, we experimented with foreign currency exchange rate of US dollar, British Pound, Japanese Yen, Singapore dollar, New Zealand dollar and Swiss Franc against Australian dollar from January 1991 to July 2002. The available data was divided in training and test set. In total 565 weekly data was considered of which first 500 weekly data was used as training set and the remaining 56 weekly data as test set to evaluate the model. Since no analytical method is available to determine the most suitable kernel for a particular data set, kernel type is arbitrarily chosen by the user. We experimented with four different kernel functions, namely, linear, polynomial, radial basis and spline, on the same data set to investigate the effect of kernel type. Other aim of this study is to investigate the variation of performance with respect to regularization parameter C. In this experiment C was varied from a very small value (0.1) to very large value (10^5) and ε was arbitrarily chosen to be 10^{-3}.

In the first set of our experiment, NSME, MAE, DS, CU and CD were calculated using the forecast obtained by SVM and the available historical (/test) data over 35 weeks and 65 weeks, for each of six different currency rates against Australian dollars, using four different kernel functions (linear, polynomial, radial Basis, and spline). Figure 1(a)~(e) illustrates these performance metrics over 35 weeks and Figure 2(a)~(e) illustrates those over 65 weeks. As found in Fig. 1 & 2, no single kernel function dominates all currency prediction. This outcome encourages us to analyze each currency independently.

First of all, we consider JPY which is the most fluctuating currency. The actual exchange rate of JPY is much lower at the end compared to the beginning of the period with many sharp jumps and drops in between. Based on NSME and MAE, Spline kernel seems performing better though polynomial kernel looks also promising for NSME only. A plot of historical data shows that the actual end of period rates of other currencies are also lower, but not as low as JPY compared to their start rates. The gap between the start rates of USD and GBP is higher than their gap between the end rates. However the change in rates for both USD and GBP looks like slow but random fluctuation with no sharp up and down. Based on the predicted error, the linear kernel is the best for USD. On the other hand, the performances of linear and polynomial kernels are very close for GBP. The actual start rates of NZD and SGD are very close, and the CHF rate is lower than these two. The end rates of SGD and CHF are somewhat close, but the NZD rate is much higher than these two currencies. Interestingly, the rates of these three currencies are almost same for 30-40 weeks at the middle of the time horizon. These three rates favor polynomial kernel based on the predicted error. That means, the polynomial kernel can be recognized as the suitable kernel in predicting exchange rate for all currencies except US dollar in this experiment. This trend in predicted error over 35 weeks (Fig. 1(a)~(b)) is very much consistent with the same over 65 week prediction (Fig. 2(a)~(b)).

Figure 1(c)~(e) show that, in term of trend prediction, linear kernel is not clearly superior in any of the cases. With respect to directional change, Fig. 1(c) shows that radial basis kernel yields best result for JPY, NZD and CHF whereas polynomial kernel produces better result for USD and SGD. The maximum difference in term of correct directional changes produced by radial basis and polynomial kernel is about 2.8%. Fig. 1(d)~(e) show that radial basis and polynomial kernels performs equally in case of three currencies in term of CU and four currencies in term of CD. Similar trend is also observed for 65 weeks prediction as illustrated in Fig. 2(c)~(d). From the directional accuracy point of view, it appears that radial basis or polynomial would be a better choice of kernel function.

Based on all the performance metrics, there is no single winner for kernel function. This can not be a convincing conclusion for practitioners. Ideally, a SVM that minimizes the prediction errors while maximizing the coverage of directional matching would be the most attractive method. However, in practice, it may happen one of the following: 1) The minimum possible prediction errors but lower coverage of directional matching than one or more kernel functions, 2) The maximum possible directional accuracy but higher prediction errors than one or more kernel functions.

In addition, it could be more complicated when one prediction error is minimum and the other is not. Similar situation can be thought for the directional indicators too. The directional indicators check only the matching of trends in each every time unit/week irrespective of their deviations. Suppose the actual trend in a given week is upward and the forecast trend is also upward with a deviational error E_1. As per the deviational indicators, this is a 100% coverage/ success for the given week. Now suppose the forecast trend is downward with a deviational error E_2. That means there is no success (0%) in terms of deviational indicators. If $E_2 <$ E_1, the predicted error indicators would favour the later case. However, from the practical point of view, the forecast in the first case is still showing gain whereas the second case is showing loss. This is not a good situation for short term forecasting. In the long term forecasting, if the predicted error is minimum and the directional indicators are accurate for most time units, then the forecast can be accepted. In our case study, the coverage of DS, CU and CD is more than 80% for most cases and no one is less than 73%.

Although the polynomial kernel performs better than the other three kernels for most currencies considered in this study, we believe the kernel function should be chosen based on the pattern of individual currency rate. In other words, no single kernel is suitable for forecasting all currency rates.

Figure 3 (a)~(c) illustrates prediction error of Japanese Yen vs regularization error C with linear kernel. Fig. 3(a) shows that NMSE drops from 0.06 to 0.035 when C is increased from 0.5 to 50. For any value larger than 50, NMSE remains the same. MAE exhibits the similar behaviour in Fig. 3(b). Fig. 3(c) shows that DS varies from

75.4% to 83.0% when C is increased from 0.5 to 7.0, later DS remains 81.54% as C increases further. Similar behaviour is observed for other kernels also. This indicates little impact on variation of prediction error with respect to regularization parameter.

5. Conclusions

This paper investigates the performance of support vector machine for Australian forex forecasting in terms of kernel type and sensitivity of free parameters selection. In reducing total prediction error (MNSE and AME) polynomial kernel produced the best result while in predicting trend (DS, CU and CD) radial basis and polynomial kernel produced equally good results. In general radial basis and polynomial kernel appeared to be a better choice in forecasting forex market in this study. However, kernel function should be chosen based on the behavior of the pattern of historical rates of individual currency. Over a wide range of values for regularization parameter C, support vectors remain exactly the same and hence do not affect the performance at all, however, showed some sensitivity over a small range of value. Further improvement in performance may be achieved by selecting complex or mixed kernel function and is currently under investigation.

6. References

[1] G. E. P. Box and G. M. Jenkins, *Time Series Analysis: Forecasting and Control*, Holden-Day, San Francisco, CA.

[2] L. Cao and F. Tay, "Financial forecasting using support vector machines," *Neural Comput & Applic*, vol. 10, pp.184-192, 2001.

[3] T. Gestel *et. al.*, "Financial time series prediction using least squares support vector machines within the evidence framework," *IEEE trans. Neural Network*, vol. 12, no.4, 2001.

[4] T. Hill, M. O'Connor and W. Remus, "Neural network models for time series forecasts," *Management Science*, vol. 42, pp 1082-1092, 1996.

[5] W. C. Jhee and J. K. Lee, "Performance of neural networks in managerial forecasting," *Intelligent Systems in Accounting, Finance and Management*, vol. 2, pp 55-71, 1993.

[6] J. kamruzzaman and R. Sarker, "Forecasting of currency exchange rate: a case study," to appear in *Proc. IEEE International Conference on Neural Networks & Signal Processing (ICNNSP'03)*, Nanjing,, 2003.

[7] J. kamruzzaman and R. Sarker, "Application of support vector machine to Forex monitoring," submitted to 3rd Int. Conf.on Hybrid Intelligent Systems HIS03, Melbourne, 2003.

[8] C. Medeiros, A. Veiga and C. Pedreira, "Modeling exchange rates: smooth transitions, neural networks, and linear models," *IEEE Trans. Neural Networks*, vol. 12, no. 4, pp. 755-764, 2001.

[9] Z. Tang and P. A. Fishwich, "Back-Propagation neural nets as models for time series forecasting," *ORSA Journal on Computing*, vol. 5(4), pp 374-385, 1993.

[10] V. Vapnik, *Statistical Learning Theory*. New York: Wiley, 198.

[11] J. H.Wang and J. Y. Leu, "Stock market trend prediction using ARIMA-based neural networks," *Proc. of IEEE Int. Conf. on Neural Networks*, vol. 4, pp. 2160-2165, 1996.

[12] J. Yao and C.L. Tan, "A case study on using neural networks to perform technical forecasting of forex," *Neurocomputing*, vol. 34, pp. 79-98, 2000.

[13] H. Zimmermann, R. Neuneier and R. Grothmann, "Multi-agent modeling of multiple FX-markets by neural networks," *IEEE Trans. Neural Networks*, vol. 12, no. 4, pp. 735-743, 2001.

[14] G. Zhang and M. Y. Hu, "Neural network forecasting of the British Pound/US Dollar exchange rate," *OMEGA: Int. Journal of Management Science*, 26, pp 495-506, 1998.

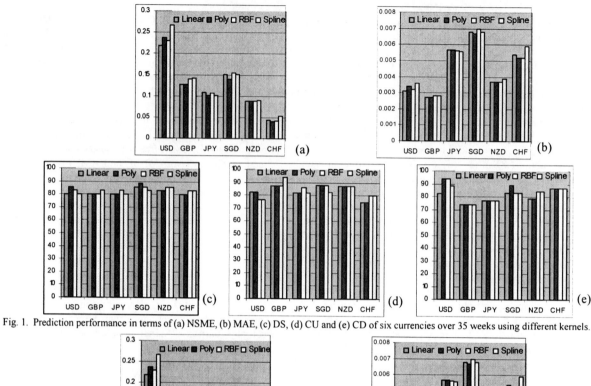

Fig. 1. Prediction performance in terms of (a) NSME, (b) MAE, (c) DS, (d) CU and (e) CD of six currencies over 35 weeks using different kernels.

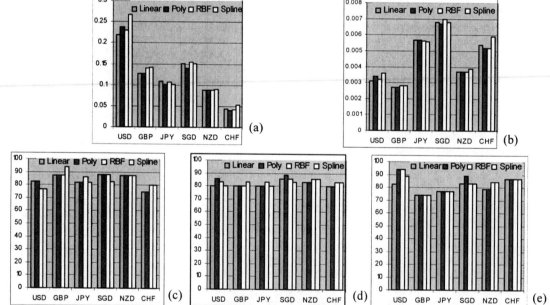

Fig. 2. Prediction performance in terms of (a) NSME, (b) MAE, (c) DS, (d) CU and (e) CD of six currencies over 65 weeks using different kernels.

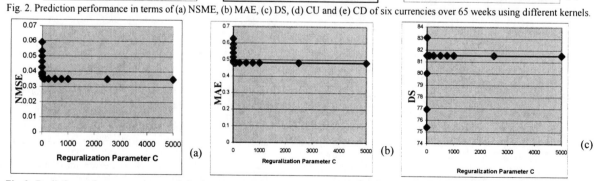

Fig. 3. Prediction performance versus regularization parameter C with linear kernel for predicting Japanese Yen exchange rate.

Facilitating Fuzzy Association Rules Mining by Using Multi-Objective Genetic Algorithms for Automated Clustering

Mehmet KAYA
Department of Computer Engineering
Fırat University
23119, Elazığ, Turkey
kaya@firat.edu.tr

Reda ALHAJJ
ADSA Lab, Department of Computer Science
University of Calgary
Calgary, Alberta, Canada
alhajj@cpsc.ucalgary.ca

Abstract

In this paper, we propose an automated clustering method based on multi-objective genetic algorithms (GA); the aim of this method is to automatically cluster values of a given quantitative attribute to obtain large number of large itemsets in low duration (time). We compare the proposed multi-objective GA-based approach with CURE-based approach. In addition to the autonomous specification of fuzzy sets, experimental results showed that the proposed automated clustering exhibits good performance over CURE-based approach in terms of runtime as well as the number of large itemsets and interesting association rules.

1. Introduction

An association rule is an implication $X \Rightarrow Y$, where both X and Y are sets of attributes or items; it is interpreted as: "for a specified fraction of the existing transactions, a particular value of X determines the value of Y as another particular value under a certain confidence". Support and confidence are the major factors in measuring the significance of an association rule. Simply, support is the percentage of transactions that contain both X and Y, while confidence is the ratio of the support of $X \cup Y$ to the support of X. So, the problem can be stated as: *find interesting association rules that satisfy user-specified minimum support and confidence.*

Quantitative association rules mining is essential because numerical attributes typically take many distinct values. The support for any particular value is likely low, while the support for intervals is much higher, e.g., [5, 6, 8]. However, existing quantitative mining algorithms either ignore or over-emphasize elements near the boundary of an interval. The use of sharp boundary intervals is also not intuitive with respect to human perception.

Some work has recently been done on the use of fuzzy sets in discovering association rules for quantitative attributes, e.g., [1, 4, 9, 10, 12]. However, in existing approaches fuzzy sets are either supplied by an expert or determined by applying an existing clustering algorithm. The former is not realistic, in general, because it is extremely hard for an expert to specify fuzzy sets. The latter approaches have not produced satisfactory results. They have not considered the optimization of membership functions; a user specifies the number of fuzzy sets and membership functions are tuned accordingly.

Motivated by this, we propose a clustering method that employs multi-objective GA for the automatic discovery of membership functions used in determining fuzzy quantitative association rules. Our approach optimizes the number of fuzzy sets and their ranges according to multi-objective criteria in a way to maximize the number of large itemsets with respect to a given minimum support value. So, we defined two objective parameters in terms of large itemsets and the time required to determine fuzzy sets. Actually, these two parameters are in conflict with each other. So, we use a GA with multiple objective optimization capabilities known as *Pareto GA* [11].

Experimental results on 100K transactions extracted from the adult data of United States census in year 2000 show the efficiency and effectiveness of the proposed approach. Also, we have demonstrated the superiority of the proposed approach, in terms of the number of produced large itemsets and interesting association rules, over semi-automated CURE clustering based approach [2].

The rest of this paper is organized as follows. Fuzzy quantitative association rule is defined in Section 2. Our approach of utilizing GA to determine membership functions is described in Section 3. Determining membership functions for CURE clustering is discussed in Section 4. The fuzzy association rules mining process is presented in Section 5. Experimental results are given in Section 6. Section 7 includes a summary and the conclusions.

2. Fuzzy Association Rules

Consider a database of transactions $T=\{t_1, t_2,...,t_n\}$, where each transaction t_j represents the j-th tuple in T. We use $I=\{i_1, i_2,...,i_m\}$ to represent all attributes that appear in T; each quantitative attribute i_k is associated with at least two fuzzy sets. The degree of membership of each value of attribute i_k in any of the fuzzy sets specified for i_k is directly based on the evaluation of the membership function of the particular fuzzy set with the value of i_k as input. The obtained value falls in the interval [0, 1], with the lower bound 0 strictly indicates "not a member", while the upper bound 1 indicates "total membership"; all other values between 0 and 1, exclusive, specify a "partial membership" degree. Finally, we use the following form for fuzzy association rules.

If $Q=\{u_1, u_2, ..., u_p\}$ is $F_1=\{ f_{1_1}, f_{1_2}, ..., f_{1_p} \}$ then

$R=\{v_1, v_2, ..., v_q\}$ is $F_2=\{ f_{2_1}, f_{2_2}, ..., f_{2_q} \}$, where $Q \subset I$ and $R \subset I$ are itemsets with $Q \cap R = \phi$, F_1 and F_2, respectively, contain the fuzzy sets associated with corresponding attributes in Q and R, i.e., f_{1i} is a fuzzy set related to attribute u_i and f_{2j} is related to attribute v_j.

Finally, for a rule to be interesting, it should have enough support and high confidence value. The basic step in the whole process is specifying corresponding fuzzy sets for each quantitative attribute. Our approach to automate this process is described next in Section 3.

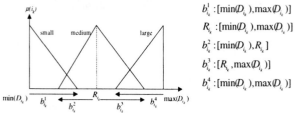

Figure 1 Membership functions and base variables of attribute i_k

3. Multi-Objective GA for Automated Clustering

In general a multi-objective optimization problem includes a set of a parameters (called decision variables), a set of b objective functions, and a set of c constraints; objective functions and constraints are functions of the decision variables. The optimization goal is expressed as:

$$\text{min/ max} \quad y = f(x) = (f_1(x), f_2(x),..., f_b(x))$$
$$\text{subject to} \quad e(x) = (e_1(x), e_2(x),..., e_c(x)) \le 0$$
$$\text{where} \quad x = (x_1, x_2,..., x_a) \in X$$
$$y = (y_1, y_2,..., y_b) \in Y$$

where, x is the decision vector, y is the objective vector, X is the decision space, and Y is the objective space; the constraints $e(x) \le 0$ determine the set of feasible solutions.

In this paper, we considered the number of large itemsets and the gain of time, inverse of the time required to find all large itemsets in a given database as objective functions. It is assumed that each of the n components of the objective vector is to be maximized. A solution defined by corresponding decision vector can be *better* than, *worse*, or *equal* to; but also *indifferent* from another solution with respect to the objective values. Here, *better* means a solution is at least better in one objective and not worse in any objective than another solution. Using this concept, an optimal solution can be defined as: *a solution not dominated by any other solution in the search space*. Such a solution is called *Pareto optimal*, and the entire set of optimal trade-offs is called *Pareto-optimal set* [11].

In our approach, each individual represents the base values of membership functions for a quantitative attribute from the given database. In our experiments, we used membership functions in triangular shape.

To illustrate the encoding scheme utilized in this study, consider a quantitative attribute, say i_k, having 3 fuzzy sets, the corresponding membership functions and their base variables are shown in Figure 1. Each base variable takes finite values. For instance, the search space of the base value

$b_{i_k}^1$ lies between the minimum and maximum values of attribute i_k, denoted $\min(D_{i_k})$ and $\max(D_{i_k})$, respectively. Enumerated next to Figure 1 are the search intervals of all the base values and the intersection point R_{i_k} of attribute i_k.

We used 8 quantitative attributes in the experiments of this study and assumed that each attribute can have at most 7 fuzzy sets. So, a chromosome consisting of the base lengths and the intersecting points is represented in the form:

$$w_{i_1}b_{i_1}^1b_{i_1}^{12}R_{i_1}^1b_{i_1}^2b_{i_1}^3R_{i_1}^2b_{i_1}^4b_{i_1}^5R_{i_1}^3b_{i_1}^6b_{i_1}^7R_{i_1}^4b_{i_1}^8b_{i_1}^9R_{i_1}^5b_{i_1}^{10}b_{i_1}^{11}...w_{i_8}b_{i_8}^1b_{i_8}^{12}...R_{i_8}^5b_{i_8}^{10}b_{i_8}^{11}$$

where gene w_{i_j} denotes the number of fuzzy sets for attributes i_j. If the number of fuzzy set is 2, then while decoding the individual, the first two base variables are considered and the others are omitted. However, if w_{i_j} is 3, then the next three variables are also taken into account. So, as long as the number of fuzzy set increases, the number of variables to be taken into account is enhanced too.

According to this encoding method, the number of variables needed to be found for each attribute can be generalized as $3(w-2)+2$, where w be the number of fuzzy sets for a given attribute. For instance, two variables need to be tuned for a quantitative attribute with $w=2$ fuzzy sets; and for the case of $w=3$ fuzzy sets, the number of variables to be tuned increases to 5, as illustrated by the above example.

In this study, we used real-valued coding, where chromosomes are represented as floating point numbers and their genes are the real parameters. While the value of a gene is reflected under its own search interval, the following formula is employed:

$$b_{i_j}^k = \min(b_{i_j}^k) + \frac{g}{g_{max}}(\max(b_{i_j}^k) - \min(b_{i_j}^k))$$

where g is the value of the gene in search, g_{max} is the maximum value that gene g may take, $\min(b_{i_j}^k)$ and $\max(b_{i_j}^k)$ are the minimum and the maximum values of the reflected area, respectively. Also, we used Pareto-based ranking procedure, where the rank of an individual is the number of solutions encoded in the population by which its corresponding decision vector is dominated, as illustrated in Figure 2. Note that Pareto-based techniques seem to be most popular and effective in the field of evolutionary multi-objective optimization.

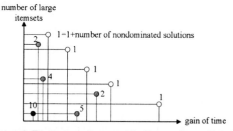

Figure 2 Fitness assignment in Pareto-based ranking

Individuals who are strong according to parent selection policy are candidates to form a new population. Many selection procedures are currently in use. However, we adapted the *elitism* policy in our experiments. Finally, after selecting chromosomes with respect to the evaluation function, genetic operators such as, crossover and mutation, are applied to these individuals.

Crossover takes as input 2 individuals, selects a random point, and exchanges the subindividuals behind the selected point to form new individuals. Since the length of the chromosomes is considerably large in our approach, we used the multi-point crossover strategy with the crossover points determined randomly. On the other hand, mutation means a random change in the information of an individual. It is traditionally performed in order to increase the diversity of the genetic information. A probability test depends on the following condition to determine whether a mutation will be carried out or not.

4. Specifying Membership Functions for CURE

The process of CURE can be summarized as follows. Starting with individual values as individual clusters, at each step the closest pair of clusters are merged to form a new cluster. This is repeated until only k clusters are left. As a result, the values of each attribute in the database are distributed into k clusters. The centroids of the k clusters are the set of midpoints of the fuzzy sets for the corresponding attribute. Here, note that in the process to obtain the membership functions by CURE clustering algorithm, the number of clusters, i.e., number of fuzzy sets should be given by the user beforehand. To overcome this restriction, we integrated a GA with CURE clustering approach.

A GA finds the most appropriate number of clusters according to a predefined fitness function. In the GA process used in this study, each variable holds the number of fuzzy sets only. This is because CURE clustering algorithm itself adjusts the base value of the membership functions.

5. Mining Fuzzy Association Rules

To generate fuzzy association rules, all sets of items that have a support above a user specified threshold should be determined first. Itemsets with at least a minimum support are called frequent or large itemsets. The process alternates between the generation of candidate and frequent itemsets until all large itemsets are identified. The following formula is used to calculate the fuzzy support value of itemset Z and its corresponding set of fuzzy sets F, denoted $S_{<Z,F>}$:

$$S_{<Z,F>} = \frac{\sum_{t_i \in T} \prod_{z_j \in Z} \mu_{z_j}(f_j \in F, t_i[z_j])}{|T|},$$ where $|T|$ denotes the

number of transactions in database T.

This way, the problem of mining all fuzzy association rules converts to generating each rule whose confidence is larger than the user specified minimum confidence. Explicitly, each large itemset, say L, is used in deriving all association rules $(L-S) \Rightarrow S$, for each $S \subset L$. The strong association rules discovered are chosen from among all the generated possible association rules by considering only rules with confidence over a pre-specified minimum confidence. However, not all of these rules are interesting enough to be presented to the user. Whether a rule is interesting or not can be judged either subjectively or objectively. Ultimately, only the user can judge if a given rule is interesting or not, and this judgment, being subjective, may differ from one user to another. However, objective interestingness criterion based on the statistics behind the data can be used as one step towards the goal of weeding out presenting uninteresting rules to the user. To help filtering out misleading strong association rules and to give each rule a more precise characterization, the interestingness of a rule $Q \Rightarrow R$, denoted $I(Q \Rightarrow R)$, is defined as: $I(Q \Rightarrow R) = \frac{S(Q,R)}{S(Q)S(R)}$

A rule is filtered out if its interestingness is less than 1, since the nominator is the actual likelihood of both Q and R being present together and the denominator is the likelihood of having the two attributes being independent. This process will help in returning only rules having positive interestingness, and hence the size of the result is reduced.

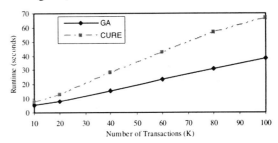

Figure 3 The runtime required to find all large itemsets

6. Experimental Results

We conducted some experiments to demonstrate the effectiveness of the proposed multi-objective GA-based clustering method. Further, the superiority of the new approach has been demonstrated by a comparison with CURE clustering based approach. All of the experiments have been conducted on a Pentium III, 1.4 GHz CPU with 512 MB of memory and running Windows 2000. As experiment data, we used 100K transactions from the adult data of United States census in 2000; we concentrated our analysis on 8 quantitative attributes. Further, in all the experiments, the GA process started with a population of 80 individuals for the GA-based approach and 30 individuals for the CURE-based approach. The maximum number of generations has been fixed at 500 as the termination criteria for the developed GA programs. Finally, in all the experiments in which GA have been used, the minimum support is set to 10%, unless otherwise specified, and the maximum number of fuzzy sets has been specified as 7.

The first experiment compares the runtime of the two clustering approaches to find large itemsets for different numbers of transactions, varying from 10K to 100K. The runtime here represents the duration, i.e., the time required to find all large itemsets after the number and ranges for the fuzzy sets have been determined by employing the corresponding method. The results are reported in Figure 3, where the two approaches are labeled as GA and CURE, to represent the proposed multi-objective GA-based clustering approach and CURE clustering based approach, respectively.

The former approach employs multi-objective GA to decide on the number of fuzzy sets as well as to optimize the ranges of membership functions, while the latter uses GA only to find the number of fuzzy sets. As a result of this experiment, it has been observed that the GA-based solution outperforms the CURE-based solution for all numbers of transactions, and both methods are scalable on the number of transactions.

The second experiment compares the total runtime required for both methods to find optimum fuzzy sets for different numbers of transactions. The results are reported in Figure 4, which demonstrates that both approaches scale well on the number of transactions. Extra runtime in the proposed method is spent on optimizing membership functions.

The third experiment utilized all the 100K transactions to compare the change in the number of large itemsets for different values of minimum support. The results are reported by the curves plotted in Figure 5, where it can be easily observed that the GA-based approach finds larger number of large itemsets than CURE based approach; this is quite consistent with our intuition, simply because the GA-based approach puts more effort on the optimization process and this has been reflected into finding better results than classical clustering approaches, like CURE.

The last experiment investigates the correlation between minimum confidence and the number of interesting association rules discovered. The results are plotted in Figure 6; the same interpretation stated for the curves of the large itemsets experiments is valid and can be repeated here.

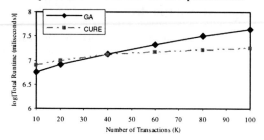

Figure 4 Total runtime required to find optimum fuzzy sets

7. Summary and Conclusions

In this paper, we proposed a multi-objective GA based clustering method, which automatically adjusts the fuzzy sets to provide large number of large itemsets in low duration. This is achieved by tuning together, for each quantitative attribute, the number of fuzzy sets and the base values of the membership functions. In addition, we demonstrated through experiments that using multi-objective GA has 3 important advantages over CURE. First, the number of clusters for each quantitative attribute is determined automatically. Thus, we implemented an autonomous structure for mining fuzzy association rules. Second, the GA-based approach optimizes membership functions of quantitative attributes for a given minimum support value. So, it is possible to obtain more appropriate solutions by changing the minimum support value in the desired direction. Finally, the number of large itemsets and interesting association rules obtained using the

GA-based approach are larger than those obtained by applying CURE. As a result, all these advantages show that multi-objective GA is more appropriate and can be used more effectively to achieve optimal solutions than the classical clustering algorithms described in the literature.

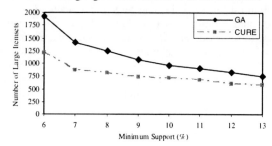

Figure 5 Number of large itemsets found

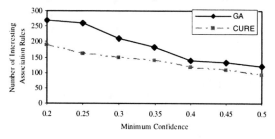

Figure 6 Number of association rules found

References

[1] K.C.C. Chan and W.H. Au, "Mining Fuzzy Association Rules," *Proc. of ACM CIKM,* pp.209-215, 1997.
[2] S. Guha, R. Rastogi and K. Shim, "CURE: An Efficient Clustering Algorithm for Large Databases," *Information Systems,* Vol.26, No.1, pp.35-58, 2001.
[3] J.H. Holland, Adaptation in Natural and Artificial Systems, The MIT Press, Cambridge, MA, MIT Press edition, 1992.
[4] T.P. Hong, C.S. Kuo and S.C. Chi, "Mining Association Rules from Quantitative Data," *Intelligent Data Analysis,* Vol.3, pp.363-376, 1999.
[5] B. Lent, A. Swami and J. Widom, "Clustering Association Rules," *Proc. of IEEE ICDE,* pp.220-231, 1997.
[6] R.J. Miller and Y. Yang, "Association Rules over Interval Data," *Proc. of the ACM SIGMOD,* pp.452-461, 1997.
[7] R. Ng and J. Han. "Efficient and effective clustering methods for spatial data mining," *Proc. of VLDB,* 1994.
[8] R. Srikant and R. Agrawal. "Mining Quantitative Association Rules in Large Relational Tables," *Proc. of ACM SIGMOD,* pp.1-12, 1996.
[9] R.R. Yager, "Fuzzy Summaries in Database Mining," *Proc. of Artificial Intelligence for Application,* pp.265-269, 1995.
[10] W. Zhang, "Mining Fuzzy Quantitative Association Rules," *Proc. of IEEE ICTAI,* pp.99-102, 1999.
[11] E. Zitzler and L. Thiele, "Multi-objective Evolutionary Algorithms: A Comparative Case Study and the Strength Pareto Approach," *IEEE TEC,* Vol.3, pp.257-271, 1999.
[12] M. Kaya, R. Alhajj, F. Polat and A. Arslan, "Efficient Automated Mining of Fuzzy Association Rules," *Proc. of DEXA,* 2002.

PixelMaps: A New Visual Data Mining Approach for Analyzing Large Spatial Data Sets

Daniel A. Keim, Christian Panse, Mike Sips
University of Konstanz, Germany
{keim, panse, sips}@informatik.uni-konstanz.de

Stephen C. North
AT&T Shannon Laboratory, Florham Park, NJ, USA
north@research.att.com

Abstract

PixelMaps *are a new pixel-oriented visual data mining technique for large spatial datasets. They combine kernel-density-based clustering with pixel-oriented displays to emphasize clusters while avoiding overlap in locally dense point sets on maps. Because a full evaluation of density functions is prohibitively expensive, we also propose an efficient approximation,* **Fast-PixelMap**, *based on a synthesis of the quadtree and gridfile data structures.*

1 Introduction

Progress in technology now allows computer systems to store and exchange datasets that were, until recently, considered extraordinarily vast. Almost all transactions of everyday life (purchases made with credit cards, web pages visited, and telephone calls made) are recorded by computers. This data is collected because of its potential to provide a competitive advantage to its holders. Finding valuable details that reveal fine structures hidden in the data, however, is difficult.

In many application domains, data is collected and referenced by its geo-spatial location. Consider, for example, a credit card purchase transaction record that describes products, quantities, time, and addresses of both the customer and merchant. There are many ways of approaching analysis of this data, including creating statistical models, clustering, and finding association rules, but often it is just as important to find relationships involving geographic location.

Automated data mining algorithms are indispensable for analyzing large geo-spatial data sets, but often fall short of completely satisfactory results. Although automatic approaches have been developed for mining geo-spatial data

[3], they are often no better than simple visualizations of the data on a map. Interactive data mining based on a synthesis of automatic and visual data mining may not only yield better results, but offer a higher degree of user satisfaction and confidence in the findings [3]. Presenting data in an interactive, graphical form often fosters new insights, encouraging the formation and validation of new hypotheses to the end of better problem-solving and gaining deeper domain knowledge. Analysis may involve multiple parameters, shown on multiple maps. If all maps in such a collection show the data in the same way, it may be easier to relate the parameters and to detect local correlations, dependencies, and other interesting patterns. On the other hand, when large data sets are drawn on maps, the problem of identifying local patterns is greatly confounded by undesired overlap of data points in densely populated areas, while lightly populated areas are almost empty.

Previous Approaches There are several approaches to coping with dense geographic data already in common use. One popular method is a 2.5D visualization showing data points aggregated up to map regions. This technique is commercially available in systems such as VisualInsight's In3D [1] and ESRI's ArcView [2]. Another approach, showing more detail, is the visualization of individual data points as bars on a map. This technique is embodied in systems such as SGI's MineSet [5] and AT&T's Swift 3D [6]. An alternative that does not aggregate data, and still avoids overlap in the two-dimensional display, is the Gridfit method [7]. The idea of Gridfit is to automatically reposition pixels that would overlap, an idea we also adopt in this contribution.

Our Approach In this paper we describe PixelMaps, a new approach to the display of dense point sets on maps, which combines clustering and visualization. PixelMaps are novel in several ways: First, they provide a new tool for exploratory data analysis with large point sets on maps, and thus augment the flexibility, creativity, and domain knowledge of human data analysts. Second, they combine advanced clustering algorithms with pixel-oriented visualization, and thus exploit the computational and graphics capabilities of current computer systems.

2 Problem Definition

The problem of visualizing geo-spatial data can be described as a mapping of input data points, with their original positions and associated statistical data values, to unique positions on an output map. Let A be the set of original data points $A = \{a_0, \ldots, a_{N-1}\}$, where $a_i = (a_i^x, a_i^y)$ is the original position of a data point, and $S_1(a_i), \ldots, S_k(a_i)$ are statistical parameters associated with a point. Since A is assumed to be large, it is likely that many data points i and j have the same original positions, i.e. $a_i = a_j$. Let the data display space DS be defined as $DS = \{0, \ldots, x_{max} - 1\} \times \{0, \ldots, y_{max} - 1\}$, where x_{max} and y_{max} are the extents of the display region. Our goal is to determine a mapping function f from the original data set to a solution set $B = \{b_0, \ldots, b_{N-1}\}$, $0 \leq b_i^x \leq x_{max} - 1$, $0 \leq b_i^y \leq y_{max} - 1$ such that $f : A \to B$, $f(a_i) = b_i$ $\forall i = \{0, \ldots, N-1\}$, i.e. f determines the new position b_i of a_i. The mapping function must satisfy three constraints:

1. **No overlap Constraint**

    The first and most important constraint is that all data points must be visible, which means that each one must be assigned to a unique position. Formally, this means
    $$i \neq j \Rightarrow b_i \neq b_j \quad \forall i, j \in \{1, \ldots, N-1\}$$

2. **Position Preservation Constraint**

    The second constraint is that the new positions should be as close as possible to the original ones. We measure this objective by summing the absolute distances of the data points from their original positions $\sum_{i=0}^{N-1} d(a_i, b_i) \longrightarrow min$ or the relative distances between the data points $\sum_{i=0}^{N-1} \sum_{j=0, i \neq j}^{N-1} (d(b_i, b_j) - d(a_i, a_j))^2 \longrightarrow min$. The distance function d can be defined by a L^m-norm ($m = 1$ or $m = 2$). This constraint ensures that the display closely represents the original data. The specific data analysis task at hand probably determines whether an absolute or relative metric is more suitable.

3. **Clustering Constraint**

    The third constraint involves clustering on one of the statistical attributes $S_i, i \in \{0, \ldots, k\}$. The idea is to present the data points such that those with high similarity in S_i are close to each other[1]. In other words, points in a neighborhood of any given

    ---
    [1] We assume that the clustering depends on the statistical attribute $S \in \{S_0, \ldots, S_k\}$.

data point should have similar values, so the output has pixel coherence. This can be expressed as: $\sum_{i=0}^{N-1} \sum_{b_j \in \mathcal{NH}(b_i)} d_S(S(b_i), S(b_j)) \longrightarrow min$. Note that this depends on the definition of the neighborhood $\mathcal{NH}$ of data points a_i, and the distance function d_S on the statistical attribute S.

Trade-Offs and Complexity While it is not too hard to find a good solution for any of these three constraints taken individually, they are difficult to optimize simultaneously. Since we give priority to constraint 1 (no overlap), the other two constraints often conflict. If constraint 2 is optimized, the location information is retained as much as possible but there may be little pixel coherence in the display. If constraint 3 is satisfied, the data is clustered according to S but the location information may be destroyed. Therefore, our goal is to find a good trade-off between constraints 2 and 3. This is a complex optimization problem that is likely to be NP-hard.

3 The PixelMap Algorithm

In this section, we describe an algorithm for making PixelMaps by optimizing the objectives described previously. The PixelMap algorithm solves the optimization problem by kernel density estimation and an iterative local repositioning scheme. It starts by computing a kernel-density-estimation-based clustering in the three dimensions $(a_i^x, a_i^y, S(a_i))$. Kernel density is a way of estimating the density of a statistical value $(S(a_i))$ at all locations in a region based on (a_i^x, a_i^y). The clustering defines sets of related pixels determined by the two spatial dimensions and the additional statistical parameter. The idea is to place all data points belonging to the same cluster in proximate display pixels. The next step is a second kernel density estimation based clustering on the two geographical dimensions (a_i^x, a_i^y). The information obtained in the two clustering steps is used for iterative positioning of the data points. Starting with the densest region, all data points belonging to one cluster are placed at neighboring pixels without overwriting previously placed ones. If multiple clusters are in the same area, the smallest cluster is positioned first. After all pixels in an area are positioned, the algorithm applies the same procedure to the clusters of the next densest region, until all the data points are positioned. Outliers and very small clusters, which would otherwise be treated as noise, are at last positioned at the remaining free pixels.

Complexity of the PixelMap Algorithm. Since our goal is to cluster many points locally according to a statistical parameter, we must anticipate a large number ($O(n)$) of relatively small clusters. This requires the kernel density estimation to be computed at a fine grain, with many peaks that must be discovered (such as by hill-climbing). In addition, the smoothness (σ) of the kernel function needs to vary with spatial density, and different kernel functions are needed for the spatial and statistical dimensions. These problems make it computationally prohibitive to directly implement the PixelMap algorithm for large data sets.

4 Fast-PixelMap - An Efficient Solution of the PixelMap Problem

The basic idea of Fast-PixelMap is to rescale certain map regions to better fit dense point clouds to unique positions on the output map. The *Fast-PixelMap*-algorithm is an efficient heuristic approximation to the *PixelMap*-algorithm, combining some of the advantages of grid-files and quadtrees in a new data structure to approximate the kernel density functions and enable placement of data points at unique output map positions. This data structure supports, first, the recursive partitioning of both the geo-spatial data set and the Euclidean 2D display space to enable an efficient distortion of the map regions, second, an automatic smoothing depending on the x-y density, and third, an array-based 3D density estimation.

The above mentioned recursive partitioning can be efficiently stored as a binary tree in each case, and the combination of both binary trees within a single multidimensional array. This combination is realized through the storage of the coordinates of the two different arising split points (in the data and in the display space) in each top-down construction step. Note, that our data structure uses midden split-operations according to different parameters. In case of the geo-spatial data set, a gridfile-like midden-split, and in case of the display space, a quadtree-like midden split operation is performed. The gridfile-like partitioning of geo-spatial data sets applies split operations within the 10% surrounding neighborhood of the middle point (left+right)/2 of the arising geo-spatial partition. The recursion terminates if the maximal split level is reached, or if a partition contains fewer than four data points. The goal is to find dense areas in the spatial dimensions (a_i^x, a_i^y) and to allocate enough pixels to place all the points of these dense regions at unique positions. The Fast-PixelMap data structure enables, in a second step, the efficient distortion of certain map regions in the 2D display space, by relocating all data points within the old boundaries of the quadtree partition to new positions within new boundaries of the quadtree partition. After rescaling all data points to the new boundaries, the iterative positioning of data points starts with the densest region. Within a region, the smallest cluster is chosen first. The iterative pixel position heuristic places all data points belonging to one cluster at adjacent pixels without overwriting existing ones.

Complexity The time complexity of the proposed approach is $O(n\log^2 n)$. The additional space overhead, $0(n + \log n)$, is negligible. This additional space is needed by the Fast-PixelMap data structure to store the original data points with a constant number of split-operations (which depends on the maximal split-level).

5 Application and Evaluation

We experimentally compared the Fast-PixelMap algorithm with a genetic algorithm for multi-objective optimization [8], and with PixelMap (based on the DenClue clustering algorithm [4]). We evaluated them with respect to time efficiency and the objectives presented in section 2. The experiments were run using a sample of 30000 points from the U.S. Year 2000 Census Household Income Database, on a 700 MHz Pentium computer with 1GByte of main memory. **Efficiency and Effectiveness** Figure 2 shows time-performance curves of all three methods, with varying degrees of input point overlap. The efficiency results show that the average number of data points assigned to the same position plays an important role in the performance of all three methods. The results indicate that the Fast-PixelMap algorithm outperforms the other two methods for all degrees of overlap, and is computationally practical for large spatial data sets. Effectiveness can be measured with respect to the three optimization goals defined in section 2. Figure 3 shows measured error curves for the three optimization goals. In summary, the results show that Fast-PixelMap is an effective approximation for the pixel placement problem, and is practical for visually exploring large geo-spatial statistical data sets in search of local correlations.

Visual Evaluation and Applications Formal measures of effectiveness are only meaningful if they lead to useful visualizations. Figure 1 shows a sample from the U.S. Year 2000 Census Median Household Income Database for the State New York, which in general validates the mathematically defined effectiveness criteria.

6 Conclusions

We presented the PixelMap algorithm, which combines kernel-density-based- clustering with a novel pixel-based visualization technique. It avoids loss of information due to overplotting of data points. It assigns each input data point to a unique pixel in 2D screen space, and balances the trade-off of spatial locality (absolute and relative position preservation) with clustering to achieve pixel coherence. We also described the Fast-PixelMap heuristic that provides efficient approximate solutions to the PixelMap optimization problem, and is of practical value for exploring geo-spatial statistical data.

Acknowledgments We thank Carmen Sanz Merino and Hartmut Ziegler for their great support. We thank Dave Belanger and Mike Wish for encouraging this investigation.

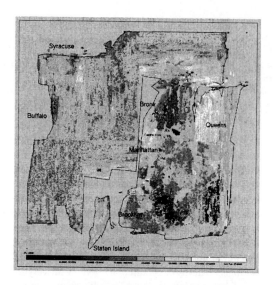

Figure 1. New York State Year 1999 Median Household Personal Income - PixelMap displays cluster regions. Note high-income clusters on the East side of Manhattan's Central Park, and low-income clusters on the West end of Brooklyn.

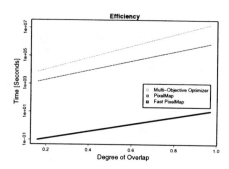

Figure 2. Comparison of the efficiency of Fast-PixelMap, PixelMap, and a multi-objective genetic optimization algorithm (log-scale)

References

[1] I. Advizor Solutions. Visual insight in3d. http://www.advizorsolutions.com/, Aug 26 15:19 2003.

[2] ESRI. An esri white paper: Arcview 3d analyst features, 1998. http://www.esri.com/library/whitepapers/pdfs/3danalys.pdf, Aug 26 15:13 2003.

[3] J. Han and M. Kamber. *Data Mining: Concepts and Techniques*. Morgan Kaufmann Publishers, 2001.

[4] A. Hinneburg and D. A. Keim. An efficient approach to clustering in large multimedia databases with noise. In *Knowledge Discovery and Data Mining*, pages 58–65, 1998.

[5] S. M. Homepage. Sgi mineset. http://www.sgi.com/software/mineset.html, Aug 26 15:13 2003.

[6] D. Keim, E. Koutsofios, and S. C. North. Visual exploration of large telecommunication data sets. In *Proc. Workshop on User Interfaces In Data Intensive Systems (Invited Talk), Edinburgh, UK*, pages 12–20, 1999.

[7] D. A. Keim and A. Herrmann. The gridfit algorithm: An efficient and effective approach to visualizing large amounts of spatial data. pages 181–188, 1998.

[8] E. Zitzler and L. Thiele. Multiobjective optimization using evolutionary algorithms - a comparative case study. parallel problem solving from nature. In *PPSN-V*, pages 292–301, September 1998.

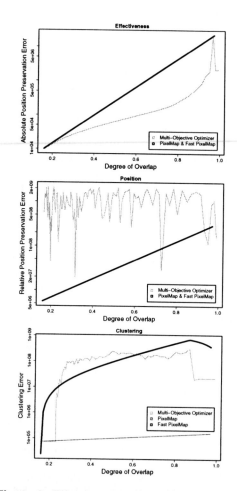

Figure 3. Effectiveness Measurement of the defined optimization constraints 1, 2, and 3 in section 2 (log-scale)

Effectiveness of Information Extraction, Multi-Relational, and Semi-Supervised Learning for Predicting Functional Properties of Genes

Mark-A. Krogel
University of Magdeburg
FIN/IWS, PO Box 4120
39016 Magdeburg, Germany
krogel@iws.cs.uni-magdeburg.de

Tobias Scheffer
Humboldt University, Berlin
Department of Computer Science,
10099 Berlin, Germany
scheffer@informatik.hu-berlin.de

Abstract

We focus on the problem of predicting functional properties of the proteins corresponding to genes in the yeast genome. Our goal is to study the effectiveness of approaches that utilize all data sources that are available in this problem setting, including unlabeled and relational data, and abstracts of research papers. We study transduction and co-training for using unlabeled data. We investigate a propositionalization approach which uses relational gene interaction data. We study the benefit of information extraction for utilizing a collection of scientific abstracts. The studied tasks are KDD Cup tasks of 2001 and 2002. The solutions which we describe achieved the highest score for task 2 in 2001, the fourth rank for task 3 in 2001, the highest score for one of the two subtasks and the third place for the overall task 2 in 2002.

1 Introduction

A principle challenge of bioinformatics is to generate models which describe the relation between genetic information and corresponding cellular processes. Such models have to explain – and can be derived from – available experimental data. We focus on a set of related problems of functional genomics. We aim at predicting the high-level function and the localization of the protein corresponding to a given yeast gene, and at predicting whether a given gene is involved in the regulation of the aryl hydrocarbon receptor (AhR) signaling pathway (for the available data, this has been determined in a gene deletion experiment).

The data which we use have been provided for the KDD Cups 2001 [3] and 2002 [4]. Besides attributes such as function, localization, and protein class for each gene, the data include relational gene interaction information and abstracts of relevant research papers in MEDLINE. Focusing on the

goal of building as accurate a model of the biological system as possible, we explore the effectiveness of several approaches that allow us to utilize these available sources of unlabeled, multi-relational, and textual data.

Approaches to utilizing relational data (in our case, gene interactions) in machine learning algorithms include inductive logic programming and *propositionalization* (originating from ILP) – *i.e.*, casting of a controlled amount of relational information into attributes (*e.g.*, [7, 9]). Because of scalability issues, we follow the latter approach. For the focused problem, unlabeled data is inexpensive and readily available. Approaches to semi-supervised learning include transduction [6] and the co-training algorithm [1]. Abstracts of scientific papers in the MEDLINE collection contain information that can be helpful for model building. Algorithms have been studied that extract information from literature [10, 5], based on dictionary-based extractors (*e.g.*, [5]), rule learners, or hidden Markov models [10].

This paper is organized as follows. We discuss the application and experimental setting in Section 2, and our propositionalization approach in Section 3. Section 4 focuses on our studies on text mining, while Section 5 presents results on semi-supervised learning. A discussion of our competition results and lessons learned is sketched in Section 6.

2 Problem Description

Our task is to predict properties of the proteins corresponding to a given yeast gene. These properties are (1) one (or several) of 15 categories of protein functions, (2) the localization (one of 15 different parts of the cell), and (3) the involvement in the regulation of the AhR signaling pathway. The AhR is a basic helix-loop-helix transcription factor with the ability to bind both synthetic chemicals such as dioxins and naturally-occurring phytochemicals, sterols and heme breakdown products. This receptor plays an important developmental and physiological role. Problems (1) and (2) have been addressed in KDD Cup 2001 whereas problem (3) is one of the tasks of KDD Cup 2002.

The available training data for problem (1) and (2) contains 862 training and 381 test instances [3]. Besides attributes that characterize the individual gene, a relation specifies which genes interact with one another. We have to limit our comparative studies to the three most frequent classes as the minority classes contain too few instances to obtain performance estimates.

The data for problem (3) has been obtained in experiments with yeast strains using a gene deletion array [4]. Each instance in the data set represents a trial in which a single gene is knocked out and the activity of a target system (AhR signaling) is measured. We distinguish genes whose deletion affects the target system (class "change"), affects the entire cell ("control"), or does not have an effect ("no change"). We learn two discriminators: *change* vs. *control* and *no change* ("narrow positive class" problem) and *change* and *control* vs. *no change* ("broad positive class").

The data contains 3,018 training and 1,489 test examples. 2,934 fall into the class *no change*, 38 into *change* and 45 into *control*. The attributes (with many missing values) describe function, localization and protein class of each gene (hierarchical attributes with four to five levels). Again, a relation describes gene interactions. A table relates genes to 15,235 relevant abstracts in the MEDLINE repository.

We use the area under the *Receiver Operating Characteristic* (ROC) curve to assess hypotheses. [2] This area (the *AUC performance*) is equal to the probability that, when we draw one positive and one negative example at random, the decision function assigns a higher value to the positive than to the negative example. We estimate the standard deviation of the AUC performance, using the Wilcoxon statistics [2].

We selected the Support Vector Machine SVM^{light} as core machine learning algorithm. In order to study the benefit of some attribute x generated by one of the discussed approaches, we compare the performance of the attribute configuration with highest cross validation performance with and without the focused attribute.

3 Propositionalization

The gene interaction data contains pairs of gene names. In order to integrate this data into our solutions, we have to generate attributes from this relation. We use the RE-LAGGS algorithm that extends the usual framework of propositionalization [7] by first computing user specified joins, and then aggregating the result into a table with a single line per instance [9].

The following example illustrates this process. We have a table *train-class* with attributes *gene-id* and *class*, a table *interaction* with *gene-id1* and *gene-id2* and, slightly simplified, a table *localization* with attribute *gene-id* and an

Table 1. Function and localization prediction with and without relational information.

Class	without	with
function growth	0.872 ± 0.01	0.882 ± 0.014
function transcription	0.886 ± 0.005	0.899 ± 0.011
function transport	0.893 ± 0.01	0.918 ± 0.013
localization cytoplasm	0.861 ± 0.008	0.865 ± 0.014
localization mitochondria	0.909 ± 0.013	0.948 ± 0.01
localization nucleus	0.941 ± 0.005	0.944 ± 0.011

Table 2. AhR prediction with and without relational information.

class	without	first level	second level	third level
narrow	0.62 ± 0.06	0.71 ± 0.05	0.69 ± 0.05	0.65 ± 0.06
broad	0.60 ± 0.04	0.60 ± 0.05	0.63 ± 0.04	0.60 ± 0.04

additional attribute for each possible value, including *mitochondria* and *cytoplasm* (this easily allows us to handle set-valued attributes). Gene "1" interacts with genes "2" and "3", where "2" has value 1 for attribute *mitochondria* and 0 for *cytoplasm*, and "3" has value 1 both for *mitochondria* and *cytoplasm*. After joining the three tables, we obtain two lines for gene "1"; the first has value 1 for *mitochondria* and 0 for *cytoplasm*, the second has value 1 for both.

We now collapse these two lines into one by applying aggregation functions such as *min, max, avg,* or *sum*; in this case, *sum* is appropriate. This leads to one line with values 2 and 1 for attributes *mitochondria* and *cytoplasm*, respectively, indicating that gene "1" interacts with two genes localizing in the mitochondria and one in the cytoplasm. The RELAGGS outputs consisted for all problems of single tables with about 1,000 columns each. This high number is caused by the number of different values for functions, localizations, and protein classes.

For problems (1) and (2), we compare the decision functions with and without the interaction attributes, generated by the RELAGGS algorithm in Table 1 (using 10-fold cross validation). The observed AUC performance obtained when using the interaction is in every single case higher; the improvement exceeds two standard deviations in two cases and one standard deviation in two more cases. These data rule out the null hypothesis that the interaction information does not influence recognition performance. For problem (3), we compare the performance without and with attributes that reflect first, second, and third level interactions in Table 2. We see that first level interactions perform best for the narrow, and second level interactions are best for the broad positive class. A significant improvement ($p \approx 0.05$) is achieved for the narrow class, we see a smaller, insignificant improvement for the broad class.

Table 3. Additional information from information extraction.

	without	with	IE only
narrow	0.590 ± 0.061	0.685 ± 0.052	0.654 ± 0.055
broad	0.597 ± 0.040	0.630 ± 0.039	0.510 ± 0.044

Table 4. Transduction results for (1) and (2).

Class	SVM	TSVM
function growth, 150 positives	0.84 ± 0.006	0.82 ± 0.008
location cytoplasm, all data	0.83 ± 0.010	$0.71pm0.016$
function growth, 5 positives	0.67 ± 0.005	0.55 ± 0.007
location cytoplasm, 5 positives	0.62 ± 0.007	0.55 ± 0.011

4 Information Extraction

The attributes of the original data set contain very many missing values. We therefore want to study whether an information extraction algorithm can effectively be used to find missing values in the 15,000 MEDLINE abstracts. We follow a dictionary-based approach [5]. From the hierarchical text files that contain possible values for the attributes function, localization, and protein class, we manually define a thesaurus that lists, for each of the possible values of these attributes, a number of plausible terms that can be used to refer to this value. Terms are constructed by adding synonyms, paraphrased variants, and plural forms, and splitting compound phrases (see [8] for more details).

Table 3 shows that the extractor yields a substantial performance improvement for problem (3). Surprisingly, the problem can even be solved to some degree using *only* the information extracted from the abstracts ("IE only"). Applying the information extractor to problems (1) and (2) raises an interesting problem. The extractor identifies both, function and localization of genes in the scientific abstracts. Hence, it solves the functional genomics problem. However, this solution would not be practically useful because it could not possibly predict function and localization values that have not previously published.

5 Semi-Supervised Learning

The transductive SVM [6] maximizes the margin between hyper-plane and both, labeled and unlabeled data; but only for the labeled data, it is required that they lie on a specific side. For problems (1) and (2), Table 4 compares 10-fold cross validation results of the "vanilla SVM" to the TSVM. In both cases, transduction *significantly decreases* performance although it has additional information (the unlabeled hold-out instances) available. Given our previous positive experience with TSVM, we hypothesized that transduction is only beneficial if only few labeled data are available. We averaged 10 iterations in which we drew only 5 labeled positive examples (and 12 and 20 negatives, respectively) and used all remaining instances as unlabeled data. Table 4 shows that transduction still dramatically decreases classifier performance, refuting our hypothesis.

For problem (3), the transductive SVM decreased the AUC for the broad class from 0.63 (± 0.04) to 0.60 (± 0.04)

and increased AUC for the narrow class from 0.685 (± 0.05) to 0.695 (± 0.05). Both differences are well below the standard deviations. The transductive SVM dramatically increases computation time.

Blum and Mitchell [1] have proposed the co-training algorithm which splits the available attributes into disjoint subsets; a labeled example (x, a) is then viewed as (x_1, x_2, a). The co-training algorithm learns two classifiers $f_1(x_1)$ and $f_2(x_2)$ which bootstrap each other by providing labels for the unlabeled data. When the views are *compatible – i.e.,* $\exists f_1, f_2$ such that $f_1(x_1) = f_2(x_2) = f(x)$ – and *independent* given the class labels – $P(x_1|f(x), x_2) = P(x_1|f(x))$ – then the co-training algorithm labels unlabeled examples in a way that is essentially equivalent to drawing labeled data at random [1].

For problems (1) and (2), we split the available attributes randomly. In each experiment, we averaged ten co-training curves for distinct attribute splits. Figure 1 shows that the performance of the decision functions remains unchanged when we use all available labeled examples, (topmost curve), or 150 labeled examples (second curve, plot for "function") whereas performance *decreases* over the co-training iterations when we use only 5 positive examples.

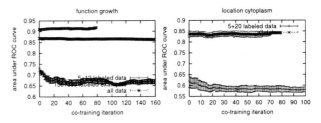

Figure 1. Co-training results for (1) and (2).

For problem (3) we tried to minimize dependency between the two attribute sets by splitting into attributes extracted from the abstracts together with the relational attributes, and all other attributes (the "natural" split). As control strategy, we randomly partition the attributes.

Figure 2 (left) shows the AUC over 200 iterations of co-training using the "natural" split. The performance does not improve; the standard deviations are around 0.05. The combined decision function (the average of two decision functions) is significantly worse than one single decision func-

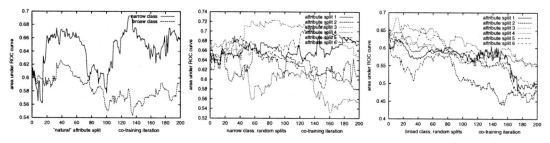

Figure 2. Co-training results for (3).

tion. For random attribute partitioning (Figure 2, center and right), the average AUC decreases significantly over the co-training iterations ($p < 0.05$) for the broad and seems to decrease for the narrow class.

6 Competition Results and Lessons Learned

For KDD Cup 2001, tasks 2 and 3, (here, problems 1 and 2) Krogel [3] submitted a solution that used the interaction attributes. Since the gene names were anonymized, we could not use text mining results; we did not use transduction or co-training either. The submission achieved the highest score for function prediction, and the fourth highest score for localization prediction [3]. Our solution for KDD Cup 2002, task 2 (here, problem 3) used second-level interactions, and entries won by information extraction. We did not include transduction or co-training. We achieved the third highest result (the highest for the narrow positive class); retrospectively, we can now obtain better performances than any team could within the tight competition time frame.

From our experience in the KDD Cup and retrospective studies, we draw a number of lessons learned. (i) In functional genomics, the interactions between genes play a crucial role. Effective utilization of the interaction information was the key success factor for both competitions. Using RELAGGS to propositionalize the data proved to be effective and scalable. (ii) Semi-supervised learning techniques such as the transductive SVM and co-training are less generally applicable than – at least we – expected. Our expectation was that taking unlabeled data into account should not decrease performance, and should at least be beneficial when only few labeled examples are available. For functional gene classification, neither of these assumptions is true. (iii) MEDLINE abstracts contain important knowledge that can help to build better models and thus to perform better on classification tasks. Our data shows that even simple, dictionary-based extractors can generate attributes that substantially improve classification performance.

Acknowledgements

We would like to thank David Page and Mark Craven. Thanks to Marco Landwehr and Marcus Denecke for their contributions to the KDD Cup 2002 entry. Tobias Scheffer is supported by Emmy Noether Fellowship SCHE540/10-1 of the German Science Foundation (DFG).

References

[1] A. Blum and T. Mitchell. Combining labeled and unlabeled data with co-training. In *Proceedings of the Workshop on Computational Learning Theory*, 1998.

[2] A. Bradley. The use of the area under the ROC curve in the evaluation of machine learning algorithms. *Pattern Recognition*, 30(7):1145–1159, 1997.

[3] J. Cheng, C. Hatzis, H. Hayashi, M.-A. Krogel, S. Morishita, D. Page, and J. Sese. KDD Cup 2001 Report. *SIGKDD Explorations*, 3(2):47–64, 2002.

[4] M. Craven. The 2002 KDD Cup competition results for gene regulation prediction. *SIGKDD Explorations*, 4(2), 2003.

[5] K. Fukuda, T. Tsunoda, A. Tamura, and T. Takagi. Towards information extraction: Identifying protein names from biological papers. In *Proceedings of the Pacific Symposium on Biocomputing*, 1998.

[6] T. Joachims. Transductive inference for text classification using support vector machines. In *Proceedings of the International Conference on Machine Learning*, 1999.

[7] S. Kramer, N. Lavrač, and P. A. Flach. Propositionalization Approaches to Relational Data Mining. In *Relational Data Mining*. Springer, 2001.

[8] M.-A. Krogel and T. Scheffer. Effectiveness of information extraction, multi-relational and multi-view learning for predicting gene deletion experiments. In *BIOKDD*, 2003.

[9] M.-A. Krogel and S. Wrobel. Transformation-Based Learning Using Multirelational Aggregation. In *Proceedings of the Eleventh International Conference on Inductive Logic Programming (ILP)*. Springer, 2001.

[10] T. Leek. Information extraction using hidden Markov models. Master's thesis, UCSD, 1997.

Tractable Group Detection on Large Link Data Sets

Jeremy Kubica
Carnegie Mellon University
Robotics Institute
Pittsburgh, PA 15213
jkubica@ri.cmu.edu

Andrew Moore
Carnegie Mellon University
School of Computer Science
Pittsburgh, PA 15213
awm@cs.cmu.edu

Jeff Schneider
Carnegie Mellon University
School of Computer Science
Pittsburgh, PA 15213
schneide@cs.cmu.edu

Abstract

Discovering underlying structure from co-occurrence data is an important task in a variety of fields, including: insurance, intelligence, criminal investigation, epidemiology, human resources, and marketing. Previously Kubica et. al. presented the group detection algorithm (GDA) - an algorithm for finding underlying groupings of entities from co-occurrence data. This algorithm is based on a probabilistic generative model and produces coherent groups that are consistent with prior knowledge. Unfortunately, the optimization used in GDA is slow, potentially making it infeasible for many large data sets. To this end, we present k-groups - an algorithm that uses an approach similar to that of k-means to significantly accelerate the discovery of groups while retaining GDA's probabilistic model. We compare the performance of GDA and k-groups on a variety of data, showing that k-groups' sacrifice in solution quality is significantly offset by its increase in speed.

1 Introduction

Co-occurrence data is an increasingly important and abundant source of data in many fields. In one general form the input consists of a series of *links*. Each link is an unordered set of entities that have been joined by some event, co-occurrence, or relation. For example, in the co-authorship domain each paper can define a link containing its authors as entities. It is important to appreciate that our definition of a link may vary from other usages, such as a link on a webpage. We do not assume any directionality or restrict links to contain a fixed number of entities.

One important task is the identification of underlying structure buried within large amounts of noisy link data. Below we examine the group detection algorithm (GDA), an algorithm that attempts to find underlying groups of entities [5]. GDA is based on a probabilistic generative model, in the form of a Bayesian network, that assumes that links are

the result of underlying groups. GDA has been found to produce groups that are consistent with prior knowledge. Unfortunately GDA makes use of heuristic optimization techniques that may be slow, making it potentially infeasible for many real world data sets.

We propose k-groups, an algorithm that uses a probabilistic model similar to GDA but uses localized updates to improve both speed and convergence properties. We compare its performance to that of GDA on a variety of data. We show that k-groups' sacrifice in solution quality is offset by its increase in speed. This trade-off makes group detection tractable on significantly larger data sets.

2 The Group Detection Algorithm (GDA)

The group detection algorithm (GDA) uses maximum likelihood estimation to find groupings of entities from two input data sets [5]. The first is demographics data (DD), which contains the N_P entities and their demographic information. The word "demographic" should not be interpreted too narrowly as it can include any information about the entities. For example in the co-authorship domain, demographics may include an author's title or affiliation. We denote a single entity as e_i and the set of all entities as ξ. The second data set is the link data (LD), which consists of a listing of N_L separate links. We denote individual links as sets $L_i \subseteq \xi$ containing $|L_i|$ entities. From these data sets GDA learns K groups, each denoted $g_i \subseteq \xi$.

GDA assumes a probabilistic generative model in the form of a Bayesian network with five components. This model defines a recipe for data generation. Initially K groups are created from the entities' demographics data (DD) and an underlying demographics model (DM). Each entity/group membership is considered with the DM indicating the probability the entity is a member of the group given its demographics. From the underlying groups N_L separate links are generated and stored in a link data set (LD). The exact model for link generation is described below. The link model (LM) controls the amount of noise added to links of various types.

The goal is to learn the *LM*, *DM*, and groupings from the two input data sets (*DD* and *LD*). The primary component of interest is the chart (*CH*), which indicates entities' memberships in groups. Unlike traditional clustering models, an entity can simultaneously be a full member of several groups. Heuristic optimization is used to find the chart that produces the highest loglikelihood. As shown in [5] the Bayesian network structure allows the likelihood to be factored into two main components for optimization: the probability of the groups given the demographics $P(CH|DD,DM)$ and the probability of the links given the groups $P(LD|LM,CH)$. For the purposes of the k-groups algorithm we focus on optimizing $P(LD|LM,CH)$ and thus on the components of the model that relate to link generation from the groups.

The model assumes that links are generated individually by choosing a group g and uniformly sampling members from it. The amount of noise in a link is determined by the *LM*. We say that a link L contains noise if it was generated by some group g and there is some entity $e \in L$ such that $e \notin g$. During link generation, this corresponds to choosing each entity in the link directly from g or with some probability P_R as noise (from $\xi - g$). We can then break down the link size as $|L| = M_R + M_G$, where M_G is the number of entities in the link that are also in the generating group g and M_R is the number of entities that are noise (i.e. not in g).

In addition, with some probability P_I the link is completely random and all of its entities are chosen from ξ. In this case we define the *world group*, $G_W = \{e_j : 1 \leq j \leq N_P\}$, as the link's generating group. We then define $\Omega = \{g_1, \ldots, g_K, G_W\}$ as the set of all possible link generators. In other words, a link can be created by any of the K groups or be completely random (created by G_W).

Assuming the links are i.i.d. and the priors for each group are equal:

$$\log(P(LD|LM,CH)) = \sum_{i=1}^{N_L} \log P(L_i|LM,CH)$$
$$= \sum_{i=1}^{N_L} \left[\sum_{g \in \Omega} P(L,g|LM) \right] \quad (1)$$

where

$$P(L,g|LM) = \begin{cases} \frac{P_I}{\binom{N_P}{|L|}} & \text{if } g = G_W \\ \frac{(1-P_I)}{K} P(L|LM,g) & \text{if } g \neq G_W \end{cases} \quad (2)$$

and (if $g \neq G_W$)

$$P(L|g,LM) = \left(\frac{(P_R)^{M_R}(1-P_R)^{M_G}\binom{M_G+M_R}{M_R}}{\binom{|g|}{M_G}\binom{N_P-|g|}{M_R}} \right) \quad (3)$$

An important approximation to the above equations is (4), which creates the concept of a group "owning" a link.

$$\log(P(L|LM,CH)) \approx \log \left(\max_{g \in \Omega} P(L|g,LM) \right) \quad (4)$$

3 The K-groups Algorithm

The k-groups algorithm focuses on the task of learning the underlying groups directly from the link data. That is to say, it optimizes $P(LD|LM,CH)$ and does not consider the demographics information in the inner loop.

Intuitively k-groups optimizes $P(LD|LM,CH)$ in a fashion similar to that of the k-means algorithm. Since the groups formed by k-groups are not disjoint, the k-means approach must be adapted by noting that the max approximation forces groups to "own" links. If we let LG_g be the set of links owned by a group $g \in \Omega$:

$$\log(P(LD|LM,CH)) = \sum_{g \in \Omega} \log(P(LG_g,g|LM))$$
$$= \sum_{g \in \Omega} \sum_{L \in LG_g} \log(P(L,g|LM)) \quad (5)$$

Similar to the k-means algorithms, k-groups can alternate (until convergence) between two greedy steps:

1. For each link, determine which group owns it.

2. For each group g, determine which entities form g so as to optimize $P(LG_g|g,LM)$.

3.1 Determining Group Ownerships

The first step of the k-groups algorithm is to determine which links each group owns. This can be done quickly with a single linear scan through the links using the approximation in (4):

$$LG_g = \{L : g = \underset{g' \in \Omega}{argmax} P(L,g'|LM)\} \quad (6)$$

3.2 Updating the Groups

The second step of k-groups is to find the "optimal" groups given their links. Since we are considering only the links owned by the current group we wish to optimize $P(LG_g,g|LM)$ for each g. We can do this locally by using (3) and (5) to examine the effect of adding or removing a single entity. Let $\Delta_g^A(e)$ and $\Delta_g^R(e)$ denote the change in $\log P(LG_g,g|LM)$ if we add entity e to group g and remove entity e from group g respectively. Then by algebra:

$$\Delta_g^A(e) = \begin{cases} \sum_{L \in LG_g} \left[\log \left(\frac{(|g| - M_G + 1)(N - |g|)}{(N - |g| - M_R)(|g| + 1)} \right) \right] + \\ \sum_{L \in LG_g : e \in L} \left[\log \left(\frac{(1 - P_R)(N - |g| - M_R)}{P_R(|g| - M_G + 1)} \right) \right] & e \notin g \\ \\ 0 & e \in g \end{cases}$$
(7)

with a similar result for $\Delta_g^R(e)$.

Using these observations we can define a second, inner greedy procedure to optimize $P(LG_g | g, LM)$:

1. For each $e \in LG_g$ calculate $\Delta_g^A(e)$ and $\Delta_g^R(e)$.

2. If there exists some entity e such that $\Delta_g^A(e) > 0$ (or $\Delta_g^R(e) > 0$) then add (or remove) the entity that would lead to the greatest improvement.

3. If $\Delta_g^A(e) \leq 0$ and $\Delta_g^R(e) \leq 0 \ \forall e$, terminate.

This procedure greedily adds/removes entities until it no longer results in an improvement. This approach has two major computational advantages. First, we do not have to recalculate $P(LG_g, g | LM)$ for each change that we wish to evaluate. This allows us to rapidly try each entity exhaustively. Second, k-groups only needs to consider a subset of links and a subset of entities when updating a group. It is important to appreciate that this search is localized and therefore may not find groups that optimize the overall likelihood of the data.

3.3 Convergence and Local Minima

One important advantage of k-groups is that it provably converges to a local optimum in a finite number of steps [4]. Despite this guarantee, k-groups may get trapped in a local optimum. We use two simultaneous strategies for "getting unstuck": a step similar to Split-Merge EM [7] and a step that adds a small amount of noise to the solution. Both serve to perturb the solution before k-groups is rerun, making each convergence a single iteration of the overall k-groups algorithm.

4 Comparison with GDA

The key advantage of k-groups is that it finds "better" solutions faster than GDA. We examined this improvement on a variety of real-world and synthetic data. Due to space considerations the experiments on the synthetic data sets are omitted. Results and analysis can be found in [4].

The tests on the real world data sets, summarized in Table 1, consisted of tracking the optimization performance

DATA SET	N_P	N_L	K	# RUNS
LAB	115	94	20	24
INSTITUTE	456	1738	100	24
DRINKS	136	5325	50	24
MANUAL	4088	5581	25	8
CITESEER	104801	181395	50	1

Table 1. Summaries of the data sets.

DATA SET	K-GROUPS 1 ITR. LL	K-GROUPS TIME	GDA TIME	TIMES SPEEDUP
LAB	-726	0.13	145	1163.2
INSTITUTE	-18847	16.00	667	41.7
DRINKS	-42664	23.25	349	15.0
MANUAL	-86509	9.38	5033	536.9
CITESEER	-4763400	1319.00	N/A	N/A

Table 2. The average loglikelihood after one iteration of k-groups and the average time (in seconds) to reach that loglikelihood.

(loglikelihood) versus the time for both algorithms. The data sets consist of links built from co-authorship (lab, citeseer, and institute), co-occurrence (manual and drinks), advisor/advisee relations (institute) and common research interests (institute). The group sizes and parameters were heuristically chosen, but constant across algorithms. Both algorithms were run multiple times on each data set.

Figure 1 shows the results of some of the runs. At each time step the plot indicates the mean loglikelihood and the bounds of the 95% confidence interval on performance. No confidence intervals were included on the Citeseer results. As the results illustrate, k-groups can offer a significant speedup. As the size of the data sets increase (number of links and entities) this speedup can become more pronounced and also more important. For example, on the Citeseer data set k-groups was able to converge to a local minima in under 22 minutes that was better than any solution found by GDA within 24 hours.

The above results lead to another natural question: "How good is the first local minima found by k-groups?" For each data set we examined the average loglikelihood after a single iteration of k-groups (convergence to the first local minima) and the average time iteration took. This was then compared to the average time it took GDA to reach this loglikelihood. The results, shown in Table 2, indicate that a single iteration often performs relatively well and is *much* faster than finding a equally good solution using GDA.

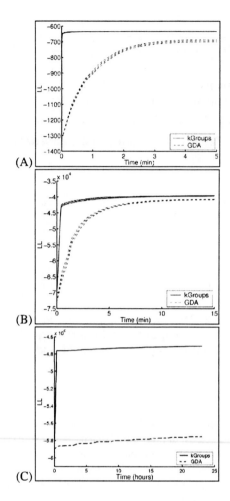

Figure 1. Loglikelihood versus time for (A) Lab, (B) Drinks, and (C) Citeseer data.

5 Related Work

The k-groups algorithm is an improvement of the GDA algorithm [5]. In addition there are a variety of similar algorithms that extract different types of structure from link data. Descriptions of these algorithms and how they compare to the GDA algorithm can be found in [4].

K-groups is similar to, and inspired by, the k-means algorithm [2]. Both algorithms use hard clustering for group membership and use only members to update the group. The two algorithms differ significantly on their domains and optimization criteria. The use of a split/merge operation was proposed by Ueda *et. al.* for use in EM optimization of mixture models [7].

When rephrased as the problem of assigning link ownerships to groups, our work becomes similar to approaches that cluster the links themselves [1, 3, 6]. There are sev-

eral key differences between these approaches and our own. First, we are using a relatively novel underlying generative model. Second, we are primarily interested in the resulting "clusters" of entities, which we restrict to be hard assignments. Finally, k-groups uses a novel greedy approach that is designed for both this model and the hard, but nonexclusive, assignments of entities to groups.

6 Conclusions

Above we presented k-groups, an algorithm that uses localized updates to improve both speed and convergence properties while still using GDA's probabilistic model. We motivating the derivation of the algorithm using the same properties as k-means and compared k-groups' performance to that of GDA on several data sets.

There are several remaining questions that we plan to investigate in future research. The first is to learn K while learning the underlying groups by using a measure such as AIC or BIC. The second is to incorporate the demographics into the localized update steps. Finally, it is possible that by combining (or alternating) the GDA and k-groups optimization steps, the resulting optimization could ultimately find even better solutions quickly.

Acknowledgements

Jeremy Kubica is supported by a grant from the Fannie and John Hertz Foundation. This research is supported by DARPA under award number F30602-01-2-0569. The authors would like to thank Alex Gray for his helpful comments and Steve Lawrence for providing the Citeseer data.

References

[1] D. M. Blei, A. Y. Ng, and M. I. Jordan. Latent dirichlet allocation. *Journal of Machine Learning Research*, 3, 2003.

[2] A. Gersho and R. M. Gray. *Vector Quantization and Signal Compression*. Communications and Information Theory. Kluwer Academic Publishers, Norwell, MA, USA, 1992.

[3] S. Guha, R. Rastogi, and K. Shim. ROCK: A robust clustering algorithm for categorical attributes. *Information Systems*, 25(5):345–366, 2000.

[4] J. Kubica, A. Moore, and J. Schneider. K-groups: Tractable group detection on large link data sets. In *CMU Tech. Report 03-32*, 2003.

[5] J. Kubica, A. Moore, J. Schneider, and Y. Yang. Stochastic link and group detection. In *AAAI*, pages 798–804. ACM Press, Jul 2002.

[6] K. Nigam, A. K. McCallum, S. Thrun, and T. M. Mitchell. Text classification from labeled and unlabeled documents using EM. *Machine Learning*, 39(2/3):103–134, 2000.

[7] N. Ueda, R. Nakano, Z. Ghahramani, and G. E. Hinton. SMEM algorithm for mixture models. *Neural Computation*, 12(9):2109–2128, 2000.

Tree-structured Partitioning Based on Splitting Histograms of Distances

Longin Jan Latecki
Computer and Inf. Sciences Dept.
Temple University, Philadelphia, PA 19122
latecki@temple.edu

Rajagopal Venugopal
Computer and Inf. Sciences Dept.
Temple University, Philadelphia, PA 19122
vrajagop@temple.edu

Marc Sobel
Dept. of Statistics
Temple University, Philadelphia, PA 19122
sobel@sbm.temple.edu

Steve Horvath
Dept. of Human Genetics and Biostatistics
Univ. of California, Los Angeles, CA 90095-1772
SHorvath@mednet.ucla.edu

Abstract

We propose a novel clustering algorithm that is similar in spirit to classification trees. The data is recursively split using a criterion that applies a discrete curve evolution method to the histogram of distances. The algorithm can be depicted through tree diagrams with triple splits. Leaf nodes represent either clusters or sets of observations that can not yet be clearly assigned to a cluster. After constructing the tree, unclassified data points are mapped to their closest clusters. The algorithm has several advantages. First, it deals effectively with observations that can not be unambiguously assigned to a cluster by allowing a "margin of error". Second, it automatically determines the number of clusters; apart from the margin of error the user only needs to specify the minimal cluster size but not the number of clusters. Third, it is linear with respect to the number of data points and thus suitable for very large data sets. Experiments involving both simulated and real data from different domains show that the proposed method is effective and efficient.

1 Introduction and Related Work

Clustering is a division of data into groups of similar objects. Each group (or cluster) consists of similar objects; objects in different clusters are dissimilar. Here we discuss clustering under the assumption that clusters are connected regions with a relatively high density of points separated from other clusters by sparse regions [2]. Common clustering methods include: k-means clustering, k-medoid also known as partitioning around medoids (PAM) clustering [7], self-organizing maps, hierarchical clustering, and mixture model clustering. For a survey of different clustering algorithms see for example [12].

We briefly review data partitioning algorithms. These algorithms divide data into several subsets (clusters) based on optimizing an objective function that often is a function of pairwise distances, e.g. it may measure inter- or intra-cluster relations. Because checking all possible subset systems is computationally infeasible, greedy heuristics are used to iteratively optimize the objective function. This results in different relocation schemes that iteratively re-assign points between the k clusters. In iterative schemes pairwise computations may quickly become computationally too expensive. Using unique cluster representatives (centroids) resolves the problem: now computation becomes linear in the number of objects. Depending on how centroids are constructed, iterative optimization partitioning algorithms are subdivided into k-medoid (PAM) and k-means methods. A medoid is the data point that minimizes the sum of its distances to all other data points. Representation by medoids has the advantage that it presents no limitations on the attribute type and only requires the specification of a distance measure. When the features are quantitative one may also represent a cluster by the mean of its points. In k-medoid (PAM) clustering, one minimizes the median of the distances between cluster centers and the constituent elements of their associated clusters. Most partitioning algorithms do not have built-in margins of error allowing for the possibility of uncertain cluster assignments at various stages of the algorithm. For example, PAM clustering must assign an observation to a particular cluster, irrespective of its distances from the different cluster medoids. Here we propose a partitioning algorithm that succeeds in building in a margin of error by allowing for 'unclassified' nodes.

Liu et al. [11] framed clustering as a supervised learning problem that uses decision trees to distinguish observed observations from synthetic observations, which are drawn from the null distribution of no cluster structure. We pursue a different strategy which is reminiscent of using classification trees but it does not involve synthetic observations or class labels. The processing flow of our algorithm is similar to the flow of classification tree algorithms [1]. At each level of the tree, the data is partitioned into subsets (also called nodes); splits (also called branches) describe how 'parent' nodes are partitioned into 'child' nodes. The node without a parent is called the root node; nodes without child nodes are called leaf nodes or terminal nodes [17]. Classification trees recursively split the data by selecting an optimal feature and corresponding cut-off value. Tree construction involves starting with a split at the root node and continuing the splits of resulting child nodes until splitting stops; the child nodes which have not been split at the end of this process become terminal or leaf nodes. Commonly used node splitting criterion are the Gini index [1] or the information gain criterion [13]. These splitting criteria partition the data by hyperplanes that are perpendicular to the coordinate axes in the feature space. We propose a different splitting criterion which does not correspond to perpendicular hyperplanes. Instead of splitting based on a single feature, our splitting criterion considers all features simultaneously by taking as input distances. Thus we propose a novel heuristic for relocating points which is based on applying a discrete curve evolution method to the histogram of distances between cluster members and centroids. Even if the histogram of distances contains more than two modes the discrete curve evolution robustly finds a cut-off point that divides data into two parts. The cut-off point is found based on the shape of the histogram function as 'the most significant local minimum' of the histogram function. The discrete curve evolution has been successfully applied in Computer Vision to obtain shape descriptors [10] and to characterize video trajectories [9]. Note that alternative statistical methods such as a mixture model involving two Gaussians may fail to divide data into two meaningful parts when there are more than 2 modes.

2. Tree-structured Partitioning

The proposed clustering algorithm consists of two major steps:

1. **Recursive Splitting Step:** A discrete curve evolution method (see below) is applied to histograms of distances to assign observations to two or one temporary cluster. In case of two temporary clusters, we use a Voronoi splitting with a margin to obtain two clusters and a margin data set of unclassified points. If we have only one temporary cluster, the data is not split, and this cluster becomes a leaf node.

2. **Remapping Step:** After the tree is built, ambiguous observations are mapped to the closest cluster centroids. This is similar to clustering by k-medoids algorithms such as PAM (Partitioning Around Medoids) [7].

We will now present our tree-structured partitioning algorithm. Section 2.2 describes the new node splitting criterion. Finally, Section 2.3 describes how unclassified data points are remapped. In binary classification trees a parent node gets split into two child nodes. Our algorithm follows the same pattern but splits a parent node into three child nodes. The reason for this modification is to deal with ambiguous observations (outliers), which cannot yet be clearly assigned to a cluster. Let us be more specific. The parent node is split into left, right and unclassified (uc) child nodes. At least two of the three child nodes must be present or the parent node will not be split. The unclassified node is a terminal node, which contains the ambiguous data points. If the left and right child nodes are terminal nodes, they contain all the data points belonging to a particular cluster.

Each node (except the root node) in the resulting tree structure has two attributes: (a) the membership information of the data points and (b) the distances of all the data points in that node from the representative of the parent node. For the root node the centroid of the data is selected as the representative. For each other node N, we select the representative point with respect to its parent node representative pr as follows. We first compute the mean of the distances of data points in N from pr. The representative data point for N is the data point in N whose distance to pr is closest to this mean. Ties are broken by random sampling. For the version of our algorithm that takes a distance matrix as input, we compute the medoid instead of the mean. Recall that the medoid is defined to be the data point that minimizes the sum of its distances to all other data points.

2.1. Algorithmic Details

The input to our algorithm is either a set of attributes or a distance matrix that contains all pairwise distances between the data points. Let $A = \{a_i\}$, for $i = 1, .., n$, be a set of data points in an m dimensional feature space, i.e., each feature is denoted by index a_{ij} for $j = 1, ..., m$. Let $a \in A$ be one of the data points. *The distance projection* function d_a is defined as $d_a(x) = d(a, x)$, which denotes the distance between x and $a \in A$. Thus a distance projection function represents the distance of the data points from a singled out data point.

Algorithm $Createtree(A)$

1) Normalize the data A (optional)

2) Compute the centroid (mean or medoid) $\bar{A}$ of the data A.

3) Define the distance projection with respect to $\bar{A}$: $d(a_i) = d(\bar{A}, a_i)$ (for $i = 1, ..., n$).

5) Create a root node (r), with attributes $\bar{A}$ and d.

6) Apply the function $splitnode(r)$ (see Section 2.2) to non-terminal nodes.

7) Let N be a non-terminal node computed in (6) that is either (lc) or (rc) type node. Let $pr(N)$ be the representative point of the parent node of N:

a) Find the mean m of distances $d(pr(N), x)$ of the data points $x \in N$

b) Select a data point $a_i \in N$ for which $|d(pr(N), a_i) - m|$ is the smallest as the *representative* of N and label it $r(N)$.

c) Define the distance projection function $dnew$ of all the data points in N with respect to $r(N)$, i.e., $dnew() = d_{r(N)}()$.

d) Replace d with $dnew$ for that node.

8) Go back to line (6) substituting non-terminal nodes for the input parameter

9) Compute the centroids for all the clusters

10) Data points in the terminal node that contains the unclassified (ambiguous) observations get assigned to the cluster that corresponds to the closest centroid.

In lines 1-5 a root node is created. For each of the non terminal nodes returned by the split function (line 6), the distance values are updated in lines 7a),b),c),d). Each of the updated non terminal nodes are split in step 8. Lines 6,7,8 are repeated until all leaf nodes are found. In lines 9,10 data points labelled unclassified are mapped to the cluster closest to them.

2.2. Node Splitting by Discrete Curve Evolution

Let $N = \{x_i\}$, for $i = 1, .., z$ be a set of data points in a node (N) and d_i, for $i = 1, .., z$ be a set of distances $d_i = d(pr(N), x_i)$, where $pr(N)$ is the representative point of the

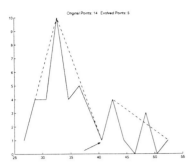

Figure 1: The initial cut-off point obtained by the discrete curve evolution for NIC41 data described in Section 3.

parent node of N. The algorithm for splitting a node in the tree is outlined below. It computes the function $splitnode(N)$.

There are two user defined inputs mnp and $percentage$. The input mnp defines the minimum number of data points the user wants to see in a cluster and acts as criterion to stop splitting. The parameter $percentage$ defines the area in between the two representative points as "danger zone". All data points falling in this area are considered to be outliers and become an unclassified terminal node.

The user does not need to specify the number of clusters since the algorithm determines the number of clusters on the basis of mnp and $percentage$. We have found that $percentage$ has minor effect on the resulting number of clusters. In our experiments we set $percentage$ to vary from 0.01 (1%) to 0.1 (10%) of the data in a given node. A good default setting is 0.1. But it is obvious that mnp will in general have a major effect on the resulting number of clusters. For example setting $mnp = 500$ will result in clusters with a minimum cluster size of 500.

The basic idea of splitting a node consists of three steps

1. Find an initial cut-off point: We first plot the histogram of distances $\{d_i\}$. We use discrete curve evolution (DCE) [10, 9] to find a temporary cut point. We treat the graph of the distance histogram as a polygonal curve P. DCE ellows us to recursively delete the vertices of P until only 5 vertices remain that best interpolate the shape of P Figure 1 shows a sample histogram (frequency plot) and the temporary cut point (marked with the arrow). The histogram plot of the distances of all the data points in a node from the representative is shown as a solid line and the evolved curve resulting from using the discrete curve evolution is shown as a dashed line. The first local minimum point in the evolved curve is chosen as the cut point.

2. Adjust the data partition: After splitting the data temporarily into two child nodes (*child1* and *child2*) the final split is found based on three criteria.

I) If the number of data points in one of the child nodes *child1* or *child2* is zero, the parent node N is labelled as a cluster and no further splitting is performed.

II) If criterion **I)** is not satisfied, then two representative points c_1, c_2 of the temporarily split data are computed. c_1 is a closest data point in *child1* to the mean of the distances $d(pr(N), a_i)$ of points a_i in *child1* to the representative of the parent node $pr(N)$. Similarly we determine c_2.

III) We declare a point x_i in N ambiguous, if it is is within the margin region

$$|d(x_i, c_1) - d(x_i, c_2)| \leq percentage * d(c_1, c_2).$$

If it is not ambiguous and closer to c_1 than to c_2, then it is mapped to cluster *newchild1* else to *newchild2*.

3. Tests on minimal number of points:
Finally we eliminate clusters that have less points than mnp.

2.3. Remapping

This is the final stage of our algorithm. We arrive here when all nodes are terminal leaf nodes. The centroids of all terminal leaf nodes (lc) and (rc) are computed and the data points from the leaf nodes labeled unclassified (uc) are mapped to their closest centroids in the feature space.

3 Comparison to PAM Clustering

Here we apply our partitioning method to 3 different data sets. On all of these data sets the proposed method performs better than PAM clustering. For our analysis we used the PAM function in the cluster library of the freely available software R (url: http://cran.r-project.org/). PAM takes as input a dissimilarity matrix between the observations and requires that the user specify the number of clusters k to be generated. In all of our analysis we used the Euclidean distance metric between the observations as dissimilarity matrix.

Our first test data set will be referred to as *ChallengeIII*. This simulated data set contains 2 clusters. Each cluster contains 50 observations. There are 4 features but only the first 2 features contain a signal while features 3 and 4 are random draws from a standard normal distribution. For cluster 1 and cluster 2 observations, the first 2 features are random draws from a beta distribution with shape parameters (2,5) and (5,2), respectively. When choosing input parameters $mnp = 30$ and $percentage = 0.05$, our proposed method misclassifies only one point. The adjusted Rand index [14] between assigned clusters and ground truth is .96 which reflects the very high agreement between cluster label and ground truth.

When using the same distance matrix in $k = 2$ medoid (PAM) clustering we find that 3 observations are misclassified which lowers the adjusted Rand index to .88. Thus our proposed method outperforms PAM on this data set.

The second data set is a subset of the NCI60 gene expression data from the National Cancer Institute (see [15] and http://genome-www.stanford.edu/nci60). We considered only 6 kinds of cancers and used the gene expression values of the 1375 genes that were available in the data set referred to as "T matrix". Our data set which could be referred to as NCI41 consisted of 41 cancer cell lines (a classical multi-dimensional scaling (MDS) plot is shown in Figure 2): 6 central nervous system (denoted by CN), 7 colon (CO), 6 leukemia (LE), 8 melanoma (M), 6 ovarian (O), and 8 renal (R) cancer cell lines.

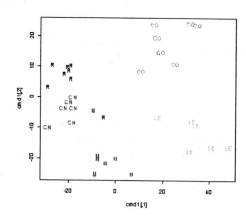

Figure 2: Classical MDS plot of the 41 samples in NIC41.

	CN	CO	LE	M	O	R
1	5	0	0	0	0	0
2	0	6	0	0	3	0
3	0	0	6	0	0	0
4	0	0	0	7	0	0
5	0	1	0	0	4	0
6	1	0	0	1	2	8

Figure 3: Our algorithm disagrees with the ground truth information for NIC41 in only five points.

We normalized the features so that they have mean zero and variance one. Our algorithm with the parameters $mnp = 3$ and $percentage = 0.01$ is very close to the ground truth: it misclassified 5 points resulting in an adjusted Rand index of .82; see Figure 3, where the rows correspond to the obtained clusters and the columns show the ground truth.

We also applied our partitioning method to the Euclidean distance matrix of the normalized feature space. With the parameters $mnp = 1$ and $percentage = 0.05$ the clustering method misclassified 9 points which resulted in an adjusted Rand index of .58. When applying PAM clustering (k=6) to the same distance measure we found that PAM misclassifies 12 observations, which lowered the adjusted Rand index to .47. Thus our proposed method outperforms PAM on this data set.

The third data set is the classical data set called Irises. It is composed of 150 observations with 4 feature measurements. As ground truth we have three clusters, each with 50 points. There is one clearly separated cluster A and two clusters B and C that are hard to distinguish. We applied our algorithm to the distance matrix of the data computed without feature normalization. It misclassified 10 observations from clusters B and C with a corresponding adjusted Rand index of .82. The results obtained with the parameters $mnp = 25$ and $percentage = 0.01$ are summarized in the table shown in Fig. 4, where the rows correspond to the obtained clusters and the columns show the ground truth.

When using the same distance measure in PAM $k = 3$ clustering, we find 16 misclassifications and a the adjusted Rand

	1	2	3
1	50	0	0
2	0	49	9
3	0	1	41

Figure 4: Our algorithm disagrees with the ground truth information for Irises data in 10 points. Adjusted Rand index is .82.

index was lowered to .73. Again, our proposed method outperforms PAM. Matlab source code of our algorithm can be found at www.cis.temple.edu/~latecki/Clustering.

References

[1] Breiman, Leo, Friedman, J.H., Olshen, R.A., and Stone, C.J. *Classification and Regression Tree's.* Wadsworth, 1984.

[2] B.S.Everitt Cluster analysis *Heinemann, London* 1974.

[3] C. Hennig and L. J. Latecki. The choice of vantage objects for image retrieval *Pattern Recognition* 36, pp. 2187-2196, 2003.

[4] Hand, D.J. *Discrimination and Classification.* Wiley, 1981.

[5] Hand, D.J. *Construction and Assessment of Classification Rules.* Wiley, 1997.

[6] Hartigan, J. *Clustering Algorithms.* Wiley, 1975.

[7] L. Kaufman and P.J. Rousseeu. *Finding Groups in Data.* Wiley, New York, 1989.

[8] Kohonen, T. *Self-Organizing Maps.* Springer, Berlin, 1995.

[9] L. J. Latecki and D. de Wildt. Automatic Recognition of Unpredictable Events in Videos *Proc. ICPR*, Vol. 2, 2002.

[10] L. J. Latecki and R. Lakamper Shape Similarity Measure Based on Correspondence of Visual Parts *IEEE Trans. Pattern Analysis and Machine Intelligence (PAMI)* 22, pp. 1185-1190, 2000.

[11] Bing Liu, Yiyuan Xia and Philip S. Yu. CLTree - Clustering through decision tree construction *IBM Research Report* RC21695, 20/3/2000.

[12] B. Pavel. Survey of clustering data mining techniques. *Accrue Software Inc* 2002.

[13] J. R. Quinlan. C4.5: program for machine learning *Morgan Kaufmann* 1992.

[14] W.M. Rand. Objective criteria for the evaluation of clustering methods. *J. of the American Statistical As.* 66, 846-850, 1971.

[15] D. T. Ross, U. Scherf, M. B. Eisen, C. M. Perou, P. Spellman, V. Iyer, S.S. Jeffrey, M. V de Rijn, M. Waltham, A. Pergamenschikov. Systematic variation in gene expression patterns in human cancer cell lines. *Nat Genet* 24, 227–234, 2000.

[16] Classification Trees *Electronic Statistic Textbook, Statsoft Inc.* "http://www.statsoftinc.com/textbook/ stathome.html"

[17] Classification Trees: Slide notes "http://medg.lcs.mit.edu/hamish/6872LECT/sld001.htm"

CoMine: Efficient Mining of Correlated Patterns *

Young-Koo Lee, Won-Young Kim, Y. Dora Cai, and Jiawei Han

University of Illinois at Urbana-Champaign, Illinois, U.S.A.

{yklee, wykim, doracai, hanj}@uiuc.edu

Abstract

Association rule mining often generates a huge number of rules, but a majority of them either are redundant or do not reflect the true correlation relationship among data objects. In this paper, we re-examine this problem and show that two interesting measures, all_confidence (denoted as α) and coherence (denoted as γ), both disclose genuine correlation relationships and can be computed efficiently. Moreover, we propose two interesting algorithms, CoMine(α) and CoMine(γ), based on extensions of a pattern-growth methodology. Our performance study shows that the CoMine algorithms have high performance in comparison with their Apriori-based counterpart algorithms.

1. Introduction

Association rule mining is a widely studied topic in data mining research. Its popularity can be attributed to the simplicity of the problem statement and the efficiency of its initial algorithms, such as Apriori [1]. Unfortunately, association mining with real data sets is not so simple. If the *min_support* threshold is high, only commonsense "knowledge" will be found. However, when *min_support* is set low, a huge number of association rules will usually be generated, a majority of which are redundant or noninformative. The true correlation relationships among data objects are buried deep among a large pile of useless rules.

To overcome this difficulty, *correlation* has been adopted as an interesting measures since most people are interested in not only association-like co-occurrences but also the possible strong correlations

implied by such co-occurrences. Brin et al. [2] introduced *lift* (called *interest* there) and a χ^2 correlation measure and developed methods for mining such correlations. However, since these measures based on sophisticated statistical computations do not have the *downward closure property* [1], some approximate similarity measures has to be proposed to explore efficient computation. Ma and Hellerstein [5] proposed a mutually dependent patterns and an Apriori-based mining algorithm. Recently, Omiecinski [7] introduced two interesting measures, called *all_confidence* and *bond*. Both have the downward closure property. Experimental results on some real data sets show that these measures are appealing since they reduce significantly the number of patterns mined, and the patterns are coherent.

In this study, we contribute to mining strongly correlated patterns in two aspects. First, several popularly used measures related to correlation mining are re-examined. Our discussion shows that both *all_confidence* (denoted as α) and *coherence* (called *bond* in [7]) (denoted as γ here) are good measures and in most cases are better than the popularly used *lift* and χ^2 measures. Second, we develop two interesting algorithms, CoMine(α) and CoMine(γ), by extension of a pattern-growth mining methodology [3]. Our experimental and performance study shows that both CoMine algorithms generate truly interesting correlation patterns and have better performance over their Apriori-based counterpart algorithms, Partition [7].

2 What measures are good for mining correlated patterns?

In this section, we examine which of these four measures: *all_confidence*, *coherence*, *lift*, and χ^2, is more suitable at expressing correlations among items in a transactional database. We proceed by first introducing a few concepts.

Let $I = \{i_1, i_2, \ldots, i_m\}$ be a set of items, and DB be a database that consists of a set of transactions. Each

*The work was supported in part by National Science Foundation under Grant No. 02-09199, the Univ. of Illinois, and an IBM Faculty Award. Any opinions, findings, and conclusions or recommendations expressed in this material are those of the author(s) and do not necessarily reflect the views of the funding agencies.

transaction T consists of a set of items such that $T \subseteq I$. Each transaction is associated with an identifier, called *TID*. Let A be a set of items, referred to as an *itemset*. An itemset that contains k items is a *k-itemset*. A transaction T is said to *contain* A if and only if $A \subseteq T$. The *support* of an itemset X in DB, denoted as $sup(X)$, is the number of transactions in DB containing X. An itemset X is *frequent* if it occurs no less frequent than a user-defined *min_support* threshold.

Definition 2.1 *Given an itemset $X = \{i_1, i_2, \ldots, i_k\}$, the universe, the max_item_sup, all_confidence, and the coherence of X are defined as,*

$$universe(X) = \{t_i \in DB | \exists i_j \in X (i_j \in t_i)\} \qquad (1)$$

$$max\_item\_sup(X) = max\{sup(i_j) | \forall i_j \in X\} \qquad (2)$$

$$all\_conf(X) = \frac{sup(X)}{max\_item\_sup(X)} \qquad (3)$$

$$coh(X) = \frac{sup(X)}{|universe(X)|} \qquad (4)$$

Two other measures, *lift* and χ^2, have been popularly used. χ^2 follows the standard definition in statistics [6], whereas the *lift* of two itemsets A and B is defined as [2],

$$lift(AB) = \frac{sup(AB)}{sup(A)sup(B)} \qquad (5)$$

Given a transaction database *DB*, a *minimum support* threshold *min_support*, a *minimum all_confidence* threshold *min_α*, and a *minimum coherence* threshold *min_γ*, a frequent itemset X is **all_confident** if $all\_conf(X) \geq min\_\alpha$; and it is **coherent** if $coh(X) \geq min\_\gamma$.

Example 1 The correlation relationships between the purchases of two items, *milk* and *coffee*, can be examined by summarizing their purchase history in the form of Table 1, a 2×2 contingency table, where an entry such as *mc* represents the number of transactions containing both milk and coffee. Table 1 shows the concrete contingency tables and the four measures for a set of transaction database A_1 to A_4. From the table, one can see that m and c are strongly positively correlated in A_1 but strongly negatively correlated in A_2. However, λ (lift) and χ^2 are very poor indicators, whereas α and γ are very good ones. Similarly, A_3 is negatively correlated, which cannot be shown by λ and χ^2 but clearly shown by α and γ values. Finally, values in A_4 are independent, which is correctly shown in λ, α, and χ^2 and approximated in γ. The reason that λ and χ^2 are so poor in many cases is because they are strongly

influenced by the value of $\overline{mc}$ which is usually big and across a wide range (many people may buy neither m nor c). On the other hand, the definitions of α and γ remove the influence of $\overline{mc}$, playing a similar role as Jaccard coefficient in cluster analysis [4]. ■

Our experiments using a real database called the CRIME data set[1] show that mining for all_confident or coherent patterns generates a much smaller set but truly correlated patterns in real databases. We omit the details due to lack of space.

3. Mining All_Confident Patterns

Given *min_support* and *min_α*, the set of all_confident patterns can be computed in the spirit of the Apriori algorithm. However, as many studies have shown [3], Apriori may not be very efficient when a database is large and/or when patterns to be mined are numerous and/or long because it may generate a huge set of candidate patterns. Therefore, we will examine how to develop more efficient methods for evaluation of such measures. This leads to the development of CoMine algorithms by extension of the pattern-growth methodology, represented by FP-growth [3].

Algorithm CoMine(α) is described briefly as follows. First, we build an FP-tree, in which the labels on each path in FP-tree and the entries in a header table of the tree are ordered in the f_list order, the order of descending support counts [3]. Then, we perform tree mining by traversing down the header table. Algorithm 1 shows the tree mining algorithm for the α conditional FP-tree. For each item in the header of the tree, repeat the following. Examine the items in the header in a top-down manner. In Algorithm 1, Line 2 generates the all_confidence pattern β. Since the FP-tree is constructed in such a way that every β becomes an all_confidence pattern, we do not need to check whether β satisfies the conditions. Lines 3 and 4 compute count for each item in β-projected database. Lines 5–8 conduct pruning based on *min_support* and *min_α*. Thus, β's conditional database contains only the items b_j's such that βb_j satisfies both the minimum support and all_confidence thresholds.

When computing count for each item in β-projected database, CoMine(α) reduces the search space using the properties of the all_confidence measure. In the β-conditional database, for item x to be included in an all_confidence pattern, the support of αx (= the

[1] The CRIME data set can be obtained from a crime report database from a Web site related to NIBRS (National Incident-Based Reporting System) (http://www.icpsr.umich.edu/NACJD/NIBRS)

	milk	¬milk	row_sum
coffee	mc	$\overline{m}c$	c
¬coffee	$m\overline{c}$	$\overline{m}\,\overline{c}$	$\overline{c}$
col_sum	m	$\overline{m}$	Σ

DB	mc	$\overline{m}c$	$m\overline{c}$	$\overline{m}\,\overline{c}$	λ	α	γ	χ^2
A_1	1000	100	100	10,000	9.26	0.91	0.83	9055
A_2	100	1000	1000	100,000	8.44	0.09	0.05	670
A_3	1000	100	10000	100,000	9.18	0.09	0.09	8172
A_4	1000	1000	1000	1000	1	0.5	0.33	0

Table 1. Contingency tables and a few measures.

Algorithm 1 CoMine(α): Mining all_confidence patterns by extending the FP-growth method

Procedure FP-mine($Tree$, α)

1: **for** each a_i in the header of $Tree$ **do**
2:     generate pattern $\beta = \alpha \cup a_i$ with all_conf = $sup(\beta)/max\_item\_sup(\beta)$; $\{sup(\beta) = sup(a_i)$ in α-projected database$\}$
3:     get a set I_β of items to be included in β-projected database;
4:     for each item in I_β, compute its count in β-projected database;
5:     **for** each b_j in I_β **do**
6:        if $sup(\beta b_j) < min\_support$, delete b_j from I_β; $\{$pruning based on minimum support$\}$
7:        if $all\_conf(\beta b_j) < min\_\alpha$, delete b_j from I_β; $\{$pruning based on minimum all_confidence$\}$
8:     **end for**
9:     construct β-conditional FP-tree with items in I_β $Tree_\beta$;
10:     **if** $Tree_\beta \neq \emptyset$ **then**
11:        call FP-mine($Tree_\beta$, β)
12:     **end if**
13: **end for**

---

support of x in the α-conditional database) should be no less than $min\_\alpha \times max\_item\_sup(\beta x)$. With this pruning rule, we can reduce the set of items I_β to be counted and, thus, reduce the number of nodes visited when traversing the FP-tree to count each item in I_β.

4. Mining Coherent Patterns

In this section we present an efficient coherent pattern mining algorithm, called CoMine(γ). Unlike the extension of FP-growth for mining all_confidence patterns, the extension for mining coherent patterns has a challenging problem: computing the cardinalities of the universes for given itemsets using the FP-tree.

We present a novel method for computing the cardinality values by exploiting the characteristics of the FP-tree. Let $X = a_1 a_2 \ldots a_n$ be an itemset and A_i be the TID set for item a_i. We can compute $|universe(a_1, a_2, \ldots, a_n)|$ by computing

Data set	#Tuples	#Items	ATL/MTL
gazelle	59602	497	2.5/267
pumsb	49046	2113	74/74

Table 2. Characteristics of Real Data sets.

$|universe(a_1, a_2, \ldots, a_{n-1})| + |A_n| - |(A_1 \cup A_2 \cup \ldots \cup A_{n-1}) \cap A_n|$. Here, $|universe(a_1, a_2, \ldots, a_{n-1})|$ has been computed in the previous step since we follow the top-down approach. $|A_n|$ can be obtained by maintaining the support for each item. We can compute $|(A_1 \cup A_2 \cup \ldots \cup A_{n-1}) \cap A_n|$ by adding the values of the nodes of label a_n that has any of the item $a_1, a_2, \ldots a_{n-1}$ as an ancestor using node-link and parent link of FP-tree[3].

Although we can compute the size of the universe using the FP-tree, the cost is still non-negligible. We can reduce the number of computations by first checking the following condition: $\frac{sup(X)}{|universe(a_1, a_2, \ldots, a_{n-1})|} \geq min\_\gamma$. If this condition fail, there is no need to compute the size of universe.

5. Experiments

In this section, we report our experimental results on the performance of CoMine in comparison with an efficient Apriori-based counterpart algorithm, *Partition* algorithm[7]. Our implementation of Partition algorithms also contains optimization techniques proposed in [5, 8]. The result shows that CoMine outperforms *Partition*, and it is efficient and scalable for mining correlated patterns in large databases. Experiments were performed on a 2.2GHz Pentium IV PC with 512MB of memory, running Windows 2000. Algorithms were coded with Visual C++.

Our experiments were performed on real data sets as shown in Table 2. Gazelle comes from click-stream data from Gazelle.com and pumsb is obtained from www.almaden.ibm.com. The gazelle is rather sparse in comparison with pumsb, which is very dense so that it produces many long frequent itemsets even for very high values of support.

Let us compare the relatively efficiency the Partition

and CoMine methods on a transactional data set. Figure 1 shows the performance on the gazelle data set when min_sup is fixed at 0.1% and min_conf varies. As we can see in these figures, CoMine always outperforms counterpart Partition for the coherence and all_confidence measures over the entire range of confidence threshold. This is because as the support or confidence threshold goes down, the number as well as the length of frequent itemsets increases and FP-growth-based methods have better scalability than Apriori-based methods under these circumstances.

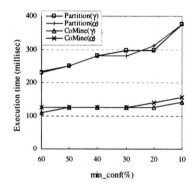

Figure 1. Gazelle when $min\_sup = 0.1\%$.

Figure 2 shows the execution time on the pumsb data set using different confidence threshold when the min_sup is fixed at 5%. It also shows that CoMine algorithms always outperform Partition algorithms. When min_conf is less than 75%, Partition algorithms run out of memory and cannot finish. At min_conf 80%, CoMine(α) can be more than 300 times faster than Partition(α) and CoMine(γ) can be more than 1000 times faster than Partition(γ). Figure 2 indicates that the gaps between CoMine(γ) and CoMine(α) are quite small compared with that of Partition(γ) and Partition(α) (Notice that the vertical axis is on a log scale). This is because CoMine(γ) uses the efficient algorithm of computing cardinalities of universes and pruning rules.

6. Conclusions

In this paper, we show that mining all_confidence and coherent patterns generates highly correlated patterns and are better measures than association-based confidence measure and two other claimed correlation measures: lift and χ^2. For efficient mining of the two kinds of correlation patterns, we proposed a new method, called CoMine, which consists of two algorithms CoMine(α) and CoMine(γ) for computing

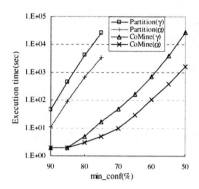

Figure 2. Pumsb when $min\_sup = 5\%$.

all_confident and coherent patterns respectively. For CoMine(γ), the proposed method can compute the cardinality of the universe efficiently using the FP-tree structure only. Several pruning methods are also developed that reduce the search space. Our extensive performance study shows that CoMine generates desirable correlation patterns and outperforms the previously proposed Apriori-based algorithms.

References

[1] R. Agrawal and R. Srikant. Fast algorithms for mining association rules. In *Proc. VLDB*, Sept. 1994.

[2] S. Brin, R. Motwani, and C. Silverstein. Beyond market basket: Generalizing association rules to correlations. In *Proc. SIGMOD*, May 1997.

[3] J. Han, J. Pei, and Y. Yin. Mining frequent patterns without candidate generation. In *Proc. SIGMOD*, May 2000.

[4] L. Kaufman and P. J. Rousseeuw. *Finding Groups in Data: an Introduction to Cluster Analysis*. John Wiley & Sons, 1990.

[5] S. Ma and J. L. Hellerstein. Mining mutually dependent patterns. In *Proc. ICDM*, Nov. 2001.

[6] S. Morishita and J. Sese. Traversing itemset lattice with statistical metric pruning. In *Proc. PODS*, May 2001.

[7] E. Omiecinski. Alternative interest measures for mining associations. *IEEE Trans. Knowledge and Data Engineering*, 15:57–69, 2003.

[8] H. Xiong, P.-N. Tan, and V. Kumar. Mining hyperclique patterns with confidence pruning. In *Tech. Report*, Univ. of Minnesota, Minneapolis, March 2003.

Ensembles of Cascading Trees

Jinyan Li   Huiqing Liu

Institute for Infocomm Research

21 Heng Mui Keng Terrace, Singapore 119613

{jinyan,huiqing}@i2r.a-star.edu.sg

Abstract

We introduce a new method, called CS4, to construct committees of decision trees for classification. The method considers different top-ranked features as the root nodes of member trees. This idea is particularly suitable for dealing with high-dimensional bio-medical data as top-ranked features in this type of data usually possess similar merits for classification. To make a decision, the committee combines the power of individual trees in a weighted manner. Unlike Bagging or Boosting which uses bootstrapped training data, our method builds all the member trees of a committee using exactly the same set of training data. We have tested these ideas on UCI data sets as well as recent bio-medical data sets of gene expression or proteomic profiles that are usually described by more than 10,000 features. All the experimental results show that our method is efficient and that the classification performance are superior to C4.5 family algorithms.

1 Introduction

Ensemble methods—such as constructing committees of decision trees as described in this paper—have been shown to improve the accuracy of single base classifiers with significant effectiveness [2, 3, 1, 5, 4]. The instability of base learning algorithms provides room for ensemble methods to improve the performance of the base classifiers. For example, Bagging [2] and Boosting [5] —two of the most widely used ensemble approaches that improve performance through manipulating original training data— explore the instability that small changes to the training data can lead to large changes in the learned classifier. They construct multiple base trees, each time using a bootstrapped replicate of the original training data.

Our new ideas to construct committees of decision trees were inspired by two interesting observations from our previous studies [9, 7, 8, 11] on gene expression and proteomic profiling data:

1. We found that many ensembles constructed by the Boosting method were singletons. This is due to a stopping criteria that is used to terminate the sequential construction of base classifiers in Boosting. If the training error of a current classifier is zero, then Boosting will not proceed to generate any more new classifiers.

2. We also found that many top-ranked features possess similar discriminating merits with little difference for classification.

The first observation indicates that it is necessary to break the constraint of the stopping criteria of Boosting. Otherwise, the ensemble method will have no difference from a base classifier in some cases. The second observation suggests that it is worthwhile to employ different top-ranked features as the root nodes for building multiple decision trees. These motivations have led to our cascading approach described below.

In our method, we first rank all features of a training set according to their gain ratios [10] (or by other measures such as entropy). Denote $ftr^1, ftr^2, \cdots, ftr^k$ as top k ranked features. Then in a *cascading* manner, we force ftr^i to be the root node of the ith tree. All the other nodes are then constructed as usual. We call such decision trees *cascading trees*, emphasizing that the selection of the root nodes is from the highest position to a lower kth position feature. In this way, we distinguish our cascading trees from those generated by the Bagging [2], Boosting [5], or Randomization method [4].

Note that our method makes use of the instability of base classifiers unlike Bagging and Boosting: Instead of manipulating the training data, we keep the original training data unchanged but change the learning phase of base classifiers. So, our cascading method solves another problem that often occurs with bio-data analysis using Bagging or Boosting. The problem is that: Rules induced from bootstrapped training data may not be correct when applied to the original data as some samples are duplicated and some are removed during training. This is of a critical concern in bio-medical applications such as the understanding and diagnosis of a disease. Although the approach may help to improve the resulting classifiers' accuracy, the Bagging or Boosting rules have to be understood with caution. However, rules from cascading trees are required to be all true with the training data, leading to a more exact understanding of the data.

Cascading trees usually have different structures and contain different features, yet these diversified trees can perform almost equally well on both training and test data. So, the cascading idea can be used to build tree committees such that they contain many "experts". Thus, the committees would bring large potential to improve the performance of the base classifiers. To combine these cascading trees for classification, we *share* the rules in the trees of a committee in a weighted manner. Basically, we compare important global rules with those rules that are locally satisfied by specific test samples, then we integrate these comparisons into a classification score. Together, the cascading idea guides the construction of tree committees while the sharing idea aggregates the decisions made by those individual trees. For convenience, we therefore name our classifier CS4: *cascading-and-sharing for* constructing decision tree ensembles.

Our cascading idea is related to but different from the randomization idea used in [4]. Like cascading trees, randomized trees are also derived from the same original training data rather than from bootstrapped training data. Unlike cascading trees, all randomized trees in a committee may share one and only one root node though their internal nodes could be different in a manner of random choice from a set of candidate features. Therefore the diversity of cascading trees has larger potential than that of randomized trees.

In this paper, we also introduce a new data set repository. We used data in this repository to evaluate the performance of our new classifier CS4. This repository is named Kent Ridge Bio-medical Data Set Repository. It can be accessed via `http://sdmc.i2r.a-star.edu.sg/GEDatasets/Datasets.html`. Currently we have stored 10 data sets in this repository that are gene expression data, protein profiling data, or genomic sequence data published recently in prestigious journals such as *Science*, *Nature* and so on for diagnostic or prognostic cancer studies. A distinctive characteristic of these data sets is: while their volume is not large, containing about only hundreds of samples, the data are of high dimensions, usually having more than 10,000 features. This characteristic is in contrast to the data sets stored at the widely used UCI machine learning repository where many of the data sets are described by less than 20 features.

In Section 3, we give one example of the performance of our CS4 classifier. For comparison, we also report the performance of single C4.5 trees, C4.5 Bagging committees, and C4.5 Boosting committees as they are the closest algorithm family to our method. Non-linear kernel-based support vector machines and instance-based k-nearest neighbours are very accurate classifiers. We compare our results with theirs to obtain a fuller picture about the performance of our CS4 method. The results will show that CS4 is indeed an accurate classifier that has consistently better performance than the C4.5 family algorithms and k-nearest neighbour, and that it has a comparable performance to support vector machines.

Other issues such as speed efficiency, ways to extend our cascading idea, as well as alternative ways to integrate the power of a committee are discussed in our full paper [6].

2 Cascading and an Illustrating Example

We show a typical example of our tree committees, and explain why tree committees are needed for classification and why cascading is a good approach.

2.1 Cascading: A new method to construct committees of trees

Suppose n number of features describe a given data. To construct k ($k \leq n$) number of trees, we use following steps: (a) Use gain ratios to rank all the features into an ordered list with the best feature at the first position; (b) $i = 1$; (c) Use the ith feature as root node to construct the ith tree; (d) Increase i by 1 and go to Step 3, until $i = k$.

Usually we set the number of trees k as 20. Steps (a) and (b) reflect our cascading idea: The root node of the trees shifts from the most important feature to the kth most important feature.

2.2 An example

We illustrate our main ideas using a real example here with an aim to show: (1) Whether top-ranked features have similar gain ratios; (2) Whether our cascading trees have similar training performance; (3) Whether they have similar, but perhaps not perfect accuracy on test data; (4) Whether their combinations converge to the true optimal function—that is, whether the expanding tree committees reduce the test errors gradually.

The data used here are a collection of gene expression profiles of 143 cells used to differentiate the subtype `Hyperdip>50` against some other subtypes of the childhood leukemia disease [11]. There are 12558 features describing the data profiles. Details about the 94 training samples and 49 test samples are shown in Table 1.

The gain ratios of the 20 top-ranked features in this data set are close to each other. The first 10 features' gain ratios are: 0.39, 0.36, 0.35, 0.33, 0.33, 0.33, 0.33, 0.32, 0.31, and 0.30; The second 10 features' gain ratios are: 0.30,

Table 1. Training and test data for differentiation between the subtype Hyperdip>50 and some other subtypes of childhood leukemia.

Class	# of Training Samples	# of Test Samples	# of Features
Hyperdip>50	42	22	12558
Others	52	27	12558

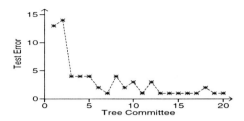

Figure 1. The performance trend when the committee is expanded by adding our cascading trees one by one. The test error becomes almost stable at the level of one mistake after the 13th tree is added into the committee.

0.30, 0.30, 0.29, 0.29, 0.28, 0.28, 0.28, 0.28, and 0.28. The biggest difference of the ratios, between the first and the 20th feature, is only 0.11—in fact, these two features' partitionings are different in only a few samples. Naturally, we should try each of them as root nodes to construct decision trees.

Using the cascading idea on these top-ranked features, we constructed a committee of 20 trees. Table 2 shows the training errors (i.e. number of samples wrongly classified over the training data) and test errors (i.e. number of samples wrongly classified over the test data) of the 20 trees.

Clearly, the performance of these trees were not perfect and fluctuated very much even on the training samples. So, each of them is far from the true optimal function. In particular, observe that the first tree, which was rooted by the best feature, made no training errors but 13 test errors. However, the 6th tree, which was *not* rooted by the best feature, made no training errors but only 5 test errors. This observation supports the following two points:

1. The first tree does not always have the best performance.

2. Alternative trees rooted by other top-ranked features may have better performance than the first tree.

In fact, from our previous experience, this phenomenon occurs quite often in bio-medical data. We randomly examined ten pairs of our first and second trees, and found 4 pairs where the first tree won, 3 pairs where the second tree won, and 3 pairs where the two trees got a tie in performance. This is also a reason why the cascading idea is a good idea to construct tree committees.

Next, we combine the trees to form committees and to see whether there is a convergence path of test errors. When combining the first two trees, the committee made 14 mistakes on the test data. After adding the third, the test errors were reduced to 4. Sequentially adding one by one until the 20th tree, the corresponding tree committees made 4, 4, ⋯, 1 and finally only one mistake on the 49 test samples. Note also that all the committees made no mistake on the training data. Figure 1 shows the error reduction curve when the tree committees were expanded by adding our cascading trees, indicating a perfect convergence route to the true function.

In comparison, Bagging and Boosting made 2 and 13 test errors respectively on this data set. In this case, Bagging also significantly reduced the error numbers of the single decision trees, just like our method, but we will show later that our overall accuracy is better than Bagging on a wide range of datasets. Boosting made the same number of mistakes as the single C4.5 tree did—a poor performance of 13 errors. This is because the first tree of the Boosting committee made no mistakes on the training data, causing the algorithm to stop generating other base classifiers. As a result, this Boosting committee is a singleton, unable to take real committee power.

This example tells us that while a single tree may explain the data, there exist many alternative sets of good features and trees that can also explain the data equally well. To handle complex high-dimensional data, a single tree is too thin. Furthermore, the mutual-exclusivity of rules in a tree cuts off many inherent relations and interactions among the data, particularly when applied to high-dimensional data sets. Thus, we need multiple trees to represent the data and allow every data point to be explained by many rules. Together, the multiple cross-supportive rules or trees can strengthen the power of prediction, and then eliminate possible biased decisions.

For classification, a simple way to combine the cascading trees of a committee is to equally vote them, just as Bagging usually does. However, in equal voting, rules no matter significant or trivial, play the same weight of roles in the prediction. We therefore introduce a voting method that distinguish the roles of significant and trivial rules based on the concept of *coverage*. Note that the *coverage* of a rule in a tree is the percentage of the samples in its class satisfying the rule. The main purpose of this weighted-voting combination method is to avoid the situations where the trivial rules play a decisive role. Detailed description of this weighting method is given in our full paper [6].

Table 2. The training and test errors of our 20 single cascading decision trees on the Hyperdip>50 vs Others data set that consist of 94 training and 49 test samples.

Tree No.	1	2	3	4	5	6	7	8	9	10	11	12	13	14	15	16	17	18	19	20
Training Errors	0	3	1	2	1	**0**	1	1	1	1	1	0	3	2	1	2	2	1	2	1
Test Errors	13	9	7	12	12	**5**	8	11	9	7	14	8	12	10	6	6	9	8	8	8

Table 3. The error numbers (Cancer : Normal) of 10-fold cross validation by five classification algorithms on the ovarian disease data set.

Methods	CS4	C4.5		
		Single	Bagging	Boosting
Errors	0 (0:0)	10 (4:6)	7 (3:4)	10 (4:6)

3 Results on an Ovarian Disease Data Set

The data is about the diagnosis of the ovarian disease using proteomic mass/charge ratios. The data consist of 253 serum samples, 91 of them are from non-cancer patients and the rest 162 from ovarian cancer patients. Each data sample is described by 15,154 features, namely, the relative amplitudes of the intensities at 15,154 molecular mass/charge (M/Z) identities.

We have conducted 10-fold cross-validations to evaluate the classification algorithms. Our CS4 classifier made no mistake on the entire sample set, giving a truely perfect diagnosis accuracy for ovarian cancer based on proteomic serum data in this case. However, the C4.5 family algorithms made at least 7 mistakes—see Table 3 for the results.

For each of the 10 folds, we found that the single C4.5 tree made no mistake on the training data. As a result, the Boosting committees were all singletons. Thus, they made the same number of mistakes as the single C4.5 trees.

The k-nearest neighbour method did not perform well, making a total of 15 mistakes (6 in Cancer and 9 in Normal). On the other hand, SVM made no mistake, also achieving the perfect 100% accuracy as ours. However, let us discuss the structure of the classification models in further details. SVM has used all the 15,154 input features together with 40 support vectors and 8,308 kernel evaluations in its decisions. It is a complicated model, making it difficult to derive any understandable explanations for each diagnostic decision made by this system. In comparison, our method used only 20 trees and less than 100 rules, with each rule containing about three features. Clearly, the understandability of CS4 is much more acceptable to the medical doctors.

Another interesting observation here is that SVM was unable to reach 100% accuracy in the 10-fold cross validation if only the top 20 or 30 features were used. Similar numbers of mistakes were also made by C4.5, Bagging and Boosting, no matter whether top 20, 30, 50, 100, or 200 features were used. It indicates that some very lower-ranked features can play a necessary role in perfect classification.

Acknowledgment: We thank Dr. See-Kiong Ng and Dr. Limsoon Wong for kindly giving useful comments on a draft of this paper.

References

[1] E. Bauer and R. Kohavi. An empirical comparison of voting classification algorithms: Bagging, boosting, and variants. *Machine Learning*, 36:105–139, 1999.

[2] L. Breiman. Bagging predictors. *Machine Learning*, 24:123–140, 1996.

[3] L. Breiman. Random forest. *Machine Learning*, 45:5–32, 2001.

[4] T. G. Dietterich. An experimental comparison of three methods for constructing ensembles of decision trees: Bagging, boosting, and randomization. *Machine Learning*, 40:139–158, 2000.

[5] Y. Freund and R. E. Schapire. Experiments with a new boosting algorithm. In L. Saitta, editor, *Machine Learning: Proceedings of the Thirteenth International Conference*, pages 148–156, Bari, Italy, July 1996. Morgan Kaufmann.

[6] J. Li and H. Liu. CS4: Ensembles of cascading trees. In *http://sdmc.i2r.a-star.edu.sg/jinyan*, pages 1–15, 2003.

[7] J. Li, H. Liu, J. R. Downing, A. E.-J. Yeoh, and L. Wong. Simple rules underlying gene expression profiles of more than six subtypes of acute lymphoblastic leukemia (ALL) patients. *Bioinformatics*, 19:71–78, 2003.

[8] J. Li, H. Liu, S.-K. Ng, and L. Wong. Discovery of significant rules for classifying cancer diagnosis data. *Bioinformatics*, 19:To appear, 2003.

[9] J. Li and L. Wong. Identifying good diagnostic gene groups from gene expression profiles using the concept of emerging patterns. *Bioinformatics*, 18:725–734, 2002.

[10] J. R. Quinlan. *C4.5: Programs for Machine Learning*. Morgan Kaufmann, San Mateo, CA, 1993.

[11] E.-J. Yeoh, M. E. Ross, S. A. Shurtleff, W. K. Williams, D. Patel, R. Mahfouz, F. G. Behm, S. C. Raimondi, M. V. Relling, A. Patel, C. Cheng, D. Campana, D. Wilkins, X. Zhou, J. Li, H. Liu, C.-H. Pui, W. E. Evans, C. Naeve, L. Wong, and J. R. Downing. Classification, subtype discovery, and prediction of outcome in pediatric acute lymphoblastic leukemia by gene expression profiling. *Cancer Cell*, 1:133–143, 2002.

Using Discriminant Analysis for Multi-class Classification

Tao Li[*]   Shenghuo Zhu[†]   Mitsunori Ogihara[‡]

Abstract

Discriminant analysis is known to learn discriminative feature transformations. This paper studies its use in multi-class classification problems. The performance is tested on a large collection of benchmark datasets.

1 Introduction

Classification is an important machine learning problem. Support vector machines (SVMs) [20] have shown superb performance in binary classification and they are accurate and robust. However, the elegant theory behind SVMs cannot be easily extended to multi-class classification problems. A number of resolutions have been proposed. One-versus-the-rest method, pairwise comparison [6], and error-correcting output coding [3, 1] are techniques for decomposing multi-class problems into a collection of binary problems. Unfortunately, these techniques are not without limitations [1]. Also, training is slow in SVMs ($O(n^\alpha)$ for some $\alpha \in [1.7, 2.1]$ [7]. So, it is worth searching for other techniques that can directly handle multi-class classification problems.

In statistical pattern recognition discriminant analysis has been well studied [5]. Fisher discriminant analysis finds a discriminative feature transformation as the collection eigenvectors of matrix $T = \hat{\Sigma}_w^{-1}\hat{\Sigma}_b$ where $\hat{\Sigma}_w$ is the intra-class covariance matrix and $\hat{\Sigma}_b$ is the inter-class covariance matrix. It has been shown [18] that the decision hyperplanes for binary classification obtained by SVMs is equivalent to the solution obtained by Fisher's linear discriminant on the set of support vectors. Although Fisher's discriminant analysis was originally developed for two classes, it can be easily extended so as to deal with more than two classes via multiple discriminant analysis [8]. In fact, discriminant

analysis has been widely used in face recognition [5], but the datasets for face recognition are generally very small.

We present a comprehensive study of the use of linear discriminant analysis for multi-class classification using a large collection of benchmark datasets. The experiments show that discriminant analysis is simple, fast, easy to implement, and accurate.

2 Linear Discriminant Analysis(LDA)

2.1 Two-class LDA

Fisher's idea behind LDA is to transform the multivariate observations $\mathbf{x}$ to univariate observations $\mathbf{y}$ such that the $\mathbf{y}$'s derived from the two classes were separated as much as possible. Suppose that we have a set of m p-dimensional samples $\mathbf{x_1}, \mathbf{x_2}, \cdots, \mathbf{x_m}$ (where $\mathbf{x_i} = (x_{i1}, \cdots, x_{ip})$) belonging to two different classes, c_1 and c_2. For the two classes, the scatter matrices are given as

$$S_i = \sum_{\mathbf{x} \in c_i} (\mathbf{x} - \bar{\mathbf{x}_i})(\mathbf{x} - \bar{\mathbf{x}_i})',$$

where $\bar{\mathbf{x}_i} = \frac{1}{m_i}\sum_{\mathbf{x} \in c_i} \mathbf{x}$ and m_i is the number of samples in c_i. Hence the total intra-class scatter matrix is given by

$$\hat{\Sigma}_w = S_1 + S_2 = \sum_i \sum_{\mathbf{x} \in c_i} (\mathbf{x} - \bar{\mathbf{x}_i})(\mathbf{x} - \bar{\mathbf{x}_i})'. \quad (1)$$

The inter-class scatter matrix is given by

$$\hat{\Sigma}_b = (\bar{\mathbf{x}_1} - \bar{\mathbf{x}_2})(\bar{\mathbf{x}_1} - \bar{\mathbf{x}_2})'.$$

Fisher's criterion suggested the linear transformation Φ that maximizes the ratio of the determinant of the inter-class scatter matrix of the projected samples to the intra-class scatter matrix of the projected samples:

$$\mathcal{J}(\Phi) = \frac{|\Phi^T\hat{\Sigma}_b\Phi|}{|\Phi^T\hat{\Sigma}_w\Phi|}. \quad (2)$$

If $\hat{\Sigma}_w$ is non-singular, eq. 2 can be solved as a conventional eigenvalue problem and Φ is given by the eigenvectors of matrix $\hat{\Sigma}_w^{-1}\hat{\Sigma}_b$.

---

[*]Department of Computer Science, University of Rochester, Rochester, NY 14627-0226. email: *taoli@cs.rochester.edu*.

[†]Current Affiliation: Amazon.com, Inc. email: *zsh@cs.rochester.edu*.

[‡]Supported in part by NSF grants EIA-0080124, DUE-9980943, and EIA-0205061, and by NIH grant P30-AG18254. Department of Computer Science, University of Rochester, Rochester, NY 14627-0226. email: *ogihara@cs.rochester.edu*.

2.2 Multi-class LDA

A natural extension of Fisher Linear discriminant that deals with more than two classes exists [8], which uses multiple discriminant analysis. As in the binary case, the projection is from high dimensional space to a low dimensional space and the transformation sought is the one that maximizes the ratio of intra-class scatter to the inter-class scatter. Unlike the binary case, the maximization should be done among several competing classes.

Suppose that there are n classes. The intra-class matrix is defined a formula similar to eq. 1:

$$\hat{\Sigma}_w = S_1 + \cdots + S_n = \sum_{i=1}^n \sum_{\mathbf{x} \in c_i} (\mathbf{x} - \bar{\mathbf{x}_i})(\mathbf{x} - \bar{\mathbf{x}_i})',$$

but the inter-class scatter matrix is slightly different:

$$\hat{\Sigma}_b = \sum_{i=1}^n m_i (\bar{\mathbf{x}_i} - \bar{\mathbf{x}})(\bar{\mathbf{x}_i} - \bar{\mathbf{x}})'.$$

Here m_i is the number of training samples for each class, $\bar{\mathbf{x}_i}$ is the mean for each class and $\bar{\mathbf{x}}$ is total mean vector given by $\bar{\mathbf{x}} = \frac{1}{m} \sum_{i=1}^n m_i \bar{\mathbf{x}_i}$. After obtaining $\hat{\Sigma}_b$ and $\hat{\Sigma}_w$, the linear transformation Φ we want should still maximize eq. 2. It can be shown that the transformation Φ can be obtained by solving the generalized eigenvalue problem:

$$\hat{\Sigma}_b \Phi = \lambda \hat{\Sigma}_w \Phi. \tag{3}$$

It is easy to prove that the upper bounds of the rank of $\hat{\Sigma}_w$ and $\hat{\Sigma}_b$ are respectively $m - n$ and $n - 1$. Multiple discriminant analysis provides an elegant way for classification using discriminant features.

Once the transformation Φ is given, the classification can be performed in the transformed space based on some distance measures d such as Euclidean distance. The new instance, $\mathbf{z}$, is classified to

$$\underset{k}{\arg\min}\, d(\mathbf{z}\Phi, \bar{\mathbf{x}}_k \Phi),$$

where $\bar{\mathbf{x}}_k$ is the centroid of k-th class.

3 Discussions on LDA

3.1 Fisher Criterion and its non-optimality

Although practical evidence has been shown that discriminant analysis is effective (and also will be demonstrated in our experimental study in Section 4), significant separation does not necessarily imply good classification. Multi-class discriminant analysis is concerned with the search for a linear transformation that reduces the dimension of a given n-class, p-dimensional statistical model to

$n - 1$ dimensions while preserving the maximum amount of discriminative information in the lower-dimensional model. In general, using the Bayes error directly as a criterion is too complicated and Fisher's criterion is easy to solve but it only provides suboptimal solutions. Fisher's criterion can be solved by an eigenvalue decomposition of $\hat{\Sigma}_w^{-1} \hat{\Sigma}_b$ and taking the rows of the transformation matrix to be the eigenvectors corresponding to the $n - 1$ largest eigenvalues. However, it has been shown that, for multi-class problem, Fisher's criterion is actually maximizing the mean square distance between the classes in the lower-dimensional space and is clearly different from minimizing classification error [11]. When maximizing the mean square distance, class pairs having large distances completely dominate the eigenvalue decomposition. The resulting transformation preserves the distances of already well separated classes. As a consequence, there is a large overlap among the remaining classes, which leads to suboptimal classification with low accuracy rate.

3.2 When the Inner Scatter Matrix is Singular

There are at most $n - 1$ nonzero generalized eigenvectors of $\hat{\Sigma}_w^{-1} \hat{\Sigma}_b$, and so an upper bound of dimension d in the transformed space is $n - 1$. At least $p + n$ samples are required to guarantee that $\hat{\Sigma}_w$ does not become singular. In practice, especially in text categorization and pattern recognition, the number of samples m is small and/or the dimensionality p is large. In such cases, $\hat{\Sigma}_w$ is usually singular. Methods for dealing with the singularity of $\hat{\Sigma}_w$ have been proposed:

- Regularization [13, 21]: Here, the matrix $\hat{\Sigma}_w$ is regularized by biasing the diagonal components by

$$\hat{\Sigma}_w' = \hat{\Sigma}_w + \delta I$$

  where δ is a relatively small parameter such that $\hat{\Sigma}_w'$ is positive definite. In practice, δ can be set to the average of the diagonal elements of $\hat{\Sigma}_w$ multiplied by a small constant k.

- Subspace [19, 12]: The subspace method uses a nonsingular intermediate space of $\hat{\Sigma}_w$ obtained by removing the null space of $\hat{\Sigma}_w$ to compute the transformation.

3.3 Time Complexity of Training

The training consists of computation of the inter-class and intra-class covariance matrices, eigenvalue decomposition, and selection of discriminative features. The time complexity for the first part is mp^2. If we use SVD to decompose the matrices, we can directly use the feature vectors and avoid the multiplications in evaluating covariance matrices. The time complexity of the second part is $ab\min(a, b)$ for a matrix of dimension $a \times b$. In our case, a and b are respectively the number of instances and the number of features. The time complexity of the last part is almost linear in p. Thus, the time complexity of training is $O(mp\min(m, p))$.

4 Experiments on Benchmark Datasets

4.1 Datasets

The datasets used in the experiments are summarized in Table 1. When available, we use the original partition of the datasets into training and test sets. For the other datasets, if not specified, we use ten-fold cross validation method to evaluate results. We implemented regularization and subspace to deal with the singularity of inner scatter matrix. For regularization method, we set δ to twice the average of the diagonal components of the inner scatter matrix [9]. When the inner matrix is singular, the results reported to be the best one obtained by the two methods.

4.2 Results

In this section, we present and discuss our experimental results. All of our experiments were performed on a P4 2GHz machine with 512M memory running Linux 2.4.9-31.

Whenever possible, we compare our experimental results with those presented in [1] since most of them were regarded to be state-of-the-art. If we can not find corresponding results from [1], we try to compare our results with the documented usage or other reported results.

For Dermatology, Satimage, Glass, Ecoli, Pendigits, Yeast, Vowel and Soybean datasets, we compare our experimental results with those presented in [1] using the support vector machine algorithm as the base binary learner. We included the results of sparse code and one-versus-the-rest using loss-based decoding for comparison. For Isolet, Letter, Audiology and Segmentation, datasets with those using AdaBoost and loss-based decoding from [1]. For Iris, Waveform, Wine, Car and Heart datasets, several state-of-the-art methods for constructing ensembles of classifiers with stacking are evaluated in [4] Stacking with Multi-response Model Tree (SMM5) achieves the best performance in their reported experiments. Therefore, we refer their results with SMM5 for comparison. For Vehicle and Shuttle datasets, we compare our results with those recorded results in [17]. For Covertype and Optdigits datasets, we compare our results with those documented results in [2]. For DNA, we compare our results with that from [15]. For Coil-100 dataset, we use the same experiment strategy as [16]. In

Dataset	#Train	#Test	Dim.	Size
ALL-AML	72	-	7129	3
DNA	2000	1186	180	3
Iris	150	-	4	3
Waveform	300	5000	21	3
Wine	178	-	13	3
car	1728	-	6	4
Vehicle	846	-	18	4
Heart	294	-	76	5
Pageblock	5473	-	10	5
Dermatology	366	-	34	6
ALL	215	112	12558	6
Satimage	4435	2000	36	6
Glass	214	-	9	7
Shuttle	3866	1934	9	7
Segmentation	2310	-	19	7
Zoo	101	-	18	7
Covertype	581012	-	54	8
Ecoli	336	-	8	8
Optdigits	3823	1797	64	10
Pendigits	7494	3498	16	10
Yeast	1484	-	8	10
Vowel	528	462	10	11
WaterTreatment	527	-	38	13
Soybean	307	376	35	19
Audiology	226	-	69	24
Isolet	6238	1559	617	26
Letter	16000	4000	16	26
Coil-100	800	6400	160	100

Table 1. Datasets.

this paper, we only present the result of an experiment using 1/9 of all the images for training, the rest for testing. For ALL-AML, Page-blocks, All, Zoo and water datasets, we compare the results on LDA with those obtained using our available implementations of SVM methods with one-against-all reductions. The detailed results are presented in Table 2.

The results of LDA on DNA, Iris, Wine, Dermatology, Ecoli, Audiology and Coil-100, outperform their counterparts. For Car, Heart, Segmentation, Covertype, Pendigits and Letter, LDA results are inferior to their counterparts. The main reason is that the number of attributes of these datasets is relatively low with respect to the size of large training sets. One possible solution is to increase dimensionality of datasets, such as using kernel functions [14]. Other results are generally comparable.

Discriminant analysis is very efficient and most experiments only took less than a second [1].

---

[1] Due to space limitation, we could not include the time table here.

Datasets	Past Usage	Past Results	LDA
ALL-AML	-	0.944	0.914
DNA	[15]	0.937	0.947
Iris	[4]	0.948	0.980
Waveform	[4]	0.8652	0.858
Wine	[4]	0.9798	0.994
Car	[4]	0.9868	0.81
Vehicle	[17]	0.85/0.448	0.785
Heart	[4]	0.8415	0.521
Page-blocks	-	0.930	0.931
Dermatology	[1]	0.969/0.967	0.970
ALL	-	0.941	0.970
Satimage	[1]	0.867/0.591	0.828
Glass	[1]	0.676/0.624	0.593
Shuttle	[17]	0.9999/0.9328	0.946
Segmentation	[1]	0.993/1.00	0.916
Zoo	-	0.970	0.930
Covertype	[2]	0.70	0.581
Ecoli	[1]	0.852/0.849	0.827
Optdigits	[2]	0.9755/0.98	0.938
Pendigits	[1]	0.973/0.975	0.829
Yeast	[1]	0.528/0.271	0.517
Vowel	[1]	0.530/0.491	0.447
Water	-	0.970	0.970
Soybean	[1]	0.910/0.790	0.89
Audiology	[1]	0.669/0.808	0.818
Isolet	[1]	0.902/0.947	0.941
Letter	[1]	0.734/0.854	0.681
Coil-100	[16]	0.8923	0.963

Table 2. Comparisons of Accuracy. Fraction shows the range of accuracy presented in the corresponding paper.

5 Conclusions and Future Work

In this paper, we investigate the use discriminant analysis for multi-class classification. Our experiments have shown that LDA is a simple efficient yet accurate approach for multi-class classification problems.

In [10], we have used Generalized Singular Value Decomposition(GSVD) to overcome the singularity problem and achieved good performance on text databasess. One of our future work is to test the technique on general benchmark datasets.

References

[1] E. L. Allwein, R. E. Schapire, and Y. Singer. Reducing multiclass to binary: A unifying approach for margin classifiers. JMLR, 1:113–141, 2000.

[2] C. Blake and C. Merz. UCI repository of machine learning databases, 1998.

[3] T. G. Dietterich and G. Bakiri. Solving multiclass learning problems via error-correcting output codes. Journal of Artificial Intelligence Research, 2:263–286, 1995.

[4] S. Dzeroski and B. Zenko. Stacking with multi-response model trees. In Proceedings of The Third International Workshop on Multiple Classifier Systems, MCS, pages 201–211. Springer-Verlag, 2002.

[5] K. Fukunaga. Introduction to statistical pattern recognition. Academic Press, 1990.

[6] T. Hastie and R. Tibshirani. Classification by pairwise coupling. In M. I. Jordan, M. J. Kearns, and S. A. Solla, editors, Advances in Neural Information Processing Systems, volume 10. The MIT Press, 1998.

[7] T. Joachims. Making large-scale support vector machine learning practical. In Advances in Kernel Methods: Support Vector Machines. 1998.

[8] R. A. Johnson and D. W. Wichern. Applied Multivariate Statistical Analysis. Prentice Hall, 1988.

[9] T. Kawatani. Topic difference factor extraction between two document sets of its application to text categorization. In SIGIR 2002, pages 137–144, 2002.

[10] T. Li, S. Zhu, and M. Ogihara. Efficient multi-way text categorization via generalized discriminant analysis. In CIKM'03, 2003.

[11] M. Loog, R. Duin, and R.Haeb-Umbach. Multiclass linear dimension reduction by weighted pairwise fisher criteria. IEEE Transaction on Pattern Analysis and Machine Intelligence, 23(7):762–766, 2001.

[12] A. M. Martinez and A. C. Kak. PCA versus LDA. IEEE Transactions on Pattern Analysis and Machine Intelligence, 23(2):228–233, 2001.

[13] G. J. McLachlan. Discriminant Analysis and Statistical Pattern Recognition. John Wiley & Sons, Inc., 1992.

[14] S. Mika, G. Rätsch, J. Weston, B. Schölkopf, and K.-R. Müller. Fisher discriminant analysis with kernels. In Y.-H. Hu, J. Larsen, E. Wilson, and S. Douglas, editors, Neural Networks for Signal Processing IX, pages 41–48. IEEE, 1999.

[15] M. O. Noordewier, G. G. Towell, and J. B. Shavlik. Training knowledge-based neural networks to recognize genes. In Advances in Neural Information Processing Systems, 1991.

[16] D. Roth, M. Yang, and N. Ahuja. Learning to recognize objects. In CVPR, pages 724–731, 2000.

[17] SGI. MLC++: Datasets from UCI. http://www.sgi.com/tech/mlc/db/.

[18] A. Shashua. On the equivalence between the support vector machine for classification and sparsified fisher's linear discriminant. Neural Processing Letters, 9(2):129–139, 1999.

[19] D. L. Swets and J. Weng. Using discriminant eigenfeatures for image retrieval. IEEE Transactions on Pattern Analysis and Machine Intelligence, 18(8):831–836, 1996.

[20] V. N. Vapnik. Statistical Learning Theory. Wiley, New York, 1998.

[21] W. Zhao, R. Chellappa, and P. Phillips. Subspace linear discriminant analysis for face recognition. Technical Report CAR-TR-914., University of Maryland, College Park, 1999.

Interpretations of Association Rules by Granular Computing

Yuefeng Li [a] and Ning Zhong [b]

[a]*School of Software Engineering & Data Communications*
Queensland University of Technology, Brisbane, OLD 4001, Australia
E-mail: y2.li@qut.edu.au
[b]*Department of Systems and Information Engineering*
Maebashi Institute of Technology, Maebashi 371-0816, Japan
E-mail: zhong@maebashi-it.ac.jp

Abstract

This paper presents interpretations for association rules. It first introduces Pawlak's method, and the corresponding algorithm of finding decision rules (a kind of association rules). It then uses extended random sets to present a new algorithm of finding interesting rules. It proves that the new algorithm is faster than Pawlak's algorithm. The extended random sets are easily to include more than one criterion for determining interesting rules. They also provide two measures for dealing with uncertainties in association rules.

1. Introduction

Mining association rules has received much attention currently [7]. The frequency of occurrence is a well-accepted criterion for mining association rules. Apart from the frequency, the rules should reflect real world patterns [1] [4]. It is desirable to use some mathematical models to interpret association rules in order to obtain real world patterns.

The patterns hidden in data can be characterized by rough set theory [6], in which the premises of association rules (or called decision rules in [6]) are interpreted as condition granules, and the post-conditions are interpreted as decision granules. The measure of uncertainties for decision rules is based on well-established statistical models. This only reveals the objective aspect of decision rules. However, knowledge in some applications is based on "subjective" judgments.

In this paper, we use granular computing to interpret association rules. We first introduce Pawlak's method [6] and formally describe the corresponding algorithm for determining strengths and certainty factors of decision rules. We then present a new interpretation of association rules using extended random sets [3]. An effective algorithm of finding interesting rules is proposed using the new interpretation. We also show that an extended

random set can be interpreted as a probability function (which can provide an "objective" interpretation) or a belief function (which can provide a "subjective" interpretation).

2. Databases to Decision Tables

Let U be a non-empty finite set of objects (a set of records), and A be a set of attributes (or fields). We call a pair $S = (U, A)$ an *information table* if there is a function for every attribute $a \in A$ such that $a: U \rightarrow V_a$, where V_a is the set of all values of a. We call V_a the domain of a.

Let B be a subset of A. B determines a binary relation $I(B)$ on U such that $(x, y) \in I(B)$ if and only if $a(x) = a(y)$ for every $a \in B$, where $a(x)$ denotes the value of attribute a for element $x \in U$. it is easy to prove that $I(B)$ is an equivalence relation, and the family of all equivalence classes of $I(B)$, that is a partition determined by B, is denoted by $U/I(B)$ or simply by U/B. The classes in U/B are referred to as *B-granules* or *B-elementary sets*. The class which contains x is called *B-granule* induced by x, and is denoted by $B(x)$.

A user may use some attributes of a database. We can divide the user used attributes into two groups: condition attributes and decision attributes, respectively. We call the tripe (U, C, D) a *decision table* of (U, A) if $C \cap D = \varnothing$ and $C \cup D \subseteq A$, where (U, C, D) is a set of classes and each class is the representative of a group of records.

For example, we assume that there is an information table (relation) that includes 1000 records of vehicle accidents, where the set of attributes is $A = \{driver, vehicle\ type, weather, road, time, accident\}$. If the user only uses 4 attributes and let $C = \{weather, road\}$, and $D = \{time, accident\}$. $C \cup D$ determines a binary relation $I(C \cup D)$ on U, and U is classified into 7 equivalence classes, as shown in Table 1 (i.e. a decision table), where N is the number of records in the corresponding class.

Using Table 1, we also can get the set of condition granules, $U/C = \{\{1,7\}, \{2,5\}, \{3,6\}, \{4\}\}$, and decision granules, $U/D = \{\{1\}, \{2,3,7\}, \{4\}, \{5,6\}\}$, respectively.

In the following we let $U/C = \{c_1, c_2, c_3, c_4\}$ and $U/D = \{d_1, d_2, d_3, d_4\}$.

Table 1. A decision table

Class	Weather	Road	Time	Accident	N
1	Misty	Icy	Day	Yes	80
2	Foggy	Icy	Night	Yes	140
3	Misty	Not icy	Night	Yes	40
4	Sunny	Icy	Day	No	500
5	Foggy	Icy	Night	No	20
6	Misty	Not icy	Night	No	200
7	Misty	Icy	Night	Yes	20

3. Pawlak's Method

Every class in a decision table can be mapped into an association rule (or called decision rule in [6]), e.g., class 2 in Table 1 can be read as "*if the weather is foggy **and** road is icy **then** the accident occurred at night*" in 140 cases.

For our convenience, we assume $A = \{a_1,..., a_k, a_{k+1}, ..., a_m\}$, $C = \{a_1, ..., a_k\}$, and $D = \{a_{k+1}, ..., a_m\}$, where $k>0$, and $m>k$. Every class f determines a sequence $a_1(f), ..., a_k(f), a_{k+1}(f), ..., a_m(f)$. The sequence can determine a decision rule:

$$a_1(f), ..., a_k(f) \rightarrow a_{k+1}(f), ..., a_m(f)$$

or in short $f(C) \rightarrow f(D)$.

The strength of the decision rule $f(C) \rightarrow f(D)$ is defined as $|C(f) \cap D(f)| / |U|$; and the certainty factor of the decision rule is defined as $|C(f) \cap D(f)| / |C(f)|$.

According to the above definitions, we can use the following algorithm to calculate strengths and certainty factors for all decision rules, where we assume N_i denotes the number of records in class i, and UN denotes the total number of records in U.

Algorithm 1.
1. let $UN = 0$;
2. for ($i = 1$ to n) // n is the number of classes
   $UN = UN + N_i$;
3. for ($i = 1$ to n)
   $\{strength(i) = N_i/UN; CN = N_i;$
   for ($j = 1$ to n)
   if (($j \neq i$) and ($f_j(C) == f_i(C)$))
   $CN = CN + N_j$;
   $certainty\_factor(i) = N_i/CN; \}$.

If we assume the basic operation is the comparison between two classes (i.e., $f_j(C) == f_i(C)$), then the time complexity is $(n-1) \times n = O(n^2)$, where n is the number of

classes in the decision table. It also needs a similar algorithm to determine interesting rules for Pawlak's method.

4. Extended Random Sets

Let U/C be the set of condition granules and U/D be the set of decision granules. To describe the relationship between condition granules and decision granules, we can rewrite the decision rules in Table 1 as follows:

$$c_1 \rightarrow \{ (d_1, 80/100), (d_2, 20/100) \}$$
$$c_2 \rightarrow \{ (d_2, 140/160), (d_4, 20/160) \}$$
$$c_3 \rightarrow \{ (d_2, 40/240) (d_4, 200/240) \}$$
$$c_4 \rightarrow \{ (d_3, 500/500) \}.$$

These determine a mapping Γ from U/C to $2^{(U/D) \times [0,1]}$, such that

$$\sum_{(fst,snd) \in \Gamma(c_i)} snd = 1 \text{ for all } c_i \in U/C$$

where $\Gamma(c_i)$ is a set of decision-granule numeral pairs.

Now we consider the support degree for each condition granule. The obvious way is to use the frequency in the decision table, that is,

$$w(c_i) = \sum_{x \in c_i} N_x \qquad (1)$$

for every condition granule c_i, where N_x is the number of records in class x. By normalizing, we can get a probability function P on U/C such that

$$P(c_i) = \frac{w(c_i)}{\sum_{c_j \in U/C} w(c_j)}$$

for all $c_i \in U/C$.

Based on the above analysis, we can use a pair (Γ, P) to represent what we can obtain from an information table. We call the pair (Γ, P) an *extended random set*.

According to the definitions in the previous section, we can obtain the following decision rules:

$$c_i \rightarrow fst_{i,1}, c_i \rightarrow fst_{i,2}, ..., \text{and } c_i \rightarrow fst_{i,|\Gamma(c_i)|}$$

for a given condition granule c_i, where

$$\Gamma(c_i) = \{(fst_{i,1}, snd_{i,1}), ..., (fst_{i,|\Gamma(c_i)|}, snd_{i,|\Gamma(c_i)|})\} \qquad (2)$$

We call $P(c_i) \times snd_{i,1}, ..., P(c_i) \times snd_{i,|\Gamma(c_i)|}$ the strengths of these decision rules, respectively; and $snd_{i,1}, ..., snd_{i,|\Gamma(c_i)|}$ the certainty factors, respectively.

From the above definitions, we have

$$snd_{i,j} = \frac{|c_i \cap fst_{i,j}|}{|c_i|}.$$

The above definitions about strengths and certainty factors are the same as Pawlak's definitions.

5. Determining Interesting Rules

Given an extended random set (Γ, P), it can provide a new representation for decision rules. Figure 1 shows a such example for representing the extended random set that is obtained from Table 2, where U/C is the set of condition granules, and $\Gamma(c_i)$ is the set of conclusions of premise c_i ($i = 1, ..., |U/C|$). Algorithm 2 shows the process of creating extended random sets, and the process of calculating of strengths and certainty factors of the decision rules.

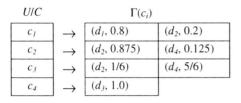

U/C		$\Gamma(c_i)$	
c_1	$\rightarrow$	$(d_1, 0.8)$	$(d_2, 0.2)$
c_2	$\rightarrow$	$(d_2, 0.875)$	$(d_4, 0.125)$
c_3	$\rightarrow$	$(d_2, 1/6)$	$(d_4, 5/6)$
c_4	$\rightarrow$	$(d_3, 1.0)$	

Figure 1. An extended random set

Algorithm 2.
1. let $UN = 0$, $U/C = \varnothing$;
2. for ($i = 1$ to n)
   $UN = UN + N_i$;
3. for ($i = 1$ to n do) // create the data structure
   if ($f_i(C) \in U/C$)
     $insert((f_i(D), N_i))$ to $\Gamma(f_i(C))$;
   else
     $add(f_i(C))$ into U/C, and set $\Gamma(f_i(C))=\varnothing$;
4. for ($i = 1$ to $|U/C|$)
   $P(c_i) = (1/UN) \times \left(\sum_{(fst.snd) \in \Gamma(c_i)} snd \right)$;
5. for ($i = 1$ to $|U/C|$) // normalization
   { $temp = 0$;
     for ($j = 1$ to $|\Gamma(c_i)|$)
       $temp = temp + snd_{i,j}$;
     for ($j = 1$ to $|\Gamma(c_i)|$)
       $snd_{i,j} = snd_{i,j}/temp$; }
6. for ($i = 1$ to $|U/C|$) // calculate rule strengths
   for ($j = 1$ to $|\Gamma(c_i)|$)
     { $strength(c_i \rightarrow fst_{i,j}) = P(c_i) \times snd_{i,j}$;
       $certainty\_factor(c_i \rightarrow fst_{i,j}) = snd_{i,j}$; }.

Because steps 4, 5, and 6 all traverse pairs in $\Gamma(c_i)$ ($i = 1, ..., |U/C|$), and the number of pairs in all $\Gamma(c_i)$ ($i = 1, ..., |U/C|$) is just n (the number of classes in the decision table), the time complexity of this algorithm is determined by step 3. In step 3, checking $f_i(C) \in U/C$ takes $O(|U/C|)$, so the time complexity of the algorithm is $O(n \times |U/C|)$, where the basic operation is still the comparison between classes. Since $|U/C| \leq n$, Algorithm 2 is better than Algorithm 1 for the time complexity.

A decision rule $c_i \rightarrow fst_{i,j}$ is an *interesting rule* if $pr(fst_{i,j} \mid c_i) - pr(fst_{i,j})$ is greater than a suitable constant.

From the definition of mapping Γ, we have $pr(fst_{i,j} \mid c_i) = snd_{i,j}$. To decide the probability on the set of decision granules, we present the following function:

$$pr : (U/D) \rightarrow [0,1] \quad \text{such that}$$
$$pr(d) = \sum_{c_i \in (U/C),(d,snd) \in \Gamma(c_i)} P(c_i) \times snd \quad (3)$$

We can prove that pr is a probability function on (U/D). The algorithm of determining pr is only to traverse the data structure as showed in Figure 1.

Table 2. Probability function on decision granules

Decision Granule	Description	pr
d_1	Accident occurred at night	0.08
d_2	Accident occurred in daytime	0.20
d_3	Accident not occurred in daytime	0.50
d_4	Accident not occurred at night	0.22

Table 2 shows the probability function on the set of decision granules. From Figure 1 and Table 2 we can obtain the probability of $pr(fst_{i,j} \mid c_i)$ for every decision rule $c_i \rightarrow fst_{i,j}$, where $fst_{i,j} \in \{d_1, d_2, d_3, d_4\}$. We can get 4 interesting rules (seeTable 3) if we assume that a decision rule $c_i \rightarrow fst_{i,j}$ is an interesting rule iff $pr(fst_{i,j} \mid c_i) - pr(fst_{i,j}) > 0$.

Table 3. Interesting rules

Rule Description	$pr(fst_{i,j} \mid c_i)$	$pr(fst_{i,j})$	Interesting rule
$c_1 \rightarrow d_1$	0.8	0.08	Yes
$c_2 \rightarrow d_2$	0.875	0.20	Yes
$c_3 \rightarrow d_2$	0.167	0.20	No
$c_4 \rightarrow d_3$	1	0.5	Yes
$c_2 \rightarrow d_4$	0.125	0.22	No
$c_3 \rightarrow d_4$	0.833	0.22	Yes
$c_1 \rightarrow d_2$	0.20	0.20	No

6. Discussions

In this section, we discuss other advantages of our approach except the time complexity. We first discuss the weight functions for condition granules. We also introduce another uncertain measure on decision granules.

6.1 Weight Functions for Condition Granules

The extended random sets are easily to include other criteria apart from the well-accepted criterion "frequencies" when determining association rules.

Although the frequency is a well-accepted criterion for data mining, it is not the only criterion for support degree because some condition granules with high frequencies may be meaningless. For example, when we use keywords to represent the meaning of documents, we usually consider both keywords frequency and inverse document frequency (e.g., the popular technique $tf*idf$ in information retrieval) because some words (like "information") may have high frequencies in a document but they may appear in most documents in a collection (e.g., "information" may appears in most documents in the information table collection).

In order to use the above idea, we assume there is a collection which contains many databases. Given a decision table (U, C, D) of a database, we can define a new weight function w on U/C to instead of the weight function in Eq. (1), which satisfies

$$w(c_i) = (\sum_{x \in c_i} N_x) \times log(M/n_i)$$

for every $c_i \in (U/C)$, where M is the total number of databases, and n_i is the number of databases which contain the given condition granule c_i. It is easy to do so because this definition does not affect the rest calculation of decision rules.

6.2 Uncertain Measures on Decision Granules

The obvious way to measure the uncertainty of a set of decision granules is using a probability function. For a given set of decision granules $X = \{d_1, \ldots, d_s\}$, we may use $\sum_{x \in X} pr(x)$ to represent the probability of $(d_1$ or … or $d_s)$. However, this measure is very sensitive to the frequencies of records.

To consider a relative stable measure, we consider a random set (ξ, P) (see [2] [5]) which is derived from the extended random set (Γ, P):

$\xi : U/C \to 2^{U/D}$ such that

$\xi(c_i) = \{fst|(fst, snd) \in \Gamma(c_i)\}$ for every $c_i \in (U/C)$.

The random set (ξ, P) determines a Dempster-Shafer mass function (see [2]) m_P on U/D such that

$$m_P(X) = P(\{c_i|c_i \in (U/C), \xi(c_i) = X\}) \qquad (4)$$

for every $X \subseteq U/D$.

This mass function can decide a belief function and plausibility function (see [2]) as well. They are defined as follows:

$bel_m : 2^{U/D} \to [0,1]$, $pl_m : 2^{U/D} \to [0,1]$ and

$$bel_m(X) = \sum_{Y \subseteq X} m_P(Y), \quad pl_m(X) = \sum_{Y \cap X \neq \varnothing} m_P(Y) \qquad (5)$$

for every $X \subseteq U/D$.

We can prove that

$$bel_m(X) \leq \sum_{x \in X} pr(x) \leq pl_m(X) \text{ for every } X \subseteq U/D.$$

Domain experts can use the interval $[bel_m, pl_m]$ to check if their "subjective" judgments for some descriptions are correct. Table 4 shows the uncertainty measures for some descriptions.

Table 4. Uncertain measures

Description	Subset	Pr	m_P	$[bel_m, pl_m]$
"d_1 or d_2"	$\{d_1, d_2\}$	0.28	0.1	[0.1, 0.5]
"d_3 or d_4"	$\{d_3, d_4\}$	0.72	0.0	[0.5, 0.9]
"d_2 or d_3"	$\{d_2, d_3\}$	0.70	0.0	[0.5, 1.0]
"d_1 or d_4"	$\{d_1, d_4\}$	0.30	0.0	[0.0, 0.5]

7. Conclusions

This paper uses granular computing to interpret association rules. The main contribution of this paper is that the concept of extended random sets is used to describe the relationships between condition granules and decision granules. It presents a new efficient algorithm to find interesting rules in databases. Apart from the "frequencies", the extended random sets are easily to include other criteria when determining association rules. The extended random sets also provide more than one measure for dealing with uncertainties in the association rules significantly.

References

[1] E. Cohen, et al., Finding interesting associations without support pruning, *IEEE Transactions on Knowledge and Data Engineering*, 2001, 13(1): 64-78.

[2] R. Kruse, E. Schwecke and J. Heinsoln, *Uncertainty and vagueness in knowledge based systems (Numerical Methods)*, Springer-Verlag, New York, 1991.

[3] Y. Li, Extended random sets for knowledge discovery in information system, in Proc. *the 9th International Conference on Rough Sets, Fuzzy Sets, Data Mining and Granular Computing*, China, 2003, 524-532.

[4] T. Y. Lin, The lattice structure of database and mining multiple level rules, *Bulletin of International Rough Set Society*, 2002, 6(1/2): 11-16.

[5] D. Liu and Y. Li, The interpretation of generalized evidence theory, *Chinese Journal of Computers*, 1997, 20(2): 158-164.

[6] Z. Pawlak, In pursuit of patterns in data reasoning from data, the rough set way, *3rd International Conference on Rough Sets and Current Trends in Computing*, USA, 2002, 1-9.

[7] R. Rastogi and K. Shim, Mining optimized association rules with categorical and numeric attributes, *IEEE Transactions on Knowledge and Data Engineering*, 2002, 14(1): 29-50.

Algorithms for Spatial Outlier Detection

Chang-Tien Lu
Dept. of Computer Science
Virginia Polytechnic Institute
and State University
7054 Haycock Road
Falls Church, VA 22043
ctlu@vt.edu

Dechang Chen
Preventive Medicine and
Biometrics
Uniformed Services University
of the Health Sciences
Bethesda, MD 20814
dchen@usuhs.mil

Yufeng Kou
Dept. of Computer Science
Virginia Polytechnic Institute
and State University
7054 Haycock Road
Falls Church, VA 22043
ykou@vt.edu

Abstract

A spatial outlier is a spatially referenced object whose non-spatial attribute values are significantly different from the values of its neighborhood. Identification of spatial outliers can lead to the discovery of unexpected, interesting, and useful spatial patterns for further analysis. One drawback of existing methods is that normal objects tend to be falsely detected as spatial outliers when their neighborhood contains true spatial outliers. In this paper, we propose a suite of spatial outlier detection algorithms to overcome this disadvantage. We formulate the spatial outlier detection problem in a general way and design algorithms which can accurately detect spatial outliers. In addition, using a real-world census data set, we demonstrate that our approaches can not only avoid detecting false spatial outliers but also find true spatial outliers ignored by existing methods.

1 Introduction

Outliers have been informally defined as observations in a data set which appear to be inconsistent with the remainder of that set of data [1, 5], or which deviate so much from other observations so as to arouse suspicions that they were generated by a different mechanism [4]. The identification of outliers can lead to the discovery of useful knowledge and has a number of practical applications in areas such as credit card fraud detection, athlete performance analysis, voting irregularity analysis, and severe weather prediction [6, 11, 16]. In a spatial context, local anomalies are of paramount importance. Spatial outliers are spatially referenced objects whose non-spatial attribute values are significantly different from those of other spatially referenced objects in their spatial neighborhoods. Informally, a spatial outlier is a local instability, or an extreme observation with respect to its neighboring values, even though it may not be significantly different from the entire population. Detecting spatial outliers is useful in many applications of geographic information systems, including transportation, ecology, public safety, public health, climatology, and location based services [12].

Recent work by Shekhar et al. introduced a method for detecting spatial outliers in graph data set [13, 14]. The method is based on the distribution property of the difference between an attribute value and the average attribute value of its neighbors. Several spatial outlier detection methods are also available in the literature of spatial statistics. These methods can be generally grouped into two categories, namely graphic approaches and quantitative tests. Graphic approaches are based on visualization of spatial data which highlights spatial outliers. Example methods include variogram clouds and pocket plots [3, 10]. Quantitative methods provide tests to distinguish spatial outliers from the remainder of data. Scatterplot [2, 8] and Moran scatterplot [9] are two representative approaches.

One major drawback of the existing detection approaches is that their application will lead to some true spatial outliers being ignored and some false spatial outliers being identified. To minimize such defect, we propose two iterative algorithms that detect spatial outliers by multi-iterations. Each iteration identifies only one outlier and modifies the attribute value of this outlier so that this outlier will not impact the subsequent iterations negatively. We also propose a non-iterative algorithm which uses the median as the neighborhood function, thus reducing the negative impact caused by the presence of neighboring points with very high/low attribute values. Using a real-world census data, we show that our algorithms can avoid detecting false spatial outliers and can find true spatial outliers ignored by existing methods when the expected number of spatial outliers is limited.

2 Problem Formulation

Given a set of spatial points $X = \{x_1, x_2, \ldots, x_n\}$ in a space with dimension $p \geq 1$, an attribute function f is defined as a mapping from X to R (the set of real number). Attribute function $f(x_i)$ represents the attribute value of spatial point x_i. For a given point x_i, let $NN_k(x_i)$ denote the k nearest neighbors of point x_i, where $k = k(x_i)$ depends on the value of x_i for $i = 1, 2, \ldots, n$. A neighborhood function g is defined as a map from X to R such that for each x_i, $g(x_i)$ returns a summary statistic of attribute values of all the spatial points inside $NN_k(x_i)$. For example, $g(x_i)$ can be the average attribute value of the k nearest neighbors of x_i. To detect spatial outliers, we compare the attribute value of each point x_i with those attribute values of its neighbors $NN_k(x_i)$. Such comparison is done through a comparison function h, which is a function of f and g. There are many choices for the form of h. For example, h can be the difference $f - g$ or the ratio f/g. Let $y_i = h(x_i)$ for $i = 1, 2, \ldots, n$. Given the attribute function f, function k, neighborhood function g, and comparison function h, a point x_i is a spatial outlier or simply S-outlier if y_i is an extreme value of the set $\{y_1, y_2, \ldots, y_n\}$. We note that the definition depends on the choices of functions k, g and h.

The definition given above is quite general. As a matter of fact, outliers involved in various existing spatial outlier detection techniques are special cases of S-outliers [15]. These include outliers detected by z algorithm [13], Scatterplot [2,8], Moran scatterplot [9] and pocket plots [3,10].

3 Proposed Algorithms

We state our algorithms to detect S-outliers. For simplicity, the description assumes all $k(x_i)$ are equal to a fixed number k. The algorithms can be easily generalized by replacing fixed k with dynamic $k(x_i)$. As seen above, outlier detection algorithms depend on the choices of the neighborhood function g and comparison function h. Selection of g and h determines the performance of each algorithm. In Algorithm 1 below, the neighborhood function g evaluated at a spatial point x is taken to be the average attribute value of all the k nearest neighbors of x. Comparison function $h(x)$ is taken to be the ratio of $f(x)$ to $g(x)$. Very large or very small value $h(x)$ (detected by the threshold θ) is an indication that x might be an S-outlier. Algorithm 1 is also termed as an iterative r(ratio) algorithm, since iterations are coupled with the ratios.

Algorithm 1 (Iterative r Algorithm)

1. Given a spatial data set $X = \{x_1, x_2, \ldots, x_n\}$, an attribute function f, a number k of nearest neighbors, and an expected number m of spatial outliers. For each spatial point x_i, compute the k nearest neighbor set $NN_k(x_i)$, the neighborhood function $g(x_i)$ $= \frac{1}{k} \sum_{x \in NN_k(x_i)} f(x)$ and the comparison function $h_i = h(x_i) = \frac{f(x_i)}{g(x_i)}$.

2. Let h_q or h_q^{-1} denote the maximum of $h_1, h_2, \ldots, h_n$, $h_1^{-1}, h_2^{-1}, \ldots, h_n^{-1}$. For a given threshold θ, if h_q or $h_q^{-1} \geq \theta$, treat x_q as an S-outlier.

3. Update $f(x_q)$ to be $g(x_q)$. For each spatial point x_i whose $NN_k(x_i)$ contains x_q, update $g(x_i)$ and h_i.

4. Repeat steps 2 and 3 until either the threshold condition is not met or the total number of S-outliers equals m.

In Algorithm 2 below, the neighborhood function g is the same as in Algorithm 1. But the comparison function $h(x)$ is chosen to be the difference $f(x) - g(x)$. Applying such an h to the n spatial points leads to the sequence $\{h_1, h_2, \ldots, h_n\}$. A spatial point x_i is treated as a candidate of S-outlier if its corresponding value h_i is extreme among the data set $\{h_1, h_2, \ldots, h_n\}$. Let μ and σ denote the sample mean and sample standard deviation of $\{h_1, h_2, \ldots, h_n\}$. The standardized value for each h_i is $y_i = \frac{h_i - \mu}{\sigma}$, and so the standardized data set becomes $\{y_1, y_2, \ldots, y_n\}$. Now it is clear that x_i is extreme in the original data set iff h_i is extreme in the standardized data set. Correspondingly, x_i is a possible S-outlier if $|y_i|$ is large enough (again detected by θ).

Algorithm 2 (Iterative z Algorithm)

1. For each spatial point x_i, compute the k nearest neighbor set $NN_k(x_i)$, the neighborhood function $g(x_i)$ $= \frac{1}{k} \sum_{x \in NN_k(x_i)} f(x)$, and the comparison function $h_i = h(x_i) = f(x_i) - g(x_i)$.

2. Let μ and σ denote the sample mean and sample standard deviation of the data set $\{h_1, h_2, \ldots, h_n\}$. Standardize the data set and compute the absolute value $y_i = |\frac{h_i - \mu}{\sigma}|$ for $i = 1, 2, \ldots, n$. Let y_q denote the maximum of $y_1, y_2, \ldots, y_n$. For a given threshold θ, if $y_q \geq \theta$, treat x_q as an S-outlier.

3. Update $f(x_q)$ to be $g(x_q)$. For each spatial point x_i whose $NN_k(x_i)$ contains x_q, update $g(x_i)$ and h_i.

4. Recalculate μ and σ of the data set $\{h_1, h_2, \ldots, h_n\}$. For $i = 1, 2, \ldots, n$, update $y_i = |\frac{h_i - \mu}{\sigma}|$.

5. Repeat steps 2, 3, and 4 until either the threshold condition is not met or the total number of S-outliers equals m.

The simplest choice of θ in Algorithm 1 is $\theta = 1$. It can be larger than 1 depending on different scenarios. A common value of θ in Algorithm 2 may be taken to be 2 or 3.

598

This is based on the result that in Algorithm 2 the comparison function h is normally distributed if the attribute function f is normally distributed [15]. There is no clear guideline on which of the two algorithms (iterative r and z algorithms) should be selected in applications. If the attribute function f can take negative values, then it is obvious that the iterative r algorithm should not be used due to the current description of the algorithm. If the attribute function f is non-negative, the selection depends on the properties of the practical applications. In general, we recommend that both algorithms be used.

In both Algorithms 1 and 2, once an S-outlier is detected, some corrections are made immediately. These include replacing the attribute value of the outlier by the average attribute value of its neighbors and some subsequent updating computation. The effect of these corrections is to avoid normal points close to the true outliers to be claimed as possible outliers. There is a direct method to reduce the risk of overstating the number of outliers without replacing the attribute value of the detected outlier, as describe in Algorithm 3. The method in Algorithm 3 defines the neighborhood function differently. Instead of the average attribute value, $g(x_i)$ is chosen to be the median of the attribute values of the points in $NN_k(x_i)$. The motivation of using median is the fact that median is a robust estimator of the "center" of a sample.

Algorithm 3 (Median Algorithm)

1. For each spatial point x_i, compute the k nearest neighbor set $NN_k(x_i)$, the neighborhood function $g(x_i) = $ median of the data set $\{f(x) : x \in NN_k(x_i)\}$, and the comparison function $h_i = h(x_i) = f(x_i) - g(x_i)$.

2. Let μ and σ denote the sample mean and sample standard deviation of the data set $\{h_1, h_2, \ldots, h_n\}$. Standardize the data set and compute the absolute values $y_i = |\frac{h_i - \mu}{\sigma}|$ for $i = 1, 2, \ldots, n$.

3. For a given positive integer m, let $i_1, i_2, \ldots, i_m$ be the m indices such that their y values in $\{y_1, y_2, \ldots, y_n\}$ represent the m largest. Then the m S-outliers are $x_{i_1}, x_{i_2}, \ldots, x_{i_m}$.

A quick illustration of Algorithms 1, 2, and 3 is to apply them to the data in Figure 1. Table 1 shows the results using the three algorithms with parameters $k = m = 3$, compared with the existing approaches. As can be seen, all the three proposed algorithms accurately detect $S1$, $S2$, and $S3$ as spatial outliers, but z algorithm, Scatterplot, and Moran Scatterplot, falsely identify $E1$ and $E2$ as spatial outliers. In this table, the rank of the outliers is defined in an obvious way. For example, in iterative r and z algorithms, the rank is the order of iterations, while in both z and Median algorithms, the rank is determined by the y value.

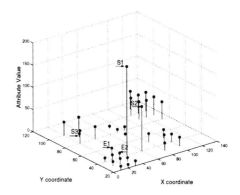

Figure 1. A spatial data set. Objects are located in the $X - Y$ plane. The height of each vertical line segment represents the attribute value of each object.

Rank	Methods					
	Scatter-plot	Moran Scatterplot	z Alg.	Iterative z Alg.	Iterative r Alg.	Median Alg.
1	E1	S1	S1	S1	S1	S1
2	E2	E1	E1	S2	S2	S2
3	S2	E2	E2	S3	S3	S3

Table 1. The top three spatial outliers detected by Scatterplot, Moran scatterplot, z, iterative z, iterative r, and median algorithms.

4 Experiments

We empirically compared the detection performance of our proposed methods with the z algorithm through mining a real-life census data set. The experiment results indicate that our algorithms can successfully identify spatial outliers ignored by the z algorithm and can avoid detecting false spatial outliers. In this experiment, we tested various attributes from census data compiled by U.S. Census Bureau [17]. The attributes tested include population, population density, percent of white persons, percent of black or African American persons, percent of American Indian persons, percent of Asian persons, and percent of female persons. We first ran the four algorithms (z, iterative r, iterative z, and median algorithms) to detect which counties have abnormal population. There are 3192 counties in the USA. We show the top 10 counties which are most likely to be the spatial outliers.

Table 2 provides the experimental results for all four spatial outlier detection algorithms. For the top 10 spatial outlier detected by z, iterative z, and median algorithms, most of them are the same with slightly different order. In fact, there are eight spatial outliers in common detected by the

Rank	Methods			
	z Alg.	Iterative z Alg.	Median Alg.	Iterative r Alg.
1	Los Angeles,CA,9637494.0	Los Angeles,CA,9637494.0	Los Angeles,CA,9637494.0	Kenedy,TX,413.0
2	Cook,IL,5350269.0	Cook,IL,5350269.0	Cook,IL,5350269.0	Loving,TX,70.0
3	Harris,TX,3460589.0	Harris,TX,3460589.0	Harris,TX,3460589.0	Treasure,MT,802.0
4	Maricopa,AZ,3194798.0	Maricopa,AZ,3194798.0	Maricopa,AZ,3194798.0	Lincoln,NV,4198.0
5	Ventura,CA,770630.0	Dallas,TX,2245398.0	Miami-Dade,FL,2289683.0	Falls Church city,VA,10612.0
6	Dallas,TX,2245398.0	Miami-Dade,FL,2289683.0	Dallas,TX,2245398.0	La Paz,AZ,19759.0
7	Miami-Dade,FL,2289683.0	Wayne,MI,2045473.0	Wayne,MI,2045473.0	Alpine,CA,1192.0
8	Wayne,MI,2045473.0	Bexar,TX,1417501.0	Clark,NV,1464653.0	Hudspeth,TX, 3318.0
9	Bexar,TX,1417501.0	King,WA,1741785.0	Bexar,TX,1417501.0	Fairfax city,VA,21674.0
10	King,WA,1741785.0	San Diego,CA,2862819.0	Tarrant,TX,1486392.0	Gilpin, CO,4823.0

Table 2. The top ten spatial outliers detected by z, iterative z, iterative r, and Median algorithms.

three algorithms. Further examination shows that the top 10 counties selected by iterative z and median algorithms are true outliers. But Ventura Co. in California was falsely detected by the non-iterative z algorithm. This falsely detected outlier was avoided by both the iterative z and median algorithms. The last column of the table shows the top ten candidate outliers from the iterative r algorithm. Although these 10 candidates are true outliers from a practical examination, they are very different from those obtained from the other three methods. This difference is due to the fact that the iterative r algorithm focuses on the ratio between the attribute value and the averaged attribute value of neighbors.

Experimental results from other attributes also show that the iterative algorithms and median method are more accurate than the non-iterative algorithm in terms of falsely detected spatial outliers. For running the algorithms and generating more results, we refer interested readers to [7], where we developed one software package which implements all the existing and proposed algorithms.

5 Conclusion

In this paper we propose three spatial outlier detection algorithms to analyze spatial data: two algorithms based on iteration and one algorithm based on median. The experimental results confirm the effectiveness of our approach in reducing the risk of falsely claiming regular spatial points as outliers, which exists in commonly used detection methodologies. Furthermore, it carries the important bonus of ordering the spatial outliers with respect to their degree of outlierness.

References

[1] V. Barnett and T. Lewis. *Outliers in Statistical Data.* John Wiley, New York, 3rd edition, 1994.

[2] R. Haining. *Spatial Data Analysis in the Social and Environmental Sciences.* Cambridge University Press, 1993.

[3] J. Haslett, R. Brandley, P. Craig, A. Unwin, and G. Wills. Dynamic Graphics for Exploring Spatial Data With Application to Locating Global and Local Anomalies. *The American Statistician*, 45:234–242, 1991.

[4] D. Hawkins. *Identification of Outliers.* Chapman and Hall, 1980.

[5] R. Johnson. *Applied Multivariate Statistical Analysis.* Prentice Hall, 1992.

[6] E. Knorr and R. Ng. Algorithms for Mining Distance-Based Outliers in Large Datasets. In *Proc. 24th VLDB Conference*, 1998.

[7] C.-T. Lu, H. Wang, and Y. Kou. http://europa.nvc.cs.vt.edu/~ctlu/Project/MapView/index.htm.

[8] A. Luc. Exploratory Spatial Data Analysis and Geographic Information Systems. In M. Painho, editor, *New Tools for Spatial Analysis*, pages 45–54, 1994.

[9] A. Luc. Local Indicators of Spatial Association: LISA. *Geographical Analysis*, 27(2):93–115, 1995.

[10] Y. Panatier. *Variowin. Software For Spatial Data Analysis in 2D.* New York: Springer-Verlag, 1996.

[11] I. Ruts and P. Rousseeuw. Computing Depth Contours of Bivariate Point Clouds. In *Computational Statistics and Data Analysis, 23:153–168*, 1996.

[12] S. Shekhar and S. Chawla. *A Tour of Spatial Databases.* Prentice Hall, 2002.

[13] S. Shekhar, C.-T. Lu, and P. Zhang. Detecting Graph-Based Spatial Outlier: Algorithms and Applications(A Summary of Results). In *Proc. of the Seventh ACM-SIGKDD Int'l Conference on Knowledge Discovery and Data Mining*, Aug 2001.

[14] S. Shekhar, C.-T. Lu, and P. Zhang. Detecting Graph-Based Spatial Outlier. *Intelligent Data Analysis: An International Journal*, 6(5):451–468, 2002.

[15] S. Shekhar, C.-T. Lu, and P. Zhang. A Unified Approach to Spatial Outliers Detection. *GeoInformatica, An International Journal on Advances of Computer Science for Geographic Information System*, 7(2), June 2003.

[16] T. Johnson and I. Kwok and R. Ng. Fast Computation of 2-Dimensional Depth Contours. In *Proceedings of the Fourth International Conference on Knowledge Discovery and Data Mining*, pages 224–228. AAAI Press, 1998.

[17] U.S. Census Burean, United Stated Department of Commence. http://www.census.gov/.

Learning Rules for Anomaly Detection of Hostile Network Traffic

Matthew V. Mahoney and Philip K. Chan
Department of Computer Sciences
Florida Institute of Technology
Melbourne, FL 32901
{mmahoney,pkc}@cs.fit.edu

Abstract

We introduce an algorithm called LERAD that learns rules for finding rare events in nominal time-series data with long range dependencies. We use LERAD to find anomalies in network packets and TCP sessions to detect novel intrusions. We evaluated LERAD on the 1999 DARPA/Lincoln Laboratory intrusion detection evaluation data set and on traffic collected in a university departmental server environment.

1. Introduction and Related Work

An important component of computer security is intrusion detection--knowing whether a system has been compromised or if an attack is occurring. Hostile activity can sometimes be inferred by examining inbound network traffic, operating system events, or changes to the file system, either for patterns signaling known attacks (signature detection), or for unusual events signaling possible novel attacks (anomaly detection). Anomaly detection has the advantage that it can sometimes detect previously unknown attacks, but has the disadvantage that it issues false alarms, because unusual events are not always hostile. Often both approaches are used. For example, a virus detector might scan files for strings signaling known viruses, and might also test for modifications of executable files as indications of possible new viruses.

Network anomaly detection is a particularly difficult problem because higher level (application) protocols are complex and difficult to model, and because data must be processed at high speed. A common approach is to use a firewall with rules programmed by a network administrator to block and/or log packets based on lower level features such as IP addresses and port numbers. This technique can detect or block port scans and unauthorized access to private services (e.g. *ssh*) from untrusted clients. However, detection of attacks on public services such as

HTTP (web), SMTP (email), and DNS (host name lookup) currently rely on signature detection systems such as SNORT [10] or Bro [8] to scan for strings signaling known attacks. The rule set is quite large (SNORT has over 1800) and must be updated frequently. This would not be an effective defense against novel attacks or fast spreading worms. Network anomaly detection systems such as ADAM [2], SPADE [3], and eBayes [11], use machine learning approaches to model normal network traffic in order to identify unusual events as suspicious, but they model low-level (firewall-like) features such as addresses and port numbers, rather than application protocols.

We introduce an efficient, randomized algorithm called LERAD (Learning Rules for Anomaly Detection), which can discover relationships among attributes in order to model application protocols. LERAD differs from association mining approaches such as APRIORI [1] in that it finds enough rules with a small set of allowed values in the consequent to describe the data, rather than *all* rules (allowing only one value) above a support/confidence threshold. We believe this form is more appropriate for "bursty" (non-Poisson) time series data with long range dependencies, a characteristic of network traffic [4, 9].

2. Rule Learning Algorithm

LERAD learns conditional rules over nominal attributes in a time series (e.g. a sequence of inbound client packets or TCP sessions), in which the antecedent is a conjunction of equalities, and the consequent is a set of allowed values, e.g. *if port = 80 and word3 = HTTP/1.0 then word1 = GET or POST*. A value is allowed if it is observed in at least one training instance satisfying the antecedent. If in testing a disallowed value is observed, then an anomaly score of tn/r is generated, where t is the time since the last anomaly by this rule, n is the support (number of training instances satisfying the antecedent), and r is the number of allowed values (2 in this example). The idea is to identify rare events: those which have not occurred for a long time (large *t*) and where the average rate of "anomalies" in training is low (small *r/n*). If the total anomaly score summed over all violated rules exceeds a threshold, then an alarm is generated.

LERAD is a two pass algorithm. In the first pass, a candidate rule set is generated from a random sample *S* of the training data (attack-free network traffic). In the second pass, the rules are trained by collecting the set of allowed values for each antecedent. After training the rules are validated on a portion of the training data (e.g. the last 10%) to remove "poor" rules where the training data is not representative of the test data (Fig. 1). For example, the set of client IP addresses contacting a web server would be expected to grow steadily over time, so we would not wish to restrict the set to only those clients observed during a training period. On the other hand, a set of local server addresses or ports would not be expected to grow after a short training period, so this would be a "good" rule.

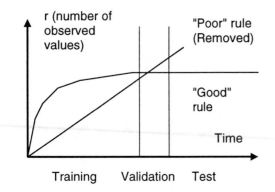

Figure 1. Growth of *r* for "good" and "poor" rules

The LERAD rule algorithm is as follows:

1. Rule generation. Randomly sample *L* pairs of training instances from a random subset *S* of the training data, and generate up to *M* rules per pair that satisfy both instances with *n/r* = 2/1, generating rule set *R*.
2. Coverage test. Discard rules from *R* to find a minimal (but not optimal) subset of rules that cover all instance-values in *S*, favoring rules with higher *n/r* over *S*.
3. Training, pass 2. Set the consequent of each rule in *R* to all values observed at least once in the training data when the antecedent is satisfied.
4. Validation. If a validation instance satisfies the antecedent but not the consequent of a rule (a violation), then remove the rule from *R*.
5. Test. For each instance, assign an anomaly score of Σ *tn/r* summed over the violations.

LERAD requires two passes over the training data, one to sample *S* uniformly prior to generating rule antecedents, and a second pass to assign the consequents. We cannot simply use the beginning of the training data for *S* because attribute values are not Poisson distributed, so *S* would not representative of the rest of the training data.

In the rule generation step, we pick pairs of training samples and suggest rules based on the matching values. The algorithm is as follows:

> Repeat *L* times
>   Randomly pick two instances S_1 and S_2 from *S*
>   Set *A* = {*a*: $S_1[a] = S_2[a]$} (*matching attributes*)
>   For *m* = 1 to *M* and *A* not empty do
>   Randomly remove *a* from *A*
>   If *m* = 1 then create rule r_i = "*a* = $S_1[a]$"
>   Else add $S_1[a] = a$ to r_i's antecedent
>   Add r_i to rule set *R*

For example, suppose that we randomly pick the first two instances of Table 1 as S_1 and S_2. Then the set of matching attributes is *A* = {*word1, port, word3*}. Suppose *M* = 4 and we randomly choose the attributes *a* in the order listed above. Then we generate the following rules:

- R_1: *word1 = GET*
- R_2: *if port = 80 then word1 = GET*
- R_3: *if port = 80 and word3 = HTTP/1.0 then word1 = GET*

Table 1. Example training sample S

Port	Word1	Word2	Word3
80	GET	/	HTTP/1.0
80	GET	/index.html	HTTP/1.0
25	HELO	pascal	

In the coverage test (step 2), we remove "redundant" rules, those which predict values in *S* already predicted by another rule with higher *n/r* over *S* (i.e. a rule which would probably generate higher anomaly scores in testing). The procedure is as follows:

> Update the consequents in *R* over *S*
> Sort *R* by decreasing *n/r*
> For each rule R_i in *R* in decreasing order of *r/n*
>   Mark the values predicted by R_i
>   If no new values can be marked, remove R_i

For example, consider the rules above. After training over *S* and sorting by *n/r* these become:

- R_2: *if port = 80 then word1 = GET* (*n/r* = 2/1)
- R_3: *if port = 80 and word3 = HTTP/1.0 then word1 = GET* (*n/r* = 2/1)
- R_1: *word1 = GET or HELO* (*n/r* = 3/2)

(Note that the ordering of R_2 and R_3 is arbitrary, and R_1 has changed). R_2 marks the two *GET* values in S. R_3 would mark the same two values and no new values, so we remove it. R_1 marks the *HELO* in the third instance, in addition to the previously marked values, so we retain this rule.

3. Experimental Evaluation

Evaluation details are available from [7] and source code from [6]. To summarize, we tested LERAD using two attribute sets, one for IP packets and one for TCP connections. For packets, the attributes were the first 24 byte pairs (as 16-bit nominal values), beginning with the 10 pairs of bytes from the IP header. For TCP connections, the attributes were the source and destination port numbers, the individual bytes of the source and destination addresses, the connection length (in bytes), duration (in seconds), the TCP flags of the first and last two packets, and the first 8 words of the application payload (delimited by white space). We used a sample size of $|S| = 100$ (20 to 500 work well) and drew $L = 1000$ sample pairs, generating up to $M = 4$ candidate rules per pair, which are sufficient to generate 50 to 100 final rules for good results. Using larger L and M do not add significantly more rules.

We tested LERAD using two data sets: the 1999 DARPA/Lincoln Laboratory intrusion detection evaluation (IDEVAL) [5], and 623 hours of traffic collected from a university departmental server over 10 weeks in which we previously identified six attacks. We examine only inbound client (unsolicited) traffic, rate limited to 16 packets per connection per minute, and further truncated TCP connections after 256 bytes of the first payload packet. This filtering removes 98-99% of traffic, greatly speeding up LERAD with minimal effect on detection accuracy.

For IDEVAL, we trained LERAD on 7 days of attack-free traffic from inside sniffer week 3, and tested on 9 days of traffic from weeks 4 and 5, which contains evidence of 146 simulated probes, denial of service, and remote to local (R2L) attacks against four "victim" machines running SunOS, Solaris, Linux, and Windows NT. We evaluated LERAD according to the same criteria used in the 1999 blind evaluation, which requires only that we identify the target address and the attack time within 60 seconds at a threshold allowing 100 false alarms (10 per day). We exclude U2R (user to root) attacks, as allowed by the evaluation criteria, because these attacks exploit operating system weaknesses rather than network protocols, and would be difficult to detect in network traffic.

The second test was on switched Ethernet traffic collected on a Sun Ultra-AX i2 running Solaris 5.9 as a file, web, and mail server. We used SNORT and manual inspection to identify six attacks that eluded the university firewall: an inside port/security scan, three HTTP worms (*Code Red II, Nimda,* and *Scalper*), an HTTP proxy scan and a DNS version probe.

We used a stricter evaluation criteria: LERAD must identify at least one packet or TCP session involved in the attack. We counted multiple instances of a worm probe from different sources as a single attack, since a detection is likely to lead to a rule being added to an accompanying signature detection system. Lacking attack-free training data, we tested LERAD by dividing the traffic into 10 one-week periods and tested each week after training on the previous week. An attack in the training or validation data might mask a similar attack in the test data, but at least the first attack ought to be detected in the previous training/test pair. We allowed 250 false alarms, or 10 per 24 hours. Results averaged over 5 runs with different random number seeds are shown in Table 2.

Table 2. Number and percent of attacks detected at 10 false alarms per day in IDEVAL and university traffic

Data	Packets	TCP
IDEVAL	48.2 (33%)	95.2 (64%)
Univ.	1.4 (23%)	2.4 (40%)

LERAD using TCP attributes detects 64% of 146 attacks in IDEVAL, compared to 40% to 55% detected by the top four (of 18) systems in the original blind 1999 evaluation [5], even though most of those systems combined both signature and anomaly detection using both host and network based attributes. However, the comparison is biased in our favor because we had access to all of the test data during development. In the 1999 evaluation, participants were provided only with the first three weeks of data, containing a subset of the labeled attacks for development.

In IDEVAL we identified five categories of anomalies in the detected attacks.

- User behavior anomalies, e.g. unusual destination ports as part of a port scan, or client IP address anomalies in a password guessing attack.

- Anomalies due to exploitation of bugs in legal but seldom used (and therefore poorly tested) features of the protocol, for example, IP fragmentation in *teardrop* and *land*, which exploit bugs in IP reassembly code in a denial of service attack.

- Anomalies due to the failure to reproduce the idiosyncrasies of normal clients, for example, omitting the opening SMTP *HELO/EHLO* handshake (which is not required) in the *sendmail* buffer overflow root shell exploit.

- Anomalies deliberately introduced in an attempt to hide the attack signature at a higher protocol level, for example, scanning with FIN packets (with a missing ACK flag) to avoid having the probe logged by the server.
- Anomalies from the victim after a successful attack, for example, interrupted TCP connections from a crashed host.

In the university traffic, all of the anomalies are due to idiosyncratic variations, mostly at the application layer, for example, generic values in the HTTP *host* field for *Nimda, Scalper*, and the proxy scan, and an unusual backslash in the port/security scan: *GET / HTTP\1.0*. The one anomaly at the network layer was the unusual TCP segmentation in the Code Red HTTP command *GET default.ida?NNNNN...* in which *GET* appears in its own packet. The actual buffer overflow exploit code was truncated during filtering.

Our implementations process 10,000 packets or 3500 TCP sessions per second (after filtering) on a 750 MHz PC. The 8.9 GB of IDEVAL traffic was filtered in 7 minutes and processed by LERAD in under two minutes.

4. Concluding Remarks

LERAD differs from conventional network anomaly detection in that it models application protocols, allowing it to detect novel attacks on public servers. Application protocols are complex, but LERAD is able to learn important relationships between attributes given only rudimentary syntactic knowledge (e.g. tokens are separated by white space). It detects both simulated and real attacks, although there is a tradeoff between detection accuracy and a low false alarm rate. The false alarm problem is fundamental to anomaly detection because unusual events are not necessarily hostile.

Many of the anomalies detected by LERAD are not due to hostile code, but rather to legal but unusual protocol implementations. Unfortunately, this makes it difficult to understand the nature of the attack from the anomaly alone, or even to decide if an alarm should be dismissed as false. We could identify no consistent differences between true and false alarms.

One may argue that many attacks could be trivially modified to elude detection. Nevertheless, idiosyncratic anomalies are common in attacks in both of the data sets we used. We argue that writing an attack to elude detection is difficult because an attacker would not be able to test it in the target environment prior to launching it.

Future work includes a single-pass version of LERAD, research into better tokenization techniques in order to parse binary protocols such as DNS, and testing on additional data sets.

Acknowledgments

This work is partially funded by DARPA (F30602-00-1-0603).

References

[1] R. Agrawal & R. Srikant, "Fast Algorithms for Mining Association Rules", *Proc. 20th Intl. Conf. Very Large Data Bases*, 1994.

[2] D. Barbara, J. Couto, S. Jajodia, L. Popyack, & N. Wu, "ADAM: Detecting Intrusions by Data Mining", *Proc. IEEE Workshop on Information Assurance and Security*, 2001, pp. 11-16.

[3] J. Hoagland, SPADE, Silicon Defense, http://www.silicondefense.com/software/spice/, 2000.

[4] W. E. Leland, M. S. Taqqu, W. Willinger, & D. W. Wilson, "On the Self-Similar Nature of Ethernet Traffic", *Proc. ACM SIGComm*, 1993.

[5] R. Lippmann, J. W. Haines, D. J. Fried, J. Korba, & K. Das (2000), "The 1999 DARPA Off-Line Intrusion Detection Evaluation", *Computer Networks 34(4)*, 2000, pp. 579-595.

[6] M. Mahoney. Source code for PHAD, ALAD, LERAD, NETAD, SAD, EVAL3, EVAL4, EVAL and AFIL.PL is available at http://cs.fit.edu/~mmahoney/dist/

[7] M. Mahoney & P. K. Chan, " Learning Rules for Anomaly Detection of Hostile Network Traffic", Florida Tech. technical report CS-2003-16, 2003.

[8] V. Paxson, "Bro: A System for Detecting Network Intruders in Real-Time", *Proc. 7'th USENIX Security Symposium*, 1998.

[9] V. Paxson, S. Floyd, "The Failure of Poisson Modeling", IEEE/ACM Transactions on Networking (3) , 1995, pp. 226-244.

[10] M. Roesch, "Snort - Lightweight Intrusion Detection for Networks", *Proc. USENIX Lisa*, 1999.

[11] A. Valdes & K. Skinner, "Adaptive, Model-based Monitoring for Cyber Attack Detection", *Proc. RAID*, 2000, pp. 80-92.

An Algorithm for the Exact Computation of the Centroid of Higher Dimensional Polyhedra and its Application to Kernel Machines

Frederic Maire

Smart Devices Laboratory,
School of SEDC, IT Faculty,
Queensland University of Technology,
2 George Street, GPO Box 2434,
Brisbane Q 4001, Australia.

Abstract

The Support Vector Machine (SVM) solution corresponds to the centre of the largest sphere inscribed in version space. Alternative approaches like Bayesian Point Machines (BPM) and Analytic Centre Machines have suggested that the generalization performance can be further enhanced by considering other possible centres of version space like the centroid (centre of mass) or the analytic centre. We present an algorithm to compute exactly the centroid of higher dimensional polyhedra, then derive approximation algorithms to build a new learning machine whose performance is comparable to BPM. We also show that for regular kernel matrices (Gaussian kernels for example), the SVM solution can be obtained by solving a linear system of equalities.

1. Introduction

In the Kernel Machine framework [5, 8], a feature mapping $x \mapsto \phi(x)$ from an input space to a feature space is given (generally, implicitly via a kernel function), as well as a training set T of pattern vectors and their class labels $\left\{(x^1, y_1), \ldots, (x^m, y_m)\right\}$ where the class labels are in $\{-1, +1\}$. The learning problem is formulated as a search problem for a linear classifier (a weight vector w) in the feature space. Because only the direction of w matters for classification purpose, without loss of generality, we can restrict the search for w to the unit sphere. The set of weight vectors w that classify correctly the training set is called *version space* and denoted by $\mathcal{V}(T)$. Version space is the region of feature space defined as the intersection of the unit sphere and the polyhedral cone of the feature space $\left\{w | \forall i \in [1, m], \ \langle w, y_i \phi(x^i) \rangle \geq 0\right\}$.

The training algorithm of a Support Vector Machine

(SVM) returns the central direction w_{svm} (a unit vector) of the largest spheric cone contained in the polyhedral cone $\left\{w | \forall i \in [1, m], \ \langle w, y_i \phi(x^i) \rangle \geq 0\right\}$. The weight vector w_{svm} can be expressed as a linear combination of the vectors $y_i \phi(x^i)$'s. That is, there exist $(\alpha_1, \ldots, \alpha_m)$ such that $w_{\text{svm}} = \sum_{i=1}^{m} \alpha_i y_i \phi(x^i)$.

The Kernel trick is that for some feature spaces and mappings ϕ, there exist easily computable kernel functions k defined on the input space such that $k(x, y) = \langle \phi(x), \phi(y) \rangle$. A new input vector x is classified with the sign of

$$\langle w_{\text{svm}}, x \rangle = \sum_{i=1}^{m} \alpha_i y_i \langle \phi(x^i), \phi(x) \rangle = \sum_{i=1}^{m} \alpha_i y_i k(x^i, x)$$

With a kernel function k, the computation of inner products $\langle \phi(x), \phi(y) \rangle$ does not require the explicit knowledge of ϕ. In fact for a given kernel function k, there may exist many suitable mappings ϕ.

Bayes Point Machines (BPM) are a well-founded improvement over to SVM which approximate the Bayes-optimal decision by the centroid (also known as the centre of mass or barycentre) of version space. It happens that the Bayes point is very close to the centroid of version space in high dimensional spaces. The Bayes point achieves better generalization performance in comparison to SVM [6, 9, 1, 10].

An intuitive way to see why the centroid is a good choice is to view version space as a (infinite) committee of experts who all are consistent with the training set. A new and unlabelled input vector corresponds to a hyperplane in feature space that may split version space in two. It is reasonable to use the opinion of the majority of the experts that were consistent with the training set to predict the class label of a new pattern. The expert that agrees the most with the majority vote on new inputs is precisely the Bayesian point. In a standard committee machine, for each new input we seek the opinions of a finite number of experts then take a majority vote, whereas with a BPM, the expert that most often agrees with the majority vote of the infinite committee (version space) is delegated the task of classifying the new inputs.

Following Rujan [7], Herbrich and Graepel [2] introduced two algorithms to stochastically approximate the centroid of version space; a billiard sampling algorithm and a sampling algorithm based on the well known perceptron algorithm.

In this paper, we present an algorithm to compute exactly the centroid of a polyhedron in high dimensional spaces. From this exact algorithm, we derive an algorithm to approximate a centroid position in a polyhedral cone. We show empirically that the corresponding machine presents better generalization capability than SVMs on a number a benchmark data sets.

In Section 2, we introduce an algorithm to compute exactly the centroid of higher dimensional polyhedra. In Section 3, we show a simple algorithm to compute the SVM solution of regular kernels. In Section 4, we sketch the idea of Balancing Board Machines. In Section 5, some implementation issues are considered and some experimental results are presented.

2. Exact Computation of the Centroid of a Higher Dimensional Polyhedron

A polyhedron P is the intersection of a finite number of half-spaces. It is best represented by a system of non redundant linear inequalities $P = \{x \mid Ax \leq b\}$. Recall that the 1-volume is the length, the 2-volume is the surface and the 3-volume is the every-day-life volume. The algorithm that we introduce for computing the centroid of an n-dimensional polyhedron is an extension of the work by Lasserre [4] who showed that the n-dimensional volume $V(n, A, b)$ of a polyhedron P is related to the $(n - 1)$-dimensional volumes of its facets and the row vectors of its matrix A by the following formula;

$$V(n, A, b) = \frac{1}{n} \sum_i \frac{b_i}{\|a_i\|} \times V_i(n - 1, A, b)$$

where a_i denotes the ith row of A and $V_i(n - 1, A, b)$ denotes the $(n - 1)$-dimensional volume of the ith facet $P \cap \{x \mid a_i^T x = b_i\}$. We obtain the centroid and the $(n-1)$-volume of a facet by variable elimination. Geometrically, this amounts to projecting the facet onto an axis parallel hyperplane, then computing the volume and the centroid of this projection recursively in a lower dimensional space. From the volume and centroid of the projected facet, we can derive the centroid and volume of the original facet.

The n-volume V and the centroid G of a cone rooted at 0 are related to the $(n - 1)$-volume V_h and the centroid

G_h of its intersection with the hyperplane $x_n = h$ by the following equalities;

$$V = \int_0^h V_x dx = \int_0^h V_h \times \left(\frac{x}{h}\right)^{n-1} dx = \frac{h}{n} \times V_h$$

$$V \times \overrightarrow{OG} = \int_0^h \overrightarrow{OG_x} \times V_x \times dx$$

$$\overrightarrow{OG} = \frac{n}{n + 1} \times \overrightarrow{OG_h}$$

The above formulae were derived by considering the n-fold integral defining the n-dimensional volume. These formulae allow a recursive computation of the centroid of a polyhedron P by partitioning P into polyhedral cones generated by its facets.

It is useful to observe that the computation of the volume and the centroid of a $(n - 1)$-dimensional polyhedron in a n-dimensional space is identical to the computation of the volume and the centroid of a facet of a n-dimensional polyhedron.

Algorithm 1 $[G, V]$=measurePolyhedron(P)

Require: $P = \{x \mid Ax \leq b\}$ non-empty and irredundant
Ensure: G is the centroid of P, and V its volume
  {m is the number of rows of A, n is its number of columns}
  for $i = 1$ to m **do**
    {Compute recursively the centroids G_{F_i} and the $(n - 1)$-volumes V_{F_i} of each facet F_i of P}
    $[G_{F_i}, V_{F_i}]$=measurePolyhedron(F_i)
  end for
  {Compute G_E, the centroid of the envelope of P}
  $G_E = \sum_i \frac{V_{F_i}}{\sum_j V_{F_j}} \times G_{F_i}$
  for $i = 1$ to m **do**
    {Compute recursively the centroids G_{C_i} and the $(n - 1)$-volumes V_{C_i} of each cone $C_i = \text{cone}(G_E, F_i)$ rooted at G_E and generated by F_i}
    Compute h_i, the distance form G_E to the hyperplane containing F_i
    $V_{C_i} = \frac{h_i}{n} \times V_{F_i}$
    $\overrightarrow{G_E G_{C_i}} = \frac{n}{n+1} \times \overrightarrow{G_E G_{F_i}}$
  end for
  $V = \sum_i V_{C_i}$
  $G = \sum_i \frac{V_{C_i}}{V} \times G_{C_i}$

The Matlab code for this algorithm is available at
`http://www.fit.qut.edu.au/~maire/G`

3. Computing the Spheric Centre of a Polyhedral Cone Derived from a Non Singular Mercer Kernel Matrix

Let $P = \{x \,|\, Ax \leq 0\}$ be the non-empty polyhedral cone derived from a non-singular kernel matrix. The matrix A is square ($m = n$). Without loss of generality, we assume that its rows are normalized. Recall that the centre of the largest spheric cone contained in the polyhedral cone P is the SVM solution w_{svm}. Because A is square and non-singular, each facet of the polyhedral cone touches the spheric cone. If each facet is moved by a distance of one in the direction of its normal vector, the new cone obtained is a translation of the original cone in the direction of w_{svm}. That is w_{svm} can be obtained by simply solving $Ax = -\vec{1}$ instead of solving the traditional constrained quadratic optimization problem.

4. Balancing Board Machines

The point of contact of a board posed in equilibrium on a sphere (assumed to be the only source of gravity) is the centroid of the board. This observation is the basis of our *balancing board algorithm*. In the rest of this paper, the term *board* will refer to the intersection of the polyhedral cone of version space with a hyperplane normal to a unit vector of version space. This definition implies that if the polyhedral cone is n-dimensional then a board will be a $(n-1)$-dimensional polyhedron tangent to the unit sphere. In the algorithm we propose, the approximation of the centroid direction of the polyhedral cone of $\mathcal{V}(T)$ is refined by computing the centroid of the board normal to a current estimate w, and then rotating w towards the centroid of the board (stopping at a local minimum of the volume of the board in a line search).

Once we know an orthonormal basis U of V the vector subspace generated by $\{\phi(x^1), \ldots, \phi(x^m)\}$ (the orthonormality is with respect to the inner product in feature space corresponding to the kernel function in the input space), we can express the polyhedral cone inequalities with respect to this orthonormal basis. Then we can apply the formulae of Section 2 to compute the centroid of any polyhedron expressed in this orthonormal basis. The kernel PCA basis is a suitable orthonormal basis U of V. The vectors of the kernel PCA basis U are the eigenvectors of the kernel matrix $K = \big(k(x^i, x^j)\big)_{i,j}$. By expressing the polyhedral cone defined by the training examples in the orthonormal basis U, we will be able to approximate a centroid direction with the board balancing algorithm sketched above.

The complexity of the algorithm of Section 2 to compute exactly the centroid is unfortunately exponential. The computational cost of the exact calculation of the centroid is too high even for medium size data sets. However, the recursive

formulae allow us to derive an approximation of the volume and the centroid of a polyhedron once we have approximations for the volumes and the centroids of its facets.

Because the balancing board algorithm requires several board centroid estimations, it is desirable to recycle intermediate results as much as possible to achieve a significant reduction in computation time. Because the intersection of a hyperplane and a spheric cone is an ellipsoid, we estimate the volume and the centroid of the intersection of the board and a facet of the polyhedral cone (this intersection is (n-2)-dimensional) with the volume and the centroid of the intersection of the board and the largest spheric cone contained in the facet (this spheric cone is (n-1)-dimensional). The computation of the largest spheric cones contained in each facet of the polyhedral cone is done only once. The centre of the ellipsoid and its quadratic matrix is easily derived from the centre and radius of the spheric cone.

To simplify the computations, we have restricted our study to non-singular kernel matrices (like those obtained from Gaussian kernels). This way, we were able to use the geometric trick of Section 3 to compute the centres of the spheric cones.

The change of basis is performed as follows. Let w_B be the coordinates of w with respect to B. Recall that the Kernel PCA basis U is made of the eigenvectors of the symmetric matrix K. Let w_U be the coordinates of w with respect to the basis U. We have $w_B = U w_U$. We are looking for w_B such that

$$\begin{cases} -\text{diag}(y) K w_B \leq 0 \\ \langle w, w \rangle = 1 \end{cases}$$

and w near the centroid direction of the polyhedral cone. Here, $\text{diag}(y)$ represents the diagonal matrix made with the entries of vector y. As we have $\langle w, w \rangle = (w_U)^T w_u$, in practice, we look for the centroid direction of

$$\begin{cases} -\text{diag}(y) K U w_U \leq 0 \\ (w_U)^T w_U = 1 \end{cases}$$

5. Implementation Issues and Experimental Results

We have implemented the exact computation of the centroid and the volume in Matlab. A direct recursive implementation of Lasserre formula would be very inefficient as faces of dimension k share faces of dimension $k-1$. Our implementation caches the volumes and centroids of the lower dimensional faces in a hash-table.

Our algorithm has been validated by comparing the values returned with a Monte-Carlo method.

The kernel matrix of a Gaussian kernel can only be singular when identical input vectors occur more than once the training set. We remove repeated occurrences of the same input vector and assign the most common label for this input vector to the occurrence that we leave in the training set.

The table that follows summarises generalization performance (percentage of correct predictions on test sets) of the Balancing Board Machine (BBM) on 6 standard benchmarking data sets from the UCI Repository, comparing results for illustrative purposes with equivalent hard margin support vector machines. In each case the data was randomly partitioned into 20 training and test sets in the ratio 60% 40%.

Data set	SVM	BBM
heart disease	58.36	58.40
thyroid	94.34	95.23
diabetes	66.89	67.68
waveform	83.50	83.50
sonar	85.06	85.78
ionosphere	86.79	86.86

Table 1. UCI benchmark Data Sets

The results obtained with a BBM are comparable to those obtained with a BPM, but the improvement is not always as dramatic as those reported in [3]. We observed that the improvement was generally better for smaller data sets. We suspect that this is due to the fact the volumes considered become very small in high dimensional spaces. In fact, on a PC, unit spheres "vanish" when their dimension exceed 340. The volume of a unit sphere of dimension 340 is $4.5 \ 10^{-223}$. This is why we consider the logarithm of the volume in our programs.

6. Conclusions

The exact computation algorithm can be useful for benchmarking to people developing new centroid approximation algorithms. We do not claim that our BBM approach is superior to any other given that the computational cost is in the order of times the cost of a SVM computation (where is the number of training examples).

Replacing the ellipsoids with a more accurate estimation would probably give better results, but deriving the volume and the centroid of the intersection of a facet and a board from the volume and the centroid of the intersection of the same facet with another board seems to be a hard problem.

The computation of the SVM point presented in Section 3 provides an efficient learning algorithm for Gaussian kernels.

Acknowledgement

I would like to thank Professor Tom Downs and Professor Peter Bartlett for their valuable comments on a previous

version of the BBM algorithm. This work was partially supported by an ATN grant.

References

[1] T. Graepel, R. Herbrich, and C. Campbell. Bayes point machines: Estimating the bayes point in kernel space. In *in Proc. of IJCAI Workshop Support Vector Machines*, pages 23–27, 1999.

[2] R. Herbrich and T. Graepel. Large scale bayes point machines. In *in Advances in Neural Information System Processing 13*, pages 528–534, 2001.

[3] R. Herbrich, T. Graepel, and C. Campbell. Bayes point machines. *Journal of Machine Learning Research, 1*, pages 245–279, 2001.

[4] J. Lasserre. An analytical expression and an algorithm for the volume of a convex polyhedron in r^n. *Journal of Optimization Theory and Applications, Vol 39, No 3*, pages 363–377, 1983.

[5] K. Muller, S. Mika, G. Ratch, K. Tsuda, and B. Scholkopf. An introduction to kernel-based learning algorithmss. *IEEE Trans. on NN, vol 12, no 2*, 2001.

[6] M. Opper and D. Haussler. Generalization performance of bayes optimal classification algorithm for learning a perceptron. *Phys. Rev. Lett. vol. 66*, pages 26–77, 1991.

[7] P. Rujn. Playing billiard in version space. *Neural Comput. , vol. 9*, pages 197–238, 1996.

[8] B. Scholkopft and A. Smola. *Learning with Kernels*. The MIT Press, Cambridge, Massachusetts, London, England, 2002.

[9] J. Shawe-Taylor and R. C. Williamson. A pac analysis of a bayesian estimator. Technical report, Royal Holloway, Univ. London,, 1997. R Tech. Rep. NC2-TR-1997-013.

[10] T. Watkin. Optimal learning with a neural network. *Europhys. Lett., vol. 21*, pages 871–877, 1993.

Simple Estimators for Relational Bayesian Classifiers

Jennifer Neville, David Jensen and Brian Gallagher

Knowledge Discovery Laboratory, Department of Computer Science,
University of Massachusetts Amherst, 140 Governors Drive, Amherst, MA 01003 USA
{jneville | jensen | bgallag}@cs.umass.edu

Abstract

In this paper we present the Relational Bayesian Classifier (RBC), a modification of the Simple Bayesian Classifier (SBC) for relational data. There exist several Bayesian classifiers that learn predictive models of relational data, but each uses a different estimation technique for modeling heterogeneous sets of attribute values. The effects of data characteristics on estimation have not been explored. We consider four simple estimation techniques and evaluate them on three real-world data sets. The estimator that assumes each multiset value is independently drawn from the same distribution (INDEPVAL) achieves the best empirical results. We examine bias and variance tradeoffs over a range of data sets and show that INDEPVAL's ability to model more multiset information results in lower bias estimates and contributes to its superior performance.

1. Introduction

This paper presents a modification of the Simple Bayesian Classifier (SBC) for relational data. The power of relational data lies in combining intrinsic information about objects in isolation with information about related objects and the connections between those objects. However, the data often have irregular structures and complex dependencies, which contradict the assumptions of conventional modeling techniques. In particular, the heterogeneous structure of relational data precludes direct application of a SBC model, which operates on attribute-value data. We consider several approaches to modeling data with a relational Bayesian classifier (RBC) and evaluate performance on three data sets. The approach that follows the spirit of SBC and assumes conditional attribute value independence appears to work best. (See [9] for an expanded version of this paper.)

The simplicity of the SBC stems from its assumption that attributes are independent given the class—an assumption rarely met in practice. Research investigating the effects of this assumption on performance has helped to better understand the range of applicability of the SBC. For example, Domingos and Pazzani [2] showed that the SBC performs well under zero-one loss even when the

independence assumption is violated by a wide margin. This paper studies similar questions for relational data. We empirically evaluate four different techniques on several real-world data sets. We explore the techniques on simulated data sets, decomposing loss into bias and variance estimates [1]. Our experiments show that characteristics of relational data can bias certain estimators and that using estimators with decreased bias improves model performance.

2. Modeling Relational Data

Relational data violate two assumptions of conventional classification techniques. First, algorithms for propositional data assume that the data instances are recorded in homogeneous structures (e.g. a fixed set of fields for each object), but relational data "instances" are consist of sets of heterogeneous records. Second, algorithms for propositional data assume that the data instances are independent and identically distributed (i.i.d.), but relational data have dependencies both through direct relations and through chaining multiple relations together. In this paper, we evaluate simple algorithms for learning models of data sets with heterogeneous instances. We do not attempt to exploit dependencies among related instances.

Relational data often have complex structures that are more difficult to model than homogeneous instances. For example, in order to predict the box-office success of a movie, a relational model might consider not only the attributes of the movie, but also attributes of the movie's actors, director, producers, and the studio that made the movie. A model might even consider attributes of indirectly related objects such as other movies made by the director. Each movie may have a different number of related objects, resulting in diverse structures. For example, some movies may have 10 actors and others may have 1000. When trying to predict the value of an attribute based on the attributes of related objects, a relational classification technique must consider *multisets* of attribute values. For example, we might model the likelihood of movie success given the multiset of gender values from the movie's actors.

There are a number of approaches to modeling sets of attribute values. *Propositionalization* is a common technique to transform heterogeneous data instances into homogenous records, mapping sets of values into single values with aggregation functions. A second approach is to treat the set of values independently and aggregate the resulting probability distributions using combining rules such as *noisy-or* or *average* [4]. A third approach is to model the sets directly with multinomials [7] or complex set-valued estimators [6].

This paper considers four estimation techniques from the range of approaches outlined above. Recent work has demonstrated the feasibility of these approaches for statistical models of relational data, but the choice of technique for any one model has been approached in a relatively ad-hoc manner. A thorough understanding of the effects of relational data characteristics on estimator performance will improve parameter estimation for relational data and should inform the development of more complex statistical models.

Figure 1. Relational data represented as (a) a subgraph, and (b) decomposed by attribute.

3. Relational Bayesian Classifiers

The RBC represents heterogeneous examples as homogenous sets of attribute multisets. For example, a movie subgraph contains information about a number of related objects, such as actors and studios (e.g. Figure 1a). Transformed examples contain a multiset of values for each attribute, such as actor-age and studio-location (e.g. Figure 1b). This enables a SBC approach, where learning a model consists of estimating conditional probabilities for each attribute. However, estimation techniques for these data will need to model multisets of varying cardinality and high dimensionality. We refer to techniques used to estimate these probabilities as *estimators*. We will evaluate three approaches to estimation and four approaches to inference.

Average Value—The average value estimator (AVGVAL) corresponds to propositionalizing the data by averaging. During estimation, each multiset is replaced with its average value (for continuous attributes) or modal value (for discrete attributes). The average values are used in a standard maximum-likelihood estimator and probabilities are inferred from average/modal values as well. AVGVAL estimators are commonly used in probabilistic relational models (PRMs) to model dependencies where the "parent" consists of a set of attribute values [3]. We hypothesize that AVGVAL should perform well if the multiset values are highly correlated, so the multiset is no more informative than the average.

Random Value—The random value estimator (RANDVAL) is similar to AVGVAL. However, instead of deterministically choosing the most prevalent value from the set, RANDVAL chooses a representative value stochastically. This allows the estimation to differentiate between relatively uniform sets of values and highly skewed sets. This approach is equivalent to the *stochastic-mode* aggregation used in PRMs for classification [10]. Although RANDVAL may be more sensitive to the distribution of values in the sets, it may also experience greater variance if multiset values are distributed uniformly over a large range.

Independent Value—The independent value estimator (INDEPVAL) assumes each multiset value is independently drawn from the same distribution. This estimator is designed to mirror the independence assumption of SBC—now in addition to attribute independence, there is also an assumption of *attribute value* independence given the class. INDEPVAL models the multiset with a multinomial distribution where the size of the set is independent of the class. INDEPVAL should perform well if the multiset can be used to reduce variance, when there is little correlation among attribute values.

Average Probability—The fourth estimator (AVGPROB) aggregates probability distributions. It is an inference technique only (INDEPVAL is used for estimation). During inference, each multiset value's probability is computed independently and then the set of probabilities is averaged. This approach is one of the combining rules used in Bayesian logic programs (BLPs) to integrate probabilities into logic programs [4]. AVGPROB computes an arithmetic average of probabilities. If the set values are dependent, geometric averaging (used in INDEPVAL) will push the probabilities to extreme values. However, geometric averaging is more robust to irrelevant values, which pull arithmetic averages toward the center and wash out the effects of the useful values.

4. Empirical Data Experiments

The experiments reported below evaluate the claim that RBC models using INDEPVAL estimators will outperform RBC models using AVGVAL, RANDVAL or AVGPROB estimators. We compare the performance of each estimator on three real-world classification tasks. To compare the approaches, we recorded accuracy and area under the ROC curve using ten-fold cross-validation.

4.1. Classification Tasks

The first data set, drawn from the Internet Movie Database (IMDb) (www.imdb.com), is a sample of all movies released in the United States from 1996 to 2001, with opening weekend box-office receipt data. The sample contains 1383 movies and related actors, directors, producers, and studios. The task was to predict whether a movie made more than $2mil in opening weekend receipts ($P(+)=0.45$). Nine attributes were supplied to the models, including studio country and actor birth-year.

The second data set, drawn from Cora [8], is a sample of 4330 machine-learning papers and associated authors, journals/books, publishers, and cited papers. The task was to predict whether a paper's topic is *Neural Networks* ($P(+)=0.32$). Ten attributes were available to the models, including journal affiliation and paper venue.

The third data set contains information about 1243 genes in the yeast genome and 1734 interactions among their associated proteins (www.cs.wisc.edu/~dpage/kddcup2001/). The task was to predict whether a gene's functions include *Transcription* ($P(+)=0.31$). Fourteen attributes where supplied to the models, including gene phenotype, motif, and interaction type.

4.2. Results

Figure 2 shows AUC results for each of the models on the three classification tasks, averaged over the ten folds. Accuracy results are comparable [9]. We used two-tailed, paired t-tests to assess the significance of the ten-fold cross-validation results, comparing INDEPVAL to each of the other estimators. Asterisks in Figure 2 indicate a significant difference in performance compared to INDEPVAL (p-value < 0.001).

On the IMDb and Cora classification tasks, INDEPVAL's AUC results are superior to any of the other approaches. The performance of AVGVAL and RANDVAL indicates that propositionalizing relational data (even stochastically) to apply conventional models may not always be a good approach. On the Gene task, all approaches perform equivalently.

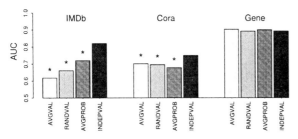

Figure 2: Results of empirical data experiments for IMDb, Cora, and Gene databases.

5. Synthetic Data Experiments

We use synthetic data to explore the effects of linkage, attribute correlation, and multiset distributions on estimator performance. Relational data sets often exhibit concentrated linkage, where certain object types have a large number of relations. For example, papers in Cora link to a few journals, and movies in the IMDb link to a small number of studios. Uniformity among attribute values of objects that share a common neighbor is also common in relational data. For example, in the gene data,

proteins located in the same place in the cell often have highly correlated functions.

5.1. Methodology

Our synthetic data sets are comprised of bipartite graphs, each containing a single core object (e.g. a movie) linked to zero or more peripheral objects (e.g. actors). Note that each actor links to exactly one movie. Each movie has a binary class label, $C=\{+,-\}$, and each actor has a binary attribute, $A=\{1,0\}$. The number of actors per movie is distributed normally with mean equal to |actors|/|movies|. The default experimental parameters were 100 movies, 500 actors, $P(C=+)=0.5$, and $P(A=1|C=+)=P(A=0|C=-)=0.75$. Variations from these defaults are described for each experiment below.

We measured average zero-one loss and squared-loss for each RBC estimator across 100 pairs of training/test sets and decomposed loss into bias and variance [1]. Bias and variance estimates were calculated for each test example using 100 different training sets and averaged over the entire test set. This was repeated for 100 test sets and averaged. The zero-one loss results are presented in Figure 3. Squared-loss results are similar [9].

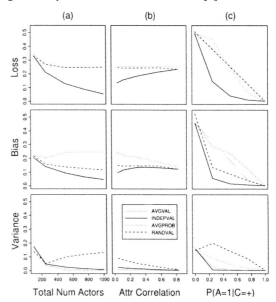

Figure 3: Results of synthetic data experiments.

5.2. Results

The experiment shown in Figure 3a varied the total number of actors in each data set from 100 to 1000. In this experiment AVGVAL and INDEPVAL are nearly indistinguishable, as are AVGPROB and RANDVAL. For all estimators except RANDVAL, increasing degree reduces variance. This was expected, as the variance of the random value selection increases with set size. AVGPROB's arithmetic averaging cannot exploit the extra information in larger sets, which results in higher bias.

The experiment in Figure 3b varied the correlation among linked actor attribute values from [0.05,0.85]. Again, AVGVAL and INDEPVAL are indistinguishable. As attribute correlation increases, the bias of the INDEPVAL estimator increases, indicating that INDEPVAL's probability estimates may be skewed in data with high attribute correlations.

The experiment in Figure 3c varied $P(A=1|C=+)$ from [0,1] while holding $P(A=1|C=-)$ constant at 0. This is the first experiment to show a difference between AVGVAL and INDEPVAL, illustrating performance when rare attribute values determine the class. Since INDEPVAL shows lower bias than either of the other estimators we can attribute its higher accuracy to this reduction in bias.

Given these results, the relative strength of INDEPVAL appears to lie in the estimator's ability to make use of rare attribute values, as well as multiple predictive values within a multiset. To determine if these types of multisets occur in practice, we examined multisets from the IMDb. We calculated the correlation of each attribute value with the class label using chi-square, assessed significance after adjusting for multiset size [5], and then determined the number of unique correlated attribute values per movie. Figure 4 shows the frequency distribution of these counts across movies for three example attributes. A large number of movie subgraphs have more than one unique attribute value correlated with the class. In this situation, estimators that can capture more multiset information (e.g. INDEPVAL) will outperform estimators that propositionalize to a single value (e.g. AVGVAL).

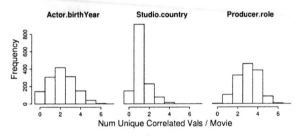

Figure 4: Count of unique significantly correlated values in each subgraph, for three attributes in the IMDb.

6. Conclusions

We have identified a simple approach to estimation for relational data. Adhering to the spirit of SBC simplicity, the RBC model that assumes conditional independence of both attributes and multiset attribute values (INDEPVAL) is successful in a variety of real-world classification tasks. This model is easy to implement and efficient to use, making it a good baseline for evaluation of more complex relational learning techniques.

INDEPVAL estimators have low bias and variance over a wide range of synthetic data sets. AVGVAL has low variance over a number of conditions, but it is easy to identify situations in which AVGVAL is a biased estimator. We can infer that INDEPVAL's superior performance on the real-world classification tasks is a result of lower overall bias—due to its ability to exploit information contained in both rare values and multiple correlated values within the sets. AVGPROB appears to be biased over a number of data sets, but it performs quite well on the IMDb. This reveals that our synthetic data experiments have not clearly identified the circumstances in which AVGPROB is a good approach to estimation.

Future work will include further analysis of the effects of relational data characteristics on complex multiset estimators [e.g. 6] and development of models that select attribute estimators based on data characteristics.

7. Acknowledgments

We thank Ross Fairgrieve for his contributions to an earlier draft of this work. This research is supported by DARPA and AFRL, AFMC, USAF under contract numbers F30602-00-2-0597 and F30602-01-2-0566.

8. References

[1] Domingos, P. A Unified Bias-Variance Decomposition for Zero-One and Squared Loss. *Proceedings of the 17th National Conference on Artificial Intelligence*, 2000.

[2] Domingos, P. and M. Pazzani. On the optimality of the simple Bayesian classifier under zero-one loss. *Machine Learning*, 29:103-130, 1997.

[3] Getoor, L., N. Friedman, D. Koller, and A. Pfeffer. Learning probabilistic relational models. *Relational Data Mining*, Dzeroski and Lavrac, Eds., Springer-Verlag, 2001.

[4] Kersting, K. and L. De Raedt. Basic principles of learning Bayesian logic programs. Tech Report 174, University of Freiburg, Germany, June 2002.

[5] Jensen, D., J. Neville and M. Hay. Avoiding bias when aggregating relational data with degree disparity. *Proc. of the 20th International Conf. on Machine Learning*, 2003.

[6] Lachiche, N. and P. Flach 1BC2: a true first-order Bayesian Classifier. *Proceedings of the 12th International Conference on Inductive Logic Programming*, 2002.

[7] McCallum, A. and K. Nigam. A comparison of Event Models for Naive Bayes Text Classification. In *AAAI-98 Workshop on Learning for Text Categorization*, 1998.

[8] McCallum, A., K. Nigam, J. Rennie and K. Seymore. A Machine Learning Approach to Building Domain-specific Search Engines. *Proceedings of the 19th International Joint Conference on Artificial Intelligence*, 1999.

[9] Neville, J., D. Jensen and B. Gallagher. Simple Estimators for Relational Bayesian Classifiers. University of Massachusetts, Technical Report 03-04.

[10] Taskar, B., E. Segal, and D. Koller. Probabilistic Classification and Clustering in Relational Data. *Proceedings of the 17th Intl Joint Conference on Artificial Intelligence*, 2001.

Protecting Sensitive Knowledge By Data Sanitization*

Stanley R. M. Oliveira[1,2]
[1]Embrapa Informática Agropecuária
13083-886 - Campinas, SP, Brasil
oliveira@cs.ualberta.ca

Osmar R. Zaïane[2]
[2]Department of Computing Science
University of Alberta, Edmonton, Canada
zaiane@cs.ualberta.ca

Abstract

In this paper, we address the problem of protecting some sensitive knowledge in transactional databases. The challenge is on protecting actionable knowledge for strategic decisions, but at the same time not losing the great benefit of association rule mining. To accomplish that, we introduce a new, efficient one-scan algorithm that meets privacy protection and accuracy in association rule mining, without putting at risk the effectiveness of the data mining per se.

1 Introduction

Despite its benefit in marketing, modern business, medical analysis and many other applications, association rule mining can also pose a threat to privacy and information security if not done or used properly. There are a number of realistic scenarios in which privacy and security issues in association mining arise. We describe one challenging scenario as follows:

Two or more companies have a very large dataset of records of their customers' buying activities. These companies decide to cooperatively conduct association rule mining on their datasets for their mutual benefit since this collaboration brings them an advantage over other competitors. However, some of these companies may not want to share some strategic patterns hidden within their own data (also called restrictive association rules) with the other parties. They would like to transform their data in such a way that these restrictive associations rules cannot be discovered. Is it possible for these companies to benefit from such collaboration by sharing their data while still preserving some restrictive association rules?

In this paper, we address the problem of transforming a database into a new one that conceals some strategic patterns (restrictive association rules) while preserving the general patterns and trends from the original database. The procedure of transforming an original database into a sanitized one is called data sanitization The sanitization process acts on the data to remove or hide a group of restrictive association rules that contain sensitive knowledge. On the one hand, this approach slightly modifies some data, but this is perfectly acceptable in some real applications [2, 6, 4]. On the other hand, an appropriate balance between a need for privacy and knowledge discovery must be guaranteed. Our contribution in this paper is two-fold. First, we introduce an efficient one-scan algorithm, called Sliding Window Algorithm (SWA). This algorithm requires only one pass over a transactional database regardless of the database size and the number of restrictive association rules that must be protected. This represents a significant improvement over the previous algorithms presented in the literature [2, 6, 3], which require various scans depending on the number of association rules to be hidden. Second, we compare our proposed algorithm with the similar counterparts in the literature. Our experiments demonstrate that our algorithm is effective, scalable, and achieves significant improvement over the other approaches presented in the literature. We also introduce the notion of disclosure threshold for every single pattern to restrict. In other words, rather than having one unique threshold ψ for the whole sanitization process, we can have a different threshold ψ_i for each pattern i to restrict. This provides a greater flexibility allowing an administrator to put different weights for different rules.

This paper is organized as follows. Related work is reviewed in Section 2. In Section 3, we describe our heuristic to improve the balance between privacy and knowledge discovery. In Section 4, we present the experimental results. Section 5 presents our conclusions and a discussion.

2 Related Work

The idea behind data sanitization was introduced in [1]. Atallah et al. considered the problem of modifying a given database so that the support of a given set of sensitive rules decreases below the minimum support value. The authors

---
*S. Oliveira was partially supported by CNPq, Brazil, and O.R. Zaïane by NSERC, Canada. We would like to thank Y. Saygin and E. Dasseni for providing us with the code of their respective algorithms.

focused on the theoretical approach and showed that the optimal sanitization is an NP-hard problem. In [2], the authors investigated confidentiality issues of a broad category of association rules and proposed some algorithms to preserve privacy of such rules above a given privacy threshold. In the same direction, Saygin et al. [6] introduced some algorithms to obscure a given set of sensitive rules by replacing known values with unknowns, while minimizing the side effects on non-sensitive rules. Like the algorithms in [2], these algorithms are CPU-intensive and require various scans depending on the number of association rules to be hidden. Oliveira and Zaïane [3] introduced a framework for protecting restrictive patterns composed of sanitizing algorithms that require only two scans over the database. The first scan is required to build an index (inverted file) for speeding up the sanitization process, while the second scan is used to sanitize the original database.

The work presented here differs from the related work in some aspects, as follows: First, we study the effectiveness of SWA and the counterpart algorithms by quantifying how much information is preserved after sanitizing a database. So, our focus is not only on hiding restrictive association rules but also on maximizing the discovery of rules after sanitizing a database. Second, in terms of balancing between privacy and disclosure, our approach is very flexible since one can adjust a disclosure threshold for every single association rule to be restricted. Another advantage is that SWA is not a memory-based algorithm and therefore can deal with very large databases. This represents a significant improvement over the previous algorithms [2, 6, 3].

3 Heuristic Approach

Before introducing our heuristic for data sanitization, we present some preliminary concepts. The explicit definitions can be found in [5].Restricted association rules are rules that need to be hidden. In other words applying an algorithm such as *Apriori* should not lead to the discovery of such rules. We note such rules as R_R. $\tilde{}R_R$ are the non restricted rules such as $\tilde{}R_R \cup R_R = R$ the set of all association rules in a transactional database D. A group of restrictive association rules is mined from a database D based on a special group of transactions, referred to sensitive transactions. Sensitive transactions are transactions that contain items involved in any restricted association rule.

For each restrictive association rule, we have to identify a candidate item that should be removed from its sensitive transactions. We refer to this item as the *victim item*. In many cases, a group of restrictive rules share one or more items. In this case, the selected victim item is one shared item. The rationale behind this selection is that by removing the victim item from a sensitive transactions that contains a group of rules, such rules would be hidden in one step.

Our heuristic approach has essentially five steps as follows. These steps are applied to every group of K transactions (window size) read from the original database D.

Step1: For each transaction read from a database D, we identify if it is sensitive. If not, the transaction is copied directly to the sanitized database D'. Otherwise, it must be sanitized.

Step2: We select the victim item the one in the restrictive association rules related to the current sensitive transaction, with the highest frequency. Otherwise, the victim item is selected randomly.

Step3: Given the disclosure threshold ψ, we compute the number of transactions to be sanitized.

Step4: We sort, in ascending order of size, the sensitive transactions computed in the previous step, for each restrictive rule. Thus, we start marking the shortest transactions to be sanitized since shortest transactions have less combinations of association rules. This will minimize the impact on the sanitized database.

Step5: Every restrictive rule has now a list of sensitive transaction IDs with their respective selected victim item. Every time we remove a victim item from a sensitive transaction, we perform a look ahead procedure to verify if that transaction has been selected as a sensitive transaction for other restrictive rules. If so, and the victim item we just removed from the current transaction is also part of this other restrictive rule, we remove that transaction from the list of transaction IDs marked in the other rules. In doing so, the transaction will be sanitized, and then copied to the sanitized database D'. This look ahead procedure is done only when the disclosure threshold is 0%. This is because the look ahead improves the misses cost but could significantly degrade the hiding failure. When $\psi = 0$, there is no hiding failure (i.e. all restrictive rules are hidden) and thus there is no degradation possible but an improvement in the misses cost.

The intuition behind the Sliding Window Algorithm (SWA) is that SWA scans a group of K transactions, at a time. Then, SWA sanitizes the set of sensitive transactions, denoted by R_R, considering a disclosure threshold ψ. For each restrictive association rule there is a disclosure threshold assigned to it. We refer to the set of mappings of a restrictive association rule into its corresponding disclosure threshold as the set of mining permissions, denoted by M_P, in which each mining permission mp is characterized by an ordered pair, defined as $mp = <rr_i, \psi_i>$, where $\forall i$ $rr_i \in R_R$ and $\psi_i \in [0 \ldots 1]$.

The sketch of SWA and the proof of its runtime complexity are given in [5].

4 Experimental Results

We compare SWA with respect to the following benchmarks: (1) the result of Apriori algorithm without transformation; (2) the results of similar algorithms in the literature.

We compare the effectiveness and scalability of SWA with a similar one proposed in [2] to hide rules by reducing support, called Algo2a. The algorithm GIH designed by Saygin et al. [6] is similar to Algo2a. The basic difference is that in Algo2a some items are removed from sensitive transactions, while in GIH a mark "?" (unknowns) is placed instead of item deletions. We also compare SWA with the Item Grouping Algorithm (IGA), our best algorithm so far published and presented in [3].

We performed two series of experiments: the first to measure the effectiveness of SWA, IGA, and Algo2a, and the second to measure the efficiency and scalability of these algorithms. All the experiments were conducted on a PC, AMD Athlon 1900/1600 (SPEC CFP2000 588), with 1.2 GB of RAM running a Linux operating system. To measure the effectiveness of the algorithms, we used a dataset generated by the IBM synthetic data generator to generate a dataset containing 500 different items, with 100K transactions in which the average size per transaction is 40 items. The effectiveness is measured in terms of the number of restrictive association rules effectively hidden, as well as the proportion of legitimate rules accidentally hidden due to the sanitization. We selected a set of ten restrictive association rules from the dataset ranging from two to five items in length, with support ranging from 20% to 42% and confidence ranging from 80% to 99% in the database. With our ten original restrictive association rules, 94701 rules became restricted in the database since any association rule that contains restrictive rules should also be restricted.

4.1 Measuring effectiveness

We measure the effectiveness Algo2a taking into account the performance measures introduced in [3]. We summarize such performance measures as follows: (1) *Hiding Failure (HF):* measures the amount of restrictive association rules that are disclosed after sanitization; (2) *Misses Cost (MC):* measures the amount of legitimate association rules that are hidden by accident after sanitization; (3) *Artifactual Patterns (AP):* measure the artificial association rules created by the addition of noise in the data; and (4) *Dif(D, D'):* difference between the original and sanitized databases, i.e., information loss.

We evaluated the effect of window size with respect to the difference of the original database D and the sanitized one D'. To do so, we varied K from 500 to 10000 transactions with the disclosure threshold $\psi = 15\%$. Figure 1A shows that up to 3000 transactions the difference between

the original and the sanitized database improves slightly. After 3000 transactions, the difference remains the same. Similarly, Figure 1B shows that after 3000 transactions the values of misses cost (MC) and hiding failure (HF) tend to be constant. This shows that on our example database, a window size representing 3% of the size of the database suffices to stabilize the misses cost and hiding failure.

The distribution of the data may affect these values. However, we have observed that the larger the window size the better the results. The reason is that when the heuristic is applied to a large number of transactions, the impact in the database is minimized. Consequently, the value of misses cost and the difference between D and D' improve slightly.

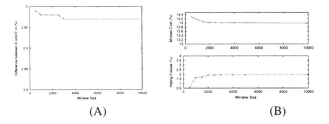

(A)   (B)

Figure 1. Effect of window size on (A): dif(D,D') (B): MC and HF

To measure the misses cost, we set the the disclosure threshold ψ to 0%. This means no restrictive rule is allowed to be mined from the sanitized database. In this situation, 18.30% of the legitimate association rules in the case of SWA, 20.08% in the case of IGA, and 24.76% in the case of Algo2a are accidentally hidden. We intentionally selected restrictive association rules with high support in the reported experiments to accentuate the differential between the sizes of the original database and the sanitized database and thus to better illustrate the impact of the sanitization on the mining process. SWA and IGA are the ones that impact the least on the database. In this particular case, 3.55% of the database is lost in the case of SWA and IGA, and 5.24% in the case of Algo2a.

Figure 2 shows the effect of the disclosure threshold ψ on the hiding failure and the misses cost for SWA and IGA, considering the minimum support threshold $\sigma = 5\%$. Since Algo2a doesn't allow the input of a disclosure threshold, it is not compared in this figure with our algorithms. As can be observed, when ψ is 0%, no restrictive association rule is disclosed for both algorithms. However, 20.08% of the legitimate association rules in the case of IGA, and 18.30% in the case of SWA are accidentally hidden. What can also be observed is that the impact of SWA on the database is smaller and the misses cost of SWA is slightly better than that of IGA. Moreover, the hiding failure for SWA is slightly better than that for IGA in all the cases, except at $\psi = 50\%$.

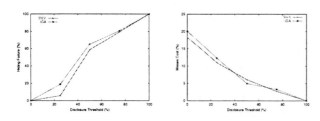

Figure 2. Effect of ψ on HF and MC

4.2 CPU Time for the Sanitization Process

We tested the scalability of our sanitization algorithms vis-à-vis the size of the database as well as the number of rules to hide. Our comparison study also includes the algorithm Algo2a. We varied the size of the original database D from 20K transactions to 100K transactions, while fixing the disclosure threshold $\psi = 0$ and the support threshold $\sigma = 5\%$, and keeping the set of restrictive rules constant (10 original patterns). We set the window size for SWA with $K = 20000$. Figure 3A shows that IGA and SWA increase CPU time linearly with the size of the database, while the CPU time in Algo2a grows fast. This is due the fact that Algo2a requires various scans over the original database, while IGA requires two, and SWA requires only one.

Although IGA requires 2 scans, it is faster than SWA. The main reason is that IGA clusters restrictive association rules in groups of rules sharing the same itemsets. Then by removing the victim item from the sensitive transactions related to the rules in the group, all sensitive rules in the group would be hidden in one step. As can be observed, SWA increases CPU linearly, even though its complexity in main memory is not linear.

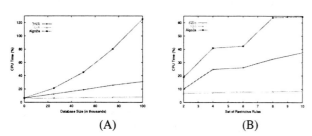

(A)   (B)

Figure 3. Results of CPU time

We also varied the number of restrictive rules to hide from approximately 6000 to 29500, while fixing the size of the database to 100K transactions and fixing the support and disclosure thresholds to $\psi = 0\%$. Figure 3B shows that our algorithms scale well with the number of rules to hide. We varied the size of the original set of restricted rules from 2 to 10. This makes the set of all restricted rules range from approximately 6097 to 29558. This scalability is mainly

due to the inverted files we use in our approaches for indexing the sensitive transaction IDs per restrictive rules. There is no need to scan the database again whenever we want to access a transaction for sanitization purposes. The inverted file gives direct access with pointers to the relevant transactions. The CPU time for Algo2a is more expensive due the number of scans over the database.

5 Conclusions

In this paper, we have introduced an efficient algorithm that improves the balance between protection of sensitive knowledge and pattern discovery, called Sliding Window Algorithm (SWA). This algorithm is useful for sanitizing large transactional databases based on a disclosure threshold (or a set of thresholds) controlled by a database owner. The experimental results revealed that SWA is effective and can achieve significant improvement over the other approaches presented in the literature. SWA slightly alters the data while enabling flexibility for someone to tune it. A strong point of SWA is that it does not introduce false drops to the data. In addition, SWA has the lowest misses cost among the known sanitizing algorithms. It is important to note that our sanitization method is robust in the sense that there is no de-sanitization possible. Moreover, there is no encryption involved. There is no possible way to reproduce the original database from the sanitized one.

References

[1] M. Atallah, E. Bertino, A. Elmagarmid, M. Ibrahim, and V. Verykios. Disclosure Limitation of Sensitive Rules. In *Proc. of IEEE Knowledge and Data Engineering Workshop*, pages 45–52, Chicago, Illinois, November 1999.

[2] E. Dasseni, V. S. Verykios, A. K. Elmagarmid, and E. Bertino. Hiding Association Rules by Using Confidence and Support. In *Proc. of the 4th Information Hiding Workshop*, pages 369–383, Pittsburg, PA, April 2001.

[3] S. R. M. Oliveira and O. R. Zaïane. Privacy Preserving Frequent Itemset Mining. In *Proc. of the IEEE ICDM Workshop on Privacy, Security, and Data Mining*, pages 43–54, Maebashi City, Japan, December 2002.

[4] S. R. M. Oliveira and O. R. Zaïane. Algorithms for Balancing Privacy and Knowledge Discovery in Association Rule Mining. In *Proc. of the 7th International Database Engineering and Applications Symposium (IDEAS'03)*, Hong Kong, China, July 2003.

[5] S. R. M. Oliveira and O. R. Zaïane. An Efficient One-Scan Sanitization For Improving The Balance Between Privacy And Knowledge Discovery. Technical report, TR03-15, Computer Science Department, University of Alberta, Canada, June 2003.

[6] Y. Saygin, V. S. Verykios, and C. Clifton. Using Unknowns to Prevent Discovery of Association Rules. *SIGMOD Record*, 30(4):45–54, December 2001.

Mining Frequent Itemsets in Distributed and Dynamic Databases

M. E. Otey   C. Wang   S. Parthasarathy
Computer and Information Science Dept.
The Ohio-State University
{otey, wachao, srini}@cis.ohio-state.edu

A. Veloso   W. Meira Jr.
Computer Science Dept.
Universidade Federal de Minas Gerais
{adrianov, meira}@dcc.ufmg.br

Abstract

Traditional methods for frequent itemset mining typically assume that data is centralized and static. Such methods impose excessive communication overhead when data is distributed, and they waste computational resources when data is dynamic. In this paper we present what we believe to be the first unified approach that overcomes these assumptions. Our approach makes use of parallel and incremental techniques to generate frequent itemsets in the presence of data updates without examining the entire database, and imposes minimal communication overhead when mining distributed databases. Further, our approach is able to generate both local and global frequent itemsets. This ability permits our approach to identify high-contrast frequent itemsets, which allows one to examine how the data is skewed over different sites.

1   Introduction

Advances in computing and networking technologies have resulted in distributed and dynamic sources of data. A classic example of such a scenario is found in the warehouses of large national and multinational corporations. Such warehouses are often composed of disjoint databases located at different sites. Each database is continuously updated with new data as transactions occur. The update rate and ancillary properties may be unique to a given site.

A user may be interested in generating a global model of the database, thus the sites must exchange some information about their local models. However, the information exchange must be made in a way that minimizes the communication overhead. The frequency at which the global model is updated may vary from the frequency at which each local model is updated. Furthermore, in such a distributed scenario, the user may be interested in not only knowing the global model of the database, but also the differences (or contrasts) between the local models.

Analyzing these distributed and dynamic databases requires approaches that make proper use of the distributed resources, minimize communication requirements and reduce work replication. In this paper we present an efficient frequent itemset mining approach when data is both distributed and dynamic. The main contributions of our paper are:

1. A parallel algorithm based on the ZIGZAG incremental approach, which is used to update the local model;

2. A distributed mining algorithm that minimizes the communication costs for mining over a wide area network, which is used to update the global model;

3. Novel interactive extensions for computing high contrast frequent itemsets;

4. Experimentation and validation on real databases.

Related Work. In [1] three distributed approaches were proposed. COUNT DISTRIBUTION is a simple distributed implementation of APRIORI. DATA DISTRIBUTION generates disjoint candidate sets on each site. CANDIDATE DISTRIBUTION partitions the candidates during each iteration, so that each site can generate disjoint candidates independently of the other sites. [9] presents another distributed algorithm, PARECLAT, which is based on the concept of *equivalence classes*. These techniques are devised to scale up a given algorithm (e.g., APRIORI, ECLAT, etc.). They perform excessive communication operations and are not efficient when data is geographically distributed.

Some effort has also been devoted to incrementally mining frequent itemsets [5, 7, 8, 2, 4] in dynamic databases. The DELI algorithm was proposed in [5]. It uses statistical sampling methods to determine when the current model is outdated. A similar approach [4] monitors changes in the data stream. An efficient algorithm called ULI [7], strives to reduce I/O requirements for updating the frequent itemsets by maintaining the previous frequent itemsets and the *negative border* along with their supports.

The rest of the paper is organized as follows. In Section 2 we describe the algorithms and novel interactive extensions. In Section 3 we validate the algorithms through extensive evaluation. Concluding remarks are made in Section 4.

2 Parallel, Distributed Incremental Mining

In this section we describe our parallel and distributed incremental mining algorithms. Specifically, the idea is that within a local domain one can resort to parallel mining approaches (either within a node or within a cluster) and across domains one can resort to distributed mining approaches (across clusters). The key distinction between the two scenarios is the cost of communication.

Problem Definition. Let $\mathcal{I}$ be a set of distinct items. Let $\mathcal{D}$ be a database of transactions, where each transaction has a unique identifier (*tid*) and contains a set of items. A set of exactly k items is called a *k-itemset*. The *tidset* of an itemset C corresponds to the set of all transaction identifiers (*tids*) where the itemset C occurs. The *support* of C, is the number of transactions of $\mathcal{D}$ in which it occurs as a subset. The itemsets that meet a user-specified *minimum support* are referred to as *frequent* itemsets. A frequent itemset is *maximal* if it is not subset of any other frequent itemset.

Using $\mathcal{D}$ as a starting point, a set of new transactions d^+ is added forming Δ ($\mathcal{D} \cup d^+$). Let $s_{\mathcal{D}}$ be the minimum support used when mining $\mathcal{D}$, and $F_{\mathcal{D}}$ be the set of frequent itemsets obtained. Let Π be the information kept from the current mining that will be used in the next operation (in our case, Π consists of $F_{\mathcal{D}}$). An itemset C is frequent in Δ if its support is no less than s_{Δ}. If a frequent itemset in $\mathcal{D}$ remains frequent in Δ it is called a *retained* itemset.

The database Δ can be divided into n partitions, $\delta_1, ..., \delta_n$. Each partition δ_i is assigned to a site S_i. Let $C.sup$ and $C.sup_i$ be the respective support of C in Δ (global support) and δ_i (local support). Given s_{Δ}, C is *global frequent* if $C.sup \geq s_{\Delta} \times |\Delta|$; correspondingly, C is *local frequent* at δ_i, if $C.sup_i \geq s_{\Delta} \times |\delta_i|$. The set of all maximal global frequent itemsets is denoted as MFI_{Δ}, and the set of maximal local frequent itemsets at δ_i is denoted as MFI_{δ_i}. The task of mining frequent itemsets in distributed and dynamic databases is to find F_{Δ}.

The ZIGZAG Incremental Algorithm. The main idea behind the algorithm is to incrementally compute MFI_{Δ} using Π. This avoids the generation of many unnecessary candidates. Having MFI_{Δ} is sufficient to know which itemsets are frequent; their exact support are then obtained by examining d^+ and using Π, or, where this is not possible, by examining Δ. ZIGZAG employs a backtracking search to find MFI_{Δ} which is explained in [8].

The support computation is based on the associativity of itemsets — let $\mathcal{L}(\mathcal{C}_k)$ be the tidset of $\mathcal{C}_k$. The support of any itemset is obtained by intersecting the tidsets of its subsets. To avoid replicating work done before, ZIGZAG first verifies if the candidate is a retained itemset. If so, its support can be computed by using d^+ and Π.

Parallel Search for the MFI_{Δ}. The main idea of our parallel approach is to assign distinct backtrack trees to distinct processors. Note that there is no dependence among the processors, because each tree corresponds to a disjoint set of candidates. Since each processor can proceed independently there is no synchronization while searching for MFI_{Δ}. To achieve a suitable level of load-balancing, the trees are assigned to the processors by using the scheme of *bitonic partitioning* [3]. The bitonic scheme is a greedy algorithm, which first sort all the w_i (the work load due to tree i). w_i is calculated based on our ideas for estimating the number candidates using correlation measures, presented in [8]. Next it extracts the tree with maximum w_i, and assign it to processor 0. The next highest workload tree is assigned to processor 1 and so on.

2.1 Distributed Algorithm

Lemma 1 – **A global frequent itemset must be local frequent in at least one partition.** ∎

Lemma 2 – $\bigcup_{i=1}^{n} \text{MFI}_{\delta_i}$ **determines** F_{Δ}. ∎

First, each site S_i independently performs a parallel and incremental search for MFI_{δ_i}, using ZIGZAG on its database δ_i. After all sites finish their searches, the result will be the set $\{\text{MFI}_{\delta_1}, \text{MFI}_{\delta_2}, ... , \text{MFI}_{\delta_i}\}$. This information is sufficient for determining all global frequent itemsets. Next, the algorithm starts after all local MFIs were found. Each site sends its local MFI to the other sites, and then they join all local MFIs. Now each site knows the set $\bigcup_{i=1}^{n} \text{MFI}_{\delta_i}$, which is an upper bound for MFI_{Δ}. In the next step each site independently performs a top down incremental enumeration of the potentially global frequent itemsets, as follows. Each itemset present in the upper bound $\bigcup_{i=1}^{n} \text{MFI}_{\delta_i}$ is broken into k subsets of size $(k - 1)$. This process iterates generating smaller subsets and incrementally computing their supports until there are no more subsets to be checked. At the end of this step, each site will have the same set of potentially global frequent itemsets.

The final step makes a reduction on the local supports of each itemset, to verify which of them are globally frequent. The process starts with site S_1, which sends the supports of its itemsets to S_2. S_2 sums the support of each itemset with the value of the same itemset obtained from S_1, and sends the result to S_3. This procedure continues until site S_n has the global supports of all potentially global frequent itemsets. Then site S_n finds all itemsets that have support greater than or equal to s_{Δ}, which constitutes F_{Δ} (by Lemma 2).

2.2 Interactive Issues

High-Contrast Frequent Itemsets. An important issue when mining Δ is to understand the differences between $\delta_1, \delta_2, ..., \delta_n$. *An effective way to understand such differences is to find the high-contrast frequent itemsets.* The supports of such itemsets vary significantly across the databases. We use the well-established notion of entropy to detect how the support of a given itemset is distributed across the databases. For a random variable, the entropy is a measure of the non-uniformity of its probability distribution. Given an itemset $\mathcal{C}$, the value $p_{\mathcal{C}}(i) = \frac{\mathcal{C}.sup_i}{\mathcal{C}.sup}$ is the probability of occurrence of $\mathcal{C}$ in δ_i. $\sum_{i=1}^{n} p_{\mathcal{C}}(i) = 1$, and $H(\mathcal{C}) = -\sum_{i=1}^{n}(p_{\mathcal{C}}(i) \times log(p_{\mathcal{C}}(i)))$ is a measure of how the local supports of $\mathcal{C}$ is distributed across the databases. Note that $0 \leq H(\mathcal{C}) \leq log(n)$, and so $0 \leq E(\mathcal{C}) = \frac{log(n) - H(\mathcal{C})}{log(n)} \leq 1$. If $E(\mathcal{C})$ is greater than or equal to a given minimum entropy threshold, then $\mathcal{C}$ is classified as high-contrast frequent itemset.

Query Response Time. One of the goals of the algorithm is to minimize response time to a query for F_{Δ} in a dynamic, distributed database. Since Δ is dynamic, each site is incrementally updating its local frequent itemsets. The time it takes to update the local frequent itemsets is proportional to $\mid d^+ \mid$. We can view the updates to the database as a queue containing zero or more such blocks. If a query arrives while a block is being processed, there cannot be a response until the calculation of the local frequent itemsets is completed. An obvious approach to reducing response time is to decrease the size of d^+. However, because of overhead, the time it takes to do two increments of size $\mid d^+ \mid$ is longer than the time it takes to do a single increment of size $2 \times \mid d^+ \mid$ ($n > 1$). So there is a trade-off: *The larger d^+ is, the more up-to-date F_{Δ} will be, since it incorporates a greater number of changes to Δ, but the longer the response time to the query will be.*

3 Experimental Evaluation

Our experimental evaluation was carried out on two clusters. The first cluster consists of dual PENTIUM III 1GHz nodes with 1GB of main memory. The second cluster consists of single PENTIUM III 933 MHz nodes with 512 MB of main memory. We assume that each database is distributed between the clusters, and that each node in the cluster has access to its cluster's portion of the database. Within each cluster, we have implemented the parallel program using the MPI message-passing library (MPICH), and for communication between clusters we have used sockets. We used a real database for testing the performance of our algorithm. The WCup database is generated from the clickstream log of the 1998 World Cup web site. This database is 645 MB in size and contains 7,618,927 transactions. Additional experiments on other real and synthetic databases can be found in [6].

Intra-Cluster Evaluation. Figure 1(a) shows the execution times obtained for the WCup dataset in parallel and incremental configurations. As we can see, better execution

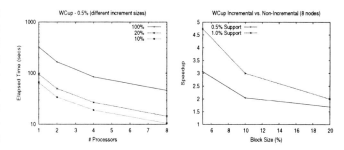

Figure 1. (a) Total Execution Times, and (b) Speedups on Different Incremental Configurations.

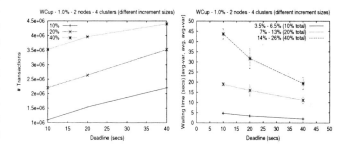

Figure 2. (a) Number of Transactions Processed, and (b) Query response time.

times are obtained when we combine both parallel and incremental approaches. Furthermore, for the same parallel configuration, the execution time is better for smaller block sizes, as Figure 1(b) shows.

Inter-Cluster Evaluation. The next experiment examines how the size of a block and the time at which a query arrives (the deadline) affects the amount of data used to build F_{Δ}. The lines on the graph represent different block sizes, which are given here as percentages of the database on each cluster. Figure 2(a) shows that the more time that elapses before the query arrives, the more data that is incorporated into the model, which is to be expected. It also shows that as the block size decreases, fewer transactions can be processed before the query arrives. *This is because there is more overhead involved in processing a large number of small blocks than there is in processing a small number of large blocks.* We also investigated the performance of our algorithm in experiments for evaluating the query response time (the amount of time a user must wait before F_{Δ} is computed). Figure 1(a) shows that as the increment size decreases, the time to wait for a response also decreases. However, the time at which a query arrives affects the waiting time in a somewhat random manner. This is because

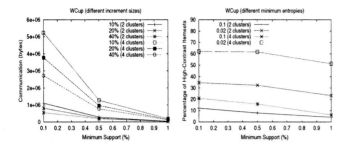

Figure 3. (a) Communication Overhead, and (b) High-Contrast Frequent Itemsets.

a query can arrive at any point during the processing of a block. The time remaining to compute the local frequent itemsets therefore varies. Figure 2(b) shows the query response time averaged over five runs, and the vertical bars represent the variance in the runs. The trade-off between block size and query response time is apparent: as the block size increases, the number of transactions processed also increases, but the response time increases as well. This shows that we can assign larger blocks to less powerful clusters, the basic idea being that the local model can be updated less frequently, but in response, smaller query response times can be obtained.

We also performed a set of experiments to analyze the communication overhead imposed by our algorithm. We examined the number of bytes transferred between clusters when we varied the minimum support, the block size, and the number of clusters involved in the computation. The results can be seen in Figure 3(a). As is expected, as the minimum support decreases, the number of candidates will increase, and will therefore increase the number of bytes that must be transferred between the clusters, since our algorithm must exchange the supports of every candidate processed. Also, as the block size increases, the amount of communication decreases. The reason is that for smaller block sizes the number of candidates processed tends to be greater. Finally, the amount of communication required increases when more clusters are involved in the process.

The last set of experiments concerns high-contrast frequent itemsets. We varied three parameters: the minimum support, the number of clusters involved in the process, and the minimum entropy. The results are showed in Figure 3(b). As we can observe, very different results were obtained from each database. The percentage of high-contrast frequent itemsets is interesting here because *it reveals the skewness of the database*. Usually the percentage of high-contrast frequent itemsets will diminish as the minimum support threshold increases. This is quite understandable considering that when the support threshold is

low, there will be a large number of global frequent itemsets generated, and many of these itemsets become global frequent only because they are frequent in some small number of sites, resulting in many high-contrast frequent itemsets. In contrast, as the support threshold increases, it becomes harder for a local frequent itemset to become global frequent, which results in a smaller number of high-contrast frequent itemsets. Meanwhile, the more clusters on which the data distributed, the greater the possibility of skewness in the data.

4 Conclusions

In this paper we considered the problem of mining frequent itemsets in dynamic and distributed databases. We presented an efficient distributed and parallel incremental algorithm to deal with this problem. Our experiments examined the trade-offs involved in minimizing the query response time (whether to sacrifice query response time in order to incorporate more transactions in the model) and the amount of data transferred between clusters. Future work involves using sampling techniques to minimize the query response time and investigating how to minimize query response time in wide-area networks, where communication latencies tend to be relatively large.

References

[1] R. Agrawal and J. Shafer. Parallel mining of association rules. In *IEEE Trans. on Knowledge and Data Engg.*, volume 8, pages 962–969, 1996.

[2] D. Cheung, J. Han, and et al. Maintenance of discovered associations in large databases: An incremental updating technique. In *Proc. of the Int'l. Conf. on Data Engineering*, 1996.

[3] M. Cierniak, M. Zaki, and W. Li. Compile-time scheduling algorithms for a heterogeneous network of workstations. In *The Computer Journal*, volume 40, pages 356–372.

[4] V. Ganti and J. G. et al. Demon: Mining and monitoring evolving data. In *Proc. of the 16th Int'l Conf. on Data Engineering*, pages 439–448, San Diego, USA, 2000.

[5] S. Lee and D. Cheung. Maintenance of discovered associations: When to update? In *Research Issues on Data Mining and Knowledge Discovery*, 1997.

[6] M. E. Otey, A. Veloso, C. Wang, S. Parthasarathy, and W. Meira. Mining frequent itemsets in distributed and dynamic databases. In *OSU-CISRC-9/03-TR48*, 2003.

[7] S. Thomas, S. Bodagala, K. Alsabti, and S. Ranka. An efficient algorithm for the incremental updation of association rules. In *Proc. of the 3rd Int'l Conf. on Knowledge Discovery and Data Mining*, August 1997.

[8] A. Veloso and W. M. J. et al. Mining frequent itemsets in evolving databases. In *Proc. of the Int'l Conf. on Data Mining*, Arlington, USA, 2002.

[9] M. Zaki and S. P. et al. New parallel algorithms for fast discovery of association rules. *Data Mining and Knowledge Discovery: An International Journal*, 4(1):343–373, 1997.

Structure Search and Stability Enhancement of Bayesian Networks

Hanchuan Peng   and   Chris Ding

Computational Research Division, Lawrence Berkeley National Laboratory,
University of California, Berkeley, CA, 94720, USA
Email: hpeng@lbl.gov, chqding@lbl.gov

Abstract

Learning Bayesian network structure from large-scale data sets, without any expert-specified ordering of variables, remains a difficult problem. We propose systematic improvements to automatically learn Bayesian network structure from data. (1) We propose a linear parent search method to generate candidate graph. (2) We propose a comprehensive approach to eliminate cycles using minimal likelihood loss, a short cycle first heuristic, and a cut-edge repairing. (3) We propose structure perturbation to assess the stability of the network and a stability-improvement method to refine the network structure. The algorithms are easy to implement and efficient for large networks. Experimental results on two data sets show that our new approach outperforms existing methods.

1. Introduction

The rapidly increasing quantity of data in many data mining fields allows a great opportunity to model and understand the relationships among a large number of variables. Bayesian Networks (BNs) [13][6][8][1] provide a consistent framework to model the probabilistic dependencies among variables, e.g. in medical image mining [15]. A BN [6][8] is a Directed Acyclic Graph (DAG) $G = (V, E)$ that models the probabilistic dependencies among a group of variables (nodes). The joint distribution can be factorized into the product of conditional probabilities of every variable given its parents: $P(\{g\}) = \Pi_{g \in V} P(g | \pi_g)$, where g stands for a variable, π_g is the parents of g; the directed edges among nodes encode the respective conditional distributions.

Directly identifying the BN structures from input data D remains a challenge. The problem is NP-hard [3][6]. Many heuristic search methods have been proposed (for reviews see [8][1]). If there is a predefined ordering of variables, the well-known K2 algorithm [6] can efficiently determine the structure. For many applications where there is no sufficient knowledge to provide such an ordering, the BN-learning methods, e.g. conditional independence test based method [2], often have at least $O(n^4)$ complexity. Other Monte Carlo methods have even larger complexity, e.g. the search method based on random-sampling and model averaging in the space of ordering [7]. Clearly, an efficient algorithm to identify BN structures, without requiring ordering of variables, is particularly important. There exist several methods/software. For example, the WinMine software of Chickering [4] has the strength to learn large BN structure. Cheng designed PowerConstructor [[1]] and won data mining contest KDD-Cup-2001.

We propose a new $O(n^2)$ algorithm to infer locally stable Bayesian networks without requiring predefined ordering of vari-

ables or predefined thresholds to terminate the model search. Our algorithm consists of three main steps. (1) We develop an efficient algorithm to search optimal parents, which form a candidate graph (See §2). (2) We propose a new graph-based method to eliminate possible cycles in the candidate graph that would violate the acyclic assumption of BNs (See §3). (3) We evaluate the network stability using structural perturbation. The structural perturbation can detect unstable local structures; an algorithm for improving the stability is proposed (See §4).

We assume a uniform prior of the structure of G. The posterior (log-likelihood) of G given the data D, $\ell(G) = \log P(G|D) \propto \log P(D|G)$, is used to judge the optimality of G. The posterior can be evaluated using different scores, including the Bayesian score [6] and its variant [5], MDL [1], BDe [8], etc. In this paper, we use the Bayesian score, but other scores can be equally well adopted in our structure identification algorithms.

2. Candidate Graph

The candidate graph G_c is a directed graph containing important associations of variables where the redundancy of associations should be minimized. Our approach is to identify the optimal parent set for each node based on the Bayesian score ℓ. Here our emphasis is on how to efficiently search for optimal parent set, $\pi = \{g^*_i, i=1,\ldots,m\}$. The locally optimal parent set is similar to dependency graph of Heckerman *et al* [9][11]; the difference is that they used regression to determine the dependency while we directly search based on the Bayesian score.

Our algorithm is an extension of K2 algorithm [6]. K2 uses a simple incremental search strategy: it first searches for the best singleton parent g^*_1, i.e., $g^*_1 = \text{argmax}_i \ell(g_i \rightarrow g)$, and $\ell(g_i \rightarrow g) > \ell(g) + \ell(g_i)$. It then searches for further parent(s) to maximize the score increase in each step, until no better score can be found.

We extend K2 in two directions. (*a*) We constrain the search in the most probable space to reduce the computational complexity. Note that once a parent or parents are found, many of the rest nodes are rendered conditionally independent. Thus in searching for the second parent g^*_2, we do not need to search through all the rest variables, $\Omega_1 = \{V \setminus g^*_1\}$; instead we need only search

$$\Omega_1^+ = \{g_i \in V \mid g_i \neq g^*_1, \ell(g_i \rightarrow g) > \ell(g_i) + \ell(g)\}. \quad (1)$$

Note that Ω_1^+ is obtained automatically when searching for g^*_1. Similarly, when searching for g^*_3, we need only search Ω_2^+, instead of $\Omega_2 = \{V \setminus \{g^*_1, g^*_2\}\}$; etc. This restriction saves a large fraction of the searched space.

(*b*) We systematically search a larger space than K2. In K2, g^*_1 corresponds to the largest $\ell(g_i \rightarrow g)$. Denote the respective parent set as $\pi^{(1)}$. We can search another set of parents beginning with the second largest $\ell(g_i \rightarrow g)$, denoted as $\pi^{(2)}$. If $\pi^{(2)}$ leads to better score than $\pi^{(1)}$, then we take $\pi^{(2)}$ as the final parent set. We call this 2-max search. This can be extended to k-max search. Clearly, the Bayesian score of $\pi^{(k)}$ increases monotonically with k, at the expense of linearly enlarged complexity.

We call this modified method the K2+ algorithm. It has the complexity O(αkmn), where α counts for the reduction using $\Omega_1^+, \Omega_2^+, \ldots, \Omega_m^+$ instead of $\Omega_1, \Omega_2, \ldots, \Omega_m$ (often Ω_i^+ contains a much smaller number of variables than Ω_i). Accordingly, the complexity to construct the whole candidate graph is O(n^2).

3. Cycle Elimination

Since the candidate graph G_c is generated via local optimal search, it is possible that G_c contains many cycles that violate the basic acyclic assumption of BNs.

A simple approach is to enumerate all possible DAGs that could emerge from G_c and select the one with the largest score. However, this method is impractical due to its exponential complexity. Approximation methods based on random edge cut [12] have been studied. A heuristic decision-tree based approach has also been studied in [11]. In this paper, we resolve this problem via graph algorithmic approach. Our comprehensive approach consists of three methods that can be implemented efficiently.

Any cycle must lie in a Strongly Connected Component (SCC) of the graph. An efficient O(n) algorithm based on depth-first search can locate SCCs in a directed graph. We first find all the SCCs in G_c, and eliminate cycles within each SCC.

3.1 Bayesian Likelihood Loss Function

If a SCC contains one cycle, we can break one cycle at a time. We break cycles based on loss function. For each edge $g_i \to g_j$, we define the loss as the reduction of Bayesian log-likelihood for g_j due to the loss of one of its parent

$$w(g_i \to g_j) = \ell(g_j \mid \pi) - \ell(g_j \mid \pi \setminus g_i). \quad (2)$$

Note that $w(g_i \to g_j) \neq w(g_i \leftarrow g_j)$. Although mutual information might be another possible choice as the loss, it does not reflect the joint association between different parents and g_j.

If a SCC contains several cycles, sometimes they share one or more common edges, such as the cycles in Figure 1. For example, in Figure 1(a) the edge $g_2 \to g_3$ is shared by the cycles C_{1231} (i.e. $g_1 \to g_2 \to g_3 \to g_1$) and C_{2342}.

There are several criteria to break the cycles. (a) We can simply cut edges with the smallest loss. (b) We can identify the common edges and cut the one shared by most cycles. In Figure 1 (b), cutting the common edge $g_2 \to g_3$ will eliminate two cycles. (c) The loss function criterion indicates there could be better choices. Suppose $g_1 \to g_2$ and $g_3 \to g_4$ are the edges with the minimal loss in cycles C_{1231} and C_{2342}. If the condition

$$w(g_1 \to g_2) + w(g_3 \to g_4) < w(g_2 \to g_3) \quad (3)$$

holds, then we break edges $g_1 \to g_2$ and $g_3 \to g_4$; otherwise, we break the edge $g_2 \to g_3$.

Figure 1 (b) illustrates a more complicated SCC with four 3-node cycles $C_{2312}, C_{2342}, C_{2542}, C_{2642}$. The edge $g_2 \to g_3$ is shared 2 times and the edge $g_4 \to g_2$ is shared 3 times. We start cycle elimination from the most-shared edge (i.e. $g_4 \to g_2$) and use a minimal-likelihood-loss strategy similar to Eq.(3). If the edge $g_4 \to g_2$ is cut, then only C_{2312} remains and we will further cut its minimal loss

edge; otherwise we use Eq.(3) to decide which edge(s) in cycles C_{2312} and C_{2342} should be broken.

This minimal-likelihood-loss criterion is summarized as follows. If there is no nested cycle, for each cycle we break the edge with the minimal loss. When several cycles nest among themselves, we identify the edge e_{ij} shared by most cycles and compare its loss with the sum of the minimal loss edges in participating cycles; if breaking e_{ij} leads to less loss, we cut e_{ij}; otherwise we cut the minimal loss edges in every participating cycle.

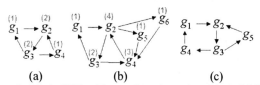

(a)　　　　(b)　　　　(c)

Figure 1. (a) A SCC with two 3-node cycles. (b) A SCC with four 3-node cycles. (c) A SCC with a 3-node cycle and a 4-node cycle. Multiplicities of nodes are shown in parentheses.

3.2 Short-Cycle-First Heuristic

Finding the set of cut edges with regarding to the minimal-likelihood-loss criterion could be complicated due to the existence of many cycles and the large number of common edges they share. We propose a short-cycle-first heuristic to minimize the complexity (for both computation and implementation):

(*a*) In BNs, information propagates multiplicatively because of the probability calculation. Along a fixed path of m edges, the influence of the starting node on the ending node is $P_1 P_2 \cdots P_m$ approximately. Therefore, in general, a long cycle violates the acyclic assumption less severely than a short cycle. If a SCC contains cycles of different lengths, our short-cycle first heuristic breaks the 2-node cycle first, and the 3-node cycle second, etc. In Figure 1 (c), we first break the 3-node cycle C_{2352}. Afterwards, we break the cycle C_{12341} if it still exists.

(*b*) When cycles of different lengths share edges, it is typically more efficient to break the shorter cycle first. For example, suppose two cycles C_a and C_b (with lengths a and b, respectively) share one common edge, and the cut-edge-loss-function is homogeneous. Approximately there is $1/a$ chance to break the common edge in C_a, and $1/b$ chance to break it in C_b. If $a<b$, then it is more likely (i.e. $1/a > 1/b$) that first breaking C_a (the shorter one) will simultaneously break C_b.

3.3 Cycle Identification by Matrix Multiplication

Short-cycle-first heuristic can be efficiently implemented through a matrix multiplication method. Let A be the adjacency matrix of a SCC. Diagonal elements of A are zeros. We compute A^m with the smallest m such that nonzero elements appear at matrix diagonal; with some elementary algebra, we can show that (1) nodes corresponding to nonzero diagonal elements in A^m must involve in m-node cycles; thus finding these cycles are restricted to the subgraph induced by these nodes; (2) the multiplicity of node i (i.e. value of $(A^m)_{ii}$) equals the number of times a cycle pass through node i (for example, in Figure 1 (a) and (b) the multiplicity of nodes are indicated by red numbers in parentheses). (3) Starting from the node with the highest multiplicity using breadth-first-search algorithm, restricting on the subgraph, we can easily traverse all m-node cycles and identify the most-shared edges. For example, in Figure 1 (b), we can start from g_2 and quickly identify the most-shared edge e_{42}. We use the likelihood loss criterion to break cycles. Note that A is usually very sparse and the sparse matrix multiplications often involve much less computation than dense matrixes.

After one or more edges are cut, we re-run the SCC-detection algorithm to identify the new SCCs and the matrix multiplication method to identify shortest remaining cycles. This is repeated until all cycles are eliminated.

3.3 Repair of Local Structures

Once an edge $g_i{\to}g_j$ in the candidate graph G_c is cut, there is a loss of the likelihood of $\ell(g_j|\pi_j)$ because now g_j's parent set π_j is less optimal. Hence, we use K2+ parent-search to repair the parent set of each node whose incident edges have been cut. The repair is done locally, i.e., all other parents of g_j are retained during the repair of π_j. In addition, the repair is subject to the acyclic condition, i.e. the best replacement edge cannot cause cycles.

Suppose in cycle elimination, M edges are cut and the local structures of the involved nodes need repair. We notice the first-repaired local structures will give extra-constraints on the space of the later-repaired local structures due to the acyclic condition (i.e. potentially the search-space of the later-repaired local structures would be shrunk). By comparing the candidate graph G_c and the DAG G returned from cycle elimination, we first locate the nodes whose local structures need repair. We calculate the likelihood loss of a node due to the cutting of incident edges. We sort these loss values from large to small, and repair the nodes according to this ordering. This maximal-loss-first heuristic is consistent with the minimal-likelihood-loss criterion. Clearly, during the course of repair, the DAG after each local repair will always have a higher likelihood score than the DAG before this local repair. This repair algorithm has the complexity of O(βn), where β is the number of nodes whose parent-sets are repaired.

4. Structure Perturbation and Stability Enhancement

To assess the quality of the obtained network G, we perform local structural perturbations to assess its stability. Here we consider the Edge Perturbation ("EP"), i.e., we attempt to eliminate an edge $e_{ij} = g_i{\to}g_j$ to see if the Bayesian likelihood is improved. A "brute force" perturbation is to simply cut e_{ij}. However, after e_{ij} is cut, g_j's parent-set is no longer optimal. For this reason, we use the K2+ algorithm to find the new optimal parents for g_2, excluding the cut edge (but keeping all other parents if any). We calculate $\Delta \ell_e^{EP}$ and the percentage of stable edges

$$r^{EP} = \frac{1}{|E|} \sum_{e \in E} \delta(\Delta \ell_e^{EP}), \quad \Delta \ell = \ell(\hat{G}) - \ell(G) = \log \frac{P(D \mid \hat{G})}{P(D \mid G)}, \quad (5)$$

where $\hat{G}$ is the perturbed structure, $\delta(x) = 1$ if $x \le 0$ and 0 otherwise. The more negative $\Delta \ell_e^{EP}$, the more "stable" the edge e is. r^{EP} indicates the local stability of G. A stable G has $r^{EP} \sim 1$.

By using perturbation, we can identify those unstable edges whose replacements lead to better likelihood scores. We may improve the network structure by replacing these unstable edges with their replacements. The edge-stability-improvement algo-

rithm first sorts the $\Delta \ell_e^{EP}$ of all unstable edges. Similar to the repair algorithm in §3.3, it then goes through all unstable edges following the sorted ordering (starting with the most unstable edge). For a given unstable edge e, the optimal replacement found in EP is first tried to see if there is cycle caused. If no, then the optimal replacement is used; otherwise, the K2+ search algorithm is invoked to search the best replacement (similar to §3.3, the search is subject to the acyclic condition, and all other parents of the current node are retained.). By applying the edge-stability-improvement algorithm, the Bayesian likelihood score of G is improved while the number of unstable edges is reduced.

Our goal is to detect and repair unstable edges to improve a single structure. This differs from other edge quality assessments, e.g. averaging over a large number of structures [14], where the edge importance is not associated with a particular structure.

5. Experiments

We use two data sets in this paper. The first is the well-known Alarm data set [6] (37 variables, 10000 samples). The intrinsic ordering of these variables is not used since our major concern is how to detect the network structure without the ordering information. We use the Alarm data accompanying the PowerConstructor software [2]. We compare our results with WinMine [4][11] (because it can generate DAGs without ordering of variables) and the best/mean results of random-sampling method in the space of variable ordering [7].

The second data set is a yeast genome [10] (481 real-valued gene variables, 300 data points). The variables are discretized to 3-states via thresholding at $\mu \pm 0.4\sigma$ (σ - standard deviation, μ - mean). These states correspond to the over-expression, baseline, and under-expression of genes.

Beside the Bayesian score, we also compute the (normalized) data likelihood L based on the learned structure and conditional probabilities. We further compute the cross-validated likelihood (10-fold CV) L_{CV}, which is a better indicator for generalization.

5.1 Results on Alarm Data Set

The results on the Alarm data set are shown in Table 1. Results of our algorithms, WinMine, and ordering-space-search, are shown, together with those of the true Alarm structure and the null model (i.e. without edges). The k-max search in K2+ clearly improves the quality-measures ℓ, L, L_{CV} and r^{EP} (i.e. the 3-max search results are better than the 1-max search results). The edge stability algorithm of §3.3 clearly improves all the ℓ, L, L_{CV}, and r^{EP}. r^{EP} becomes 1 afterwards.

Compared to true model results, our best results (i.e. 3-max with improved stability) are very close. Remember that the ordering of variables is assumed unknown, thus it is highly unlikely that the true structure can be recovered from data. Hence, these results indicate our network can model the data almost equivalent to the true model, with a different network structure (57 edges in our model versus 46 edges in the true model).

We run WinMine using three different κ values, 0.01 (default value), 0.002, and 8e-12, to adjust the network to have the same number of edges as our results or as the true model. The quality metrics of these structures are not as good as our results.

When variables' ordering is unknown, one may generate many

random orderings, use K2 to learn structures, and select the best ones [7]. We perform this ordering-space-search for 100 random trials. Both the mean and best results are listed in Table 1. They are substantially worse than both our and WinMine's results, indicating it is hard to generate good models from random orderings of variables, even at great computation expense.

Table 1. Results on the Alarm data set. (ℓ, L, L_{CV} are all normalized by nN; κ is the WinMine parameter controlling the complexity of network structure. "ImpStab" means improving stability algorithm in §4.)

Method	Parent Search Method	Learning (all data)				CV (10-fold)
		ℓ	L	r^{EP}	$\lvert E\rvert$	L_{CV}
Our method (Before ImpStab)	1-max	-0.2587	-0.2543	0.9123	57	-0.2554
	3-max	-0.2581	-0.2539	0.9298	56	-0.2550
Our method (After ImpStab)	1-max	-0.2566	-0.2522	1.0000	56	-0.2533
	3-max	-0.2562	-0.2519	1.0000	57	-0.2530
True Model		-0.2555	-0.2517	0.9783	46	-0.2526
WinMine	$\kappa = 0.01$ (Default)	-0.2593	-0.2551	1.0000	57	-0.2561
	$\kappa = 0.002$	-0.2593	-0.2551	1.0000	57	-0.2561
	$\kappa = 8e\text{-}12$	-0.2655	-0.2622	0.9783	46	-0.2630
Search of Ordering Space (100 trials)	Best results	-0.2633	-0.2578	0.8730	63	-0.2592
	Mean results	-0.2701 ±0.0026	-0.2631 ±0.0023	0.8765 ±0.0521	74.0 ±5.4	-0.2650 ±0.0003
Null Model		-0.5822	-0.5813	---	0	-0.5815

5.2 Results on Yeast Gene Expression Data Set

Table 2 compares the results on the yeast gene data. In both our BNs and WinMine's results, there are more than 1600 edges for the 481 nodes. For learning, Table 2 shows that k-max search in K2+ improves ℓ, L, and r^{EP}. The edge-stability-improvement algorithm leads to steady improvements in all quality-measures.

We also run WinMine for a variety of parameter κ. The best results are obtained by setting κ to its maximal value, i.e. 1.0. Table 2 shows that in the best case, WinMine results are worse than that of 3-max, i.e. smaller ℓ, smaller r^{EP}, and less generalization strength L_{CV}. It is interesting to see that the training likelihood L of WinMine result is higher than that of 3-max, however L_{CV} of WinMine is lower than that of 3-max; this implies that the best network of WinMine might overfit data slightly.

Table 2 also lists the time (on PIII 1G CPU) of each method. A plus "+" in our results means the time spent for the current step for edge stability improvement. (Our algorithms were implemented in Matlab and C++, while WinMine was in C++). Our method uses less than 16 minutes to generate an initial BN, and 1 hour or so to refine the network structure. In contrast, WinMine takes about 4 hours to generate a network with the similar performance. These timing results show that our methods are much faster than WinMine, due to our algorithm's O(n^2) complexity.

6. Discussions

A characteristic of the networks in our results is that they are rather sparse, which partially explains the high local stability of the obtained structures regarding to the perturbations. We use local structural perturbations to systematically assess the roles of individual edges in the network. Based on them, one could build larger subnet-level perturbations using clustering, seed growing, etc. This could help to detect sub-structures of BNs [16].

Acknowledgements: We thank Edward Herskovits for discussions on Bayesian learning, David Maxwell Chickering for discussion on using WinMine, and Dana Pe'er for providing the list of 481 genes. This work is supported by Department of Energy, Office of Science, under contract No. DE-AC03-76SF00098.

Table 2. Results on the Yeast gene expression data. b is the number of iterations in stability enhancement.

Search Method and Parameters			Learning (All Data)					CV (10-fold)
	k-max	b	ℓ	L	r^{EP}	E	T (min)	L_{CV}
Our Method	1-max	0	-0.9770	-0.8269	0.6222	1326	9	-0.9420
		1	-0.9691	-0.7831	0.8451	1517	+44	-0.9303
		2	-0.9662	-0.7687	0.9426	1586	+25	-0.9255
		3	-0.9654	-0.7640	0.9863	1611	+ 8.7	-0.9242
		4	-0.9651	-0.7627	0.9951	1620	+ 1.8	-0.9237
	3-max	0	-0.9710	-0.8019	0.7077	1433	16	-0.9338
		1	-0.9654	-0.7689	0.8901	1583	+40	-0.9250
		2	-0.9639	-0.7624	0.9579	1614	+27	-0.9226
		3	-0.9635	-0.7612	0.9821	1620	+14	-0.9220
		4	-0.9634	-0.7606	0.9889	1624	+ 6.2	-0.9218
		5	-0.9631	-0.7588	0.9957	1634	+ 0.09	-0.9212
	κ		ℓ	L	r^{EP}	E	T (min)	L_{CV}
WinMine	0.01 (Default)		-1.0218	-0.9918	0.2868	272	57	-1.0063
	0.50		-0.9916	-0.9373	0.4944	627	115	-0.9683
	0.99		-0.9644	-0.7744	0.9064	1528	229	-0.9239
	0.999		-0.9638	-0.7591	0.9468	1616	235	-0.9224
	1.00		-0.9636	-0.7554	0.9494	1641	268	-0.9220
Null Model			-1.1079	-1.0918	---	0	0	-1.0987

References

[1] Buntine, W., "A guide to the literature on learning probabilistic networks from data," *IEEE Trans KDE*, 8(2): 195-210, 1996.

[2] Cheng, J., Bell, DA, Liu, W., "Learning belief networks from data: an information theory based approach," *6th ACM Int Conf on Information and Knowledge Management*, 1997.

[3] Chickering, D., Geiger, D., and Heckerman, D., "Learning Bayesian Networks is NP-Hard," *MSR-TR-94-17*, Microsoft Research, 1994.

[4] Chickering, D.M., "The WinMine toolkit," *MSR-TR-2002-103*, Microsoft Research, 2002.

[5] Cooper, G.F., and Yoo, C., "Causal discovery from a mixture of experimental and observational data," *UAI-1999*: 116-125, 1999.

[6] Cooper, G.F., and Herskovits, E., "A Bayesian method for the induction of probabilistic networks from data," *Machine Learning*, 9: 309-347, 1992.

[7] Friedman, N., and Koller, D., "Being Bayesian about network structure: a Bayesian approach to structure discovery in Bayesian networks," *Machine Learning*, 2002.

[8] Heckerman, D., "A tutorial on learning with Bayesian networks," in M.I. Jordan (Ed.) *Learning in Graphical Models*: 301-354, MIT Press, 2000.

[9] Heckerman, D., Chickering, D.M., Meek, C., Rounthwaite, R., and Kadie, C. "Dependency networks for inference, collaborative filtering, and data visualization," *J. Machine Learning Research, 1*: 49-75, 2000.

[10] Hughe, T.R., et al. "Functional discovery via a compendium of expression profiles," *Cell, 102*: 109-126, 2000.

[11] Hulten, G., Chickering, D.M., and Heckerman, D., "Learning Bayesian networks from dependency networks: a preliminary study," *AI & Statistics 2003*: 54-61, 2003.

[12] Larranaga, P., Poza, M., Yurramendi, Y., Murga, R.H., and Kuijpers, C.M., "Structural learning of Bayesian networks by genetic algorithms: a performance analysis of control parameters," *IEEE Trans. PAMI. 18*: 912-926, 1996.

[13] Pearl, J., *Probabilistic Reasoning in Intelligent Systems: Networks of Plausible Inference*, San Mateo, CA: Morgan Kaufmann, 1988.

[14] Pe'er, D., Regev, A., Elidan, G., and Friedman, N., "Inferring subnetworks from perturbed expression profiles," *Bioinformatics, 17*: 215S-224S, 2001.

[15] Peng, H.C., Herskovits E, and Davatzikos C. "Bayesian clustering methods for morphological analysis of MR images," IEEE Int'l Symp on Medical Imaging: Macro to Nano: 875-878, 2002.

[16] Peng, H.C., and Ding, C., "An efficient algorithm for detecting modular regulatory networks using Bayesian subnets of co-regulated genes," LBNL Technical Report 53734, Aug 2003.

Privacy-Preserving Collaborative Filtering Using Randomized Perturbation Techniques*

Huseyin Polat and Wenliang Du
Systems Assurance Institute
Department of Electrical Engineering and Computer Science
Syracuse University, 121 Link Hall, Syracuse, NY 13244
E-mail: {hpolat,wedu}@ecs.syr.edu

Abstract

Collaborative Filtering (CF) techniques are becoming increasingly popular with the evolution of the Internet. To conduct collaborative filtering, data from customers are needed. However, collecting high quality data from customers is not an easy task because many customers are so concerned about their privacy that they might decide to give false information. We propose a randomized perturbation (RP) technique to protect users' privacy while still producing accurate recommendations.

1. Introduction

With the amount of the information available for individuals growing steadily, information overload has become a major problem for users. To make the information to serve users better, information filtering and recommendation schemes become more and more important. Collaborative filtering (CF) is a recent technique for such filtering and recommendation purposes.

With the number of users accessing the Internet growing, CF techniques are becoming increasingly popular as part of online shopping sites. These sites incorporate recommendation systems that suggest products to users based on products that like-minded users have ordered before. CF has many important applications [4, 5] in e-commerce, direct recommendations, and search engines. Users can get recommendations about many of their daily activities.

The goal of CF is to predict the preferences of one user, referred to as the active user, based on the preferences of a group of other users. The key idea is that the active user

*Portions of this work were supported by Grants IIS-0312366 and IIS-0219560 from the National Science Foundation. The extended version of this paper can be downloaded from http://www.cis.syr.edu/~wedu/Research/paper/ppcf03.pdf

will prefer those items that like-minded users prefer, or that dissimilar users do not.

Today's CF systems have a number of disadvantages [4, 5]. The most important is that they are a serious threat to individual privacy. There is a great potential for individuals to share all kinds of information about places and things to do, see and buy, but the privacy risks are severe. Most online vendors collect buying information and preferences about their customers and make reasonable efforts to keep this data private. However, customer data is a valuable asset and it has been sold when some e-companies suffered bankruptcy.

Some people might be willing to selectively divulge information if they can get benefit in return. However, a significant number of people are not willing to divulge their information because of privacy concerns. The challenge is *how can users contribute their personal information for CF purposes without compromising their privacy?*

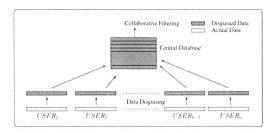

Figure 1. Privacy preserving CF

One way to achieve privacy is to use anonymous techniques [1, 8], which allow users to disclose their personal information without disclosing their identities. The biggest problem of using anonymous techniques is that there is no guarantee on the quality of the dataset. Canny shows another way to conduct CF without disclosing each user's private data [4, 5].

We propose a new scheme (Fig. 1), in which each user

first disguises his/her personal data, and then sends to a central place (the data collector), such that the data collector cannot derive the truthful information about a user's private information. We propose to use *Randomized Perturbation (RP)* techniques to disguise private data.

We hypothesize that *by combining the RP techniques with CF algorithms, we can achieve a decent degree of accuracy for the privacy-preserving collaborative filtering (PPCF)*. To verify this hypothesis, we implemented the RP technique for a CF algorithm, which was proposed by [6]. We compared the predictions that are calculated based on original data with the predictions on randomized data.

2. Related Work

Canny proposes two schemes for PPCF [4, 5]. In these schemes, users control all of their own private data; a community of users can compute a public "aggregate" of their data without disclosing individual users' data. The aggregate allows personalized recommendations to be computed by members of the community, or by outsiders. Each user uses local computation to get personalized recommendations.

While Canny's work focuses on the peer-to-peer framework, in which users actively participate in the CF process, our work focuses on another framework, in which users do not participate in the CF process; only the central place needs to conduct CF.

There are two general classes of CF algorithms (memory-based and model-based) [3]. The task in CF is to predict the votes of a particular user (the active user) based on a database of user votes from a population of other users (the user database) [3]. The user database consists of a set of votes v_{ij} corresponding to the vote for user i on item j.

GroupLens introduced an automated collaborative filtering system using a neighborhood-based algorithm [7, 9]. An extension of the GroupLens algorithm, which we use in our study in here was proposed by [6]. If the v_{ij} is user i's vote on item j, $\overline{v_i}$ is the mean vote of the user i, and σ_i is the standard deviation for the user i, then the z-scores (z_{ij}) can be defined as: $z_{ij} = (v_{ij} - \overline{v_i})/\sigma_i$. Herlocker et al. [6] account for the differences in spread between users' rating distributions by converting ratings to z-scores, and compute a weighted average of the z-scores:

$$p_{aq} = \overline{v_a} + \sigma_a \cdot \frac{\sum_{i=1}^{n} w_{ai} \cdot z_{iq}}{\sum_{i=1}^{n} w_{ai}}, \qquad w_{ai} = \sum_{k} z_{ak} \cdot z_{ik} \quad (1)$$

where k is the counter that shows the number of items that both the active user a and the user i have rated. σ_a and σ_i

are standard deviations of the active user a's ratings and the user i's ratings, respectively. z_{ak} and z_{ik} are z-score values for active user a and the user i, respectively.

Randomized perturbation scheme was used by Agrawal and Srikant to solve privacy-preserving data mining problems [2]. The paper shows that it is possible to build decision tree classifiers if data is disguised using the RP scheme. Our work solves a different but related problem.

3. Privacy Preserving CF Using RP

There are several ways to hide numbers or information. To hide a number a, a simple way is to add a random number r to it. Although we cannot do anything to a since it is disguised, we can conduct certain computations if we are interested in the aggregate data, rather than each individual data.

The basic idea of RP is to perturb the data in such a way that certain computations can be done while preserving users' privacy. Although information from each individual user is scrambled, if the number of users is significantly large, the aggregate information of these users can be estimated with decent accuracy. Such property is useful for computations that are based on aggregate information. Scalar product and sum are among such computations and used in CF algorithms.

Let A and B be the original vectors, where $A = (a_1, \ldots, a_n)$ and $B = (b_1, \ldots, b_n)$. A is disguised by $R = (r_1, \ldots, r_n)$, and B is disguised by $V = (v_1, \ldots, v_n)$, where r_i and v_i are uniformly distributed in domain $[-\alpha, \alpha]$. Let $A' = A + R$ and $B' = B + V$ be the disguised data that are known. Since R and V are independent and r_i and v_i are uniformly distributed in domain $[-\alpha, \alpha]$, the scalar product of A and B can be estimated from A' and B' and the sum of the values of vector A can be estimated from A'.

$$A' \cdot B' = \sum_{i=1}^{n}(a_i b_i + a_i v_i + r_i b_i + r_i v_i) \approx \sum_{i=1}^{n} a_i b_i \quad (2)$$

$$\sum_{i=1}^{n}(a_i + r_i) = \sum_{i=1}^{n} a_i + \sum_{i=1}^{n} r_i \approx \sum_{i=1}^{n} a_i \quad (3)$$

In the long run, the values of $\sum_{i=1}^{n} a_i v_i$, $\sum_{i=1}^{n} r_i b_i$, $\sum_{i=1}^{n} r_i v_i$, and $\sum_{i=1}^{n} r_i$ will converge to zero.

3.1. CF with privacy using RP techniques

Our goal of CF using RP techniques is to achieve privacy and produce recommendations with high accuracy. However, achieving privacy and producing accurate recommendations are two conflicting goals. We propose a technique to achieve a good balance between the privacy and the accuracy.

Without privacy concerns, the server, which has a central database containing ratings from all users can calculate the p_{aq} (predicted vote for active user a on item q) based on active user's known ratings and the query (for which item he/she is looking for prediction) using the Eq. (1).

With the privacy concerns, the server should not know the true data of each user including the active users. We use the RP technique to achieve data disguise. In our approach, users add a random number to each of their actual ratings that they want to disguise, and send the results to the server. The server should not be able to find the true values of the ratings because of the random numbers. If we simplify the Eq. (1) and replace w_{ai} with $\sum_k z_{ak} \cdot z_{ik}$, then we get:

$$p_{aq} = \overline{v_a} + \sigma_a \cdot p'_{aq}, \quad p'_{aq} = \frac{\sum_k z_{ak} \cdot \left[\sum_{i=1}^{n} z_{ik} \cdot z_{iq} \right]}{\sum_k z_{ak} \cdot \left[\sum_{i=1}^{n} z_{ik} \right]} \quad (4)$$

Since the active user and the other users have not rated all items, the counter, k, is different from user to user. Only those items that have been rated by both the active user a and the user i are involved in computations. The entries for those items that have not been rated are zero.

Notice that the nominator part consists of a scalar product between vector $Z_k = (z_{1k}, \ldots, z_{nk})$ and vector $Z_q = (z_{1q}, \ldots, z_{nq})$. If the server can compute the scalar products for all k's, it can send the results of the scalar products to the active user who can easily compute the nominator part. The denominator part is even simpler. All the server needs to do is to send the result of $\sum_{i=1}^{n} z_{ik}$ for each k to the active user.

We develop the following scheme that preserves the privacy while still allowing the producing accurate recommendations. First, the server decides on a range $[-\alpha, \alpha]$, and let each user know. Then, each user i calculates the z-scores z_{ij} for the items that he/she has rated. Finally, each user i creates n_i uniformly-random numbers r_{ij} in the range $[-\alpha, \alpha]$, where n_i is the total number of items that user has rated. User i then generates the disguised z-scores $z'_{ij} = z_{ij} + r_{ij}$ and sends the results (n_i disguised z-scores) to the server.

After getting all the disguised z-scores z'_{ij} from many users, the server can now provide CF services to active users based on the following facts from Eq. (2) and (3):

$$\sum_{i=1}^{n} z_{ik} \cdot z_{iq} \approx \sum_{i=1}^{n} z'_{ik} \cdot z'_{iq}, \quad \sum_{i=1}^{n} z_{ik} \approx \sum_{i=1}^{n} z'_{ik} \quad (5)$$

To get a recommendation for item q, the active user computes the z-scores z_{ak} for those items that he/she has rated before. Then, the server sends the results of $\sum_{i=1}^{n} z'_{ik} \cdot z'_{iq}$ and

$\sum_{i=1}^{n} z'_{ik}$ for all k to the active user who uses Eq. (4) and (5) to compute p'_{aq} and p_{aq}.

To protect the private data, the range of the random numbers is critical. To understand how the range affects the accuracy, we associate the range with the distribution of the original data. When the distribution is standard normal distribution, i.e. the distribution is a normal distribution with the mean (μ) being 0 and the standard deviation (σ) being 1, the ranges for certain percentiles can be looked up from a table. From now on, we use γ to represent the percentile.

There are several ways we can disguise the original data. In fixed range scheme, we use a fixed range to generate random numbers. In random range scheme, after deciding on the range of the random numbers, each user randomly generates a number α within this range, and then uses $[-\alpha, \alpha]$ as the range to generate uniform random numbers.

4. Experimental Results

Although we use Jester and MovieLens datasets in our experiments, we only show the results of MovieLens (ML) million dataset. There are two ML datasets (ML public data and ML million data) available. ML million data consists of approximately 1 million ratings for approximately 3,500 movies made by 7,463 users. Ratings are made on a 5-star scale. We use the *Mean Absolute Error (MAE)* and the *standard deviation (σ)* as criteria in our evaluation.

4.1. Methodology

The outline of our procedure can be described as follows. First, we randomly selected 3,000 users for training and 300 users for testing from ML million dataset. Then, for each active user selected randomly from the testing dataset, we randomly select an item and use our randomized-perturbation-based scheme and the original algorithm, respectively, to predict the ratings on this item for this active user. Finally, we calculate the difference of these two ratings and run this prediction procedure for 100 times and calculate the mean absolute error and standard deviation of the errors.

We hypothesize that the privacy and accuracy depend on several factors including the selection of α (fixed or random α), the γ values (50%, 75%, 85%, or 95%) that affect the range of the random numbers (α), the total number of users, and the total number of items. Therefore, we conducted several experiments to show how these factors affect accuracy.

We hypothesize that the RP techniques give more accurate results when the number of users and/or items increases. To test this hypothesis, we conducted three groups of experiments: for the first and the second groups, we try to keep the number of users the same while changing the number of items; for the second and the third groups, we try to keep the number of items the same while changing the number of users. Since the third group needs to involve a large number of users, we conduct the third group of experiments on dense datasets.

4.2. Experimental results

Fig. 2 and Fig. 3 depict our results on ML million dataset. The results get much better when we use the random-α scheme to generate the random numbers. When the range of the random numbers is random from $[0, \beta]$, the distribution of all the random numbers is not uniform in range $[-\beta, \beta]$; the probability of choosing a number near 0 is larger than the probability of choosing a number near β or $-\beta$. The smaller the random number, the more accurate the result.

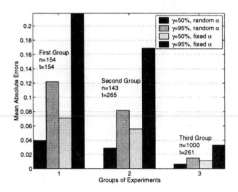

Figure 2. The mean absolute errors

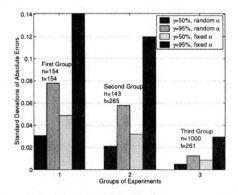

Figure 3. Standard deviations of the errors

The results also get better when we choose a smaller γ value. When γ is small, the range of random numbers is also small. As we know, when the range is small, we have less randomness; thus the accuracy can be improved.

The results are better when we increase the value of n (the total number of users) and t (the total number of items). In our scheme, increasing n and t is equivalent to increasing the amount of data involved in the sum and the scalar product computations. The more data we have for these two computations, the more accurate the approximation will be.

5. Conclusion and Future Work

We have presented a solution to the PPCF problem using the RP scheme. Our solution makes it possible for servers to collect private data from users for CF purposes without compromising users' privacy requirements. Our experiments have shown that our solution can achieve accurate prediction compared to the prediction based on the original data.

We believe that accuracy of our scheme can be further improved if more aggregate information is disclosed along with the disguised data, especially those aggregate information whose disclosure does not compromise much of users' privacy.

References

[1] Anonymizer.com: http://www.anonymizer.com.

[2] R. Agrawal and R. Srikant. Privacy-preserving data mining. In *Proceedings of the 2000 ACM SIGMOD on Management of Data*, pages 439–450, Dallas, TX USA, May 15 - 18 2000.

[3] J. Breese, D. Heckerman, and C. Kadie. Empirical analysis of predictive algorithms for collaborative filtering. In *Proceedings of the Fourteenth Conference on Uncertainty in Artificial Intelligence*, pages 43–52, Madison,WI, July 1998.

[4] J. Canny. Collaborative filtering with privacy. In *IEEE Symposium on Security and Privacy*, pages 45–57, Oakland, CA, May 2002.

[5] J. Canny. Collaborative filtering with privacy via factor analysis. In *Proceedings of the 25th annual international ACM SIGIR conference on Research and development in information retrieval*, pages 238–245, Tampere, Finland, August 2002.

[6] J. Herlocker, J. Konstan, A. Borchers, and J. Riedl. An algorithmic framework for performing collaborative filtering. In *Proceedings of the 1999 Conference on Research and Development in Information Retrieval*, August 1999.

[7] J. A. Konstan, B. N. Miller, D. Maltz, J. L. Herlocker, L. R. Gordon, and J. Riedl. Grouplens: Applying collaborative filtering to usenet news. In *Communications of the ACM*, pages 77–87, March 1997.

[8] M. K. Reiter and A. D. Rubin. Crowds: anonymity for web transaction. *ACM Transactions on Information and System Security*, 1(1):Pages 66–92, 1998.

[9] P. Resnick, N. Iacovou, M. Suchak, P. Bergstrom, and J. Riedl. Grouplens: An open architecture for collaborative filtering of netnews. In *Proceedings of the ACM Conference on Computer Supported Cooperative Work*, pages 175–186, 1994.

Semantic Role Parsing: Adding Semantic Structure to Unstructured Text[*]

Sameer Pradhan, Kadri Hacioglu, Wayne Ward, James H. Martin, Daniel Jurafsky
Center for Spoken Language Research,
University of Colorado, Boulder, CO 80303

Abstract

There is a ever-growing need to add structure in the form of semantic markup to the huge amounts of unstructured text data now available. We present the technique of shallow semantic parsing, the process of assigning a simple WHO did WHAT to WHOM, etc., structure to sentences in text, as a useful tool in achieving this goal. We formulate the semantic parsing problem as a classification problem using Support Vector Machines. Using a hand-labeled training set and a set of features drawn from earlier work together with some feature enhancements, we demonstrate a system that performs better than all other published results on shallow semantic parsing.

1. Introduction

Automatic, accurate, wide-coverage techniques that can annotate naturally occurring text with semantic roles can facilitate the discovery of patterns of information in large text collections [15]. Shallow semantic parsing is a process for producing such a markup. In shallow semantic parsing, semantic tags are assigned to the arguments, or case roles, associated with each predicate in the sentence. This technique is used widely in Information Extraction, and is being evaluated for use in Summarization, Question Answering and Machine Translation.

We treat the problem of tagging parsed constituents as a multi-class classification problem, where the classifier is trained in a supervised manner from human-annotated data using Support Vector Machines [17]. The next section describes our training and test corpora. Rest of the paper describes our system in detail, compares it to other systems, presents some analysis, and points to future work.

2. Semantic Annotation and Corpora

There are many possible approaches to specifying the roles to be used for the markup. Two corpora are available for de-

veloping and testing semantic annotation – FrameNet[1] [1] and PropBank[2] [11]. FrameNet uses predicate specific labels such as JUDGE and JUDGEE. PropBank uses predicate independent labels – ARG0, ARG1, etc. In this paper, we will be reporting on results using PropBank, a one million word corpus in which predicate argument relations are marked for every occurrence of every verb in the Wall Street Journal (WSJ) part of the Penn TreeBank [13]. The arguments of a verb are labeled sequentially from ARG0 to ARG5, where ARG0 is usually the subject of a transitive verb; ARG1, its direct object, etc. In addition to these "core arguments," additional "adjunctive arguments," for example, ARGM-LOC, for locatives, and ARGM-TMP, for temporals, are also marked. We will refer to these as ARGMs. An example PropBank style markup:

1. [ARG0 Merrill Lynch Co.] refuses to [predicate perform] [ARG1 index arbitrage trades] for [ARG2 clients.]

All experiments in this paper are performed on the July 2002 release of PropBank. In these experiments, the test set is Section-23 of the WSJ data. Section-02 through Section-21 are used for training. The training set comprises approximately 51,000 sentences with 132,000 arguments, and the test set comprises approximately 2,700 sentences with 7,000 arguments.

3. System Architecture

The basic steps of our shallow semantic parser are similar to those outlined by Gildea & Jurafsky (G&J) [6]:

procedure *Parse(Sentence)*
- Generate a full syntactic parse for the *Sentence*
- Identify all verb *predicates*
for *predicate* ∈ *Sentence* **do**
  - Extract a set of features for each node in the tree relative to the *predicate*
  - Classify each node as NULL, or as one of the PropBank arguments
  - Generate Parse
end for

---

[*]This research was partially supported by the ARDA AQUAINT program via contract OCG4423B and by the NSF via grant IIS-9978025

[1] http://www.icsi.berkeley.edu/~framenet/
[2] http://www.cis.upenn.edu/~ace/

The features used by the classifier are:

Predicate – The predicate itself is used as a feature.

Path – The syntactic path through the parse tree from the governing predicate to the parse constituent being classified. For example, in Figure 1, the path from ARG0 – "The lawyers" to the predicate "went", is represented with the string NP↑S↓VP↓VBD.

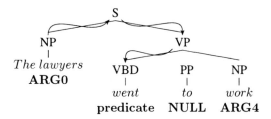

Figure 1. Illustration of path NP↑S↓VP↓VBD

Phrase Type – The syntactic category (NP, PP, S, etc.) of the phrase corresponding to the semantic role.

Position – Whether the phrase is before or after the governing predicate.

Voice – Whether the governing predicate is realized as an active or passive construction.

Head Word – The syntactic head of the phrase.

Sub-categorization – This is the phrase structure rule expanding the predicate's parent node in the parse tree. For example, in Figure 1, the sub-categorization for the predicate "went" is VP→VBD-PP-NP.

We use SVM as the classifier in the ONE *vs* ALL formalism, where an SVM is trained for each class (ARG0-5, ARGMs, and NULL) to discriminate between that class and all others. We found it efficient to divide the classification process into three stages:

1. A binary NULL *vs* NON-NULL classifier labels each node as NULL or as being some argument class. A threshold is set so that nodes with very high confidence of being NULL are pruned.

2. In a second pass, each node not pruned in the first stage is classified as one of the set of argument classes or as NULL using the ONE *vs* ALL strategy. In this collection of binary classifiers, the NULL *vs* NON-NULL classifier is trained on nodes that weren't pruned by the first pass, and so is different than the one in the first pass.

3. Overlapping argument assignments are disallowed. Since there are no overlapping roles in the training set, this is another constraint that can be enforced and results in a significant increase in precision with little or no reduction in recall.

4. Experimental Configurations and Results

For our experiments, we used tinySVM[3] along with Yam-Cha[4] as the SVM training and test software. The system was optimized on three parameters: a) The kernel function used - polynomial with degree 2; b) The cost per unit violation of the margin ($C=1$), and c) Tolerance of the termination criterion ($e=0.001$).

As a baseline, we trained a system using the set of features listed earlier. The Precision, Recall and F_1 measure are shown in the Baseline row of Table 1. We also tested four new features, Verb Clusters, Named Entities, Partial-Path and Head Word Part-of-Speech[5].

Verb clustering – In order to improve performance on verbs that are unseen in the training set, we clustered verbs into 64 classes using the probabilistic co-occurrence model of Hofmann [10] and using a distance function derived from Lin's database of verb-direct object relations [12]. The verb class of the current predicate was added as a feature. The performance improvement is shown in Table 1.

	No Overlaps		
	P	R	F_1
Baseline	85	79	82
With verb clusters	86	81	84

Table 1. Improvement on adding verb-cluster

Named Entities in the constituents – Another obvious improvement was considering the presence of named entities present in the constituents. We tagged 7 named entities (PERSON, ORGANIZATION, LOCATION, PERCENT, MONEY, TIME, DATE) using Identifinder [2] and added them as binary features. This feature is true if the entity is contained in the constituent. On the task of assigning labels to constituents known to represent either "core" or "adjunctive" arguments, adding this feature increased the accuracy from 87.74% to 88.24%. The most significant improvement was for adjunct roles like temporals (ARGM-TMP) and locatives (ARGM-LOC) as shown in Table 2. Named Entities are used in the argument classifiers but not in the NULL *vs* NON-NULL classifier. We found the classifier degraded when this feature was added.

	ARGM-LOC			ARGM-TMP		
	P	R	F_1	P	R	F_1
Without NE	64	55	59	80	85	82
With NE	71	67	69	84	87	85

Table 2. Improvement using Named Entities

Partial Path – We tried generalizing the Path feature by setting its value to the part of the original Path feature that goes from the constituent to the common parent. Partial

---

[3]http://cl.aist-nara.ac.jp/~talus-Au/software/TinySVM/
[4]http://cl.aist-nara.ac.jp/~taku-Au/software/yamcha/
[5]Unless mentioned otherwise, the test set comprises perfect hand-corrected, "gold-standard" parses.

Path for the Path illustrated in Figure 1 is NP↑S. On the task of assigning labels to constituents known to represent "core arguments", adding this feature increased the accuracy from 93.7% to 94%.

Head Word Part-of-Speech (POS) – Adding the Head Word POS improved NULL *vs* NON-NULL classification accuracy from 91% to 92%

4.1. Alternative Pruning Strategies. A preliminary error analysis suggested that the biggest confusion was between NULL and NON-NULL roles, therefore we decided to re-examine our strategy of filtering out nodes that have a high likelihood of being NULL in a first pass. To do this, we converted the raw SVM scores to probabilities by fitting a sigmoid function [14]. We trained and tested systems for three conditions:

1. System I, a one pass system where all ONE *vs* ALL classifiers are trained on all the data. This has considerably higher training time as compared to the other two.
2. System II, which uses a NULL *vs* NON-NULL classifier in a first pass. The difference is that here, all nodes labeled NULL are filtered (not just high confidence ones.)
3. System III, which also uses a NULL *vs* NON-NULL classifier, but filters out nodes with high confidence of being NULL in a first pass.

A detailed description of all possible formulations, are described at length in [9, 8]

Table 3 shows performance on the task of identifying and labeling PropBank arguments. The two-stage System III performs the best. It slightly outperforms the system trained on all the data. The fact that about 80% of the nodes in a tree are NULL, and we have to train only one classifier on the entire data, there is a considerable saving in training time. Therefore, we decided to continue using this strategy.

	No Overlaps		
	P	R	F$_1$↑
SVM System I	87	80	83.3
SVM System II	84	80	81.9
SVM System III	86	81	83.4

Table 3. Comparing Pruning Strategies

5. Comparing Performance with Other Systems

We evaluated our system in a number of ways. First, we compare it against 4 other shallow parsers in the literature. Second, we compare the performance of our system when using gold-standard parses versus when using an more realistic parser – Charniak Parser [3]. Finally, we compare the performance of our parser on "core arguments" (ARG0-ARG5).

In comparing systems, results are reported for tree types of tasks:

1. *Argument Identification* - Given a (correct) parse tree, label each node as NULL or as being some argument (the NULL - NON-NULL discrimination).
2. *Argument Classification* - Given the (correct) set of nodes in the tree that are arguments, label each node with the argument class label.
3. *Combined Identification and Classification* - This is the real usage scenario where the system must classify nodes as NULL or some specific argument.

5.1. Description of the Systems.

5.1.1 The Gildea and Palmer (G&P) System. This system uses the same features used by G&J [6], which are the ones that we started with. They report results on the December 2001 release of PropBank.

5.1.2 The Surdeanu *et al*. System. Surdeanu *et al*. [16] report results on two systems. One that uses exactly the same features as the G&J [6] system. We call this "Surdeanu System I." [16] They then show improved performance of another system – "Surdeanu System II," [16] which uses some additional features. They use the July 2002 release of PropBank.

5.1.3 The Gildea and Hockenmaier (G&H) System. The G&H [5] system uses features extracted from Combinatory Categorial Grammar (CCG) corresponding to the features that were used by G&J [6] and G&P [7] systems. They use a slightly newer – November 2002 release of Prop-Bank. We will refer to this as "G&H System I". They also report performance on the Treebank-based data – "G&H System II."

5.1.4 The Chen and Rambow (C&R) System. Chen and Rambow report on two different systems. The first "C&R System I" uses surface syntactic features much like the G&P [7] system. The second "C&R System II" uses additional syntactic and semantic representations that are extracted from a Tree Adjoining Grammar (TAG).

5.2. Role Classification Using Known Boundaries. Table 4 compares the role classification accuracies of various systems, and at various levels of classification granularity, and parse accuracy. It can be seen that the SVM System performs significantly better than all the other systems on all PropBank arguments.

"C&R System II" [4] uses some additional syntactic features extracted from TAG. The "C&R System I" [4] that uses the almost the same features as the SVM System performs considerably worse. The test sets of the "C&R System I" [4] and SVM System are not identical, but nevertheless, the rough comparison is valuable.

5.3. Argument Identification (NULL **vs** NON-NULL). Table 5 compares the results of the task of identifying the parse constituents that represent semantic arguments. As expected, the performance degrades considerably when we

Classes	System	Gold Accuracy	Automatic Accuracy
ARG0-5 + ARGMs	SVM	88	87
	G&P	77	74
	Surdeanu System II	84	-
	Surdeanu System I	79	-
CORE ARGUMENTS (ARG0-5)	SVM	93.9	90
	C&R System II	93.5	-
	C&R System I	92.4	-

Table 4. Argument classification

extract features from an automatic parse as opposed to a gold-standard parse. This indicates that the syntactic parser performance directly influences the role boundary identification performance. This could be attributed to the fact that the two features, viz., Path and Head Word that have been seen to be good discriminators of the semantically salient nodes in the syntax tree, are derived from the syntax tree.

Classes	System	Gold			Automatic		
		P	R	F_1	P	R	F_1
ARG0-5 + ARGMs	SVM	94	90	92	89	80	84
	Surdeanu System II	-	-	89	-	-	-
	Surdeanu System I	85	84	85	-	-	-

Table 5. Argument identification

5.4. Argument Identification and Tagging. Table 6 shows the results for the task where the system first identifies candidate argument boundaries and then labels them with the most likely role as discussed in Sections 3 and 4. This is the hardest of the three tasks outlined earlier. SVM does a very good job of generalizing in both stages of processing.

Classes	System	Gold			Automatic		
		P	R	F_1	P	R	F_1
ARG0-5 + ARGMs	SVM System III	86	81	83	82	73	77
	G&H System I	76	68	72	71	63	67
	G&H System II	79	70	74	73	61	66
	G&P	71	64	67	58	50	54
ARG0-5	SVM System III	89	85	87	85	77	81
	G&H System I	82	79	80	76	73	75
	G&H System II	85	82	84	76	70	73
	C&R System II	-	-	-	65	75	70

Table 6. Identification and classification

6. Conclusions

We have extended the work of Gildea and Jurafsky [6] on shallow semantic role labeling. We first made a number of small augmentations to their system which generalizes the statistical power of the original algorithm, improving the precision and recall significantly on test data. We then replaced the probability estimators of the original system with an SVM. This resulted in a substantial improvement the system's overall performance. A detailed comparison of our results with those reported by other groups working on similar tasks indicate that ours outperforms all. One drawback of the current system is that it labels each argument in a sentence independent of the others. We plan to overcome

this by converting the SVM output into an n-best lattice and using other features such as role language model score.

We would like to thank Ralph Weischedel and Scott Miller of BBN Inc. for letting us use their named entity tagger – IdentiFinder; Daniel Gildea for providing the source for his parser; Martha Palmer for providing us with the PropBank data; Valerie Krugler and Karin Kipper for mapping the PropBank arguments to thematic roles.

References

[1] C. F. Baker, C. J. Fillmore, and J. B. Lowe. The Berkeley FrameNet project. In *COLING/ACL-98*, Montreal, 1998. ACL.

[2] D. M. Bikel, R. Schwartz, and R. M. Weischedel. An algorithm that learns what's in a name. *Machine Learning*, 34:211–231, 1999.

[3] E. Chaniak. Immediate-head parsing for language models. In *Proceedings of the 39th ACL*, Toulouse, France, 2001.

[4] J. Chen and O. Rambow. Use of deep linguistics features for the recognition and labeling of semantic arguments. In *Proceedings of the EMNLP*, Sapporo, Japan, 2003.

[5] D. Gildea and J. Hockenmaier. Identifying semantic roles using combinatory categorial grammar. In *Proceedings of the EMNLP*, Sapporo, Japan, 2003.

[6] D. Gildea and D. Jurafsky. Automatic labeling of semantic roles. *Computational Linguistics*, 28(3):245–288, 2002.

[7] D. Gildea and M. Palmer. The necessity of syntactic parsing for predicate argument recognition. In *Proceedings of the 40th ACL*, Philadelphia, PA, 2002.

[8] K. Hacioglu, S. Pradhan, W. Ward, J. Martin, and D. Jurafsky. Shallow semantic parsing using support vector machines. Technical Report TR-CSLR-2003-1, Center for Spoken Language Research, Boulder, Colorado, 2003.

[9] K. Hacioglu and W. Ward. Target word detection and semantic role chunking using support vector machines. In *Proceedings of the Human Language Technology Conference*, Edmonton, Canada, 2003.

[10] T. Hofmann and J. Puzicha. Statistical models for co-occurrence data. Memo, Massachussetts Institute of Technology Artificial Intelligence Laboratory, Feb. 1998.

[11] P. Kingsbury and M. Palmer. From Treebank to PropBank. In *Proceedings of the LREC*, Las Palmas, Canary Islands, Spain, 2002.

[12] D. Lin. Automatic retrieval and clustering of similar words. In *Proceedings of the COLING-ACL*, Montreal, Canada, 1998.

[13] M. Marcus, G. Kim, M. A. Marcinkiewicz, R. MacIntyre, A. Bies, M. Ferguson, K. Katz, and B. Schasberger. The penn treebank: Annotating predicate argument structure, 1994.

[14] J. Platt. Probabilities for support vector machines. In A. Smola, P. Bartlett, B. Scolkopf, and D. Schuurmans, editors, *Advances in Large Margin Classifiers*. MIT press, Cambridge, MA, 2000.

[15] G. N. Sean Wallis. Knowledge discovery in grammatically analysed corpora. *Data Mining and Knowledge Discovery*, 5(4):305–335, 2001.

[16] M. Surdeanu, S. Harabagiu, J. Williams, and P. Aarseth. Using predicate-argument structures for information extraction. In *Proceedings of the ACL*, Sapporo, Japan, 2003.

[17] V. Vapnik. *The Nature of Statistical Learning Theory*. Springer-Verlag, New York, 1995.

Mining Semantic Networks for Knowledge Discovery

K. Rajaraman
Institute for Infocomm Research
21 Heng Mui Keng Terrace
Singapore 119613
kanagasa@i2r.a-star.edu.sg

Ah-Hwee Tan
School of Computer Engineering
Nanyang Technological University
Singapore 639798
asahtan@ntu.edu.sg

Abstract

This paper addresses the problem of mining a class of semantic networks, called Concept Frame Graphs (CFG's), for knowledge discovery from text. This new representation is motivated by the need to capture richer text content so that non-trivial mining tasks can be performed. We first define the CFG representation and then describe a rule-based algorithm for constructing a CFG from text documents. Treating the CFG as a networked knowledge base, we propose new methods for text mining. On a specific task of discovering the top companies in an area, we observe that our approach leads to simpler content mining algorithms, once the CFG has been constructed. Moreover, exploiting the network structure of CFG results in significant improvements in precision and recall.

1. Introduction

Text Mining or Knowledge Discovery from Text refers to "the nontrivial extraction of implicit, previously unknown, and potentially useful information from unstructured (or semi-structured) text data" [2]. Most text mining methods, however, deal with the problem of organizing document collections and providing interactive user interfaces for intelligent access to the documents. Relatively few works concern the problem of analyzing documents at the content level for extracting useful knowledge. In this paper we investigate techniques for text content mining via a semantic network approach. We propose an enriched semantic network representation, called the Concept Frame Graph (CFG), and present mining algorithms by analysing this representation. The following two steps outline our approach: *Concept Frame Graph (CFG) Construction*, where the text documents are processed using a rule-based system to extract a CFG, and *CFG Mining* where we propose and apply new mining techniques on the CFG for discovering useful knowledge.

2. Concept Frame Graph Representation

Definition 2.1 *A concept frame is an object (*NAME, SYNSET, RELS, CONTEXTS*) where:*
NAME *is the name of the concept*
SYNSET *is a set of synonyms of the concept*
RELS *is a set that describes the relations of this concept with other concepts. Each element of this set is a relation tuple of the form (AgentCF,rel,ObjectCF), where 'AgentCF' and 'ObjectCF' are pointers to concept frames (one of which is 'Self' - the concept frame being defined) and 'rel' is a relation between them.*
and
CONTEXTS *is an (optional) set of text segments corresponding to each relation tuple in* RELS. *The text segment is the portion of text from which the corresponding relation was extracted from.*

Remark 2.1 *In the relation tuples* RELS, *either AgentCF or ObjectCF point to Self (sometimes denoted as '*'). In the former case, the relation would be an OUT relation and the latter case leads to an IN relation. It is possible that one of AgentCF or ObjectCF is empty. In this case, the relation would be monadic. The rel field, however, cannot be empty.*
The CONTEXTS *field is intended to clarify the right sense of the relations in* RELS.

As an example, the 'Computer Virus' concept could be represented by a concept frame as follows:

NAME: Computer Virus

SYNSET: virus, worm, trojan horse

RELS: (*,infect,**computer**), (**hacker**,create,*), (*,spread by,**email**)

CONTEXTS: "a deadly virus has infected computers worldwide", "hackers have been creating worms lately","the worms spread by emails"

where "computer", "hacker" and "email" stand for pointers to the respective concept frames. Through the RELS field,

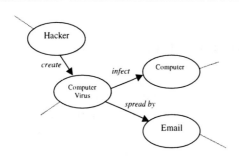

Figure 1. Example of a CFG.

a set of relationships of a concept frame with other concept frames is defined. This in turn defines the concept frame graph. Formally,

Definition 2.2 *Given a set of concept frames*
$F_i = (Name_i, Synset_i, Rels_i, Contexts_i)$, *with* $Rels_i = \{(a_{ij}, r_{ij}, o_{ij}), j = 1, \cdots, M_i\}$, $i = 1, \cdots, N$, *the Concept Frame Graph(CFG) is a finite, directed, edge-labeled graph in which* F_i *and every* a_{ij}, o_{ij} *other than 'Self', define the nodes and the pairs* (a_{ij}, o_{ij}) *define the corresponding edges with* r_{ij} *as the edge label.*

For example, the CFG of the 'Computer Virus' concept frame would look like the one in Figure 1.

CFG is structurally similar to a Conceptual Graph[5]. A basic difference is that conceptual graph is a bipartite graph whereas CFG uses labeled edges. In addition, information of the form of synset or contexts is not explicitly embedded in conceptual graphs.

3. CFG Construction

Given a document collection, the set of concept frames that completely describes this collection would form a CFG, according to Definition 2.2. Below we describe an algorithm for learning a class of CFG's from a set of text documents.

Pre-processing: The documents are first pre-processed to remove menu bars (as found on web pages) or formatting specifications such as HTML tags so that only the main body of the content is retained.

Name Entity (NE) Recognition: This step extracts all entities such as person names and company names. Different variations of an entity are identified through a co-reference resolution algorithm[6]. The variations are reduced to a standard form and the documents annotated using this standard form for further processing.

NVN 3-tuples extraction: An NVN 3-tuple is of the form (NC, VC, NC), where NC is a Noun Clause and VC is a Verb Clause. NC and VC are extended forms of Noun

Phrase and Verb Phrase respectively, defined by the regular expressions

NC :- $(ADJP)?(NP)^+((IN|VBG)^*(ADJP|NP))^*$
VC :- $(ADVP)?(VP)^+(IN|ADVP)^*(VP)^*$

where ADJP is an adjective, NP is a noun phrase, IN is a preposition, VBG is a Verb gerund, ADVP is an adverb and VP is a verb phrase. The NVN 3-tuples will be ultimately used to generate the Synset and Rels parts of the concept frames.

As a first step in the extraction, text is tagged using an in-house developed Part-of-Speech (POS) tagger. Then we employ a rulebase to extract the NVN 3-tuples. (The rulebase is constructed through interactive learning.) Then, the NC's are sense disambiguated and then the synsets learned through a concept unification algorithm, as described below.

Sense Disambiguation: Our word sense disambiguation (WSD) algorithm is a variant of the Lesk's algorithm [3], one of the best performing unsupervised WSD algorithms. The algorithm chooses the sense of the target word whose dictionary definition and the context of the word in the given text passage have the most number of words in common.

Concept Unification: In this step, we group the disambiguated NC's and VC's through clustering. We employ a fuzzy ART[1] based clustering algorithm. A fuzzy ART system consists of a field F_1 that receives both bottom-up input from the input field and top-down input from a field, F_2, that represents the active code or category. Fuzzy ART formulates recognition categories of input patterns by encoding each input pattern into a category node in an unsupervised manner. Thus each category node in F_2 field encodes a cluster of patterns. Hence, the clustering problem translates to the problem of the creation of new categories in the F_2 field as more patterns are presented. In our problem, the input patterns correspond to the NC's. Each NC is converted to a vector form for processing by ART. All key terms (omitting stop words) are extracted from the part-of-speech information to form a weight vector, $\mathbf{c} = (c_1, c_2, \ldots, c_M)$, where M denotes the number of features extracted and c_i denotes the term frequency for term $i, i = 1, \cdots, M$. The vector is then normalized by dividing all elements with $max_i\{c_i\}$.

Frame Filling: Each cluster generated above is mapped to a concept frame through a Frame Filling algorithm. In this algorithm, the cluster members are first collected to form the synset. Then, by identifying the synset to which the agent and object NC's of an NVN tuple belong to and replacing them with the corresponding cluster ID's, the NVN 3-tuples are generalized to form the Rels. The Contexts field is formed by collecting the sentence fragments corresponding to each relation tuple. A key subphrase is extracted from the most dominant member of the synset as the name of the frame.

Step 1. Let $G = \{F_1, F_2, ..., F_M\}$, where F_i denotes the i-th concept frame, be the CFG to be mined.

Step 2. Let t be the term denoting the area and N be the number of top companies desired.

Step 3. For each $i = 1, ..., M$
Begin
  - score t against every element in the Synset of F_i
  - let s_i be the average score
End

Step 4. Let $m = arg\ min_i\ s_i$

Step 5. Let L be a list of all organization entities in the Synset and Rels of F_m, along with their term frequencies.

Step 6. Sort the entities in L based on term frequency.

Step 7. Output the top N entities having frequency ≥ 2, as the top companies.

Table 1. Algorithm TopOrgs1.

4. CFG Mining

The graph structure of CFG can be manipulated directly to perform a variety of knowledge discovery tasks. In this paper we investigate this aspect of CFG on a specific task of discovering the top companies in an area. That is, given an area, say *Linux*, the task is to mine the CFG to come up with a list of top N companies in this area. Table 1 presents an algorithm to accomplish this task. The idea behind the algorithm is to identify the concept that best matches the area and analyze this concept and relationships with its neighbours.

Note that the mining task becomes much simpler to tackle, once we have captured the text content in the form of a CFG.

Algorithm TopOrgs1 explores the matched concept and its immediate neighbours. If a target company name appears along with the area name in the same sentence, then this relation would have been captured (assuming there is a rule match) in the CFG and hence the company accounted for. However, if the company and area relationship spans across sentences, then this algorithm will miss out these companies. In fact, if the No. 1 company appears more often in such indirect relations and the No. 2 company appears more often in first-order relations, then the ranking done by this algorithm will be incorrect.

To overcome this limitation, we propose another algorithm, called TopOrgs2, that attempts to capture the second-order relations. It is presented in Table 2.

Algorithm TopOrgs2 is identical to Algorithm TopOrgs1 except for an additional step (Step 6) before sorting the entities. In this step, the list of candidate companies is enlarged

Step 1. Let $G = \{F_1, F_2, ..., F_M\}$, be the CFG to be mined.

Step 2. Let t be the term denoting the area and N be the number of top companies desired.

Step 3. For each $i = 1, ..., M$
Begin
  - score t against every element in the Synset of F_i
  - let s_i be the average score
End

Step 4. Let $m = arg\ min_i\ s_i$

Step 5. Let L be a list of all organization entities in the Synset and Rels of F_m, along with their term frequencies.

Step 6. For each rel in Rels of F_m
If rel is from/to an organization or person concept,
  - Add all organization entities from this concept to L and update it.
End If

Step 7. Sort the entities in L based on term frequency.

Step 8. Output the top N entities having frequency ≥ 2, as the top companies.

Table 2. Algorithm TopOrgs2.

by expanding the immediate neighbours and analyzing their synsets and rels. During this expansion, we consider only the neighbours that correspond to organization and person entities. The reason is to minimize spurious terms companies being added to the candidate list.

5. Experiments

In our experiments, we first evaluate the ability of CFG to accurately capture selected concepts and relations from the text collection. We then investigate the effectiveness of analyzing the CFG for knowledge discovery. The experiments have been done on a SUN UltraSPARC 60 workstation.

We have chosen to perform the experiments on a custom built technology news collection grabbed from CNet Asia (http://asia.cnet.com). We have tagged the documents using a schema that captures the concepts of organizations, locations, products and employees, and their inter-relations. The corpus is available for free download[4].

5.1. CFG Extraction

5.1.1. Concept Extraction In this task, we consider the problem of extracting three classes of concepts, namely ORGANIZATION, PERSON, and LOCATION, from the text collection. Given a set of text documents, the system is evaluated on its ability to correctly identify these entities. The

Entity	Precision	Recall
ORGANIZATION	0.43	0.66
PERSON	0.64	0.54
LOCATION	0.51	0.77

Table 3. Performance in extracting concepts.

Relation	Precision	Recall
EMPLOYEE-OF	0.85	0.41
LOCATION-OF	0.63	0.30

Table 4. Performance in extracting relations.

system performance was measured by *precision* (the portion of correct entities among the entities identified), and *recall* (the portion of entities identified among the target entities). The performance for extracting ORGANIZATION, PERSON, and LOCATION concepts are summarized in Table 3. We note that the precision and recall scores are average, and not so encouraging. As concept extraction relies heavily on the black-box Name Entity Recognition (NER) engine, we believe a significant performance improvement can be obtained if we can customize the NER engine using the training documents of the domain.

5.1.2. Relation Extraction In this task, we investigate the ability of our system in extracting two classes of relations, namely EMPLOYEE-OF and LOCATION-OF. The performance results for this task are presented in Table 4. Whereas there is a significant drop in *recall*, *precision* has improved dramatically, compared with those for concept extraction. This indicates that the system is capable of identifying at least a portion of the relations with a reasonable level of accuracy.

5.2. CFG Mining

Here we investigate the performance of Algorithms TopOrgs1 and TopOrgs2 on our corpus.

We first ranked all the ORGANIZATION entities by counting their occurrences in the whole of test set. Then we selected five technology areas and identified the top five companies in each area from ranked list by manual inspection. The top companies identified for each area are presented in Table 5. With this as the reference, we compute precision and recall for the top five companies discovered by algorithms TopOrgs1 and TopOrgs2. The results are presented in Table 6.

We observe that algorithm TopOrgs1 performed at an overall precision of 0.64 and recall of 0.56. Algorithm TopOrgs2, which makes use of the graph structure of CFG, performed at 0.76 precision and 0.76 recall, showing a 18

Area	Companies
Chip	Intel, AMD, Nvidia, Lucent, Texas Instruments
PDA	Palm, HP, Compaq, HandSpring, Fossil
Linux	Red Hat, Lindows, SuSe, Turbolinux, Montavista
Music	Napster, Real Networks, Kazaa, Music city, Lime Wire
Mobile Phone	Nokia, Motorola, Samsung, Ericsson, Siemens

Table 5. Reference Top companies.

Area	TopOrgs1		TopOrgs2	
	P	R	P	R
Chip	0.8	0.6	0.8	0.8
PDA	0.6	0.4	0.8	0.8
Linux	0.6	0.6	0.8	0.8
Music	0.4	0.4	0.6	0.6
Mobile phone	0.8	0.8	0.8	0.8
Average	0.64	0.56	0.76	0.76

Table 6. Summary of performance on mining top companies.

% improvement in precision and 35 % improvement in recall. Thus we conclude that exploiting the graph structure of CFG can indeed lead to better mining performance.

References

[1] G. A. Carpenter, G. Grossberg, and D. B. Rosen. Fuzzy ART: Fast stable learning and categorization of analog patterns by an adaptive resonance system. *Neural Networks*, 4:759–771, 1991.

[2] R. Feldman and I. Dagan. Knowledge discovery in textual databases. In *Proceedings, KDD*, pages 112–117, 1995.

[3] M. Lesk. Automatic sense disambiguation using machine readable dictionaries: How to tell a pine cone from an ice cream cone. In *Proceedings, SIGDOC*, pages 24–26, 1986.

[4] K. Rajaraman. I2R TM corpus. URL: http://textmining.i2r.a-star.edu.sg/people/kanagasa/tmcorpus, 2002.

[5] J. F. Sowa. *Conceptual Structures: Information Processing in Mind and Machine*. Addison-Wesley, MA, 1984.

[6] G. Zhou and J. Su. Named entity recognition using a HMM-based chunk tagger. In *Proceedings, ACL*, pages 473–480, 2002.

Impact Studies and Sensitivity Analysis in Medical Data Mining with ROC-based Genetic Learning

Michèle Sebag   Jérôme Azé   Noël Lucas

PCRI, CNRS UMR 86-23, Université Paris-Sud Orsay, 91405 France

{ Michele.Sebag, Jerome.Aze, Noel.Lucas} @lri.fr

Abstract

ROC curves have been used for a fair comparison of machine learning algorithms since the late 90's. Accordingly, the area under the ROC curve (AUC) is nowadays considered a relevant learning criterion, accommodating imbalanced data, misclassification costs and noisy data.

This paper shows how a genetic algorithm-based optimization of the AUC criterion can be exploited for impact studies and sensitivity analysis.

The approach is illustrated on the Atherosclerosis Identification problem, PKDD 2002 Challenge.

1 Introduction

A novel criterion has been proposed in the late 90's for evaluating and comparing classifiers, based on the Receiver Operating Characteristics (ROC) curve [2, 11, 9].

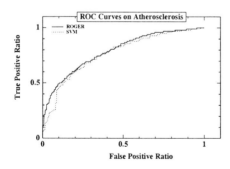

Figure 1. ROC Curves of *ROGER* **and SVM-Torch on Atherosclerosis Identification**

ROC curves, originated from signal processing and popularized from Medical Data Analysis, represent the tradeoff between the true positive rate *vs* the false positive rate over the (interpretations of) hypotheses (Fig. 1). Though ROC curves have been extended to multi-class concepts [8], only binary concepts will be considered in the rest of the paper.

It comes naturally to define the best hypothesis, as the hypothesis with maximal area under the ROC curve (AUC). Note that the optimization of the AUC criterion is a mixed, continuous and combinatorial, optimization problem. This optimization problem has been tackled using greedy search, learning decision trees [4], and genetic algorithms, learning neural nets [7] or linear hypotheses [12].

This paper focuses on providing the expert with Impact Study and Sensitivity Analysis facilities, describing how the various factors/descriptors of the problem contribute to the concept at hand. The point is to build an easy-to-interpret and yet precise picture of the factor impacts, as a first step toward Visual Data Mining.

To this aim, we exploit a genetic ROC-based learner named *ROGER*, first described in [12], which is briefly summarized in Section 2 for the sake of self-containedness. The Impact Study facilities are illustrated in Section 3, on the Atherosclerosis Identification problem presented for the PKDD Challenge 2002, showing the influence of the tobacco and alcohol factors on the risk of atherosclerosis and cardio-vascular diseases.

The paper ends with some perspectives for further research. The approach is believed to be particularly appropriate to Medical Data Mining for two reasons. On one hand, by construction ROC curves do not suffer from difficulties such as imbalanced class distributions, noisy examples, and cost-sensitive problems, which are commonly encountered in medical domains (and in other domains as well, see [6]). On the other hand, medical experts are used to handle and interpret ROC curves.

2 Learning with AUC

This section presents the *ROGER* algorithm, referring the interested reader to [12] for more details.

Let the dataset be noted $\mathcal{E} = \{(x_i, y_i), i = 1 \ldots n, x_i \in X, y_i \in \{1, -1\}\}$, where X denotes the instance space.

The hypothesis space $\mathcal{H}$ considered in the following, inspired from margin-oriented learners such as Support Vector Machines [14] or bagging [3] and boosting [13], is the set of real-valued hypotheses, mapping the instance space X onto $\mathbb{R}$. Each hypothesis h in $\mathcal{H}$ induces by thresholding a family of binary classifiers $\{h_t, t \in \mathbb{R}\}$, with $h_t(x) = 1$ if $h(x) > t$ and -1 otherwise.

It is straightforward to see that the true positive and the false positive rates of h_t monotonically increase as t decreases. Let us define the performance of the real-valued hypothesis h as the area under the ROC curve (AUC) associated to the set of binary classifiers h_t.

Learning can thus be achieved by optimizing the AUC criterion, which is a mixed, continuous and combinatorial optimization problem as the ROC curve depends on the order induced by h on the examples.

This optimization problem is therefore tackled using evolutionary computation techniques, which are population-based stochastic optimization algorithms, roughly inspired from the natural evolution of biological populations and Darwinian principles [1].

Assuming the reader's familiarity with canonical genetic algorithms (GA), we only detail *ROGER* specificities for the sake of reproducibility.

The fitness function computing the AUC criterion is described in Table 1 (normalization is omitted as of no effect on the optimization problem).

Fitness function of hypothesis h

Input
Data set $\mathcal{E} = \{(x_i, y_i), i = 1 \ldots n, x_i \in X, y_i \in \{1, -1\}\}$
Hypothesis $h : X \mapsto \mathbb{R}$
Init
Sort $\mathcal{E} = \{(x_i, y_i)\}$ by decreasing order, where $i > j$
iff $(h(x_i) > h(x_j))$ or $((h(x_i) = h(x_j)$ and $(y_i > y_j))$.
$p = 0$
$\mathcal{F} = 0$
For $i = 1$ to n
if $y_i = 1$, increment p;
else $\mathcal{F} = \mathcal{F} + p$
EndFor
Return $\mathcal{F}$

Table 1. Area Under the Roc Curve of h

At the moment, *ROGER* is restricted to attribut-value languages and linear hypotheses. Its extension to more complex instance and hypothesis languages is a perspective for further research. Formally, the instance space X is set to $\mathbb{R}^d$, where any nominal attribute with k modalities is handled as k boolean attributes. The hypothesis search space $\mathcal{H}$ is similarly set to $\mathbb{R}^d$; hypothesis h, a weighted sum of the attributes, is a vector in $\mathbb{R}^d$.

The optimisation of the fitness function $\mathcal{F}$ on $\mathcal{H} = \mathbb{R}^d$ is performed using evolution strategies (ES) [1]. The main difference compared to canonical GAs regards the mutation operator, specifically tailored to numerical optimization. Mutation, used with probability 1, perturbs the i-th component of individual h by addition of a Gaussian noise $\mathcal{N}(0, \sigma_i)$. We used self-adaptive mutation, where the genetic material of the individual incorporates the standard deviations σs (the individual thus belongs to $\mathbb{R}^{2d}$); this way, evolution automatically adjusts the mutation amplitude along generations, for each individual. The reader is referred to [1] for an exhaustive presentation of self adaptive mutation.

We use the $(\mu + \lambda) - ES$ selection/replacement mechanism; μ parents generate λ offspring, and the best individuals among the μ parents + λ offspring are selected as parents for the next generation.

For space limitations, the interested reader is referred to [12] for a comparative validation on benchmark problems from the Irvine repository; compared to Support Vector Machines, *ROGER* show similar performances within a fraction of the computational effort.

3 Impact Studies and Sensitivity Analysis

This section focuses on exploiting the by-products of *ROGER* for a visual inspection of the data, particularly the impact of various factors on the concept at hand. The approach is illustrated on the PKDD 2002 Challenge page[1], concerned with the identification of risk factors for atherosclerosis and cardio-vascular diseases (CVD).

3.1 The data and learning goal

Two databases have been made publicly available for the PKDD2002 Challenge. The Entry database describes the personal and family case for 1419 middle aged men. These men are classified into three groups; the pathologic group includes all men with manifested cardio-vascular or other malignant diseases; other men are respectively classified in the normal or high risk group, depending on their (family-related or personal) risk factors.

This database involves 219 attributes, most of which are sparingly informed (e.g. a Myocardial Infarction for the patient's Fourth Sister appears 4 times in the whole dataset). The data preparation, summarizing the family case, toxicological (alcohol and tobacco) ingestion, and bio-chemical exams into 28 boolean and numerical attributes, has been described in detail in [10].

The Control database presents the longitudinal study over 20 years of a sample of men belonging to the normal and high risk groups.

---

[1] http://lisp.vse.cz/challenge/ecmlpkdd2002/

3.2 Experimental setting

Using the medical expertise of the third author, all men were divided into three classes according to their health state at the end of the medical campaign: healthy, ill, and other (the later includes all men not considered in the Control database, and those who disappeared from the study)[2].

Eventually the goal is to predict from the individual description given in the Entry database, his health state after twenty years.

The dataset is splitted into a 2/3 training set and 1/3 test set with same class distribution as the global dataset, and 11 independent splits are considered.

On each training set, 21 independent *ROGER* runs are launched (with same parameters as for all benchmark problems, given in Table 2). The ROC curve of the best hypothesis extracted by *ROGER* is evaluated on the test set, and the median of all ROC curves is displayed in Fig 1. The baseline reference is given by the state-of-the art SVMTorch algorithm, with default parameters and linear kernel. The separating hyperplane $h(\vec{x}) = \vec{w}.\vec{x} + b$ is also evaluated from its median ROC curve on the test sets (Fig. 1).

As already noted by [11], the representativity of the median ROC curve is difficult to assess since different portions of the curve correspond to distinct hypotheses. However, the general trend is confirmed from the comparison of the min and max ROC curves obtained for both algorithms.

population size	# parents μ	10
	# offspring λ	50
max nb evaluations		10,000
crossover	uniform	rate .6
mutation	self-adaptive	rate 1

Table 2. *ROGER* parameters

ROGER shows good performances, with an average AUC of .79 $\pm$.012 to be compared with .76 $\pm$.045 for SVMTorch.

Interestingly, the main difference between the two curves occurs close to the origin. It appears that some negative examples are classified as positive with high confidence by SVMTorch. Indeed, SVMs make no difference between misclassified examples provided that their confidence is above the cost threshold; and one would not increase the cost threshold too much, as this would increase the sensitivity to noise of the algorithm. In contrast, the AUC criterion offers a finer-grained evaluation of misclassifications, as the cost of an error actually depends on its rank; improving the example order, even in extreme regions, is rewarded. Accordingly, the *True Positive* rate increases abruptly at the beginning of the *ROGER* curve: individuals classified as the

---

[2]The prepared dataset is available at http://www.lri.fr/~aze/PKDD2002/.

most at risk are on average in bad shape. In medical terms, the sensibility of the *ROGER* hypothesis is better compared to SVMTorch on this problem.

3.3 Impact Studies

A well known limitation of SVMs (also incurred by *ROGER*) is that it does not provide an easy-to-read hypothesis, although in many domains the expert needs a readable hypothesis about the concept at hand even more than an accurate predictor.

An alternative to the analytic inspection of hypotheses is offered by diagrammatic representations, as investigated in Visual Data Mining [5]. Along these lines, we explore some graphical interpretations of the *ROGER* hypotheses.

A first graphical exploitation concerns the impact study, analyzing the contribution of a given feature on the concept under examination; this contribution is classically measured by its correlation with the concept or its quantity of information.

It is shown that *ROGER* hypotheses (and more generally, any ordered hypothesis) provide a more detailed, intuitive and yet precise picture, about the contribution of a feature (attribute, function of attributes). As an example, let us investigate the impacts of the tobacco and alcohol intoxication on atherosclerosis risk factors.

These impacts are graphically assessed, using the following protocol.

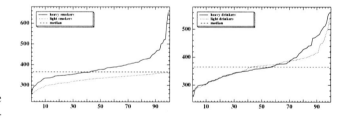

Figure 2. Comparative influence of Tobacco and Alcohol on Atherosclerosis

For each feature (here, an attribute), the 10% individuals in the test set with maximal (resp. minimal) values for this attribute, are considered. In both subsets, the individuals are ranked by increasing value of h, and the curves $(i, h(x_i))$ are displayed.

Each curve shows globally the risk range for the individuals with high (resp. low) intoxication (though the risk might be due to other factors, correlated with the intoxication). It is believed that such curves convey a lot more information than the correlation factor or quantity of information.

Furthermore, they allow for an intuitive and straight forward comparison of the factors, by superposing the curves. For instance, the impact of tobacco can be argued from the fact that the non-smoking individuals all lie in the better half of the population (their risk is less than the median risk). The heavy smoker risk is always higher than for non-smokers; 2/3 of the heavy smokers show an above-average risk and the risk rises sharply for the worst 20% of the heavy smokers.

The apparently lesser impact of alcohol must be taken with care. On one hand, it is true that a small amount of red wine was found beneficial against some cardio-vascular diseases. On the other hand it appears that, the population considered as "light drinker" ... was not so lightly drinking.

3.4 Sensitivity Analysis

The multiplicity of optimal solutions for the AUC criterion and/or the variability of stochastic optimization, can also be exploited for feature selection and more generally sensitivity analysis. Let us represent a model h as a curve i, w_i, where i stands for the index of the attribute and w_i is the associated weight. Fig. 3 displays the 21 models learned from the total dataset, showing that some attributes play a major role for the target concept (typically the tobacco factor, attribute 9). Conversely, some other attributes can be considered as weakly relevant at best. Last, the inspection of the curves suggests that some attributes might be inversely correlated, hinting at the creation of compound attributes.

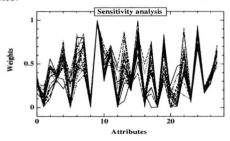

Figure 3. Sensitivity analysis

4 Conclusion and Perspectives

This paper presents some exploitations of the genetic ROC-based learner *ROGER*, allowing for a visual inspection of the hypotheses. The inspection is at the moment limited to the impact studies and sensitivity analysis. It has been argued that such a visual inspection provides a harvest of precise information in a compact and readable way.

Further research is concerned with extending *ROGER* to more complex instance and hypothesis languages, using for instance kernel representations. In parallel, the sensitivity analysis will be exploited for feature selection and construction.

Acknowledgment

Our thanks go to Dr Maria Temeckova and R. Collobert, for their valuable data and algorithm free resources.

We also warmly thank M.-C. Jaulent, Dr. I. Colombet, Dr. F. Gueyffier and Pr. G. Chatellier, for strong pluridisciplinary interactions.

References

[1] T. Bäeck. *Evolutionary Algorithms in theory and practice*. New-York:Oxford University Press, 1995.

[2] A. Bradley. The use of the area under the ROC curve in the evaluation of machine learning algorithms. *Pattern Recognition*, 1997.

[3] L. Breiman. Arcing classifiers. *Annals of Statistics*, 26(3):801–845, 1998.

[4] P. Flach, C. Ferri and J. Hernández-Orallo. Learning decision trees using the area under the ROC curve. In *Proc. of the 19th Int. Conf. on Machine Learning*, pages 179–186, Morgan Kaufmann, 2002.

[5] S. K. Card, J. D. Mackinlay, and B. Shneiderman. *Information Visualization: Using vision to think*. Morgan Kaufmann, 1999.

[6] P. Domingos. Meta-cost: A general method for making classifiers cost sensitive. In *Knowledge Discovery from Databases*, pages 155–164. Morgan Kaufmann, 1999.

[7] D. B. Fogel, E. C. Wasson, E. M. Boughton, V. W. Porto, and P. J. Angeline. Linear and neural models for classifying breast cancer. *IEEE Trans. Medical Imaging*, 17(3):485–488, 1998.

[8] D. Hand and R. Till. A simple generalisation of the area under the ROC curve for multiple class classification problems. *Machine Learning*, 45(2):171–186, 2001.

[9] C. Ling, J. Hunag, and H. Zhang. Auc: a better measure than accuracy in comparing learning algorithms. In *Proc. of 16th Canadian Conference on AI 2003*, 2003.

[10] N. Lucas, J. Azé, and M. Sebag. Atherosclerosis risk identification and visual analysis. In *Discovery Challenge ECML-PKDD*. http://lisp.vse.cz/challenge/ecmlpkdd2002/, 2002.

[11] F. Provost, T. Fawcett, and R. Kohavi. The case against accuracy estimation for comparing classifiers. In *Proc. of the 15th Int. Conf. on Machine Learning*, pages 445–553. Morgan Kaufmann, 1998.

[12] M. Sebag, J. Azé, and N. Lucas. Roc-based evolutionary learning. Application to medical data mining. In P. Liardet et al., editors, *Artificial Evolution'03*. Springer Verlag, 2004.

[13] R. Shapire, Y. Freund, P.Bartlett, and W. Lee. Boosting the margin: a new explanation for the effectiveness of voting methods. In *Proc. of the 14th Int. Conf. on Machine Learning*, pages 322–330. Morgan Kaufmann, 1997.

[14] V. N. Vapnik. *Statistical Learning Theory*. Wiley, 1998.

K-D Decision Tree:
An Accelerated and Memory Efficient Nearest Neighbor Classifier

Tomoyuki Shibata, Takekazu Kato and Toshikazu Wada
Faculty of Systems Engineering, Wakayama University
{shibata,twada,tkato}@vrl.sys.wakayama-u.ac.jp

Abstract

Most nearest neighbor (NN) classifiers employ NN search algorithms for the acceleration. However, NN classification does not always require the NN search. Based on this idea, we propose a novel algorithm named k-d decision tree (KDDT). Since KDDT uses Voronoi condensed prototypes, it is less memory consuming than naive NN classifiers. We have confirmed that KDDT is much faster than NN search based classifiers through the comparative experiment (from 9 to 369 times faster).

1. Introduction

The nearest neighbor (NN) classifier [1] was proposed in 1967, and it still has the following attractive properties.

1. Its error probability is less than the twice of ideal Bayesian error probability, if sufficient number of training samples are given.
2. It does not require the knowledge on the pattern distribution.
3. As contrasted with Support Vector Machine (SVM) [12] and ADA Boosting [13], it performs maximum-margin classification without using predetermined kernel functions or base classifiers.
4. It can naturally be applied to multiclass classification problems.

However, the NN classifier is not regarded as a practical classifier, because of its inefficient memory use and poor classification speed.

Basically, the NN classifier stores all training samples for better classification. The solution of this wasteful memory consumption is investigated in two directions [11]. Condensing[9][10] removes prototypes while keeping the classification performance, and editing [3][4][5][6][7][8] attempts to remove erroneous training samples. The classification speed, however, is not drastically improved by these methods.

For the acceleration, a NN search engine, such as, k-d tree [14], is employed as shown in Figure 1. In this realization of the NN classifier, the prototype nearest to

the input pattern is found by the search engine. Then, the input is classified into the same class with that prototype. This is sufficient but somewhat redundant.

This paper presents an accelerated and memory efficient Nearest Neighbor (NN) classifier named k-d decision tree (KDDT). KDDT is based on the box decomposition of the pattern space (Figure 2). Each decomposed box is labeled *"unsafe"* or *"safe"* depending on whether the classification boundary intersects with the box or not. Since the class labels are embedded in the safe boxes, input patterns that fall into them are immediately classified. Those input patterns captured by unsafe boxes are classified by *local NN search* that finds the nearest prototype to the input pattern in the local prototype set, which defines the local decision boundary.

The box decomposition is represented by a binary tree, which is used for searching the box that includes the input pattern. In this binary search, a higher tree consumes longer search time. For solving this problem, our method merges the adjacent safe boxes into a bigger box. This reduces the depths of the safe leaves and the search time.

As described above, KDDT simply performs binary search, and local NN search is additionally performed for special patterns. This enables drastic speedup of the NN pattern classification. Furthermore, KDDT is less memory consuming than the naive NN classifiers, because it uses Voronoi condensed prototypes [9] and the prototypes in the safe boxes are removed after the tree construction.

In the following sections, KDDT is introduced in Section 2, and experimental results are shown in Section 3.

2. KDDT and its components

In this section, we describe the components of KDDT.

2.1. Box Decomposition

The box decomposition employed in KDDT is based on the balanced box-decomposition (BBD) tree 0. The BBD recursively partitions a given box by performing not

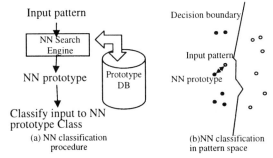

Input pattern

NN Search Engine

NN prototype

Prototype DB

Classify input to NN prototype Class

(a) NN classification procedure

Decision boundary

Input pattern

NN prototype

(b) NN classification in pattern space

Figure 1: NN search based classifier

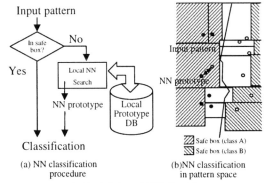

Input pattern

In safe box?

No

Yes

Local NN Search

NN prototype

Local Prototype DB

Classification

(a) NN classification procedure

Input pattern

NN prototype

Safe box (class A)
Safe box (class B)

(b) NN classification in pattern space

Figure 2: KDDT based NN classifier

only *splitting* but also *shrinking*, which creates nested boxes. Since our purpose is disjoint decomposition of the pattern space, we don't use the shrinking operation. For the splitting, a rule called *sliding-midpoint rule* provided by the ANN library 0 is employed.

The *midpoint split rule* simply cuts the current box through its midpoint orthogonal to the longest side. If the split operation produces empty and non-empty boxes, then the splitting plane is translated so that the empty box becomes non-empty box. This rule is called *sliding-midpoint rule..*

By applying the above splitting method, the pattern space containing training samples is partitioned into disjoint boxes that include each single training samples.

2.2. Safe/Unsafe Labeling

As shown in Figure 3 (a), the classification boundary is determined by mutually nearest prototypes belonging to different classes. These prototypes can be found by Voronoi condensing that extract the generators of adjacent Voronoi regions belonging to different classes.

In Figure 3 (a), training samples on a dotted circle are mutually nearest points belonging to different classes. Centers of these dotted circles coincide with the corner points of the decision boundary. We call these points *knots*. Of course, knots are the subset of Voronoi vertices.

Since the knots are on the classification boundary, it is clear that

a) All boxes involving knots are unsafe (see Figure 3(b)).

An unsafe box detected by this rule stores all prototypes nearest to the knot as local prototypes.

Since the Voronoi condensed prototypes define the classification boundary, the following property stands.

b) Boxes that do not contain Voronoi condensed prototypes are safe (Box1,2,4 in Figure3 (a)).

There is another type of unsafe box having no Voronoi vertex inside (see Figure 3 (c)). For analyzing this case, we use the following notations:

● Distance between point P_1 and P_2 : $d(P_1, P_2)$,

● Point inside the box: P_b,

● Box vertices: v_{bi} $(i = 1, 2, \cdots)$,

● Points connected with P_b by each single Delauney edges having different class label(s): P_{ok} $(k = 1, 2, \cdots)$.

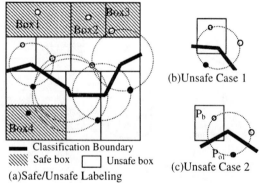

Figure 3: Safe and Unsafe Boxes

(a)Safe/Unsafe Labeling

■ Classification Boundary
▨ Safe box ☐ Unsafe box

(b)Unsafe Case 1

(c)Unsafe Case 2

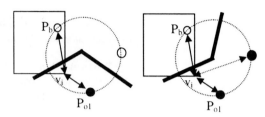

Figure 4: Unsafe Case2

● Hyperplane orthogonal to the line segment $\overline{P_1 P_2}$ and passing its mid point: $H(P_1, P_2)$,

NN classifier has a piecewise linear classification boundary consists of hyperplanes. The hyperplanes nearest to P_b are denoted as $H(P_b, P_{ok})$ $(k = 1, 2, \cdots)$.

In the case that a box includes P_b, if all the box vertices v_{bi} $(i = 1, 2, \cdots)$ are located in the same half space separated by $H(P_b, P_{ok})$, the hyperplane does not intersect with this box. This property can be applied to determining the safe box. Practically, we use the following equivalent rule for determining the unsafe box.

c)   If $^{\exists i,k} d(v_{bi}, P_b) \geq d(v_{bi}, P_{ok})$ then the box is unsafe (see Figure 4).

In this case, all P_{ok} satisfying the above inequation and P_b are stored as prototypes for local NN search.

From the property (b), we can focus on the Voronoi condensed prototypes for detecting unsafe boxes. By applying the rules (a) and (c), we can extract unsafe boxes.

2.4. Merging safe boxes

In our approach, we can merge safe boxes if they form a bigger safe box. As a result of merging, the depths of the safe leaves are reduced, and hence, the binary search will be accelerated. The mergeable box is detected as a subtree in the binary tree whose leaves are all safe and labeled the same class.

2.4. Classification

Most of the NN search algorithm first guesses a NN candidate by a simple binary search. Next, it searches nearer point to the input (query point) than the current candidate. In the case of BBD tree, this verification process is called *priority search*. Figure 5 illustrates the priority search. The box containing the query point q can be found using the binary search. The data point P_b

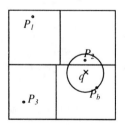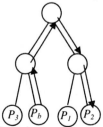

Figure 5: Priority Search

contained in this box is selected as the initial NN candidate. Other nearer neighbor may lie within the circle centered on q and passing through P_b. The priority search moves to the parent node and checks the possibility of the closer neighbor in the other child. If no closer neighbor can exist in the other child, it immediately moves up to a further level, otherwise it recursively explore the child.

Fortunately, for the classification task, we don't have to perform the priority search. Instead, KDDT examines whether the box found by the binary search is safe or unsafe. If the box is safe, it simply returns the class label embedded in the box. Otherwise, it performs local NN search for the input data with the local prototypes stored in the box.

3. Experimental Results

In the experiment, we compared the following methods:

NAIVE: NN search based classifier using all training samples as prototypes. The NN search engine is ANN.

CONDENSED: NN search based classifier using Voronoi condensed prototypes. The NN search engine is ANN.

KDDT: Proposed algorithm.

Training and test samples are generated randomly using isotropic normal distributions. The standard deviation is $\sigma = 10$ for each dimension. In all experiments we don't use the feasible error for ANN, i.e., $\varepsilon = 0$. We use the following settings as default:

Distance: Euclid Distance
Number of classes: 2
Spatial dimensions: 10
Number of training samples: 3000 (1500 for each)
Number of test samples: 100000
Distance between the distribution centers: 50 (5σ)

Except we specify the value, the above settings are used.

All experimental results described here are obtained on Pentium4 PC, 2 GHz CPU, 1 Gigabyte memory using Microsoft Visual C++.

3.1. Speed against spatial dimensions

In this experiment, we measured the elapsed time of the classifiers by changing the spatial dimensions from 2 to 20. The total elapsed time for 100000 test data is measured and the result is divided by 100000. The result is shown in Figure 6. From this figure, we can notice the following properties.

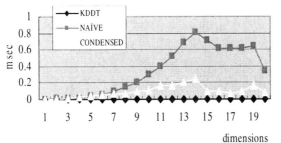

Figure 6: Elapsed time against spatial dimensions

1) NAIVE and CONDENSED classifiers slow down while the dimension increases up to 14-D. At higher dimensions than 15-D, the classification times are improved. This is because the prototypes form sparse distributions at higher dimensions and the elapsed time for priority search is reduced.

2) KDDT is incomparably faster than others. The classification time at 2-D space increases only four times at 20-D space. This implies that the classification speed of KDDT is almost insensitive to the spatial dimensions.

This might be the result of the leaf node reduction by merging safe nodes. Comparing with other methods, at 13-D, KDDT is 369 times faster than NAIVE classifier and 111 times faster than CONDENSED classifier. Even in the worst case at 2-D, KDDT is 11 times faster than NAIVE and 9 times faster than CONDENSED.

3.2. Speed against number of training samples

In this experiment, we measured the elapsed time by changing the number of training samples from 1000 to 10000. Figure 7 shows the result of this experiment.

From this figure, we can notice that the elapsed times of NAIVE and CONDENSED classifiers almost linearly increase by the number of training samples. However, the elapsed time of KDDT is almost flat. Actually, the elapsed time of KDDT is 0.00253ms for 1000 training samples and 0.00203 for 10000 training samples. Elapsed time of KDDT for all data is less than 0.00281ms. These imply that the classification speed of KDDT is insensitive to the number of training samples.

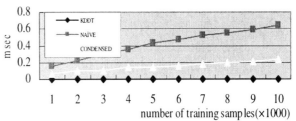

Figure 7: Elapsed time against the number of training samples

3.3. Speed against distribution proximity

In this experiment, we measured the elapsed time by changing the distance between the centers of distributions from σ to 10σ. Figure 8 shows the result. All classifiers slow down at proximal pattern distributions.

At a small distance, randomly generated training samples are mixed in wide area, and the density of

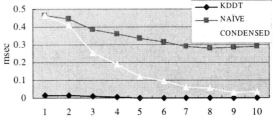

Figure 8: Elapsed time against distribution proximity

training samples between two distributions will be increased. As a result, complex classification boundary is generated.

In the case of NAIVE classifier, high density sample distribution produces higher binary tree and the elapsed time of both binary search and priority search increases. In the case of CONDENSED classifier, since Voronoi condensing cannot reduce most of the training samples at proximal pattern distributions, the classification speed is almost equivalent to the NAIVE classifier. But, in more separable case, condensing reduces useless training samples, and the classification speed becomes faster than NAIVE classifier. In the case of KDDT, the total amount of safe boxes will be shrunk and the merging seldom work at proximal pattern distributions. Even though, it is much faster than NAIVE and CONDENSED classifiers (32 times faster at σ). This might be the result of the local NN search.

Figure 9 shows the probability that input data falls into the safe boxes. This probability is computed based on the total volumes of safe and unsafe boxes. As we mentioned above, most of the input patterns fall into unsafe boxes at proximal distributions, however, at separable distributions most input patterns are captured by safe boxes. Also, the average number of local prototypes stored in a single box is 26 at σ , and 2.7 at 10σ .

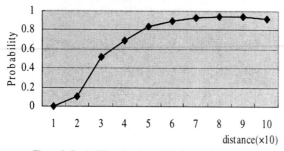

Figure 9: Probability that input falls into safe boxes

3.3. Result for other data

KDDT is also applied to Iris data (4D, 150 samples) and Wisconsin Breast Cancer Diagnosis (30D, 569 samples). In both cases, 4/5 samples are used for training and 1/5 for testing. Comparing with NAIVE classifier, KDDT is 6.4 times faster for former data and 4.2 times faster for latter.

4. Discussion

Through these experiments, we can summarize the following acceleration properties of KDDT:

Local NN search: The local NN search sustains the base performance of KDDT, which is revealed in the worst case, i.e., proximal pattern distributions. Its advantage over the standard NN search is that it can avoid time consuming verification process, such as, priority search. It simply performs brute force NN search on 26-2.7 prototypes.

Safe box labeling: In normal cases, safe box labeling accelerates KDDT algorithm by skipping local NN search.

Safe box merging: By merging the safe boxes, the depth of the safe leaf nodes is reduced. This reduction accelerates the binary search.

The combination of these three acceleration properties produces drastic speed up of NN classification.

5. Conclusions

In this paper, we propose an accelerated NN classifier, KDDT algorithm. As shown in Section 3, we have confirmed the following properties.

1) KDDT is incomparably faster than NN search based classifiers.
2) KDDT can keep almost constant speed against the spatial dimensions (2-20) and number of training samples (1000-10000).
3) KDDT slightly slows down for proximal pattern distributions, but it is still much faster than others.

These properties demonstrate the incomparable speed of the KDDT algorithm. KDDT makes the NN classifier much faster keeping its superior classification power. It means that NN classifier can be applied to real-time and/or vast data classification tasks.

KDDT still has a potential margin for further accelerations, i.e., enlarging the safe zone by adding dummy data and by changing the partitioning algorithm, and reducing the tree height by modifying the merging algorithm. These works will be done in the future works.

7. References

[1]B.K.B T.M. Cover and P.E. Hart: Nearest neighbor pattern classification, IEEE Transactions on Information Theory, Vol. IT-13, No.1, pp.21-27, (1967)

[3]P.E. Hart: The condensed nearest-neighbor rule, IEEE Transactions on Information Theory, Vol. IT-4, No. 5, pp.515-516, (1968)

[4]G. W. Gates: The Reduced Nearest Neighbor Rule, IEEE Trans. on Information Theory, Vol. IT-18, No. 3, pp.431-433, 1972

[5]G. L. Ritter, H. B. Woodruff, S. R. Lowry, and T. L. Isenhour: An algorithm for a selective nearest neighbor decision rule, IEEE Trans. on Information Theory, Vol. 21, pp. 665-669, 1975

[6]I. Tomek: A generalization of the k-nn rule, IEEE Trans. on Systems, Man and Cybernetics, Vol. 6, pp. 121-126, 1976

[7]D. W. Aha and D. Kibler: Noise-Tolerant Instance-Based Learning Algorithms, Proc. of 11th IJCAI, pp.794-799, 1989

[8]D. W. Aha, D. Kibler and M. Albert: Instance-Based Learning Algorithms, Machine Learning, Vol.6, pp. 37-66, 1991

[9]Bhattacharya, R. S. Poulsen,, G. T. Toussaint: Application of Proximity Graphs to Editing Nearest Neighbor Decision Rule, International Symposium on Information Theory, Santa Monica, (1981)

[10]B.V. Dasarathy: Minimal consistent set (MCS) identification for optimal nearest neighbor decision systems design, IEEE Transactions on Systems, Man and Cybernetics, Vol. 24, No. 3, pp.511-517, (1994)

[11]B.V. Dasarathy, J. S. Sanchez and S. Townsend: Nearest Neighbour Editing and Condensing Tools–Synergy Exploitation, Pattern Analysis & Applications, Vol. 3, pp.19-30, 2000

[12]V. N. Vapnik: The Nature of Statistical Learning Theory, Splinger, 1995

[13]Y. Freund and R. E. Schapire: A decision-theoretic generalization of on-line learning and an application to boosting, Journal of Computer and System Sciences, Vol. 55, No. 1, pp. 119-139, 1997

[14]J. L. Bentley: Multidimensional binary search trees used for associative searching, Communications of the ACM, Vol.18, No.9, 1975

[15]S. Arya, D. M. Mount, N. S. Netanyahu, R. Silverman, and A. Y. Wu, ``An optimal algorithm for approximate nearest neighbor searching,'' Journal of the ACM, Vol.45, pp. 891-923, 1998

[16]ANN: Library for Approximate Nearest Neighbor Searching (http://www.cs.umd.edu/~mount/ANN/)

Mining the Web to Discover the Meanings of an Ambiguous Word

Raz Tamir
The Hebrew University of Jerusalem
imr@netvision.net.il

Reinhard Rapp
Johannes Gutenberg-Universität Mainz
rapp@mail.fask.uni-mainz.de

Abstract[1]

In information retrieval and text mining, information on word senses is usually taken from dictionaries or lexical databases that have been prepared by lexicographers. In this paper we propose an automatic method for word sense induction, i.e. for the discovery of a set of sense descriptors to a given ambiguous word. The approach is based on the statistics of word co-occurrence as derived from web pages. The underlying assumption is that the senses of an ambiguous word are best described by terms that, although bearing a strong association to this word, are mutually exclusive, i.e. whose association strength within the retrieved web pages is as weak as possible. Measuring association strength is based upon a novel Confidence Gain approach that relates the observed co-occurrence frequency for two sense descriptor candidates to an average co-occurrence frequency for pairs of arbitrary words. The proposed approach is fully unsupervised and takes into account the contemporary meanings of words, as reflected in texts from the internet. Our results are evaluated using a list of ambiguous words commonly referred to in the literature.

1. Introduction

An important characteristic of natural languages is that they are ambiguous at many levels of processing, e.g. at the phonological, the morphological, the syntactic, and the semantic levels. Ambiguity is the main and still unresolved problem that makes the computer processing of natural languages so difficult. In comparison, the processing of programming languages, which are unambiguous by design, appears simple.

The topic of this paper is semantic ambiguity. Semantic ambiguity arises from coding two or more concepts by a single term. It is dynamic in nature as new concepts that evolve are often coded using existing terms. But ambiguity not only changes with time, it also very much depends on the domain of a text or an utterance. For these reasons, ambiguity cannot be looked at as a problem that can be solved once and for all, but that requires continuous learning. The question is how humans accomplish this, and the challenge to approach the problem by machine.

Due to the importance of the problem, many publications have dealt with the task of ambiguity resolution. Concerning word semantics, important contributions have been made, for example, in the framework of SENSEVAL, a competition where a number of word sense disambiguation systems were compared and evaluated [1]. Given an ambiguous word in context, the aim of these systems was to choose among a number of predefined senses the one that best described the semantic role of the word in the particular context. In such systems, the sets of senses are usually taken from dictionaries such as the *Longman Dictionary of Contemporary English*, or from lexical databases such as *WordNet*. These dictionaries and databases are constructed manually by lexicologists and linguists.

However, only few attempts have been made to derive the sets of possible senses automatically from corpora. Probably the first to do so was Arns [2]. On the basis of a simple co-occurrence measure, she clustered typical associations to ambiguous words and hoped to obtain clusters corresponding to each meaning. This method seemed to work in principle, but the results were insufficient for practical purposes. We believe that other measures for associative strength, such as TF/IDF, log-likelihood, mutual information [3] and in particular the confidence gain measure that we introduce here, can yield significantly better results, especially if applied to very large corpora.

Whereas Arns clustered only typical associations to an ambiguous word (local clustering [4]), other researchers – most notably Pantel and Lin [5] – tried to cluster all words in a corpus (global clustering) according to some semantically motivated distance measure. These attempts can be interpreted as inducing word senses, as long as the clustering algorithm used allows a word to belong to more than one cluster. In this case, each cluster to which a word belongs can be considered as one of its senses.

The approach suggested here is to discard the clustering for a method based on the assumption that terms related to the different meanings of a given ambiguous word have low mutual association strength. To give an example, let us look at the ambiguous word *bank* with its *money* and *river* senses. We observe that the context of bank contains words representative for both meanings, e.g. *institute*, *interest*, and *account* for the *money* sense and *sand*, *water*, and *beach* for the *river* sense. We now assume that the meanings of an ambiguous word are best

---

[1] This research was in part supported by the DFG.

described by those of its significant associates whose association strength to each other is as low as possible, because in those contexts of *bank* where the word *money* occurs it is unlikely that we also find the word *river* and vice versa. So it can be expected that word pairs that belong to different senses, e.g. *money – river* or *interest – beach*, have a low mutual association strength. It turns out that this approach works surprisingly well, as will be shown in the remainder of this paper.

2. Measuring association strength

Since the algorithm is based on a similarity measure relying on word co-occurrences, textual data is required from which the co-occurrence counts can be derived. A valuable source of such data that is constantly updated and expanded is the World Wide Web. Since the number of documents in the web is so large and since web pages have a considerable variation concerning topic and style, it is likely that the senses that we are looking for are actually represented in the web.

A difficulty with measuring association strength between pairs of words is that word frequencies can vary over several orders of magnitude, which makes it problematic to use the co-occurrence counts directly. For this reason, many previous studies somehow relate the observed co-occurrence frequencies to some theoretically expected co-occurrence frequency. Possible measures are, for example, TF/IDF, the log-likelihood ratio, and mutual information [3]. However, all these measures have the disadvantage that for the computation of the expected co-occurrence frequencies certain theoretical assumptions on the statistical distribution of the words in a language have to be made, e.g. statistical independence between words, normal distribution, Poisson distribution, or the like. The problem with these assumptions is that they are not well justified, as the statistical distribution that underlies human language is still under discussion [6].

Our conclusion from this situation is that since no well-justified theory is available, we should try to find a measure that is not based on a theoretically expected distribution but instead uses distributional data extracted from the corpus. For implementation of this idea, a novel measure called *Confidence Gain* was developed [7]. Simply speaking, it compares the observed co-occurrence frequency for a particular pair of words to an average co-occurrence frequency for a representative sample of other word pairs. A formal description of the confidence gain measure is derived below.

Given a stimulus word X and another word Y (called *associative response*), two well defined measures describe the degree of support (Supp) and confidence (Conf) of the association between them:

[1]
$$Supp(X \Rightarrow Y) = Supp(X \cup Y) = \frac{\|X \& Y\|}{w}$$
$$Conf(X \Rightarrow Y) = \frac{Supp(X \cup Y)}{Supp(X)}$$

In this formula, w is the total number of scanned web pages, $\|X \& Y\|$ is the number of web pages containing both X and Y, and Supp(X) is the fraction of pages in the world wide web that contain word X. For a fixed stimulus, Conf is a function of all possible responses Y.

The average confidence of response Y, $\overline{Conf(Y)}$, is calculated as follows:

[2]
$$\overline{Conf(Y)} = \frac{1}{n} \sum_{i=1}^{n} \frac{Supp(I_i \cup Y)}{Supp(I_i)}$$

Hereby, n is the number of valid instances. An instance is valid if support and confidence are above certain thresholds. Given the above definitions, the confidence gain measure (CG) is a function of both X and Y:

[3]
$$CG(X \Rightarrow Y) = \frac{Conf(X \Rightarrow Y)}{Conf(Y)} = n \cdot \frac{\dfrac{Supp(X \cup Y)}{Supp(X)}}{\sum_{i=1}^{n} \dfrac{Supp(I_i \cup Y)}{Supp(I_i)}}$$

This formula implies that the co-occurrence frequency of a stimulus/response pair is compared to an average co-occurrence frequency of other word pairs. In these other word pairs the response is always the original one and only the stimulus varies. It cannot be the other way round because our aim is to get a ranked list of responses to a given stimulus word. The asymmetry in the formula leads to asymmetric association strengths, i.e. using X as stimulus and Y as response yields a different CG-value from using Y as stimulus and X as response. This is in agreement with human associative behavior, which has also been found to be asymmetric [8].

3. Algorithm for word sense induction

Our algorithm uses the API of the well-known *Google* search engine for retrieving relevant documents from the World Wide Web. Words that frequently occur in these documents are considered as sense descriptor candidates. Assuming that the given ambiguous word has two main senses, all possible candidate pairs[2] are created and ranked according to the following formula:

---

[2] Please note that by considering triples, quadruples, etc. the method could also be applied to words with three or more senses. However, since the problem of sense induction is hard enough for two senses, in this paper we restrict ourselves to two-fold ambiguous words.

$$TC(X, Y \mid S) = \frac{\exp[CG(S \Rightarrow X)] \times \exp([CG(S \Rightarrow Y)]}{\exp[CG(X \Rightarrow Y)] \times \exp[CG(Y \Rightarrow X)]}$$

[4]

$$= \exp[CG(S \Rightarrow X) + CG(S \Rightarrow Y) - CG(X \Rightarrow Y) - CG(Y \Rightarrow X)]$$

Hereby, TC is the so called *term complementarity*; S is the stimulus term and X and Y are possible sense descriptor candidates.

By computing the quotient between the association strengths among different pairs of words, formula 4 (first line) implements the previously stated notion that good sense descriptors should be weakly associated to each other but nevertheless be strongly associated to the ambiguous word. With CG being our measure for association strength, the numerator holds the strength of the stimulus word S to both of the candidates X and Y. The denominator holds the mutual association strength between the candidates. Since – as stated in the previous section – CG is an asymmetric formula, both directions are represented in the denominator. The exponential function was chosen since it behaves well (no singular values when denominator components are zero).

Having introduced the main credentials of our algorithm, namely the CG and TC measures, these are the details of our implementation:

1. By using the Google-API, search and scan the first 500 web pages retrieved by Google that contain the ambiguous word.
2. Select the top 200 words that occur in as many of these documents as possible.[3] It is assumed that this list includes the strongest associations to the ambiguous word.
3. Generate all possible 40,000 pairs[4] of the 200 candidates.
4. Exclude from the list words that appear in the same document.[5] Compute the confidence gain measure for each of the remaining pairs.
5. Compute the TC measure for all pairs of candidates and rank them in descending order.

After performing stage 4 of the algorithm, the number of remaining pairs decreases from 40,000 (at stage 3) to typically 15,000. As intended, this algorithm is capable of successfully identifying those words as sense descriptors that are each strongly associated to the ambiguous word but whose mutual association is as weak as possible.

---

[3] Function words and web-specific technical terms are excluded beforehand.

[4] Please note that due to the asymmetric nature of the CG-measure, the order of the words in a pair is relevant.

[5] This step implements the *one-sense-per-document* assumption [9], which is based on the observation that in most cases an ambiguous word will occur in only a single coherent meaning in a specific document. Therefore, when looking for candidates representing different meanings of a word, these are unlikely to be found in the same document.

4. Results

In order to quantitatively evaluate our results in sense induction we took the list of 12 ambiguous words used by Yarowsky [9]. Each of these words is considered to have two main senses, and for each sense he provides a word characteristic of that sense. This information is provided in the first two columns of table 1. The third column shows the best two sense descriptor pairs as automatically computed for each of the 12 ambiguous words.[6] Pairs that we judge to agree with Yarowsky's senses are printed in italics and pairs that correspond to other plausible senses are printed as small capitals. To justify our decisions, where appropriate comments were added in the fourth column of table 1.

Table 1. Computed results

WORD	EXPECTED SENSES	COMPUTED SENSES	COMMENTS
axes	grid tools	*normalized – hatchets* *coordinates – hatchets*	
bass	fish music	*fishing – guitar* *hunting – guitar*	
crane	bird machine	*sandhill – hoist* *sandhill – hydraulic*	sandhill crane = bird
drug	medicine narcotic	*pharmacy – ecstasy* *pharmacy – arrests*	
duty	tax obligation	ACCESSORIES – JUROR ENGINE – JUROR	heavy duty
motion	legal physical	SERVO – ANIMATION VELOCITY – PICTURES	servo motor cinema
palm	tree hand	*clie – springs* HOTSYNC – SPRINGS	CLIE = handheld Palm Springs
plant	living factory	*systems – flower* *laboratory – flower*	
poach	steal boil	SIMMER – OPPONENT SIMMER – DOUBLES	strike in tennis doubles match
sake	benefit drink	GOD – GINJO HEAVEN – GINJO	ginjo sake = high grade sake
space	volume outer	BROWSER – ORBIT *hosting – orbit*	space in computing
tank	vehicle container	*septic – turret* *septic – infantry*	turret = tower on a tank

The results look encouraging. In all cases the algorithm points us to different senses of the seed word, i.e. it never occurs that both words of a pair belong to the same sense. According to our (subjective) judgment, 14 of the 24 result pairs correspond to the two main senses as provided by Yarowsky. Another 10 pairs correspond to other sense distinctions, that are not in agreement with

---

[6] Please note that word order of the computed sense pairs is arbitrary, as is word order for Yarowsky's sense descriptors. So an agreement in order can not be expected.

Yarowsky's sense distinctions, but are nevertheless plausible (see comments in the right column of table 1 for interpretations). In some cases, as for example with *poach*, we had not been aware of some meanings pointed to by the algorithm, but a Google search specifying the ambiguous word and the sense descriptor in question quickly led us to the respective web pages.

Since cases where an algorithm fails or produces unexpected results are often interesting to examine, let us have a closer look at the results for the words *palm*, *sake*, and *space*. These words have more than two main senses and the algorithm happened to choose a different sense pair than proposed by Yarowsky. For example, in the case of *palm* the dominant sense in the web is *handheld computer*, which is reflected in the results. The same bias of the web towards computer related terms can be observed with *space*, where one of the computed meanings reflects the sense *memory space* or *disk space* rather than *physical space*. With *sake*, which is commonly used in collocations like *God's sake* or *heaven's sake*, it is not surprising when words like *God* or *heaven* instead of *benefit* are chosen as sense descriptors.

5. Discussion, conclusions, and prospects

Considering the difficulty of the problem, the results that we presented look surprisingly good. On the one hand our algorithm sometimes produced word pairs that do not well reflect the two main senses of the ambiguous words as given by Yarowsky. On the other hand, the task of unsupervised sense induction is certainly difficult and research in this field is at an early stage. Unfortunately, we are not aware of related work close enough to ours that we could have compared our results with.

The good performance of the system was achieved despite the following problems and limitations: First, the sense descriptors chosen by Yarowsky are somewhat arbitrary. Second, the bias of the internet towards new technology is of course reflected in our results (e.g. the interpretation of *palm* as a handheld computer). Third, the top 500 documents retrieved by Google may not contain enough occurrences of some of the expected senses. Fourth, our approach does not take into account the syntactic usage, that is the one-sense-per-collocation-constraint formulated by Yarowsky [9]. If one sense is much more frequent than the other, but there is a clear distinction in syntactic usage, then neglecting this distinction means neglecting crucial information.

The current version of our algorithm has a tendency to identify less common words as sense descriptors. This has to do with the one-sense-per-document assumption (step 4 of the algorithm), but the main reason is that there are many more rare words in the vocabulary of a language than there are frequent words. Thus it is more likely that a sense is best described by a rare word rather than a fre-quent word. If for certain applications, e.g. as an aid for second language learners, the use of better known words as sense descriptors is desirable, this could be accomplished in a straightforward way by restricting candidate selection using a positive list of familiar words, e.g. the controlled vocabulary of about 2000 words (called "defining senses") used in the *Longman Dictionary of Contemporary English* for describing the meanings of all dictionary entries.

Despite some limitations, the approach that we presented looks promising. Since it utilizes the web, changes in language over time are automatically accounted for, and a reasonable amount of data should be available even for rare words. Current experiments retrieving more documents from the web indicate that by only increasing the amount of data further advances should be possible. Our plans for the future include extending the algorithm towards identifying more than two senses, to admit multiword terms, to restrict the possible sense descriptors to a controlled vocabulary, to apply the algorithm to texts from limited domains, and to perform a quantitative evaluation based on association norms for a large number of ambiguous words [10].

6. References

[1] A. Kilgarrif and M. Palmer, *International Journal of Computers and the Humanities. Special Issue on SENSEVAL*, 34(1-2), 2000.

[2] U. Arns, *Sprachstatistische Analysen lexikalischer Mehrdeutigkeiten.* Diplomarbeit an der Universität-GH Paderborn, Germany, Fachbereich Psychologie, 1994.

[3] C.D. Manning and H. Schütze, *Foundations of Statistical Natural Language Processing.* Cambridge, MA: MIT Press, 1999.

[4] D.B. Neill, *Fully Automatic Word Sense Induction by Semantic Clustering.* Cambridge University, Master's Thesis, M.Phil. in Computer Speech, 2002.

[5] P. Pantel and D. Lin, Discovering Word Senses from Text. In: *Proceedings of ACM SIGKDD Conference on Knowledge Discovery and Data Mining*, Edmonton, 613–619, 2002.

[6] K.W. Church and W.A. Gale, Poisson Mixtures. In: *Natural Language Engineering* 1, 163–190, 1995.

[7] R. Tamir, *Association Generation Using Confidence Gain over Internet Pages.* Manuscript of doctoral dissertation, 2003.

[8] R. Rapp, *Die Berechnung von Assoziationen.* Hildesheim: Olms, 1996.

[9] D. Yarowsky, Unsupervised word sense disambiguation rivaling supervised methods. In: *Proceedings of the 33rd Annual Meeting of the Association for Computational Linguistics*, Cambridge, MA, 189–196, 1995.

[10] D.L. Nelson, C.L. McEvoy, J.R. Walling, and J.W. Wheeler, The University of South Florida homograph norms. *Behavior Research Methods and Instrumentation*, 12, 16–37, 1980.

A Hybrid Data-Mining Approach in Genomics and Text Structures

Horia-Nicolai Teodorescu[*]
* Romanian Academy, Iasi, Romania
hteodor@etc.tuiasi.ro

Lucian Iulian Fira[**]
** Technical University of Iasi, Romania
lfira@etc.tuiasi.ro

Abstract

We introduce a genetic sequence identifier based on a hierarchical system using fuzzy and classic (crisp) neural networks. The system is based on a set of predictors and on a decision network. The prediction of the structure of the genes is addressed using a new method and tools, involving the sequence of distances between bases and neuro-fuzzy predictors. The method and system have been successful in predicting genomic sequences and text structures.

1. Introduction

A large effort has been made during the last decades to unveil the genome for humans, some species of mammals, viruses, and bacteria. Many genome databases exist today, which include huge sets of data to be processed. Consequently, genomics apply on the software community a serious pressure for new, faster, and highly reliable systems able to sequence and identify specific sequences in the genomes. Among others, essential tasks for the computer scientist is to develop programs able to find specific patterns in the sequence and to predict a sequence. The prediction, at the current stage, is used to help the analysis of the structure, taking into account the huge amount of data that is to be analyzed.

There are numerous approaches today for sequencing, analyzing and predicting genomic sequences, including fuzzy, statistical, Markov models, and neural networks [1-4]. We present a genome representation method and a related hybrid tool to mine and identify genomic sequences. The tool is based on a combination of crisp neural network (NN) and fuzzy neural networks (FNN).

2. Coding the genomic sequences

The standard codes of the genes are letters and have no numerical representation. In order to use a numerical analysis/prediction algorithm, we have to produce a "translation" from the symbol to numbers for the sequence. The method of numerical coding is important, as the analysis/prediction results may heavily depend on it. We applied a new method, first used for the prediction of words in natural languages [5]. Namely, we coded the sequence as a set of four sequences, each constituted by the distances between successive occurrences of the basis.

Then, we may use the set of four sequences and the initial occurrence positions of the four bases to characterize the overall sequence. In particular, we develop predictors to generate each of the four sequences A,C,G, and T. In fact, we are not interested in the prediction itself, but in building systems that thoroughly learn genomic sequences. A good predictor will work well only on the desired type of sequences, and will flag by poor prediction results any unknown type of sequence.

Subsequently, we present the general architecture and details on the neuro-fuzzy predictor used in the analyzing system. Other details are presented in [6], [7].

3. A neuro-fuzzy tool for sequence identification

Changes in the learned statistics of a sequence may reveal different segments or may indicate the occurrence of an unknown segment. A method to identify changes of the statistics is to determine if some "agent" able to predict (and thus recognize) a segment becomes "unaware" of another segment that it cannot recognize (predict). Tools to recognize species based on genomes, to identify genomes, or to identify and locate mutations are in demand. Such means are needed to perform extensive research on large genomic databases for thousands of organisms.

The trend today is to learn the role of any genome. However, to do so, a large number of genomes from the diseased cells have to be investigated and compared to "normal" genomes. Direct comparison might be a way to determine differences. However, this requires a large number of accesses to the memory, and a large, fast memory to store the information of the "normal" templates and the investigated genomes. The space complexity is large for direct comparisons (at least twice that of the genome). Moreover, because the registers used to store sections of the compared strings are rather small, the number of accesses to the memory is proportional to the genome length, too. One of the systems currently used (see [8]) basically operates using a set of templates to which the actual genome sections are contrasted.

An alternate system, which operation would involve a similar time complexity, but a smaller space complexity, might be achieved. Indeed, if a system or a set of systems is highly trained to "learn" normal genome sections, it will be able to pinpoint that the analyzed genome section is – or is not – the one learned. Such a system may use a NN, or a fuzzy NN (FNN), knowing that NNs and FNNs are able to learn a specific context and to flag when they operate in a different context.

Instead of using FNN-based systems, other predictors could be considered too. However, linear predictors and simple NN predictors can be expected to require a larger number of inputs, to efficiently learn the series. This is a major drawback when small DNA sequences are available. Moreover, a FNN has the advantage of having a significantly larger number of parameters available for training, for the same order of the predictor, compared to linear or NN predictors. This is an intrinsic advantage for the available equivalent memory per unit of order of the predictor (per leg), to store the information on the learned sequence.

The suggested structure for the hybrid, hierarchical Fuzzy-NN to perform the analysis/recognition task is shown in Figure 1. The decision block is itself a (crisp) NN. Its role is to best determine the situations when a recognition score is high enough to decide the sequence has been recognized. This NN should be trained on a large number of sequences, to insure that the sequences not of the desired type are rejected.

The decision-making NN should receive extra inputs, one of them for the type of sequence recognized, or, equivalently, for the type of FNN to which it applies. A code can be assigned to each FNN, to be used as input to the decision-making NN (DM-NN). Moreover, the DM-NN might receive input information on the organism and chromosome under investigation (when known). Taking into account these requirements, the structure of the suggested DM-NN is like in Figure 2.

The fuzzy-NN predictor has been adopted from the literature and we developed the basic gradient-descent training algorithm, which reflects the classic algorithm used in NNs, with a few improvements. A convenient FNN predictor is composed of several Sugeno fuzzy logic systems with derivable input RBF membership functions. Sugeno-type fuzzy systems are simple enough and do not require complex computations, like the Mamdani-type systems. Recall that a Sugeno system (also named TSK system) is a fuzzy system mapping input fuzzy sets to real

numbers, based on a knowledge base consisting in rules like "If input is $\tilde{A}$ (here $\tilde{A}$ is a fuzzy set), then output is x, where x is a real number. The Gauss functions are preferred for the RBF membership functions.

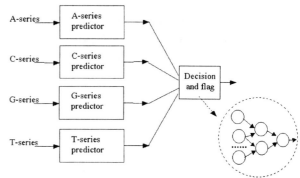

Figure 1. The multi-fuzzy-predictor and decision-making block for pattern recognition in genomic sequences. The individual predictors may be of any type, but FNN predictors have several advantages

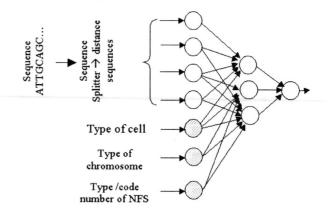

Figure 2. The overall structure of the genomic sequence identification agent

The NNs (and FNNs alike) are insensitive to small variations of sequences (a desired feature, when minute mutations are acceptable), moreover NNs are insensitive to frame shift errors (a highly desirable feature). On the other hand, the method will operate poorer on short exons. The NN method is close in effect with HMMs, as both carry statistical information on the global sequence and use information in the vicinity of the current point (several steps around or behind.)

The FNN method may be used in conjunction with other methods, either as the basic recognition method, or as a complementary method. The proposed method significantly differs from the NN methods presented in the literature (e.g., [4]) in several respects, beyond the use of fuzzy NNs.

We have used a neuro-fuzzy predictor, who has been developed and tested, in our group during the previous years, e.g. [9]. The architecture for one step predictive system is shown that presented in [7] and has a finite-response predictor topology using Sugeno systems for the "weights". There are twelve fuzzy systems acting as "multipliers" of the delayed basis samples. The Sugeno fuzzy system with single input and single output was chosen for these cells. The overall architecture is that of a neuro-fuzzy system. The input of fuzzy systems is characterized by seven Gaussian type membership functions. Technical details on the membership functions are presented in [7].

The gradient algorithm for adaptation of the neuro-fuzzy predictor is used. The prediction is one-step ahead.

4. Results

For testing the neuro-fuzzy predictor, we have used the data available at Los Alamos National Laboratory, http://hiv-web.lanl.gov/content/hiv-db/align_current/ align-index.html. Namely, we used the nucleotide sequence from the region ENV from HIV-1 "B.FR.83.HXB2". The basic statistic of the distances for the basis A is shown in Table 1. The statistics of the four bases are highly asymmetric, with averages spanning a range larger than 1:2.

Table 1. Statistical properties of the sequence of distances between subsequent occurrences of the basis A, C, G, T.

	A Basis series	C Basis series	G Basis series	T Basis series
Average	2.776	6.026	4.327	4.107
Spreading	2.445	6.201	4.117	3.871
Mode	1	1	1	1
Median	2	4	3	3
Skewness	3.160	2.200	2.021	2.418
Max	24	46	25	27

Any time series may include a slowly changing component, usually named the trend component, an almost periodical component, usually named cyclic or seasonal component, and a non-periodic, fast variable component, originating from a stochastic or nonlinear dynamic process.

Using a predictor for each of the components is known to significantly enhance the prediction outcome. Therefore, we have first decomposed the time series into the trend component $y_t[n]$, the cyclic component $y_c[n]$, and the fast varying component $y_a[n]$. The trend component is obtained by a moving average procedure.

Because the cyclic component has been found insignificant by applying the self-correlation procedure, the result of the subtraction $y[n] - y_t[n]$ has been dealt with as a random component. After normalization, these two series have been separately predicted using the same number of samples for the train and test periods. The values are then de-normalized, such that the results obtained from the two predictions are compatible. The denormalized results of the two independent predictions have been added to obtain the original series prediction. An example of results is shown in Figure 3, which show the actual distance sequences (solid lines) and the predicted sequences (dashed lines). The average error (normalized mean square error – NMSE) in distance prediction has been 0.513 for the A basis, 0.927 for the T basis, 0.488 for the G basis.

The results obtained with several prediction methods available in this software are significantly poorer than the results obtained with our predictor.

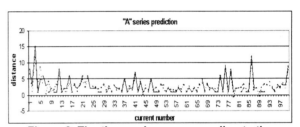

Figure 3. The time series corresponding to the distances for the A basis and the result of its one-step ahead prediction

For comparison, we have used the prediction software package [10], freely available on the Internet.

Table 2. Comparison between neuro-fuzzy predictor and prediction performed with VRA

Basis	Error type	NFP	VRA
A	NMSE	0.513	1.195
	RMSE	1.127	2.69
C	NMSE	0.566	1.057
	RMSE	1.930	7.201
T	NMSE	0.927	1.107
	RMSE	1.803	3.72
G	NMSE	0.488	0.965
	RMSE	1.214	4.602

A normalized error about 1.195 for test period in case of basis A, 1.107 in case of basis T and 0.965 for basis G. That was the best performance we obtained with the VRA package. A comparison between the performance of the neuro-fuzzy predictor and prediction with VRA is presented in Table 2, where RMSE denotes the root mean square error. The quality of the predictor is proved by the symmetrical, almost Gauss histogram of the prediction errors.

The same tool has been used to predict distances between successive occurrences of words in texts. The results have been equally promising and show the tool developed may be used, with appropriate training of the predictors, in various data-mining applications, including texts. For example, we have been quite successful in determining where the next "and" word will occur in the Bible and in various other texts. (Other words, like "not", "or" etc., have been also tested with similar results.) As the "and" word is showing connections between parts of the discourse, we can confidently say that our system is successful in inferring how specific talkers will generate a connective between two parts of their thinking process.

5. Discussion and conclusions

A hybrid – crisp plus fuzzy neural network structure – tool to mine genomic sequences has been introduced. The tool is believed suitable for mass analysis of genomic sequences. The proposed genomic identification system is based on a set of fuzzy neural network predictors and a decision-making neural network.

We proposed a modified method to deal with the prediction of bases sequences, converting the sequence of bases in several sequences, each for a single basis. Moreover, we use a neuro-fuzzy predictor for prediction; then, the distances are converted back to current positions of the individual bases, and the complete sequence is reconstructed. The method yields better results than those obtained with several other predictors.

We have found that the conversion to distances much enhances the results. Actually, we also tried the method of first converting the bases symbols into numerical values like A$\rightarrow$ 1, C$\rightarrow$2, G$\rightarrow$3, T$\rightarrow$4 moreover A$\rightarrow$1, C$\rightarrow$2, G$\rightarrow$4, T$\rightarrow$8, but the results obtained were poor.

As expected, the separation of the trend and fast varying components plays an important role. Indeed, we have tried another the prediction directly for the distance series between bases, with very poor results.

The introduced method for representation and a neuro-fuzzy predictor to derive the sequence of genes has been tested on the HIV virus genome. The use of the distance representation and of the neuro-fuzzy predictor looks promising, at least compared to other prediction methods reported in the literature.

Further work is needed to train the predictors and the decision-making NN on large sets of genomic sequences of different type and to improve the overall system performance.

Finally, the method has been tested with very promising results on texts to determine specific characteristics of the texts, like the writer, or the domain to which the text applies. Further results will be reported elsewhere.

6. References

[1] E. Uberbacher, *Computing the Genome*, http://www.ornl.gov/ORNLReview/v30n3-4/genome.htm.

[2] S. Tomida, T. Hanai, H. Honda, T. Kobayashi, "Gene Expression Analysis Using Fuzzy ART", *Genome Informatics*, 12: 245–246 (2001) 245.

[3] A.P. Gasch, B. M. Eisen, "Exploring the conditional coregulation of yeast gene expression through fuzzy k-means clustering", *Genome Biol.* 2002; 3 (11): research0059.1– research0059.22. http://www.pubmedcentral.nih.gov/ articlerender.fcgi?tool=pubmed&pubmedid=12429058.

[4] R. Hugheygif, A. Kroghgif, "Hidden Markov models for sequence analysis: extension and analysis of the basic method". *CABIOS* 12(2):95-107, 1996. Reprint: http://www.cse.ucsc.edu /research/compbio/html_format_papers/hughkrogh96/cabios.

[5] H.N. Teodorescu, *The Dynamics of the Words.* Invited Plenary Lecture, The 11th Conference on Applied and Industrial Mathematics (CAIM 2003): 29-31 May, 2003. University of Oradea, Romania, http://caim2003.rdsor.ro/.

[6] H.N. Teodorescu, L.I. Fira, "Predicting the Genome Bases Sequences by means of distance sequences and a Neuro-Fuzzy Predictor", *Fuzzy Systems & A.I. – Reports and Letters*, vol. 7 (2003) (to appear).

[7] L.I. Fira, H.N. Teodorescu, "Genome Bases Sequences Characterization by a Neuro-Fuzzy Predictor", *Proceedings IEEE-EMBS 2003 Conference*, 17-21 September, Cancun, Mexico.

[8] M.A. Martý-Renom, A.C. Stuart, A. Fiser, R. Sanchez, F. Melo, A. Ali, "Comparative Protein Structure modeling of Genes and Genomes", *Annu. Rev. Biophys. Biomol. Struct.* 2000. 29:291–325.

[9] T. Yamakawa, H.N. Teodorescu, "Neuro-Fuzzy Systems: Hybrid configurations". In vol. M.J. Patyra, D. Mlynek (Eds.): *Fuzzy Logic. Implementation and applications.* Wiley & Teubner, 1996, pp. 267-298.

[10] E. Kononov, Visual Recurrence Analysis - version 4.2, http://home.netcom.com/~eugenek/download.html.

Model Stability:
A key factor in determining whether an algorithm produces an optimal model from a matching distribution

Kai Ming Ting and Regina Jing Ying Quek
KaiMing.Ting@infotech.monash.edu.au
Gippsland School of Computing and Information Technology
Monash University, Victoria 3842, Australia.

Abstract

This paper investigates the factors leading to producing suboptimal models when training and test class distributions (or misclassification costs) are matched. Our result shows that model stability plays a key role in determining whether the algorithm produces an optimal model from a matching distribution (cost). The performance difference between a model trained from the matching distribution (cost) and the optimal model generally increases as the degree of model stability decreases. The practical implication of our result is that one should only follow the conventional wisdom of using a training class distribution (cost) that matches the test class distribution (cost) to train a classifier if the learning algorithm is known to be stable.

1. Introduction

A common tacit assumption in classifier induction is that the class distribution of the training set must match the class distribution of the test set. This intuitive assumption is believed to produce the optimal model for a given learning algorithm. However, recent research [5,8] has shown that this conventional wisdom can produce suboptimal models for decision tree learning algorithms. The empirical evidence demonstrates that the performance difference in terms of expected cost between a model trained from a matching distribution and the optimal model can be more than 50% [5]. Despite this evidence, there is no explanation as to why the intuitive assumption has misled classifier induction so badly in practice. Because the assumption is applied so commonly, it is imperative that the reasons for its failure to produce the optimal model be investigated and understood.

This paper contributes towards this aim. In investigating the condition under which an algorithm will or will not produce an optimal model from a matching distribution, we

find that the model stability is a key factor, and the size of the model space has a direct influence on model stability. We show that by controlling the size of the model space to vary the degree of model stability, the performance of the model trained from a matching distribution also changes accordingly, with respect to the performance of the optimal model. This is shown using decision trees in which the size of the model space can be controlled by the allowable maximum depth of the tree. We also show that while the cost sensitivity of a decision tree splitting criterion has an influence on model stability, it has much less impact than the size of the model space.

In contrast to decision trees, Naive Bayesian classifiers are shown to be totally insensitive to cost or prior probability. We thus have a complete range of models that have varying degrees of model stability (decision trees) and Naive Bayes which is totally stable or cost insensitive. They are used in this paper to show how model stability influences the performance of the model trained from a matching distribution.

The terminologies used in this paper are defined in the next section. We report the experimental result in Section 3. followed by conclusions.

2. Terminology

2.1. Expected cost and cost ratio

Throughout this paper, the performance of a model is measured in terms of expected cost $E[C]$, defined as follows as in [2,3] for ROC curves and cost curves.

$$E[C] = (1 - TP)\, p(+)C(-|+) + FP\, p(-)C(+|-),$$

where TP is the true positive rate, FP is the false positive rate, $p(a)$ is the prior probability of a given example being in class a, and $C(a|b)$ is the cost of misclassifying a class b example as being in class a.

We are interested in using data with unbalanced distribution in this study, as such data occurs in many real-world applications. We denote the minority class as $+$ and the majority class as $-$. The cost ratio (M) is defined as the ratio of the cost of misclassifying the minority class and the cost of misclassifying the majority class, that is $C(-|+)/C(+|-)$. Note that the expected cost reduces to error rate when $M=1$. While the cost ratio reflects the operating condition for the given data, one can use this information in training a model. This is what we do by using M as a training parameter in cost sensitive learning. We will only use $M \geq 1$, first to balance the initial unbalanced distribution and then to bias the minority class.

Since doubling $p(b)$ has the same effect of doubling $C(a|b)$ in terms of expected cost defined above, we use cost or prior interchangably and the cost ratio to also denote the relative class distribution between the two classes in the rest of this paper. To improve readability in the previous introductory section, we have used only class distribution; but the assumption applies to misclassification cost as well.

2.2 Optimal model for an operating condition

An optimal model for an operating condition M in a domain is the best performing model produced by the learning algorithm by searching over the model space with varying cost ratios using a fixed set of learning parameters[1].

Given a pair of training and testing sets, the optimal model for an operating condition can be produced by an exhaustive search over all models that can be induced from all cost ratios, and having other learning parameters constant. The search is *exhaustive* with respect to the set granularity within the specified range. For example, with a granularity of one, an exhaustive search will generate 100 models within the range of cost ratio, $M=1\text{-}100$; and the best performing model is selected to be the the optimal model.

Note that we also allow the decision threshold of each model to vary. A decision threshold is the cut-off level used to decide the final prediction of a classification model. In a two-class problem, the final prediction is class positive if the model's posterior probability of a test example is above the threshold; otherwise it is class negative. When the threshold is changed, the model's performance also changes. A search for the optimal threshold is conducted for each model.

We regard this process as having an oracle informing us which is the optimal model at any operating condition in which a model will be used.

[1]Note that it does not refer to the optimal model for the domain. To produce the optimal model for the domain, one needs to search using different sets of learning parameters.

2.3. Model Stability

Model stability is defined as the "structural" sensitivity of the models produced from a learning algorithm, i.e., the degree to which the models differ from one another when training misclassification cost or class distribution changes. Note that this definition is a special case of the usual meaning of the term in which the structural sensitivity is due to any (non-specific) changes in the training data.

There are a number of factors that influence the model stability of a learning algorithm. The model space of a learning algorithm is the total number of distinct models that can be produced. If the size of the model space increases, one can expect the degree of model instability to increase because the probability of inducing a different model increases. However, the search method used in a learning algorithm determines the actual size of the model subspace to be included in the search. For models in which attribute selection and pruning are an integral part of the search process, the cost sensitivity of the attribute selection criterion and the effect of pruning also influence the model stability.

We will study the effect of model space, attribute selection criterion and pruning using a decision tree learning algorithm. The algorithm is a good candidate for our investigation because the model space can be easily controlled by limiting the maximum allowable depth to which a tree can grow, and the attribute selection criterion can be easily changed from one which is more cost sensitive to one which is less, and pruning can be turned on or off.

3. Experiment

We use twelve data sets obtained from the UCI repository [1]. The minority prior spans from 50% to 1%, that is from balanced to highly skewed distributions; and the data sizes range from 1000 to about 49000. They are coding, kr-vs-kp, abalone, german, adult, splice, satellite, pendigits, hypothyroid, letter-a, nursery and nettalk. A stratified 10-fold cross-validation is conducted for each data set.

We use the decision tree induction algorithm C4.5 [4] and its default setting, while taking the following modifications into consideration. The algorithm is modified to take cost ratio into consideration in the training process. For example, with $M=2$, every minority class training instance will be weighted twice as high as every majority class instance during the tree induction process [6]. Cost sensitive pruning is done in accordance with the modified weights, though the default pruning method of C4.5 is used unaltered. The Laplace estimate is used to compute the class posterior probability for a leaf of the tree. This allows us to compute all pairs of $\{TP, FP\}$ in one pass using the algorithm in [3]. We also added the DKM splitting criterion which is claimed to be totally cost insensitive [2]. A levelled tree is obtained from C4.5 by imposing a maximum depth limit in the tree growing process with no pruning.

An experiment is conducted to examine whether the best performing model is different from that induced from the matching distribution. An exhaustive search of 100 models is conducted using M=1-100. The optimal model obtained from the search is used to compare with the model induced from the matching distribution.

We measure the percentage difference in terms of the expected cost at an operating point corresponding to M, between the tree trained with M and the optimal tree, using the former tree as the base model ($D = [E_M - E_O]/E_M$). A large difference means that a better performing model can be induced from a condition different from the operating condition, contrary to the conventional wisdom.

In the following sections, we show the effect of model stability on the quality of the models trained from a matching distribution, first using models of different degrees of stability which consist of levelled unpruned trees and pruned trees, then using a totally cost insensitive model, Naive Bayesian classifiers.

3.1. Levelled unpruned trees and pruned trees

To show that the quality of the models trained from a matching distribution changes with the size of the model space in decision trees, we gradually increase the maximum allowable depth of levelled trees from 1, 5, 10, and then to 25, and also pruned trees, as induced by C4.5. The performance differences D for these trees are measured and compared. The DKM and gain ratio splitting criteria which have different degrees of cost sensitivity are used.

Figure 1(a) shows the maximum of average performance difference in each data set, for levelled trees at four different maximum depths and pruned trees. Each bar is an average over twelve data sets. It is a summarised result from the detailed results, which can be found in [7].

The summarised result shows that the performance difference increases as the model space increases—a direct result of tree maximum depth increases. This happens to both splitting criteria, despite the fact that one criterion is less cost sensitive than the other. Though DKM has lower average maximum performance difference than that of gain ratio, the gap between the two decreases as the maximum depth increases; and it is further reduced with pruning from about 6% (at maximum depth = 25) to 4.5%.

It is important to point out that the claim that DKM is independent of priors is misleading. If 'DKM is completely insensitive to cost/priors' [2], then only one unpruned tree will be produced independent of cost/prior. This is not true even in their own paper in which different costs produce different unpruned trees, shown as different points in the ROC curves. Our experiments using levelled unpruned trees

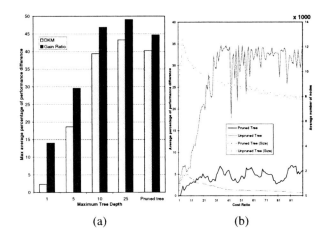

Figure 1. (a) Maximum average percentage of performance difference for levelled trees of maximum depth = 1, 5, 10, 25, and pruned trees trained using DKM and gain ratio. Each bar is an average over all twelve data sets. (b)Comparing pruned trees to unpruned trees in terms of performance difference and tree size in the adult data set.

also show the same result. This is despite the fact that DKM might be less sensitive to priors than other criteria. We show that the proof provided by [2] is incorrect in [7].

Pruning has the effect of reducing the model space and thus increases the model stability. However, the effect is less significant unless the tree size is significantly reduced. This is indicated in the small reduction of the maximum average percentage of performance difference from unpruned trees to pruned trees in Figure 1(a). An example of a significantly reduced pruned tree is in adult, in which the total number of decision nodes reduces from about 12000 to 2000, at maximum size. Figure 1(b) shows the performance difference and the number of nodes in this data set using gain ratio where a significant reduction of performance difference (from 35% to 7% at peak difference) is due to significant model size reduction by pruning.

For pruned trees, both gain ratio and DKM exhibit a quite similar level of performance difference. The majority is a double digit performance degradation compared to the optimal model. See [7] for details.

3.2. Naive Bayesian Classifiers

Naive Bayesian classifiers are different from decision trees in one important aspect which is not always mentioned in the literature: the model is completely insensitive to cost or prior. This is because Naive Bayesian classifiers are modeling the class conditional probability density function $P(x|C)$ in which the probability of x within each class remains the same even if the relative cost between classes changes. The estimation of $P(C)$ can be delayed until classification time to match that of the test data.

Derived from the Bayes rule, Naive Bayesian classifiers use the following Bayes decision rule to make prediction:

$$\text{Predict class } + \text{ if } P(x|+)P(+) > P(x|-)P(-), \qquad (1)$$

otherwise predict class $-$.

Re-arranging (1) gives

$$\text{Predict class } + \text{ if } \frac{P(x|+)}{P(x|-)} > \frac{P(-)}{P(+)}. \qquad (2)$$

The term $\frac{P(-)}{P(+)}$ determines the decision threshold. Thus, changing the decision threshold of Naive Bayes is equivalent to changing the class distribution. It can be easily shown that it is also equivalent to changing the cost ratio.

This implies that a Naive Bayesian model $P(x|C)$ induced from a given cost/prior can be used for a different cost/prior by using an appropriate threshold. Thus, no re-training of a model is required under changing operating conditions as suggested by the matching distribution assumption. In other words, *Naive Bayesian model is totally insensitive to cost/prior*. In practice, the threshold is determined from the priors estimated from the training data which has a class distribution that matches that of the testing data. The experimental results can be found in [7].

4. Conclusions

The requirement of matching distribution conventionally used to mean to re-train a new model every time the operating condition changes. We identify that they are two separate, albeit related issues.

For unstable models such as decision trees, we show that following this requirement does not produce the optimal model. With regard to the issue of re-training, previous results [5] have shown that only a small number of models are required in each data set because each of these models is optimal in a wide range of operating points. For example, a decision tree trained with $M=2$ is optimal for an operating range of $M=1$-50, and another optimal tree for the rest of the operating range. This means only those few optimal models need to be identified and trained for a task.

For stable models, our result shows that re-training of a model is not a requirement at all, and this does not only apply to Naive Bayesian classifiers but all induction algorithms which are modeling the class conditional probability density function since changes in cost/priors has no effect on the modeling process. However, matched distribution shall be used to estimate the priors during classification.

The level of performance difference measures the degree of divergence from the conventional requirement of matching distribution. Using this measure, we show that model

stability is one key factor in determining whether the divergence takes place—the more unstable is the learning algorithm, the more likely it is to diverge from the conventional wisdom. We demonstrate this using models with varying degrees of stability: from levelled unpruned trees of varying maximum depth and different splitting criteria, and pruned trees, to Naive Bayesian classifiers.

Our result shows that the level of performance difference generally increases as the model space increases. The cost sensitivity of the splitting criterion is found to have much lesser influence on the model stability than the size of the model space in decision trees. Because pruning reduces the model space, the significance of its influence is proportional to the degree of model size reduction by pruning in a particular data set.

Acknowledgements

Geoff Webb provides many valuable suggestions for the initial draft. Ross Quinlan provides C4.5. Mark Micallef helps to conduct some experiments.

References

[1] Blake, C. & Merz, C.J. *UCI Repository of machine learning databases*. [http://www.ics.uci.edu/~mlearn/MLRepository.html]. Irvine, CA: University of California. 1998.

[2] Drummond C. & Holte R. Exploiting the Cost (In)sensitivity of Decision Tree Splitting Criteria. *Proceedings of The 17th International Conference on Machine Learning*. Morgan Kaufmann. San Francisco. 2000. pp. 239-246.

[3] Provost, F. & Fawcett, T. Robust Classification for Imprecise Environments. *Machine Learning* 42, 2001. pp. 203-231.

[4] Quinlan, J.R. *C4.5: Program for Machine Learning*. Morgan Kaufmann. 1993.

[5] Ting, K.M. Issues in Classifier Evaluation using Optimal Cost Curves. *Proceedings of The 19th International Conference on Machine Learning*. Morgan Kaufmann. San Francisco. 2002. pp. 642-649.

[6] Ting, K.M. An Instance-Weighting Method to Induce Cost-Sensitive Trees. *IEEE Transactions on Knowledge and Data Engineering*. Vol. 14, No. 3. 2002. pp. 659-665.

[7] Ting, K.M. & Quek, R.J.Y. Model Stability: A key factor in determining whether an algorithm produces an optimal model from a matching distribution. *TR-2003/3*. GSCIT, Monash University. http://www.gscit.monash.edu.au/~kmting/. 2003.

[8] Weiss, G. & Provost, F. The Effect of Class Distribution on Classifier Learning: An Empirical Study. *TR ML-TR-44*, Dept of Computer Sc., Rutgers University. 2001.

Enhancing Techniques for Efficient Topic Hierarchy Integration*

Jyh-Jong Tsay   Chi-Feng Chang
Hsuan-Yu Chen   Ching-Han Lin
Department of Computer Science and Information Engineering
National Chung Cheng University
Chiayi, Taiwan 62107, ROC. Email: tsay@cs.ccu.edu.tw

Abstract

In this paper, we study the problem of integrating documents from different sources into a comprehensive topic hierarchy. Our objective is to develop efficient techniques that improve the accuracy of traditional categorization methods by incorporating categorization information provided by data sources into categorization process. Notice that in the World-Wide Web, categorization information is often available from information sources. We present several enhancing techniques that use categorization information to enhance traditional methods such as naive Bayes and support vector machines. Experiment on collections from Openfind and Yam, and Google and Yahoo!, well-known popular web sites in Taiwan and USA, respectively, shows that our techniques significantly improve the classification accuracy from, for example, 55% to 66% for Naive Bayes, and from 57% to 67% for SVM for the data set collected from Yam and Openfind.

1 Introduction

In this paper, we study the problem of topic hierarchy integration whose purpose is to integrate documents categorized by different source topic hierarchies into a common target topic hierarchy. In particular, we consider the case in which we are given a source hierarchy H_1 and a target hierarchy H_2 each consisting of a hierarchy of topics, and document collections D_1 and D_2 categorized by H_1 and H_2, respectively. We are asked to classify all documents in D_1 to topics in H_2. Our objective is to develop efficient enhancing techniques that explore relations between topics in H_1 and H_2, and can be used to extend traditional methods to incorporate categorization information into the classification process.

Traditional approaches for text categorization such as, for example, linear classifiers produced by Rocchio algorithms [6], Bayesian probabilistic approaches[15], decision trees[2], k Nearest Neighbors(kNN)[15], neural networks[9], and Support Vector Machines(SVM)[5], mainly relies on the contents of the documents to predict their class labels. Usually, no categorization information from other topic hierarchies is assumed. However, in the World-Wide Web, categorization information is often available from information sources. For example, news from newspapers, books from publishers, items from electronic commercial sites, or even web pages archived by web information portals are categorized. Observe that many of the topic hierarchies adopted by current information sources are highly related. We believe that categorization information can be used to improve classification accuracy. We propose the following approaches.

- Probabilistic Enhancement that uses categorization information to enhance probabilistic classifiers such as naive Bayes(NB) classifiers.

- Topic Restriction that uses categorization information to restrict the set of candidate classes for classifiers such as SVM that does not explicitly output a probability.

Experiment on collections from Openfind and Yam, and Google and Yahoo!, well-known popular web sites in Taiwan and USA, respectively, shows that our approaches significantly improve traditional approaches such as NB and SVM that do not utilize categorization information. For data set from Opendfind and Yam, probabilistic enhancement improves the classification accuracy of NB from 55% to 66%, and topic restriction improves the classification accuracy of SVM from 57% to 67%.

There are several recent papers [1, 3, 13] studying problems that can be formulated as topic hierarchy integration. In [1], Agrawal and Srikant proposed an enhancement of NB classifiers which introduces similar idea developed in

*This research is supported in part by the National Science Council, Taiwan, ROC, under grant NSC-92-2213-E-194-021.

our probabilistic enhancement. Topic restriction is a new technique proposed by this paper.

2 Preliminaries

A *topic hierarchy* H consists of a set of topics (or classes) organized as a tree in which each node is associated with a topic, and the topic associated to a node is a sub-topic of the topic associated to its parent node if it exists. For each topic $v \in H$, let $I(v)$ denote the instance space of topic v, i.e. the set of all possible documents that are assigned to topic v. We assume that $I(v)$ contains but may not be equal to $\cup_{u \in Child(v)} I(u)$, where $Child(v)$ denote the set of topics associated to the children of the node of topic v. Namely, a document in topic v may be related to but not properly belong to any of its sub-topics. Let $I(H)$ denote the instance space of hierarchy H, i.e. $I(H) = \cup_{v \in H} I(v)$. The topic (or class label), denoted as $c_H(x)$, of document $x \in I(H)$ in hierarchy H is defined to be the topic $v \in H$ so that $x \in I(v)$ but $x \notin I(u)$ for all $u \in Child(v)$. Notice that $c_H : I(H) \to H$ is a mapping that assigns topics to documents in $I(H)$.

In this paper, we study the topic hierarchy integration problem in which we are given a source hierarchy H_1 and a target hierarchy H_2, and we are asked to build a model for computing $c_{H_2}(x)$ for each $x \in I(H_1)$, provided that $c_{H_1}(x)$ is also given as part of the input. Let D_1 be a collection of documents labelled by H_1, and D_2 be another collection of documents labelled by H_2. We are asked to build, using D_1 and D_2 as training examples, an assignment $\hat{c}_{H_2} : I(H_1) \times H_1 \to H_2$, which assigns topics in H_2 to documents in $I(H_1)$, and can be used to integrate D_1 into D_2.

3 Probabilistic Enhancement(PE)

Let x be a document in the source collection D_1, and s be the class label of x in source hierarchy H_1. Let v_t be the label of a class in target hierarchy H_2. In probabilistic enhancement, we assign to document x the class v_t that maximizes the posterior probability $P(v_t|x, s)$. Let $v_{PE}(x)$ denote the class assigned to document x in probabilistic enhancement.

$$v_{PE}(x) = \arg \max_{v_t \in H_2} P(v_t|x, s)$$

By Bayes theorem and independent assumptions, we can derive the following equation.

$$P(v_t|x, s) = \frac{P(v_t|x)P(v_t|s)}{P(v_t)} \frac{P(x)P(s)}{P(x, s)}$$

Since for input instance (x, s), $\frac{P(x)P(s)}{P(x,s)}$ is a constant, we therefore have the following equation for v_{PE}.

$$v_{PE}(x) = \arg \max_{v_t \in H_2} \frac{P(v_t|x)P(v_t|s)}{P(v_t)}$$

3.1 Enhanced Naive Bayes (ENB)

In NB, $P(v_t|x)$ is estimated as follows.

$$P(v_t|x) = \frac{P(v_t) \prod_{w_i \in x} P(w_i|v_t)^{TF(w_i, x)}}{P(x)},$$

where w_i is a term appearing in x, and $TF(w_i, x)$ is the term frequency of w_i in x. NB assigns the following topic to x.

$$v_{NB}(x) = \arg \max_{v_t \in H_2} P(v_t) \prod_{w_i \in x} P(w_i|v_t)^{TF(w_i, x)}$$

When class label of x in H_1 is given as part of input, we have the following NBC (Naive Bayes with Categorization information) classifier as developed in PE.

$$v_{NBC}(x) = \arg \max_{v_t \in H_2} P(v_t|s) \prod_{w_i \in x} P(w_i|v_t)^{TF(w_i, x)}$$

We propose the following enhanced version of NBC, denoted as ENB (Enhanced Naive Bayes), which takes into account the distribution of class s in hierarchy H_2.

$$v_{ENB}(x) = \arg \max_{v_t \in H_2} P(v_t|s)^{\lambda(s, H_2)} \prod_{w_i \in x} P(w_i|v_t)^{TF(w_i, x)},$$

where $\lambda(s, H_2)$ is supposed to be proportional to the degree of concentration of class s in H_2. When documents in class s is highly concentrated in some target classes, we will assign large value to $\lambda(s, H_2)$. On the contrary, when documents in class s is highly scattered in the target hierarchy, we will assign small value to $\lambda(s, H_2)$. We use a tuning set to find the value of $\lambda(s, H_2)$ for every source class.

3.2 Estimation of $P(v_t|s)$ in ENB

For any class label v in hierarchy H_1, resp. H_2, let $D_1(v)$, resp. $D_2(v)$, be the subset of documents in D_1, resp. D_2, that is labelled as class v. A straightforward estimation of $P(v_t|s)$ is defined as follows.

$$P(v_t|s) = \frac{|D_2(v_t) \cap D_1(s)|}{|D_1(s)|}$$

We propose the following enhanced estimation that is expected to be more robust.

$$P(v_t|s) = \frac{|D_2(v_t)|^{\alpha(s, H_2)} \times |D_2(v_t) \cap D_1(s)|}{\sum_{v \in H_2} |D_2(v)|^{\alpha(s, H_2)} \times |D_2(v) \cap D_1(s)|}$$

	source hierarchy	target hierarchy
I	Yam	Openfind
II	Yam.Business_and_Economics	Openfind.Business_and_Economics
III	Google.Business	Yahoo!.Business_and_Economics

Figure 1. Data Sets

	classes in source	classes in target	links in source	links in target	links in common
I	274	275	167,070	171,286	40,205
II	82	96	33,834	35,747	14,508
III	84	103	167,070	118,750	14,378

Figure 2. Statistics of Data Sets

Notice that $0 \leq \alpha(s, H_2) \leq 1$. When $\alpha(s, H_2) = 0$, the estimation is equivalent to the straightforward estimation. When $\alpha(s, H_2) = 1$, the estimation is almost equivalent to $P(v_t)$. We use a tuning set to choose the value of $\alpha(s, H_2)$ for every source class s in H_1.

3.3 ENB-Related Methods

In [1], Agrawal and Srikant proposed an algorithm, called AS for short, similar to ENB presented in last section. AS returns the class $v_{AS}(x)$ defined as below.

$$v_{AS}(x) = \arg \max_{v_t \in H_2} P(v_t|s)P(x|v_t)$$

Estimation of $P(v_t|s)$ in AS does not rely on the intersection between source and target collections. Instead, they run NB to estimate $P(v_t|s)$ as follows. Let $NB(s, v)$ denote the set of documents that are in $D_1(s)$ and are predicted to be in target class v by the NB classifier. In AS, $P(v|s)$ is estimated as follows.

$$P(v_t|s) = \frac{|D_2(v_t)| \times |NB(s, v_t)|^{w(s, H_2)}}{\sum_{v \in H_2} |D_2(v)| \times |NB(s, v)|^{w(s, H_2)}}$$

Notice that when $w(s, H_2) = 0$, categorization information provided by H_1 is completely ignored, and $P(v_t|s) = P(v_t)$.

4 Comparison of NB-Based Methods

We compare the performance of NB, NBC, ENB, and AS on data sets collected from Yam and Openfind, and Yahoo! and Google. From the collections downloaded from above portals, we compile 3 data sets I, II and III as given in Figure 1. Notice that most of the documents downloaded from Yam and Openfind are Chinese. We follow the approaches proposed in [12] to preprocess Chinese documents. Figure 2 gives statistics of each data set.

In each data set, we partition the common links into 3 sets: (i)training set for estimating the probability $P(v|s)$, (ii)tuning set for choosing parameters α, λ and w, and (iii) testing set for measuring classification accuracy.

Figure 3 gives the statistics of λ and w for Data Set I. Notice that ENB tends to select large λ that implies that the influence of categorization information in ENB is very

λ or w	0	1	3	10	30	100	300
λ in ENB	63	72	4	5	7	624	0
w in AS	513	6	27	37	76	91	23

Figure 3. Distribution of λ and w

strong. Most of w in AS is 0 that implies that categorization is mostly ignored by AS.

Figure 4, gives the classification accuracy of NB-based methods on data set I, II and III. All of the extensions NBC, ENB and AS significantly improves NB. ENB achieves the best classification accuracy, and outperforms NBC and AS in all of the 3 data sets. The performance of AS is slightly worse than NBC. This may be due to the poor performance of NB as AS relies on NB in parameter estimation.

5 Topic Restriction

Topic restriction is a general approach to integrate categorization information into any traditional classifiers such as SVM that does not necessarily return a probability for each candidate class. The main idea is to use the categorization information of a test document to identify a small subset of classes as candidates, and restrict classification of that document to consider only those classes identified as candidates. Topic restriction can be static or dynamic. In static topic restriction (STR), each source class is associated with a small subset of candidates that is determined at learning stage. Let $s \in H_1$ be a source class, and $R(s, H_2)$ be the subset of target classes in T that contains documents from source class s. Namely, $R(s, H_2) = \{v_t \in H_2 | I(s) \cap I(v_t) \neq \emptyset\}$. The basic idea of STR is to restrict

Data Set	NB	NBC	ENB	AS
I	41.12%	62.58%	77.58%	46.53%
II	55.47%	57.63%	66.15%	59.12%
III	67.38%	73.24%	83.42%	71.24%

Figure 4. Accuracy of NB-Based Methods

Data Set	NB	STR NB	SVM	STR SVM
II	55.47%	59.96%	57.62%	57.8%
III	67.38%	79.62%	76.49%	76.62%

Figure 5. Accuracy of STR

	NB+SVM	ENB+SVM
k=1	55.47%	66.15%
k=2	60.51%	67.00%
k=3	60.69%	66.47%
k=4	61.19%	66.56%
k=5	61.55%	66.06%
k=6	61.69%	66.06%

Figure 6. Accuracy of Cascaded SVM

the classification of any document with source class s by considering only the target classes in $R(s, T)$. We compute an approximation $\hat{R}(s, H_2)$ of $R(s, H_2)$ as follows.

$$\hat{R}(s, H_2) = \{v_t \in H_2 | \Psi(D_1(s), D_2(v_t)) \geq \delta\}$$

, where Ψ defines a measure between $D_1(s)$ and $D_2(v_t)$, and δ is a threshold. In this paper, we simply define $\Psi(D_1(s), D_2(v_t)) = |D_1(s) \cap D_2(v_t)|$. Figure 5 shows that STR significantly improves NB, and slightly improves SVM.

In dynamic topic restriction, candidates are selected dynamically for each test document at its classification stage. Notice that simple classifiers such as NB-based methods achieve very high top k measure for small k such as 3 and 4. We will use those top k classes ranked by NB-based methods as candidates, and then apply SVM to determine the final prediction. Notice that candidate classes are ranked by their posterior probabilities computed by NB-based methods. Once candidate classes are provided, SVM is applied to determine the final prediction as follows. It checks each candidate class in the order of their ranks given by the candidate selector, and pick the first class that passes the check, i.e. whose score is higher than a predetermined threshold. If none of them passes the check, it simply outputs the class ranked 1st by the candidate selector. Figure 6 gives the performance of SVM cascaded with NB and ENB for Data Set II. Notice that cascading ENB and SVM improves the classification accuracy of both ENB and SVM, and achieves the best classification accuracy when $k = 2$. It also reduces the classification time of SVM as it examines only k of the m classes, where m is the number of classes in the target hierarchy. The time reduction will be crucial in applications that requires on-line response.

6 Conclusion and Further Remarks

In this paper, we present a probabilistic enhancement approach to enhancing probabilistic classifiers such as naive Bayes, and a topic restriction approach that is a general approach for cascading any classifiers. Experiment shows that our approaches significantly improve the performance of traditional methods that ignore the categorization information. Notice that categorization information can be viewed as external annotation provided by information portals. One of our on-going research is to extend our approaches to applications where external annotations are available.

References

[1] Rakesh Agrawal, Ramakrishnan Srikant. *On Integrating Catalogs*. Int'l World Wide Web Conference, Hong Kong, 2001.

[2] C. Apte, F. Damerau, S. Weiss. *Text mining with decision rules and decision trees*. Proc. of Automated Learning and Discovery, 1998.

[3] V. Boyapati *Towards a Comprehensive Topic Hierarchy for News*. Master Thesis, 2000.

[4] S. Chakrabarti, B. Dom, R. Agrawal, P. Raghavan. *Scalable feature selection, classification and signature generation for organizing large text databases into hierarchical topic taxonomies*. VLDB'98.

[5] T. Joachims. *Text Categorization with Support Vector Machines: Learning with Many Relevant Features*. ECML'98.

[6] D. Lewis, R. Schapire, J. Callan, R. Papka. *Training Algorithms for Linear Text Classifiers*. SIGIR'96.

[7] A. McCallum, R. Rosenfeld, T. Mitchell, A. Ng. *Improving Text Classification by Shrinkage in a Hierarchy of Classes*. ICML'98.

[8] T. Mitchell. *Machine Learning*. McGraw-Hill, 1997.

[9] H.T. Ng, W.B. Goh, K.L. Low. *Feature selection, perceptron learning, and a usability case study for text categorization*. SIGIR'97.

[10] R.E. Schapire, Y. Singer. *BoosTexter: A Boosting-based System for Text Categorization*. Machine Learning, 39(2/3):135-168, 2000.

[11] D. Susan, C. Hao. *Hierarchical Classification of Web Content*. SIGIR'00.

[12] J.-J. Tsay, J.-D. Wang. *Design and Evaluation of Approaches for Automatic Chinese Text Categorization*, Journal of Computational Linguistics and Chinese Language Processing, Vol. 5, No. 2, pp. 43-58, August, 2001.

[13] J.-J. Tsay, K.-J. Wu. *Learning Between Class Hierarchies for Text Categorization*. Technical Report, Dept of CSIE, National Chung Cheng University, 2001.

[14] K. Wang, S. Zhou, C. C. Liew. *Building hierarchical classifier using class proximity*. VLDB'99.

[15] Y. Yang *An evaluation of statistical approaches to text categorization*. Journal of Information Retrieval, 1(1/2):67-88, 1999.

Pattern Discovery based on Rule Induction and Taxonomy Generation

Shusaku Tsumoto and Shoji Hirano
Department of Medical Informatics,
Shimane University, School of Medicine,
Enya-cho Izumo City, Shimane 693-8501 Japan
tsumoto@computer.org, hirano@ieee.org

Abstract

One of the most important problems with rule induction methods is that they cannot extract rules, which plausibly represent experts' decision processes. In this paper, the characteristics of experts' rules are closely examined and a new approach to extract plausible rules is introduced, which consists of the following three procedures. First, the characterization of decision attributes (given classes) is extracted from databases and the concept hierarchy for given classes is calculated. Second, based on the hierarchy, rules for each hierarchical level are induced from data. Then, for each given class, rules for all the hierarchical levels are integrated into one rule.

1. Introduction

One of the most important problems in data mining is that extracted rules are not easy for domain experts to interpret. One of its reasons is that conventional rule induction methods[5] cannot extract rules, which plausibly represent experts' decision processes[7]. For example, rule induction methods, including C4.5[4], induce the following common rule for muscle contraction headache from databases on differential diagnosis of headache:

[*location* = *whole*] ∧[Jolt Headache = *no*]
∧[Tenderness of M1 = *yes*]
→ muscle contraction headache.

This rule is shorter than the following rule given by medical experts.

[Jolt Headache = *no*]
∧([Tenderness of M0 = *yes*] ∨[Tenderness of M1 = *yes*]
∨[Tenderness of M2 = *yes*])
∧[Tenderness of B1 = *no*] ∧[Tenderness of B2 = *no*]
∧[Tenderness of B3 = *no*]
∧[Tenderness of C1 = *no*] ∧[Tenderness of C2 = *no*]
∧[Tenderness of C3 = *no*] ∧[Tenderness of C4 = *no*]
→ muscle contraction headache

where [Tenderness of B1 = *no*] and [Tenderness of C1 = *no*] are added.

One of the main reasons why rules are short is that these patterns are generated only by one criteria, such as high accuracy or high information gain. The comparative studies[7, 9] suggest that experts should acquire rules not only by one criteria but by the usage of several measures. Those characteristics of medical experts' rules are fully examined not by comparing between those rules for the same class, but by comparing experts' rules with those for another class[7].

For example, the classification rule for muscle contraction headache given in Section 1 is very similar to the following classification rule for disease of cervical spine:

[Jolt Headache = *no*]
∧([Tenderness of M0 = *yes*] ∨[Tenderness of M1 = *yes*]
∨[Tenderness of M2 = *yes*])
∧([Tenderness of B1 = *yes*] ∨[Tenderness of B2 = *yes*]
∨[Tenderness of B3 = *yes*]
∨[Tenderness of C1 = *yes*] ∨[Tenderness of C2 = *yes*]
∨[Tenderness of C3 = *yes*]
∨[Tenderness of C4 = *yes*])
→ disease of cervical spine

The differences between these two rules are attribute-value pairs, from tenderness of B1 to C4. Thus, these two rules are composed of the following three blocks:

$$A_1 \wedge A_2 \wedge \neg A_3 \quad \rightarrow \quad \textit{muscle contraction headache}$$
$$A_1 \wedge A_2 \wedge A_3 \quad \rightarrow \quad \textit{disease of cervical spine,}$$

where A_1, A_2 and A_3 are given as the following formulae: A_1 = [Jolt Headache = *no*], A_2 = [Tenderness of M0 = *yes*] ∨ [Tenderness of M1 = *yes*] ∨ [Tenderness of M2 = *yes*], and A_3 = [Tenderness of C1 = *no*] ∧ [Tenderness of C2 = *no*] ∧ [Tenderness of C3 = *no*] ∧ [Tenderness of C4 = *no*]. The first two blocks (A_1 and A_2) and the third one (A_3) represent the different types of differential diagnosis. The first one A_1 shows the discrimination between muscular type and vascular type of headache. Then, the second part shows that between headache caused by neck and head muscles. Finally, the third formula A_3 is used to make a differential diagnosis between muscle contraction headache and disease of cervical spine. Thus, medical experts first select several diagnostic candidates, which are very similar to each other, from many diseases and then make a final diagnosis from those candidates.

In this paper, the characteristics of experts' rules are closely examined from the viewpoint of hiearchical decision steps. Then, extraction of diagnostic taxonomoy from medical datasets is introduced, which consists of the following three procedures. First, the characterization set of each decision attribute (a given class) is extracted from databases. Then, similarities between characterization sets are calculated. Finally, the concept hierarchy for given classes is calculated from the similarity values.

2. Rough Set Theory: Preliminaries

In the following sections, we use the following notations introduced by Grzymala-Busse and Skowron[6], which are based on rough set theory[3].

Let U denote a nonempty, finite set called the universe and A denote a nonempty, finite set of attributes, i.e., $a : U \to V_a$ for $a \in A$, where V_a is called the domain of a, respectively. Then, a decision table is defined as an information system, $A = (U, A \cup \{d\})$.

The atomic formulae over $B \subseteq A \cup \{d\}$ and V are expressions of the form $[a = v]$, called descriptors over B, where $a \in B$ and $v \in V_a$. The set $F(B, V)$ of formulas over B is the least set containing all atomic formulas over B and closed with respect to disjunction, conjunction and negation.

For each $f \in F(B, V)$, f_A denote the meaning of f in A, i.e., the set of all objects in U with property f, defined inductively as follows.

1. If f is of the form $[a = v]$, then $f_A = \{s \in U | a(s) = v\}$
2. $(f \wedge g)_A = f_A \cap g_A; (f \vee g)_A = f_A \vee g_A;$
   $(\neg f)_A = U - f_a$

By the use of the framework above, classification accuracy and coverage, or true positive rate is defined as follows.

Definition 1
Let R and D denote a formula in $F(B, V)$ and a set of objects which belong to a decision d. Classification accuracy and coverage(true positive rate) for $R \to d$ is defined as:

$$\alpha_R(D) = \frac{|R_A \cap D|}{|R_A|} (= P(D|R)), \text{ and}$$
$$\kappa_R(D) = \frac{|R_A \cap D|}{|D|} (= P(R|D)),$$

where $|S|$, $\alpha_R(D)$, $\kappa_R(D)$ and P(S) denote the cardinality of a set S, a classification accuracy of R as to classification of D and coverage (a true positive rate of R to D), and probability of S, respectively.

It is notable that $\alpha_R(D)$ measures the degree of the sufficiency of a proposition, $R \to D$, and that $\kappa_R(D)$ measures the degree of its necessity.

According to the definitions, probabilistic rules with high accuracy and coverage are defined as:

$$R \xrightarrow{\alpha, \kappa} d \ s.t. \quad R = \vee_i R_i = \vee \wedge_j [a_j = v_k],$$
$$\alpha_{R_i}(D) \geq \delta_\alpha \text{ and } \kappa_{R_i}(D) \geq \delta_\kappa,$$

where δ_α and δ_κ denote given thresholds for accuracy and coverage, respectively.

3. Characterization Sets

In order to model medical reasoning, a statistical measure, coverage plays an important role in modeling, which is a conditional probability of a condition (R) under the decision (D) (P(R—D)). Let us define a characterization set of D, denoted by $L(D)$ as a set, each element of which is an elementary attribute-value pair R with coverage being larger than a given threshold, δ_κ. That is,

Definition 2 Let R denote a formula in $F(B, V)$. Characterization sets of a target concept (D) is defined as:

$$L_{\delta_\kappa}(D) = \{R | \kappa_R(D) \geq \delta_\kappa\}$$

Then, three types of relations between characterization sets can be defined as follows:

Independent type: $L_{\delta_\kappa}(D_i) \cap L_{\delta_\kappa}(D_j) = \phi$,
Overlapped type: $L_{\delta_\kappa}(D_i) \cap L_{\delta_\kappa}(D_j) \neq \phi$, and
Subcategory type: $L_{\delta_\kappa}(D_i) \subseteq L_{\delta_\kappa}(D_j)$.

All three definitions correspond to the negative region, boundary region, and positive region, respectively, if a set of the whole elementary attribute-value pairs will be taken as the universe of discourse.

Tsumoto focuses on the subcategory type in [8] because D_i and D_j cannot be differentiated by using the characterization set of D_j, which suggests that D_i is a generalized disease of D_j. Then, Tsumoto generalizes the above rule induction method into the overlapped type, considering rough inclusion[9]. However, both studies assumes two-level diagnostic steps: focusing mechanism and differential diagnosis, where the former selects diagnostic candidates from the whole classes and the latter makes a differential diagnosis between the focused classes.

The proposed method below extends these methods into multi-level steps.

In the subsequent sections, we consider the special case of characterization sets in which the thresholds of coverage

procedure *Total Process*;
  var inputs
    L_D : *List*; /* A list of Target Concepts */
  begin
        Calculate a list of grouping L_g; (Fig. 2)
        /* Generation of Diagnostic Taxonomy */
        Induce a set of rules for L_g: L_r;
        Combine Rules in L_r for each D_i;
  end {*Total Process*}

Figure 1. An Algorithm for Total Process

is equal to 1.0. That is,

$$L_{1.0}(D) = \{R_i | \kappa_{R_i}(D) = 1.0\}.$$

4. Generation of Diagnostic Taxonomy

4.1. Intuitive Ideas

As discussed in Section 2, When the coverage of R for a target concept D is equal to 1.0, R is a necessity condition of D. That is, a proposition $D \to R$ holds and its contrapositive $\neg R \to \neg D$ holds. Thus, if R is not observed, D cannot be a candidate of a target concept. Thus, if two target concepts have a common formula R whose coverage is equal to 1.0, then $\neg R$ supports the negation of two concepts, which means these two concepts belong to the same group. Furthermore, if two target concepts have similar formulae $R_i, R_j \in L_{1.0}(D)$, they are very close to each other with respect to the negation of two concepts. In this case, the attribute-value pairs in the intersection of $L_{1.0}(D_i)$ and $L_{1.0}(D_j)$ give a characterization set of the concept that unifies D_i and D_j, D_k. Then, compared with D_k and other target concepts, classification rules for D_k can be obtained. When we have a sequence of grouping, classification rules for a given target concepts are defined as a sequence of subrules. It is notable that these characteristics will hold when the relation between $L_{1.0}(D_i)$ and $L_{1.0}(D_j)$ is overlapped type. In the case of subcategory type, the intersection between two sets will be equal to smaller sets. We should pay attention to the case when $|L_{1.0}(D_i)| << |L_{1.0}(D_j)|$, because the similarity becomes very small if we do not take the effect into account.

Figure 1 shows the total process of a rule induction algorithm with grouping target concepts.

4.2. Algorithm

From these ideas, an algorithm on grouping target concepts can be described as follows (Figure 2). First, this algorithm first calculates $L_{1.0}(D_i)$ for $\{D_1, D_2, \cdots, D_k\}$. Second, from the list of characterization sets, it calculates

procedure *Grouping* ;
  var inputs
    L_c : *List*; /* A list of Characterization Sets */
    L_{id} : *List*; /* A list of Intersection */
    L_s : *List*; /* A list of Similarity */
  var outputs
    L_{gr} : *List*; /* A list of Grouping */
  var
    k : *integer*;
    L_g, L_{gr} : *List*;
  begin
    $L_g := \{\}$;
    $k := n$ /* n: A number of Target Concepts*/
    Calculate a set of characterization set L_c;
    Calculate a set of intersection L_{id};
      Calculate a list of similarity measures L_s;
      Sort L_s with respect to similarities;
    Take a set of (D_i, D_j), L_{max}
    with maximum similarity values;
    k:= k+1;
    forall $(D_i, D_j) \in L_{max}$ **do**
    begin
      Group D_i and D_j into D_k;
      $L_c := L_c - \{(D_i, L_{1.0}(D_i)\}$;
        $L_c := L_c - \{(D_j, L_{1.0}(D_j)\}$;
          $L_c := L_c + \{(D_k, L_{1.0}(D_k)\}$;
          Update L_{id} for DD_k;
        Update L_s;
      $L_{gr} := (Grouping$ for L_c, L_{id}, and L_s) ;
      $L_g := L_g + \{\{(D_k, D_i, D_j), L_g\}\}$;
    end
  return L_g;
  end {*Grouping*}

Figure 2. An Algorithm for Grouping

the intersection between $L_{1.0}(D_i)$ and $L_{1.0}(D_j)$ and stores it into L_{id}. Third, the procedure calculates the similarity (matching number)of the intersections and sorts L_{id} with respect of the similarities. Finally, the algorithm chooses one intersection $(D_i \cap D_j)$ with maximum similarity (highest matching number) and group D_i and D_j into a concept DD_i. These procedures will be continued until all the grouping is considered.

4.3. Similarity

To measure the similarity between two characterization sets, we can apply several indices of two-way contingency tables. Table 1 gives a contingency table for two rules, $L_{1.0}(D_i)$ and $L_{1.0}(D_j)$. The first cell a (the intersection of the first row and column) shows the number of matched attribute-value pairs. From this table, several kinds of similarity measures can be defined. The best similarity mea-

| | | $L_{1.0}(D_j)$ | | |
		Observed	Not Observed	Total
$L_{1.0}(D_i)$	Observed	a	b	$a+b$
	Not observed	c	d	$c+d$
	Total	$a+c$	$b+d$	$a+b$ $+c+d$

Table 1. Contingency Table for Similarity

sures in the statistical literature are four measures shown in Table 2[2, 1]. It is notable that these indices satisfies the property on symmetry. As discussed in Section 3, a single-

(1)	Matching Number	a
(2)	Jaccard's coefficient	$a/(a+b+c)$
(3)	χ^2-statistic	$N(ad-bc)^2/M$
(4)	point correlation coefficient	$(ad-bc)/\sqrt{M}$
(5)	Kulczynski	$\frac{1}{2}(\frac{a}{a+b}+\frac{a}{a+c})$
(6)	Ochiai	$\frac{a}{\sqrt{(a+b)(a+c)}}$
(7)	Simpson	$\frac{a}{min\{(a+b),(a+c)\}}$
(8)	Braun	$\frac{a}{max\{(a+b),(a+c)\}}$

$$N = a+b+c+d, M = (a+b)(b+c)(c+d)(d+a)$$

Table 2. A List of Similarity Measures

valued similarity becomes low when $L_{1.0}(D_i) \subset L_{1.0}(D_j)$ and $|L_{1.0}(D_i)| << |L_{1.0}(D_j)|$. For example, let us consider when $|L_{1.0}(D_i)| = 1$. Then, match number is equal to 1.0, which is the lowest value of this similarity. In the case of Jaccard's coefficient, the value is $1/1 + b$ or $1/1 + c$: the similarity is very small when $1 << b$ or $1 << c$. Thus, these similarities do not reflect the subcategory type. Thus, we should check the difference between $a + b$ and $a + c$ to consider the subcategory type. One solution is to take an interval of maximum and minimum as a similarity, which we call an interval-valued similarity.

For this purpose, we combine Simpson and Braun similarities and define an interval-valued similarity:

$$\left[\frac{a}{max\{(a+b),(a+c)\}}, \frac{a}{min\{(a+b),(a+c)\}} \right]$$

If the difference between two values is large, it would be better not to consider this similarity for grouping in the lower generalization level. For example, when $a + c = 1(a = 1, c = 0)$, the above value will be: $\left[\frac{1}{1+b}, 1\right]$ If $b >> 1$, then this similarity should be kept as the final candidate for the grouping.

The disadvantage is that it is difficult to compare these inverval values. In this paper, the maximum value of a given interval is taken as the representative of this similarity when the difference between min and max are not so large. If the maximum values are equal to the other, then the minimum value will be compared. If the minimum value is larger than the other, the large one is selected.

5. Conclusion

In this paper, the characteristics of experts' rules are closely examined, whose empirical results suggest that grouping of diseases is very important to realize automated acquisition of medical knowledge from clinical databases. Thus, we focus on the role of coverage in focusing mechanisms and propose an algorithm for grouping of diseases by using this measure. The above example shows that this method generates a grouping reasonable to medical experts' reasoning. This research is a preliminary study on a rule induction method with grouping and it will be a basis for a future work to compare the proposed method with other rule induction methods by using real-world datasets.

Acknowledgments

This work was supported by the Grant-in-Aid for Scientific Research (13131208) on Priority Areas (No.759) "Implementation of Active Mining in the Era of Information Flood" by the Ministry of Education, Science, Culture, Sports, Science and Technology of Japan.

References

[1] T. Cox and M. Cox. *Multidimensional Scaling*. Chapman & Hall/CRC, Boca Raton, 2nd edition, 2000.

[2] B. Everitt. *Cluster Analysis*. John Wiley & Son, London, 3rd edition, 1996.

[3] Z. Pawlak. *Rough Sets*. Kluwer Academic Publishers, Dordrecht, 1991.

[4] J. Quinlan, editor. *C4.5 - Programs for Machine Learning*. Morgan Kaufmann, Palo Alto, 1993.

[5] J. Shavlik and T. Dietterich, editors. *Readings in Machine Learning*. Morgan Kaufmann, Palo Alto, 1990.

[6] A. Skowron and J. Grzymala-Busse. From rough set theory to evidence theory. In R. Yager, M. Fedrizzi, and J. Kacprzyk, editors, *Advances in the Dempster-Shafer Theory of Evidence*, pages 193–236. John Wiley & Sons, New York, 1994.

[7] S. Tsumoto. Automated induction of medical expert system rules from clinical databases based on rough set theory. *Information Sciences*, 112:67–84, 1998.

[8] S. Tsumoto. Extraction of experts' decision rules from clinical databases using rough set model. *Intelligent Data Analysis*, 2(3), 1998.

[9] S. Tsumoto. Extraction of hierarchical decision rules from clinical databases using rough sets. *Information Sciences*, 2003.

Active Sampling for Feature Selection

Sriharsha Veeramachaneni   Paolo Avesani

ITC-IRST, Via Sommarive 18 - Loc.Pantè, I-38050 Povo, Trento, Italy
E-mail: {sriharsha,avesani}@irst.itc.it

Abstract

In knowledge discovery applications, where new features are to be added, an acquisition policy can help select the features to be acquired based on their relevance and the cost of extraction. This can be posed as a feature selection problem where the feature values are not known in advance. We propose a technique to actively sample the feature values with the ultimate goal of choosing between alternative candidate features with minimum sampling cost. Our heuristic algorithm is based on extracting candidate features in a region of the instance space where the feature value is likely to alter our knowledge the most. An experimental evaluation on a standard database shows that it is possible outperform a random subsampling policy in terms of the accuracy in feature selection.

1 Introduction

In many knowledge discovery applications the step of data analysis is often followed by further data acquisition (new instances and/or new features). Our contribution deals with cost-constrained acquisition of new features. This work is motivated by a research project (SMAP) in the domain of agriculture dealing with the Apple Proliferation disease in apple trees[1]. The scenario [3, 6, 5] is the following: biologists monitor a distributed collection of apple trees affected by the disease; the goal is to characterize the conditions for infection spreading. An archive is arranged with a finite set of records each describing a single apple tree. All the instances are labeled as infected or not infected. Every summer the archive is updated extending each record with new features. Each year the biologists propose new candidate features that could be extracted (or measured) and at the end of summer the past and new data are analyzed. Since the data collection on the field can be very expensive or time consuming the biologists have to arrange a data acquisition plan at the beginning of summer by selecting a

subset of the most relevant candidate features that should really be acquired.

Given a sample of labeled instances described by a set of features, the problem is to rank the new candidate features in order of relevance to the class label given the previous features. Clearly the usual feature selection approaches that are conceived as a posteriori tasks performed on a database with a large number of features that are fully extracted on the set of instances are inappropriate in our case. We propose a myopic look-ahead strategy for feature selection. The basic idea is to prescribe an iterative policy that chooses the next instance on which the candidate features are to be probed. The goal is to trade-off the accuracy of the assessment of the feature relevance and the cost associated to the acquisition of the feature values. An optimum solution would produce the same ranking as a fully informed method, but with a small subsample of the feature values. If all the candidate features have unit cost, this is equivalent to minimizing the size of the subsample. Notice that when we conduct an exhaustive sampling, we fall into the traditional framework of feature selection [1, 4].

2 Related Work

Although feature selection is a well studied problem in machine learning [1, 4], the traditional feature selection methods are unapplicable because in our case the assessment of feature relevance must be performed in conjunction with acquiring the feature values.

Our work on the active sampling for feature selection is inspired by earlier work on active learning [2, 10, 7, 11]. In contrast to the conventional active learning paradigm, where the class labels of unlabeled samples are probed to quickly ascertain the best predictor of the class from the features, our problem is to choose from a set of class-labeled samples on which candidate features are to be extracted while trying to learn their relevance.

Zheng and Padmanabhan [12] address the problem of active feature extraction albeit for the purpose of cost-constrained generation of an accurate classifier. Their algorithm guesses the feature value for every instance and picks

---

[1]This work is funded by Fondo Progetti PAT, SMAP (Scopazzi del Melo - Apple Proliferation), art. 9, Legge Provinciale 3/2000, DGP n. 1060 dd. 04/05/01.

the one which yields the most accurate classifier. In contrast our method averages the conditional entropy over all possible values of the candidate feature and probes the instance where the change from the current entropy is the maximum.

Although the influence of the cost model on a learning process has been studied (see the works on cost-sensitive learning [8, 9]), we currently ignore this aspect for our active sampling approach by assuming unit cost for feature extraction.

3 Active Sampling of Feature Values

Consider a set of monitored pattern instances (or subjects) $S = \{s_i\}_{i=1,...,N}$. Let the random variable corresponding to the class label be denoted by $\mathbf{C}$ taking values in $\mathcal{C}$. We assume that the class labels $\{c_i\}_{i=1,...,N}$ for all the instances are known. $\mathbf{X}, \mathbf{Y}_1, \ldots, \mathbf{Y}_M$ are discrete valued features that can be extracted on any pattern taking on values in $\mathcal{X}, \mathcal{Y}_1, \ldots \mathcal{Y}_M$ respectively. Assume that feature $\mathbf{X}$ is extracted for all the subjects and therefore the feature values $\{x_i\}_{i=1,...,N}$ are known. Therefore the estimated probability distribution $\hat{p}_N(c, x)$ on $\mathcal{C} \times \mathcal{X}$ is assumed be accurate (the subscript N represents the number of samples used for estimation). Initially none of the instances have features $\mathbf{Y}_1, \ldots, \mathbf{Y}_M$ extracted. The objective is to rank the candidate features $\mathbf{Y}_1, \ldots, \mathbf{Y}_M$ according to relevance for classification problem given the feature $\mathbf{X}$. At the same time cost incurred for feature extraction has to be minimized. In the following discussion we assume that all features are nominal valued with multinomial probability densities.

The feature extraction policy considers each candidate feature separately. Let $\mathbf{Y}$ denote the candidate feature whose relevance we are trying to learn. We define the set of all pattern instances s_i with $(c_i, x_i) = (\alpha, \beta)$ as region $R_{\alpha\beta}$.

Whereas a random feature extraction scheme (denoted π_R) chooses an instance randomly from all the instances on which $\mathbf{Y}$ is not extracted, our active sampling strategy (denoted π_A) decides on the most *profitable* subset (or region) $R_{\alpha\beta}$ of instances for feature extraction. Then the candidate feature is extracted on a randomly chosen instance from this region.

Let $\overline{S}_k = \{(c_{i_1}, x_{i_1}, y_{i_1}), \ldots, (c_{i_{k-1}}, x_{i_{k-1}}, y_{i_{k-1}})\}$ be the current set of samples with $\mathbf{Y}$ extracted (i.e., with complete descriptions). Then $\pi_A(\overline{S}_k, \hat{p}(c, x)) = (c^\star, x^\star) \in \mathcal{C} \times \mathcal{X}$ is the result of the active policy. The active sampling scheme is an iterative process that proposes at each step the class label and the value taken by the previous feature of the samples on which it is most beneficial to probe the candidate feature.

The algorithm for active feature extraction for a particular candidate feature is presented in Figure 1. Here θ is the estimator for the conditional density $p_k(y|c, x)$ and

function ActiveSample($\mathbf{Y}$, MaxSamples, $\hat{p}_N(c, x)$)
$\overline{S}_1 := \{\}$
for k=1 **to** MaxSamples
$\quad \hat{p}_k(y|c, x) := \theta(\overline{S}_k; c, x, y)$
$\quad \hat{p}_k(c, x, y) := \hat{p}_k(y|c, x)\hat{p}_N(c, x)$
$\quad H_k(\mathbf{C}|\mathbf{X}, \mathbf{Y}) := -\sum_{\mathcal{C}, \mathcal{X}, \mathcal{Y}} \hat{p}_k(c, x, y) \log \hat{p}_k(c|x, y)$
$\quad$ **foreach** $(\alpha, \beta) \in \mathcal{C} \times \mathcal{X}$
$\qquad q_\gamma(c, x, y) := \hat{p}_N(c, x)\theta(\overline{S}_k \cup (\alpha, \beta, \gamma); c, x, y)$
$\qquad \hat{H}_{k+1}(\mathbf{C}|\mathbf{X}, \mathbf{Y}) := -\sum_{\gamma \in \mathcal{Y}} \hat{p}_k(\mathbf{Y} = \gamma|\alpha, \beta) \cdot$
$\qquad\qquad\qquad\qquad\qquad\qquad \sum_{\mathcal{C}, \mathcal{X}, \mathcal{Y}} q_\gamma(c, x, y) \log q_\gamma(c|x, y)$
$\qquad B(\alpha, \beta) := |\hat{H}_{k+1}(\mathbf{C}|\mathbf{X}, \mathbf{Y}) - H_k(\mathbf{C}|\mathbf{X}, \mathbf{Y})|$
$\quad$ **end-foreach**
$\quad (c^\star, x^\star) := \underset{(c, x) \in \mathcal{C} \times \mathcal{X}}{\operatorname{argmax}} B(c, x)$
$\quad \overline{S}_k := \overline{S}_k \cup$ new random sample in the region $R_{c \cdot x}$.
end-for

Figure 1. Pseudo-code for the active feature extraction algorithm for a particular candidate feature.

$q_\gamma(c, x, y)$ is the estimate of the joint density after the inputed sample (α, β, γ) is added to the current data. H_k is the current estimate of the conditional entropy and $\hat{H}_{k+1}$ is the expected conditional entropy if an instance from the region $R_{\alpha\beta}$ were to be probed. $B(\alpha, \beta)$ is the expected *benefit* of sampling in the region $R_{\alpha\beta}$.

Thus the active decision is based upon the absolute change between the current estimate of the entropy in the class given the previous feature and the candidate feature and the expected entropy in the class after the candidate feature is extracted from a sample in the said region. The expectation is over the possible values that the candidate feature can assume and the probabilities used in calculation of the expectation are the current estimates. The algorithm iterates until the candidate feature is extracted on a specified number of instances denoted L ($L = |\overline{S}_Y|$, where $\overline{S}_Y$ is the final subsample). L is problem dependent and is determined by the cost constraints (for feature extraction).

As mentioned earlier our active learning algorithm considers each candidate feature separately. Therefore the candidate features $\mathbf{Y}$ and $\mathbf{Z}$ are not necessarily extracted on the same subsample of the instances.

After the candidate feature is extracted on the specified number (L) of samples or after the cost budget is exhausted, we can construct a Bayes maximum a posteriori classifier $\phi_L : \mathcal{X} \times \mathcal{Y} \to \mathcal{C}$ using the final estimate $\hat{p}_L(c, x, y) = \hat{p}_L(y|c, x)\hat{p}_N(c, x)$ of the joint distribution. The features are ranked based upon the error rates of these classifiers estimated according to $p_e(L) = \{1 - \sum_{x,y} \hat{p}_N(x, y|\mathbf{C} = \phi_L(x, y))\} * 100$. In reality, however, we cannot extract the candidate feature for all the samples to estimate the error rates. We can circumvent this problem by obtaining a small random subsample for testing.

4 Experimental evaluation

To compare the active feature sampling strategy and the random feature extraction scheme for feature evaluation we use two performance measures.

The first is based on the mean square error between the estimated error rate at a particular sample size and the "true" error rate for a given feature. For us the true error rate represents the estimated error rate of the classifier trained after extracting the candidate feature on all N samples in the training set (denoted $p_e(N)$), i,e, the error rate of the classifier designed using $\hat{p}_N(c, x, y)$ (the estimate of the probability densities from all N samples).

The quantity $mse = \mathrm{E}\{(p_e(N) - p_e(L))^2\}$ is a measure of the correctness in the estimated error rate for a feature after the given number of samples were extracted. We compute the error rate of the classifier for several runs of the learning scheme for the given sample size to compute the mean square error. For a particular learning scheme and for each feature the mean square error can be plotted against the sample size.

The second performance measure which is based on the Spearman rank-order correlation more directly indicates the efficacy of a sampling scheme for feature ranking and therefore for feature selection.

For each sample size we compute the error rate (as described above) for every candidate feature which are then ranked accordingly. The rank-order correlation between this ranking and the *true* ranking (based on $p_e(N)$ for all candidates) is computed and its average value over many iterations of the learning scheme is plotted against the sample size.

We chose the *mushroom* database from the UCI machine learning repository for experimentation because it contains a large number of instances with several nominal features whose relevance to the class varies widely. The 8124 instances are almost evenly distributed between 2 classes (edible and poisonous) and there are 22 features extracted of which feature 11 (stalk-root) has several missing values and was therefore deleted from the database leaving 21 features for each instance. Feature 5 (odor) is the most relevant and feature[2] 15 (veil-type) is the least relevant for classification. We only use $N = 4000$ randomly chosen samples for experimentation. We vary the number of samples extracted L from 0 through 100 for the plots.

To compare the performance of the active and the random learning schemes given previous features we partitioned the 21 features into seven sets of three. This was

---

[2]Feature 16 before deleting the stalk-root feature

X	1,2,3	4,5,6	7,8,9	10,11,12	13,14,15	16,17,18	19,20,21
E	30.9	2.3	12.8	17.5	24.7	21.3	11.1

Table 1. Classifier error (E) rates (%) for each set of previous features $\mathbf{X} = (\mathbf{X}_1, \mathbf{X}_2, \mathbf{X}_3)$.

done instead of experimenting with all possible $\binom{21}{3}$ combinations for simplicity. Each of these sets was fixed as the previous feature set $\mathbf{X}$ and the remaining $M = 18$ features were evaluated as candidates. The error rates for the classifier trained on each of previous feature set (i.e, before the candidate feature is extracted on any sample) is given in Table 1.

Figure 2(1-7) shows the behaviour of the rank-order correlation coefficient (y-axis) between the vector of error rates estimated after a specific number of samples (x-axis) are extracted and the true error rates. The different plots correspond to different sets of previous feature vectors $\mathbf{X}$ indicated on the top of each subplot. Our active feature extraction strategy converges more quickly to the correct ranking of the features than the random scheme. When $\mathbf{X} = (4, 5, 6)$ the difference is not significant. This can be attributed to the fact that feature 5 individually leads to a very low error rate and therefore the candidate features have to be extracted on a large number of samples to be confidently ranked.

For each set of previous features we plotted the mean square difference between the true error rate and the estimated error rate (y-axis) after the candidate feature is extracted on a specific number of samples (x-axis). Figure 2(8-14) shows the plot for feature where the active policy proffered the most advantage over the random scheme. The plots indicate that the active policy can be used to lower the cost for feature evaluation.

5 Conclusions and Future Work

We have dealt with the problem of cost-constrained feature selection in a knowledge discovery process. An active strategy that selects the instances for feature extraction is proposed to aid in choosing the most relevant features among a set of candidate features. We provided empirical evidence on a standard dataset for the dominance of the active sampling scheme over a random policy for subsample selection for feature evaluation. The choice is based upon the absolute change between the current estimate of the entropy in the class before and the predicted entropy after the candidate feature value acquisition.

The promising results, although restricted to a specific dataset, encourage more study. Our current method does not scale to large number of previous features because of the necessity to estimate full class-conditional distributions (we

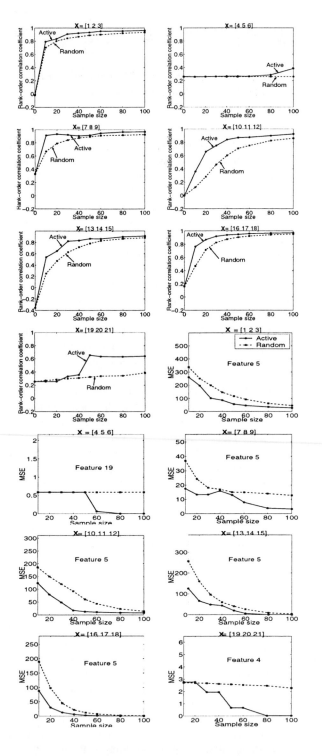

Figure 2. (1-7) The plot against sample size of the Spearman rank-order correlation between estimated error rates and the true error rates. (8-14) The plot of the mean square difference between estimated error rate and the true error rate, for best feature only.

do not assume any feature independence). Moreover the current design of solution is strongly related to the specific classifier, i.e. the Bayes classifier with class-conditional multinomial feature distributions. A general solution should be independent of the specific classifier and suitable for both nominal and real valued features.

References

[1] A.Blum and P.Langley. Selection of Relevant Features and Examples in Machine Learning. *Artificial Intelligence*, 97(1-2):245–271, 1997.

[2] D.A.Cohn, L.Atlas, and R.E.Ladner. Improving Generalization with Active Learning. *Machine Learning*, 15(2):201–221, 1994.

[3] G.Hughes. Sampling for Decision Making in Crop Loss Assessment and Pest Management: Introduction. In *Symposium on Sampling for Decision Making in Crop Loss Assessment and Pest Management*, pages 1080–1083, 1999.

[4] I.Guyon and A.Elisseefi. An Introduction to Variable and Feature Selection. *Journal of Machine Learning Research*, 3:1157–1182, 2003.

[5] J.P.Nyrop, M.R.Binns, and W. der Werf. Sampling for IPM Decision Making: Where Should We Invest Time and Resources. In *Symposium on Sampling for Decision Making in Crop Loss Assessment and Pest Management*, pages 1104–1111, 1999.

[6] L.V.Madden and G.Hughes. Sampling for Plant Disease Incidence. In *Symposium on Sampling for Decision Making in Crop Loss Assessment and Pest Management*, pages 1088–1103, 1999.

[7] M.Saar-Tsechansky and F.Provost. Active Sampling for Class Probability Estimation and Ranking. In *Proc. 7th International Joint Conference on Artificial Intelligence*, pages 911–920, 2001.

[8] P.Domingos. MetaCost: A General Method for Making Classifiers Cost-Sensitive. In *Knowledge Discovery and Data Mining*, pages 155–164, 1999.

[9] P.D.Turney. Cost-sensitive Classification: Empirical Evaluation of a Hybrid Genetic Decision Tree Induction Algorithm. *Journal of Artificial Intelligence Research*, 2:369–409, 1995.

[10] N. Roy and A. McCallum. Toward optimal active learning through sampling estimation of error reduction. In *Proc. 18th International Conf. on Machine Learning*, pages 441–448. Morgan Kaufmann, San Francisco, CA, 2001.

[11] S.Tong and D.Koller. Support vector machine active learning with applications to text classification. In *Proceedings of the International Conference on Machine Learning*, pages 999–1006, 2000.

[12] Z.Zheng and B.Padmanabhan. On active learning for data acquisition. In *Proceedings of the International Conference on Datamining*, pages 562–570, 2002.

Combining the web content and usage mining to understand the visitor behavior in a web site

Juan Velásquez, Hiroshi Yasuda and Terumasa Aoki
Research Center for Advanced Science and Technology, University of Tokyo, Japan
E-mail:{jvelasqu,yasuda,aoki}@mpeg.rcast.u-tokyo.ac.jp

Abstract

A web site is a semi structured collection of different kinds of data, whose motivation is show relevant information to visitor and by this way capture her/his attention.

Understand the specifics preferences that define the visitor behavior in a web site, is a complex task. An approximation is suppose that it depend the content, navigation sequence and time spent in each page visited. These variables can be extracted from the web log files and the web site itself, using web usage and content mining respectively.

Combining the describe variables, a similarity measure among visitor sessions is introduced and used in a clustering algorithm, which identifies groups of similar sessions, allowing the analysis of visitors behavior.

In order to prove the methodology's effectiveness, it was applied in a certain web site, showing the benefits of the described approach.

1 Introduction

To understand the processes in the web visitor browsing, can be the key in order to improve both, the respective web content and understanding of visitor pattern [8]. This way, an organization can assure its success in Internet.

From all the possibly available data, three variables are analyzed: content, navigation sequence and time spent in each page visited. They can to get from the web log files and web site itself [7].

In the web site, is possible to find a lot of contents. The question is which of them are interesting for the visitor?

Using web mining techniques [2], is possible to find hidden knowledge about the visitor preferences [7]. In this work, we combine web usage and content mining approach [2], through the definition of a similarity measure among visitor session.

The proposed methodology was applied for analysis of a certain web site. The particular results show the method's

effectiveness, suggesting changes in content and structure of web site.

This paper is organized as follows. In section 2 the web mining proposition is introduced. Section 3 describe the data preparation process, which is necessary for comparison of visitor sessions (section 4). Section 5 describes the application of our work to the case of a Chilean bank. Section 6 concludes this work and points at future work.

2 Web content and usage mining proposition

The web mining techniques, can be categorized in three areas: Web Content Mining (WCM), Web Structure Mining (WSM) and Web Usage Mining (WUM) [2].

In order to discover hidden knowledge about the visitor behavior in the web site, we used WCM and WUM techniques with clustering algorithms [7], [8].

It aims to combine the philosophies behind WCM and WUM through providing a complemented vision of both techniques [5].

Using WUM is possible to understand the visitor browsing behavior, but is not directly which content is interesting for the visitor. It is possible to review using WCM, specify specifically sub area related to the semantics of the Web.

One first approach is the definition of a measurement that allows to compare behaviors between two visitor sessions, through the analysis of visitor preferences, i.e., at first time what pages visited and soon, what contains were more interesting for him.

The final idea is to use the measurement in a cluster algorithm in order to find group of visitor sessions with closed behavior and using this information, make prediction about the preferences of the future web site's visitors.

3 Data preparation process

We propose to consider two kinds of data sources that are easily available: Web log registers and Web pages.

The web log registers contain information about the browsing behavior of the web site visitors, in particular the page navigation sequence and the spent time in each page visited. The data from web logs is based on the structure given by W3C (http://www.rfc-editor.org/rfc/rfc2616.txt).

The second data source is the web site itself. Each web page is defined by its content. Here, we are only interested in the content of the pages, particularly its words.

3.1 Web log data preparation process

A web log file contains information on the access of all visitors to a particular Web site in chronological order. Then, we have to determine for each visitor, the sequence of web pages visited in his/her session. This process is known as **sessionization** [3]. It considers a maximum time duration given by a parameter, which is usually 30 minutes in the case of total session time.

3.2 Web page content data processing

A web page contains a variety of tags and words that do not have direct relation with the content of the page we want to study. Therefore we have to filter the text and to eliminate the following types of words: HTML Tags, Stop words (e.g. pronouns, prepositions, conjunctions, etc.) and Word stemming. Process of suffix removal, to generate word stems.

After filtering, we represent a document (web page) by a vector space model [1], in particular by vectors of words.

Let R be the number of different words in a Web site and Q be the number of its pages. A vectorial representation of the web site would then be a matrix M of dimension RxQ with:

$$M = (m_{ij}) \quad i = 1, \ldots, R \quad and \quad j = 1, \ldots, Q \quad (1)$$

where m_{ij} is the weight of word i in page j.

We propose to estimate these weights using equation 2, which is based on the *tfxidf-weighting* [1].

$$m_{ij} = f_{ij}(1 + \frac{sw(i)}{TR}) * \log(\frac{R}{n_i}) \quad (2)$$

f_{ij} is the number of occurrences of word i in page j and n_i is the total number of times the word i appears in the entire Web site. Additionally, we propose to augment word importance if a user searches for a specific word. This is done by sw (special words) which is an array with dimension R. It contains in component i the number of times that a user searches word i during a given period (e.g.: one month). TR is the total number of times that a user searches words in the Web site during the same period. If TR is zero, $\frac{sw(i)}{TR}$ is defined as zero, i.e. if there has not been any word searching, the weight m_{ij} depends just on the number of occurrences of words.

3.2.1 Distance measure between two pages

With the above definitions we can use vectorial linear algebra, in order to define a distance measure between two web pages.

Definition 1 (Word Pages Vectors)
$\mathbf{WP^k} = (wp_1^k, \ldots, wp_R^k) = (m_{1k}, \ldots, m_{Rk})$ *with* $k = 1, \ldots, Q$.

We define $dp_{ij} = dp(WP^i, WP^j)$ as the similarity between page vectors of the web site. It is the angle's cosine between two page vectors.

3.3 Web page sequence data processing

The sequence navigation can be represented by a graph like shown in figure 1. Each page is identified by an identification number. We denoted by $E(G)$ the edges set in the graph G. In the case of figure 1, $G_1 = \{1 \rightarrow 2, 2 \rightarrow 6, 2 \rightarrow 5, 5 \rightarrow 8\}$ and $G_2 = \{1 \rightarrow 3, 3 \rightarrow 6, 3 \rightarrow 7\}$ then $E(G_1) = \{1, 2, 6, 5, 8\}$ and $E(G_2) = \{1, 3, 6, 7\}$ with $\| E(G_1) \| = 5$ and $\| E(G_2) \| = 4$ respectively.

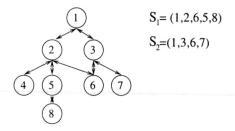

$S_1 = (1,2,6,5,8)$

$S_2 = (1,3,6,7)$

Figure 1. A web site with two navigation sequences

3.3.1 Comparing navigation graphs

Is necessary to define a measure that considerate the common or intersected sub sequences. The equation 3 introduce a simple way to compare to navigation sequences [6].

$$dG(G_1, G_2) = 2 \frac{\| E(G_1) \cap E(G_2) \|}{\| E(G_1) \| + \| E(G_2) \|} \quad (3)$$

Notice that $dG \in [0, 1]$ and if $G_1 = G_2$, we have $dG(G_1, G_2) = 1$. In the case of disjoint graphs, $dG(G_1, G_2) = 0$ because $\| E(G_1) \cap E(G_2) \| = 0$.

In order to calculate $\| E(G_1) \cap E(G_2) \|$ we have to determine how similar two sequences are, considering the order in which the nodes are visited.

Both sequences in figure 1 can be represented by a string of tokens [6] such as $S_1 = "12658"$ and $S_2 = "1367"$. We need to know how similar or different are both sequences in its string representation. The *Levenshtein distance* [4], also well known like *edit distance*, determine the number of transformations necessaries to convert S_1 in S_2. Then can be used as dissimilarity measure for sequences.

4 Comparing visitor sessions in a web site

We propose a model for visitor behavior using three variables: the sequence of visited pages, their content and the time spent in each one of them. The model is represented by a vector with dimension n and two parameters in each component.

Definition 2 (Visitor Behavior Vector)
$v = [(p_1, t_1) \ldots (p_n, t_n)]$, *being* (p_i, t_i) *parameters that represent the page and the time spent on it respectively in the* i^{th} *visit. In this expression,* p_i *is the page identifier.*

For instance, using the browsing navigation showed in figure 1, we have $v_1 = [(1,3), (2,40), (6,5), (5,16), (8,15)]$.

Let α, β be two visitor behavior vectors with cardinality C^α and C^β respectively and $\Gamma(\cdot)$ a function that applied over α or β returns the respective navigation sequence.

The proposed similarity measure is introduced in equation 4 as:

$$sm(\alpha, \beta) = dG(\Gamma(\alpha), \Gamma(\beta)) \frac{1}{\eta} \sum_{k=1}^{\eta} \tau_k * dp(p_{\alpha.k}^h, p_{\beta.k}^h) \quad (4)$$

where $\eta = \min\{C^\alpha, C^\beta\}$, p_k^h is the pairwise relation between k^{th} page and its content.

The first element of equation 4 is the sequence distance introduced in the equation 3.

As second element, $\tau_k = \min\{\frac{t_k^\alpha}{t_k^\beta}, \frac{t_k^\beta}{t_k^\alpha}\}$ is indicating the visitor's interest for the pages visited. We assume that the time spent on a page is proportional to the interest the visitor has in its content. In this way, if the times by visitors α and β on k^{th} page visited are close to each other, the value of the expression will be near **1**. In the opposite case, it will be near **0**.

The third element is dp because it is possible that two users visit different web pages in the web site, but the content is similar, e.g., one page contains information about classic rock and another one about progressive rock. In both cases the users have interest in music, specifically in rock.

5 Practical application

The web site selected[1], is about the first Chilean virtual bank, i.e., it doesn't have physical branches and all the

---

[1] http://www.tbanc.cl/

transactions are made using electronic means, like e-mails, portals, etc.

We have the following information about the web site: written in Spanish, contains 217 static web pages and approximately eight million web logs registers, correspond to the period January to March, 2003.

5.1 Sessionization process

Only 16% of the visitors visit 10 or more pages and 18% less than 4. The average of visited pages is 6. With these data, we fix 6 as maximum number of components in a visitor behavior vector, i.e. the parameter $H = 6$.

Finally, applying the above described filters, approximately 400,000 vectors were identified.

5.2 Web page content processing

Applying web page text filters, we find that the complete web site contains 710 different words for our analysis ($R=710$). Regarding word weights, especially the special words (see equation 2), we applied the following procedure.

The web site offers visitors the option to send e-mails to the call center platform. Then the text sent is a source to identified the most useful words. In this case, only 20 special words were used for page vector calculation.

5.3 Applying Self-Organizing Feature Maps

We used an artificial neural network of the Kohonen type (Self-organizing Feature Map; SOFM), in order to mining the visitor behavior vector and get knowledge [7] about the visitor preferences.

The notion of neighborhood among the neurons provides diverse topologies. In this case the thoroidal topology was used [7], which means that the neurons closest to the ones of the superior edge, are located in the inferior and lateral edges.

The SOFM used has 6 input neurons and 32 output neurons. The thoroidal topology maintains the continuity in clusters [8], which allows to study the transition among the preferences of the visitor from one cluster to another.

5.4 Results

From figure 2, we can identify four clusters as shown in the following table. The second and third column of table 1 contain the center neurons (winner neuron) of each of the clusters, representing the visited pages and the time spent in each one of them.

The pages in the web site were labelled with a number to facilitate its analysis. Table 2 shows the main content of each page.

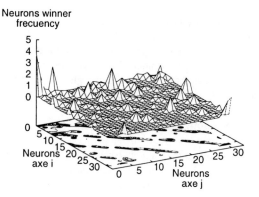

Figure 2. Clusters among visitor behavior vectors

Cluster	Pages Visited	Time spent in seconds
1	(1,3,8,9,147,190)	(40,67,175,113,184,43)
2	(100,101,126,128,30,58)	(20,69,40,63,107,10)
3	(70,86,150,186,137,97)	(4,61,35,5,65,97)
4	(157,169,180,101,105,1)	(5,80,121,108,30,5)

Table 1. Visitor behavior clusters

A detailed cluster analysis, revealed the following results:

- Cluster 1. Products and services offered by the bank.

- Cluster 2. Information about credit cards.

- Cluster 3. Agreements between the bank and other institutions.

- Cluster 4. Investments and remote services offered by the bank

Reviewing the clusters found, it can be inferred that the visitors show interest in the promotions with others institutions, investments and services. Based on our analysis we have proposed changes of the structure of the Web site, privileging the described information.

Pages	Content
1	Home page
$2, \ldots, 65$	Products and Services
$66, \ldots, 98$	Agreements with other institutions
$99, \ldots, 115$	Remote services
$116, \ldots, 130$	Credit cards
$131, \ldots, 155$	Promotions
$156, \ldots, 184$	Investments
$185, \ldots, 217$	Different kinds of credits

Table 2. Pages and their content

6 Conclusions

We proposed a way to study the visitor behavior in a Web site, based in web content and usage mining. The result is the definition of a new similarity measure based on three characteristics derived from the visitor sessions: the sequence of visited pages, their content and the time spent in each one of them. Using this similarity in a self organizing map, we found clusters from visitor sessions, which allow us to study the user behavior in the web.

The similarity introduced, can be very useful to increase the knowledge about the visitor behavior in the web. As future work, it is proposed to improve the presented methodology introducing advanced variables derived from visitor sessions.

References

[1] R. Baeza-Yates, B. Ribeiro-Neto, Modern Information Retrieval, chapter 2. *Addison-Wesley* 1999

[2] B. Berendt, A. Hotho and G. Stumme, Towards Semantic Web Mining, *Procs. in First Int. Semantic Web Conf.*, pages 264-278, Sardinia, Italy, June 9-12, 2002.

[3] R. Cooley, B. Mobasher, J. Srivastava. Data Preparation for Mining World Wide Web Browsing Patterns. *Journal of Knowlegde and Information Systems* Vol. 1, pages 5-32, 1999.

[4] V.I. Levenshtein, Binary codes capable of correcting deletions, insertions and reversals, *Sov. Phys. Dokl.*, pages 705-710, 1966

[5] B. Mobasher,T. Luo, Y. Sung, and J. Zhu, Integrating Web Usage and Content Mining for More Effective Personalization, *In Procs. of the Int. Conf. on E-Commerce and Web Technologies*, September, Greenwich, UK, 2000

[6] T.A. Runkler and J.C. Bezdek, Web mining with Relational Clustering December, 2001.

[7] J. Velásquez, H. Yasuda, T. Aoki and Richard Weber, Acquiring Knowledge About User's Preferences in a Web Site, *In Procs. of the IEEE Int. Conf. on Information Technology: Research and Education*, pages 375-379, Newark, New Jersey, USA,August 2003

[8] J. Velásquez, H. Yasuda, T. Aoki and Richard Weber, Using Self Organizing Feature Maps to Acquire Knowledge About Visitor Behavior in a Web Site, *In Procs. of the Knowledge-Based Intelligent Information & Engineering Systems*, to appear, University of Oxford, UK, September, 2003

Class Decomposition via Clustering: A New Framework for Low-Variance Classifiers

Ricardo Vilalta, Murali-Krishna Achari, and Christoph F. Eick
Department of Computer Science
University of Houston
Houston TX, 77204-3010, USA
{vilalta, amkchari, ceick}@cs.uh.edu

Abstract

We propose a pre-processing step to classification that applies a clustering algorithm to the training set to discover local patterns in the attribute or input space. We demonstrate how this knowledge can be exploited to enhance the predictive accuracy of simple classifiers. Our focus is mainly on classifiers characterized by high bias but low variance (e.g., linear classifiers); these classifiers experience difficulty in delineating class boundaries over the input space when a class distributes in complex ways. Decomposing classes into clusters makes the new class distribution easier to approximate and provides a viable way to reduce bias while limiting the growth in variance. Experimental results on real-world domains show an advantage in predictive accuracy when clustering is used as a pre-processing step to classification.

1 Introduction

Our study explores how classification algorithms can benefit from class density information that is obtained using clustering. Such information can be exploited to improve the quality of the decision boundaries during classification and enhance the prediction accuracy of simple classifiers. We demonstrate how using classification and clustering techniques in conjunction addresses key issues in learning theory (e.g., bias vs variance) and provides an attractive new family of classification models.

Our goal is to exploit the information derived from a clustering algorithm to increase the complexity of simple classifiers characterized by low variance and high bias. These algorithms, commonly referred to as model-based or parametric-based, encompass a small class of approximating functions and exhibit limited flexibility in their decision boundaries. Examples include linear classifiers, prob-

abilistic classifiers based on the attribute-independence assumption (e.g., Naive Bayes), and single logical rules. The question we address is how to increase the complexity of these classifiers to trade-off bias for variance in an effective manner. Since these models start off with simple representations, increasing their complexity is expected to improve their generalization performance while still retaining their ability to output models amenable to interpretation.

Our approach extends previous work [6] in which we increase the degree of complexity of the decision boundaries of a simple classifier by augmenting the number of boundaries per class. The idea is to transform the classification problem by decomposing each class into clusters. By relabelling the examples covered by each cluster with a new class label, the simple classifier generates an increased number of boundaries per class, and is then armed to cope with complex distributions where classes cover different regions of the input space. In this paper we add a new step in which we explore the space of possible new class assignments in a greedy manner maximizing predictive accuracy.

We test our methodology on twenty datasets from the University of California at Irvine repository, using two simple classifiers: Naive Bayes and a Support Vector Machine with a polynomial kernel of degree one. Empirical results support our goal statement that *pre-identifying local patterns in the data through clustering is a helpful tool in improving the performance of simple classifiers.*

The paper organization is described next. Section 2 introduces background information and our problem statement. Section 3 details our class decomposition approach. Section 4 reports our empirical results. Finally, Section 5 states our summary and future work.

2 Problem Statement

Let $(X_1, X_2, \cdots, X_n)$ be an n-component vector-valued random variable, where each X_i represents an attribute or feature; the space of all possible attribute vectors is called the attribute or input space $\mathcal{X}$. Let $\{y_1, y_2, \cdots, y_k\}$ be the possible classes, categories, or states of nature; the space of all possible classes is called the output space $\mathcal{Y}$. A classifier receives as input a set of training examples $T = \{(\mathbf{x}, y)\}$, where $\mathbf{x} = (x_1, x_2, \cdots, x_n)$ is a vector or point in the input space (x_i is the value of attribute X_i) and y is a point in the output space. The outcome of the classifier is a function h (or hypothesis) mapping the input space to the output space, $h : \mathcal{X} \rightarrow \mathcal{Y}$.

2.1 Simple Discriminant Functions

We consider the case where a classifier defines a discriminant function for each class $g_j(\mathbf{x})$, $j = 1, 2, \cdots, k$ and chooses the class corresponding to the discriminant function with highest value (ties are broken arbitrarily):

$$h(\mathbf{x}) = y_m \text{ iff } g_m(\mathbf{x}) \geq g_j(\mathbf{x}) \quad (1)$$

Possibly, the simplest case is that of a linear discriminant function, where the approximation is based on a linear model:

$$g_j(\mathbf{x}) = w_0 + \sum_{i=1}^{n} w_i x_i \quad (2)$$

where each $w_i, 0 \leq i \leq n$, is a coefficient that must be learned by the classification algorithm.

We will also consider probabilistic classifiers where the discriminant functions are proportional to the posterior probabilities of a class given the input vector $\mathbf{x}$, $P(y_j|\mathbf{x})$. The classifier, also known as Naive Bayes, assumes feature independence given the class:

$$g_j(\mathbf{x}) = P(y_j)\Pi_i^n P(x_i|y_j) \quad (3)$$

where $P(y_j)$ is the a priori probability of class y_j, and $\Pi_i^n P(x_i|y_j)$ is a simple product approximation of $P(\mathbf{x}|y_j)$, called the likelihood or class-conditional probability.

2.2 The Bias-Variance Trade-Off

Simple discriminant functions tend to output poor function approximations when the data distributes in complex ways. Our goal is to increase the complexity of simple classifiers to obtain better function approximations. Since our training set comprises a limited number of examples and we do not know the form of the true target distribution, our goal is inevitably subject to the bias-variance dilemma in statistical inference [4, 5]. The dilemma is based on the fact that prediction error can be decomposed into a bias and a variance component[1]; ideally we would like to have classifiers

---

[1]A third component, the *irreducible error* or *Bayes error*, cannot be eliminated.

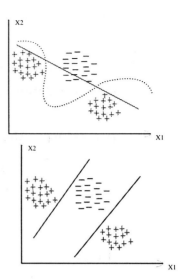

Figure 1. (top) A high-order polynomial improves the classification of a linear classifier at the expense of increased variance. (bottom) Increasing the number of linear discriminants guided by local patterns increases complexity with lower impact on variance.

with low bias and low variance but these components are inversely related.

Our problem statement can be rephrased as follows: how can we decrease the bias (i.e., increase the complexity) of our simple classifiers without drastically increasing the variance component? Notice our goal sets forth in a direction orthogonal to combination methods like bagging [2] and boosting [3] where the goal is to reduce the variance component in generalization error by voting on classifiers obtained from variants of the training data.

2.3 Increasing Complexity Through Additional Boundaries

Our solution is to exploit information about the distribution of examples through a pre-processing step that identifies natural clusters in data. As an illustration, Figure 1 shows a two dimensional input space with two classes (positive + and negative −). The distribution of examples precludes a simple linear classifier attaining good performance (Figure 1-top, bold line). One way to increase the complexity of the classifier is to enlarge the original space of linear combinations to allow for more flexibility on the decision boundaries, for example by adding higher order polynomials (Figure 1-top, dashed line). But this comes at the expense of increased variance and possibly data overfitting.

Alternatively, one can retain the same space of linear functions but increase the number of decision boundaries per class (Figure 1-bottom). This increases the complexity of the classifier but with less impact on variance. The trick lies on identifying regions of high class density within subsets of examples of the same class which we accomplish through clustering. The next sections provide a detail description of our approach.

3   Class Decomposition via Clustering

Our solution comprises three steps: A) a decomposition of classes into clusters; B) a search for an optimal class assignment configuration; and C) a function mapping predictions to the original set of class labels. We explain each step in turn.

A. Class Decomposition. Our first step pre-processes the training data by clustering examples that belong to the same class. We proceed by first separating dataset T into sets of examples of the same class. That is T is separated into different sets of examples $T = \{T_j\}$, where each T_j comprises all examples in T labelled with class y_j, $T_j = \{(\mathbf{x}, y) \in T | y = y_j\}$.

For each set T_j we apply a clustering algorithm C to find sets of examples (i.e., clusters) grouped together according to some distance metric over the input space. Let $\{c_i^j\}$ be the set of such clusters. We map the set of examples in T_j into a new set T_j' by renaming every class label to indicate not only the class but also the cluster to which each example belongs. One simple way to do this is by making each class label a pair (a, b), where the first element represents the original class and the second element represents the cluster that the example falls into. In that case, $T_j' = \{(\mathbf{x}, y_j')\}$, where $y_j' = (y_j, i)$ whenever example $\mathbf{x}$ is assigned to cluster c_i^j. Finally the new dataset T' is simply the union of all sets of examples of the same class relabelled according to the cluster to which each example belongs, $T' = \bigcup_{j=1}^{k} T_j'$.

An illustration of the transformation above is shown in Figure 2. We assume a two-dimensional input space where examples belong to either class positive (+) or negative (−). Let's suppose the clustering algorithm separates class positive into two clusters, while class negative is grouped into one single cluster. The transformation relabels every example to encode class and cluster label. As a result, dataset T' has now three different classes.

B. A Search for Class Assignments. Increasing the number of classes according to the number of induced clusters may result in an excessive number of classes. Our second step extends previous work [6] by exploring the space of possible ways to merge clusters derived from the first step. Following the same notation as before, a class label will be a pair (a, b), where the first element represents the original class label and the second element represents the cluster that the example falls into; but the difference now is that two or

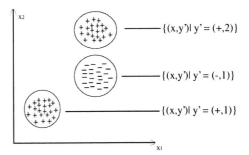

Figure 2. The mapping process relabels examples to encode both class and cluster.

more clusters may correspond to the same second element (i.e., element b), which can be interpreted as having clusters merged into a single cluster.

Our goal is to explore the space of possible ways to merge clusters obtained during the first step, until we find a configuration that maximizes predictive accuracy (over a validation set different from the training set). The space of possible configurations corresponds to the space of all subsets of clusters, with each subset being assigned the same cluster index (i.e., being assigned the same class label). Obviously one cannot explore this space exhaustively. If class y_j is decomposed into n_j clusters, the number of different configurations has an upper bound of $\mathcal{O}(2^{n_j})$. To avoid an exhaustive search we follow a heuristic greedy approach. The search starts by evaluating predictive accuracy assuming each cluster is mapped to a separate index. Next we start looking for pairs of clusters (e.g. $\{c_1^j, c_2^j\}$) and compute predictive accuracy assuming the two clusters of each pair are mapped to the same index. We then take those pairs for which predictive accuracy increased and rank them accordingly. To enforce a mutually exclusive list of clusters we prune every cluster pair where at least one cluster appears on another pair with higher rank. The algorithm keep merging clusters until no new cluster sets of higher cardinality can be produced from the cluster sets in the previous iteration. At that point we assign the clusters on each subset the same index (i.e., the same class label).

C. Classification of Examples. Our last step serves to assess the performance of the linear classifier over the extended output space. This is necessary during the search over the space of subsets of clusters, and while estimating final predictive accuracy. During learning, the simple classifier is trained over dataset T' producing a hypothesis h' mapping points from input space $\mathcal{X}$ to the new output space $\mathcal{Y}'$. During classification, hypothesis h' will output a prediction consisting of a class label and a cluster label, $h'(\mathbf{x}) = (a, b)$. To know the actual prediction in the original output space $\mathcal{Y}$ we simply remove the cluster index.

Essentially, we predict class label y_j whenever example $\mathbf{x}$ is assigned to any of the clusters (or subsets of clusters) of class y_j.

4 Experiments

Our experiments include as simple classifiers a naive probabilistic classifier that assumes feature independence given the class (known as Naive Bayes), and a support vector machine (SVM) with a polynomial of degree one as the kernel function. The clustering algorithm follows the Expectation Maximization (EM) technique. The number of clusters is estimated using cross-validation. On each run we use 50% of the examples for training, 25% for validation, and 25% for testing. Reports on accuracy are the average of ten runs (over the testing set). An asterisk at the top right of a number implies the difference is significant at the $p = 0.01$ level (using a t-student distribution). Our datasets can be obtained from the University of California at Irvine Repository [1]

4.1 Results

Table 1 displays our results. The second column reports the mean accuracy of Naive Bayes, and the third column reports the increase in accuracy using our proposed approach. The fourth and fifth columns show the corresponding performance and increase in accuracy for the linear classifier. There is a clear gain in performance with the probabilistic classifier. The average increase in accuracy for Naive Bayes is 4.56%. There is statistically significant enhancement met in eight domains. No performance improvement indicates our algorithm has merged all clusters of each class into a single cluster; such configuration is equivalent to the original dataset and thus produces no change in performance. Compared to previous work [6], we find that merging clusters into single classes (Step 2, Section 3) is indeed effective, but the need for a validation step reduces the number of available training examples, resulting in some performance impact.

The average increase in accuracy for the linear classifier is of 0.89%. Performance is almost the same between our proposed approach and the standard version, except for two domains (vehicle and vowel) where the difference is significant. In some cases there is a decrease in performance (not significant), indicating an apparent increase in accuracy on the validation set, but an actual decrease on the testing set.

5 Summary and Future Work

We propose an approach to improve the accuracy of simple classifiers through a pre-processing step that applies a clustering algorithm over examples belonging to the same

Table 1. Predictive accuracy on real-world domains.

Domain	Naive Bayes	Δ Acc	Linear Classifier	Δ Acc
Anneal	82.21	9.98*	88.13	0.42
Balance-Scale	89.88	0.0	87.83	0.0
Breast-Cancer	73.52	0.38	72.96	0.63
Breast-W	96.19	0.16	96.87	0.0
Colic	79.44	1.92	83.39	−0.22
Credit-a	77.87	3.71*	85.04	0.15
Credit-g	78.17	0.0	76.02	−0.23
Diabetes	76.81	0.0	78.07	0.0
Heart-c	83.40	0.44	85.96	−0.53
Heart-h	86.84	0.0	83.48	0.61
Hypothyroid	90.22	1.02	72.88	0.63
Letter	59.68	1.04*	56.23	0.05
Mushroom	92.91	6.45*	99.93	0.04
Segment	80.18	8.57*	91.88	0.0
Sick	86.36	4.82*	92.19	0.0
Soybean	90.17	0.00	94.11	0.00
Splice	96.88	0.00	93.99	0.00
Vehicle	42.52	25.24*	66.86	4.88*
Vote	89.17	6.02*	97.49	−0.09
Vowel	59.92	21.53*	72.17	11.53*

class. We demonstrate the resulting knowledge can be exploited to improve the quality of the class decision boundaries. Our algorithm explores the space of possible class assignments over the induced clusters searching to maximize accuracy. Our experiments show that our proposed approach results in either equal or increased accuracy on most of the real-world domains used for analysis.

Future work will try to explain why performance improvement is evident in the probabilistic classifier but not in the linear classifier. We will also look for ways to improve the computational cost of finding the best class-assignment configuration.

References

[1] C. Blake and M. C.J. UCI, Repository of machine learning databases. *University of California, Irvine, Dept. of Information and Computer Sciences*, 1998.

[2] L. Breiman. Bagging predictors. *Machine Learning Journal*, 24:123–140, 1996.

[3] Y. Freund and R. E. Schapire. Experiments with a new boosting algorithm. pages 148–156, 1996.

[4] S. Geman, E. Bienenstock, and R. Doursat. Neural networks and the bias/variance dilemma. *Neural Computation*, pages 1–58, 1992.

[5] T. Hastie, R. Tibshirani, and J. Friedman. *The elements of statistical learning; data mining, inference, and prediction.* Springer-Verlag, 2001.

[6] R. Vilalta and I. Rish. A decomposition of classes via clustering to explain and improve naive bayes. *14th European Conference on Machine Learning*, 2003.

Bootstrapping Rule Induction

Lemuel R. Waitman, Douglas H. Fisher*, Paul H. King
Department of Biomedical Engineering
*Department of Electrical Engineering and Computer Science
Vanderbilt University, Nashville, TN 37235
lemuel.r.waitman@, douglas.h.fisher@, paul.h.king@vanderbilt.edu

Abstract

Most rule learning systems posit hard decision boundaries for continuous attributes and point estimates of rule accuracy, with no measures of variance, which may seem arbitrary to a domain expert. These hard boundaries/points change with small perturbations to the training data. Moreover, rule induction typically produces a large number of rules that must be filtered and interpreted by an analyst. This paper describes a method of combining rules over multiple bootstrap replications of rule induction so as to reduce the total number of rules presented to an analyst and to provide measures of variance to continuous attribute decision boundaries and accuracy-point estimates. The method is illustrated with perioperative data.

1. Introduction

Rule induction [1] identifies conditions that are associated with particular outcomes. For example, in the domain of perioperative medicine (i.e., the process of preoperative evaluation, providing anesthesia, and managing postoperative recovery), 34,926 "outcomes" (generally adverse events) have been identified [2] and are used to evaluate post-surgical status of patients in cases that involve general anesthesia. Rule induction from data in this setting results in rules like:

```
IF Height < 158 AND Age < 49 AND ASAClass >= 3
     THEN NauseaVomit = Significant
IF Hypertension = yes AND Phase1Recovery >= 84
     AND Age < 49 THEN Pain = Severe
IF Age >= 61 AND BloodLoss >= 100
     AND BloodPressureVariability >= 16.7371
     THEN ExtendedPhase1Recovery = yes
```

Since there may be multiple adverse outcomes/incidents for some patients, but most patients are free of any given

adverse outcome, perioperative KDD seeks to identify sub-populations at risk so that preoperative safeguards can be taken. Rule induction fits this objective because induced rules focus on positive examples that "represent some surprising occurrence or anomaly we wish to monitor" [3]. This is in contrast to the classification of positive and negative examples by classifiers that cover all data, typically with respect to mutually-exclusive outcomes. If the majority of the examples are negative, a classifier may be constructed to optimize overall classification at the expense of creating branches that isolate the abnormalities [4].

Though rule induction represents a good starting point for analyzing perioperative data and like domains, current systems have drawbacks, which include: a) No measure of variance around a rule's accuracy and no variance around continuous attribute decision boundaries (e.g., Height < 158), which can diminish a domain expert's trust in discovered knowledge. If the boundary for a rule involving weight is 67 kilograms, it's valuable to know the standard deviation is 3 kilograms instead of 10. It is also useful to know that one rule might have lower accuracy but a smaller standard deviation than another rule. b) The discovery of a large number of rules that are difficult for a domain expert to filter. This paper describes a method of combining rules over multiple bootstrap replications of rule induction so as to mitigate these problems.

Section 2 describes Brute, which we use as the basic rule induction system. Section 3 describes bootstrapping rule induction. Section 4 presents experimental results with the bootstrapped-Brute system, indicating substantial reduction in the number of discovered rules and providing variability information that is helpful in rule interpretation.

2. The Brute System for Rule Induction

Brute version 1.2 [3, 5] was chosen to discover rules over which summary rules would eventually be induced across multiple bootstrap replications. Theoretically, Brute can exhaustively search the space of conjunctive rules (antecedents), but has a variety of options to limit the search in practice. Options include limiting the depth of search (i.e., the number of conjuncts that can occur in a rule's antecedent) and rejecting rules that cover less than a certain percentage of positive examples. Brute has other filters to eliminate some rules from consideration.

Of the rules discovered in the constrained search, Brute returns the best N rules according to an objective function. We modified Brute to use extended Laplace Accuracy [6]. If n is the number of examples in the (test) data set for which the antecedent of the rule holds and e is the number of examples for which the consequent and the antecedent holds, then extended Laplace accuracy is

$$A_{LE} = \frac{e + k + A_D}{n + k} (1)$$

where A_D is the proportion of positive examples in the data and k is a small integer, commonly set to 2 or the depth of search. Extended Laplace accuracy is centered on the frequency of positive examples in the data instead of 50%, which is an implicit assumption of regular Laplace accuracy. All of the clinical datasets in our studies had positive data proportions below 50%, typically 10% to 20%.

3. Bootstrapping Rule Induction

Our work reduces the number of discovered rules and assigns variance values to decision boundaries and point estimates. To achieve these goals, we repeatedly apply rule induction using Brute to different, but overlapping subsets of the available data, and abstract rules that occur across multiple rule-induction trials.

3.1 Bootstrapping

The bootstrap was introduced by Efron and Tibshirani [7] as a computer-based method to estimate the standard error of a parameter. Bootstrap samples, also called replications, are created by uniformly sampling n times with replacement from a dataset of size n. Some instances in the original data set will appear zero times while others will appear multiple times. The bootstrap samples are used for rule induction. For large sample sizes, approximately 36.8% of the original samples will not be included in the bootstrap sample. These are reserved for testing. The bootstrap estimate, often referred to as the 0.632-bootstrap estimate, combines the accuracies from the testing and training sets as

$$acc^{.632} = \frac{1}{b}\Sigma_{i=1}^{b}(0.632 * acc_i^{test} + 0.368 * acc_i^{train})(2)$$

where b is the number of bootstrap samples, `acctrain` is the accuracy of the classifier or rule on the training data (i.e.,

the bootstrap sample) and `acctest` is the accuracy on the test data (i.e., data not included in the bootstrap sample). Bootstrap sampling underlies the machine learning method of bagging (or bootstrap aggregating) classifiers [8]. Bootstrapping rule induction is different, however, than bootstrapping a classifier. Bootstrapping a classifier has the goal of characterizing the repeatability of a method's classification performance, and often to increase accuracy. Unless a decision list [9] is generated, there is no equivalent overall accuracy criterion for bootstrapping rule induction. Each rule independently classifies only a portion of the data. A rule found during one bootstrap replication might not appear in another replication. A rule with the same attributes might exist in other replications but the attribute values (or value ranges) differ. Instead of maximizing overall classification accuracy, we seek to find rules whose basic form persists across bootstrap replications. These rules are combined into summary rules, which reflect variability in rule accuracy and antecedent conditions.

3.2 Summary Rule Generation

Once all bootstrap replications are complete, the best N (e.g., 50) rules, if that many are found, are compared to the rules from the remaining replications. For this study, the criterion for determining the best rules was the 0.632 bootstrap estimate (Equation 2) of the rule's extended Laplace accuracy (Equation 1). Ten bootstrap replications are performed. "Nearly identical" rules across the replications are identified. For a given rule, the rules from other replications must involve the same attributes with identical relational operators. For discrete attributes, the attribute value must be identical. For continuous attributes, the attribute values are allowed to vary. For example,

```
IF CPTCode = 29 AND Height < 164 AND
HeartRateVariability >= 28.6 THEN Nause-
aGreaterThanMild = yes
```
is nearly identical to
```
IF CPTCode = 29 AND Height < 158 AND
HeartRateVariability >= 25.7 THEN Nause-
aGreaterThanMild = yes
```
but is not nearly identical to
```
IF CPTCode = 29 AND Height >= 140 AND
HeartRateVariability >= 21.3 THEN Nause-
aGreaterThanMild = yes
```
and also not nearly identical to
```
IF CPTCode <> 27 AND Height < 164 AND
HeartRateVariability >= 31.5 THEN Nause-
aGreaterThanMild = yes
```

If nearly identical rules exist across multiple replications, a summary rule is created. The summary rule stores the mean and standard deviation of the summary rule's bootstrap extended Laplace accuracy and coverage (i.e., percentage of cases that satisfy the rule's antecedent) and the number of replications that contained a nearly identical rule that support the summary rule. The summary rule also contains basic statistics regarding the variability of the continuous attributes and variability of accuracy across the base rules used to construct the summary.

Consider the summary rule:

SourceRuleID: `NVPreo0048005115, SummaryRuleID:`
`7851 IF Height >= 158.6 (1.2) AND Height`
`< 162.9 (0.7) AND Phase2Recovery < 29.4`
`(6.24) THEN NauseaGreaterThanMild = Yes`
`(2.89x as likely) Accuracy:  51.7 (8.0),`
`Coverage:  6.6 (2.6), 10/10`

The continuous attribute means are followed by the standard deviations in parentheses. The bootstrap extended Laplace accuracy and coverage are shown in parentheses on the following line The odds-ratio, shown just prior to accuracy, indicates how many times as likely the outcome occurs for the subpopulation satisfying the rule's antecedent, relative to the data as a whole.

Summary rules that contain the same continuous attribute twice were further filtered. For example, consider the summary rule above, which specifies upper and lower boundaries for Height. In this case, there is concern that the distance between the upper and lower boundaries on Height is small, but the small standard deviations suggest that the summary rule is significant. In this case, we would choose to retain the rule, but we wish to eliminate rules in which the specified range is meaningless due to a large standard deviation relative to the distance between the lower and upper boundaries as determined by a test for the difference between means [10].

4. Experimental Studies

We applied bootstrapped rule induction to perioperative databases developed and utilized at Vanderbilt University Medical Center. Data with preoperative attributes and different outcomes were created. The outcomes were high intraoperative heart rate variability (533 out of 3655 instances; 14.6%), postoperative pain (198 with no pain and 231 with severe pain out of 1583 instances; 12.5% and 14.6%, respectively), postoperative nausea and vomiting (494 greater than mild and 270 greater than moderate out of 2533 instances; 19.5% and 10.7%, respectively), and long recovery time (1615 out of 8248 instances; 19.6%). These outcomes were chosen because they are clinically meaningful for ambulatory patients, are reliably recorded in the perioperative database, and occur with moderate frequency. The attributes included 8 Boolean, 4 other categorical, 4 small-integer-range, and 8 other numeric attributes.

For this study, all data mining was done to a depth of three conjuncts and the minimum positive coverage was five percent. Iterative depth first search was used. The best 900 rules, as measured by extended Laplace accuracy, were saved. Brute's standard filters (Section 2) were employed with default settings. Ten bootstrap replications were made for each data set.

After completing all 10 replications of a data set, the top 50 rules (of the 900 stored) for each replication were examined, in turn. For each top-50 rule of a replication, all 900 rules of each alternate replication were examined for nearly identical rules from which a summary rule could be constructed. If one or more nearly identical rules were found for a top-50 rule, then a summary rule was generated and stored, along with the base rules that support it. Thus, a rule ranked 32 in replication 4, together with a rule ranked 431 in replication 2, and rule 128 in replication 6, might all support a single summary rule with 3/10 support. Each summary rule must have at least one top-50 rule in support. Reducing summary rule discovery costs was the primary motivation for the top-50 restriction. By focusing on summary rules, the number of rules to be analyzed is reduced significantly. We illustrate this with two representative outcomes.

We show the total number of rules discovered during the ten bootstrap replications , the number of summary rules with any level of support (2/10 through 10/10), and the number of fully (10/10) supported summary rules. For `Heart Rate Variability` the results are:

Sample Size	#RulesFound (Ave per Replication)	#SummaryRules SummaryRules	#10/10
3655	6068 (607)	129	16

and for `Long Recovery` are:

Sample Size	#RulesFound (Ave per Replication)	#SummaryRules SummaryRules	#10/10
8248	9000 (900)	152	56

Remember that Brute was configured to find up to 900 statistically significant rules. This limit was reached for the long recovery data set. On average, across all outcomes, focusing on the summary rules reduces the number of rules to be analyzed by a factor of 4 and evaluating only fully supported rules (10/10 replications) reduces the number of rules by a factor of 20.

Table 1 shows 3 of the 16 summary rules for high heart rate variability that persisted across all ten bootstrap replications. It is provided to give an idea of the kinds of rules that were found. All the rules include low preoperative pulse as an attribute. Most of the rules share another common attribute such as age, weight, or blood pressure.

Table 1. Summary Rules for high heart rate variability
SourceRuleID: `HRHigh0009001014, SummaryRuleID:`
`1445 Height < 177.7 (2.869) AND Age <`
`47.1 (10.999) AND Pulse < 58.9 (3.9) THEN`
`HRVarOver30 = yes (4.398x as likely) Accu-`
`racy:  64.572 (4.3879), Coverage:  4.3287`
`(1.0141), 10/10`

SourceRuleID: HRHigh0009001010, SummaryRuleID: 1443 PreopSysBP < 115.5 (6.916) AND Age < 46.3 (9.719) AND Pulse < 61 (4.853) THEN HRVarOver30 = yes (4.066x as likely) Accuracy: 59.707 (7.5339), Coverage: 4.9437 (1.2526), 10/10

SourceRuleID: HRHigh0009001083, SummaryRuleID: 1473 IF PreopECGAssess = none AND Weight < 68.65 (5.457) AND Pulse < 64.9 (5.507) THEN HRVarOver30 = yes (3.354x as likely) Accuracy: 49.246 (6.3210), Coverage: 5.4851 (1.6223), 10/10

5. Conclusion

Rule induction is well suited for problem domains with a multitude of risks and events. Conjunctive rules are easy to understand but the absolute boundaries of the rules and their sheer number invite skepticism from domain experts. Summary rules display the variability in accuracy and conjunct boundaries expected by the domain expert and reduce the number of rules that must be analyzed. Highly supported, stable summary rules give greater confidence that this knowledge is not just an artificial, over-fitted construct of the machine-learning algorithm.

More generally, we are concerned with advancing strategies for analyst exploration of discovered rules. In this endeavor, we [10] have also defined similarity between summary rules, and exploited similarity for visualizing the space of summary rules using multidimensional scaling (MDS). Analyst exploration can be directed to disparate portions of the summary rule space, and similarity can also be exploited for characterizing algorithm stability.

The disadvantage of the summary rule approach is increased computation time. All work was accomplished with identical Intel Pentium III 500 MHz computers with 256MB. One computer contained the database and carried the computational burden of running stored procedures, storing, and retrieving data. The other computer acted as an analysis workstation by executing the Brute algorithm and other client applications. Rule induction at a depth of three and rule storage for a single bootstrap replication took between ten seconds and three hours depending of the dataset. Preliminary experimentation with some datasets took over twelve hours to mine to a depth of four. Calculating and retrieving summary rules took between one minute and two hours.

Future research should focus on advancing understanding of induced rule stability in larger datasets, and reducing computational cost.

6. References

[1] Van Den Eijkel,G.C. 1999. Rule Induction. In Intelligent Data Analysis: An Introduction. Springer-Verlag, Berlin. pp. 195-216.

[2] Forrest,J.B., Rehder,K., Cahalan,M.K., and Goldsmith,C.H. 1992. Multicenter Study of General Anesthesia III. Predictors of Severe Perioperative Adverse Outcomes. Anesthesiology 76: 3-15.

[3] Riddle,P., Segal,R., and Etzioni,O. 1994. Representation Design and Brute-force Induction in a Boeing Manufacturing Domain. Applied Artificial Intelligence 8: 125-147.

[4] Kubat,M., Holte,R.C., and Matwin,S. 1998. Machine learning for the detection of oil spills in satellite radar images. Machine Learning 30: 195-215.

[5] Segal,R.B. Machine learning as massive search. 1997. University of Washington. Ref Type: Thesis/Dissertation

[6] Good, I. J. The Estimation of Probabilities: An Essay on Modern Bayesian Methods. Research monograph 30. MIT Press, 1965.

[7] Efron,B. and Tibshirani,R.J. 1993. An Introduction to the Bootstrap. Chapman and Hall, New York, NY.

[8] Breiman,L. 1996. Bagging Predictors. Machine Learning 24: 123-140.

[9] Segal,R. and Etzioni,O. 1994. Learning Decision Lists Using Homogeneous Rules. In AAAI-94.

[10] Waitman, L. R., Fisher, D., & King, P. (2001) http://www.vuse.vanderbilt.edu/ dfisher/waitman2001.doc

Center-Based Indexing for Nearest Neighbors Search

Arkadiusz Wojna

Institute of Informatics, Warsaw University
ul. Banacha 2, 02-097 Warsaw, Poland
wojna@mimuw.edu.pl

Abstract

The paper addresses the problem of indexing data for the k nearest neighbors (k-nn) search. It presents a tree-based top-down indexing method that uses an iterative k-means algorithm for tree node splitting and combines three different search pruning criteria from BST, GHT and GNAT into one. The experiments show that the presented indexing tree accelerates the k-nn searching up to several thousands times in case of large data sets.

1 Introduction

In the similarity based searching problem first a distance measure is defined on data objects and next the problem is to find k objects from a database that are nearest to a given query object. The problem is important for multimedia, machine learning and data mining applications. To reduce the cost of searching one can construct an indexing tree. Such a tree is built using the top-down strategy starting with the whole data set at the root of a tree and recursively at each node splitting data objects into a fixed number k of smaller clusters. The search algorithm traverses the constructed tree in the depth-first order and tries to discard some nodes from searching.

Great number of indexing methods (R-, R*-, R+-, X-, TV-, SS-, M-trees) described in the literature concern the case when data are stored on disk [6]. However, one of the most popular application of the k-nn method is object classification. It requires fast access to data and often the only solution is to assume that data are kept in the main memory. With growing size of the main memory in data servers this case attracts more and more attention of researchers working in other application areas too. In the paper we focus on this case.

The first main memory based indexing structures for k-nn searching are k-d- and quad-trees [1, 4]. They use iso-oriented hyperplanes to split objects at each node of an indexing tree. BST [8] and GHT [10] use a more advanced algorithm for splitting nodes. It selects randomly two child node centers among objects in the parent node and assigns each object to the nearest center. This procedure may produce splitting hyperplanes in an arbitrary direction, what is more effective for the search process. Both trees have the same construction but different search pruning criteria are used: the covering radius in BST and the hyperplane cut in GHT. GNAT [3] is a more advanced version of the BST/GHT tree. To balance the tree GNAT computes the number of child nodes for each node separately. It uses the same splitting procedure as in BST and GHT but the centers for child nodes are selected more carefully. Finally, it uses more sophisticated search pruning criterion.

Our method differs from the above indexing structures in two ways. First, we use an iterative splitting procedure instead of a one-step procedure. Second, as a search pruning criterion we propose the combination of three different criteria from BST [8], GHT [10] and GNAT [3]. The experiments with real-life data show that the indexing tree with the iterative k-means based splitting procedure and the complex search pruning criteria is several times faster than the tree with a one-step splitting procedure and any single criterion. Hence, in case of large databases it can accelerate searching even up to several thousands times in comparison to the linear search.

2 Indexing

We assume that data objects are represented by vectors from a d-dimensional vector space $\mathbb{X}$ with a distance function $\rho : \mathbb{X}^2 \to \mathbb{R}_{\geq 0}$ satisfying the triangular inequality. In the paper we use a metric specialized for decision systems, i.e., we assume that a training data set $\mathbb{U}$ is provided to induce a metric and each data object $x \in \mathbb{U}$ is labeled with a decision. The metric combines the distances specialized for numerical and for symbolic attributes [7]. For numerical attributes we use the difference between attribute values normalized by the largest observed attribute value difference and for symbolic attributes the VDM metric (two symbolic values are similar if they have similar decision

Figure 1. Search pruning: (a) the covering radius (b) the hyperplane cut (c) the rings

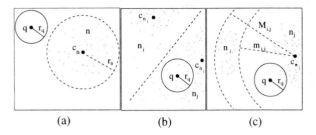

| (a) | (b) | (c) |

distribution). In the second phase of the metric induction process the weights of attributes are adjusted to optimize the performance of the metric on the training set $\mathbb{U}$. The results in [7] show that this metric with the k-nn algorithm gives classification accuracy at least as good as other widely used classification methods such as C5.0.

To construct an indexing tree we use an indexing strategy introduced in [5]. It starts with the whole training data set $\mathbb{U}$ and recursively splits data objects into a fixed k smaller clusters. After each split the new child nodes are inserted to the global priority queue and the node with the largest weight is selected from the queue to be split as the next. Each tree node has the center and the weight of a node is defined as the sum of the distances between the node members and the center. The algorithm stops when the number of leaf nodes exceeds $\frac{1}{5}$ of the size of the training set $|\mathbb{U}|$, in other words when the average size of the leaf nodes is 5. This stopping criterion reflects the trade-off between the optimality of searching and the additional memory usage.

For node splitting procedure we use the k-means algorithm. Initially, it selects k objects from the parent node as the centers of the child nodes. Then it assigns each object in the parent node to the child node with the nearest center and computes the means of the child nodes as the new centers. It iterates the assignment procedure until the same set of centers is obtained in two subsequent iterations.

For initial centers selection in the k-means algorithm we use the following global method. First the mean of a node is computed. As the first seed the farthest object from the mean is picked. Then the farthest object from this one is picked. Then the object that is farthest from these two is chosen, i.e., such that the minimum distance from the previous two seeds is the greatest one among all unchosen objects. Then the one farthest from these three is picked and so on until there are k data objects chosen. The computational cost is $O(ndk^2)$ where n is the size of the node and d is the number of attributes. For small values of k this cost is still acceptable. The above global method provides a little better results than the GNAT sampled and the random methods and this method was used in our experiments.

3 Searching

The searching algorithm is assumed to find a fixed number k of data objects nearest to a query object q. It traverses an indexing tree in the depth-first order and stores the k nearest data objects from already visited nodes in $nearestQueue$. The objects in $nearestQueue$ are sorted in the increasing order of the distance to the query q. The algorithm starts with the empty $nearestQueue$ and visits tree nodes unconditionally as long as $nearestQueue$ contains less than k objects. Since then the algorithm checks at each tree node n with search pruning criteria whether n is to be visited, i.e., whether n can contain an object that is closer to the query q than any other previously found nearest neighbor in $nearestQueue$. If not, the whole subtree of the node n is discarded from searching. Otherwise, if the node n is a leaf, it compares each data object $x \in n$ against data objects in $nearestQueue$ and replaces the farthest object y from $nearestQueue$ if x is closer to the query q than y. In case when the node n is an inner node it visits child nodes in the increasing order of the distance between the center of a child node and the query q. This heuristics guides the algorithm first to child nodes that are more probable to have data object close to the query q, what makes the searching considerably more effective than random order of visiting.

There are different search pruning criteria described in the literature and all of them are based on the triangular inequality. Figure 1 presents three different criteria for pruning tree nodes. The value r_q denotes the distance $\rho(q, x)$ between the query q and the farthest from q object $x \in nearestQueue$. The most common criterion applied in BST [8] uses the covering radius (Figure 1a). Each node n keeps the center c_n and the covering radius r_n:

$$r_n := \max_{x \in n} \rho(c_n, x).$$

A node n is discarded if the intersection between the ball around q containing all nearest neighbors from $nearestQueue$ and the ball containing all members of the node n is empty:

$$\rho(c_n, q) > r_q + r_n$$

Uhlmann proposed another criterion for his Generalized Hyperplane Tree (GHT) [10] based on the assumption that the splitting procedure assigns each object to the node with the nearest center. It uses the hyperplanes separating the child nodes of the same parent (Figure 1b). A node n_i is discarded if there is a brother node n_j of n_i (another child node of the same parent node as n_i) such that the whole query ball is placed beyond the hyperplane separating n_i and n_j on the side of the brother node n_j:

$$\rho(c_{n_i}, q) - r_q > \rho(c_{n_j}, q) + r_q.$$

GNAT pruning criterion [3] is also based on mutual relation among brother nodes (Figure 1c). If the degree of a tree is k then each child node n_i keeps the minimal $m_{i,1}, \ldots, m_{i,k}$ and the maximal $M_{i,1}, \ldots, M_{i,k}$ distances from its elements to the centers of the remaining brother nodes:

$$m_{i,j} = \min_{x \in n_i} \rho(c_{n_j}, x) \text{ and } M_{i,j} = \max_{x \in n_i} \rho(c_{n_j}, x).$$

A node n_i is discarded if there is a brother node n_j such that the query ball is entirely placed outside the ring around the center of n_j containing all members of n_i:

$$\text{either } \rho(c_{n_j}, q) + r_q < m_{i,j} \text{ or } \rho(c_{n_j}, q) - r_q > M_{i,j}.$$

The covering radius and the hyperplane criteria require from each node n only to store the center c_n and the covering radius r_n. The criterion based on rings requires more memory: each node stores the $2(k-1)$ distances to the centers of brother nodes.

4 Experimental results

We have performed experiments with different indexing and search methods for 6 benchmark data sets from the UCI repository [2] (the indexed and the query set sizes are given in parenthesis): *census94* (30162, 15060), *census94-95* (199523, 99762), *covertype* (387308, 193704), *letter* (15000, 5000), *nursery* (8640, 4320), *pendigits* (7494, 3498). The data sets provided as a single file (*covertype, nursery*) have been randomly split into an indexed and a query parts with the ratio 2 to 1, the others have been tested with the originally provided partition.

The k-means splitting procedure used in our method selects initial centers, assigns each data object to the nearest center and computes the means as the new centers of clusters. Then assignment of data objects to the centers and computation of new cluster centers is iterated until the same set of cluster centers is generated in two subsequent iterations. The one-step splitting procedure used in the other indexing trees (BST, GHT and GNAT) stops after the first iteration and uses the initial centers as the final. The interesting question is how much the search process profits from the additional cost due to the iterative k-means splitting procedure and the combined search pruning criterion in comparison to the one-step case with a single pruning criterion. To answer this question we tested the iterative k-means based and the one-step k-centers based trees.

First we analyzed the performance of the k-means indexing tree as a function of the degree k by testing all values in the range $2 \leq k \leq 9$. The experiment showed that the best performance is for small values of k but greater than 2. Assuming k equal to 3, 4 or 5 one may have the confidence that they get almost optimal performance. In farther experiments we have used the degree $k = 3$ in the k-means

Figure 2. The average number of distance computations per single object of the 1-nn (the upper graph) and the 100-nn (the lower graph) search in different indexing trees.

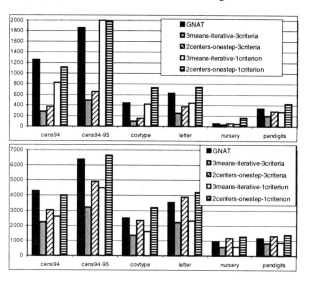

based indexing tree. A similar experiment was performed for the one-step k-centers based tree, for which $k = 2$ was the optimal.

Figure 2 presents the cost of searching in the trees with the iterative k-means and the one-step k-centers splitting procedures. The performance of searching is presented for two cases: with all 3 pruning criteria and with a single covering radius criterion. We chose this single criterion for comparison since it has the best performance among all three tested criteria. For comparison we also present the performance of the GNAT tree [3]. We implemented different structures from the literature [3, 8, 10] and GNAT had the best performance among them. To make the results comparable all indexing trees were tested with the same distance function and the same partition for each data set.

While comparing the performance of the iterative 3-means (the second column) and the one-step 2-centers (the third column) procedures the profit from applying the iterative procedure is visible: it ranges from 20% to 50% and is similar for the 1-nn and the 100-nn search. The good experimental performance of the tree with the k-means procedure may result from the theoretical property proved by Savaresi and Boley [9]. They show that in an infinite theoretical model of data the 2-means procedure with random selection of initial centers converges to the partition orthogonal to the principal direction, what is in a sense the optimal partition of data.

The comparison of the second and the fourth column shows that the application of the combined pruning criterion also accelerates the performance of the k-nn search in relation to a single criterion. In case of the 1-nn search the acceleration is visible for all data sets and reaches up to several times for the largest sets. In case of the 100-nn search the difference is visible only for three larger data sets (*census94, census94-94, covertype*) and is much smaller than in the 1-nn case. It indicates that the less number of neighbors k and the greater size of a data set, the improvement is more significant. We have compared the performance of all combinations among the three presented criteria and in both cases of the 1-nn and the 100-nn search adding the memory consuming criterion based on rings does not improve the combination of the remaining two. This result may suggest that the covering radius and the hyperplane cut provide the optimal pruning combination and there is no need to search for more sophisticated pruning mechanisms.

The experimental results show that the tree with the iterative 3-means splitting procedure and the combined search pruning criteria (the second column) is up to several times as effective as the one-step based tree with a single criterion (the fifth column). A particularly advanced acceleration level in comparison to the linear search has been reached in case of the largest tested data sets. The presented structure has reduced the 1-nn search cost 4000 times in case of the data set *covertype* and 400 times in case of the data set *census94-95*. For the 100-nn search the reductions in cost are 300 and 60 times, respectively. Such good performance has been reached both due to the improved splitting procedure and the complex search criterion.

The question arises whether the cost of constructing the k-means based tree is not too large in comparison to the cost of searching. We have compared the average cost of indexing a single object to the average cost of searching for nearest neighbors of a single object. In case of a small number of neighbors the results are not uniformly interpretable and the usefulness of the presented structure depends on individual properties of a data set and on the number of queries to be performed. However, while estimating the optimal size of a neighborhood or searching for geometrical properties in a data set, there is a need to search for a large number of nearest neighbors and in this case the presented tree keeps the appropriate balance between the costs of construction and searching: for all tested data sets the average cost of indexing a single object was lower than the average cost of the 100-nn search, usually several times lower. It means that if the size of an indexed database and the number of queries are of the same order the main workload remains on the side of the search process. The cost of indexing increases while increasing the degree of a tree k. The cost of searching is stable for $k \geq 3$. It indicates that the best trade-off between the indexing cost and the search performance is obtained at $k = 3$ and by increasing the value of k the cost of indexing is increased without any profit for searching.

5 Summary

In the paper we present the searching tree with the iterative k-means splitting procedure and the combined search pruning criteria that is up to several times better than the one-step based tree with a single criterion and is particularly effective while indexing very large data sets. The effectiveness of indexing structures is measured by the average number of distance computations in a single k-nn search what allows us to measure the acceleration of searching in comparison to the linear search. Almost 100% of run-time is used by distance computation operations and the measured acceleration factors correspond directly to the real-time acceleration. The presented tree is used for the k-nn classifier included in RSES system (http://logic.mimuw.edu.pl/˜rses).

Acknowledgments. The author is very grateful to professor Andrzej Skowron for useful remarks on this presentation. This work was supported by the grants 8 T11C 009 19 and 4 T11C 040 24 from the Polish State Committee for Scientific Research and by the grant from Ministry of Scientific Research and Information Technology.

References

[1] J. L. Bentley. Multidimensional binary search trees used for associative searching. *Communications of the ACM*, 18(9):509–517, 1975.

[2] C. L. Blake and C. J. Merz. UCI repository of machine learning databases. http://www.ics.uci.edu/˜mlearn/MLRepository.html, Department of Information and Computer Science, University of California, Irvine, CA, 1998.

[3] S. Brin. Near neighbor search in large metric spaces. In *Proceedings of the Twenty First International Conference on Very Large Databases*, pages 574–584, 1995.

[4] R. Finkel and J. Bentley. Quad-trees: a data structure for retrieval and composite keys. *ACTA Informatica*, 4(1):1–9, 1974.

[5] K. Fukunaga and P. M. Narendra. A branch and bound algorithm for computing k-nearest neighbors. *IEEE Transactions on Computers*, 24(7):750–753, 1975.

[6] V. Gaede and O. Gunther. Multidimensional access methods. *ACM Computing Surveys*, 30(2):170–231, 1998.

[7] G. Góra and A. G. Wojna. RIONA: a new classification system combining rule induction and instance-based learning. *Fundamenta Informaticae*, 51(4):369–390, 2002.

[8] I. Kalantari and G. McDonald. A data structure and an algorithm for the nearest point problem. *IEEE Transactions on Software Engineering*, 9(5):631–634, 1983.

[9] S. M. Savaresi and D. L. Boley. On the performance of bisecting K-means and PDDP. In *Proceedings of the First SIAM International Conference on Data Mining*, pages 1–14, Chicago, USA, 2001.

[10] J. Uhlmann. Satisfying general proximity/similarity queries with metric trees. *Information Processing Letters*, 40(4):175–179, 1991.

Postprocessing Decision Trees to Extract Actionable Knowledge

Qiang Yang and Jie Yin
Department of Computer Science
Hong Kong University of Science and Technology
Clearwater Bay, Kowloon Hong Kong
{qyang, yinjie}@cs.ust.hk

Charles X. Ling and Tielin Chen
Department of Computer Science
The University of Western Ontario
London, Ontario, Canada N6A 5B7
{ling, tchen}@csd.uwo.ca

Abstract

Most data mining algorithms and tools stop at discovered customer models, producing distribution information on customer profiles. Such techniques, when applied to industrial problems such as customer relationship management (CRM), are useful in pointing out customers who are likely attritors and customers who are loyal, but they require human experts to postprocess the mined information manually. Most of the postprocessing techniques have been limited to producing visualization results and interestingness ranking, but they do not directly suggest actions *that would lead to an increase the objective function such as profit. In this paper, we present a novel algorithm that suggest actions to change customers from an undesired status (such as attritors) to a desired one (such as loyal) while maximizing objective function: the expected net profit. We develop these algorithms under resource constraints that are abound in reality. The contribution of the work is in taking the output from an existing mature technique (decision trees, for example), and producing novel, actionable knowledge through automatic postprocessing.*

1. Introduction

Extensive research in data mining has been done on discovering distributional knowledge about the underlying data. Models such as the Bayesian models, decision trees, support vector machines and association rules have been applied to various industrial applications such as customer relationship management (CRM) [6, 1]. Despite such phenomenal success, most of these techniques stop short of the final objectives of data mining, such as maximizing profit while reducing costs, relying on such postprocessing techniques as visualization and interestingness ranking [2, 3, 5]. While these techniques are essential to move the data mining result to the eventual application, they nevertheless require a great deal of human manual work by experts.

In this paper, we present a novel postprocessing technique to mine actionable knowledge from decision trees. To illustrate our techniques, we focus on the application in CRM. Like most data mining algorithms today, a common problem in current applications of data mining in intelligent CRM is that people tend to focus on, and be satisfied with, building up the models and interpreting them, but not to use them to get profit explicitly. This knowledge is useful but it does not directly benefit the enterprise. To improve customer relationship, the enterprise must know what *actions* to take to change customers from an undesired status (such as attritors) to a desired one (such as loyal customers). To our best knowledge, no data mining algorithms have been made widely available to accomplish this important task in intelligent CRM.

In this paper, we present novel algorithms for postprocessing decision trees in order to extract *actions* to maximize a profit-based objective function. We consider two cases, one corresponds to unlimited resources, and the other limited resource constraints. In both cases, our aim is to maximize the expected net profit of all the customers. We show that finding the optimal solution for the limited resource problem is NP-complete, and design a greedy heuristic algorithm to solve it efficiently. We compare the performance of the exhaustive search algorithm with a greedy heuristic algorithm, and show that the greedy algorithm is efficient while achieving results with quality very close to the optimal ones.

2. Action Mining in Decision Trees under Unlimited Resources

Given a decision tree as input, our `leaf-node search` algorithm searches for optimal actions to transfer each leaf node to another leaf node with a higher probability of being in a more desirable class. After a customer profile is built in the form of a decision tree, the resulting decision tree can be used to classify, and more importantly, provide probability of customers in the desired status such as being loyal or high-spending. When a customer, who can be either an training example used to build the decision tree or an unseen testing example, falls into a particular leaf node with a certain probability of being in the desired status, the algorithm tries to "move" the customer into other leaves with higher probabilities of being in the desired status. The probability gain can then be converted into an expected gross profit.

However, moving a customer from one leaf to another means some attribute values of the customer must be changed. This change, in which an attribute A's value is transformed from v_1 to v_2, corresponds to an action. These actions incur costs. The cost of all changeable attributes are defined in a cost matrix by a domain expert. The `leaf-node search` algorithm searches all leaves in the tree so that for every leaf node, a best destination leaf node is found to move the customer to. The collection of moves are required to maximize the net profit, which equals the gross profit minus the cost of the corresponding actions.

Based on a domain-specific cost matrix for actions, we define the net profit of an action to be as follows.

$$P_N = P_E \times P_{gain} - \sum_i COST_i \qquad (1)$$

where P_N denotes the net profit, P_E denotes the total profit of the customer in the desired status, P_{gain} denotes the probability gain, and $COST_i$ denotes the cost of each action involved.

The `leaf-node search` algorithm for searching the best actions can thus be described as follows:

Algorithm `leaf-node search`

1. For each customer c, do
2.   Let L be the leaf node in which c falls into;
3.   Let S be a leaf node for c the maximum net profit P_N;
4.   Output (L, S, P_N);

To illustrate, consider an example shown in Figure 1, which represents an overly simplified, hypothetical decision tree as the customer profile of loyal customers built from a bank. The tree has five leaf nodes (A, B, C, D, and E), each with a probability of customers' being loyal. The probability of attritors is simply 1 minus this probability.

Consider a customer Jack who has the following attributes: Service (service level) = L (low), Sex = M (male), and Rate (mortgage rate) = L. The customer is classified by the decision tree. Clearly, Jack falls into the leaf B, which predicts that Jack will have only 20% chance of being loyal (or Jack will have 80% chance to churn in the future). The algorithm will now search through all other leaves (A, C, D,

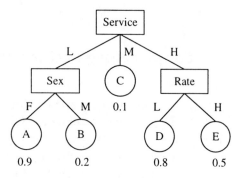

Figure 1. An example of customer profile

E) in the decision tree to see if Jack can be "replaced" into a best leaf with the highest net profit.

1. Consider leaf A. It does have a higher probability of being loyal (90%), but the cost of action would be very high (Jack should be changed to female), so the net profit is a negative infinity.

2. Consider leaf C. It has a lower probability of being loyal, so the net profit must be negative, and we can safely skip it.

3. Consider leaf D. There is a probability gain of 60% (80% − 20%) if Jack falls into D. The action needed is to change Service from L (low) to H (high). Assume that the cost of such a change is $200 (given by the bank). If the bank can make a total profit of $1000 from Jack when he is 100% loyal, then this probability gain (60%) is converted into $600 (1000 × 0.6) of the expected gross profit. Therefore, the net profit would be $400 (600 − 200).

4. Consider leaf E. The probability gain is 30% (50% − 20%), which transfers to $300 of the expected gross profit. Assume that the cost of the actions (change Service from L to H and change Rate from L to H) is $250, then the net profit of moving Jack from B to E is $50 (300 − 250).

Clearly, the node with the maximal net profit for Jack is D, with suggested action of changing Service from L to H.

In our discussion so far, we assume that attribute-value changes will incur costs. These costs can only be determined by domain knowledge and domain experts. For each attribute used in the decision tree, a cost matrix is used to represent such costs. In many applications, the values of many attributes such as sex, address, number of children cannot be changed with any reasonable amount of money. Those attributes are called "hard attributes". For hard attributes, users must assign a very large number to every entry in the cost matrix.

If, on the other hand, some value changes are possible with reasonable costs, then those attributes such as the Service level, interest rate, promotion packages are called "soft attributes". Note that the cost matrix needs not to be symmetric. One can assign $200 as the cost of changing service level from low to high, but infinity (a very large number) as the cost from high to low, if the bank does not want to "degrade" service levels of customers as an action.

One might ask why hard attributes should be included in the tree building process in the first place, since they can prevent customers from being moved to other leaves. This is because that many hard attributes are important in accurate probability estimation of the leaves. When the probability estimation is inaccurate, the reliability of the prediction would be low, or the error margin of the prediction would be high.

3. Post-processing Decision Trees: the Limited Resource Case

Our previous case considered each leave node of the decision tree to be a separate customer group. For each such customer group, we were free to design actions to act on it in order to increase the net profit. However, in practice, a company may be limited in its resources. For example, a mutual fund company may have a limited number k (say three) of account managers, each manager can take care of only one customer group. Thus, when such limitations exist, it is a difficult problem to merge all leave nodes into k segments, such that each segment can be assigned to an account manager. To each segment, the responsible manager can apply actions to increase the overall profit.

This limited resources problem can be formulated as a precise computational problem. Our input is as follows:

1. a decision tree built from training examples

2. a pre-specified constant k ($k \leq m$)

3. a set of testing examples

Given these, our problem is to find k customer groups and their corresponding action sets from a decision tree such that when these actions are applied to the corresponding group in testing examples, the total net profit is maximized.

To illustrate, consider an example in Figure 2. Assume that for leaf nodes L_1 to L_4, the probability values of being in the desired class are 0.9, 0.2, 0.8, 0.5, respectively. Now consider the task of transforming all leaf nodes from a lower probability value node to a higher one, such that the net benefit of such transformation is maximized. To illustrate this point, consider a test data set such that there is exactly one member that falls in each leaf node in this decision tree.

In order to calculate the net profit, we assume all leaf nodes to have a profit of one. We also assume that the cost

of transferring a customer is equal to the number of attribute value changes multiplied by 0.1. Thus, to change from L_2 to L_1, we need to modify the value of the attribute Status, with a profit gain of $(0.9 - 0.2) \times 1 - 0.1 = 0.6$.

To illustrate the limited resources problem, consider again our decision tree in Figure 2. Suppose that we wish to find one single customer segment ($k = 1$). One such group is $\{L_2, L_4\}$, with a selected action set $\{Service \leftarrow H, Rate \leftarrow C\}$ which can be applied on it. Assume L_2 and L_4 only contain one example. If we consider transferring this group to leaf node L_3, L_2 has a profit gain of $(0.8 - 0.2) \times 1 - 0.2 = 0.4$ and L_4 has a profit gain of $(0.8 - 0.5) \times 1 - 0.1 = 0.2$. Thus the net benefit for this group is $0.2 + 0.4 = 0.6$.

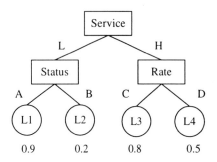

Figure 2. An example decision tree

How difficult is it to find an optimal solution for any value of k? Below, we show that when there is limited resources, the problem NP-Complete to solve. Because this problem requires that the number of customer segments to be limited, we call it the bounded segmentation problem (BSP).

To solve the problems optimally, it requires an exponential search. To avoid the computational complexity, we have developed a greedy algorithm which can reduce the computational cost but also guarantee the quality of the solution at the same time. Consider the following generalization of the maximum coverage problem. Given a set with m leaf nodes $L_s = \{L_1, L_2, \ldots, L_m\}$, each associated with a different profit P_{ij} ($P_{ij} \geq 0$) for each action set A_j, $1 \leq j \leq n$. Each A_j can be denoted as a subset of L_s which only contains the covered leaf nodes L_i for $P_{ij} \neq 0$, $1 \leq i \leq m$. The goal is to choose k action sets so as to maximize the net profit of covered leaf nodes. We can solve this problem using a greedy algorithm which is a variation of a set covering algorithm. We call it the Greedy-BSP algorithm below.

We evaluated our algorithm using a dataset from an insurance company in Canada. It consists of over 25,000 records for customers who have the status of "stay" or "leave" the insurance company. We will refer to them as positive and negative respectively. The dataset is described by over 60 attributes, many of which are not hard attributes.

About 20 attributes are soft attributes with reasonable costs for value changes.

Since the data distribution in the training set is highly unbalanced, we first perform data sampling with the ratio of positive and negative examples is about one to one [4], in order to prevent the decision tree from predicting all the customers to be negative. In this setting, we have built a decision tree with 153 leaf nodes. 87 of them are considered as negative leaf nodes because their probability of being positive is less than 50%, while the other 66 as positive leaf nodes. Furthermore, we have constructed a cost matrix for each attribute contained in the dataset according to their semantics in the real domain. The testing set consists of about 300 examples. We use the built decision tree to classify them into corresponding leaf nodes.

To compare the performance of the Greedy-BSP algorithm and the Optimal-BSP algorithm, we have again carried out experiments on the dataset from the insurance company. We apply Greedy-BSP and Optimal-BSP respectively to find the pre-specified k action sets with maximal net profit.

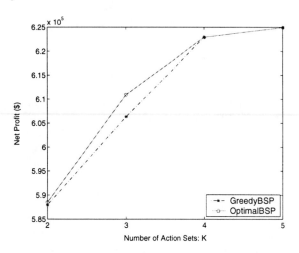

Figure 3. Net Profit vs. Number of action sets

Figure 3 shows the net profit obtained by the two algorithms over the number of action sets k. As shown in the figure, the net profit increases for both Greedy-BSP and Optimal-BSP with increasing number of action sets k. This is because if more customers are transformed to a desired status, it is more possible to obtain higher profit. In addition, an important property to note is that, for a specific k, the net profit obtained by Greedy-BSP is very close to or the same as that by Optimal-BSP, which can guarantee the quality of solution provided by Greedy-BSP.

For Greedy-BSP, The runtime is always around 0.20 seconds irrespective of the number of action sets k. On the other hand, the runtime for Optimal-BSP increases exponentially with the increasing number of action sets k. This is because it needs to compare much more combinations for larger k in order to obtain maximal net profit.

We conclude from our experiments that, Greedy-BSP can find k action sets with maximal net profit, which is very close to those found by Optimal-BSP, at least for small values of k for which Optimal-BSP terminates in a reasonable amount of time. At the same time, Greedy-BSP can scale well with the increasing number of action sets k, which is more efficient than Optimal-BSP.

4. Conclusions and Future Work

Intelligent CRM improves customer relationship from the data about customers. This paper contributed to the data mining field by considering mining the best k action groups to maximize the net profit. We formulated two versions of the problem and described a greedy algorithm that efficiently discovers the best k groups efficiently. The results discussed in this paper offer effective solutions to intelligent CRM for Enterprises. In our future work, we will research on other forms of limited resources problem as a result of postprocessing data mining models, and evaluate the effectiveness of our algorithms in the real-world deployment of the action-oriented data mining.

Acknowledgment   Qiang Yang and Jie Yin are supported by a Hong Kong Government RGC grant. Charles X. Ling and Tielin Chen are supported by a Canadian NSERC grant.

References

[1] R. Agrawal and R. Srikant. Fast algorithms for mining association rules. In *Proceedings of 20th International Conference on Very Large Data Bases(VLDB'94)*, pages 487–499. Morgan Kaufmann, September 1994.

[2] D. Keim and H. Kriegel. Issues in visualizing large databases, 1995.

[3] D. A. Keim and H.-P. Kriegel. Visualization techniques for mining large databases: A comparison. *Transactions on Knowledge and Data Engineering, Special Issue on Data Mining*, 8(6):923–938, 1996.

[4] C. X. Ling and C. Li. Data mining for direct marketing – specific problems and solutions. In *Proceedings of Fourth International Conference on Knowledge Discovery and Data Mining (KDD-98)*, pages 73 – 79. 1998.

[5] B. Liu, W. Hsu, L.-F. Mun, and H.-Y. Lee. Finding interesting patterns using user expectations. *Knowledge and Data Engineering*, 11(6):817–832, 1999.

[6] P. S. Usama Fayyad, Gregory Piatetsky-Shapiro. From data mining to knowledge discovery in databases. *AI Magazine*, 17(11), Fall 1996.

Frequent-Pattern based Iterative Projected Clustering *

Man Lung Yiu and Nikos Mamoulis
Department of Computer Science and Information Systems
University of Hong Kong
Pokfulam Road, Hong Kong
{mlyiu2,nikos} @csis.hku.hk

Abstract

Irrelevant attributes add noise to high dimensional clusters and make traditional clustering techniques inappropriate. Projected clustering algorithms have been proposed to find the clusters in hidden subspaces. We realize the analogy between mining frequent itemsets and discovering the relevant subspace for a given cluster. We propose a methodology for finding projected clusters by mining frequent itemsets and present heuristics that improve its quality. Our techniques are evaluated with synthetic and real data; they are scalable and discover projected clusters accurately.

1. Introduction

Clustering is typically used to partition a collection of data samples into a set of clusters (i.e., groups) such that the similarity between objects within a cluster is large and the objects from different clusters are dissimilar. Typical applications include customer segmentation, image processing, biology, document classification, indexing, etc.

It was shown in [5] that the distance of any two records is almost the same in high dimensional spaces for a large class of common distributions. Thus, the widely used distance measures are more meaningful in subsets (i.e., *projections*) of the high dimensional space. It is more likely for the data to form dense, meaningful clusters in a dimensional subspace, especially in real datasets, where irrelevant, noise attributes exist. The effects of dimensionality can be reduced by a dimensionality reduction technique [7] but information from all dimensions is uniformly transformed and relevant information for some clusters may be reduced. Also, clusters in the transformed space may be hard to interpret.

Therefore, *projected clustering* methods have been developed to find the clusters together with their associated

---
*This research was supported by grant HKU 7380/02E from Hong Kong RGC.

subspaces. These methods disregard the noise induced by irrelevant dimensions and also provide interpretable descriptions for the clusters. CLIQUE [3], one of the first projected clustering algorithms, finds the dense regions (clusters) in a level-wise manner, based on the Apriori principle. However, this algorithm does not scale well with data dimensionality. In addition, the formed clusters have large overlap, and this may not be acceptable for some applications (e.g., classification) which require disjoint partitions.

PROCLUS [1] and ORCLUS [2] employ alternative techniques. They are much faster than CLIQUE and they can discover disjoint clusters. In PROCLUS, the dimensions relevant to each cluster are selected from the original set of attributes. ORCLUS is more general and can select relevant attributes from the set of arbitrary directed orthogonal vectors. PROCLUS fails to identify clusters with large difference in size and requires their dimensionality to be in a predefined range. ORCLUS may discover clusters that are hard to interpret.

DOC [10] is a simple, density-based, projected clustering algorithm. A projected cluster C is defined by (i) the set of points in C (also denoted by C), (ii) a set D of relevant dimensions. In addition, three parameters w, α, and β are defined. w controls the extent of the clusters; the distances between records in the same cluster in each relevant dimension are bounded by w. $\alpha \in (0, 1]$ is the minimum *density* of the discovered clusters; each cluster should have at least $\alpha \cdot |S|$ points, where $|S|$ is the database size. $\beta \in (0, 1]$ reflects the importance of the size of the subspace over the size of the cluster. DOC discovers one cluster at a time. At each step, it picks a random point p from the database S and attempts to discover the cluster centered at p. For this, it runs an inner loop that selects a set of samples $X \subset S$. A set of dimensions D, where *all* points in X are within distance w from p is selected. Then, a cluster C for X is approximated by a bounding box of width $2w$ around p in the relevant dimensions. C is defined by the set of points from S in this box. The process is repeated for a number of random points p and samples X for each p. Among all discovered

C, the cluster with the highest *quality* is finally selected. The quality of a cluster C is defined by $\mu(a, b) = a \cdot (1/\beta)^b$, where a is the number of points in C and b is the dimensionality of C. After one cluster has been discovered, the records in it are removed from the sample and the process is iteratively applied to the rest of the points. With this approach the number of clusters k can be automatically found. Moreover, small clusters can be identified. However, DOC only produces approximate results and requires a lot of time to discover clusters of high accuracy.

In this paper, we propose an algorithm that improves DOC in several ways. First, we draw some analogues between mining frequent itemsets and discovering the relevant subspace for a given cluster. Then, we adapt a data mining technique [9] to systematically find the optimal cluster. Second, we propose techniques that improve the quality of the clusters. The resulting algorithm is much faster than DOC, while producing clusters of high quality.

The outline of the paper is as follows. Our methodology is presented in Section 2. Section 3 presents experimental comparisons between projected clustering techniques. Finally, Section 4 concludes the paper and discusses issues for future work.

2. Projected Clustering

2.1. Mining relevant dimensions

Given a random medoid $p \in S$, we can transform the problem of finding the best projected cluster that contains p, to the problem of mining frequent itemsets in transactional databases as shown in Figure 1. The original dataset S is shown in Figure 1a. We consider each dimension i as one attribute a_i. Assume that the record marked in bold is the medoid p. We replace each point $q \in S$ by an itemset as follows. If and only if the value of q in dimension i is bounded by p with respect to width w (here, w=2), we include a_i in the corresponding itemset, as shown in Figure 1b. Observe that all frequent itemsets (i.e., combinations of dimensions) with respect to $min\_sup = \alpha \cdot |S|$ are candidate clusters for medoid p.

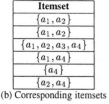

a_1	a_2	a_3	a_4
1	2	4	8
2	1	9	6
3	**2**	**7**	**3**
4	8	1	2
9	6	2	1
7	3	3	2

Itemset
$\{a_1, a_2\}$
$\{a_1, a_2\}$
$\{a_1, a_2, a_3, a_4\}$
$\{a_1, a_4\}$
$\{a_4\}$
$\{a_2, a_4\}$

(a) Original table   (b) Corresponding itemsets

Figure 1. Transforming dataset to itemsets

/* Table header entries (hl) are in descending order of support */
Algorithm $\mu Growth(\mathcal{T}, \mathcal{I}_{cond}, \mathcal{I}_{best})$
1   **if** $\mathcal{T}$ has a single path **then**
2         $\mathcal{I} := \mathcal{I}_{cond}$;
3   **for** l:=1 to $\mathcal{T}.hl.length$
4            $\mathcal{I} := \mathcal{I} \cup \{\mathcal{T}.hl[l].item\}$; $sup(\mathcal{I}) := \mathcal{T}.hl[l].support$;
5   update $\mathcal{I}_{best}$ if $\mu(\mathcal{I}) > \mu(\mathcal{I}_{best})$;
6   **else**
7         $\mathcal{I} := \mathcal{I}_{cond} \cup \{\mathcal{T}.hl[\mathbf{1}].item\}$; $sup(\mathcal{I}) := \mathcal{T}.hl[\mathbf{1}].support$;
8   update $\mathcal{I}_{best}$ if $\mu(\mathcal{I}) > \mu(\mathcal{I}_{best})$;
9   **for** l:=$\mathcal{T}.hl.length$ down to 2
10        $\mathcal{I} := \mathcal{I}_{cond} \cup \{\mathcal{T}.hl[l].item\}$;
11   **if** $\mu(\mathcal{T}.hl[l].support, dim(\mathcal{I}_{cond}) + l) > \mu(\mathcal{I}_{best})$ **then**
12   construct $\mathcal{I}$'s conditional pattern base;
13   create $\mathcal{I}$'s conditional FP-Tree $\mathcal{T}_{\mathcal{I}}$;
14   **if** $(\mathcal{T}_{\mathcal{I}} \neq \emptyset)$ **then** $\mu Growth(\mathcal{T}_{\mathcal{I}}, \mathcal{I})$;

Figure 2. The $\mu Growth$ algorithm

Therefore, the problem of finding the best projected cluster for a random medoid p can be transformed to the problem of finding the best itemset in a transformation of S (like the one of Figure 1b), where goodness is defined by the μ function. Instead of discovering it in an non-deterministic way [10], we apply a systematic data mining algorithm on S. The frequent itemset mining problem was first proposed in [4]. Recently, there is an more efficient algorithm, the FP-growth method [9]. We adopt it for subspace clustering. However, our objective is to find the frequent itemset with maximum μ value, rather than finding *all* frequent subspaces with respect to p.

Assume that $\mathcal{I}_{best}$ is the itemset with the maximum μ value found so far and let $dim(\mathcal{I}_{best})$ and $sup(\mathcal{I}_{best})$ be its dimensionality and support, respectively. Let $\mathcal{I}_{cond}$ be the current conditional pattern of the FP-growth process. Its support $sup(\mathcal{I}_{cond})$ gives an upper bound for the supports of all patterns containing it. Moreover, the dimensionality of the itemsets that contain $\mathcal{I}_{cond}$ is at most $dim(\mathcal{I}_{cond}) + l$, where l is the number of items above the items in $\mathcal{I}_{cond}$ in the header table. Therefore if:

$$\mu(sup(\mathcal{I}_{cond}), dim(\mathcal{I}_{cond}) + l) \leq \mu(\mathcal{I}_{best}), \quad (1)$$

we can avoid constructing the conditional FP-tree for $\mathcal{I}_{cond}$, since that tree cannot generate a better pattern than $\mathcal{I}_{best}$. This bound can help prune the search space of the original mining process, effectively.

The $\mu Growth$ process is shown in Figure 2. It can replace the randomized inner loop of DOC to systematically discover the best subspace for a given medoid p. Moreover, it can accelerate a given phase of DOC. The best μ found so far is kept, allowing further pruning in subsequent iterations. In other words, if a good p is found in early iterations, it can help prune FP-trees for other medoids in subsequent iterations. With this modification, DOC can converge to a good solution fast.

2.2. The MineClus algorithm

Our clustering algorithm (*MineClus*) has four phases. In the *iterative* phase, the process described in Section 2.1 is applied to generate iteratively one cluster at a time. It is possible that the resulting cluster may be part of a large cluster that spreads outside the bounding rectangle. By using the Manhattan segmental distance [1], we also assign records having distance at most max_dist from the cluster centroid. max_dist is defined by the distance of the farthest point from the centroid, currently in the cluster. In the *pruning* phase, clusters having μ values significantly lower than the rest are pruned. First, we sort the clusters according to their μ values in descending order. Then, we find the position pos such that $\mu_{pos}/\mu_{pos+1} \geq \mu_i/\mu_{i+1} \ \forall i$. This position divides the clusters into a set of *strong* clusters C_i ($i \leq pos$), and a set of *weak* clusters C_i ($i > pos$). The weak clusters are pruned and their records are added back to S. The *merging* phase is applied only when the user wants at most k clusters in the result. In this case, the strong clusters are merged in an agglomerative way until k clusters remain. Given clusters C_x and C_y, the merged cluster is $C_x \cup C_y$, its subspace is $D_x \cap D_y$, its spread[1] is $R(C_x \cup C_y, D_x \cap D_y)$ and its μ value is $\mu(|C_x \cup C_y|, |D_x \cap D_y|)$. A good cluster should have small spread and large μ value (i.e., large subspace), so we use both measures to determine the next pair to merge. We consider two rankings of the cluster pairs; one with respect to spread and one with respect to μ value. Then the pair with the highest sum of ranks in both orderings is merged. In the *refinement* phase, we further improve the clusters by assigning the remaining records in the dataset (considered as outliers so far) to clusters. We use a similar algorithm to the refinement phase of PROCLUS [1].

3. Experimental Evaluation

In this section, we experimentally evaluate the effectiveness and efficiency of MineClus by comparing it with DOC[2] and PROCLUS, under various settings, for synthetic and real data. The performance measures are accuracy, percentage of outliers, and running time. Clustering accuracy corresponds to the number of correctly classified samples as a percentage of the total number of clustered data (excluding outliers). Outlier percentage is defined by the number of records assigned to no clusters as a percentage of the database size. First, we compare the performance of the methods on synthetic data and study their scalability on large datasets. Then, we compare them on real datasets.

---

[1]the *spread* $R(C, D)$ of a cluster C is defined by the mean squared distance between its points and its centroid, considering only the relevant dimensions D [2].

[2]We also implemented FastDOC [10], a faster variant of DOC, but found that the clusters generated failed to satisfy the α constraint most of the cases and it was sensitive to outliers.

We have implemented a synthetic data generator similar to the one in [1]. The outlier percentage is 5%. The generated datasets contain $k = 5$ clusters with random subspaces comprising from 5 to 10 dimensions. The smallest cluster size is $0.1 \cdot |S|$, where $|S|$ is the size of the database S. In the experiments that involve synthetic data, the results are averaged over 5 runs in order to smoothen the effects of randomness in the algorithms. All algorithms were implemented in Java. The experiments were run on a PC with a Pentium 4 CPU of 2.3GHz and 512MB RAM.

First, we compare the accuracy of MineClus, DOC, and PROCLUS, for various types of synthetic data. The input parameters for MineClus and DOC are $\alpha = 0.08, \beta = 0.25, w = 0.2$. For PROCLUS, we set $k = 5$ and the average subspace dimensionality $l = 7$. The running time of DOC is too high when the number of inner iterations m is high. We set $m = 2^{10}$ for DOC because it has quite high accuracy with this value, and its running time is in the same order as MineClus and PROCLUS.

Figure 3 shows accuracy as a function of α and β, on the same synthetic dataset. Entries in the tables are of the form X/Y, where X is the accuracy percentage and Y is the outlier percentage. In general, both MineClus and DOC have high accuracy. When $\alpha = 0.12$, the accuracy of MineClus decreases as the smallest cluster with $0.1 \cdot |S|$ records was missed. MineClus is not sensitive to β because of the deterministic behavior of the $\mu Growth$ algorithm. The accuracy of DOC decreases significantly as β increases, because DOC picks a larger discriminating set and smaller subspaces are likely to be discovered. Observe that DOC misclassifies many points as outliers in both experiments. Figure 4 compares the accuracy of all three algorithms as a function of data dimensionality. Observe that the accuracy of MineClus (and PROCLUS) is insensitive to dimensionality. On the other hand, the accuracy of DOC decreases when the dimensionality increases. This is explained by the fact that DOC applies a fixed number m of inner iterations and the chance to select an appropriate sample in each iteration decreases with dimensionality.

Next, we compare the scalability of the algorithms on various dataset sizes. Figure 5 shows their running time in seconds. They are all scalable to the database size. However, DOC is very expensive compared to the other methods, even for the smallest value of m, where its accuracy is low. MineClus is the fastest technique due to the efficiency of the $\mu Growth$ algorithm.

Finally, we compare the effectiveness of the three algorithms on real datasets from the UCI Machine Learning Repository [6]. The Iris dataset has only numerical attributes and the rest have only categorical attributes so we set $w = 0.5$ for Iris dataset and $w = 0$ for the rest in both DOC and MineClus. These datasets have no outliers so we turned off the outlier removal mechanism. The number of clusters k is set to the number of classes, except from the mushroom dataset where k is set to 20 (as suggested in [8]). For PROCLUS, we set the average subspace dimensionality l to be the average subspace size of the actual clusters. For DOC and MineClus, we set $\beta = 0.25$ and $\alpha = 0.2, 0.2, 0.4, 0.01$ for the Iris, Soybean, Votes, and Mushroom datasets respectively. DOC becomes too slow for the Mushroom dataset, so no result is given. In general, MineClus and DOC have high accuracy but DOC declares too many points as outliers. In summary, MineClus is highly accurate and robust.

α	MineClus	DOC,$m = 2^{10}$
0.04	95.57/0.60	99.05/16.00
0.06	95.76/0.80	100.00/15.04
0.08	95.12/1.60	99.72/26.40
0.10	95.38/0.40	99.54/12.40
0.12	89.88/1.2	99.53/15.00

(a) Dependency on α

β	MineClus	DOC,$m = 2^{10}$
0.1	95.84/0.87	100.00/50.80
0.2	96.04/1.08	100.00/24.80
0.3	94.53/3.32	88.70/13.00
0.4	95.68/0.72	50.60/6.00

(b) Dependency on β

Figure 3. Accuracy and outlier percentage

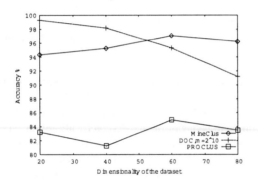

Figure 4. Accuracy w.r.t. dimensionality

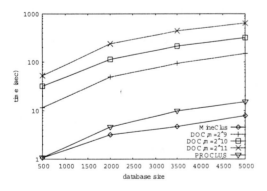

Figure 5. Scalability w.r.t. database size

4. Conclusions

In this paper, we presented an efficient and effective projected clustering algorithm. First, we identified the similar-

Dataset	MineClus	DOC,$m = 2^{10}$	PROCLUS
Iris	92.66/0.00	94.80/22.00	87.87/0.00
Soybean	97.87/0.00	81.30/8.50	84.97/0.00
Votes	86.67/0.00	99.60/28.00	84.41/0.00
Mushroom	96.41/0.59	-/-	97.68/0.00

Figure 6. Performance on real datasets

ity between mining frequent itemsets and discovering the best projected cluster for a pivot point p. Then, we proposed an adaptation of FP-growth that exploits the properties of the μ function and employs branch-and-bound techniques to reduce the search space significantly. We extended the cluster definition of [10] to consider more appropriate distance and quality measures for projected clustering. The quality of the results was further improved by (i) pruning small clusters of low quality, (ii) merging clusters close to each other with similar subspaces, and (iii) assigning points close to some cluster, else considered as outliers. We evaluated the efficiency and effectiveness of MineClus by comparing it with DOC [10] and PROCLUS [1] using synthetic and real data, under various conditions. It was shown that MineClus is more efficient, robust and scalable. In the future, we hope to devise additional heuristics for improving the discovered clusters.

References

[1] C. C. Aggarwal, J. L. Wolf, P. S. Yu, C. Procopiuc, and J. S. Park. Fast algorithms for projected clustering. In *ACM SIGMOD*, 1999.

[2] C. C. Aggarwal and P. S. Yu. Finding generalized projected clusters in high dimensional spaces. In *ACM SIGMOD*, 2000.

[3] R. Agrawal, J. Gehrke, D. Gunopulos, and P. Raghavan. Automatic subspace clustering of high dimensional data for data mining applications. In *ACM SIGMOD*, 1998.

[4] R. Agrawal and R. Srikant. Fast algorithms for mining association rules in large databases. In *VLDB*, 1994.

[5] K. S. Beyer, J. Goldstein, R. Ramakrishnan, and U. Shaft. When is "nearest neighbor" meaningful? In *ICDT*, 1999.

[6] C. Blake and C. Merz. UCI repository of machine learning databases, www.ics.uci.edu/~mlearn/mlrepository.html, 1998.

[7] C. Faloutsos and K.-I. Lin. Fastmap: A fast algorithm for indexing, data-mining and visualization of traditional and multimedia datasets. In *ACM SIGMOD*, 1995.

[8] S. Guha, R. Rastogi, and K. Shim. Rock: A robust clustering algorithm for categorical attributes. In *IEEE ICDE*, 1999.

[9] J. Han, J. Pei, and Y. Yin. Mining frequent patterns without candidate generation. In *ACM SIGMOD*, 2000.

[10] C. M. Procopiuc, M. Jones, P. K. Agarwal, and T. M. Murali. A monte carlo algorithm for fast projective clustering. In *ACM SIGMOD*, 2002.

General MC: Estimating Boundary of Positive Class from Small Positive Data

Hwanjo Yu
hwanjoyu@cs.uiuc.edu
Department of Computer Science
University of Illinois at Urbana-Champaign
Urbana, IL 61801 USA

Abstract

Single-Class Classification (SCC) seeks to distinguish one class of data from the universal set of multiple classes. We propose a SCC method called General MC *that estimates an accurate classification boundary of positive class from small positive data using the distribution of unlabeled data. Our theoretical and empirical analyses show that, as long as the distribution of unlabeled data is not highly skewed in the feature space, General MC significantly outperforms other recent SCC methods when the positive data set is highly under-sampled.*

1. Introduction

Single-Class Classification (SCC) seeks to distinguish one class of data from the universal set of multiple classes. (e.g., distinguishing apples from fruits, identifying "waterfall" pictures from image databases, or classifying personal homepages from the Web) (Throughout the paper, we call the target class *positive* and the complement set of samples *negative*.)

The recently proposed *Mapping Convergence (MC)* algorithm and *Support Vector Mapping Convergence (SVMC)* have shown superior performance over most other SCC methods [2]. (SVMC is a little modification of MC for fast training, but we denote MC for both MC and SVMC throughout the paper since both have the same properties in the context of our analysis.)[1]

In this paper, however, we theoretically and experimentally disclose that MC has the *"over-iteration"* problem, which degrades the performance significantly when the positive data is highly under-sampled and no wide gaps exist between positive and negative data in the feature space, which is common in real-world problems. The positive training data often do not cover the user's intended concept

---

[1] Refer to [2] for other related work on SCC in details.

in the feature space. For instance, assume that a user wants to build a Web page classifier of his/her interest by bookmarking such pages from the Internet. While Web page classification involves the feature space of thousands of dimensions and thus usually requires a large number of training data to cover such high dimensional spaces [3], users are not likely to bookmark more than tens of Web pages before they start training a classifier, in which the classifier suffers from the under-sampled positive training data.

Here we propose a new algorithm, called *General MC*, which bypasses the *over-iteration* problem even under such environments to generate more reliable boundary with fewer positive training data. Computing a reliable boundary of positive class becomes a very hard problem when positive training data is very few. Based on the assumption that the distribution of unlabeled data is not highly skewed in the feature space, General MC generates reliable boundaries using the unlabeled data in a systematic way. Additionally, we argue that many real data sets tend not highly skewed such that General MC generates absurdly poor results. Our experiments on two common data sets – the Reuter data set for text classification and the letter recognition from UCI repository for pattern recognition – show that General MC performs similar to MC when positive data are quite large, and it significantly outperformed MC and other recent SCC methods when the positive data is highly under-sampled.

2. MC Overview

The key idea of MC is to exploit the natural "gap" between positive and negative data in the feature space by incrementally labeling negative data from U using a margin maximization algorithm Ψ_2. The MC algorithm can be divided into two parts as follows:

1. First, MC identifies "strong negatives" from U using algorithm Ψ_1 with P and U. *Strong negatives* denote the negative data located far from the positive class in the feature space. For instance, consider a resume

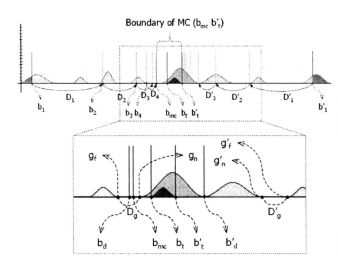

Boundary of MC (b_{mc} b'_t)

Figure 1. MC process

page classification from the Web. Suppose there are two negative data objects (i.e., two non-resume pages) – "how to write a resume" page, and "how to write an article" page. In the feature space, "how to write an article" page is considered more distant from the boundary of the resume class because "how to write a resume" page has more features relevant to the resume class (e.g., the word "resume" in text) though it is not a true resume page. Ψ_1 can be any algorithms that can identify the strong negatives from P and U as noted in [2]. (In [2], OSVM is used for Ψ_1.)

2. In Figure 1, let the strong negatives that algorithm Ψ_1 identifies be the data outside of b_1 and b'_1 to left and right side respectively, which are located far from the positive data set in the feature space. At each iteration, Ψ_2 includes the data within D_i into $\hat{N}$ as illustrated in Figure 1 where i is the number of iterations and b_i is the starting point of ith iteration in the feature space. Since Ψ_2 maximizes the margin at each iteration (SVM is used for Ψ_2 in [2].), D_1 has the margin of half of that between b_1 and b_t, and D_{i+1} has the half margin of D_i. (e.g., In Figure 1, D_2 has the half margin of D_1.) However, if there exists a gap around the boundary after i iteration, b_{i+1} will draw back to the point that there exists a data, because the data within D_i merged into $\hat{N}$ will be the nearest negative data points of the newly constructed boundary, and Ψ_2 (e.g., SVM) maximizes the margin between the nearest data points (called *Support Vectors*). (e.g., In Figure 1, b_4 draws back a little from the boundary after 3rd iteration.) If there exist no data at all within D_i, the convergence stops because nothing will be accumulated into $\hat{N}$ and thus more iterations after that

will not change the location of boundary. (e.g., the final boundary in the left side of Figure 1 will be b_{mc} because there is no data within D_4.)

When positive class is composed of multiple sub-classes, MC still performs well by (1) Ψ_1 initiating "strong negatives" in multiple places and (2) Ψ_2 (i.e., SVM) transforming into high dimensional space where the positive class is linearly separable [4, 2].

3. General MC

In this section, we first analyze MC to disclose its previously-"hidden" properties, which formally identify the problems of MC, and then propose more reliable boundary estimation method – *General MC*.

3.1. MC Analysis

MC will stop the convergence and locate the boundary close to optimum if the positive data set is large and there exists a wide gap between positive and negative data. (e.g., b_{mc} is close to b_d in the zoomed-in figure of Figure 1.) However, if those two conditions are not satisfied (e.g., right side of Figure 1), the MC boundary will "over-iterate" and end up converging into the tight boundary (e.g., b'_t in Figure 1).

How wide gaps or how large positive set are needed to avoid the "over-iteration" problem? Let D_g be the size of the gap ($= |g_n - g_f|$) where g_n and g_f are the two ending points of the gap respectively near and far from the positive class. (See the zoomed-in figure of Figure 1.) Then we have the following theorem.

Theorem 1. *In order to MC to avoid of $b_{mc} = b_t$, there must exist at least one gap of $D_g (= |g_f - g_n|)$ such that $|g_f - g_n| > |g_n - b_t|$.*

Proof. Suppose that at ith iteration, there exist a gap of $|g_f - g_n| > |g_n - b_t|$ where g_f is located within D_i. If b_i is located farther than g_f from b_t, b_{i+1} will be equal to g_f because b_{i+1} will draw back to the point that some data exist as we discussed in Section 2. When b_i becomes equal to g_f, b_{i+1} also will be equal to g_f because the boundary of i iteration maximize the margin between g_f and b_t and thus nothing will be merged into $\hat{N}$ since the gap $D_g (= |g_f - g_n|)$ will be larger than D_{i+1}.

$\square$

From Theorem 1, we can deduce the following observations:

- MC is not likely to locate the boundary exorbitantly far from the true boundary unless U is extremely sparse because larger gaps ($|g_f - g_n|$) are needed as the nearer

Input:	- positive data set P, unlabeled data set U
	- a parameter k $(k > 1)$
Output:	- a boundary function of positive class

Ψ_1: an algorithm identifying "strong negatives" from U
(e.g., OSVM, Rocchio)

Ψ_2: a supervised learning algorithm that maximizes the margin
(e.g., SVM)

Algorithm:
1. Use Ψ_1 with P and U to extract "strong negatives" from U and put the strong negatives into $\hat{N}_0$
2. i = 0
3. Do loop
   3.1. $U = U - \hat{N}_i$; $\hat{N} = \hat{N} \cup \hat{N}_i$
   3.2. Use Ψ_2 with P and $\hat{N}$ to construct the boundary that maximize the margin between them
   3.3. Classify U and put the negatively labeled data into $\hat{N}_{i+1}$
   3.4. Exit the loop if $i > 0$ and ($\hat{N}_i = \emptyset$ or $\frac{|\hat{N}_{i-1}| * |\hat{N}_{i+1}|}{|\hat{N}_i|^2} > k$)
   3.5. i = i + 1

Figure 2. General MC algorithm

ending point of the gap (g_n) is becoming farther from b_t.

- The more P is under-sampled, the larger gaps are needed between positive and negative data to avoid the over-iteration, because the degree of under-sampling of P determines $|g_n - b_t|$ as the boundary approaches to the positive class.

From the above observations, we see that MC is likely to generate near-optimal boundary when P is not under-sampled and wide gaps exist between P and N in the feature space. However, as we discussed in Section 1, in practice, positive data set is likely under-sampled, and no wide gaps exist between positive and negative classes. The General MC algorithm we present in the following section generates more reliable classification boundary even under such environments.

3.2. General MC (GMC) Algorithm

The basic idea of the General MC (GMC) algorithm is to monitor the changes of the rate of the accumulation of the negative data at each iteration of MC to detect the desirable position of the boundary of the positive class.

To guarantee the performance of GMC, we need to make the following assumption.

Assumption 1. *P covers every peak point of the distribution of positive class.*

In other words, when the positive class is composed of multiple clusters, P should not miss any of the cluster peak points in the feature space. Estimating the boundary of positive class from very few P is a very hard problem. The above assumption is the minimum requirement of P for GMC to generate a reliable boundary. Our experiments in Section 4 show that this assumption is not strong in practice such that GMC actually generates very reliable boundaries with very small randomly chosen positive data. The necessity of this assumption will be cleared through this section.

Steps 1 to 3 of the GMC algorithm in Figure 2 are essentially the same as the MC algorithm, except that the GMC algorithm has an additional loop-stopping condition, $\frac{|\hat{N}_{i-1}| * |\hat{N}_{i+1}|}{|\hat{N}_i|^2} > k, (k > 1)$. The following is the rationale for this stopping condition.

- When U is *uniformly distributed* in the feature space, $|\hat{N}_i| \approx 2 * |\hat{N}_{i+1}|^m$ where m is the number of dimensions of the feature space, and thus normally $\frac{|\hat{N}_i|}{|\hat{N}_{i+1}|} >> 1$, and $\frac{|\hat{N}_{i-1}|}{|\hat{N}_i|} \approx \frac{|\hat{N}_i|}{|\hat{N}_{i+1}|}$, thus $\frac{|\hat{N}_{i-1}| * |\hat{N}_{i+1}|}{|\hat{N}_i|^2} \approx 1$.

- Let b_p be the boundary of the positive data distribution in U. (e.g., In the zoomed-in figure of Figure 1, $b_p = g_n$ to the left side, and $b_p = b'_d$ to the right side.) When the boundary at ith iteration b_i passes through b_p in the GMC algorithm, $\frac{|\hat{N}_i|}{|\hat{N}_{i+1}|}$ will drop abruptly because: the data distribution from b_p to the cluster peak point of positive class will monotonically increase since P covers every peak point (by Assumption 1). Thus, $\frac{|\hat{N}_{i-1}| * |\hat{N}_{i+1}|}{|\hat{N}_i|^2} >> 1$ at that point.

The new stopping condition is still not likely to locate the boundary exorbitantly far from the true boundary unless U is extremely skewed toward the positive class in the feature space, because the margin of one iteration increases exponentially as it is farther from the positive class, and thus the "monotonically increasing data distribution area" has to be exponentially larger as it is farther from the positive class to satisfy the stopping criterion.

The stopping criteria will become unstable when data set has a highly skewed distribution in the feature space. However, we argue that many real data sets tend not highly skewed such that GMC generates absurdly poor results. Our experiments on two common data sets – the Reuter data set and the letter recoginition from UCI repository – show that, with a reasonable range of k (i.e., $2.5 \leq k \leq 4$), GMC significantly outperformed other recent SCC methods when the positive data is under-sampled.

Class	α	F_1, accuracy(%)						
		MC	GMC	OSVM	SVM_NN	S-EM	NB_NN	ISVM
earn	0.7	**0.965, 99.2**	0.952, 99.1	0.841, 96.3	0.007, 89.2	0.815, 96.2	0.815, 96.2	0.986, 99.7
	0.5	**0.964, 99.2**	0.950, 99.1	0.847, 96.7	0.007, 89.2	0.790, 95.8	0.790, 95.8	0.982, 99.6
	0.3	0.367, 91.5	**0.943, 99.0**	0.876, 97.4	0.004, 89.2	0.766, 95.6	0.766, 95.6	0.977, 97.7
grain	0.3	0.649, 99.4	**0.729, 99.4**	0.535, 99.2	0.027, 98.8	0.000, 98.8	0.000, 98.8	0.762, 99.5
wheat	0.3	0.667, 99.7	**0.701, 99.7**	0.624, 99.6	0.055, 99.5	0.000, 99.4	0.000, 99.4	0.726, 99.8
corn	0.3	0.487, 99.7	**0.580, 99.7**	0.469, 99.6	0.000, 99.6	0.000, 99.6	0.000, 99.6	0.602, 99.7
crude	0.3	0.432, 98.9	**0.625, 99.1**	0.525, 98.8	0.000, 98.5	0.000, 98.5	0.000, 98.5	0.721, 99.3
letter "A"	0.7	**0.963, 99.8**	0.962, 99.8	0.083, 97.3	0.063, 97.3	0.461, 94.4	0.461, 94.4	0.972, 99.9
	0.5	**0.941, 99.8**	0.941, 99.7	0.038, 97.3	0.043, 97.3	0.618, 97.8	0.618, 97.8	0.953, 99.8
	0.3	0.928, 99.7	**0.929, 99.7**	0.024, 97.6	0.024, 97.6	0.662, 98.2	0.662, 98.2	0.939, 99.7
	0.1	0.325, 97.8	**0.767, 99.0**	0.000, 97.2	0.007, 97.2	0.629, 98.2	0.629, 98.2	0.827, 99.2
letter "B"	0.1	0.385, 98.0	**0.727, 98.9**	0.024, 97.4	0.008, 97.4	0.179, 91.6	0.179, 91.6	0.777, 99.1
letter "C"	0.1	0.540, 98.5	**0.726, 98.8**	0.008, 97.5	0.009, 97.6	0.253, 90.7	0.253, 90.7	0.886, 99.5
letter "D"	0.1	0.218, 97.5	**0.617, 98.4**	0.000, 97.2	0.007, 97.2	0.062, 96.3	0.062, 96.3	0.719, 98.8
letter "E"	0.1	0.259, 97.7	**0.668, 98.3**	0.000, 97.2	0.008, 97.4	0.195, 95.1	0.195, 95.1	0.752, 99.0

Table 1. Performance with small positive training data. (The unlabeled data is used for testing.)

The stopping criteria also avoid the over-iteration problem when P is under-sampled and there are no wide gaps in the feature space as long as P covers the cluster peak point of positive class, because the stopping condition is not dependent on $|g_f - g_n|$ or $|g_n - b_t|$ that respectively implicate the size of gaps and the degree of under-sampling of P.

4. Experimental Evaluation

Due to the space limitations, we only report main results. We compare seven methods – *MC, GMC, OSVM, SVM_NN, S-EM, NB_NN, ISVM*.

OSVM is One-Class SVM. (Refer to [2] for details.)

SVM_NN is standard SVM trained using positive data, with unlabeled data as a subsitute for negative data. This is not unreasonable, as the unlabeled data can be thought of as a good approximation of negative data.

S-EM is a recently published SCC method. (Refer to http://www.cs.uic.edu/~liub/S-EM/readme.html)

NB_NN (Naive Bayes with Noisy Negatives) also uses the unlabeled data as negative data.

ISVM is the Ideal SVM trained from completely labeled data (P, with true N whi ch is manually classified from U). ISVM shows the ideal performance when the unlabeled data are labeled.

We used Reuters-21578[2] for text classification and the letter recognition data set from the UCI machine learning repository[3] for pattern recognition.

We vary the number of labeled positive data for training. We randomly sampled $\alpha\%$ from the previous positive set, and used those as P, with the same U, for training. Table 1

[2] http://www.daviddlewis.com/resources/testcollections/reuters21578
[3] http://www.ics.uci.edu/ mlearn/MLRepository.html

show that as α decreases, the performance of MC decreases slowly, and *the performance of MC drops abruptly at some point (e.g., $\alpha = 0.3$ and 0.1 respectively for "earn" and letter "A") that the boundary becomes highly overfit.* However, *the performance of GMC is less susceptible to a low α so that it significantly outperforms all other methods when the positive data set is highly under-sampled.*

SVM_NN gives very low F_1 scores due to the low recall. The small number of false positives in SVM_NN are likely to affect the support vectors (SVs) of the boundary, which hurts the recall performance.

S-EM shows the same performance as NB_NN. As noted in [1], S-EM outperforms NB_NN only when the positive data form a significant fraction of the universal set. (i.e., when $|P|$ is significantly large compared to $|U|$.) ([1] gives an example of "the class of movies we may enjoy watching" as a dominant positive class where S-EM could outperform NB_NN.)

References

[1] B. Liu, W. S. Lee, P. S. Yu, and X. Li. Partially supervised classification of text documents. In *Proc. 19th Int. Conf. Machine Learning (ICML'02)*, pages 387–394, Sydney, Australia, 2002.

[2] H. Yu. SVMC: Single-class classification with support vector machines. In *Proc. Int. Joint Conf. on Articial Intelligence (IJCAI-03)*, Acapulco, Maxico, 2003.

[3] H. Yu, J. Han, and K. C. Chang. PEBL: Positive-example based learning for Web page classification using SVM. In *Proc. 8th Int. Conf. Knowledge Discovery and Data Mining (KDD'02)*, pages 239–248, Edmonton, Canada, 2002.

[4] H. Yu, J. Han, and K. C.-C. Chang. PEBL: Web page classification without negative examples. *to appear IEEE Transactions on Knowledge and Data Engineering*, 2004.

Clustering Item Data Sets with Association-Taxonomy Similarity

Ching-Huang Yun*, Kun-Ta Chuang+ and Ming-Syan Chen*+
Department of Electrical Engineering*
Graduate Institute of Communication Engineering+
National Taiwan University
Taipei, Taiwan, ROC
E-mail: chyun@arbor.ee.ntu.edu.tw, doug@arbor.ee.ntu.edu.tw, mschen@cc.ee.ntu.edu.tw

Abstract

We explore in this paper the efficient clustering of item data. Different from those of the traditional data, the features of item data are known to be of high dimensionality and sparsity. In view of the features of item data, we devise in this paper a novel measurement, called the association-taxonomy similarity, *and utilize this measurement to perform the clustering. With this association-taxonomy similarity measurement, we develop an efficient clustering algorithm, called algorithm* AT *(standing for Association-Taxonomy), for item data. Two validation indexes based on association and taxonomy properties are also devised to assess the quality of clustering for item data. As validated by the real dataset, it is shown by our experimental results that algorithm AT devised in this paper significantly outperforms the prior works in the clustering quality as measured by the validation indexes, indicating the usefulness of association-taxonomy similarity in item data clustering.*

1 Introduction

Data clustering is an important technique for exploratory data analysis. Data clustering is an application dependent issue and certain applications may call for their own specific requirements. Different from those of the traditional data, the features of market-basket data are known to be of high dimensionality and sparsity. There are several clustering technologies which addressed the issue of clustering market-basket data [2][3][4][5].

Explicitly, the support of item i is defined as the percentage of transactions which contain i. Note that in mining association rules, a *large item* is basically an item with frequent occurrence in transactions. Thus, item i is called a large item if the support of item i is larger than the pre-given minimum support threshold. In market-basket data, the taxonomy of items defines the generalization relationships for the concepts in different abstraction levels.

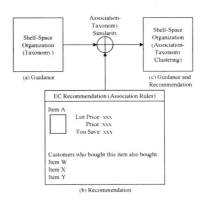

Figure 1. An example for taking guidance and recommendation into consideration.

In this paper, we devise the techniques of clustering item data sets for fulfilling both the guidance and recommendation purposes which is shown in Figure 1. By using the taxonomy of items, it is shown in Figure 1(a) that shelf-space is intuitively organized to guide customers to find the items according to the corresponding categories. In addition, it is shown in Figure 1(b) that association rules of items are used for item recommendation in the electronic commerce environments. In view of the features of item data, it is shown in Figure 1(c) that we devise in this paper a novel measurement, called the *association-taxonomy similarity*, and utilize this measurement to perform the clustering for shelf-space organization. With this association-taxonomy similarity measurement, we develop an efficient clustering algorithm, called algorithm *AT* (standing for *Association Taxonomy*), for item data in the following.

2 Preliminaries

In market-basket data, a database of transactions is denoted by $D = \{t_1, t_2, ..., t_v\}$, where each transaction t_h is a set of items $\{i_1, i_2, ..., i_w\}$. In mining association rules [1], the minimum support Sup is given to identify the large itemsets. In addition, the support of an itemset in database D is defined as the number of transactions which contain this itemset in database D. An itemset is called a *large itemset* if its support is larger than or equal to the minimum support Sup. In this paper, an *association itemset* is defined as a large itemset that contains at least two items and is not contained by any other large itemset. The set of association itemsets is denoted by $L_A = \{I_1, I_2, ..., I_m\}$. Items in the transactions can be generalized to multiple concept levels of the taxonomy and represented as a taxonomy tree. In the taxonomy tree, the leaf nodes are called the *item nodes* and the internal nodes are called the *category nodes*.

In view of the features of item data, the items are categorized into three kinds of items which are *association items* (represented as I_A), *single large items* (represented as I_S), and *rare items* (represented as I_R). An association item is an item which appears in at least one association itemset. A single large item is a large item but not an association item. In essence, a single large item can be viewed as a large 1-item which is not contained by any large 2-itemset. A rare item is not a large item (i.e., not frequently purchased). Explicitly, the rare item is an item whose support is smaller than the minimum support.

In this paper, a clustering $U = <C_1, C_2, ..., C_k>$ is a partition of items into k clusters, where C_j is a cluster consisting of a set of items. Note that purchasing relationships (i.e., association) and taxonomy relationships are important for the shelf-space organization. In this paper, the objective of clustering item data is to cluster the items with high association relationships and high taxonomy relationships together.

In view of the features of item data, we propose association index and taxonomy index, which are defined below, to assess the qualities of the clustering results.

Definition 1: (Association Index) The association index of the clustering U is defined as:

$$AI(U) = \frac{\sum_{C_p \in U}\left(\frac{\sum_{(i_x, i_y) \in C_p} A(i_x, i_y)}{\frac{1}{2}(|C_p|)(|C_p|-1)}\right)}{|U|},$$

where $A(i_x, i_y)$ is the association value of item i_x and item i_y. Explicitly, $A(i_x, i_y) = 1$, if i_x and i_y are in the same association itemset based on the minimum support Sup, and $A(i_x, i_y) = 0$, otherwise.

Definition 2: (Taxonomy Index) The taxonomy index of the clustering U is defined as:

$$TI(U) = \frac{\sum_{C_p \in U}\left(\frac{\sum_{(i_x, i_y) \in C_p} T(i_x, i_y)}{\frac{1}{2}(|C_p|)(|C_p|-1)}\right)}{|U|},$$

where $T(i_x, i_y)$ is the taxonomy value of item i_x and item i_y. Explicitly, $T(i_x, i_y) = 1$, if i_x and i_y are in the same category under the cluster level Lev^C, and $T(i_x, i_y) = 0$, otherwise. In this paper, the cluster level Lev^C is defined as the level where the number of categories is equal to the number of clusters k.

3 Design of Algorithm AT (Association Taxonomy)

In this paper, we devise algorithm AT for clustering item data. The similarity measurement of AT will be described in Section 3.1. Section 3.2 describes the procedure of AT.

3.1 Similarity Measurement

The similarity measurement employed by algorithm AT is called association-taxonomy similarity which consists of the association similarity and the taxonomy similarity. As described before, the set of association itemsets is denoted by $L_A = \{I_1, I_2, ..., I_m\}$. For each association itemset, the association relationships of items can be represented as a complete graph $I_p = \{V_p, E_p\}$, consisting of a set of vertices V_p and a set of edges E_p. In each complete graph, each vertex represents an item in the association itemset and each edge represents the association between two items. In mining association rules, an association rule $i_x \rightarrow i_y$ holds in transaction database D with confidence $Con(i_x \rightarrow i_y)$ if $Con(i_x \rightarrow i_y)$ of transactions in D that contain i_x also contain i_y. In this paper, we use *co-confidence* as the measurement of the association between two items. Here the co-confidence between i_x and i_y is defined as:

$$
\begin{aligned}
e(i_x, i_y) &= \frac{1}{2}(Con(i_x \rightarrow i_y) + Con(i_y \rightarrow i_x)) \\
&= \frac{1}{2}\left(\frac{Sup(i_x i_y)}{Sup(i_x)} + \frac{Sup(i_x i_y)}{Sup(i_y)}\right),
\end{aligned}
$$

where $Sup(i_x)$ is the support of item i_x. The co-confidence $e(i_x, i_y)$ represents the association between item i_x and item i_y.

Each association itemset is viewed as a cluster of items (i.e., $C_p = I_p$). For notational simplicity, the union cluster of C_p and C_q is denoted as $C_{p,q}$. The set of overlapped items in $C_{p,q}$ is denoted as $C_{p,q}^o$ and the set of non-overlapped items in $C_{p,q}$ is denoted as $C_{p,q}^n$. In addition, $E_{C_{p,q}}$ denotes the set of edges in $C_{p,q}$, $E_{C_{p,q}}^{oo}$ denotes the set of edges connecting the overlapped items in $C_{p,q}$, $E_{C_{p,q}}^{on}$ denotes the set of edges connecting the overlapped items and non-overlapped items in $C_{p,q}$, and $E_{C_{p,q}}^{nn}$ denotes the set of edges connecting the non-overlapped items in $C_{p,q}$. Similarly, the association similarity between overlapped items of C_p and C_q is defined as:

$$AS_{oo}(C_p, C_q) = \frac{\sum\limits_{i_x \in C^o_{p,q}, i_y \in C^o_{p,q}} e(i_x, i_y)}{|E^{oo}_{C_{p,q}}| + |E^{nn}_{C_{p,q}}|}.$$

Moreover, the association similarity between overlapped items and non-overlapped items of C_p and C_q is defined as:

$$AS_{on}(C_p, C_q) = \frac{\sum\limits_{i_x \in C^o_{p,q}, i_z \in C^n_{p,q}} e(i_x, i_z)}{|E^{on}_{C_{p,q}}| + |E^{nn}_{C_{p,q}}|}.$$

Note that $|E^{nn}_{C_{p,q}}|$ is a normalization factor for considering the effect of the edges of non-overlapped items in decreasing the similarity between two clusters. Explicitly, the existence of non-overlapped items represents the dissimilarity between two clusters. Thus, an edge between the non-overlapped items increases the association dissimilarity between two clusters.

Definition 3: (Association Similarity) The association similarity between C_p and C_q is defined as:

$$AS(C_p, C_q) = \alpha_{oo} * AS_{oo}(C_p, C_q) + \alpha_{on} * AS_{on}(C_p, C_q),$$

where α_{oo} is the weight of the association similarity between overlapped items and α_{on} is the weight of the association similarity between overlapped items and non-overlapped items.

In view of the factor of the taxonomy similarity, the similarity for different properties are thus conducted. The taxonomy similarity of overlapped item i_x to union cluster $C_{p,q}$ is defined as:

$$T_o(i_x, C_{p,q}) = \sum_{k=1}^{N^{Lev}} \frac{|C_{p,q}(i_x, k)|}{k},$$

where N^{Lev} is the number of levels in the taxonomy tree and $C_{p,q}(i_x, k)$ is the set of items which is in the same category with item i_x in level k in $C_{p,q}$. Similarly, the taxonomy similarity of overlapped items of C_p and C_q is defined as:

$$TS_o(C_p, C_q) = \frac{\sum\limits_{i_x \in C^o_{p,q}} T_o(i_x, C_{p,q})}{|C^o_{p,q}| * (|C_{p,q}| - 1)}.$$

Moreover, let i_y be an item in C_p and i_y is not overlapped with any item in C_q. The taxonomy similarity of non-overlapped item i_y in cluster C_p to cluster C_q is defined as:

$$T_n(i_y, C_q) = \sum_{k=1}^{N^{Lev}} \frac{|C_q(i_y, k)|}{k},$$

where $C_q(i_y, k)$ is the set of items which is in the same category with item i_y in level k in C_q. As a result, the taxonomy similarity of non-overlapped items of C_p and C_q is defined as:

$$TS_n(C_p, C_q) = \frac{\sum\limits_{i_y \in C^n_p} T_n(i_y, C_q) + \sum\limits_{i_z \in C^n_q} T_n(i_z, C_p)}{|C^n_p| * |C_q| + |C^n_q| * |C_p|}.$$

Definition 4: (Taxonomy Similarity) The taxonomy similarity between C_p and C_q is defined as:

$$TS(C_p, C_q) = \beta_o * TS_o(C_p, C_q) + \beta_n * (TS_n(C_p, C_q) - \frac{1}{N^{Lev}}),$$

where β_o is the weight of the taxonomy similarity of overlapped items and β_n is the weight of the taxonomy similarity of non-overlapped items. If each item in C_p and each item in C_q only have the root node as the same category, C_p is totally dissimilar to C_q according to the taxonomy tree and $TS(C_p, C_q)$ should be zero. Hence, because there are no overlapped item between C_p and C_q, the constant $\frac{1}{N^{Lev}}$ is subtracted in the non-overlapped part for normalization purpose.

Definition 5: (Association-Taxonomy Similarity) The association-taxonomy similarity between C_p and C_q is denoted as $SIM(C_p, C_q)$ defined as:

$$SIM(C_p, C_q) = \varpi_A * AS(C_p, C_q) + \varpi_T * TS(C_p, C_q),$$

where ϖ_A is the weight of the association similarity and ϖ_T is the weight of the taxonomy similarity. The determination of values of ϖ_A and ϖ_T is in fact application-dependent.

3.2 Procedure of Algorithm AT

Algorithm AT is designed to consist of three phases: the segmentation phase, the association-taxonomy phase, and the pure-taxonomy phase. Note that the association items consist of the elements in association itemsets. The overall procedure of algorithm AT is outlined as follows.

Procedure of Algorithm AT (Association-Taxonomy)

(1) The Segmentation Phase:

Step 1. Identify the set of association itemsets, the set of single large items, and the set of rare items.

(2) The Association-Taxonomy Phase:

Step 2. For each pair in the set of the association itemsets, calculate the corresponding association-taxonomy similarity.

Step 3. Merge the pair which has the largest association-taxonomy similarity as a new cluster.

Step 4. Repeat Step 2 and Step 3 until the dendrogram is constructed.

(3) The Pure-Taxonomy Phase:

Step 5. Identify k clusters in the dendrogram.

Step 6. For each single large item, allocate it to the cluster with the largest taxonomy similarity.

Step 7. For each rare item, allocate it to the cluster with the largest taxonomy similarity.

Step 8. Repeat Step 6 and Step 7 until no item is moved between clusters.

The advantageous features of algorithm AT are twofold. The first one is on employing the association-taxonomy similarity to effectively improve the quality of clustering association items. The second one is to allocate the single large items and rare items into clusters by calculating the taxonomy similarity. As such, these items can be efficiently and effectively allocated into the clusters. Note that the numbers of single large items and rare items are usually large as compared to the number of association itemsets. If we take each single large item (or each rare item) as a cluster and put them into the procedure from Step 2 to Step 4, the execution time will be prohibitive. In addition, lack of large association similarity with other clusters, these clusters with only one single large item (or one rare item) would never be merged until most of the association itemsets are merged. These problems are avoided in algorithm AT.

4 Experimental Studies

To assess the efficiency of AT, we conducted experiments to compare AT with the k-modes algorithm [3] and the ROCK algorithm [2]. For the lack of space, we merely use the real market-basket data from a large bookstore company for performance study and the analytical comparison from synthetic data will be conducted in our future extesion. In this real data set, there are $|D| = 100K$ transactions, $|I| = 58909$ items, and $N^{Lev} = 3$ levels. In addition, the number of the taxonomy level in this real data set is 3. In the real data, the items with the same category are usually purchased together. Thus, the association relationships and taxonomy relationships are related to each other.

Figure 2 shows the relative quality of clustering results of AT, ROCK, and k-modes in real data set where the database size $|D|$ varies from 20K to 100K. When we vary $|D|$ from 20K to 100K in ROCK, the numbers of clusters are, respectively, 576, 524, 468, 413, and 519. With association-taxonomy similarity measurement, AT significantly outperforms other algorithms as validated by $AI(U)$ in Figure 2(a) and by $TI(U)$ in Figure 2(b). In this real data set, because the items with high taxonomy relationships are usually purchased together while the items with low taxonomy relationships are not, AT has higher taxonomy index than association index, i.e., $AI(U) > AI(U)$.

5 Conclusion

In this paper, with the association-taxonomy similarity measurement proposed, we developed algorithm AT for item data. Two validation indexes based on association and

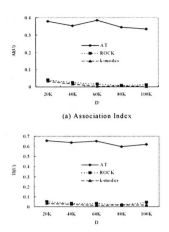

(a) Association Index

(b) Taxonomy Index

Figure 2. $AI(U)$ **and** $TI(U)$ **for algorithms when** $|D|$ **varies.**

taxonomy features of items was also devised in this paper to assess the quality of clustering for item data. As validated by real data, it was shown by our experimental results that algorithm AT devised in this paper significantly outperforms the prior works in the clustering quality of item data.

Acknowledgement

The authors are supported in part by the Ministry of Education Project No. 89-E-FA06-2-4, and the National Science Council Project No. NSC 91-2213-E-002-034 and NSC 91-2213-E-002-045, Taiwan, Republic of China.

References

[1] R. Agrawal and R. Srikant. Fast Algorithms for Mining Association Rules in Large Databases. *Proceedings of the 20th International Conference on Very Large Data Bases*, pages 478–499, September 1994.

[2] S. Guha, R. Rastogi, and K. Shim. ROCK: A Robust Clustering Algorithm for Categorical Attributes. *Proceedings of the 15th International Conference on Data Engineering*, 1999.

[3] Z. Huang. Extensions to the k-Means Algorithm for Clustering Large Data Sets with Categorical Values. *Data Mining and Knowledge Discovery*, 2(3):283–304, September 1998.

[4] K. Wang, C. Xu, and B. Liu. Clustering Transactions Using Large Items. *Proceedings of ACM CIKM International Conference on Information and Knowledge Management*, 1999.

[5] C.-H. Yun, K.-T. Chuang, and M.-S. Chen. Using Category-Based Adherence to Cluster Market-Basket Data. *Proceedings of the 2nd IEEE International Conference on Data Mining (ICDM 2002)*, Dec. 2002.

Dimensionality Reduction Using Kernel Pooled Local Discriminant Information

Peng Zhang & Jing Peng
EECS Department
Tulane University
New Orleans, LA 70118
{zhangp,jp}@eecs.tulane.edu

Carlotta Domeniconi
ISE Department
George Mason University
Fairfax, VA 22030
carlotta@ise.gmu.edu

Abstract

We study the use of kernel subspace methods for learning low-dimensional representations for classification. We propose a kernel pooled local discriminant subspace method and compare it against several competing techniques: generalized Fisher discriminant analysis (GDA) and kernel principal components analysis (KPCA) in classification problems. We evaluate the classification performance of the nearest-neighbor rule with each subspace representation. The experimental results demonstrate the efficacy of the kernel pooled local subspace method and the potential for substantial improvements over competing methods such as KPCA in some classification problems.

1 Introduction

Subspace analysis methods such as GDA and KPCA play an important role in classification and data mining. In data visualization and classification the principal modes are extracted and utilized for description, detection, and classification. Using these "principal modes" to represent data can be found in data preprocessing [5, 10] and linear discriminant analysis [7].

Subspace analysis often significantly simplifies tasks such as regression, classification, and density estimation by computing low-dimensional subspaces having statistically uncorrelated or independent variables. PCA [9] is a prime example that employs eigenvector-based techniques to reduce dimensionality and extract features. KPCA [12]

and GDA [1] extend these linear techniques in a nonlinear fashion. In this paper we propose a kernel pooled local Fisher discriminant subspace method for learning low-dimensional representations for classification. We perform a nonlinear global dimensionality reduction by pooling local discriminant dimension information in feature space and applying the kernel trick [4] to capture nonlinearity. The resulting subspaces are nonlinear, discriminant and compact, whereby better classification performance and greater computational efficiency can be expected.

2 Subspace Methods

The objective of subspace analysis is to represent high-dimensional data in a low-dimensional subspace according to some optimality criteria. Classification then takes place on the chosen subspace. Here we briefly describe several methods for computing both linear and nonlinear subspaces and highlight their corresponding characteristics. We assume that the data can be captured by a compact and connected subspace, which is often the case, for example, in face recognition.

Kernel PCA is a nonlinear version of PCA [12]. KPCA applies a nonlinear mapping to the input $\phi(\mathbf{x}) : \Re^q \to \Re^N$ and then solve for a linear PCA in the induced feature space $\Re^N$, where $N \gg q$ and possibly infinite. In KPCA, the mapping ϕ is made implicit by the use of kernel functions satisfying Mercer's theorem [3] $k(\mathbf{x}, \mathbf{y}) = \phi(\mathbf{x}) \cdot \phi(\mathbf{y})$. Since computing covariance involves only dot-products, performing a PCA in the feature space can be formulated with kernels in the input space without the explicit (and possibly prohibitive) direct computation of ϕ. A major advan-

701

tage of KPCA over principal curves is that KPCA does not require nonlinear optimization. On the other hand, selecting the optimal kernel (and its associated parameters) remains an engineering problem.

Similar to KPCA, GDA [1] is a kernelized version of Fisher discriminant analysis (FDA). The basic idea is to maximize the ratio of the between sum-of-squares matrix to the within sum-of-squares matrix in the feature space. The major problem associated with GDA (or FDA) is that the within sum-of-squares matrix is usually degenerated in practice. Often this problem is solved by using techniques such as pseudo inverse or PCA to remove the null space of the within sum-of-squares matrix. However, it can be shown that the null space potentially contains significant discriminant information [2].

3 Kernel Pooled local Discriminant Subspace Method

3.1 Pooled Local Subspace Method

Hastie and Tibshrani [8] propose a global dimension reduction technique by pooling local dimension information. For each training point, local pooling calculates the local centroid deviations $\tilde{\mathbf{x}}_j(i) = \bar{\mathbf{x}}_j^{(i)} - \bar{\mathbf{x}}^{(i)}$, where $\bar{\mathbf{x}}_j^{(i)}$ denotes the mean of class j points in a neighborhood of the ith training point, and $\bar{\mathbf{x}}^{(i)}$ the overall mean. Then it seeks a subspace that is close in average weighted squared distance to all these deviations. If U denotes an orthonormal basis for the subspace, this subspace can be computed by minimizing the total weighted residual sum of squares $RSS(U) = \sum_{i=1}^{l} \sum_{j=1}^{J} \pi_j(i) \tilde{\mathbf{x}}_j^t(i)(I - UU^t)\tilde{\mathbf{x}}_j(i)$, where $\pi_j(i)$ represents the local class membership proportions, l the number of training samples, and J the number of classes.

It turns out, as shown in [8], that this subspace is spanned by the largest eigenvectors of the average between-sum of squares matrix: $B = \frac{1}{l} \sum_{i=1}^{l} B_i$, where B_i denotes the local between-sum of squares matrices at the ith training point: $B_i = \sum_{j=1}^{J} \pi_j(i)(\bar{\mathbf{x}}_j^{(i)} - \bar{\mathbf{x}}^{(i)})(\bar{\mathbf{x}}_j^{(i)} - \bar{\mathbf{x}}^{(i)})^t$. The experimental results presented in [8] show that the pooled local subspace method is very promising.

It is important to note that local pooling does not sphere the data locally before calculating the centroid deviations.

An argument given in [8] is that any local spherical window containing two classes will likely have a linear decision boundary orthogonal to the line joining the two means. As a result, local pooling will not suffer the small size sample problem (degenerate within class matrices) facing FDA or GDA [1, 2]. It is interesting to note that locally linear embedding also uses pooled locally linear constraints to compute a global subspace [11].

3.2 Kernel Pooled Local Subspace Analysis

We now show how to compute a nonlinear pooled local discriminant subspace by using the kernel trick [4]. Let $\phi : \mathbf{x} \to \phi(\mathbf{x})$ be the nonlinear mapping from $\Re^q$ to $\Re^N$. Also, let $\bar{\phi}_j(\mathbf{x}^{(i)}) = \frac{1}{l_{ij}} \sum_{y_k=j} \phi(\mathbf{x}_k^{(i)})$ be the mean of class j samples in a neighborhood of the ith training point in the feature space, and $\bar{\phi}(\mathbf{x}^{(i)}) = \frac{1}{l_i} \sum_{k=1}^{l_i} \phi(\mathbf{x}_k^{(i)})$ be the overall mean in the same neighborhood, where l_{ij} represents the number of class j training samples in the neighborhood of the ith training point, and l_i the total number of training samples in the neighborhood. Then the local between-sum of squares matrix at the ith training point in the feature space is $B_i^{\phi} = \frac{1}{J} \sum_{j=1}^{J} (\bar{\phi}_j(\mathbf{x}^{(i)}) - \bar{\phi}(\mathbf{x}^{(i)}))(\bar{\phi}_j(\mathbf{x}^{(i)}) - \bar{\phi}(\mathbf{x}^{(i)}))^t$. The pooled local subspace method seeks a discriminant subspace that is close to all of B_is. The average between-sum of squares matrix B in the feature space is

$$B^{\phi} = \frac{1}{l} \sum_{i=1}^{l} B_i^{\phi} = \frac{1}{lJ} \sum_{i=1}^{l} \sum_{j=1}^{J} \tilde{\phi}_j(\mathbf{x}^{(i)}) \tilde{\phi}_j(\mathbf{x}^{(i)})^t \quad (1)$$

where $\tilde{\phi}_j(\mathbf{x}^{(i)}) = \bar{\phi}_j(\mathbf{x}^{(i)}) - \bar{\phi}(\mathbf{x}^{(i)})$.

Similar to KPCA [12], we have the eigenvector equation $\lambda \mathbf{v} = B^{\phi} \mathbf{v}$. Clearly all solutions must lie in the span of $\phi(\mathbf{x}_1), \cdots, \phi(\mathbf{x}_l)$. Therefore, there exist coefficients α_i $(i = 1, \cdots, l)$ such that

$$\mathbf{v} = \sum_{i=1}^{l} \alpha_i \phi(\mathbf{x}_i). \quad (2)$$

It is also true that for all $k = 1, \cdots, l$ we have

$$\lambda(\phi(\mathbf{x}_k) \cdot \mathbf{v}) = (\phi(\mathbf{x}_k) \cdot B^{\phi} \mathbf{v}) \quad (3)$$

Substituting (2) and (1) into (3), we obtain, the left hand side of (3) $\lambda(\phi(\mathbf{x}_k) \cdot \mathbf{v}) = \lambda \sum_{i=1}^{l} \alpha_i \phi(\mathbf{x}_k) \cdot \phi(\mathbf{x}_i)$. For the right hand side of (3), we have $\sum_{j=1}^{J} [\phi(\mathbf{x}_k) \cdot$

$\tilde{\phi}_j(\mathbf{x}^{(1)}) \cdots \phi(\mathbf{x}_k) \cdot \tilde{\phi}_j(\mathbf{x}^{(l)})]K_j\alpha$, for all $k = 1, \cdots, l$.
Here $\alpha = (\alpha_1, \cdots, \alpha_l)^t$ and

$$K_j = \begin{pmatrix} \tilde{\phi}_j(\mathbf{x}^{(1)}) \cdot \phi(\mathbf{x}_1) & \cdots & \tilde{\phi}_j(\mathbf{x}^{(1)}) \cdot \phi(\mathbf{x}_l) \\ \cdots & \cdots & \cdots \\ \tilde{\phi}_j(\mathbf{x}^{(l)}) \cdot \phi(\mathbf{x}_1) & \cdots & \tilde{\phi}_j(\mathbf{x}^{(l)}) \cdot \phi(\mathbf{x}_l) \end{pmatrix}.$$

$$(4)$$

Define

$$K = [k_{ij}] = [\phi(\mathbf{x}_i) \cdot \phi(\mathbf{x}_j)] \qquad (5)$$

and $\tilde{K} = \sum_{j=1}^{J} K_j^t K_j$. We obtain

$$(lJ)\lambda K\alpha = \tilde{K}\alpha \qquad (6)$$

which is a generalized eigenvector problem [6]. By solving (6), the ith principal component u_i of $\mathbf{x}$ can be calculated according to: $u_i = \mathbf{v}_i \cdot \phi(\mathbf{x}) = \sum_{k=1}^{l} \alpha_k^i k(\mathbf{x}, \mathbf{x}_k)$, where $\mathbf{v}_i$ denotes the ith eigenvector of the feature space.

3.3 Centering in Feature Space

Computing both K and $\tilde{K}$ requires centering the data in feature space. This is done as follow. Let $\Phi(\mathbf{x}_k) = \phi(\mathbf{x}_k) - \frac{1}{l}\sum_{i=1}^{l}\phi(\mathbf{x}_i)$ and $\mathbf{1}_l$ as a $l \times l$ matrix with entries $(\mathbf{1}_N)_{ij} := 1/l$. Then the Gram matrix K on the left side of (6) becomes $K^c = K - \mathbf{1}_l K - K\mathbf{1}_l + \mathbf{1}_l K\mathbf{1}_l$. On the other hand, $\tilde{\Phi}_j(\mathbf{x}^{(i)}) = \bar{\Phi}_j(\mathbf{x}^{(i)}) = \tilde{\phi}_j(\mathbf{x}^{(i)}) - \bar{\phi}_j(\mathbf{x}^{(i)})$. It follows that the centered matrix $\tilde{K}$ becomes $\tilde{K}^c = \sum_{j=1}^{J}(K_j^c)^t K_j^c$, where $K_j^c = K_j - K_j\mathbf{1}_l$. Thus the generalized eigenvector problem (6) becomes

$$(lJ)\lambda K^c\alpha = \tilde{K}^c\alpha \qquad (7)$$

4 Experimental Results

Figure 1 Here we use a 2D toy example to illustrate subspace computation by KPooLS using Gaussian kernels. The left panel shows the 2D example, where the two class data are uniformly distributed in two dimensions, separated by a sinusoidal decision boundary. The middle panel shows the projection of the data onto the first two eigenvectors of the feature space computed by KPooLS, while the right panel shows the intensity values of the first principal component when the 2D space is projected onto the first eigenvector of the feature space.

In the following we use two data sets to examine the classification performance of the nearest neighbor rule (3NN)

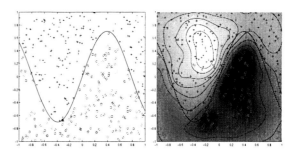

Figure 1. Left panel: 2D toy example. Right panel: First principal component values of KPooLS.

with each subspace representation, i.e., PCA, KPCA, and the proposed KPooLS algorithm. Since our focus here is on subspace methods, a simple classifier is prefered.

For each data set, we randomly select 60% of the data as training and remaining 40% as testing. This process is repeated 20 times and the average error distributions are reported. The dimensions of subspaces computed by each method are determined so that only eigenvectors remain whose eigenvalues are great than or equal to $0.1\lambda_{max}$ are retained. Also, we use Gaussian kernels for all nonlinear subspace methods and kernel parameters are determined through cross-validation.

Glass Data: This data set is taken from UCI Machine Learning Repository. It consists of $q = 9$ chemical attributes measured for each of $N = 214$ data of $J = 6$ classes. The left panel in Figure 2 shows the error distributions of each subspace methods.

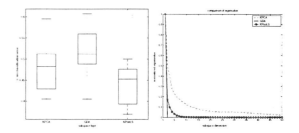

Figure 2. Left panel: Error distributions by each subspace method on the Glass data. Right panel: Normalized eigenvalues

The error distributions clearly favor KPooLS. It is interesting to note that while the normalized eigenvalues of the principal subspaces computed by KPooLS and GDA follow a similar trend (right panel), KPooLS performed better than GDA. On average, both KPooLS and GDA used three principal modes to represent the subspace. In contrast, KPCA used 12. GDA performed slightly worse than KPCA. However, KPCA used substantially larger subspaces (12 dimensions on average).

Cat and Dog Image Data: In this experiment, the data set is composed of one hundred images of cat faces and dog faces. Each image is a black-and-white 64×64 pixel image, resulting in 4096 dimensional measurement space. These images have been registered by aligning the eyes.

The left panel in Figure 3 shows the error distributions obtained by each method on the cat and dog image data. KPooLS and GDA registered similar performance. However, KPCA performed significantly worse, as expected.

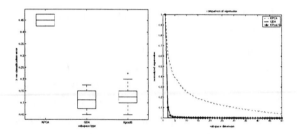

Figure 3. Left panel: Error distributions by each subspace method on the cat and dog data. Right panel: Normalized eigenvalues.

The right panel in Figure 3 shows normalized eigenvalues calculated by each method. The eigenvalues of the principal spaces computed by both KPooLS and GDA again decrease rapidly. On average, the subspaces computed by KPooLS and GDA were represented by two principal components. In contrast, KPCA used 30 principal components to represent the subspaces. It is rather surprising to see that KPCA failed to achieve significant dimensionality reduction.

5 Summary

This paper presents a kernel pooled local discriminant subspace method for learning low-dimensional representations for classification. This method performs a nonlinear global dimensionality reduction by pooling local dimension information and applying the kernel trick to capture nonlinearity. The resulting Subspaces are nonlinear, discriminant and compact, whereby better classification performance and greater computational efficiency can be achieved. The experimental results show that the KPooLS algorithm can learn discriminant subspaces that are much more compact than that computed by KPCA and can outperform competing methods such as GDA in some classification problems.

References

[1] G. Baudat and F. Anouar. Generalized discriminant analysis using akernel approach. *Neural Computation*, 12:2385–2404, 2000.

[2] L. Chen and et al. A new lda-based face recognition system which can solve the small samplesize problem. *Pattern Recognition*, 33:1713–1726, 2000.

[3] R. Courant and D. Hilbert, editors. *Methods of Mathematical Physiacs, vol. 1*. Interscience, New York, 1953.

[4] N. Cristianini and J. Shawe-Taylor. *An Introduction to Support Vector Machines and other kernel-based learning methods*. Cambridge University Press, Cambridge, UK, 2000.

[5] M. Dash and H. Liu. Feature selection methods for classification. *Intelligent Data Analysis: An International Journal*, 1, 1997.

[6] R. O. Duda and P. E. Hart. *Pattern Classification and Scene Analysis*. John Wiley & Sons, Inc., 1973.

[7] K. Etemad and R. Chellappa. Discriminant analysis for recognition of human faces. In *Proc. Int'l Conf. Acoustics, Speech, and Signal Processing*, pages 2148–2151, 1996.

[8] T. Hastie and R. Tibshirani. Discriminant adaptive nearest neighbor classification and regression. In D. S. Touretzky, M. C. Mozer, and M. E. Hasselmo, editors, *Advances in Neural Information Processing Systems*, volume 8, pages 409–415. The MIT Press, 1996.

[9] I. Jolliffe. *Principal Component Analysis*. New York: Springer-Verlag, 1986.

[10] J. Neter, M. Kutner, C. Nachtsheim, and L. Wasserman. *Applied Linear Statistical Models, 4th Edition*. Irwin, Chicago, 1996.

[11] S. T. Roweis and L. K. Saul. Nonlinear dimensionality reduction bylocally linear embedding. *Science*, 290:2323–2326, 2000.

[12] B. Scholkopf, A. Smola, and K.-R. Muller. Nonlinear component analysis as a kernel eigenvalue problem. *Neural Computation*, 10:1299–1319, 1998.

A Feature Selection Framework for Text Filtering

Zhaohui Zheng   Rohini Srihari   Sargur Srihari
CEDAR, Department of Computer Science and Engineering
University at Buffalo, The State University of New York
{zzheng3,rohini,srihari}@cedar.buffalo.edu

Abstract

This paper presents a new framework for local feature selection in text filtering. In this framework, a feature set is constructed per category by first selecting a set of terms highly indicative of membership (positive set) and another set of terms highly indicative of non-membership (negative set), and then combining these two sets. This feature selection framework not only unifies several standard feature selection methods, but also facilitates the proposal of a new method that optimally combines the positive and negative sets. The experimental comparison between the proposed method and standard methods was conducted on six feature selection metrics: chi-square, correlation coefficient, odds ratio, GSS coefficient and two proposed variants of odds ratio and GSS coefficient: OR-square and GSS-square respectively. The results show that the proposed feature selection method improves text filtering performance.

1. Introduction

Several feature selection measures have been explored in the text filtering literature including Document Frequency (DF), Information Gain (IG), Mutual Information (MI), Ghi-square (CHI), Correlation Coefficient (CC), Odds Ratio (OR) and GSS Coefficient (GSS) [1, 2, 3, 4, 5, 7]. Out of the seven features, CHI, CC, OR and GSS seem to be the most effective based on the experiments reported so far. We will focus on the four measure in this study.

This paper presents a feature selection framework, in which the terms highly indicative of membership and non-membership are selected separately, and then combined explicitly afterwards. Several standard methods are unified by this framework and a new method is proposed that combines the terms most indicative of membership and non-membership for each category in a way such that the optimal performance, e.g. F1 measure, will be obtained on a validation set. The features indicative of membership and non-membership are also referred to as the positive and neg-

ative features respectively.

2. Related work

In this section, we will present six feature selection measures (four known measures and two proposed variants), and then describe the imbalanced data problem and its impacts on feature selection.

2.1. Feature selection measures

Chi-square (CHI)   Chi-square measures the lack of independence between a term t and a category c_i and can be compared to the chi-square distribution with one degree of freedom to judge extremeness [7, 5]. It is defined as:

$$\chi^2(t, c_i) = \frac{N[P(t, c_i)P(\bar{t}, \overline{c_i}) - P(t, \overline{c_i})P(\bar{t}, c_i)]^2}{P(t)P(\bar{t})P(c_i)P(\overline{c_i})}$$

Correlation coefficient (CC)   Correlation coefficient of a word t with a category c_i was defined by Ng et al. as [3, 5]

$$CC(t, c_i) = \frac{\sqrt{N}[P(t, c_i)P(\bar{t}, \overline{c_i}) - P(t, \overline{c_i})P(\bar{t}, c_i)]}{\sqrt{P(t)P(\bar{t})P(c_i)P(\overline{c_i})}}$$

It is a variant of the CHI metric, where $CC^2 = \chi^2$. CC can be viewed as a "one-sided" chi-square metric. The positive values correspond to features indicative of membership, while negative values indicate non-membership. Feature selection using CC selects the terms with maximum CC values. The rationale behind is that terms coming from the non-relevant texts of a category are considered useless. On the other hand, CHI is non-negative, whose value indicates either membership or non-membership of a term to one cateogry. Accordingly the ambiguous features will be ranked lower. In contrast with CC, CHI considers the terms coming from both the relevant and non-relevant texts.

Odds ratio (OR)   Odds ratio was proposed originally by Van Rijsbergen et al. for selecting terms for relevance feedback [4]. The basic idea is that the distribution of features on the relevant documents is different from the distribution of features on the non-relevant documents. It has been used by Mladenic for selecting terms in text categorization [2]. It is defined as follows:

$$OR(t, c_i) = log \frac{P(t|c_i)[1 - P(t|\overline{c_i})]}{[1 - P(t|c_i)]P(t|\overline{c_i})}$$

GSS coefficient (GSS)   GSS coefficent is another simplified variant of the statistics χ^2 proposed by Galavotti et al. [1], which is defined as:

$$GSS(t, c_i) = P(t, c_i)P(\overline{t}, \overline{c_i}) - P(t, \overline{c_i})P(\overline{t}, c_i)$$

Similar to CC, OR and GSS only consider the positive features.

OR-square (ORS) and GSS-square (GSSS)   In spirit of relationship between CHI and CC, we propose two variants of OR and GSS: OR-square (ORS) and GSS-square (GSSS) respectively as follows:

$$ORS(t, c_i) = OR^2(t, c_i),$$

$$GSSS(t, c_i) = GSS^2(t, c_i)$$

Similar to CHI, ORS or GSSS is non-negative, whose value represents the strength of a term indicating membership or non-membership, e.g. non-ambiguity. CC, OR and GSS can be considered as "one-sided" CHI, ORS and GSSS respectively.

In summary, local feature selection using CC, OR and GSS pick out the terms most indicative of membership. They will never consider negative features unless all the positive features have already been selected. On the other hand, local feature selection using CHI, ORS and GSSS do not differentiate between the terms indicative of membership and non-membership by comparing their squared CC, OR and GSS values respectively (e.g. CHI, ORS and GSSS vlaues respectively). Among those terms with positive/negative CC (OR or GSS) values, the greater/smaller the value is, the more likely it will be selected by the standard method using CHI (ORS or GSSS respectively). Therefore, they implicitly combine the terms most indicative of membership and non-membership. The size ratio between the positive and negative features is internally and implicitly decided by thresholding on the number of features with the highest squared values, e.g., the size of feature set.

2.2. Imbalanced data problem

When training a text filtering system for a category, we use all the documents in the training corpus that belong to that category as relevant training data and all the documents in the training corpus that belong to all the other categories as non-relevant training data. It is ofen the case that there is an overwhelming number of non-relevant training documents, which is typically an "imbalanced data problem".

The impacts of imbalanced data problem on the standard feature selection for text filtering can be illustrated as follows:

1. For the methods using the positive features only (e.g. CC, OR and GSS), the non-relevant documents are subject to misclassification. It will be even worse for the imbalanced data problem, where non-relevant documents dominate. How to confidently reject the non-relevant documents is very important in that case.

2. When applying to the imbalanced data the methods implicitly combining the positive and negative features (e.g. CHI, ORS and GSSS), the positive features usually have much higher values than the negative features according to the definition of the three metrics and our previous experiments. Therefore, the positive features will dominate in the feature set. The similar situation occurs as described above.

3. The feature selection framework

3.1. The general formulation

In local feature selection, we consider all the terms as either positive or negative. As mentioned in Section 2.1.3, the basic idea behind OR is that the distribution of positive features is different from the distribution of negative features. In light of this theory and the two illustrations in Section 2.2, we suggest separate handling of positive and negative features in the following framework:

For each category c_i :

- generate a positive-feature set F_i^+ of size l_1 by selecting the l_1 terms with highest $\Im(t, c_i)$. $l_1, 0 < l_1 \leq l$, is a nature number.

- generate a negative-feature set F_i^- of size l_2 by selecting the l_2 terms with highest $\Im(t, \overline{c_i})$. $l_2 = l - l_1$ is a non-negative integer.

- $F_i = F_i^+ \cup F_i^-$.

where: l is the predefined size of feature set. $l_1/l, 0 < l_1/l \leq 1$, is the key parameter of the framework to be set.

The function $\Im(\cdot, c_i)$ should satisfy that the larger $\Im(t, c_i)$ is, the more likely the term t belongs to the category c_i. Obviously, CC, OR and GSS can serve as such functions, while CHI, ORS and GSSS cannot.

In the first step, we intend to pick out those terms most indicative of membership of c_i, while those terms most indicative of non-membership are selected as well in the second step. The final feature set will be the union of the two.

Based on their definition, we can easily obtain:

$$CC(t, \overline{c_i}) = -CC(t, c_i),$$

$$OR(t, \overline{c_i}) = -OR(t, c_i),$$

$$GSS(t, \overline{c_i}) = -GSS(t, c_i).$$

Accordingly, the second step can be rewritten as:

- generate a negative-feature set F_i^- of size l_2 by selecting the l_2 terms with smallest $\Im(t, c_i)$.

Therefore, the framework combines the l_1 terms with largest $\Im(\cdot, c_i)$ and the $l - l_1$ terms with smallest $\Im(\cdot, c_i)$.

3.2. Two special cases

The standard feature selection methods can be forced into two groups:

1. select the positive features only, e.g. CC, OR and GSS. For convenience, we will use CC as the representative of this group.

2. implicitly but not optimally combine the positive and negative features, e.g. CHI, ORS and GSSS. CHI will be chosen to represent the this group.

The two groups are two special cases of our feature selection framework. The standard feature selection using CC corresponds to the case where $\Im = CC$, $l_1/l = 1$. The standard method using CHI corresponds to the case where $\Im = CC$, and l_1/l is implicitly and internally set by thresholding as mentioned in Section 2.1.

3.3. Optimally combining positive and negative features

The above analysis and our previous work [8] indicate:

1. The negative features are also useful and should be included in the feature set. The presence of negative features in a document is a good indicator of its non-membership. Thus the text filtering performance can be improved through condifent rejection of non-relevant documents.

2. Implicit combination of positive and negative features is not necessarily optimal especially for imbalanced data set, in which the values of positive features are usually much larger than negative features. CHI, ORS or GSSS might select the positive features only (equivalent to CC, OR or GSS based approach respectively) when the size of feature set is small.

3. The feature selection framework facilitates us the manipulation on explicitly combining the positive and negative features through the parameter l_1/l.

Based on the above three observations, we propose a new method in the framework, which empirically chooses l_1/l such that the optimal text filtering performance is obtained on a validation set. Therefore, it allows the size of the feature set to be as small as needed while guaranteeing that the system uses both positive and negative features in an optimal way.

4. Experimental results and analysis

We use the ApteMod version of Reuters-21578 as described by Yang [6, 7]. When learning the category specific parameters, e.g. size ratio in feature selection and relevance score threshold in classification, we use two thirds of the training set for training and the remaining one third as "validation". After obtain these parameters, the classifiers will be retrained on the entire training set for classification.

In order to compare our proposed feature selection methods with the standard methods, we apply them to naïve Bayes classifiers. Three groups of feature selection methods are considered:

- Standard CHI, Standard CC and improved CC. The three methods are referred as CHI, CC, iCC respectively for notational simplicity.

- Standard ORS, Standard OR and improved OR, referred as ORS, OR and iOR respectively.

- Standard GSSS, Standard GSS and improved GSS, referred as GSSS, GSS and iGSS respectively.

where: standard CHI, CC, ORS, OR, GSSS and GSS represent the standard local feature selection using CHI, CC, ORS, OR, GSSS and GSS measures respectively, while the improved CC, OR and GSS are the proposed feature selection methods using CC, OR and GSS measures respectively (e.g. $\Im = CC, OR$ and GSS respectively). Typical size of a local feature set is between 10 and 50 [5]. In this paper, the performance are reported at a much wider range: $10 \sim 1000$.

Table 1 lists the micro-averaged F1 values for naive Bayes classifiers with the nine different feature selection

Table 1. Micro-averaged F1 values for naïve Bayes classifiers with the nine feature selection methods at different sizes of features.

$|F_i|$	CHI	CC	iCC	ORS	OR	iOR	GSSS	GSS	iGSS
10	.771	.76	.781	.621	.628	.641	.738	.733	.774
20	.767	.763	.803	.635	.644	.661	.738	.74	.78
30	.782	.765	.816	.649	.654	.671	.762	.74	.797
40	.778	.76	.812	.658	.669	.687	.763	.74	.797
50	.784	.769	.82	.674	.689	.712	.768	.734	.797
100	.779	.751	.819	.696	.721	.762	.778	.734	.802
200	.769	.719	.823	.752	.738	.773	.784	.733	.821
500	.786	.708	.816	.763	.726	.805	.796	.725	.813
1000	.79	.673	.816	.754	.701	.802	.792	.70	.811

methods (as listed in the first row) at different sizes of feature set ranging from 10 to 1000 (as listed in the first column).

Accordingly, we can rank the nine methods within the three groups in term of their micro-averaged F1 values as follows:

$$iCC > CHI > CC;$$

$$iOR > ORS > OR;$$

$$iGSS > GSSS > GSS.$$

This confirms:

- the usefulness of negative features. That is, the inclusion of negative features improves performance;

- explicit and empirically optimal combination of positive and negative features is better than implicit combination. The positive and negative features should be separately handled. Simply comparing their squared values (e.g. CHI, ORS and GSSS values.) without differentiating between the positive and negative features is not appropriate.

5. Conclusion

A new feature selection framework was presented, in which the positive and negative features are separately selected and explicitly combined. We explored three special cases of the framework:

1. use the positive set only;

2. internally and implicitly combine the positive and negative features by thresholding on the size of feature set, but the size ratio is not necessarily optimal;

3. combine the two explicitly and the size ratio is empirically chosen such that optimal performance is obtained on a validation set.

The first two cases are known and standard, and the last one is new. The main conclusions are:

- The terms indicative of non-membership (negative features) are useful and should be considered in local feature selection.

- By optimally setting the size ratio of the positive and negative set, the text filtering performance was improved.

References

[1] F. Galavotti, L. Sebastiani and M. Simi. Experiments on the use of feature selection and negative evidence in automated text categorization. *Proceedings of ECDL-00, 4th European Conference on Research and Advanced Technology for Digital Libraries*, pages 59–68, 2000.

[2] D. Mladeni. *Machine Learning on non-homogeneous, distributed text data*. PhD Dissertation, University of Ljubljana, Slovenia, 1998.

[3] W. Ng, H. Goh and K. Low. Feature selection, perceptron learning, and a usability case study for text categorization. *ACM SIGIR Conference on Research and Developement in Information Retrieval*, pages 67–73, 1997.

[4] V. Rijsbergen. *Information Retrieval*. Butterworths, London, 1979.

[5] F. Sebastiani. Machine learning in automated text categorization. *ACM Computing Surveys*, 34(1):1–47, 2002.

[6] Y. Yang. An evaluation of statistical approaches to text categorization. *Journal of Information Retrieval*, 1(1/2):67–88, 1999.

[7] Y. Yang and J. Pedersen. A comparative study on feature selection in text categorization. *The Fourteenth International Conference on Machine Learning*, pages 412–420, 1997.

[8] Z. Zheng and R. Srihari. Optimally combining positive and negative features for text categorization. *Learning from Imbalanced Data Sets II workshop at The Twentieth International Conference on Machine Learning*, 2003.

A K-NN Associated Fuzzy Evidential Reasoning Classifier
with Adaptive Neighbor Selection

Hongwei Zhu, Otman Basir
Department of Systems Design Engineering, University of Waterloo
200 University Ave. W., Waterloo, Ontario, N2L 3G1, Canada
h4zhu@engmail.uwaterloo.ca, obasir@uwaterloo.ca

Abstract

The paper presents a fuzzy evidential reasoning algorithm in light of the Dempster-Shafer evidence theory and the K-nearest neighbor algorithm for pattern classification. Given an input pattern to be classified, each of its K nearest neighbors is viewed as an evidence source, in terms of a fuzzy evidence structure. The distance between the input pattern and each of its K nearest neighbors is used for mass determination while the contextual information of the nearest neighbor in the training sample space is formulated by a fuzzy set in determining a fuzzy focal element. Therefore, pooling evidence provided by neighbors is realized by a fuzzy evidential reasoning, where feature selection is further considered through ranking and adaptive combination of neighbors. A fast implementation scheme of the fuzzy evidential reasoning is also developed. Experimental results of classifying multi-channel remote sensing images have shown that the proposed approach outperforms the K-nearest neighbor (K-NN) algorithm [1], the fuzzy K-nearest neighbor (F-KNN) algorithm [2], the evidence-theoretic K-nearest neighbor (E-KNN) algorithm [3], and the fuzzy extended version of E-KNN (FE-KNN) [4], in terms of the classification accuracy and insensitivity to the number K of nearest neighbors.

1. Introduction

Pattern classification has been applied to various application domains, such as data mining, remote sensing. Many approaches have been proposed for pattern classification, of which the K-nearest neighbor (K-NN) algorithm is a very simple but effective method. K-NN assigns an input pattern to the majority class according to distances between the pattern and its K-nearest neighbors in the training data space. In addition to possessing some pleasing properties [1], K-NN is often seen to result in very good classi-

fication performances in many practical applications. However, it still suffers some problems, such as high sensitivity to the choice of value K, lack of capability in dealing with the presence of overlapped classes, and unreasonableness of equal treatment to neighbors. To deal with these, some alternatives of K-NN have been proposed. One is called the fuzzy K-nearest neighbor (F-KNN) algorithm which introduces fuzziness to K-NN based on the fuzzy set theory [2]. Another typical variation is called the evidence-theoretic K-nearest neighbor algorithm (E-KNN) [3], and its fuzzy extended version [4], referred to as FE-KNN, both taking advantage of the Dempster-Shafer evidence theory [5].

Following the concepts from E-KNN and FE-KNN, we propose a new K-NN associated fuzzy evidential reasoning classifier with adaptive neighbor selection, referred to as FE-NN (Fuzzy Evidential reasoning associated Nearest Neighbor algorithm). In FE-NN, each nearest neighbor is considered to provide a fuzzy evidence structure for the assignment of class label to an input pattern. Rather than unconditionally combining all K neighbor associated fuzzy evidence structures, each neighbor is evaluated and ranked in a certain manner, and they are combined adaptively. An efficient scheme is proposed for implementing the fuzzy evidential reasoning. Experimental results of classifying the Feltwell remote sensing image dataset have shown that FE-NN outperforms K-NN, F-KNN, E-KNN, and FE-KNN, in terms of the classification accuracy and insensitivity to the number K of nearest neighbors. Worth mentioning is that K-NN has been reported to result in better classification accuracy on the same data set than following popular classifiers: Bayes classifier, the multi-layer perceptron neural network, the radial basis function neural network, and probabilistic neural network [6].

The remainder is organized as follows. The Dempster-Shafer evidence theory (DSET) and its fuzzy extended version fuzzy evidential reasoning (FDS) are briefly reviewed in Section 2. Section 3 details the proposed FE-NN. The experimental results are presented in Section 4, and final remarks are concluded in Section 5.

2. DSET and FDS

The Dempster-Shafer evidence theory (DSET) provides a framework to aggregate evidence from multiple information sources [5], by dealing with uncertainty and imprecision in three levels: representing evidence by foal elements and masses, combing evidence by the Dempster's rule of combination, and making decisions.

A *mass function* is a mapping $m : 2^\Omega \rightarrow [0,1]$, satisfying $\sum_{A \subseteq \Omega} m(A) = 1$, and $m(\emptyset) = 0$, where $\Omega = \{\omega_1, \cdots, \omega_c\}$ is called a frame of discernment, and 2^Ω the power set. Subset A with non-zero mass is called a *focal element* (focal for short). Focal elements and their masses construct an *evidence structure*, expressed in the form: $\{(A, m(A)) | A \subseteq \Omega, m(A) > 0\}$. Based on the assumption of independence between sources, the Dempster's rule combines multiple sources by

$$\oplus_{i=1}^{n} m_i(A) = N \sum_{\cap_{i=1}^{n} A^i = A} \prod_{i=1}^{n} m_i(A^i), \qquad (1)$$

$$\oplus_{i=1}^{n} m_i(\emptyset) = 0,$$

$$N^{-1} = 1 - \sum_{\cap_{i=1}^{n} A^i = \emptyset} \prod_{i=1}^{n} m_i(A^i);$$

where $\oplus$ denotes the combination operator. A^i designates the focal in source i, and $m_i(A^i)$ is the corresponding mass. $\cap_{i=1}^{n} A^i$ denotes the intersection of focals A^1 through A^n. Some common evidential measures are belief, plausibility and commonality, among which the commonality is defined by $Q(A) = \sum_{A \subseteq B} m(B)$, where $B \subseteq \Omega$, $A \subseteq \Omega$.

Making fuzzy sets replace crisp focal elements leads to the fuzzy Dempster-Shafer evidential reasoning (FDS). Correspondingly, a *fuzzy evidence structure* is expressed by

$$FS = \{(A, m(A), \mu_A(x)) | A \subseteq \Omega, x \in U\}, \qquad (2)$$

where A denotes a fuzzy focal element with membership $\mu_A(x)$ for its element $x \in U$ (universe of discourse).

Multiple fuzzy evidence structures can be also combined by the Dempster's rule after they are decomposed into crisp evidence structures as follows. Given a piece of fuzzy evidence: $(A, m(A), \mu_A(x))$, fuzzy focal A is decomposed into its α-cuts using the resolution principle in the fuzzy set theory: $A = \sum_{\mu_A(x_j)} A'_{\alpha_j}$, where $\sum$ denotes the set union operation (max), and A'_{α_j} denotes a fuzzy set associated with an α-cut of A, $A_{\alpha_j} = \{x_1, \cdots, x_j\}$ at level $\mu_A(x_j)$, given that $\mu_A(x_1) \geq \mu_A(x_2) \cdots \geq \mu_A(x_n)$, where $j = 1, \cdots, n$. $\mu_{A'_{\alpha_j}}(x) = \mu_A(x_j)$ if $x \in A_{\alpha_j}$; 0 otherwise. The mass of fuzzy focal A is then distributed to its α-cuts by

$$m(A_{\alpha_j}) = \frac{m(A)}{\max_x \mu_A(x)} (\mu_A(x_j) - \mu_A(x_{j+1})). \qquad (3)$$

3. The proposed FE-NN

A fuzzy evidence structure model

Given a training data set $S = \{s_1, \cdots, s_i, \cdots, s_n\}$ composed of n labelled samples, with $s_i \in R^p$ denoting i^{th} training sample pattern of p dimensions, a pattern classification problem aims to assign an input pattern $s \in R^p$ to one of c classes, $\omega_j \in \Omega = \{\omega_1, \cdots, \omega_c\}$. Let $\mathcal{N}(s)$ of cardinality K be the set of K-nearest neighbors of s in terms of the Euclidean distance measure. Let $\mathcal{N}_j(s)$ consist of the neighbors belonging to class ω_j in $\mathcal{N}(s)$. Any $s_k \in \mathcal{N}_j(s)$ is assumed to provide a fuzzy evidence structure in form of

$$FS_k = \{(\{\omega_j\}, \alpha_{kj}), (F_k, 1 - \alpha_{kj})\}, \qquad (4)$$

where $\alpha_{kj} = \alpha_0 \exp(-\gamma_j d(s, s_k)^\beta)$ is the mass assigned to singleton focal $\{\omega_j\}$. $d(s, s_k) = \|s - s_k\|$ is the Euclidean distance. $\alpha_0 \in (0,1)$, $\beta \in \{1, 2, \cdots\}$, and $\gamma_j > 0$. The amount $1 - \alpha_{kj}$ is assigned to a fuzzy set $F_k \subseteq \Omega$: $F_k = \left\{ \frac{\mu_{k1}}{\omega_1}, \frac{\mu_{k2}}{\omega_2}, \cdots, \frac{\mu_{kc}}{\omega_c} \right\}$, where μ_{kl} denotes the membership to class ω_l for $l = 1, \cdots, c$. The motivation of using fuzzy set F_k is to exploit the local information of neighbor s_k in the training sample space. Memberships in F_k are determined in a similar manner as the mass determination for the singleton focal in (4): $\mu_{kl} = \exp\left(-\gamma_j \times \min_{s_i \in \mathcal{N}_l(s_k), s_i \neq s_k} d^\beta(s_k, s_i)\right)$. Note that for the class s_k belongs to, its membership is avoided to be 1. This is not strange because the contribution of membership of s_k has been accounted for in mass α_{kj}, thus it is not double taken into account when its local context information is considered. As a result of fuzzy evidence construction, K nearest neighbors provide a set FS $= \{FS_k | k = 1, \cdots, K\}$ for input pattern s. FE_k's are further combined and reasoned.

Adaptive fusing fuzzy evidence

In multi-source classification problems, it is well recognized that not all available evidence needs to be combined for achieving good performance, in terms of high classification accuracy, good robustness, or less computation cost. In cooperating with the fuzzy evidence structure model (4) and the transformation scheme (3), FE-NN is designed to take into account evidence ranking and adaptive combination through following steps.

Step 1: Apply scheme (3) to fuzzy evidence structure FE_k and obtain crisp evidence structure ES_k for $k = 1, \cdots, K$.

Step 2: Crisp evidence structures in ES $= \{ES_k | k = 1, \cdots, K\}$ are ranked in a non-decreasing order in terms of the mass of the frame of discernment: $m_k(\Omega) = \frac{(1 - \alpha_{kj}) \min(\mu_{F_k}(\omega_l))}{\max(\mu_{F_k}(\omega_l))}$ for $k = 1, \cdots, K$, and the ranked crisp evidence structure set is expressed by ES$' = \{ES'_k | k = 1, \cdots, K\}$.

Step 3: ES$'$ keeps combined one by one in an iterative and accumulated manner, starting with the first evidence structure, until an information measure, called the pignistic Shannon entropy H_{pig} of intermediate combined evidence structure does not decrease. $H_{\text{pig}} = \sum_{\omega_l \in \Omega} -P_{\text{pig}}(\{\omega_l\}) log_2 P_{\text{pig}}(\{\omega_l\})$, and the pignistic probability $P_{\text{pig}}(\{\omega_l\}) = \sum_{\omega_l \in A, A \subseteq \Omega} \frac{m(A)}{|A|}$, where $|A|$ denotes the cardinality of focal A with mass $m(A)$ in the combined evidence structure.

Step 4: Finally, a decision is made by the maximum commonality principle: $\omega = \arg\max_{\omega_l} Q(\{\omega_l\})$, where $Q(\{\omega_l\}$ is computed on the combined evidence structure corresponding to the first local minimum H_{pig} (or the fully combined evidence structure of K fuzzy evidence if H_{pig} continues to decrease as new evidence structures are combined).

Fast implementation of FE-NN

The above fuzzy evidential reasoning process can be realized by an efficient equivalent process without the decomposition of fuzzy evidence structures and Dempster's combination. Using the correspondence between the general fuzzy evidence structure (2) and the proposed fuzzy evidence structure model (4) (x denotes class $\omega_l \in \Omega$, and $U = \Omega$; A is either a singleton set or a fuzzy set), for fuzzy evidence FS_k in (4), the commonality of singleton $\{\omega_l\}$ is thus

$$Q_k(\{\omega_l\}) = \frac{(1 - \alpha_{kj})}{\max(\mu_{F_k}(\omega_{l'}))} \times \mu'_{F_k}(\omega_l), \qquad (5)$$

where

$$\mu'_{F_k}(\omega_l) = \begin{cases} \mu_{F_k}(\omega_l), & \text{if } l \neq j \\ \mu_{F_k}(\omega_l) + \frac{\alpha_{kj} \max(\mu_{F_k}(\omega_{l'}))}{1 - \alpha_{kj}}, & \text{if } l = j \end{cases} \qquad (6)$$

Due to our previous work [7], we have the property:

Theorem 1 *Given the K-nearest neighbor set $\{s_k | k = 1, \cdots, K\}$ of input pattern s, if a fuzzy evidence structure FS_k is constructed by (4) for neighbor s_k, and FS_k is further transferred to a crisp evidence structure ES_k by scheme (3), then the commonality of a singleton class set in the combined evidence structure ES (which is obtained by applying the Dempster's rule to ES_k's) is proportional to the product of confidence measures computed by (6), i.e.,*

$$Q(\{\omega_l\}) \propto \prod_{l=1}^{K} \mu'_{F_k}(\omega_l).$$ *Consequently, finding the single-ton set with the maximum commonality measure in ES is equivalent to finding the class with the maximum product of confidence measures, i.e.,*

$$\arg\max_{\omega_l} Q(\{\omega_l\}) \Leftrightarrow \arg\max_{\omega_l} \left(\prod_{k=1}^{K} \mu'_{F_k}(\omega_l) \right).$$

In above, K fuzzy evidence structures are used for illustration. In fact, less than K fuzzy evidence structures are usually involved due to the adaptive capability of FE-NN. One issue is that the true pignistic Shannon entropy on

intermediate combined evidence structures is not available. Yet, we turn to a decomposition-like scheme, where a product result of fuzzy evidence structures is treated as a fuzzy like focal with mass 1, and it is further decomposed into a crisp evidence structure in the same manner as (3). Moreover, pignistic Shannon entropy is computed based on the derived crisp evidence structure.

4. Experimental results

Experiments are carried out on the remote sensing Feltwell data set, one benchmark commonly used in the GRSS-DFC. The Feltwell data set consists of 15 images of size 250×350 (6 ATM images and 9 SAR images). As an example, one ATM image and one of SAR image are shown in Fig. 1 (a), (b) respectively, together with the ground truth map in Fig. 1 (c). 10944 pixels belonging to five agricultural classes (i.e., sugar beets, stubble, bare soil, potatoes, and carrots) were prepared with a randomly subdivided training set (5124 pixels) and a test set (5820 pixels) [6]. Pixel intensities from the fifteen images form one attribute vector associated with one physical ground unit.

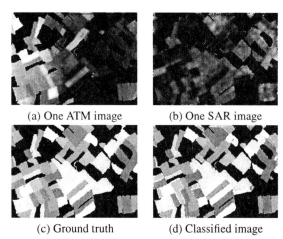

(a) One ATM image   (b) One SAR image

(c) Ground truth   (d) Classified image

Figure 1. Feltwell images and classified image

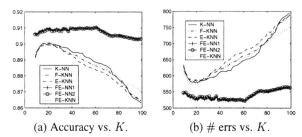

(a) Accuracy vs. K.   (b) # errs vs. K.

Figure 2. Classification results on test data

A set of experiments are performed for comparison, based respectively on K-NN [1], F-KNN [2], E-KNN [3],

FE-KNN [4], and two versions of FE-NN, referred to as FE-NN1 and FE-NN2. FE-NN1 is based on the standard Demspter's rule and the true pignistic Shannon entropy. FE-NN2 is based on the fast implementation scheme and the approximate pignistic Shannon entropy. 6 classifiers are correspondingly involved, denoted also by K-NN, F-KNN, E-KNN, FE-KNN, FE-NN1 and FE-NN2.

In K-NN, if a tie appears to a pattern, it is broken by choosing randomly one of tied classes. Parameters involved in E-KNN, FE-NN1/FE-NN2 are set as: $\alpha_0 = 0.95$, $\beta = 1.0$, and $\gamma_j = \frac{1}{\sigma_j}$, where σ_j is the standard deviation of distances between all possible pairs of training data belonging to ω_j. For E-KNN, an crisp evidence structure is constructed in a similar manner as FE-NN1/FE-NN2, except that Ω takes the place of F_k in (4). In FE-KNN, a fuzzy evidence structure for s_k are constructed by: $\text{FS}_k = \{(F_k, \alpha_{kj}), (\Omega, 1 - \alpha_{kj})\}$, where α_{kj} and F_k are determined similarly as in FE-NN1/FE-NN2 except that $\mu_{kj} = 1$ for FE-KNN if $\omega(s_k) = \omega_j$.

Different values of K, from $K = 9$ to $K = 99$ by steps equal to 2, are examined (in total 46 values of K) for the 6 classifiers. Classification accuracies, as summarized in Table 1, are plotted in Fig. 2 (a) while numbers of misclassified pixels are given in 2 (b). Fig. 2 (a) shows that FE-NN1 and FE-NN2 perform best no matter what values K takes with about 2% of accuracy gain on average. If looking at the numbers of errors in Fig. 2 (b), the average number of errors resulted from FE-KNN1 and FE-KNN2 over 46 experiments are 537.91 and 539.85 respectively while average numbers of errors are 652.65, 659.67, 667.15, and 651.09 respectively for K-NN, F-KNN, E-KNN, and FE-KNN. Compared with the other classifiers, both FE-NN classifiers decrease errors by at least near 17% on average. In terms of the classification accuracies of the non FE-NN classifiers, FE-NN > K-NN > F-KNN > E-KNN, where '>' denotes 'better than'. Worth mentioning is that K-NN has been reported to perform better than on the same data set than Bayes classifier, the multi-layer perceptron neural network, the radial basis function neural network, and probabilistic neural network [6]. The experiments show that our FE-NN classifier outperforms K-NN.

Table 1. Accuracy summary on test data (%)

Classifier	Min	mean	max	std
K-NN	86.32	88.79	90.07	1.13
F-KNN	86.46	88.67	89.95	1.06
E-KNN	86.44	88.54	90.07	1.11
FE-KNN	87.06	88.81	90.17	0.94
FE-NN1	90.33	90.76	91.05	0.24
FE-NN2	90.29	90.72	91.03	0.23

When FE-NN1 and FE-NN2 are compared, their accuracy curves are almost overlapped in Fig. 2. This indicates the proposed fast implementation scheme works well, both

in equivalent combination scheme and the use of approximate pignistic Shannon entropy. Fig. 2 shows also that all non FE-NN classifiers are much sensitive to the choice of K than both FE-NN classifiers whose result curves are much flatter with small variations. The sensitivity can also be discerned from the maximum and minimum accuracies and standard deviations (std) of accuracies in Table 1.

A classification image is shown in Fig. 1 (d), which is resulted from the FE-NN2 classifier with $K = 61$. Comparing with the ground truth image in Fig. 1 (c), the classification is good from our visual justification.

5. Conclusions

In this paper, we have proposed a K-NN associated fuzzy evidential reasoning classifier with adaptive neighbor selection. A fuzzy evidence structure model is proposed using the notation of nearest neighbor algorithm; an effective and efficient adaptive neighbor selection scheme is developed; comparative experiments have demonstrated that our algorithm performs best in terms of the accuracy and the insensitivity to the number K of nearest neighbors.

Acknowledgments

The authors would like to appreciate Prof. F. Roli, University of Cagliari for providing us the Feltwell remote sensing data set.

References

[1] T.M. Cover, P. E. Hart. Nearest neighbor pattern classification. *IEEE Trans. Information Theory*, 12:21-27, 1967.

[2] J.M. Keller, M.R. Gray, J.A. Givens. A fuzzy K-nearest neighbor algorithm. *IEEE Trans. Syst. Man, Cybern.*, SMC-15 (4):580-585, July 1985.

[3] T. Denoex. A k-nearest neighbor classification rule based on Dempster-Shafer theory. *IEEE Trans. Syst. Man, Cybern.*, 25(5):804-813, May 1995.

[4] L.M. Zouhal, T. Denoeux. Generalizing the evidence-theoretic k-NN rule to fuzzy pattern recognition. In *Proc. of 2nd Int. ICSC Symposium on Fuzzy Logic and Applications*, pages 294-300, Zurich, Switzerland, Feb. 1997.

[5] G. Shafer. *A Mathematic Theory of Evidence*. Princeton University Press, Priceton, NJ, 1976.

[6] G. Giacinto, F. Roli, L. Bruzzone. Combination of neural and statistical algorithms for supervised classification of remote-sensing images. *Pattern Recognit. Lett.*, 21(5):385-397, May 2000.

[7] H. Zhu, O. Basir. A scheme for constructing evidence structures in Dempster-Shafer evidence theory for data fusion. In *Proc. of 5th IEEE Int. Symposium on Computational intelligence in Robotics and Automation*, Japan, July 2003.

Industry-Track Papers

Findings from a Practical Project Concerning Web Usage Mining

Prof. Dr. Frank Dellmann   Dipl.-Kfm. Holger Wulff   Dipl.-Betriebw. Stefan Schmitz
Fachhochschule Münster   *Fachhochschule Münster*   *Fachhochschule Münster*
dellmann@fh-muenster.de   *h.wulff@freenet.de*   *stefanschmitz@muenster.de*

Abstract

In a practical project a statistical analysis of the Web log files of the domain www.volkswagen.de was carried out by using the CRISP-DM procedure. For the preprocessing phase, more profound findings could be gained than are usually described in many studies. Since the aim was to deduce significant statements while measuring the effect, tests of significance for e-metrics were used in addition to the commonly described procedure.

1. Introduction

Most companies use the internet to communicate with their customers as well as, in some cases, to sell their products. Therefore, it is necessary to measure the intended effect of this marketing tool and deduce certain procedures accordingly.

This challenge is met with the help of Web usage mining which does not only aim at measuring the intended effect but also at recognising patterns of user conduct in order to develop new marketing measures. Another aim is an increased customer attraction and commitment through the improvement of structure and content of the Web site.

It is against this background that Web log files of the domain www.volkswagen.de were analysed statistically within a practical project in cooperation with the BBDO Interactive GmbH by using the CRISP-DM procedure [1]. www.volkswagen.de serves as a communication and distribution channel. The distribution function includes a car configurator (not analysed in this case since it is operated by another server) with the help of which the customer can create an individual automobile and then email the configuration to the car dealer. The findings gained from this project will be described in this paper.

Several authors have dealt with preprocessing in Web Usage Mining (e.g. [2] with preprocessing in general and [3] with the recognition of robots).

Some contributions as to how to measure the success of Web sites using e-metrics exist, but they only deal with descriptive, not inferential statistical methods (e.g. [4]).

However, the application of tests of significance to patterns of navigation is described in [2] and [5].

In addition to the studies already mentioned, this paper will focus specifically on the use of status codes and non-pages, especially frames, as well as on the application of tests of significance to the calculated e-metrics [6].

The structure of the paper follows the steps of the CRISP-DM procedure beginning with the business understanding in chapter 2 and ending with the interpretation of the results (chapter 6) and an outlook on further possible analyses (chapter 7).

2. Business Understanding

It is vital for the development of a purposeful investigation to be familiar with the situation and aims of the company whose data will be analysed. Volkswagen finds itself within a stagnant, heavily fragmented market. Slow growth, fierce competition and high costs are characterizing the company situation. In this environment it is crucial for the Volkswagen group that all steps, which have already been taken or are planned for the future, pass a critical evaluation concerning their effectiveness and efficiency in order to satisfy clients and shareholders.

Therefore the task was to check Volkswagen's internet profile with regard to the fulfilment of its communication and distribution function and to work out measures to improve the employment of resources.

3. Data Understanding

For the investigation of www.volkswagen.de, log files are used in unformatted ASCII text. These log files contain the requests of the static html pages of the web server were accessed including the starting of the configurator.

The server stores three main files (transfer, agent and referrer log) in which visitors' activities are registered using the Common Log File Format. These files were then fed into SPSS and put together correctly. This means that the individual lines have to be identifiable with the help of a specific key. The IP address (remotehost) in connection with the date serves as the key in this case. The referrer log data cannot be used due to the absence of the IP address. Entries which have the same IP address in transfer log and agent log and have been registered in the same second do not cause problems of compatibility since these lines can definitely be allocated to the right session. After the files had been put together, eight files in SPSS format were available, each referring to one particular day. They will be put together at a later stage of preprocessing.

The files of the individual days in the domain www.volkswagen.de consist of approximately five million lines each. The size of the file is about 2 GB per day. The average size of traffic within the domain www.volkswagen.de is 12.625 GB per day.

The well known cache and proxy problems and the difficulties caused by dynamic IP addresses and company networks still persist (see [2], p. 47f.).

4. Data Preprocessing

4.1. Data Cleaning

All transactions of the Web server are registered in the log files. However, only those entries depicting activities of actual or potential clients are interesting from a marketing point of view. Therefore extensive data cleaning has to be performed.

The status code describes the success or failure of a transaction. Within this Web usage mining project it has become clear that the status codes 200, 206 and 304 are of particular interest.

The log file does not only contain access of actual or potential clients but also of members of staff (e.g. administrators) as well as crawlers/spiders and robots which have to be deleted with regard to the marketing aim. While own members of staff can be easily recognised by the familiar IP address, it is necessary to rely on lists (See http://www.spiderhunter.com/spiderlist/spider-info.txt, http://info.webcrawler.com/mak/projects/robots/active/) and heuristics in relation to the mentioned programmes. Certain entries in the agent point to spiders (cf. [3], p. 13f.). Furthermore, spiders and robots can be identified by the way they access the Web site. [3] describe the use of patterns of navigation in a classification algorithm in order to recognise robots.

Analogously, entries from programmes have to be deleted which store the complete Web site locally (e.g. SiteSnagger). These access all pages of the site once, which is uncharacteristic of user conduct. In the project they were discovered during the calculation of e-metrics. This recognition is impossible with programmes for automatic data cleaning and calculation of e-metrics.

Furthermore, a log file does not only register actual access to web pages and downloads but also requests which only result from user activities indirectly, such as automatically loaded graphics, frames, applets, scripts and stylesheets. These non-pages have to be eliminated from the log file because they are called up automatically during a request and therefore do not represent active user conduct. In many studies it is suggested to delete all entries with graphic suffixes, such as gif or jpg (see [7], p. 16). However, on some web pages this could lead to graphics being deleted by mistake which the user has intentionally called up. Therefore the site has to be checked for such graphic files which can be activated by the user so that these can remain within the cleared log file.

However, some html entries have to be deleted because they represent automatically loaded frames. All requests with an "_.html" have to be deleted because, according to the programming agreement at BBDO Interactive, they signify frames.

So it is necessary to have a thorough knowledge of the Web site when cleaning the non-pages, in order to carry out eliminations correctly in certain contexts.

In order to obtain reliable results in the sequence analysis it is also necessary to adapt the entries in the request field because what the user enters is stored case-sensitively. This means that www.VolksWagen.de and www.volkswagen.de would be registered as two different pages in the sequence analysis. In addition, all entries which are led to the starting page www.volkswagen.de are changed accordingly (e.g. www.autolernwerkstatt.info). During this step however, the original entries are stored separately for further analyses, e.g. for the statistics of the starting pages.

Through data cleaning 96% of lines have been deleted in www.volkswagen.de (out of approximately 40 million only 1.6 million remain).

4.2. User / Session Identification

If there are no entries in the "authuser" space and no cookies have been used, identical users can only be registered with the help of heuristics. If the same IP address and the same agent have been registered, this is considered one user (cf. [8], p. 452). An unequivocal user identification can be prevented through dynamic IP addresses, anonymisation programmes and standardised agents and identical IP addresses (Firewall) in company networks (cf. [7], p. 17). These problems could be reduced through cookies or some kind of user authentication. However, it has to be remembered that the user can de-activate cookies, and in addition the need for authentication could deter visitors from the site.

With regard to session identification, timeout intervals between 15 and 30 minutes are suggested. If the user remains inactive during this time, a new session begins (cf. [7], p. 17). In this project the timeout interval is 15 minutes.

In order to solve most of the problems of user/session identification session-IDs could be used. This however may cause deficiencies in server performance.

4.3. Path Completion

Not all user activities are registered in a log file since some activities do not lead to a request to the Web server. These include access from the local or proxy cache. In order to analyse complete click paths in the sequence analysis, a path completion by backtracking or shortest path completion is necessary (cf. [7], p. 19).

4.4. Data Structuring

The cleared data with the labelled sessions can be used for the sequence analysis together.

However, a new file has to be established for classification. This file has to depict one session in each line instead of one request. Additional variables are also added, such as dichotomous variables which mark the visit to certain pages and the use of certain paths, and a goal variable for the classification algorithm.

5. Modelling

Within this project, e-metrics were calculated and tests of significance were applied to them. In addition, click paths were investigated through sequence analysis. Different classification procedures were carried out for the sessions. Segmentation of the data did not produce useful results for marketing in this project.

5.1. E-Metrics / Tests of Significance

Descriptive statistics were formed for a series of so called e-metrics (e.g. clicks, pageviews, visits) in order to obtain a first overview over the quantitative use of the internet profile.

In order to validate the statements derived from the indicators they were examined with regard to significance. A nonparametric, distribution-free test of significance for two independent samples, the Mann-Whitney U test, was applied [9]. Significantly more traffic/pageviews/clicks/visits on weekdays than at weekends resulted for www.volkswagen.de while the duration rate was sig-

nificantly higher at weekends than on weekdays for www.volkswagen.de ($\alpha = 0.05$).

How useful the application of tests of significance can be becomes clear when dealing with the efficiency of individual marketing measures. By examining whether the number of visits has increased significantly after putting the measures into practice or not, tests of significance could show whether an online or offline measure for the promotion of the domain was effective.

5.2. Sequence Analysis

The click paths taken by users have been examined with regard to rules and recurring patterns with the help of sequence analysis. The aim of the investigation was the identification of typical user conduct.

A total of 51 rules could be established with a support factor of 1% and minimum confidence of 25%.

One interesting rule shows that in 16,273 sessions (3.946% of all sessions) the car configurator was activated directly via the Menu "Modelle" from the starting page. These users already know the page well and use it purposefully. It can be assumed that their involvement is very high and that there is a specific intention to buy a car. Another rule indicates that a user has chosen the link to the Touareg model from the starting page. Instead of choosing a different link from there, the starting page for Touareg is called up once more. This indicates that the users possibly tried to get back to the starting page www.volkswagen.de with the back button of their browser. But the back button calls up the previously loaded page, in this case the file "touareg_29_04_02.htm" which loads the files compiling the Touareg page. That is the reason why it is impossible to get back to www.volkswagen.de and the Touareg page is reloaded.

5.3. Classification

A decision tree algorithm has been used for classification. For www.volkswagen.de the goal variable indicates whether or not the user has started the configuration.

In order to explain the goal variable in the domain www.volkswagen.de, the variables clicks, pageviews, bytes and duration of the session were included as input in the model. Variables were added which indicated the use of carline pages, the access to information about the company and downloading of files. The analysis has been carried out by applying the CART algorithm based on the Gini index [10]. The data was divided into 20% training data and 80% test data. This model has proved to be the most successful. After running the model a binary tree could be generated.

The first split was done with the variable clicks. An improvement of the model performance is achieved through further splits on the following steps. The variables bytes, duration per session and the carline pages were used as splitting variables. With the help of this classification it is possible to predict whether or not the user will start a configuration during a session using the information from the user's activities in a realtime application. Variables as clicks must be counted during a session for realtime classification. Those users who are predicted to start a configuration and are therefore regarded as motivated to buy a car could thus be provided on dynamic pages with special offers and information, e.g. on financing. This would give them further incentives to buy the product.

The hitting rate of this classification model is 62%. Without the application of the model however the rate only amounts to 16.4%. 87.5% of sessions could be classified correctly by the model in total.

6. Evaluation

Only when it is proved that the findings are suitable for the formulation of concrete recommendations, Web usage mining will gain the status of a valuable planning and controlling instrument.

Within this practical project specific measures were worked out to improve the communication and distribution function of the internet profile. Within www.volkswagen.de, the car configurator has an important distribution function. The aim of all supporting activities therefore lies in an increased number of started configurations. For 16.4% of the sessions which include a configuration it would be advisable to provide additional adverts and special incentives in order to support the configurator. This could include a discount when the configurator is used and an automobile is bought subsequently.

The analysis of the click paths has given indications for www.volkswagen.de to improve the programming which simplifies user navigation.

With the help of the decision tree analysis, it was possible to classify users of www.volkswagen.de into those who started a configuration and those who did not. This provides the possibility to introduce one-to-one marketing on dynamic pages and supply the user with the information and offers relevant to his needs. This would also step up customer attraction and commitment.

7. Outlook

This project was realised with log files of static html pages. In the case of dynamic html pages, such as in Con-

tent Management Systems, the Web usage mining analyses have to be extended to the application log as well. In order to avoid problems of compatibility it is advisable to use a session-ID for session identification for the static as well as the dynamic pages. Very interesting marketing ideas for future research projects can be gained with the help of log files which emerge from the dynamic pages.

For a more detailed version of this paper including the analysis for www.vw-club.de see www.fh-muenster.de/FB9/person/dellmann.

References

[1] Chapman et al. (2000): Chapman, P.; Clinton, J.; Kerber, R.; Khabaza, T.; Reinartz, T.; Shearer, C.; Wirth, R.: CRISP-DM 1.0: Step-by-step data mining guide. http://www.crisp-dm.org/CRISPWP-0800.pdf.

[2] Cooley (2000): Cooley, R.: Web Usage Mining: Discovery and Application of Usage Patterns from Web Data. Diss., University of Minnesota, 2000.

[3] Tan/Kumar (2002): Tan, P.-N. ; Kumar, V.: Discovery of Web Robot Sessions Based on their Navigational Patterns. In: Data Mining and Knowledge Discovery, Vol. 6, Issue 1, 2002, p. 9-35.

[4] Spiliopoulou/Pohle (2001): Spiliopoulou, M.; Pohle, C.: Data Mining for Measuring and Improving the Success of Web Sites. In: Data Mining and Knowledge Discovery, Vol. 5, No. 1/2, 2001, p. 85-114.

[5] Berendt (2002): Berendt, B.: Using Site Semantics to Analyze, Visualize, and Support Navigation. In: Data Mining and Knowledge Discovery, Vol. 6, Issue 1, 2002, p. 37-59.

[6] Dellmann (2001): Dellmann, F.: Análisis de la utilización de sitios web con métodos de estadística inferencial en la práctica. 36° Asamblea Anual del Consejo Latinoamericano de Escuelas de Administración CLADEA: Los nuevos modelos de negocios ante la globalización. Mexico City, 25.-28.9.2001. http://www.fh-muenster.de/FB9/person/dellmann/articulocladea.pdf (german version: http://www.fh-muenster.de/FB9/person/dellmann/artikelcladea.pdf).

[7] Cooley et al. (1999): Cooley, R.; Mobasher, B.; Srivastan, J.: Data Preparation for Mining World Wide Web Browsing Patterns. In: Knowledge and Information Systems, Vol. 1, No. 1, 1999, p. 5-32.

[8] Pitkow (1997): Pitkow, J.: In Search of Reliable Usage Data on the WWW. In: Sixth International World Wide Web Conference, Santa Clara, CA, 1997, p. 451-463. http://www.scope.gmd.de/info/www6/technical/paper126/paper126.html.

[9] Mann/Whitney (1947): Mann, H. B.; Whitney, D. R. (1947): On a test of whether one of two random variables is stochastically larger than the other. In: Annals of Mathematical Statistics, Vol. 18, p. 50-60.

[10] Breiman et al. (1984): Breiman, L.; Friedman, J. H.; Olshen, R. A.; Stone, C. J.: Classification and Regression Trees. Wadsworth International Group, 1984.

Predicting distribution of a new forest disease using one-class SVMs

Qinghua Guo[1], Maggi Kelly[1], Catherine Graham[2]

[1]*Dept. of Envi. Sci., Pol. and Mgmt., Univ. of California, Berkeley, CA*
[2]*Museum of Vertebrate Zoology, Univ. of California, Berkeley, CA*
{gqh, mkelly}@nature.berkeley.edu, cgraham@uclink.berkeley.edu

Abstract

In California, a newly discovered virulent pathogen (Phytophthora ramorum) has killed thousands of native oak trees. Mapping the potential distribution of the pathogen is essential for decision makers to assess the risk of the pathogen and aid in preventing its further spread. Most methods used to map potential ranges of species (e.g. multivariate or logistic regression) require both presence and absence data, the latter of which is not always feasibly collected. In this study, we present the one-class Support Vector Machine (SVM) to predict the potential distribution of Sudden Oak Death in California. The model was developed using presence data collected throughout the state, and tested for accuracy using a 5-fold cross-validation approach. The model performed well, and provided 91% predicted accuracy. We believe one-class SVM when coupled with Geographical Information Systems (GIS) will become a very useful method to deal with presence-only data in ecological analysis over a range of scales.

1. Introduction

In the central California coastal forests, a newly discovered virulent pathogen (*Phytophthora ramorum*) has killed hundreds of thousands of native trees including tanoak (*Lithocarpus densiflorus*), coast live oak (*Quercus agrifolia*), and black oak (*Quercus kelloggii*) [1]. This phenomenon is often referred as "Sudden Oak Death" (SOD), and has caused public attention worldwide. The state has dedicated millions of dollars for management of the disease, and a monitoring system has been implemented for the state's forests. As more becomes known about the mechanisms assisting the dispersal of the pathogen, prediction of its distribution can be performed. Predicting the potential distribution of the disease in California remains an urgent demand of regulators and scientists alike.

The existence and dispersal of a pathogen is likely influenced by environmental conditions such as humidity, temperature, and elevation. Niche models combine known localities of a given species with layers of meaningful niche dimension to extrapolate suitable environmental parameters for a given species. Researchers have demonstrated that environmental niche models are powerful tools for predicting the potential distribution and spread of a disease or invasive species [2] [3]. Methods used to predict species distribution consist of various statistical approaches such as linear, multivariate and logistic regression, generalized linear modeling and generalized additive modeling, discriminant analysis, classification and regression tree analysis, and artificial neutral networks. These methods require data on species presence and absence to establish a statistical relationship [4]. In reality, many types of ecological datasets (e.g. those collected by museums, or on wildlife surveys) lack reliable absence data. Such is the case with SOD. Confirmation of *P. ramorum* is a time-consuming process that involves culturing the pathogen from material removed from the border of an infected canker. After about a week, the pathogen can be identified based on morphological traits [5]. However, while negative samples are reported, these are not used in a regulatory sense due to the large potential for false negatives caused by seasonality of sample, species of host and time to lab. Hence, negative samples are not proxies for absence data in this case. Therefore, we sought to develop a method that utilized presence-only data to predict the potential SOD distribution.

Support vector machines (SVMs), originally developed by Vapnik [6], are considered a new generation of learning algorithms. SVM comes with several appealing characteristics such as a statistically based model rather than loose analogies with natural learning systems, and it theoretically guarantees performance [7]. Typically, SVM is designed for two-class problem where both positive and negative objects exist. In ecology, many museum-collected records exist in presence-only forms, and we are interested in using these data to predict the potential distribution of species. These are common one-class problems, which need to separate the target class from the rest of feature space. Recently, Scholkopf et al. [8] developed one-class SVM to deal with this one-class problem. Applications of the one-class SVM include handwriting recognition, document classification, texture segmentation, and image retrieval.

In this paper we map the potential distribution of SOD in California using one-class SVM.

2. Method and Materials

2.1. Data

The training data used in this study were locations of confirmed *P. ramorum* in California. These data are routinely provided to the monitoring community as part of the management and regulatory function of the California Oak Mortality Task Force (COMTF). As of February 2003 there were over 300 confirmed samples of *P. ramorum* in 12 California counties (Alameda, Contra Costa, Humboldt, Marin, Mendocino, Monterey, Napa, San Mateo, Santa Clara, Santa Cruz, Solano and Sonoma). A hand-held GPS was used in the field with each sample to collect location information. Accuracy was reported with the sample, and when an offset greater than 100m was reported, a second visit with a GPS was completed. All spatial location data are stored in a common projection system. Spatial distribution of host species was provided by the California GAP dataset. These include Big leaf maple, California bay laurel, California black oak, California buckeye, California coffeeberry, California hazelnut, Canyon live oak, Cascara, Coast live oak, Huckleberry, Madrone, Rhododendron, Tanoak and Toyon.

Our goal was to predict if trees in presently uninfested areas are potentially likely to be infected by the pathogen. We thus made the assumption that if the host plants share similar conditions (both environmental and anthropogenic conditions) with those in areas with confirmed SOD, they are more likely to be potential targets for *P. ramorum*. We used 14 environmental variables to train the model and predict the potential distribution for the pathogen. There variables included: annual mean temperature, annual mean precipitation, mean temperature in January, April, July and October, mean precipitation in January, April, July, and October, annual mean solar radiation, distance to main roads, distance to the edge of patches of hosted oak, coexistence of other hosts and elevation. California climate data was extracted from the Daymet conterminous United States database (www.daymet.org).

2.2. One-class SVM

Assuming we have l training points x_i (i=1, 2,...,l), we want to find a hypersphere as small as possible to contain the training points in multidimensional space.

Meanwhile, we also allow a small portion of outliers to exist using a slack variable (ζ_i):

$$\text{Min } R^2 + \frac{1}{vl}\sum_i \zeta_i \qquad (1)$$

Subject to

$$(x_i - c)^T (x_i - c) \le R^2 + \zeta_i, \ \zeta_i \ge 0, \ i \in [l] \qquad (2)$$

Where c and R are the center and radius of the sphere, and $v \in [0, 1]$ is the trade-off between volume of the sphere and the number of training points rejected. When v is large, the volume of the sphere is small so more training points will be rejected than when v is small, where more training points will be contained within the sphere. v can be roughly explained as the percentage of outliers in the training dataset [8]. Scholkopf [8] used v =0.05 to distinguish the handwritten digits and got 91% recognition accuracy with a fairly moderate Type II errors (false-positive) rate of 7%. In this study, we choose v to be 0.05 in order to contain more training points in the sphere. In doing so, we minimize the Type I errors (potential SOD that is rejected) because the risk of SOD is our most important concern. It should be noted that lower probability of committing Type I errors are associated with higher probability of committing Type II errors. Because we lack absence data, it is difficult to estimate Type II errors.

This optimization problem can be solved by the Lagrangian:

$$L(R,\xi,c,a_i,\beta_i) = R^2 + \frac{1}{vl}\sum_{i=1}^{l}\zeta_i$$
$$- \sum_{i=1}^{l} a_i \left\{R^2 + \zeta_i - (x_i^2 - 2cx_i + c^2)\right\} - \sum_{i=1}^{l}\beta_i\zeta_i \qquad (3)$$

where $a_i \ge 0$ and $\beta_i \ge 0$. Setting the partial derivative of L with respect to R, a_i, c equal to 0, we get:

$$\sum_{i=1}^{l} a_i = 1 \qquad (4)$$

$$0 \le a_i \le \frac{1}{vl} \qquad (5)$$

$$c = \sum_{i=1}^{l} a_i x_i \qquad (6)$$

Substituting equation (4)-(6) to equation (3), we have the dual problem:

$$\min_{a} \sum_{i,j} a_i a_j (x_i \cdot x_j) - \sum_i a_i (x_i, x_i) \qquad (7)$$

Subject to: $0 \le a_i \le \frac{1}{vl}$, $\sum_{i=1}^{l} a_i = 1$

To determinate whether or not a test point (x) is within the sphere, we can calculate the distance between the test point and the center C. It can be expressed as:

$$(x \cdot x) - 2\sum_i a_i(x \cdot x_i) + \sum a_i a_j(x_i \cdot x_j) \le R^2 \qquad (8)$$

So far, we have assumed that the data are spherically distributed. In reality, the data are often not spherically distributed. To make the method more flexible to account for this issue and capture the non-linearity such as multi-mode distribution, Kernels function $K(x_i, x_j)$ can be introduced. Basically, we express the inner product in equation 8 as the Kernel function:

$$K(x,x) - 2\sum_i a_i k(x,x_i) + \sum_{i,j} a_i a_j K(x_i,x_j) \le R^2 \qquad (9)$$

There are two often-used Kernels as following:
Polynomial Kernal:

$$K(x_i,x_j) = (x_i \cdot x_j + 1)^n \qquad (10)$$

where n is the free parameter. Usually this kernel dose not produce a tight description of the data [9]. Moreover, when n is high, the results will be very sensitive to outliers. A more robust way is to construct the Gaussian Kernel:

$$K(x,y) = e^{-(x-y)^2 / S^2} \qquad (11)$$

The Gaussian Kernel was applied in this study. It should be noted that the method above was proposed by Tax and Duin [9], another approach proposed by Scholkopf et al [8] is to find some hyperplane to separate the training data from the origin with maximum margin. For the Gaussian Kernel, these two methods are equivalent [8]. We implemented the one-class SVM by the modified version of LIBSVM-a library for support vector machines developed by Chang and Lin [10]. Further information about one-class SVM can be found in [8] [9] [10]. A 5-fold cross-validation method was used to estimate the accuracy of the predicted model.

3. Results

The average accuracy of the 5-fold cross-validation was 91%. Figure 1 shows the potential distribution of SOD in California mapped according to this method. The results show what was expected; the majority of SOD are predicted to occur in coastal areas. We predict the disease will continue to spread northward through Mendocino County and then sparsely through the tanoak/redwood and coastal forests of Humboldt and Del Norte Counties. The disease will also likely invade Southern California. Specifically, the disease will likely continue its southward march through Monterey County's redwood/tanoak forests into San Luis Obispo and Santa Barbara Counties which have extensive areas of oak woodlands. These two counties share very similar environmental niches with the northern California counties that are already infested. There are small areas of likely infestation through San Diego County. Interestingly, our model shows a potential for the disease in the foothills of the Sierra Nevada

mountain ranges. These contain oak woodlands comprised largely of black oaks – one of the hosts for *P. ramorum*. In 2001, *P. ramorum* was cultured from a sample taken from the Sierra foothills, but the results have not been repeated to date.

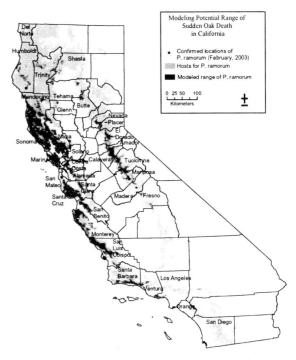

Figure 1. Potential distribution of SOD in California

4. Discussion and Conclusions

The SOD epidemic has the potential to affect biodiversity, fire risk, soil erosion and aesthetic value of oak landscapes [11]. Sudden Oak Death is an example of a biological invasion that may have a human component to its introduction and spread. Such introductions of plants and animals across the globe have dramatic consequences on global ecosystems, and are considered by many to be an important component of environmental change. Invasive species are devastating ecological systems by reducing biodiversity, altering ecosystem processes, changing genetic diversity and community structure, and functioning as vectors of disease. As such, the mechanisms underlying the dispersal of pathogens are critical issues being pursued from a variety of approaches and spatial scales, and spatial modeling of these dispersal pathways remains and important pursuit. Indeed, developing a spatially-explicit model of potential spread is an important step in unraveling the nature of the epidemic. Other types of research can be done "on top" of this spatially explicit prediction of where the pathogen can survive and can be dispersed.

It is important to note that mapped potential distribution of the pathogen does not necessary mean that an area will become infected. High probability of distribution indicates that those areas share similar environmental niches with confirmed SOD, and therefore are possible locales for *P. ramorum* to survive. Thus, there are several management implications for results like these: targeted monitoring in uninfested but highly likely sites could be developed, citizen groups in areas likely to host *P. ramorum* could be alerted to watch for symptoms of the disease, and quarantine regulations could be strengthened in areas of greater risk while lessened in areas without the necessary environmental factors for harboring the disease.

Researchers have developed various methods to predict the potential distribution of invasive species. Many of those methods (e.g. multivariate or logistic regression) require both presence and absence data, the latter of which is not always feasibly collected. In this study, we presented an alternative method to those traditional statistical approaches by using the one-class SVM. Compared with traditional statistical or learning models in predicting species distribution using presence-only data, one-class SVM has several main advantages. Firstly, the method only requires one-class data (presence data) for training and predicting. Consequently, it does not need to generate any pseudo-absence data. That is particularly suitable for the study of invasive species or animals, because the absence data for those cases are very difficult to obtain and assumptions about generating pseudo-absence data are not well sustained. Secondly, the method provides a flexible way to jointly analyze multiple types of data such as categorical data and continuous data. Thirdly, the method is easy to use. Unlike many other machine learning algorithms, which rely on creativity and extensive tuning parameters by users, one-class SVM only requires a minimum tuning [7]. Lastly, because the method is a theoretically-based model, combining optimization, statistics and functional analysis to achieve maximum separation, it has many appealing characteristics: it is free from local mimima, it is computationally efficient and it provides outstanding performance [7].

In this study, we used one-class SVM to predict the potential distribution of Sudden Oak Death in California. The model performed well, and provided 91% predicted accuracy based on a 5-fold cross-validation test. We believe one-class SVM when coupled with GIS will become a very useful method to deal with presence-only data in ecological analysis over a range of scales. We plan to compare the results of this work with the other SOD modeling approaches in the near future.

5. Acknowledgements

We thank Michael Jordan and Chih-Jen Lin for their comments on the manuscript. This work was supported in part by a NASA New Investigator Program award and a grant from the California Department of Forest and Fire Protection, both to M. Kelly.

6. References

[1] D. Rizzo, M. Garbelotto, J.M. Davidson, G.W. Slaughter, and S.T. Koike, "*Phytophthora ramorum* as the cause of extensive mortality of *Quercus spp.* and *Lithocarpus densiflorus* in California", *Plant Disease*, 2002, pp. 205-213.

[2] A.T. Peterson, and D. A. Vieglais, "Predicting species invasions using ecological niche modeling: new approaches from bioinformatics attack a pressing problem", *Bioscience*, 2001, pp. 363-371.

[3] E. Welk, K. Schubert, and M.H. Hoffmann, "Present and potential distribution of invasive garlic mustard (Alliaria petiolata) in North America", *Diversity and Distributions*, 2002, pp. 219-233.

[4] R. Dettmers, and J. Bart, "A GIS modeling method applied to predicting forest songbird habitat", *Ecological Applications*, 1999, pp. 152-163.

[5] M. Garbelotto, P. Svihra, and D. Rizzo, "Sudden oak death syndrome fells three oak species", *California Agriculture*, 2001, pp. 9-19.

[6] V. Vapnik, *The Nature of Statistical Learning Theory*, Springer-Verlag, New York, 1995.

[7] N. Cristianini, and B. Scholkopf, "Support vector machines and kernel methods - The new generation of learning machines". *Ai Magazine*, 2002, pp. 31-41.

[8] B. Scholkopf, J.C. Platt, J. Shawe-Taylor, A.J. Smola, and R.C. Williamson, "Estimation the support of a high-dimensional distribution", *Neural Computation*, 2001, pp.1443-1471.

[9] D. Tax, and E. Duin, "Support vector domain description", *Pattern Recognition Letters*, 1999, pp. 1191-1199.

[10] C. Chang, and C. Lin, *LIBSVM: a library for support vector machines*, Software available at http://www.csie.ntu.edu.tw/~cjlin/libsvm, 2001.

[11] M. Kelly, and R.K. Meentemeyer, "Landscape dynamics of the spread of Sudden Oak Death", *Photogrammetric Engineering & Remote Sensing*, 2002, pp. 1001-1009.

Understanding *Helicoverpa armigera* Pest Population Dynamics related to Chickpea Crop Using Neural Networks

Rajat Gupta
*IIIT, Hyderabad
India*

BVL Narayana
*IIIT, Hyderabad
India*

P.Krishna Reddy
*IIIT, Hyderabad, India
E-mail:pkreddy@iiit.net*

G.V.Ranga Rao
*ICRISAT,
Patancheru, India*

CLL Gowda
ICRISAT, Patancheru, India

YVR Reddy
ICRISAT, Patancheru, India

G.Rama Murthy
IIIT, Hyderabad, India

Abstract

Insect pests are a major cause of crop loss globally. Pest management will be effective and efficient if we can predict the occurrence of peak activities of a given pest. Research efforts are going on to understand the pest dynamics by applying analytical and other techniques on pest surveillance data sets. In this study we make an effort to understand pest population dynamics using Neural Networks by analyzing pest surveillance data set of Helicoverpa armigera or Pod borer on chickpea (Cicer arietinum L.) crop. The results show that neural network method successfully predicts the pest attack incidences for one week in advance.

1. Introduction

Insect pests are well known as the major constraint to crop production. One of the problems in addressing pest management is inadequate knowledge about the factors influencing pest population dynamics. To understand pest dynamics, scientists collect pest surveillance data and related agricultural operations regarding crops, farming practices and other weather parameters. These databases contain details of pest incidence, climatic, soil, agricultural practices and serve as repositories of information. Correlations between some of these factors and pest incidence based on statistical models have been developed. However, a functionally viable model for pest forecast is still needed by farmers for efficient and effective pest management.

Pod borer, *Helicoverpa armigera* is one of the key pests causing severe yield losses, infesting several crops such as cereals, pulses, cotton, vegetables and fruit crops as well as wild hosts [5]. Ecological and Physiological features like high fecundity, multi-voltinism, ability to migrate long distances and diapause during unfavorable conditions contribute for it's severity in different situations. The climatic data follows a gradual seasonal pattern that repeats almost every year. The *Helicoverpa armigera* incidence, on the other hand, show a certain pattern in terms of population dynamics. However the peaks can change abruptly from one week to the other. In other words the overlapping generations of the pest lead to unpredictable biological events. This non-linear and complex nature of *Helicoverpa* population dynamics makes it difficult to predict population densities using traditional forecasting models.

In this paper, an effort has been made to understand the *Helicoverpa* population dynamics on the chickpea (*Cicer arietinum L.*) crop using data mining [4] techniques such as neural networks.

Literature Review:

A great deal of work on forecast models has been done especially on regression modeling and simulation models. The studies conducted by Trivedi et al., (1998) [8] have proposed a multinomial regression model to predict the impending attack of *Helicoverpa armigera*. However the model seems to be working well only when the pest population were moderate in years like 1992-1994. Whereas when there was an unusual spurt in the pest populations during 1995 the model outputs were not up to the expectations. Pimbert and Srivastava (1991) [6] analyzed the *Helicoverpa* larval counts, light trap data and related parameters over six years and showed that rainfall deficit year favor *Helicoverpa* population in Andhra Pradesh, India. Regression analysis techniques were used by Das et al., (2001) [1] to explore the relationship between rainfall and pest abundance in different years and the cumulative effect of drought on the abundance of *Helicoverpa*. Kruskal-Wallis [2] one way analysis of variance by ranks was used to compare the pest abundance in normal and rainfall deficient years. In their experiment they regressed rainfall versus larval count for a period of 9 years from 1983-1989. Their results hold good for most of the period between but fail for 87/88 where there is a departure in the usual behavior of *Helicoverpa* from the original trend. Zhao and Shen [9] discussed about building a Monte Carlo simulation model based on variance and did not use the deviations. They used the nonlinear least square regression for simulating insect stochastic population rather than methods in simulation of differential equations and estimating parameters of nonlinear equations. This innovation made simulation easy to use for plant protectionists. The results of simulation seemed to be the best till date and are better than regression models. However they are far from the required accuracy which necessitates the exploration of new techniques to address the pest problem.

Therefore, the present study was initiated to enhance the predictability of *Helicoverpa* population using neural networks. In the next section we explain about the data set. Next, we explain experimental procedure and discuss the results. The last section contains conclusions.

2. Data set

As a part of investigation to understand *Helicoverpa armigera* population dynamics, scientists at the International Crops Research Institute for the Semi-Arid Tropics (ICRISAT) [3], Patancheru, near Hyderabad, India, have collected pest surveillance data. ICRISAT focuses on improving the productivity and production of the farming systems of the semi-arid tropical areas of the developing world and conducts research on the following crops: sorghum, pearl millet, groundnut, chickpea, and pigeonpea. Pest surveillance data collected at ICRISAT for chickpea crop on *Helicoverpa* pest contains a set of daily and weekly recordings about weather and pest incidence at various locations in the farm. We briefly describe these recordings.

- **Date and Week**
  - **Date**: The date of survey for a particular event. There were some missing values in the data, which were indicated as nulls in the database.
  - **Standard Week**: The weeks in a year are mapped to integer values by considering first week of January as first standard week.
- **Weather**
  - **Minimum and Maximum Temperature (Tmin and Tmax)**: The lowest and highest temperatures (°c) recorded on ICRISAT campus on the date of survey respectively.
  - **Humidity:** The relative humidity recorded on ICRISAT campus on the date of survey.
  - **Rainfall:** The amount of rainfall (mm) recorded on ICRISAT campus on the date of survey.
- **Pest Incidence**
  - **Larvae/Plant:** The mean number of *Helicoverpa* larvae present per plant. Larval counts are based on 30-50 randomly picked plants per hectare.
  - **Eggs/Plant:** It is an estimate of the number of *Helicoverpa* eggs present per plant.

- **Light and Pheromone Trap Catchs:** Number of *Helicoverpa* moths caught by Light trap and Pheromone traps.
- **Location**
  - **Zone:** ICRISAT farm was divided into various zones. So this attribute indicate the zone of the observation.
  - **Location:** Location of the observation in a particular zone.
  - **Season:** Two main seasons in Indian agriculture: Kharif (rainy) and Rabi (post-rainy).
  - **Area Surveyed:** The farm size surveyed in hectares.
  - **Plant Protection Type:** Different types of plant protection practices that are undertaken on farm.
  - **Observer:** The scout's name who has collected that particular information.

3. Pest attack prediction

A Neural network [7] is an interconnected set of input/output units where each connection has a weight associated with it. During the learning phase, the network learns by adjusting the weights so as to able to predict the call label of input samples during testing phase. Neural networks posses high tolerance to noisy data as well as ability to identify patterns on which they were not trained. However, a deep problem in the use of neural network techniques involves regularization, complexity adjustment, or model selection, that is, selecting (or adjusting) the complexity of the network. Even though the number of inputs and outputs is given by the feature space, the total number of weights or parameters in the network is not known directly.

3.1 Data Preprocessing and neural network training

From the chickpea data set, weather parameters and larvae/plant information is selected and other information was ignored. We have decreased the granularity of the data set by taking weekly mean of Tmin, Tmax, rainfall, humidity and larvae/plant. The reasons for doing this are as follows: Daily data was having lots of gaps in it. Because, sometimes, it was not possible to collect the data on a particular day due to bad weather or absence of scout. Null values (about 2 %) have been ignored. We have used z-score normalization to scale the attribute data to fall within a small specified range [4].

Discrete Fourier transform (DFT) was used to convert the time domain periodic data into the frequency domain. DFT gives the set of complex numbers for the normalized data set. We have designed separate feed-forward neural networks for real values and imaginary values. Bayesian Regularization in combination with Levenberg-Marquardt algorithm (Gauss Newton) [7] is used for training. The typical performance function used by the feed-forward neural networks is the mean sum of squares of network errors. The neural network architecture is having two hidden layers. We have used hyperbolic tangent sigmoid function in both of these hidden layers. In the outer layer we have used linear transfer function.

3.2 Experiments and results

The pest surveillance data set for the chickpea crop was collected over a period of 11 years (1991-2001) and contains 2372 daily recordings. In this data set, eight years (1991-1998) data was selected for training and three years data (1999-2001) for testing. Each tuple in the data set is of the form <Tmin, Tmax, Humidity (H), Rainfall (RF), Larvae/plant (L)>, where each value represents the weekly mean. After reducing the data set into weekly means, the number of tuples comes to 380. Let us term this as a base data set. For prediction, we have generated four kinds of data sets from the base data set. Let the notation advance(x), where x = 0, 1,2, and 3, denote the data set. In the advance(0) data set, the L value is a function of corresponding Tmin, Tmax, H, R values of the same week, i.e., it is same as base data set. In advance(1), advance(2) and advance(3) data sets, the L value is a function of previous first, second and third week's Tmin, Tmax, H, and R values respectively. Experiments were conducted on advance(x) data set to predict Larvae for x-weeks advance.

Table 1. Results

Data set	Correl -ation	Hits	Misses	False hits
Advance(0)	0.91	27	4	6
Advance(1)	0.96	27	3	4
Advance(2)	0.91	27	2	11
Advance(3)	0.75	22	6	11

Each data set was transformed into complex domain through DFT. Two networks are being trained: one for predicting the real value, another for predicting the imaginary value. After the prediction, these predicted complex values are remapped back to corresponding values in time domain through inverse DFT. By starting with different initial values, the experiment was conducted fifteen times for each data set. Each neural network to predict both real and imaginary part of complex value consists of an input layer (four variables), two hidden layers and an output layer (one variable). For the neural network to predict the real value, first hidden layer consists of twelve neurons and second hidden layer consists of six neurons. And, for the neural network to predict complex value, first hidden layer consists of nine neurons and second hidden layer consists of six neurons.

Analysis: Figures 1, 2, 3 and 4 show the real and prediction curves for advance(0), advance(1), advance(2),

and advance(3) data sets respectively. The standard week was plotted on X-axis and the corresponding mean L-values of fifteen experiments on Y-axis. In these figures the horizontal thick line indicates the threshold larvae/plant value for the pest emergence which is equal to 1.2. Whenever the actual value is greater than or equal to 1.2, we term it as a *real peak*. Whenever the predicted value is greater than or equal to 1.2, we term it as a *predicted peak*. The performance of neural network is measured by the number of real peaks it predicts.

Table 1 shows the correlation coefficients of actual and predicted curves, the number of hits, misses and false hits results corresponding to Figures 1-4. Here, a hit means, the network is able to predict the real peak. A miss means the network is unable to predict the peak. A false hit means, there is no real peak, but there is a predicted peak.

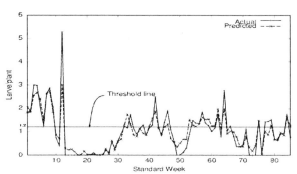

Figure 1. Advance(0) data set.

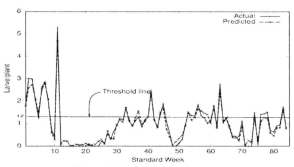

Figure 2. Advance(1) data set

Figure 1 shows the results for advance(0) data set. Given the weather parameters of a particular week, this experiment predicts the larvae/plant value of the same week. Out of 31 peaks, 27 peaks are being predicted and 4 peaks are being missed with 6 false hits.

Figure 2 shows the results for advance(1) data set. Given the weather parameters of a particular week, this experiment predicts the larvae/plant value of the next week. The correlation coefficient is 0.96. Surprisingly, it can be observed that we are getting an improved correlation over advance(0) data set (see Table 1). It means that the weather parameters of the current week are influencing more the larvae of the next week over the larvae of the current week. This is indeed a fact as it takes a four to five days for the eggs to hatch and convert into larvae. So this result agrees with the pattern of pest growth. Out of 30 peaks, 27 peaks are being predicted and 3 peaks are being missed with 4 false hits. This result shows that the neural network is able to predict the pest attack in one week advance with high accuracy.

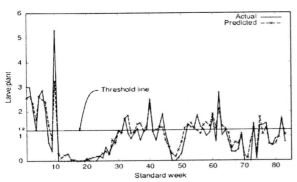

Figure 3. Advance(2) data set.

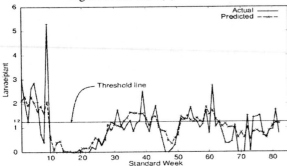

Figure 4. Advance(3) data set.

Figure 3 shows the results for advance(2) data set. Given the weather parameters of the particular week, this experiment predicts the larvae/plant value of the next two weeks. The correlation coefficient (0.91) is decreased over advance(1) data set. So the performance of neural network is decreasing with the delay. Out of 29 peaks, 27 peaks are being predicted and 2 peaks are being missed with 11 false hits. This result shows that the neural network is able to predict the pest attack two weeks advance with high accuracy, however with more number of false hits.

Figure 4 shows the results for advance(3) data set. Given the weather parameters of the particular week, this experiment predicted the larvae/plant value of the next three weeks. Here the correlation coefficient (0.75) is decreased significantly over advance(2) and

advance(1) data sets. So the decrease in the performance continues with the increase in the delay as expected.

4. Summary and Conclusions

Experiments were conducted to predict pest attack by extracting pest dynamics patterns using climatic data and pest surveillance databases of *Helicoverpa armigera* pest dynamics on chickpea using neural network technique. The experimental results show that it is possible to predict the pest attack with high probability for one week in advance. These predictions would help the farmers in pest management programs by avoiding the crop losses with improved environment quality, as it can avoid unnecessary sprays of chemical pesticides.

Bibliography

1. D.K.Das, T.P.Trivedi and C.P.Srivastava. 2001. Simple rules to predict attack of *Helicoverpa armigera* on crops growing in Andhra Pradesh, Indian Journal of Agricultural Sciences 71: 421-423.

2. Dean W. Wichern and Richard Arnold Johnson, Applied Multivariat Statistical Analysis, Prentice Hall, 2002.

3. International Crop Research Institute for Semi-Arid tropics: ICRISAT, URL: www.icrisat.org, April 2003.

4. Jiawei Han and Micheline Kamber, Data Mining Concepts and Techniques, Morgan Kaufmann, 2001.

5. T.M.Manjunath, V.S.Bhatnagar, C.S.Pawar, and S.Sithnantham. 1989. Economic importance of *Helicoverpa* spp. In India and an assessment of their natural enemies and host plants. In King EG, Jackson RD, eds. Proceeding of the workshop on Biological Control of *Helicoverpa:* Increasing the Effectiveness of natural Enemies, Far Eastern Regional Research Office, United States Department Agriculture, New Delhi. pp. 197-228.

6. M.P.Pimbert, C.P.Srivastava. 1991. The influence of rainfall deficits on the abundance of *Helicoverpa armegira* in Andhra Pradesh, India. Biological Agriculture and Horticulture, 8:153-176.

7. Simon Haykin, Neural Networks: A Comprehensive Foundation, Pearson Education, 2001.

8. T.P.Trivedi, D.K.Das, A.Dhandapani, and A.K.Kanojia, 2002. Models for Pests and Disease Forecasting, Resources Management in Plant Protection, Volume I, Plant Protection Association of India, Hyderabad, India, 2002.

9. Zhongua Zhao, Zuorui Shen. Theories and their applications of Stochastic Simulation Models for Insect population Dynamics. Department of Entomology, The China Agricultural University, Feb.2003.

Text Mining for a Clear Picture of Defect Reports: A Praxis Report

Jutta Kreyss
IBM Deutschland Entwicklung
kreyss@de.ibm.com

Steve Selvaggio
IBM Silicon Valley Laboratory
selvagg@us.ibm.com

Michael White
IBM Silicon Valley Laboratory
mjew@us.ibm.com

Zach Zakharian
IBM Silicon Valley Laboratory
kzakhar@us.ibm.com

Abstract

We applied the text mining categorization technology, in the publicly available, IBM Enterprise Information Portal V8.1 to more than 15,000 customer reported, product problem records. We used a proven software quality category set to categorize these problem records into different areas of interest. Our intent was to develop a clear picture of potential areas for quality improvement in each of the software products reviewed, and to provide this information to development's management.

The paper presents the benefits that can be gained from categorizing problem records, as well as the limitations.

1. Introduction

The quality of software is one of the significant criteria for its breakthrough, acceptance, and continued use in the market place. Software quality is paramount in achieving and maintaining customer satisfaction.

The goal of the study was to make a significant contribution to the business objectives of increasing customer satisfaction by enhancing long-term product quality. The study relies on the idea that increased product quality can be realized by enhancing the effectiveness of development groups by directing resources to areas of the products that are objectively shown to be in need of quality improvement.

To determine the areas that are most in need of improvement, the complete set of problem records for each software product should be analyzed with the main areas of weaknesses given as feedback to development. By using this categorization data, development managers can use the information as an objective guideline to concentrate and direct efforts and resources onto areas of the product that have the most significant impact on the number of identified problem areas. The mining technology aids in efficiency by automatically assigning problem records into the categories of interest.

The summarized question is: "Which product area(s) are problematic and require development focus in order to improve both product quality and customer satisfaction?"

This paper presents the results of our problem record analysis using the text mining categorization technology in the IBM Enterprise Information Portal V8.1.

2. Proven quality criteria for software

CUPRIMDSO is a set of categories that IBM uses as one of the quality measurements during the software development cycle. It is used during product planning and as a customer satisfaction measurement tool. The categories are: *Capability, Usability, Performance, Reliability, Installability, Maintainability, Documentation, Serviceability* and *Overall*. [1, 4]. Each product is ranked against these categories and future development steps are planned according to the rankings.

Since the CURPIMDSO categories reflect IBM's best practice to establish, track, and sustain product quality, these criteria were used to apply the text mining categorization technology against actual problem records.

2.1 Problem Management Records

If a customer detects an issue using IBM software they can report it by opening a "Problem Management Record" (Problem Record). A problem record is stored in a database as free-form text mixed with control information. The problem record contains all of the information about a problem from its first reporting, up to and including its resolution. In addition, problem records contain header information and signatures and frequently contain excerpts of error logs, programming code, SQL Statements, etc. 95% of the problem records in our data set contained more than 7500 characters.

2.2 Categorization hurdles due to data format

Categorization of problem records was hindered by the format of the data source. The control information (such as time stamps) is intermixed with the free-form text in the body of the problem record. Other non-formatting issues also hindered categorization:

- A single product problem may actually straddle or involve other products.
- A single problem record may actually contain or encompass more than one product issue.
- A product problem may be the result of 3rd party software interactions or dependencies, or may be caused by the operating system.

For control reasons, problem records cannot be edited after being entered. Because of this limitation, problem records will include any incorrect or misleading information that was entered. It will also contain any possible fixes that were unsuccessful.

3. Categorization to clear the defect picture

The decision to improve the quality of an existing product has to be driven by the current status of the product. An initial analysis of the strengths and weaknesses of the product should be used to determine the baseline of the product. Problem records can be used to obtain the needed information in detail about reported product problems.

To manually classify thousands of problem records according to their content can be overwhelming; due to the time involved, the amount of work required, and the large number of existing and incoming problem records. An overwhelming amount of work and a continuous effort is required to maintain a manual classification process.

The application of the text mining categorization technology provides one the access to the classified problem records while reducing the effort of processing the problem records. Instead of an ongoing manual process, the technology requires only initial effort to configure the desired categories and to train the classification engine. Therefore, automatic classification can fit easily into almost any process structure and is able to satisfy the information requirements of the development management in determining where focus is needed in the product to improve product quality.

4. Categorization

The presented study applied the categorization approach available in Enterprise Information Portal (EIP)

V8.1 [3]. The underlying technology is special due to the combination of a fast decision tree induction algorithm especially suited to text data and a new method for converting a decision tree to a rule set that is simplified but still logically equivalent to the original tree.

The following paragraphs provide a summary of the underlying technology, for more information refer to [2]. A set of training documents is indexed by consecutive integers. For each integer i in the index set, the ith document is transformed into a numeric vector $x_i = (x_{i,1},...,x_{i,d})$ whose components are counts of the numbers of occurrences of words or features in the ith document. For each category a label $y_i \in \{0,1\}$ is determined which indicates that the ith document belongs to the category or for $y_i = 0$ if the ith document does not belong to the category. The construction of the decision tree which is the base for the algorithm contains two phases: tree growing and tree smoothing. These phases take advantage of the sparse structure presented in text documents to select the best partition. The special feature of the chosen categorization approach in EIP V8.1 is the writing of the decision tree as an equivalent set of human interpretable rules. In general, the advantage of human interpretable rules is threefold:

- It is easier for a human user to understand and modify a rule set than a decision tree.
- The rule set is logically equivalent to the corresponding decision tree. Therefore, any mathematical analysis of the overall performance of the decision tree, with respect to text categorization, carries over to the rule set.
- Since a person can write logical rules, it can be envisioned that handwritten rule sets could be incorporated with machine-generated rule sets.

5. Categorization results

Some of the benefits of categorization are:
1. Extraction of unique views and trends.
2. Detection of the distributions of topics in records that are stored as unstructured text documents.
3. Compare products quickly and easily.

The following sections focus on these benefits.

5.1 Unique view of trends

In more detail, trend information can be observed and validated. Analysis and comparisons can be used to determine whether the same trends are also valid for different products or across different operating systems. An example for a unique view of a trend is the comparison of problem records for different products or different product versions across differing platform.

5.2 Detection of distribution

After the training phase, more than 9000 documents were categorized into the CUPRIMDSO categories.

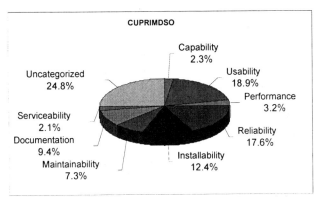

Figure 1: Distribution (>9000 Problem Records)

Figure 1 is the combined distributions of four products using CUPRIMDSO categories, which gives an overview of where improvements should be considered. For more detail, the categorization set was expanded into subcategories.

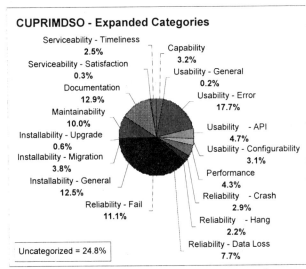

Figure 2: Distribution including subcategories for four products (> 9000 Problem Records)

Figure 2 uses the same data set as Figure 1 and also gives an expanded view of the CUPRIMDSO categories by incorporating subcategories. The additional subcategories allow one to better view problematic areas of a product.

5.3 Comparing versions / products

The application of automatic categorization makes it easy to study objective comparisons between products.

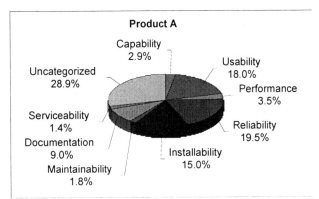

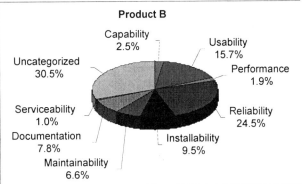

Figure 3: Comparison of two different products (>5000 Product Records)

Figure 3 shows a product-to-product comparison using the CUPRIMDSO categories.

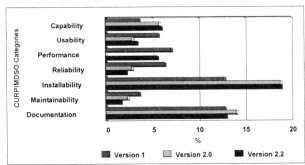

Figure 4: Comparison percentage of problems among different versions of Product C

Figure 4 provides a comparison of different versions of the same product. This high level overview is a good starting point for an analysis of how a product changed from version to version. Further categorization and analysis could focus on single categories to study how those areas changed between versions. The "Documentation" category could be drilled into to learn more about what improved, or "Installability" can be analyzed to get more information about which installation areas need additional focus to get back to, or improve over, the quality of version 1.

5.4 The categorization rules

According to the benefits of the categorization approach in EIP V8.1, the system generates a set of rules in XML format. Below is a section of the rule set that was generated for Figure 1. Each category is defined by its own set of these rules.

```
<?xml version="1.0" encoding="UTF-8" ?>
- <rules>
    <global_comment />
  - <rule active="yes">
    - <antecedent>
      - <condition>
          <feature>disappointed</feature>
          <operator>></operator>
          <count>0</count>
        </condition>
      </antecedent>
- <consequent>
      <category>Serviceability</category>
      <confidence>0.9</confidence>
    </consequent>
  </rule>
  - <rule active="yes">
    - <antecedent>
      - <condition>
          <feature>critsit</feature>
          <operator>></operator>
          <count>0</count>
        </condition>
      </antecedent>
- <consequent>
      <category>Serviceability</category>
      <confidence>0.92</confidence>
    </consequent>
  </rule>
+ <rule active="yes">
+ <rule active="yes">
+ <rule active="yes">
</rules>
```

6. Handling uncategorized documents

The study coped with the issue of a high percentage of problem records that could not be categorized. The overall uncategorized percentage of the sample set is 24.8%. The uncategorized documents are due to a huge variance of the problem record's text length. The uncategorized documents have a very small amount of text that consists of very little product or problem information, whereas successfully categorized documents had more information in the body of the problem record. The longer documents also contained more specific information used to diagnose the customer's issue. By discarding extremely small problem records, categorization results improved dramatically as shown in Figure 5, which demonstrates the positive impact of setting the minimal size of the document.

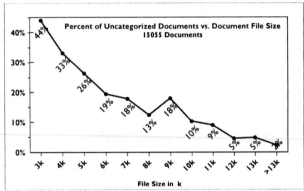

Figure 5: Uncategorized documents related to different minimal document file size

7. References

[1] Chulani, S., P. Santhanam, D. Moore, B. Leszkowicz, & G. Davidson: Deriving a Software Quality View from Customer Satisfaction and Service Data. European Software Control and Metrics conference, 2001

[2] http://www.escom.co.uk/conference2001/index.shtml

[3] Enterprise Information Portal V8.1: http://www.ibm.com/software/data/eip

[4] Johnson, D. E., F. J. Oles, T. Zhang & T. Goetz: A decision-tree-based symbolic rule induction system for text categorization. IBM Systems Journal 41:3 (March 2002)

[5] Venkataraman, B. K. & W. A. Ward, Jr: An Introduction to Software Quality, June 1999, TR ITL-99-4, http://www.wes.army.mil/ITL/itlpubl.html

Mining Production Data with Neural Network & CART

Mingkun Li[1], Shuo Feng[1], Ishwar K. Sethi[1], Jason Luciow[2], Keith Wagner[2]

[1] *Intelligent Information Engineering Lab*
Oakland University
Rochester, MI 48309
{li, sfeng, isethi}@oakland.edu

[2]*Guardian Industries Corp. Science & Tech.*
14511 Romine Road
Carleton, MI 48117
{jluciow, kwagner}@Guardian.com

Abstract

This paper presents the preliminary results of a data mining study of a production line involving hundreds of variables related to mechanical, chemical, electrical and magnetic processes involved in manufacturing coated glass. The study was performed using two nonlinear, nonparametric approaches, namely neural network and CART, to model the relationship between the qualities of the coating and machine readings. Furthermore, neural network sensitivity analysis and CART variable rankings were used to gain insight into the coating process. Our initial results show the promise of data mining techniques to improve the production.

1. Introduction

Traditionally, the industrial engineers use a set of statistical test and inference procedures, known as Six Sigma techniques [11]; these work well for a few variables and a few hundred observations when the underlying production processes are well understood. However, many production processes often have hundreds of control and quality measurement variables, involving chemical, mechanical, electrical and magnetic processes. These processes are generally controlled by complex nonlinear relationships, often not completely understood by operators and plant engineers. Furthermore, the collected data is noisy. In such situations, data mining has emerged as an alternative approach to relate quality with process variables. Many applications of data mining for process quality monitoring have been reported in recent years [7, 8, 9].

In this paper, we describe the results of a data mining pilot project to coated glass manufacturing. The glass coating involves mechanical, chemical, electrical and magnetic processes with over one hundred variables. Currently the settings for process variables are achieved through a trial and error process. The project was aimed at understanding the influence of different process variables on the qualities of the glass coating to minimize the trial and error process of variable setting. The neural network and CART approaches were applied to model the

relationship and analyze the coating process. The initial results are promising.

The organization of the paper is as follows. In Section 2, background knowledge and the goal of our project are described. Data extraction and cleaning methods are discussed in Section 3. Section 4 presents a neural network approach and results. The CART method and results are given in Section 5. Section 6 presents our variable analysis results. The last section consists of a summary.

2. Industrial background & project goal

The glass coating involves deposition of several layers of metal materials on raw glass surface. The coating could improve the mechanical, optical and chemical properties of the glass. Currently, sputtering is the most advanced technique of glass coating [2]. The glass coating assembly line considered in this project consists of six coaters. Each coater has five cathodes. All cathodes are independent of each other and are controlled by chemical, electrical and mechanical variables for easy setup and control. During the production and initial setup, some samples are taken to the laboratory for various quality tests, the results of which the operators use to tune up the coaters.

The whole coating process is affected by numerous chemical, electrical and mechanical measurement variables. The result of the process is characterized by optical quality variables (Figure 1). The involved variables can be grouped into three categories:

1) Machine settings: The set points of the coater system. These include electrical set points such as voltage and power, chemical set points like gas pressure and distribution, and mechanical set points like line speed. The set points are adjusted when the machine is turned on, during the period of replacing the coating material, and when the quality of the glass is outside of the industry specification. There are 147 machine setting variables.

2) Machine readings: The readings record the actual state of the production line. The readings follow the change of settings immediately. There are 175 machine reading variables. The sensors record data

every ten minutes to create a huge database of the machine readings.

3) Quality measurements: The quality of the sputtered glass is mainly measured in three tests, namely glass side reflectance, film side reflectance and transmission. Scale and spectrum data are captured when a sample glass is taken off the production line to the laboratory. Total, there are 129 quality measurements.

The ultimate goal of this project is to improve the glass coating process by giving guidance on adjustments to the machine settings, resulting in shorter setup time and better glass coating quality. Thus, we need to develop a model which could accurately predict the quality of glass given the machine settings and target consumptions. Since the response time is very short, the readings are used as inputs to the model instead of the machine settings. The scale and spectrum qualities are the output of the model.

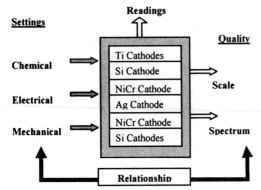

Figure 1. System diagram of the coating process

3. Data Extraction and Preprocessing

The data in this project was collected during a six-month production period. The data was made available to us in the form of a database of 29 tables storing more than 700 variables with 2 gigabytes data. The database can be divided into two parts: one storing processing data and the other storing quality data. This division lies in the methods of collecting data: the processing data is automatically recorded in the assemble line every 10 minutes; the quality data is manually entered in the laboratory with around 25 samples everyday. Thus, we need to relate the quality data with its corresponding processing data. For each quality data, there is a time stamp to record when the test is performed and an id number to record the glass. All processing data is associated with a time stamp, recording when the data was collected. The quality and processing time stamps of the same glass should be in the same day. The glass id number and time stamps determine when the glass enters and exits the coater. It was found that most glass stays in

the coater less than 10 minutes, which means at most there is one set of processing data recorded when the glass is in the coater. Considering that the process data is not changing much in a short time, such as 10 minutes, we extract the processing data before the glass enters the coater, when the glass is in the coater if there is a processing data at that time and after the glass exits the coater. Then we averaged them to get the corresponding processing data.

The process data and quality data are characterized by noise and missing values. These errors result from operator errors, machine malfunctions, measurement errors, etc. First, any observations with missing fields were discarded. From the initial data statistical analysis, we found that the data is Gaussian distributed with some noise. By consulting with domain experts, the noise is iteratively removed using the Gaussian distribution. Figure 2 shows the process: the left picture presents the original data distribution; the center shows the distribution after removing outliers one standard deviation away from the mean from the left picture; the right picture shows the results after removing the outliers two standard deviations away from the new mean. The black line is the Gaussian curve with the same mean and standard deviation as the samples.

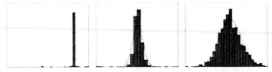

Figure 2. Iterative noise removal: original distribution (left), first outlier removal (center), and second outlier removal (right). The black line is the Gaussian curve.

There are more than one hundred process variables, but not all of them play the same important role. From the initial analysis, the process variables are classified into three categories: frequent large changing variables, less frequent small changing variables, and almost constant variables (Figure 3). According to the domain and statistical knowledge, the frequent large changing variables play a dominant role in the coating process. In our initial experiment, 74 frequent large changing variables were chosen as the input of the model.

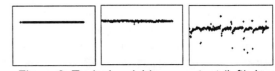

Figure 3. Typical variables: constant (left), less frequent small changing (center), and frequent large changing (right).

4. Neural Network Based Approach and Results

In this section, we describe how the neural network approach using the feed-forward network was applied.

The input variables are highly correlated in the coating process. For example, if we slow the assembly line speed, we need to lower the electric voltage and the gas density to obtain the same quality of coating. To get the compact representation of the input variables, principle component analysis is applied to the input variables. The 11 new components account for around 80% variance of the original 74 variables. The main advantage of dimension reduction is a dramatic reduction of neural network complexity; simple network requires less training examples. Additionally, a simple network reduces the search space of network configuration, which is crucial for the success of a neural network approach.

The data set is randomly permuted first to reduce the effect of the ordering of patterns. Then data is normalized to zero mean and one standard deviation. After performing principle component analysis, the dataset is divided into two sets: training set and test set. Training set is used for the neural network to learn the mapping and the test set is used to validate the neural network. The conjugate gradient algorithm is implemented to train the neural network for its complexity and performance [4]. After extensive experiments, the network architecture 11x5x3x1 was found to have good performance.

Figure 4 shows typical prediction results on test set. The typical predication errors are given in Table 1. The error distributions were thoroughly analyzed. All the errors are within the manufacturer quality specification. Thus, our model can be implemented to improve the real production process.

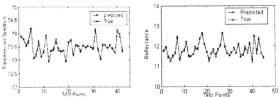

Figure 4. Prediction results of test set for transmission spectrum

5. CART Modeling and Results

Since the tree-based approach offers a way of generating models that are easily comprehensible, it was decided to build a tree-based regression model using the CART (Classification and Regression Tree) [6] methodology.

The entire data set is randomly divided into two subsets: 80% for training set, and 20% for testing set. The frequent large changing variables are used as the input to the CART method. In the training stage, the proper decreasing ratio is set to grow the tree; then the tree is pruned to achieve the best performance by avoiding over fitting with the training set. One typical tree model has 10 layers and 16 terminal nodes. Other models have similar structure. The typical relationship between the predicted and the true value is shown in Figure 5. Similar to the neural network approach, most of the error lies within the manufacture's quality specification.

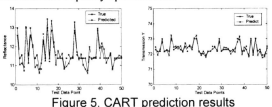

Figure 5. CART prediction results

Table 1. Relative root mean square errors of models

Quality Variables	Training data		Test data	
	CART	NN	CART	NN
Trans. Y	0.0066	0.0053	0.0072	0.0062
Trans. Spec.	0.0043	0.0053	0.0074	0.0061
GS ref. spec.	0.0389	0.032	0.0495	0.0402
FS ref. spec.	0.0487	0.0443	0.0523	0.0518

Four models were built to predict the transmission Y value, the transmission spectrum, the glass side reflectance spectrum, and the film side reflectance spectrum. The relative root mean square errors of the two approaches are listed in Table 1. Both approaches achieve similar results. The performance of the neural network models is slightly better than models built using the CART approach.

6. Variable Analysis

Engineers do not easily accept the results without a good explanation. Indeed, it is one of main goal of data mining to gain insight into the underlying process. Since our models can predict the results with high accuracy, we can use them to rank the variables to figure out the important variables.

6.1 Neural networks

The technique used is neural network sensitivity analysis [10]. Basically, neural network sensitivity analysis calculates the derivatives of output with respect to the input variables on trained neural network. The important input variables should show larger derivatives. Since the derivatives are changing with the input samples, the average value on our data set is used as the metric. The formula is given in (1), where y is the network output and I_K is the kth input sample. We further analyzed the effect of the different data sets such as electricity and gas, the different materials such as silicon, silver, nickel chromium, etc.

$$A_i = \frac{1}{N} \sum_{k=1}^{N} \left| \frac{\partial y(I_k)}{\partial x_l} \right| \quad (1)$$

Table 2(a) gives the top 10 important variables for transmission. The scores are normalized by dividing the largest derivative. The variable name is given by the coater sputtering the material followed by the data type. From this table, we can see that the silver coater plays a dominant role for the transmission property of the glass. Another thing is that target consumption variables are very important. The engineers validated our results. Our sensitivity analysis also added new understanding to the coating process. At the same time, the correctness of the sensitivity analysis proves the correctness of neural network models.

Table 2. Top variables for transmission.

(a) Neural network		(b) CART	
Variables	**Score**	**Variables**	**Score**
Ag. coater vtank	1.0000	Ag. coater target	100.0
Ag. coater target	0.9883	Si coater vtank	75.52
Ag. coater vos	0.9746	Si coater VOS	65.48
Ti. coater 2 target	0.8962	Ti coater 3 Press.	56.70
Si coater 1 target	0.7996	NiCr Coater VOS	54.57
Ti coater 3 target	0.7768	Si coater 1 target	45.40
Ti coater 1 target	0.7516	Ti coater 2 target	40.77
Ti coater 5 vtank	0.7208	Ti coater 1 O2	40.69
Ti coater 1 O2	0.7193	Si coater 5 press.	33.71
NiCr coater press.	0.6893	NiCr coater target	30.99

6.2. CART

CART provides not only regression capabilities, but also methods on determining the relative importance of the variables. Each variable in the CART tree has an importance score based on how often and with what significance it served as a primary or surrogate splitter throughout the tree.

Top 10 variables are ranked in Table 2(b) for transmission. The top ten variables in the neural network approach and CART are not exactly the same and in the same order; however, the important variables from one approach rank highly in the other approach. It is well known that silver layer should be the dominant layer to control the transmission of the glass, which is confirmed by the results: the top three variables are all from the silver coater. The importance score of the gas and electricity variables in different layers can guide the

engineers to change the machine setting when they need to adjust the quality of the glass.

7. Conclusion

The experience of applying data mining in a production improvement has been discussed in this paper Two widely used and powerful nonparametric approaches, neural networks and CART, were used to model the relationships between production line machine readings and quality measurements. Both models achieved an error within the tolerance range given by the quality specification guide. Additionally, neural network sensitivity analysis and CART variable ranking were employed to rank the variables to gain insight into the coating process and to verify the models. Currently we are working on using our results to improve the production process. The most direct usage of our models is to give a quantitative guideline to the assembly line operator to shorten the set up time and improve the quality of the glass.

8. References

[1] J. Han and M. Kamber, *Data Mining: Concepts and Techniques*, Morgan Kaufmann Publishers, 2001

[2] R. J. Hill and S. J. Nadel, *Coated Glass Applications and Markets, BOC Coating Technology*, 1999

[3] R. O. Duda, P. E. Hart, and D. G. Stork, *Pattern Classification*, 2nd, John Wiley & Sons, 2001

[4] S. Haykin, *Neural Networks: A Comprehensive Foundation*, Macmillan, 1994

[5] V. N. Vapnik, *The Nature of Statistical Learning Theory*, 2nd, Springer, 1999

[6] L. Breiman, J. Friedman, R. Olshen, and C.J. Stone, *Classification and Regression Trees*, Wadsworth Int.l Group, Belmont, CA, 1984.

[7] Q. g. Ali and Y. Chen, "Design Quality and Robustness with Neural Networks", *IEEE Transactions on Neural Networks*, pp 1518-1527, Vol. 10, No. 6, November 1999

[8] R. H. Kewley, M. J. Embrechts, and C. Breneman, "Data Strip Mining for the Virtual Design of Pharmaceuticals with Neural Networks", *IEEE Transactions on Neural Networks*, pp 668-769, Vol. 11, No. 3, May 2000

[9] A. Dhond, A. Gupta, and S. Vadhavkar, "Data Mining Techniques for Optimizing Inventories for Electronic Commerce", pp 480-486, KDD 2000, Boston

[10] L. M. Belue, and K. W. Bauer, "Determining input features for multilayer perceptrons", *Neurocomputing*, 7 (1995) 111-121

[11] T. Pyzdek, "Six Sigma, Data Mining and Dead Customer Accounts", *Quality Digest*, Apr. 1999

[12] M. Li, S. Feng, I. K. Sethi, Data Mining on Guardian Glass Coating Process, Technical Report, Science and Technology Center of Guardian Industries Corp, March, 2003

Inference of Protein-Protein Interactions by Unlikely Profile Pair

Byung-Hoon Park, George Ostrouchov, Gong-Xin Yu,
Al Geist, Andrey Gorin, and Nagiza F. Samatova

Computational Biology Group, Computer Science and Mathematics Division,
Oak Ridge National Laboratory
{parkbh, samatovan}@ornl.gov

Abstract

We note that a set of statistically "unusual" protein-profile pairs in experimentally determined database of protein-protein interactions can typify protein-protein interactions, and propose a novel method called PICUPP that sifts such protein-profile pairs using a statistical simulation. It is demonstrated that unusual Pfam and InterPro profile pairs can be extracted from the DIP database using a bootstrapping approach. We particularly illustrate that such protein-profile pairs can be used for predicting putative pairs of interacting proteins. Their prediction accuracies are around 86% and 90% when InterPro and Pfam profiles are used, respectively at 75% confidence level.

1. Introduction

Protein-protein interactions are fundamental to cellular processes. They are responsible for phenomena like DNA replication/transcription, regulation of metabolic pathways, immunologic recognition, signal transduction, etc. The identification of interacting proteins is therefore an important prerequisite step in understanding its physiological function. From a computational standpoint, the problem is how we can predict that two proteins interact from their structures or sequence information. Various computational methods using genomic context alone have recently been designed to address this problem (see reviews in [1, 2]). They are based on gene fusion events [3, 4], conservation of gene-order or co-occurrence of genes in potential operons [5, 6], and presence/absence of genes in different species [7]. All these methods attempt to identify functionally associated genes (for example, involvement in the same biochemical pathway or similar gene regulation). However, they provide only a small coverage of direct physical interactions [8], which is more inherent to experimental approaches.

In parallel to genomic context based developments, a number of computational methods that attempt to "learn" from experimental data of interacting proteins have been reported in the literature [9, 10]. Sprinzak and Margalit [10] tried to learn what typifies interacting protein pairs by analyzing over-representation of sequence-signature pairs derived from available experimental data of interacting proteins. Bock and Gough [9] attempted to learn correlations between biochemical patterns of sequence pairs derived from experimentally verified positive set and artificially manufactured "negative" set (a set of putative "non-interacting" protein pairs).

Protein Interaction Classification by Unlikely Profile Pair (PICUPP) - our proposed method - extracts protein interaction indicators from positive protein-protein interaction data (no negative instances). It particularly seeks to identify correlated protein-profile pairs as indicators of protein-protein interactions. A profile describes a protein domain or family that may perform biologically important functions. Here "correlated" indicates that co-occurrence of the two given profiles accounts for an interaction. We particularly choose to use *unusual* protein profile pairs, which are derived from statistical simulation using interacting protein pairs, as such correlated pairs. A pair of profiles is then identified as a correlated pair, if its occurrence(s) in the data is statistically unusual relative to its occurrence generated by random (independent) protein pairings. Whenever the context is clear, we will use *correlated* and *unusual* interchangeably henceforth. The proposed approach is investigated with various protein profiles: Pfam domains [11], InterPro signatures [12] and Blocks motifs [13] using the Database of Interacting Protein (DIP) [14] of June 16, 2002.

2. Methods

A protein sequence is typically associated with multiple profiles. Thus each interacting protein pair may contribute to a number of profile pairs. A set of protein pairs creates a table, where each cell denoted by a row and column contains the frequency count of a profile pair. Note that it is different from an ordinary contingency table, because each protein pair would not contribute to exactly one cell of the table. Therefore significance analysis would not follow standard contingency table theory with a closed form solution [15]. Because of the non-standard setting of multiple cell contributions we evaluate significance by simulation.

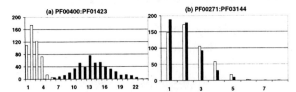

Figure 1: Example count distributions of unusual (a) and usual (b) Pfam profile pairs. In each case, white bars and black bars represent d_r and d_p distributions, respectively. X and Y axes represent count and its frequency.

The frequency counts in a profile pair table are random variables that are generated by the simulation. For each protein pair (pr_k, pr_l) in D, a set of profile pairs is identified by all pair-wise combinations of profiles between pr_k and pr_l. For example, let proteins pr_k and pr_l be associated with profiles (s_1, s_2) and (s_3, s_4), respectively. Then, any combination (s_i, s_j) $\in$ (s_1, s_2) $\times$ (s_3, s_4), where $\times$ denotes Cartesian product operator, is identified as a profile pair. Since a meaningful evaluation of a random variable can only be made through its distribution, we bootstrap the table cell distributions by resampling the protein pair data D and computing many instances of tables: one from bootstrapped samples of the same protein interaction data and the other from bootstrapped samples of the random protein pairings. This provides two count samples for each cell of the table: an interacting pairs sample, c_p, and a random pairs sample, c_r. We denote the corresponding empirical count distribution as d_p and d_r, respectively. The amount of overlap between d_p and d_r determines the usualness of the pair compared to what is expected at random. That is, PICUPP finds a profile pair (a cell in the table) to be unusual (or, correlated) if its frequency distribution constructed from interacting protein pair samples is significantly different from what

is constructed from random protein pairings. Computationally, PICUPP only keeps track of the d_p and d_r distributions for non-zero counts. Technically, the confidence score, or the degree of correlation of a profile pair (s_i, s_j) is computed from its two count distributions d_p and d_r as:

$$S(d_p, d_r) = max_a(\frac{1}{2}P(X_r \leq a) + \frac{1}{2}P(X_p \geq a) \;) \quad (1)$$

where X_r and X_p are random variables of d_p and d_r, respectively. Given a set of identified unusual protein-profile pairs, PICUPP determines a possible interaction between a pair of proteins (pr_k, pr_l), if any of its profile pair is unusual. An example of unusual and usual profile pair distribution is shown in Figure 1.

3. Results

PICUPP is modeled by comparing statistics of the given protein interaction pairs with those expected by random pairing of proteins. Therefore, it is expected to be sensitive to the positive protein interactions while being insensitive to those random protein couples. In this section, we report the sensitivity of PICUPP when InterPro and Pfam profiles are used over protein interactions in DIP database. We also discuss how different sizes of bootstrap samples and different confidence levels affect the overall performance.

DIP database contains a rich set of protein interactions from several species. From approximately 17,000 total protein interactions, we selected proteins that have Swiss-Prot annotations. As a result, the 7,655 and 6,652 protein interactions are left available for the experiment for cases with InterPro and Pfam, respectively. Figure 2 illustrates sensitivity to positive and randomly coupled interactions at the confidence levels of 0.7 and 0.8 with the different bootstrapped sample sizes. In both cases with (a) InterPro and (b) Pfam profiles, PICUPP shows high sensitivity to positive interactions, whereas low to randomly coupled protein pairs. With confidence of 80%, the sensitivity of PICUPP to positive interactions is around 82% (InterPro) and 75% (Pfam) from the simulation of size 1,000. On the other hand, it is around 17% (InterPro) and 13% (Pfam) to randomly coupled protein pairs. The result illustrates that PICUPP effectively identifies protein-protein interactions.

We also measured the performance of PICUPP when it is applied to a list of interacting protein pairs that is left out during the training stage. For this, we excluded all interactions of Yeast from DIP database and trained PICUPP. Then the sensitivity (or, accuracy) of PICUPP to the interacting protein pairs in Yeast was measured. Likewise, the sensitivity to protein pairs in E-coli was

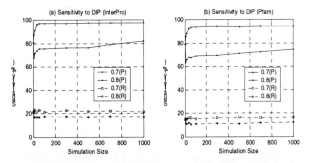

Figure 2: The sensitivity to protein interactions in DIP when PICUPP is trained with InterPro and Pfam respectively. In each figure, the sensitivities at confidence levels of 0.7 and 0.8 are shown to both positive (P) and randomly coupled (R) interactions.

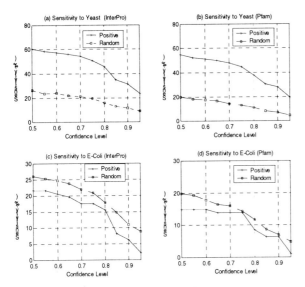

Figure 3: Cross coverage of PICUPP. Sub-figures (a),(b) and (c),(d) illustrate the sensitivities to yeast subset and *E-coli* when InterPro and Pfam are used. In each case, the solid line illustrates sensitivity to positive interactions at different threshold level, whereas dashed line illustrates sensitivity to randomly coupled interactions .

measured. Figure 3-(a) and (b) shows the sensitivity (coverage) of PICUPP to Yeast protein pairs in case of InterPro and Pfam, respectively. Similarly Figures 3-(c) and (d) show the coverage of E-coli protein pairs. As clearly illustrated in the Figures, PICUPP was able to differentiate interacting protein pairs from randomly coupled pairs in Yeast around 57% at confidence level of 70%. However, it is around 20% for interacting pairs in E-coli at the same confidence level, which indicate the unusual profile pairs that typify interaction in E-coli were not found by the process and may be different from what are observed in the remaining data. This can be understood by the fact that DIP database is largely biased toward Eukaryotes. Although the bacterium *Escherichia coli* (E-coli) is the most dominant non-eukaryote proteome in DIP database, it only accounts for 1.3% of the proteins therein [9].

4. Discussion

Approximately 108 pairs of Pfam domains are identified unusual at a confidence level of 98%. A case-by-case investigation discovered many well-established Pfam-Pfam associations among these interactions. The SH3 domain is perhaps the best-characterized member of protein-interaction modules. It plays a vital role in a wide variety of biological processes. It increases the local concentration or altering the subcellular

localization of components of signaling pathways, and mediates the assembly of large multiprotein complexes [16]. The SH3 is found to be correlated with Actin in our analysis. In fact it has been verified that this domain is often closely associated with Actin (in cytoskeletal proteins, such as fodrin and yeast actincytoskeletal proteins, such as fodrin and yeast actin binding protein ABP-1 [17]).

G-protein beta WD-40 repeat (G-β), another well-known interaction module, is one of the three subunits (α, β, and gamma) of the guanine nucleotide-binding proteins (G proteins) which act as intermediaries in the transduction of signals generated by transmembrane receptors. The α subunit binds to and hydrolyzes GTP; the β and gamma subunits seem to be required for the replacement of GDP by GTP as well as for membrane anchoring and receptor recognition. We found that this domain is highly coupled with Small nuclear ribonucleoprotein (sm protein) in our analysis. This finding is consistent with previous research results [18]. Both the sm proteins and G-β possibly mediate regulated protein-protein interactions essential for the functions of small nuclear ribonucleoproteins (snRNPs). Additional well-known Pfam pairs found in our prediction include actin and Cofilin/tropomyosin-type actin-binding protein [19], Protein kinase domain and Fibroblast growth factor [20], and EF hand and Myosin head (motor domain) [21].

5. Conclusion

A statistical approach to identify correlated protein-profile pairs that account for protein interactions is presented with experimental validation. We demonstrate that the proposed approach, PICUPP, effectively maximizes statistical confidences given to correlated protein-profile pairs by applying a bootstrapping approach to an incomplete data. We show that a set of unusual protein-profile pairs inferred from experimentally determined protein interactions can indeed epitomize putative protein-protein interactions. Such unusual protein-profile pairs reveal interacting domains and uncover relationships between highly correlated/uncorrelated domains for protein interactions.

PICUPP needs to be further refined in several ways. First, its performance highly depends on the quality of the experimental data. Unfortunately genome-scale experimental methods, such as protein arrays and two-hybrid system, have many limitations intrinsic to the experimental design. Another limitation, and even more restrictive, is the binary nature of some of those experimental approaches, which potentially excludes many of the cellular machines that are multi-protein complexes. Moreover, transient (short-living) protein complexes probably comprising a significant fraction of all regulatory interactions in the cell may need additional stabilization for detection by these experimental methods. Thus, expanding the training set with various types of annotated protein interactions will potentially address this problem. Second, an accurate understanding of interactions between protein profiles and how these interactions affect interactions between proteins is very limited. A possible solution may involve moving away from somewhat "ad hoc" utilization of protein profiles to more systematic approaches leading to a comprehensive understanding of relationships between interacting protein profiles and interacting proteins.

Acknowledgements

This work was funded in part or in full by the US Department of Energy's Genomes to Life program (www.doegenomestolife.org) under project, "Carbon Sequestration in Synechococcus Sp.: From Molecular Machines to Hierarchical Modeling," (www.genomes-to-life.org). The work of G.O. was sponsored by the Laboratory Directed Research and Development Program of Oak Ridge National Laboratory. This research used resources of the Center for Computational Sciences at Oak Ridge National Laboratory.

6. References

[1] Y. a. X. D. Chen, "Computational Analyses of High-Throughput Protein-Protein Interaction Data," *Current Protein and Peptide Science*, vol. 4, 2003.

[2] A. Valencia and F. Pazos, "Computational methods for the prediction of protein interactions," *Current Opinion in Structural Biology*, vol. 12, pp. 368-373, 2002.

[3] A. J. Enright, et al., "Protein interaction maps for complete genomes based on gene fusion events," *Nature*, vol. 402, pp. 86-90, 1999.

[4] E. M. Marcotte, et al., "Detecting protein function and protein-protein interactions from genome sequences," *Science*, vol. 285, pp. 751-3., 1999.

[5] R. Overbeek, Fonstein, M., D'Souza, M., Pusch, G.D., Maltsev, N., "Use of contiguity on the chromosome to predict functional coupling," *In Silico Biol.*, vol. 1, pp. 93-108, 1999.

[6] T. Dandekar, et al., "Conservation of gene order: a fingerprint of proteins that physically interact," *Trends in Biochemical Sciences*, vol. 23, pp. 324-328, 1998

[7] M. Pellegrini, et al., "Assigning protein functions by comparative genome analysis: protein phylogenetic profiles," *Proc Natl Acad Sci U S A*, vol. 96, pp. 4285-8., 1999.

[8] M. Huynen, et al., "Predicting protein function by genomic context: Quantitative evaluation and qualitative inferences," *Genome Research*, vol. 10, pp. 1204-1210, 2000.

[9] J. R. Bock and D. A. Gough, "Predicting protein--protein interactions from primary structure," *Bioinformatics*, vol. 17, pp. 455-60., 2001.

[10] E. Sprinzak and H. Margalit, "Correlated sequence-signatures as markers of protein-protein interaction," *J Mol Biol*, vol. 311, pp. 681-92., 2001.

[11] A. Bateman, et al., "The Pfam protein families database," *Nucleic Acids Res*, vol. 30, pp. 276-80., 2002.

[12] N. J. Mulder, et al., "The InterPro Database, 2003 brings increased coverage and new features," *Nucleic Acids Research*, vol. 31, pp. 315-318, 2003.

[13] J. G. Henikoff, et al., "Blocks-based methods for detecting protein homology," *Electrophoresis*, vol. 21, pp. 1700-6. [pii], 2000.

[14] I. Xenarios, et al., "DIP, the Database of Interacting Proteins: a research tool for studying cellular networks of protein interactions," *Nucleic Acids Research*, vol. 30, pp. 303-305, 2002.

[15] S. E. Fienberg, "Analysis of Cross-Classified Categorical Data," *Notices of the American Mathematical Society*, vol. 23, pp. A619-A619, 1976.

[16] T. Pawson and J. Schlessinger, "Sh2 and Sh3 Domains," *Current Biology*, vol. 3, pp. 434-442, 1993.

[17] D. G. Drubin, et al., "Homology of a Yeast Actin-Binding Protein to Signal Transduction Proteins and Myosin-I," *Nature*, vol. 343, pp. 288-290, 1990.

[18] T. Achsel, et al., "The human U5-220kD protein (hPrp8) forms a stable RNA-free complex with several US-specific proteins, including an RNA unwindase, a homologue of ribosomal elongation factor EF-2, and a novel WD-40 protein," *Molecular and Cellular Biology*, vol. 18, pp. 6756-6766, 1998.

[19] E. Nishida, et al., "Cofilin, a Protein in Porcine Brain That Binds to Actin- Filaments and Inhibits Their Interactions with Myosin and Tropomyosin," *Biochemistry*, vol. 23, pp. 5307-5313, 1984.

[20] F. Taniguchi, et al., "Activation of mitogen-activated protein kinase pathway by keratinocyte growth factor or fibroblast growth factor-10 promotes cell proliferation in human endometrial carcinoma cells," *Journal of Clinical Endocrinology and Metabolism*, vol. 88, pp. 773-780, 2003.

[21] N. Messer and J. Kendrickjones, "Chimeric Myosin Regulatory Light-Chains - Subdomain Switching Experiments to Analyze the Function of the N-Terminal Ef Hand," *Journal of Molecular Biology*, vol. 218, pp. 825-835, 1991.

Regulatory Element Discovery Using Tree-structured Models

Tu Minh Phuong, Doheon Lee, Kwang Hyung Lee

Department of BioSystems, Korea Advanced Institute of Science and Technology
373-1 Guseong-dong Yuseong-gu Daejeon 305-701, Korea
{phuong, dhlee, khlee}@bioif.kaist.ac.kr

Abstract

Computational discovery of transcriptional regulatory regions in DNA sequences provides an efficient way to broaden our understanding of how cellular processes are controlled. In this paper, we formulate the regulatory element discovery problem in the regression framework with regulatory regions treated as predictor variables and gene expression levels as responses. We use regression tree models to identify structural relationships between predictors and responses. The regression tree methodology is extended to handle multiple responses from different experiments by modifying the split function. We apply this method to two data sets of the yeast Saccharomyces cerevisiae. The method successfully identifies most of regulatory motifs that are known to control gene transcription under the given experimental conditions. Our method also suggests several putative motifs that can present novel regulatory motifs.

1. Introduction

Regulation of gene expression is crucial for the function and development of cells. Central to gene expression regulation are proteins called transcription factors (TF), which bind to specific short DNA sequences in the promoter regions of genes and activate or inhibit their transcription. The expression pattern of a gene is largely determined by short sequences (motifs) that serve as TF binding sites. Hence identification of regulatory motifs is important for understanding gene expression regulation. In this paper we focus on computational approaches to solving this problem.

A popular approach to finding regulatory elements is to look for conserved motifs upstream of genes that are believed to be co-regulated (reviewed in [10]). First, genes are clustered based on expression patterns over experiments. Then a motif discovery algorithm looks for DNA motifs that are common to the set of genes within each cluster. In spite of success in identifying many regulatory motifs, this approach presupposes that the clustering is correct and results in many false positives.

Another approach to regulatory motif discovery is based on association of gene expression values with motif abundances [2,5,8]. Taking gene expression levels for a single experiment, this method enumerates all words in the promoter regions of genes and use linear regression to check whether the words contribute to changes in the gene expression levels. The underlying assumption here is that if a word represents a binding site for an active TF then presence of the word contributes additively to the expression level of the gene.

In this paper, we propose a method to identify regulatory elements from sequence and expression data using a regression tree model. The tree-based regression paradigm was introduced by Breiman et al. [1] for dealing with a single continuous response and later was extended for handling multiple responses by Segal [12]. When used for multiple responses, it is called multivariate regression tree. The multivariate regression trees are useful when the goal is to identify strata with common covariates values and homogeneous multiple outcomes [12, 14].

Our approach is similar to the works [2,5,8] in that it considers candidate motifs as predictors or explanatory variables (covariates), gene expression levels as responses and formulates the problem in the regression framework. However, unlike these works, the tree-structured model we use does not require the linearity assumption or any assumption about relationships between variables. More importantly, using multivariate regression tree model, our approach can handle expression data collected over multiple experiments at once. This would reduce the negative effect of noise and missing data.

In sections 2 we give a brief overview of the regression tree techniques. Section 3 details the way we apply regression tree model to identify regulatory motifs from real biological data sets and provides experimental results. Section 4 concludes the paper.

2. Regression trees

2.1. Tree-based techniques for a single response

In this subsection we give a brief introduction to the tree-based models. The reader is referred to [1] for more details.

Suppose that there are p predictor variables $X_1, X_2,..., X_p$ and a response Y. The values of X_j and Y are observed for n learning cases.

A regression tree is a binary tree constructed by repeatedly splitting (sub)sets of learning cases into two descendant subsets. Each node of a tree contains a subset of cases. A node that does not have descendant nodes is a terminal node. The root node comprises the entire sample. The left and right child nodes contains disjoint subsets of the parent content and are defined by splitting the parent node. Splitting is a critical step in tree-based techniques. Briefly, suppose that a predictor X_i is an ordered variable. Two subgroups result from answering the question "is $x_i \leq c$?" The cases with answer "yes" go to the left node, and the cases with "no" go to the right node. The cutoff value c is in the range of observed values of x_i. Given the number of predictor variables and the number of cutoff values, there may be many allowable splits. A tree-growing algorithm chooses the best split for each node based on a split function $\phi(s,g)$ that can be evaluated for each split s in each node g. A split is chosen such that the distributions of responses in child nodes are most homogeneous or equivalently least heterogeneous. The two split functions discussed in [1] are *least squares* (LS) and *least absolute deviation* (LAD). Here we will focus only on LS.

Assume that g is a node containing a subgroup of cases $\{(\mathbf{x}_i, y_i)\}$, where $\mathbf{x}_i^t = (x_{i1},...,x_{ip})$. Let n_g be the total number of cases in g. The within node sum-of-square is given by

$$SS(g) = \sum_{i \in g} (y_i - \bar{y}(g))^2 \qquad (1)$$

where $\bar{y}(g) = (\sum_{i \in g} y_i)/n_g$

For a split s that partitions g into left and right child nodes g_L and g_R, the LS split function is

$$\phi(s,g) = SS(g) - SS(g_L) + SS(g_R) \qquad (2)$$

The best split s^* is such a split that maximizes $\phi(s,g)$. The algorithm proceeds recursively until some stop criteria are met. Typical, a minimum node size is specified or the algorithm stops when split function drops below a certain threshold.

2.2. Multiple responses

Now consider a multivariate regression setting, in which more than one response is observed. That is, beside the vector of predictor variables, each learning case has a vector of responses $\mathbf{y}_i^t = (y_{i1},...,y_{iq})$.

In [12], Segal proposed to generalize the within node sum-of-square in (1) to

$$SS(g) = \sum_{i \in g} (\mathbf{y}_i - \bar{\mathbf{y}}(g))^t \mathbf{V}^{-1} (\mathbf{y}_i - \bar{\mathbf{y}}(g)) \qquad (3)$$

where $\mathbf{V}$ is the covariance matrix of $\mathbf{y}_i$ in the root node

and $\bar{\mathbf{y}}(g)$ is the average of $\mathbf{y}_i$ within node g. The split function remains the same as in (2)

$$\phi_1(s,g) = SS(g) - SS(g_L) + SS(g_R) \qquad (4)$$

Another obvious way to measure within node homogeneity is to use similarity between $\mathbf{y}_i$ of the node. Taking Euclidean distance as a measure of similarity, we can define the heterogeneity of a node g as

$$SE(g) = \sum_{i \in g} \| \mathbf{y}_i - \bar{\mathbf{y}}(g) \|^2 = \frac{1}{2n_g} \sum_{i \in g} \sum_{j \in g} \| \mathbf{y}_i - \mathbf{y}_j \|^2 \qquad (5)$$

where $\|.\|$ is the Euclidean norm. Using (5) we derive another split function as follows

$$\phi_2(s,g) = SE(g) - SE(g_L) - SE(g_R) \qquad (6)$$

With the new generalized split functions the recursive algorithm proceeds as in the case with a single response.

2.3. Determining tree size

A crucial aspect of constructing a tree is avoiding overfitting and undefitting, that is avoiding trees with too many nodes or too few nodes. Breiman *et al.* [1] proposed a pruning algorithm that determines the tree size as follows: (a) Grow a large tree initially; (b) Starting with the initial tree, define a nested sequence of its subtrees using cost-complexity; (c) Select an optimal subtree from this sequence by cross-validation.

For step (b) to be carried out, a tree cost-complexity must be defined. For the case of multiple responses, the following cost functions $R(G)$ are used for $\phi_1(s,g)$ and $\phi_2(s,g)$. ($R_1(G)$ is borrowed from [15])

$$R_1(G) = \sum_{g \in \tilde{G}} \sum_{i \in g} (\mathbf{y}_i - \bar{\mathbf{y}}(g))^t \mathbf{V}^{-1} (\mathbf{y}_i - \bar{\mathbf{y}}(g)) \qquad (7)$$

$$R_2(G) = \sum_{g \in \tilde{G}} \sum_{i,j \in g} \| \mathbf{y}_i - \mathbf{y}_j \|^2 \qquad (8)$$

where $\tilde{G}$ is the set of the terminal nodes, $\mathbf{V}$ and $\tilde{\mathbf{y}}(g)$ are estimated from the learning sample.

3. Identification of regulatory motifs using tree-based model

When transcription factors bind to appropriate motifs, they regulate the expression levels of the respective genes. Thus, motifs can be considered as predictor or explanatory variables that explain changes in responses, which are expression levels in this case. For a gene i, we introduce a vector of predictor variables $\mathbf{x}_i^t = (x_{i1},...,x_{ip})$, where x_{ij} is the number of times motif j appears in the promoter region of i. The vector of responses for i is $\mathbf{y}_i^t = (y_{i1},...,y_{iq})$, where y_{ij} is the logarithm base two of the expression level of gene i in sample point j.

To build the tree model, first we need to decide which sequence motifs will be motif candidates and therefore will be predictor variables in the model. The simplest way is to enumerate all the sequences in the promoter regions of genes as potential motifs [2,8]. The number of all possible sequences in this case is very large, most of them are not present in the final models while they can make noise that affect the model selection process.

Here, we follow a more reasonable way to choose motif candidates to build the model from. Our method of choosing motif candidates is similar to the method proposed in [5]. In particular, we take only sequences that conserve over genes. The details of selecting motif candidates will be given below.

3.1. Data sets

Motif candidates. For experiments, we used the set of motif candidates from [11]. This set contains 356 motifs. The motif matrices are derived by applying the motif finding program AlignACE [7] to the upstream regions of genes in the MIPS [9] functional categories. From 356 motifs, 25 are known motifs that have been described in the biological literature. The motif lengths are between 5 and 20 nucleotides. The details of collecting motifs and the list of all the motifs can be found at [15].

For each motif, the number of the motif's instances in the promoter regions of a gene is counted by applying program ScanACE [7]. This program takes a motif matrix and scans target sequences to find similar motifs. When applying ScanACE to the gene promoters of *Saccharomyces cerevisiae*, the authors of [11] found 4483 promoter regions that contain motifs from the above set. We counted x_{ij} from those data.

Microarray data. We tested the tree model on two sets of microarray data for the yeast *S. cerevisiae*: the mitotic cell cycle data [3] and the sporulation data [4].

Cho *et al.* [3] collected gene expression levels at 17 time points with 10 minutes intervals across two full cell cycles. Following Tavazoie *et al.* [13], we discarded two time points (90 min and 100 min) due to less efficient labeling of their mRNA. From all 6220 genes, 3000 most variable genes were selected. The metric of variation was the ratio between standard variation and mean of expression levels of each gene across time points. From 3000 genes retained, only 2584 genes contain motifs from our set of motif candidates. The expression data were then transformed so that the sum of squared values for each gene was unit. This transformation is a common preprocessing procedure for microarray data. We selected only genes that have observed data for at least 80% of sample points. The missing values were replaces with the mean of the observed data over sample points.

The second data set was downloaded from http://cmgm.stanford.edu/pbrown/sporulation. This data set contains expression levels for about 6200 genes over 10 sample points during meiosis and spore formation. According to [6] we selected 2467 most variable genes

and applied selection and transformation procedures as described above to this data matrix.

3.2. Results

During the growing phase we do not partition any node with less than 60 genes. In addition, we do not consider splits that result in nodes with less than 30 genes.

In spite of some difference in topology of trees constructed with $\phi_1(s,g)$ and $\phi_2(s,g)$, these trees share the most important splits. Thus, we consider them equally useful for our purpose of motif identification. Due to lack of space we show only trees constructed with $\phi_1(s,g)$. The trees constructed for the cell cycle and sporulation datasets are shown in Figure 1a and 1b respectively.

The numbers inside circles are node indices. The split used for a node is shown below the circle and has form "*motif i name* $<= n$", which means that genes with more than n instances of motif i in the promoters go to the right, other genes go to the left. For putative motifs with long names we show only the motif number. The names of these motifs are given in the appendix.

The trees tend to grow leftward with less numbers of genes going to the right child node for each split. It is normal for our application where functional regulatory motifs present only in small numbers of gene promoters. The most important splits in Figure 1a contain regulatory motifs MCB, SCB, MCM1, RAP1, mRRPE, SFF, PAC, MET31-32, ABF1, ECB, SFF'. From 19 non-terminal nodes of the tree in Figure 1a, 14 nodes are split based on known motifs that have been biologically verified.

For the sporulation data set, the most important motifs identified by regression trees in Figure 1b are: MCB, URS1, Ntd80(MSE), mRRPE(M3A), CSRE, SFF, PAC and two new putative motifs number 287 and 304 (see appendix).

The trees also include some putative motifs. These motifs are new motifs that have not yet been identified by biological studies.

4. Conclusion

Our approach to discover regulatory elements is based on regression trees. The tree model does not require any assumption about linearity or other structure of these relationships. To deal with expression data from multiple experiments we have adopted the approach proposed by Segal [12]. This approach extends traditional tree model to cases with multiple responses by using generalized split functions. Using the cell cycle and sporulation data sets as examples, we reconfirmed most of motifs found in other works and discovered several new motifs. Filtering motif candidates used to build tree reduces computational complexity and increases the specificity of results.

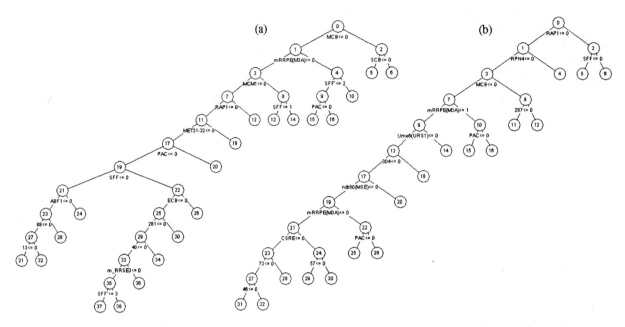

Figure 1: Regression trees for the cell cycle data set (a) and the sporulation data set (b)

References

[1] L. Breiman, J.H. Friedman, R.A. Olshen, C.J. Stone. *Classification and regression tree*. Wadsworth, 1984.

[2] H.M. Bussemaker, H. Li, E.R. Siggia, "Regulatory element detection using correlation with expression", *Nature genetics*, 2001, 27, pp 167-171.

[3] R.J. Cho, *et al*. "A genome-wide transcription analysis of the mitotic cell cycle", *Molecular Cell*, 1998 2, pp 65-73.

[4] S. Chu, *et al.*, "The Transcriptional Program of Sporulation in Budding Yeast", *Science*, 1998, 282, pp 699-705.

[5] E.M. Conlon, X.S. Liu, J.D. Lieb, J.S. Liu, "Integrating regulatory motif discovery and genome-wide expression analysis", *Proceedings of National Academy of USA*, 2003, 100(6), pp 3339-3344.

[6] M.B. Eisen, P.T.Spellman, P.O. Brown, D. Botstein. "Cluster analysis and display of genome-wide expression patterns", *Proceedings of National Academy of USA*, 1998, 95, pp 14863-14868.

[7] J.D. Hughes, P.W. Estep, S. Tavazoie, G.M. Church. "Computational identification of cis-regulatory elements associated with groups of functionally related genes in S . Cerevisiae". *Journal of Molecular Biology*, 2000, Vol 296, p 1205-1214.

[8] S. Keles, M. van der Laan, M. Eisen, "Identification of regulatory elements using a feature selection method", *Bioinformatics*, Oxford press, 2002, 18(9), pp 1167-1175.

[9] H.W. Mewes et al. "MIPS: a database for genomes and protein sequences", *Nucleic acids research*, 2000, 28, pp 37-40.

[10] U. Ohler, H. Niemann, "Identification and analysis of eukaryotic promoters: recent computational approaches". *Trends Genetics* 2001, *17*, pp 56-60.

[11] Y. Pilpel *et al.*, "Identifying regulatory networks by combinatorial analysis of promoter elements", *Nature Genetics*, 2001, 29(2), pp 153-159.

[12] M.R.Segal, "Tree-structured methods for longitudinal data". *Journal of American Statistical Association*, 1992, 87(418), pp 407-418

[13] S. Tavazoie *et al.*, "Systematic determination of genetic network architecture",. *Nature Genetics*, 1999, 22, pp 281-285.

[14] H. Zhang, "Classification trees for multiple binary responses", *Journal of American Statistical Association*, 1998, 93(441),pp 180-193.

[15] http://genetics.med.harvard.edu/~tpilpel/MotComb.html

Appendix

Names of motifs discovered by the tree models
(Full list of motifs and sequences are available at [15])

	Motif name
13	m_ion_transporters_orfnum2SD_n7
40	m_biogenesis_of_cytoskeleton_orfnum2SD_n5
46	m_breakdown_of_lipids_fatty_acids_and-isoprenoids_orfnum2SD_n8
57	m_lipid_and_fatty-acid_transport_orfnum2SD_n11
73	m_metal_ion_transporters_orfnum2SD_n10
88	m_regulation_of_lipid_fatty-acid_and_isoprenoid_biosynthesis_orfnum2SD_n8.scn
281	m_other_energy_generation_activities_orfnum2SD_n4
287	m_g-proteins_orfnum2SD_n11
304	m_other_protein-destination_activities_orfnum2SD_n7

Applying Noise Handling Techniques to Genomic Data: A Case Study*

Choh Man Teng
Institute for Human and Machine Cognition
40 South Alcaniz Street, Pensacola FL 32501, USA

Abstract

Osteogenesis Imperfecta (OI) is a genetic collagenous disease associated with mutations in one or both of the genes COLIA1 and COLIA2. There are at least four known phenotypes of OI, of which type II is the severest and often lethal. We identified three approaches to noise handling, namely, robust algorithms, filtering, and polishing, and evaluated their effectiveness when applied to the problem of classifying the disease OI based on a data set of amino acid sequences and associated information of point mutations of COLIA1. Preliminary results suggest that each noise handling mechanism can be useful under different circumstances. Filtering is stable across all cases. Pruning with robust c4.5 increased the classification accuracy in some cases, and polishing gave rise to some additional improvement in classifying the lethal OI phenotype.

1. Approaches to Noise Handling

Imperfections in a data set can be dealt with in three broad ways. We may leave the noise in, filter it out, or correct it. On the first approach, the data set is taken as is, with the noisy instances left in place. Algorithms that make use of the data are designed to be *robust*; that is, they can tolerate a certain amount of noise in the data. Robustness is typically accomplished by avoiding overfitting, so that the resulting classifier is not overly specialized to account for the noise. This approach is taken by, for example, c4.5 [7] and CN2 [1].

On the second approach, the data is *filtered* before being used. Instances that are suspected of being noisy according to certain evaluation criteria are discarded [4, 2]. A classifier is then built using only the retained instances in the smaller but cleaner data set.

On the third approach, the noisy instances are identified, but instead of tossing these instances out, they are repaired by replacing the corrupted values with more appropriate ones. These corrected instances are then reintroduced into the data set. An example of this approach is polishing [8].

There are pros and cons to adopting each of these three approaches to noise handling. Robust algorithms do not require preprocessing of the data, but each algorithm has to institute its own noise handling routine, duplicating the effort required even if the same data set is used in each case. In addition, the noise in the data may interfere with the mechanism, affecting the performance of the resulting classifier.

By filtering out the noisy instances from the data, there is a tradeoff between the amount of information available for building the classifier and the amount of noise retained in the data set. Filtering is not information-efficient; the more noisy instances we discard, the less data remains.

Noise correction, when carried out correctly, would preserve the maximal information available in the data set. A classifier built from this corrected data should have a higher predictive power and a more compact representation. However, we may also inadvertently introduce undesirable features into the data during the process of correction.

In this paper we evaluate the effectiveness of the three noise handling approaches on a research problem in the biomedical domain: the classification of the genetic disease *Osteogenesis Imperfecta* based on a data set of amino acid sequences and associated information of point mutations. Let us first describe the problem domain.

2 *Osteogenesis Imperfecta* (OI)

Osteogenesis Imperfecta (OI) is a genetic disorder characterized by bones that fracture easily for little reason. This disorder is linked to mutations in one or both of the genes COLIA1 and COLIA2, which are associated with the production of peptides of type I collagen. There are at least four known phenotypes of OI, namely, types I, II, III and IV. Type II is the severest form of OI and is often lethal. While OI may be diagnosed with collagenous or DNA tests, the relevant structure and the relationship between the point mutations and the types of OI are still under investigation [3, 6, for example].

The data set we used consists of information on se-

*This work was supported by NASA NCC2-1239 and ONR N00014-03-1-0516.

quences of amino acids, each with a point mutation in CO-LIA1. Each instance contains the following attributes.

$A_1, \ldots, A_{29}$: a sequence of 29 amino acids.

These are the amino acids at and around the site of the mutation. The mutated residue is centered at A_{15}, with 14 amino acids on each side. Four attributes provide supplementary information regarding hydrogen bonds in the molecules:

S-W : # solute hydrogen bonds (wild);
S-M : # solute hydrogen bonds (mutated);
SS-W : # solute-solvent hydrogen bonds (wild);
SS-M : # solute-solvent hydrogen bonds (mutated).

These are the numbers of hydrogen bonds of the specified types that are present in the wild (un-mutated) and mutated protein molecules more than 80% of the time.

The class of each instance can be one of two values: lethal (type II) or non-lethal (types I, III, or IV).

A number of characteristics of the data suggest that this data set is in need of noise handling and is amenable to the methods to be investigated in this study. First of all, the amino acid sequence and associated information are prone to noise arising from the clinical procedures. Thus, there is a need for an effective measure for noise handling.

While the precise relationship between the different amino acid blocks in a sequence is not clear, we do know that they interact, and this inter-relationship can be exploited to locate potentially noisy values in the data. In addition, the conformation of collagen molecules is exceptionally linear, and thus we can expect that each attribute may be predicted to a certain extent by considering only the values of the neighboring attributes in the sequence.

3. Algorithms

Representative mechanisms of the three noise handling approaches were identified and their performances on the OI data set were compared experimentally. We used the decision tree builder c4.5 [7] to provide our basic classifiers. The three noise handling mechanisms are as follows.

Robust : c4.5, with its built in mechanisms for avoiding overfitting. These include, for instance, post-pruning and stop conditions that prevent further splitting of a leaf node.

Filtering : Instances that have been misclassified by the initial decision tree are discarded, and a new tree is built using the remaining data. This is similar to the approach taken in [4].

Polishing : Instances in the data set are polished, and a tree is built using the polished data.

Let us briefly describe below the relatively novel data correction method *polishing*.

3.1 Polishing

Polishing takes advantage of the interdependency between the components of a data set to identify noisy elements and suggest appropriate replacements. Rather than utilizing the features only to predict the target concept, we in addition utilize the target together with selected features to predict the value of another feature. This provides a means for noise correction.

The basic algorithm of polishing consists of two phases: prediction and adjustment. In the *prediction* phase, elements in the data that are suspected of being noisy are identified together with nominated replacement values. In the adjustment phase, we selectively incorporate the nominated changes into the data set. In the first phase, the predictions are carried out by systematically swapping the target and particular features of the data set, and performing a tenfold classification to predict the feature values. If the predicted value of a feature in an instance is different from the stated value in the data set, the location of the discrepancy is flagged and recorded together with the predicted value. This information is passed on to the next phase, where we institute the actual adjustments.

Since the polishing process itself is based on imperfect data, the predictions obtained in the first phase can contain errors as well. We should not indiscriminately incorporate all the nominated changes. Rather, in the second phase, the *adjustment* phase, changes are selectively adopted from those predicted in the first phase, using a number of strategies to identify the best combination of changes that will improve the fitness of a datum.

Polishing has been shown to improve the performance of classifiers in a number of situations. Further details, including parameter selection and adjustment heuristics, can be found in [8]. Experimental evaluation of polishing on a number of test data sets, as well as some preliminary work on the OI data set, can be found in [9, 10].

4. Experiments

We performed ten-fold cross-validation on the OI data set, using each of the three noise handling mechanisms described in Section 3 (robust, filtering, polishing). In each trial, nine parts of the data were used for training and a tenth part was reserved for testing. The training data was subject to each of the three mechanisms and a decision tree was constructed in each case. The unseen (and untreated) instances in the test set were classified according to this tree. The results are reported below.

4.1. Classifier Characteristics

The average classification accuracy and size of the un-pruned and pruned decision trees constructed using the

Table 1. Average classification accuracy and tree size, using all attributes available.

	Unpruned		Pruned	
	Accuracy	Size	Accuracy	Size
Robust	46.5%	91.4	60.0%	11.6
Filtering	60.0%	11.6	60.0%	11.6
Polishing	53.0%	94.8	66.0%	11.4

Table 2. Relevant attributes

Robust; Filtering		Polishing	
Attribute	Occurrence	Attribute	Occurrence
S-M	33.3%	A_{15}	50.0%
S-W	16.7%	A_{11}, A_{14}	25.0%
A_{15}, A_{20}, A_{22}	16.7%		

Table 3. Average percentages of instances and attributes that have been adjusted in the data used as input for building the classifiers.

	% Instances	% Attributes
Robust	0.0%	–
Filtering	29.0%	–
Polishing	73.5%	7.1%

three mechanisms are reported in Table 1.

The differences between the classification accuracies of the pruned trees constructed using polishing and those constructed using both the robust and filtering methods are statistically significant at the 0.05 level, using a one-tailed paired t-test. This suggests that, when combined with pruning, polishing was effective in improving the quality of the training data such that more accurate classifiers could be built.

We noted that the trees built in three of the cases have similar characteristics: robust pruned trees built from the original data, and both unpruned and pruned trees built from the filtered data. Pruning using the original data gave results similar to pruning using the filtered data. Combining the two methods seemed to have little effect on the results.

The tree sizes resulting from the three approaches do not differ much, with the exception of the unpruned trees built from the filtered data. Filtering has the effect of making the data set smaller and more uniform, by discarding some of the instances, and thus fewer nodes should be needed to represent the resulting data set.

4.2. Relevant Attributes

We are interested in identifying the relevant features contributing to the lethal phenotype of OI and the relationship between these features. We used the number of trees involving a particular attribute as an indicator of the relevance of that attribute. Table 2 gives the normalized percentages of occurrence of the attributes, averaged over the cross validation trials, obtained from the pruned decision trees constructed using the three noise handling mechanisms.

Whereas there are 33 attributes altogether in each instance, the number of attributes used in building the decision trees is relatively small, as indicated by both the number of relevant attributes in Table 2 and the small (pruned) tree size reported in Table 1. This suggests that a small number of attributes determined the classification generated.

Both robust and filtering methods picked out the same set of relevant attributes, while polishing gave rise to a different set. We expected A_{15}, the attribute denoting the mutated amino acid in the molecule, to play a significant role in the classification of OI disease types. This is supported by the

findings in Table 2. We also noted that A_{15} was used more frequently in the decision trees constructed from the polished data than in those constructed using both of the other two methods (50.0% versus 16.7%). The stronger emphasis placed on this attribute may partially account for the increase in the classification accuracy obtained by polishing.

The other attributes that were picked out as being relevant from using the three mechanisms were dissimilar. Domain expertise is needed to further interpret the implications of these results.

4.3. Adjustment Level

By comparing the original, filtered, and polished data, we can quantify the amount of change that has occurred in each case. An attribute is counted as having been adjusted if its value in the data used for constructing the trees differs from the value in the original data. This measure only applies to polishing, as neither the robust method nor filtering makes changes to the individual attributes in an instance.

In the case of filtering, an instance is counted as having been adjusted if it has been eliminated from the data set used to construct the trees. In the case of polishing, an instance is counted as having been adjusted if at least one of its attributes has been adjusted. In the robust case, the percentage of adjustment is 0 since the whole original data set was used as input for building the trees.

The average percentages of instances and attributes that have been adjusted are reported in Table 3. On average filtering discarded 29.0% of the original data, building the trees using only the remaining 71.0% of the data.

We observed that although a fairly high percentage of instances (73.5%) were polished, the average percentage of attributes adjusted in each such instance is considerably lower (7.1%). This again suggests that only a small number

Table 4. Average classification accuracy and tree size, using only the relevant attributes.

	Unpruned		Pruned	
	Accuracy	Size	Accuracy	Size
Robust	71.0%	34.4	62.0%	16.7
Filtering	60.0%	7.4	60.0%	7.4
Polishing	73.5%	76.4	66.0%	8.8

of attributes are relevant to the classification task and polishing can be effective even when concentrating on only a select few of the attributes.

4.4. Rebuilding with Relevant Attributes

As we discussed above, the results in Table 2 indicated that only a few of the attributes were used in the decision trees. Even though the rest of the attributes were not present in the resulting trees, they nonetheless entered into the computation, and may have a distracting effect on the tree building process.

We "thinned" the data by removing those attributes that were not used, and then rebuilding the trees using the thinned data. This is a kind of feature selection [5]. Instead of removing entire instances as in pruning and filtering, portions of each instance are uniformly removed.

The classification accuracy and size of the decision trees built using the thinned original, filtered, and polished data are reported in Table 4. The attributes deemed relevant and thus retained in each case are those that were used in building the classifiers in the first pass (whose results were given in Tables 1–3). The difference between the corresponding classification accuracies of the unpruned trees constructed using polishing and the robust method are significant at the 0.05 level, using a one-tailed paired t-test.

Neither pruning nor selecting the relevant attributes had much effect on the trees built from the filtered data. The pruned results using the selected attributes are similar to those obtained using all attributes for the three mechanisms (reported in Table 1), perhaps because the data set has already been cleaned to some extent by the various preprocessing procedures. In the unpruned robust and polished cases, using only the relevant attributes gave rise to classification accuracies that are higher than any of those obtained with the three methods when all the attributes were included. With additional pruning, however, the advantages thus gained can be offset.

5. Remarks

We studied three different noise handling techniques and their application to the problem of characterizing the genetic disease *osteogenesis imperfecta*. Experimental results suggested that each can be useful under different circumstances. Filtering is stable across all cases. Pruning with robust c4.5 increased the classification accuracy in some cases, and polishing gave rise to some additional improvement in the results.

The number of possible values for many of the attributes of interest is fairly large, resulting in a data set that is sparse with little redundancy. This makes it more desirable to use an information-efficient mechanism such as polishing (as opposed to filtering) for noise handling, since discarding any data is likely to lose some information that is not duplicated in the remaining portion of the data set. This loss of information may account for some of the differences between the results obtained using filtering and polishing.

While each of these noise handling mechanisms can be an effective measure against the presence of noise in the data, a straightforward combination of the methods may not always give an additional increase in performance. It would be very helpful to explore the connections between these approaches and their possible interaction.

References

[1] P. Clark and T. Niblett. The CN2 induction algorithm. *Machine Learning*, 3(4):261–283, 1989.

[2] D. Gamberger, N. Lavrač, and S. Džeroski. Noise elimination in inductive concept learning: A case study in medical diagnosis. In *Proceedings of the Seventh International Workshop on Algorithmic Learning Theory*, pages 199–212, 1996.

[3] L. Hunter and T. E. Klein. Finding relevant biomolecular features. In *Proceedings of the International Conference on Intelligent Systems for Molecular Biology*, pages 190–197, 1993.

[4] G. H. John. Robust decision trees: Removing outliers from databases. In *Proceedings of the First International Conference on Knowledge Discovery and Data Mining*, pages 174–179, 1995.

[5] H. Liu and H. Motoda, editors. *Feature Selection for Knowledge Discovery and Data Mining*. Kluwer Academic Publishers, 1998.

[6] S. D. Mooney, C. C. Huang, P. A. Kollman, and T. E. Klein. Computed free energy differences between point mutations in a collagen-like peptide. *Biopolymers*, 58:347–353, 2001.

[7] J. R. Quinlan. *C4.5: Programs for Machine Learning*. Morgan Kaufmann, 1993.

[8] C. M. Teng. Correcting noisy data. In *Proceedings of the Sixteenth International Conference on Machine Learning*, pages 239–248, 1999.

[9] C. M. Teng. A comparison of noise handling techniques. In *Proceedings of the Fourteenth International Florida Artificial Intelligence Research Society Conference*, pages 269–273, 2001.

[10] C. M. Teng. Noise correction in genomic data. In *International Conference on Intelligent Data Engineering and Automated Learning*. Springer-Verlag, 2003. Forthcoming.

Detecting Patterns of Change Using Enhanced Parallel Coordinates Visualization[1]

Kaidi Zhao, Bing Liu
Department of Computer Science
University of Illinois at Chicago
851 S. Morgan St., Chicago, IL 60607
{kzhao, liub}@cs.uic.edu

Thomas M. Tirpak
Motorola Advanced Technology Center
1301 E. Algonquin Rd. Room 1014,
Schaumburg, IL. 60196
T.Tirpak@motorola.com

Andreas Schaller
MATC-Europe
Heinrich-Hertz-Str.1
65232 Taunusstein, Germany
Andreas.Schaller@motorola.com

Abstract

Analyzing data to find trends, correlations, and stable patterns is an important problem for many industrial applications. In this paper, we propose a new technique based on parallel coordinates visualization. Previous work on parallel coordinates methods has shown that they are effective only when variables that are correlated and/or show similar patterns are displayed adjacently. Although current parallel coordinates tools allow the user to manually rearrange the order of variables, this process is very time-consuming when the number of variables is large. Automated assistance is needed. This paper proposes an edit-distance based technique to rearrange variables so that interesting patterns can be easily detected. Our system, *V-Miner*, includes both automated methods for visualizing common patterns and a query tool that enables the user to describe specific target patterns to be mined/displayed by the system. Following an overview of the system, a case study is presented to explain how Motorola engineers have used V-Miner to identify significant patterns in their product test and design data.

Keywords: change patterns, parallel coordinate visualization.

1. Introduction

This paper describes a multi-variable visualization tool called V-Miner (for Visual Miner) designed for mining product design and test data. The goal is to discover useful, actionable knowledge from mobile phone testing data that can be provided as feedback to design engineers, who will use the knowledge to identify opportunities for improving both the product design and the design process. In this way, the design cycle of new products can be reduced. To better understand the challenges faced by designers and test engineers, we first give a short description of the typical design process for consumer electronic products, such as mobile phones.

1.1 Design Process

A high-level characterization of the process of designing a mobile phone is as follows:

1. Engineers, who are experts in mechanical, electrical, software, aspects of mobile phones, design their specific section based on previous designs, new product specifications, and general design guidelines.
2. After the mechanical, electrical and software designs are finalized, some prototypes are built.
3. A set of tests is performed on the prototypes to ensure that the product fulfills the requirements. According to the test results, the engineers can verify whether the design meets the requirements. If it does not, the design engineers have to modify the existing design, which leads to the next design cycle, i.e., step 1.

The above three steps are repeated until the design meets the required specifications (then the design is finalized). In order to reduce the engineering costs and cycle time associated with the design process, we have developed a method and a software tool for mining useful knowledge from test data that can be used to guide decision making of the mobile phone designers.

1.2 The Data

We analyzed the test result data with our proposed parallel coordinates visualization technique. For this project, Motorola engineers performed an extensive set of tests on one new type of mobile phone. After each design change, all the test variables were measured. There are more than 100 test variables that characterize the performance of a mobile phone. Each variable takes numeric values, and has the following characteristics:

1. It has an *upper limit* and a *lower limit*. Any value that exceeds either of the limits is considered unacceptable (the variable fails the test). A design modification is

---

[1] We would like to thank Thorsten Hoefer and Knut Moeller of the Motorola Personal Communications Sector in Flensburg, Germany, for performing the mobile phone tests, collecting and organizing the data used in this paper, and providing us with feedback on the use of our system. We also thank Weimin Xiao for many insightful discussions, and Tom Babin for his review of this manuscript, MATC 2003810M-19.

needed to bring the failed variable to its normal range.

2. It also has an ideal value, which is called the *target value*. The closer the value of the variable is to its target value the better it is.

Table 1 shows a sample test dataset. *Value for change i* is the measured value for each variable after the *i*th component change to the phone.

Table 1. Sample electrical test data.

Test variable	Target value	Lower limit	Upper limit	Value unit	Value for change 1	......
Variable 1	0	- 4	4	Voltage	0.9	......
Variable 2	50000	50000	55000	HZ	495830	......
......	......	......	......	......	......	......

Understanding the sequence of values for change 1, 2, ... is a significant part of our analyses. Note that the tests were done after each component change, and that once a change was made to the design, it was not changed back to its original component. Thus, we can view each change of a component on the phone as a new design, and subsequent changes are based on earlier changes. Thus, the data can be treated as a time series or sequential data set.

With the testing data, product designers are typically interested in the following:

- Prominent (or significant) changes in variable values after some design changes.
- The cause of these significant value changes.
- Stable variables whose values are not affected by design changes.
- Patterns of values changes and failures.

1.3 Using Traditional Rule Mining Systems

It is easy to think of ways to use some classic data mining algorithms to mine patterns from the data. For example, Motorola engineers have used association rule mining [1] or a decision tree method [8] to find failure patterns. However, these algorithms are inadequate for the following reasons:

1. Due to the large number of variables (more than 100), association mining generates too many rules (more than 20,000 for our data set).

2. The decision tree method has the problem that it only finds a subset of the patterns that exist in data. In some cases, the discovered patterns may not be the ones that are interesting to the users. It was also tedious to run a decision tree program because each failed variable has to be set as the class variable in order to find patterns related to its failure.

In our approach, we use an enhanced parallel coordinates visualization, which gives an intuitive view of the data, thereby enabling the user to identify interesting patterns quickly. Feedback from Motorola engineers, who carried out the data mining using our system, confirmed this.

1.4 Parallel Coordinates

Figure 1 shows a typical parallel coordinates visualization.

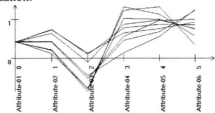

Figure 1. An illustration of parallel coordinates

Using the classic parallel coordinates technique directly is not suitable for our task for two main reasons:

1. It does not consider the data sequence.
2. It does not consider the ordering of the variables. Thus, vertical axes are ordered in an arbitrary manner.

We have enhanced the parallel coordinates technique on both aspects in order to meet our need. Details of these two enhancements are discussed in Section 3.

2. Related Work

Parallel coordinates techniques are widely used for multi-variable visualization [4][5][6]. Most existing systems are not designed for sequential data as in our application.

Our work is related to shape querying [2]. However, the approach in [2] does not allow approximate matching. In our work, we use edit distance in the similarity matching. We allow the user to specify a query shape either by indicating an example point or by explicitly specifying the shape of interest. In [7], an algorithm for ordering categorical values in parallel coordinates is proposed. The basic idea is to make sure that the most similar variables are placed next to each other after the rearrangement. Our work is different as we wish to allow the user to issue approximate queries. We believe that doing a single sorting for the best global result is not flexible and not always effective, because users have different interests, and their interests change with time.

3. The Enhanced Parallel Coordinates

In our work, we have extended the basic parallel coordinates technique in two significant ways.

3.1 Trend Figures

In our product testing application, the data sequence is significant. For this reason, we extend the classical parallel coordinates method by adding a small figure for each variable above its coordinate. In this small figure, as shown at the top of Figure 2, the horizontal axis reflects the sequence of the data record, and the vertical axis shows its value in each data record. We call these graphs *trend figures*. They make it possible to quickly see the variables that change in similar ways, by noting their similar trend figures.

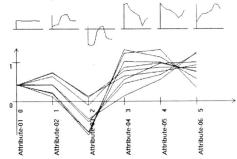

Figure 2. Parallel coordinates with trend figures.

3.2 Edit Distance Based Querying and Sorting

Our second major enhancement to traditional parallel coordinates visualization allows the user to query shapes based on approximate pattern matching. After the matching is completed, sorting of variables is performed to enable the user to view those most interesting patterns in nearby sections of the horizontal axis.

Two important types of patterns are the *value change pattern* and the *failure pattern*. For our mobile phone design application, the value change pattern of a variable shows how the variable's value changes over different design changes. After a design change, if a variable value increases compared to its previous value, we say its value is "up", and we denote it with the character "3" in its value change pattern. If its value decreases after a design change, we say it is "down" and use the character "1" to represent it. If its value stays stable after a design change, we use "2" (stable) to represent it in the value change pattern. With these representations, the behavior history of the variable can be summarized using a value change pattern string. For example, the string "331" means that the value becomes larger after the first and the second changes, and then goes down after the 3rd change. Queries can be issued using such value change strings.

The failure pattern of a variable shows whether or not its value falls outside the upper or lower limit after a design modification. If the variable value is outside the normal range, we say that it fails. The letter "F" denotes the failure. If the value is within the normal range, we mark it with an "O" (OK). An example of a failure pattern is "OOOFFF", which means that the variable is within the normal range for the first three design changes, but fails from the fourth design change onward. Our system allows the user to query failure patterns.

The value change pattern and failure pattern convert the numerical comparison task to string comparison, which is more convenient and intuitive for human users. Our system allows the user to issue queries by supplying the above two types of string patterns. We employ the edit distance [3] for string comparison. Ordering of

variables in parallel coordinates visualization is done according to the comparison results. The query can be formed either by indicating an example data point or by specifying the shape of interest explicitly.

4. Product Test Application

We now describe how our enhanced visualization tool V-Miner has been used by Motorola engineers to discover useful knowledge from phone testing data.

4.1 Data Normalization

Traditional data normalization methods are not applicable in our application for two reasons:
1. They do not consider any user-specified target value.
2. They do not consider the lower and upper limits.
We have designed a normalization method that clearly separates the values that are within the normal range from those that are out of the normal range. Variables whose values are out of range will be normalized to either larger than 1 or less than −1. Those values close to 0 are the ones that are close to the target values. In our interviews with Motorola engineers who used V-Miner, we found that this intuitive normalization was one of their favorite features of the software.

4.2 A Typical Scenario

We now present a typical knowledge discovery scenario. After normalization and loading data into V-Miner, the user can see the visualization as shown in Figure 3. Due to confidentiality, the test variable (attribute) names have been replaced with generic names Test-Attribute-*i*.

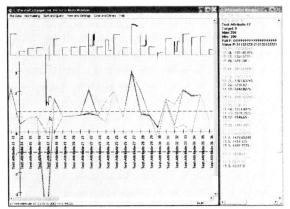

Figure 3. Initial Display of the Test Data

In Figure 3, the main window on the left displays the parallel coordinates visualization of the data. Most of the user interactions with the system are performed in this window. The horizontal axis shows all the test variables. Their names are displayed below the horizontal axis. The vertical axis displays the normalized value of each variable after every component or design change.

The information window on the right displays the

detailed information as the user moves the mouse cursor over points in the main window.

The key features of the visualization include:

1. Data from different designs (component changes) are visualized using different colors. The same color schema is also used on the right information window so that the user can easily relate the visual clues found in the left window to the detailed information shown in the information window on the right.
2. For each test variable, a trend figure is drawn at the top of the screen. These small figures complement the main visualization in that they show the correlation of component changes and value changes of each test variable. Those test variables which have similar change patterns will have similar figures.
3. There are two dashed lines on the vertical axes at Y = 1 and Y = -1 for both the parallel coordinate diagram and the trend figures above. Due to the way that the data are normalized, these two lines enable the user to clearly and instantly identify the out-of-range values.
4. The querying mechanism discussed in Section 3 allows the user to sort the variables in order to see interesting patterns and facts conveniently.

After loading data into V-Miner, the user can identify some significant characteristics from the visualization (Figure 3):

1. The user can see which values of a variable are out of the range and which are within range. Only those values that are between -1 and 1 are within the normal range of a variable, e.g., test variables 19, 20, etc.
2. From the trend figures on top of each variable, it is possible to see that some variables have very similar behaviors, e.g., variables 33 and 34. This suggests that there are some correlations among these variables.
3. Some variables have stable values over all the tests.

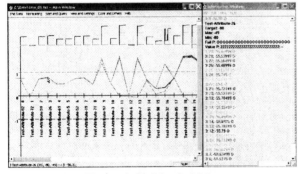

Figure 4. Stable variables

Now suppose that the user want to identify stable variables. The user can issue a "222…" query to obtain this information. Figure 4 shows the query result. The variables on the horizontal axis are sorted in such a way that stable variables come first on the left.

V-Miner includes a rich set of options and operations. Due to space limitations, we are unable to give all the

details. Interested readers, refer to the full paper [9].

4.4. Application Feedback

V-miner was used by engineers and researchers at the Motorola Personal Communications Sector in Flensburg, Germany, and at Motorola Labs in the U.S.A for approximately three months. During this time, they provided us many insights regarding the application of V-Miner and reported that the tool indeed helped them to find useful patterns and information from their product test data.

- Due to the enhanced normalization and visualization, it is easy to identify variables with prominent changes with a single glance of the V-Miner screen.
- It is easy to see the failure patterns of variables and to group related variables.
- Querying and sorting functions are used frequently to find ad hoc patterns of interest to the decision makers.

5. Conclusions

In this paper, we have introduced the V-Miner system and its initial application in mobile phone design and testing. This tool implements two major extensions to classical parallel coordinates visualization. Experimental results and feedback from Motorola engineers, who have used the system for several months, confirmed that the proposed enhancements are both powerful and easy to use.

6. Reference

[1] R. Agrawal and R. Srikant. "Fast algorithm for mining association rules" *VLDB-94*, 1994.

[2] R. Agrawal, Giuseppe Psaila, Edward L. Wimmers, Mohamed Zait. "Querying Shapes of Histories". *VLDB-95*.

[3] R.A. Baeza-Yates. "Algorithms for string matching: A survey". *ACM SIGIR Forum*, 23(3-4):34--58, 1989.

[4] A. Goel, C. Baker, C. Shaffer, B. Grossman, R. Haftka, W. Mason, and L. Watson. "VizCraft: A Multidimensional Visualization Tool for Aircraft Configuration Design". *IEEE Visualization'99*, 1999.

[5] A. Inselberg, B. Dimsdale. "Parallel Coordinates for Visualizing Multi-Dimensional Geometry". *In Proceedings of the Computer Graphics Intl. Conf.* 1987.

[6] D. Keim and H.-P. Kriegel. "VisDB: Database Exploration using Multidimensional Visualization". *IEEE Computer Graphics and Applications*, 14(5):40--49, 1994.

[7] S. Ma, J. Hellerstein. "Ordering Categorical Data to Improve Visualization". *InfoVis99*. 1999.

[8] J. Quinlan. "C4.5: program for machine learning". *Morgan Kaufmann*, 1993.

[9] K. Zhao, B. Liu, T. Tirpak, and A. Schaller. "Detecting patterns of change using enhanced parallel coordinates visualization". *UIC-CS technical report, 2003*.

Invited Talks

Sequential Supervised Learning: General Methods for Sequence Labeling and Segmentation
Thomas G. Dietterich, Oregon State University, USA

Grand Challenges on the Road to Practical Data Mining Systems
Usama M. Fayyad, DMX Group, LLC, USA

Global Structure from Sequences
Heikki Mannila, University of Helsinki, Finland

Pattern Discovery for Genomics
Gene W. Myers, University of California, Berkeley, USA

Real-Time Monitoring and Surveillance Using Data Stream Mining
Philip S. Yu, IBM T. J. Watson Research Center, USA

Tutorials

Workshops

Clustering Large Data Sets
Organizers: Daniel Boley, Inderjit Dhillon, Joydeep Ghosh, and Jacob Kogan

Data Mining for Computer Security (DMSEC '03)
Organizers: Philip Chan, Vipin Kumar, Wenke Lee, and Srinivasan Parthasarathy

Foundations and New Directions in Data Mining
Organizers: T. Y. Lin (Co-Chair), S. Ohsuga (Co-Chair), Tony Hu, and C. J. Liau

Frequent Itemset Mining Implementations (FIMI '03)
Organizers: Bart Goethals and Mohammed J. Zaki

Privacy Preserving Data Mining (PPDM)
Organizers: Wenliang Du (Chair) and Chris Clifton (Co-Chair)

VDM@ICDM2003: The 3rd International Workshop on Visual Data Mining
Organizers: Simeon J. Simoff, Monique Noirhomme-Fraiture, and Michael H. Bvhlen

Author Index

IEEE Computer Society Publications

The world-renowned IEEE Computer Society publishes, promotes, and distributes a wide variety of authoritative computer science and engineering texts. These books are available from most retail outlets. Visit the CS Store at *http://computer.org* for a list of products.

IEEE Computer Society Proceedings

The IEEE Computer Society also produces and actively promotes the proceedings of more than 160 acclaimed international conferences each year in multimedia formats that include hard and soft-cover books, CD-ROMs, videos, and on-line publications.

For information on the IEEE Computer Society proceedings, please e-mail to csbooks@computer.org or write to Proceedings, IEEE Computer Society, P.O. Box 3014, 10662 Los Vaqueros Circle, Los Alamitos, CA 90720-1314. Telephone +1-714-821-8380. Fax +1-714-761-1784.

Additional information regarding the Computer Society, conferences and proceedings, CD-ROMs, videos, and books can also be accessed from our web site at *http://computer.org/cspress*

Revised 11 March 2002